DICTIONARY OF

American History

Third Edition

EDITORIAL BOARD

DICTIONARY OF
American History

Third Edition

Stanley I. Kutler, *Editor in Chief*

Volume 9
Archival Maps and Primary Sources

CHARLES SCRIBNER'S SONS®

New York • Detroit • San Diego • San Francisco • Cleveland • New Haven, Conn. • Waterville, Maine • London • Munich

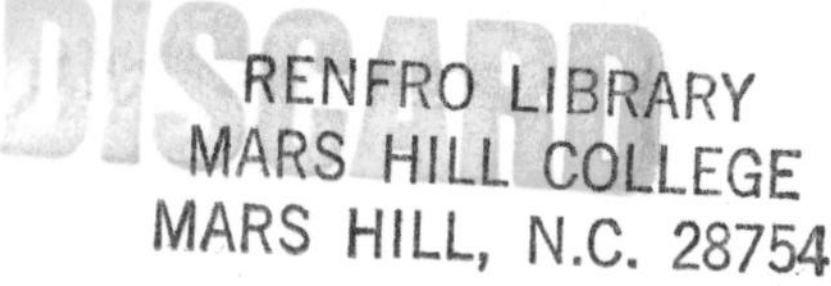

Dictionary of American History, Third Edition

Stanley I. Kutler, *Editor*

Charles Scribner's Sons is an imprint of The Gale Group, Inc., a division of Thomson Learning, Inc.

Charles Scribner's Sons® and Thomson Learning™ are trademarks used herein under license.

For more information, contact
Charles Scribner's Sons
An imprint of the Gale Group
300 Park Avenue South
New York, NY 10010

LIBRARY OF CONGRESS CATALOGING-IN-PUBLICATION DATA
Dictionary of American history / Stanley I. Kutler-- 3rd ed.
p. cm.
Includes bibliographical references and index.
ISBN 0-684-80533-2 (set : alk. paper)
1. United States--History--Dictionaries. I. Kutler, Stanley I.
E174 .D52 2003
973'.03 --dc21

Printed in United States of America
10 9 8 7 6 5 4 3 2 1

CONTENTS

Section I: Archival Maps . . . 1

U.S. History through Maps and Mapmaking . . . *1*

Early Maps of the New World . . . *6*

Fig. 1. Die Nüw Welt. Sebastian Munster, c. 1550 . . . *6*
Fig. 2. Mondo Nuovo. Tomaso Porcacchi. Venice, 1576 . . . 7
Fig. 3. Norumbega et Virginia. Cornelius van Wytfliet . . . *8*
Fig. 4. Provinciae Borealis Americae non itapridem dete ctae avt magis ab europaeis excvitae. Heinrich Scherer . . . *9*
Fig. 5. Carte systematique des pays septentrionaux de l'Asie et de l'Amérique . . . *11*

The Colonies . . . *12*

Fig. 6. Virginiae partis australis, et Floridae partis orientalis, interjacentiumq regionum Nova Descriptio. Arnoldus Montanus . . . *12*
Fig. 7. A Map of Virginia and Maryland . . . *13*
Fig. 8. A Map of New England, Being the first that was ever here cut . . . *14*
Fig. 9. A Mapp of New England by John Seller Hydrographer to the King . . . *15*
Fig. 10. A New Map of the Most Considerable Plantations of the English in America Dedicated to His Highness William Duke of Glocester . . . *16*
Fig. 11. New England, New York, New Jersey and Pensilvania. By H. Moll Geographer. An Account of ye Post of ye Continent of Nth America as they were Regulated by ye Postmasters Genl of ye Post House . . . *17*
Fig. 12. An Accurate Map of the English Colonies in North America bordering on the River Ohio . . . *18*

Exploration of the American Continent . . . *19*

Fig. 13. Unidentified French manuscript map of the Mississippi River, c. 1683 . . . *19*
Fig. 14. A Map of Louisiana and of the River Mississippi . . . *20*
Fig. 15. Carte de la Louisiane et du Cours du Mississippi . . . *21*
Fig. 16. A New Map of the River Mississippi from the Sea to Bayagoulas . . . *22*
Fig. 17. Louisiana, as formerly claimed by France, and now containing part of British America to the East & Spanish America to the West of the Mississipppi . . . *23*
Fig. 18. Carte de la Californie et des Pays Nord-ouest separés de l'Asie par le détroit d'Anian . . . *24*

Colonial Wars . . . *25*

Fig. 19. Plan of the City & Fortifications of Louisburg, from a Survey made by Richard Gridley, Lieut. Col. of the Train of Artillery in 1745 [with] A Plan of the City and Harbour of Louisburg . . . *25*
Fig. 20. Map of that part of America which was the Principal Seat of War in 1756 . . . *27*
Fig. 21. A Plan of the River St. Lawrence, from the Falls of Montmorenci to Sillery; with the Operations of the Siege of Quebec . . . *28*

The Revolutionary War . . . *29*

Fig. 22. Plan of the Town and Harbour of Boston and the Country adjacent with the Road from Boston to Concord Shewing the Place of the late Engagement between the King's Troops & the Provincials . . . *29*
Fig. 23. A Map of Part of Rhode Island, Showing the Positions of the American and British Armies at the Siege of Newport . . . 1778 . . . *31*
Fig. 24. A Plan of the Town of Boston with the Intrenchments &c of His Majesty's Forces in 1775 . . . *32*
Fig. 25. Plan of the Battle of Bunkers Hill June 17th, 1775 . . . *33*
Fig. 26. A Map of the Country which was the scene of operations of the Northern Army; including the Wilderness through which General Arnold marched to attack Quebec . . . *34*
Fig. 27. A Map of the United States of America, As settled by the Peace of 1783 . . . *35*

The Early Republic . . . *37*

Fig. 28. A Plan of the Boundary Lines between the Province of Maryland and the Three Lower

Counties of Delaware with Part of The Parallel of Latitude which is the boundary between the provinces of Maryland and Pennsylvania; A Plan of the West Line or Parallel of Latitude, which is the Boundary between the Provinces of Maryland and Pennsylvania. . . . *38*
Fig. 29. A Chorographical Map of the Northern Department of North America. Engraved Printed and Sold at New Haven . . . *39*
Fig. 30. An Exact Map of North America from the Best Authorities . . . *40*
Fig. 31. America, c. 1806 . . . *41*

The War of 1812 . . . *42*

Fig. 32. Plan of the Attack and Defence of the American Lines below New Orleans on the 8th January, 1815 . . . *43*
Fig. 33. Plan showing the Attack made by a British Squadron on Fort Bowyer at Mobile Point on the 15th September 1814 . . . *44*

The United States Expands . . . *45*

Fig. 34. North America, 1812 . . . *46*
Fig. 35. A Map of the eclipse of Feb.y 12th (1831) in its passage across the United States . . . *47*
Fig. 36. Map of the Western Territory &c., 1834 . . . *48*
Fig. 37. Map of the Northern parts of Ohio, Indiana and Illinois with Michigan, and that part of the Ouisconsin Territory Lying East of the Mississippi River, 1836 . . . *49*
Fig. 38. North America, 1851 . . . *50*
Fig. 39. Sketch of the Lower portion of the White Fish River by John Palliser, Esq. 1857 . . . *51*

Texas and the Mexican War . . . *52*

Fig. 40. Map of Texas and the Country Adjacent, 1844 . . . *53*
Fig. 41. Ornamental Map of the United States & Mexico, 1848 . . . *54*
Fig. 42. Untitled map of U.S. and Mexico, 1849 . . . *55*

Transportation . . . *56*

Fig. 43. Map of the Country between the Atlantic & Pacific Oceans . . . shewing the proposed route of a Rail Road from the Mississippi Valley to the ports of St. Diego, Monterey, & St. Francisco, 1848 . . . *56*
Fig. 44. A Complete Map of the Feather & Yuba Rivers, with Towns, Ranches, diggings, Roads, distances, 1851 . . . *57*
Fig. 45. Map of the United States Shewing the principal Steamboat routes and projected Railroads connecting with St. Louis, 1854 . . . *58*

Gold Rush in California . . . *59*

Fig. 46. Run for Gold, from all nations, Geographically Explained, 1849 . . . *60*
Fig. 47. Map of the Gold Regions of California, 1849 . . . *61*
Fig. 48. Plan of Benicia, California; Founded by Thomas O. Larkin and R. Simple Esq'rs. 1847 . . . *62*
Fig. 49. California, 1855 . . . *63*

The Civil War . . . *65*

Fig. 50. Sketch of The Country occupied by the Federal & Confederate Armies on the 18th & 21st July 1861 . . . *65*
Fig. 51. Plan of Cantonment Sprague near Washington, D.C. May 1851 . . . *66*
Fig. 52. White House to Harrison's Landing, 1862 . . . *68*
Fig. 53. Map of the United States, Showing the Territory in Possession of the Federal Union, January 1864 . . . *69*

New York—The Development of a City . . . *70*

Fig. 54. Plan de Manathes ou Nouvelle Yorc, c. 1675 . . . *70*
Fig. 55. Reproduction of A Plan of the City of New York from an actual Survey, Made by James Lyne, 1728 . . . *71*
Fig. 56. Plan of the City of New York for the Use of Strangers, 1831 . . . *72*
Fig. 57. A map of Manhattan copyrighted by the Aug. R. Ohman Map Co. of New York in 1913 and issued as a publicity brochure by the Navarre Hotel . . . *74*
Fig. 58. Bird's Eye View of Manhattan . . . *75*
Fig. 59. *Washington Post*—The Day After . . . *76*

Section II: Primary Source Documents . . . 79

The Colonial Period . . . *81*

The Origin of the League of Five Nations . . . *81*
Charter to Sir Walter Raleigh . . . *82*
Starving in Virginia . . . *84*
The Mayflower Compact . . . *86*
Trial of Anne Hutchinson at Newton . . . *87*
An Act Concerning Religion . . . *89*
Untitled Poem . . . *91*
Massachusetts School Law . . . *92*
Evidence Used Against Witches . . . *93*
Excerpt from *Voyages of the Slaver St. John* . . . *95*
Earliest American Protest Against Slavery . . . *97*
Powhatan's Speech to John Smith . . . *98*
A Dialogue Between Piumbukhou and His Unconverted Relatives . . . *99*
Captivity Narrative of a Colonial Woman . . . *101*
Logan's Speech . . . *103*
Excerpt from *Life and Adventures of Colonel Daniel Boon* . . . *104*
Letter Describing Catholic Missions in California . . . *107*

Excerpt from *The History and Present State of Virginia* . . . *109*
Letter Describing Plantation Life in South Carolina . . . *111*
Spanish Colonial Official's Account of Triangular Trade with England . . . *112*
Maxims from *Poor Richard's Almanack* . . . *113*
Indentured "White Slaves" in the Colonies . . . *114*
The Writ of Assistance . . . *116*
Stamp Act . . . *117*
Patrick Henry's Resolves as Printed in the *Maryland Gazette* . . . *120*
Townshend Revenue Act . . . *121*
Massachusetts Circular Letter . . . *122*
The Continental Association . . . *123*

The Revolutionary War . . . *127*

"The Pennsylvania Farmer's Remedy" . . . *127*
Eyewitness Account of the Boston Massacre . . . *128*
Slave Andrew's Testimony in the Boston Massacre Trial . . . *130*
Declaration and Resolves of the First Continental Congress . . . *132*
Address of the Continental Congress to Inhabitants of Canada . . . *134*
The Virginia Declaration of Rights . . . *135*
Excerpt from "Common Sense" . . . *137*
Declaration of Independence . . . *139*
Paul Revere's Account of His Ride . . . *141*
Battle of Lexington, American and British Accounts . . . *143*
Letters of Abigail and John Adams . . . *144*
A Soldier's Love Letter . . . *146*
Life at Valley Forge . . . *147*
Letters of Eliza Wilkinson . . . *150*
Correspondence Leading to Surrender . . . *152*

The Early Republic . . . *153*

Treaty with the Six Nations . . . *153*
Shays's Rebellion . . . *154*
From Annapolis to Philadelphia . . . *156*
The Call for Amendments . . . *159*
Constitution of the United States . . . *169*
Washington's Farewell Address . . . *179*
Madison's War Message . . . *183*

Expansion . . . *187*

Message on the Lewis and Clark Expedition . . . *187*
The Journals of the Lewis and Clark Expedition . . . *191*
Sleep Not Longer, O Choctaws and Chickasaws . . . *199*
Excerpt from *Glimpse of New Mexico* . . . *201*
The Monroe Doctrine and the Roosevelt Corollary . . . *204*
Life of Ma-ka-tai-me-she-kai-kiak, or Black Hawk . . . *210*
The Story of Enrique Esparza . . . *212*
Americans in Their Moral, Social and Political Relations . . . *215*
Mexican Minister of War's Reply to Manuel de la Peña y Peña . . . *218*
Message on the War with Mexico . . . *219*
National Songs, Ballads, and Other Patriotic Poetry, Chiefly Relating to the War of 1846 . . . *221*
Excerpt from *The Oregon Trail* . . . *222*
Excerpt from *Memories of the North American Invasion* . . . *224*
Fort Laramie Treaty . . . *227*
Excerpt from *Across the Plains to California in 1852* . . . *229*
Excerpt from *An Expedition to the Valley of the Great Salt Lake of Utah* . . . *233*
A Pioneer Woman's Letter Home . . . *238*
Constitution of the Committee of Vigilantes of San Francisco . . . *239*
Excerpt from *The Vigilantes of Montana* . . . *240*
American Party Platform . . . *242*
Speech of Little Crow on the Eve of the Great Sioux Uprising . . . *243*
Excerpt from *My Army Life* . . . *244*
Excerpt from *Roughing It* . . . *248*
Account of Battle at Little Bighorn . . . *253*
Excerpt from *Half a Century* . . . *255*
Excerpt from *A Century of Dishonor* . . . *257*
A Letter from Wovoka . . . *259*
Women in the Farmers' Alliance . . . *260*
A Soldier's Account of the Spanish-American War . . . *261*
Anti-Imperialist League Platform . . . *263*
Gentlemen's Agreement . . . *264*

Slavery, Civil War, and Reconstruction . . . *267*

Text of the Pro-Slavery Argument . . . *267*
Excerpt from *Notes Illustrative of the Wrong of Slavery* . . . *269*
Excerpt from *Running a Thousand Miles for Freedom* . . . *272*
On the Underground Railroad . . . *274*
Excerpt from *Sociology for the South* . . . *276*
Excerpt from *The Impending Crisis of the South: How to Meet It* . . . *280*
A House Divided . . . *284*
John Brown's Last Speech . . . *286*
The Nat Turner Insurrection . . . *287*
Excerpt from "The Crime Against Kansas" Speech . . . *288*
South Carolina Declaration of Causes of Secession . . . *292*
Benjamin Butler's Report on the Contrabands of War . . . *294*
A Confederate Blockade-Runner . . . *296*

Letter to President Lincoln from Harrison's Landing . . . *298*
Address to President Lincoln by the Working-Men of Manchester, England . . . *299*
Emancipation Proclamation . . . *300*
Gettysburg Address . . . *302*
Head of Choctaw Nation Reaffirms His Tribe's Position . . . *302*
Letters from Widows to Lincoln Asking for Help . . . *303*
Prisoner at Andersonville . . . *304*
Robert E. Lee's Farewell to His Army . . . *308*
President Lincoln's Second Inaugural Address . . . *308*
Congress Debates the Fourteenth Amendment . . . *310*
President Andrew Johnson's Civil Rights Bill Veto . . . *317*
Black Code of Mississippi . . . *319*
Police Regulations of Saint Landry Parish, Louisiana . . . *323*

Women's Rights . . . *325*

Excerpt from "On the Equality of the Sexes" . . . *325*
Human Rights Not Founded on Sex . . . *327*
When Woman Gets Her Rights Man Will Be Right . . . *329*
What If I Am a Woman? . . . *331*
Seneca Falls Declaration of Rights and Sentiments . . . *332*
Excerpt from *Path Breaking* . . . *334*

Industry and Labor . . . *339*

Civil Disobedience . . . *339*
Mill Worker's Letter on Hardships in the Textile Mills . . . *340*
Excerpt from *The Principles of Scientific Management* . . . *342*
Excerpt from *The Theory of the Leisure Class* . . . *347*
In the Slums . . . *351*
The Pullman Strike and Boycott . . . *353*
Women in Industry (Brandeis Brief) . . . *357*
Conditions in Meatpacking Plants . . . *360*
Bartolomeo Vanzetti's Last Statement . . . *361*

World War I . . . *363*

Excerpt from "The War in Its Effect upon Women" . . . *363*
Lyrics of "Over There" . . . *364*
Excerpt from *Peace and Bread in Time of War* . . . *365*
Letters from the Front, World War I . . . *367*
The Fourteen Points . . . *368*
Dedicating the Tomb of the Unknown Soldier . . . *370*

Great Depression . . . *375*

Advice to the Unemployed in the Great Depression . . . *375*
Letter to Franklin Roosevelt on Job Discrimination . . . *376*
Fireside Chat on the Bank Crisis . . . *377*
Excerpt from *Land of the Spotted Eagle* . . . *379*
Living in the Dust Bowl . . . *384*
Ford Men Beat and Rout Lewis . . . *385*
Excerpt from *Power* . . . *388*
Proclamation on Immigration Quotas . . . *390*

World War II . . . *393*

"America First" Speech . . . *393*
War Against Japan . . . *396*
Women Working in World War II . . . *397*
Hobby's Army . . . *398*
Total Victory . . . *401*
"War and the Family" Speech . . . *403*
The Japanese Internment Camps . . . *405*
Pachucos in the Making . . . *407*

The Cold War . . . *411*

Excerpt from "American Diplomacy" . . . *411*
The Testimony of Walter E. Disney Before the House Committee on Un-American Activities . . . *413*
A Personal Narrative of the Korean War . . . *417*
"War Story" . . . *419*
The History of George Catlett Marshall . . . *424*
General Douglas MacArthur's Speech to Congress . . . *427*
Censure of Senator Joseph McCarthy . . . *428*
Excerpt from *The Blue Book of the John Birch Society* . . . *429*
Eisenhower's Farewell Address . . . *434*
"Voice from Moon: The Eagle Has Landed" . . . *435*

Civil Rights . . . *445*

The Arrest of Rosa Parks . . . *445*
Student Nonviolent Coordinating Committee Founding Statement . . . *446*
An Interview with Fannie Lou Hamer . . . *447*
"Black Power" Speech . . . *452*

The Vietnam War . . . *455*

Excerpt from *The Pentagon Papers* . . . *455*
Statement by Committee Seeking Peace with Freedom in Vietnam . . . *459*
Lyndon B. Johnson's Speech Declining to Seek Re-election . . . *462*
Vietnamization and Silent Majority . . . *467*
Excerpts from *Dear America: Letters Home from Vietnam* . . . *473*
Nixon's Letter to Nguyen Van Thieu . . . *474*
The Christmas Bombing of Hanoi was Justified . . . *475*
The Fall of Saigon . . . *477*
Pardon for Vietnam Draft Evaders . . . *479*

The Late Twentieth Century . . . *481*

NOW Statement of Purpose . . . *481*
Excerpt from "Chicano Nationalism: The Key to Unity for La Raza" . . . *484*
Nixon's Watergate Investigation Address . . . *486*
"Constitutional Faith" Speech . . . *489*
Proclamation 4311, Nixon Pardon . . . *491*
Address on the Energy Crisis . . . *492*
Interrogation of an Iran Hostage . . . *494*
Excerpt from *The New Right: We're Ready to Lead* . . . *495*
Deming's Fourteen Points for Management . . . *499*
Excerpt from *The New American Poverty* . . . *500*
Report on the Iran-Contra Affair . . . *504*
Excerpt from *Maya in Exile: Guatemalans in Florida* . . . *509*
Address to the Nation: Allied Military Action in the Persian Gulf . . . *515*
Gulf War Story . . . *518*
Gulf War Letter . . . *520*
Clinton's Rose Garden Statement . . . *522*
Responses to Supreme Court Decision in *Bush v. Gore* . . . *523*
George W. Bush, Address to a Joint Session of Congress and the American People . . . *526*

Acknowledgments . . . 531

Section I

ARCHIVAL MAPS

ARCHIVAL MAPS

U.S. HISTORY THROUGH MAPS AND MAPMAKING

Maps are key documents that tell us important stories. They are a form of communication that speaks across the centuries. We have to listen with a careful ear because their messages are rarely simple or clear. They have been described as the "slippery witnesses" of history.

Maps are often unwitting witnesses because they tell two stories: the story in the map and the story of the map. The story in the map is the physical and social depictions it contains. The story of the map is the history of its production and consumption. A map meant for one purpose, such as a French map of the eighteenth century intended to advance an imperial agenda, is now a revealing document of imperial rivalry over contested territory. Maps tell us more than one story.

Maps reveal much about imagined worlds, past worlds, and contemporary worlds. They tell us of the worlds we have lost and the worlds in which we now live. Maps indicate much about the history as well as the geography of a land and its peoples. A series of maps of the same territory at different times provide us with a transect through time and space. The geographic representation of the United States, as in other countries, is concerned not only with the depiction of place but also the understanding of the physical world and the social hierarchy. Maps reflect physical space and embody social order.

Maps are neither mirrors of nature nor neutral transmitters of universal truths. They are social constructions, narratives with a purpose, stories with an agenda. They contain silences as well as articulations, secrets as well as knowledge, lies as well as truth. They are biased, partial and selective. Traditional histories of maps and mapmaking tended to focus on the accuracy of maps. The driving narrative was the movement to increasing accuracy through time; it was a triumphalist view of cartographic evolution. In recent years the history of mapmaking has been enlivened and enlarged by scholars who view maps as texts to be decoded. Maps are no longer seen as value-free, socially neutral depictions, links in a chain of increasing accuracy, but rather as social constructions that bear the marks of power and legitimation, conflict and compromise. Maps are not just technical products, they are social products, and mapping is not only a technical exercise, but also a social and political act.

Maps are rhetorical devices that do not only neutrally describe territory, but also make arguments, advance claims, justify and legitimize. To look at a map is to view a complex argument, a sophisticated rhetorical device.

Maps are complex. A map is not just an inscription to be decoded. It is also a theory, a story, a claim, a hope, a scientific document, an emotional statement, an act of imagination, a technical document, a lie, a truth, an artifact, an image, an itinerary. A map, like a speech and musical event, can also be performed. The drawing of boundary lines, for example, creates the context for very different experiences either side of the cartographic line.

Understanding maps is not an easy task. The meaning of it is never fixed. Even if the makers of the map had a simple message, creative readers can produce complex readings: A map of national boundaries reveals to us now the extent of national power and political compromise; a map of landholdings indicates to a contemporary audience the dispossession and commodification of what used to be Native American land. Maps are capable of multiple readings. We need to use maps with much care and attention.

Although each map in this volume tells its own story in a distinctive voice, there are seven general running narratives that distinguish this series of maps. The first is the story of discovery and appropriation. The vast bulk of the maps were drawn by and for those moving East to West, those moving in rather than already here. We will be looking at the maps made by the invaders.

The New World was coveted and desired as well as mapped and traversed. The New World was claimed by European powers, and these claims were represented in maps. These maps were an integral part of European rivalry for they contained imperial claims and challenges. The colonial maps are not so much simple descriptions of territory as claims to ownership, acts of domination, a cartographic legitimization of control. The mapping of the New World was never innocent of political agendas. The New World was both appropriated and understood through mapping. The maps became the documents of scientific understanding as well as political control. To map was to incorporate scientific understanding and political ambitions. The British and the French struggled for dominance, and we will see in the plethora of colonial mappings maps embodying imperial claims in a changing geopolitical order. The colonial maps were acts of military surveillance, claims to land ownership, and representations of the native other.

It is important to bear in mind, however, that the maps did not result solely from the gaze of the Western observer. In fact, the maps of early North America bear witness to a major native contribution. Despite the traditional view that Europeans created maps of the continent on their own, Native Americans helped in the mapping of North America. It is more accurate to consider the notion of cartographic encounters involving Europeans and Native Americans, rather than a simple cartographic appropriation by only Europeans. The mapping of the continent was underpinned by native knowledge. There are hidden strata of Native American geographical knowledge that are only now being uncovered. The European depiction of the lay of the land was the product of a series of cartographic encounters between two peoples: the indigenous people with detailed spatial knowledge of the land and the colonialists seeking to obtain this land.

The second narrative, in fact woven throughout the first, is the story of national expansion as the country became the United States of America and expanded its territorial control to its continental limits. Many of the maps record the territorial expansion of the United States and its extension of control and power over most of the continent. Maps were the embodiment of imperial power. Manifest Destiny was both imagined and realized on maps as well as on the ground. The struggle for dominance was neither easy nor predetermined. Clashes with other imperial powers and local resistances led to a series of clashes and wars, again all recorded in maps. The changing boundaries of the United States, so clearly visible in many of the maps, record the limits of territorial expansion and the resultant compromises shaped after war and negotiation.

The mapping of the national territory, especially of its westward expansion, was replete with both political significance and scientific inquiry. The maps of westward expansion described and celebrated the drive to the Pacific, the intensification of settlement, and ultimately the closing of the frontier.

From its inception in the late eighteenth century to the close of the nineteenth century, the United States went through enormous changes: the expansion of the railway system, the industrialization of the economy, massive immigration from overseas, enormous urban growth, the creation of a national market, the growth of big business, the closing of the frontier, the increased settlement of the West, the enlargement of the federal government, and the creation of an overseas empire. In the last third of the nineteenth century the United States became a more industrial urban society, a more densely settled nation, and a more important power in world politics. These changes were recorded, embodied, and reflected in maps. Cartographic representations gave shape and form to the expanding and evolving nation. A rich variety of maps were produced and consumed: county maps, state maps, survey maps, maps of the country and of the city, maps produced by public and private agencies, maps made by small firms, maps made by large companies, maps made by local, state, and central governments. These maps were sold, read, displayed, presented, distributed, and consumed throughout the country.

The United States was created in war and its shape owes much to military engagements. To conduct war it is essential to have accurate maps. Good maps allow commanders to move their forces efficiently, to have some idea of the location of enemy forces, and to plan marches, sieges, and military maneuvers. Maps also record and commemorate historic battles and military encounters. The third narrative concerns the importance of war and individual battles in shaping the geography and history of the nation. There are numerous maps that record military campaigns: the colonial wars, the War of Independence, the War of 1812, the war with Mexico, and the Civil War. The maps of significant battles enhance our understanding of these conflicts and military campaigns. Maps also serve as a form of historic commemoration.

The fourth narrative, again running throughout the first two, is the creation of a state. Maps allowed the state to imagine the people under its dominance and the geographic territory under its control. The cartographic representation of territory has great political significance and social meaning. By mapping a territory the state reinforces its claim to power and dominance. Its claim to sovereignty is partly vindicated by its ability to map and represent the territory. The cartographic representation reinforces its claim to legitimacy. Maps of the state's territory suggest a permanence, the unfolding on paper of a "natural" organism, the picturing of a "natural" object beyond the winds of arbitrary adjustment or historical contingency. Maps record the creation of the state.

The fifth narrative involves the creation of a national community. Nations are not so much facts of race or ethnicity. Rather, they are what one commentator referred to as "imagined communities." A national identity is fostered, encouraged, and created by a shared cartographic depiction, a common cartographic understanding of the nation, its outline, and its boundaries.

In the cartographic representations of the new Republic an emphasis was placed on the construction of a national geography, a description and representation of the territory of the fledgling nation. In the last two decades of the eighteenth century and the first two of the nineteenth century, some of the most important and best-selling books were geography texts and maps that created, advanced, and codified a national geography. Such projects had a number of objectives. Nationalist concerns were bound to more purely "scientific" endeavors, such as the accurate location and description of unknown territory. Geography was part of a scientific project that sought universal truths. However, there was a special American desire to create and describe a particular American geography. Tension existed between the search for scientific universals, but also the perceived need to create a national geographic discourse. There was an ambiguity between the depiction of space and the construction of a national place: space and place, global debates and local concerns, an international language of science and the vernacular concerns of a particular nation. Although geographical matters had a connection with the general language of science, they also had a direct connection with national identity. This ambiguity was most obvious in the use of a prime meridian. There is no natural starting point establishing the 0 degree of longitude, the prime meridian. Before the end of the nineteenth century it was an arbitrary designation that varied between countries. The British established theirs at Greenwich. As we will see, the early American geographies used Greenwich, then Philadelphia, and later Washington as the prime meridian; some maps even had a dual system, with both the British and American prime meridians appearing on the same map, one at the top, the other at the bottom. The early maps of the fledgling Republic not only described national space, they also sought to promote spatial unification. The early maps and atlases, for example, by bringing the individual states onto one sheet or under one cover promoted national cohesion and national consciousness, and the many geography texts that listed all the states helped construct a national market and a national polity.

The geographical construction of the state is intimately linked to the territorial imagination of the nation. This imagining takes many forms. There was a geographical representation of the national community in such varied mapping exercises as the inscribing of a national landscape and the construction of a national economy. Cartographic images were and still are important elements of national identity. Maps were an important part of this story of territorial expansion and national identity. Many maps showed how the bounded territory was connected and the national community created. The railway maps of the nineteenth century, for example, are maps of the vital arteries of a connected economy and linked society.

A national community can even be defined by the widespread usage of the same cartographic convention. The saturation of cartographic images has created widely accepted semiotics of the country and individual states. Outline maps of the United States or of individual states of the Union, for example, are easily recognizable; they are used as symbols of these places. Maps not so much reflect or represent; they are.

These national geographies communicated many moral injunctions. With their implicit and often explicit dichotomy of nation/nonnation, these maps also had an "otherizing" quality that at times filtered into notions of moral purity, political correctness, and consequent images of spiritual cleansing and political enemies. The "others" were variously identified as Native Americans, foreigners, the Spanish, and Southerners. Women were rarely discussed. The discourse of national geography and identity was racialized, gendered, and moralized. This is most clearly demonstrated in the case of Native Americans and their cartographic representation. The sixth narrative of many of the maps under discussion is the changing depiction of Native Americans. Their presence was shown on many of the early maps; their tribal names and territories figure largely in British, French, and early U.S. maps. The maps cartographically record not only their presence, but also their eradication and dispossession. By the late nineteenth century, Native Americans rarely figured in maps as little more than blocks to westward progress; their eradication and dispossession is one of the hidden themes in many of the maps.

The seventh narrative is the story of place. Maps come in different scales. Small-scale maps may cover an entire territory. Large-scale maps, in contrast, focus on specific areas. The different scales can be seen as lenses on the world; small scales are the wide-angle lens, whereas the large-scale maps are the cartographic equivalent of close-ups. We will consider a number of large-scale maps that individually and collectively provide a series of close-ups of particular places and specific times. These maps allow us to flesh out the broad general story with the "warp and weft" of particularity and uniqueness. These maps are narratives of particular places and show how the national picture is in fact a mosaic of many different local histories and geographies. One of the places we will concentrate on is New York City. Since New York is currently the largest city in the country and one of the most heterogeneous and global of U.S. cities, we will show its cartographic evolution from the seventeenth to the twenty-first century.

Maps have played a varied role in the history of the territory that is now the United States. Our story begins with some of the earliest printed maps. They were rare and expensive items. Most of them were created for specific audiences, often in the imperial centers of Europe. A truly mass market for maps did not surface until the 1840s. In Britain in the eighteenth century a number of magazines published maps to accompany reports of battles, military campaigns, and political hotspots around the world. Many of the maps we will look at derive from this source. They were part of the world view of the educated elite in the imperial center of London.

In the early history of the United States from 1780 to 1840, there were limitations to mass production and consumption. Books and maps were expensive items; they were an important part of the material culture of the political and economic elites, but not cheap enough for mass consumption. There were also limitations on the use of illustrations and especially of maps in books. Most printed maps came from engravings on individual sheets that often were added to printed books by hand, an expensive and cumbersome method that restricted the wide use of maps in books. Of forty-nine geography texts published before 1840, twenty-four had no maps. In contrast, in the period from 1840 to 1890, when map production became much cheaper and easier, only ten of ninety-seven geography texts had no maps. After the Civil War there was a cartographic explosion as many more maps were produced and available to a wider, broader audience. The decreasing cost of cartographic images meant wider availability and maps becoming part of the national debate, the national image, and an integral part of the way the country was represented.

Maps are important texts that provide an invaluable and innovative way to illuminate wider social processes. In the following sections we will examine a range of maps or mappings and their relationship to the history of early North America and the United States. Slippery and often unwitting witnesses, maps tell us much about the past.

John Rennie Short,
Department of Geography and Environmental Systems
University of Maryland Baltimore County

Note: Except as indicated, the maps throughout this section are reproduced courtesy of the Map Collection, Yale University Library.

EARLY MAPS OF THE NEW WORLD

When Christopher Columbus landed on an island in the Caribbean on 12 October 1492, it signified a creation as well as a discovery, for the New World was invented as much as it was discovered. The cartographic construction of the New World relied as much on imagination as actual reports. Accurate and not so accurate reports from travelers and mapmakers slowly completed the story of the land. However, it could be a slow process as those moving in from the coast or traveling along one river system often had little knowledge of how it connected with other parts of the country. It took a long while for a coherent picture to develop. The coasts were first known and knowledge was accumulated slowly and fitfully from the coasts and along the rivers. The knowledge varied by colonizing powers. The Spanish settled North America in the Southwest, the French along the St. Lawrence and down the Mississippi, while the English moved in from the eastern seaboard. Geographical knowledge varied among European powers. And when all else failed the gaps in the map could be filled with fanciful images of imaginary cities such as Norumbega or imprecise rivers and mountains. The New World was made as well as uncovered.

The imaginative construction of the world is evident in the earliest European maps of the New World. The very first one we consider (fig. 1) was published in 1540. It appeared in books written by Sebastian Munster (1489–1552). Munster authored a very popular text entitled *Cosmographia*, that appeared in numerous editions between 1544 and 1628. For the literate of Europe it was the most popular and comprehensive global geography. The map's subtitle is "the new islands discovered in our times by the King of Spain in the great ocean." Central and South America are shown in greater detail, reflecting the course of Spanish exploration and colonization. North America is less well known, with only the shape of

Fig.1. Die Nüw Welt. Sebastian Munster, c.1550. From an edition of his *Cosmographia*. A version of a map first issued in 1540.

Florida bearing any resemblance to its real geography. The interior of North America is a figment of creative imagination, with only a narrow belt of land connecting Spanish Florida and French North America. At that time, the interior of North America was still a relatively unknown land to Europeans. Central and South America, in contrast, are shown in relatively more accurate terms, with Caribbean islands such as Cuba exaggerated in size. The city of Tenochtitlan is also shown in Central America.

In the northeast of the South American continent, an illustration depicts the practice of cannibalism, with body parts being shown roasting on a fire. Munster had a wonderfully rich imagination and his *Cosmographia* is full of one-eyed men and people with giant feet. He also drew upon ancient prejudice as much as contemporary reports. The cannibal scene was part of the fantastical depiction of the world outside of Europe. Just to the west of Central America, the island of Zipangri represents Japan and further west Cathay and India are shown. The Pacific is clearly undersized, embodying the hopeful belief that the New World was a convenient stepping stone to the Far East. The ship sailing through the waters of the Pacific is probably a representation of Magellan.

One of the best known earliest European depictions of the New World, this map shows North America as a hazy unknown extension of the better known, at least to the Europeans, Central and South America.

The 1576 map of the New World, *Mondo Nuovo* (fig. 2), is a fine example of sixteenth-century Italian cartography. Throughout much of the middle of the sixteenth century, Italy was a center for the dissemination of geographical knowledge and mapmaking. Rome and Venice became important publishing centers for maps. Tomaso Porcacchi (1530–1585) was cosmographer to the Venetian republic and produced many copper-engraved maps. His maps illustrated Ramusio's 1550 book *Delle Navigazione e Viaggi*, the first published account of New World travels. Porcacchi developed the idea that there was a route between North America and Asia that he called the Strait of Anian, named after Marco Polo's Kingdom of Anian. The very first map that showed the strait on a map was engraved in Venice by Bolognino Zaltieri in 1566. The 1576 map is a later variant of this map.

Fig. 2. Mondo Nuovo. Tomaso Porcacchi. Venice, 1576. From an edition of *L'Isole piu Famose del Mondo* first published in 1572.

The map depicts a New World that is coming into better focus for Europeans. It is based on European knowledge and travels, hence the exaggeration of the coastal areas. The name Florida appears on the map although there is little evidence of its telltale peninsular shape. The French incursions along the northeast coast of what is now Canada are represented in the naming of Labrador, Arcadia, and New France (*Nova Franza*). The Spanish presence in the Southwest is recorded and the Baja correctly portrayed as a peninsula; later it would be seen as an island. In the West the term *Terra Incognita* masks a monumental ignorance. The English had yet to arrive so much of the eastern seaboard was unknown and as a result, the interior region in the map is reduced to an insignificant size compared to the better known Caribbean islands.

The depiction of the New World conveys a sense of boundless commercial possibilities. It is shown as very close to Asia, with the Pacific shrunk to a navigable size; Japan, shown as the island off the coast of California named Giapan, is very close and the Strait of Anian between Asia and North America provides a quick passage around the continent. Commercial interests shaped the representation of the New World as a place of new economic opportunity, easily connected the existing system of global trading.

The map entitled *Norumbega and Virginia* and dating from 1597 (fig. 3) appeared in the very first atlas of America produced by the Antwerp lawyer and cartographer Cornelius van Wytfliet. The atlas contained eighteen regional maps of the New World. This map drew upon two sources. The first was the manuscript map of the Virginia-Carolina coastal area drawn by the artist and illustrator John White, who accompanied an English colonization enterprise sponsored by Sir Walter Raleigh. The expedition that settled briefly in Roanoke, Virginia was not a success; it was abandoned after a few short years. But from July 1585 to June 1586 John White, accompanied by the mathematician and cartographer Thomas Harriot, surveyed the outer banks and coasts of

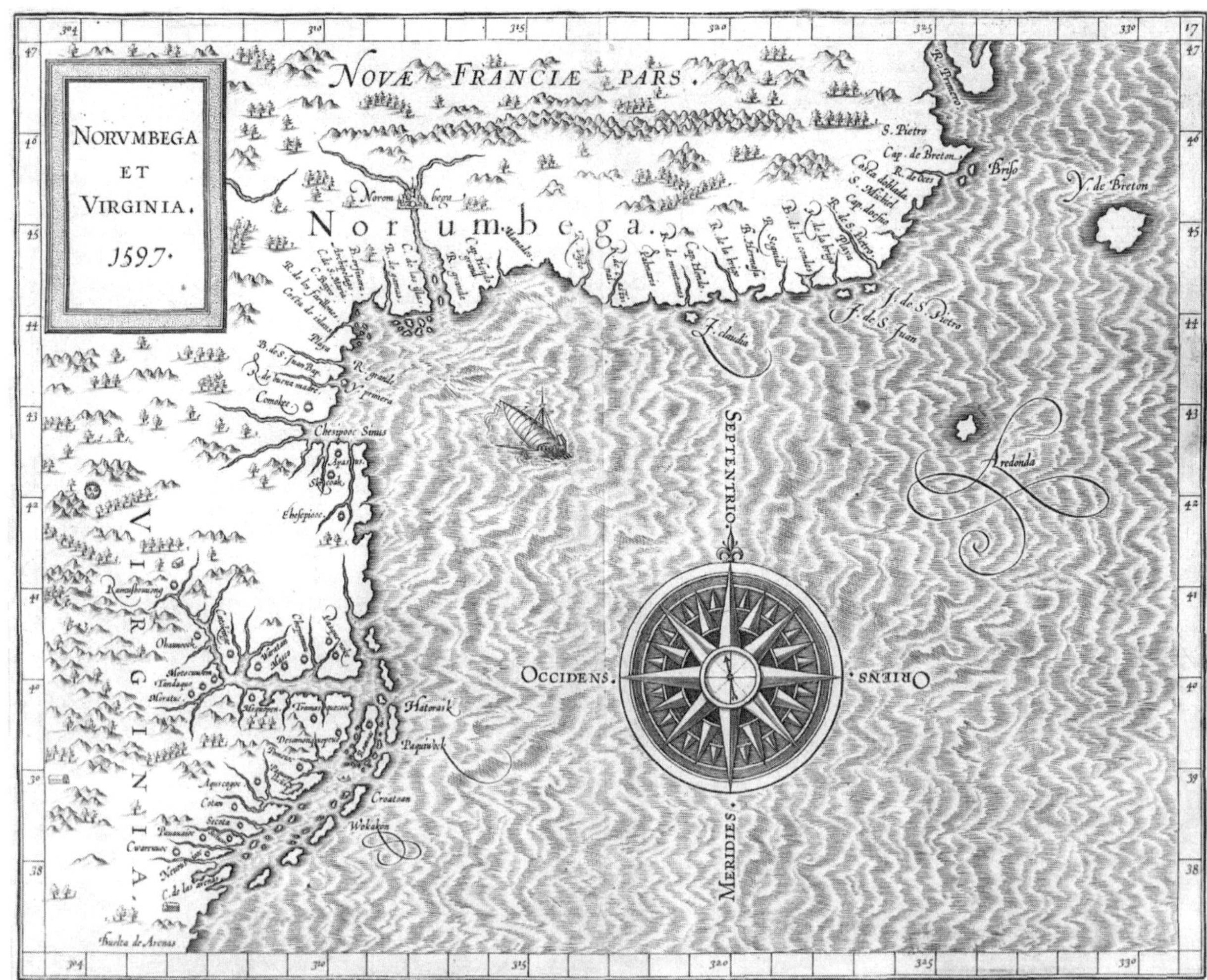

Fig. 3. Norumbega et Virginia. Cornelius van Wytfliet. From his *Descriptionis Ptolemaicae augmentum*, Louvain, 1597.

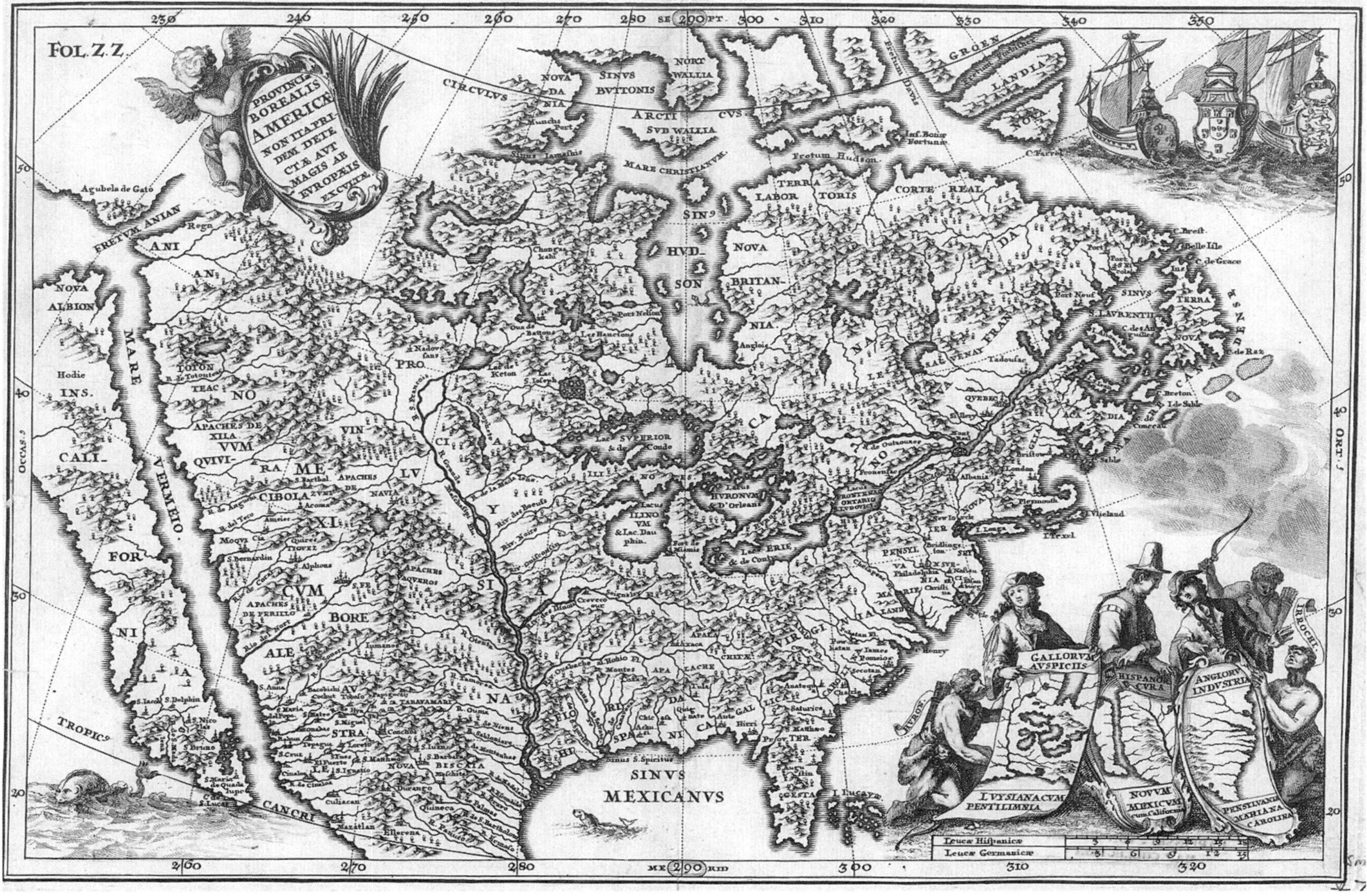

Fig. 4. Provinciae Borealis Americae non itapridem dete ctae avt magis ab europaeis excvitae. Heinrich Scherer. From Scherer's *Geographia Politica*, Munich, 1703.

what we now call Virginia. Their detailed work carefully depicts the numerous islands and Native American villages. The second source was an imaginative depiction of a mythical land named Norumbega. Between the detailed mapping of the Virginia coast and the better known New France north of Cape Breton, Wytfliet followed the lead of other mapmakers of the day who simply filled in the gap with a fanciful land with a made-up name, Norumbega, and even a mythical city located at the fork of two rivers. It would be over a decade before the Hudson River and Long Island became known to Europeans and codified in maps. Until then the mythical land of Norumbega comprised the gap between the Chesapeake Bay and Cape Breton.

The map of 1703 (fig. 4) is both a geographical text and a political document. Its geography shows an improvement over the previous maps of North America. East of the Mississippi the lay of the land has become better known. The coastline from Florida up through Virginia now includes Long Island and New England. An attempt is made to better connect the St. Lawrence to the Great Lakes, which are now shown in greater detail than in any of the earlier maps we have seen of the New World. The Mississippi River is illustrated in approximately correct orientation. West of the great river, geographical knowledge becomes hazy and imprecise. The general area is known as New Mexico, Spanish knowledge of the Southwest is expanded upon to fill in the entire western territory. And California is shown as an island, long a factor in the cosmography of early European explorers and in early maps. In 1541, however, Domingo del Castillo drew a map in which the true nature of the Baja's geography was depicted. The Baja was clearly shown in Castillo's map as a peninsula. Spanish and even some English maps made after 1542 and throughout the sixteenth century reflected the view that the Baja was a peninsula. However, the island myth did not disappear, it was simply in remission. It was resuscitated in the late sixteenth century. The New World was visualized as a collection of islands; the passage to China and the Far East was just waiting to be discovered. In the late 1570s Sir Francis Drake sailed around the world, landing somewhere in California and naming it New Albion. Drake's presence and quick return home made the Spanish believe that perhaps the Gulf of California joined with another ocean to create a Northwest Passage. This belief in a Northwest Passage beyond the tangle of islands to the fabled Far East was espoused by all European merchants, explorers, and governments. By the very early seventeenth century California was again being described as an island. The myth of a California island endured most of the seventeenth century. In 1622 a map of the world by Michiel Colijn marks the first example of the second flowering of the myth. It was not until 1700 when the doughty Jesuit Father Kino, who traveled in the area, published his map of California as a peninsula that the myth was seriously questioned and refuted. It persisted and lingered, but by the middle of the eighteenth century the myth was completely routed.

The map of 1703 is also an explicit and implicit political document. In the bottom right-hand corner of the map a group of people are shown. Three large-scale maps are unfurled. They show the imperial claims of Spain, France, and England. The French claim the Mississippi basin, the English claim the eastern seaboard, while Spain gets California and the West. The North American continent is thus divided up into outposts of the European colonial powers. The map is also an implicitly political document in the way Europeans name the continent. New France, New Spain, and New England are not just geographical descriptions; because acts of naming are also acts of possession and legitimization, and the names become territorial claims. There are some Native American words on the map. It also shows, perhaps for the first time, the name Canada on the map, but this name is located between Nova Britannia and Nova Francia.

By the late eighteenth century it was common knowledge that California was not an island, and the map of 1768 (fig. 5) reflects this understanding. The map locates North America in a wider context, showing, albeit in rudimentary geography, how the continent is close to Asia, if not the Asia depicted in the map of 1540. The map, a polar projection, depicts the Aleutian Islands in some detail, but the entire Pacific Northwest and Alaska are still hazy in outline. The Rockies do not figure at all in this map. The map shows the Asian northeast much more accurately than the North American northwest, which was still relatively unknown and uncharted by European powers. Although the interior of the continent was clearly better known at this time, the Rockies and areas west of them were still largely unknown in the knowledge centers of the East and Europe.

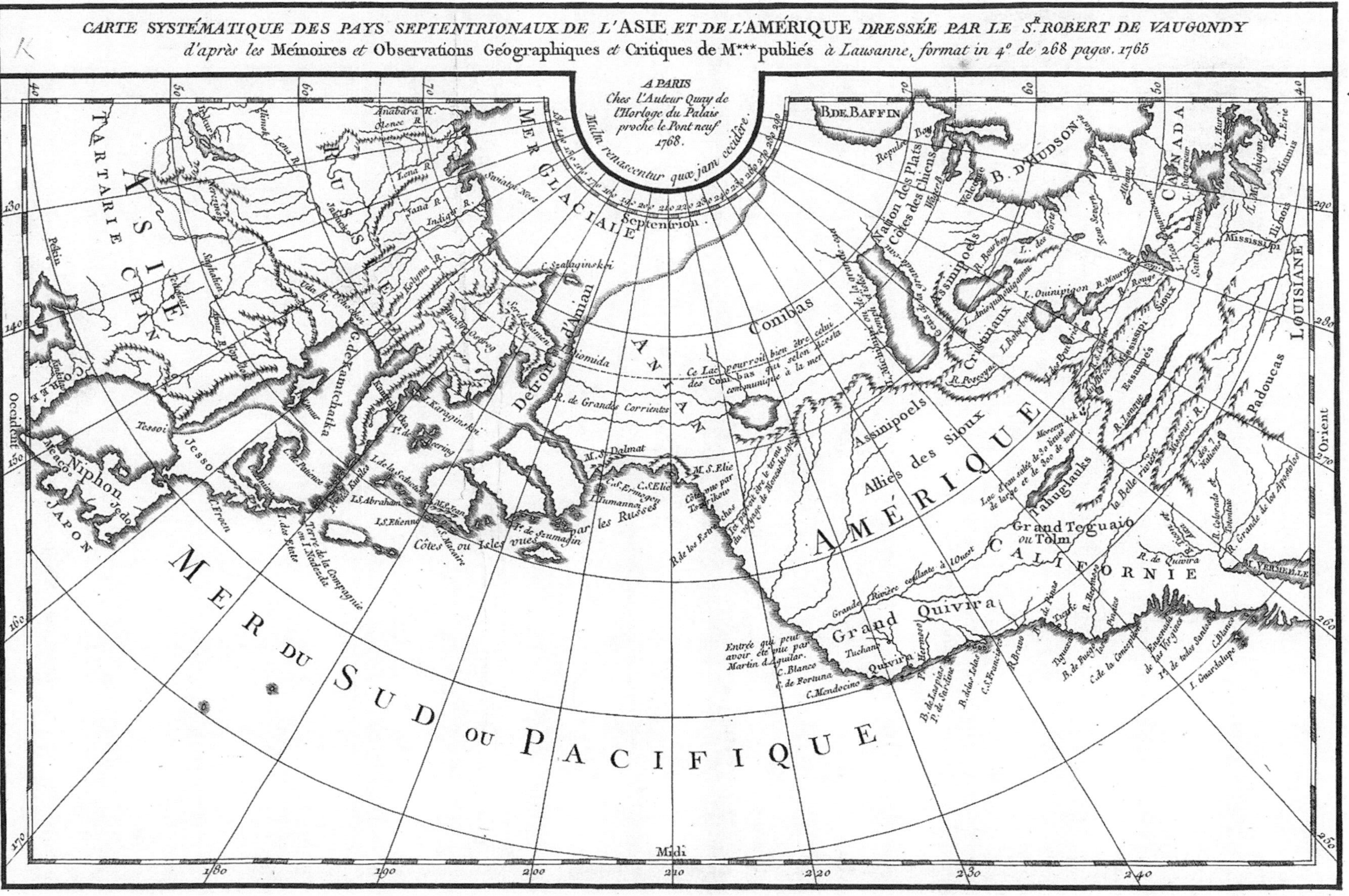

Fig. 5. **Carte systématique des pays septentrionaux de l'Asie et de l'Amérique.** Didier Robert de Vaugondy. Paris, 1768.

THE COLONIES

Maps of colonial North America are more than just descriptions of geographical areas. They are documents of possession, claims to property, and sovereign rights. The New World was claimed in and through maps. They made visible the claim, outlined the possessions, and recorded territory involved and colonization. The maps tell a story of a land already settled, the people there, how it was taken over, resettled, renamed, and brought into a wider sphere of trade and power. The maps show a contested space and the creation of a new geography. Colonial maps reflect both victory and loss, possession and dispossession, the coming of a new order.

The maps shown here are taken from the seventeenth and eighteenth centuries and show colonies along the eastern seaboard and in the interior. These maps are not just depictions of territory. They are rhetorical devices that act as claims of possession and sometimes enticements to other potential settlers. The names that speak of the Old World, such as New England and New France, were ways to both claim the new land and make it appealing to future settlers. The "New" gives a sense of promise and hope, the European name a sense of continuity and order.

Although the map of Virginia and Florida (fig. 6) is dated 1671, it draws on the information contained in older maps and reports. This was a common feature of early maps. They would repeat previous maps, mistakes and all. Maps were continually printed but only occasionally updated. This late-seventeenth-century map draws on the late-sixteenth-century reports of the

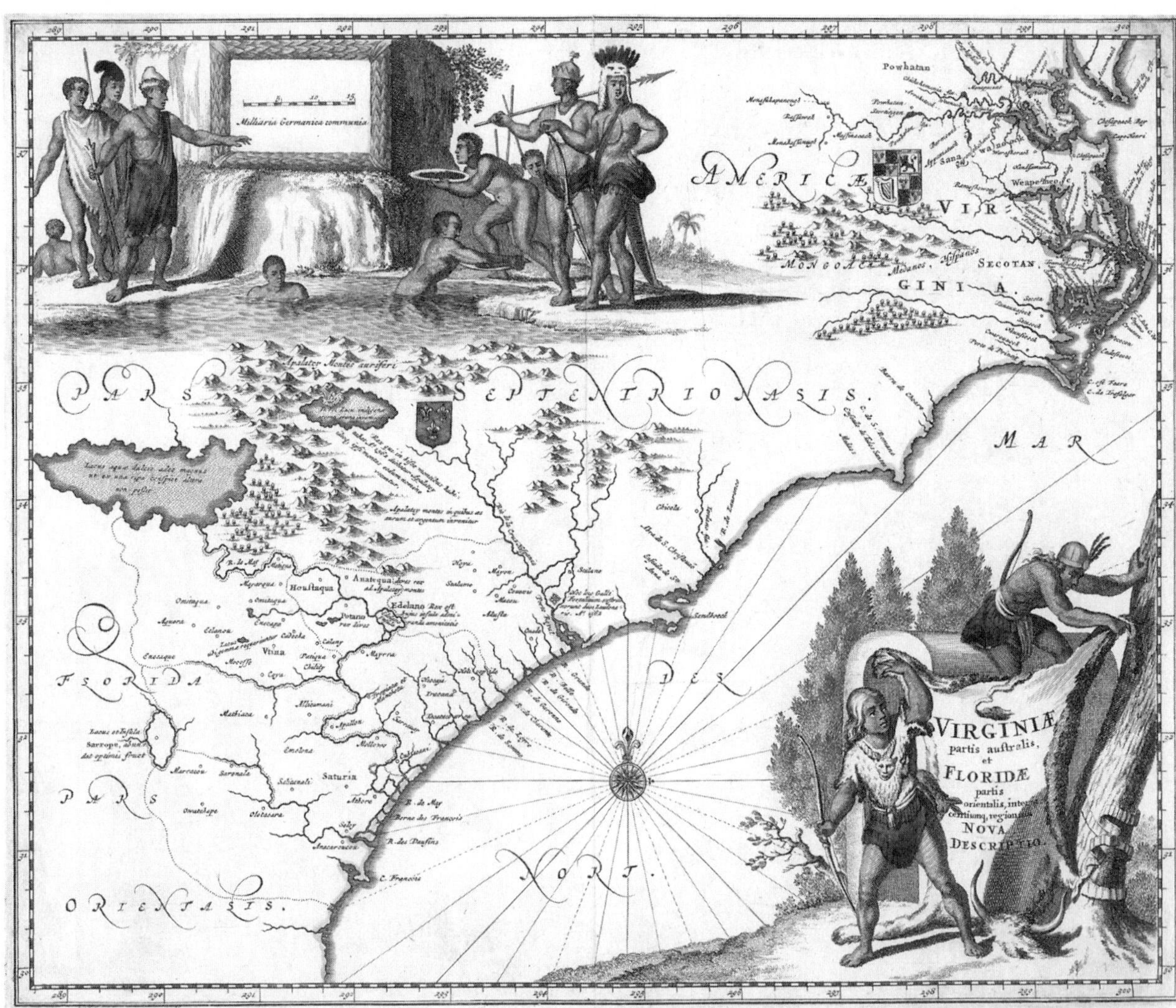

Fig. 6. Virginiae partis australis, et Floridae partis orientalis, interjacentiumq regionum Nova Descriptio. Arnoldus Montanus. A copy of the 1640 map by Willem Janszoon Blaeu, this version appeared in Montanus' *De Nieuwe en Onbekende Weereld*, Amsterdam, 1671, and in John Ogilby's *America*, London, 1676.

Englishman John White and Frenchman Jacques Le Moyne. White had made illustrations and maps on his travels to Virginia and Le Moyne had traveled with the French expedition to Florida from 1562 to 1565. Their reports and maps were the basis of a map produced in 1606. The map of 1671 is a later version of this earlier map. It shows the careful delineation of the Virginia coastline, based on the work of White. Further south, on the coast, building on the work of Le Moyne, it shows the French fort at Porto Royale. In between these better known areas, the coast is only lightly annotated, indicating the general lack of information about this region.

The earliest European settlements in North America were concentrated on the coast. A coastal location was vital to maintain the necessary links and ties with the mother country. As a general rule, European knowledge decreased further away from the coast. The Appalachian Mountains are shown inland, as well as two great lakes. The depiction hints at firm geographic realities, but the overall picture is still hazy. Inland from the better known coastal areas, myth and fancy coincided with distant reports and vague knowledge.

The map indicates a land already peopled and settled. The cartouches in the bottom right and top left of the map show Native Americans and the map is littered with the names of tribes, such as the Powhatan and Secotan in Virginia, and villages such as Saturia and Seloy in Florida. This was not an empty land.

The map of Virginia and Maryland (fig. 7) was published in the 1676 edition of John Speed's geography text *A Prospect of the Most Famous Parts of the World.* It is oriented with the west at the top. It is an extremely detailed account of the coast and immediate coastal areas. The indentations of the Chesapeake Bay are carefully delineated. Notice how English names proliferate around the bay, names such as Anne Arundel, Baltimore, Charles. This is a land that has been occupied. There is still evidence of the continued presence of Native Americans; in the bottom right of the map the names of Native American tribes, the Minquaa and Tockwoghs, are indi-

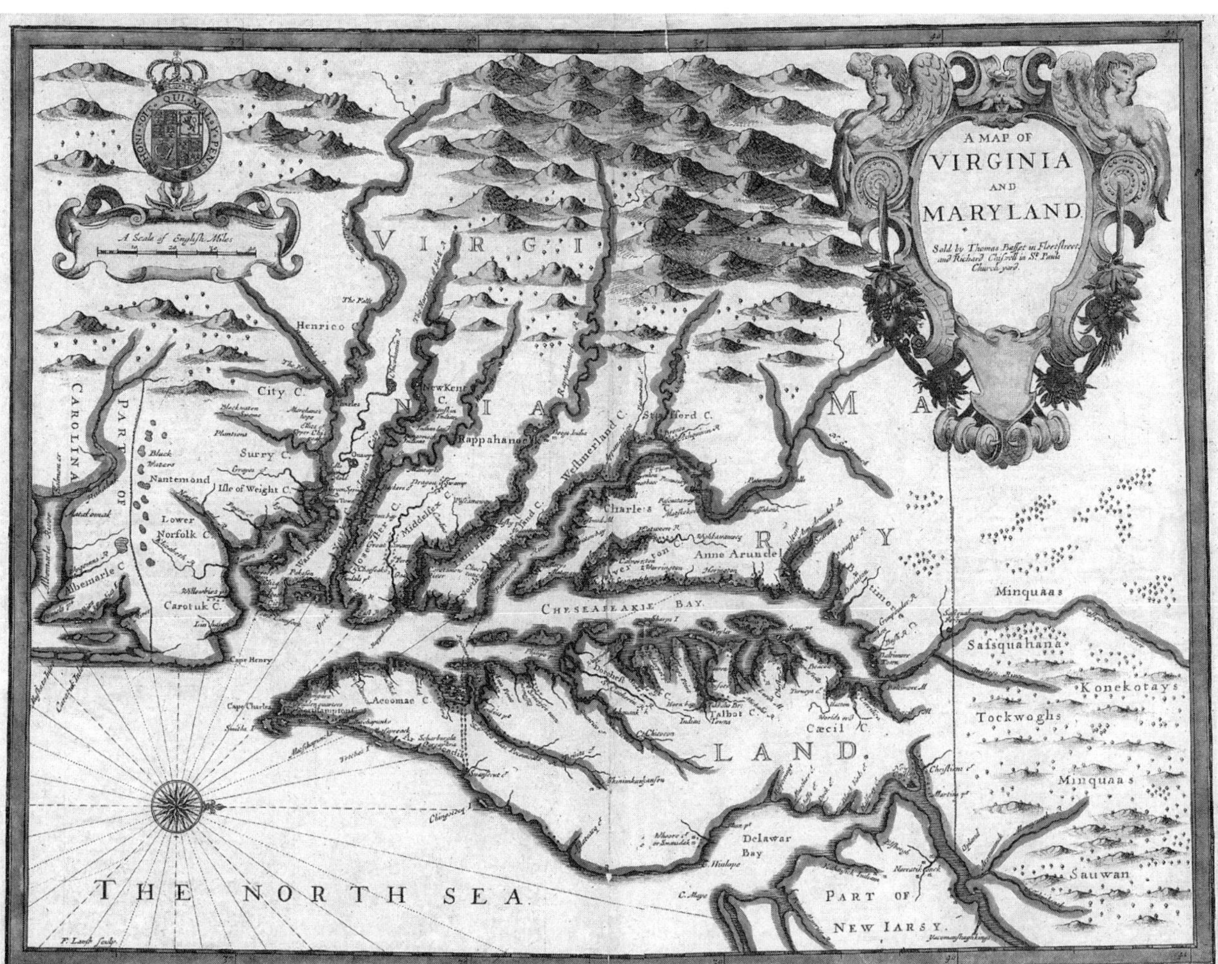

Fig. 7. A Map of Virginia and Maryland. John Speed. From an edition of his *A Prospect of the Most Famous Parts of the World,* London, 1671.

cated. But they are being pushed toward the edge of the map.

The layout of the map emphasizes the coastal areas, the main area of English control and presence. Inland the geography becomes hazy. The mapmakers use a large illustration, elaborate cartouches, and scales to fill in the interior space—all useful devices to conceal a lack of knowledge. Further from the coast the land is scarcely known; it is mainly imagined. Compared to the previous map this one records the increasing presence of the colonists in their renaming of the land and their positioning of boundary lines that divide up Carolina, Virginia, and Maryland. Their presence is still restricted to the safe haven of the coast. Further inland the colonists' ability to colonize and map is severely restricted.

The map of New England shown here (fig. 8) was the first one printed in North America; it is a truly American map. It is a large-scale map of the New England coastal area from Connecticut to Maine. The map was part of William Hubbard's book *Narrative of the Troubles with the Indians in New England* published in 1677. Hubbard was a minister and acting president of Harvard College. The title of the book speaks to the contested space that was New England at that time as colonists moved into land occupied by Native Americans. The map shows the typical coastal orientation of the early European settlements and the toponymy of the colonies embodied in such names as Deerfield, Weymouth, and Newhaven. The map also indicates Native American land holdings: Pequod Country, Naraganset, and Nipmuk are all represented. The map indicates both the causes of the conflict, with Native American inhabitants and colonists now competing for the same territory, as well as the resultant struggles. The key in the upper right of the map tells us that the numbers beside the names of towns and villages refer to the number of assaults by Indians. The map records, quite literally, the struggle between Native Americans and the colonists. It was a struggle for land and survival.

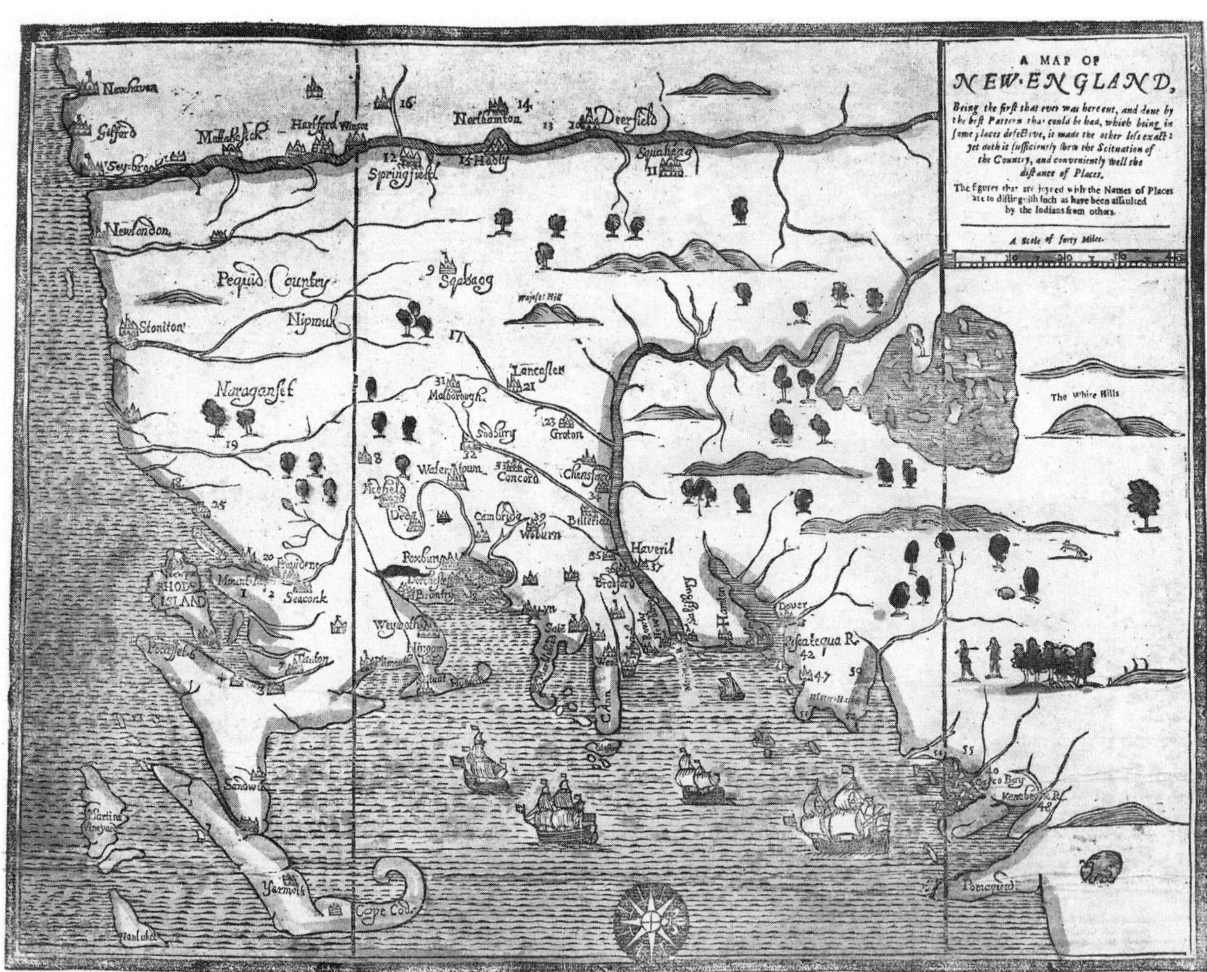

Fig. 8. A Map of New England, Being the first that was ever here cut . . . John Foster. From William Hubbard's *A Narrative of the Troubles with the Indians in New England,* Boston, 1677.

John Seller also represents the conflict between colonizers and Native Americans in his map of New England (fig. 9). First published in 1676 and reprinted with minor changes at least three more times, this map is a later variant. It depicts a broader sweep of New England than the previous map and the orientation is traditional, with north at the top, whereas the previous map was oriented with west at the top. This map takes us further into the interior and is more detailed. The landscape is dotted with hills, trees, and native animals: A turkey is depicted, as are deer, beaver, and wolves. This suggests a rich country, an often used technique in colonial maps to encourage more settlers to leave their home country. It also provides us with a picture of the ecology of the time, a well-wooded landscape rich in wildlife. That land is also a shared space. The map indicates at various places the presence of different peoples: "The Mohawks Country," "The Connecticuts Country," and "The Mohegans Country." But more prominent than these are the labels "*Plymouth Colony*" and "*Connecticut Colony*" as well as very English names such as Cape Ann and Elizabeth Isle. And at the top of the map the English crown appears, indicating the sovereign power in this land.

In the area marked as Plymouth Colony, just north of Rhode Island, a patch of land is referred to as "King Phillip Country." King Philip was chief of the Wampagnoag Indians. In 1675 he led an uprising against the colonists. The previous map indicated the extent of casualties among settlers. Part of King Philip's War is also depicted on this map; just east of the Connecticut River an encounter between Native Americans and settlers is illustrated. It is probably a reference to the defense of Hadley on 1 September 1675.

Seller's map depicts a New World rich in wildlife, with settlers moving into the territory of Native Americans. The resultant conflict is also vividly shown on the map. The map tells the story of a place of tension, a source of conflict. In August 1676 King Philip was killed. Native American resistance did not end, but his

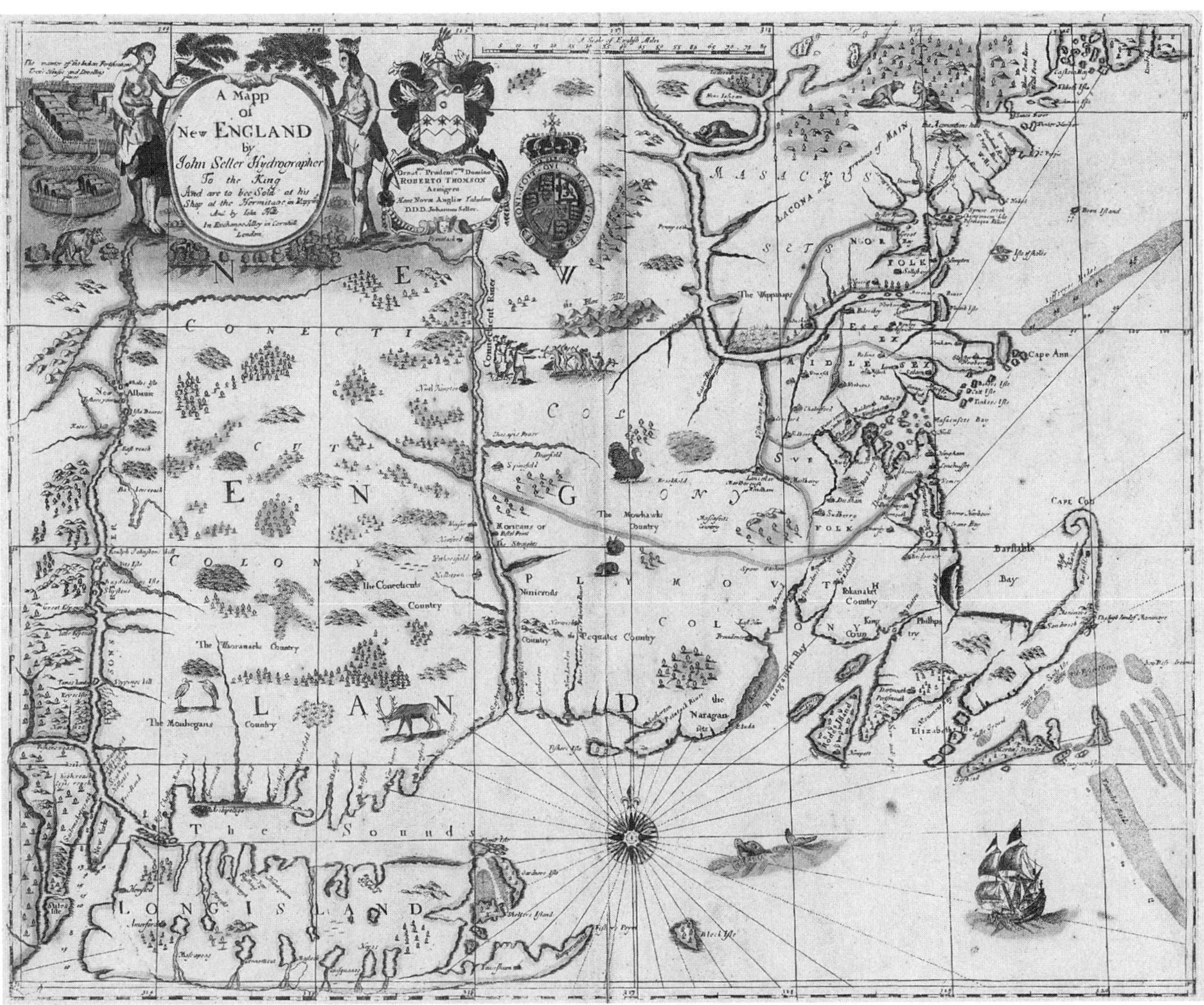

Fig. 9. **A Mapp of New England by John Seller Hydrographer to the King.** London, c. 1676.

death and the defeat of the uprising marked the beginning of the end of Native American control of land in New England.

By 1722 the map of New England (fig. 10) shows no trace of a Native American presence. What is shown is a landscape populated with English towns. Few indications of a Native American presence can be identified. "The Mohawks Country," "The Connecticuts Country," and "The Mohegans Country" have all but disappeared into the anglicized landscape.

The map also represents the separate English "plantations" as a connected whole. Plantations means English settlements rather than specific forms of agricultural production. The map visualizes the separate colonies as one whole: from New England down to Carolina with inserts of Nova Scotia, Jamaica, Bermuda, and Barbados. The map shows the English maritime empire. There were links between them: Slaves were brought from Africa to the sugar islands of Barbados, Bermuda, and Jamaica as well as the colonies of Carolina, Virginia, and Maryland. Sugar and tobacco were shipped back to Britain, and agricultural produce as well as pelts and furs also traveled from the more northerly colonies to Britain. The colonies were a vital part of a system that linked them with Britain and Africa in a triangular trade route. On one page the colonies are shown as a coherent imperial presence linked by commerce. Trade and shared sovereignty are the cement that binds these disparate areas. The map of 1722 is a map of Britain's North American commercial empire.

Hermann Moll's map of New England, New York, New Jersey, and Pennsylvania from 1736 (fig. 11) shows evidence of an expanding colony. The map now covers a larger area than just a narrow coastal fringe; colonists and thus British power are moving further inland. The area around the coast has been won. Now the expanding frontier is further inland. In western Pennsylvania and the upper Hudson the map records Iroquois, Mohawk, and Oneida tribes. And further north, Lake Champlain indicates the boundary with New France. The expand-

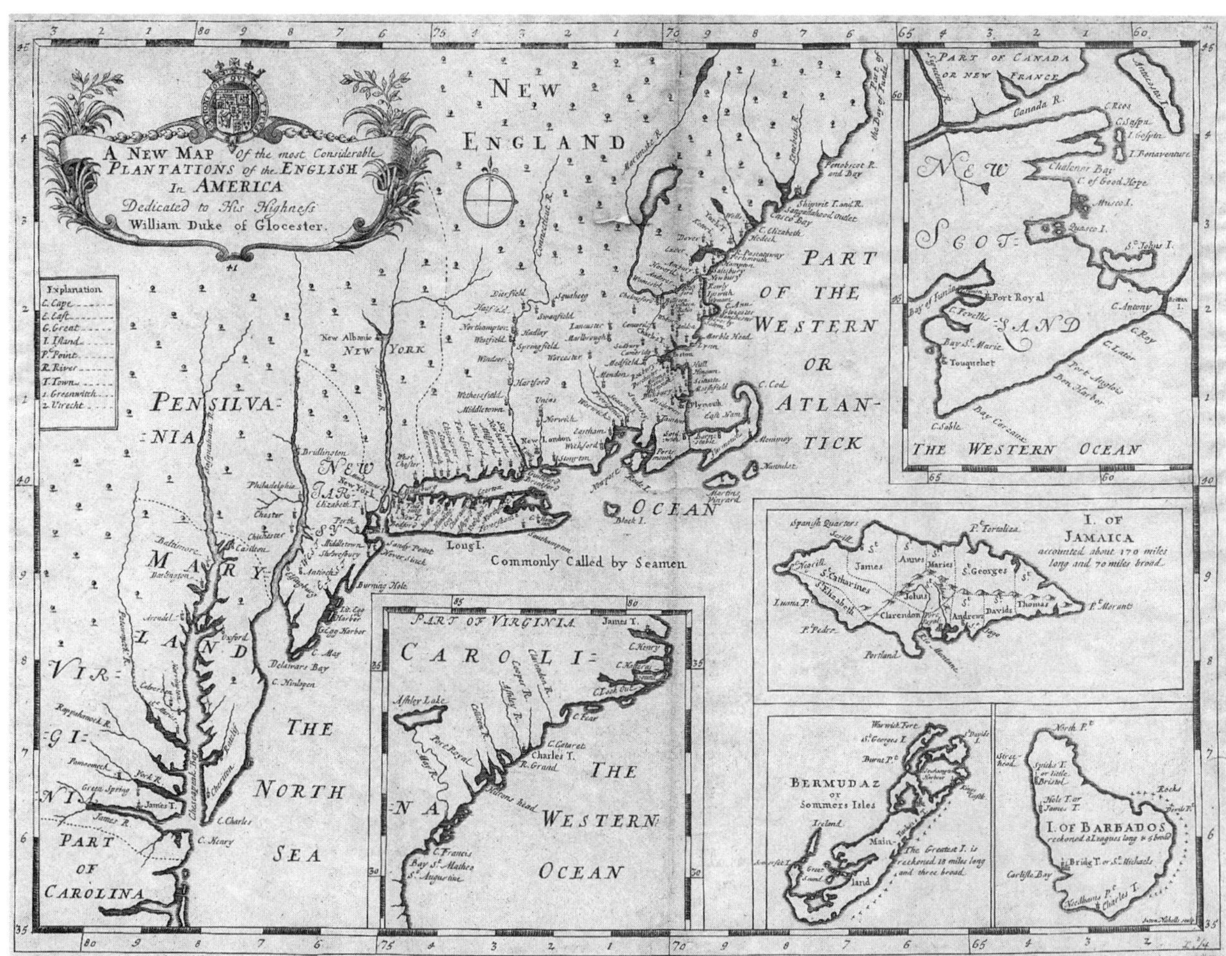

Fig. 10. A New Map of the Most Considerable Plantations of the English in America Dedicated to His Highness William Duke of Glocester. Edward Wells. From an edition of his *A New Sett of Maps, Both of Ancient and Present Geography,* London, 1722.

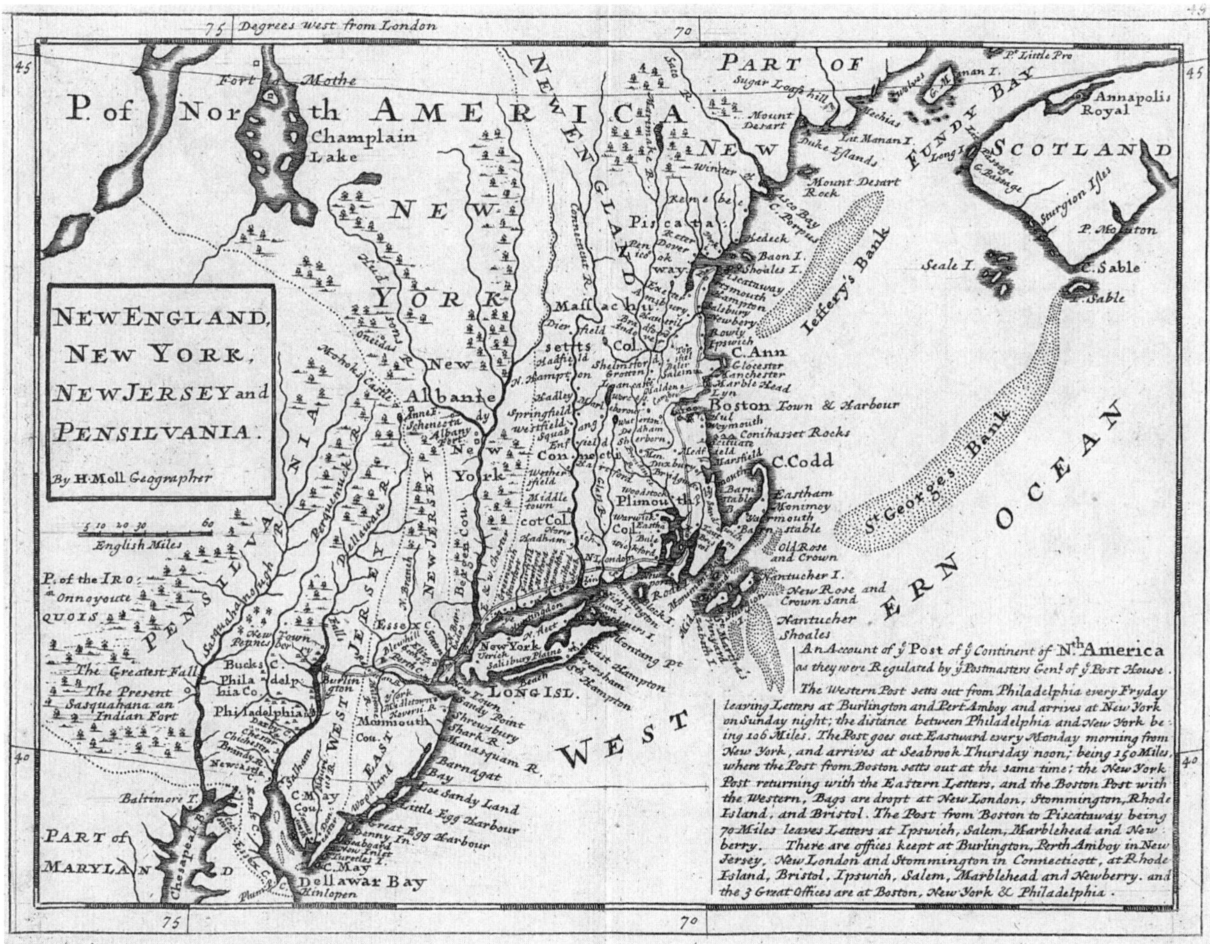

Fig. 11. New England, New York, New Jersey and Pensilvania. By H. Moll Geographer. An Account of ye Post of ye Continent of Nth. America as they were Regulated by ye Postmasters Genl of ye Post House. From an edition of Herman Moll's *Atlas Minor*, London, 1736.

ing colony is confronting new forces, new sources of conflict and tension. Inside the colony the map records the creation of an integrated society. The written account in the bottom right-hand corner of the map refers to the creation and operation of a postal service that links the main centers of Boston, New York, and Philadelphia with smaller centers around the territory. Postal service both reflects and embodies linkages between different parts of what once were separate colonies. The separate colonies are becoming more connected with the beginnings of a coherent identity, a distinctly American community still reliant on the mother country but showing the first signs of a separate identity, a North American colonial character.

The "accurate map of the English colonies" dating from 1754 (fig. 12) is less an accurate topography and more a geopolitical claim. If you look carefully you can see the boundary of each colony as dotted lines. They begin on the coast and move inland, uninterrupted in many cases to the edge of the map. The southern boundary of Virginia, for example, begins on the Atlantic coast south of Cape Henry and moves inland, through what the map refers to as the "Apalachy Mountains" and beyond the Ohio River to the west of the map. These boundaries are claims for the interior that was yet to be settled. They should be seen in the light of imperial conflict with France and Spain, the hazy nature of what was known about the interior, and which power had not only the better claim but also the military wherewithal to assert it.

Close to the coast the geography is more accurately portrayed. The coastline is recorded in some detail and the careful depiction of river mouths and coastal settlements indicate the nature of English settlement in the New World colonies; it was concentrated on the coast, where easier transport to and from the imperial center was possible. The inland waterways are described, probably through information provided by river-borne explorers and Native American informants, but south of the Great Lakes the interior is only comprehended in part.

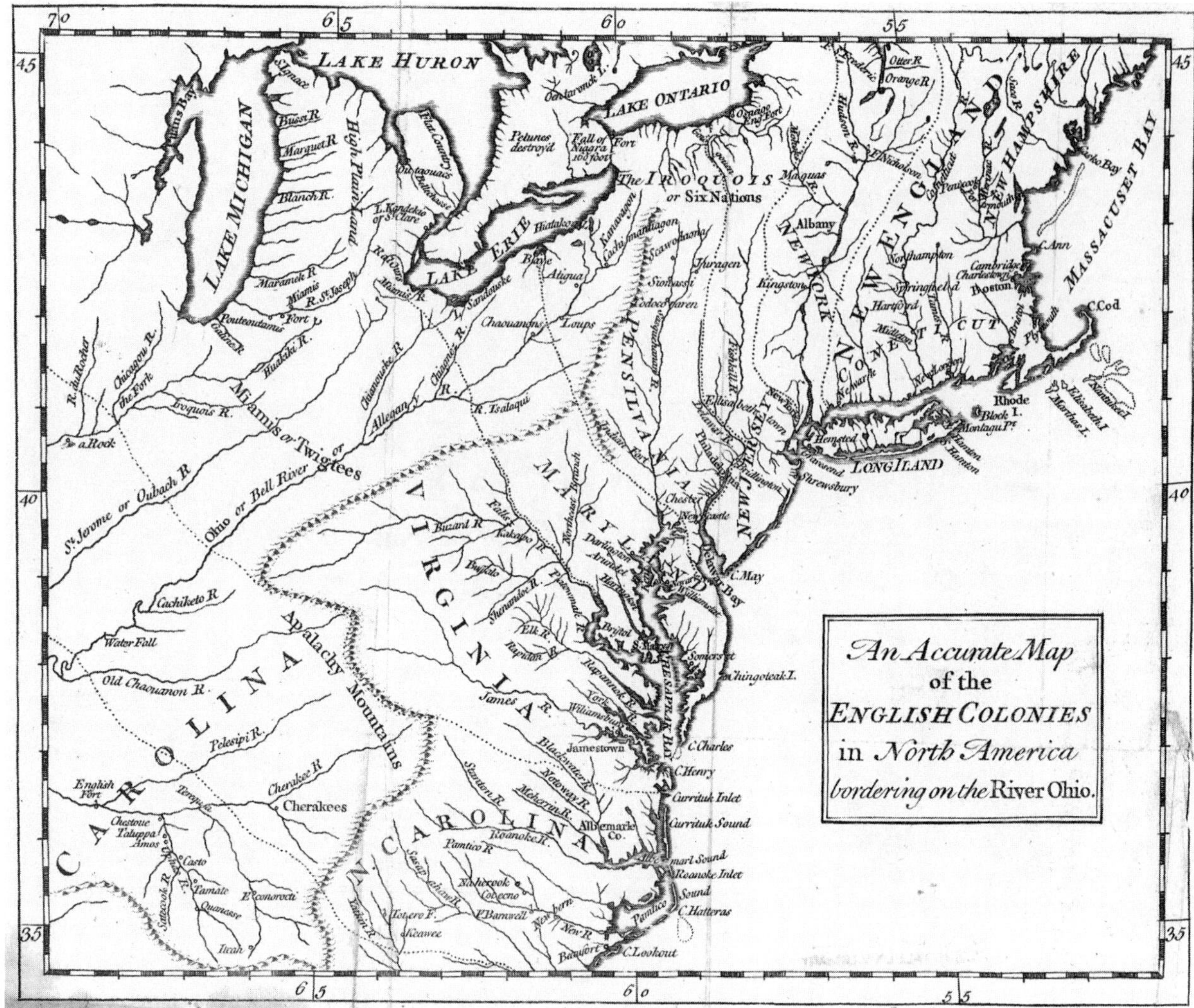

Fig. 12. An Accurate Map of the English Colonies in North America bordering on the River Ohio. From the *Universal Magazine* of December 1754.

Just south of Lake Ontario, the map records the presence of the Iroquois and accords them the dignity of the title "Six Nations." The Iroquois were a powerful force in the entire region, in control of much of the fur trade and vital allies in the struggle against France. In London the English wanted to maintain a strong alliance with the Iroquois. In colonial America, however, many of the English looked on Iroquois territory with envy and land-longing.

EXPLORATION OF THE AMERICAN CONTINENT

The North American continent was explored from various directions. The English moved inland from their footholds on the eastern seaboard, the Spanish ventured north from their empire in Mexico, while the French explored west along the St. Lawrence Seaway and south through the Mississippi. Priests and traders, soldiers and adventurers undertook these explorations over many years. European knowledge of the continent was gained fitfully and erratically, with knowledge not often shared among rival imperial powers. In this section we will consider maps produced in both manuscript and printed form, and both French and English maps, that span almost a hundred years. They show the encroachment of European power and influence further and further inland. The mapping of the interior was both a claim to sovereignty over the indigenous peoples as well as an act of imperial enlargement. To map the continent was to claim the continent.

The French manuscript map from 1683 shown here (fig. 13) records part of the Mississippi. Successive French explorers had used the great river to explore the interior. In May 1673 the fur trader Louis Jolliet and the Jesuit priest Father Jacques Marquette, along with five guides, canoed down the Mississippi River. They traveled over 600 miles and got as far as the Arkansas River, the present-day northern Louisiana border. Nine years later the French explorer Sieur de La Salle managed to reach the Gulf of Mexico.

The manuscript map is an itinerary map; it records the journey down the river as the explorers encountered the people and places. It is not drawn to accurate scale and there are no latitude and longitude. It simply represents the journey down the river.

The map draws attention to three main elements. First, it highlights the Native American presence, recording the names of the tribes and villages. Knowledge of

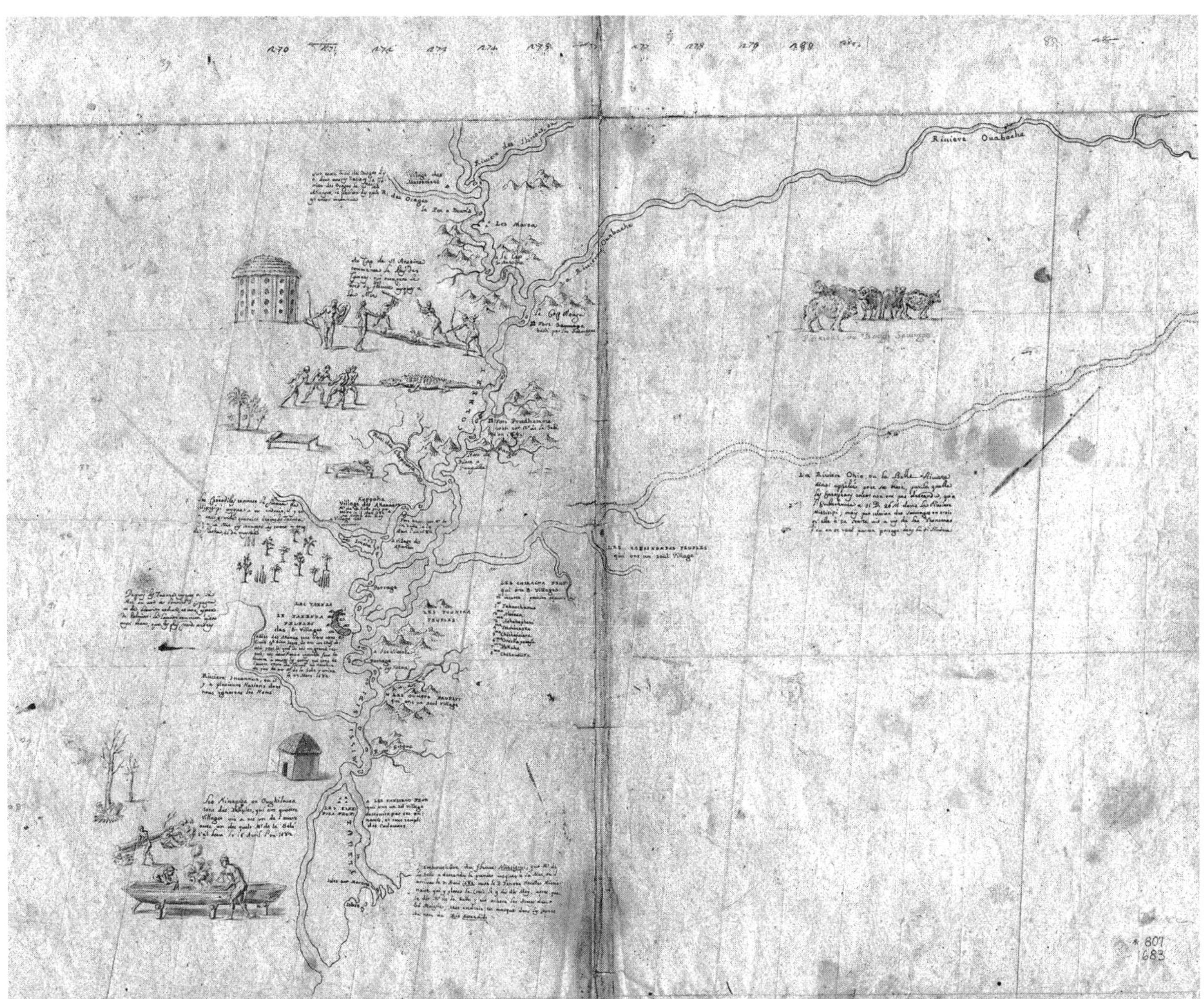

Fig. 13. Unidentified French manuscript map of the Mississippi River, c. 1683.

the local people was essential in order to conduct trade and commerce. The French were very keen to establish both commercial trade and political alliances with the local people. French intentions were less about colonizing the land than about extending their trade and broadening political alliances against the English and Spanish. The Native Americans were also souls to be converted. Missionaries played an important part in many of the French explorations. The search for land was also a search for converts to Catholicism. Second, at various stages the word *portage* is mentioned. These are references to places where canoes could be carried across land to save time and reduce distance. The map is like a present-day road map that highlights shortcuts. Finally, the map also records the French presence. At a number of stages the map identifies forts such as Fort Prudhomme, established by La Salle in 1682.

John Senex's 1721 map of Louisiana and the Mississippi River (fig. 14) is in fact a direct copy of a French map, produced by the cartographer Guillaume de L'Isle, that codified much of the reports and maps of previous French explorers of the Great Lakes and the Mississippi River. The great river basin is shown in its entirety. The text is both a history and geography as it records previous explorations as well as recent events. Thus, below Lake Erie under the label *The Nation du Chat* (note the French name giving a clue to its origin) de L'Isle notes that "it was destroyed by the Iroquois." The river basin is a scene of conflict and struggle; the key at the bottom of the map identifies nations that have been destroyed. The map records in great detail Native American villages and tribes. Further west the information is scantier, and although New Mexico is recognized, the outline of the Rockies is only hinted at.

Fig. 14. A Map of Louisiana and of the River Mississippi. John Senex. From *A New General Atlas*, London, 1721. Based on a 1718 map by Guillaume de L'Isle.

The map's strongest details refer to either side of the river system, the main point of French exploration and trade. The further from the river, the less reliable the information.

The map is also a political document. *Louisiana* is written in broad letters across the entire basin. The English colonies are compressed along the eastern seaboard.

De L'Isle's map drew on the observations of French explorers, priests, and traders. They had traveled along the rivers of the Mississippi basin, and the compilation of their knowledge led to de Isle's map being the most accurate one of the river system to date. It was immensely influential and was used as a template for almost fifty years. Thomas Jefferson had a copy of the map, and it was an important source of information for the later Lewis and Clark expedition.

The map presents a picture of a huge river basin in French possession inhabited by a variety of Native American nations with the British claims sidelined to the eastern coast.

The map entitled *Carte de la Louisiane* (fig. 15) is a later version of the de L'Isle map. In contrast to the English version, this map, published in 1730 like the de L'Isle original, notes underneath Carolina that the area was named in honor of Charles of France. This is a subtle way of undermining English claims and reinforcing French ones. The Senex map dropped this French claim. The French map also contains an insert of the mouth of the Mississippi River showing the recently established city of New Orleans. A French merchant company founded the city in 1718. Blocked in the east by the English colonies, the great river was the trading outlet of the French inland trading empire. The new city of New Orleans was founded the same year that the original de L'Isle map was published. Both represented French attempts to legitimize and secure their hold over the interior of North America.

This map draws on the observations, maps, and writings of French explorers, priests, and traders, including Bourgmont, Marquette, Louis Joliet, La Salle, Sieur Vermale, Father Jacob Le Maire, and Louis Hennepin.

Fig. 15. Carte de la Louisiane et du Cours du Mississippi. Guillaume de L'Isle. From *Atlas Noveau,* Amsterdam: Covens and Mortier, 1730. A version of de L'Isle's map of 1718.

They had all traveled extensively along the rivers of the Mississippi basin. The explorers were dependent on Native Americans to find their way and help them survive. Indian tribal names and the location of their villages were thus of supreme importance.

French economic interests lay primarily in the fur trade. They traded with the Indians and thus needed specific knowledge of their trading partners. The Indian presence is richly detailed on the map.

French interests as opposed to British holdings also guided the making of this map. Note how the British possessions are limited to the coast and surrounded by a solid wall of French possessions. The map is a record of French claims and explorations beyond the Appalachians.

The map completed in 1761 (fig. 16) is a more detailed and accurate representation of the mouth of the Mississippi River. This was a low-lying swampy area where it was often difficult to differentiate between land and water, making it hard to navigate. It was a watery wilderness. As the map records at one point, "shallow water with many small islands, very little known." Although the map is written in English it draws heavily on Spanish and French influences. The phrase "according to the Spanish charts" is used at least twice. From 1699 until 1762, first as a merchant company outpost and later as a royal province, the area was under French control. That French influence is apparent in the names on the map. It is an influence that has endured to the present in the area of this map.

The map covers an area with an interesting history as well as a relatively unknown geography. French speakers in the northern colonies of New France were pawns in the great imperial struggle between France and Britain. Beginning in 1754 they were routed from what is now Nova Scotia, but was then called Arcadia. Many of the Arcadians settled in the bayou country of the map. It provided an empty space in which to locate a displaced people. The Arcadians became the Cajuns with their distinctive language (a mixture of old provincial French and English), music, and cuisine. The watery wilderness became the setting for the formation of a uniquely American culture.

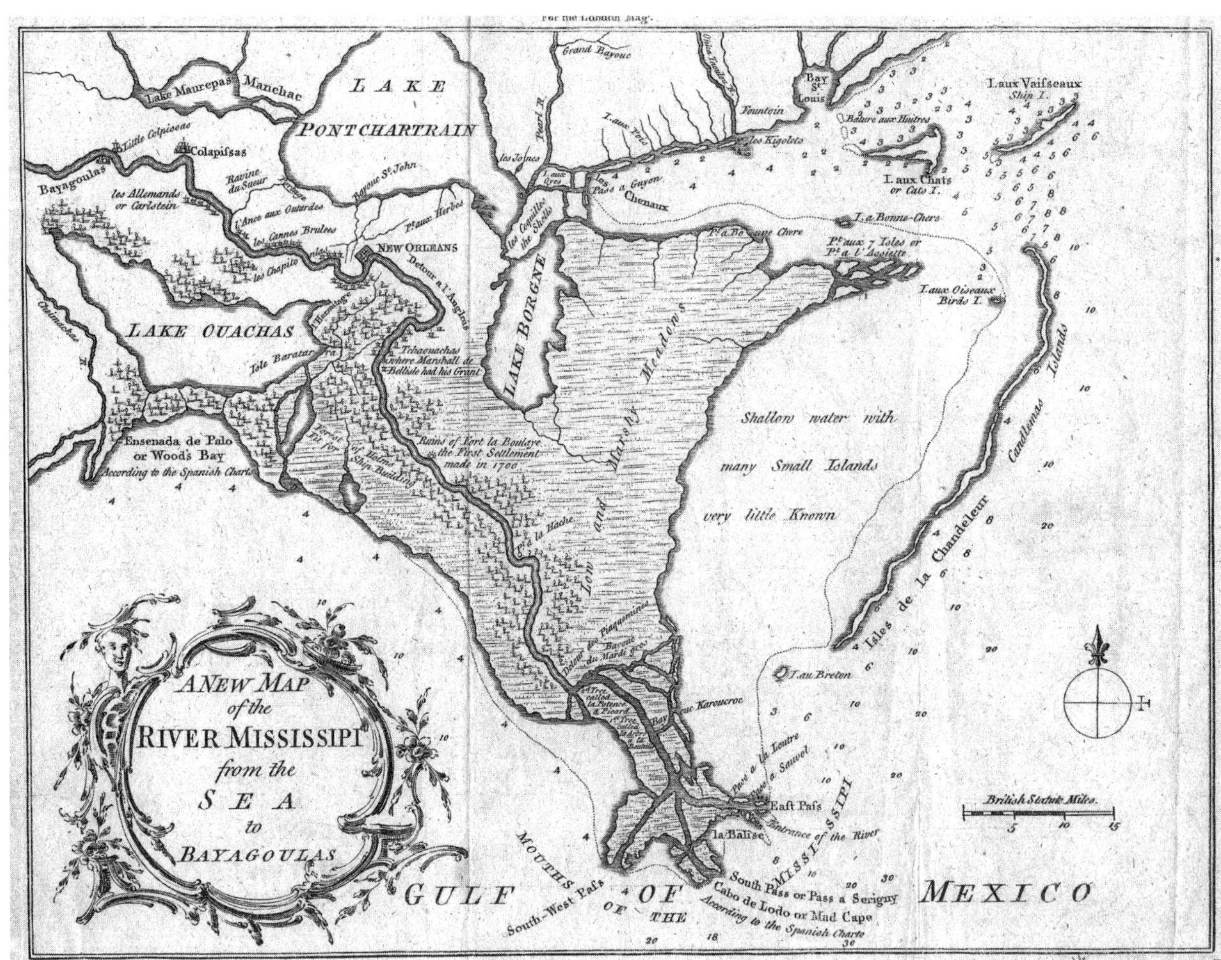

Fig. 16. A New Map of the River Mississippi from the Sea to Bayagoulas. From the *London Magazine* of March 1761.

Thomas Kitchin's map of 1765 (fig. 17) was printed after the end of the Seven Years War as it was called in Europe, also known as the French and Indian War in North America. It was a global conflict between Britain and France that was fought in Europe, Asia, and America. In North America it gave colonial gentleman like George Washington valuable wartime experience.

The British won the war and at the peace treaty signed in Paris in 1763, France ceded its North American possessions. It kept the valuable sugar islands of Martinique and Guadeloupe but gave up claims to New France and lands in the interior of North America. The land that had been explored by La Salle, Hennepin, and Le Maire and that had been mapped by de L'Isle now fell into the hands of the British. The cartouche proudly proclaims that "Louisiana, as formerly claimed by FRANCE and now containing parts of British America to the east." The great river basin of the Mississippi had been redistributed: land to the east of the river was now British, that to the west was Spanish.

The landscape of the map is populated with Native American tribes. All along the river Native American tribal names and villages are shown; further east at the edge of the map the British colonial presence is recorded in anglicized names. Between the two, the British colonies and the Native American basin, there is a gap, a lack of connection. This would not last for long as westward expansion from British colonies would soon come up against the Native American presence.

This map was published in the *London Magazine.* In the eighteenth century periodicals flourished. They published articles describing colonial struggles and imperial rivalries. Maps accompanied articles that described military campaigns, battles, and imperial struggles around the world. For the moment, two years after the Paris Treaty, readers of the magazine must have felt that British control of the land east of the Mississippi looked secure, the enduring fruits of an epic struggle with their old European rival, the French.

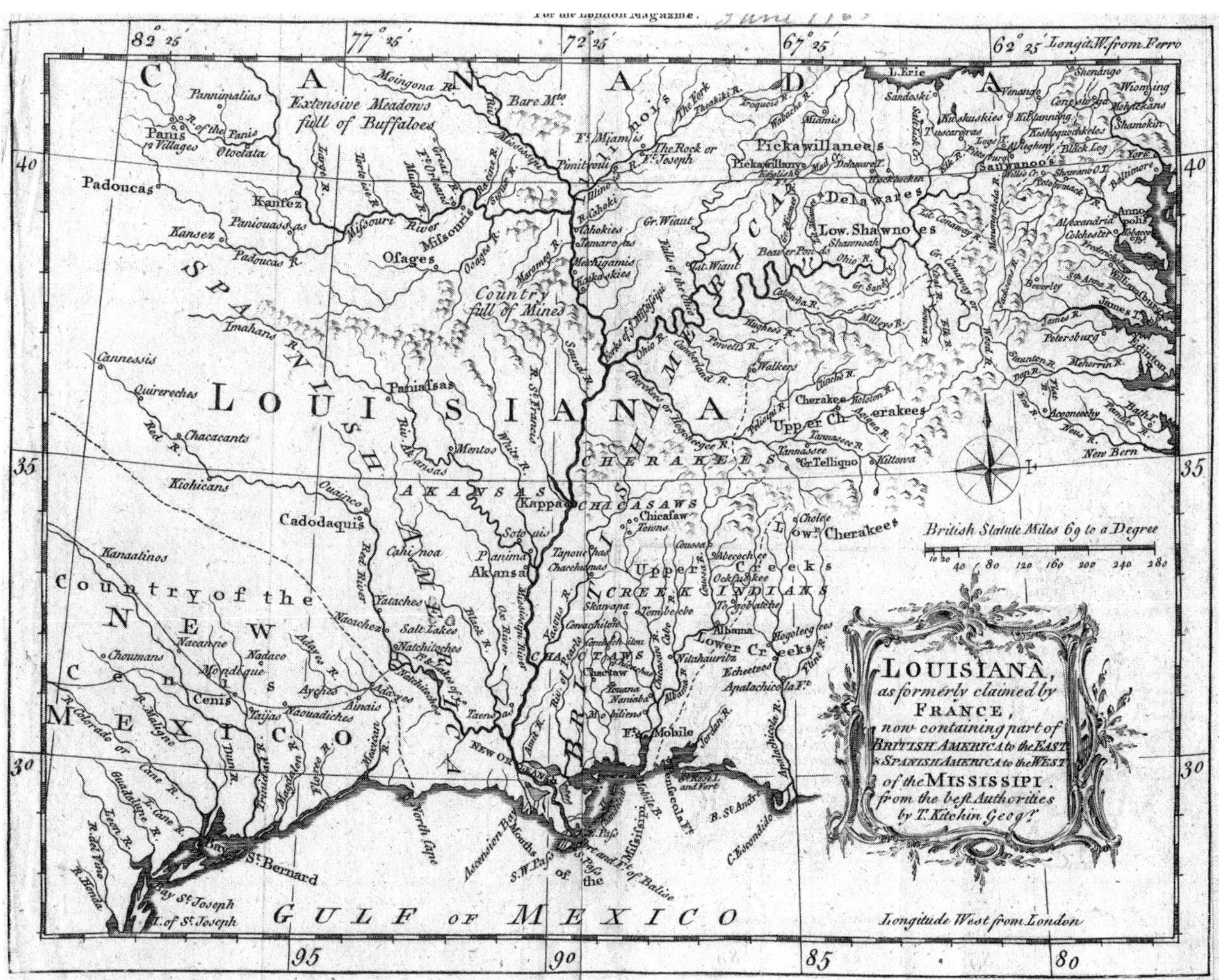

Fig. 17. **Louisiana, as formerly claimed by France, and now containing part of British America to the East & Spanish America to the West of the Mississipppi.** Thomas Kitchin. From the *London Magazine* of June 1765.

Sometimes maps tell us a great deal by what they do not show. The map completed in 1772 (fig. 18) is revealing in its inaccuracies. Hazy and imprecise, this map of the West Coast of North America lacks any real understanding of the region. The old established Spanish presence is apparent in the detail devoted to *Nova Granada* in the southern region of the map. And there is evidence of some reliance on sailing reports for the names of islands, capes, and bays are recorded on the California coast. However, in general terms it is a map that relies more on outdated historical evidence and old maps. The label *Nova Albion*, for example, is a reminder of Sir Francis Drake's trip around the world, from 1577 to 1580. In 1570 he anchored near Coos Bay in Oregon and when he returned home, the English claim to the land was noted in maps by the name New Albion. The use of this name persisted for over two hundred years.

This map shows only the names of coastal features. Although the name Sierra Nevada is noted, the interior is more of a blank space. There is no indication of the region's geography. The map is revealing because of its lack of information. Even as late as 1772 the western area of North America was little known.

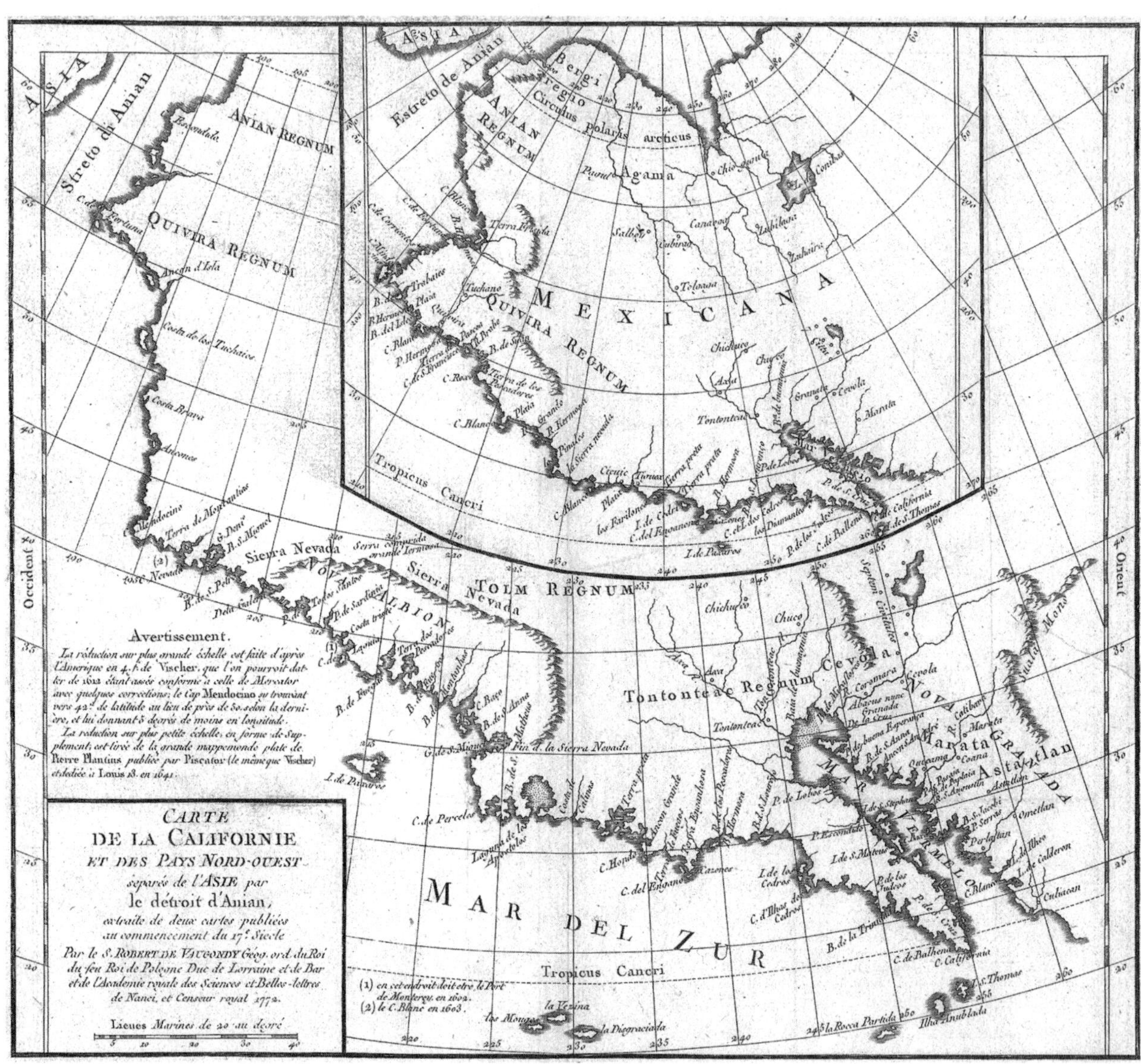

Fig. 18. Carte de la Californie et des Pays Nord-ouest separés de l'Asie par le détroit d'Anian. Didier Robert de Vaugondy, 1772.

COLONIAL WARS

In the eighteenth century Britain and France fought for global supremacy. The struggle unfolded in Europe, Asia, and the Americas. The competition between the two European powers became a global war as they fought each other in and over colonial holdings spread across the world.

Throughout most of the first half of the eighteenth century Britain and France competed and fought over territory in North America. The result of wars in Europe could mean a restructuring of colonial possessions. At the Treaty of Utrecht in 1713, after the War of the Spanish Succession, France ceded Nova Scotia, Newfoundland, and Hudson's Bay to the British. The agreement still left a large amount of land in the interior unaccounted for and hence the subject of continual conflict and friction, as in King George's War of 1744 to 1748. And conflict in North America could ignite global conflict. When George Washington, then a major in the Virginia militia, fired on a French reconnaissance force close to Fort Duquesne in 1753, it was the opening rounds in what became the Seven Years War. In North America this same conflict was referred to as the French and Indian War, which lasted from 1754 to 1763. As Voltaire noted at the time, "A cannon shot fired in America, set Europe in a blaze." The colonial wars were struggles over local territory as well as part of a broader struggle for European dominance and global supremacy.

We will consider three maps that first saw the light of day as illustrations in British journals. The eighteenth century saw an increase in the number of journals and magazines. Journals such as the *Gentleman's Magazine*, *London Magazine*, *Scots Magazine*, and *Universal Magazine* all printed maps as illustrations to articles. The maps of the colonial struggles informed readers of the fighting

Fig. 19. Plan of the City & Fortifications of Louisburg, from a Survey made by Richard Gridley, Lieut. Col. of the Train of Artillery in 1745 [with] A Plan of the City and Harbour of Louisburg. From the *Universal Magazine* of May 1758. A reduced copy of the original published by Thomas Jefferys in 1757.

taking place in distant lands. The maps of colonial wars provided a domestic audience with an understanding of overseas events.

French settlers founded Louisburg in 1713 in what is now northeastern Cape Breton Island. It was named after Louis XIV and built as a strategic fort guarding the entrance to the St. Lawrence River that led into the heart of French North American interests. It was an impressive place, built by hundreds of men over a thirty-year period. The entire harbor was heavily fortified with extra cannon placed at Royal Battery and Island Battery. Over a hundred large cannon looked down from the high ramparts. Louisburg was both a symbol and strategic element of French power. This map from 1745 (fig. 19) shows the elaborate fortifications that surrounded the grid-patterned town.

The map is made at three scales: a very detailed mapping of the town; a wider-angled view of its regional setting, which shows the unfolding story of the operation; and a little insert of Gabarus Bay.

The map tells the story of the siege of the town by the British in 1745 during King George's War, which in Europe was known as the War of Austrian Succession. The Massachusetts General Court sent 3,500 men under the command of William Pepperrell to attack the French fort. Another 1,000 soldiers came from Connecticut and New Hampshire to lend their support. On April 30 the New England forces landed to the southwest of the citadel in Gabarus Bay. Their camp is shown on the map. On May 16 a battery was erected further north, in effect encircling the fort by land. Forces then moved north to seize the cannon at Royal Battery, abandoned by the French. The captured cannon were then brought to the lighthouse opposite the harbor mouth and used to bombard the city. The fort was surrounded on all sides, and after a forty-nine-day siege and constant bombardment the French surrendered. The fort was returned to the French in 1749 with the Treaty of Aix La Chapelle.

With its three-scale map and detailed notation, the map provides good coverage of this important military event.

In 1754 hostilities between British and French interests again erupted into war. The map of 1756 shown here (fig. 20) describes the cockpit of the North American theater. The map hints at both the agreed upon and still to be determined boundaries. In the northwest part of the map the following notation appears: "This river is by the Treaty of Utrecht the limits between the English and French settlements." Further east the map notes, "The North limits of New Hampshire have not yet been described." The map depicts a place of both settled and fluid boundaries, a place where the lack of agreement is in itself a source of conflict. The map highlights military installations. Forts are depicted all over the map, especially along the geopolitical fault line north and south of Lake Champlain; to the south the British forts William Henry and Frederick; to the north the French forts St. John and Chambli. Nestled on the shores of Lake Ontario, both Fort Oswego and Fort Ontario are depicted. In 1756, the year this map was made, the French Gen. Montcalm de Saint-Veran attacked both these forts and the next year he destroyed Fort William Henry.

The map is interesting because it does more than just note the military installations. It also records the presence of the Iroquois to the immediate west of Lake Champlain and the constituent tribes along the Mohawk valley: the Tuscarora, Onondagans, Mohawks, and Cayugas. These Native Americans still "owned" the land and wielded immense power and influence throughout the entire area. They had military strength and controlled the lucrative fur trade with tribes further west. They were essential allies to the British in the struggle against the French. As powerful allies they were noted in this map.

The map also suggests the potential of the land for further settlement. The area of the Adirondacks is dismissed as "swamps and drowned lands," but an area on the other side of the St. Lawrence is described as "a great deal of good land all uncultivated." The military map also cocked one eye at the potential for further investment and economic development.

An important battle in the French and Indian Wars was the British victory at Quebec. The map shown here (fig. 21) accompanied a written report of the event published in 1759 and was used to illustrate the text. Written descriptions of battles are enhanced for the reader by the spatial depictions of the event. The map describes a place but is also like a movie, telling how events unfolded in time.

General James Wolfe led the British Forces, whose encampment is shown on the north shore of the St. Lawrence River. The previous year Wolfe had led a successful campaign against the Louisburg fortress. In failing health he returned to Britain, but was chosen by the then Prime Minister, William Pitt, to command the assault on Quebec. The city was an important French settlement strategically located at the heart and center of New France. The tide of military affairs had recently turned against France. In July 1758 they abandoned Fort Duquesne and in 1759 Fort Niagara was overrun. After years of defeat by Montcalm and the French, the British were getting ready to strike a deathblow. British ships sailed up the St. Lawrence and laid siege to the city of Quebec. British naval power controlled the river, but the city was heavily fortified at the top of an impregnable cliff. There was an unsuccessful assault by the British to the east of the city at Beauport. The British laid siege for over two months, eventually finding a way up the cliffs to the east of the city. A diversionary attack was made, as the map notes to the east of the city, while Wolfe and his troops secretly landed in the night to the west of the city

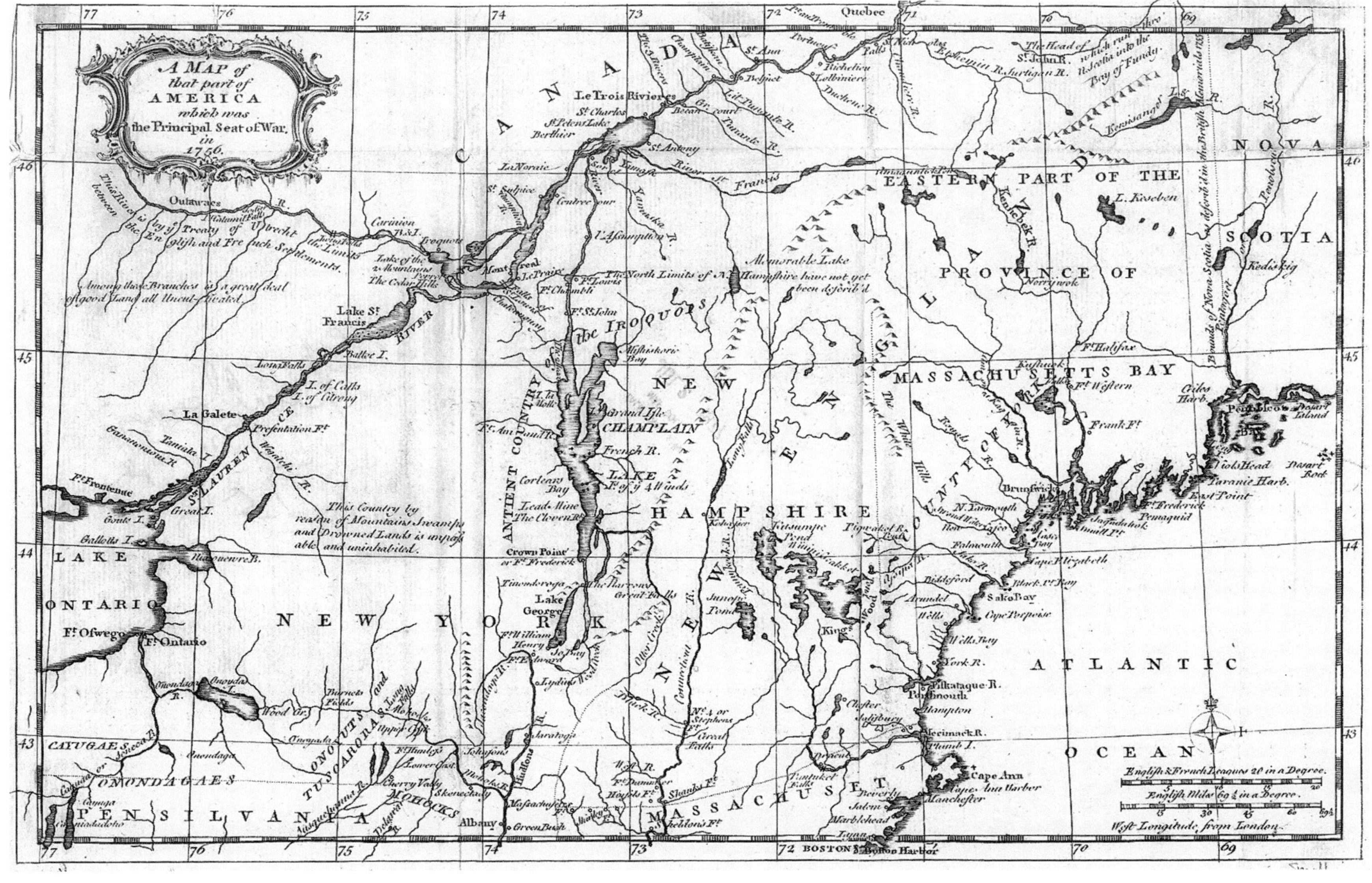

Fig. 20. Map of that part of America which was the Principal Seat of War in 1756. From *Gentleman's Magazine* of February 1757.

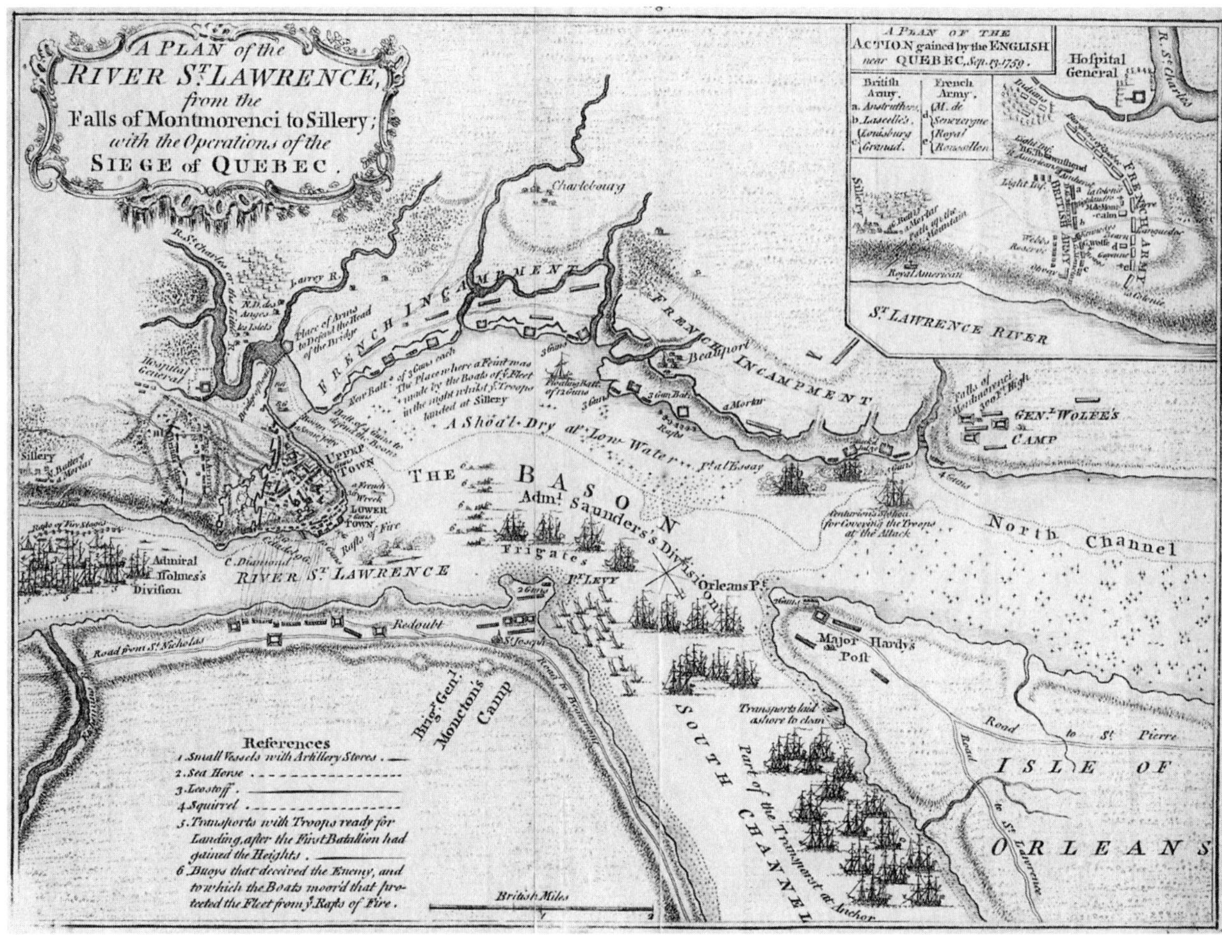

Fig. 21. A Plan of the River St. Lawrence, from the Falls of Montmorenci to Sillery; with the Operations of the Siege of Quebec. From the *London Magazine* of November 1759.

at Sillery. The next morning the British forces faced the French army that had advanced from the city led by Montcalm. The battle lines are drawn in the insert on the top right-hand side of the map. The victory was legendary. The battle lasted no more than an hour. The French were routed and Montcalm was killed. Wolfe too died in the battle and the scene of his death became an important subject for artistic representation. The battle marked the beginning of the end of French power in North America. In a few years they would no longer have any presence on the continent. The map tells the story of a major turning point in the colonial wars.

THE REVOLUTIONARY WAR

The colonial wars were the background to the Revolutionary War. The cost of the colonial military campaigns led many in Britain to feel that the colonies should shoulder a larger share of the costs for their own administration and defense. Many of the colonials, in contrast, felt that they should be given greater freedom from a crown situated on the other side of the great ocean, too far removed from their daily lives. The colonial wars also provided the necessary military experience that many patriots, most notably Gen. George Washington, would draw on in the ensuing conflict.

It is easy in hindsight to view the conflict and its result as inevitable. Hindsight tends to find in chaos and chance events a pattern recognizable after the fact. At the time of the Revolution, events could have just as easily unfolded otherwise. The lines were rarely finely drawn as there were loyalists born in America and British liberals extremely critical of the British crown.

The War of Independence was fought on many fronts. It broke out in Boston and New England, moved to New York and New Jersey, and then encompassed parts of Virginia and the Carolinas. There were few decisive battles; the fortunes of both sides waxed and waned over the years in different places. The battle of Yorktown in 1781 was the last major military engagement. Negotiations between the two sides began in April 1782 and by February 1783 a formal treaty was signed. Britain lost its thirteen colonies and the United States came into being. The following maps note some of the more significant encounters of the War of Independence.

Boston and New England were at the center of the early conflict between the Colonials and the British. The argument had been brewing for some time over the imposition of taxes. After a two-year boycott of British goods tension was in the air. Things could have gone very differently. On 5 March 1770 the British Parliament

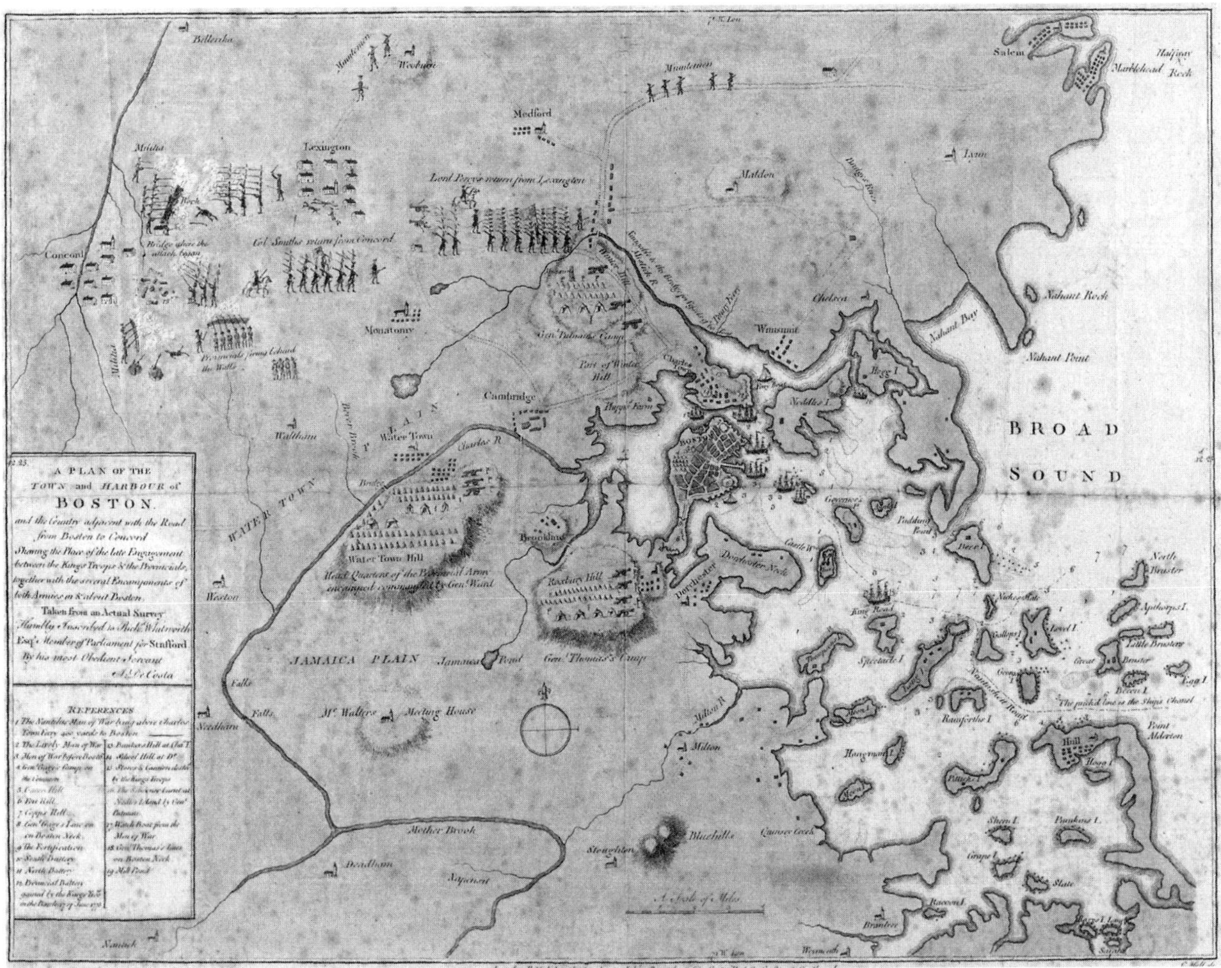

Fig. 22. Plan of the Town and Harbour of Boston and the Country adjacent with the Road from Boston to Concord Shewing the Place of the late Engagement between the King's Troops & the Provincials . . . J. De Costa. London, 1775.

repealed the unpopular duties. But on the same day a brawl took place between citizens of Boston and British troops. The troops fired on the unruly mob and three people were instantly killed and two mortally wounded. The event fueled the republican cause. Three years later tea, an item still taxed by the British, was dumped into Boston harbor. The British were goaded into action, just what the radicals wanted.

The British had naval superiority and could blockade the unruly cities. The map of 1775 reproduced here (fig. 22) shows English men-of-war ships in Boston harbor. Inland, the situation differed. In 1775 Gen. Thomas Gage sent redcoats to take control of munitions at Concord and arrest radical leaders, but they had been forewarned by Paul Revere's famous ride and call that the "British are coming."

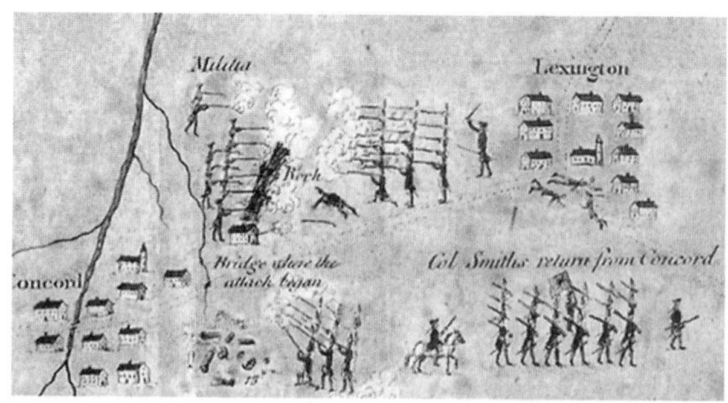

Fig. 22a. Detail of map on page 29 shows British and colonial forces at Lexington and Concord.

The map shows the engagements at Lexington when redcoats faced off against almost seven hundred Minutemen. The battle was not decisive, and fewer than ten people were killed; however, it signaled the start of armed resistance and open warfare in the colonies. It marked the formal beginning of the War of Independence. The map also shows the engagement at Concord where the British were forced to withdraw.

This is a complicated small map because it depicts not only the geography of the area, but also tries to show the recent military history in illustrative form as bands of soldiers are shown marching and fighting in the countryside around Boston. Battles are portrayed, military positions outlined, and army camps located. The map tells us about the local geography and recent military history of the area.

The war was not restricted to colonials and British. The French joined with the Americans against their British enemies. The French role in the war is clearly illustrated in this map of Rhode Island from 1778 (fig. 23). At the bottom of the map a substantial French fleet is shown just off the coast. Washington and the French leader Comte d'Estaing hatched a plan to attack the British at Newport in 1778. The city had a fine harbor and was under British control. The French were to attack the city from the west, the Colonials were to depart from Providence and take the ferry to Rhode Island from Tivertona and attack from the north. The attack was set for August 10th.

The French landed troops on Conannicut Island, just to the west of the city, while the Colonials moved south, their way made easy as the British had retired to Newport. The British defenses around the city are shown on the map. They were also reinforced by the arrival of British ships, also shown in the map in the "Maine Channel" and "Eastern Passage." For two days the British and French fleets eyed each cautiously, but strong winds blew them out of formation. The French fleet departed for Boston. The Colonials, under the command of Gen. John Sullivan, attacked the city on August 14 but were resisted. Without French support the attack petered out.

Like many a battle plan the attack on Newport was characterized by many errors, mishaps, chance events, and breakdowns in communication. The French did not put ashore 4,000 troops when they could have and sailed away too soon. Sullivan was lucky to escape from Rhode Island. The day after he left a British force of 4,000 men arrived to trap him on the island. Unfavorable winds had slowed their journey enough so that Sullivan and his men could escape.

Boston was one of the storm centers of the American Revolution. Within the city and in the surrounding area there was a significant amount of anti-British sentiment. The city portrayed in this map was a crucible of patriotic resistance. The Boston Tea Party of 1773 had initiated the formal acts of defiance against British rule in the colonies.

The map (fig. 24) was drawn in 1775 by Lt. Page of the British Corps of Engineers. They were responsible for building fortifications. The map is oriented with north at the top and shows the street plan of the city. Boston was a city of the sea. It was a merchant city; the many wharfs along the shoreline tell of commercial connections with the Caribbean, Britain, and Europe. The city is packed into a constricted land mass with a tightly congested street pattern. The British mapmaker has selected significant hills in the city, important sites for military considerations and defensive fortifications. Overlying the street pattern the mapmaker has also identified the major public buildings as well as military installations. The key at the bottom of the map identifies military and civil sites in the left and right columns, respectively.

The map was drawn at a particularly tense time. In early 1775 minutemen were beginning to surround the city. The British commander dispatched approximately seven hundred redcoats to secure munitions at Concord and to arrest patriotic leaders. After the British forces were fired upon at Lexington and forced to withdraw at

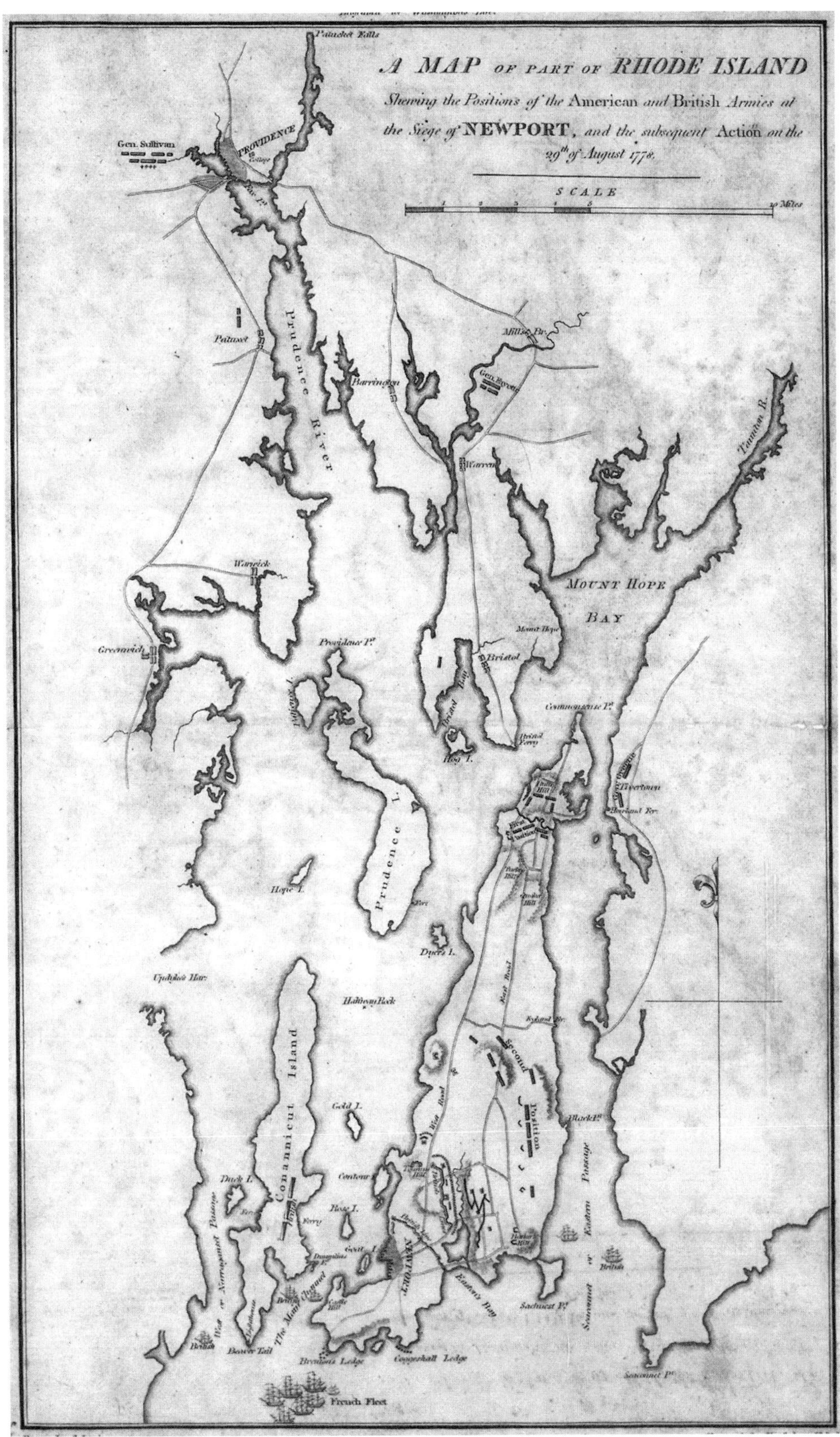

Fig. 23. A Map of Part of Rhode Island, Showing the Positions of the American and British Armies at the Siege of Newport . . . 1778. Samuel Lewis. From John Marshall's *Life of George Washington*, Philadelphia, 1804–07.

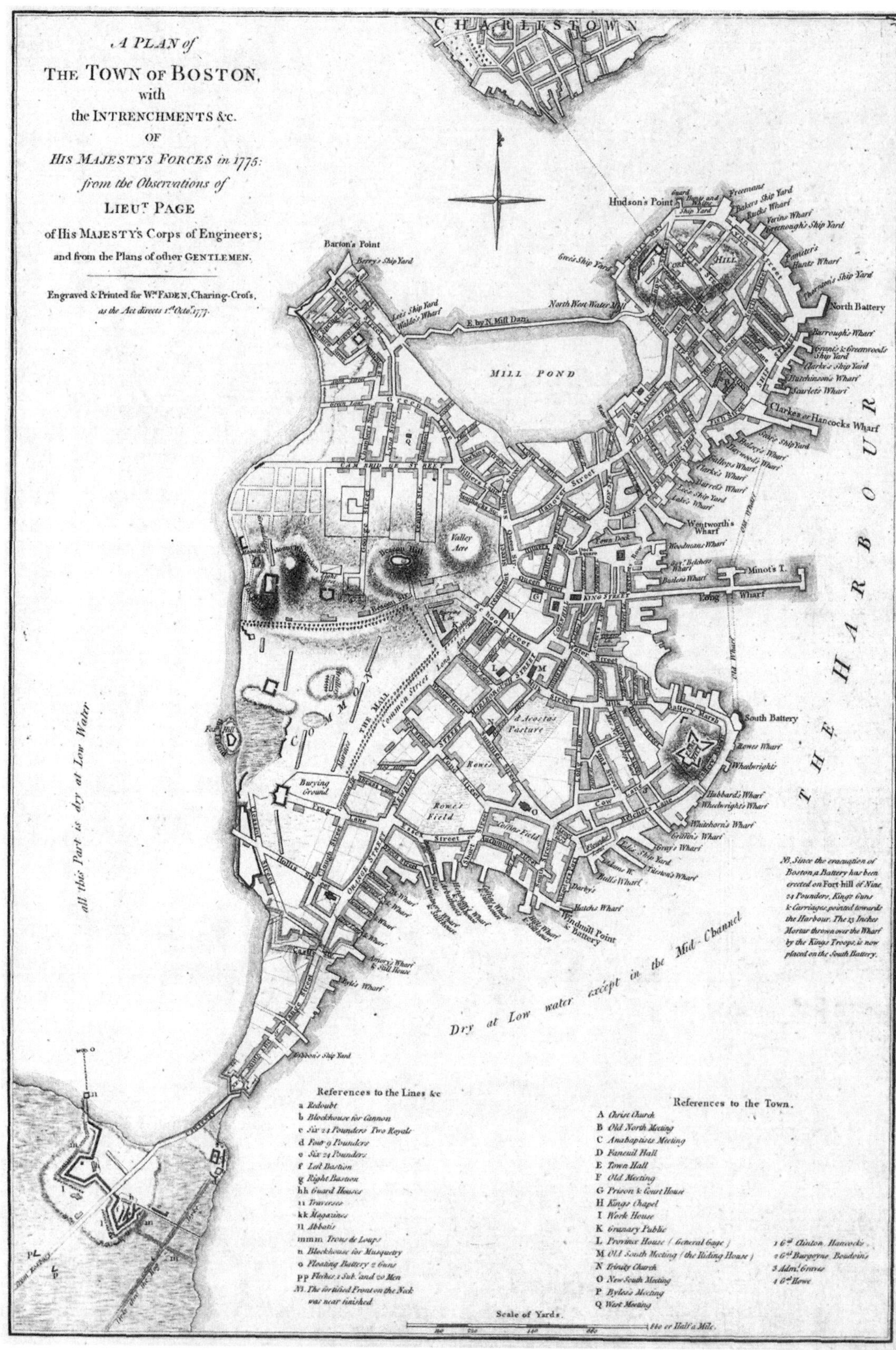

Fig. 24. A Plan of the Town of Boston with the Intrenchments &c of His Majesty's Forces in 1775; from the Observations of Lieut. Page. William Faden. London, 1777.

Concord they retreated to Boston in April 1775. It was not only the sea that surrounded the city but also anti-British patriotic sentiment. In June 1775 patriots occupied the high ground on the Charlestown Peninsula, whose southernmost edge is shown at the top of this map. It was close enough to be within artillery range. The British regained the strategic location of Bunker Hill at a heavy cost. The city remained in British hands but it was effectively besieged. Although able to move ships in and out, the British were landlocked in the city. The fortifications described in the map were the British response to the rising tide of patriotic force in the region. The next year, 1776, Washington surrounded the city and British troops were evacuated by ship to Nova Scotia.

When the British retreated from Concord and Lexington in April 1775, they returned to occupy the city of Boston. In order to secure the city they sought to occupy commanding heights around the city including Bunker's Hill on the Charlestown Peninsula. A patriotic group, the Massachusetts Committee of Safety, got wind of the plan and decided to occupy the first site. On the night of June 16, approximately one thousand patriots marched to Breed's Hill and worked tirelessly through the night to build defenses, trenches and bales of cotton and hay. The patriots also occupied and fortified Bunker Hill. The Battle of Bunker Hill is the story of how the British retook the site.

The 1775 map of the battle shown here (fig. 25) is both a geography and history. The map focuses on the Charlestown Peninsula that was a strategic location in Boston harbor. The unfolding of the battle is shown with reference to the sequence of military events noted in the key to the left of the map. The map is oriented with the north in the bottom right-hand corner of the map.

On 17 June 1775, the British assault began with a bombardment of Charlestown and the high terrain with howitzers and mortars from Boston and from the two ships, *Lively* and *Falcon*, shown on the map. British troops under the command of Gen. Richard Howe landed to the east of Bunker Hill, marked "A" on the bottom of the map. The British attacked the patriots on the hill by moving forward in two ranks. The British came to within 150 feet of the barricades before the Americans opened fire. The devastating fire caused them to withdraw. Another attack was also repulsed before the British finally captured the Hill when the Americans ran out of ammunition and fled.

Although the British won the Battle of Bunker Hill, it was a hollow victory. What the map does not show is

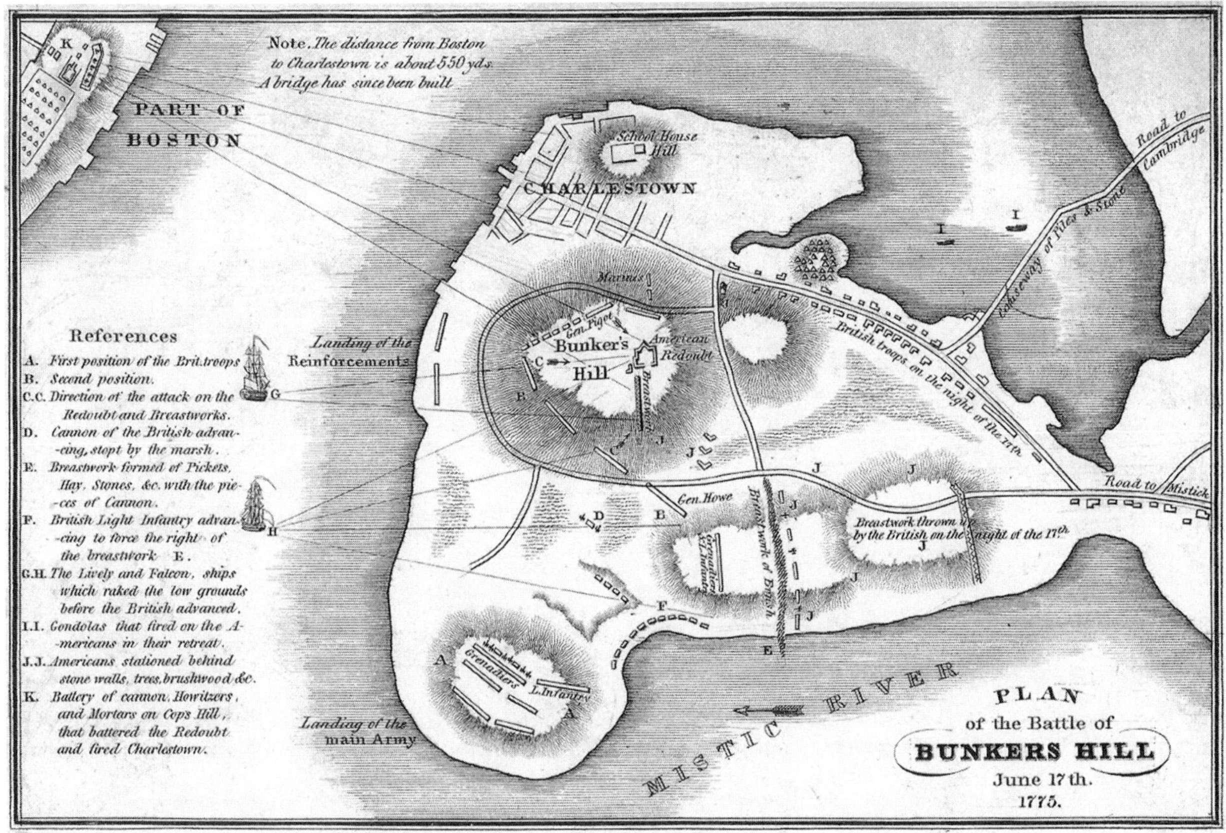

Fig. 25. Plan of the Battle of Bunkers Hill June 17th, 1775.

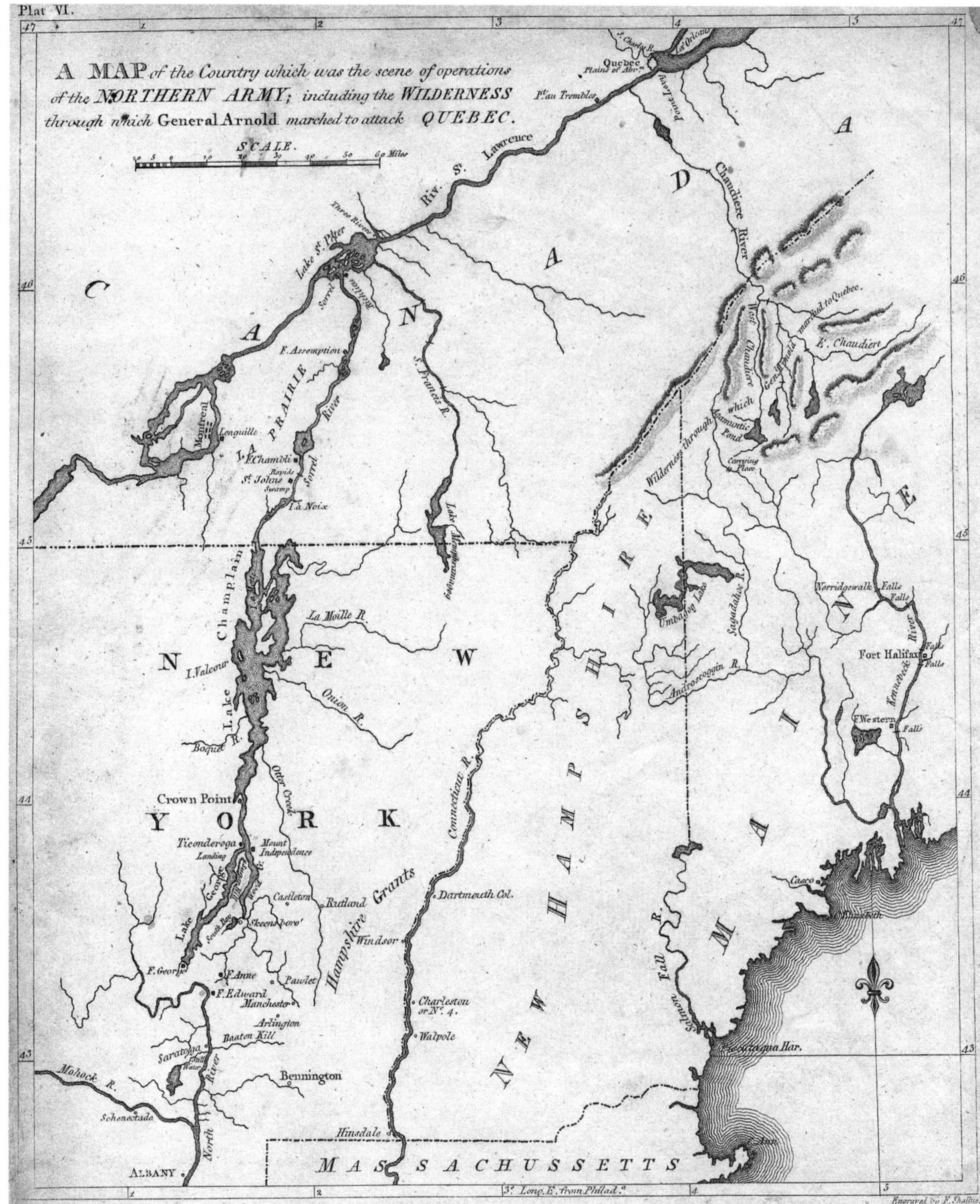

Fig. 26. A Map of the Country which was the scene of operations of the Northern Army; including the Wilderness through which General Arnold marched to attack Quebec. From John Marshall's *The Life of George Washington*, Philadelphia, 1804–07.

the immense carnage. Half of the British force of 2,500 men were casualties; an eighth of all British officers killed in the Revolutionary War died at Bunker Hill. Despite the fact that the Americans also sustained casualties, almost 450 from a total of 1,500 soldiers, they had won a psychological victory. They had demonstrated that the British were not invincible. Bunker Hill became a rallying cry for subsequent resistance to British rule and marked an end to any easy reconciliation between Britain and the patriots. A revolutionary rupture became more thinkable after the Battle of Bunker Hill.

The map from 1806 shown here (fig. 26) was published long after the event in a book to celebrate Washington's life. It is a self-conscious American map. Longitude, shown as numerical values along the top and bottom of the page, takes Philadelphia as its prime meridian. Between 1790 and 1800 Philadelphia was the capital of the new nation and, in an act of cartographic patriotism, the prime meridian on many maps published in the United States during this time was Philadelphia.

The map shows the region of upstate New York and New England as far as the St. Lawrence River. The main rivers and military fortifications are illustrated. The "Hampshire Grants" depicted on the map to the east of Ticonderoga is the future state of Vermont, which had been settled by New England farmers who had organized a de facto independent state with strong patriotic sentiments.

The map depicts an area that was a major site of military engagements. In 1777 the British, under Gen. John Burgoyne, drove south through Lake Champlain and captured Fort Ticonderoga. He slowly pushed south as far as Saratoga where he encountered an army of Patriots led by Gen. Horatio Gates. On 7 October 1777 Burgoyne led another attack on the patriot army only to

Fig. 27. A Map of the United States of America, As settled by the Peace of 1783. Published Decr. 1, 1785 by I. Fielding. From John Andrews' *History of the War with America, France, Spain, and Holland,* London, 1785–86. Variant of a map first issued in the *European Magazine and London Review* of November 1783.

be repelled. His army was surrounded, and on October 17 he surrendered and some 5,700 British troops were made prisoners of war. News of the American victory and British defeat at Saratoga persuaded the French to side with the Americans against their traditional enemy, and they officially recognized the independence of the United States and signed a commercial and military treaty with the patriots.

The title of the map refers to the exploits of Gen. Benedict Arnold who in 1775 was commanded by Washington to lead an expedition to capture Quebec. He took 700 men through what the map described as "wilderness" to attack the city. The effort was not successful and Arnold was severely wounded. Arnold distinguished himself in subsequent campaigns including Saratoga. His patriotism eventually turned to loyalist sympathies, however, and when it was revealed that he had asked the British for 20,000 pounds to give up West Point, his name became a synonym for traitorous acts. He led a British attack on New London in 1781 and later lived in London. The map describes his military campaigns while still a commander of patriotic forces.

At the Treaty of Paris in 1783 between Britain and the United States, new boundaries were established. The United States could now occupy all the land east of the Mississippi to the eastern seaboard. West of the great river lay the Spanish possession of Louisiana. In the south the boundary line with Spanish Florida ran just north of St. Augustine and south of Savannah. In the north the boundary line with British Canada started in the northwest "Lake of the Woods" and moved through the Great Lakes up to the St. Lawrence River. In its extreme northeast boundary, the British map from 1785 reproduced here (fig. 27) shows the disputed northern Maine territory as British. The Americans successfully disputed this boundary and to this day the northern part of Maine has an extended dome of territory that breaks through the straight line of Canada in the Americans' favor.

The new Republic had enlarged its boundaries from the western limit of the thirteen colonies, which is shown as a dotted line running north and south with the legend "*Ancient boundary.*" This line was originally drawn by the British to mark the westward expansion of settlers. Worried about the conflict between Native Americans, who were important allies in the war against France and the colonials, the British sought to halt settler incursions into Native American territory. The line was often breached, however, and one important factor in the War of Independence was the patriots' wish for land development and land speculation westward beyond the British line of proclamation. On the map, west of the line, the names of Native American tribes are clearly visible. The region is identified with the label "Indian Territory" with many tribal names noted, including the Illinois and Miamis in the north and the Chickasaw and Creeks in the south.

The map shows a new nation bounded by limits. Hemmed in by the British in the north and the Spanish in the south and west, even the sea boundary is marked with a line that reads "the limited boundary of the sea coast of the United States." The map speaks to boundaries and limits and the existence of Native American lands. The people of the Republic had other plans that involved the removal of Native Americans and the extension of its own boundaries. Although the British map clearly shows limits, history tells us that these were only temporary.

THE EARLY REPUBLIC

The early Republic of the United States was a mosaic of states that stretched down the eastern seaboard from what is now Maine to Georgia. It was a relatively thin sliver of coastal land hemmed in by the Line of Proclamation established by the British in 1763 to stop further settlement in Native American territory. According to the Treaty of Paris in 1783, the new country included all the land east of the Mississippi. This land was both occupied by Native American tribes and claimed by different states. Various schemes to divide it soon evolved. Thomas Jefferson proposed a fourteen-state division between the Appalachians and the Mississippi; Jefferson being an Enlightenment rationalist, the proposal was all straight lines and right angles. Many in the West argued that the scheme, while mathematically elegant, would leave some states with no river access. The most important form of transport in the West was along the great river system of the Mississippi and its many tributaries. The Northwest Ordinance of 1787 set the number of states northwest of the Ohio River at no less than three and no more than five.

Although lines could be easily drawn on a map, integrating the new territory within the structure of the New Republic was a more difficult matter. Native Americans resisted the land claims of the fledgling republic whose ability to draw maps was greater than its power to turn the map into reality on the ground. With the hindsight of history, we now know that the ground and the map would become one and the same thing as the United States expanded its power and its sovereignty further and further west.

States did not just emerge as natural objects. They were shaped and molded by older colonial divisions and new political agreements. The first map shown here and dating from 1768 (fig. 28) represents the boundary line between the two states of Maryland and Delaware. The map is extremely detailed, outlining individual houses, rivers, and roads. It covers a swathe of territory six miles wide of the boundary line. Miles are noted on the line every five miles. The level of detail was necessary to make absolutely clear where the line fell so as to avoid subsequent property disputes. The map extract is taken from where the boundary begins on the Atlantic coast.

The leaders of the surveying party were George Mason and Jeremiah Dixon, two Englishmen who earlier had been employed to settle a boundary dispute between the proprietors of certain Pennsylvania and Maryland lands. The land grants given to the Penns and the Baltimores had no agreed upon boundary line. Between 1765 and 1768 Mason and Dixon led a survey party that measured the 233 miles of border between Pennsylvania and Maryland.

The work of the surveyors in dividing Pennsylvania and Delaware from Maryland was later referred to as the Mason-Dixon Line. The name did not simply refer to neutral state divisions. Prior to the Civil War it came to mark the boundary between free and slave states. In this case the notation was actually incorrect since both Delaware and Maryland were slave states.

For many years after the Civil War the Mason-Dixon Line was seen as the divide between the North and the South. An arbritary line on a map, surveyed with precision on the ground, came to represent a sharp political and social division that was to fracture the early Republic for many years to come.

The term chorographical was used during the early Republic to refer to maps of land holdings. The chorographical map reproduced here and dating from 1780 (fig. 29) shows territory in northern New York and New England on either side of the Hudson River and Lake Champlain. It is oriented with east at the top so a second glance may be needed to see the lay of the land.

The early Republic was a rush to claim, buy, and steal land. The chaotic nature of the land claims are revealed in the written text on the top left, which tells the story of claim and counterclaim created in land allocations made by Vermont, New Hampshire, and New York, sometimes for the same piece of land.

In individual pieces of land the name of the landowner is noted. On either side of the Hudson River many of the land holdings had been divided up well before the Revolutionary War. The Manor of Renselaerswyk, shown on either side of the river, refers to land claims that were made during the Dutch colonial era in the seventeenth century.

The early Republic had significant financial problems. It owed huge debts to France and to private investors. Its only resource was land and that was often used to pay military personnel. The neat geometric boundary lines shown between Lake Champlain and Lake Ontario refer to military land grants given to officers and men serving in the Revolutionary War. During the war the state legislature of New York, for example, offered land in return for military service. Under a 1781 act, colonels were to receive 2,000 acres for three years service, captains and surgeons 1,500 acres, lieutenants 1,000 acres, and privates 500 acres. The state needed men but had little money. Land became the accepted currency. In 1782 even more generous allocations were made, and 2 million acres of land were set aside on former Iroquois territory for disbursement to military servicemen. Few ex-soldiers took advantage of the scheme; most sold their land warrants to speculators.

Notice on the map that the presence of Native Americans persists. The military tract in the Adirondacks is cited as "land purchased from the savages." And across the entire area two competing land claims are made: "Part of the State of New York" and "Coughsagrage or the beaver hunting country of the Six Nations." This was

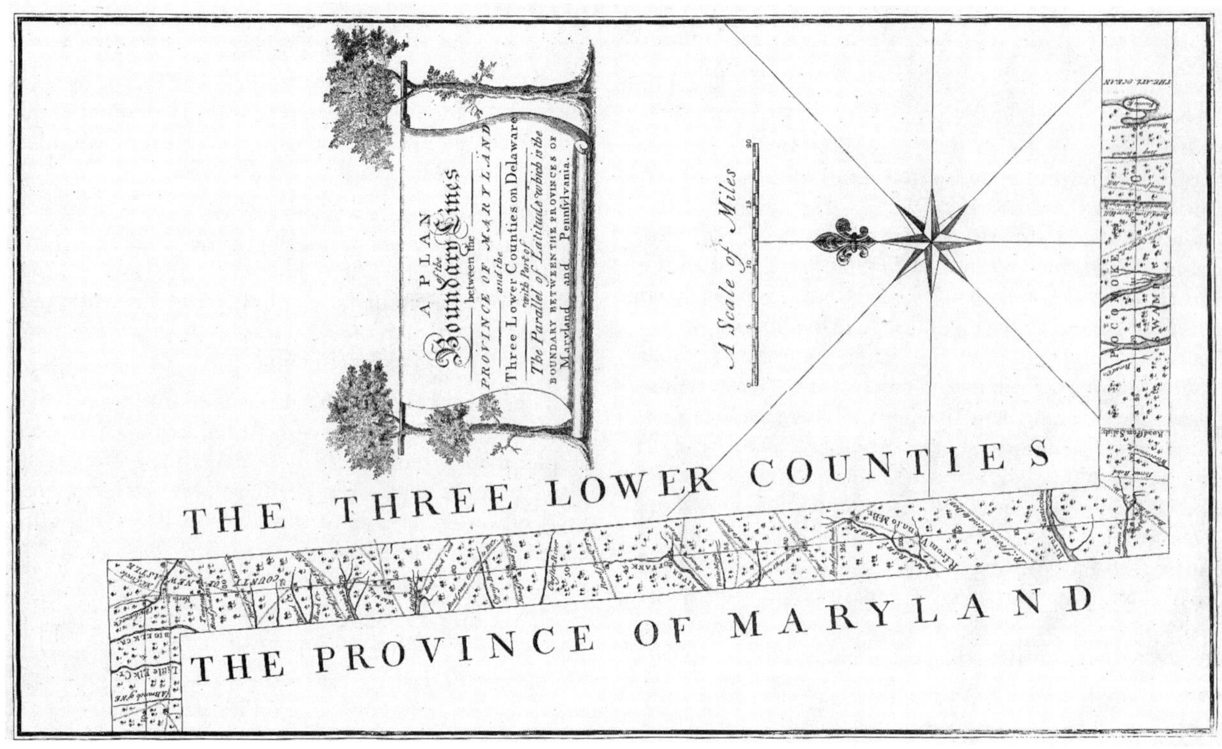

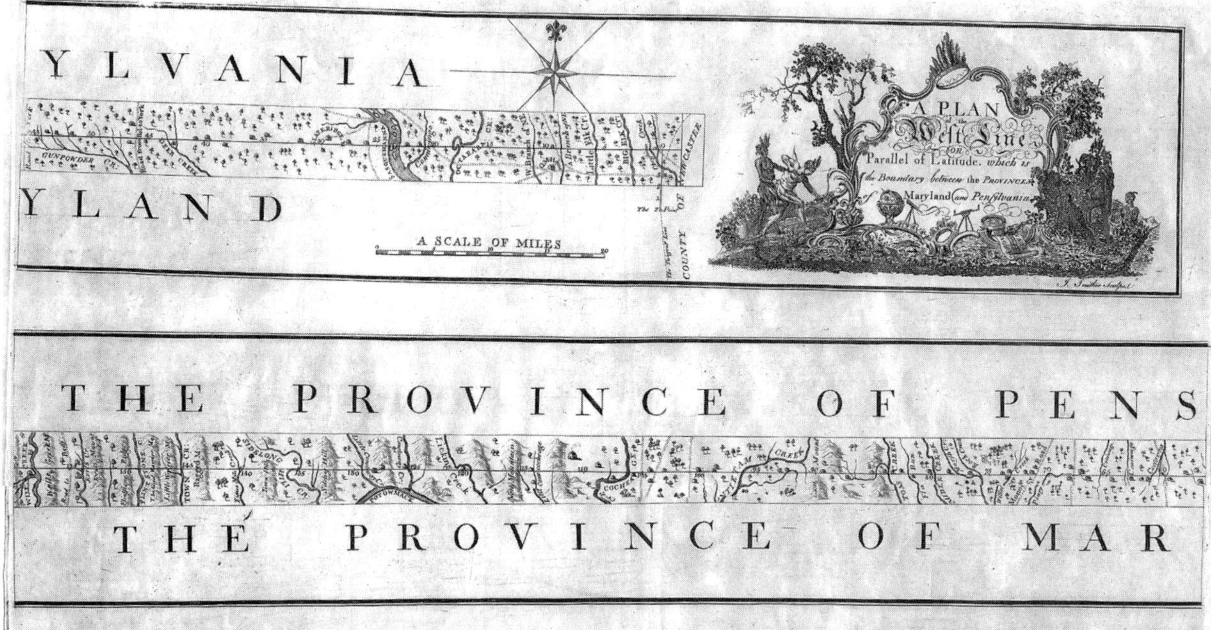

Fig. 28. A Plan of the Boundary Lines between the Province of Maryland and the Three Lower Counties of Delaware with Part of The Parallel of Latitude which is the boundary between the provinces of Maryland and Pennsylvania; A Plan of the West Line or Parallel of Latitude, which is the Boundary between the Provinces of Maryland and Pennsylvania. Charles Mason and Jeremiah Dixon. Philadelphia, 1768.

still contested land, and dubious land dealings would resurface almost two centuries later in Native American claims that the original land sales were flawed, illegal, and unfair.

The title of the 1780 British map shown here (fig. 30) is something of a misnomer. It claims to be "An Exact Map," a common claim at the time for most maps, and yet it strikes the modern reader as crude. Small-scale maps, such as this, were used to give a general impression rather than a detailed survey. But what impressions does this map give? The first is that it reflects a maritime perspective rather than a continental sensibility. The islands of the Caribbean, the Azores, Bermuda, the scatter of islands off the coast of Mexico, and even the islands of Alaska all reflect a sea power's viewpoint. Inland the picture is not so clear. Although some areas are treated in great detail, with the Great Lakes, for instance, taking on a shape very familiar to us today, much of continental North America, especially west of the Mississippi, is only vaguely conceptualized. The British claim of New Albion and the citing of "Drake's Harbour" in California all speak to ancient British claims on this part of the world. The map was drawn before the Lewis and Clark expedition and before the West was officially mapped and surveyed. In it the West is only a sketch drawn from ancient authorities, rumors, and speculation.

Across much of the continental interior the Native American presence is noted and recorded. Tribal names such as the Apaches, Sioux, and Assinboes are indicated in their approximate homelands. But the colonial legacy is also evident in the map's names: New Mexico, New South Wales, New North Wales, New England, New Britain, and New Albion all depict the New World as the property and prize of the Old World.

The map of 1806 (fig. 31) is a more detailed representation of the early Republic. Unlike the previous map, which did not illustrate political boundaries, these figure prominently in this map. The international boundary

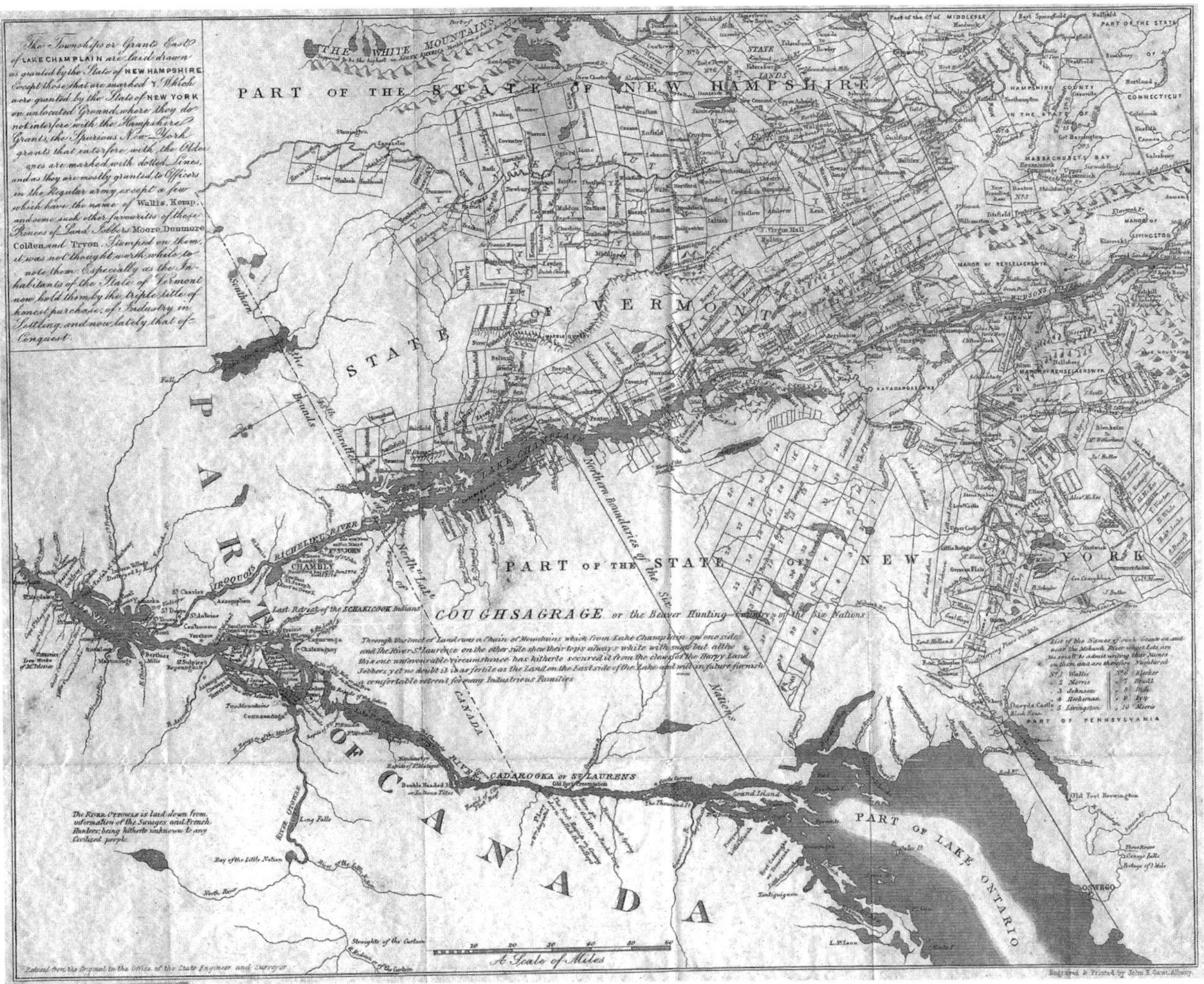

Fig. 29. A Chorographical Map of the Northern Department of North America. Engraved Printed and Sold at New Haven. Reduced from the original in the Office of the State Engineer and Surveyor. A reproduction of a map from around 1780.

between the United States and Spanish Florida is shown, as is the boundary line in the north with British Canada as far west as Lake Superior. The states are taking on a more familiar shape. After the Treaty of 1783 the United States gained land beyond the original thirteen colonies as far west as the Mississippi. This land is shown under the names of competing claims. Native American names figure prominently throughout this territory: the Choctaws and Chickasaws in the south and Illinois and Chipawas in the north. The names and location of forts throughout this area are also provided, including Fort Washington along the Ohio River, Fort Pierias along the Illinois River, and Fort St. Joseph along the river of the same name. It is a contested area with the state boundaries of Georgia, Virginia, and Kentucky merging into the territory.

The process of state formation is hinted at in the map. The states of Kentucky and Tennessee had been formed in 1792 and 1796, respectively. The state of Virginia originally claimed most of the northwestern territory. The map suggests more states will be created from this contested territory.

Along the eastern seaboard the towns and cities of a mercantile society are identified. Philadelphia, one of the largest cities and the capital of the new Republic until 1800, is shown in capital letters. The name of the new capital, Washington, is also written in capital letters. In addition, the map highlights state capitals for extra attention. Elsewhere, the signs of economic progress and urban growth are reflected in the many names of cities and towns provided. The map shows urban growth and political cohesion in the established areas along the seaboard, and territorial annexation and new state formation in the contested region on the edge of the ever-advancing frontier.

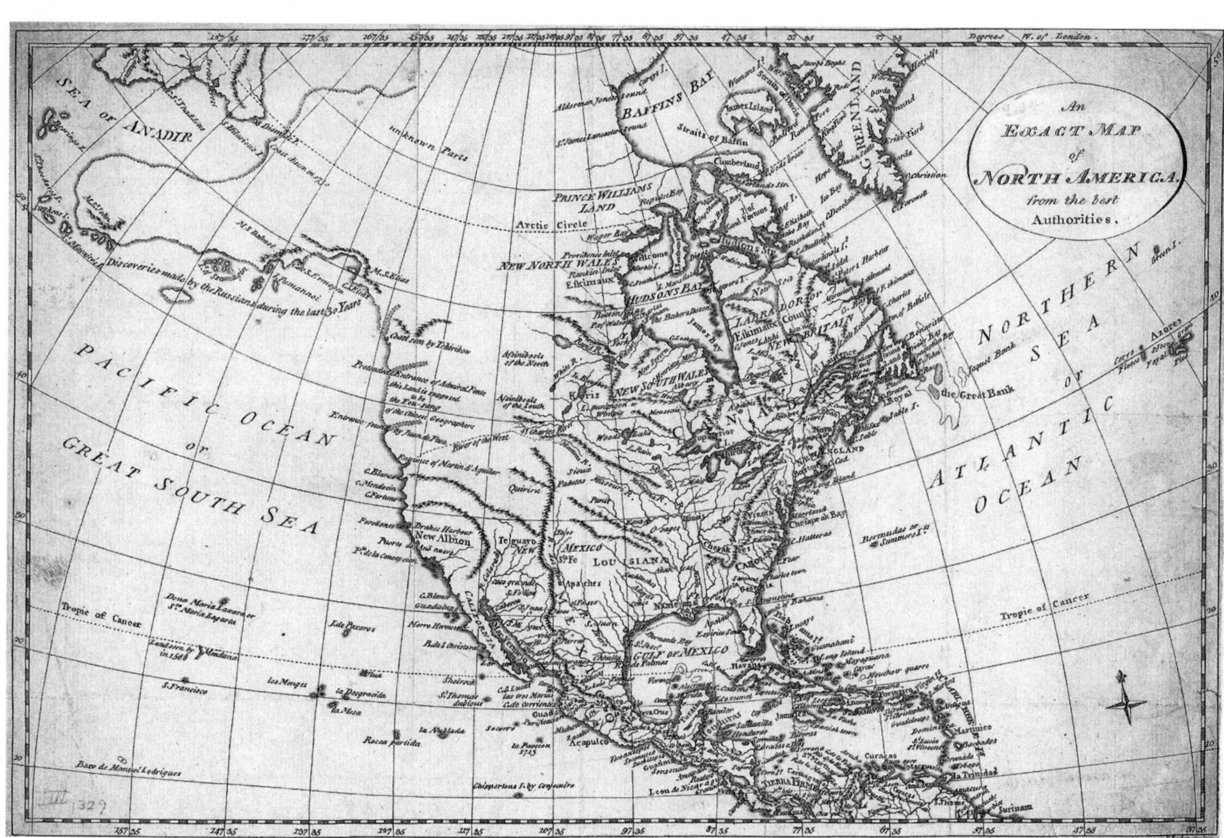

Fig. 30. **An Exact Map of North America from the Best Authorities.** c. 1780.

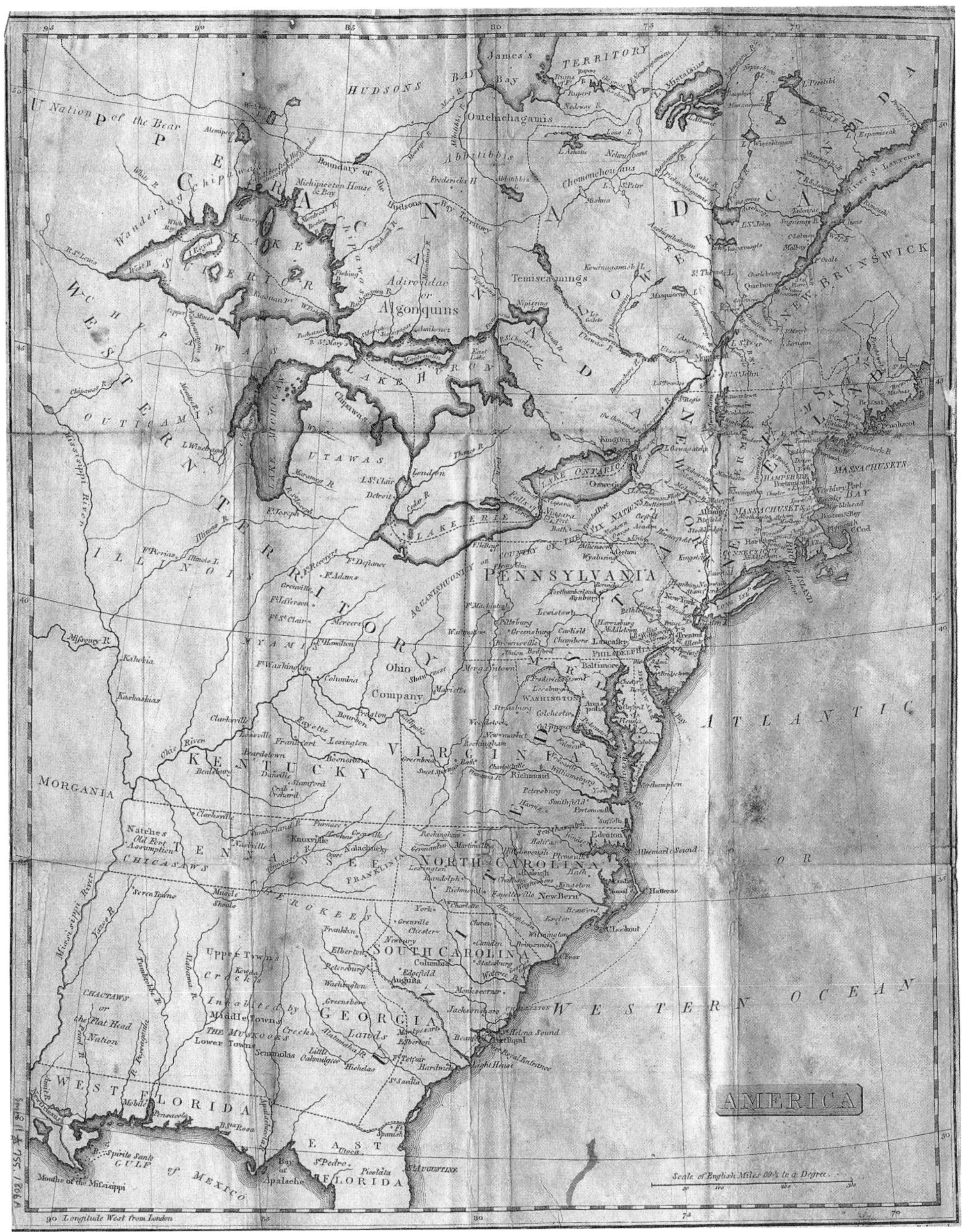

Fig. 31. America. c. 1806.

THE WAR OF 1812

Congress declared war on Great Britain in June 1812. It was part of a larger dispute between Britain and France. The United States entered the Napoleonic Wars because although both European powers sought to restrict the United States from trading with the other, the more powerful British Navy had been more effective in reducing U.S. trade. Moreover, there was still lingering hostility toward the former colonial adversary. Canada also provided a tempting target. Some in the U.S. believed that it should become part of the expanding nation.

On land the war started badly for the United States. Three attempted invasions of Canada proved disastrous. Detroit was lost, then won back. Buffalo was burned. In 1814 a British force landed in Maryland, defeated a U.S. army, and marched on the nation's new capital. The president and Congress fled, and in a humiliating blow to national self-esteem the British burned the White House to the ground. The British sailed up the Chesapeake and laid siege to Baltimore. The militiamen resisted. The struggle is immortalized in the U.S. national anthem, "The Star Spangled Banner."

In late 1814 a British force sailed from Jamaica to attack New Orleans. The city was defended by Gen. Andrew Jackson, who had been summoned from his command of forces fighting Native Americans in Florida and Alabama. The British fleet arrived on 13 December 1814, and British troops were dispatched to seize the city's outlying forts and islands. The British under the command of Gen. Edward Packenham faced Jackson's forces just south of New Orleans on 8 January 1815. The British were roundly defeated, and their heavy casualties were all the more tragic since a peace treaty between the countries had been signed two weeks earlier on December 24 in Ghent. The battle was thus unnecessary. However, the American victory signified two important developments. The first was the political career of Andrew Jackson, whose military accomplishments catapulted him into a successful run for the presidency. The second was the very first signs of potential U.S. influence as a superpower. The new Republic had defeated a global superpower, and although it did not immediately become a dominant force on the world stage, it marked the beginning of a geopolitical role that would lead the United States to assume global significance.

The map of 1814 shown here (fig. 32) refers to the opening rounds of the Battle of New Orleans. It started with an attempted British attack on Mobile. This had been Spanish territory until the United States annexed West Florida in 1813. Fort Bowyer, which guarded the entrance to Mobile Bay, was garrisoned with U.S. forces. In September 1814 the British landed marines and "Indians" to cut off the fort situated at the end of a peninsula. The British forces are marked on the coastline of the map, to the southeast of the fort. The British fleet then sailed close to the fort and bombarded it. Note how the sea depths are carefully noted on the map, a vital piece of information for military commanders. The ships are also shown and named in the channel. The engagement lasted four days; the British suffered the worst losses. They lost over 160 men as well as the HMS *Hermes*, whose explosion is graphically depicted on the map.

The map reports on an important though little known engagement in the war with Britain. The doughty defenders of Fort Bowyer saved Mobile and forced the British to direct their energies to New Orleans. Fort Bowyer set the scene for the upcoming battle.

The fort was the site of another significant conflict in February 1815 when British forces, in retreat from New Orleans, landed almost five thousand men and heavy artillery. This time the fort surrendered without a fight. The British were about to enter Mobile itself when news of the peace treaty arrived. They then abandoned the fort to U.S. possession.

The map of the Battle of New Orleans (fig. 33) from the same year is oriented with the east at the top of the page. It is a very detailed map, which allows us to identify the configuration of British and U.S. forces.

The British under the command of Gen. Edward Pakenham had landed to the east of the city and marched through the swamps. U.S. forces under the command of Gen. Andrew Jackson were positioned behind a well-fortified, five-mile-long dry canal. Gen. Jackson, a wily fighter seasoned by frontier campaigns, led the U.S. forces, while Pakenham, a brave but dim nobleman, commanded the British. The four-foot-deep and ten-foot-wide Rodriguez's Canal is referred to as "*Line Jackson*" on the map. The British had superior forces, almost 8,000 men compared to the nearly 6,000 Americans, but they were at a tactical disadvantage. Their movement was hindered in the east by the impenetrable "Cypress Swamp" and in the west by the wide Mississippi. At dawn on Sunday, 8 January 1815, the British forces marched across empty fields marked only by parallel ditches. Denied cover, they advanced into a hail of bullets. By ten in the morning the battle was over. The British had been soundly defeated. Repeated forward surges were beaten back by U.S. firepower. The United States lost only 13 men, while the British suffered staggering casualties: over 2,000 wounded, 291 dead, and almost 500 missing. Among the casualties were all three British commanding officers, including Pakenham, who was killed. The casualties were all the sadder since a treaty had already been signed on Christmas Eve 1814. However, news of the peace did not reach the combatants until March 1815.

The utter defeat of the British boosted American self-confidence and the conflict came to be known as the "Second War of Independence," projecting Jackson into national prominence.

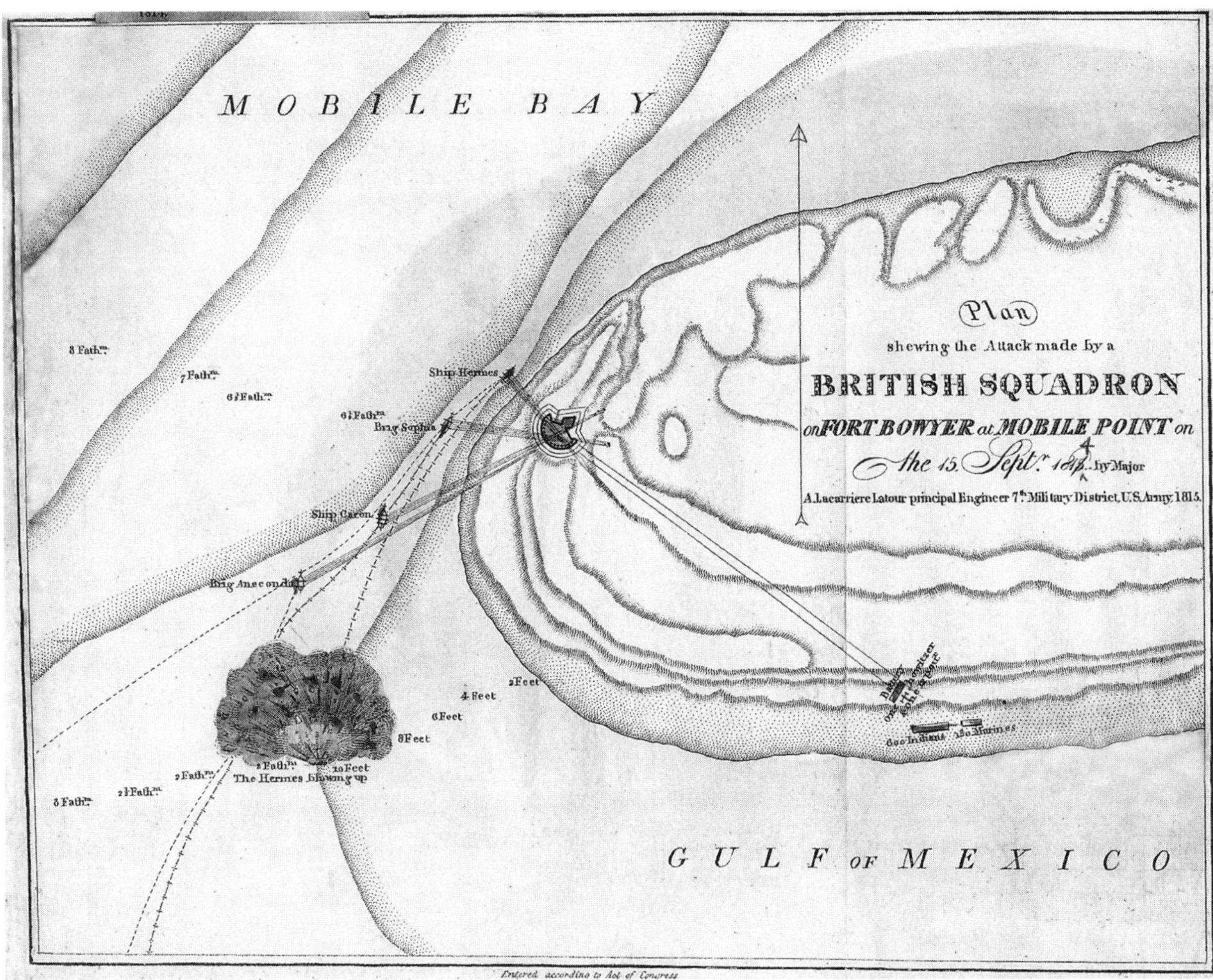

Fig. 32. Plan showing the Attack made by a British Squadron on Fort Bowyer at Mobile Point on the 15th September 1814. A. Lacarriere Latour. From his *Historical Memoir of the War in West Florida and Louisiana, 1814–15*, Philadelphia, 1816.

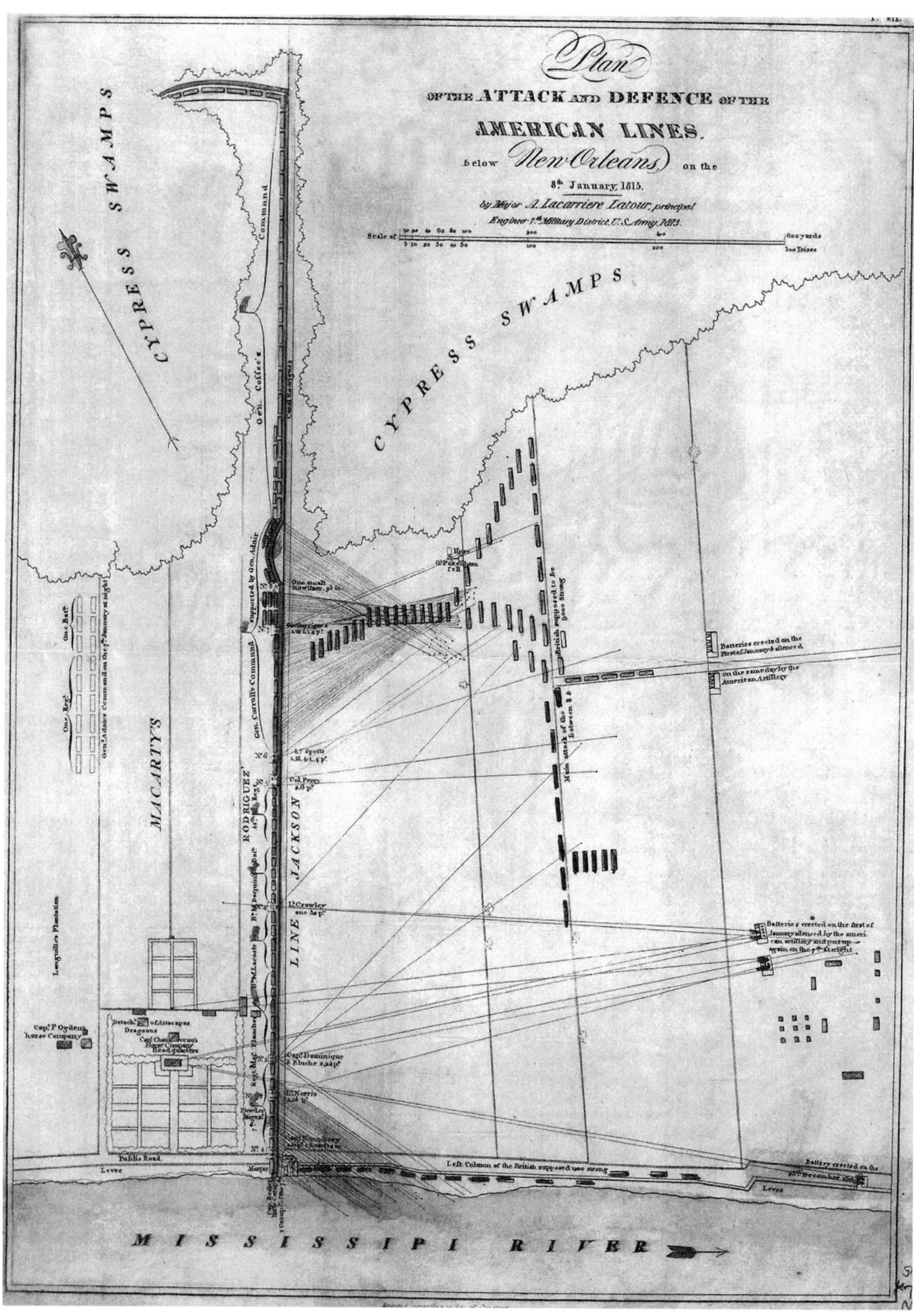

Fig. 33. Plan of the Attack and Defence of the American Lines below New Orleans on the 8th January, 1815. A. Lacarriere Latour. From his *Historical Memoir of the War in West Florida and Louisiana in 1814–15*, Philadelphia, 1816.

THE UNITED STATES EXPANDS

At its independence the United States consisted of thirteen former colonies along the coast of the Atlantic Ocean. Most settlements were on or close to the sea. Inland lay a contested land where Native Americans and other colonial powers vied for territorial control.

In a series of sales, treaties, and annexations the nation expanded its boundaries. In the Treaty of Paris in 1783 the western border was extended to the Mississippi. In 1803 the Louisiana Purchase more than doubled the size of the country. Then a series of annexations and purchases extended the country to continental proportions: the Red River Basin in 1818, Florida in 1819, Texas in 1845, Oregon Country in 1846. The Mexican cession of 1848 and the Gadsden Purchase of 1853 rounded out the continental United States. Later, the purchase of Alaska in 1867 and the annexation of Hawaii in 1898 would increase the nation to its present size.

The bounty of land came at a price. Sometimes the cost could be calculated. Louisiana was purchased for three cents an acre. But the cost to indigenous peoples was much higher. When a territory came under U.S. control, land was quickly commodified and native peoples soon came under threat from soldiers, settlers, and land speculators. The relentless commercial growth brought remote areas into the orbit of a capitalist economy. Various gold rushes, the coming of the railways, the search for minerals, and the turning of the prairie into grassland and the forests into timber stands, all wrought major changes on the land and its indigenous peoples.

The annexation of territory did not eradicate all established custom. Large sized *ranchos* became a unit of administration and landholding in southern California, the French long-lot land pattern persisted in Louisiana, and many of the native peoples throughout the West and Alaska tenaciously survived. Not everything was washed away. However many things did change as new territory became part of the expanding United States.

The boundaries of the United States are depicted boldly on the map of North America from 1812 that is reproduced here (fig. 34). Just nine years earlier the United States had extended its western edge and doubled its size with the purchase of Louisiana from France. The map embodies both uncertainties over the expansion and continuing continental aspirations. The Mississippi is still shown as a significant border, as if the annotator is not yet sure of the purchase. And indeed, the terms of the sale were murky. The area was inhabited by a rich variety of North American tribes who had settled there thousands of years earlier. They would have found it strange and incomprehensible that foreign powers could lay claim to land that was theirs. Amongst European powers, the land was claimed first by France, in part based on the exploration of its missionaries and fur traders down the Mississippi. In 1762 France ceded the land to Spain, but in 1800 Napoleon Bonaparte won it back. In 1803 France offered the land to the U.S. and a treaty was signed by both nations in May 1803, granting the United States full possession of the territory. The treaty, however, always remained vague as to the true boundary lines and size of Louisiana. In this map the boundary has been established as far west as the Pacific. This would have been news to Britain and Spain, who had claims on the same territory. The term Louisiana only refers to the area immediately west of the Mississippi, but the boundary depicted here takes into account a wider swathe of still contested land. The boundary line with Spanish possessions in the south is also drawn. At the time Spain controlled Florida and most of New Mexico.

The map is a physical geography map to which the boundaries of the expanding Republic have been added. That the boundaries lines match expectation rather than existing political realities speaks to the fluidity of territorial claims and the boldness of U.S. territorial ambitions.

The map from 1831 (fig. 35) has a dual scale of longitude. On the bottom of the map the figures record values from Greenwich. On the top the values are taken from the prime meridian of Washington. It would be over forty years before there was international agreement in 1875 on an agreed prime meridian centered in Greenwich in Britain. Until then many countries would favor national primes. Early U.S. maps, in fact, often showed Philadelphia and then Washington as the prime meridian. This map reveals a dual system: paying recognition to the dominance of Greenwich as an international standard as well as deferring to national sentiments by also using Washington, D.C.

The map shows the passage of the moon's eclipse across the national territory. It is an example of thematic mapping, illustrating a natural phenomenon. It is also a sophisticated map that uses parallel lines to indicate the extent of the eclipse in different parts of the country. But it is additionally a political map that shows the emergence of new states from the territory gained in the Treaty of 1783 and the later Louisiana Purchase. The map depicts the relatively new states of Ohio, Indiana, and Illinois as carved from the northwest territory, as well as Mississippi and Alabama in the south. And west of the Mississippi River the new states of Louisiana and Missouri have emerged from the Louisiana Purchase. The areas of Michigan, Missouri, and Arkansas that will be the site and names of future states remain marked as territories. The map shows an emerging nation as more territories become states in the Union. East of the Mississippi the map records the presence of the Creeks and Cherokees in the south and Chippewas and Shawnees in the north; west of the river the Cherokees and Osages are about to experience the full force of U.S. expansionism.

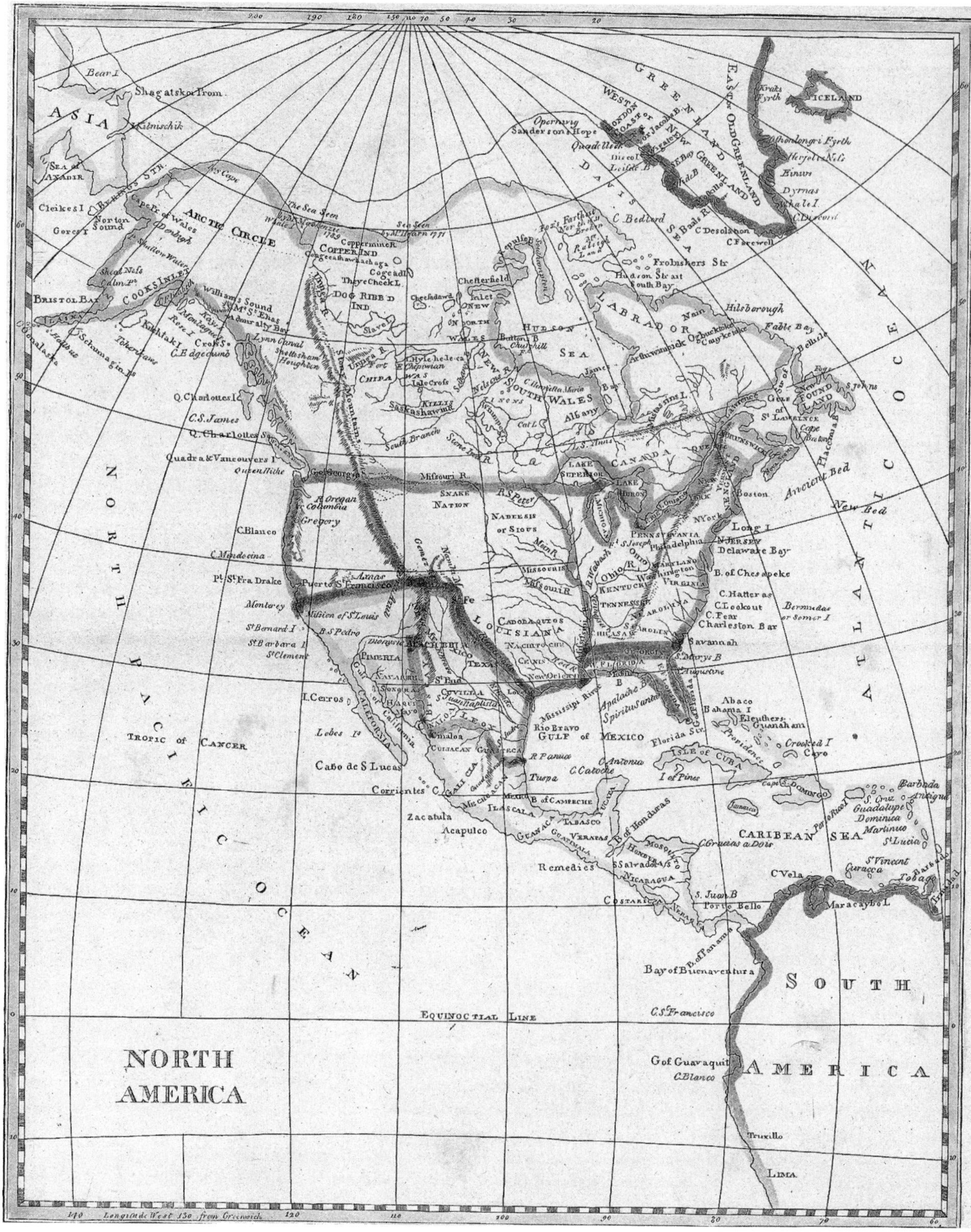

Fig. 34. North America. From an edition of Aaron Arrowsmith and Samuel Lewis' *A New and Elegant General Atlas,* Boston, 1812.

Fig. 35. A Map of the eclipse of Feb.y 12th in its passage across the United States. Boston: Gray & Bowen. [1831]. A depiction of the solar eclipse of 1831.

The map of 1834 (fig. 36) tells a sad story on the edge of the frontier. In the eastern portion of the map the states of Missouri and Arkansas are shown. They became part of the Union in 1821 and 1836, respectively. North of these states the ceding and sale of Indian lands are recorded. West and north of these new states tribal lands are shown with the names of tribes noted. Earlier we had observed the presence of such tribes as the Cherokees, Creeks, and Choctaws east of the Mississippi. What are they doing here?

The forward march of settlers was relentless. In 1830 Congress passed the Indian Removal Act. Since the time of Jefferson, it had long been a dream of U.S. politicians to remove all Indians to the west of the Mississippi. Their land was too valuable, they stood in the way of progress. One rationale behind the Louisiana Purchase was to have land readily available in the West so that Indians could be moved there from their land in the East. Their newly vacated lands would provide room for settlement and agriculture by U.S. settlers. For the eastern

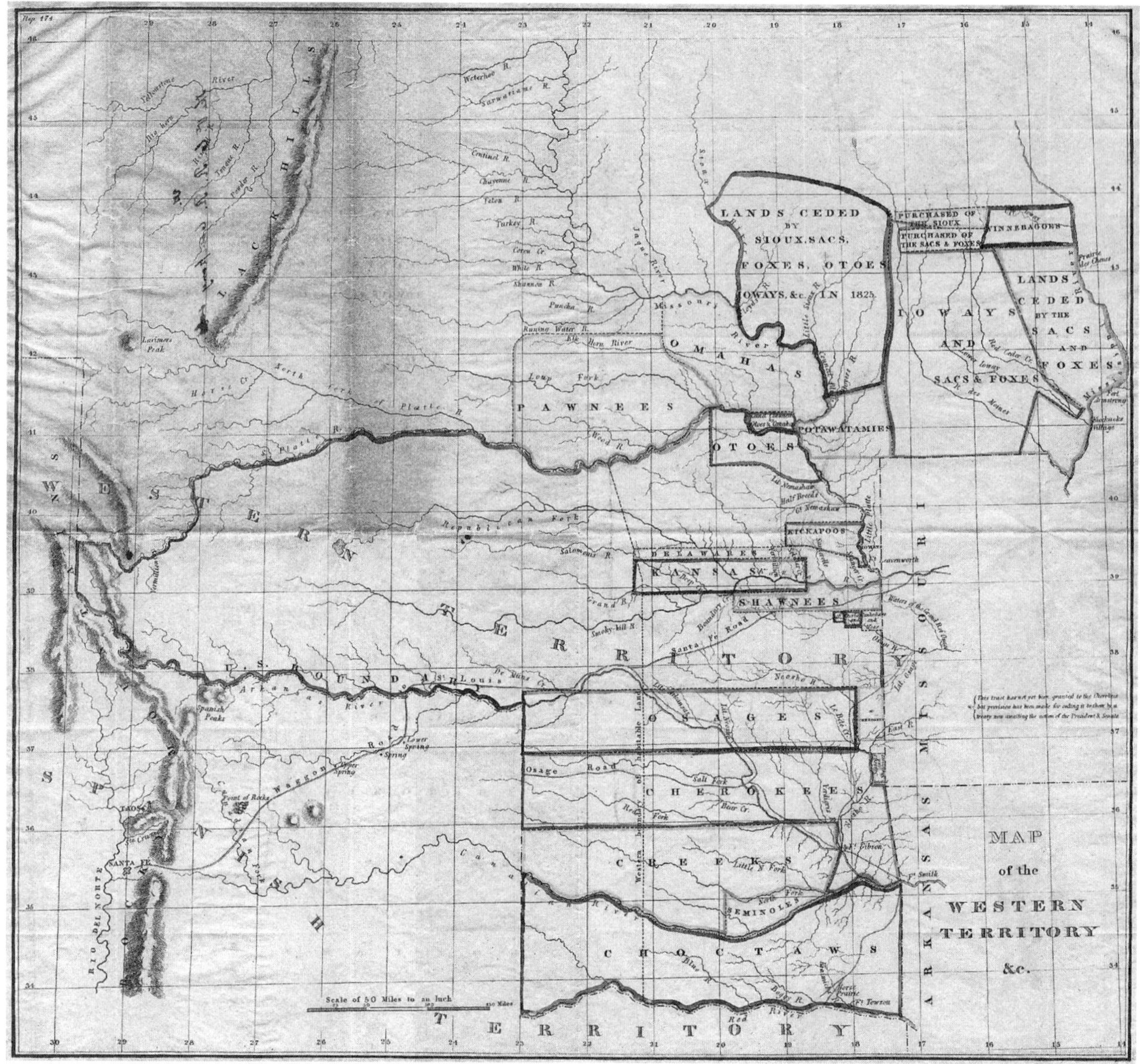

Fig. 36. Map of the Western Territory &c. Map accompanying a report from the Committee on Indian Affairs, published as House Report 474 of the 23rd Congress, 1st Session, 1834.

tribes, the Removal Act was a tragedy. Removed from their traditional lands, they were given inadequate space in a strange land. Between 1831 and 1833 some Choctaws were moved from central Mississippi to the region shown in the map.

In the map shown here the text on the right reads "This tract has not yet been granted to the Cherokees but provision has been made for ceding it to them by a treaty now awaiting the action of the President and the Senate." These simple words underlie the "Trail of Tears," the removal of the Cherokees from their traditional homelands in the East to the designated land shown on the map. Despite a Supreme Court ruling in their favor, the Cherokee were forcibly removed from their land by 7,000 U.S. troops. Between 1838 and 1839 over 15,000 Cherokee were forced to travel by foot on a 116-day journey during which 4,000 died, most of them women and children.

Not all the eastern tribes were so compliant. The Seminoles, for example, resisted their removal and Chief Osceola led a guerilla campaign against U.S. forces. His capture in 1837 ended most of the resistance. By 1842 most of the Seminole were removed to the tiny area of land noted on the map between the land set aside for the Choctaws and Creeks.

The map of the northern Midwest states dating from 1836 (fig. 37) is a very detailed example of topography. Rivers and lakes are shown in great detail. Across this

Fig. 37. Map of the Northern parts of Ohio, Indiana and Illinois with Michigan, and that part of the Ouisconsin Territory Lying East of the Mississippi River. By David Burr, Draughtsman to the House of Reps. 1836. Map accompanying House Report 380 of the 24th Congress, 1st Session on the position of the northern boundary of Ohio.

physical landscape only a few towns are illustrated. On the southwestern shore of Lake Michigan the small settlement of Chicago is depicted. The town was incorporated as a city the following year, in 1837. And next to Lake St. Clair the settlement of Detroit is shown. These urban settlements are but pinpricks in a world of rivers and lakes.

The map also depicts the relatively new states of Indiana (1816) and Illinois (1818). Michigan only became a state in 1837 and its southern boundary still looks like a set of provisional lines rather than a single fixed, agreed upon division. The final boundary with Indiana is the northernmost line with Indiana, just south of Buffalo, and with Ohio, north of Toledo.

The area on the map referred to as "Ouisconsin Territory" would be divided into the upper peninsula region of Michigan; Wisconsin, which became a state in 1848; and Minnesota, which became a state a decade later.

The map suggests that states were carved from a northern wilderness. It depicts endless rivers and lakes, a physical geography with little human settlement. However, the map fails to record the Native American presence. This was land, as we have seen in previous maps, that was populated and settled by different tribal groups such as the Fox and Sioux. Whereas older maps had shown the Chippewas, Illinois, Outaowas, Miamis, and Mascontens, this map only illustrates a physical ter-

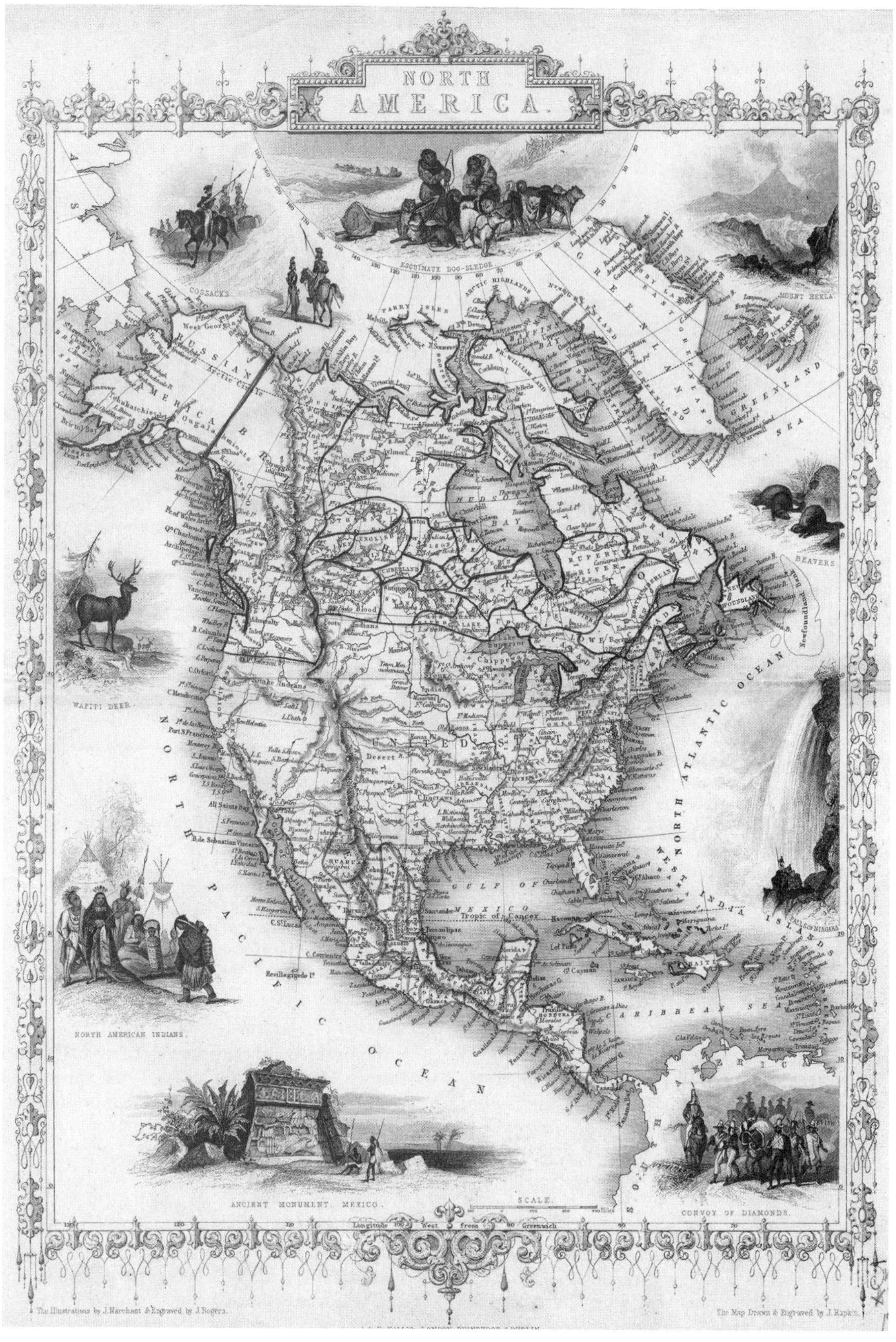

Fig. 38. North America. J. Rapkin. From the *Illustrated Atlas and Modern History of the World*, London: J. & F. Tallis, 1851.

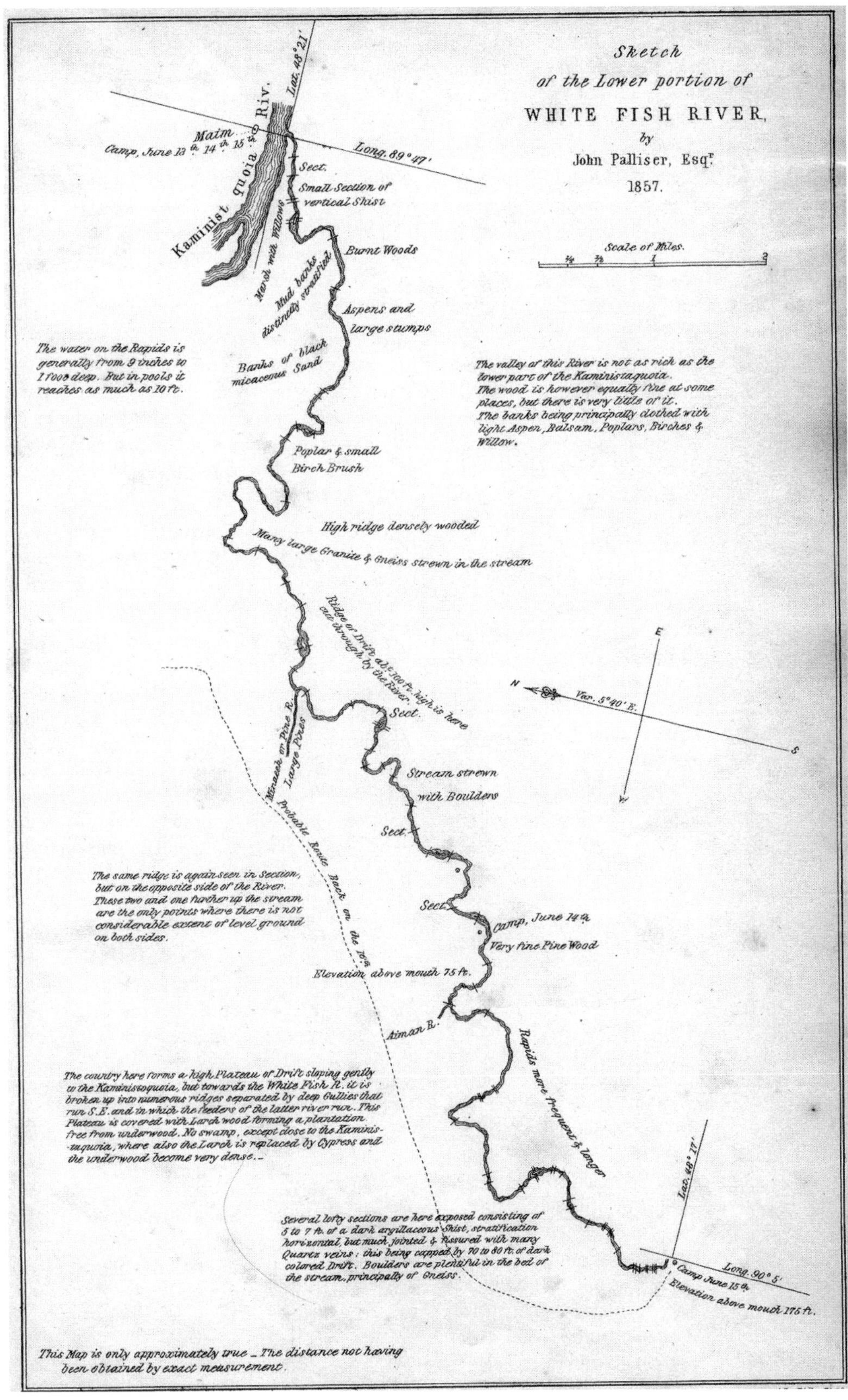

Fig. 39. Sketch of the Lower portion of the White Fish River by John Palliser, Esq. 1857. From *Exploration—British North America*, London, HMSO, 1859.

rain. The map embodies the process of Indian removal and marginalization. As they lost their land they were removed from the map. The cartographer has eliminated their presence just as they were removed physically; the map and history function in perfect synchronization.

The ornate map of North America printed in 1851 (fig. 38) depicts the United States at the end of one stage of territorial expansion and political incorporation and on the threshold of another. This is a British map and the boundaries with British Canada are highlighted in the north. Alaska is shown as "Russian Alaska" while in the Pacific Northwest British Canada extended well south of the Columbia River.

In this map the name United States is shown in block capital letters spanning the territory from the Atlantic Ocean to the Rocky Mountains. Recent states such as Florida (1845) and Texas (1845) are included, and the names of future states such as Iowa (1846) and Wisconsin (1848) also appear on the map. It shows how the United States has incorporated the land of the Louisiana Purchase and the annexation of Texas.

The boundary lines in the West are difficult to discern. This is, in part, a result of the very small symbol of dotted lines used, which make the boundaries hard to see. It is also indicative of the fluid nature of actual ownership of the land west of the Rockies. In the Pacific Northwest the British laid claim to land as far south as the Great Salt Lake. Spain and later Mexico claimed California and lands as far west as the Rocky Mountains.

The map demonstrates a much better understanding of western topography than many earlier maps. The Rocky Mountains are shown in approximate outline, and the course of the Columbia River is clearly known, as is the existence of Great Salt Lake. Although the area's physical layout is becoming better known to the general public, the geopolitical structures of the land are still in the process of crystallization.

The expansion of the United States was forever a problem for its neighbors. Both north and south, the adjoining countries feared the expansionist doctrines and policies of their neighbor. The border with Canada, especially the western border, was a source of contention for many years. In 1856 the Royal Geographical Society in London lobbied the Colonial Office to fund an exploration party to map and discover possible sites of settlement along the border zone with the United States in order to block any future American expansion. A party was dispatched led by Lt. John Palliser accompanied by a botanist, geologist, astronomer, and scientist. The group lacked a skilled mapmaker. Their travels were extensive, taking in much of the U.S.-Canadian borderland as far west as the Columbia River over the period from 1857 to 1859. They found numerous passes through the Rocky Mountains, one of which was used later as a route by the Canadian Pacific Railroad. The resultant connections between east and west Canada helped maintain its coherence as a country and effectively blocked the northward expansion of the United States.

The map shown here (fig. 39), first published in 1859 and then as part of a report in 1863, shows a part of their journey in the summer of 1857 on the White Fish River, along the border with the U.S. The explorers' campsites are marked near the watery trail, allowing the reader to note their progress. The trail is annotated with topographic reports in the form of small inserts such as "stream strewn with boulders" to more extensive descriptions of the surrounding areas.

Texas and the Mexican War

The map from 1844 (fig. 40) was produced by the War Department's Corps of Topographical Engineers. The Corps was first constituted by Thomas Jefferson for the Lewis and Clark expedition. It was the federal organization responsible for many western explorations. A number of these are both noted on the map and on its bottom left portion under the title "Authorities."

The map shows the country in the process of becoming a nation. In the upper center of the map, the phrase "Proposed Nebraska Territory" hints at newly incorporated territory and states in formation.

One significant feature of the map's text is the uppermost left notation that reads, "The present boundaries of Texas are defined by an Act of the Texas Congress approved Dec. 9th, 1836." The map describes a tense and volatile geopolitical moment. Until Texas seceded from Mexico in 1836, the border between Spain (and then Mexico when it achieved independence in 1821) and the United States was much further north at the Red River. The United States long held designs on the land. In 1821 the Mexican ambassador to the United States wrote to his superiors in Mexico City, reporting that America intended to draw its boundaries at the Rio Grande.

In 1836 an anglo rebellion in Texas rose against the Mexicans and declared a republic. The boundary was set, as the map notes, at the Rio Grande. At the time the map was published, the situation was complex and confused. Mexico saw Texas as a province in revolt, whereas the United States viewed it as an independent republic. There were those in the United States who wanted Texas to become part of the Union, while others were wary. Annexation was possible but dangerous since it would provoke Mexico into war. The antislavery lobby worried about the addition of another slave state to the Union. Slavery was part of the constitution of Texas, and the text in the left of the map records both the number of free whites and the number of slaves.

This map was produced on the eve of war between Mexico and the United States. The careful mapping of the region was not just a scientific exercise, it was also an act of military surveillance.

The ornate map of 1848 (fig. 41) was produced after the war with Mexico. In March 1845 many Texans

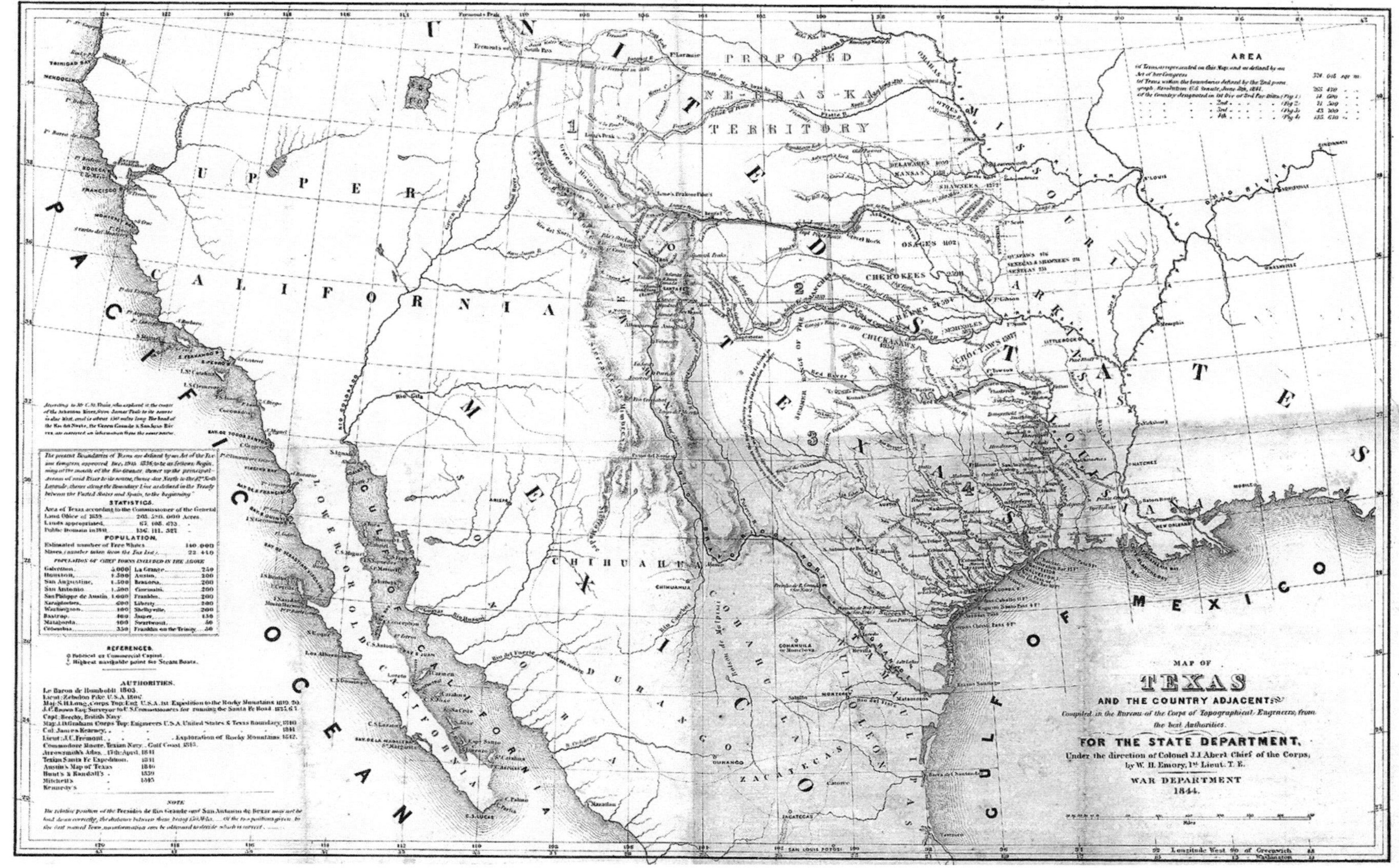

Fig. 40. Map of Texas and the Country Adjacent. William H. Emory. Washington: War Department, 1844.

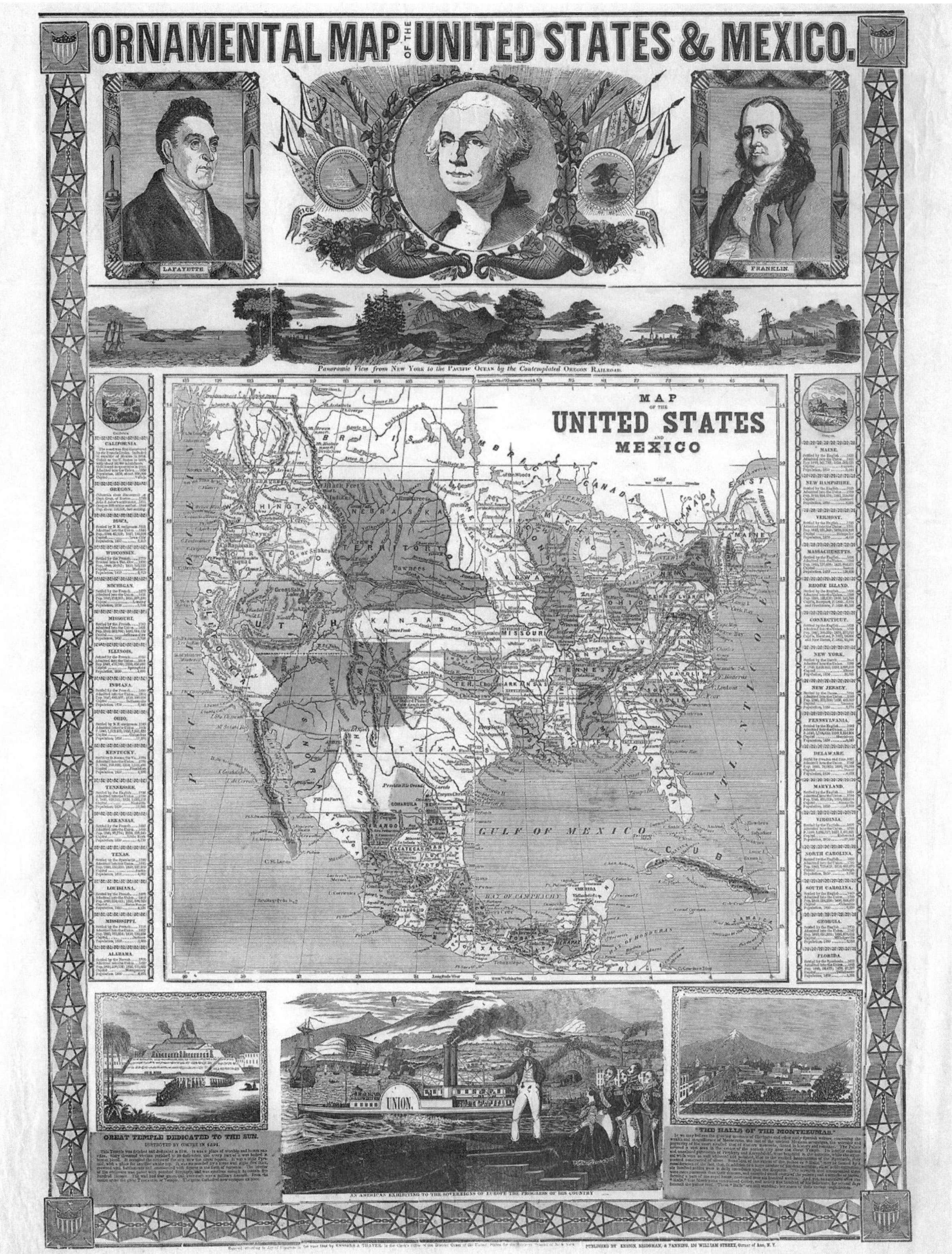

Fig. 41. Ornamental Map of the United States & Mexico. New York: Ensigns & Thayer, 1848.

Fig. 42. Untitled map of U.S. and Mexico. 1849.

refused the Mexican offer of recognition as a separate nation, and in December of that year Texas was officially admitted into the Union as a state. Hostilities between Mexico and the United States began in April 1846 and lasted until September 1847 when U.S. forces captured Mexico City. Under the Treaty of Guadalupe Hidalgo, signed in March 1848, the United States received a huge chunk of territory, including California, Arizona, New Mexico, Nevada, and Utah and parts of Wyoming, Colorado, and Oklahoma. In a major geopolitical turning point, Mexico lost half its territory and the United States became a continental power. Two years earlier in 1846 the boundary with Canada was fixed in the Pacific Northwest at the 42 parallel. The final piece of the territorial picture was concluded in 1854 when James Gadsden negotiated the purchase of land south of the Gila River in southern Arizona from Mexico. The continental United States was complete.

The map records the reality of Manifest Destiny. At the top of the map, below the portraits of George Washington, Benjamin Franklin, and the Marquis de Lafayette, a transect displays a land from sea to shining sea. Below the map, a proud American, raised higher than the European dignitaries, displays the signs and objects of social advancement and material progress: A steamboat with a U.S. flag plows through a busy harbor, a train passes through a tunnel, houses dot a well-watered agricultural landscape, and high above a balloon looks down on a prosperous land, an expanding economy, and a settled society. On either side of this picture, smaller images depict the splendors of the American past. The message is clear: they have been surpassed, the power of the ancients is eclipsed, and the United States now undertakes the mission of civilizing other lands. On either side of the map the individual states are represented. They may be separate, but they are shown as part of one great nation fulfilling its grand historic mission and ambitious territorial expansion.

The map of 1849 (fig. 42) reproduced here illustrates the U.S. international boundaries in the North and South. After years of uncertainty and limitations, the United States is now shown in its continental extent. However, it is still a land that has to be subdued and controlled. The map shows the forts used to control the newly won territory. An elaborate key distinguishes between old and new frontier stations, and a close look at the map reveals a steady westward march. As new territory is claimed and occupied, the line of the frontier forts pushes inexorably west. Some of the former frontier posts such as Fort Leavenworth and Fort Gibson continue to be occupied, whereas others, such as Fort Crawford and Fort Atkinson, have been abandoned. New forts are shown in the recently acquired lands of Texas and the Southwest and along the westward trails leading out of Fort Leavenworth. A cluster of new forts are also shown in California and the Pacific Northwest.

These forts were necessary to protect the new international borders and to subdue the local indigenous populations. They were the expression of U.S. power meant to impress and subdue those who resisted. The Native American tribes of the Great Plains, the West, and the southwest were to be surveyed, contained, and destroyed by the people of the forts. The forts mark the frontier.

The map shows both the outer limits of U.S. power and its center. Washington is displayed in bold capital letters, and the system of longitude at both the top and bottom of the map is measured from the capital. The maritime as well as the land connections between the East and West are also shown. This is a map of national territorial coherence.

Transportation

The map from 1848 shown here (fig. 43) is replete with typical railroad rhetoric. It shows a country gridded with railroads from the Atlantic to the Pacific. It also suggests that this transcontinental connection is merely one link in a global transportation system. The transcontinental railroad will, according to the text above the world map, "make us the center."

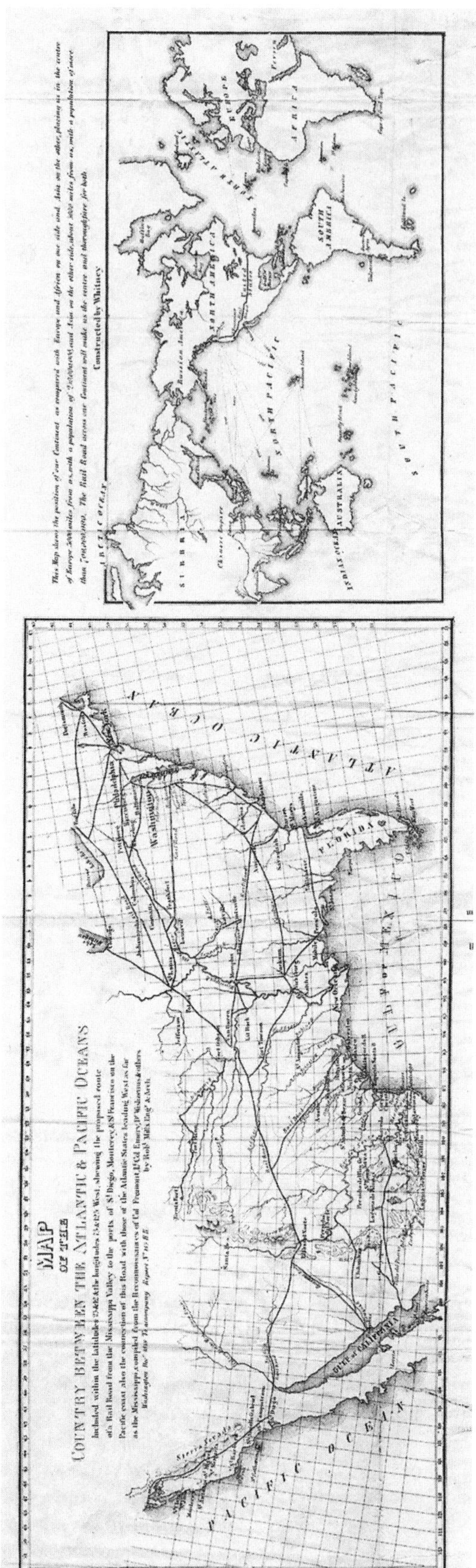

Fig. 43. Map of the Country between the Atlantic & Pacific Oceans . . . shewing the proposed route of a Rail Road from the Mississippi Valley to the ports of St. Diego, Monterey, & St. Francisco, 1848.

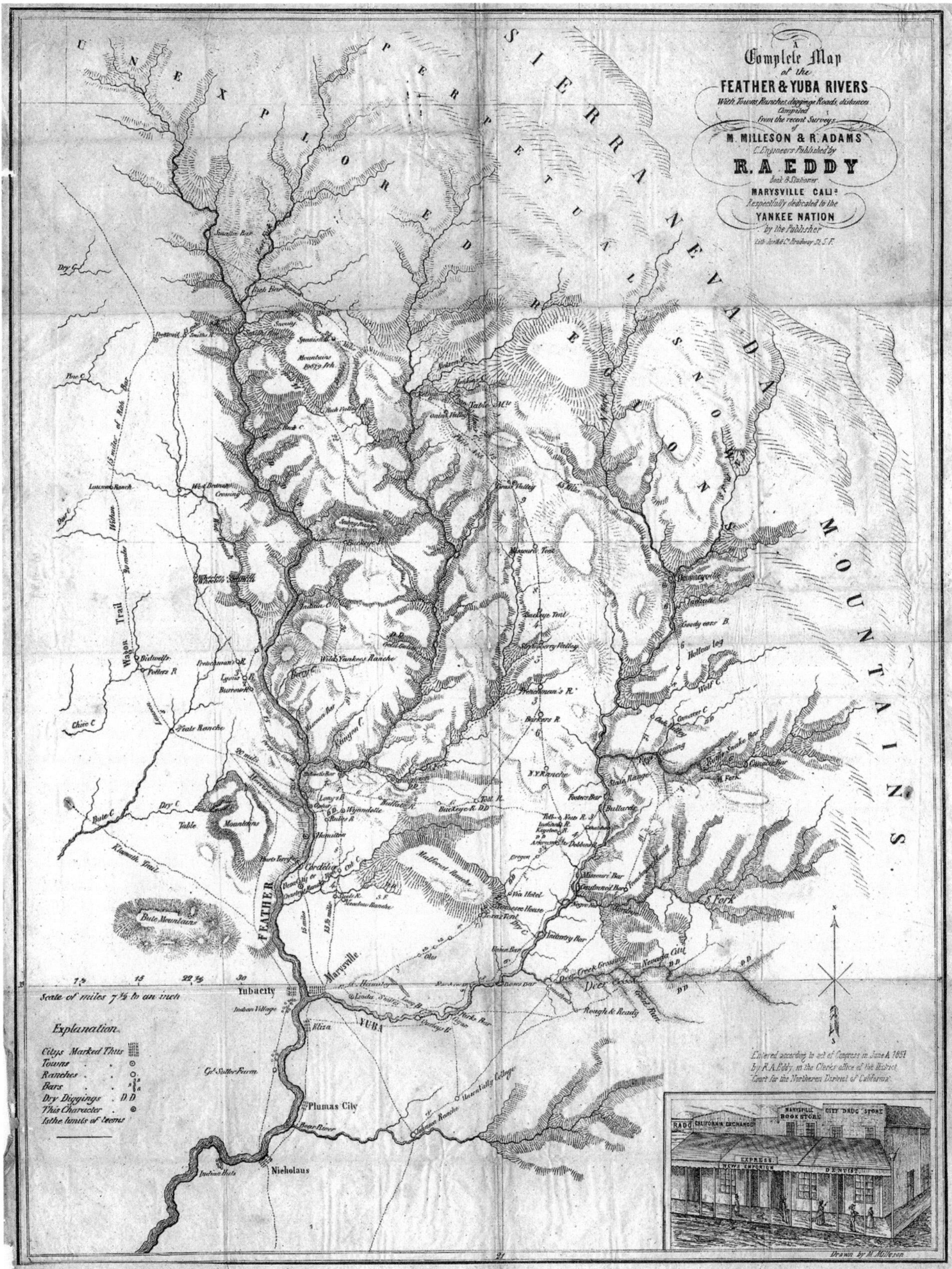

Fig. 44. **A Complete Map of the Feather & Yuba Rivers, with Towns, Ranches, diggings, Roads, distances. Compiled from the recent surveys of M. Milleson & R. Adams.** Marysville, Calif.: R. A. Eddy, 1851.

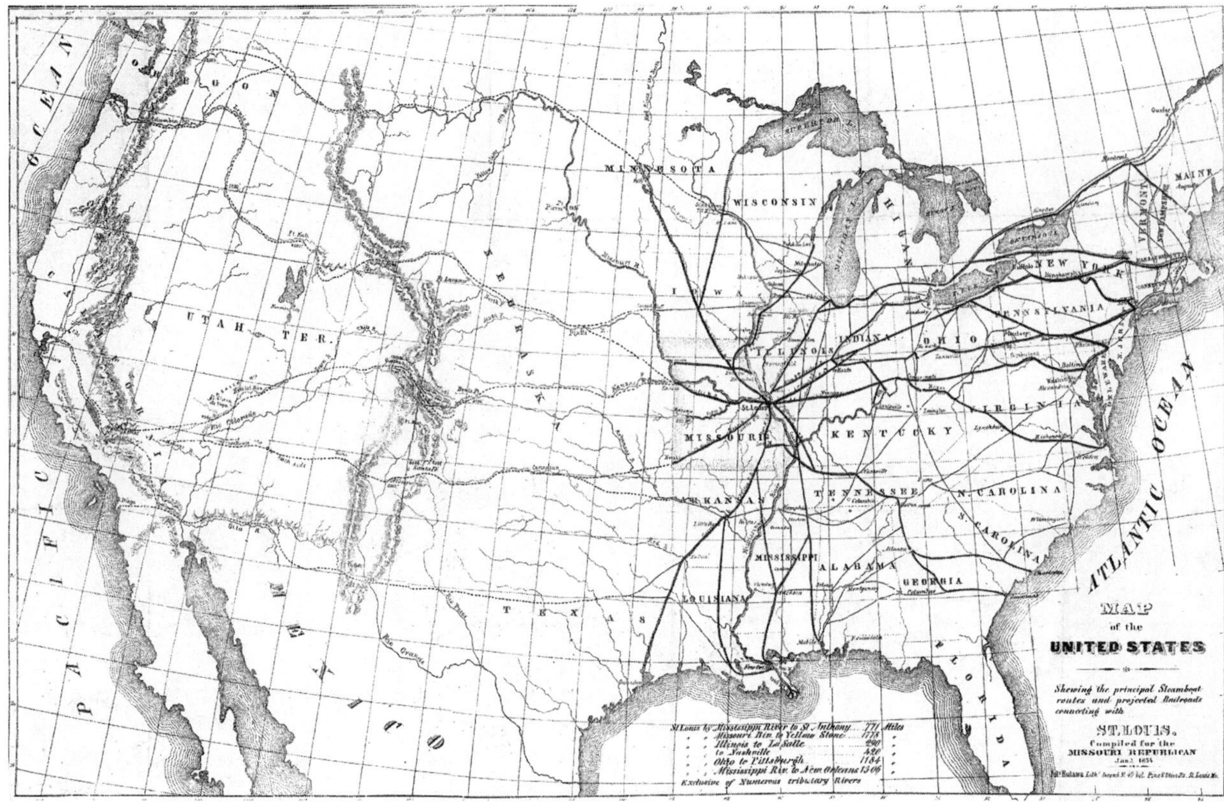

Fig. 45. Map of the United States Shewing the principal Steamboat routes and projected Railroads connecting with St. Louis. Compiled for the *Missouri Republican* Jany. 1854.

In 1848 this map was little more than a pipe dream. California was not yet a state, Oregon had become part of the continental United States just two years earlier, the railways only breached the Appalachians, and but a few lines reached the Mississippi, never mind the Rockies. The map is more of a promise than a reality. However, it was a reality that would come to pass. The territory had been assembled; the country now stretched from sea to shining sea. The map indeed depicts many of the routes that later would be built. The emphasis on East to West links rather than North to South connections that is revealed on this map would be repeated when people got around to building national railway lines.

The map also contains a profile of relief along one route from Little Rock to San Diego. It stretches all along the bottom of the page and even at a much reduced scale gives some idea of the enormity of the transcontinental project. Moving westward along the profile, as along the ground, one finally meets the formidable barrier of the southern Rocky Mountains.

Below the title of the map is a text that pays homage to the role of western explorers such as Col. John Fremont and Lt. Col. William Emory who played an important role in generating reliable topographical information on western lands beyond the settlement frontier. These explorers assembled the data that allowed engineers and laborers to build the railway lines which would come to connect the whole country.

Yuba City is located in the Sacramento Valley in northern California. It was established during the gold rush of 1849. The map of 1851 (fig. 44) is laid out at the detailed scale of 7.5 miles to 1 inch. It shows a variety of features, including the names of cities and towns, and those of newly established havens for miners such as "Rough and Ready." Gold diggings are shown on this map. Ranches are also identified, as well as a detailed topography indicated by a system of line shading known as hachures. This intricate shading has been used to good effect to show complicated river valleys, gulches, and steep-sided mountain streams.

This is a frontier area. In the north of the map the phrase "Unexplored Region" is noted.

This is very sophisticated transport map. The routes to gold diggings are clearly marked, and alongside the trails both the names of towns and ranches are shown. Between each point, the mapmaker has indicated beside a number of the trails the distance in miles. Someone traveling from Marysville to Veza City now knows that the distance is 15 miles. Since the map also suggests that the name of the town is Charley's Ranch, the weary traveler would not expect a giant metropolis.

The map caters to an incoming population eager to reach the gold fields and the towns and ranches where they can make money. This map is an early map of routes sketched in a frontier location for the brave and the greedy—just the kind of people you might meet walking along the boardwalk in Marysville, which is depicted in the insert illustration on the bottom right of the map.

In 1854 there were two principal means of mechanically transporting people and goods around the country. The first was the steamboat. Since 1807 steamboats had proved commercially viable. By 1830 steamboats could sail upstream against the flow of even the mighty Mississippi. Before the coming of the railways, and for a while afterward, they were the principal means of opening up the West to trade and settlement. St. Louis, situated on the banks of the Mississippi, was at the center of this dense network of steamboat river traffic that fanned out to Pittsburgh and down to New Orleans. Using the Mississippi and Ohio Rivers and other river arteries, steamboat traffic connected the vast interior. When the map presented here (fig. 45) was made in 1854, there were over 700 steamboats in the West, and by 1860 steamboats could travel as far upriver as Fort Benton in Montana.

The other main form of transport was the railway. Trains could travel faster than the 20-mile-per-hour steamboats and be built inland away from the large rivers. At the time of this map the railroad companies were on the eve of major expansion. Within thirty years four transcontinental lines would be built and the amount of track would increase from approximately 30,000 miles to almost 95,000 miles.

This map was made to sing the praises of St. Louis. It is positioned at the center of the steamboat traffic. The city is poised to become the hub of a transcontinental rail network, with all but one of the five future lines to travel West connecting directly there. In fact, four lines were later built across the country, and St. Louis was a major transportation center for water, rail, and eventually road and air. Their map, the work of an early advocate of St. Louis, was not far from the mark.

Gold Rush in California

In late January of 1848 gold was found in the Sacramento Valley in what was soon to become the state of California. When the gold was discovered, a peace treaty to end the war between Mexico and the United States had not yet been signed. Technically the land belonged to Mexico until the Treaty of Guadalupe Hidalgo was signed in March 1848.

News of the gold find soon spread throughout the region, across the country, and around the world. The magnetic attraction that the lure of gold had on people around the world is shown in the map of 1849 (fig. 46), which depicts the global race to reach the gold fields of the West. The single hemispheric map of the world provides a useful context in which to highlight the worldwide attraction. Lines are drawn from different parts of the world, all headed toward San Francisco and the California gold fields from across the Pacific: 13,000 from Calcutta, 8,300 from Canton, 11,000 from Sydney, and 9,500 from New Zealand. A line around the coast of the American continent signals the route of 20,000 traveling from London around the hazardous Cape Horn. The route from New York hugs the coast as far south as Panama, then across the narrow land bridge, then north along the coast. This was for wealthier travelers. Those with little money had to travel in overcrowded compartments in leaky vessels rounding the southern tip of the continent. Not shown in the map are the trails forged across the country by those traveling overland.

San Francisco was transformed almost overnight from a tiny village to a town of 25,000 and ultimately to a major metropolis. California became a magnet for people in the United States and around the world. Its attraction has scarcely dimmed over the years. Present-day routes would show airlines and motorways still luring people to California in the hope of realizing their dreams.

When people eventually arrived in California they needed to know where to go. The 1849 map of the gold regions (fig. 47) shows, albeit not in great detail, the location of gold. At this scale they give the migrant very little detailed topographic information. The map is more useful as a general picture of the entire region.

The notes in the map tell us a great deal about the routes, time, and cost of travelling to the gold fields. At the bottom left of the map distances to various points along the coastal route from New York are shown. It was a total of 5,700 long and uncomfortable miles between New York and San Francisco via the overland Panama route. The notes also record that a "railroad is in contemplation." A canal rather than a railroad was eventually built, but that would occur long after the gold rush had ended. The notes allow us to see the comparative distances and times of the different routes. From New York to San Francisco around Cape Horn was a massive 17,000 miles. The Panama route was thus quicker and more expensive. People were in a hurry. What fueled the rush was the desire to reach the gold as quickly as possible. Latecomers would find no gold; it would be taken by those who arrived there sooner. The Panama route took 30 to 35 days and cost between $300 to $420, the Cape Horn route took from 130 to 150 days and cost between $100 and $300.

The 1848 boundary line with Mexico is shown just south of San Diego. To the south the name "Old California" is listed. The implication is that land above the line is "new California." And in many ways it was a new California, a California transformed by the 1849 gold rush and the influx of people from around the country and across the world.

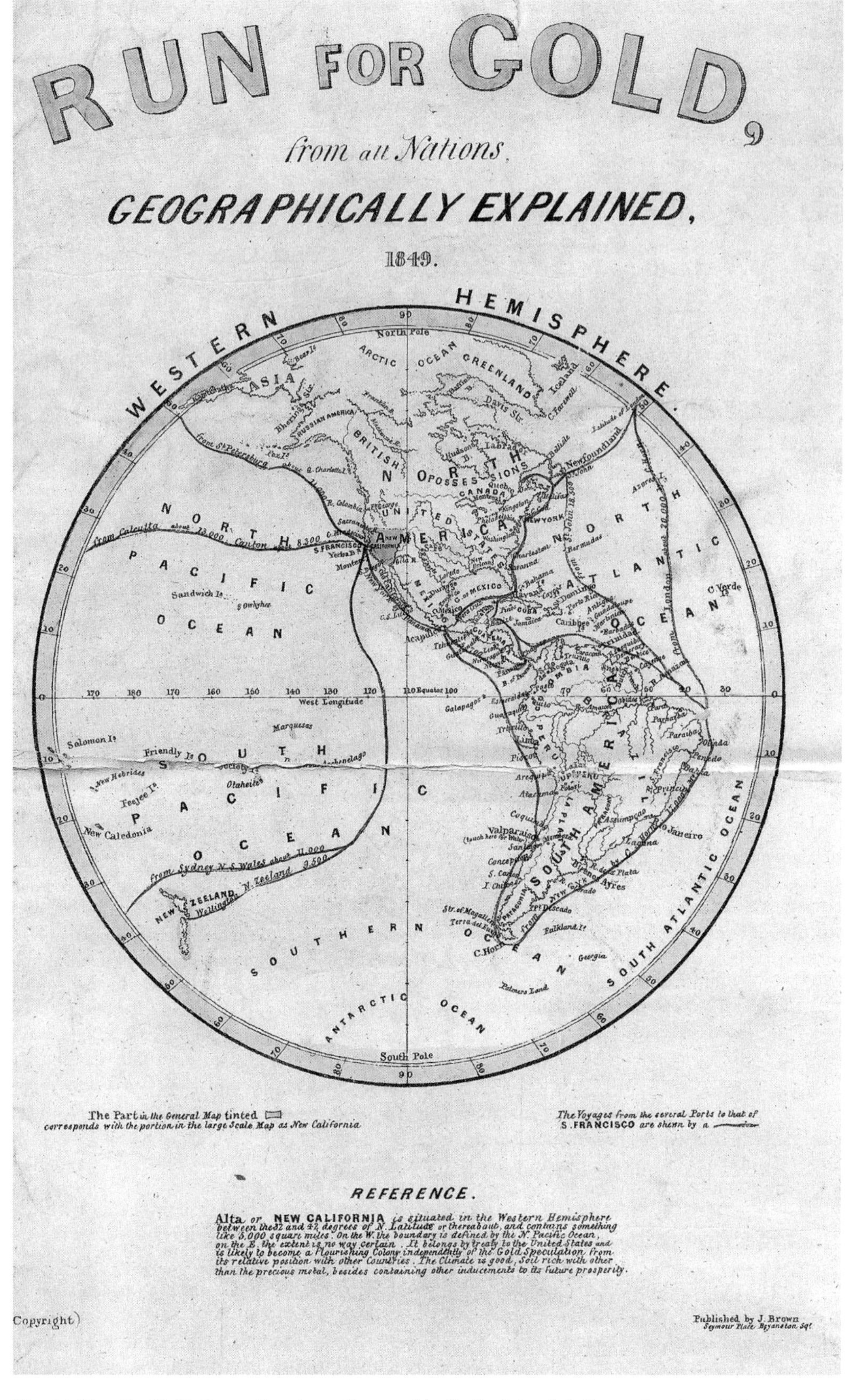

Fig. 46. Run for Gold, from all nations, Geographically Explained. J. Brown. London, 1849.

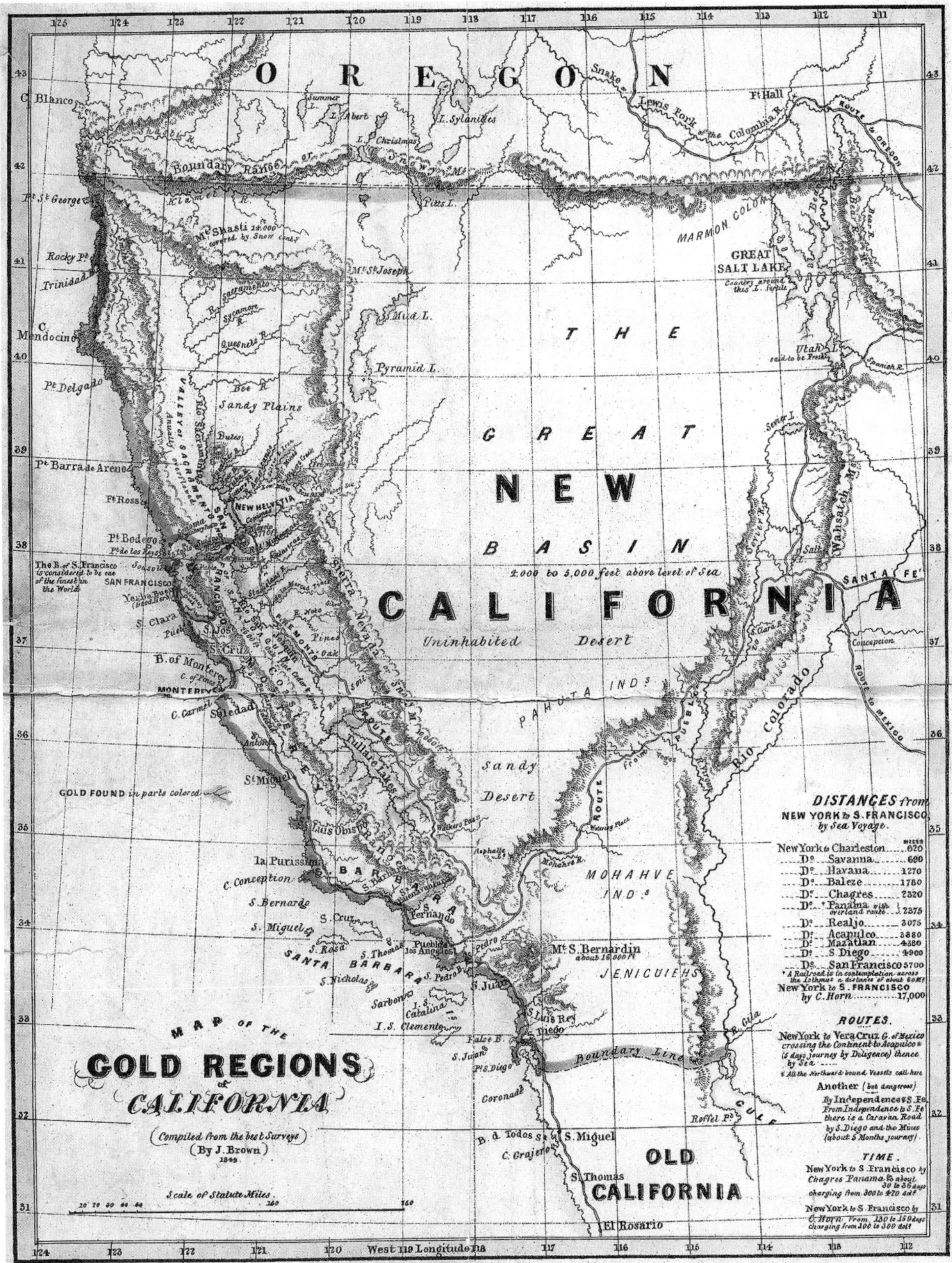

Fig. 47. Map of the Gold Regions of California, Compiled from the best Surveys by J. Brown. London, 1849.

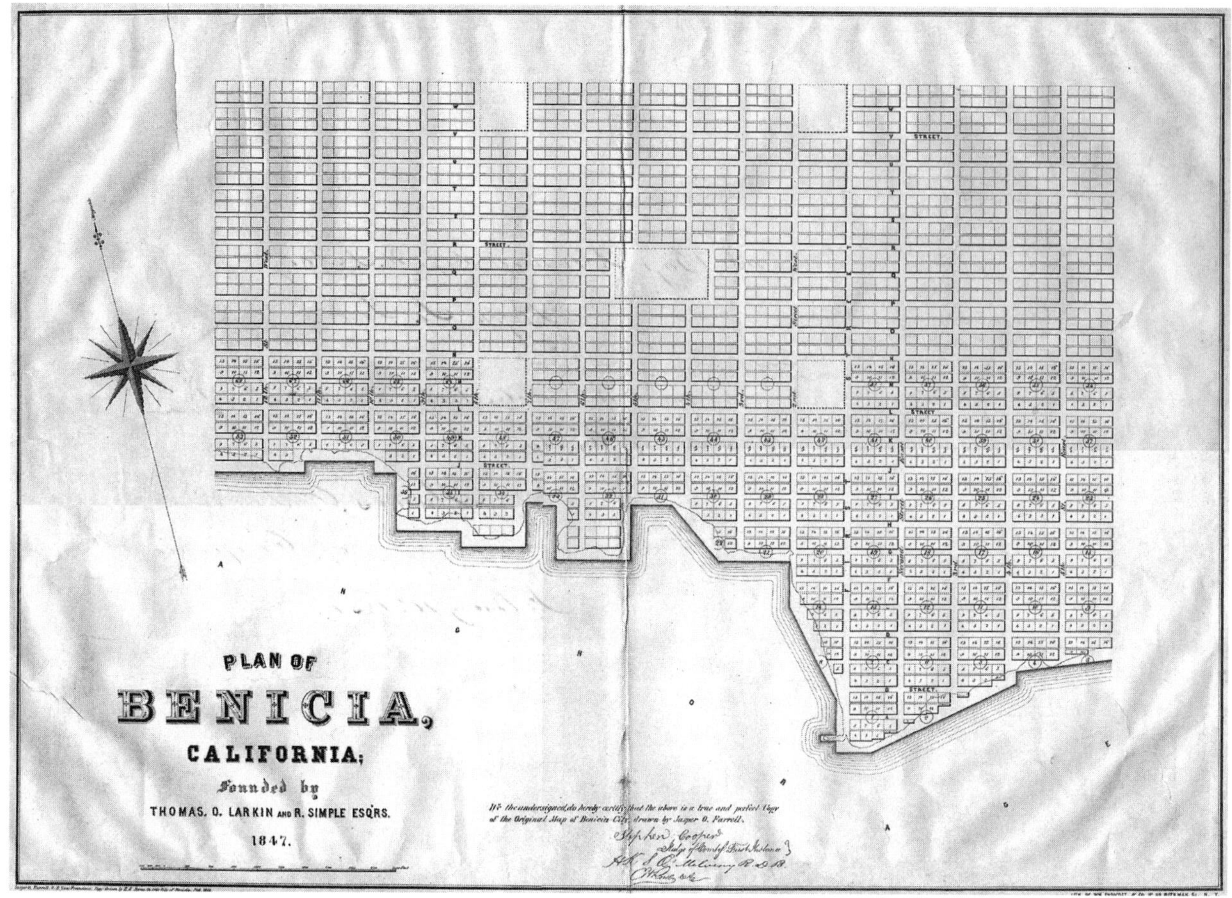

Fig. 48. Plan of Benicia, California; Founded by Thomas O. Larkin and R. Simple Esq'rs. 1847. We the undersigned hereby certify that the above is a true and perfect Copy of the Original Map of Benicia City, drawn by Jasper O. Farrell. San Francisco. Copy drawn by E. H. Rome in this City of Benicia, Feb. 1850. Lith. Of Wm. Endicott & Co. . . . N. Y.

The town of Benicia is located at the mouth of the Sacramento River where it flows into San Pablo Bay, the northern part of San Francisco Bay. The map from 1850 shown here (fig. 48) illustrates the grid-like division of the city.

The grid was a common feature of Midwestern and western towns of the nineteenth century. It was easy to draw, paid little attention to local topographies, and has been referred to as the triumph of geometry over geography. The streets are numbered east to west with letters north to south. Each block is divided into sixteen units. The unnumbered blocks are probably set aside for public spaces, schools, parks and public buildings. The grid is infinitely reproducible and seems to move relentlessly to the very edge of the map.

Within such a grid-like pattern the incredible activity of the 1849 gold rush took place. The mute lattice was the context for all kinds of wheeling and dealing. The town was for a very brief period from 1853 to 1854 the third capital of California. The town was too small to cope with the expanding functions of a rapidly growing state, and as a result of this and political shenanigans, the state government moved to Sacramento. The old capitol building is now a state park.

The name Benicia references the convoluted history of California. The founder of the town, Robert Semple, was involved in the Bear Flag Revolt, during which a group of armed Americans led by Fremont and William Ide seized the town of Sonoma and control of California from the Mexicans until Commodore John Sloat claimed the territory for the United States; he was one of those who arrested Gen. Mariano Vallejo and took him to Sacramento. According to local legend, the wily American persuaded Vallejo to grant him a piece of land where the town now stands. Vallejo's only stipulation was that the town be named after his wife. It is an interesting story. And it may even be true. Even if it is not, the name of the town nonetheless reminds us of the Hispanic influence in this part of the United States.

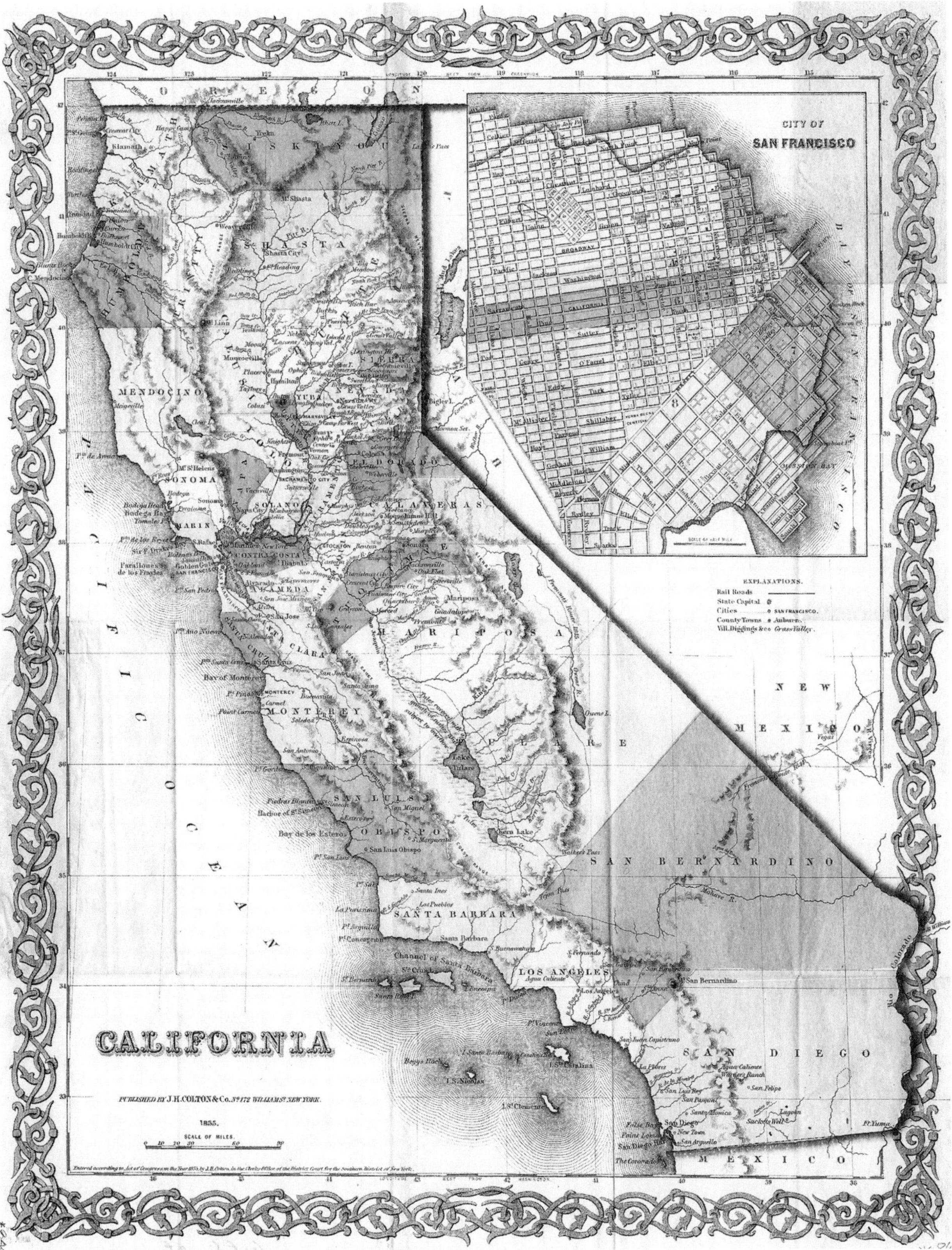

Fig. 49. **California.** New York: J. H. Colton. 1855.

The map of California from 1855 (fig. 49) shows the state's present-day boundaries. Stretching from Oregon in the north to Mexico in the south, the state had reached its full extent. At a scale of approximately 50 miles to an inch, the map covers the entire state in a single page, although at the expense of some detail. The county boundaries are depicted, including Los Angeles, San Bernardino, and Mendocino. These are large, a legacy from the extensive landholdings of the Spanish and then Mexican era. Another legacy from the Hispanic past is the line of missions, identified on the map as towns that are located throughout the state. From San Diego and San Luis Rey in the south, through San Juan Capistrano, San Gabriel, and Santa Barbara, all the way as far north as San Francisco, the missions were places of worship, social control, and agricultural production.

The map also shows towns and villages. California was only lightly settled at this time, with two major exceptions. The first was the gold towns that had grown rapidly from 1849. All over the upper Sacramento Valley there is a scatter of town names around Yuba and Marysville. Some of these grew quickly then declined. Others became ghost towns as soon as the gold ran out. The second exception was San Francisco, which was the first major port of call for the 49ers. The city grew into the largest urban area in the state. In the upper right-hand corner of the map there is an insert of the city's grid-like street pattern. Few of the buildings from this era survive, victims of time, earthquake, or fire.

The map shows the physical topography of the state, and evidence of the Hispanic presence in missions as well as many Spanish names for towns, mountains, rivers, and counties that survive to this day. It is a map that reveals the northern urban bias of the state in the wake of the gold rush. Further south only a few missions and small settlements dot the landscape. And while Los Angeles is cited on the map, it appears as an insignificant place.

THE CIVIL WAR

Slavery was a problem that would not disappear. Widespread throughout all the colonies, by the end of the eighteenth century, it was concentrated in the cotton-growing areas along the Georgia and Carolina coast. The invention of the cotton gin in 1793 allowed the wider spread of cotton production and also slavery. In 1793 only 300 bales of cotton were produced in the United States; by the time of the Civil War, the number rose to almost 4 million bales produced as far west as Texas and as far north as Virginia and Tennessee. By 1860 there were 4 million slaves and slavery had become a big business, as well as a "peculiar institution."

Slavery became an important issue in the expansion of the United States. In the Northwest Ordinance of 1787 Congress barred slavery from the states of Ohio, Indiana, Illinois, Michigan, and Wisconsin. Entry to the Union was contingent. Under the Missouri Compromise of 1820 Maine was added as a free state, while Missouri joined as a slave state. Other compromises in 1850 and 1854 determined California's free status. After the Dred Scott decision of the Supreme Court in 1857, most of the West except California was either slave or open to slavery by decision.

Although slavery was the underlying cause of the territorial rupture, the Civil War was fought over the constitutional issue of the right to secede from the Union. In December 1860 the first Southern states seceded from the Union. While a majority in Southern states voted to secede, there were also areas, such as the Appalachian South, where a majority voted against secession. By 1861 the nation was at war.

One of the first military battles took place at Bull Run. The 1861 map reproduced here (fig. 50) has a regional map on the bottom left that shows the battle was fought just southwest of Washington D.C.

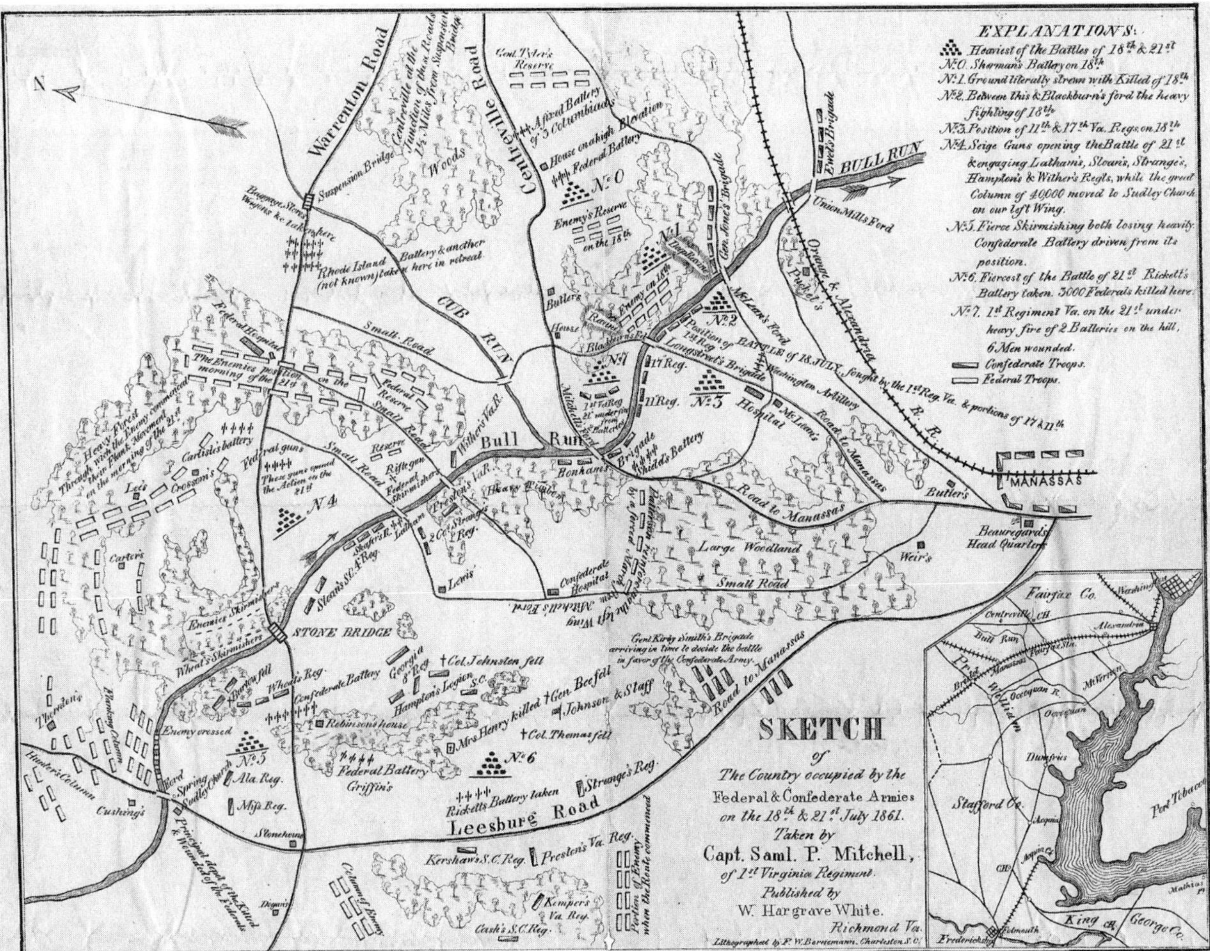

Fig. 50. Sketch of The Country occupied by the Federal & Confederate Armies on the 18th & 21st July 1861. Taken by Capt. Saml. P. Mitchell, of 1st Virginia Regiment. Richmond: W. Hargrave White, 1861.

Battles are confused affairs. This map, drawn by a Confederate soldier, Capt. Samuel Mitchell, makes some attempt to bring order out of the chaos. It is difficult to read because the map not only shows topography, but also how the battle played out over a few days. The explanation in the top right holds the key to understanding how the battle unfolded over both time and space.

On 16 July 1861 a large Union army led by Brig. Gen. Irwin McDowell moved south toward Manassas in Virginia. There they met a Confederate force. General Pierre Beauregard, whose headquarters are shown just below the end of the railway line, commanded 20,000 Confederate soldiers.

The encounter reached a head on July 21 when three Federal brigades opened fire at the Stone Bridge over Bull Run (see 4 in the map's explanation chronology). At the same time, five brigades moved on the ford just south of Stone Bridge, marked on the map beside Sudley Church. The advance did not hold, and by late afternoon Union forces began a retreat that ended as a rout.

Bull Run was the first major battle of the war. A confused affair with inexperienced troops and less than brilliant commanders, it was nonetheless a Confederate victory in that the Union army left the field. But the confederates did not take advantage of the situation by capturing men or arms. The confusion and chaos of the battlefield are captured in the map with its myriad symbols and confusing chronology.

The detailed plan of Cantonment Sprague from 1861 (fig. 51), drawn at a scale of 100 feet to 1 inch, reveals an army camp under construction. In the right center of the map, dotted lines outline army barracks being planned, while around them one sees a rural landscape affected by the war. The landscape is, in part, a bucolic scene: trees, bluffs, rivers, farm roads, the houses of local folk, including Jonathan Searer and G. W. Keatings, and the impressive mansion of Mrs. Joseph Gales. In the top right there is an illustration of the Burnside Cottage, in what could be mistaken as an innocent scene of men idly chatting away the morning. There is another landscape in this map, however: evidence of armies and war preparation, a target practice area, kitchens and commissary, stables, and a parade ground.

The capitol of the nation and the seat of federal power lay deep in the South, surrounded by slave states, and just to its south the state of Virginia that had seceded from the Union in April. The Confederacy counted

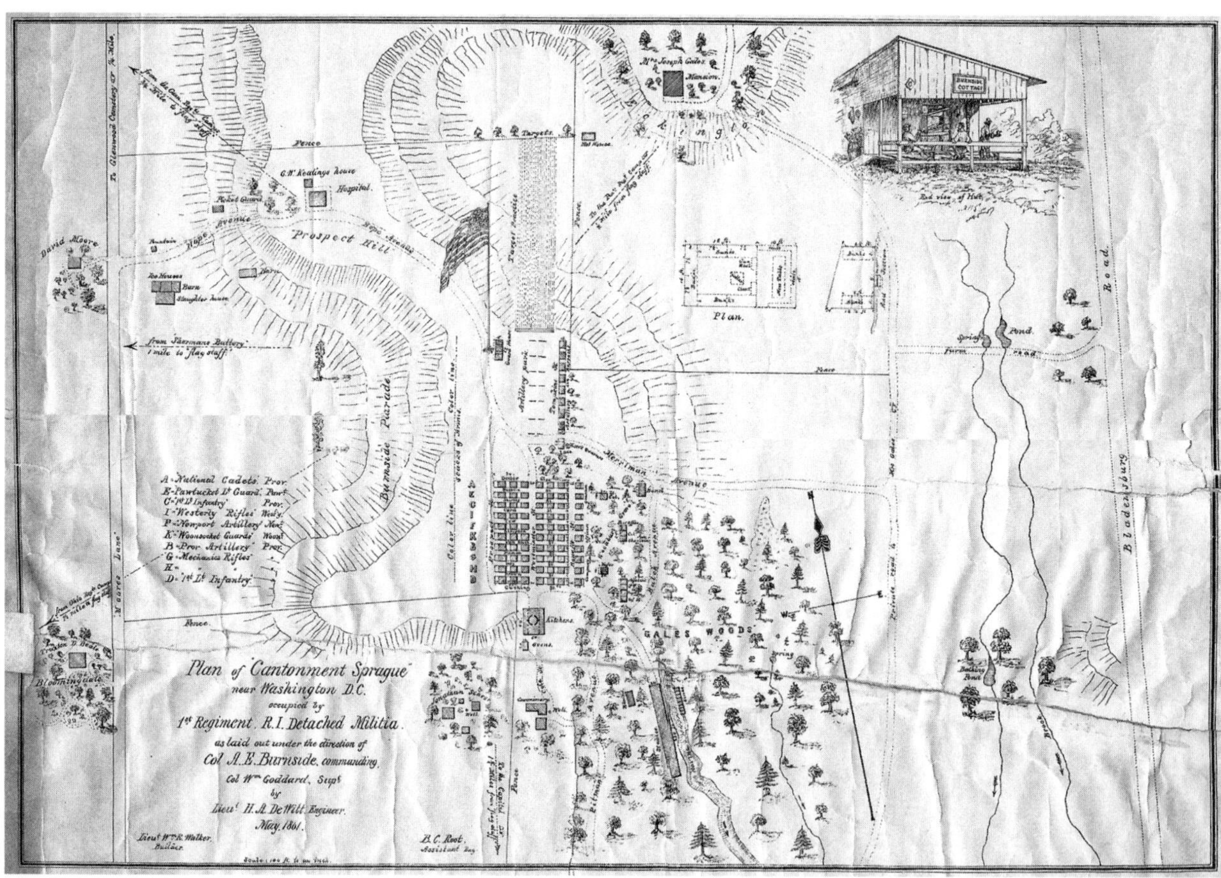

Fig. 51. Plan of Cantonment Sprague near Washington, D.C. May 1861.

100,000 volunteers by March 1861. President Abraham Lincoln, in his proclamation of 15 April 1861, called for 75,000 volunteers in three months. In two weeks 35,000 soldiers were either in Washington or on their way there. Every Northern state had a volunteer militia force. Men who had been made colonels by the state governor also raised regiments.

In the middle of the map the First Regiment of the Rhode Island Detached Militia is shown. In neat army regulation lines the camp of the cadets, riflemen, and infantry from the towns and regions of the small state is laid out. The volunteers from Newport, Providence, and Pawtucket were no doubt eager to see some action. On the edge of Gales Wood the men waited to go to war. The vast majority of troops on either side were under twenty-one. Farm boys and city men heeded the patriotic call, but also sought adventure and a chance for glory. All too soon, their desires would be met.

After the rout at Bull Run, Gen. George McClellan spent months training the Union Army of the Potomac. Its strategy focused on the capture of Richmond in Virginia. McClellan arrived at a plan to locate his men at the mouth of the peninsula formed between the York and James Rivers and then quickly move them toward Richmond. When the Confederate army in Virginia began to move further back from Washington to protect Richmond, McClellan's plan was adopted. Battles rarely unfold according to plan. The Union army was stalled at Yorktown, where McClellan besieged the town for over a month, enough time for the Confederates to increase the defenses of Richmond. The Army of the Potomac got as close as six miles to Richmond but was beaten back. On 25 June 1862, Gen. Robert E. Lee led an attack on McClellan's forces. The Seven Days' Battle succeeded in pushing back the Federal army from Richmond. McClellan's forces withdrew to Harrison's Landing on the James River where Federal gunboats provided them with protective firepower.

The Confederates saved Richmond but lost one-quarter of their men. McClellan was defeated, yet he managed to save most of his army by strategically withdrawing to Harrison's Landing.

The map shown here, drawn by command of McClellan in 1862 (fig. 52), illustrates the site of the assault on Richmond and the scene of many of the Seven Days' battles. Harrison's Landing is shown in the bottom center of the map, while Richmond appears just off the edge of the left-hand side of the map. Between them lie such places as Malvern Hill, scene of the final battle of this engagement when Federal artillery and gunboats stationed in the James River cut down 5,000 of Lee's men. The map depicts a landscape of trees, rivers, houses, and railways. What it does not show is that in the summer of 1862 the landscape was awash with blood.

The map from 1864 (fig. 53) marks a turn in the tide of events. Although the early years of the Civil War were confused, the Confederates won most of the major engagements. With fewer soldiers but smarter generals the Confederates had kept the upper hand. The year 1863, however, marked a turning point. The successful Union siege of Vicksburg and the Battle of Gettysburg foreshadowed the defeat of the Confederacy.

The map provides a graphic account of the establishment, rise, and beginning fall of the Confederacy. The original map's ingenious color-coded key allows us to see the flux of events. Areas coded purple, green, and yellow mark the territory claimed by the Confederacy in 1861, which includes Southern states south of the Mason-Dixon Line as well as Arizona, New Mexico, Texas, and the "Indian Territory." It is an area of over a million square miles with a population of 8.3 million free inhabitants and 3.9 million slaves. Although this represents the ambitious reach of the Confederacy, its military control was somewhat less. The areas marked green and yellow are the territory actually under the military command of the Confederacy. This stretch of land does not include Arizona, New Mexico, and the "Indian Territory." But it is still a significant chunk of territory.

By 1864 Federal forces had begun their successful prosecution of the war. The map highlights in green territory reclaimed by Union forces. These include a T-shaped swathe of territory up the Mississippi, with one arm going east through Kentucky and Tennessee and down into Maryland, and the other going west through Missouri. Green outliers are also shown along the Florida coastline and in South Carolina. What remains yellow is the heart of the Confederacy that by January 1864 still remained in Confederate control: an area of almost half a million square miles and a total population of almost 6 million.

The map not only depicts the space of the Civil War, but also its temporal dynamic. It is a Union map that highlights the contraction of Confederate power and by implication the expansion of Union control. In 1864 much of the South still remains defiantly Confederate, but in little more than a year even the Southern heartland would fall to Union power.

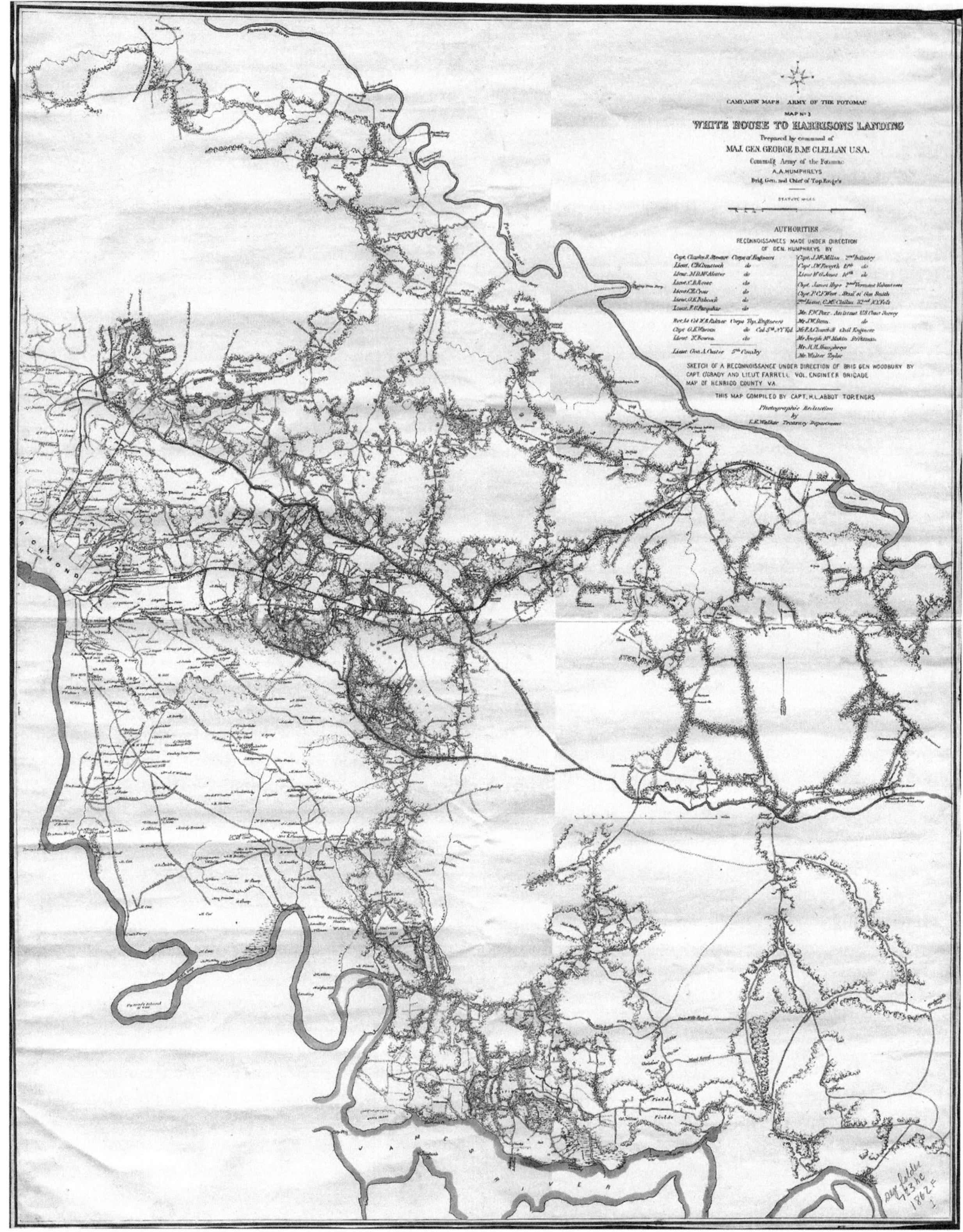

Fig. 52. White House to Harrison's Landing. Henry L. Abbot. Campaign Maps, Army of the Potomac, Map No. 3. Prepared by command of Maj. Gen. George B. McClellan. 1862.

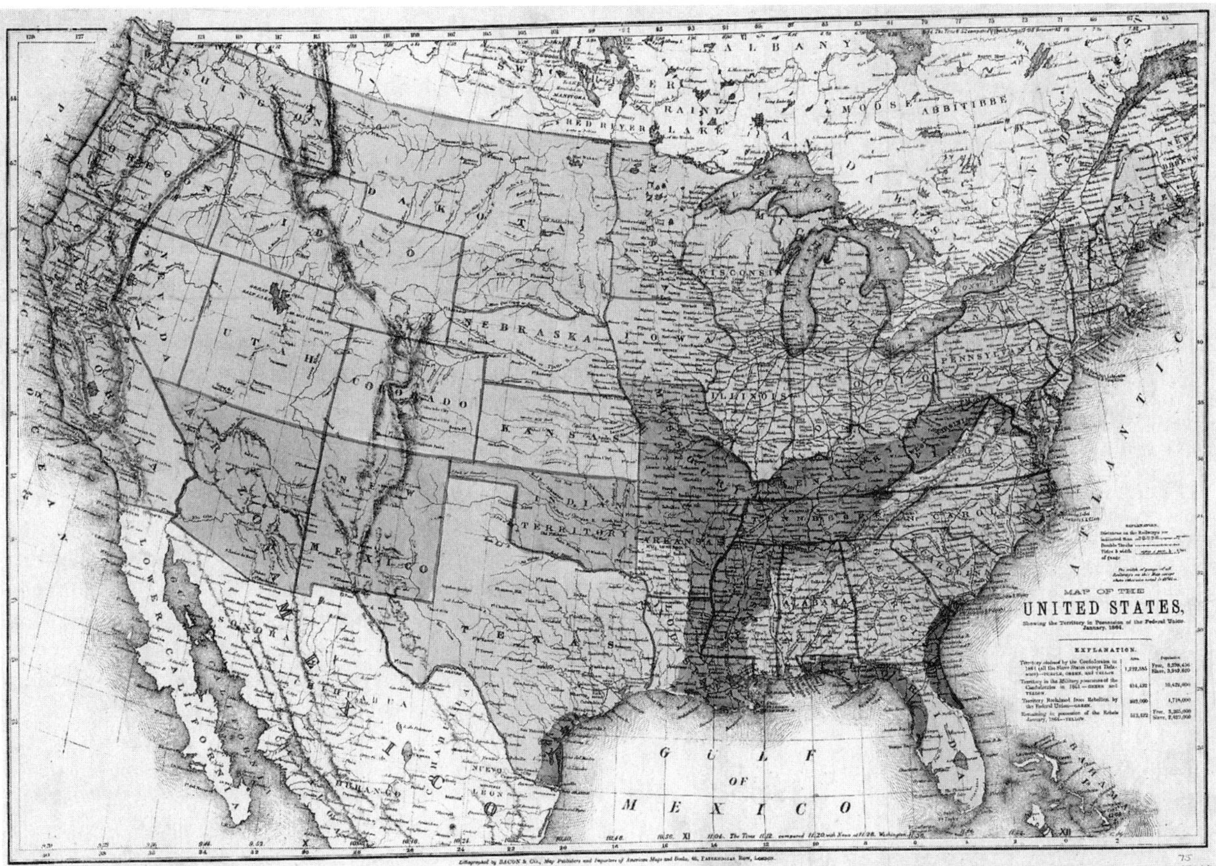

Fig. 53. Map of the United States, Showing the Territory in Possession of the Federal Union, January 1864. London: Bacon & Co., 1864.

NEW YORK—THE DEVELOPMENT OF A CITY

New York is the largest city in the United States. One of the first sites of Dutch and then English settlement, it has been continuously settled by Europeans since the early seventeenth century. It is a city that has grown to national and international significance. It is a truly global city with a population from around the world and social, economic, and political ties that span the globe.

The story of the city can be told in many ways: through the lives of its citizens, the history of its buildings and enterprises, the evolution of its politics. Here we tell the story in maps. They will show the inexorable growth of the city from a tiny foothold on the southern tip of Manhattan to a sprawling metropolis. The neat little settlement is shown in a series of cartographic snapshots extending up the island in the march of a mathematically precise grid that hides the island's topography in a predetermined geometry. The magnificent Central Park provides a welcome relief from the gridded streets.

Successive maps show the restless dynamism of the place. Railways, ferries, piers, bridges, and tunnels connect Manhattan to the expanding metropolis and the wider world.

By the end of the Twentieth Century, the city skyline had become one of the most recognized urban signatures in the world. Two contemporary maps provide a cartographic picture of New York City before and after 11 September 2001.

The French map reproduced here (fig. 54) was published in 1675, eleven years after the English takeover of the Dutch colony when New Amsterdam became New York. The map shows the settlement clinging to the tip of Manhattan Island, protected in the north by fortifications that later would be known as Wall Street.

The settlement looks orderly, the streets planned on a regular grid pattern. It is well defended with impressive fortifications and a fort. There are signs of political power: the town hall (*Maison de Ville*) and governor's residence. New York was part of the English maritime empire that was just beginning to spread its tentacles around the globe. The place was one more node in a global trading system and network of military and politi-

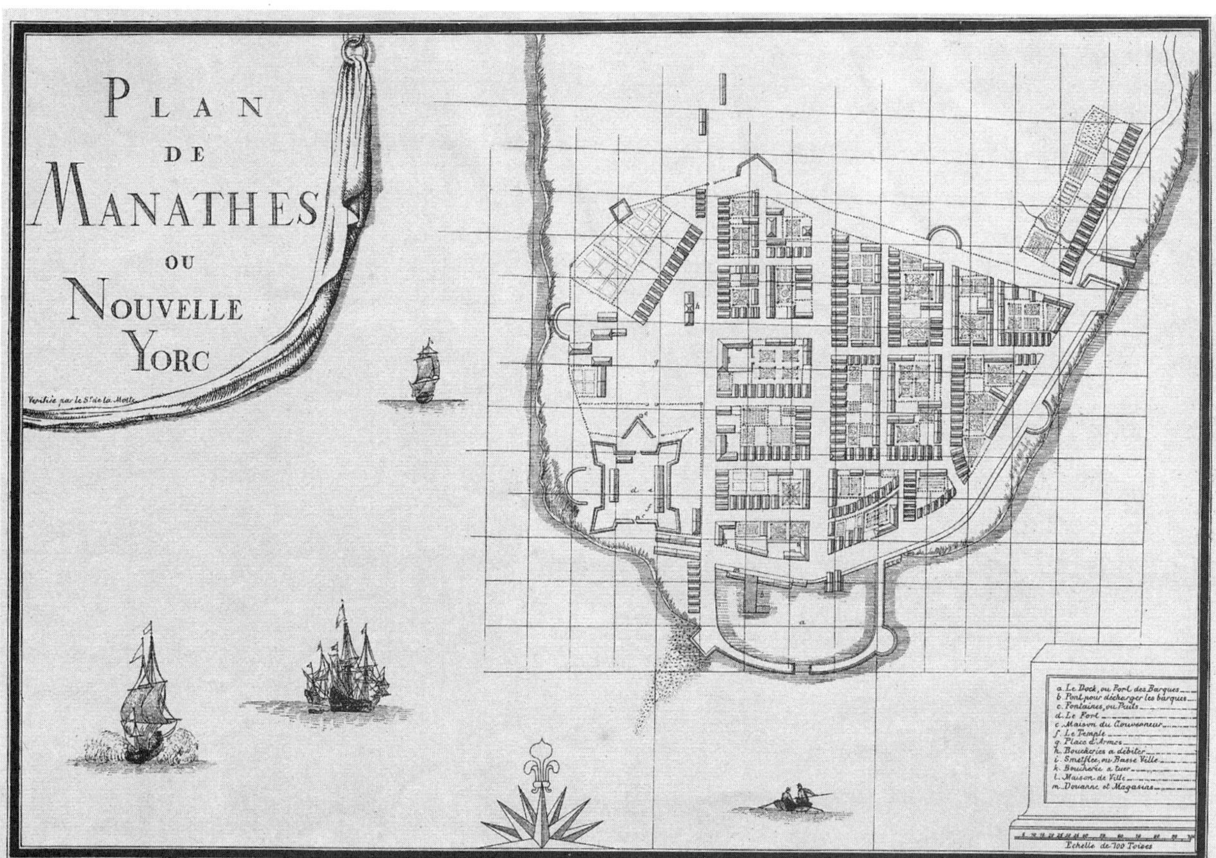

Fig. 54. Plan de Manathes ou Nouvelle Yorc. Verifiée par le Sr de la Motte. C. 1675. [Facsimile of part of "Carte de la Côte de la Nouvelle-Angleterre. . . . par J. B. L. Franquelin, hydrographe du roy." Archives du Dépôt de la Marine, Paris.]

cal power. It is a military post. However, there are also signs of an unruly urban reality. In the northeast beyond the protective but also controlling embrace of the wall, a line of houses is shown. The new developments beyond the formal boundaries are the first stirrings of an urban dynamism that would blossom in the ensuing years.

The New York of the late seventeenth century was a dense collection of buildings but a relatively small place, with kitchen gardens and green spaces behind most facades. It was more of a village than the city it was soon to become.

New York was part of a wider political and commercial network. It is situated right beside the water, and the dock is one the largest and most impressive structures in the city. The decorative illustrations show ships that link this tiny colony with a wider world. Situated on the southern tip of Manhattan, New York is obviously part of a wider global order.

In the second map of New York City (fig. 55) we can see the expansion of the city further up the island of Manhattan. By the date of this map, made in 1728, the northern line of fortifications has become Wall Street and Broadway is just beginning its relentless march up the island. The city has lost the neat gridlike regularity of the previous map. It is a more chaotic, but also a more dynamic robust-looking city that seems almost alive as we look at it. The cartographer, William Bradford, has succeeded in embodying the vitality of the city in his map.

The maritime influence is still strong—in fact, stronger than before as the growth of the city is now intimately related to places over the river and across the seas. Docks, shipyards, and keys now encircle most of the inhabited part of Manhattan. Ships and boats sail up what is now called the Hudson (North River on the map) and the East River. This is a city not only on the water, but of the water.

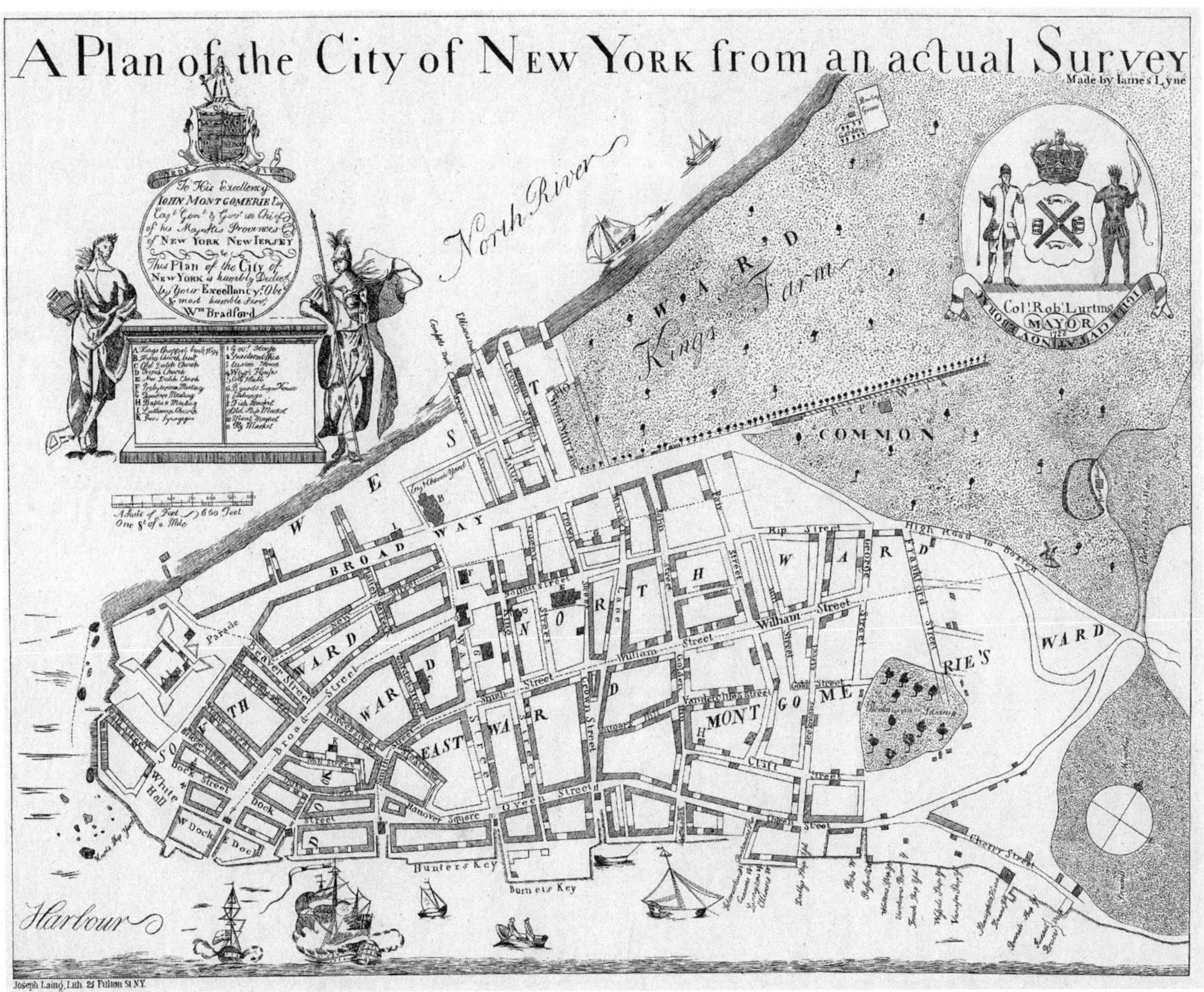

Fig. 55. Reproduction of A Plan of the City of New York from an actual Survey, Made by James Lyne. New York: William Bradford, 1728.

A city of religious observation and a city of commerce are shown in the map. The key lists churches and places of commercial exchange. There are a variety of both places of worship and places of economic transactions. The Old Dutch Church, French Church and Jew's Synagogue suggest a polyglot, variegated community, whereas the Fish Market, Meat Market, and Exchange tell of an expanding commercial life. Secular life and commercial life are shown. The city teems with life.

The plan of the city of New York (fig. 56) was first published in 1838. The city was the largest in the entire Republic. To some it seemed like the most natural place

Fig. 56. Plan of the City of New York for the Use of Strangers. Undated but similar to a map published by S. Mahon of New York in 1831.

to locate the nation's capitol. Washington D.C. had become the capital as a result of a deal struck between Alexander Hamilton and Thomas Jefferson.

The city is now taking a shape familiar to us today. Around the tip there is the skewed historic grid pattern that reflects both the earliest Dutch and English settlements. North of Washington Square is the very gridded block system. Avenues running north to south are numbered from one to ten, and streets running east to west are numbered from one upward. This grid pattern was adopted after the New York Assembly passed an act in 1807 to "lay out streets, roads, and public squares of such width and extent as them should seem most conducive for the public good." A plan was drawn up by three commissioners, Simeon DeWitt, Governeur Morris, and John Rutherford, and published in 1811. The plan spread the grid over the entire island. This map of 1838 (fig. 56) shows that the grid predates urban developments: Although the grid is on the ground, there are few buildings above 1st Street. The grid plan established the shape that later urban developments in the city would follow.

The city has grown from the making of the previous map. The list of churches is more extensive. The city is even more of a melting pot, with Episcopalians, Presbyterians, Baptists, Dutch Reformed, Methodists, Jews, and other religious groups sharing the same city but worshipping at different places. On the top right of the map the list of banks is impressive. There are also public buildings: libraries, post offices, hospitals, and asylums. Banks and almshouses tell the story of a city composed of rich and poor.

The fact that the list of churches, banks, and public buildings also includes addresses is indicative of an enlarged city beyond easy understanding.

The maritime influence on the city is also recorded in the various shipping lines listed along the river front. Look carefully along this edge of the map and you will also see the growing number of ferry companies. The city is extending beyond the island of Manhattan to such places as Hoboken and Brooklyn.

The map from 1913 (fig. 57) shows the 1811 Commissioner's plan for the city in its full fruition. The city's grid pattern now stretches up to 120th Street and beyond. The relentless geometry is only broken up by the curving lines and open space of Central Park, which takes up 840 acres. The site was cleared of buildings in 1857. A plan by the landscape architects Frederick Law Olmstead and Calvert Vaux envisaged a pastoral oasis for hard-pressed city dwellers. The park opened in 1876.

The city has grown not only over the entire island, its influence has now also spread across the rivers. A series of bridges across the East River and tunnels under the East and Hudson Rivers now connect Manhattan to an entire metropolitan region. The Brooklyn and Manhattan Bridges for example, now form a link between Manhattan and Long Island. Railways arriving into Penn Street and Grand Central and ferries docking at the tip of the island are the transport linkages of an expanding metropolis. The map also shows urban developments on the neighboring islands as well as Manhattan.

The maritime influence in still strong. Piers and docks all around the southern tip of the island tell of international connections in trade and commerce. The skyline of this island was one of the first sights in the United States seen by many of the newly arriving immigrants from Europe.

Always a commercial city, some enterprising person has used the map of the city to sell the facilities of the Hotel Navarre. Stamped across the city streets, bold black lettering tells the name and exact location of the hotel, while the text at the top and bottom of the map explains the room rates. The city—its hustle, its commercial impulse, and its press of humanity are all reflected in this map.

The bird's-eye view map (fig. 58) is an image of downtown Manhattan before 11 September 2001. The name "bird's eye" signifies a map that is drawn at an oblique angle. The technique is commonly used to depict cities because, in contrast to that of plan maps, it gives a sense of the height of buildings. Bird's-eye city views have been a staple of urban representation in the United States since the nineteenth century. They were used not only to document but also to celebrate.

The southern tip of Manhattan, the site of the original Dutch settlement, is now shown as a dense concentration of high-rise buildings. The small precarious Dutch settlement has grown into a global city with connections around the world. The area shown is the heart of the financial district. It is not only a place of local significance, but also a major cog in the global financial system. Wall Street is no longer a name that conjures up images of stockades and defenses, it presently signifies the relentless activity of financial dealings, business, and stock trading.

The tallest buildings are the giant twin towers of the World Trade Center that rise up from the mass of buildings on the middle left of the map. It is impossible to look at this map without the benefit of hindsight. The solid buildings seem more fragile now that we know both of them will collapse. The orderly urban scene of streets and buildings has a vulnerability to destruction.

The final map reproduced here (fig. 59) is a view of downtown Manhattan after 11 September. It was a beautiful cloudless morning, with bright sunshine and low humidity—one of those magical fall days. In the clear blue sky overhead, two commercial jet liners deliberately flew into the Twin Towers. Initially, the towers survived the impact, but in a few hours they crashed to the ground in a scene of devastation that was agonizing to watch.

The map shows the site the day after the attack. It is drawn at three scales. A small insert map of the region clarifies the location of Manhattan within its larger

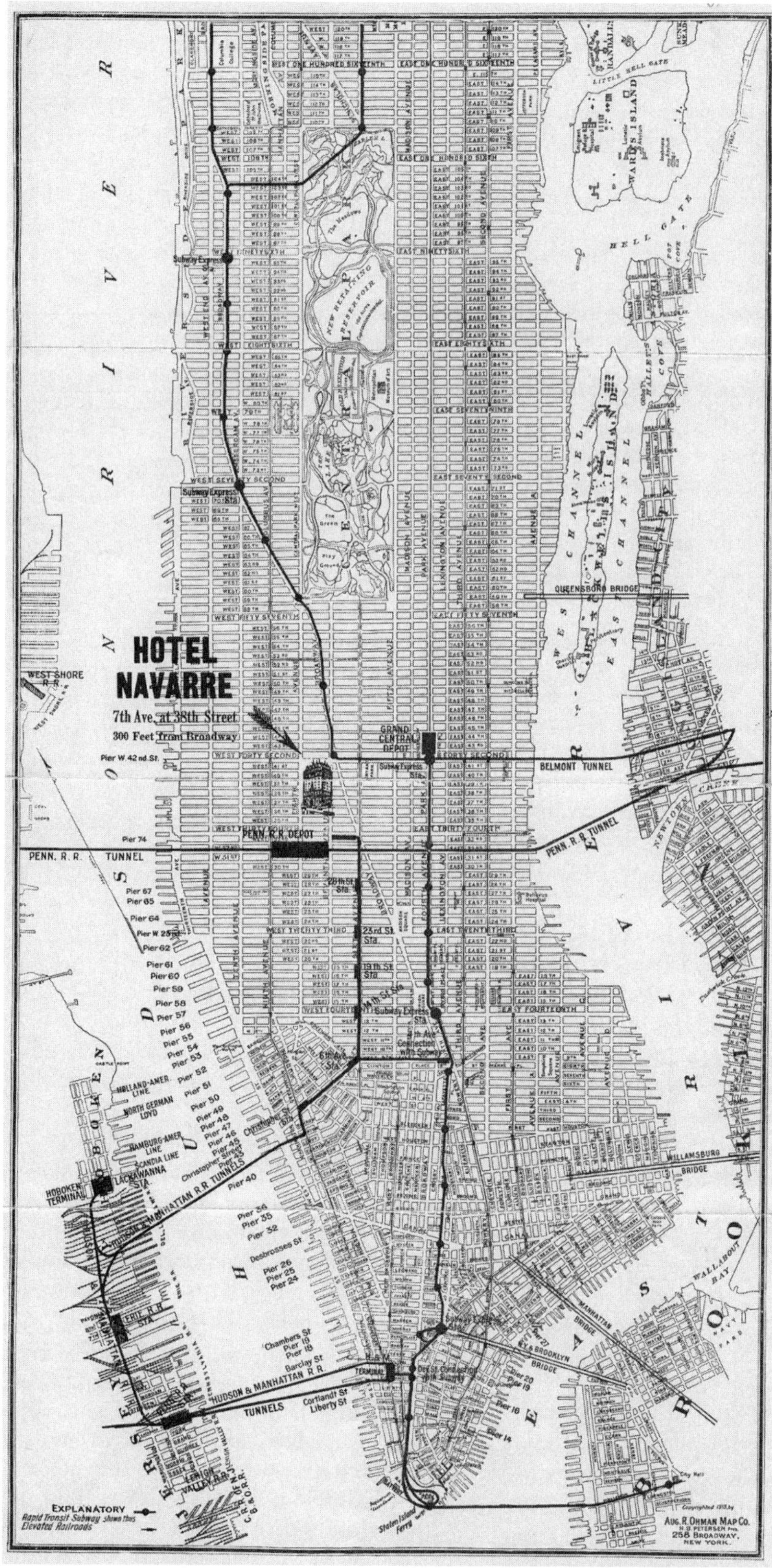

Fig. 57. A map of Manhattan copyrighted by the Aug. R. Ohman Map Co. of New York in 1913 and issued as a publicity brochure by the Navarre Hotel.

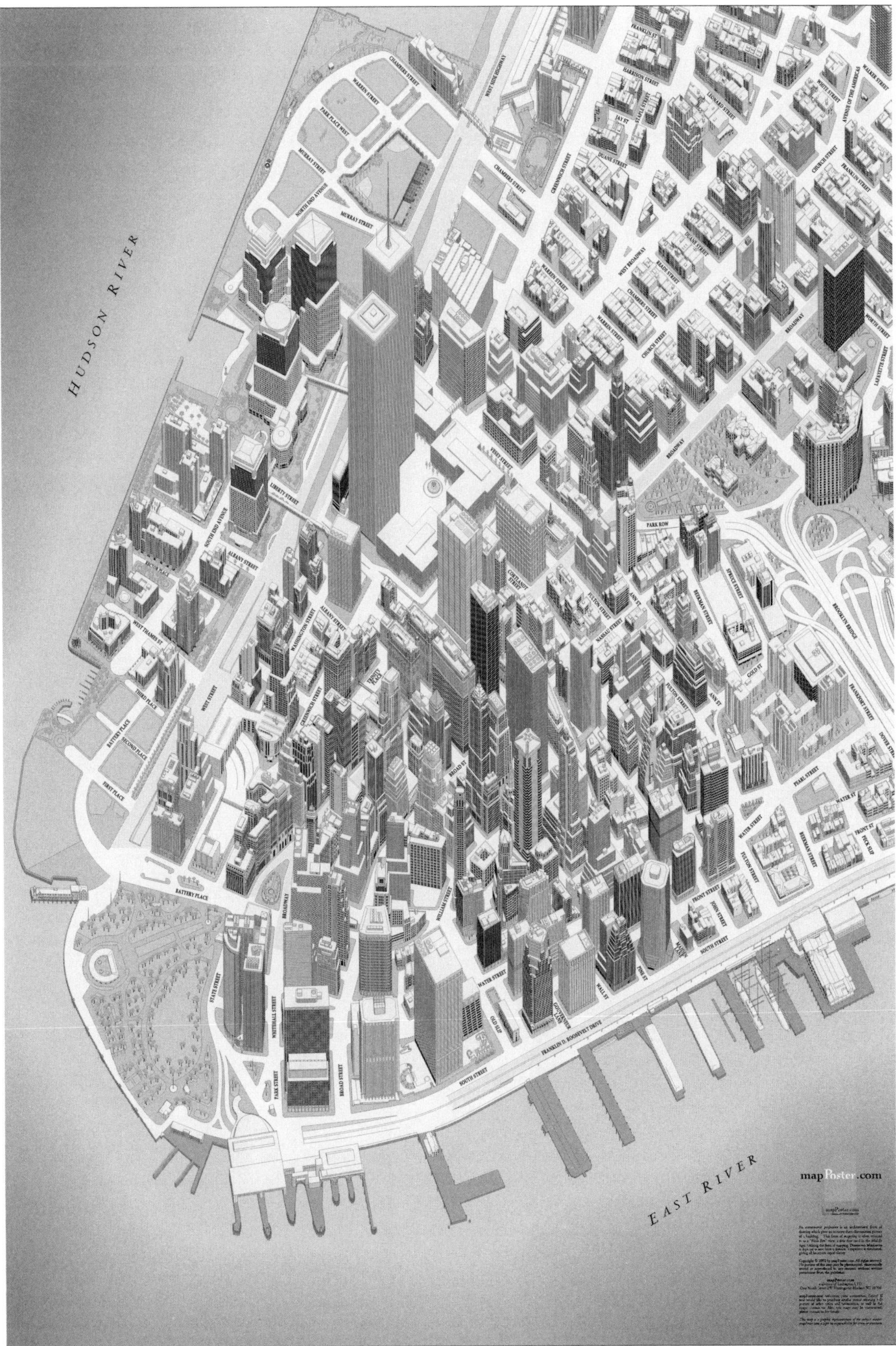

Fig. 58. Bird's Eye View of Manhattan. Reprinted with permission of mapPoster.com.

Fig. 59. *Washington Post*—The Day After. ©2001, *The Washington Post.* Reprinted with permission.

regional setting. The largest map shows the grid pattern of lower Manhattan overset with information about the immediate results of the tragedy: a traffic ban below 14th Street, the cordoning off of the city below Chambers Street, the closing of tunnels and bridges, and the bypassing of subway stops below Canal Street. This map highlights the location of hospitals and shelters. Many of the latter were quickly established to treat casualties. In the confusion of the event's immediate aftermath, the scale of the tragedy was unknown. Families and friends of the missing flocked to these hospitals and shelters, in the desperate hope that their loved ones had somehow miraculously survived.

The third map, an insert in the bottom right-hand corner, focuses on what became known as Ground Zero: the collapse of Towers 1 and 2, the collapse of Building 7, major damage to Building 5 and the Hilton Hotel, and burning fires in the Marriott Hotel. This was the center of devastation where collapsed concrete and twisted steel marked a disaster site. The area quickly turned into a rescue location and then a recovery site where the remains of over 2,500 people were eventually discovered in the rubble.

This map was produced very soon after the attack. It suggests damage and devastation, shock and tragedy. But the city is a work in progress, an endless experiment. Later maps will no doubt show the transformation of Ground Zero into something new, something different. The city endures.

Section II

PRIMARY SOURCE DOCUMENTS

THE COLONIAL PERIOD

THE ORIGIN OF THE LEAGUE OF FIVE NATIONS
(c. 1745)

At the end of the sixteenth century, five related Iroquois Nations created what was known as "The Iroquois League." To the Five Nations, represented by the Cayugas, the Mohawks, the Oneidas, the Onondagas, and the Senecas, all indigenous to the woods and hills of New York, this union was "The Great Peace." In fact, however, the benefits of the confederation were often military as well as civil. When the western-most tribe of the Iroquois, the Senecas, became avowed enemies of the Illini, their membership in the Five Nations allowed them to muster numbers of warriors much greater than those of their adversaries. And as the French began their colonization of the St. Lawrence Valley near Quebec, the Iroquois were able to fight them for land until the burgeoning French population drove them into upstate New York and the Great Lakes Basin. The Five Nations was one of the most important instances of representative intertribal governance. Its leaders, chosen by the women of the various tribes and appointed for life, were selected for their wisdom, tolerance, and generosity of spirit.

Laura M. Miller,
Vanderbilt University

See also **Civilized Tribes, Five; Indian Political Life; Iroquois.**

Where the Mohawk river empties into the Hudson in ancient times there was a Mohawk village. The people there were fierce and warlike and were continually sending out war parties against other settlements and returning would bring back long strings of scalps to number the lives they had destroyed. But sometimes they left their own scalps behind and never returned. They loved warfare better than all other things and were happy when their hands were slimy with blood. They boasted that they would eat up all other nations and so they continued to go against other tribes and fight with them.

Now among the Mohawks was a chief named Dekanawida, a very wise man, and he was very sad of heart because his people loved war too well. So he spoke in council and implored them to desist lest they perish altogether but the young warriors would not hear him and laughed at his words but he did not cease to warn them until at last dispairing of moving them by ordinary means he turned his face to the west and wept as he journeyed onward and away from his people. At length he reached a lake whose shores were fringed with bushes, and being tired he lay down to rest. Presently, as he lay meditating, he heard the soft spattering of water sliding from a skillful paddle and peering out from his hiding place he saw in the red light of sunset a man leaning over his canoe and dipping into the shallow water with a basket. When he raised it up it was full of shells, the shells of the periwinkles that live in shallow pools. The man pushed his canoe toward the shore and sat down on the beach where he kindled a fire. Then he began to string his shells and finishing a string would touch the shells and talk. Then, as if satisfied, he would lay it down and make another until he had a large number. Dekanawida watched the strange proceeding with wonder. The sun had long since set but Dekanawida still watched the man with the shell strings sitting in the flickering light of the fire that shadowed the bushes and shimmered over the lake.

After some deliberation he called out, "Kwe, I am a friend!" and stepping out upon the sand stood before the man with the shells. "I am Dekanawida," he said, "and come from the Mohawk."

"I am Haiowentha of the Onondaga," came the reply.

The Dekanawida inquired about the shell strings for he was very curious to know their import and

Haiowentha answered, "They are the rules of life and laws of good government. This all white string is a sign of truth, peace and good will, this black string is a sign of hatred, of war and of a bad heart, the string with the alternate beads, black and white, is a sign that peace should exist between the nations. This string with white on either end and black in the middle is a sign that wars must end and peace declared." And so Haiowentha lifted his strings and read the laws.

Then said Dekanawida, "You are my friend indeed, and the friend of all nations.—Our people are weak from warring and weak from being warred upon. We who speak one tongue should combine against the Hadiondas instead of helping them by killing one another but my people are weary of my advising and would not hear me."

"I, too, am of the same mind," said Haiowentha, "but Tatodaho slew all my brothers and drove me away. So I came to the lakes and have made the laws that should govern men and nations. I believe that we should be as brothers in a family instead of enemies."

"Then come with me," said Dekanawida, "and together let us go back to my people and explain the rules and laws."

So when they had returned Dekanawida called a council of all the chiefs and warriors and the women and Haiowentha set forth the plan he had devised. The words had a marvelous effect. The people were astonished at the wisdom of the strange chief from the Onondaga and when he had finished his exposition the chiefs promised obedience to his laws. They delegated Dekanawida to go with him to the Oneida and council with them, then to go onward to Onondaga and win over the arrogant erratic Tatodaho, the tyrannical chief of the Onondaga. Thus it was that together they went to the Oneida country and won over their great chief and made the people promise to support the proposed league. Then the Oneida chief went with Haiowentha to the Cayugas and told them how by supporting the league they might preserve themselves against the fury of Tatodaho. So when the Cayuga had promised allegiance Dekanawida turned his face toward Onondaga and with his comrades went before Tatodaho. Now when Tatodaho learned how three nations had combined against him he became very angry and ran into the forest where he gnawed at his fingers and ate grass and leaves. His evil thoughts became serpents and sprouted from his skull and waving in a tangled mass hissed out venom. But Dekanawida did not fear him and once more asked him to give his consent to a league of peace and friendship but he was still wild until Haiowentha combed the snakes from his head and told him that he should be the head chief of the confederacy and govern it according to the laws that Haiowentha had made. Then he recovered from his madness and asked why the Seneca had not been visited for the Seneca outnumbered all the other nations and were fearless warriors. "If their jealousy is aroused," he said, "they will eat us."

Then the delegations visited the Seneca and the other nations to the west but only the Seneca would consider the proposal. The other nations were exceedingly jealous.

Thus a peace pact was made and the Long House built and Dekanawida was the builder but Haiowentha was its designer.

Now moreover the first council of Haiowentha and Dekanawida was in a place now called Albany at the mouth of a small stream that empties into the Hudson.

SOURCE: Parker, Arthur C. *Seneca Myths and Folklore.* Buffalo, N.Y.: Buffalo Historical Society, 1923.

CHARTER TO SIR WALTER RALEIGH
(25 March 1584)

With this document began the first determined endeavor by the British Crown to colonize the North American continent. A clever administrator as well as a soldier and occasional pirate, Walter Raleigh took over the charter from his half-brother, Sir Humphrey Gilbert, who drowned in 1583 during an aborted attempt to colonize St. John's, Newfoundland. By April 1584, Raleigh had already undertaken a new expedition, and in 1585–1586, the first colony at Roanoke, Va., had been established, some twenty-two years before the founding of Jamestown and thirty-seven before the Pilgrims made their landing at Plymouth Rock, Mass. Unfortunately, life in the New World was even more difficult than Raleigh's intrepid explorers had anticipated. Plagued by supply shortages and hampered by their failure to deal intelligently with their mostly agreeable Indian neighbors, the colonists soon became disenchanted with their new way of life. They took advantage of the coincidental arrival of the explorer and pirate Sir Francis Drake as a chance to abandon the colony. Only ten months old, the Roanoke expedition came to an end. A second expedition, mounted in 1587 and consisting of some 150 women, children, and men, was discovered three years later to have vanished without a trace, save for a single word etched into a post, "Croatoan." The colonists were never heard from again, and the second disastrous attempt to secure Roanoke Island for the Crown of England remains one of the greatest, still unsolved, mysteries of North American history.

Laura M. Miller,
Vanderbilt University

See also **Colonial Charters; Raleigh, Sir Walter, Colonies of.**

ELIZABETH, by the Grace of God of England, Fraunce and Ireland Queene, defender of the faith, &c. To all people to whome these presents shall come, greeting.

Knowe yee that of our especial grace, certaine science, and meere motion, . . . we give and graunt to our trustie and welbeloved servant *Walter Ralegh*, Esquire, and to his heires assignes for ever, free libertie and licence from time to time, and at all times for ever hereafter, to discover, search, finde out, and view such remote, heathen and barbarous lands, countries, and territories, not actually possessed of any Christian Prince, nor inhabited by Christian People, as to him, . . . shall seeme good, and the same to have, holde occupie and enjoy to him, . . . for ever, with all prerogatives, . . . thereto or thereabouts both by sea and land, whatsoever we by our letters patent may graunt, . . . and the said *Walter Ralegh*, his heires and assignes, . . . shall goe or travaile thither to inhabite or remaine, there to build and fortifie, at the discretion of the said *Walter Ralegh*, . . .

And we do likewise . . . give and graunt full authoritie, libertie and power to the said *Walter Ralegh*, . . . that he . . . shall . . . have, take, and leade in the saide voyage, and travaile thitherward, or to inhabit there with him, or them, and every or any of them, such and so many of our subjects as shall willingly accompanie him or them, And further that the said *Walter Ralegh*, . . . shall have . . . all the soile of all such lands, territories, and Countreis, so to bee discovered and possessed as aforesaide, and of all such Cities, castles, townes, villages, and places in the same, with the right, royalties, franchises, and jurisdictions, as well marine as other within the saide landes, or Countreis, or the seas thereunto adjoining, to be had, or used, with full power to dispose thereof, and of every part in fee-simple or otherwise, according to the order of the lawes of England, . . .: reserving always to us our heires, and successors, for all services, duties, and demaundes, the fift part of all the oare of golde and silver, that from time to time, and at all times . . . shal be there gotten and obtained: . . .

And moreover, we doe . . . give and graunt licence to the said *Walter Ralegh*, . . . that he, . . . shall and may . . . for his and their defence, encounter and expulse, repell and resist . . . all . . . as without the especiall liking and licence of the said *Walter Ralegh*, . . . shall attempt to inhabite within the said Countreis, . . . or within the space of two hundreth leagues neere to the place or places within such Countreis, . . . where the saide *Walter Ralegh*, . . . shall within sixe yeeres . . . make their dwellings. . . . And for uniting in more perfect league and amitie, of such Countreis, landes, and territories so to bee possessed and inhabited as aforesaide with our Realmes of Englande, and Ireland, and the better incouragement of men to these enterprises: we do . . . declare that all such Countreis, so hereafter to be possessed and inhabited as is aforesaide, from thencefoorth shall bee of the allegiance of us, our heires and successours. And wee doe graunt to the saide *Walter Ralegh*, . . . and to all and every of them, . . . that they . . . being either borne within our saide Realmes of Englande, . . . shall and may have all the priviledges of free Denizens, and persons native of England. . . .

And . . . we . . . do give and graunt to the said *Walter Ralegh*, . . . that hee . . . shall, within the said mentioned remote landes . . . have full and meere power and authoritie to correct, punish, pardon, governe, and rule by their and every or any of their good discretions and pollicies, as well in causes capital, or criminall, as civil, . . . all such our subjects as shall from time to time adventure themselves in the said journies or voyages, or that shall at any time hereafter inhabite any such landes, countreis, or territories as aforesaide, . . . according to such statutes, lawes and ordinances, as shall bee by him the saide *Walter Ralegh* . . . devised, or established, for the better government of the said people as aforesaid. So always as the said statutes, lawes, and ordinances may be as neere as conveniently may be, agreeable to the forme of the lawes, statutes, government, or pollicie of England, . . .

Provided alwayes, and our will and pleasure is, and wee do hereby declare to all Christian kings, princes and states, that if the saide *Walter Ralegh*, his heires or assignes, or any of them, or any other by their licence or appointment, shall at any time or times hereafter, robbe or spoile by sea or by lande, or do any acte of unjust or unlawful hostilitie, to any of the subjects of us, our heires or successors, or to any of the subjects of any the kings, princes, rulers, governors, or estates, being then in perfect league and amitie with us, our heires and successors, and that upon such injury, or upon just complaint of any such prince, ruler, governoir, or estate, or their subjects, wee, our heires and successours, shall make open proclamation within any the portes of our Realme of England, that the saide *Walter Ralegh*, his heires and assignes, and adherents, or any to whome these our letters patents may extende, shall within the termes to be limitted, by such proclamation, make full restitution, and satisfaction of all such injuries done, so as both we and the said princes, or other so complayning, may holde us and themselves fully contented. And that if the saide *Walter Ralegh*, his heires and assignes, shall not make or cause to be made satisfaction accordingly, within such time so to be limitted, that then it shall be lawfull to us our heires and successors, to put the saide *Walter Ralegh*, his heires and assignes and adherents, and all the inhabitants of the said places to be discovered (as is aforesaide) or any of them out of our allegiance and protection, and that from and after such time of putting out of protection the said *Walter Ralegh*, his heires, assignes and adherents, and others so to be put out, and the said places within their habitation, possession and rule, shal be out of our allegeance and protection, and free for all princes and others, to pursue with hostilitie, as being not our subjects, nor by us any way to be avouched, maintained or defended, nor to be holden as any of ours, nor to our protection or dominion, or allegiance any way belonging, for that expresse mention of the cleer yeerely value of the certaintie of the premisses, or any part thereof, or of any other gift, or grant by us, or any our progenitors, or predecessors to the said *Walter Ralegh*, before this time made in these presents be not expressed, or any other grant, ordinance, provision, proclamation, or restraint to the contrarye thereof, before this time given, ordained, or provided, or any other thing, cause, or matter whatsoever, in any wise notwithstanding. In witness whereof, we have caused these our letters to be made patents. Witnesse our selves, at *Westminster*, the 25. day of March, in the sixe and twentieth yeere of our Raigne.

SOURCE: Thorpe, Francis N., ed. *The Federal and State Constitutions, Colonial Charters, and Other Organic Laws of the States, Territories, and Colonies Now or Heretofore Forming the United States of America.* Washington: Government Printing Office, 1909.

STARVING IN VIRGINIA
(1607–1610, by Captain John Smith)

The colony of Jamestown, Va., represents the first successful attempt by the British to settle the North American continent. Mounted by the Virginia Company, and with the soldier and profiteer Captain John Smith among its leaders, the expedition endured a brutal four-month ocean voyage, only to discover upon its arrival that conditions in the New World were hardly more agreeable. Unable to produce a sufficient amount of food for themselves and unsuccessful at dominating the powerful confederacy of Native Americans under the leadership of Powhatan, Smith and his party flirted occasionally with abandoning Jamestown and returning home. By 1608 the situation was desperate. Hoping to avert disaster, the colonists appointed as their leader the sometimes unpopular, self-aggrandizing Smith, who immediately instituted a strict order under which those who did not work would not eat. The rule was harsh, perhaps, but Jamestown survived and flourished. Smith himself would not remain to see it, however. In 1609, injured in an accident involving gunpowder, Captain Smith was forced to seek treatment in England, where he had fallen out of favor with the Virginia Company. He never returned to the colony that he had helped rescue from the harsh realities of the New World.

Laura M. Miller,
Vanderbilt University

See also **Chesapeake Colonies; Colonial Settlements; Starving Time.**

1607

Being thus left to our fortunes, it fortuned that within ten days scarce ten among us could either go or well stand, such extreme weakness and sickness oppressed us. And thereat none need marvel if they consider the cause and reason, which was this.

While the ships stayed, our allowance was somewhat bettered by a daily proportion of biscuits, which the sailors would pilferto sell, give, or exchange with us for money, sassafras, furs, or love. But when they departed, there remained neither tavern, beer, house, nor place of relief, but the common kettle. Had we been as free from all sins as gluttony and drunkenness, we might have been canonized for saints; but our president [Wingfield] would never have been admitted for engrossing to his private [use] oatmeal, sack, aquavitae, beef, eggs, or what not, but the kettle; that indeed he allowed equally to be distributed, and that was half a pint of wheat, and as much barley boiled with water for a man a day, and this having fried some twenty-six weeks in the ship's hold, contained as many worms as grains; so that we might truly call it rather so much bran than corn, our drink was water, our lodgings castles in the air.

With this lodging and diet, our extreme toil in bearing and planting palisades so strained and bruised us, and our continual labor in the extremity of the heat had so weakened us, as were cause sufficient to have made us as miserable in our native country, or any other place in the world.

From May to September, those that escaped lived upon sturgeon, and sea crabs. Fifty in this time we buried, the rest seeing the president's projects to escape these miseries in our pinnace by flight (who all this time had neither felt want nor sickness) so moved our dead spirits, as we deposed him, and established Ratcliffe in his place (Gosnoll being dead), Kendall deposed. Smith newly recovered, Martin and Ratcliffe was by his care preserved and relieved, and the most of the soldiers recovered with the skillful diligence of Master Thomas Wolton, our chirurgeon [surgeon] general.

But now was all our provision spent, the sturgeon gone, all helps abandoned, each hour expecting the fury of the savages; when God, the Patron of all good endeavors in that desperate extremity so changed the hearts of the savages that they brought such plenty of their fruits and provision as no man wanted.

And now where some affirmed it was ill done of the Council to send forth men so badly provided, this incontradictable reason will show them plainly they are too ill advised to nourish such ill conceits. First, the fault of our going was our own; what could be thought fitting or necessary we had; but what we should find, or want, or where we should be, we were all ignorant, and supposing to make our passage in two months, with victual to live and the advantage of the spring to work. We were at sea five months, where we both spent our victual and lost the opportunity of the time and season to plant, by the unskillful presumption of our ignorant transporters, that understood not at all what they undertook. . . .

And now, the winter approaching, the rivers became so covered with swans, geese, ducks, and cranes that we daily feasted with good bread, Virginia peas, pumpions [pumpkins], and putchamins [persimmons], fish, fowl, and diverse sorts of wild beasts as fat as we could eat them; so that none of our tuftaffety humorists desired to go for England. . . .

1609

The day before Captain Smith returned for England with the ships, Captain Davis arrived in a small pinnace, with some sixteen proper men more. To these were added a company from Jamestown, under the command of Captain John Sickelmore, alias Ratcliffe, to inhabit Point Comfort. Captain Martin and Captain West, having lost their boats and near half their men among the savages, were returned to Jamestown; for the savages no sooner understood Smith was gone but they all revolted, and did spoil and murder all they encountered.

Now we were all constrained to live only on that Smith had only for his own company, for the rest had consumed their proportions. And now they had twenty residents with all their appurtenances. Master Piercie, our new president, was so sick he could neither go nor stand. But ere all was consumed, Captain West and Captain Sickelmore, each with a small ship and thirty or forty men well appointed, sought abroad to trade. Sickelmore, upon the confidence of Powhatan, with about thirty others as careless as himself, were all slain; only Jeffrey Shortridge escaped; and Pocahontas, the king's daughter, saved a boy called Henry Spilman, that lived many years after, by her means, among the Patawomekes. Powhatan still, as he found means, cut off their boats, denied them trade; so that Captain West set sail for England.

Now we all found the loss of Captain Smith; yea, his greatest maligners could now curse his loss. As for corn provision and contribution from the savages, we had nothing but mortal wounds, with clubs and arrows. As for our hogs, hens, goats, sheep, horses, or what lived, our commanders, officers, and savages daily consumed them; some small proportions sometimes we tasted, till all was devoured. Then swords, arms, pieces, or anything we traded with the savages, whose cruel fingers were so oft imbrued in our blood, that what by their cruelty, our governor's indiscretion, and the loss of our ships, of 500 within six months after Captain Smith's departure there remained not past 60 men, women, and children—most miserable and poor creatures. And those were preserved for the most part by roots, herbs, acorns, walnuts, berries, now and then a little fish. They that had starch in these extremities made no small use of it; yea, even the very skins of our horses.

Nay, so great was our famine that a savage we slew and buried, the poorer sort took him up again and ate him; and so did diverse one another boiled and stewed with roots and herbs. And one among the rest did kill his wife, powdered [salted] her, and had eaten part of her before it was known; for which he was executed, as he well deserved. Now, whether she was better roasted, boiled, or carbonadoed [broiled] I know not; but of such a dish as powdered wife I never heard.

This was that time, which still to this day, we called the starving time. It were too vile to say, and scarce to be believed, what we endured; but the occasion was our own for want of providence, industry, and government, and not the barrenness and defect of the country, as is generally supposed. For till then in three years, for the numbers were landed us, we had never from England provision sufficient for six months, though it seemed by the bills of lading sufficient was sent us, such a glutton is the sea, and such good fellows the mariners. We as little tasted of the great proportion sent us as they of our want and miseries, yet, notwithstanding, they ever overswayed and ruled the business, though we endured all that is said, and chiefly lived on what this good country naturally afforded. Yet had we been even in Paradise itself with these governors, it would not have been much better with us; yet there was among us, who, had they had the government as Captain Smith appointed, but that they could not maintain it, would surely have kept us from those extremities of miseries. This in ten days more would have supplanted us all with death.

1610
But God, that would not this country should be unplanted, sent Sir Thomas Gates and Sir George Sommers with 150 people most happily preserved by the Bermudas to preserve us. Strange it is to say how miraculously they were preserved in a leaking ship....

SOURCE: Smith, John. *The Generall Historie of Virginia, New England and the Summer Isles: Together with The True Travels, Adventures and Observations and A Sea Grammar.* Glasgow: James MacLehose and Sons, 1907.

THE MAYFLOWER COMPACT
(11 November 1620)

Dissatisfied with the Church of England, the Pilgrims, a group of poor, largely uneducated English religious separatists, had already relocated to Amsterdam and Leiden in Holland before deciding in 1617 to emigrate to the New World. On 16 September 1620, having secured an essential patent from the London Company, 102 passengers began their historic sixty-five-day voyage aboard a single ship, the 180-ton *Mayflower.* Originally intended by William Bradford and others to discourage the formation of splinter colonies, the Mayflower Compact, a church covenant modified for civic use, represents an early attempt to establish written laws in an American colony. It would become the foundation for the settlement's government.

Laura M. Miller,
Vanderbilt University

***See also* Colonial Charters; Mayflower Compact; Pilgrims; Plymouth Colony.**

In the Name of God, Amen. We, whose names are underwritten, the Loyal Subjects of our dread Sovereign Lord King *James*, by the Grace of God, of *Great Britain, France*, and *Ireland*, King, *Defender of the Faith*, &c. Having undertaken for the Glory of God, and Advancement of the Christian Faith, and the Honour of our King and Country, a Voyage to plant the first colony in the northern Parts of Virginia; Do by these Presents, solemnly and mutually in the Presence of God and one another, covenant and combine ourselves together into a civil Body Politick, for our better Ordering and Preservation, and Furtherance of the Ends aforesaid; And by Virtue hereof do enact, constitute, and frame, such just and equal Laws, Ordinances, Acts, Constitutions, and Offices, from time to time, as shall be thought most meet and convenient for the general Good of the Colony; unto which we promise all due Submission and Obedience. In WITNESS whereof we have hereunto subscribed our names at *Cape Cod* the eleventh of *November*, in the Reign of our Sovereign Lord King *James of England, France*, and *Ireland*, the eighteenth and of *Scotland*, the fifty-fourth. *Anno Domini*, 1620

Mr. John Carver
Mr. William Bradford
Mr. Edward Winslow
Mr. William Brewster
Isaac Allerton
Miles Standish
John Alden
John Turner
Francis Eaton
James Chilton
John Craxton
John Billington
Joses Fletcher
John Goodman
Mr. Samuel Fuller
Mr. Christopher Martin
Mr. William Mullins
Mr. William White
Mr. Richard Warren
John Howland
Mr. Stephen Hopkins
Digery Priest
Thomas Williams
Gilbert Winslow
Edmund Margesson
Peter Brown
Richard Bitteridge
George Soule
Edward Tilly
John Tilly
Francis Cooke
Thomas Rogers
Thomas Tinker
John Ridgate
Edward Fuller
Richard Clark
Richard Gardiner
Mr. John Allerton
Thomas English
Edward Doten
Edward Liester

SOURCE: Cheever, George B., ed. *The Journal of the Pilgrims at Plymouth in New England, in 1620, etc., etc.*, second ed. New York: J. Wiley, 1849.

THE TRIAL OF ANNE HUTCHINSON AT NEWTON (1637)

Anne Hutchinson was born in 1591 in England into the large family of a freethinking Anglican clergyman. She was intelligent and consumed with religious issues. After marrying merchant William Hutchinson, Anne bore twelve children. While living at Alford, England, she came under the influence of the Reverend John Cotton, a Puritan minister who believed in a "covenant of grace" rather than a "covenant of works," which went against the standards of outward behavior then advocated by the Church of England. When Rev. Cotton was forced to leave England for the new Puritan colony at Massachusetts Bay, Anne convinced her husband and family that they must follow him to America. The family settled in Boston, where Anne began to promote and lecture on Rev. Cotton's beliefs to local women. The "covenant of grace" she espoused appealed to so many men and women that she was soon leader of a religious movement, which brought her to the attention of the Massachusetts Bay authorities.

John Winthrop, the most respected citizen of the Massachusetts Bay Colony, was its governor in 1637. The Massachusetts Puritans sought to build their religious commonwealth on order and conformity. Anne taught that the covenant that an individual had with God had little outward manifestation; rather it was an inward conversion, a wholly individual experience. There was very little room for duty, order, and power in such a belief. As a consequence of her teachings, Anne was put on trial for going beyond her domestic sphere to become an unlawful spiritual leader who could destroy the order and hierarchy of Puritan society and government.

During the trial Winthrop's attempts to prevail upon Anne to abandon her quest to change the religious standards of the colony fell on deaf ears. She refused to budge. Her claim that her conscience was law threatened disorder and anarchy. Citing the letters of the Apostle Paul, Anne also claimed her right to counsel women in religion, which threatened the male hierarchy of the colony.

After being sentenced to exile, Anne Hutchinson and children joined her husband at a new settlement in Rhode Island. After her husband's death, she moved to New Netherland, where Indians killed her in 1643.

Russell Lawson,
Bacone College

***See also* General Court, Colonial; Massachusetts Bay Colony; Puritans and Puritanism.**

MR. WINTHROP GOVERNOR. Mrs. Hutchinson, you are called here as one of those that have troubled the peace of the commonwealth and the churches here; you are known to be a woman that hath had a great share in the promoting and divulging of those opinions that are causes of this trouble, and to be nearly joined not only in affinity and affection with some of those the court had taken notice of and passed upon, but you have spoken divers things as we have been informed very prejudicial to the honour of the churches and ministers thereof, and you have maintained a meeting and an assembly in your house that hath been condemned by the general assembly as a thing not tolerable nor comely in the sight of God nor fitting for your sex, and notwithstanding that was cried down you have continued the same, therefore we have thought good to send for you to understand how things are, that if you be in an erroneous way we may reduce you that so you may become a profitable member here among us, otherwise if you be obstinate in your course that then the court may take such course that you may trouble us no further, therefore I would entreat you to express whether you do not assent and hold in practice to those opinions and factions that have been handled in court already, that is to say, whether you do not justify Mr. Wheelright's sermon and the petition.

MRS. HUTCHINSON. I am called here to answer before you but I hear no things laid to my charge.

GOV. I have told you some already and more I can tell you. (*Mrs. H.*) Name one Sir.

GOV. Have I not named some already?

MRS. H. What have I said or done?

GOV. Why for your doings, this you did harbour and countenance those that are parties in this faction that you have heard of. (*Mrs. H.*) That's matter of conscience, Sir.

GOV. Your conscience you must keep or it must be kept for you.

MRS. H. Must not I then entertain the saints because I must keep my conscience....

GOV. You have joined with them in the faction.

MRS. H. In what faction have I joined with them?

GOV. In presenting the petition.

MRS. H. Suppose I had set my hand to the petition what then? (*Gov.*) You saw that case tried before.

MRS. H. But I had not my hand to the petition.

GOV. You have councelled them. (*Mr H.*) Wherein?

GOV. Why in entertaining them.

MRS. H. What breach of law is that Sir?

GOV. Why dishonouring of parents.

MRS. H. But put the case Sir that I do fear the Lord and my parents may not I entertain them that fear the Lord because my parents will not give me leave?

GOV. If they be the fathers of the commonwealth, and they of another religion, if you entertain them then you dishonour your parents and are justly punishable. . . .

GOV. Why do you keep such a meeting at your house as you do every week upon a set day?

MRS. H. It is lawful for me so to do, as it is all your practices and can you find a warrant for yourself and condemn me for the same thing? The ground of my taking it up was, when I first came to this land because I did not go to such meetings as those were, it was presently reported that I did not allow of such meetings but held them unlawful and therefore in that regard they said I was proud and did despise all ordinances, upon that a friend came unto me and told me of it and I to prevent such aspersions took it up, but it was in practice before I came therefore I was not the first. . . .

MRS. H. I conceive their lyes a clear rule in Titus, that the elder women should instruct the younger and then I must have a time wherein I must do it.

GOV. All this I grant you, I grant you a time for it, but what is this to the purpose that you Mrs. Hutchinson must call a company together from their callings to come to be taught of you?

MRS. H. Will it please you to answer me this and to give me a rule for then I will willingly submit to any truth. If any come to my house to be instructed in the ways of God what rule have I to put them away? . . .

MRS. H. . . . Do you think it not lawful for me to teach women and why do you call me to teach the court?

GOV. We do not call you to teach the court but to lay open yourself.

MRS. H. I desire you that you would then set me down a rule by which I may put them away that come unto me and so have peace in so doing.

GOV. You must shew your rule to receive them.

MRS. H. I have done it.

GOV. I deny it because I have brought more arguments than you have.

MRS. H. I say, to me it is a rule.

MR. ENDICOT. You say there are some rules unto you. I think there is a contradiction in your own words. What rule for your practice do you bring, only a custom in Boston.

MRS. H. No Sir that was no rule to me but if you look upon the rule in Titus it is a rule to me. If you convince me that it is no rule I shall yield.

GOV. You know that there is no rule that crosses another, but rule crosses that in the Corinthians. But you must take it in this sense that elder women must instruct the younger about their business and to love their husbands and not to make them to clash.

MRS. H. I do not conceive but that it is meant for some publick times. . . .

GOV. Well, we see how it is we must therefore put it away from you or restrain you from maintai[n]ing this course.

MRS. H. If you have a rule for it from God's word you may.

GOV. We are your judges, and not you ours and we must compel you to it. . . .

DEP. GOV. I would go a little higher with Mrs. Hutchinson. About three years ago we were all in peace. Mrs. Hutchinson from that time she came hath made a disturbance, and some that came oyer with her in the ship did inform me what she was as soon as she was landed. I being then in place dealt with the pastor and teacher of Boston and desired them to enquire of her, and then I was satisfied that she held nothing different from us, but within half a year after, she had vented divers of her strange opinions and had made parties in the country, and at length it comes that Mr. Cotton and Mr. Vane were of her judgment, but Mr. Cotton hath cleared himself that he was not of that mind, but now it appears by this woman's meeting that Mrs. Hutchinson hath so forestalled the minds of many by their resort to her meeting that now she hath a potent party in the country. Now if all these things have endangered us as from that foundation and if she in particular hath disparaged all our ministers in the land that they have preached a covenant of works, and only Mr. Cotton a covenant of grace, why this is not to be suffered, and therefore being driven to the foundation and it being found that Mrs. Hutchinson is she that hath depraved all the ministers and hath been the cause of what is fallen out, why we must take away the foundation and the building will fall.

MRS. H. I pray Sir prove it that I said they preached nothing but a covenant of works.

DEP. GOV. Nothing but a covenant of works, why a Jesuit may preach truth sometimes.

MRS. H. Did I ever say they preached a covenant of works then?

DEP. GOV. If they do not preach a covenant of grace clearly, then they preach a covenant of works.

MRS. H. No Sir, one may preach a covenant of grace more clearly than another, so I said.

D. GOV. We are not upon that now but upon position.

MRS. H. Prove this then Sir that you say I said.

D. GOV. When they do preach a covenant of works do they preach truth?

MRS. H. Yes Sir, but when they preach a covenant of works for salvation, that is not truth. . . .

D. GOV. Likewise I will prove this that you said the gospel in the letter and words holds forth nothing but a covenant of works and that all that do not hold as you do are in a covenant of works.

MRS. H. I deny this for if I should so say, I should speak against my own judgment.

MR. ENDICOT. I desire to speak seeing Mrs. Hutchinson seems to lay something against them that are to witness against her.

GOVER. Only I would add this. It is well discerned to the court that Mrs. Hutchinson can tell when to speak and when to hold her tongue. Upon the answering of a question which we desire her to tell her thoughts of she desires to be pardoned.

MRS. H. It is one thing for me to come before a public magistracy and there to speak what they would have me to speak and another when a man comes to me in a way of friendship privately there is difference in that....

DEP. GOV. I called these witnesses and you deny them. You see they have proved this and you deny this, but it is clear. You said they preached a covenant of works and that they were not able ministers of the new testament; now there are two other things that you did affirm which were that the scriptures in the letter of them held forth nothing but a covenant of works and likewise that those that were under a covenant of works cannot be saved.

MRS. H. (*Gov.*) Did you say so?

MRS. H. Prove that I said so.

GOV. Did you say so? No Sir it is your conclusion....

GOV. What say you to this, though nothing be directly proved yet you hear it may be.

MRS. H. I acknowledge using the words of the apostle to the Corinthians unto him, that they that were ministers of the letter and not the spirit did preach a covenant of works. Upon his saying there was such scripture, then I fetched the bible and shewed him this place 2 Cor. iii. 6. He said that was the letter of the law. No said I it is the letter of the gospel.

GOV. You have spoken this more than once then.

MRS. H. Then upon further discourse about proving a good and holding it out by the manifestation of the spirit he did acknowledge that to be the nearest way, but yet said he, will you not acknowledge that which we hold forth to be a way too wherein we may have hope; no truly if that be a way it is a way to hell.

GOV. Mrs. Hutchinson, the court you see hath laboured to bring you to acknowledge the error of your way that so you might be reduced, the time now grows late, we shall therefore give you a little more time to consider of it and therefore desire that you attend the court again in the morning....

SOURCE: Hutchinson, Thomas. *The History of the Province of Massachusetts Bay*. . . Boston: 1767.

AN ACT CONCERNING RELIGION
(1649)

During the 1600s, the Stuart kings of England granted proprietorships of American lands to loyal supporters, thus forming close attachments with the aristocracy as well as directing the settlement of the American colonies. A proprietor was given title and control to a set parcel of land. King Charles I, for example, granted the lands of the upper Chesapeake to Lord Baltimore, George Calvert, who was a Catholic at a time when the official church of England was the Anglican Church. Anglicans and Puritans sometimes persecuted Catholics in England and America. Lord Baltimore hoped to make his proprietorship, which he named Maryland, a place where Catholics could worship unimpeded by opposition from Protestants. Even so, the colony attracted more Protestants than Catholics, which impelled Lord Baltimore into proposing an act for the toleration of all expressions of Christianity.

"An Act Concerning Religion," the Maryland Toleration Act, was passed by the Maryland Assembly in 1649. The Act imposed harsh penalties on any persons who denied Christianity or broke such Old Testament Commandments as worshipping other gods or taking the Lord's name in vain. The requirement to honor "the Blessed Virgin Mary" was an obvious Catholic sentiment. The Act set forth punishments for not honoring the Sabbath, and for abusive name calling for the sake of religion. At the same time, the Maryland Toleration Act called for freedom of conscience among all Christians, Protestants as well as Catholics. The Act was significant in countering the tendency in Europe, England, and other American colonies to proclaim one expression of Christianity the truth and all others error, deserving punishment.

Russell Lawson,
Bacone College

See also **Chesapeake Colonies; Religious Liberty.**

Acts and Orders of Assembly assented vnto

Enacted and made at a Genall Sessions of the said Assembly held at St Maries on the one and twentieth day of Aprill Anno Dm 1649 as followeth viz.:

An Act concerning Religion

fforasmuch as in a well governed and Xpian Comon Weath matters concerning Religion and the honor of God ought in the first place to bee taken, into serious consideracon and endeavoured to bee settled. Be it therefore ordered and enacted by the Right Hoble Cecilius Lord Baron of Baltemore absolute Lord and Proprietary of this Province with the advise and consent of this Generall Assembly. That whatsoever pson or psons within this Province and the Islands thereunto belonging shall from henceforth blaspheme God, that is Curse him, or deny our Saviour Jesus Christ to bee the sonne of God, or shall deny the holy Trinity the ffather sonne and holy Ghost, or the Godhead of any of the said Three psons of the Trinity or the Vnity of the Godhead, or shall use or utter any reproachfull Speeches, words or language concerning the said Holy Trinity, or any of the said three psons thereof, shalbe punished with death and confiscaton or forfeiture of all his or her lands and goods to the Lord Proprietary and his heires, And bee it also Enacted by the Authority and with the advise and assent aforesaid. That whatsoever pson or psons shall from henceforth use or utter any reproachfull words or Speeches concerning the blessed Virgin Mary the Mother of our Saviour or the holy Apostles or Evangelists or any of them shall in such case for the first offence forfeit to the said Lord Proprietary and his heirs Lords and Proprietaries of this Province the sume of ffive pound Sterling or the value thereof to be Levyed on the goods and chattells of every such pson soe offending, but in case such Offender or Offenders, shall not then have goods and chattells sufficient for the satisfyeing of such forfeiture, or that the same bee not otherwise speedily satisfyed that then such Offender or Offenders shalbe publiquely whipt and bee ymprisoned during the pleasure of the Lord Proprietary or the Leivet or cheife Governor of this Province for the time being. And that every such Offender or Offenders for every second offence shall forfeit tenne pound sterling or the value thereof to bee levyed as aforesaid, or in case such offender or Offenders shall not then haue goods and chattells within this Province sufficient for that purpose then to be publiquely and severely whipt and imprisoned as before is expressed. And that every pson or psons before mentioned offending herein the third time, shall for such third Offence forfeit all his lands and Goods and bee for ever banished and expelled out of this Province. And be it also further Enacted by the same authority advise and assent that whatsoever pson or psons shall from henceforth vppon any occasion of Offence or otherwise in a reproachful manner or Way declare call or denominate any pson or psons whatsoever inhabiting residing traffiqueing trading or comerceing within this Province or within any the Ports, Harbors, Creeks or Havens to the same belonging an heritick, Scismatick, Idolator, puritan, Independent, Prespiterian popish prest, Jesuite, Jesuited papist, Lutheran, Calvenist, Anabaptist, Brownist, Antinomian, Barrowist, Roundhead, Sepatist, or any other name or terme in a reproachfull manner relating to matter of Religion shall for every such Offence forfeit and loose the some or tenne shillings sterling or the value thereof to bee levyed on the goods and chattells of every such Offender and Offenders, the one half thereof to be forfeited and paid unto the person and persons of whom such reproachfull words are or shalbe spoken or vttered, and the other half thereof to the Lord Proprietary and his heires Lords and Proprietaries of this Province, But if such pson or psons who shall at any time vtter or speake any such reproachfull words or Language shall not have Goods or Chattells sufficient and overt within this Province to bee taken to satisfie the penalty aforesaid or that the same bee not otherwise speedily satisfyed, that then the pson or persons soe offending shalbe publickly whipt, and shall suffer imprisonmt. without baile or maineprise vntill hee shee or they respectively shall satisfy the party soe offended or greived by such reproachfull Language by asking him or her respectively forgivenes publiquely for such his Offence before the Magistrate or cheife Officer or Officers of the Towne or place where such Offence shalbe given. And be it further likewise Enacted by the Authority and consent aforesaid That every person and persons within this Province that shall at any time hereafter pphane the Sabbath or Lords day called Sunday by frequent swearing, drunkennes or by any uncivill or disorderly recreacon, or by working on that day when absolute necessity doth not require it shall for every such first offence forfeit 2s.6d sterling or the value thereof, and for the second offence 5s sterling or the value thereof, and for the third offence and soe for every time he shall offend in like manner afterwards 10s sterling or the value thereof. And in case such offender and offenders shall not have sufficient goods or chattels within this Province to satisfy any of the said Penalties respectively hereby imposed for prophaning the Sabbath or Lords day called Sunday as aforesaid, That in Every such case the ptie soe offending shall for the first and second offence in that kinde be imprisoned till hee or shee shall publickly in open Court before the cheife Commander Judge or Magistrate, of that Country Towne or precinct where such offence shalbe committed acknowledg the Scandall and offence he hath in that respect given against God and the good and civill Governemt. of this Province And for the third offence and for every time after shall also bee publickly whipt. And where as the inforceing of the conscience in matters of Religion hath frequently fallen out to be of dangerous Consequence in those commonwealthes where it hath been practised, And for the more quiett and peaceable governemt. of this Province, and the better to pserve mutuall Love and amity amongst the Inhabitants thereof. Be it Therefore also by the Lo: Proprietary with the advise and consent of this Assembly Ordeyned & enacted (except as in this psent Act is before Declared and sett forth) that noe person or psons whatsoever within this Province, or the Islands, Ports, Harbors, Creekes, or havens thereunto belonging professing to believe in Jesus Christ, shall from henceforth bee any waies troubled, Molested or discountenanced for or in respect of his or her religion nor in the free exercise thereof within this Province or the Islands thereunto belonging nor any way compelled to the beleife or exercise of any other Religion against his or her consent, soe as they be not unfaithfull to the Lord Proprietary, or molest or conspire against the civill Governemt, established or to bee established in this Province vnder him or his heires. And that all & every pson and psons that shall presume Contrary to this Act and the true intent and meaning thereof directly or indirectly either in person or estate willfully to wrong disturbe trouble or molest any person whatsoever within this Province professing to believe in Jesus Christ for or in respect of his or her religion or the free exercise thereof within this Province other than is provided for in this Act that such pson or psons soe offending, shalbe compelled to pay trebble damages to the party soe wronged or molested, and for every such offence shall also forfeit 20s sterling in money or the value thereof, half thereof for the vse of the Lo: Proprietary, and his heires Lords and Proprietaries of this Province, and the other half for the vse of the party soe wronged or molested as aforesaid, Or if the ptie soe offending as aforesaid shall refuse or bee vnable to recompense the party soe wronged, or to satisfy such ffyne or forfeiture, then such Offender shalbe severely punished by publick whipping &imprisonmt. during the pleasure of the Lord Proprietary, or his Leivetenat or cheife Governor of this Province for the tyme being without baile or maineprise. And bee it further alsoe Enacted by the authority and consent aforesaid That the Sheriff or other Officer or Officers from time to time to bee appointed & authorized for that purpose, of the County Towne or precinct where every particular offence in this psent Act conteyned shall happen at any time to bee comitted and wherevppon there is hereby a fforfeiture ffyne or penalty imposed shall from time to time distraine and seise the goods and estate of every such pson soe offending as aforesaid against this psent Act or any pt thereof, and sell the same or any part thereof for the full satisfaccon of such forfeiture, ffine, or penalty as aforesaid, Restoring vnto the ptie soe offending the Remainder or over-plus of the said goods or estate after such satisfaccon soe made as aforesaid.

The ffreemen haue assented. Tho: Hatton Enacted by the Governor Willm Stone

SOURCE: Browne, William H., ed. *Proceedings and Acts of the General Assembly of Maryland, January 1637/8–September 1664.* Baltimore: 1883.

UNTITLED POEM
(1643, by Anne Bradstreet)

Anne Dudley Bradstreet was perhaps the most famous and accomplished seventeenth-century Massachusetts Puritan wife and mother. She was born in 1612 in England, immigrated to the Massachusetts Bay Colony along with her husband and parents in the *Arbella* under the leadership of John Winthrop in 1630, and lived and wrote and raised children in Massachusetts until her death in 1672. Married to Simon Bradstreet, a leader of the colony, Anne had no leadership position, but rather lived a domestic life in rural New England. Her intelligence and need to express herself about life, family, and God led her to pen poems for her own (and her family's) pleasure. These were unexpectedly published in London in 1650, titled, "The Tenth Muse Lately Sprung Up in America."

Bradstreet's untitled poem, written in 1643, reflects the Puritan preoccupation with morality, character, duty, prayer, and death. Puritan ministers called on their parishioners to imitate the character of Christ in piety, acceptance of one's role and status in life, and charity toward others; to subordinate their own feelings to the will of God, expressed in the authorities of family, government, and church; to engage in constant prayer so to prepare for the inevitability yet unexpectedness of death. Bradstreet's poem reads as an epitaph for her own life and that of many other Puritan matrons of seventeenth-century Massachusetts.

Russell Lawson,
Bacone College

See also **Colonial Society; Literature.**

Here lyes
A Worthy Matron of unspotted life,
A loving Mother and obedient wife,
A friendly Neighbor, pitiful to poor,
Whom oft she fed, and clothed with her store;

To Servants wisely aweful, but yet kind,
And as they did, so they reward did find:
A true Instructer of her Family,
The which she ordered with dexterity.

The publick meetings ever did frequent,

And in her Closet constant hours she spent;
Religious in all her words and wayes,
Preparing still for death, till end of dayes:
Of all her Children, Children liv'd to see,
Then dying, left a blessed memory.

SOURCE: Bradstreet, Anne. "Untitled." In *The Tenth Muse Lately Sprung Up in America*. London: 1650.

MASSACHUSETTS SCHOOL LAW
(April 14, 1642)

English Puritans founded the colony of Massachusetts Bay in 1630 upon the belief that they could create a model commonwealth in the New World based on the Christian principles of faith in God and obedience to His will. They believed that Church and State worked best when linked closely together. Suffrage was granted only to those males who had "owned the covenant" before a congregation of "saints," the community of believers who cared for and watched over each other. Personal liberty was subordinate to civil liberty, which was the right of the individual to conform to the laws of the commonwealth. It was of utmost importance, then, that children be raised in proper ways to become useful, obedient members of the commonwealth.

The Puritans believed that the best approach to educating the young was prayer and work. Masters who had charge of children apprenticed to them until they reached maturity were just as responsible as parents to inculcate proper Christian beliefs and respect for the civil authorities. In 1642, the General Court of Massachusetts assumed the responsibility of overseeing masters and parents in the education and employment of their apprentices and children. To the English Puritans of Massachusetts, such firmness seemed the only way to guarantee order in a religious commonwealth.

Russell Lawson,
Bacone College

See also **Colonial Society; Education; Massachusetts Bay Colony.**

This Co^{rt}, taking into consideration the great neglect of many parents & masters in training up their children in learning & labo^{r}, & other implyments which may be proffitable to the common wealth, do hereupon order and decree, that in euery towne ye chosen men appointed for managing the prudentiall affajres of the same shall henceforth stand charged with the care of the redresse of this evill, so as they shalbee sufficiently punished by fines for the neglect thereof, upon presentment of the grand iury, or other information or complaint in any Court within this iurisdiction; and for this end they, or the greater numbe^{r} of them, shall have power to take account from time to time of all parents and masters, and of their children, concerning their calling and implyment of their children, especially of their ability to read & understand the principles of religion & the capitall lawes of this country, and to impose fines upon such as shall refuse to render such accounts to them when they shall be required; and they shall have power, with consent of any Court or the magistrate, to put forth apprentices the children of such as they shall (find) not to be able & fitt to employ and bring them up. They shall take ... that boyes and girles be not suffered to converse together, so as may occasion any wanton, dishonest, or immodest behavio^{r}; & for their better performance of this trust committed to them, they may divide the towne amongst them, appointing to every of the said townesmen a certaine number of families to have special oversight of. They are also to provide that a sufficient quantity of materialls, as hemp, flaxe, ec^{ra}, may be raised in their severall townes, & tooles & implements provided for working out the same; & for their assistance in this so needfull and beneficiall imploym^{t}, if they meete wth any difficulty or opposition wch they cannot well master by their own power, they may have reco^r^se to some of the ma^trats^, who shall take such course for their help & incuragm^t^ as the occasion shall require according to iustice; & the said townesmen, at the next Co^r^t in those limits, after the end of their year, shall give a briefe account in writing of their proceedings herein, provided that they have bene so required by some Co^r^t or magistrate a month at least before; & this order to continew for two yeares, & till the Co^r^t shall take further order.

SOURCE: *The Charters and General Laws of the Colony and Province of Massachusetts Bay.* Boston: T. B. Wait, 1814.

EVIDENCE USED AGAINST WITCHES
(1693, by Increase Mather)

After becoming concerned that innocent people were being convicted and executed for witchcraft, Massachusetts Puritan clergyman Increase Mather (1639–1723) argued against the use of "spectral evidence" and the "vulgar probation" in the prosecution of those accused of witchcraft. Mather's elaborately argued disquisition, delivered during a meeting with his fellow Boston clergymen in 1692, represents a philosophical change from his previous writings, which had been used by witch hunters during the earliest days of the Salem hysteria. The change in his views is thought by many to have been prompted by rumors that his own wife would soon join the unhappy ranks of the accused. Whatever his motivation, Mather's words helped solidify the growing public opinion against the trials, which ended in May 1693 after nineteen hangings and one death caused by the accused being crushed with rocks.

Laura M. Miller,
Vanderbilt University

See also **Massachusetts Bay Colony; Salem Witch Trials; Witchcraft.**

If the things which have been mentioned are not infallible proofs of guilt in the accused party, it is then queried: Whether there are any discoveries of this crime which jurors and judges may with a safe conscience proceed upon to the conviction condemnation of the persons under suspicion?

Let me here premise two things:

1. The evidence in this crime ought to be as clear as in any other crimes of a capital nature. The Word of God does nowhere intimate that a less clear evidence, or that fewer or other witnesses may be taken as sufficient to convict a man of sorcery, which would nor be enough to convict him were he charged with another evil worthy of death. If we may not take the oath of a distracted person, or of a possessed person in a case of murder, theft, felony of any sort, then neither may we do it in the case of witchcraft.
2. Let me premise this also, that there have been always of trying witches long used in many nations, especially in the dark times of paganism and popery, which the righteous God never approved of, but which (as judicious Mr. Perkins expresseth it in plain English) were invented by the devil, that so innocent persons might be condemned and some notorious witches escape. Yea, many superstitious and magical experiments have been used to try witches by. Of this sort is that of scratching the witch . . . yea, and that way of discovering witches by trying their hands and feet, and casting them on the water to try whether they will sink or swim. I did publicly bear my testimony against this superstition in a book printed at Boston eight years past.

I hear that of late some in a neighbor colony have been playing with this diabolical invention. It is to be lamented that, in such a land of uprightness as New England once was, a practice which Protestant writers generally condemn as sinful, and which the more sober and learned men among papists themselves have not only judged unlawful but (to express it in their own terms) to be no less than a mortal sin, should ever be heard of. Were it not that the coming of Christ to judge the earth draweth near, I should think that such practices are an unhappy omen that the devil and pagans will get these dark territories into their possession again. But that I may not be thought to have no reason for my calling the impleaded experiment into question, I have these things further to allege against it.

1. It has been rejected long agone by Christian nations as a thing superstitious and diabolical. In Italy and Spain it is wholly disused, and in the Low Countries and in France, where the judges are men of learning. In some parts of Germany old paganism customs are observed more than in other countries; nevertheless, all the academies throughout Germany have disapproved of this way of purgation.

2. The devil is in it, all superstition is from him; and when secret things or latent crimes are discovered by superstitious practices, some compact and communion with the devil is the cause of it, as Austin has truly intimated. And so it is here; for if a witch cannot be drowned, this must proceed either from some natural cause, which it doth not, for it is against nature for human bodies, when hands and feet are tied, not to sink under the water. Besides, they that plead for this superstition say that if witches happen to be condemned for some other crime and not for witchcraft, they will not swim like a cork above water, which, cause showeth that the cause of this natation is not physical. And if not, then either it must proceed from a divine miracle to save a witch from drowning; or, lastly, it must be a diabolical wonder.

This superstitious experiment is commonly known by the name of "The Vulgar Probation," because it was never appointed by any lawful authority, but from the suggestion of the devil taken up by the rude rabble. And some learned men are of opinion that the first explorator (being a white witch) did explicitely covenant with the devil that he should discover latent crimes in this way. And that it is by virtue of that first contract that the devil goeth to work to keep his servants from sinking when this ceremony of his ordaining is used. Moreover, we know that *Diabolus est Dei simia*, the devil seeks to imitate divine miracles. We read in ecclesiastical story that some of the martyrs, when they were by persecutors ordered to be drowned, proved to be immersible. This miracle would the devil imitate in causing witches, who are his martyrs, not to sink when they are cast into the waters.

3. This way of purgation is of the same nature with the old ordeals of the pagans. If men were accused with any crime, to clear their innocency, they were to take a hot iron into their hands, or to suffer scalding water to be poured down their throats; and, if they received no hurt, thereby they were acquitted. This was the devil's invention, and many times (as the devil would have it) they that submitted to these trials suffered no inconvenience. Nevertheless, it is astonishing to think what innocent blood has been shed in the world by means of this satanical device. Witches have often (as Sprenger observes) desired that they might stand or fall by this trial by hot iron, and sometimes come off well.

Indeed, this ordeal was used in other cases, and not in cases of witchcraft only. And so was "The Vulgar Probation" by casting into the water practised upon persons accused with other crimes as well as that of witchcraft. How it came to be restrained to that of witchcraft I cannot tell; it is as supernatural for a body whose hands and feet are tied to swim above the water as it is for their hands not to feel a red hot iron. If the one of these ordeals is lawful to be used, then so is the other too. But as for the fiery ordeal it is rejected and exploded out of the world; for the same reason then the trial by water should be so.

4. It is a tempting of God when men put the innocency of their fellow creatures upon such trials; to desire the Almighty to show a miracle to clear the innocent or to convict the guilty is a most presumptuous tempting of Him. Was it not a miracle when Peter was kept from sinking under the water by the omnipotency of Christ? As for Satan, we know that his ambition is to make his servants believe that his power is equal to God's, and that therefore he can preserve whom he pleaseth. I have read of certain magicians who were seen walking on the water. If then guilty persons shall float on the waters, either it is the devil that causes them to do so (as no doubt it is), and what have men to do to set the devil on work; or else it is a divine miracle, like that of Peter's not sinking, or that of the iron that swam at the word of Elisha. And shall men try whether God will work a miracle to make a discovery? If a crime cannot be found out but by miracle, it is not for any judge on earth to usurp that judgment which is reserved for the Divine Throne.

5. This pretended gift of immersibility attending witches is a most fallible deceitful thing; for many a witch has sunk under water.... Besides, it has sometimes been known that persons who have floated on the water when the hangman has made the experiment on them, have sunk down like a stone, when others have made the trial.

6. The reasons commonly alleged for this superstition are of no moment. It is said they hate the water; whereas they have many times desired that they might be cast on the water in order to their purgation. It is alleged that water is used in baptism, therefore witches swim. A weak fancy; all the water in the world is not consecrated water. Cannot witches eat bread or drink wine, notwithstanding those elements are made use of in the Blessed Sacrament? But (say some) the devils by sucking of them make them so light that the water bears them; whereas some witches are twice as heavy as many an innocent person. Well, but then they are possessed with the devil. Suppose so; is the devil afraid if they should sink that he should be drowned with them? But why then were the Gadaren's hogs drowned when the devil was in them?

These things being premised, I answer the question affirmatively: There are proofs for the conviction of witches which jurors may with a safe conscience proceed upon so as to bring them in guilty. The Scripture which saith, "Thou shalt not suffer a witch to live," clearly implies that some in the world may be known and proved to be witches. For until they be so, they may and must be suffered to live. Moreover, we find in Scripture that some have been convicted and executed for witches. "For Saul cut off those that had familiar spirits, and the wizards out of the land" (I Sam. 28:9)....

But then the inquiry is: What is sufficient proof?

This case has been with great judgment answered by several divines of our own, particulary by Mr. Perkins and Mr. Bernard. Also Mr. John Gaul, a worthy minister at Staughton, in the county of Huntington, has published a very judicious discourse called, "Select Cases of Conscience touching Witches and Witchcrafts," printed at London A.D. 1646, wherein he does with great prudence and evidence of Scripture lightly handle this and other cases. Such jurors as can obtain those books, I would advise them to read, and seriously as in the fear of God to consider them, and so far as they keep to the law and to the testimony, and speak according to that word, receive the light which is in them. But the books being now rare to be had, let me express my concurrence with them in these two particulars.

1. That a free and voluntary confession of the crime made by the person suspected and accused after examination is a sufficient ground of conviction.

Indeed, if persons are distracted or under the power of frenetic melancholy, that alters the case, but the jurors that examine them, and their neighbors that know them, may easily determine that case; or if confession be extorted, the evidence is not so clear and convictive; but if any persons out of remorse of conscience, or from a touch of God in their spirits, confess and show their deeds, as the converted magicians in Ephesus did, nothing can be more clear. Suppose a man to be suspected for murder, or for committing a rape, or the like nefarious wickedness, if he does freely confess the accusation, that's ground enough to condemn him. The Scripture approveth of judging the wicked servant out of his own mouth. It is by some objected that persons in discontent may falsely accuse themselves. I say, if they do so, and it cannot be proved that they are false accusers of themselves, they ought to die for their wickedness, and their blood will be upon their own heads; the jury, the judges, and the land is clear....

2. If two credible persons shall affirm upon oath that they have seen the party accused speaking such words, or doing things which none but such as have familiarity with the devil ever did or can do, that's a sufficient ground for conviction.

Some are ready to say that wizards are not so unwise as to do such things in the sight or hearing of others, but it is certain that they have very often been known to do so. How often have they been seen by others using enchantments? Conjuring to raise storms? And have been heard calling upon their familiar spirits? And have been known to use spells and charms? And to show in a glass or in a show stone persons absent? And to reveal secrets which could not be discovered but by the devil? And have not men been seen to do things which are above human strength, that no man living could do without diabolical assistances?...

The devil never assists men to do supernatural things undesired. When, therefore, such like things shall be testified against the accused party, not by specters, which are devils in the shape of persons either living or dead, but by real men or women who may be credited, it is proof enough that such a one has that conversation and correspondence with the devil as that he or she, whoever they be, ought to be exterminated from among men. This notwithstanding I will add: It were better that ten suspected witches should escape than that one innocent person should be condemned.

SOURCE: Stedman, Edmund C., and Ellen M. Hutchinson, eds. *A Library of American Literature from the Earliest Settlement to the Present Time.* New York: C. L. Webster, 1889.

EXCERPT FROM *VOYAGES OF THE SLAVER ST. JOHN (1659)*

The accidental discovery of the New World during the fifteenth century brought with it an enormous and rapidly expanding demand for human labor. Indentured whites, transported convicts, and conquered Native Americans temporarily filled the need. But indentured servants and convicts eventually satisfied their contracts and had to be set free, and the natives were too susceptible to foreign ailments and too prone to escape or to mounting organized revolts to be reliable. Eager to find a solution to the problem and to increase their profits, European merchants turned their eyes toward the western shores of Africa with a vengeance. From the sixteenth to the nineteenth century, some nine to fifteen million Africans were kidnapped and brought against their wills to the Americas. During the deadly "Middle Passage" across the Atlantic Ocean to either the plantations of the West Indies or the English colonies, conditions on slave ships were barbarously cruel. In order to maintain high profit margins, slavers crammed their human cargo into tiny, poorly ventilated spaces between decks and fed them only the poorest foods. Among the countless malicious indignities visited upon captured slaves was the practice called "bed warming," wherein women dragged from the hold were raped and beaten by officers eager to keep the night chill from their sheets. The mortality rate of such crossings sometimes exceeded twenty percent.

Laura M. Miller,
Vanderbilt University

See also **Slave Ships; Slave Trade.**

[March 4, 1659] We Weighed anchor, by order of the Honorable Director, *Fohan Valcken-borch*, and the Honorable Director *Fasper van Heussen*, to proceed on our Voyage from *Elmina* to *Rio Reael*, to trade for Slaves for the Honorable Company.

[March 8] Saturday. Arrived with our ship before *Arda*, to take on board the Surgeon's mate and a Supply of Tamarinds for the Slaves; sailed again next day on our Voyage to *Rio Reael.*

[March 17] Arrived at *Rio Reael* in front of a village called *Bany* where we found the Company's Yacht, named the *Peace*, which was sent out to assist us to trade for Slaves.

[April] Nothing was done except to trade for Slaves.

[May 6] One of our seamen died; his name was *Claes van Diemen*, of *Durgerdam.*

[May 22] Again weighed Anchor and ran out of *Rio Reael* accompanied by the Yacht *Peace;* purchased there *two hundred* and *nineteen* head of Slaves, men, women, boys and girls, and proceeded on our course for the High land of *Ambosius*, for the purpose of procuring food there for the Slaves, as nothing was to be had at *Rio Reael.*

[May 26] Monday. Arrived under the High land of *Ambosius* to look there for Victuals for the Slaves, and spent *seven* days there, but with difficulty obtained enough for the daily consumption of the Slaves, so that we resolved to run to *Rio Cammerones* to see if any food could be had there for the Slaves.

[June 5] Thursday. Arrived at the *Rio Commerones* and the Yacht *Peace* went up to look for provisions for the Slaves. This day died our cooper, named *Peter Claessen*, of *Amsterdam.*

[June 29] Sunday. Again resolved to proceed on our Voyage, as but little food was to be had for the Slaves in consequence of the great Rains which fell every day, and because many of the Slaves were suffering from the Bloody Flux in consequence of the bad provisions we were supplied with at *El Mina*, amongst which were several barrels of Groats, wholly unfit for use.

We then turned over to *Adriaen Blaes*, the Skipper, *One hundred* and *ninety five* Slaves, consisting of *Eighty one* **Men**, *One hundred* and *five* **Women**, *six* boys and *three* girls for which Bills of lading were signed and sent, one by the Yacht *Peace* to *El Mina* with an account of, and receipts for, remaining Merchandize.

[July 25] Arrived at *Cabo de Loop de Consalvo* for wood and water.

[July 27] Our Surgeon, named *Martin de Lanoy*, died of the Bloody Flux.

[August 10] Arrived the Company's Ship *Raven* from *Castle St. George d'el Mina*, homeward bound.

[August 11] Again resolved to pursue our Voyage towards the Island of *Annebo*, in order to purchase there Supplies for the Slaves. We have lain *Sixty* days at *Cabo de Loop* hauling wood and water. Among the Water barrels, forty were taken to pieces to be refitted, as our Cooper died at *Rio Cammerones*, and we had no other person capable of repairing them.

[August 15] Arrived at the *Island Annebo* where we purchased *One hundred* half tierces of little Beans, *twelve* Hogs, *five thousand* Cocoa nuts, *five thousand* Oranges, besides some other stores.

[August 17] Again hoisted Sail to prosecute our Voyage to the Island of *Curacao.*

[September 21] The Skipper called the Ships officers aft, and resolved to run for the Island of *Tobago* and to procure Water there; otherwise we should have perished for want of water, as many of our Water casks had leaked dry.

[September 24] Friday. Arrived at the Island of *Tobago* and shipped Water there, also purchased some Bread, as our hands had had no ration for three weeks.

[September 27] Again set sail on our Voyage to the Island of *Curacao*, as before.

[November 2] Lost our ship on the Rifts of *Rocus*, and all hands immediately took to the Boat, as there was no prospect of saving the Slaves, for we must abandon the Ship in consequence of the heavy Surf.

[November 4] Arrived with the Boat at the Island of *Curacao;* the Honorable Governor *Beck* ordered two sloops to take the Slaves off the wreck, one of which sloops with *eighty four* slaves on board, was captured by a Privateer.

SOURCE: O'Callaghan, E. B., trans. *Voyages of the Slavers St. John and Arms of Amsterdam, 1659, 1663: Together with Additional Papers Illustrative of the Slave Trade under the Dutch.* Albany, N.Y.: J. Munsell, 1867.

EARLIEST AMERICAN PROTEST AGAINST SLAVERY
(February, 1688, drawn up by Mennonite Germans)

William Penn's establishment of the principle of religious toleration in his proprietorship of Pennsylvania attracted a variety of religious sects from Europe. Along with the Quakers, Moravians, Lutherans, and Dunkers were the Mennonites, a strongly cohesive group that practiced a basic form of Christianity focusing on simplicity, individualism, hard work, and prayer. These German immigrants believed that all humans were equal, being children of God the Creator. They practiced toleration in all of its forms. They opposed any restrictions on human rights and liberty.

The Mennonites gave expression to these beliefs in 1688. They argued that Blacks and Whites were essentially equal, that it was unjust and a contradiction of Christianity to enslave them. They pointed out that Christian slave-owners were no better than the "Turks," or Muslims, who practiced slavery in Asia and Africa. They appealed to the consciences of slave-owners, asking them to realize that the sin of slavery led to many other sins, such as adultery when the master lay with the female slave. The consequence of this sinful union was the birth of a child rejected and enslaved by the master, who denied all that was right and true by denying his own flesh and blood. The Mennonites believed that all social relations should be based on the Golden Rule, to treat others as you would have them treat you.

Russell Lawson,
Bacone College

See also **Antislavery; Mennonites.**

This is to the Monthly Meeting held at Rigert Worrell's.

These are the reason why we are against the traffic of mens-body as follows: Is there any that would be done or handled at this manner, viz., to be sold or made a slave for all the time of his life? How fearful and fainthearted are many on sea when they see a strange vessel, being afraid it should be a Turk, and they should be taken and sold for slaves in Turkey. Now what is this better done as Turks do? Yea, rather is it worse for them which say they are Christians, for we hear that the most part of such Negroes are brought hither against their will and consent, and that many of them are stolen. Now, though they are black, we cannot conceive there is more liberty to have them slaves as it is to have other white ones. There is a saying that we shall do to all men like as we will be done ourselves, making no difference of what generation, descent, or color they are. And those who steal or rob men, and those who buy or purchase them, are they not all alike? Here is liberty of conscience, which is right and reasonable. Here ought to be likewise liberty of the body, except of evildoers, which is another case. But to bring men hither, or to rob and sell them against their will, we stand against.

In Europe there are many oppressed for conscience sake; and here there are those oppressed which are of a black color. And we, who know that men must not commit adultery, some do commit adultery in others, separating wives from their husbands and giving them to others, and some sell the children of those poor creatures to other men. Oh! do consider well this thing, you who do it, if you would be done at this manner, and if it is done according [to] Christianity? You surpass Holland and Germany in this thing. This makes an ill report in all those countries of Europe, where they hear of that the Quakers do here handle men like they handle there the cattle. And for that reason some have no mind or inclination to come hither.

And who shall maintain this your cause or plead for it? Truly we cannot do so except you shall inform us better hereof, viz., that Christians have liberty to practise these things. Pray! What thing in the world can be done worse toward us than if men should rob or steal us away and sell us for slaves to strange countries, separating husbands from their wives and children.

Being now this is not done at that manner we will be done at, therefore, we contradict and are against this traffic of mens-bodies. And we who profess that it is not lawful to steal must likewise avoid to purchase such things as are stolen, but rather help to stop this robbing and stealing if possible and such men ought to be delivered out of the hands of the robbers and set free as well as in Europe. Then is Pennsylvania to have a good report; instead it has now a bad one for this sake in other countries. Especially whereas the Europeans are desirous to know in what manner the Quakers do rule in their province, and most of them do look upon us with an envious eye. But if this is done well, what shall we say is done evil?

If once these slaves (which they say are so wicked and stubborn men) should join themselves, fight for their freedom and handle their masters and mistresses as they did handle them before, will these masters and mistresses take the sword at hand and war against these poor slaves, like we are able to believe some will not refuse to do? Or have these Negroes not as much right to fight for their freedom as you have to keep them slaves?

Now consider well this thing, if it is good or bad. And in case you find it to be good to handle these blacks at that manner, we desire and require you hereby lovingly that you may inform us herein, which at this time never was done, viz., that Christians have liberty to do so, to the end we shall be satisfied in this point, and satisfy likewise our good friends and acquaintances in our native country, to whom it is a terror or fearful thing that men should be handled so in Pennsylvania.

SOURCE: *The Pennsylvania Magazine of History and Biography*, Vol. 4, 1880.

POWHATAN'S SPEECH TO JOHN SMITH *(1607)*

In his speech, Powhatan (1547–1618), the father of Pocahontas, makes a plea for peace to John Smith, a leader of the English settlers at Jamestown. From the very beginning, relations between the Native Americans and the settlers were uncertain at best. When John Smith and his fellows from the Virginia Company arrived on the shores of the New World in 1607, they faced an uncertain future. The landscape was unforgiving and alien. The local Algonquian tribe hoped to run the settlers off by raiding their settlement and stealing essential supplies, gunpowder, and tools. When in 1607 native hunters captured Smith, they presented him to Powhatan for judgment. What occurred next has been the subject of considerable conjecture and revisionist speculation. Whatever the facts, Smith, a proud and boastful man prone to exaggeration, became convinced that Powhatan's eleven-year-old daughter, Pocahontas, was responsible for his survival. He was made a subordinate chief in the tribe and released a month later. Powhatan was a powerful chief, the leader of a confederacy of some thirty tribes and eight thousand people from his capital in Werowocomoco. His words here reflect the anxiety and doubt surrounding the arrival of white settlers in the New World and presage the generations of conflict and bloodshed between Europeans and Native Americans that would darken much of the history of both peoples for the next three hundred years.

Laura M. Miller,
Vanderbilt University

See also: **Chesapeake Colonies**

I am now grown old, and must soon die; and the succession must descend, in order, to my brothers, *Opitchapan*, *Opekankanough*, and *Catataugh*, and then to my two sisters, and their two daughters. I wish their experience was equal to mine; and that your love to us might not be less than ours to you. Why should you take by force that from us which you can have by love? Why should you destroy us, who have provided you with food? What can you get by war? We can hide our provisions, and fly into the woods; and then you must consequently famish by wronging your friends. What is the cause of your jealousy? You see us unarmed, and willing to supply your wants, if you will come in a friendly manner, and not with swords and guns, as to invade an enemy. I am not so simple, as not to know it is better to eat good meat, lie well, and sleep quietly with my women and children; to laugh and be merry with the English; and, being their friend, to have copper, hatchets, and whatever else I want, than to fly from all, to lie cold in the woods, feed upon acorns, roots, and such trash, and to be so hunted, that I cannot rest, eat, or sleep. In such circumstances, my men must watch, and if a twig should but break, all would cry out, "*Here comes Capt. Smith;*" and so, in this miserable manner, to end my miserable life; and, Capt. Smith, this *might* be soon your fate too, through your rashness and unadvisedness. I, therefore, exhort you to peaceable councils; and, above all, I insist that the guns and swords, the cause of all our jealousy and uneasiness, be removed and sent away.

SOURCE: Drake, Samuel G. *Biography and History of the Indians of North America.* Boston: O. L. Perkins, 1834.

A DIALOGUE BETWEEN PIUMBUKHOU AND HIS UNCONVERTED RELATIVES
(c. 1671, by John Eliot)

For many Christian British and European settlers to the Americas, attaining personal religious freedom was not tantamount to securing the Kingdom of Heaven. Necessary also was an effort to win new souls, in this case those belonging to the New World's native inhabitants. The proselytizing ethic is the impetus behind the unusual work seen here. Educated at Cambridge University in England, the missionary John Eliot (1604–1690) settled in colonial Massachusetts in 1631, whereupon he flung himself into the difficult task of reconstructing the local Indian population. To this end and with the help of the British Parliament, Eliot established some fourteen villages so that his "praying Indians" could live apart from harmful pagan influences. Most of these villages would eventually be taken over by white settlers, eager always for more space. Eliot's several *Dialogues,* written from the perspective of successful converts, were intended as guide books to aid in the challenge of swaying the spirits of the often-dubious Native Americans. An accomplished pamphleteer and a contributor to the *Bay Psalm Book,* the self-styled "Apostle to the Indians" went so far as to render the Bible into the native language Massachuset (sometimes called Natick), thus producing, in translation, the first Bible printed in North America.

Laura M. Miller,
Vanderbilt University

***See also Bay Psalm Book;* Indian Missions; Indian Religious Life; Praying Towns.**

KINSMAN: I had rather that my actions of love should testify how welcome you are, and how glad I am of this your kind visitation, than that I should say it in a multitude of words. But in one word, you are very welcome into my heart, and I account it among the best of the joys of this day, that I see your face, and enjoy your company in my habitation.

KINSWOMAN: It is an addition to the joys of this day, to see the face of my loving kinsman. And I wish you had come a little earlier, that you might have taken part with us in the joys of this day, wherein we have had all the delights that could be desired, in our merry meeting, and dancing.

And I pray cousin, how doth your wife, my loving kinswoman, is she yet living? And is she not yet weary of your new way of praying to God? And what pleasure have you in those ways?

PIUMBUKHOU: My wife doth remember her love to you. She is in good health of body, and her soul is in a good condition. She is entered into the light of the knowledge of God, and of Christ. She is entered into the narrow way of heavenly joys, and she doth greatly desire that you would turn from these ways of darkness in which you so much delight, and come taste and see how good the Lord is.

And whereas you wish I had come sooner, to have shared with you in your delights of this day. Alas, they are no delights, but griefs to me, to see that you do still delight in them. I am like a man that have tasted of sweet wine and honey, which have so altered the taste of my mouth, that I abhor to taste of your sinful and foolish pleasures, as the mouth doth abhor to taste the most filthy and stinking dung, the most sour grapes, or most bitter gall. Our joys in the knowledge of God, and of Jesus Christ, which we are taught in the Book of God, and feel in our heart, is sweeter to our soul, than honey is unto the mouth and taste.

KINSWOMAN: We have all the delights that the flesh and blood of man can devise and delight in, and we taste and feel the delights of them, and would you make us believe that you have found out new joys and delights, in comparison of which all our delights do stink like dung? Would you make us believe that we have neither eyes to see, nor ears to hear, nor mouth to taste? Ha, ha, he! I appeal to the sense and sight and feeling of the company present, whether this be so.

ALL: You say very true. Ha, ha, he!

PIUMBUKHOU: Hearken to me, my friends, and see if I do not give a clear answer unto this seeming difficulty. Your dogs take as much delight in these meetings, and the same kinds of delight as you do. They delight in each others company. They provoke each other to lust, and enjoy the pleasures of lust as you do. They eat and play and sleep as you do. What joys have you more than dogs have to delight the body of flesh and blood?

But all mankind have an higher and better part than the body. We have a soul, and that soul shall never die. Our soul is to converse with God, and to converse in such things as do concern God, and heaven, and an eternal estate, either in happiness with God, if we walk with him and serve him in this life, or in misery and torment with the Devil, if we serve him in this life. The service of God doth consist in virtue, and wisdom, and delights of the soul, which will reach to heaven, and abide forever.

But the service of the Devil is in committing sins of the flesh, which defile both body and soul, and reach to hell, and will turn all to fire and flame to torment your souls and bodies in all eternity.

Now consider, all your pleasures and delights are such as defile you with sin, and will turn to flame, to burn and torment you. They provoke God to wrath, who hath created the prison of hell to torment you, and the more you have took pleasure in sin, the greater are your offences against God, and the greater shall be your torments.

But we that pray to God repent of our old sins, and by faith in Christ we seek for, and find a pardon for what is past, and grace and strength to reform for time to come. So that our joys are soul joys in godliness, and virtue, and hope of glory in another world when we die.

Your joys are bodily, fleshly, such as dogs have, and will all turn to flames in hell to torment you.

KINSMAN: If these things be so, we had need to cease laughing, and fall to weeping, and see if we can draw water from our mournful eyes to quench these tormenting flames. My heart trembles to hear theses things. I never heard so much before, nor have I any thing to say to the contrary, but that these things may be so. But how shall I know that you say true? Our forefathers were (many of them) wise men, and we have wise men now living. They all delight in these our delights. They have taught us nothing about our soul, and God, and heaven, and hell, and joy and torment in the life to come. Are you wiser than our fathers? May not we rather think that *English* men have invented these stories to amaze us and fear us out of our old customs, and bring us to stand in awe of them, that they might wipe us of our lands, and drive us into corners, to seek new ways of living, and new places too? And be beholding to them for that which is our own, and was ours, before we knew them.

ALL: You say right.

PIUMBUKHOU: The Book of God is no invention of Englishmen. It is the holy law of God himself, which was given unto man by God, before Englishmen had any knowledge of God; and all the knowledge which they have, they have it out of the Book of God. And this book is given to us as well as to them, and it is as free for us to search the scriptures as for them. So that we have our instruction from a higher hand, than the hand of man. It is the great Lord God of heaven and earth, who teacheth us these great things of which we speak. Yet this is also true, that we have great cause to be thankful to the English, and to thank God for them. For they had a good country of their own, but by ships sailing into these parts of the world, they heard of us, and of our country, and of our nakedness, ignorance of God, and wild condition. God put it into their hearts to desire to come hither, and teach us the good knowledge of God; and their King gave them leave so to do, and in our country to have their liberty to serve God according to the word of God. And being come hither, we gave them leave freely to live among us. They have purchased of us a great part of those lands which they possess. They love us, they do us right, and no wrong willingly. If any do us wrong, it is without the consent of their rulers, and upon our complaints our wrongs are righted. They are (many of them, especially the ruling part) good men, and desire to do us good. God put it into the heart of one of their ministers (as you all know) to teach us the knowledge of God, by the word of God, and hath translated the holy Book of God into our language, so that we can perfectly know the mind and counsel of God. And out of this book have I learned all that I say unto you, and therefore you need no more doubt of the truth of it, then you have cause to doubt that the heaven is over our head, the sun shineth, the earth is under our feet, we walk and live upon it, and breathe in the air. For as we see with our eyes these things to be so, so we read with our own eyes these things which I speak of, to be written in God's own book, and we feel the truth thereof in our own hearts.

KINSWOMAN: Cousin, you have wearied your legs this day with along journey to come and visit us, and you weary your tongue with long discourses. I am willing to comfort and refresh you with a short supper.

ALL: Ha, ha, he. Though short, if sweet that has good favor to a man that is weary. Ha, ha, he.

KINSWOMAN: You make long and learned discourses to us which we do not well understand. I think our best answer is to stop your mouth, and fill your belly with a good supper, and when your belly is full you will be content to take rest yourself, and give us leave to be at rest from these gastering and heart-trembling discourses. We are well as we are, and desire not to be troubled with these new wise sayings.

SOURCE: Bowden, Henry W., and James P. Ronda. *John Eliot's Indian Dialogues.* Westport, Conn.: Greenwood, 1981. Reproduces dialogues by Eliot originally published by M. Johnson in Cambridge, Mass., 1671.

CAPTIVITY NARRATIVE OF A COLONIAL WOMAN (February, 1675, by Mary Rowlandson)

Mary White Rowlandson was born in 1635 in England, emigrated to Salem, Mass., with her family, then migrated west to Lancaster, Mass., where she met and married the Reverend Joseph Rowlandson and assumed the duties of a pastor's wife in a small frontier town. She bore four children. In 1675, when King Philip's War began, the New England frontier was the site of battles and atrocities committed by the Indians as well as the colonists. Mary Rowlandson, her children, and friends experienced the horrors of war when raiders descended upon the small town of Lancaster. Mary and her children were captured, the mother and her daughter Sarah being wounded. Sarah died within a week as the Indians forced the captives to travel west then north. Mary and her other two children were separated, and forced to work as slaves to their captives. Eventually Rev. Rowlandson, who had been absent during the raid and had since sought the means to free his wife and children, ransomed his family. The reunited Rowlandsons lived in Boston, then Wethersfield, Conn. At some point Mary penned a narrative of her captivity, which was published in Boston in 1682.

The themes of Mary Rowlandson's *The Soveraignty & Goodness of God, Together, with the Faithfulness of His Promises Displayed; Being a Narrative of the Captivity and Restauration of Mrs. Mary Rowlandson* were typical for the time and place. Merciless savages and heathens, opponents of all that is true and good, oppose Christians. Yet God watches over his suffering servants, and eventually redeems them from captivity, rather like the redemption of the Hebrews from the Egyptians. God's providence controls all things—Mary Rowlandson's struggle to survive and be released from bondage was, in short, in conformity with the will of God.

Russell Lawson,
Bacone College

See also **Captivity Narratives.**

On the tenth of February 1675, Came the Indians with great numbers upon Lancaster: Their first coming was about Sun-rising; hearing the noise of some Guns, we looked out; several Houses were burning, and the Smoke ascending to Heaven. There were five persons taken in one house, the Father, and the Mother and a sucking Child, they knockt on the head; the other two they took and carried away alive. Their were two others, who being out of their Garison upon some occasion were set upon; one was knockt on the head, the other escaped: Another their was who running along was shot and wounded, and fell down; he begged of them his life, promising them Money (as they told me) but they would not hearken to him but knockt him in head, and stript him naked, and split open his Bowels. Another seeing many of the Indians about his Barn, ventured and went out, but was quickly shot down. There were three others belonging to the same Garison who were killed; the Indians getting up upon the roof of the Barn, had advantage to shoot down upon them over their Fortification. Thus these murtherous wretches went on, burning, and destroying before them.

At length they came and beset our own house, and quickly it was the dolefullest day that ever mine eyes saw. The House stood upon the edg of a hill; some of the Indians got behind the hill, others into the Barn, and others behind any thing that could shelter them; from all which places they shot against the House, so that the Bullets seemed to fly like hail; and quickly they wounded one man among us, then another, and then a third, About two hours (according to my observation, in that amazing time) they had been about the house before they prevailed to fire it (which they did with Flax and Hemp, which they brought out of the Barn, and there being no defence about the House, only two Flankers at two opposite corners and one of them not finished) they fired it once and one ventured out and quenched it, but they quickly fired it again, and that took. Now is the dreadfull hour come, that I have often heard of (in time of War, as it was the case of others) but now mine eyes see it. Some in our house were fighting for their lives, others wallowing in their blood, the House on fire over our heads, and the bloody Heathen ready to knock us on the head, if we stirred out. Now might we hear Mothers and Children crying out for themselves, and one another, Lord, What shall we do? Then I took my Children (and one of my sisters, hers) to go forth and leave the house: but as soon as we came to the dore and appeared, the Indians shot so thick that the bulletts rattled against the House, as if one had taken an handfull of stones and threw them, so that we were fain to give back. We had six stout Dogs belonging to our Garrison, but none of them would stir, though another time, if any Indian had come to the door, they were ready to fly upon him and tear him down. The Lord hereby would make us the more to acknowledge his hand, and to see that our help is always in him. But out we must go, the fire increasing, and coming along behind us, roaring, and the Indians gaping before us with their Guns, Spears and Hatchets to devour us. No sooner were we out of the House, but my Brother in Law (being before wounded, in defending the house, in or near the throat) fell down dead, wherat the Indians scornfully shouted, and hallowed, and were presently upon him, stripping off his cloaths, the bulletts flying thick, one went through my side, and the same (as would seem) through the bowels and hand of my dear Child in my arms. One of my elder Sisters Children, named William, had then his Leg broken, which the Indians perceiving, they knockt him on head. Thus were we butchered by those merciless Heathen, standing amazed, with the blood running down to our heels. My eldest Sister being yet in the House, and seeing those wofull sights, the Infidels haling Mothers one way, and Children another, and some wallowing in their blood: and her elder Son telling her that her Son William was dead, and my self was wounded, she said, And, Lord, let me dy with them; which was no sooner said, but she was struck with a Bullet, and fell down dead over the threshold. I hope she is reaping the fruit of her good labours, being faithfull to the service of God in her place. In her younger years she lay under much trouble upon spiritual accounts, till it pleased God to make that precious Scripture take hold of her heart, 2 Cor. 12. 9. *And he said unto me, my Grace is sufficient for thee.* More then twenty years after I have heard her tell how sweet and comfortable that place was to her. But to return: The Indians laid hold of us, pulling me one way, and the Children another, and said, Come go along with us; I told them they would kill me: they answered, If I were willing to go along with them, they would not hurt me.

Oh the dolefull sight that now was to behold at this House! *Come, behold the works of the Lord, what dissolations he has made in the Earth.* Of thirty seven persons who were in this one House, none escaped either present death, or a bitter captivity, save only one, who might say as he, Job 1. 15, *And I only am escaped alone to tell the News.* There were twelve killed, some shot, some stab'd with their Spears, some knock'd down with their Hatchets. When we are in prosperity, Oh the little that we think of such dreadfull sights, and to see our dear Friends, and Relations ly bleeding out their heart-blood upon the ground. There was one who was chopt into the head with a Hatchet, and stript naked, and yet was crawling up and down. It is a solemn sight to see so many Christians lying in their blood, some here, and some there, like a company of Sheep torn by Wolves, All of them stript naked by a company of hell-hounds, roaring, singing, ranting and insulting, as if they would have torn our very hearts out; yet the Lord by his Almighty power preserved a number of us from death, for there were twenty-four of us taken alive and carried Captive.

I had often before this said, that if the Indians should come, I should chuse rather to be killed by them then taken alive but when it came to the tryal my mind changed; their glittering weapons so daunted my spirit, that I chose rather to go along with those (as I may say) ravenous Beasts, then that moment to end my dayes; and that I may the better declare what happened to me during that grievous Captivity, I shall particularly speak of the severall Removes we had up and down the Wilderness.

The First Remove

Now away we must go with those Barbarous Creatures, with our bodies wounded and bleeding, and our hearts no less than our bodies. About a mile we went that night, up upon a hill within sight of the Town, where they intended to lodge. There was hard by a vacant house (deserted by the English before, for fear of the Indians). I asked them whither I might not lodge in the house that night to which they answered, what will you love English men still? this was the dolefullest night that ever my eyes saw. Oh the roaring, and singing and danceing, and yelling of those black creatures in the night, which made the place a lively resemblance of hell. And as miserable was the wast that was there made, of Horses, Cattle, Sheep, Swine, Calves, Lambs, Roasting Pigs, and Fowl (which they had plundered in the Town) some roasting, some lying and burning, and some boyling to feed our merciless Enemies; who were joyful enough though we were disconsolate. To add to the dolefulness of the former day, and the dismalness of the present night: my thoughts ran upon my losses and sad bereaved condition. All was gone, my Husband gone (at least separated from me, he being in the Bay; and to add to my grief, the Indians told me they would kill him as he came homeward) my Children gone, my Relations and Friends gone, our House and home and all our comforts within door, and without, all was gone, (except my life) and I knew not but the next moment that might go too. There remained nothing to me but one poor wounded Babe, and it seemed at present worse than death that it was in such a pitiful condition, be-speaking Compassion, and I had no refreshing for it, nor suitable things to revive it. Little do many think what is the savageness and bruitishness of this barbarous Enemy, even those that seem to profess more than others among them, when the English have fallen into their hands.

Those seven that were killed at Lancaster the summer before upon a Sabbath day, and the one that was afterward killed upon a week day, were slain and mangled in a barbarous manner, by one-ey'd John, and Marlborough's Praying Indians, which Capt. Mosely brought to Boston, as the Indians told me.

The Second Remove

But now, the next morning, I must turn my back upon the Town, and travel with them into the vast and desolate Wilderness, I knew not whither. It is not my tongue, or pen can express the sorrows of my heart, and bitterness of my spirit, that I had at this departure: but God was with me, in a wonderfull manner, carrying me along, and bearing up my spirit, that it did not quite fail. One of the Indians carried my poor wounded Babe upon a horse, it went moaning all along, I shall dy, I shall dy. I went on foot after it, with sorrow that cannot be exprest. At length I took it off the horse, and carried it in my armes till my strength failed, and I fell down with it: Then they set me upon a horse with my wounded Child in my lap, and there being no furniture upon the horse back, as we were going down a steep hill, we both fell over the horses head, at which they like inhumane creatures laught, and rejoyced to see it, though I thought we should there have ended our dayes, as overcome with so many difficulties. But the Lord renewed my strength still, and carried me along, that I might see more of his Power; yea, so much that I could never have thought of, had I not experienced it.

After this it quickly began to snow, and when night came on, they stopt: and now down I must sit in the snow, by a little fire, and a few boughs behind me, with my sick Child in my lap; and calling much for water, being now (through the wound) fallen into a violent Fever. My own wound also growing so stiff, that I could scarce sit down or rise up; yet so it must be, that I must sit all this cold winter night upon the cold snowy ground, with my sick Child in my armes, looking that every hour would be the last of its life; and having no Christian friend near me, either to comfort or help me. Oh, I may see the wonderful power of God, that my Spirit did not utterly sink under my affliction: still the Lord upheld me with his gracious and mercifull Spirit, and we were both alive to see the light of the next morning.

SOURCE: Rowlandson, Mary. *The Soveraignty and Goodness of God . . . Being a Narrative of the Captivity of Mrs. Mary Rowlandson.* Cambridge, Mass.: 1682.

LOGAN'S SPEECH
(1774)

The atmosphere of the Ohio River valley in the years before the American War for Independence featured atrocities committed on both sides by American settlers and Indian warriors. Logan, or Tahgahjute, was a Mingo chief who sought revenge for the gruesome torture and murder of his family by vengeful Americans on the Ohio River in 1773. A year later Logan led Shawnee and Mingo raiders to the Clinch River settlements in Kentucky, where after some minor successes, they were defeated. Logan, overwhelmed with the desire for vengeance, refused to surrender.

Logan's letter points out the friendship that once existed between the Mingo tribe and British Americans. The code of hospitality was extremely important to Indians, and they expected the like in return. But war had existed for so long in the trans-Appalachian region between French, English, Indians, and Americans, that memories of wrongs committed against friends and families smoldered beneath periods of apparent calm, only to erupt once again into violence.

Russell Lawson,
Bacone College

See also **Dunmore's War; Wars with Indian Nations.**

IN THE SPRING of the year 1774, a robbery was committed by some Indians on certain land adventurers on the River Ohio. The whites in that quarter, according to their custom, undertook to punish this outrage in a summary way. Captain Michael Cresap, and a certain Daniel Greathouse, leading on these parties, surprized, at different times, travelling and hunting parties of the Indians, having their women and children with them, and murdered many. Among these were unfortunately the family of Logan, a chief celebrated in peace and war, and long distinguished as the friend of the whites. This unworthy return provoked his vengeance. He accordingly signalized himself in the war which ensued. In the autumn of the same year a decisive battle was fought at the mouth of the Great Kanhaway, between the collected forces of the Shawanese, Mingoes and Delawares, and a detachment of the Virginia militia. The Indians were defeated and sued for peace. Logan, however, disdained to be seen among the suppliants. But lest the sincerity of a treaty should be distrusted, from which so distinguished a chief absented himself, he sent, by a messenger [General Gibson], the following speech, to be delivered to lord Dunmore.

I appeal to any white man to say, if ever he entered Logan's cabin hungry, and he gave him not meat: if ever he came cold and naked, and he cloathed him not. During the course of the last long and bloody war Logan remained idle in his cabin, an advocate for peace. Such was my love for the whites, that my countrymen pointed as they passed, and said, 'Logan is the friend of white man.' I had even thought to have lived with you, but for the injuries of one man. Colonel Cresap, the last spring, in cold blood, and unprovoked, murdered all the relations of Logan, not even sparing my women and children. There runs not a drop of my blood in the veins of any living creature. This called on me for revenge. I have sought it: I have killed many: I have fully glutted my vengeance: for my country I rejoice at the beams of peace. But do not harbour a thought that mine is the joy of fear. Logan never felt fear. He will not turn on his heel to save his life. Who is there to mourn for Logan?—Not one.

SOURCE: Jefferson, Thomas. *Notes on the State of Virginia. With an Appendix Relative to the Murder of Logan's Family.* Trenton, N.J.: Wilson & Blackwell, 1803.

EXCERPT FROM *LIFE AND ADVENTURES OF COLONEL DANIEL BOON (1769–1778)*

Daniel Boone, born in 1734, was famous for his leadership before and during the War of American Independence in settling Kentucky. Boone made his living as a hunter; on long hunts he explored the Appalachian Mountains and rediscovered the Cumberland Gap through the mountains. In 1773, he led his and other families through the Gap to Kentucky, encountering resistance from the Shawnees along the way. The forests of Kentucky teemed with wildlife, and the soil was especially rich, which promised good lives for American settlers—if they could foil Indian resistance. The settlement and fortress of Boonesborough was founded in 1775 to protect their wives and children and to serve as a vanguard of penetration into Kentucky. The fort was under frequent attack, which led to such incidents as the kidnapping of Boone's daughter and subsequent rescue, and Boone's own capture and adoption into an Indian family. Boone served in the Revolution with distinction, rising to the rank of colonel. After the war, Kentucky had so many settlers that Boone decided to move further west, settling on the Ohio River, and eventually crossing the Mississippi to the Missouri River, where he died in 1820.

Boone's fame derived from a brief biography that was appended to John Filson's *Discovery, Settlement and Present State of Kentucke,* published in 1784. Filson interviewed Boone, who told the author the basics of his life, which Filson embellished into an amazing story of courage and adventure. One may assume that the general incidents described by Filson are true. But Boone—a frontiersman rather than a philosopher—would hardly have employed such romantic eloquence in his description of his life and the lands he settled. Hence, this document describes John Filson's Daniel Boone, a hero of imagination built up from the true struggles, victories, and defeats of daily life.

Russell Lawson,
Bacone College

See also **Expeditions and Explorations: U.S.; Frontier.**

It was on the first of May 1769, that I resigned my domestic happiness, and left my family and peaceable habitation of the Yadkin river, in North Carolina, to wander through the wilderness of America, in quest of the country of Kentucky, in company with John Finley, John Stuart, Joseph Holden, James Money, and William Cool.

On the 7th of June, after travelling through a mountainous wilderness, in a western direction, we found ourselves on Red River, where John Finley had formerly been trading with the Indians, and, from the top of an eminence, saw with pleasure the beautiful level of Kentucky. For some time we had experienced the most uncomfortable weather. We now encamped, made a shelter to defend us from the inclement season, and began to hunt and reconnoitre the country. We found abundance of wild beasts in this vast forest. . . . The buffaloes were more numerous than cattle on other settlements, browzing on the leaves of the cane, or cropping the herbage on those extensive plains. We saw hundreds in a drove; and the numbers about the salt springs were amazing. In the forest, the habitation of beasts of every American kind, we hunted with great success until December.

On the 22d of December, John Stuart and I had a pleasing ramble; but fortune changed the day at the close of it. We had passed through a great forest, in which stood myriads of trees, some gay with blossoms, others rich with fruits. Nature was here a series of wonders and a fund of delight. Here she displayed her ingenuity and industry in a variety of flowers and fruits, beautifully coloured, elegantly shaped, and charmingly flavored; and we were diverted with numberless animals, presenting themselves perpetually to our view. In the decline of the day, near Kentucky river, as we ascended the brow of a small hill, a number of Indians rushed out of a thick cane brake, and made us prisoners. The Indians plundered us, and kept us in confinement seven days.... During this, we discovered no uneasiness or desire to escape, which made them less suspicious; but in the dead of night, as we lay by a large fire, in a thick cane brake, when sleep had locked up their senses, my situation not disposing me to rest, I gently awoke my companion. We seized this favorable opportunity, and departed, directing our course towards our old camp, but found it plundered, and our company dispersed or gone home.

About this time my brother, Squire Boon, with another adventurer, who came to explore the country shortly after us, was wandering through the forest, and accidentally found our camp. Notwithstanding our unfortunate circumstances, and our dangerous situation, surrounded with hostile savages, our meeting fortunately in the wilderness, gave us the most sensible satisfaction.

Soon after this, my companion in captivity, John Stuart, was killed by the savages: and the man that came with my brother returned home by himself. We were then in a dangerous, helpless situation, exposed daily to perils and death, among savages and wild beasts, not a white man in the country but ourselves.

Thus many hundred miles from our families in the howling wilderness, we did not continue in a state of indolence, but hunted every day, and prepared a little cottage to defend us from the winter storms. We met with no disturbance through the winter.

On the first of May 1770, my brother returned home by himself, for a new recruit of horses and ammunition, leaving me alone, without bread, salt, or sugar, or even a horse or dog. I passed a few days uncomfortably. The idea of a beloved wife and family, and their anxiety on my account, would have disposed me to melancholy, if I had further indulged the thought.

One day I undertook a tour through the country, when the diversity and beauties of nature I met with, in this charming season, expelled every gloomy thought. Just at the close of day, the gentle gales ceased; a profound calm ensued; not a breath shook the tremulous leaf. I had gained the summit of a commanding ridge, and looking round with astonishing delight, beheld the ample plains and beautious tracts below. On one hand I surveyed the famous Ohio, rolling in silent dignity, and marking the western boundary of Kentucky with inconceivable grandeur. At a vast distance, I beheld the mountains lift their venerable brows, and penetrate the clouds. All things were still. I kindled a fire, near a fountain of sweet water, and feasted on the loin of a buck, which a few hours before I had killed. The shades of night soon overspread the hemisphere, and the earth seemed to gasp after the howering moisture. My excursion had fatigued my body, and amused my mind. I laid me down to sleep, and awoke not until the sun had chased away the night. I continued this tour, and in a few days explored a considerable part of the country, each day equally pleased as at first after which I returned to my old camp, which had not been disturbed in my absence. I did not confine my lodging to it, but often reposed in thick cane brakes to avoid the savages, who, I believe, often visited my camp, but, fortunately for me, in my absence. No populous city, with all the varieties of commerce and stately structures, could afford so much pleasure to my mind, as the beauties of nature I found in this country.

Until the 27th of July, I spent the time in an uninterrupted scene of sylvan pleasures, when my brother, to my great felicity, met me according to appointment, at our old camp. Soon after we left the place, and proceeded to Cumberland river, reconnoitring that part of the country, and giving names to the different rivers.

In March 1771, I returned home to my family, being determined to bring them as soon as possible, at the risk of my life and fortune, to reside in Kentucky, which I esteemed a second paradise.

On my return I found my family in happy circumstances. I sold my farm at Yadkin, and what goods we could not carry with us; and, On the 25th of September 1773, we bade farewell to our friends, and proceeded on our journey to Kentucky, in company with five more families, and forty men that joined us in Powell's Valley, which is 150 miles from the now settled parts of Kentucky, but this promising beginning was soon overcast with a cloud of adversity.

On the 10th of October, the rear of our company was attacked by a number of Indians, who killed six and wounded one man. Of these my eldest son was one that fell in the action. Though we repulsed the enemy, yet this unhappy affair scattered our cattle, brought us into extreme difficulty, and so discouraged the whole company, that we retreated forty miles to Clench river. We had passed over two mountains, Powell's and Walden's, and were approaching Cumberland mountain, when this adverse fortune overtook us. These mountains are in the wilderness, in passing from the old settlements in Virginia to Kentucky, are ranged in a south-west and north-east direction, are of great length and breadth, and, not far distant from each other. Over them nature hath formed passes less difficult than might be expected from the view of such huge piles. The aspect of these cliffs is so wild and horrid, that it is impossible to behold them without terror.

Until the sixth of June, 1774, I remained with my family on the Clench when I and Michael Stoner were solicited by governor Dunmore, of Virginia, to conduct a number of surveyors to the falls of Ohio. This was a tour of near eight hundred miles, and took us sixty-two days.

On my return, governor Dunmore gave me the command of three garrisons, during the campaign against the Shawanese.

In March, 1775, at the solicitation of a number of gentlemen, of North-Carolina, I attended their treaty at Wataga, with the Cherokee Indians, to purchase the lands on the south-side of Kentucky river. After this, I undertook to mark out a road in the best passage from the settlements, through the wilderness to Kentucky.

Having collected a number of enterprizing men, well armed, I soon began this work. We proceeded until we came within fifteen miles of where Boonsborough now stands, where the Indians attacked us, and killed two, and wounded two more.

This was the 20th of March, 1775. There days after, they attacked us again; we had two killed and three wounded. After this we proceeded on to Kentucky river without opposition.

On the 1st of April, we began to erect the fort of Boons-borough, at a salt-lick, sixty yards from the river, on the south side.

On the 4th, they killed one of our men.

On the 14th of June, having finished the fort, I returned to my family, on the Clench. Soon after I removed my family to the fort; we arrived safe; my wife and daughter being the first white women that stood on the banks of Kentucky river.

December 24th. The Indians killed one man, and wounded another, seeming determined to persecute us for erecting this fort.

July 14th 1776. Two of col. Calway's daughters, and one of mine, were taken prisoners near the fort. I immediately pursued the Indians, with only 18 men.

On the 16th, I overtook them, killed two of them, and recovered the girls.

The Indians had divided themselves into several parties, and attacked, on the same day, all our settlements and forts, doing a great deal of mischief. The husbandman was shot dead in the field, and most of the cattle were destroyed. They continued their hostilities until The 15th of April, 1777, when a party of 100 of them attacked Boonsborough and killed one man, and wounded four.

July 4th, they attacked it again with 200 men, and killed us one and wounded two. They remained 48 hours, during which we killed seven of them. All the settlements were attacked at the same time.

July 19th. Col. Logan's fort was besieged by 200 Indians: they did much mischief; there were only fifteen men in the fort; they killed two, and wounded four of them. Indians' loss unknown.

July 25. Twenty-five men came from Carolina. About August 20th, colonel Bowman arrived with 100 men from Virginia. Now we began to strengthen, and had skirmishes with the Indians almost every day. The savages now learned the superiority of the LONG KNIFE, as they call the Virginians; being outgeneraled in almost every battle. Our affairs began to wear a new aspect; the enemy did not now venture open war, but practised secret mischief.

January 1, 1778. I went with thirty men to the Blue Licks, on Licking river, to make salt for the different garrisons.

February 7th. Hunting by myself, to procure meat for the company, I met a party of 102 Indians and two Frenchmen, marching against Boonsborough. They pursued and took me; and next day I capitulated for my men, knowing they could not escape. They were 27 in number, three having gone home with salt. The Indians, according to the capitulation, used us generously. They carried us to Old Chelicothe, the principal Indian town on Little Miami.

On the 18th of February we arrived there, after an uncomfortable journey, in very severe weather.

On the 10th of March, I and ten of my men were conducted to Detroit.

On the 30th, we arrived there, and were treated by governour Hamilton, the British commander at that post, with great humanity. The Indians had such an affection for me, that they refused 1001. sterling offered them by the governor, if they would leave me with the others, on purpose that he might send me home on my parole. Several English gentlemen there, sensible of my adverse fortune, and touched with sympathy, generously offered to supply my wants, which I declined with many thanks, adding that I never expected it would be in my power to recompence such unmerited generosity. The Indians left my men in captivity with the British at Detroit.

On the 10th of April, they brought me towards Old Chelicothe, where we arrived on the 25th day of the same month. This was a long and fatiguing march, through an exceeding fertile country, remarkable for fine springs and streams of water. At Chelicothe, I spent my time as comfortable as I could expect; was adopted, according to their custom, into a family, where I became a son, and had a great share in the affection of my new parents, brothers, sisters, and friends. I was exceedingly familiar and friendly with them, always appearing as cheerful and satisfied as possible, and they put great confidence in me. I often went a hunting with them, and frequently gained their applause for my activity at our shooting matches. I was careful not to exceed many of them in shooting; for no people are more envious than they in this sport. I could observe in their countenance and gestures the greatest expressions of joy when they exceeded me; and, when the reverse happened, of envy. The Shawanese king took great notice of me, and treated me with profound respect, and entire friendship, often entrusting me to hunt at my liberty. I frequently returned with the spoils of the woods, and as often presented some of what I had taken to him, expressive of duty to my sovereign. My food and lodging was in common with them, not so good indeed as I could desire; but necessity made everything acceptable.

I now began to meditate an escape, but carefully avoided giving suspicion.

Until the 1st day of June I continued at Old Chelicothe, and then was taken to the salt springs on Sciota, and kept their ten days making salt. During this time, I had hunted with them, and found the land, for a great extent above this river, to exceed the soil of Kentucky, if possible, and remarkably well watered.

On my return to Chelicothe, four hundred and fifty of the choicest Indian warriors were ready to march against Boonsborough, painted and armed in a fearful manner. This alarmed me, and I determined to escape.

On the 16th of June, before sunrise, I went off secretly, and reaching Boonsborough on the 20th, a journey of one hundred and sixty miles, during which I had only one meal. I found our fortress in a bad state, but we immediately repaired our flanks, gates, posterns, and formed double bastions, which we completed in ten days. One of my fellow prisoners escaping after me, brought advice, that on account of my flight, the Indians had put off their expedition for three weeks.

About August 1st, I set out with 19 men to surprise Point Creek Town on Sciota. Within 4 miles we fell in with 30 Indians going against Boonsborough. We fought, and the enemy gave way. We suffered no loss. The enemy had 1 killed, and 2 wounded. We took 3 horses and all their baggage. The Indians having evacuated their town and gone all together against Boonsborough, we returned, passed them on the 6th day, and on the 7th arrived safe at Boonsborough.

On the 8th, the Indian army, 444 in number, commanded by capt. Duquesne, and 11 other Frenchmen, and their own chiefs, came and summoned the fort. I requested two days consideration, which they granted. During this, we brought in through the posterns all the horses and other cattle we could collect.

On the 9th, in the evening, I informed their commander, that we were determined to defend the fort, while a man was living. They then proposed a treaty, and said if we sent out 9 men to conclude it, they would withdraw. The treaty was held within 60 yards of the fort, as we suspected the savages. The articles were agreed to and signed; when the Indians told us, it was their custom for 2 Indians to shake hands with every white man in the treaty, as an evidence of friendship. We agreed to this also. They immediately grappled us to take us prisoners, but we cleared ourselves of them, though surrounded by hundreds, and gained the fort safe, except one that was wounded by a heavy fire from their army. On this they began to undermine the fort, beginning at the water-mark of Kentucky river, which is 60 yards from the fort. We discovered this by the water being made muddy with the clay and countermined them by cutting a trench across their subteranean passage. The enemy discovering this, by the clay we threw out of the fort, desisted.

On the 20th of August, they raised the siege.

During this dreadful siege, we had 2 men killed, and 4 wounded. We lost a number of cattle. We killed 37 of the enemy, and wounded a great number. We picked up 125 pounds of their bullets, besides what struck in the logs of the fort.

Soon after this I went into the settlement, and nothing worthy of notice passed for some time.

SOURCE: Filson, John. *The Discovery, Settlement and Present State of Kentucke.* Wilmington, Del.: James Adams, 1784.

LETTER DESCRIBING CATHOLIC MISSIONS IN CALIFORNIA
(1774, by Fray Junipero Serra)

Spain controlled up to two-thirds of the present continental United States for over two hundred years. California, which was not incorporated into the United States until the 1840s, was one of the prized possessions of the Spanish Empire in North America. Besides the fertile soil in a temperate climate were wonderful ports such as San Francisco, which guaranteed a lucrative trade. Spain, like the other imperialist powers in North America, Great Britain and France, demanded that its American colonies be a benefit and not a detriment to the empire as a whole. An economically weak and dependent colony was of little use.

Like France, Spain was a Roman Catholic country. It was assumed by the church, and obligatory to the Spanish colonial power, that the spread of Christianity and Christian values of prayer, work, peace, and faith, be inculcated among the people at large. Hence, the Spanish put much energy into creating missions that would convert the Native Americans of the Southwest to Christianity and ensure their devotion to the Catholic Church. The activities of Fray Junipero Serra were important in this regard.

Father Serra was a Franciscan priest who risked his life on numerous occasions to journey north to California, where he established almost two dozen Catholic missions to minister to the spiritual and bodily needs of the Indians. Father Serra died in 1784.

Russell Lawson,
Bacone College

***See also* Catholicism; Indian Missions.**

Hail Jesus, Mary and Joseph!
My greatly venerated, most excellent Sir:

I have just written at length to Your Excellency by a courier whom Captain Don Fernando Rivera, four days since, dispatched for California, and in answer to the letter of Your Excellency bearing date 25th May, which, on the 6th August, was received by conduct and hand of the said captain by Father Lector Fray Francisco Palou, who is my companion here. In that letter I gave an account of further events at these missions, and with it sent the diary of one of the two religious who accompanied the naval expedition dispatched by Your Excellency under the command of Don Juan Perez, an officer of the navy. The reason for sending these letters and documents by a means usually rather tardy was this: The naval expedition having arrived at this port on the 27th of August last, in the frigate Santiago, and on board of her in safety the two chaplains (God be thanked!), her captain informed us that he had a mind to remain at this port until the middle of October, by which time it is probable that the families expected by Don Fernando will be here, and then to make the exploration of the port of San Francisco, with a view to the founding of the mission, or missions, which may seem necessary, in order that the region about that port be occupied in accordance with the orders of Your Excellency and the intention of our catholic monarch. And it having so to be—with which circumstance I and all were very content—it seemed that the only way of giving desired information to Your Excellency consisted in sending it by way of California. Since then Don Juan Perez has come to a new determination—that is, to sail for San Blas with the frigate under his command; and, although Father Palou and myself have besought him earnestly that, were it possible, he adhere to his prior determination, in order that the matter of the occupation of San Francisco might be attended to at this time, he has utterly refused to do so, saying that he has many reasons for not delaying and for resolving on a speedy departure. And, considering that this letter will reach you before the arrival of those already sent, I proceed to relate, with the brevity made necessary by this sudden notice and the little time remaining in which to do so, some portions of that which has been written already. And, first: As to the cattle for the two missions of San Francisco and Santa Clara, mindful of the directions contained in the said letter of Your Excellency, Captain Don Fernando turned the cattle over to me on the 16th of August, without renewed demand, in accordance with the disposition of the Royal Junta and the orders of Your Excellency; and that same day we branded them here. I gave a receipt, and now nothing remains to be done in that matter, which was arranged very much to the liking and satisfaction of both parties.

I wrote also, that, on the day after receiving the said letter of Your Excellency, taking it with me to the royal presidio, I communicated its contents to the Captain, for the purpose of learning whether he would resolve to do anything in the matter of the port of San Francisco. But he replied to my request that he found himself without men, or even arms, for any undertaking, as Captain Anza had not left him a single soldier and the families had not arrived. It is a pity that when we do have them here then there will be no longer any vessel available; and I recognize a far greater inclination to employ them in establishing a new presidio, at a distance of four or five leagues from the port and six from this mission, rather than in founding any new mission. This is a matter concerning which I was about to present to Your Excellency a written memorial, at the time I was in that city, when I learned that the new official proposed making such a demand; but, as I was told that any failure to protect the port would not be allowed, nor any such change of plan, I abandoned that design. Yet I afterwards repented of this, when in Guadalajara, Tepic, and other places, I found that tidings had gone abroad to the effect that the new captain was about to move the presidio—as though this were the principal object of his appointment. Still, for one reason this would not grieve me, and that is because at the distance of a league farther—on the road to San Francisco, be it understood—we might plant a new mission; and in this way the new presidio would be easily and in a perfectly fitting way provided with spiritual food, and the heathen of both sexes of those parts would become parishioners of the missionary fathers and not of the soldiers. Such mission would be at a distance of seven leagues from this one—which is not a matter of slight importance when it is considered that such an establishment would be likely to be of service in the prevention of disadvantages which I fancy might arise from a different condition of things. Were it not a matter connected with the missions I would not speak of it; but, being such, and to so great a degree, it does not seem to me that in this proposition I am advocating anything not within the scope of my clerical functions. And in this matter I conform to what Your Excellency may consider most fitting. It is a grevious thing for me, Most Excellent Sir, to find myself well provided with religious and with provisions, while no steps are taken in one way or another, towards some new spiritual labor; and I should fear to fatigue Your Excellency with this my oft-repeated importunity were I not sure that my desires are so much in accord with those of Your Excellency.

I gave to Your Excellency, also, the agreeable tidings that these new christians, following the example set by some of the workmen of the vessels whose services I managed to secure, are learning how to apply themselves to labor, hoe in hand and with the bar and in making adobes, in reaping or harvesting the wheat and in carting these crops, as well as in other work in which they take part. I reported, also, that this year there have been harvested at this mission, in addition to twenty fanegas of barley, one hundred and twenty-five of wheat, some horse-beans and a greater quantity of kidney-beans, and together with continuous help from the vegetable garden—in the consumption of which all share. There is reason for expecting a fair return from the maize sown, and it is well-grown and in good condition, and there will be obtained a goodly number of fish from the abundance of sardines which, for twenty consecutive days, have been spawning along the beach near this mission, and a reasonable harvest from the spiritual advancement we are experiencing each day—thanks be to God! At all the missions they are making preparation for more extensive sowings in the coming year, and I trust God that a happy outcome may attend the work.

Concerning the diary that I remitted to Your Excellency, I said that no copy remained here for transmission to our college at a suitable time, and to that effect I wrote to the Reverend Father Guardian of said college, because, when I had finished and signed the letter, I came to the conclusion that time to copy it was wanting; but, as it fell out, there was time, and it was copied in great haste. Now that I doubt not those of the navigating officers will be sent to Your Excellency, I remit it to the Reverend Father Guardian; that of the other religious will go later. I have already told the Reverend Father Guardian that, despite the other diaries, if Your Excellency desires he will place them in your hands; supposing that this will be done, I am not now sending it directly to you.

For the rest I refer to my said letters, which I trust in God, will not fail to reach your hands somewhat later. Since dispatching them nothing noteworthy has happened, other than that the volunteers who remained here at the time Don Pedro Fages left have taken passage in the ship, excepting the six whose permits I asked for, and of whom three have married here while the other three are about to marry—although one of them, I hear, is going away too. With this letter there goes, also, to Your Excellency one of Father Palou, who sends again his affectionate regards to Your Excellency and the assurance of his prayers for you. And I continue praying that God our Lord guard the health, life and prosperity of Your Excellency for many years in His holy grace. From this mission favored by Your Excellency of San Carlos de Monterey, Sept. 9, 1774.

Most Excellent Sir:—Your most affectionate and humble servant and chaplain, who venerates and loves you, kisses the hands of Your Excellency.

Fray Junipero Serra

SOURCE: Tibesar, Antonine, ed. *Writings of Junipero Serra.* Vol. 1. Washington, D.C.: Academy of American Franciscan History, 1955.

EXCERPT FROM *THE HISTORY AND PRESENT STATE OF VIRGINIA* *(1705, by Robert Beverley)*

The need for human labor in Great Britain's North American settlements was a never-ebbing tide. By the beginning of the eighteenth century, with booming regional economies necessitating greater and greater numbers to assist with the harvest of staple crops like tobacco and indigo, some two hundred thousand African slaves had been kidnapped and transported across the Atlantic Ocean to the New World. Exceeding even this, however, was the number of white indentured servants, bonded for a set number of years as the personal property of the masters who held their contracts. A wealthy planter and local official, Robert Beverly, who was concerned with the legal distinctions between the two classes of servitude, composed

The History and Present State of Virginia because he was dissatisfied with a similar book by an English author. The book was an enormous hit and was reprinted several times.

Laura M. Miller,
Vanderbilt University

See also **Indentured Servants; Slavery; Virginia.**

Of the Servants and Slaves in Virginia

Their servants they distinguish by the names of slaves for life and servants for a time.

Slaves are the Negroes and their posterity following the condition of the mother, according to the maxim partus sequitur ventrem. They are called slaves in respect of the time of their servitude because it is for life.

Servants are those which serve only for a few years, according to the time of their indenture or the custom of the country. The custom of the country takes place upon such as have no indentures. The law in this case is that if such servants be under nineteen years of age, they must be brought into court to have their age adjudged, and from the age they are judged to be of they must serve until the reach four and twenty. But if they be adjudged upwards of nineteen, they are then only to be servants for the term of five years.

The male servants and slaves of both sexes are employed together in tilling and manuring the ground, in sowing and planting tobacco, corn, etc. Some distinction, indeed, is made between them in their clothes and food, but the work of both is no other than what the overseers, the freemen, and the planters themselves do.

Sufficient distinction is also made between the female servants and slaves, for a white woman is rarely or never put to work in the ground if she be good for anything else. And to discourage all planters from using any women so, their law imposes the heaviest taxes upon female servants working in the ground, while it suffers all other white women to be absolutely exempted. Whereas on the other hand, it is a common thing to work a woman slave out of doors; nor does the law make any distinction in her taxes, whether her work be abroad or at home.

Because I have heard how strangely cruel and severe the service of this country is represented in some parts of England, I can't forbear affirming that the work of their servants and slaves is no other than what every common freeman does. Neither is any servant required to do more in a day than his overseer. And I can assure you with a great deal of truth that generally their slaves are not worked near so hard nor so many hours in a day as the husbandmen and day laborers in England. An overseer is a man that having served his time has acquired the skill and character of an experienced planter and is therefore entrusted with the direction of the servants and slaves.

But to complete this account of servants I shall give you a short relation of the care their laws take that they be used as tenderly as possible.

By the Laws of Their Country

1. All servants whatsoever have their complaints heard without fee or reward, but if the master be found faulty the charge of the complaint is cast upon him, otherwise the business is done ex officio.
2. Any justice of peace may receive the complaint of a servant and order everything relating thereto till the next county court, where it will be finally determined.
3. All masters are under the correction and censure of the county courts to provide for their servants good and wholesome diet, clothing, and lodging.
4. They are always to appear upon the first notice given of the complaint of their servants, otherwise to forfeit the service of them until they do appear.
5. All servants' complaints are to be received at any time in court without process and shall not be delayed for want of form. But the merits of the complaint must be immediately inquired into by the justices, and if the master cause any delay therein the court may remove such servants if they see cause until the master will come to trial.
6. If a master shall at any time disobey an order of court made upon any complaint of a servant, the court is empowered to remove such servant forthwith to another master who will be kinder, giving to the former master the produce only (after fees deducted) of what such servants shall be sold for by public outcry.
7. If a master should be so cruel as to use his servant ill that is fallen sick or lame in his service and thereby rendered unfit for labor, he must be removed by the church wardens out of the way of such cruelty and boarded in some good planter's house till the time of his freedom, the charge of which must be laid before the next county court, which has power to levy the same from time to time upon the goods and chattels of the master. After which the charge of such boarding is to come upon the parish in general.
8. All hired servants are entitled to these privileges.
9. No master of a servant can make a new bargain for service or other matter with his servant without the privity and consent of a justice of peace, to prevent the master's overreaching or scaring such servant into an unreasonable compliance.
10. The property of all money and goods sent over thither to servants, or carried in with them, is

reserved to themselves and remain entirely at their disposal.

11. Each servant at his freedom receives of his master fifteen bushels of corn (which is sufficient for a whole year) and two new suits of clothes, both linen and woolen, and then becomes as free in all respects and as much entitled to the liberties and privileges of the country as any other of the inhabitants or natives are.
12. Each servant has then also a right to take up fifty acres of land, where he can find any unpatented; but that is no great privilege, for anyone may have as good a right for a piece of eight.

This is what the laws prescribe in favor of servants, by which you may find that the cruelties and severities imputed to that country are an unjust reflection. For no people more abhor the thoughts of such usage than the Virginians, nor take more precaution to prevent it.

SOURCE: Beverly, Robert. *The History and Present State of Virginia.* London: R. Parker, 1705. Edited by Louis B. Wright. Chapel Hill: Published for the Institute of Early American History and Culture by the University of North Carolina Press, 1947.

LETTER DESCRIBING PLANTATION LIFE IN SOUTH CAROLINA
(2 May 1740, by Eliza Lucas Pinckney)

Of all Great Britain's colonies in the New World, South Carolina held most dear the "peculiar institution" of slavery. In an economy based primarily on the cultivation of rice and indigo, the colony's planters relied so heavily on unwilling human labor, in fact, that by the time of Ms. Pinckney's correspondence, slaves actually outnumbered free whites, accounting for some sixty percent of the population. South Carolina was the only colony so distinguished. The letter presented here is a look into a world in which landed white masters, often women, pined to visit fashionable cities like Charleston and to leave for a while the work of managing their sprawling plantations to overseers and hired hands. The commitment of Ms. Pinckney and her fellow citizens to an institution of forced labor would have long-lasting consequences, nationally as well as locally. Partly in deference to the wishes of South Carolina, the Second Continental Congress excoriated a condemnation of slavery from Thomas Jefferson's original draft of the Declaration of Independence. Following the American Civil War, during which it was first to secede from the Federal Union, South Carolina endured an especially difficult and tumultuous period of Reconstruction.

Laura M. Miller,
Vanderbilt University

See also **Plantation System of the South; South Carolina.**

To my good friend Mrs. Boddicott
Dear Madam,

I flatter myself it will be a satisfaction to you to hear I like this part of the world, as my lott has fallen here—which I really do. I prefer England to it, 'tis true, but think Carolina greatly preferable to the West Indias, and was my Papa here I should be very happy.

We have a very good acquaintance from whom we have received much friendship and Civility. Charles Town, the principal one in this province, is a polite, agreeable place. The people live very Gentile and very much in the English taste. The Country is in General fertile and abounds with Venison and wild fowl; the Venison is much higher flavoured than in England but 'tis seldom fatt.

My Papa and Mama's great indulgence to me leaves it to me to chose our place of residence either in town or Country, but I think it more prudent as well as most agreeable to my Mama and self to be in the Country during my Father's absence. We are 17 mile by land and 6 by water from Charles Town—where we have about 6 agreeable families around us with whom we live in great harmony.

I have a little library well furnished (for my papa has left me most of his books) in which I spend part of my time. My Musick and the Garden, which I am very fond of, take up the rest of my time that is not imployed in business, of which my father has left me a pretty good share—and indeed, 'twas inavoidable as my Mama's bad state of health prevents her going through any fatigue.

I have the business of 3 plantations to transact, which requires much writing and more business and fatigue of other sorts than you can imagine. But least you should imagine it too burthensom to a girl at my early time of life, give me leave to answer you: I assure you I think myself happy that I can be useful to so good a father, and by rising very early I find I can go through much business. But least you should think I shall be quite moaped with this way of life I am to inform you there is two worthy Ladies in Charles Town, Mrs. Pinckney and Mrs. Cleland, who are partial enough to me to be always pleased to have me with them, and insist upon my making their houses my home when in town and press me to relax a little much oftener than 'tis in my honor to accept of their obliging intreaties. But I some times am with one or the other for 3 weeks or a month at a time, and then enjoy all the pleasures Charles Town affords, but nothing gives me more than subscribing my self

Dear Madam,
Yr. most affectionet and most obliged humble Servt.
Eliza. Lucas

Pray remember me in the best manner to my worthy friend Mr. Boddicott.

SOURCE: Pinckney, Eliza. *The Letterbook of Eliza Lucas Pinckney, 1739–1762.* Chapel Hill, N.C.: Univ. of North Carolina, 1972.

SPANISH COLONIAL OFFICIAL'S ACCOUNT OF THE TRIANGULAR TRADE WITH ENGLAND *(c. 1726)*

In the triangle trade system, English ships loaded with trade goods sailed to the west coast of Africa and exchanged their merchandise for African blacks, then made the deadly "Middle Passage" to either the plantations of the West Indies or the English colonies, where the slaves would be bartered for sugar or other agricultural products. The ships then returned to England, once again filled with valuable cargo. Conditions on these slave ships were preternaturally cruel with slaves crammed into tiny spaces between decks and fed only the poorest foods to maintain high profits margins. The mortality rate of such crossings sometimes exceeded twenty percent.

Laura M. Miller,
Vanderbilt University

See also **Middle Passage; Slave Trade; Triangular Trade.**

On June 21 of the same year (1721) the Southern Fleet of galleons left Cadiz under the command of Lieutenant General Baltasar de Guevara. Upon its arrival at Porto Bello in time for the annual Fair it encountered the *Royal George,* the first of the English license ships. Though allowed no more than 650 tons of cargo by the treaty of 1716, the vessel actually carried 975. General de Guevara forthwith intrusted to three license masters of the fleet the duty of measuring the hold of the English ship, but they could not prove the excess. Their failure was due in part to a confusion of the measurement in geometric feet, by which the dimensions of vessels are gauged, with the cubic handbreadths by which the tonnage is determined.

In part, also, another circumstance is responsible for the failure of the Spanish officers to detect any evidence of fraud, assuming, of course, the absence of collusion on their side. Apparently the vessel had no greater carrying capacity than 650 tons, but persons who are expert in the rules of naval construction know very well that the steerage, commonly called "between-decks," equals in capacity a third of the hold, and the cabin a sixth of it; so when all three have been filled,—hold, steerage, and cabin,—the gross tonnage will be 975. The English ship always carried a cargo of this size. Indeed it was laden so heavily that its very gunwales were awash. Bundles and packages filled the hold, the steerage space was crowded with huge chests, and the cabin bulged with boxes and bales.

The English claimed that the materials stored in the steerage and cabin were furniture for the use of their trading houses, cloth goods for their agents and employees, and medicines and drugs for accidents and cures, but all of it was salable merchandise. Some things they could not conceal from the commander and the commercial representatives of the galleons. For example, many of the bales and bundles had not been pressed, the stitches in their seams were recent, and the ink of their lettering was still fresh. Hundreds of items, also, were lacking in the order of enumeration, which, if they had not been thrown overboard to lighten the ship during the course of the voyage, must have been put ashore somewhere. The proof soon appeared when the Spanish commissioner of trade asked to see the original bill of lading so that he might know by this means whether the cargo was in excess of the amount permitted. On the ground that the treaty had authorized no such procedure, the request was denied.

During the course of the Fair the agents of the *Royal George* sold their goods to the colonial tradesmen thirty percent cheaper than the Spanish merchants of the galleons could do. This advantage came from the fact that they had been able to bring the commodities directly from the place of manufacture, exempt from Spanish customs duties, convoy charges, transportation expenses, commissions, and the like. Even after the original contents of the ship had been disposed of, the supply was kept up by secret consignments of goods of English and European manufacture received from the packet boats and sloops engaged ostensibly in the slave trade.

Instead of bringing the negroes in the slave hulks directly from Africa to the ports specified in the Asiento, the English cunningly devised the plan of landing them first at their colony of Jamaica. Here the slaves were packed, along with divers kinds of merchandise, into small boats that made frequent sailings. Not only was the cargo of the *Royal George* thus replenished as rapidly as it was exhausted, but trade could be surreptitiously carried on at times when the Fair was not in progress, and the treasure of the Spanish colonies duly gathered into English hands.

Nor was this all of their duplicity. On the pretext that a number of bales and boxes stored in the warehouse at Porto Bello were an unsold residue of the cargo, the governor of Panama was asked for the privilege of bringing them to that city. In this fashion the English could legitimize goods that had already been smuggled into the warehouses at Panama and then proceed to sell them to the merchants of New Granada and to the traders on the vessels that plied along the Pacific coast. On one occasion in 1723, at the instance of the Spanish commissary, ten loads of twenty bales each of the supposed residue of the cargo of the *Royal George* were opened on the way from Porto Bello to Panama and found to contain nothing but stones, sticks, and straw.

A knavish trick connected with the slave trade should now be described. Having brought the negroes in a number of small boats to out-of-the-way places not authorized for the purpose in the Asiento, the English traders sold them for a third less than the prices at the regular trading stations. But since the treaty empowered them to seize, as smuggled goods, slaves brought in by individuals of other nations, they posted guards and sentinels in the outskirts of the spot where the sale had just taken place, and had the purchasers arrested. Many a thrifty-minded Spaniard who relished the thought of buying slaves at cheap rates fell into a snare from which he could not escape until he had paid the regular price in addition to what he had already given. In order to obscure the facts of these fraudulent transactions as thoroughly as possible, the English contrived a scheme craftier than any hitherto related. It seems that the Asiento had allowed them to appoint "judges-conservators" whose business it should be to defend their privileges against unlawful interference. In the exercise of this right they appointed to the office the local governors of the ports where the traffic was carried on, and gave them a salary of two thousand dollars a year, supplemented by special gratifications in the shape of European furniture, jewels, and delicacies. Thus were the officials pledged to connivance and silence. If any of the governors should decline to be bribed, he was threatened with political destruction by the letters and complaints which the English minister at the Spanish court would surely present to the home authorities. Few there were under such circumstances who were able to resist the frauds, preserve their honor, and uphold their good name.

MAXIMS FROM *POOR RICHARD'S ALMANACK* *(1733, by Benjamin Franklin)*

A compilation of stories, adages, and folksy wisdom published annually by Benjamin Franklin from 1732 to 1757, *Poor Richard's Almanack* was an important contribution to the development of a unique American idiom based on independence, practicality, temperance, and plain-spoken honesty. The son of a Boston soap maker, Franklin (1706–1790) would go on to become a major figure in American and international politics as delegate to the Continental Congress, Postmaster General, and appointee to the committee that drafted the Declaration of Independence. His standing in England was high, even during the troubled days leading up to the American Revolution, and following the war, the French came to regard him as an important philosopher and a significant influence on revolutionary thought. *The Almanack,* sold in 1757, continued publication under a different title until 1796 and is still available in many modern editions.

Laura M. Miller,
Vanderbilt University

See also* Almanacs; *Poor Richard's Almanack.

The Good And Virtuous Life

A long life may not be good enough, but a good life is long enough.
A lie stands on one leg, truth on two.

Blessed is he that expects nothing, for he shall never be disappointed.
Eat to live, and not live to eat.

There are three things extremely hard, steel, a diamond, and to know one's self.

Industry, Frugality, And Thrift

Little strokes fell great oaks.
Early to bed and early to rise,
Makes a man healthy, wealthy, and wise.

Follies And Faults; Vanities And Vices

E'er you remark another's sin,
Bid your conscience look within.

Success has ruined many a man.
Glass, china, and reputation are easily cracked, and never well mended.

He is a governor that governs his passions, and he a servant that serves them.
Fools need advice most, but wise men only are the better for it.

He that lieth down with dogs shall rise up with fleas.
Love your enemies, for they tell you your faults.

When reason preaches, if you don't hear her she'll box your ears.

Women And Marriage

Love, cough, and a smoke can't well be hid.
Where there's marriage without love, there will be love without marriage.

People

To err is human, to repent divine; to persist devilish.
A mob's a monster; heads enough but no brains.

War brings scars.
Fish and visitors smell in three days.

Men and melons are hard to know.

Wit And Wisdom

Three may keep a secret, if two of them are dead.
Dost thou love life? Then do not squander time; for that's the stuff life is made of.

Great talkers, little doers.
God helps them that help themselves.

In the affairs of this world, men are saved not by faith but by the want of it.

SOURCE: Franklin, Benjamin (as Richard Saunders). *Poor Richard, 1734: An Almanack* and following years. Philadelphia: B. Franklin, 1733 ff.

INDENTURED "WHITE SLAVES" IN THE COLONIES
(1770, by William Eddis)

By the eighteenth century indentured servants outnumbered African slaves in the North American colonies. Unlike the situation endured by slaves, however, the state was an impermanent one for indentured servants. Initially an attempt to alleviate severe labor shortages in New World settlements, the system of indenture comprised not only willing English women, children, and men, but also convicts, religious separatists, and political prisoners. Indentured servants labored a set number of years (usually four to seven, though the period for convicts could be considerably longer), during which time they were considered the personal property of their masters. Couples were often prevented from marrying, and women from having children. If a woman did become pregnant and was unable to work, an equivalent amount of time was added to her period of servitude. Upon their release, indentured servants were not only given clothing, tools, and, often, even land; they also were usually freed of the stigma of having been a servant at all. In 1665, half of Virginia's House of Burgesses was made up of former indentured servants.

Laura M. Miller,
Vanderbilt University

See also **Indentured Servants.**

PERSONS in a state of servitude are under four distinct denominations: negroes, who are the entire property of their respective owners: convicts, who are transported from the mother country for a limited term: indented servants, who are engaged for five years previous to their leaving England; and free-willers, who are supposed, from their situation, to possess superior advantages. . . .

Persons convicted of felony, and in consequence transported to this continent, if they are able to pay the expense of passage; are free to pursue their fortune agreeably to their inclinations or abilities. Few, however, have means to avail themselves of this advantage. These unhappy beings are, generally, consigned to an agent, who classes them suitably to their real or supposed qualifications; advertises them for sale, and disposes of them, for seven years, to planters, to mechanics, and to such as choose to retain them for domestic service. Those who survive the term of servitude, seldom establish their residence in this country: the stamp of infamy is too strong upon them to be easily erased: they either return to Europe, and renew their former practices; or, if they have fortunately imbibed habits of honesty and industry, they remove to a distant situation, where they may hope to remain unknown, and be enabled to pursue with credit every possible method of becoming useful members of society. . . .

The generality of the inhabitants in this province are very little acquainted with those fallacious pretenses, by which numbers are continually induced to embark for this continent. On the contrary, they too generally conceive an opinion that the difference is merely nominal between the indented servant and the convicted felon: nor will they readily believe that people, who had the least experience in life, and whose characters were unexceptionable, would abandon their friends and families, and their ancient connections, for a servile situation, in a remote appendage to the British Empire. From this persuasion they rather consider the convict as the more profitable servant, his term being for seven, the latter, only for five years; and, I am sorry to observe, that there are but few instances wherein they experience different treatment. Negroes being a property for life, the death of slaves, in the prime of youth or strength, is a material loss to the proprietor; they are, therefore, almost in every instance, under more comfortable circumstances than the miserable European, over whom the rigid planter exercises an inflexible severity. They are strained to the utmost to perform their allotted labor; and, from a prepossession in many cases too justly founded, they are supposed to be receiving only the just reward which is due to repeated offenses.

There are doubtless many exceptions to this observation. Yet, generally speaking, they groan beneath a worse than Egyptian bondage. By attempting to enlighten the intolerable burden, they often render it more insupportable. For real or imaginary causes, these frequently attempt to escape, but very few are successful; the country being intersected with rivers, and the utmost vigilance observed in detecting persons under suspicious circumstances, who, when apprehended, are committed to close confinement, advertised, and delivered to their respective masters; the party who detects the vagrant being entitled to a reward. Other incidental charges arise. The unhappy culprit is doomed to a fevered chastisement; and a prolongation of servitude is decreed in full proportion to expenses incurred, and supposed inconveniences resulting from a desertion of duty.

The situation of the free-willer is, in almost every instance, more to be lamented than either that of the convict or the indented servant; the deception which is practiced on those of this description being attended with circumstances of greater duplicity and cruelty. Persons under this denomination are received under express conditions that, on their arrival in America, they are to be allowed a stipulated number of days to dispose of themselves to the greatest advantage. They are told, that their services will be eagerly solicited, in proportion to their abilities; that their reward will be adequate to the hazard they encounter by courting fortune in a distant region; and that the parties with whom they engage will readily advance the sum agreed on for their passage; which, being averaged at about nine pounds sterling, they will speedily be enabled to repay, and to enjoy, in a state of liberty, a comparative situation of ease and affluence.

With these pleasing ideas they support with cheerfulness, the hardships to which they are subjected during the voyage; and with the most anxious sensations of delight, approach the land which they consider as the scene of future prosperity. But scarce have they contemplated the diversified objects which naturally attract attention; scarce have they yielded to pleasing reflection, that every danger, every difficulty, is happily surmounted, before their fond hopes are cruelly blasted, and they find themselves involved in all the complicated miseries of a tedious, laborious and unprofitable servitude.

Persons resident in America being accustomed to procure servants for a very trifling consideration, under absolute terms, for a limited period, are not often disposed to hire adventurers, who expect to be gratified in full proportion to their acknowledged qualifications; but, as they support authority with a rigid hand, they little regard the former situation of their unhappy dependants.

This disposition, which is almost universally prevalent, is well known to the parties, who on your side of the Atlantic engage in this iniquitous and cruel commerce.

It is, therefore, an article of agreement with these deluded victims, that if they are not successful in obtaining situations, on their own terms, within a certain number of days after their arrival in the country, they are then to be sold, in order to defray the charges of passage, at the discretion of the master of the vessel, or the agent to whom he is consigned in the province.

SOURCE: Eddis, William. *Letters from America, Historical and Descriptive: Comprising Occurrences from 1769 to 1777 Inclusive.* London: 1792.

THE WRIT OF ASSISTANCE *(1762)*

By 1761, cracks were appearing in the relationship between Great Britain and her colonies in the New World. At issue were frequent disputes over judicial tenure in the colonial courts, the nullification of measures passed in popular domestic assemblies, and, perhaps especially, the adoption of so-called Writs of Assistance. A sort of blanket search warrant, such a writ granted royal customs agents unimpeded authority to search houses for smuggled goods, with or without just cause. Many colonists, already suspicious of legislative decisions made in London, regarded the writs as a direct assault on one of the fundamental principles of liberty and law, that a man's home was his castle. The issuance of the Writs was one of the specific grievances named in the Declaration of Independence. Later, when the Bill of Rights was crafted, the Fourth Amendment banned such general search warrants in order to protect the people from unreasonable search and seizure.

Laura M. Miller,
Vanderbilt University

***See also* Colonial Policy, British; Writs of Assistance.**

George the third by the grace of God of Great Britain France & Ireland King Defender of the faith &c.

To all & singular our Justices of the peace Sheriffs Constables and to all other our Officers and Subjects within our said Province and to each of you Greeting.

Know ye that whereas in and by an Act of Parliament made in the thir[four]teenth year of [the reign of] the late King Charles the second it is declared to be [the Officers of our Customs & their Deputies are authorized and impowered to go & enter aboard any Ship or Vessel outward or inward bound for the purposes in the said Act mentioned and it is also in & by the said Act further enacted & declared that it shall be] lawful [to or] for any person or persons authorized by Writ of assistants under the seal of our Court of Exchequer to take a Constable Headborough or other publick Officer inhabiting near unto the place and in the day time to enter & go into any House Shop Cellar Warehouse or Room or other place and in the case of resistance to break open doors chests trunks & other package there to seize and from thence to bring any kind of goods or merchandize whatsoever prohibited & uncustomed and to put and secure the same in his Majestys [our] Storehouse in the port next to the place where such seizure shall be made.

And whereas in & by an Act of Parliament made in the seventh & eighth year of [the reign of the late] King William the third there is granted to the Officers for collecting and managing our revenue and inspecting the plantation trade in any of our plantations [the same powers authority for visiting & searching of Ships & also] to enter houses or warehouses to search for and seize any prohibited or uncustomed goods as are provided for the Officers of our Customs in England by the said last mentioned Act made in the fourteenth year of [the reign of] King Charles the Second, and the like assistance is required to be given to the said Officers in the execution of their office as by the said last mentioned Act is provided for the Officers in England.

And whereas in and by an Act of our said Province of Massachusetts bay made in the eleventh year of [the reign of] the late King William the third it is enacted & declared that our Superior Court of Judicature Court of Assize and General Goal delivery for our said Province shall have cognizance of all matters and things within our said Province as fully & amply to all intents & purposes as our Courts of King's Bench Common Pleas & Exchequer within our Kingdom of England have or ought to have.

And whereas our Commissioners for managing and causing to be levied & collected our customs subsidies and other duties have [by Commission or Deputation under their hands & seal dated at London the 22 day of May in the first year of our Reign] deputed and impowered Charles Paxton Esquire to be Surveyor & Searcher of all the rates and duties arising and growing due to us at Boston in our Province aforesaid and [in & by said Commission or Deputation] have given him power to enter into [any Ship Bottom Boat or other Vessel & also into] any Shop House Warehouse Hostery or other place whatsoever to make diligent search into any trunk chest pack case truss or any other parcell or package whatsoever for any goods wares or merchandize prohibited to be imported or exported or whereof the Customs or other Duties have not been duly paid and the same to seize to our use In all things proceeding as the Law directs.

Therefore we strictly Injoin & Command you & every one of you that, all excuses apart, you & every one of you permit the said Charles Paxton according to the true intent & form of the said commission or deputation and the laws & statutes in that behalf made & provided, [as well by night as by day from time to time to enter & go on board any Ship Boat or other Vessel riding lying or being within or coming to the said port of Boston or any Places or Creeks thereunto appertaining such Ship Boat or Vessel then & there found to search & oversee and the persons therein being strictly to examine touching the premises aforesaid & also according to the form effect and true intent of the said commission or deputation] in the day time to enter & go into the vaults cellars warehouses shops & other places where any prohibited goods wares or merchandizes or any goods wares or merchandizes for which the customs or other duties shall not have been duly & truly satisfied and paid lye concealed or are suspected to be concealed, according to the true intent of the law to inspect & oversee & search for the said goods wares & merchandize. And further to do and execute all things which of right and according to the laws & statutes in this behalf shall be to be done. And we further strictly Injoin & Command you and every one of you that to the said Charles Paxton Esqr you & every one of you from time to time be aiding assisting & helping in the execution of the premises as is meet. And this you or any of [you] in no wise omit at your perils. Witness Thomas Hutchinson Esq at Boston the day of December in the Second year of our Reign Annoque Dom 1761.

By order of Court

N. H. Cler.

STAMP ACT
(22 March 1765)

Maintaining order in the New World proved to be an expensive business. The end of the French and Indian War in 1763 greatly increased Great Britain's material holdings in North America, but it also brought under the watchful eye of the King's army large numbers of the defeated and disaffected. To meet the desperate need for fresh soldiers and new garrisons, the London Parliament leveled the Stamp Act, the first direct tax ever imposed on the American colonies. A duty on printed material, such as pamphlets, newspapers, and commercial documents (all of which were emblazoned with a special stamp), the Stamp Act of 1765 inflamed the colonists, who were not allowed to elect members of Parliament, and led to boycotts of British goods, petitions to the King, and a formal declaration of American grievances and rights from a body calling itself the Stamp Act Congress. Surprised by such harsh reaction, Parliament repealed the Act in 1766 (along with a restatement of its dominance over the colonies "in all cases whatsoever"), but the damage had already been done, and the groundwork for the American Revolution had been laid.

Laura M. Miller,
Vanderbilt University

See also **Colonial Policy, British; Stamp Act; "Taxation Without Representation."**

An act for granting and applying certain stamp duties, and other duties, in the British *colonies and plantations in* America, *towards further defraying the expences of defending, protecting, and securing the same; and for amending such parts of the several acts of parliament relating to the trade and revenues of the said colonies and plantations, as direct the manner of determining and recovering the penalties and forfeitures therein mentioned.*

Whereas by an act made in the last session of parliament, several duties were granted, continued, and appropriated, towards defraying the expences of defending, protecting, and securing, the British *colonies and plantations in* America: *and whereas it is just and necessary, that provision be made for raising a further revenue within your Majesty's dominions in* America, *towards defraying the said expences:* . . . be it enacted . . . , That from and after [November 1, 1765,] there shall be raised, levied, collected, and paid unto his Majesty, his heirs, and successors, throughout the colonies and plantations in *America* which now are, or hereafter may be, under the dominion of his Majesty, his heirs and successors,

For every skin or piece of vellum or parchment, or sheet or piece of paper, on which shall be ingrossed, written or printed, any declaration, plea, replication, rejoinder, demurrer, or other pleading, or any copy thereof, in any court of law within the *British* colonies and plantations in *America*, a stamp duty of three pence.

For every skin . . . on which shall be ingrossed . . . any donation, presentation, collation, or institution of or to any benefice, or any writ or instrument for the like purpose, or any register, entry, testimonial, or certificate of any degree taken in any university, academy, college, or seminary of learning . . . a stamp duty of two pounds. . . .

For every skin . . . on which shall be ingrossed . . . any note or bill of lading, bill of lading, which shall be signed for any kind of goods, wares, or merchandize, to be exported from, or any cocket or clearance granted within the said colonies and plantations, a stamp duty of four pence. . . .

For every skin . . . on which shall be ingrossed . . . any grant, appointment, or admission of or to any publick beneficial office or employment, for the space of one year, or any lesser time, of or above the value of twenty pounds *per annum* sterling money, in salary, fees, and perquisites . . . , (except commissions and appointments of officers of the army, navy, ordnance, or militia, of judges, and of justices of the peace) a stamp duty of ten shillings. . . .

For every skin . . . on which shall be ingrossed . . . any licence for retailing of spirituous liquors, to be granted to any person who shall take out the same . . . , a stamp duty of twenty shillings. . . .

For every skin . . . on which shall be ingrossed . . . any probate of a will, letters of administration, or of guardianship for any estate above the value of twenty pounds sterling money; within the *British* colonies and plantations upon the continent of *America*, the islands belonging thereto, and the *Bermuda* and *Bahama* islands, a stamp duty of five shillings. . . .

For every skin . . . on which shall be ingrossed . . . any bond for securing the payment of any sum of money, not exceeding the sum of ten pounds sterling money, within the *British* colonies and plantations upon the continent of *America*, the islands belonging thereto, and the *Bermuda* and *Bahama* islands, a stamp duty of six pence. . . .

For every skin . . . on which shall be ingrossed . . . any order or warrant for surveying or setting out any quantity of land, not exceeding one hundred acres, issued by any governor, proprietor, or any publick officer alone, or in conjunction with any other person or persons, or with any council, or any council and assembly, within the *British* colonies and plantations in *America*, a stamp duty of six pence. . . .

For every skin . . . on which shall be ingrossed . . . any such original grant . . . by which any quantity of land not exceeding one hundred acres shall be granted . . . within all other parts of the *British* dominions in *America*, a stamp duty of three shillings. [Further provision for larger grants.]

For every skin . . . on which shall be ingrossed . . . any grant, appointment, or admission, of or to any publick beneficial office or employment, not herein before charged, above the value of twenty pounds *per annum* sterling money in salary, fees, and perquisites, or any exemplification of the same, within the *British* colonies and plantations upon the continent of *America*, the islands belonging thereto, and the *Bermuda* and *Bahama* islands (except commissions of officers of the army, navy, ordnance, or militia, and of justices of the peace) a stamp duty of four pounds. . . .

For every skin . . . on which shall be ingrossed . . . any indenture, lease, conveyance, contract, stipulation, bill of sale, charter party, protest, articles of apprenticeship, or covenant (except for the hire of servants not apprentices, and also except such other matters as are herein before charged) within the *British* colonies and plantations in *America*, a stamp duty of two shillings and six pence. . . .

For every skin . . . on which shall be ingrossed . . . any notarial act, bond, deed, letter of attorney, procuration, mortgage, release, or other obligatory instrument, not herein before charged . . . , a stamp duty of two shillings and three pence. . . .

And for and upon every pack of playing cards, and all dice, which shall be sold or used . . . , the several stamp duties following (that is to say)

For every pack of such cards, the sum of one shilling.

And for every pair of such dice, the sum of ten shillings.

And for and upon every paper, commonly called a *pamphlet*, and upon every news paper . . . and for and upon such advertisements as are herein after mentioned, the respective duties following (that is to say)

For every such pamphlet and paper contained in half a sheet, or any lesser piece of paper . . . , a stamp duty of one half-penny, for every printed copy thereof.

For every such pamphlet and paper (being larger than half a sheet, and not exceeding one whole sheet) . . . , a stamp duty of one penny, for every printed copy thereof.

For every pamphlet and paper being larger than one whole sheet, and not exceeding six sheets in octavo, or in a lesser page, or not exceeding twelve sheets in quarto, or twenty sheets in folio . . . , a duty after the rate of one shilling for every sheet of any kind of paper which shall be contained in one printed copy thereof.

For every advertisement to be contained in any gazette, news paper, or other paper, or any pamphlet . . . , a duty of two shillings.

For every almanack or calendar, for any one particular year, or for any time less than a year, which shall be written or printed on one side only of any one sheet, skin, or piece of paper parchment, or vellum . . . , a stamp duty of two pence.

For every other almanack or calendar for any one particular year . . . , a stamp duty of four pence. And for every almanack or calendar written or printed . . . , to serve for several years, duties to the same amount respectively shall be paid for every such year.

For every skin . . . on which any instrument, proceeding, or other matter or thing aforesaid, shall be ingrossed . . . , in any other than the *English* language, a stamp duty of double the amount of the respective duties before charged thereon. . . .

II. And also a duty of one shilling for every twenty shillings, in any sum exceeding fifty pounds, which shall be given, paid, contracted, or agreed, for, with, or in relation to any such clerk or apprentice. . . .

V. And be it further enacted . . . , That all books and pamphlets serving chiefly for the purpose of an almanack, by whatsoever name or names intituled or described, are and shall be charged with the duty imposed by this act on almanacks, but not with any of the duties charged by this act on pamphlets, or other printed papers. . . .

VI. Provided always, that this act shall not extend to charge any bills of exchange, accompts, bills of parcels, bills of fees, or any bills or notes not sealed for payment of money at sight, or upon demand, or at the end of certain days of payment. . . .

XII. And be it further enacted . . . , That the said several duties shall be under the management of the commissioners, for the time being, of the duties charged on stamped vellum, parchment, and paper, in *Great Britain:* and the said commissioners are hereby impowered and required to employ such officers under them, for that purpose, as they shall think proper. . . .

XVI. And be it further enacted . . . , That no matter or thing whatsoever, by this act charged with the payment of a duty, shall be pleaded or given in evidence, or admitted in any court within the said colonies and plantations, to be good, useful, or available in law or equity, unless the same shall be marked or stamped, in pursuance of this act, with the respective duty hereby charged thereon, or with an higher duty. . . .

LIV. And be it further enacted . . . , That all the monies which shall arise by the several rates and duties hereby granted (except the necessary charges of raising, collecting, recovering, answering, paying, and accounting for the same and the necessary charges from time to time incurred in relation to this act, and the execution thereof) shall be paid into the receipt of his Majesty's exchequer, and shall be entered separate and apart from all other monies, and shall be there reserved to be from time to time disposed of by parliament, towards further defraying the necessary expences of defending, protecting, and securing, the said colonies and plantations. . . .

LVII. . . . offences committed against any other act or acts of Parliament relating to the trade or revenues of the said colonies or plantations; shall and may be prosecuted, sued for, and recovered, in any court of record, or in any court of admiralty, in the respective colony or plantation where the offence shall be committed, or in any court of vice admiralty appointed or to be appointed, and which shall have jurisdiction within such colony, plantation, or place, (which courts of admiralty or vice admiralty are hereby respectively authorized and required to proceed, hear, and determine the same) at the election of the informer or prosecutor. . . .

SOURCE: "Authentic account of the proceedings of the Congress held at New-York in 1765, on the subject of the American Stamp Act," 1767. Courtesy of The Huntington Library, San Marino, CA.

PATRICK HENRY'S RESOLVES AS PRINTED IN THE *MARYLAND GAZETTE* *(4 July 1765)*

A failure as a shopkeeper and farmer, Patrick Henry entered Virginia's House of Burgesses only shortly before the London Parliament imposed upon its North American Colonies the much-detested Stamp Act of 1765. In response, Henry, already famous for his impassioned rhetoric in defense of colonial rights, composed the radical resolutions seen here, in which he denounced the ultimate authority of the Parliament over domestic legislatures and reiterated the rallying cry of "no taxation without representation." Mysteriously, although the House of Burgesses rejected some of Henry's complaints as too harshly critical of the King, what finally appeared in the Maryland Gazette on 4 July contains strong language that seems to belong neither to Henry nor the House. Electrified by such straightforwardness, whatever its origin, more colonies rushed to follow suit, and Patrick Henry became famous throughout North America and Great Britain as a powerful influence on revolutionary thought.

Laura M. Miller,
Vanderbilt University

See also **Revolution, American: Political History; "Taxation Without Representation."**

Resolves of the House of Burgesses in Virginia, June 1765.

That the first Adventurers & Settlers of this his Majesty's Colony and Dominion of Virginia, brought with them, and transmitted to their Posterity, and all other his Majesty's Subjects since inhabiting in this his Majesty's Colony, all the Liberties, Privileges, Franchises, and Immunities, that at any Time have been held, enjoyed, and possessed, by the People of Great Britain.

That by Two Royal Charters, granted by King James the First, the Colonies aforesaid are Declared Entitled, to all Liberties, Privileges and Immunities, of Denizens and Natural Subjects (to all Intents and Purposes) as if they had been Abiding and Born within the Realm of England.

That the Taxation of the People by Themselves, or by Persons Chosen by Themselves to Represent them, who can only know what Taxes the People are able to bear, or the easiest Method of Raising them, and must themselves be affected by every Tax laid upon the People, is the only Security against a Burthensome Taxation; and the Distinguishing Characteristic of British freedom; and, without which, the ancient Constitution cannot exist.

That his Majesty's Liege People of this his most Ancient and Loyal Colony, have, without Interruption, the inestimable Right of being Governed by such Laws, respecting their internal Polity and Taxation, as are derived from their own Consent, with the Approbation of their Sovereign, or his Substitute; which Right hath never been Forfeited, or Yielded up; but hath been constantly recognized by the Kings and People of Great Britain.

Resolved therefore, That the General Assembly of this Colony, with the Consent of his Majesty, or his Substitute, Have the Sole Right and Authority to lay Taxes and Impositions upon It's Inhabitants: And, That every Attempt to vest such Authority in any other Person or Persons whatsoever, has a Manifest Tendency to Destroy American Freedom.

That his Majesty's Liege People, Inhabitants of this Colony, are not bound to yield Obedience to any Law or Ordinance whatsoever, designed to impose any Taxation upon them, other than the Laws or Ordinances of the General Assembly as aforesaid.

That any Person who shall, by Speaking, or Writing, assert or maintain, That any Person or Persons, other than the General Assembly of this Colony, with such Consent as aforesaid, have any Right or Authority to lay or impose any Tax whatever on the Inhabitants thereof, shall be Deemed, an Enemy to this his Majesty's Colony.

SOURCE: Henry, Patrick. "Resolves of the House of Burgesses in Virginia." *Maryland Gazette*, July 4, 1765.

TOWNSHEND REVENUE ACT
(29 June 1767)

One of four legislative statutes called after the Crown's Chancellor of the Exchequer Charles Townshend (1725–1767) and intended to help cover the rapidly growing expense of North American colonization, the Townshend Revenue Act imposed import duties on material goods such as lead, tea, paper, and paint. The other Townshend Acts sanctioned blanket search warrants called Writs of Assistance, established courts without juries, created a board of customs commissioners in Boston, and suspended the New York assembly when it publicly disputed the Quartering Act of 1765. Outraged colonial reaction included more petitions to the King, boycotts of British goods, and increased violence by groups like the radical Sons of Liberty. Upbraided, the Parliament repealed the duties in 1770 except, disastrously for the Crown, the one on tea.

Laura M. Miller,
Vanderbilt University

See also **Colonial Policy, British; Townshend Acts.**

An act for granting certain duties in the British *colonies and plantations in* America; *for allowing a drawback of the duties of customs upon the exportation from this kingdom, of coffee and cocoa nuts of the produce of the said colonies or plantations; for discontinuing the drawbacks payable on china earthen ware exported to America; and for more effectually preventing the clandestine running of goods in the said colonies and plantations.*

Whereas *it is expedient that a revenue should be raised, in your Majesty's dominions in* America, *for making a more certain and adequate provision for defraying the charge of the administration of justice, and the support of civil government, in such provinces as it shall be found necessary; and towards further defraying the expenses of defending protecting and securing the said dominions;* ... be it enacted.... That from and after the twentieth day of *November,* one thousand seven hundred and sixty seven, there shall be raised, levied, collected, and paid, unto his Majesty, his heirs, and successors, for upon and the respective Goods here in after mentioned, which shall be imported from *Great Britain* into any colony or plantation in *America* which now is or hereafter may be, under the dominion of his Majesty, his heirs, or successors, the several Rates and Duties following; that is to say,

For every hundredweight avoirdupois of crown, plate, flint, and white glass, four shillings and eight pence.

For every hundred weight avoirdupois of red lead, two shillings.

For every hundred weight avoirdupois of green glass, one shilling and two pence.

For every hundred weight avoirdupois of white lead, two shillings.

For every hundred weight avoirdupois of painters colours, two shillings.

For every pound weight avoirdupois of tea, three pence.

For every ream of paper, usually called or known by the name of *Atlas fine,* twelve shillings....

IV. ... and that all the monies that shall arise by the said duties (except the necessary charges of raising, collecting, levying, recovering, answering, paying, and accounting for the same) shall be applied, in the first place, in such manner as is herein after mentioned, in making a more certain and adequate provision for the charge of the administration of justice, and the support of civil government in such of the said colonies and plantations where it shall be found necessary; and that the residue of such duties shall be payed into the receipt of his Majesty's exchequer, and shall be entered separate and apart from all other monies paid or payable to his Majesty ...; and shall be there reserved, to be from time to time disposed of by parliament towards defraying the necessary expense of defending, protecting, and securing, the *British* colonies and plantations in *America.*

V. And be it further enacted ..., That his Majesty and his successors shall be, and are hereby, impowered, from time to time, by any warrant or warrants under his or their royal sign manual or sign manuals, countersigned by the high treasurer, or any three or more of the commissioners of the treasury for the time being, to cause such monies to be applied, out of the produce of the duties granted by this act, as his Majesty, or his successors, shall think proper or necessary, for defraying the charges of the administration of justice, and the support of the civil government, within all or any of the said colonies or plantations....

X. *And whereas by an act of parliament made in the fourteenth year of the reign of King Charles the Second,* intituled, An act for preventing frauds, and regulating abuses, in his Majesty's customs, *and several other acts now in force, it is lawful for any officer of his Majesty's customs, authorized by writ of assistance under the seal of his Majesty's court of exchequer, to take a constable, head-borough, or other public officer inhabiting near unto the place, and in the daytime to enter and go into any house, shop cellar, warehouse, or room or other place and, in case of resistance, to break open doors, chests, trunks, and other pakage there, to seize, and from thence to bring, any kind of goods or merchandise whatsoever prohibited or uncustomed, and to put and secure the same in his Majesty's storehouse next to the place where such seizure shall be made; and whereas by an act made in the seventh and eighth years of the reign of King William the Third, intituled* An act for preventing frauds, and regulating abuses, in the plantation trade, *it is, amongst otherthings, enacted, that the officers for collecting and managing his Majesty's revenue, and inspecting the plantation trade, in America, shall have the same powers and authorities to enter houses or warehouses, to search or seize goods prohibited to be imported or exported into or out of any of the said plantations, or for which any duties are payable, or ought to have been paid; and that the like assistance shall be given to the said officers in the execution of their office, as, by the said recited act of the fourteenth year of King Charles the Second, is provided for the officers of* England: *but, no authority being expressly given by the said act, made in the seventh and eighth years of the reign of King William the Third, to any particular court to grant such writs of assistance for the officers of the customs in the said plantations, it is doubted whether such officers can legally enter houses and other places on land, to search for and seize goods, in the manner directed by the said recited acts*: To obviate which doubts for the future, and in order to carry the intention of the said recited acts into effectual execution, be it enacted . . . , That from and after the said twentieth day of *November*, one thousand seven hundred and sixty seven, such writs of assistance, to authorize and impower the officers of his Majesty's customs to enter and go into any house, warehouse, shop, cellar, or other place, in the *British* colonies or plantations in *America*, to search for and seize prohibited and uncustomed goods, in the manner directed by the said recited acts, shall and may be granted by the said superior or supreme court of justice having jurisdiction within such colony or plantation respectively. . . .

SOURCE: Pickering, D., ed. *Statutes at Large*. Vol. XXVII.

MASSACHUSETTS CIRCULAR LETTER
(11 February 1768, by Samuel Adams)

Enraged by the Townshend Acts of 1767, which among other things imposed new duties on tea and paper and established vice-admiralty courts unchecked by juries, and having petitioned George III himself, Samuel Adams and the Massachusetts legislature drafted the so-called Circular Letter to alert the other colonies of their activities. Adams, the son of a wealthy brewer, was already well-known for his fiery rhetoric and for his hand in founding the radical and sometimes violent Sons of Liberty. Reaction by the Crown was swift. General Gage was ordered to send a regiment to Boston, and vessels of war sailed into the harbor. On 1 July 1768, Parliament dissolved the Massachusetts Legislature.

Laura M. Miller,
Vanderbilt University

See also **Massachusetts Circular Letter; Revolution, American: Political History; "Taxation Without Representation."**

SIR,

The House of Representatives of this Province, have taken into their serious Consideration, the great difficulties that must accrue to themselves and their Constituents, by the operation of several acts of Parliament, imposing Duties & Taxes on the American colonys. As it is a Subject in which every Colony is deeply interested, they have no reason to doubt but your Assembly is deeply impressed with its importance, & that such constitutional measures will be come into, as are proper . . .

The House have humbly represented to the ministry, their own Sentiments that his majesty's high Court of Parliament is the supreme legislative Power over the whole Empire; That in all free States the Constitution is fixed; & as the supreme Legislative derives its Power & Authority from the Constitution, it cannot overleap the Bounds of it, without destroying its own foundation; That the constitution ascertains & limits both Sovereignty and allegiance, & therefore, his Majesty's American Subjects, who acknowledge themselves bound by the Ties of Allegiance, have an equitable Claim to the full enjoyment of the fundamental Rules of the British

Constitution: That it is in an essential unalterable Right, in nature, ungrafted into the British Constitution, as a fundamental Law, & ever held sacred & irrevocable by the Subjects within the Realm, that what a man has honestly acquired is absolutely his own, which he may freely give, but cannot be taken from him without his consent: That the American Subjects may, therefore, exclusive of any Consideration of Charter Rights, with a decent firmness, adapted to the Character of free men & subjects assert this natural and constitutional Right.

It is, moreover, their humble opinion, which they express with the greatest Deferrence to the Wisdom of the Parliament, that the Acts made there, imposing Duties on the People of this province, with the sole & express purpose of raising a Revenue, are Infringements of their natural & constitutional Rights: because, as they are not represented in the British Parliament, his Majesty's Commons in Britain, by those grant their Property without their consent.

This House further are of Opinion, that their Constituents, considering their local Circumstances cannot by any possibility, be represented in the Parliament, & that it will forever be impracticable, that they should be equally represented there, & consequently not at all; being separated by an Ocean of a thousand leagues: and that his Majesty's Royal Predecessors, for this reason, were graciously pleased to form a subordinate legislature here, that their subjects might enjoy the unalienable Right of a Representation: Also that considering the utter impracticability of their ever being fully & equally represented in parliament, & the great Expence that must unavoidably attend even a partial representation there, this House think that a taxation of their Constituents, even without their Consent, grievous as it is, would be preferable to any Representation that could be admitted for them there.

Upon these principles, & also considering that were the right in Parliament ever so clear, yet, for obvious reasons, it would be beyond the rules of Equity that their Constituents should be taxed, on the manufactures of Great Britain here, in Addition to the dutys they pay for them in England, & the other advantages arising to G Britain from the Acts of trade, this House have preferred a humble, dutifull, & loyal Petition, to our most gracious Sovereign, & made such Representations to his Majesty's Ministers, as they apprehended would fend to obtain redress.

They have also submitted to Consideration whether any People can be said to enjoy any degree of Freedom if the Crown in addition to its undoubted Authority of constituting a Governor, should appoint him such a Stipend as it may judge proper, without the Consent of the people & at their expence; & whether, while the Judges of the Land & other Civil officers hold not their Commissions during good Behaviour, their having salarys appointed for them by the Crown independent of the people hath not a tendency to subvert the principles of Equity & endanger the Happiness and Security of the Subject . . .

These are the Sentiments & proceedings of this House; & as they have too much reason to believe that the enemys of the Colonies have represented them to his Majestys Ministers & the parliament as factious disloyal & having a disposition to make themselves independent of the Mother Country, they have taken occasion, in the most humble terms, to assure his Majesty & his Ministers that with regard to the People of this province, & as they doubt not, of all the colonies the charge is unjust.

The House is fully satisfied, that your Assembly is too generous & liberal in sentiment, to believe, that this Letter proceeds from an Ambition to take the lead, or dictating to the other Assemblys: They freely submit their opinions to the Judgment of others, & shall take it kind in your house to point out to them any thing further, that may be thought necessary.

This House cannot conclude, without expressing their firm Confidence in the King our common head & Father, that the united & dutifull Supplications of his distressed American Subjects will meet with his Royal & favorable Acceptance.

SOURCE: Cushing, Harry A., ed. *The Writings of Samuel Adams.* New York: 1904.

THE CONTINENTAL ASSOCIATION
(1774)

By the fall of 1774, Great Britain's North American colonies were ready to rattle the fetters forged by their cross-oceanic masters. Spurred to action by the so-called Intolerable Acts, and inspired in part by the Stamp Act Congress of 1765, the First Continental Congress gathered in Carpenter's Hall, Philadelphia, to express their grievances to the Crown and not, as would happen in two years, to seriously consider the still-radical idea of separation. What emerged from their labors was the Continental Association, a list of objections and reactions to perceived British injustice. Among its many caveats, the Association called for an immediate ban on the importation and use of British-made goods, as well as the termination of the colonial slave trade. An important step in the long road toward revolution, versions of the Continental Association were eventually adopted by twelve colonies, most of which enforced its dictates by coercion and the careful manipulation of public opinion against violators. Finished with its work, the First Continental Congress adjourned on 26 October 1774.

Laura M. Miller,
Vanderbilt University

***See also* Colonial Commerce; Nonimportation Agreements; Revolution, American: Political History.**

We, his majesty's most loyal subjects, the delegates of the several colonies of New-Hampshire, Massachusetts-Bay, Rhode-Island, Connecticut, New-York, New-Jersey, Pennsylvania, the three lower counties of Newcastle, Kent, and Sussex on Delaware, Maryland, Virginia, North-Carolina, and South-Carolina, deputed to represent them in a continental Congress, held in the city of Philadelphia, on the 5th day of September, 1774, avowing our allegiance to his majesty, our affection and regard for our fellow-subjects in Great-Britain and elsewhere, affected with the deepest anxiety, and most alarming apprehensions, at those grievances and distresses, with which his Majesty's American subjects are oppressed; and having taken under our most serious deliberation, the state of the whole continent, find, that the present unhappy situation of our affairs is occasioned by a ruinous system of colony administration, adopted by the British ministry about the year 1763, evidently calculated for enslaving these colonies, and, with them, the British Empire. In prosecution of which system, various acts of parliament have been passed, for raising a revenue in America, for depriving the American subjects, in many instances, of the constitutional trial by jury, exposing their lives to danger, by directing a new and illegal trial beyond the seas, for crimes alleged to have been committed in America: And in prosecution of the same system, several late, cruel, and oppressive acts have been passed, respecting the town of Boston and the Massachusets-Bay, and also an act for extending the province of Quebec, so as to border on the western frontiers of these colonies, establishing an arbitrary government therein, and discouraging the settlement of British subjects in that wide extended country; thus, by the influence of civil principles and ancient prejudices, to dispose the inhabitants to act with hostility against the free Protestant colonies, whenever a wicked ministry shall chuse so to direct them.

To obtain redress of these grievances, which threaten destruction to the lives, liberty, and property of his majesty's subjects, in North-America, we are of opinion, that a non-importation, non-consumption, and non-exportation agreement, faithfully adhered to, will prove the most speedy, effectual and peaceable measure; And, therefore, we do, for ourselves, and the inhabitants of the several colonies, whom we represent, firmly agree and associate, under the sacred ties of virtue, honour and love of our country, as follows:

1. That from and after the first day of December next, we will not import, into British America, from Great-Britain or Ireland, any goods, wares, or merchandize whatsoever, or from any other place, any such goods, wares, or merchandise, as shall have been exported from Great-Britain or Ireland; nor will we, after that day, import any East-India tea from any part of the world; nor any molasses, syrups, paneles, coffee, or pimento, from the British plantations or from Dominica; nor wines from Madeira, or the Western Islands; nor foreign indigo.
2. We will neither import nor purchase any slave imported after the first day of December next; after which time, we will wholly discontinue the slave trade, and will neither be concerned in it ourselves, nor will we hire our vessels, nor sell our commodities or manufactures to those who are concerned in it.
3. As a non-consumption agreement, strictly adhered to, will be an effectual security for the observation of the non-importation, we as above, solemnly agree and associate, that from this day, we will not purchase or use any tea, imported on account of the East-India company, or any on which a duty hath been or shall be paid; and from and after the first day of March next, we will not purchase or use any East-India tea whatever; nor will we, nor shall any person for or under us, purchase or use any of those goods, wares, or merchandize, we have agreed not to import, which we shall know, or have cause to suspect, were imported after the first day of December, except such as come under the rules and directions of the tenth article hereafter mentioned.
4. The earnest desire we have not to injure our fellow-subjects in Great-Britain, Ireland, or the West-Indies, induces us to suspend a non-exportation, until the tenth day of September, 1775; at which time, if the said acts and parts of acts of the British parliament herein after mentioned, are not repealed, we will not directly or indirectly, export any merchandize or commodity whatsoever to Great-Britain, Ireland, or the West-Indies, except rice to Europe.
5. Such as are merchants, and use the British and Irish trade, will give orders, as soon as possible, to their factors, agents and correspondents, in Great-Britain

and Ireland, not to ship any goods to them, on any pretence whatsoever, as they cannot be received in America; and if any merchant, residing in Great-Britain or Ireland, shall directly or indirectly ship any goods, wares or merchandize, for America, in order to break the said non-importation agreement, or in any manner contravene the same, on such unworthy conduct being well attested, it ought to be made public; and, on the same being so done, we will not, from thenceforth, have any commercial connexion with such merchant.

6. That such as are owners of vessels will give positive orders to their captains, or masters, not to receive on board their vessels any goods prohibited by the said non-importation agreement, on pain of immediate dismission from their service.

7. We will use our utmost endeavours to improve the breed of sheep, and increase their number to the greatest extent; and to that end, we will kill them as seldom as may be, especially those of the most profitable kind; nor will we export any to the West-Indies or elsewhere; and those of us, who are or may become overstocked with, or can conveniently spare any sheep, will dispose of them to our neighbours, especially to the poorer sort, on moderate terms.

8. We will, in our several stations, encourage frugality, economy, and industry, and promote agriculture, arts and the manufactures of this country, especially that of wool; and will discountenance and discourage every species of extravagance and dissipation, especially all horse-racing, and all kinds of gaming, cock fighting, exhibitions of shews, plays, and other expensive diversions and entertainments; and on the death of any relation or friend, none of us, or any of our families will go into any further mourning-dress, than a black crape or ribbon on the arm or hat, for gentlemen and a black ribbon and necklace for ladies, and we will discontinue the giving of gloves and scarves at funerals.

9. Such as are venders of goods or merchandize will not take advantage of the scarcity of goods, that may be occasioned by this association, but will sell the same at the rates we have been respectively accustomed to do, for twelve months last past.—And if any vender of goods or merchandize shall sell such goods on higher terms, or shall, in any manner, or by any device whatsoever, violate or depart from this agreement, no person ought, nor will any of us deal with any such person, or his or her factor or agent, at any time thereafter, for any commodity whatever.

10. In case any merchant, trader, or other person, shall import any goods or merchandize, after the first day of December, and before the first day of February next, the same ought forthwith, at the election of the owner, to be either re-shipped or delivered up to the committee of the country or town, wherein they shall be imported, to be stored at the risque of the importer, until the non-importation agreement shall cease, or be sold under the direction of the committee aforesaid; and in the last-mentioned case, the owner or owners of such goods shall be re-imbursed out of the sales, the first cost and charges, the profit, if any, to be applied towards relieving and employing such poor inhabitants of the town of Boston, as are immediate sufferers by the Boston port-bill; and a particular account of all goods so returned, stored, or sold, to be inserted in the public papers; and if any goods or merchandizes shall be imported after the said first day of February, the same ought forthwith to be sent back again, without breaking any of the packages thereof.

11. That a committee be chosen in every county, city, and town, by those who are qualified to vote for representatives in the legislature, whose business it shall be attentively to observe the conduct of all persons touching this association; and when it shall be made to appear, to the satisfaction of a majority of any such committee, that any person within the limits of their appointment has violated this association, that such majority do forthwith cause the truth of the case to be published in the gazette; to the end, that all such foes to the rights of British-America may be publicly known, and universally contemned as the enemies of American liberty; and thenceforth we respectively will break off all dealings with him or her.

12. That the committee of correspondence, in the respective colonies, do frequently inspect the entries of their customhouses, and inform each other, from time to time, of the true state thereof, and of every other material circumstance that may occur relative to this association.

13. That all manufactures of this country be sold at reasonable prices, so that no undue advantage be taken of a future scarcity of goods.

14. And we do further agree and resolve, that we will have no trade, commerce, dealings or intercourse whatsoever, with any colony or province, in North-America, which shall not accede to, or which shall hereafter violate this association, but will hold them as unworthy of the rights of freemen, and as inimical to the liberties of their country.

And we do solemnly bind ourselves and our constituents, under the ties aforesaid, to adhere to this association, until such parts of the several acts of parliament passed since the close of the last war, as impose or continue duties on tea, wine, molasses, syrups, paneles, coffee, sugar, pimento, indigo, foreign paper, glass, and painters' colours, imported into America, and extend the powers of the admiralty courts beyond their ancient limits, deprive the American subject of trial by jury, authorize the judge's certificate to indemnify the prosecutor from damages, that he might otherwise be liable to from a trial by his peers, require oppressive security from a claimant of ships or goods seized, before he shall be allowed to defend his property, are repealed.—And until that part of the act of 12 G. 3. ch. 24, entitled "An act for the better securing his majesty's dock-yards, magazines, ships, ammunition, and stores," by which any persons charged with committing any of the offences therein described, in America, may be tried in any shire or county within the realm, is repealed—and until the four acts, passed the last session of parliament, viz. that for stopping the port blocking up the harbour of Boston—that for altering the charter and government of the Massachusetts-Bay—and that which is entitled "An act for the better administration of justice, &c."—and that "for extending the limits of Quebec, &c." are repealed. And we recommend it to the provincial conventions, and to the committees in the respective colonies, to establish such farther regulations as they may think proper, for carrying into execution this association.

The foregoing association being determined upon by the Congress, was ordered to be subscribed by the several members thereof; and thereupon, we have hereunto set our respective names accordingly.

IN CONGRESS, PHILADELPHIA, October 20, 1774.

Signed, PEYTON RANDOLPH, President.

SOURCE: *Journals of the American Congress from 1774 to 1788.* Washington: 1823.

THE REVOLUTIONARY WAR

"THE PENNSYLVANIA FARMER'S REMEDY" *(1768, by John Dickinson)*

Not everyone in Great Britain's North American colonies champed at the bit of revolution. Some 500,000, almost twenty percent of the white population, actively opposed independence. Many more were probably silent Royalists, and some, such as John Dickinson, argued passionately for colonial rights while advocating conciliation with the Crown. A revolutionary pamphleteer and Philadelphia trial lawyer, Dickinson protested the Stamp Act of 1765 in the so-called Stamp Act Congress but advocated only commercial reprisal. Not until the Battle of Lexington did he become convinced of the necessity for armed resistance. Later, as a member of the Continental Congress, Dickinson helped to draft the Articles of Confederation and was instrumental in the fight for ratification of the Federal Constitution in Delaware. His widely read letters made him famous both in the colonies and in England.

Laura M. Miller,
Vanderbilt University

See also **Independence; Revolution, American: Political History.**

I hope, my dear countrymen, that you will in every colony be upon your guard against those who may at any time endeavour to stir you up, under pretences of patriotism, to any measures disrespectful to our sovereign and other mother country. Hot, rash, disorderly proceedings, injure the reputation of a people as to wisdom, valour and virtue, without procuring them the least benefit. I pray God, that he may be pleased to inspire you and your posterity to the latest ages with that spirit, of which I have an idea, but find a difficulty to express; to express in the best manner I can, I mean a spirit that shall so guide you, that it will be impossible to determine, whether an *American's* character is most distinguishable for his loyalty to his sovereign, his duty to his mother country, his love of freedom, or his affection for his native soil.

Every government, at some time or other, falls into wrong measures; these may proceed from mistake or passion. —But every such measure does not dissolve the obligation between the governors and the governed; the mistake may be corrected; the passion may pass over.

It is the duty of the governed, to endeavour to rectify the mistake, and appease the passion. They have not at first any other right, than to represent their grievances, and to pray for redress, unless an emergence is so pressing, as not to allow time for receiving an answer to their applications which rarely happens. If their applications are disregarded, then that kind of position becomes justifiable, which can be made without breaking the laws, or disturbing the public peace. This consists in the prevention of the oppressors reaping advantage from their oppressions, and not in their punishment. For experience may teach them what reason did not; and harsh methods, cannot be proper, till milder ones have failed.

If at length it become undoubted, that an inveterate resolution is formed to annihilate the liberties of the governed, the English history affords frequent examples of resistance by force. What particular circumstances will in any future case justify such resistance, can never be ascertained till they happen. Perhaps it may be allowable to say, generally, that it never can be justifiable, until the people are FULLY CONVINCED, that any further submission will be destructive to their happiness.

When the appeal is made to the sword, highly probable it is, that the punishment will exceed the offence; and the calamities attending on war out weigh those preceding it. These considerations of justice and prudence, will always have great influence with good and wise men.

To these reflections on this subject, it remains to be added, and ought for ever to be remembred; that resistance in the case of colonies against their mother country, is extremely different from the resistance of a people against their prince. A nation may change their King or race of Kings, and retain[ing] their ancient form of government, be gainers by changing. Thus Great-Britain, under the illustrious house of Brunswick, a house that seems to flourish for the happiness of mankind, has found a felicity, unknown in the reigns of the Stuarts. But if once we are separated from our mother country, what new form of government shall we accept, or when shall we find another Britain to supply our loss? Torn from the body to which we are united by religion, liberty, laws, affections, relations, language, and commerce, we must bleed at every vein.

In truth, the prosperity of these provinces is founded in their dependance ante on Great-Britain; and when she returns to "her old good humour, and old good nature," as Lord Clerendon expresses it, I hope they will always esteem it their duty and interest, as it most certainly will be, to promote her welfare by all the means in their power.

We cannot act with too much caution in our disputes. Anger produces anger; and differences that might be accommodated by kind and respectful behaviour, may by imprudence be changed to an incurable rage. In quarrels between countries, as well as in those between individuals, when they have risen to a certain heighth, the first cause of dissention is no longer remembred, the minds of the parties being wholly engaged in recollecting and resenting the mutual expressions of their dislike. When feuds have reached that fatal point, all considerations of reason and equity vanish; and a blind fury governs, or rather confounds all things. A people no longer regards their interest, but the gratification of their wrath. The sway of the Cleon's, and Clodius's, the designing and detestable flatter[er] of the prevailing passion, become confirmed.

Wise and good men in vain oppose the storm, and may think themselves fortunate, if, endeavouring to preserve their ungrateful fellow citizens, they do not ruin themselves. Their prudence will be called baseness; their moderation, guilt; and if their virtue does not lead them to destruction, as that of many other great and excellent persons has done, they may survive, to receive from their expiring country, the mournful glory of her acknowledgment, that their councils, if regarded, would have saved her.

The constitutional modes of obtaining relief, are those which I would wish to see pursued on the present occasion, that is, by petitioning of our assemblies, or, where they are not permitted to meet, of the people to the powers that can afford us relief.

We have an excellent prince, in whose good dispositions towards us we may confide. We have a generous, sensible, and humane nation, to when we may apply. They may be deceived: they may, by artful be provoked to anger against us; but I cannot yet believe they will be cruel or unjust; or that their anger will be implacable. Let us behave like dutiful children, who have received unmerited blows from a beloved parent. Let us complain to our parents; but let our complaints speak at the same time, the language of affliction and veneration.

If, however, it shall happen by an unfortunate course of affairs, that our applications to his Majesty and the parliament for the redress, prove ineffectual, let us then take another step, by witholding from Great-Britain, all the advantages she has been used to receive from us. Then let us try, if our ingenuity, industry, and frugality, will not give weight to our remonstrances. Let us all be united with one spirit in one cause. Let us invent; let us work; let us save; let us at the same time, keep up our claims, and unceasingly repeat our complaints; but above all, let us implore the protection of that infinite good and gracious Being, "by whom kings reign and princes decree justice."

"Nil desperandum."

Nothing is to be despaired of.

A FARMER.

EYEWITNESS ACCOUNT OF THE BOSTON MASSACRE *(1770)*

The so-called Boston Massacre of 5 March 1770 created the greatest schism to that date in the already stormy relationship between Great Britain and her Colonies. The contemporary account presented here by an anonymous author is typical of the time. The British are portrayed as villains, while the anger of the colonial mob is not mentioned at all; according to the account, some young boys throwing a few harmless snowballs touched off the "horrid murder." In fact, the conflict had been brewing for some time. In 1768, four regiments of British regulars were dispatched to Boston to protect the much-hated collectors of customs duties for the Crown. This action by the British crown enraged a population already deeply involved in fighting for the right to tax and govern themselves. In the aftermath of the massacre, British troops were removed from Boston. John Adams successfully defended the soldiers who had fired the shots that killed three Bostonians outright, including the rope-maker and former slave Crispus Attucks. But by the end of the short trial in late 1770, the event had already impressed itself as an outrage in the minds of innumerable colonists, heightening their fear and hatred of the British and their army, and moving the colonists ever more quickly down the path toward revolution.

Laura M. Miller,
Vanderbilt University

See also **Boston Massacre.**

On Monday Evening the 5th current, a few Minutes after 9 O'Clock a most horrid murder was committed in King Street before the Customhouse Door by 8 or 9 Soldiers under the Command of Capt Thos Preston drawn of from the Main Guard on the South side of the Townhouse.

This unhappy affair began by Some Boys & young fellows throwing Snow Balls at the sentry placed at the Customhouse Door. On which 8 or 9 Solders Came to his assistance. Soon after a Number of people colected, when the Capt commanded the Soldiers to fire, which they did and 3 Men were Kil'd on the Spot & several Mortaly Wounded, one of which died next morning. The Capt soon drew off his Soldiers up to the Main Guard, or the Consequencis mite have been terable, for on the Guns fiering the people were alarm'd & set the Bells a Ringing as if for Fire, which drew Multitudes to the place of action. Levt Governor Hutchinson, who was commander in Chefe, was sent for & Came to the Council Chamber, w[h]ere som of the Magistrates attended. The Governor desired the Multitude about 10 O'Clock to sepperat & go home peaceable & he would do all in his power that Justice shold be don &c. The 29 Rigiment being then under Arms on the south side of the Townhouse, but the people insisted that the Soldiers should be ordered to their Barracks 1st before they would sepperat, Which being don the people sepperated aboute 1 O'Clock.—Capt Preston was taken up by a warrent given to the high Sherif by Justice Dania & Tudor and came under Examination about 2 O'clock & we sent him to Goal soon after 3, having Evidence sufficient, to committ him, on his ordering the soldiers to fire: So aboute 4 O'clock the Town became quiet. The next forenoon the 8 Soldiers that fired on the inhabitants was allso sent to Goal. Tuesday A. M. the inhabitants mett at Faneuil Hall & after som pertinant speches, chose a Committee of 5 Gentlemn to waite on the Levt. Governor in Council to request the immediate removeal of the Troops. The message was in these Words. That it is the unanimous opinion of this Meeting, that the inhabitants & soldiery can no longer live together in safety; that nothing can Ratonaly be expected to restore the peace of the Town & prevent blood & Carnage, but the removal of the Troops: and that we most fervently pray his Honor that his power & influence may be exerted for their instant removal. His Honor's Reply was. Gentlmen I am extreemly sorry for the unhappy difference & especially of the last Evening & Signifieng that it was not in his power to remove the Troops &c &c.

The Above Reply was not satisfactory to the Inhabitants, as but one Regiment should be removed to the Castle Barracks. In the afternoon the Town Adjourned to Dr Sewill's Meetinghouse, for Fanieul Hall was not large enough to hold the people, their being at least 3,000, som supos'd near 4,000, when they chose a Committee to waite on the Levt. Governor to let him & the Council Know that nothing less will satisfy the people, then a total & immediate removal of the Troops oute of the Town.—His Honor laid before the Council the Vote of the Town. The Council thereon expressed themselves to be unanimously of opinion that it was absolutely Necessary for his Majesty service, the good order of the Town &c that the Troops Should be immeditly removed oute of the Town.—His Honor communicated this advice of the Council to Col Dalrymple & desir'd he would order the Troops down to Castle William. After the Col. had seen the Vote of the Council He gave his Word & honor to the Town's Committe that both the Rigiments should be remov'd without delay. The Comte return'd to the Town Meeting & Mr Hancock, chairman of the Comte Read their Report as above, which was Received with a shoute & clap of hands, which made the Meeting-house Ring: So the Meeting was dessolved and a great number of Gentlemen appear'd to Watch the Center of the Town & the prison, which continued for 11 Nights and all was quiet again, as the Soldiers was all moved of to the Castle.

(Thursday) Agreeable to a general request of the Inhabitants, were follow'd to the Grave (for they were all Buried in one) in succession the 4 Bodies of Messs Saml Gray[,] Saml Maverick[,] James Caldwell & Crispus Attucks, the unhappy Victims who fell in the Bloody Massacre. On this sorrowfull Occasion most of the shops & stores in Town were shut, all the Bells were order'd to toll a solom peal in Boston, Charleston, Cambridge & Roxbery. The several Hearses forming a junction in King Street, the Theatre of that inhuman Tradgedy, proceeded from thence thro' the main street, lengthened by an immence Concourse of people, So numerous as to be obliged to follow in Ranks of 4 & 6 abreast and brought up by a long Train of Carriages. The sorrow Visible in the Countenances, together with the peculiar solemnity, Surpass description, it was suppos'd that the Spectators & those that follow'd the corps amounted to 15000, som supposed 20,000. Note Capt Preston was tried for his Life on the affare of the above Octob[r] 24 1770. The Trial lasted 5 Days, but the Jury brought him in not Guilty.

SLAVE ANDREW'S TESTIMONY IN THE BOSTON MASSACRE TRIAL
(1770)

The trials of the soldiers involved in the Boston Massacre of 5 March 1770 were short ones, lasting no longer than a few days in October and December. The counsel for the defense, John Adams (1735–1826), emphasized the violence of the colonial mob and the instigation of the British soldiers by the sailor and runaway slave Crispus Attucks. In an attempt to play on the prejudices of many of his fellow colonists, Adams, later the second president of the United States, decried the throng of Bostonians as having been incited by a "rabble of Negroes" and Irish. The ploy, in conjunction with the graphic evidence presented here, was successful. Captain Thomas Preston, leader of the British, and four of his men were acquitted outright. Two soldiers were convicted of the lesser charge of manslaughter, branded on the hands with the letter "M," and released.

Laura M. Miller,
Vanderbilt University

See also **Boston Massacre.**

On the evening of the fifth of March I was at home. I heard the bells ring and went to the gate. I stayed there a little and saw Mr. Lovell coming back with his buckets. I asked him where was the fire. He said it was not fire.

After that, I went into the street and saw one of my acquaintances coming up . . . holding his arm. I asked him, "What's the matter?"

He said the soldiers were fighting, had got cutlasses, and were killing everybody, and that one of them had struck him on the arm and almost cut it off. He told me I had best not go down. I said a good club was better than a cutlass, and he had better go down and see if he could not cut some too.

I went to the Town House, saw the sentinels. Numbers of boys on the other side of the way were throwing snowballs at them. The sentinels were enraged and swearing at the boys. The boys called them, "Lobsters, bloody backs," and hollered, "Who buys lobsters!"

One of my acquaintance came and told me that the soldiers had been fighting, and the people had drove them to Murray's barracks. I saw a number of people coming from Murray's barracks who went down by Jackson's corner into King Street.

Presently I heard three cheers given in King Street. I said, "We had better go down and see what's the matter." We went down to the whipping post and stood by Waldo's shop. I saw a number of people 'round the sentinel at the Custom House.

There were also a number of people who stood where I did and were picking up pieces of sea coal that had been thrown out thereabout and snowballs, and throwing them over at the sentinel. While I was standing there, there were two or three boys run out from among the people and cried, "We have got his gun away and now we will have him!"

Presently I heard three cheers given by the people at the Custom House. I said to my acquaintance I would run up and see whether the guard would turn out. I passed round the guard house and went as far as the west door of the Town House.

I saw a file of men, with an officer with a laced hat on before them. Upon that, we all went to go towards him, and when we had got about half way to them, the officer said something to them, and they filed off down the street.

Upon that, I went in the shadow towards the guard house and followed them down as far as Mr. Peck's corner. I saw them pass through the crowd and plant themselves by the Custom House. As soon as they got there, the people gave three cheers.

I went to cross over to where the soldiers were and as soon as I got a glimpse of them, I heard somebody huzza and say, "Here is old Murray with the riot act"—and they began to pelt snowballs.

A man set out and run, and I followed him as far as Philips's corner, and I do not know where he went. I turned back and went through the people until I got to the head of Royal Exchange Lane right against the soldiers. The first word I heard was a grenadier say to a man by me, "Damn you, stand back."

QUESTION. How near was he to him?

ANSWER. He was so near that the grenadier might have run him through if he had stepped one step forward. While I stopped to look at him, a person came to get through betwixt the grenadier and me, and the soldier had like to have pricked him. He turned about and said, "You damned lobster, bloody back, are you going to stab me?"

The soldier said, "By God, will I!"

Presently somebody took hold of me by the shoulder and told me to go home or I should be hurt. At the same time there were a number of people towards the Town House who said, "Come away and let the guard alone. You have nothing at all to do with them."

I turned about and saw the officer standing before the men, and one or two persons engaged in talk with him. A number were jumping on the backs of those that were talking with the officer, to get as near as they could.

QUESTION. Did you hear what they said?

ANSWER. No. Upon this, I went to go as close to the officer as I could. One of the persons who was talking with the officer turned about quick to the people and said, "Damn him, he is going to fire!" Upon that, they cried out, "Fire and be damned, who cares! Damn you, you dare not fire," and began to throw snowballs and other things, which then flew pretty thick.

QUESTION. Did they hit any of them?

ANSWER. Yes, I saw two or three of them hit. One struck a grenadier on the hat. And the people who were right before them had sticks, and as the soldiers were pushing their guns back and forth, they struck their guns, and one hit a grenadier on the fingers.

At this time, the people up at the Town House called again, "Come away! Come away!" A stout man who stood near me and right before the grenadiers as they pushed with their bayonets the length of their arms, kept striking on their guns.

The people seemed to be leaving the soldiers and to turn from them when there came down a number from Jackson's corner huzzaing and crying, "Damn them, they dare not fire!" "We are not afraid of them!"

One of these people, a stout man with a long cordwood stick, threw himself in and made a blow at the officer. I saw the office try to fend off the stroke. Whether he struck him or not, I do not know. The stout man then turned round and struck the grenadier's gun at the Captain's right hand and immediately fell in with his club and knocked his gun away and struck him over the head. The blow came either on the soldier's cheek or hat.

This stout man held the bayonet with his left hand and twitched it and cried, "Kill the dogs! Knock them over!" This was the general cry. The people then crowded in and, upon that, the grenadier gave a twitch back and relieved his gun, and he up with it and began to pay away on the people. I was then betwixt the officer and this grenadier. I turned to go off. When I had got away about the length of a gun, I turned to look towards the officer, and I heard the word, "Fire!" I thought I heard the report of a gun and, upon hearing the report, I saw the same grenadier swing his gun and immediately he discharged it.

QUESTION. Did the soldiers of that party, or any of them, step or move out of the rank in which they stood to push the people?

ANSWER. No, and if they had they might have killed me and many others with their bayonets.

QUESTION. Did you, as you passed through the people towards Royal Exchange Lane and the party, see a number of people take up any and everything they could find in the street and throw them at the soldiers?

ANSWER. Yes, I saw ten or fifteen round me do it.

QUESTION. Did you yourself. . . .

ANSWER. Yes, I did.

QUESTION. After the gun fired, where did you go?

ANSWER. I run as fast as I could into the first door I saw open . . . I was very much frightened.

DECLARATION AND RESOLVES OF THE FIRST CONTINENTAL CONGRESS
(14 October 1774)

When the First Continental Congress convened in Carpenter's Hall, Philadelphia, on September 5, 1774, one of its first actions was to articulate colonial grievances against the crown of Great Britain. Among its several complaints, Congress demanded the abolition of the so-called Intolerable Acts passed by Parliament early in the year in response to the Boston Tea Party. Widely detested, one of these allowed a change of venue to another colony or to the Mother Country for crown officers charged with capital crimes in the execution of their sanctioned duties, while another, the Quartering Act, empowered civil officers to commandeer private residences or empty buildings to house royal troops when no alternative was available. Perhaps more important than these protestations, the Declaration laid out the principle, dearly held, of self-governance or governance by consent, and was the blueprint for later documents such as the Continental Association and, in a matter of fewer than two years, the Declaration of Independence.

Laura M. Miller,
Vanderbilt University

See also **Continental Congress; Revolution, American: Political History.**

Whereas, since the close of the last war, the British parliament, claiming a power, of right, to bind the people of America by statutes in all cases whatsoever, hath, in some acts, expressly imposed taxes on them, and in others, under various presences, but in fact for the purpose of raising a revenue, hath imposed rates and duties payable in these colonies, established a board of commissioners, with unconstitutional powers, and extended the jurisdiction of courts of admiralty, not only for collecting the said duties, but for the trial of causes merely arising within the body of a county.

And whereas, in consequence of other statutes, judges, who before held only estates at will in their offices, have been made dependent on the crown alone for their salaries, and standing armies kept in times of peace. And it has lately been resolved in parliament, that by force of a statute, made in the thirty-fifth year of the reign of King Henry the Eighth, colonists may be transported to England, and tried there upon accusations for treasons and misprisions, or concealments of treasons committed in the colonies, and by a late statute, such trials have been directed in cases therein mentioned.

And whereas, in the last session of parliament, three statutes were made; one entitled, "An act to discontinue, in such manner and for such time as are therein mentioned, the landing and discharging, lading, or shipping of goods, wares and merchandise, at the town, and within the harbour of Boston, in the province of Massachusetts-Bay in New England;" another entitled, "An act for the better regulating the government of the province of Massachusetts-Bay in New England;" and another entitled, "An act for the impartial administration of justice, in the cases of persons questioned for any act done by them in the execution of the law, or for the suppression of riots and tumults, in the province of the Massachusetts-Bay in New England;" and another statute was then made, "for making more effectual provision for the government of the province of Quebec, etc." All which statutes are impolitic, unjust, and cruel, as well as unconstitutional, and most dangerous and destructive of American rights.

And whereas, assemblies have been frequently dissolved, contrary to the rights of the people, when they attempted to deliberate on grievances; and their dutiful, humble, loyal, and reasonable petitions to the crown for redress, have been repeatedly treated with contempt, by his Majesty's ministers of state:

The good people of the several colonies of New-Hampshire, Massachusetts-Bay, Rhode Island and Providence Plantations, Connecticut, New-York, New Jersey, Pennsylvania, Newcastle, Kent, and Sussex on Delaware, Maryland, Virginia, North Carolina and South Carolina, justly alarmed at these arbitrary proceedings of parliament and administration, have severally elected, constituted, and appointed deputies to meet, and sit in general Congress, in the city of Philadelphia, in order to obtain such establishment, as that their religion, laws, and liberties, may not be subverted:

Whereupon the deputies so appointed being now assembled, in a full and free representation of these colonies, taking into their most serious consideration, the best means of attaining the ends aforesaid, do, in the first place, as Englishmen, their ancestors in like cases have usually done, for asserting and vindicating their rights and liberties, declare,

That the inhabitants of the English colonies in North-America, by the immutable laws of nature, the principles of the English constitution, and the several charters or compacts, have the following RIGHTS:

Resolved, N.C.D.

1. That they are entitled to life, liberty and property: and they have never ceded to any foreign power whatever, a right to dispose of either without their consent.
2. That our ancestors, who first settled these colonies, were at the time of their emigration from the mother country, entitled to all the rights, liberties, and immunities of free and natural-born subjects, within the realm of England.
3. That by such emigration they by no means forfeited, surrendered, or lost any of those rights, but that they were, and their descendants now are, entitled to the exercise and enjoyment of all such of them, as their local and other circumstances enable them to exercise and enjoy.
4. That the foundation of English liberty, and of all free government, is a right in the people to participate in their legislative council: and as the English colonists are not represented, and from their local and other circumstances, cannot properly be represented in the British parliament, they are entitled to a free and exclusive power of legislation in their several provincial legislatures, where their right of representation can alone be preserved, in all cases of taxation and internal polity, subject only to the negative of their sovereign, in such manner as has been heretofore used and accustomed. But, from the necessity of the case, and a regard to the mutual interest of both countries, we cheerfully consent to the operation of such acts of the British parliament, as are bona fide, restrained to the regulation of our external commerce, for the purpose of securing the commercial advantages of the whole empire to the mother country, and the commercial benefits of its respective members; excluding every idea of taxation internal or external, for raising a revenue on the subjects, in America, without their consent.
5. That the respective colonies are entitled to the common law of England, and more especially to the great and inestimable privilege of being tried by their peers of the vicinage, according to the course of that law.
6. That they are entitled to the benefit of such of the English statutes, as existed at the time of their colonization; and which they have, by experience, respectively found to be applicable to their several local and other circumstances.
7. That these, his Majesty's colonies, are likewise entitled to all the immunities and privileges granted and confirmed to them by royal charters, or secured by their several codes of provincial laws.
8. That they have a right peaceably to assemble, consider of their grievances, and petition the king; and that all prosecutions, prohibitory proclamations, and commitments for the same, are illegal.
9. That the keeping a standing army in these colonies, in times of peace, without the consent of the legislature of that colony, in which such army is kept, is against law.
10. It is indispensably necessary to good government, and rendered essential by the English constitution, that the constituent branches of the legislature be independent of each other; that, therefore, the exercise of legislative power in several colonies, by a council appointed, during pleasure, by the crown, is unconstitutional, dangerous and destructive to the freedom of American legislation.

All and each of which the aforesaid deputies, in behalf of themselves, and their constituents, do claim, demand, and insist on, as their indubitable rights and liberties, which cannot be legally taken from them, altered or abridged by any power whatever, without their own consent, by their representatives in their several provincial legislature.

In the course of our inquiry, we find many infringements and violations of the foregoing rights, which, from an ardent desire, that harmony and mutual intercourse of affection and interest may be restored, we pass over for the present, and proceed to state such acts and measures as have been adopted since the last war, which demonstrate a system formed to enslave America.

Resolved, That the following acts of parliament are infringements and violations of the rights of the colonists; and that the repeal of them is essentially necessary, in order to restore harmony between Great Britain and the American colonies, viz.

The several acts of 4 Geo. III, ch. 15, and ch. 34; 5 Geo. III, ch. 25; 6 Geo. III, ch. 52; 7 Geo. III, ch. 41 and ch. 46; 8 Geo. III. ch. 22; which impose duties for the purpose of raising a revenue in America, extend the power of the admiralty courts beyond their ancient limits, deprive the American subject of trial by jury, authorize the judges certificate to indemnify the prosecutor from damages, that he might otherwise be liable to, requiring oppressive security from a claimant of ships and goods seized, before he shall be allowed to defend his property, and are subversive of American rights.

Also 12 Geo. III. ch. 24, entitled, "An act for the better preserving his majesty's dockyards, magazines, ships, ammunition, and stores," which declares a new offence in America, and deprives the American subject of a constitutional trial by jury of the vicinage, by authorizing the trial of any person, charged with the committing any offence described in the said act, out of the realm, to be indicted and tried for the same in any shire or county within the realm.

Also the three acts passed in the last session of parliament, for stopping the port and blocking up the harbour of Boston, for altering the charter and government of Massachusetts-Bay, and that which is entitled, "An act for the better administration of justice, etc."

Also the act passed in the same session for establishing the Roman Catholic religion, in the province of Quebec, abolishing the equitable system of English laws, and erecting a tyranny there, to the great danger (from so total a dissimilarity of religion, law and government) of the neighbouring British colonies, by the assistance of whose blood and treasure the said country was conquered from France.

Also the act passed in the same session, for the better providing suitable quarters for officers and soldiers in his majesty's service, in North-America.

Also, that the keeping a standing army in several of these colonies, in time of peace, without the consent of the legislature of that colony, in which such army is kept, is against law.

To these grievous acts and measures, Americans cannot submit, but in hopes their fellow subjects in Great Britain will, on a revision of them, restore us to that state, in which both countries found happiness and prosperity, we have for the present, only resolved to pursue the following peaceable measures: 1. To enter into a non-importation, non-consumption, and non-exportation agreement or association. 2. To prepare an address to the people of Great Britain, and a memorial to the inhabitants of British America: and 3. To prepare a loyal address to his majesty, agreeable to resolutions already entered into.

SOURCE: *Journals of the American Congress from 1774 to 1788.* Washington: 1823.

ADDRESS OF THE CONTINENTAL CONGRESS TO INHABITANTS OF CANADA
(29 May 1775)

When the Second Continental Congress convened in Philadelphia on 10 May 1775, the battles of Lexington and Concord had been waged and the American Revolutionary War begun. As hopes of reconciliation with the Crown of Great Britain quickly fell away, many in the Congress began to entertain the idea of a permanent American-Canadian union, and adopted the appeal seen here on 29 May. Unfortunately for the Americans, the Canadians simply were not interested. Frustrated by their northern neighbor's refusal to answer, Congress dispatched soldiers under the command of General Richard Montgomery and a brilliant young officer named Benedict Arnold to force the issue. The undertaking was a debacle. Montgomery attacked and captured Montreal, Fort Chambly, and Fort Saint John, but on 31 December 1775, he was killed during the disastrous assault on Quebec. In spite of these humiliations, many in Congress remained hopeful of an eventual merger between the two nations, and provided for such an occurrence when they drafted the Articles of Confederation in November 1777.

Laura M. Miller,
Vanderbilt University

***See also* Canada, Relations with; Continental Congress; Revolution, American: Political History.**

Alarmed by the designs of an arbitrary Ministry, to extirpate the Rights and liberties of all America, a sense of common danger conspired with the dictates of humanity, in urging us to call your attention, by our late address, to this very important object.

Since the conclusion of the late war, we have been happy in considering you as fellow-subjects, and from the commencement of the present plan for subjugating the continent, we have viewed you as fellow-sufferers with us. As we were both entitled by the bounty of an indulgent creator to freedom. And being both devoted by the cruel edicts of a despotic administration, to common ruin, we perceived the fate of the protestant and catholic colonies to be strongly linked together, and therefore invited you to join with us in resolving to be free, and in rejecting, with disdain, the fetters of slavery, however artfully polished.

We most sincerely condole with you on the arrival of that day, in the course of which, the sun could not shine on a single freeman in all your extensive dominion. Be assured, that your unmerited degradation has engaged the most unfeigned pity of your sister colonies; and we flatter ourselves you will not, by tamely bearing the yoke, suffer that pity to be supplanted by contempt.

When hardy attempts are made to deprive men of rights, bestowed by the almighty when avenues are cut thro' the most solemn compacts for the admission of despotism, when the plighted faith of government ceases to give security to loyal and dutiful subjects, and when the insidious stratagems and manoeuvres of peace become more terrible than the sanguinary operations of war, it is high time for them to assert those rights, and, with honest indignation, oppose the torrent of oppression rushing in upon them.

By the introduction of your present form of government, or rather present form of tyranny, you and your wives and your children are made slaves. You have nothing that you can call your own, and all the fruits of your labour and industry may be taken from you, whenever an avaritious governor and a rapacious council may incline to demand them. You are liable by their edicts to be transported into foreign countries to fight Battles in which you have no interest, and to spill your blood in conflicts from which neither honor nor emolument can be derived: Nay, the enjoyment of your very religion, in the present system, depends on a legislature in which you have no share, and over which you have no controul, and your priests are exposed to expulsion, banishment, and ruin, whenever their wealth and possession furnish sufficient temptation. They cannot be sure that a virtuous prince will always fill the throne, and should a wicked or a careless king concur with a wicked ministry in extracting the treasure and strength of your country, it is impossible to conceive to what variety and to what extremes of wretchedness you may, under the present establishment, be reduced.

We are informed you have already been called upon to waste your lives in a contest with us. Should you, by complying in this instance, assent to your new establishment, and a war break out with France, your wealth and your sons may be sent to perish in expeditions against their islands in the West Indies.

It cannot be presumed that these considerations will have no weight with you, or that you are so lost to all sense of honor. We can never believe that the present race of Canadians are so degenerated as to possess neither the spirit, the gallantry, nor the courage of their ancestors. You certainly will not permit the infamy and disgrace of such pusillanimity to rest on your own heads, and the consequences of it on your children forever.

We, for our parts, are determined to live free, or not at all; and are resolved, that posterity shall never reproach us with having brought slaves into the world.

Permit us again to repeat that we are your friends, not your enemies, and be not imposed upon by those who may endeavor to create animosities. The taking of the fort and military stores at Ticonderoga and Crown-Point, and the armed vessels on the lake, was dictated by the great law of self-preservation. They are intended to annoy us, and to cut off that friendly intercourse and communication, which has hitherto subsisted between you and us. We hope it has given you no uneasiness, and you may rely on our assurances, that these colonies will pursue no measures whatever, but such as friendship and a regard for our mutual safety and interest may suggest.

As our concern for your welfare entitles us to your friendship, we presume you will not, by doing us injury, reduce us to the disagreeable necessity of treating you as enemies.

We yet entertain hopes of your uniting with us in the defence of our common liberty, and there is yet reason to believe, that should we join in imploring the attention of our sovereign, to the unmerited and unparalleled oppressions of his American subjects, he will at length be undeceived, and forbid a licentious Ministry any longer to riot in the ruins of the rights of Mankind.

SOURCE: *Journals of the American Congress from 1774 to 1788.* Washington: 1823.

THE VIRGINIA DECLARATION OF RIGHTS
(1776)

One of America's fundamental political documents, Virginia's Declaration of Rights was ratified by the Virginia Constitutional Convention on 12 June 1776, and not long after was used as a model by Thomas Jefferson during the composition of the Declaration of Independence. Parts of it were later copied by other colonies, and many of its concerns helped to inspire the Constitutional Bill of Rights. Its author, the revolutionary thinker George Mason, would later serve as a member of the Constitutional Convention in 1787. Ironically, though he was instrumental in drafting the Constitution, Mason, a bitter opponent of slavery (for which he blamed the English) and the centralization of government, remained true to his principles and refused to sign.

Laura M. Miller,
Vanderbilt University

See also **Bill of Rights in U.S. Constitution; Virginia Declaration of Rights.**

I. That all men are by nature equally free and independent, and have certain inherent rights, of which, when they enter into a state of society, they cannot, by any compact, deprive or divest their posterity; namely, the enjoyment of life and liberty, with the means of acquiring and possessing property, and pursuing and obtaining happiness and safety.

II. That all power is vested in, and consequently derived from, the people; that magistrates are their trustees and servants, and at all times amenable to them.

III. That government is, or ought to be, instituted for the common benefit, protection, and security of the people, nation or community; of all the various modes and forms of government that is best, which is capable of producing the greatest degree of happiness and safety and is most effectually secured against the danger of maladministration; and that, whenever any government shall be found inadequate or contrary to these purposes, a majority of the community hath an indubitable, unalienable, and indefeasible right to reform, alter or abolish it, in such manner as shall be judged most conducive to the public weal.

IV. That no man, or set of men, are entitled to exclusive or separate emoluments or privileges from the community, but in consideration of public services; which, not being descendible, neither ought the offices of magistrate, legislator, or judge be hereditary.

V. That the legislative and executive powers of the state should be separate and distinct from the judicative; and, that the members of the two first may be restrained from oppression by feeling and participating the burthens of the people, they should, at fixed periods, be reduced to a private station, return into that body from which they were originally taken, and the vacancies be supplied by frequent, certain, and regular elections in which all, or any part of the former members, to be again eligible, or ineligible, as the laws shall direct.

VI. That elections of members to serve as representatives of the people in assembly ought to be free; and that all men, having sufficient evidence of permanent common interest with, and attachment to, the community have the right of suffrage and cannot be taxed or deprived of their property for public uses without their own consent or that of their representatives so elected, nor bound by any law to which they have not, in like manner, assented, for the public good.

VII. That all power of suspending laws, or the execution of laws, by any authority without consent of the representatives of the people is injurious to their rights and ought not to be exercised.

VIII. That in all capital or criminal prosecutions a man hath a right to demand the cause and nature of his accusation to be confronted with the accusers and witnesses, to call for evidence in his favor, and to a speedy trial by an impartial jury of his vicinage, without whose unanimous consent he cannot be found guilty, nor can he be compelled to give evidence against himself; that no man be deprived of his liberty except by the law of the land or the judgement of his peers.

IX. That excessive bail ought not to be required, nor excessive fines imposed; nor cruel and unusual punishments inflicted.

X. That general warrants, whereby any officer or messenger may be commanded to search suspected places without evidence of a fact committed, or to seize any person or persons not named, or whose offense is not particularly described and supported by evidence, are grievous and oppressive and ought not to be granted.

XI. That in controversies respecting property and in suits between man and man, the ancient trial by jury is preferable to any other and ought to be held sacred.

XII. That the freedom of the press is one of the greatest bulwarks of liberty and can never be restrained but by despotic governments.

XIII. That a well regulated militia, composed of the body of the people, trained to arms, is the proper, natural, and safe defense of a free state; that standing armies, in time of peace, should be avoided as dangerous to liberty; and that, in all cases, the military should be under strict subordination to, and be governed by, the civil power.

XIV. That the people have a right to uniform government; and therefore, that no government separate from, or independent of, the government of Virginia, ought to be erected or established within the limits thereof.

XV. That no free government, or the blessings of liberty, can be preserved to any people but by a firm adherence to justice, moderation, temperance, frugality, and virtue and by frequent recurrence to fundamental principles.

XVI. That religion, or the duty which we owe to our Creator and the manner of discharging it, can be directed by reason and conviction, not by force or violence; and therefore, all men are equally entitled to the free exercise of religion, according to the dictates of conscience; and that it is the mutual duty of all to practice Christian forbearance, love, and charity toward each other.

Adopted unanimously June 12, 1776 Virginia Convention of Delegates drafted by Mr. George Mason

SOURCE: Thorpe, Francis N., ed. *The Federal and State Constitutions, Colonial Charters, and Other Organic Laws of the States, Territories, and Colonies Now or Heretofore Forming the United States of America.* Washington: Government Printing Office, 1909.

EXCERPT FROM "COMMON SENSE"
(1776, by Thomas Paine)

With the publication of *Common Sense* early in the winter of 1776 came also the inevitability of war between Great Britain and her colonies in North America. All that had been needed, it seems, was a voice to finally forcefully articulate the patriot's case against the mother country and to insist upon the impossibility of reconciliation with the Crown. Penned anonymously by the English-born Thomas Paine, who had immigrated to America at the urging of Benjamin Franklin, the tract was an astonishing sensation, selling some 120,000 copies during its first three months, and nearly a half-million throughout the years of the Revolution. George Washington himself commended the power of its reasoning. Paine became a hero in the colonies and was, at least for a time, considered one of America's foremost revolutionary thinkers. Later, his "Crisis" pamphlets would be an inspiration to many throughout the long, difficult years of the war.

Laura M. Miller,
Vanderbilt University

***See also Common Sense*; Revolution, American: Political History.**

A Call for Independence

LEAVING the moral part to private reflection, I shall chiefly confine my further remarks to the following heads:

First, That it is the interest of America to be separated from Britain.

Secondly, Which is the easiest and most practicable plan, reconciliation or independence? with some occasional remarks.

In support of the first, I could, if I judged it proper, produce the opinion of some of the ablest and most experienced men on this continent; and whose sentiments, on that head, are not yet publicly known. It is in reality a self-evident position: For no nation, in a state of foreign dependence, limited in its commerce, and cramped and fettered in its legislative powers, can ever arrive at any material eminence. America does not yet know what opulence is; and although the progress which she has made stands unparalleled in the history of other nations, it is but childhood, compared with what she would be capable of arriving at, had she, as she ought to have, the legislative powers in her own hands. England is, at this time, proudly coveting what would do her no good, were she to accomplish it; and the continent hesitating on a matter, which will be her final ruin if neglected. It is the commerce, and not the conquest of America, by which England is to be benefited, and that would in a great measure continue, were the countries as independent of each other as France and Spain; because in many articles, neither can go to a better market. But it is the independence of this country on Britain or any other, which is now the main and only object worthy of contention, and which, like all other truths discovered by necessity, will appear clearer and stronger every day.

First. Because it will come to that one time or other.

Secondly. Because the longer it is delayed, the harder it will be to accomplish.

I have frequently amused myself both in public and private companies, with silently remarking the specious errors of those who speak without reflecting. And among the many which I have heard, the following seems the most general, viz. that had this rupture happened forty or fifty years hence, instead of now, the Continent would have been more able to have shaken off the dependence. To which I reply, that our military ability at this time, arises from the experience gained in the late war, and which in forty or fifty years time, would have been totally extinct. . . .

Should affairs be patched up with Britain, and she to remain the governing and sovereign power of America, (which as matters are now circumstanced, is giving up the point entirely) we shall deprive ourselves of the very means of sinking the debt we have, or may contract. The value of the back lands, which some of the provinces are clandestinely deprived of, by the unjust extension of the limits of Canada, valued only at five pounds sterling per hundred acres, amount to upwards of twenty-five millions, Pennsylvania currency; and the quit-rents at one penny sterling per acre, to two millions yearly. . . .

I proceed now to the second head, viz. Which is the easiest and most practicable plan, Reconciliation or Independence; with some occasional remarks.

He who takes nature for his guide, is not easily beaten out of his argument, and on that ground, I answer generally, that independence being a single simple line, contained within ourselves; and reconciliation, a matter of exceedingly perplexed and complicated, and in which, a treacherous capricious court is to interfere, gives the answer without a doubt.

The present state of America is truly alarming to every man who is capable of reflection. Without law, without government, without any other mode of power than what is founded on, and granted by courtesy. Held together by an unexampled concurrence of sentiment, which, is nevertheless subject to change, and which, every secret enemy is endeavoring to dissolve. Our present condition is, legislation without law; wisdom without a plan; a Constitution without a name; and, what is strangely astonishing, perfect independence, contending for dependence. The instance is without a precedent; the case never existed before; and who can tell what may be the event? The property of no man is secure in the present unbraced system of things. The mind of the multitude is left at random, and seeing no fixed object before them, they pursue such as fancy or opinion starts. Nothing is criminal; there is no such thing as treason; wherefore, every one thinks himself at liberty to act as he pleases. The Tories would not have dared to assemble offensively, had they known that their lives, by that act, were forfeited to the laws of the State. A line of distinction should be drawn between English soldiers taken in battle, and inhabitants of America taken in arms. The first are prisoners, but the latter traitors. The one forfeits his liberty, the other his head....

Put us, say some, upon the footing we were on in sixty-three.... To be on the footing of sixty-three, it is not sufficient, that the laws only be put on the same state, but that our circumstances, likewise be put on the same state; our burnt and destroyed towns repaired or built up, our private losses made good, our public debts (contracted for defense) discharged; otherwise we shall be millions worse than we were at that enviable period. Such a request, had it been complied with a year ago, would have won the heart and soul of the Continent, but now it is too late. "The Rubicon is passed."

Besides, the taking up arms, merely to enforce the repeal of a pecuniary law, seems as unwarrantable by the divine law, and as repugnant to human feelings, as the taking up arms to enforce the obedience thereto. The object, on either side, does not justify the means; for the lives of men are too valuable, to be cast away on such trifles. It is the violence which is done and threatened to our persons; the destruction of our property by an armed force; the invasion of our country by fire and sword, which conscientiously qualifies the use of arms: And the instant, in which such a mode of defense became necessary, all subjection to Britain ought to have ceased; and the independency of America, should have been considered, as dating its era from, and published, by the first musket that was fired against her. This line is a line of consistency; neither drawn by caprice, nor extended by ambition; but produced by a chain of events, of which the colonies were not the authors.

I shall conclude these remarks, with the following timely and well intended hint. We ought to reflect that there are three different ways, by which an independency may hereafter be effected; and that one of those three, will one day or other, be the fate of America, viz. By the legal voice of the people in Congress; by a military power; or by a mob. It may not always happen that our soldiers are citizens, and the multitude a body of reasonable men; virtue, as I have already remarked, is not hereditary, neither is it perpetual. Should an independency be brought about by the first of those means, we have every opportunity and every encouragement before us, to form the noblest purest constitution on the face of the earth. We have it in our power to begin the world over again. A situation, similar to the present, has not happened since the days of Noah until now. The birthday of a new world is at hand, and a race of men, perhaps as numerous as all Europe contains, are to receive their portion of freedom from the event of a few months. The reflection is awful and in this point of view, how trifling, how ridiculous, do the little paltry cavilings, of a few weak or interested men appear, when weighed against the business of a world....

In short, independence is the only bond that can tie and keep us together. We shall then see our object, and our ears will be legally shut against the schemes of an intriguing, as well as a cruel enemy. We shall then too be on a proper footing to treat with Britain; for there is reason to conclude, that the pride of that court will be less hurt by treating with the American states for terms of peace, than with those she denominates "rebellious subjects," for terms of accommodation. It is our delaying it that encourages her to hope for conquest, and our backwardness tends only to prolong the war. As we have, without any good effect therefrom, withheld our trade to obtain a redress of our grievances, let us now try the alternative, by independently redressing them ourselves, and then offering to open the trade. The mercantile and reasonable part in England will be still with us; because, peace with trade, is preferable to war without it. And if this offer is not accepted, other courts may be applied to. On these grounds I rest the matter. And as no offer hath yet been made to refute the doctrine contained in the former editions of this pamphlet, it is a negative proof, that either the doctrine cannot be refuted, or, that the party in favor of it are too numerous to be opposed. Wherefore instead of gazing at each other with suspicious or doubtful curiosity, let each of us hold out to his neighbor the hearty hand of friendship, and unite in drawing a line, which, like an act of oblivion, shall bury in forgetfulness every former dissension. Let the names of Whig and Tory be extinct; and let none other be heard among us, than those of a good citizen, an open and resolute friend, and a virtuous supporter of the rights of mankind and of the free and independent states of America.

SOURCE: Paine, Thomas. "Common Sense." Philadelphia: self-published pamphlet, 1776.

DECLARATION OF INDEPENDENCE
(1776)

Originally designed to influence the sometimes reluctant and uncertain public opinion, both in the colonies and abroad (particularly in France, a potential military ally), the Declaration of Independence was written by Thomas Jefferson and ratified shortly after by the Second Continental Congress on 4 July 1776, two days after that body had officially severed its ties to Great Britain.

In composing this greatest, most famous of legal documents, Jefferson, already well regarded as an essayist, drew heavily not only on the ideas of his fellow patriots, but also on the natural-rights theories of John Locke and the Swiss legal philosophy of Emerich de Vattel. Although Jefferson's bitter attack on the institution of slavery was rejected by the convention in deference to South Carolina and Georgia, the principles set forth in the Declaration, among them the revolutionary notion that human beings had rights which even governments and kings could not take from them, would nevertheless become a rallying cry not only for Jefferson and his New World contemporaries, but also for many people at all times in the United States and around the world.

Laura M. Miller,
Vanderbilt University

See also **Continental Congress; Declaration of Independence; Revolution, American: Political History.**

WHEN in the Course of human Events, it becomes necessary for one People to dissolve the Political Bands which have connected them with another, and to assume among the Powers of the Earth, the separate and equal Station to which the Laws of Nature and of Nature's God entitle them, a decent Respect to the Opinions of Mankind requires that they should declare the causes which impel them to the Separation.

WE hold these Truths to be self-evident, that all Men are created equal, that they are endowed by their Creator with certain unalienable Rights, that among these are Life, Liberty and the Pursuit of Happiness—That to secure these Rights, Governments are instituted among Men, deriving their just Powers from the Consent of the Governed, that whenever any Form of Government becomes destructive of these Ends, it is the Right of the People to alter or to abolish it, and to institute new Government, laying its Foundation on such Principles, and organizing its Powers in such Form, as to them shall seem most likely to effect their Safety and Happiness. Prudence, indeed, will dictate that Governments long established should not be changed for light and transient Causes; and accordingly all Experience hath shewn, that Mankind are more disposed to suffer, while Evils are sufferable, than to right themselves by abolishing the Forms to which they are accustomed. But when a long Train of Abuses and Usurpations, pursuing invariably the same Object, evinces a Design to reduce them under absolute Despotism, it is their Right, it is their Duty, to throw off such Government, and to provide new Guards for their future Security. Such has been the patient Sufferance of these Colonies; and such is now the Necessity which constrains them to alter their former Systems of Government. The History of the present King of Great-Britain is a History of repeated Injuries and Usurpations, all having in direct Object the Establishment of an absolute Tyranny over these States. To prove this, let Facts be submitted to a candid World.

HE has refused his Assent to Laws, the most wholesome and necessary for the public Good.

HE has forbidden his Governors to pass Laws of immediate and pressing Importance, unless suspended in their Operation till his Assent should be obtained; and when so suspended, he has utterly neglected to attend to them.

HE has refused to pass other Laws for the Accommodation of large Districts of People, unless those People would relinquish the Right of Representation in the Legislature, a Right inestimable to them, and formidable to Tyrants only.

HE has called together Legislative Bodies at Places unusual, uncomfortable, and distant from the Depository of their public Records, for the sole Purpose of fatiguing them into Compliance with his Measures.

HE has dissolved Representative Houses repeatedly, for opposing with manly Firmness his Invasions on the Rights of the People.

HE has refused for a long Time, after such Dissolutions, to cause others to be elected; whereby the Legislative F, incapable of the Annihilation, have returned to the People at large for their exercise; the State remaining in the mean time exposed to all the

Dangers of Invasion from without, and the Convulsions within.

HE has endeavoured to prevent the Population of these States; for that Purpose obstructing the Laws for Naturalization of Foreigners; refusing to pass others to encourage their Migrations hither, and raising the Conditions of new Appropriations of Lands.

HE has obstructed the Administration of Justice, by refusing his Assent to Laws for establishing Judiciary Powers.

HE has made Judges dependent on his Will alone, for the Tenure of their Offices, and the Amount and Payment of their Salaries.

HE has erected a Multitude of new Offices, and sent hither Swarms of Officers to harrass our People, and eat out their Substance.

HE has kept among us, in Times of Peace, Standing Armies, without the consent of our Legislatures.

HE has affected to render the Military independent of and superior to the Civil Power. HE has combined with others to subject us to a Jurisdiction foreign to our Constitution, and unacknowledged by our Laws; giving his Assent to their Acts of pretended Legislation:

FOR quartering large Bodies of Armed Troops among us;

FOR protecting them, by a mock Trial, from Punishment for any Murders which they should commit on the Inhabitants of these States:

FOR cutting off our Trade with all Parts of the World:

FOR imposing Taxes on us without our Consent:

FOR depriving us, in many Cases, of the Benefits of Trial by Jury:

FOR transporting us beyond Seas to be tried for pretended Offences:

FOR abolishing the free System of English Laws in a neighbouring Province, establishing therein an arbitrary Government, and enlarging its Boundaries, so as to render it at once an Example and fit Instrument for introducing the same absolute Rules into these Colonies:

FOR taking away our Charters, abolishing our most valuable Laws, and altering fundamentally the Forms of our Governments:

FOR suspending our own Legislatures, and declaring themselves invested with Power to legislate for us in all Cases whatsoever.

HE has abdicated Government here, by declaring us out of his Protection and waging War against us.

HE has plundered our Seas, ravaged our Coasts, burnt our Towns, and destroyed the Lives of our People.

HE is, at this Time, transporting large Armies of foreign Mercenaries to compleat the Works of Death, Desolation, and Tyranny, already begun with circumstances of Cruelty and Perfidy, scarcely paralleled in the most barbarous Ages, and totally unworthy the Head of a civilized Nation.

HE has constrained our fellow Citizens taken Captive on the high Seas to bear Arms against their Country, to become the Executioners of their Friends and Brethren, or to fall themselves by their Hands.

HE has excited domestic Insurrections amongst us, and has endeavoured to bring on the Inhabitants of our Frontiers, the merciless Indian Savages, whose known Rule of Warfare, is an undistinguished Destruction, of all Ages, Sexes and Conditions.

IN every stage of these Oppressions we have Petitioned for Redress in the most humble Terms: Our repeated Petitions have been answered only by repeated Injury. A Prince, whose Character is thus marked by every act which may define a Tyrant, is unfit to be the Ruler of a free People.

NOR have we been wanting in Attentions to our British Brethren. We have warned them from Time to Time of Attempts by their Legislature to extend an unwarrantable Jurisdiction over us. We have reminded them of the Circumstances of our Emigration and Settlement here. We have appealed to their native Justice and Magnanimity, and we have conjured them by the Ties of our common Kindred to disavow these Usurpations, which, would inevitably interrupt our Connections and Correspondence. They too have been deaf to the Voice of Justice and of Consanguinity. We must, therefore, acquiesce in the Necessity, which denounces our Separation, and hold them, as we hold the rest of Mankind, Enemies in War, in Peace, Friends.

WE, therefore, the Representatives of the UNITED STATES OF AMERICA, in GENERAL CONGRESS, Assembled, appealing to the Supreme Judge of the World for the Rectitude of our Intentions, do, in the Name, and by Authority of the good People of these Colonies, solemnly Publish and Declare, That these United Colonies are, and of Right ought to be, FREE AND INDEPENDENT STATES; that they are absolved from all Allegiance to the British Crown, and that all political Connection between them and the State of Great-Britain, is and ought to be totally dissolved; and that as FREE AND INDEPENDENT STATES, they have full Power to levy War, conclude Peace, contract Alliances, establish Commerce, and to do all other Acts and Things which INDEPENDENT STATES may of right do. And for the support of this Declaration, with a firm Reliance on the Protection of divine Providence, we mutually pledge to each other our Lives, our Fortunes, and our sacred Honor.

John Hancock.

GEORGIA, *Button Gwinnett, Lyman Hall, Geo. Walton.*

NORTH-CAROLINA, *Wm. Hooper, Joseph Hewes, John Penn.*
SOUTH-CAROLINA, *Edward Rutledge, Thos Heyward, junr., Thomas Lynch, junr., Arthur Middleton.*
MARYLAND, *Samuel Chase, Wm. Paca, Thos. Stone, Charles Carroll, of Carrollton.*
VIRGINIA, *George Wythe, Richard Henry Lee, Ths. Jefferson, Benja. Harrison, Thos. Nelson, jr., Francis Lightfoot Lee, Carter Braxton.*
PENNSYLVANIA, *Robt. Morris, Benjamin Rush, Benja. Franklin, John Morton, Geo. Clymer, Jas. Smith, Geo. Taylor, James Wilson, Geo. Ross.*
DELAWARE, *Caesar Rodney, Geo. Read.*
NEW-YORK, *Wm. Floyd, Phil. Livingston, Frank Lewis, Lewis Morris.*
NEW-JERSEY, *Richd. Stockton, Jno. Witherspoon, Fras. Hopkinson, John Hart, Abra. Clark.*
NEW-HAMPSHIRE, *Josiah Bartlett, Wm. Whipple, Matthew Thornton.*
MASSACHUSETTS-BAY, *Saml. Adams, John Adams, Robt. Treat Paine, Elbridge Gerry.*
RHODE-ISLAND AND PROVIDENCE, *C. Step. Hopkins, William Ellery.*
CONNECTICUT, *Roger Sherman, Saml. Huntington, Wm. Williams, Oliver Wolcott.*
IN CONGRESS, JANUARY 18, 1777.

SOURCE: *Journals of the American Congress from 1774 to 1788.* Washington: 1823.

PAUL REVERE'S ACCOUNT OF HIS RIDE
(1775)

Like the Boston Massacre or Washington crossing the Delaware, the midnight ride of the Boston silversmith and printmaker Paul Revere (1734–1818) has become one of the most enduring and misrepresented images of the American Revolution. Asked by his friend, the political activist and fellow Mason Dr. Joseph Warren, to carry news of the British landing and advance toward Lexington, Massachusetts, Revere set out from Boston at around ten o'clock on 18 April 1775. He and his two companions, William Dawes and Dr. Samuel Prescott, were detained by British troops just outside Lexington. Although all three eventually escaped, Revere was left without a mount and had to continue toward Concord afoot. Revere himself would compose several versions of the incident throughout his life, but it was not until 1861 and the publication of William Wordsworth Longfellow's commemorative poem in the *Atlantic Monthly,* that Revere's reputation expanded beyond the local. That poem made him a figure of lasting national prominence, a symbol of all things American, intrepid, and fleet.

Laura M. Miller,
Vanderbilt University

See also **Revere's Ride.**

I, PAUL REVERE, of Boston, in the colony of the Massachusetts Bay in New England; of lawful age, do testify and say; that I was sent for by Dr. Joseph Warren, of said Boston, on the evening of the 18th of April, about 10 o'clock; when he desired me, "to go to Lexington, and inform Mr. Samuel Adams, and the Hon. John Hancock Esq. that there was a number of soldiers, composed of light troops, and grenadiers, marching to the bottom of the common, where was a number of boats to receive them; it was supposed, that they were going to Lexington, by the way of Cambridge River, to take them, or go to Concord, to destroy the colony stores."

I proceeded immediately, and was put across Charles River and landed near Charlestown Battery; went in town, and there got a horse. While in Charlestown, I was informed by Richard Devens Esq. that he met that evening, after sunset, nine officers of the ministerial army [British regulars], mounted on good horses, and armed, going towards Concord.

I set off, it was then about 11 o'clock, the moon shone bright. I had got almost over Charlestown Common, towards Cambridge, when I saw two officers on horse-back, standing under the shade of a tree, in a narrow part of the road. I was near enough to see their holsters and cockades. One of them started his horse towards me, the other up the road, as I supposed, to head me, should I escape the first. I turned my horses short about, and rode upon a full gallop for Mistick Road, he followed me about 300 yards, and finding he could not catch me, returned. I proceeded to Lexington, through Mistick, and alarmed Mr. Adams and Col. Hancock.

After I had been there about half an hour Mr. Daws arrived, who came from Boston, over the Neck.

We set off for Concord, and were overtaken by a young gentleman named Prescot, who belonged to Concord, and was going home. When we had got about half way from Lexington to Concord, the other two stopped at a house to awake the man, I kept along. When I had got about 200 yards ahead of them, I saw two officers as before. I called to my company to come up, saying here was two of them, (for I had told them what Mr. Devens told me, and of my being stopped). In an instant I saw four of them, who rode up to me with their pistols in their bands, said "G—d d—n you, stop. If you go an inch further, you are a dead man." Immediately Mr. Prescot came up. We attempted to get through them, but they kept before us, and swore if we did not turn in to that pasture, they would blow our brains out, (they had placed themselves opposite to a pair of bars, and had taken the bars down). They forced us in. When we had got in, Mr. Prescot said "Put on!" He took to the left, I to the right towards a wood at the bottom of the pasture, intending, when I gained that, to jump my horse and run afoot. Just as I reached it, out started six officers, seized my bridle, put their pistols to my breast, ordered me to dismount, which I did. One of them, who appeared to have the command there, and much of a gentleman, asked me where I came from; I told him. He asked what time I left it. I told him, he seemed surprised, said "Sir, may I crave your name?" I answered "My name is Revere. "What" said he, "Paul Revere"? I answered "Yes." The others abused much; but he told me not to be afraid, no one should hurt me. I told him they would miss their aim. He said they should not, they were only waiting for some deserters they expected down the road. I told him I knew better, I knew what they were after; that I had alarmed the country all the way up, that their boats were caught aground, and I should have 500 men there soon. One of them said they had 1500 coming; he seemed surprised and rode off into the road, and informed them who took me, they came down immediately on a full gallop. One of them (whom I since learned was Major Mitchel of the 5th Reg.) clapped his pistol to my head, and said he was going to ask me some questions, and if I did not tell the truth, he would blow my brains out. I told him I esteemed myself a man of truth, that he had stopped me on the highway, and made me a prisoner, I knew not by what right; I would tell him the truth; I was not afraid. He then asked me the same questions that the other did, and many more, but was more particular; I gave him much the same answers. He then ordered me to mount my horse, they first searched me for pistols. When I was mounted, the Major took the reins out of my hand, and said "By G—d Sir, you are not to ride with reins I assure you;" and gave them to an officer on my right, to lead me. He then ordered 4 men out of the bushes, and to mount their horses; they were country men which they had stopped who were going home; then ordered us to march. He said to me, "We are now going towards your friends, and if you attempt to run, or we are insulted, we will blow your brains out." When we had got into the road they formed a circle, and ordered the prisoners in the center, and to lead me in the front. We rode towards Lexington at a quick pace; they very often insulted me calling me rebel, etc., etc. After we had got about a mile, I was given to the sergeant to lead, he was ordered to take out his pistol, (he rode with a hanger,) and if I ran, to execute the major's sentence.

When we got within about half a mile of the Meeting House we heard a gun fired. The Major asked me what it was for, I told him to alarm the country; he ordered the four prisoners to dismount, they did, then one of the officers dismounted and cut the bridles and saddles off the horses, and drove them away, and told the men they might go about their business. I asked the Major to dismiss me, he said he would carry me, let the consequence be what it will. He then ordered us to march.

When we got within sight of the Meeting House, we heard a volley of guns fired, as I supposed at the tavern, as an alarm; the Major ordered us to halt, he asked me how far it was to Cambridge, and many more questions, which I answered. He then asked the sergeant, if his horse was tired, he said yes; he ordered him to take my horse. I dismounted, and the sergeant mounted my horse; they cut the bridle and saddle of the sergeant's horse, and rode off down the road. I then went to the house were I left Messrs. Adams and Hancock, and told them what had happened; their friends advised them to go out of the way; I went with them, about two miles across road.

After resting myself, I set off with another man to go back to the tavern, to inquire the news; when we got there, we were told the troops were within two miles. We went into the tavern to get a trunk of papers belonging to Col. Hancock. Before we left the house, I saw the ministerial troops from the chamber window. We made haste, and had to pass through our militia, who were on a green behind the Meeting House, to the number as I supposed, about 50 or 60, I went through them; as I passed I heard the commanding officer speak to his men to this purpose; "Let the troops pass by, and don't molest them, without they begin first." I had to go across road; but had not got half gunshot off, when the ministerial troops appeared in sight, behind the Meeting House. They made a short halt, when one gun was fired. I heard the report, turned my head, and saw the smoke in front of the troops. They immediately gave a great shout, ran a few paces, and then the whole fired. I could first distinguish irregular firing, which I supposed was the advance guard, and then platoons; at this time I could not see our militia, for they were covered from me by a house at the bottom of the street. And further saith not.

PAUL REVERE.

BATTLE OF LEXINGTON, AMERICAN AND BRITISH ACCOUNTS
(26 April 1775)

Here the opposing tactics and perceptions of the two sides in the American Revolutionary War are laid bare. On 18 April 1775 in Boston, British General Thomas Gage was ordered to destroy weapons and ammunition being stored in Concord, fifteen miles away. Gage mustered some 700 to 900 light infantrymen and grenadiers from the Boston Garrison and placed them under the command of Lieutenant Colonel Francis Smith. Unfortunately for the British, along the way they encountered a waiting colonial militia, exchanged shots with them (though it is unclear who fired first), and only a little while later were in full retreat, enduring terrible casualties along the way. Smith's inexperienced soldiers were unaccustomed to facing guerilla tactics. When the colonists refused to form a firing line for them to shoot at, the British lost their courage and broke ranks, fleeing back to Boston. The American Revolutionary War had begun. The battle would come to stand as an important propaganda victory for the separatists, who used it to sway the large majority of colonists, some two-thirds, still loyal to the Crown.

Laura M. Miller,
Vanderbilt University

***See also* Lexington and Concord, Battles of; Revolution, American: Military History.**

In provincial congress of Massachusetts, to the inhabitants of Great Britain

Friends and fellow subjects—Hostilities are at length commenced in this colony by the troops under the command of general Gage, and it being of the greatest importance, that an early, true, and authentic account of this inhuman proceeding should be known to you, the congress of this colony have transmitted the same, and from want of a session of the hon. continental congress, think it proper to address you on the alarming occasion.

By the clearest depositions relative to this transaction, it will appear that on the night preceding the nineteenth of April instant, a body of the king's troops, under the command of colonel Smith, were secretly landed at Cambridge, with an apparent design to take or destroy the military and other stores, provided for the defence of this colony, and deposited at Concord—that some inhabitants of the colony, on the night aforesaid, whilst travelling peaceably on the road, between Boston and Concord, were seized and greatly abused by armed men, who appeared to be officers of general Gage's army; that the town of Lexington, by these means, was alarmed, and a company of the inhabitants mustered on the occasion—that the regular troops on their way to Concord, marched into the said town of Lexington, and the said company, on their approach, began to disperse—that, notwithstanding this, the regulars rushed on with great violence and first began hostilities, by firing on said Lexington company, whereby they killed eight, and wounded several others—that the regulars continued their fire, until those of said company, who were neither killed nor wounded, had made their escape—that colonel Smith, with the detachment then marched to Concord, where a number of provincials were again fired on by the troops, two of them killed and several wounded, before the provincials fired on them, and provincials were again fired on by the troops, produced an engagement that lasted through the day, in which many of the provincials and more of the regular troops were killed and wounded.

To give a particular account of the ravages of the troops, as they retreated from Concord to Charlestown, would be very difficult, if not impracticable; let it suffice to say, that a great number of the houses on the road were plundered and rendered unfit for use, several were burnt, women in child-bed were driven by the soldiery naked into the streets, old men peaceably in their houses were shot dead, and such scenes exhibited as would disgrace the annals of the most uncivilized nation.

These, brethren, are marks of ministerial vengeance against this colony, for refusing, with her sister colonies, a submission to slavery; but they have not yet detached us from our royal sovereign. We profess to be his loyal and dutiful subjects, and so hardly dealt with as we have been, are still ready, with our lives and fortunes, to defend his person, family, crown and dignity. Nevertheless, to the persecution and tyranny of his cruel ministry we will not tamely submit—appealing to Heaven for the justice of our cause, we determine to die or be free....

By order,
Joseph Warren, President

English account of the battle of Lexington: Report of Lieutenant-Colonel Smith to Governor Gage

22 April 1775

SIR,—In obedience to your Excellency's commands, I marched on the evening of the 18th inst. with the corps of grenadiers and light infantry for Concord, to execute your

Excellency's orders with respect to destroying all ammunition, artillery, tents, &c, collected there, which was effected, having knocked off the trunnions of three pieces of iron ordnance, some new gun-carriages, a great number of carriage-wheels burnt, a considerable quantity of flour, some gun-powder and musquet-balls, with other small articles thrown into the river. Notwithstanding we marched with the utmost expedition and secrecy, we found the country had intelligence or strong suspicion of our coming, and fired many signal guns, and rung the alarm bells repeatedly; and were informed, when at Concord, that some cannon had been taken out of the town that day, that others, with some stores, had been carried three days before, which prevented our having an opportunity of destroying so much as might have been expected at our first setting off.

I think it proper to observe, that when I had got some miles on the march from Boston, I detached six light infantry companies to march with all expedition to seize the two bridges on different roads beyond Concord. On these companies' arrival at Lexington, I understand, from the report of Major Pitcairn, who was with them, and from many officers, that they found on a green close to the road a body of the country people drawn up in military order, with arms and accoutrements, and, as appeared after, loaded; and that they had posted some men in a dwelling and Meeting-house. Our troops advanced towards them, without any intention of injuring them, further than to inquire the reason of their being thus assembled, and, if not satisfactory, to have secured their arms; but they in confusion went off, principally to the left, only one of them fired before he went off, and three or four more jumped over a wall and fired from behind it among the soldiers; on which the troops returned it, and killed several of them. They likewise fired on the soldiers from the Meeting and dwelling-houses.... Rather earlier than this, on the road, a countryman from behind a wall had snapped his piece at Lieutenants Adair and Sutherland, but it flashed and did not go off. After this we saw some in the woods, but marched on to Concord without anything further happening. While at Concord we saw vast numbers assembling in many parts; at one of the bridges they marched down, with a very considerable body, on the light infantry posted there. On their coming pretty near, one of our men fired on them, which they returned; on which an action ensued, and some few were killed and wounded. In this affair, it appears that, after the bridge was quitted, they scalped and otherwise ill-treated one or two of the of the men who were either killed or severely wounded. . . . On our leaving Concord to return to Boston, they began to fire on us from behind the walls, ditches, trees. &c., which, as we marched, increased to a very great degree, and continued without intermission of five minutes altogether, for, I believe, upwards of eighteen miles; so that I can't think but it must have been a preconcerted scheme in them, to attack the King's troops the first favorable opportunity that offered, otherwise, I think they could not, in so short a time from our marching out, have raised such a numerous body, and for so great a space of ground. Notwithstanding the enemy's numbers, they did not make one gallant attempt during so long an action, though our men were so very much fatigued, but kept under cover.

I have the honor, &c.,
F. Smith, Lieutenant-Colonel 10th Foot

SOURCE: Niles, Hezekiah, ed. *Principles and Acts of the Revolution in America.* Baltimore: W. O. Niles, 1822.

LETTERS OF ABIGAIL AND JOHN ADAMS
(1776)

Abigail Adams was thirty-one years old and her husband John was forty-one when they exchanged these letters. Abigail was the daughter of the Reverend William and Elizabeth Quincy Smith of Weymouth, Massachusetts. She had been a well-read young woman, which attracted the attention of John Adams of Braintree, a graduate of Harvard College, schoolteacher, and lawyer-in-training. They married in 1764. They kept their farm in Braintree even as John's law practice grew and they relocated to Boston. Abigail kept house, bore five children, and supported John in his efforts to make the rule of law the foundation for government and society in America. John became a very vocal advocate for American rights, yet his defense of the British soldiers involved in the Boston Massacre showed that his concern for justice was equally great. He represented Massachusetts in the First Continental Congress in 1774, followed by the Second Continental Congress a year later. This latter Congress was still meeting in Philadelphia when Abigail wrote John in March 1776.

Abigail's love for John and the wit of her personality surface in letters echoing the formal standards of the epistle. The elegance of the correspondent's handwriting matched the artistry of words and sentences. Abigail's letter shows that she completely understood the political situation of the spring of 1776. The thirteen colonies were loosely united by a common enemy, otherwise the middle-class farmers and merchants of New England would want little to do with the arrogant aristocrats of the South who enslaved other human beings even as they proclaimed the God-given rights of equality and freedom. Abigail was tongue in cheek in chastising John not to forget the "ladies" and their rights, which she clearly considered to be equal to their husbands.

The standards of eighteenth-century letter writing were to respond to each topic in the order presented in a letter. John knew Abigail was his intellectual equal, and he treated her accordingly, responding to each of her queries as he would any male correspondent. He responded in kind to her playful yet wholly serious comments about women's rights, arguing that his wife and other "saucy" colonial dames have the power in fact if not in name.

Russell Lawson,
Bacone College

See also **Gender and Gender Roles; Revolution, American: Political History.**

The first letter is from Abigail Adams to her husband John Adams. The second is his reply.

Braintree, 31 March 1776

I wish you would ever write me a letter half as long as I write you, and tell me, if you may, where your fleet are gone; what sort of defence Virginia can make against our common enemy; whether it is so situated as to make an able defense. Are not the gentry lords, and the common people vassals? Are they not like the uncivilized vassals Britain represents us to be? I hope their riflemen, who have shown themselves very savage and even bloodthirsty, are not a specimen of the generality of the people. I am willing to allow the colony great merit for having produced a Washington; but they have been shamefully duped by a Dunmore.

I have sometimes been ready to think that the passion for liberty cannot be equally strong in the breasts of those who have been accustomed to deprive their fellow-creatures of theirs. Of this I am certain, that it is not founded upon that generous and Christian principle of doing to others as we would that others should do unto us. . . .

I feel very differently at the approach of spring from what I did a month ago. We knew not then whether we could plant or sow with safety, whether when we had tilled we could reap the fruits of our own industry, whether we could rest in our own cottages or whether we should be driven from the seacoast to seek shelter in the wilderness; but now we feel a temporary peace, and the poor fugitives are returning to their deserted habitations. . . .

Though we felicitate ourselves, we sympathize with those who are trembling lest the lot of Boston should be theirs. But they cannot be in similar circumstances unless pusillanimity and cowardice should take possession of them. They have time and warning given them to see the evil and shun it.

I long to hear that you have declared an independency. And, by the way, in the new code of laws which I suppose it will be necessary for you to make, I desire you would remember the ladies and be more generous and favorable to them than your ancestors. Do not put such unlimited power into the hands of the husbands. Remember, all men would be tyrants if they could. If particular care and attention is not paid to the ladies, we are determined to foment a rebellion, and will not hold ourselves bound by any laws in which we have no voice or representation.

That your sex are naturally tyrannical is a truth so thoroughly established as to admit of no dispute; but such of you as wish to be happy willingly give up the harsh title of master for the more tender and endearing one of friend. Why then, not put it out of the power of the vicious and the lawless to use us with cruelty and indignity with impunity? Men of sense in all ages abhor those customs which treat us only as the vassals of your sex: regard us then as beings placed by providence under your protection, and in imitation of the Supreme Being make use of that power only for our happiness.

14 April

You justly complain of my short letters, but the critical state of things and the multiplicity of avocations must plead my excuse. You ask where the fleet is? The inclosed papers will inform you. You ask what sort of defense Virginia can make? I believe they will make an able defense. Their militia and minute-men have been some time employed in training themselves, and they have nine battalions of regulars, as they call them, maintained among them, under good officers, at the Continental expense. They have set up a number of manufactories of firearms, which are busily employed. They are tolerably supplied with powder, and are successful and assiduous in making saltpetre. Their neighboring sister, or rather daughter colony of North Carolina, which is a warlike colony, and has several battalions at the Continental expense, as well as a pretty good militia, are ready to assist them, and they are in very good spirits and seem determined to make a brave resistance. The gentry are very rich, and the common people very poor. This inequality of property gives an aristocratical turn to all their proceedings, and occasions a strong aversion in their patricians to "Common Sense." But the spirit of these Barons is coming down, and it must submit. It is very true, as you observe, they have been duped by Dunmore. But this is a common case. All the colonies are duped, more or less, at one time and another. A more egregious bubble was never blown up than the story of Commissioners coming to treat with the Congress, yet it has gained credit like a charm, not only with, but against the clearest evidence. I never shall forget the delusion which seized our best and most sagacious friends, the dear inhabitants of Boston, the winter before last. Credulity and the want of foresight are imperfections in the human character, that no politician can sufficiently guard against. . . .

Your description of your own *gaiete de coeur* charms me. Thanks be to God, you have just cause to rejoice, and may the bright prospect be obscured by no cloud. As to declarations of independency, be patient. Read our privateering laws and our commercial laws. What signifies a word?

As to your extraordinary code of laws, I cannot but laugh. We have been told that our struggle has loosened the bonds of government everywhere; that children and apprentices were disobedient; that schools and colleges were grown turbulent; that Indians slighted their guardians and negroes grew insolent to their masters. But your letter was the first intimation that another tribe more numerous and powerful than all the rest, were grown discontented. This is rather too coarse a compliment, but you are so saucy, I won't blot it out.

Depend upon it, we know better than to repeal our masculine systems. Although they are in full force, you know they are little more than theory. We dare not exert our power in its full latitude. We are obliged to go fair and softly, and, in practice, you know we are the subjects. We have only the name of masters, and rather than give up this, which would completely subject us to the despotism of the petticoat, I hope General Washington and all our brave heroes would fight.

SOURCE: Adams, Charles Francis, ed. *Familiar Letters of John Adams and His Wife Abigail Adams During the Revolution.* New York: Hurd and Houghton, 1876.

A SOLDIER'S LOVE LETTER
(8 June 1777, by Alexander Scammell)

Alexander Scammell was the scion of a prominent Massachusetts family, a general in the Continental Army, and popularly the first patriot officer to bring down a British "Jack." In this letter, he wrote to his love Abigail Bishop to describe duties that include maintaining the spirits of his men through illness and scarcity, as well as the unpleasant task of trying his fellow soldiers in courts-martial. The letter, composed in the formal address common among the educated of the day, allows a peek into the private life, hopes, and fears of a colonist during the earliest days of the Revolution. Sadly, Scammell's pretty vision of himself at Abigail's side was not to be. Despite his reputation and status, his proposal of marriage was coldly received. In July 1778, during the siege of Yorktown on a routine reconnoiter of abandoned British positions, he was surprised by a patrol of Hessian soldiers and killed.

Laura M. Miller,
Vanderbilt University

See also **Revolution, American: Military History.**

June 8th 1777.

My Dearest Naby.

After a very severe march one hundred miles of the way on foot, through the woods in an excessive miry Road, wet, rainy weather accompanied with Snow and Hail, I arrived the 20th of May at Ticonderoga. Am now stationed at what is called the French Lines, where the british army last year met with such a fatal defeat, and lost so many men—and if they make an attempt upon us in the same place I nothing doubt we shall be able by the smiles of superintendant Providence to give them as fatal an overthrow— Our men are well supplied, and I am of opinion will behave well— The blood of our murder'd countrymen cry for Vengence on those british Villains and I hope we shall be the just Instruments of revenge. Tho I should much rather be able to retire to enjoy the sweets of Liberty and domestick happiness, but more especially the pleasing Charms of your dear Company. But so long as my Country demands my utmost Exertions, I must devote myself entirly to it's Service— Tho accustomed to the Service, I am now enter'd upon a new scene, I have an agreable and worthy sett of Officers— But my men are undisciplin'd, they are expos'd to severe Duty, many of them sick—and but poorly coverd. They look up to me as a common

Father—and you may well Judge of my disagreable Sensations, when I am unable to afford them, or procure wherewithal to make them comfortable— However I shall endeavor to do all that I can for them, and if possible make them pay me ready and implicit Obedience, through Love and Affection, rather than through Fear and Dread— We at present have a very agreable, & healthy Situation—In good Spirits, and have good provisions— And hope early next Fall or Winter to do myself the pleasure of waiting upon you at Mistic unless you should forbid it.

The tender moments which we have spent together still, and ever will, remain fresh in my memory— You are ever present in my enraptur'd heart—& a mutual return of Affection from you, I find more and more necessary to my Happiness—cherish the Love my dearest Nabby, which you have so generously professed for me— Altho I am far distant from you, still remember that I am your constant, and most affectionate admirerer—I should have wrote you sooner, but being orderd upon the disagreable Command of sitting as president of a Genl.-Court martial to try men for their Lives, many of which have justly forfeited them—and to try several Villains who have attempted to spread the small Pox— I assure you that it is a most trying Birth, and has worried my mind more than any command I was ever upon—But hope I shall ever be able to discharge my Duty in such a manner as never to be subject to any disagreable Reflections—I have been upon said Court steady since my arrival and this is the first opportunity I had of writing to you—I hope therefore that you will not impute any neglect to me But ever consider me unalterably thine— My Lovely Girl, write every Opportunity to

Y[s]
Alexd Scammell

Write to me every Opportunity.

Miss Naby Bishop.

PS—I long for the time when through you I can send my dutiful Regards to your Hon[d] Parents by the tender Name of Father & Mother—June 23[d] 1777.

I congratulate you upon the Cause of your Fear being remov'd as Burgoyne is going to attack Ticonderoga & not Boston. I hope we shall be able to keep him off.

LIFE AT VALLEY FORGE
(1777–1778, by Albigence Waldo)

General Washington's army, already exhausted from battles, long marches, and a persistent dearth of supplies, arrived at Valley Forge, Pa., on 19 December 1777. The winter was a difficult one, and the land offered little in the way of shelter or food. The diary of the surgeon, Washington's personal physician, Albigence Waldo, is graphic testimony of the hardships endured by the amateur Continental Army throughout the long winter. The woes were seemingly endless. A dozen men were forced to share a 16′ × 14′ log hut with dirt floors and little more than cloth rags to serve as doors. Because there were no nearby wells, water had to be brought from the Schuylkill River and nearby creeks where the soldiers and their animals often relieved themselves. Disease was so rampant that Washington ordered his men inoculated against smallpox, a controversial and much-distrusted procedure. Accounts of the winter's death toll vary, with some estimates as high as three thousand. What emerged from that suffering, however, was a newly hardened, more disciplined Continental Army than the British had ever encountered, one that had at last undertaken a strict training regimen and was now prepared to meet its enemy openly on the field of conflict.

Laura M. Miller,
Vanderbilt University

See also **Valley Forge.**

Dec. 12th [1777]. — A Bridge of Waggons made across the Schuylkill last Night consisting of 36 waggons, with a bridge of Rails between each. Some Skirmishing over the River. Militia and draggoons brought into Camp several Prisoners. Sun Set.—We are order'd to march over the River—It snows—I'm Sick—eat nothing—No Whiskey–No Baggage—Lord—Lord—Lord. The Army were 'till Sun Rise crossing the River—some at the Waggon Bridge, & some at the Raft Bridge below. Cold & Uncomfortable.

Dec. 13th. — The Army march'd three miles from the West side the River and encamp'd near a place call'd the Gulph and not an improper name neither— For this Gulph seems well adapted by its situation to keep us from the pleasure & enjoyments of this World, or being conversant with any body in it—It is an excellent place to raise the Ideas of a Philosopher beyond the glutted thoughts and Reflexions of an Epicurian. His Reflexions will be as different from the Common Reflexions of Mankind as if he were unconnected with the world, and only conversant with material beings. It cannot be that our Superiors are about to hold consult[t]ation with Spirits infinitely beneath their Order—by bringing us into these utmost regions of the Terraqueous Sphere. No—it is, upon consideration, for many good purposes since we are to Winter here—1st There is plenty of Wood & Water. 2dly There are but few families for the soldiery to Steal from—tho' far be it from a Soldier to Steal—4^{ly} There are warm sides of Hills to erect huts on. 5^{ly} They will be heavenly Minded like Jonah when in the belly of a great Fish. 6^{ly}. They will not become home Sick as is sometimes the Case when Men live in the Open World—since the reflections which must naturally arise from their present habitation, will lead them to the more noble thoughts of employing their leizure hours in filling their knapsacks with such materials as may be necessary on the Jorney to another Home.

Dec. 14th. — Prisoners & Deserters are continually coming in. The Army who have been surprisingly healthy hitherto—now begin to grow sickly from the continued fatigues they have suffered this Campaign. Yet they still show spirit of Alacrity & Contentment not to be expected from so young Troops. I am Sick—discontented—and out of humour. Poor food—hard lodging—Cold Weather—fatigue—Nasty Cloaths—nasty Cookery—Vomit half my time—smoak'd out of my senses—the Devil's in't—I can't Endure it—Why are we sent here to starve and freeze—What sweet Felicities have I left at home;—A charming Wife—pretty Children—Good Beds—good food—good Cookery—all agreeable—all harmonious. Here, all Confusion—smoke Cold—hunger & filthyness—A pox on my bad luck. Here comes a bowl of beef soup—full of burnt leaves and dirt, sickish enough to make a hector spue,—away with it Boys—I'll live like the Chameleon upon Air. Poh! Poh! crys Patience within me—you talk like a fool. Your being sick Covers your mind with a Melancholic Gloom, which makes every thing about you appear gloomy. See the poor Soldier, when in health—with what chearfullness he meets his foes and encounters every hardship—if barefoot—he labours thro' the Mud & Cold with a Song in his mouth extolling War & Washington—if his food be bad—he eats it notwithstanding with seeming content—blesses God for a good Stomach—and Whis[t]les it into digestion. But harkee Patience—a moment—There comes a Soldier—His bare feet are seen thro' his worn out Shoes—his legs nearly naked from the tatter'd remains of an only pair of stockings—his Breeches not sufficient to cover his Nakedness—his Shirt hanging in Strings—his hair dishevell'd—his face meagre—his whole appearance pictures a person forsaken & discouraged. He comes, and crys with an air of wretchedness & dispair—I am Sick—my feet lame—my legs are sore—my body cover'd with this tormenting Itch—my Cloaths are worn out—my Constitution is broken—my former Activity is exhausted by fatigue—hunger & Cold—I fail fast I shall soon be no more! and all the reward I shall get will be—"Poor Will is dead." . . .

Dec. 18th. — Universal Thanksgiving—a Roasted Pig at Night. God be thanked for my health which I have pretty well recovered. How much better should I feel, were I assured my family were in health—But the same good Being who graciously preserves me—is able to preserve them—& bring me to the ardently wish'd for enjoyment of them again.

Rank & Precedence make a good deal of disturbance & confusion in the American Army. The Army are poorly supplied with Provision, occationed it is said by the Neglect of the Commissary of Purchases. Much talk among Officers about discharges. Money has become of too little consequence. . . .

Dec. 22st. — Preparations made for hutts. Provision Scarce. Mr. Ellis went homeward—sent a Letter to my Wife. Heartily wish myself at home—my Skin & eyes are almost spoil'd with continual smoke.

A general cry thro' the Camp this Evening among the Soldiers—"No Meat!—No Meat!"—the Distant vales Echo'd back the melancholly sound—"No Meat! No Meat!" Immitating the noise of Crows & Owls, also, made a part of the confessed Musick.

What have you got for our Dinners Boys? "Nothing but Fire Cake & Water, Sir." At night—"Gentlemen the Supper is ready." What is your Supper, Lads? "Fire Cake & Water Sir."

Dec. 22d. — Lay excessive Cold & uncomfortable last Night—my eyes are started out from their Orbits like a Rabbit's eyes, occation'd by a great Cold—and Smoke.

What have you got for Breakfast, Lads? "Fire Cake & Water, Sir." The Lord send that our Commissary of Purchases may live on, Fire Cake & Water. . . .

Our Division are under Marching Orders this morning. I am ashamed to say it, but I am tempted to steal Fowls if I could find them—or even a whole Hog—for I feel as if I could eat one. But the Impoverish'd Country about us, affords but little matter to employ a Thief—or keep a Clever Fellow in good humour—But why do I talk of hunger & hard usage, when so many in the World have not even fire Cake & Water to eat. . . .

Dec. 23d. — The Party that went out last evening not Return'd to Day. This evening an excellent Player on the Violin in that soft kind of Musick, which is so finely adapted to stirr up the tender Passions, while he was playing in the next Tent to mine, these kind of soft Airs—it immediately called up in remembrance all the endearing expressions—the Tender Sentiments—the sympathetic friendship that has given so much satisfaction and sensible pleasure to me from the first time I gained the heart & affections of the tenderest of the Fair. . . .

Dec. 24th. — Party of the 22^d^ returned. Hutts go on Slowly—Cold & Smoke make us fret. But mankind are always fretting, even if they have more than their proportion of the Blessings of Life. We are never Easy—allways repining at the Providence of an Allwise & Benevolent Being—Blaming Our Coutry—or faulting our Friends. But I don't know of any thing that vexes a man's Soul more than hot smoke continually blowing into his Eyes—& when he attempts to avoid it, is met by a cold and piercing Wind. . . .

Dec. 25th, Christmas. — We are still in Tents—when we ought to be in huts—the poor Sick, suffer much in Tents this cold Weather—But we now treat them differently from what they used to be at home, under the inspection of Old Women & Doct. Bolus Linctus. We give them Mutton & Groggy—and a Capital Medicine once in a While—to start the Disease from its foundation at once. We avoid—Piddling Pills, Powders, Bolus's Linctus's—Cordials—and all such insignificant matters whose powers are Only render'd important by causing the Patient to vomit up his money instead of his disease. But very few of the sick Men Die.

Dec. 26th. — Party of the 22^d^ not Return'd. The Enemy have been some Days the west Schuylkill from Opposite the City to Derby—There intentions not yet known. The City is at present pretty Clear of them—Why don't his Excellency rush in & retake the City, in which he will doubtless find much Plunder?—Because he knows better than to leave his Post and be catch'd like a . . . fool cooped up in the City. He has always acted wisely hitherto—His conduct when closely scrutinised is uncensurable. Were his Inferior Generals as skillfull as him self—we should have the grandest Choir of Officers ever God made. . . .

Dec. 28th. — Yesterday upwards of fifty Officers in Gen^l^Green's Division resigned their Commissions—Six or Seven of our Regiment are doing the like to-day. All this is occation'd by Officers Families being so much neglected at home on account of Provisions. Their Wages will not by considerable, purchase a few trifling Comfortables here in Camp, & maintain their families at home, while such extravagant prices are demanded for the common necessaries of Life—What then have they to purchase Cloaths and other necessaries with? It is a Melancholly reflection that what is of the most universal importance, is most universally, neglected—I mean keeping up the Credit of Money.

The present Circumstances of the Soldier is better by far than the Officer— for the family of the Soldier is provided for at the public expence if the Articles they want are above the common price—but the Officer's family, are obliged not only to beg in the most humble manner for the necessaries of Life—but also to pay for them afterwards at the most exhorbitant rates—and even in this manner, many of them who depend entirely on their Money, cannot procure half the material comforts that are wanted in a family—this produces continual letters of complaint from home. . . .

Dec. 31st. — Ajutant Selden learn'd me how to Darn Stockings—to make them look like knit work—first work the Thread in a parallel manner, then catch these over & over as above. . . .

1778. January 1st. — New Year. I am alive. I am well.

Hutts go on briskly, and our Camp begins to appear like a spacious City. . . .

Bought an embroidered Jacket.

How much we affect to appear of consequence by a superfluous Dress,—and yet Custom—(that law which none may fight against) has rendered this absolutely necessary & commendable. An Officer frequently fails of being duly noticed, merely from the want of a genteel Dress. . . .

Sunday, Jan. 4th. — Properly accouter'd I went to work at Masonry—None of my Mess were to dictate me—and before Night (being found with Mortar & Stone) I almost compleated a genteel Chimney to my Magnificent Hutt—however, as we had short allowance of food & no Grogg—my back ached before Night.

I was call'd to relieve a Soldier tho't to be dying—he expir'd before I reach'd the Hutt. He was an Indian—an excellent Soldier—and an obedient good natur'd fellow. . . .

LETTERS OF ELIZA WILKINSON
(c. 1780)

Eliza Wilkinson, a South Carolina matron and patriot, experienced one of the most humiliating defeats suffered by the Americans during the Revolutionary War. British strategy in the South paid off with victories in South Carolina, including the spectacular fall of Charleston in the spring of 1780. In the aftermath, British soldiers and American Tories (the Loyalists, or as Wilkinson called them, "liars") taunted and abused the South Carolinians and looted their homes. Their avariciousness knew no bounds, according to the story related by Wilkinson in the first letter. What was worse, the Tories had no respect for elderly Americans (the "grey hairs"), and stole from them and humiliated them at will.

The second letter relates more details about the British occupation of South Carolina. Wherever there were large bodies of troops, smallpox and other diseases were not far behind. Wilkinson was lucky to escape the pox with her life and, she predicted, no scars. The American soldiers captured at South Carolina were being held in a prison ship. Wilkinson received a letter from two prisoners, who kept their spirits amid suffering, just as she did. Her solace was poetry and philosophy, and the conviction that justice would in the end reign supreme.

Russell Lawson,
Bacone College

See also **Revolution, American: Military History.**

I seem to have an inexhaustible fund just now for letter writing; but it will amuse your leisure hours, and that hope encourages me to proceed. Without further preamble, I will present you with another scene, where my Father noted Mother were spectators, and also sufferers. It was likewise on the 3d of June that my Father, with an old man who lived a few miles from him, and whose head was silvered o'er with age, (one Mr. Byrant,) was sitting in the Piazza, when they saw a liar party of men—some in red, others in green, coming up to the house furiously; the moment they arrived, they jumped from their horses, and ran into the house with drawn swords and pistols, and began to curse and abuse Father and the other man very much; indeed, took his buckles from his shoes, searched his pockets, and took all they found there; they then went to search Mr. Bryant's pockets; he threw his top jacket aside, and producing his under-one, "Here," said he,"I'm a poor old man," (he was so, sure enough.) They searched but I believe found nothing, for by a lucky thought the "poor old man" saved several hundred pounds, by carelessly casting aside his top jacket, as if it had no pockets in it. They then went in the rooms up and down stairs, demolished two sets of drawers, and took all they could conveniently carry off. One came to search Mother's pockets too, (audacious fellow!) but she resolutely threw his hand aside. "If you must see what's in my pocket, I'll show you myself," and she took out a threadcase, which had thread, needles, pins, tape, &c. &c. The mean wretch took it from her. They even took her two little children's caps, hats, &c. &c.; and when they took Mother's thread, &c. she asked them what they did with such things, which must be useless to them? "Why, Nancy would want them." They then began to insult Father again in the most abusive manner. "Aye," says one, "I told you yesterday how you'd be used if you did not take a protection! But you would not hear me; you would not do as I told you, now you see what you have got by it." "Why," said Mother, in a jeering way, "is going about plundering women and children, taking the State?" "I suppose you think you are doing your king a great piece of service by these actions, which are very noble, to be sure; but you are mistaken—'twill only enrage the people; I think you'd much better go and fight the men, than go about the country robbing helpless women and children; that would be doing something." "O! you are all, every one of you, rebels! and, old fellow," (to Father,) "I have a great mind to blow my pistol through your head." Another made a pass at him, (inhuman monsters—I have no patience to relate it,) with his sword, swearing he had "a great mind," too, to run him through the body.

What callous-hearted wretches must these be, thus to treat those who rather demanded their protection and support. Grey hairs have always commanded respect and reverence until now; but these vile creatures choose the aged and helpless for the objects of their insults and barbarity. But what, think you, must have been my Father's feelings at the time! used in such a manner. and not having it in his power to resent it; what a painful conflict must at that instant have filled his breast. He once or twice, (I heard him say afterwards,) was on the verge of attempting to defend himself and property; his breast was torn with the most violent agitations; but when he considered his helpless situation, and that certain death must ensue, he forbore, and silently submitted to their revilings and insults. It reminds me of poor old Priam, King of Troy, when the says,

As for my sons! I thank ye, Gods—'twas well—
Well—they have perished, for in fight they fell.
Who dies in youth and vigor, dies the best,
Cover'd with wounds, all honest, on the breast,
But when the Fates, in fury of their rage,
Spurn the hoar head of *unresisting age*,
This, this is misery, the last, the worst,
That man can feel—man fated to be curst.

I think those are the lines; it is a great while since I read them.

But to proceed. After drinking all the wine, rum, &c. they could find, and inviting the negroes they had with them, who were very insolent, to do the same; they went to their horses, and would shake hands with Father and Mother before their departure. Did you ever hear the like? Fine amends, to be sure! a bitter pill covered with gold, and so a shake of the hand was to make them ample satisfaction for all their sufferings! But the "iron hand of Justice" will overtake them sooner or later. Though *slow*, it is *sure*.

After they were gone, poor old Bryant began to bless his stars for saving his money, and to applaud himself for his lucky invention; he was too loud with it; Father admonished him to speak lower, for, should any of the servants about the house hear him, and another party come, he might stand a chance to lose it after all; but still the old man kept chatting on, when lo! another company of horsemen appeared in view: the poor soul was panic-struck, he looked aghast, and became mute: these were M'Girth's men, who had just left *us*. They did not behave quite so civil to Mother as they did to us; for they took sugar, flour, butter, and such things from her; but not much. These particulars I had from Mother. And now, my dear, I'll conclude here; I expect company to spend the day, so will defer ending my long story till the next leisure hour, and will then bare another epistolary chat with you. Adieu.

Eliza.

Mount Royal, May 19, 1781.

Hang dull life, 'tis all a folly,
Why should we be melancholy?

Aye, why should we? Does it answer one good purpose? or will it be any alleviation to our present misfortune? No. Very well, then, I will e'en banish it, and make the best of what I cannot prevent. To indulge melancholy, is to afflict ourselves, and make the edge of calamity more keen and cutting; so I will endeavor to maintain a calm, let what will happen. I will summon philosophy, fortitude, patience, and resignation to my aid; and sweet hope, which never forsakes us, will be one chief support. Let us, by anticipation, be happy; and though we may have cause to mourn, let it not be with despair.

I have just got the better of the small-pox, thanks be to God for the same. My face is finely ornamented, and my nose *honored with thirteen spots*. I must add, that I am pleased they will not pit, for as much as I revere the number, I would not choose to have so conspicuous a mark. I intend, in a few days, to introduce my spotted face in Charlestown. I hear there are a number of my friends and acquaintances to be exiled, and I must see them before they are. Oh! Mary, who can forbear to execrate these barbarous, insulting *red-coats?* I despise them most cordially and hope *their* day of suffering is not far off. I have received a long epistle from on board the prison ship; it is dated from the "Pack Horse, or Wilful Murder," and signed by two of its inhabitants. They first congratulate me on my recovery from the small-pox, and then proceed to a detail of their sufferings, and a description of their present habitation. But I am very much pleased to see by their style, that they bear all with fortitude, and are still in high spirits. I have also had a letter from Capt. ****; he advises me to take care whom I speak to, and not to be very saucy; for the two Miss Sarazens were put in Provost, and very much insulted for some trifle or other. Did you ever hear the like! Do the Britons imagine that they will conquer America by such actions? If they do, they will find themselves much mistaken. I will answer for that. We may be *led*, but we never will be *driven!* He also writes me, that the Britons were making great preparations to celebrate the anniversary of the day that Charlestown capitulated, and that, what with the *grand parade* and one thing or other, a poor rebel had not the least chance to walk the streets without being insulted; but, in opposition to all that, he had hoisted a very large *union* in his hat, and would brave it out; that the rebel ladies were obliged to compose their phizzes before they dared to venture in the streets; and concludes in as high spirits as he began. How it pleases me to see our prisoners bear it as they do. They live in the greatest harmony together, and are in high favor with the ladies; which, I dare say, gives the proud conquerors the heart-burn. Bless me! here is a whole troop of British horse coming up to the house; get into my bosom, letter;—how I tremble! I won't finish it until I return from Charlestown. Adieu, till then.

SOURCE: Wilkinson, Eliza. *Letters During the Invasion and Possession of Charleston, S.C., by the British in the Revolutionary War.* New York: S. Colman, 1839.

CORRESPONDENCE LEADING TO SURRENDER
(1781)

George Washington, commander in chief of the American Continental Army, had taken a rocky road to the surrender of Lord Cornwallis at Yorktown. The British army and navy were the greatest powers in the world, whereas the Continental army could scarcely supply itself with adequate clothing and weapons. The British soldiers, the regulars, were the best fighters in the world, highly disciplined killers. The American soldier was typically a farmer who was serving a six-month enlistment, yearning the whole time to get back to hearth and home. Washington's great accomplishment was not the winning of battles, rather merely keeping an army together to oppose the British. But by will and perseverance it was Washington who was preparing to accept the surrender of Cornwallis, and not the other way around.

Lord Charles Cornwallis was in command of five thousand troops. He had enjoyed success in the British southern campaign against the rebellious colonies. But he had not expected the arrival of such a large force of American and French troops. He hunkered down at Yorktown, Va., hoping to be supported and rescued by the British navy, only to discover the French navy sailing off the coast of Virginia. Resistance was futile. Lord Cornwallis accepted Washington's terms of surrender.

Although the Americans were known to use guerrilla tactics in fighting the British, the Battle of Yorktown was a more traditional battle befitting eighteenth-century conceptions of the logic and honor of, and proper behavior during, war. Washington continued to refer to Cornwallis as "your Lordship," respecting his opponent's aristocratic standing even in defeat. Both men ended their letters with traditional salutations that were generally meaningless yet required in formal society. Neither man hinted that the surrender of Cornwallis to Washington was the beginning of the end of British attempts to prevent American independence.

Russell Lawson,
Bacone College

See also **Revolution, American: Military History; Yorktown Campaign.**

SIR,

I propose a cessation of hostilities for twenty-four hours, and that two officers may be appointed by each side, to meet at Mr. Moore's house, to settle terms for the surrender of the posts of York and Gloucester.

I have the honor to be, &c
Cornwallis

My Lord,

I have had the honor of receiving your Lordship's letter of this date. An ardent desire to spare the further effusion of blood will readily incline me to listen to such terms for the surrender of your posts of York and Gloucester, as are admissible.

I wish, previously to the meeting of commissioners, that your Lordship's proposals in writing may be sent to the American lines, for which purpose a suspension of hostilities, during two hours from the delivery of this letter, will be granted.

I have the honor to be, &c.
George Washington

THE EARLY REPUBLIC

TREATY WITH THE SIX NATIONS
(1784)

Native Americans of the St. Lawrence, Ohio, Mississippi, and Mohawk River valleys played an important role during the century of warfare from the 1680s to the 1780s, when the French, English, and Americans fought for control of North America. During the last great contest, the War for American Independence (1775–1783), most Indian tribes allied with the English. This opposition to the American patriots was true of the Six Nations of the Iroquois. The Treaty of Paris of 1783 ending the war gave the new United States control of the region from the Appalachian Mountains to the Mississippi River, which included countless Indian villages and thousands of warriors. The new government of the United States organized under the Articles of Confederation gave Congress the power to make treaties with Indian nations. In 1784, Congress appointed Oliver Wolcott, Richard Butler, and Arthur Lee to negotiate a treaty with the defeated Cayuga, Seneca, Mohawk, Oneida, Tuscarora, and Onondaga tribes of upstate New York. The resulting treaty, signed by the American commissioners and representatives of the tribes, set forth the boundaries of the Indian nations, demanded Indian hostages be turned over to American authorities, and agreed to bring supplies to the beleaguered natives. This treaty, like many treaties before and after signed by the United States and North American Indian tribes, would be short-lived. War would again occur during the next ten years until the Indians were soundly defeated at Fallen Timbers in 1794.

Russell Lawson,
Bacone College

See also **Indian Treaties; Iroquois.**

Articles concluded at Fort Stanwix, on the twenty-second day of October, one thousand seven hundred and eighty-four, between Oliver Wolcott, Richard Butler, and Arthur Lee, Commissioners Plenipotentiary from the United States, in Congress assembled, on the one Part, and the Sachems and Warriors of the Six Nations, on the other.

The United States of America give peace to the Senecas, Mohawks, Onondagas and Cayugas, and receive them into their protection upon the following conditions:

Article I.
Six hostages shall be immediately delivered to the commissioners by the said nations, to remain in possession of the United States, till all the prisoners, white and black, which were taken by the said Senecas, Mohawks, Onondagas and Cayugas, or by any of them, in the late war, from among the people of the United States, shall be delivered up.

Article II.
The Oneida and Tuscarora nations shall be secured in the possession of the lands on which they are settled.

Article III.
A line shall be drawn, beginning at the mouth of a creek about four miles east of Niagara, called Oyonwayea, or Johnston's Landing-Place, upon the lake named by the Indians Oswego, and by us Ontario; from thence southerly in a direction always four miles east of the carrying-path, between Lake Erie and Ontario, to the mouth of Tehoseroron or Buffaloe Creek on Lake Erie; thence south to the north boundary of the state of Pennsylvania; thence west to the end of the said north boundary; thence south along the west boundary of the said state, to the river Ohio; the said line from the mouth of the Oyonwayea to the Ohio, shall be the western boundary of the lands of the Six Nations, so that the Six Nations shall and do yield to the United States, all claims

to the country west of the said boundary, and then they shall be secured in the peaceful possession of the lands they inhabit east and north of the same, reserving only six miles square round the fort of Oswego, to the United States, for the support of the same.

Article IV.

The Commissioners of the United States, in consideration of the present circumstances of the Six Nations, and in execution of the humane and liberal views of the United States upon the signing of the above articles, will order goods to be delivered to the said Six Nations for their use and comfort.

Oliver Wolcott, [L.S.]
Richard Butler, [L.S.]
Arthur Lee, [L.S.]

Mohawks:

Onogwendahonji, his x mark, [L.S.]
Touighnatogon, his x mark, [L.S.]

Onondagas:

Oheadarighton, his x mark, [L.S.]
Kendarindgon, his x mark, [L.S.]

Senekas:

Tayagonendagighti, his x mark, [L.S.]
Tehonwaeaghrigagi, his x mark, [L.S.]

Oneidas:

Otyadonenghti, his x mark, [L.S.]
Dagaheari, his x mark, [L.S.]

Cayuga:

Oraghgoanendagen, his x mark, [L.S.]

Tuscaroras:

Ononghsawenghti, his x mark, [L.S.]
Tharondawagon, his x mark, [L.S.]

Seneka Abeal:

Kayenthoghke, his x mark, [L.S.]

Witnesses:

Sam. Jo. Atlee,
Wm. Maclay,
Fras. Johnston,

Pennsylvania Commissioners.

Aaron Hill,
Alexander Campbell,
Saml. Kirkland, missionary,
James Dean,
Saml. Montgomery,
Derick Lane, captain,
John Mercer, lieutenant,
William Pennington, lieutenant,
Mahlon Hord, ensign,
Hugh Peebles.

SOURCE: "Treaty with the Six Nations, 1784." In *Indian Treaties, 1778–1883*. Edited by Charles J. Kappler. Washington, DC: 1904.

SHAYS'S REBELLION
(1786)

The great debate among Americans before, during, and after the War for American Independence was whether a state based on liberty and freedom made unnecessary a central power, or whether liberty and freedom were inherent rights frequently trampled upon by others, hence demanding an orderly government to secure and protect them. In western Massachusetts, where the Berkshire Mountains and huge stands of virgin forest separated the few small towns of farmers, the feeling was, the less government the better. These people struggled to make ends meet, to provide the basic essentials for their families. Their desire for self-sufficiency led to a fierce independence. They had no love for government, and indeed feared that the natural tendency of government to order and secure the lives of the majority would take away their freedoms. These farmers, such as Daniel Gray and Thomas Grover, grew angry in the mid-1780s as the State of Massachusetts imposed more taxes to pay its debts, and allowed local law enforcement officials—sheriffs, constables, justices of the peace—the power to enforce the will of the government, to arrest those who refused to pay taxes and fomented rebellion, and to imprison those who were in debt and had no means to pay their creditors.

The exasperated farmers of western Massachusetts found their hero, as it were, in one Daniel Shays, who led them to desperate measures, intending to take the matters of self-government into their own hands. The result was Shays's Rebellion. Starting in Boston, this was an attempt to wrestle control from the State of Massachusetts. The rebellion was ruthlessly put down, and order secured in western Massachusetts. Yet Shays's Rebellion served as a reminder to conservative statesmen that the Articles of Confederation did not give enough authority to the central government, thus encouraging such anarchy.

Russell Lawson,
Bacone College

See also **Debt, Imprisonment for; Shays's Rebellion.**

An ADDRESS to the People of the several towns in the country of Hampshire, now at arms.

GENTLEMEN,

We have thought proper to inform you of some of the principal causes of the late risings of the people, and also of their present movement, viz.

1st. The present expensive mode of collecting debts, which by reason of the great scarcity of cash, will of necessity fill our gaols with unhappy debtors; and thereby a reputable body of people rendered incapable of being serviceable either to themselves or the community.

2d. The monies raised by impost and excise being appropriated to discharge the interest of governmental securities, and not the foreign debt, when these securities are not subject to taxation.

3d. A suspension of the writ of Habeas Corpus, by which those persons who have stepped forth to assert and maintain the rights of the people, are liable to be taken and conveyed even to the most distant part of the Commonwealth, and thereby subjected to an unjust punishment.

4th. The unlimited power granted to Justices of the Peace and Sheriffs, Deputy Sheriffs, and Constables, by the Riot Act, indemnifying them to the prosecution thereof; when perhaps, wholly actuated from a principle of revenge, hatred, and envy.

Furthermore, Be assured, that this body, now at arms, despise the idea of being instigated by British emissaries, which is so strenuously propagated by the enemies of our liberties: And also wish the most proper and speedy measures may be taken, to discharge both our foreign and domestick debt.

Per Order,
DANIEL GRAY, Chairman
of the Committee.

2. To the Printer of the Hampshire Herald. SIR,

It has some how or other fallen to my lot to be employed in a more conspicuous manner than some others of my fellow citizens, in stepping forth on defence of the rights and privileges of the people, more especially of the country of Hampshire.

Therefore, upon the desire of the people now at arms, I take this method to publish to the world of mankind in general, particularly the people of this Commonwealth, some of the principal grievances we complain of, . . .

In the first place, I must refer you to a draught of grievances drawn up by a committee of the people, now at arms, under the signature of Daniel Gray, chairman, which is heartily approved of; some others also are here added, viz.

1st. The General Court, for certain obvious reasons, must be removed out of the town of Boston.

2d. A revision of the constitution is absolutely necessary.

3d. All kinds of governmental securities, now on interest, that have been bought of the original owners for two shillings, and the highest for six shillings and eight pence on the pound, and have received more interest than the principal cost the speculator who purchased them—that if justice was done, we verily believe, nay positively know, it would save this Commonwealth thousands of pounds.

4th. Let the lands belonging to this Commonwealth, at the eastward, be sold at the best advantage to pay the remainder of our domestick debt.

5th. Let the monies arising from impost and excise be appropriated to discharge the foreign debt.

6th. Let that act, passed by the General Court last June by a small majority of only seven, called the Supplementary Act, for twenty-five years to come, be repealed.

7th. The total abolition of the Inferiour Court of Common Pleas and General Sessions of the Peace.

8th. Deputy Sheriffs totally set aside, as a useless set of officers in the community; and Constables who are really necessary, be empowered to do the duty, by which means a large swarm of lawyers will be banished from their wonted haunts, who have been more damage to the people at large, especially the common farmers, than the savage beasts of prey.

To this I boldly sign my proper name, as a hearty wellwisher to the real rights of the people.

THOMAS GROVER
Worcester, December 7, 1786.

SOURCE: Minot, George R. *The History of the Insurrections in Massachusetts in the Year 1786 and The Rebellion Consequent Thereon*, second ed. Boston: James W. Burditt, 1810.

FROM ANNAPOLIS TO PHILADELPHIA
(1786–1787)

During the summer of 1786 representatives of five of the thirteen states united under the Articles of Confederation met at Annapolis, Maryland to discuss and remedy the "defects" of the Confederation. Congress had proposed the convention based on the inadequacy of the central government to meet the changing needs of a new nation still struggling to remedy the effects on the economy of an eight-year war. Commerce between the states and with other nations was hampered by the lack of a uniform trade policy. Each state issued its own currency of varying and fluctuating worth. Commerce was also seriously threatened by Spain's aggressive act of closing the port of New Orleans to American shipping. Spain controlled the region west of the Mississippi River and the traffic of the river itself. The Spanish realized that American settlers west of the Appalachian Mountains required the Mississippi to ship their goods to eastern ports. By closing the Mississippi to American trade, the Spanish intended to split the United States, creating independent republics in such territories as Kentucky, hence weakening the United States and allowing easy Spanish domination.

The commissioners at Annapolis knew that something had to be done, but they felt powerless to recommend significant revisions in the government. However, they did feel compelled to recommend to the Congress that another convention be formed in the following year that would have full representation from all of the states and the power to recommend significant changes in the Confederation government. Congress took up the issue in February 1787. Alexander Hamilton of New York took the lead in requesting from Congress the formation of a convention "for the purpose of revising the Articles of Confederation and perpetual Union between the United States of America and reporting to the United States in Congress assembled and to the States respectively such alterations and amendments of the said Articles of Confederation as the representatives met in such convention shall judge proper and necessary to render them adequate to the preservation and support of the Union." But the Congress, particularly southern representatives, was hesitant to grant such power to such a convention. Supporters of a stronger government from Massachusetts submitted another resolution requesting that a convention meet for "the sole and express purpose of revising the Articles of Confederation." This slight change of wording, limiting the power of the convention to simple revisions of the Confederation, gained the majority support of Congress. The convention would take place in Philadelphia in May 1787.

Russell Lawson,
Bacone College

***See also* Annapolis Convention; Articles of Confederation.**

PROCEEDINGS OF COMMISSIONERS TO REMEDY DEFECTS OF THE FEDERAL GOVERNMENT (THE ANNAPOLIS CONVENTION REPORT)

Report of Proceedings in Congress, Wednesday February 21, 1787

Proceedings of Commissioners to Remedy Defects of The Federal Government
Annapolis in the State of Maryland

September 11th. 1786

At a meeting of Commissioners, from the States of New York, New Jersey, Pennsylvania, Delaware and Virginia—

Present

New York

Alexander Hamilton
Egbert Benson

New Jersey

Abraham Clarke
William C. Houston
James Schuarman
Tench Coxe

Pennsylvania

George Read
John Dickinson

Delaware

Richard Bassett
Edmund Randolph
James Madison, Junior

Virginia

Saint George Tucker

Mr. Dickinson was unanimously elected Chairman.

The Commissioners produced their Credentials from their respective States; which were read.

After a full communication of Sentiments, and deliberate consideration of what would be proper to be done by the Commissioners now assembled, it was unanimously agreed: that a Committee be appointed to prepare a draft of a Report to be made to the States having Commissioners attending at this meeting—Adjourned 'till Wednesday Morning.

Wednesday September 13th. 1786
Met agreeable to Adjournment.

The Committee, appointed for that purpose, reported the draft of the report; which being read, the meeting proceeded to the consideration thereof, and after some time spent therein, Adjourned 'till tomorrow Morning.

Thursday Septr. 14th. 1786
Met agreeable to Adjournment.

The meeting resumed the consideration of the draft of the Report, and after some time spent therein, and amendments made, the same was unanimously agreed to, and is as follows, to wit.

To the Honorable, the Legislatures of Virginia, Delaware, Pennsylvania, New Jersey, and New York—

The Commissioners from the said States, respectively assembled at Annapolis, humbly beg leave to report.

That, pursuant to their several appointments, they met, at Annapolis in the State of Maryland, on the eleventh day of September Instant, and having proceeded to a Communication of their powers; they found that the States of New York, Pennsylvania, and Virginia, had, in substance, and nearly in the same terms, authorised their respective Commissioners "to meet such Commissioners as were, or might be, appointed by the other States in the Union, at such time and place, as should be agreed upon by the said Commissioners to take into consideration the trade and Commerce of the United States, to consider how far an uniform system in their commercial intercourse and regulations might be necessary to their common interest and permanent harmony, and to report to the several States such an Act, relative to this great object, as when unanimously ratified by them would enable the United States in Congress assembled effectually to provide for the same."

That the State of Delaware, had given similar powers to their Commissioners, with this difference only, that the Act to be framed in virtue of those powers, is required to be reported "to the United States in Congress assembled, to be agreed to by them, and confirmed by the Legislatures of every State."

That the State of New Jersey had enlarged the object of their appointment, empowering their Commissioners, "to consider how far an uniform system in their commercial regulations and other important matters, might be necessary to the common interest and permanent harmony of the several States," and to report such an Act on the subject, as when ratified by them "would enable the United States in Congress assembled, effectually to provide for the exigencies of the Union."

That appointments of Commissioners have also been made by the States of New Hampshire, Massachusetts, Rhode Island, and North Carolina, none of whom however have attended; but that no information has been received by your Commissioners, of any appointment having been made by the States of Connecticut, Maryland, South Carolina or Georgia.

That the express terms of the powers to your Commissioners supposing a deputation from all the States, and having for object the Trade and Commerce of the United States, Your Commissioners did not conceive it advisable to proceed on the business of their mission, under the Circumstance of so partial and defective a representation.

Deeply impressed however with the magnitude and importance of the object confided to them on this occasion, your Commissioners cannot forbear to indulge an expression of their earnest and unanimous wish, that speedy measures may be taken, to effect a general meeting, of the States, in a future Convention, for the same, and such other purposes, as the situation of public affairs, may be found to require.

If in expressing this wish, or in intimating any other sentiment, your Commissioners should seem to exceed the strict bounds of their appointment, they entertain a full confidence, that a conduct, dictated by an anxiety for the welfare, of the United States, will not fail to receive an indulgent construction.

In this persuasion, your Commissioners submit an opinion, that the Idea of extending the powers of their Deputies, to other objects, than those of Commerce, which has been adopted by the State of New Jersey, was an improvement on the original plan, and will deserve to be incorporated into that of a future Convention; they are the more naturally led to this conclusion, as in the course of their reflections on the subject, they have been induced to think, that the power of regulating trade is of such comprehensive extent, and will enter so far into the general System of the federal government, that to give it efficacy, and to obviate questions and doubts concerning its precise nature and limits, may require a correspondent adjustment of other parts of the Federal System.

That there are important defects in the system of the Federal Government is acknowledged by the Acts of all those States, which have concurred in the present Meeting; That the defects, upon a closer examination, may be found greater and more numerous, than even these acts imply, is at least so far probable, from the embarrassments which characterise the present State of our national affairs, foreign and domestic, as may reasonably be supposed to merit a deliberate and candid discussion, in some mode, which will unite the Sentiments and Councils of all the States. In the choice of the mode, your Commissioners are of opinion, that a Convention of Deputies from the different States, for the special and sole purpose of entering into this investigation, and digesting a plan for supplying such defects as may be discovered to exist, will be entitled to a preference from considerations, which will occur, without being particularised.

Your Commissioners decline an enumeration of those national circumstances on which their opinion respecting the propriety of a future Convention, with more enlarged powers, is founded; as it would be an useless intrusion of facts and observations, most of which have been frequently the subject of public discussion, and none of which can have escaped the penetration of those to whom they would in this instance be addressed. They are however of a mature so serious, as, in the view of your Commissioners to render the situation of the United States delicate and critical, calling for an exertion of the united virtue and wisdom of all the members of the Confederacy.

Under this impression, Your Commissioners, with the most respectful deference, beg leave to suggest their unanimous conviction, that it may essentially tend to advance the interests of the union, if the States, by whom they have been respectively delegated, would themselves concur, and use their endeavours to procure the concurrence of the other States, in the appointment of Commissioners, to meet at Philadelphia on the second Monday in May next, to take into consideration the situation of the United States, to devise such further provisions as shall appear to them necessary to render the constitution of the Federal Government adequate to the exigencies of the Union; and to report such an Act for that purpose to the United States in Congress assembled, as when agreed to, by them, and afterwards confirmed by the Legislatures of every State, will effectually provide for the same.

Though your Commissioners could not with propriety address these observations and sentiments to any but the States they have the honor to Represent, they have nevertheless concluded from motives of respect, to transmit Copies of this Report to the United States in Congress assembled, and to the executives of the other States.

By order of the Commissioners.

Dated at Annapolis

September 14th, 1786

Resolved, that the Chairman sign the aforegoing Report in behalf of the Commissioners.

Then adjourned without day—

Egbt. Benson
Alexander Hamilton New York
Abra: Clark
Wm Ch.l.l. Houston New Jersey
Js. Schureman
Tench Coxe Pennsylvania
Geo: Read
John Dickinson Delaware
Richard Bassett
Edmund Randolph
Js. Madison Jr. Virginia
St. George Tucker

Report of Proceedings in Congress, Wednesday Feby. 21, 1787

Congress assembled as before.

The report of a grand comee. consisting of Mr. Dane Mr. Varnum Mr. S. M. Mitchell Mr. Smith Mr. Cadwallader Mr. Irwine Mr. N. Mitchell Mr. Forrest Mr. Grayson Mr. Blount Mr. Bull & Mr. Few, to whom was referred a letter of 14 Septr. 1786 from J. Dickinson written at the request of Commissioners from the States of Virginia Delaware Pensylvania New Jersey & New York assembled at the City of Annapolis together with a copy of the report of the said commissioners to the legislatures of the States by whom they were appointed, being an order of the day was called up & which is contained in the following resolution viz "Congress having had under consideration the letter of John Dickinson esqr. chairman of the Commissioners who assembled at Annapolis during the last year also the proceedings of the said commissioners and entirely coinciding with them as to the inefficiency of the federal government and the necessity of devising such farther provisions as shall render the same adequate to the exigencies of the Union do strongly recommend to the different legislatures to send forward delegates to meet the proposed convention on the second Monday in May next at the city of Philadelphia"

The delegates for the state of New York thereupon laid before Congress Instructions which they had received from their constituents, & in pursuance of the said instructions moved to postpone the farther consideration of the report in order to take up the following proposition to wit

"That it be recommended to the States composing the Union that a convention of representatives from the said States respectively be held at—on—for the purpose of revising the Articles of Confederation and perpetual Union between the United States of America and reporting to the United States in Congress assembled and to the States respectively such alterations and amendments of the said Articles of Confederation as the representatives met in such convention shall judge proper and necessary to render them adequate to the preservation and support of the Union"

On the question to postpone for the purpose above mentioned the yeas & nays being required by the delegates for New York.

Massachusetts:

Mr. King ay
Mr. Dane ay

Connecticut:

Mr. Johnson ay
Mr. S. M. Mitchell no

New York:

Mr. Smith ay
Mr. Benson ay

New Jersey:

Mr. Cadwallader ay
Mr. Clarke no
Mr. Schurman no

Pensylvania:

Mr. Irwine no
Mr. Meredith ay
Mr. Bingham no

Delaware:

Mr. N. Mitchell no

Maryland:

Mr. Forest no

Virginia:

Mr. Grayson ay
Mr. Madison ay

North Carolina:

Mr. Blount no
Mr. Hawkins no

South Carolina:

Mr. Bull no
Mr. Kean no
Mr. Huger no
Mr. Parker no

Georgia:

Mr. Few ay
Mr. Pierce no

So the question was lost.

A motion was then made by the delegates for Massachusetts to postpone the farther consideration of the report in order to take into consideration a motion which they read in their place, this being agreed to, the motion of the delegates for Massachusetts was taken up and being amended was agreed to as follows

Whereas there is provision in the Articles of Confederation & perpetual Union for making alteration therein by the assent of a Congress of the United States and of the legislatures of the several States; And whereas experience hath evinced that there are defects in the present Confederation, as a mean to remedy which several of the States and particularly the State of New York by express instructions to their delegates in Congress have suggested a convention for the purposes expressed in the following resolution and such convention appearing to be the most probable mean of establishing in these states a firm national government.

Resolved that in the opinion of Congress it is expedient that on the second Monday in May next a Convention of delegates who shall have been appointed by the several states be held at Philadelphia for the sole and express purpose of revising the Articles of Confederation and reporting to Congress and the several legislatures such alterations and provisions therein as shall when agreed to in Congress and confirmed by the states render the federal constitution adequate to the exigencies of Government & the preservation of the Union.

SOURCE: Elliot, Jonathan, ed. *The Debates in the Several State Conventions on the Adoption of the Federal Constitution, etc., etc.,* second ed. Philadelphia: Lippincott, 1861.

THE CALL FOR AMENDMENTS *(1787–1788)*

Article 7 of the Constitution states simply that each of the thirteen states form a convention of delegates to approve or disapprove the proposed new government. If in 1787 nine of the thirteen states voted for approval, the Constitution would become the fundamental law of the land. This process of ratification took several months. In each state the supporters of the Constitution, the Federalists, lauded the creation of a single sovereign power, *the people,* to oversee the functions of government. Opponents of the Constitution believed that the rights of individuals and local government were ignored. But at the same time, these Antifederalists realized that the process of amendment could change the Constitution to fit the needs of the people.

Antifederalists, such as Melancton Smith of New York, argued that since the Constitution does not state that the people retain all power not explicitly granted to the federal government, it must be amended with such explicit statements, a Bill of Rights. Federalists, such as

Alexander Hamilton and Noah Webster, countered that an implicit recognition that the ultimate authority rests with the people, who are sovereign, is sufficient; that an explicit list of powers would, in fact, curtail the rights of the people by putting limits on their own power; that for a sovereign people to list their rights implies that they question their sovereignty, and creates a division between the rulers and the ruled.

Eventually, the Federalists agreed to the Antifederalist demand to adopt ten amendments to guarantee the rights of Americans. In turn, the Antifederalists agreed to support the Constitution, which was ratified in 1788, became the law of the land in 1789, and was amended with the Bill of Rights in 1791.

Russell Lawson,
Bacone College

See also* Bill of Rights in U.S. Constitution; Constitution of the United States; *Federalist Papers.

Letters from the Federal Farmer, Melcanton Smith (?), January 20, 1788

Federalist Papers, No. 84, Alexander Hamilton

"Giles Hickory" (or "On the Absurdity of a Bill of Rights"), Noah Webster, December 1787

LETTERS FROM THE FEDERAL FARMER

January 20, 1788.

Dear Sir,

Having gone through with the organization of the government, I shall now proceed to examine more particularly those clauses which respect its powers. I shall begin with those articles and stipulations which are necessary for accurately ascertaining the extent of powers, and what is given, and for guarding, limiting, and restraining them in their exercise. We often find, these articles and stipulations placed in bills of rights; but they may as well be incorporated in the body of the constitution, as selected and placed by themselves. The constitution, or whole social compact, is but one instrument, no more or less, than a certain number of articles or stipulations agreed to by the people, whether it consists of articles, sections, chapters, bills of rights, or parts of any other denomination, cannot be material. Many needless observations, and idle distinctions, in my opinion, have been made respecting a bill of rights. On the one hand, it seems to be considered as a necessary distinct limb of the constitution, and as containing a certain number of very valuable articles, which are applicable to all societies: and, on the other, as useless, especially in a federal government, possessing only enumerated power—nay, dangerous, as individual rights are numerous, and not easy to be enumerated in a bill of rights, and from articles, or stipulations, securing some of them, it may be inferred, that others not mentioned are surrendered. There appears to me to be general indefinite propositions without much meaning—and the man who first advanced those of the latter description, in the present case, signed the federal constitution, which directly contradicts him. The supreme power is undoubtedly in the people, and it is a principle well established in my mind, that they reserve all powers not expressly delegated by them to those who govern; this is as true in forming a state as in forming a federal government. There is no possible distinction but this founded merely in the different modes of proceeding which take place in some cases. In forming a state constitution, under which to manage not only the great but the little concerns of a community: the powers to be possessed by the government are often too numerous to be enumerated; the people to adopt the shortest way often give general powers, indeed all powers, to the government, in some general words, and then, by a particular enumeration, take back, or rather say they however reserve certain rights as sacred, and which no laws shall be made to violate: hence the idea that all powers are given which are not reserved: but in forming a federal constitution, which ex vi termine, supposes state governments existing, and which is only to manage a few great national concerns, we often find it easier to enumerate particularly the powers to be delegated to the federal head, than to enumerate particularly the individual rights to be reserved; and the principle will operate in its full force, when we carefully adhere to it. When we particularly enumerate the powers given, we ought either carefully to enumerate the rights reserved, or be totally silent about them; we must either particularly enumerate both, or else suppose the particular enumeration of the powers given adequately draws the line between them and the rights reserved, particularly to enumerate the former and not the latter, I think most advisable: however, as men appear generally to have their doubts about these silent reservations, we might advantageously enumerate the powers given, and then in general words, according to the mode adopted in the 2d art. of the confederation, declare all powers, rights and privileges, are reserved, which are not explicitly and expressly given up. People, and very wisely too, like to be express and explicit about their essential rights, and not to be forced to claim them on the precarious and unascertained tenure of inferences and general principles, knowing that in any controversy between them and their rulers, concerning those rights, disputes may be endless, and nothing certain:—But admitting, on the general principle, that all rights are reserved of course, which are not expressly surrendered, the people could with sufficient certainty assert their fights on all occasions, and establish them with ease, still there are infinite advantages in particulalarly enumerating many of the most essential rights reserved in all cases; and as to the less important ones, we may declare in general terms, that all not expressly surrendered are reserved. We do not by declarations change the nature of things, or create new truths, but we give existence, or at least establish in the minds of the people truths and principles which they might never otherwise have thought of, or soon forgot. If a nation means its systems, religious or political, shall have duration, it ought to recognize the leading principles of them in the front page of every family book. What is the usefulness of a truth in theory, unless it exists constantly in the minds of the people, and has their assent:—we discern certain rights, as the freedom of the press, and the trial by jury, &c. which the people of England and of America of course believe to be sacred, and essential to their political happiness, and this belief in them is the result of ideas at first suggested to them by a few able men, and of subsequent experience; while the people of some other countries hear these rights mentioned with the utmost indifference; they think the privilege of existing at the will of a despot much preferable to them. Why this difference amongst beings every way formed alike. The reason of the difference is obvious—it is the effect of education, a series of notions impressed upon the minds of the people by examples, precepts and declarations. When the people of England got together, at the time they formed Magna Charta, they did not consider it sufficient, that they were indisputably entitled to certain natural and unalienable rights, not depending on silent titles, they, by a declaratory act, expressly recognized them, and explicitly declared to all the world, that they were entitled to enjoy those rights; they made an instrument in writing, and enumerated those they then thought essential, or in danger, and this wise men saw was not sufficient; and therefore, that the people might not forget these rights, and gradually become prepared for arbitrary government, their discerning and honest leaders caused this instrument to be confirmed near forty times, and to be read twice a year in public places, not that it would lose its validity without such confirmations, but to fix the contents of it in the minds of the people, as they successively come upon the stage.—Men, in some countries do not remain free, merely because they are entitled to natural and unalienable rights; men in all countries are entitled to them, not because their ancestors once got together and enumerated them on paper, but because, by repeated negociations and declarations, all parties are brought to realize them, and of course to believe them to be sacred. Were it necessary, I might shew the wisdom of our past conduct, as a people in not merely comforting ourselves that we were entitled to freedom, but in constantly keeping in view, in addresses, bills of rights, in news-papers, &c. the particular principles on which our freedom must always depend.

It is not merely in this point of view, that I urge the engrafting in the constitution additional declaratory articles. The distinction, in itself just, that all powers not given are reserved, is in effect destroyed by this very constitution, as I shall particularly demonstrate—and even independent of this, the people, by adopting the constitution, give many general undefined powers to congress, in the constitutional exercise of which, the rights in question may be effected. Gentlemen who oppose a federal bill of rights, or further declaratory articles, seem to view the subject in a very narrow imperfect manner. These have for their objects, not only the enumeration of the rights reserved, but principally to explain the general powers delegated in certain material points, and to restrain those who exercise them by fixed known boundaries. Many explanations and restrictions necessary and useful, would be much less so, were the people at large all well and fully acquainted with the principles and affairs of government. There appears to be in the constitution, a studied brevity, and it may also be probable, that several explanatory articles were omitted from a circumstance very common. What we have long and early understood ourselves in the common concerns of the community, we are apt to suppose is understood by others, and need not be expressed; and it is not unnatural or uncommon for the ablest men most frequently to make this mistake. To make declaratory articles unnecessary in an instrument of government, two circumstances must exist; the rights reserved must be indisputably so, and in their nature defined; the powers delegated to the government, must be precisely defined by the words that convey them, and clearly be of such extent and nature as that, by no reasonable construction, they can be made to invade the rights and prerogatives intended to be left in the people.

The first point urged, is, that all power is reserved not expressly given, that particular enumerated powers only are given, that all others are not given, but reserved, and that it is needless to attempt to restrain congress in the exercise of powers they possess not. This reasoning is logical, but of very little importance in the common affairs of men; but the constitution does not appear to respect it even in any view. To prove this, I might cite several clauses in it. I shall only remark on two or three. By article I, section 9, "No title of nobility shall be granted by congress" Was this clause omitted, what power would congress have to make titles of nobility? in what part of the constitution would they find it? The answer must be, that congress would have no such power—that the people, by adopting the constitution, will not part with it. Why then by a negative clause, restrain congress from doing what it would have no power to do? This clause, then, must have no meaning, or imply, that were it omitted, congress would have the power in question, either upon the principle that some general words in the constitution may be so construed as to give it, or on the principle that congress possess the powers not expressly reserved. But this clause was in the confederation, and is said to be introduced into the constitution from very great caution. Even a cautionary provision implies a doubt, at least, that it is necessary; and if so in this case, clearly it is also alike necessary in all similar ones. The fact appears to be, that the people in forming the confederation, and the convention, in this instance, acted, naturally, they did not leave the point to be settled by general principles and logical inferences; but they settle the point in a few words, and all who read them at once understand them.

The trial by jury in criminal as well as in civil causes, has long been considered as one of our fundamental rights, and has been repeatedly recognized and confirmed by most of the state conventions. But the constitution expressly establishes this trial in criminal, and wholly omits it in civil causes. The jury trial in criminal causes, and the benefit of the writ of habeas corpus, are already as effectually established as any of the fundamental or essential rights of the people in the United States. This being the case, why in adopting a federal constitution do we now establish these, and omit all others, or all others, at least with a few exceptions, such as again agreeing there shall be no ex post facto laws, no titles of nobility, &c. We must consider this constitution, when adopted, as the supreme act of the people, and in construing it hereafter, we and our posterity must strictly adhere to the letter and spirit of it, and in no instance depart from them: in construing the federal constitution, it will be not only impracticable, but improper to refer to the state constitutions. They are entirely distinct instruments and inferior acts: besides, by the people's now establishing certain fundamental rights, it is strongly implied, that they are of opinion, that they would not otherwise be secured as a part of the federal system, or be regarded in the federal administration as fundamental. Further, these same rights, being established by the state constitutions, and secured to the people, our recognizing them now, implies, that the people thought them insecure by the state establishments, and extinguished or put afloat by the new arrangement of the social system, unless re-established.—Further, the people, thus establishing some few rights, and remaining totally silent about others similarly circumstanced, the implication indubitably is, that they mean to relinquish the latter, or at least feel indifferent about them. Rights, therefore, inferred from general principles of reason, being precarious and hardly ascertainable in the common affairs of society, and the people, in forming a federal constitution, explicitly shewing they conceive these rights to be thus circumstanced, and accordingly proceed to enumerate and establish some of them, the conclusion will be, that they have established all which they esteem valuable and sacred. On every principle, then, the people especially having began, ought to go through enumerating, and establish particularly all the rights of individuals, which can by any possibility come in question in making and executing federal laws. I have already observed upon the excellency and importance of the jury trial in civil as well as in criminal causes, instead of establishing it in criminal causes only; we ought to establish it generally;—instead of the clause of forty or fifty words relative to this subject, why not use the language that has always been used in this country, and say, "the people of the United States shall always be entitled to the trial by jury." This would shew the people still hold the fight sacred, and enjoin it upon congress substantially to preserve the jury trial in all cases, according to the usage and custom of the country. I have observed before, that it is the jury trial we want; the little different appendages and modifications tacked to it in the different states, are no more than a drop in the ocean: the jury trial is a solid uniform feature in a free government; it is the substance we would save, not the little articles of form.

Security against expost facto laws, the trial by jury, and the benefits of the writ of habeas corpus, are but a part of those inestimable rights the people of the United States are entitled to, even in judicial proceedings, by the course of the common law. These may be secured in general words, as in New-York, the Western Territory, &c. by declaring the people of the United States shall always be entitled to judicial proceedings according to the course of the common law, as used and established in the said states. Perhaps it would be better to enumerate the particular essential rights the people are entitled to in these proceedings, as has been done in many of the states, and as has been done in England. In this case, the people may proceed to declare, that no man shall be held to answer to any offence, till the same be fully described to him; nor to furnish evidence against himself: that, except in the government of the army and navy, no person shall be tried for any offence, whereby he may incur loss of life, or an infamous punishment, until he be first indicted by a grand jury: that every person shall have a right to produce all proofs that may be favourable to him, and to meet the witnesses against him face to face: that every person shall be entitled to obtain right and justice freely and without delay; that all persons shall have a right to be secure from all unreasonable searches and seizures of their persons, houses, papers, or possessions; and that all warrants shall be deemed contrary to this right, if the foundation of them be not previously supported by oath, and there be not in them a special designation of persons or objects of search, arrest, or seizure: and that no person shall be exiled or molested in his person or effects, otherwise than by the judgment of his peers, or according to the law of the land. A celebrated writer observes upon this last article, that in itself it may be said to comprehend the whole end of political society. These rights are not necessarily reserved, they are established, or enjoyed but in few countries: they are stipulated rights, almost peculiar to British and American laws. In the execution of those laws, individuals, by long custom, by magna charta, bills of rights &c. have become entitled to them. A man, at first, by act of parliament, became entitled to the benefits of the writ of habeas corpus—men are entitled to these rights and benefits in the judicial proceedings of our state courts generally: but it will by no means follow, that they will be entitled to them in the federal courts, and have a right to assert them, unless secured and established by the constitution or federal laws. We certainly, in federal processes, might as well claim the benefits of the writ of habeas corpus, as to claim trial by a jury—the right to have council—to have witnesses face to face—to be secure against unreasonable search warrants, &c. was the constitution silent as to the whole of them:—but the establishment of the former, will evince that we could not claim them without it; and the omission of the latter, implies they are relinquished, or deemed of no importance. These are rights and benefits individuals acquire by compact; they must claim them under compacts, or immemorial usage—it is doubtful, at least, whether they can be claimed under immemorial usage in this country; and it is, therefore, we generally claim them under compacts, as charters and constitutions.

The people by adopting the federal constitution, give congress general powers to institute a distinct and new judiciary, new courts, and to regulate all proceedings in them, under the eight limitations mentioned in a former letter; and the further one, that the benefits of the habeas corpus act shall be enjoyed by individuals. Thus general powers being given to institute courts, and regulate their proceedings, with no provision for securing the rights principally in question, may not congress so exercise those powers, and constitutionally too, as to destroy those rights? Clearly, in my opinion, they are not in any degree secured. But, admitting the case is only doubtful, would it not be prudent and wise to secure them and remove all doubts, since all agree the people ought to enjoy these valuable rights, a very few men excepted, who seem to be rather of opinion that there is little or nothing in them? Were it necessary I might add many observations to shew their value and political importance.

The constitution will give congress general powers to raise and support armies. General powers carry with them incidental ones, and the means necessary to the end. In the exercise of these powers, is there any provision in the constitution to prevent the quartering of soldiers on the inhabitants? you will answer, there is not. This may sometimes be deemed a necessary measure in the support of armies; on what principle can the people claim the right to be exempt from this burden? they will urge, perhaps, the practice of the country, and the provisions made in some of the state constitutions—they will be answered, that their claim thus to be exempt is not founded in nature, but only in custom and opinion, or at best, in stipulations in some of the state constitutions, which are local, and inferior in their operation, and can have no controul over the general government—that they had adopted a federal constitution—had noticed several rights, but had been totally silent about this exemption—that they had given general powers relative to the subject, which, in their operation, regularly destroyed the claim. Though it is not to be presumed, that we are in any immediate danger from this quarter, yet it is fit and proper to establish, beyond dispute, those fights which are particularly valuable to individuals, and essential to the permanency and duration of free government. An excellent writer observes, that the English, always in possession of their freedom, are frequently unmindful of the value of it: we, at this period, do not seem to be so well off, having, in some instances abused ours; many of us are quite disposed to barter it away for what we call energy, coercion, and some other terms we use as vaguely as that of liberty—There is often as great a rage for change and novelty in politics, as in amusements and fashions.

All parties apparently agree, that the freedom of the press is a fundamental right, and ought not to be restrained by any taxes, duties, or in any manner whatever. Why should not the people, in adopting a federal constitution, declare this, even if there are only doubts about it. But, say the advocates, all powers not given are reserved:—true; but the great question is, are not powers given, in the excercise of which this fight may be destroyed? The people's or the printers claim to a free press, is founded on the fundamental laws, that is, compacts, and state constitutions, made by the people. The people, who can annihilate or alter those constitutions, can annihilate or limit this right. This may be done by giving general powers, as well as by using particular words. No right claimed under a state constitution, will avail against a law of the union, made in pursuance of the federal constitution: therefore the question is, what laws will congress have a right to make by the constitution of the union, and particularly touching the press? By art. 1. sect. 8. congress will have power to lay and collect taxes, duties, imposts and excise. By this congress will clearly have power to lay and collect all kind of taxes whatever—taxes on houses, lands, polls, industry, merchandize, &c.—taxes on deeds, bonds, and all written instruments—on writs, pleas, and all judicial proceedings, on licences, naval officers papers, &c. on newspapers, advertisements, &c. and to require bonds of the naval officers, clerks, printers, &c. to account for the taxes that may become due on papers that go through their hands. Printing, like all other business, must cease when taxed beyond its profits; and it appears to me, that a power to tax the press at discretion, is a power to destroy or restrain the freedom of it. There may be other powers given, in the exercise of which this freedom may be effected; and certainly it is of too much importance to be left thus liable to be taxed, and constantly to constructions and inferences. A free press is the channel of communication as to mercantile and public affairs; by means of it the people in large countries ascertain each others sentiments; are enabled to unite, and become formidable to those rulers who adopt improper measures. Newspapers may sometimes be the vehicles of abuse, and of many things not true; but these are but small inconveniencies, in my mind, among many advantages. A celebrated writer, I have several times quoted, speaking in high terms of the English liberties, says. "lastly the key stone was put to the arch, by the final establishment of the freedom of the press.," I shall not dwell longer upon the fundamental rights, to some of which I have attended in this letter, for the same reasons that these I have mentioned, ought to be expressly secured, lest in the exercise of general powers given they may be invaded: it is pretty clear, that some other of less importance, or less in danger, might with propriety also be secured.

I shall now proceed to examine briefly the powers proposed to be vested in the several branches of the government, and especially the mode of laying and collecting internal taxes.

The Federal Farmer.

Federalist No. 84, Alexander Hamilton

In the course of the foregoing review of the Constitution, I have taken notice of, and endeavored to answer most of the objections which have appeared against it. There however remain a few which either did not fall naturally under any particular head or were forgotten in their proper places. These shall now be discussed; but as the subject has been drawn into great length, I shall so far consult brevity as to comprise all my observations on these miscellaneous points in a single paper.

The most considerable of these remaining objections is that the plan of the convention contains no bill of rights. Among other answers given to this, it has been upon different occasions remarked that the constitutions of several of the States are in a similar predicament. I add that New York is of this number. And yet the opposers of the new system, in this State, who profess an unlimited admiration for its constitution, are among the most intemperate partisans of a bill of rights. To justify their zeal in this matter they allege two things: one is that, though the constitution of New York has no bill of rights prefixed to it, yet it contains, in the body of it, various provisions in favor of particular privileges and rights which, in substance, amount to the same thing; the other is that the Constitution adopts, in their full extent, the common and statute law of Great Britain, by which many other rights not expressed in it are equally secured.

To the first I answer that the Constitution proposed by the convention contains, as well as the constitution of this State, a number of such provisions.

Independent of those which relate to the structure of the government, we find the following: Article 1, section 3, clause 7—"Judgment in cases of impeachment shall not extend further than to removal from office and disqualification to hold and enjoy any office of honor, trust, or profit under the United States; but the party convicted shall, nevertheless, be liable and subject to indictment, trial, judgment, and punishment according to law." Section 9, of the same article, clause 2—"The privilege of the writ of habeas corpus shall not be suspended, unless when in cases of rebellion or invasion the public safety may require it." Clause 3—"No bill of attainder or ex post facto law shall be passed." Clause 7—"No title of nobility shall be granted by the United States; and no person holding any office of profit or trust under them shall, without the consent of the Congress, accept of any present, emolument, office, or title of any kind whatever, from any king, prince, or foreign state." Article 3, section 2, clause 3—"The trial of all crimes, except in cases of impeachment, shall be by jury; and such trial shall be held in the State where the said crimes shall have been committed; but when not committed within any State, the trial shall be at such place or places as the Congress may by law have directed." Section 3, of the same article—"Treason against the United States shall consist only in levying war against them, or in adhering to their enemies, giving them aid and comfort. No person shall be convicted of treason, unless on the testimony of two witnesses to the same overt act, or on confession in open court." And clause 3, of the same section—"The Congress shall have power to declare the punishment of treason; but no attainder of treason shall work corruption of blood, or forfeiture, except during the life of the person attainted."

It may well be a question whether these are not, upon the whole, of equal importance with any which are to be found in the constitution of this State. The establishment of the writ of habeas corpus, the prohibition of ex post facto laws, and of TITLES OF NOBILITY, to which we have no corresponding provision in our Constitution, are perhaps greater securities to liberty and republicanism than any it contains. The creation of crimes after the commission of the fact, or, in other words, the subjecting of men to punishment for things which, when they were done, were breaches of no law, and the practice of arbitrary imprisonments, have been, in all ages, the favorite and most formidable instruments of tyranny. The observations of the judicious Blackstone, in reference to the latter, are well worthy of recital: "To bereave a man of life [says he] or by violence to confiscate his estate, without accusation or trial, would be so gross and notorious an act of despotism as must at once convey the alarm of tyranny throughout the whole nation; but confinement of the person, by secretly hurrying him to jail, where his sufferings are unknown or forgotten, is a less public, a less striking, and therefore a more dangerous engine of arbitrary government." And as a remedy for this fatal evil he is everywhere peculiarly emphatical in his encomiums on the habeas corpus act, which in one place he calls "the BULWARK of the British Constitution."

Nothing need be said to illustrate the importance of the prohibition of titles of nobility. This may truly be denominated the cornerstone of republican government;

for so long as they are excluded there can never be serious danger that the government will be any other than that of the people.

To the second, that is, to the pretended establishment of the common and statute law by the Constitution, I answer that they are expressly made subject "to such alterations and provisions as the legislature shall from time to time make concerning the same." They are therefore at any moment liable to repeal by the ordinary legislative power, and of course have no constitutional sanction. The only use of the declaration was to recognize the ancient law and to remove doubts which might have been occasioned by the Revolution. This consequently can be considered as no part of a declaration of rights, which under our constitutions must be intended as limitations of the power of the government itself.

It has been several times truly remarked that bills of rights are, in their origin, stipulations between kings and their subjects, abridgments of prerogative in favor of privilege, reservations of rights not surrendered to the prince. Such was MAGNA CHARTA, obtained by the barons, sword in hand, from King John. Such were the subsequent confirmations of that charter by subsequent princes. Such was the Petition of Right assented to by Charles the First in the beginning of his reign. Such, also, was the Declaration of Right presented by the Lords and Commons to the Prince of Orange in 1688, and afterwards thrown into the form of an act of Parliament called the Bill of Rights. It is evident, therefore, that, according to their primitive signification, they have no application to constitutions, professedly founded upon the power of the people and executed by their immediate representatives and servants. Here, in strictness, the people surrender nothing; and as they retain everything they have no need of particular reservations, "We, the people of the United States, to secure the blessings of liberty to ourselves and our posterity, do ordain and establish this Constitution for the United States of America." Here is a better recognition of popular rights than volumes of those aphorisms which make the principal figure in several of our State bills of rights and which would sound much better in a treatise of ethics than in a constitution of government.

But a minute detail of particular rights is certainly far less applicable to a Constitution like that under consideration, which is merely intended to regulate the general political interests of the nation, than to a constitution which has the regulation of every species of personal and private concerns. If, therefore, the loud clamors against the plan of the convention, on this score, are well founded, no epithets of reprobation will be too strong for the constitution of this State. But the truth is that both of them contain all which, in relation to their objects, is reasonably to be desired.

I go further and affirm that bills of rights, in the sense and to the extent in which they are contended for, are not only unnecessary in the proposed Constitution but would even be dangerous. They would contain various exceptions to powers which are not granted; and, on this very account, would afford a colorable pretext to claim more than were granted. For why declare that things shall not be done which there is no power to do? Why, for instance, should it be said that the liberty of the press shall not be restrained, when no power is given by which restrictions may be imposed? I will not contend that such a provision would confer a regulating power; but it is evident that it would furnish, to men disposed to usurp, a plausible pretense for claiming that power. They might urge with a semblance of reason that the Constitution ought not to be charged with the absurdity of providing against the abuse of an authority which was not given, and that the provision against restraining the liberty of the press afforded a clear implication that a power to prescribe proper regulations concerning it was intended to be vested in the national government. This may serve as a specimen of the numerous handles which would be given to the doctrine of constructive powers, by the indulgence of an injudicious zeal for bills of rights.

On the subject of the liberty of the press, as much as has been said, I cannot forbear adding a remark or two: in the first place, I observe, that there is not a syllable concerning it in the constitution of this State; in the next, I contend that whatever has been said about it in that of any other State amounts to nothing. What signifies a declaration that "the liberty of the press shall be inviolably preserved"? What is the liberty of the press? Who can give it any definition which would not leave the utmost latitude for evasion? I hold it to be impracticable; and from this I infer that its security, whatever fine declarations may be inserted in any constitution respecting it, must altogether depend on public opinion, and on the general spirit of the people and of the government.

And here, after all, as is intimated upon another occasion, must we seek for the only solid basis of all our rights.

There remains but one other view of this matter to conclude the point. The truth is, after all the declamations we have heard, that the Constitution is itself, in every rational sense, and to every useful purpose, A BILL OF RIGHTS. The several bills of rights in Great Britain form its Constitution, and conversely the constitution of each State is its bill of rights. And the proposed Constitution, if adopted, will be the bill of rights of the Union. Is it one object of a bill of rights to declare and specify the political privileges of the citizens in the structure and administration of the government? This is done in the most ample and precise manner in the plan of the convention; comprehending various precautions for the public security which are not to be found in any of the State constitutions. Is another object of a bill of rights to define certain immunities and modes of proceeding, which are relative to personal and private concerns? This we have seen has also been attended to in a variety of cases in the same plan. Adverting therefore to the substantial meaning of a bill of rights, it is absurd to allege that it is not to be found in the work of the convention. It may be said that it does not go far enough though it will not be easy to make this appear; but it can with no propriety be contended that there is no such thing. It certainly must be immaterial what mode is observed as to the order of declaring the rights of the citizens if they are to be found in any part of the instrument which establishes the government. And hence it must be apparent that much of what has been said on this subject rests merely on verbal and nominal distinctions, entirely foreign from the substance of the thing.

Another objection which has been made, and which, from the frequency of its repetition, it is to be presumed is relied on, is of this nature: "It is improper [say the objectors] to confer such large powers as are proposed upon the national government, because the seat of that government must of necessity be too remote from many of the States to admit of a proper knowledge on the part of the constituent of the conduct of the representative body." This argument, if it proves anything, proves that there ought to be no general government whatever. For the powers which, it seems to be agreed on all hands, ought to be vested in the Union, cannot be safely intrusted to a body which is not under every requisite control. But there are satisfactory reasons to show that the objection is in reality not well founded. There is in most of the arguments which relate to distance a palpable illusion of the imagination. What are the sources of information by which the people in Montgomery County must regulate their judgment of the conduct of their representatives in the State legislature? Of personal observation they can have no benefit. This is confined to the citizens on the spot. They must therefore depend on the information of intelligent men, in whom they confide; and how must these men obtain their information? Evidently from the complexion of public measures, from the public prints, from correspondences with their representatives, and with other persons who reside at the place of their deliberations. This does not apply to Montgomery County only, but to all the counties at any considerable distance from the seat of government.

It is equally evident that the same sources of information would be open to the people in relation to the conduct of their representatives in the general government, and the impediments to a prompt communication which distance may be supposed to create will be overbalanced by the effects of the vigilance of the State governments. The executive and legislative bodies of each State will be so many sentinels over the persons employed in every department of the national administration; and as it will be in their power to adopt and pursue a regular and effectual system of intelligence, they can never be at a loss to know the behavior of those who represent their constituents in the national councils, and can readily communicate the same knowledge to the people. Their disposition to apprise the community of whatever may prejudice its interests from another quarter may be relied upon, if it were only from the rivalship of power. And we may conclude with the fullest assurance that the people, through that channel, will be better informed of the conduct of their national representatives than they can be by any means they now possess, of that of their State representatives.

It ought also to be remembered that the citizens who inhabit the country at and near the seat of government will, in all questions that affect the general liberty and prosperity, have the same interest with those who are at a distance, and that they will stand ready to sound the alarm when necessary, and to point out the actors in any pernicious project. The public papers will be expeditious messengers of intelligence to the most remote inhabitants of the Union.

Among the many extraordinary objections which have appeared against the proposed Constitution, the most extraordinary and the least colorable one is derived from the want of some provision respecting the debts due to the United States. This has been represented as a tacit relinquishment of those debts, and as a wicked contrivance to screen public defaulters. The newspapers have teemed with the most inflammatory railings on this head; and yet there is nothing clearer than that the suggestion is entirely void of foundation, and is the offspring of extreme ignorance or extreme dishonesty. In addition to the remarks I have made upon the subject in another place, I shall only observe that as it is a plain dictate of common sense, so it is also an established doctrine of political law, that "States neither lose any of their rights, nor are discharged from any of their obligations, by a change in the form of their civil government."

The last objection of any consequence, which I at present recollect, turns upon the article of expense. If it were even true that the adoption of the proposed government would occasion a considerable increase of expense, it would be an objection that ought to have no weight against the plan.

The great bulk of the citizens of America are with reason convinced that Union is the basis of their political happiness. Men of sense of all parties now with few exceptions agree that it cannot be preserved under the present system, nor without radical alterations; that new and extensive powers ought to be granted to the national head, and that these require a different organization of the federal government—a single body being an unsafe depositary of such ample authorities. In conceding all this, the question of expense must be given up; for it is impossible, with any degree of safety, to narrow the foundation upon which the system is to stand. The two branches of the legislature are, in the first instance, to consist of only sixty-five persons, which is the same number of which Congress, under the existing Confederation, may be composed. It is true that this number is intended to be increased; but this is to keep pace with the increase of the population and resources of the country. It is evident that a less number would, even in the first instance, have been unsafe, and that a continuance of the present number would, in a more advanced stage of population, be a very inadequate representation of the people.

Whence is the dreaded augmentation of expense to spring? One source pointed out is the multiplication of offices under the new government. Let us examine this a little.

It is evident that the principal departments of the administration under the present government are the same which will be required under the new. There are now a Secretary at War, a Secretary for Foreign Affairs, a Secretary for Domestic Affairs, a Board of Treasury, consisting of three persons, a treasurer, assistants, clerks, etc. These offices are indispensable under any system and will suffice under the new as well as under the old. As to ambassadors and other ministers and agents in foreign countries, the proposed. Constitution can make no other difference than to render their characters, where they reside, more respectable, and their services more useful. As to persons to be employed in the collection of the revenues; it is unquestionably true that these will form a very considerable addition to the number of federal officers; but it will not follow that this will occasion an increase of public expense. It will be in most cases nothing more than an exchange of State officers for national officers. In the collection of all duties, for instance, the persons employed will be wholly of the latter description. The States individually will stand in no need of any for this purpose. What difference can it make in point of expense to pay officers of the customs appointed by the State or those appointed by the United States? There is no good reason to suppose that either the number or the salaries of the latter will be greater than those of the former.

Where then are we to seek for those additional articles of expense which are to swell the account to the enormous size that has been represented to us? The chief item which occurs to me respects the support of the judges of the United States. I do not add the President, because there is now a president of Congress, whose expenses may not be far, if anything, short of those which will be incurred on account of the President of the United States. The support of the judges will clearly be an extra expense, but to what extent will depend on the particular plan which may be adopted in practice in regard to this matter. But it can upon no reasonable plan amount to a sum which will be an object of material consequence.

Let us now see what there is to counterbalance any extra expense that may attend the establishment of the proposed government. The first thing that presents itself is that a great part of the business which now keeps Congress sitting through the year will be transacted by the President. Even the management of foreign negotiations will naturally devolve upon him, according to general principles concerted with the Senate, and subject to their final concurrence. Hence it is evident that a portion of the year will suffice for the session of both the Senate and the House of Representatives; we may suppose about a fourth for the latter and a third, or perhaps a half, for the former. The extra business of treaties and appointments may give this extra occupation to the Senate. From this circumstance we may infer that, until the House of Representatives shall be increased greatly beyond its present number, there will be a considerable saving of expense from the difference between the constant session of the present and the temporary session of the future Congress.

But there is another circumstance of great importance in the view of economy. The business of the United States has hitherto occupied the State legislatures, as well as Congress. The latter has made requisitions which the former have had to provide for. Hence it has happened that the sessions of the State legislatures have been protracted greatly beyond what was necessary for the execution of the mere local business of the States. More than half their time has been frequently employed in matters which related to the United States. Now the members who compose the legislatures of the several States amount to two thousand and upwards, which number has hitherto performed what under the new system will be done in the first instance by sixty-five persons, and probably at no future period by above a fourth or a fifth of that number. The Congress under the proposed government will do all the business of the United States themselves, without the intervention of the State legislatures, who thenceforth will have only to attend to the affairs of their particular States, and will not have to sit in any proportion as long as they have heretofore done. This difference in the time of the sessions of the State legislatures will be all clear gain, and will alone form an article of saving, which may be regarded as an equivalent for any additional objects of expense that may be occasioned by the adoption of the new system.

The result from these observations is that the sources of additional expense from the establishment of the proposed Constitution are much fewer than may have been imagined; that they are counterbalanced by considerable objects of saving; and that while it is questionable on which side the scale will preponderate, it is certain that a government less expensive would be incompetent to the purposes of the Union.

Publius

"Giles Hickory" (or "On the Absurdity of a Bill of Rights"), Noah Webster

American Magazine (New York), December 1787

One of the principal objections to the new Federal Constitution is, that it contains no Bill of Rights. This objection, I presume to assert, is founded on ideas of government that are totally false. Men seem determined to adhere to old prejudices, and reason wrong, because our ancestors reasoned right. A Bill of Rights against the encroachments of Kings and Barons, or against any power independent of the people, is perfectly intelligible; but a Bill of Rights against the encroachments of an elective Legislature, that is, against our own encroachments on ourselves, is a curiosity in government.

One half the people who read books, have so little ability to apply what they read to their own practice, that they had better not read at all. The English nation, from which we descended, have been gaining their liberties, inch by inch, by forcing concessions from the crown and the Barons, during the course of six centuries. Magna Charta, which is called the palladium of English liberty, was dated in 1215, and the people of England were not represented in Parliament till the year 1265. Magna Charta established the rights of the Barons and the clergy against the encroachments of royal prerogative; but the commons or people were hardly noticed in that deed. There was but one clause in their favor, which stipulated that, "no villain or rustic should, by any fine, be bereaved of his carts, plows and instruments of husbandry." As for the rest, they were considered as a part of the property belonging to an estate, and were transferred, as other moveables, at the will of their owners. In the succeeding reign, they were permitted to send Representatives to Parliament; and from that time have been gradually assuming their proper degree of consequence in the British Legislature. In such a nation, every law or statute that defines the powers of the crown, and circumscribes them within determinate limits, must be considered as a barrier to guard popular liberty. Every acquisition of freedom must be established as a right, and solemnly recognized by the supreme power of the nation; lest it should be again resumed by the crown under pretence of ancient prerogative; For this reason, the habeas corpus act passed in the reign of Charles 2d, the statute of the 2d of William and Mary, and many others which are declaratory of certain privileges, are justly considered as the pillars of English freedom.

These statutes are however not esteemed because they are unalterable; for the same power that enacted them, can at any moment repeal them; but they are esteemed, because they are barriers erected by the Representatives of the nation, against a power that exists independent of their own choice.

But the same reasons for such declaratory constitutions do not exist in America, where the supreme power is the people in their Representatives. The Bills of Rights, prefixed to several of the constitutions of the United States, if considered as assigning the reasons of our separation from a foreign government, or as solemn declarations of right against the encroachments of a foreign jurisdiction, are perfectly rational, and were doubtless necessary. But if they are considered as barriers against the encroachments of our own Legislatures, or as constitutions unalterable by posterity, I venture to pronounce them nugatory, and to the last degree, absurd.

In our governments, there is no power of legislation, independent of the people; no power that has an interest detached from that of the public; consequently there is no power existing against which it is necessary to guard. While our Legislatures therefore remain elective, and the rulers have the same interest in the laws, as the subjects have, the rights of the people will be perfectly secure without any declaration in their favor.

But this is not the principal point. I undertake to prove that a standing Bill of Rights is absurd, because no constitutions, in a free government, can be unalterable. The present generation have indeed a right to declare what they deem a privilege; but they have no right to say what the next generation shall deem a privilege. A State is a supreme corporation that never dies. Its powers, when it acts for itself, are at all times, equally extensive; and it has the same right to repeal a law this year, as it had to make it the last. If therefore our posterity are bound by our constitutions, and can neither amend nor annul them, they are to all intents and purposes our slaves.

But it will be enquired, have we then no right to say, that trial by jury, the liberty of the press, the habeas corpus writ and other invaluable privileges, shall never be infringed nor destroyed? By no means. We have the same right to say that lands shall descend in a particular mode to the heirs of the deceased proprietor, and that such a mode shall never be altered by future generations, as we have to pass a law that the trial by jury shall never be abridged. The right of Jury-trial, which we deem invaluable, may in future cease to be a privilege; or other modes of trial more satisfactory to the people, may be devised. Such an event is neither impossible nor improbable. Have we then a right to say that our posterity shall not be judges of their own circumstances? The very attempt to make perpetual constitutions, is the assumption of a right to control the opinions of future generations; and to legislate for those over whom we have as little authority as we have over a nation in Asia. Nay we have as little right to say that trial by jury shall be perpetual, as the English, in the reign of Edward the Confessor, had, to bind their posterity forever to decide causes by fiery Ordeal, or single combat. There are perhaps many laws and regulations, which from their consonance to the eternal rules of justice, will always be good and conformable to the sense of a nation. But most institutions in society, by reason of an unceasing change of circumstances, either become altogether improper or require amendment; and every nation has at all times, the right of judging of its circumstances and determining on the propriety of changing its laws.

The English writers talk much of the omnipotence of Parliament; and yet they seem to entertain some scruples about their right to change particular parts of their constitution. I question much whether Parliament would not hesitate to change, on any occasion, an article of Magna Charta. Mr. Pitt, a few years ago, attempted to reform the mode of representation in Parliament. Immediately an uproar was raised against the measure, as unconstitutional. The representation of the kingdom, when first established, was doubtless equal and wise; but by the increase of some cities and boroughs and the depopulation of others, it has become extremely unequal. In some boroughs there is scarcely an elector left to enjoy its privileges. If the nation feels no great inconvenience from this change of circumstances, under the old mode of representation, a reform is unnecessary. But if such a change has produced any national evils of magnitude enough to be felt, the present form of electing the Representatives of the nation, however constitutional, and venerable for its antiquity, may at any time be amended, if it should be the sense of Parliament. The expediency of the alteration must always be a matter of opinion; but all scruples as to the right of making it are totally groundless.

Magna Charta may be considered as a contract between two parties, the King and the Barons, and no contract can be altered but by the consent of both parties. But whenever any article of that deed or contract shall become inconvenient or oppressive, the King, Lords and Commons may either amend or annul it at pleasure.

The same reasoning applies to each of the United States, and to the Federal Republic in general. But an important question will arise from the foregoing remarks, which must be the subject of another paper.

SOURCE: The Call for Amendments. Letters from the "Federal Farmer," No. XVI (1787). Hamilton, Alexander. *The Federalist*, No. 84. 1788. Webster, Noah, "Giles Hickory." *American Magazine* (December 1787).

CONSTITUTION OF THE UNITED STATES
(1787–1788)

Delegates sent to Philadelphia from the thirteen states to discuss changes to the existing Confederation government formed the Constitution during the summer of 1787. The delegates tended to be well-educated, wealthy conservatives who worried about the economic and diplomatic problems facing the young United States. Shortly after the beginning of the proceedings, the delegates adopted a rule of debate behind closed doors, so that views could be expressed without fear of repercussions at home. James Madison of Virginia used this opportunity to introduce his plan for revising the government of the United States. Madison's Virginia Plan meant to scrap the Articles of Confederation, replacing it with a highly centralized government based on *federalism.* The delegates, realizing that Madison's plan answered their desire for a government that would protect liberty while ensuring order, began in earnest to create a new government of the United States.

The heart of Madison's proposal balanced and separated the three most important functions of government: a bicameral legislature, a strong executive, and an independent judiciary. The Constitution models itself on past successful republics in creating a lower house, the members of which are elected according to the respective population of the states, with authority over how money is raised and spent; and an upper house, restricted to two representatives from each state, with functions resembling that of a general court. Executive power is modeled on the consuls of the ancient Roman Republic, who had two general powers: to serve as commander in chief and to execute the laws passed by the legislative power. Madison, who realized the importance of freeing judges from the influence of significant others, created a judicial system independent of the legislative and executive branches. The resulting Constitution balances power among the varying functions of the federal government while creating a method for local, state, and federal governments to share power.

Russell Lawson,
Bacone College

See also **Constitution of the United States.**

Preamble

WE THE PEOPLE of the United States, in Order to form a more perfect Union, establish Justice, insure domestic Tranquility, provide for the common defence, promote the general Welfare, and secure the Blessings of Liberty to ourselves and our Posterity, do ordain and establish this Constitution for the United States of America.

Article One

Section 1. All legislative Powers herein granted shall be vested in a Congress of the United States, which shall consist of a Senate and House of Representatives.

Section 2. The House of Representatives shall be composed of Members chosen every second Year by the People of the several States, and the Electors in each State shall have the qualifications requisite for Electors of the most numerous Branch of the State Legislature. No Person shall be a Representative who shall not have attained to the age of twenty five Years, and been seven Years a Citizen of the United States, and who shall not, when elected, be an Inhabitant of that State in which he shall be chosen.

Representatives and direct Taxes shall be apportioned among the several States which may be included within this Union, according to their respective Numbers, which shall be determined by adding to the whole Number of free Persons, including those bound to Service for a Term of Years, and excluding Indians not taxed, three fifths of all other Persons. The actual Enumeration shall be made within three Years after the first Meeting of the Congress of the United States, and within every subsequent Term of ten Years, in such Manner as they shall by Law direct. The Number of Representatives shall not exceed one for every thirty Thousand, but each State shall have at Least one Representative; and until such enumeration shall be made, the State of New Hampshire shall be entitled to chuse three, Massachusetts eight, Rhode Island and Providence Plantations one, Connecticut five, New York six, New Jersey four, Pennsylvania eight, Delaware one, Maryland six, Virginia ten, North Carolina five, South Carolina five and Georgia three.

When vacancies happen in the Representation from any State, the Executive Authority thereof shall issue Writs of Election to fill such Vacancies.

The House of Representatives shall chuse their Speaker and other officers; and shall have the sole Power of Impeachment.

Section 3. The Senate of the United States shall be composed of two Senators from each State, chosen by the Legislature thereof, for six Years; and each Senator shall have one Vote.

Immediately after they shall be assembled in Consequence of the first Election, they shall be divided as equally as may be into three Classes. The Seats of the Senators of the first class shall be vacated at the Expiration of the second Year, of the second Class at the Expiration of the fourth Year, and of the third Class at the Expiration of the sixth Year, so that one third may be chosen every second Year; and if Vacancies happen by Resignation, or otherwise, during the Recess of the Legislature of any State, the Executive thereof may make temporary Appointments until the next Meeting of the Legislature, which shall then fill such Vacancies.

No Person shall be a Senator who shall not have attained to the Age of thirty Years, and been nine Years a Citizen of the United States, and who shall not, when elected, be an Inhabitant of that State for which he shall be chosen.

The Vice President of the United States shall be President of the Senate, but shall have no Vote, unless they be equally divided.

The Senate shall chuse their other Officers, and also a President pro tempore, in the Absence of the Vice President, or when he shall exercise the Office of President of the United States.

The Senate shall have the sole Power to try all Impeachments. When sitting for that Purpose, they shall be on Oath or Affirmation. When the President of the United States is tried, the Chief Justice shall preside: and no Person shall be convicted without the Concurrence of two thirds of the Members present.

Judgment in Cases of Impeachment shall not extend further than to removal from Office, and disqualification to hold and enjoy any Office of honor, Trust or Profit under the United States: but the Party convicted shall nevertheless be liable and subject to Indictment, Trial, Judgment and Punishment, according to Law.

Section 4. The Times, Places and Manner of holding Elections for Senators and Representatives, shall be prescribed in each State by the Legislature thereof; but the Congress may at any time by Law make or alter such Regulations, except as to the Places of chusing Senators.

The Congress shall assemble at least once in every Year, and such Meeting shall be on the first Monday in December, unless they shall by Law appoint a different Day.

Section 5. Each House shall be the Judge of the Elections, returns and Qualifications of its own Members, and a Majority of each shall constitute a Quorum to do Business; but a smaller Number may adjourn from day to day, and may be authorized to compel the Attendance of absent Members, in such Manner, and under such Penalties as each House may provide.

Each House may determine the Rules of its Proceedings, punish its Members for disorderly Behavior, and, with the Concurrence of two thirds, expel a Member.

Each House shall keep a Journal of its Proceedings, and from time to time publish the same, excepting such Parts as may in their Judgment require Secrecy; and the Yeas and Nays of the Members of either House on any question shall, at the Desire of one-fifth of those Present, be entered on the Journal.

Neither House, during the Session of Congress, shall, without the Consent of the other, adjourn for more than three days, nor to any other Place than that in which the two Houses shall be sitting.

Section 6. The Senators and Representatives shall receive a Compensation for their Services, to be ascertained by Law, and paid out of the Treasury of the United States. They shall in all Cases, except Treason, Felony and Breach of the Peace, be privileged from Arrest during their Attendance at the Session of their respective Houses, and in going to and returning from the same; and for any Speech or Debate in either House, they shall not be questioned in any other Place.

No Senator or Representative shall, during the Time for which he was elected, be appointed to any civil Office under the Authority of the United States which shall have been created, or the Emoluments whereof shall have been increased during such time; and no Person holding any Office under the United States, shall be a member of either House during his Continuance in Office.

Section 7. All Bills for raising Revenue shall originate in the House of Representatives; but the Senate may propose or concur with Amendments as on other Bills.

Every Bill which shall have passed the House of Representatives and the Senate, shall, before it become a Law, be presented to the President of the United States; if he approve he shall sign it, but if not he shall return it, with his Objections to that House in which it shall have originated, who shall enter the Objections at large on their Journal, and proceed to reconsider it. If after such Reconsideration two thirds of that House shall agree to pass the Bill, it shall be sent, together with the Objections, to the other House, by which it shall likewise be reconsidered, and if approved by two thirds of that House, it shall become a Law. But in all such Cases the Votes of both Houses shall be determined by yeas and Nays, and the Names of the Persons voting for and against the Bill shall be entered on the Journal of each House respectively. If any Bill shall not be returned by the President within ten Days (Sundays excepted) after it shall have been presented to him, the Same shall be a Law, in like Manner as if he had signed it, unless the Congress by their Adjournment prevent its Return, in which Case it shall not be a Law.

Every Order, resolution, or Vote to which the Concurrence of the Senate and House of Representatives may be necessary (except on a question of Adjournment) shall be presented to the President of the United States; and before the Same shall take Effect, shall be approved by him, or being disapproved by him, shall be repassed by two thirds of the Senate and House of Representatives, according to the Rules and Limitations prescribed in the Case of a Bill.

Section 8. The Congress shall have Power

To lay and collect Taxes, Duties, Imposts and Excises, to pay the Debts and provide for the common Defence and general Welfare of the United States; but all Duties, Imposts and Excises shall be uniform throughout the United States;

To borrow Money on the credit of the United States; To regulate Commerce with foreign Nations, and among the several States, and with the Indian Tribes;

To establish a uniform Rule of Naturalization, and uniform Laws on the subject of Bankruptcies throughout the United States;

To coin Money, regulate the Value thereof, and of foreign coin, and fix the Standard of Weights and Measures;

To provide for the Punishment of counterfeiting the Securities and current Coin of the United States;

To establish Post-Offices and post-Roads;

To promote the Progress of Science and useful Arts, by securing for limited Times to Authors and Inventors the exclusive Right to their respective Writings and Discoveries;

To constitute Tribunals inferior to the Supreme Court;

To define and punish Piracies and Felonies committed on the high Seas, and Offenses against the Law of Nations;

To declare War, grant Letters of Marque and Reprisal, and make Rules concerning Captures on Land and Water;

To raise and support Armies, but no Appropriation of Money to that Use shall be for a longer Term than two Years;

To provide and maintain a Navy;

To make Rules for the Government and Regulation of the land and naval Forces;

To provide for calling forth the Militia to execute the Laws of the Union, suppress insurrections and repel invasions;

To provide for organizing, arming, and disciplining, the Militia, and for governing such Part of them as may be employed in the Service of the United States, reserving to the States respectively, the Appointment of the Officers, and the Authority of training the Militia according to the discipline prescribed by Congress;

To exercise exclusive Legislation in all Cases whatsoever, over such District (not exceeding ten Miles square) as may, by Cession of particular States, and the Acceptance of Congress, become the Seat of the Government of the United States, and to exercise like Authority over all Places purchased by the Consent of the Legislature of the State in which the Same shall be, for the erection of Forts, Magazines, arsenals, dock-Yards, and other needful Buildings; and

To make all Laws which shall be necessary and proper for carrying into Execution the foregoing Powers, and all other Powers vested by this Constitution in the Government of the United States, or in any Department or Officer thereof.

Section 9. The Migration or Importation of such Persons as any of the States now existing shall think proper to admit, shall not be prohibited by the Congress prior to the Year one thousand eight hundred and eight, but a Tax or duty may be imposed on such Importation, not exceeding ten dollars for each Person.

The Privilege of the Writ of Habeas Corpus shall not be suspended, unless when in Cases of Rebellion or Invasion the public Safety may require it.

No bill of Attainder or ex post facto Law shall be passed.

No Capitation, or other direct Tax shall be laid, unless in Proportion to the Census or Enumeration herein before directed to be taken.

No Tax or Duty shall be laid on Articles exported from any State.

No Preference shall be given by any Regulation of Commerce or Revenue to the Ports of one State over those of another: nor shall Vessels bound to, or from, one State, be obliged to enter, clear, or pay Duties in another.

No Money shall be drawn from the Treasury, but in Consequence of Appropriations made by Law; and a regular Statement and Account of the Receipts and Expenditures of all public Money shall be published from time to time.

No Title of Nobility shall be granted by the United States: And no Person holding any Office of Profit or Trust under them, shall, without the Consent of the Congress, accept of any present, Emolument, Office, or Title, of any kind whatever, from any King, Prince or Foreign State.

Section 10. No State shall enter into any Treaty, Alliance, or Confederation; grant Letters of Marque and Reprisal; coin Money; emit Bills of Credit; make any Thing but gold and silver Coin a Tender in Payment of Debts; pass any Bill of Attainder, ex post facto Law, or Law impairing the Obligation of Contracts, or grant any Title of Nobility.

No State shall, without the Consent of the Congress, lay any Imposts or Duties on Imports or Exports, except what may be absolutely necessary for executing it's inspection Laws: and the net Produce of all Duties and Imposts, laid by any State on Imports or Exports, shall be for the use of the Treasury of the United States; and all such Laws shall be subject to the Revision and Controul of the Congress.

No State shall, without the Consent of Congress, lay any Duty of Tonnage, keep Troops, or Ships of War in time of Peace, enter into any Agreement or Compact with another State, or with a foreign Power, or engage in War, unless actually invaded, or in such imminent Danger as will not admit of delay.

Article Two

Section 1. The executive Power shall be vested in a President of the United States of America. He shall hold his Office during the Term of four Years, and, together with the Vice President chosen for the same Term, be elected, as follows:

Each State shall appoint, in such Manner as the Legislature thereof may direct, a Number of Electors, equal to the whole Number of Senators and Representatives to which the State may be entitled in the Congress: but no Senator or Representative, or person holding an Office of Trust or Profit under the United States, shall be appointed an elector.

The Electors shall meet in their respective States, and vote by Ballot for two Persons, of whom one at least shall not be an Inhabitant of the same State with themselves. And they shall make a List of all the persons voted for, and of the Number of Votes for each; which List they shall sign and certify, and transmit sealed to the Seat of the Government of the United States, directed to the President of the Senate. The President of the Senate shall, in the Presence of the Senate and House of Representatives, open all the Certificates, and the Votes shall then be counted. The Person having the greatest Number of Votes shall be the President, if such Number be a Majority of the whole Number of Electors appointed; and if there be more than one who have such Majority, and have an equal Number of Votes, then the House of Representatives shall immediately chuse by Ballot one of them for President; and if no person have a Majority, then from the five highest on the List the said House shall in like Manner chuse the President. But in chusing the President, the Votes shall be taken by States, the representation from each State having one Vote; a quorum for this Purpose shall consist of a Member or Members from two thirds of the States, and a Majority of all the States shall be necessary to a Choice. In every Case, after the Choice of the President, the Person having the greatest number of votes of the electors shall be the Vice President. But if there should remain two or more who have equal Votes, the Senate shall chuse from them by Ballot the Vice President.

The Congress may determine the time of chusing the Electors, and the Day on which they shall give their Votes; which Day shall be the same throughout the United States.

No Person except a natural born Citizen, or a Citizen of the United States, at the time of the Adoption of this Constitution, shall be eligible to the Office of President; neither shall any person be eligible to that Office who shall not have attained to the Age of thirty five Years, and been fourteen Years a Resident within the United States.

In Case of the Removal of the President from Office, or of his Death, Resignation, or Inability to discharge the Powers and Duties of the said Office, the Same shall devolve on the Vice President, and the Congress may by Law provide for the Case of Removal, Death, Resignation or Inability, both of the President and Vice President, declaring what Officer shall then act as President, and such Officer shall act accordingly, until the Disability be removed, or a President shall be elected.

The President shall, at stated Times, receive for his Services, a Compensation, which shall neither be increased nor diminished during the Period for which he shall have been elected, and he shall not receive within that Period any other Emolument from the United States, or any of them.

Before he enter on the Execution of his Office, he shall take the following Oath or Affirmation:

> "I do solemnly swear (or affirm) that I will faithfully execute the Office of President of the United States, and will to the best of my Ability, preserve, protect and defend the Constitution of the United States."

Section 2. The President shall be Commander in Chief of the Army and Navy of the United States, and of the Militia of the several States, when called into the actual service of the United States; he may require the Opinion, in writing, of the principal Officer in each of the executive Departments, upon any Subject relating to the Duties of their respective Offices, and he shall have Power to grant Reprieves and Pardons for Offenses against the United States, except in Cases of Impeachment.

He shall have Power, by and with the Advice and Consent of the Senate, to make Treaties, provided two thirds of the Senators present concur; and he shall nominate, and by and with the Advice and Consent of the Senate, shall appoint Ambassadors, other public Ministers and Consuls, Judges of the supreme Court, and all other Officers of the United States, whose appointments are not herein otherwise provided for, and which shall be established by law: but the Congress may by law vest the appointment of such inferior officers, as they think proper, in the President alone, in the Courts of Law, or in the Heads of Departments.

The President shall have Power to fill up all Vacancies that may happen during the Recess of the Senate, by granting Commissions which shall expire at the End of their next session.

Section 3. He shall from time to time give to the Congress Information of the State of the Union, and recommend to their consideration such Measures as he shall judge necessary and expedient; he may, on extraordinary Occasions, convene both Houses, or either of them, and in Case of Disagreement between them, with Respect to the Time of Adjournment, he may adjourn them to such Time as he shall think proper; he shall receive Ambassadors and other public Ministers; he shall take Care that the Laws be faithfully executed, and shall Commission all the Officers of the United States.

Section 4. The President, Vice President and all civil Officers of the United States, shall be removed from Office on Impeachment for, and Conviction of, Treason, Bribery, or other high Crimes and Misdemeanors.

Article Three

Section 1. The judicial Power of the United States, shall be vested in one supreme Court, and in such inferior Courts as the Congress may from time to time ordain and establish. The Judges, both of the supreme and inferior courts, shall hold their Offices during good Behavior, and shall, at stated times, receive for their Services, a Compensation, which shall not be diminished during their Continuance in Office.

Section 2. The judicial Power shall extend to all Cases, in Law and Equity, arising under this Constitution, the Laws of the United States, and Treaties made, or which shall be made, under their Authority; to all Cases affecting Ambassadors, other public Ministers and Consuls; to all Cases of admiralty and maritime Jurisdiction; to Controversies to which the United States shall be a Party; to Controversies between two or more States; between a State and Citizens of another State; between Citizens of different States; between Citizens of the same State claiming Lands under Grants of different States, and between a State, or the Citizens thereof, and foreign States, Citizens or Subjects.

In all Cases affecting Ambassadors, other public Ministers and Consuls, and those in which a State shall be party, the supreme Court shall have original Jurisdiction. In all the other Cases before mentioned, the supreme Court shall have appellate Jurisdiction, both as to Law and Fact, with such Exceptions, and under such Regulations as the Congress shall make.

The trial of all Crimes, except in Cases of Impeachment, shall be by Jury; and such trial shall be held in the State where the said Crimes shall have been committed; but when not committed within any State, the Trial shall be at such Place or Places as the Congress may by Law have directed.

Section 3. Treason against the United States, shall consist only in levying War against them, or in adhering to their Enemies, giving them Aid and Comfort. No Person shall be convicted of Treason unless on the Testimony of two Witnesses to the same overt Act, or on Confession in open court.

The Congress shall have Power to declare the Punishment of Treason, but no Attainder of Treason shall work Corruption of Blood, or Forfeiture except during the Life of the Person attainted.

Article Four

Section 1. Full Faith and Credit shall be given in each State to the public Acts, Records, and judicial Proceedings of every other State. And the Congress may by general Laws prescribe the Manner in which such Acts, Records and Proceedings shall be proved, and the Effect thereof.

Section 2. The Citizens of each State shall be entitled to all Privileges and Immunities of Citizens in the several States.

A person charged in any State with Treason, Felony, or other Crime, who shall flee from Justice, and be found in another State, shall on Demand of the Executive Authority of the State from which he fled, be delivered up, to be removed to the State having Jurisdiction of the Crime.

No Person held to Service or Labour in one State, under the Laws thereof, escaping into another, shall, in Consequence of any Law or Regulation therein, be discharged from such Service or Labour, but shall be delivered up on Claim of the Party to whom such Service or Labour may be due.

Section 3. New States may be admitted by the Congress into this Union; but no new States shall be formed or erected within the Jurisdiction of any other State; nor any State be formed by the Junction of two or more States, or Parts of States, without the Consent of the Legislatures of the States concerned as well as of the Congress.

The Congress shall have Power to dispose of and make all needful Rules and Regulations respecting the Territory or other Property belonging to the United States; and nothing in this Constitution shall be so construed as to Prejudice any Claims of the United States, or of any particular State.

Section 4. The United States shall guarantee to every State in this Union a Republican Form of government, and shall protect each of them against Invasion; and on Application of the Legislature, or of the Executive (when the legislature cannot be convened) against domestic Violence.

Article Five

The Congress, whenever two thirds of both Houses shall deem it necessary, shall propose Amendments to this Constitution, or, on the Application of the Legislatures of two thirds of the several States, shall call a Convention for proposing Amendments, which, in either Case, shall be valid to all intents and purposes, as part of this Constitution, when ratified by the Legislatures of three fourths of the several States, or by Conventions in three fourths thereof, as the one or the other Mode of Ratification may be proposed by the Congress; Provided that no Amendment which may be made prior to the Year One thousand eight hundred and eight shall in any Manner affect the first and fourth Clauses in the Ninth Section of the first Article; and that no State, without its Consent, shall be deprived of its equal Suffrage in the Senate.

Article Six

All Debts contracted and Engagements entered into, before the Adoption of this Constitution, shall be as valid against the United States under this Constitution, as under the Confederation.

This Constitution, and the Laws of the United States which shall be made in Pursuance thereof; and all Treaties made, or which shall be made, under the Authority of the United States, shall be the supreme Law of the Land; and the Judges in every State shall be bound thereby, any Thing in the Constitution or Laws of any State to the Contrary notwithstanding.

The Senators and Representatives before mentioned, and the Members of the several State Legislatures, and all executive and judicial Officers, both of the United States and of the several States, shall be bound by Oath or Affirmation, to support this Constitution; but no religious Test shall ever be required as a Qualification to any Office or public Trust under the United States.

Article Seven

The Ratification of the Conventions of nine States, shall be sufficient for the establishment of this Constitution between the States so ratifying the Same.

Done in Convention by the Unanimous Consent of the States present the Seventeenth day of September in the Year of our Lord one thousand seven hundred and Eighty-seven and of the Independence of the United States of America the Twelfth, In witness whereof We have hereunto subscribed our Names,

George Washington
President and deputy from Virginia

New Hampshire.

John Langdon
Nicholas Gilman

Georgia.

William Few
Abraham Baldwin

Massachusetts.

Nathaniel Gorham
Rufus King

Connecticut.

William Samuel Johnson
Roger Sherman

New Jersey.

William Livingston
David Brearley
William Paterson
Jonathan Dayton

New York.

Alexander Hamilton

Maryland.

James McHenry
Daniel Carrol
Daniel of St. Thomas Jenifer

Pennsylvania.

Benjamin Franklin
Robert Morris
Thomas FitzSimons
James Wilson
Thomas Mifflin
George Clymer
Jared Ingersoll
Gouverneur Morris

Virginia.

John Blair
James Madison Jr.

North Carolina.

William Blount
Hugh Williamson
Richard Dobbs Spaight

Delaware.

George Read
John Dickinson
Jacob Broom
Gunning Bedford Jr.
Richard Bassett

South Carolina.

John Ruttledge
Charles Pinckney
Charles Cotesworth Pinckney
Pierce Butler

Attest:

William Jackson, Secretary

Amendments

ARTICLE ONE Congress shall make no law respecting an establishment of religion, or prohibiting the free exercise thereof; or abridging the freedom of speech, or of the press; or the right of the people peaceably to assemble, and to petition the government for a redress of grievances.

ARTICLE TWO A well regulated militia, being necessary to the security of a free State, the right of the people to keep and bear arms, shall not be infringed.

ARTICLE THREE No soldier shall, in time of peace, be quartered in any house, without the consent of the owner, nor in time of war, but in a manner to be prescribed by law.

ARTICLE FOUR The right of the people to be secure in their persons, houses, papers, and effects, against unreasonable searches and seizures, shall not be violated, and no warrants shall issue, but upon probable cause, supported by Oath or affirmation, and particularly describing the place to be searched, and the persons or things to be seized.

ARTICLE FIVE No person shall be held to answer for a capital, or otherwise infamous crime, unless on a presentment or indictment of a Grand Jury, except in cases arising in the land or naval forces, or in the militia, when in actual service in time of war or public danger; nor shall any person be subject for the same offence to be twice put in jeopardy of life or limb; nor shall be compelled in any criminal case to be a witness against himself, nor be deprived of life, liberty, or property, without due process of law; nor shall private property be taken for public use, without just compensation.

ARTICLE SIX In all criminal prosecutions, the accused shall enjoy the right to a speedy and public trial, by an impartial jury of the State and district wherein the crime shall have been committed, which district shall have been previously ascertained by law, and to be informed of the nature and cause of the accusation; to be confronted with the witnesses against him; to have compulsory process for obtaining witnesses in his favor, and to have the assistance of counsel for his defence.

ARTICLE SEVEN In suits at common law, where the value in controversy shall exceed twenty dollars, the right of trial by jury shall be preserved, and no fact tried by a jury, shall be otherwise re-examined in any court of the United States, than according to the rules of the common law.

ARTICLE EIGHT Excessive bail shall not lie required, nor excessive fines imposed, nor cruel and unusual punishments inflicted.

ARTICLE NINE The enumeration in the Constitution, of certain rights, shall not be construed to deny or disparage others retained by the people.

ARTICLE TEN The powers not delegated to the United States by the Constitution, nor prohibited by it to the States, are reserved to the States respectively, or to the people.

ARTICLE ELEVEN January 8, 1798

The judicial power of the United States shall not be construed to extend to any suit in law or equity, commenced or prosecuted against one of the United States by Citizens of another State, or by citizens or subjects of any foreign State.

ARTICLE TWELVE September 25, 1804

The Electors shall meet in their respective States, and vote by ballot for President and Vice President, one of whom at least, shall not be an inhabitant of the same State with themselves; they shall name in their ballots the person voted for as President, and in distinct ballots the person voted for as Vice President, and they shall make distinct lists of all persons voted for as President, and of all persons voted for as Vice President, and of the number of votes for each, which lists they shall sign and certify, and transmit sealed to the seat of the Government of the United States, directed to the President of the Senate; the President of the Senate shall, in the presence of the Senate and House of Representatives, open all the certificates and the votes shall then be counted; the person having the greatest number of votes for President, shall be the President, if such number be a majority of the whole number of Electors appointed; and if no person have such majority, then from the persons having the highest numbers not exceeding three on the list of those voted for as President, the House of Representatives shall choose immediately, by ballot, the President. But in choosing the President, the votes shall be taken by States, the representation from each State having one vote; a quorum for this purpose shall consist of a member or members from two-thirds of the States, and a majority of all the States shall be necessary to a choice. And if the House of Representatives shall not choose a President whenever the right of choice shall devolve upon them, before the fourth day of March next following, then the Vice President shall act as President, as in the case of the death or other constitutional disability of the President. The person having the greatest number of votes as Vice President, shall be the Vice President, if such number be a majority of the whole number of Electors appointed, and if no person have a majority, then from the two highest numbers on the list, the Senate shall choose the Vice President; a quorum for the purpose shall consist of two-thirds of the whole number of Senators, and a majority of the whole number shall be necessary to a choice. But no person constitutionally ineligible to the office of President shall be eligible to that of Vice-President of the United States.

ARTICLE THIRTEEN December 18, 1865

Section 1. Neither slavery nor involuntary servitude, except as a punishment for crime whereof the party shall have been duly convicted, shall exist within the United States, or any place subject to their jurisdiction.

Section 2. Congress shall have power to enforce this article by appropriate legislation.

ARTICLE FOURTEEN July 28, 1868

Section 1. All persons born or naturalized in the United States, and subject to the jurisdiction thereof, are citizens of the United States and of the State wherein they reside. No State shall make or enforce any law which shall abridge the privileges or immunities of citizens of the United States; nor shall any State deprive any person of life, liberty, or property, without due process of law; nor deny to any person within its jurisdiction the equal protection of the laws.

Section 2. Representatives shall be apportioned among the several States according to their respective numbers, counting the whole number of persons in each State, excluding Indians not taxed. But when the right to vote at any election for the choice of Electors for President and Vice President of the United States, Representatives in Congress, the executive and judicial officers of a State, or the members of the Legislature thereof, is denied to any of the male inhabitants of such State, being twenty-one years of age, and citizens of the United States, or in any way abridged, except for participation in rebellion, or other crime, the basis of representation therein shall be reduced in the proportion which the number of such male citizens shall bear to the whole number of male citizens twenty-one years of age in such State.

Section 3. No person shall be a Senator or Representative in Congress, or Elector of President and Vice-President, or hold any office, civil or military, under the United States, or under any State, who, having previously taken an oath, as a member of Congress, or as an officer of the United States, or as a member of any State Legislature, or as an executive or judicial officer of any State, to support the Constitution of the United States, shall have engaged in insurrection or rebellion against the same, or given aid or comfort to the enemies thereof, but Congress may by a vote of two-thirds of each House, remove such disability.

Section 4. The validity of the public debt of the United States, authorized by law, including debts incurred for payment of pensions and bounties for services in suppressing insurrection or rebellion, shall not be questioned. But neither the United States nor any State shall assume or pay any debt or obligation incurred in aid of insurrection or rebellion against the United States, or any claim for the loss or emancipation of any slave; but all such debts, obligations and claims shall be held illegal and void.

Section 5. The Congress shall have power to enforce, by appropriate legislation, the provisions of this article.

ARTICLE FIFTEEN March 30, 1870

Section 1. The right of citizens of the United States to vote shall not be denied or abridged by the United States or by any State on account of race, color, or previous condition of servitude.

Section 2. The Congress shall have power to enforce this article by appropriate legislation.

ARTICLE SIXTEEN February 25, 1913

The Congress shall have power to lay and collect taxes on incomes, from whatever source derived, without apportionment among the several States and without regard to any census or enumeration.

ARTICLE SEVENTEEN May 31, 1913

The Senate of the United States shall be composed of two Senators from each State, elected by the people thereof, for six years; and each Senator shall have one vote. The electors in each State shall have the qualifications requisite for electors of the most numerous branch of the State legislature.

When vacancies happen in the representation of any State in the Senate, the executive authority of such State shall issue writs of election to fill such vacancies: Provided, That the legislature of any State may empower the Executive thereof to make temporary appointments until the people fill the vacancies by election as the legislature may direct.

This amendment shall not be so construed as to affect the election or term of any senator chosen before it becomes valid as part of the Constitution.

ARTICLE EIGHTEEN January 29, 1919

Section 1. After one year from the ratification of this article, the manufacture, sale, or transportation of intoxicating liquors within, the importation thereof into, or the exportation thereof from the United States and all territory subject to the jurisdiction thereof for beverage purposes is hereby prohibited.

Section 2. The Congress and the several States shall have concurrent power to enforce this article by appropriate legislation.

Section 3. This article shall be inoperative unless it shall have been ratified as an amendment to the Constitution by the Legislatures of the several States, as provided in the Constitution, within seven years from the date of the submission hereof to the States by Congress.

ARTICLE NINETEEN August 26, 1920

The right of citizens of the United States to vote shall not be denied or abridged by the United States or by any State on account of sex.

The Congress shall have power by appropriate legislation to enforce the provisions of this article.

ARTICLE TWENTY February 6, 1933

Section 1. The terms of the President and Vice-President shall end at noon on the twentieth day of January, and the terms of Senators and Representatives at noon on the third day of January, of the years in which such terms would have ended if this article had not been ratified; and the terms of their successors shall then begin.

Section 2. The Congress shall assemble at least once in every year, and such meeting shall begin at noon on the third day of January, unless they shall by law appoint a different day.

Section 3. If, at the time fixed for the beginning of the term of the President, the President-elect shall have died, the Vice-President-elect shall become President. If a President shall not have been chosen before the time fixed for the beginning of his term, or if the President-elect shall have failed to qualify, then the Vice-President-elect shall act as President until a President shall have qualified; and the Congress may by law provide for the case wherein neither a President-elect nor a Vice-President-elect shall have qualified, declaring who shall then act as President, or the manner in which one who is to act shall be selected, and such person shall act accordingly until a President or Vice-President shall have qualified.

Section 4. The Congress may by law provide for the case of the death of any of the persons from whom the House of Representatives may choose a President whenever the right of choice shall have devolved upon them, and for the case of the death of any of the persons from whom the Senate may choose a Vice-President whenever the right of choice shall have devolved upon them.

Section 5. Sections 1 and 2 shall take effect on the 15th day of October following the ratification of this article.

Section 6. This article shall be inoperative unless it shall have been ratified as an amendment to the Constitution by the Legislatures of three-fourths of the several States within seven years from the date of its submission.

ARTICLE TWENTY-ONE December 5, 1933

Section 1. The eighteenth article of amendment to the Constitution of the United States is hereby repealed.

Section 2. The transportation or importation into any State, Territory, or Possession of the United States for delivery or use therein of intoxicating liquors, in violation of the laws thereof, is hereby prohibited.

Section 3. The article shall be inoperative unless it shall have been ratified as an amendment to the Constitution by conventions in the several States, as provided in the Constitution, within seven years from the date of the submission hereof to the States by the Congress.

ARTICLE TWENTY-TWO February 26, 1951

Section 1. No person shall be elected to the office of the President more than twice, and no person who has held the office of President, or acted as President for more than two years of a term to which some other person was elected President shall be elected to the office of the President more than once. But this Article shall not apply to any person holding the office of President when this Article was proposed by the Congress, and shall not prevent any person who May be holding the office of President, or acting as President, during the term within which this Article becomes operative from holding the office of President or acting as President during the remainder of such term.

Section 2. This article shall be inoperative unless it shall have been ratified as an amendment to the Constitution by the Legislatures of three-fourths of the several States within seven years from the date of its submission to the States by the Congress.

ARTICLE TWENTY-THREE June 16, 1960

Section 1. The District constituting the seat of government of the United States shall appoint in such manner as the Congress may direct:

A number of electors of President and Vice-President equal to the whole number of Senators and Representatives in Congress to which the District would be entitled if it were a State, but in no event more than the least populous State; they shall be in addition to those appointed by the States, but they shall be considered, for the purposes of the election of President and Vice-President, to be electors appointed by a State; and they shall meet in the District and perform such duties as provided by the twelfth article of amendment.

Section 2. The Congress shall have power to enforce this article by appropriate legislation.

ARTICLE TWENTY-FOUR February 4, 1964

Section 1. The right of citizens of the United States to vote in any primary or other election for President or Vice-President, for electors for President or Vice-President, or for Senator or Representative in Congress, shall not be denied or abridged by the United States or any State by reason of failure to pay any poll tax or other tax.

Section 2. The Congress shall have power to enforce this article by appropriate legislation.

ARTICLE TWENTY-FIVE February 10, 1967

Section 1. In case of the removal of the President from office or of his death or resignation, the Vice-President shall become President.

Section 2. Whenever there is a vacancy in the office of the Vice-President, the President shall nominate a Vice-President who shall take office upon confirmation by a majority vote of both Houses of Congress.

Section 3. Whenever the President transmits to the President pro tempore of the Senate and the Speaker of the House of Representatives his written declaration that he is unable to discharge the powers and duties of his office, and until he transmits to them a written declaration to the contrary, such powers and duties shall be discharged by the Vice-President as Acting President.

Section 4. Whenever the Vice-President and a majority of either the principal officers of the executive departments or of such other body as Congress may by law provide, transmit to the President pro tempore of the Senate and the Speaker of the House of Representatives their written declaration that the President is unable to discharge the powers and duties of his office, the Vice-President shall immediately assume the powers and duties of the office as Acting President.

Thereafter, when the President transmits to the President pro tempore of the Senate and the Speaker of the House of Representatives his written declaration that no inability exists, he shall resume the powers and duties of his office unless the Vice-President and a majority of either the principal officers of the executive department or of such other body as Congress may by law provide, transmit within four day to the President pro tempore of the Senate and the Speaker of the House of Representatives their written declaration that the President is unable to discharge the powers and duties of his office. Thereupon Congress shall decide the issue, assembling within forty-eight hours for that purpose if not in session. If the Congress, within twenty-one days after receipt of the latter written declaration, or, if Congress is not in session, within twenty-one days after Congress is required to assemble, determines by two-thirds vote of both Houses that the President is unable to discharge the powers and duties of his office, the Vice-President shall continue to discharge the same as Acting President; otherwise, the President shall resume the powers and duties of his office.

ARTICLE TWENTY-SIX July 1, 1971

Section 1. The right of citizens of the United States, who are eighteen years of age or older, to vote shall not be denied or abridged by the United States or by any State on account of age.

Section 2. The Congress shall have power to enforce this article by appropriate legislation.

ARTICLE TWENTY-SEVEN May 7, 1992

No law, varying the compensation for the services of the Senators and Representatives, shall take effect, until an election of representatives shall have intervened.

WASHINGTON'S FAREWELL ADDRESS
(17 September 1796)

When George Washington was unanimously elected by the Constitutional Convention as the first president of the United States in 1789, the newly forged nation was still deeply uncertain of its own survival. Washington, a towering figure, legendary even in his own time, served two terms as president, but grew weary at last of public service and longed to return to his beloved farm at Mount Vernon, determined not to seek a third. No provisions for term limits had yet been considered, and Washington could almost certainly have remained president for the rest of his life. What followed, however, was perhaps as astonishing as the Revolution itself. The ruler of a nation, and its greatest military hero, voluntarily surrendered his office. For Washington, this act was the very fulfillment of the promise of the War of Independence and a sign to the rest of the world that the Revolution had not been in vain. Among its other subjects, Washington's masterful "Farewell Address," published in newspapers in 1796, warned against close alliances with foreign powers and gave birth to the sometimes controversial American tradition of Isolationism.

Laura M. Miller,
Vanderbilt University

See also **Foreign Policy; Neutrality; Washington's Farewell Address.**

United States, *September 17, 1796. Friends and Fellow-Citizens:*

The period for a new election of a citizen to administer the Executive Government of the United States being not far distant, and the time actually arrived when your thoughts must be employed in designating the person who is to be clothed with that important trust, it appears to me proper, especially as it may conduce to a more distinct expression of the public voice, that I should now apprise you of the resolution I have formed to decline being considered among the number of those out of whom a choice is to be made....

The impressions with which I first undertook the arduous trust were explained on the proper occasion. In the discharge of this trust I will only say that I have, with good intentions, contributed toward the organization and administration of the Government the best exertions of which a very fallible judgment was capable. Not unconscious in the outset of the inferiority of my qualifications, experience in my own eyes, perhaps still more in the eyes of others, has strengthened the motives to diffidence of myself; and every day the increasing weight of years admonishes me more and more that the shade of retirement is as necessary to me as it will be welcome. Satisfied that if any circumstances have given peculiar value to my services they were temporary, I have the consolation to believe that, while choice and prudence invite me to quit the political scene, patriotism does not forbid it....

Here, perhaps, I ought to stop. But a solicitude for your welfare which can not end with my life, and the apprehension of danger natural to that solicitude, urge me on an occasion like the present to offer to your solemn contemplation and to recommend to your frequent review some sentiments which are the result of much reflection, of no inconsiderable observation, and which appear to me all important to the permanency of your felicity as a people....

Interwoven as is the love of liberty with every ligament of your hearts, no recommendation of mine is necessary to fortify or confirm the attachment.

The unity of government which constitutes you one people is also now dear to you. It is justly so, for it is a main pillar in the edifice of your real independence, the support of your tranquillity at home, your peace abroad, of your safety, of your prosperity, of that very liberty which you so highly prize. But as it is easy to foresee that from different causes and from different quarters much pains will be taken, many artifices employed, to weaken in your minds the conviction of this truth, as this is the point in your political fortress against which the batteries of internal and external enemies will be most constantly and actively (though often covertly and insidiously) directed, it is of infinite moment that you should properly estimate the immense value of your national union to your collective and individual happiness; that you should cherish a cordial, habitual, and immovable attachment to it; accustoming yourselves to think and speak of it as of the palladium of your political safety and prosperity; watching for its preservation with jealous anxiety; discountenancing whatever may suggest even a suspicion that it can in any event be abandoned, and indignantly frowning upon the first dawning of every attempt to alienate any portion of our country from the rest or to enfeeble the sacred ties which now link together the various parts.

For this you have every inducement of sympathy and interest. Citizens by birth or choice of a common country, that country has a right to concentrate your affections. The name of American, which belongs to you in your national capacity, must always exalt the just pride of patriotism more than any appellation derived from local discriminations. With slight shades of difference, you have the same religion, manners, habits, and political principles. You have in a common cause fought and triumphed together. The independence and liberty you possess are the work of joint councils and joint efforts, of common dangers, sufferings, and successes.

But these considerations, however powerfully they address themselves to your sensibility, are greatly outweighed by those which apply more immediately to your interest. Here every portion of our country finds the most commanding motives for carefully guarding and preserving the union of the whole.

The *North*, in an unrestrained intercourse with the *South*, protected by the equal laws of a common government, finds in the productions of the latter great additional resources of maritime and commercial enterprise and precious materials of manufacturing industry. The *South*, in the same intercourse, benefiting by the same agency of the *North*, sees its agriculture grow and its commerce expand. Turning partly into its own channels the seamen of the *North*, it finds its particular navigation invigorated; and while it contributes in different ways to nourish and increase the general mass of the national navigation, it looks forward to the protection of a maritime strength to which itself is unequally adapted. The *East*, in a like intercourse with the *West*, already finds, and in the progressive improvement of interior communications by land and water will more and more find, a valuable vent for the commodities which it brings from abroad or manufactures at home. The *West* derives from the *East* supplies requisite to its growth and comfort, and what is perhaps of still greater consequence, it must of necessity owe the *secure* enjoyment of indispensable *outlets* for its own productions to the weight, influence, and the future maritime strength of the Atlantic side of the Union, directed by an indissoluble community of interest as *one nation*. Any other tenure by which the *West* can hold this essential advantage, whether derived from its own separate strength or from an apostate and unnatural connection with any foreign power, must be intrinsically precarious.

While, then, every part of our country thus feels an immediate and particular interest in union, all the parts combined can not fail to find in the united mass of means and efforts greater strength, greater resource, proportionably greater security from external danger, a less frequent interruption of their peace by foreign nations, and what is of inestimable value, they must derive from union an exemption from those broils and wars between themselves which so frequently afflict neighboring countries not tied together by the same governments, which their own rivalships alone would be sufficient to produce, but which opposite foreign alliances, attachments, and intrigues would stimulate and imbitter. Hence, likewise, they will avoid the necessity of those overgrown military establishments which, under any form of government, are inauspicious to liberty, and which are to be regarded as particularly hostile to republican liberty. In this sense it is that your union ought to be considered as a main prop of your liberty, and that the love of the one ought to endear to you the preservation of the other....

Is there a doubt whether a common government can embrace so large a sphere? Let experience solve it. To listen to mere speculation in such a case were criminal. It is well worth a fair and full experiment. With such powerful and obvious motives to union affecting all parts of our country, while experience shall not have demonstrated its impracticability, there will always be reason to distrust the patriotism of those who in any quarter may endeavor to weaken its bands.

In contemplating the causes which may disturb our union it occurs as matter of serious concern that any ground should have been furnished for characterizing parties by *geographical* discriminations—*Northern* and *Southern*, *Atlantic* and *Western*—whence designing men may endeavor to excite a belief that there is a real difference of local interests and views. One of the expedients of party to acquire influence within particular districts is to misrepresent the opinions and aims of other districts. You can not shield yourselves too much against the jealousies and heartburnings which spring from these misrepresentations; they tend to render alien to each other those who ought to be bound together by fraternal affection....

To the efficacy and permanency of your union a government for the whole is indispensable. No alliances, however strict, between the parts can be an adequate substitute. They must inevitably experience the infractions and interruptions which all alliances in all times have experienced. Sensible of this momentous truth, you have improved upon your first essay by the adoption of a Constitution of Government better calculated than your former for an intimate union and for the efficacious management of your common concerns. This Government, the offspring of our own choice, uninfluenced and unawed, adopted upon full investigation and mature deliberation, completely free in its principles, in the distribution of its powers, uniting security with energy, and containing within itself a provision for its own amendment, has a just claim to your confidence and your support. Respect for its authority, compliance with its laws, acquiescence in its measures, are duties enjoined by the fundamental maxims of true liberty. The basis of our political systems is the right of the people to make and to alter their constitutions of government. But the constitution which at any time exists till changed by an explicit and authentic act of the whole people is sacredly obligatory upon all. The very idea of the power and the right of the people to establish government presupposes the duty of every individual to obey the established government. . . .

Toward the preservation of your Government and the permanency of your present happy state, it is requisite not only that you steadily discountenance irregular oppositions to its acknowledged authority, but also that you resist with care the spirit of innovation upon its principles, however specious the pretexts. One method of assault may be to effect in the forms of the Constitution alterations which will impair the energy of the system, and thus to undermine what can not be directly overthrown. In all the changes to which you may be invited remember that time and habit are at least as necessary to fix the true character of governments as of other human institutions; that experience is the surest standard by which to test the real tendency of the existing constitution of a country; that facility in changes upon the credit of mere hypothesis and opinion exposes to perpetual change, from the endless variety of hypothesis and opinion; and remember especially that for the efficient management of your common interests in a country so extensive as ours a government of as much vigor as is consistent with the perfect security of liberty is indispensable. Liberty itself will find in such a government, with powers properly distributed and adjusted, its surest guardian. It is, indeed, little else than a name where the government is too feeble to withstand the enterprises of faction, to confine each member of the society within the limits prescribed by the laws, and to maintain all in the secure and tranquil enjoyment of the rights of person and property.

I have already intimated to you the danger of parties in the State, with particular reference to the founding of them on geographical discriminations. Let me now take a more comprehensive view, and warn you in the most solemn manner against the baneful effects of the spirit of party generally.

This spirit, unfortunately, is inseparable from our nature, having its root in the strongest passions of the human mind. It exists under different shapes in all governments, more or less stifled, controlled, or repressed; but in those of the popular form it is seen in its greatest rankness and is truly their worst enemy. . . .

It serves always to distract the public councils and enfeeble the public administration. It agitates the community with ill-founded jealousies and false alarms; kindles the animosity of one part against another; foments occasionally riot and insurrection. It opens the door to foreign influence and corruption, which find a facilitated access to the government itself through the channels of party passion. Thus the policy and the will of one country are subjected to the policy and will of another.

There is an opinion that parties in free countries are useful checks upon the administration of the government, and serve to keep alive the spirit of liberty. This within certain limits is probably true; and in governments of a monarchical cast patriotism may look with indulgence, if not with favor, upon the spirit of party. But in those of the popular character, in governments purely elective, it is a spirit not to be encouraged. From their natural tendency it is certain there will always be enough of that spirit for every salutary purpose; and there being constant danger of excess, the effort ought to be by force of public opinion to mitigate and assuage it. A fire not to be quenched, it demands a uniform vigilance to prevent its bursting into a flame, lest, instead of warming, it should consume.

It is important, likewise, that the habits of thinking in a free country should inspire caution in those intrusted with its administration to confine themselves within their respective constitutional spheres, avoiding in the exercise of the powers of one department to encroach upon another. The spirit of encroachment tends to consolidate the powers of all the departments in one, and thus to create, whatever the form of government, a real despotism. . . . If in the opinion of the people the distribution or modification of the constitutional powers be in any particular wrong, let it be corrected by an amendment in the way which the Constitution designates. But let there be no change by usurpation; for though this in one instance may be the instrument of good, it is the customary weapon by which free governments are destroyed. The precedent must always greatly overbalance in permanent evil any partial or transient benefit which the use can at any time yield.

Of all the dispositions and habits which lead to political prosperity, religion and morality are indispensable supports. In vain would that man claim the tribute of patriotism who should labor to subvert these great pillars of human happiness—these firmest props of the duties of men and citizens. The mere politician, equally with the pious man, ought to respect and to cherish them. A volume could not trace all their connections with private and public felicity. Let it simply be asked, Where is the security for property, for reputation, for life, if the sense of religious obligation *desert* the oaths which are the instruments of investigation in courts of justice? And let us with caution indulge the supposition that morality can be maintained without religion. Whatever may be conceded to the influence of refined education on minds of peculiar structure, reason and experience both forbid us to expect that national morality can prevail in exclusion of religious principle.

It is substantially true that virtue or morality is a necessary spring of popular government. The rule indeed extends with more or less force to every species of free government. Who that is a sincere friend to it can look with indifference upon attempts to shake the foundation of the fabric? Promote, then, as an object of primary importance, institutions for the general diffusion of knowledge. In proportion as the structure of a government gives force to public opinion, it is essential that public opinion should be enlightened.

As a very important source of strength and security, cherish public credit. One method of preserving it is to use it as sparingly as possible, avoiding occasions of expense by cultivating peace, but remembering also that timely disbursements to prepare for danger frequently prevent much greater disbursements to repel it; avoiding likewise the accumulation of debt, not only by shunning occasions of expense, but by vigorous exertions in time of peace to discharge the debts which unavoidable wars have occasioned, not ungenerously throwing upon posterity the burthen which we ourselves ought to bear....

Observe good faith and justice toward all nations. Cultivate peace and harmony with all. Religion and morality enjoin this conduct. And can it be that good policy does not equally enjoin it? It will be worthy of a free, enlightened, and at no distant period a great nation to give to mankind the magnanimous and too novel example of a people always guided by an exalted justice and benevolence. Who can doubt that in the course of time and things the fruits of such a plan would richly repay any temporary advantages which might be lost by a steady adherence to it? Can it be that Providence has not connected the permanent felicity of a nation with its virtue? The experiment, at least, is recommended by every sentiment which ennobles human nature. Alas! is it rendered impossible by its vices?

In the execution of such a plan nothing is more essential than that permanent, inveterate antipathies against particular nations and passionate attachments for others should be excluded, and that in place of them just and amicable feelings toward all should be cultivated. The nation which indulges toward another an habitual hatred or an habitual fondness is in some degree a slave. It is a slave to its animosity or to its affection, either of which is sufficient to lead it astray from its duty and its interest. Antipathy in one nation against another disposes each more readily to offer insult and injury, to lay hold of slight causes of umbrage, and to be haughty and intractable when accidental or trifling occasions of dispute occur.

So, likewise, a passionate attachment of one nation for another produces a variety of evils. Sympathy for the favorite nation, facilitating the illusion of an imaginary common interest in cases where no real common interest exists, and infusing into one the enmities of the other, betrays the former into a participation in the quarrels and wars of the latter without adequate inducement or justification. It leads also to concessions to the favorite nation of privileges denied to others, which is apt doubly to injure the nation making the concessions by unnecessarily parting with what ought to have been retained, and by exciting jealousy, ill will, and a disposition to retaliate in the parties from whom equal privileges are withheld; and it gives to ambitious, corrupted, or deluded citizens (who devote themselves to the favorite nation) facility to betray or sacrifice the interests of their own country without odium, sometimes even with popularity, gilding with the appearances of a virtuous sense of obligation, a commendable deference for public opinion, or a laudable zeal for public good the base or foolish compliances of ambition, corruption, or infatuation....

Against the insidious wiles of foreign influence (I conjure you to believe me, fellow-citizens) the jealousy of a free people ought to be *constantly* awake, since history and experience prove that foreign influence is one of the most baneful foes of republican government. But that jealousy, to be useful, must be impartial, else it becomes the instrument of the very influence to be avoided, instead of a defense against it. Excessive partiality for one foreign nation and excessive dislike of another cause those whom they actuate to see danger only on one side, and serve to veil and even second the arts of influence on the other. Real patriots who may resist the intrigues of the favorite are liable to become suspected and odious, while its tools and dupes usurp the applause and confidence of the people to surrender their interests.

The great rule of conduct for us in regard to foreign nations is, in extending our commercial relations to have with them as little *political* connection as possible. So far as we have already formed engagements let them be fulfilled with perfect good faith. Here let us stop.

Europe has a set of primary interests which to us have none or a very remote relation. Hence she must be engaged in frequent controversies, the causes of which are essentially foreign to our concerns. Hence, therefore, it must be unwise in us to implicate ourselves by artificial ties in the ordinary vicissitudes of her politics or the ordinary combinations and collisions of her friendships or enmities.

Our detached and distant situation invites and enables us to pursue a different course. If we remain one people, under an efficient government, the period is not far off when we may defy material injury from external annoyance; when we may take such an attitude as will cause the neutrality we may at any time resolve upon to be scrupulously respected; when belligerent nations, under the impossibility of making acquisitions upon us, will not lightly hazard the giving us provocation; when we may choose peace or war, as our interest, guided by justice, shall counsel.

Why forego the advantages of so peculiar a situation? Why quit our own to stand upon foreign ground? Why, by interweaving our destiny with that of any part of Europe, entangle our peace and prosperity in the toils of European ambition, rivalship, interest, humor, or caprice?

It is our true policy to steer clear of permanent alliances with any portion of the foreign world, so far, I mean, as we are now at liberty to do it; for let me not be understood as capable of patronizing infidelity to existing engagements. I hold the maxim no less applicable to public than to private affairs that honesty is always the best policy. I repeat, therefore, let those engagements be observed in their genuine sense. But in my opinion it is unnecessary and would be unwise to extend them.

Taking care always to keep ourselves by suitable establishments on a respectable defensive posture, we may safely trust to temporary alliances for extraordinary emergencies.

Harmony, liberal intercourse with all nations are recommended by policy, humanity, and interest. But even our commercial policy should hold an equal and impartial hand, neither seeking nor granting exclusive favors or preferences; consulting the natural course of things; diffusing and diversifying by gentle means the streams of commerce, but forcing nothing; establishing with powers so disposed, in order to give trade a stable course, to define the rights of our merchants, and to enable the Government to support them, conventional rules of intercourse, the best that present circumstances and mutual opinion will permit, but temporary and liable to be from time to time abandoned or varied as experience and circumstances shall dictate; constantly keeping in view that it is folly in one nation to look for disinterested favors from another; that it must pay with a portion of its independence for whatever it may accept under that character; that by such acceptance it may place itself in the condition of having given equivalents for nominal favors, and yet of being reproached with ingratitude for not giving more. There can be no greater error than to expect or calculate upon real favors from nation to nation. It is an illusion which experience must cure, which a just pride ought to discard....

Though in reviewing the incidents of my Administration I am unconscious of intentional error, I am nevertheless too sensible of my defects not to think it probable that I may have committed many errors. Whatever they may be, I fervently beseech the Almighty to avert or mitigate the evils to which they may tend. I shall also carry with me the hope that my country will never cease to view them with indulgence, and that, after forty-five years of my life dedicated to its service with an upright zeal, the faults of incompetent abilities will be consigned to oblivion, as myself must soon be to the mansions of rest.

Relying on its kindness in this as in other things, and actuated by that fervent love toward it which is so natural to a man who views in it the native soil of himself and his progenitors for several generations, I anticipate with pleasing expectation that retreat in which I promise myself to realize without alloy the sweet enjoyment of partaking in the midst of my fellow-citizens the benign influence of good laws under a free government—the ever-favorite object of my heart, and the happy reward, as I trust, of our. mutual cares, labors, and dangers.

SOURCE: Ford, Worthington C., ed. *The Writings of George Washington.* New York: Putnam, 1889–1893.

MADISON'S WAR MESSAGE
(1 June 1812)

The close of the American Revolutionary War did not signal an end to tensions and occasional hostilities between the fledgling United States and Great Britain. Annoyed by the reluctance of the British to withdraw entirely from American territory and by their support of the Indians on America's frontiers, the United States once again entered a period of disaffection and unease with its former ruler. The breaking point came in 1803 when, following hostilities between itself and France, Great Britain imposed a blockade on the European continent and in enforcing it seized several American ships and "impressed," or forced into service against their will, a number of American and British sailors. Hopeful of peace, then-president Thomas Jefferson attempted to strike back with a number of trade embargos, which were ultimately unsuccessful. Tensions continued to mount until at last, faced with the possibility of an economic depression, many Americans once again sounded the cry for war against the Crown. James Madison, who succeeded Jefferson as president, along with a congress made up partially of the so-called War Hawks, heeded the call. Shortly after delivering his war message, on 18 June 1812 James Madison signed a declaration of war, and once again the armies of the United States rose to meet the British on the field of battle.

Laura M. Miller,
Vanderbilt University

See also **War of 1812.**

Washington, *June 1, 1812.*
To the Senate and House of Representatives of the United States:

I communicate to Congress certain documents, being a continuation of those heretofore laid before them on the subject of our of our affairs with Great Britain.

Without going back beyond the renewal in 1803 of the war in which Great Britain is engaged, and omitting unrepaired wrongs of inferior magnitude, the conduct of her Government presents a series of acts hostile to the United States as an independent and neutral nation.

British cruisers have been in the continued practice of violating the American flag on the great highway of nations, and of seizing and carrying off persons sailing under it, not in the exercise of a belligerent right founded on the law of nations against an enemy, but of a municipal prerogative over British subjects. British jurisdiction is thus extended to neutral vessels in a situation where no laws can operate but the law of nations and the laws of the country to which the vessels belong, and a self-redress is assumed which, if British subjects were wrongfully detained and alone concerned, is that substitution of force for a resort to the responsible sovereign which falls within the definition of war....

The practice, hence, is so far from affecting British subjects alone that, under the pretext of searching for these, thousands of American citizens, under the safeguard of public law and of their national flag, have been torn from their country and from everything dear to them; have been dragged on board ships of war of a foreign nation and exposed, under the severities of their discipline, to be exiled to the most distant and deadly climes, to risk their lives in the battles of their oppressors, and to be the melancholy instruments of taking away those of their own brethren.

Against this crying enormity, which Great Britain would be so prompt to avenge if committed against herself, the United States have in vain exhausted remonstrances and expostulations, and that no proof might be wanting of their conciliatory dispositions, and no pretext left for a continuance of the practice, the British Government was formally assured of the readiness of the United States to enter into arrangements such as could not be rejected if the recovery of British subjects were the real and the sole object. The communication passed without effect.

British cruisers have been in the practice also of violating the rights and the peace of our coasts. They hover over and harass our entering and departing commerce. To the most insulting pretensions they have added the most lawless proceedings in our very harbors, and have wantonly spilt American blood within the sanctuary of our territorial jurisdiction....

Under pretended blockades, without the presence of an adequate force and sometimes without the practicability of applying one, our commerce has been plundered in every sea, the great staples of our country have been cut off from their legitimate markets, and a destructive blow aimed at our agricultural and maritime interests. In aggravation of these predatory measures they have been considered as in force from the dates of their notification, a retrospective effect being thus added, as has been done in other important cases, to the unlawfulness of the course pursued. And to render the outrage the more signal these mock blockade have been reiterated and enforced in the face of official communications from the British Government declaring as the true definition of a legal blockade "that particular ports must be actually invested and previous warning given to vessels bound to them not to enter."

Not content with these occasional expedients for laying waste our neutral trade, the cabinet of Britain resorted at length to the sweeping system of blockades, under the name of orders in council, which has been molded and managed as might best suit its political views, its commercial jealousies, or the avidity of British cruisers. . . .

Abandoning still more all respect for the neutral rights of the United States and for its own consistency, the British Government now demands as prerequisites to a repeal of its orders as they relate to the United States that a formality should be observed in the repeal of the French decrees nowise necessary to their termination nor exemplified by British usage, and that the French repeal, besides including that portion of the decrees which operates within a territorial jurisdiction, as well as that which operates on the high seas, against the commerce of the United States should not be a single and special repeal in relation to the United States, but should be extended to whatever other neutral nations unconnected with them may be affected by those decrees....

It has become, indeed, sufficiently certain that the commerce of the United States is to be sacrificed, not as interfering with the belligerent rights of Great Britain; not as supplying the wants of her enemies, which she herself supplies; but as interfering with the monopoly which she covets for her own commerce and navigation. She carries on a war against the lawful commerce of a friend that she may the better carry on a commerce with an enemy—a commerce polluted by the forgeries and perjuries which are for the most part the only passports by which it can succeed....

In reviewing the conduct of Great Britain toward the United States our attention is necessarily drawn to the warfare just renewed by the savages on one of our extensive frontiers—a warfare which is known to spare neither age nor sex and to be distinguished by features peculiarly shocking to humanity. It is difficult to account for the activity and combinations which have for some time been developing themselves among tribes in constant intercourse with British traders and garrisons without connecting their hostility with that influence and without recollecting the authenticated examples of such interpositions heretofore furnished by the officers and agents of that Government.

Such is the spectacle of injuries and indignities which have been heaped on our country, and such the crisis which its unexampled forbearance and conciliatory efforts have not been able to avert. . . .

Our moderation and conciliation have had no other effect than to encourage perseverance and to enlarge pretensions. We behold our seafaring citizens still the daily victims of lawless violence, committed on the great common and highway of nations, even within sight of the country which owes them protection. We behold our vessels, freighted with the products of our soil and industry, or returning with the honest proceeds of them, wrested from their lawful destinations, confiscated by prize courts no longer the organs of public law but the instruments of arbitrary edicts, and their unfortunate crews dispersed and lost, or forced or inveigled in British ports into British fleets, whilst arguments, are employed in support of these aggressions which have no foundation but in a principle equally supporting a claim to regulate our external commerce in all cases whatsoever. We behold, in fine, on the side of Great Britain a state of war against the United States, and on the side of the United States a state of peace toward Great Britain.

Whether the United States shall continue passive under these progressive usurpations and these accumulating wrongs, or, opposing force to force in defense of their national rights, shall commit a just cause into the hands of the Almighty Disposer of Events, avoiding all connections which might entangle it in the contest or views of other powers, and preserving a constant readiness to concur in an honorable re-establishment of peace and friendship, is a solemn question which the Constitution wisely confides to the legislative department of the Government. In recommending it to their early deliberations I am happy in the assurance that the decision will be worthy the enlightened and patriotic councils of a virtuous, a free, and a powerful nation. . . .

SOURCE: *A Compilation of the Messages and Papers of the Presidents, 1789–1897.* Vol. 1. New York: Bureau of National Literature, 1897.

EXPANSION

MESSAGE ON THE LEWIS AND CLARK EXPEDITION
(1803)

In 1803, the United States purchased the massive Louisiana Territory that stretched from the 49th parallel in the north to the Red River in the south, from the Mississippi River west to the Rocky Mountains. Although Louisiana had been alternately under Spanish and French control, it was a largely unsettled wilderness region inhabited by sporadic tribes of American Indians. President Thomas Jefferson (1743–1826), who had directed the purchase of Louisiana from the French, realized that the economic and political interests of the United States required full knowledge of the people, productions, and geography of the Territory. The Missouri River was the most important region demanding exploration. The land was rich in furs; Jefferson hoped the United States could monopolize the fur trade. The Indians were warlike, particularly with each other, which required careful diplomacy to bring peace to the region. Jefferson as a scientist was especially interested in finding out the natural productions of Louisiana Territory. The Missouri River reputedly originated deep within the Rocky Mountains, so that its source might be only a short distance from a westward flowing river, such as the Columbia, hence allowing for water passage through the continent.

To accomplish these goals Jefferson chose his own secretary and friend, Meriwether Lewis, to command a military expedition up the Missouri River. Jefferson's instructions to Lewis detail the hazards and uncertainty of the journey, the necessity to live off the land and rely on developing positive trade relations with the native inhabitants, and the mind-boggling list of topics to fill the pages of the daily journal to be kept in the wilderness. Jefferson's instructions reveal the lack of knowledge about the Missouri River that the most informed scientist in America had at his disposal, which was the fundamental reason for the journey of Lewis and Clark.

Russell Lawson,
Bacone College

***See also* Explorations and Expeditions: U.S.; Lewis and Clark Expedition; Western Exploration.**

Confidential Message to Congress

Gentlemen of the Senate, and of the House of Representatives:

As the continuance of the act for establishing trading houses with the Indian tribes will be under the consideration of the legislature at its present session, I think it my duty to communicate the views which have guided me in the execution of that act, in order that you may decide on the policy of continuing it, in the present or any other form, or discontinue it altogether, if that shall, on the whole, seem most for the public good.

The Indian tribes residing within the limits of the United States have, for a considerable time, been growing more and more uneasy at the constant diminution of the territory they occupy, although effected by their own voluntary sales. And the policy has long been gaining strength with them of refusing absolutely all further sale, on any conditions; insomuch that, at this time, it hazards their friendship, and excites dangerous jealousies and perturbations in their minds to make any overture for the purchase of the smallest portions of their land.

A very few tribes only are not yet obstinately in these dispositions. In order, peaceably, to counteract this policy of theirs, and to provide an extension of territory which the rapid increase of our numbers will call for, two measures are deemed expedient. First, to encourage them to abandon hunting, to apply to the raising stock, to agriculture, and domestic manufacture, and thereby prove to themselves that less land and labor will maintain them in this better than in their former mode of living. The extensive forests necessary in the hunting life, will then become useless, and they will see advantage in exchanging them for the means of improving their farms, and of increasing their domestic comforts. Second, to multiply trading houses among them, and place within their reach those things which will contribute more to their domestic comfort than the possession of extensive, but uncultivated wilds. Experience and reflection will develop to them the wisdom of exchanging what they can spare and we want, for what we can spare and they want. In leading them to agriculture, to manufactures, and civilization; in bringing together their and our settlements, and in preparing them ultimately to participate in the benefits of our governments, I trust and believe we are acting for their greatest good.

At these trading houses we have pursued the principles of the act of Congress which directs that the commerce shall be carried on liberally, and requires only that the capital stock shall not be diminished. We, consequently, undersell private traders, foreign and domestic, drive them from the competition; and, thus, with the goodwill of the Indians, rid ourselves of a description of men who are constantly endeavoring to excite in the Indian mind suspicions, fears, and irritations toward us. A letter now enclosed shows the effect of our competition on the operations of the traders, while the Indians, perceiving the advantage of purchasing from us, are soliciting, generally, our establishment of trading houses among them. In one quarter this is particularly interesting.

The legislature, reflecting on the late occurrences on the Mississippi, must be sensible how desirable it is to possess a respectable breadth of country on that river, from our southern limit to the Illinois, at least, so that we may present as firm a front on that as on our eastern border. We possess what is below the Yazoo, and can probably acquire a certain breadth from the Illinois and Wabash to the Ohio; but, between the Ohio and Yazoo, the country all belongs to the Chickasaws, the most friendly tribe within our limits, but the most decided against the alienation of lands. The portion of their country most important for us is exactly that which they do not inhabit. Their settlements are not on the Mississippi but in the interior country. They have lately shown a desire to become agricultural; and this leads to the desire of buying implements and comforts. In the strengthening and gratifying of these wants, I see the only prospect of planting on the Mississippi itself the means of its own safety.

Duty has required me to submit these views to the judgment of the legislature; but as their disclosure might embarrass and defeat their effect, they are committed to the special confidence of the two houses.

While the extension of the public commerce among the Indian tribes may deprive of that source of profit such of our citizens as are engaged in it, it might be worthy the attention of Congress, in their care of individual as well as of the general interest, to point in another direction the enterprise of these citizens, as profitably for themselves and more usefully for the public.

The River Missouri, and the Indians inhabiting it, are not as well known as is rendered desirable by their connection with the Mississippi, and consequently with us. It is, however, understood that the country on that river is inhabited by numerous tribes, who furnish great supplies of furs and peltry to the trade of another nation, carried on in a high latitude, through an infinite number of portages and lakes shut up by ice through a long season. The commerce on that line could bear no competition with that of the Missouri, traversing a moderate climate, offering, according to the best accounts, a continued navigation from its source, and possibly with a single portage, from the western ocean, and finding to the Atlantic a choice of channels through the Illinois or Wabash, the lakes and Hudson, through the Ohio and Susquehanna, or Potomac or James rivers, and through the Tennessee and Savannah rivers.

An intelligent officer, with ten or twelve chosen men, fit for the enterprise and willing to undertake it, taken from our posts, where they may be spared without inconvenience, might explore the whole line, even to the western ocean; have conferences with the natives on the subject of commercial intercourse; get admission among them for our traders; as others are admitted, agree on convenient deposits for an interchange of articles; and return with the information acquired, in the course of two summers. Their arms and accoutrements, some instruments of observation, and light and cheap presents for the Indians would be all the apparatus they could carry, and, with an expectation of a soldier's portion of land on their return, would constitute the whole expense. Their pay would be going on, whether here or there. While other civilized nations have encountered great expense to enlarge the boundaries of knowledge by undertaking voyages of discovery and for other literary purposes, in various parts and directions, our nation seems to owe to the same object, as well as to its own interests, to explore this, the only line of easy communication across the continent, and so directly traversing our own part of it.

The interests of commerce place the principal object within the constitutional powers and care of Congress, and that it should incidentally advance the geographical knowledge of our own continent cannot be but an additional gratification. The nation claiming the territory, regarding this as a literary pursuit, which is in the habit of permitting within its dominions, would not be disposed to view it with jealousy, even if the expiring state of its interests there did not render it a matter of indifference.

The appropriation of $2,500, "for the purpose of extending the external commerce of the United States," while understood and considered by the executive as giving the legislative sanction, would cover the undertaking from notice, and prevent the obstructions which interested individuals might otherwise previously prepare in its way.

Instructions to Meriwether Lewis

Your situation as secretary of the president of the United States has made you acquainted with the objects of my confidential message of Jan. 18, 1803, to the legislature. You have seen the act they passed, which, though expressed in general terms, was meant to sanction those objects, and you are appointed to carry them into execution.

Instruments for ascertaining by celestial observations the geography of the country through which you will pass, have been already provided. Light articles for barter, and presents among the Indians, arms for your attendants, say for from ten to twelve men, boats, tents, and other traveling apparatus, with ammunition, medicine, surgical instruments, and provision you will have prepared with such aids as the secretary of war can yield in his department. And from him also you will receive authority to engage among our troops, by voluntary agreement, the number of attendants above mentioned, over whom you, as their commanding officer, are invested with all the powers the laws give in such a case.

As your movements while within the limits of the U.S. will be better directed by occasional communications, adapted to circumstances as they arise, they will not be noticed here. What follows will respect your proceedings after your departure from the U.S.

Your mission has been communicated to the ministers here from France, Spain, and Great Britain, and through them to their governments; and such assurances given them as to its objects as we trust will satisfy them. The country of Louisiana having been ceded by Spain to France, the passport you have from the minister of France, the representative of the present sovereign of the country, will be a protection with all its subjects. And that from the minister of England will entitle you to the friendly aid of any traders of that allegiance with whom you may happen to meet.

The object of your mission is to explore the Missouri River, and such principal stream of it, as, by its course and communication with the water of the Pacific Ocean may offer the most direct and practicable water communication across this continent, for the purposes of commerce.

Beginning at the mouth of the Missouri, you will take observations of latitude and longitude at all remarkable points on the river, and especially at the mouths of rivers, at rapids, at islands, and other places and objects distinguished by such natural marks and characters of a durable kind, as that they may with certainty be recognized hereafter. The courses of the river between these points of observation may be supplied by the compass, the logline, and by time, corrected by the observations themselves. The variations of the compass, too, in different places should be noticed.

The interesting points of the portage between the heads of the Missouri and the water offering the best communication with the Pacific Ocean should be fixed by observation and the course of that water to the ocean, in the same manner as that of the Missouri.

Your observations are to be taken with great pains and accuracy, to be entered distinctly and intelligibly for others as well as yourself to comprehend all the elements necessary, with the aid of the usual tables to fix the latitude and longitude of the places at which they were taken, and are to be rendered to the War Office for the purpose of having the calculations made concurrently by proper persons within the U.S. Several copies of these, as well as of your other notes, should be made at leisure times and put into the care of the most trustworthy of your attendants, to guard by multiplying them against the accidental losses to which they will be exposed. A further guard would be that one of these copies be written on the paper of the birch, as less liable to injury from damp than common paper.

The commerce which may be carried on with the people inhabiting the line you will pursue renders a knowledge of these people important. You will therefore endeavor to make yourself acquainted, as far as a diligent pursuit of your journey shall admit, with the names of the nations and their numbers; the extent and limits of their possessions; their relations with other tribes or nations; their language, traditions, monuments; their ordinary occupations in agriculture, fishing, hunting, war, arts, and the implements for these; their food, clothing, and domestic accommodations; the diseases prevalent among them, and the remedies they use; moral and physical circumstance which distinguish them from the tribes they know; peculiarities in their laws, customs and dispositions; and articles of commerce they may need or furnish and to what extent.

And considering the interest which every nation has in extending and strengthening the authority of reason and justice among the people around them, it will be useful to acquire what knowledge you can of the state of morality, religion, and information among them, as it may better enable those who endeavor to civilize and instruct them to adapt their measures to the existing notions and practices of those on whom they are to operate.

Other objects worthy of notice will be: the soil and face of the country, its growth and vegetable productions, especially those not of the U.S.; the animals of the country generally, and especially those not known in the U.S.; the remains and accounts of any which may be deemed rare or extinct; the mineral productions of every kind; but more particularly metals, limestone, pit coal, and saltpeter; salines and mineral waters, noting the temperature of the last and such circumstances as may indicate their character; volcanic appearances; climate as characterized by the thermometer, by the proportion of rainy, cloudy, and clear days, by lightning, hail, snow, ice, by the access and recess of frost, by the winds, prevailing at different seasons, the dates at which particular plants put forth or lose their flowers, or leaf, times of appearance of particular birds, reptiles, or insects.

Although your route will be along the channel of the Missouri, yet you will endeavor to inform yourself, by inquiry, of the character and extent of the country watered by its branches, and especially on its southern side. The North River, or Rio Bravo, which runs into the Gulf of Mexico, and the North River, or Rio Colorado, which runs into the Gulf of California, are understood to be the principal streams heading opposite to the waters of the Missouri, and running southwardly. Whether the dividing grounds between the Missouri and them are mountains or flatlands, what are their distance from the Missouri, the character of the intermediate country, and the people inhabiting it are worthy of particular inquiry.

The northern waters of the Missouri are less to be inquired after, because they have been ascertained to a considerable degree, and are still in a course of ascertainment by English traders and travelers. But if you can learn anything certain of the most northern source of the Mississippi, and of its position relative to the Lake of the Woods, it will be interesting to us. Some account, too, of the path of the Canadian traders from the Mississippi, at the mouth of the Ouisconsin [Wisconsin] River, to where it strikes the Missouri and of the soil and rivers in its course, is desirable.

In all your intercourse with the natives, treat them in the most friendly and conciliatory manner which their own conduct will admit; allay all jealousies as to the object of your journey, satisfy them of its innocence; make them acquainted with the position, extent, character, peaceable and commercial dispositions of the U.S., of our wish to be neighborly, friendly, and useful to them, and of our dispositions to a commercial intercourse with them; confer with them on the points most convenient, as mutual emporiums and the articles of most desirable interchange for them and us. If a few of their influential chiefs, within practicable distance, wish to visit us, arrange such a visit with them, and furnish them with authority to call on our officers, on their entering the U.S., to have them conveyed to this place at the public expense. If any of them should wish to have some of their young people brought up with us and taught such arts as may be useful to them, we will receive, instruct, and take care of them. Such a mission, whether of influential chiefs or of young people, would give some security to your own party.

Carry with you some matter of the kinepox [cowpox], inform those of them with whom you may be of its efficacy as a preservative from the smallpox; and instruct and encourage them in the use of it. This may be especially done wherever you may winter.

As it is impossible for us to foresee in what manner you will be received by those people, whether with hospitality or hostility, so is it impossible to prescribe the exact degree of perseverance with which you are to pursue your journey. We value too much the lives of citizens to offer them to probable destruction. Your numbers will be sufficient to secure you against the unauthorized opposition of individuals, or of small parties; but if a superior force, authorized or not authorized, by a nation should be arrayed against your further passage, and inflexibly determined to arrest it, you must decline its further pursuit, and return. In the loss of yourselves, we should lose also the information you will have acquired. By returning safely with that, you may enable us to renew the essay with better calculated means. To your own discretion, therefore, must be left the degree of danger you may risk, and the point at which you should decline, only saying we wish you to err on the side of your safety, and to bring back your party safe, even if it be with less information.

As far up the Missouri as the white settlements extend, an intercourse will probably be found to exist, between them and the Spanish posts at St. Louis, opposite Cahokia, or St. Genevieve opposite Kaskaskia. From still further up the river, the traders may furnish a conveyance for letters. Beyond that you may perhaps be able to engage Indians to bring letters for the government to Cahokia or Kaskaskia on promising that they shall there receive such special compensation as you shall have stipulated with them. Avail yourself of these means to communicate to us at seasonable intervals a copy of your journal, notes, and observations of every kind, putting into cipher whatever might do injury if betrayed.

Should you reach the Pacific Ocean, inform yourself of the circumstances which may decide whether the furs of those parts may not be collected as advantageously at the head of the Missouri (convenient as is supposed to the waters of the Colorado and Oregon or Columbia) as at Nootka Sound or any other point of that coast; and that trade be consequently conducted through the Missouri and U.S. more beneficially than by the circumnavigation now practised. On your arrival on that coast, endeavor to learn if there be any port within your reach frequented by the sea vessels of any nation, and to send two of your trusted people back by sea, in such way as shall appear practicable, with a copy of your notes. And should you be of opinion that the return of your party by the way they went will be eminently dangerous, then ship the whole, and return by sea by way of Cape Horn or the Cape of Good Hope, as you shall be able.

As you will be without money, clothes, or provisions, you must endeavor to use the credit of the U.S. to obtain them; for which purpose open letters of credit shall be furnished you authorizing you to draw on the executive of the U.S. or any of its officers in any part of the world, in which drafts can be disposed of, and to apply with our recommendations to the consuls, agents, merchants, or citizens of any nation with which we have intercourse, assuring them in our name that any aids they may furnish you shall be honorably repaid and on demand. Our consuls, Thomas Howes at Batavia in Java, William Buchanan of the Isles of France and Bourbon, and John Elmslie at the Cape of Good Hope will be able to supply your necessities by drafts on us.

Should you find it safe to return by the way you go, after sending two of your party round by sea, or with your whole party if no conveyance by sea can be found, do so; making such observations on your return as may serve to supply, correct, or confirm those made on your outward journey.

In reentering the U.S. and reaching a place of safety, discharge any of your attendants who may desire and deserve it, procuring for them immediate payment of all arrears of pay and clothing which may have incurred since their departure; and assure them that they shall be recommended to the liberality of the legislature for the grant of a soldier's portion of land each, as proposed in my message to Congress; and repair yourself with your papers to the seat of government.

To provide, on the accident of your death, against anarchy, dispersion, and the consequent danger to your party, and total failure of the enterprise, you are hereby authorized, by any instrument signed and written in your own hand, to name the person among them who shall succeed to the command on your decease; and, by like instruments, to change the nomination from time to time, as further experience of the characters accompanying you shall point out superior fitness. And all the powers and authorities given to yourself are, in the event of your death, transferred to and vested in the successor so named, with further power to him, and his successors, in like manner, to name each his successor, who, on the death of his predecessor shall be invested with all the powers and authorities given to yourself.

SOURCE: Ford, Paul. L., ed. *The Writings of Thomas Jefferson.* New York and London: Putnam, 1892–1899.

THE JOURNALS OF THE LEWIS AND CLARK EXPEDITION *(1804)*

The Lewis and Clark Expedition across the American continent began in May 1804 and concluded over two years later in September 1806. Captain Meriwether Lewis and Lieutenant William Clark held joint command over about thirty soldiers and pilots, including the French trader Touissant Charbonneau and his wife, Sacajawea, a young Shoshone. The thirty-year-old Lewis was a native Virginian, friend of, and personal secretary to President Thomas Jefferson. He was intelligent, commanding, and given to fits of depression. Less learned, yet more at ease with the Native Americans was Clark, younger brother of the famous Revolutionary War General George Rogers Clark. William was a skilled navigator, engineer, and frontier diplomat. Lewis, more sophisticated, was the scientist of the expedition. Both men practiced medicine on their men, with mixed results. The two shared as well the responsibilities of keeping a detailed journal of observations and events. Lewis and Clark learned to become remarkable observers of human nature, anthropology, geography, natural history, and human history.

The journal excerpt records their adventures on the Missouri River in what is today North Dakota during the autumn and early winter of 1804. The Mandan, Assiniboin, and Minnetaree Indians lived in the region of the confluence of the Knife and the Missouri Rivers. The Mandans were once strong, though by 1804 weakened by disease and war, particularly with the Sioux, who lived further west up the Missouri. Lewis and Clark planned to winter at this location, building a fort, gaining the trust of the Indians, establishing trade, and encouraging the Indians to rely on the United States for protection against their enemies. The men built huts and a fort out of the cottonwood trees that grew along the Missouri River. Living with these people for several months, Lewis and Clark and the Indians of the upper Missouri grew to have mutual respect and affection. It was an auspicious beginning of the Lewis and Clark Expedition.

Russell Lawson,
Bacone College

See also **Explorations and Expeditions: U.S.; Lewis and Clark Expedition; Western Exploration.**

Lewis and Clark Penetrate the West

Tuesday 13. We this morning unloaded the boat and stowed away the contents in a storehouse which we have built. At half-past ten ice began to float down the river for the first time: in the course of the morning we were visited by the Black Cat, Poscapsahe, who brought an Assiniboin chief and seven warriors to see us. This man, whose name is Chechawk, is a chief of one out of three bands of Assiniboins who wander over the plains between the Missouri and Assiniboin during the summer, and in the winter carry the spoils of their hunting to the traders on the Assiniboin River, and occasionally come to this place: the whole three bands consist of about eight hundred men. We gave him a twist of tobacco to smoke with his people, and a gold cord for himself: the Sioux also asked for whisky, which we refused to give them. It snowed all day and the air was very cold.

Wednesday 14. The river rose last night half an inch, and is now filled with floating ice. This morning was cloudy with some snow: about seventy lodges of Assiniboins and some Knistenaux are at the Mandan village, and this being the day of adoption and exchange of property between them all, it is accompanied by a dance, which prevents our seeing more than two Indians today: these Knistenaux are a band of Chippeways, whose language they speak; they live on the Assiniboin and Saskashawan rivers, and are about two hundred and forty men. We sent a man down on horseback to see what had become of our hunters, and as we apprehend a failure of provisions we have recourse to our pork this evening. Two Frenchmen who had been below returned with twenty beaver which they had caught in traps.

Thursday 15. The morning again cloudy, and the ice running thicker than yesterday, the wind variable. The man came back with information that our hunters were about thirty miles below, and we immediately sent an order to them to make their way through the floating ice, to assist them in which we sent some tin for the bow of the periogue and a towrope. The ceremony of yesterday seems to continue still, for we were not visited by a single Indian. The swan are still passing to the south.

Friday 16. We had a very hard white frost this morning, the trees are all covered with ice, and the weather cloudy. The men this day moved into the huts, although they are not finished. In the evening some horses were sent down to the woods near us in order to prevent their being stolen by the Assiniboins, with whom some difficulty is now apprehended. An Indian came down with four buffalo robes and some corn, which he offered for a pistol, but was refused.

Saturday, November 17. Last night was very cold, and the ice in the river today is thicker than hitherto. We are totally occupied with our huts, but received visits from several Indians.

Sunday, November 18. Today we had a cold windy morning; the Black Cat came to see us, and occupied us for a long time with questions on the usages of our country. He mentioned that a council had been held yesterday to deliberate on the state of their affairs. It seems that not long ago, a party of Sioux fell in with some horses belonging to the Minnetarees, and carried them off; but in their flight they were met by some Assiniboins, who killed the Sioux and kept the horses: a Frenchman too, who had lived many years among the Mandans, was lately killed on his route to the British factory on the Assiniboin; some smaller differences existed between the two nations, all of which being discussed, the council decided that they would not resent the recent insults from the Assiniboins and Knistenaux, until they had seen whether we had deceived them or not in our promises of furnishing them with arms and ammunition. They had been disappointed in their hopes of receiving them from Mr. Evans and were afraid that we too, like him, might tell them what was not true. We advised them to continue at peace, that supplies of every kind would no doubt arrive for them, but that time was necessary to organize the trade. The fact is that the Assiniboins treat the Mandans as the Sioux do the Ricaras; by their vicinity to the British they get all the supplies, which they withhold or give at pleasure to the remoter Indians: the consequence is, that however badly treated, the Mandans and Ricaras are very slow to retaliate lest they should lose their trade altogether.

Monday 19. The ice continues to float in the river, the wind high from the northwest, and the weather cold. Our hunters arrived from their excursion below, and bring a very fine supply of thirty-two deer, eleven elk, and five buffalo, all of which was hung in a smokehouse.

Tuesday 20. We this day moved into our huts which are now completed. This place, which we call Fort Mandan, is situated in a point of low ground, on the north side of the Missouri, covered with tall and heavy cotton wood. The works consist of two rows of huts or sheds, forming an angle where they joined each other; each row containing four rooms, of fourteen feet square and seven feet high, with plank ceiling, and the roof slanting so as to form a loft above the rooms, the highest part of which is eighteen feet from the ground: the backs of the huts formed a wall of that height, and opposite the angle the place of the wall was supplied by picketing: in the area were two rooms for stores and provisions. The latitude by observation is 4 degrees 21′47″, and the computed distance from the mouth of the Missouri sixteen hundred miles.

In the course of the day several Indians came down to partake of our fresh meat; among the rest, three chiefs of the second Mandan village. They inform us that the Sioux on the Missouri above the Chayenne River threaten to attack them this winter; that these Sioux are much irritated at the Ricaras for having made peace through our means with the Mandans, and have lately ill-treated three Ricaras who carried the pipe of peace to them, by beating them and taking away their horses. We gave them assurances that we would protect them from all their enemies.

November 21. The weather was this day fine: the river clear of ice and rising a little: we are now settled in our new winter habitation, and shall wait with much anxiety the first return of spring to continue our journey.

The villages near which we are established are five in number, and are the residence of three distinct nations; the Mandans, the Ahnahaways, and the Minnetarees. The history of the Mandans, as we received it from our interpreters and from the chiefs themselves, and as it is attested by existing monuments, illustrates more than that of any other nation the unsteady movements and the tottering fortunes of the American nations. Within the recollection of living witnesses, the Mandans were settled forty years ago in nine villages, the ruins of which we passed about eighty miles below, and situated seven on the west and two on the east side of the Missouri. The two, finding themselves wasting away before the small-pox and the Sioux, united into one village, and moved up the river opposite to the Ricaras. The same causes reduced the remaining seven to five villages, till at length they emigrated in a body to the Ricara nation, where they formed themselves into two villages, and joined those of their countrymen who had gone before them. In their new residence they were still insecure, and at length the three villages ascended the Missouri to their present position. The two who had emigrated together still settled in the two villages on the northwest side of the Missouri, while the single village took a position on the southeast side. In this situation they were found by those who visited them in 1796; since which the two villages have united into one. They are now in two villages, one on the southeast of the Missouri, the other on the opposite side, and at the distance of three miles across. The first, in an open plain, contains about forty or fifty lodges, built in the same way as those of the Ricaras: the second, the same number, and both may raise about three hundred and fifty men.

On the same side of the river, and at the distance of four miles from the lower Mandan village, is another called Mahaha. It is situated in a high plain at the mouth of Knife River, and is the residence of the Ahnahaways. This nation, whose name indicates that they were "people whose village is on a hill," formerly resided on the Missouri, about thirty miles below where they now live. The Assiniboins and Sioux forced them to a spot five miles higher, where the greatest part of them were put to death, and the rest emigrated to their present situation, in order to obtain an asylum near the Minnetarees. They are called by the French, Soulier Noir or Shoe Indians; by the Mandans, Wattasoons, and their whole force is about fifty men.

On the south side of the same Knife River, half a mile above the Mahaha and in the same open plain with it, is a village of Minnetarees surnamed Metaharta, who are about one hundred and fifty men in number. On the opposite side of Knife River, and one and a half miles above this village is a second of Minnetarees, who may be considered as the proper Minnetaree nation. It is situated in a beautiful low plain, and contains four hundred and fifty warriors. The accounts which we received of the Minnetarees were contradictory. The Mandans say that this people came out of the water to the east, and settled near them in their former establishment in nine villages; that they were very numerous, and fixed themselves in one village on the southern side of the Missouri. A quarrel about a buffalo divided the nation, of which two bands went into the plains, and were known by the name of Crow and Paunch Indians, and the rest moved to their present establishment. The Minnetarees proper assert, on the contrary, that they grew where they now live, and will never emigrate from the spot; the great spirit having declared that if they moved they would all die. They also say that the Minnetarees Metaharta, that is, Minnetarees of the Willows, whose language with very little variation is their own, came many years ago from the plains and settled near them, and perhaps the two traditions may be reconciled by the natural presumption that these Minnetarees were the tribe known to the Mandans below, and that they ascended the river for the purpose of rejoining the Minnetarees proper. These Minnetarees are part of the great nation called Fall Indians, who occupy the intermediate country between the Missouri and the Saskaskawan, and who are known by the name of Minnetarees of the Missouri, and Minnetarees of Fort de Prairie; that is, residing near or rather frequenting the establishment in the prairie on the Saskaskawan. These Minnetarees indeed told us that they had relations on the Saskaskawan, whom they had never known till they met them in war, and having engaged in the night were astonished at discovering that they were fighting with men who spoke their own language. The name of Grosventres, or Bigbellies, is given to these Minnetarees, as well as to all the Fall Indians. The inhabitants of these five villages, all of which are within the distance of six miles, live in harmony with each other. The Ahnahaways understand in part the language of the Minnetarees: the dialect of the Mandans differs widely from both; but their long residence together has insensibly blended their manners, and occasioned some approximation in language, particularly as to objects of daily occurrence and obvious to the senses.

November 22. The morning was fine, and the day warm. We purchased from the Mandans a quantity of corn of a mixed color, which they dug up in ears from holes made near the front of their lodges, in which it is buried during the winter: this morning the sentinel informed us that an Indian was about to kill his wife near the fort; we went down to the house of our interpreter where we found the parties, and after forbidding any violence, inquired into the cause of his intending to commit such an atrocity. It appeared that some days ago a quarrel had taken place between him and his wife, in consequence of which she had taken refuge in the house where the two squaws of our interpreter lived: by running away she forfeited her life, which might have been lawfully taken by the husband. About two days ago she had returned to the village, but the same evening came back to the fort much beaten and stabbed in three places, and the husband now came for the purpose of completing his revenge. He observed that he had lent her to one of our sergeants for a night, and that if he wanted her he would give her to him altogether: we gave him a few presents and tried to persuade him to take his wife home; the grand chief too happened to arrive at the same moment, and reproached him with his violence, till at length they went off together, but by no means in a state of much apparent love.

November 23. Again we had a fair and warm day, with the wind from the southeast: the river is now at a stand having risen four inches in the whole.

November 25. The wind continued from the same quarter and the weather was warm: we were occupied in finishing our huts and making a large rope of elk-skin to draw our boat on the bank.

Sunday, November 25. The weather is still fine, warm and pleasant, and the river falls one inch and a half. Captain Lewis went on an excursion to the villages accompanied by eight men. A Minnetaree chief, the first who has visited us, came down to the fort: his name was Waukerassa, but as both the interpreters had gone with Captain Lewis we were obliged to confine our civilities to some presents with which he was much pleased: we now completed our huts, and fortunately too, for the next day.

Monday, November 26. Before daylight the wind shifted to the northwest, and blew very hard, with cloudy weather and a keen cold air, which confined us much and prevented us from working: the night continued very cold, and,

Tuesday 27. The weather cloudy, the wind continuing from the northwest and the river crowded with floating ice. Captain Lewis returned with two chiefs, Mahnotah, an Ahnahaway, and Minnessurraree, a Minnetaree, and a third warrior: they explained to us that the reason of their not having come to see us was that the Mandans had told them that we meant to combine with the Sioux and cut them off in the course of the winter: a suspicion increased by the strength of the fort, and the circumstance of our interpreters having been removed there with their families: these reports we did not fail to disprove to their entire satisfaction, and amused them by every attention, particularly by the dancing of the men, which diverted them highly. All the Indians whom Captain Lewis had visited were very well disposed, and received him with great kindness, except a principal chief of one of the upper villages, named Mahpahpaparapassatoo or Horned Weasel, who made use of the civilized indecorum of refusing to be seen, and when Captain Lewis called he was told the chief was not at home. In the course of the day seven of the northwest company's traders arrived from the Assiniboin River, and, one of their interpreters having undertaken to circulate among the Indians unfavorable reports, it became necessary to warn them of the consequences if they did not desist from such proceedings. The river fell two inches today and the weather became very cold.

Wednesday 28. About eight o'clock last evening it began to snow and continued till daybreak, after which it ceased till seven o'clock, but then resumed and continued during the day, the weather being cold and the river full of floating ice: about eight o'clock Poscopsahe came down to visit us, with some warriors; we gave them presents and entertained them with all that might amuse their curiosity, and at parting we told them that we had heard of the British trader, Mr. Laroche, having attempted to distribute medals and flags among them, but that those emblems could not be received from any other than the American nation without incurring the displeasure of their great father the president. They left us much pleased with their treatment. The river fell one inch today.

Thursday 29. The wind is again from the northwest, the weather cold, and the snow which fell yesterday and last night is thirteen inches in depth. The river closed during the night at the village above, and fell two feet; but this afternoon it began to rise a little. Mr. Laroche, the principal of the seven traders, came with one of his men to see us; we told him that we should not permit him to give medals and flags to the Indians; he declared that he had no such intention, and we then suffered him to make use of one of our interpreters, on his stipulating not to touch any subject but that of his traffic with them. An unfortunate accident occurred to Sergeant Pryor, who in taking down the boat's mast dislocated his shoulder, nor was it till after four trials that we replaced it.

Friday 30. About eight o'clock an Indian came to the opposite bank of the river, calling out that he had something important to communicate, and on sending for him, he told us that five Mandans had been met about eight leagues to the southwest by a party of Sioux, who had killed one of them, wounded two, and taken nine horses; that four of the Wattasoons were missing, and that the Mandans expected an attack. We thought this an excellent opportunity to discountenance the injurious reports against us, and to fix the wavering confidence of the nation. Captain Clark therefore instantly crossed the river with twenty-three men strongly armed, and circling the town approached it from behind. His unexpected appearance surprised and alarmed the chiefs, who came out to meet him, and conducted him to the village. He then told them that having heard of the outrage just committed, he had come to assist his dutiful children; that if they would assemble their warriors and those of the nation, he would lead them against the Sioux and avenge the blood of their countrymen. After some minutes conversation, Oheenaw the Chayenne arose: "We now see," said he, "that what you have told us is true, since as soon as our enemies threaten to attack us you come to protect us and are ready to chastise those who have spilled our blood. We did indeed listen to your good talk, for when you told us that the other nations were inclined to peace with us, we went out carelessly in small parties, and some have been killed by the Sioux and Ricaras. But I knew that the Ricaras were liars, and I told their chief who accompanied you, that his whole nation were liars and bad men; that we had several times made a peace with them which they were the first to break; that whenever we pleased we might shoot them like buffalo, but that we had no wish to kill them; that we would not suffer them to kill us, nor steal our horses; and that although we agreed to make peace with them, because our two fathers desired it, yet we did not believe that they would be faithful long. Such, father, was my language to them in your presence, and you see that instead of listening to your good counsels they have spilled our blood. A few days ago two Ricaras came here and told us that two of their villages were making moccasins, that the Sioux were stirring them up against us, and that we ought to take care of our horses; yet these very Ricaras we sent home as soon as the news reached us today, lest our people should kill them in the first moment of grief for their murdered relatives. Four of the Wattasoons whom we expected back in sixteen days have been absent twenty-four, and we fear have fallen. But, father, the snow is now deep, the weather cold, and our horses cannot travel through the plains: the murderers have gone off: if you will conduct us in the spring, when the snow has disappeared, we will assemble all the surrounding warriors and follow you."

Captain Clark replied that we were always willing and able to defend them; that he was sorry that the snow prevented their marching to meet the Sioux, since he wished to show them that the warriors of their great father would chastise the enemies of his obedient children who opened their ears to his advice; that if some Ricaras had joined the Sioux, they should remember that there were bad men in every nation, and that they should not be offended at the Ricaras till they saw whether these ill-disposed men were countenanced by the whole tribe; that the Sioux possessed great influence over the Ricaras, whom they supplied with military stores, and sometimes led them astray, because they were afraid to oppose them: but that this should be the less offensive since the Mandans themselves were under the same apprehensions from the Assiniboins and Knistenaux, and that while they were thus dependent, both the Ricaras and Mandans ought to keep on terms with their powerful neighbors, whom they may afterward set at defiance, when we shall supply them with arms, and take them under our protection.

After two hours' conversation Captain Clark left the village. The chief repeatedly thanked him for the fatherly protection he had given them, observing that the whole village had been weeping all night and day for the brave young man who had been slain, but now they would wipe their eyes and weep no more as they saw that their father would protect them. He then crossed the river on the ice and returned on the north side to the fort. The day as well as the evening was cold, and the river rose to its former height.

Saturday, December 1. The wind was from the northwest, and the whole party engaged in picketing the fort. About ten o'clock the half-brother of the man who had been killed came to inform us that six Sharhas or Chayenne Indians had arrived, bringing a pipe of peace, and that their nation was three days' march behind them. Three Pawnees had accompanied the Sharhas, and the Mandans, being afraid of the Sharhas on account of their being at peace with the Sioux, wished to put both them and the three Pawnees to death; but the chiefs had forbidden it as it would be contrary to our wishes. We gave him a present of tobacco, and although from his connection with the sufferer, he was more embittered against the Pawnees than any other Mandan, yet he seemed perfectly satisfied with our pacific counsels and advice. The Mandans, we observe, call all the Ricaras by the name of Pawnees; the name of Ricaras being that by which the nation distinguishes itself.

In the evening we were visited by a Mr. Henderson, who came from the Hudson Bay Company to trade with the Minnetarees. He had been about eight days on his route in a direction nearly south, and brought with him tobacco, beads, and other merchandise to trade for furs, and a few guns which are to be exchanged for horses.

Sunday, December 2. The latter part of the evening was warm, and a thaw continued till the morning, when the wind shifted to the north. At eleven o'clock the chiefs of the lower village brought down four of the Sharhas. We explained to them our intentions, and advised them to remain at peace with each other: we also gave them a flag, some tobacco, and a speech for their nation. These were accompanied by a letter to Messrs. Tabeau and Gravelines at the Ricara village, requesting them to preserve peace if possible, and to declare the part which we should be forced to take if the Ricaras and Sioux made war on those whom we had adopted. After distributing a few presents to the Sharhas and Mandans, and showing them our curiosities we dismissed them, apparently well pleased at their reception.

Monday, December 3. The morning was fine, but in the afternoon the weather became cold with the wind from the northwest. The father of the Mandan who was killed brought us a present of dried pumpkins and some pemitigon, for which we gave him some small articles. Our offer of assistance to avenge the death of his son seemed to have produced a grateful respect from him, as well as from the brother of the deceased, which pleased us much.

Tuesday 4. The wind continues from the northwest, the weather cloudy and raw, and the river rose one inch. Oscapsahe and two young chiefs pass the day with us. The whole religion of the Mandans consists in the belief of one great spirit presiding over their destinies. This being must be in the nature of a good genius since it is associated with the healing art, and the great spirit is synonymous with great medicine, a name also applied to every thing which they do not comprehend. Each individual selects for himself the particular object of his devotion, which is termed his medicine, and is either some invisible being or more commonly some animal, which thenceforward becomes his protector or his intercessor with the great spirit; to propitiate whom every attention is lavished, and every personal consideration is sacrificed. "I was lately owner of seventeen horses," said a Mandan to us one day, "but I have offered them all up to my medicine and am now poor." He had in reality taken all his wealth, his horses, into the plain, and turning them loose committed them to the care of his medicine and abandoned them forever. The horses, less religious, took care of themselves, and the pious votary traveled home on foot. Their belief in a future state is connected with this tradition of their origin: the whole nation resided in one large village under ground near a subterraneous lake: a grapevine extended its roots down to their habitation and gave them a view of the light: some of the most adventurous climbed up the vine and were delighted with the sight of the earth, which they found covered with buffalo and rich with every kind of fruits: returning with the grapes they had gathered, their countrymen were so pleased with the taste of them that the whole nation resolved to leave their dull residence for the charms of the upper region; men, women, and children ascended by means of the vine; but when about half the nation had reached the surface of the earth, a corpulent women who was clambering up the vine broke it with her weight, and closed upon herself and the rest of the nation the light of the sun. Those who were left on earth made a village below where we saw the nine villages; and when the Mandans die they expect to return to the original seats of their forefathers; the good reaching the ancient village by means of the lake, which the burden of the sins of the wicked will not enable them to cross.

Wednesday 5. The morning was cold and disagreeable, the wind from the southeast accompanied with snow: in the evening there was snow again and the wind shifted to the northeast: we were visited by several Indians with a present of pumpkins, and by two of the traders of the northwest company.

Thursday 6. The wind was violent from the north northwest with some snow, the air keen and cold. At eight o'clock A.M. the thermometer stood at ten degrees above 0, and the river rose an inch and a half in the course of the day.

Friday, December 7. The wind still continued from the northwest and the day is very cold: Shahaka the chief of the lower village came to apprise us that the buffalo were near, and that his people were waiting for us to join them in the chase: Captain Clark with fifteen men went out and found the Indians engaged in killing the buffalo, the hunters mounted on horseback and armed with bows and arrows encircle the herd, and gradually drive them into a plain or an open place fit for the movement of horse; they then ride in among them, and singling out a buffalo, a female being preferred, go as close as possible and wound her with arrows till they think they have given the mortal stroke; when they pursue another till the quiver is exhausted: if, which rarely happens, the wounded buffalo attacks the hunter, he evades his blow by the agility of his horse, which is trained for the combat with great dexterity. When they have killed the requisite number they collect their game, and the squaws and attendants come up from the rear and skin and dress the animals. Captain Clark killed ten buffalo, of which five only were brought to the fort, the rest which could not be conveyed home being seized by the Indians, among whom the custom is that whenever a buffalo is found dead without an arrow or any particular mark, he is the property of the finder; so that often a hunter secures scarcely any of the game he kills if the arrow happens to fall off; whatever is left out at night falls to the share of the wolves, who are the constant and numerous attendants of the buffalo. The river closed opposite the fort last night, an inch and a half in thickness. In the morning the thermometer stood at one degree below 0. Three men were badly frostbitten in consequence of their exposure.

Saturday 8. The thermometer stood at twelve degrees below 0, that is at forty-two degrees below the freezing point: the wind was from the northwest. Captain Lewis with fifteen men went out to hunt the buffalo; great numbers of which darkened the prairies for a considerable distance: they did not return till after dark, having killed eight buffalo and one deer. The hunt was, however, very fatiguing, as they were obliged to make a circuit at the distance of more than seven miles: the cold too was so excessive that the air was filled with icy particles resembling a fog, and the snow generally six or eight inches deep and sometimes eighteen, in consequence of which two of the party were hurt by falls, and several had their feet frostbitten.

Sunday 9. The wind was this day from the east, the thermometer at seven degrees above 0, and the sun shone clear: two chiefs visited us, one in a sleigh drawn by a dog and loaded with meat.

Monday 10. Captain Clark who had gone out yesterday with eighteen men to bring in the meat we had killed the day before, and to continue the hunt, came in at twelve o'clock. After killing nine buffalo and preparing that already dead, he had spent a cold disagreeable night on the snow, with no covering but a small blanket, sheltered by the hides of the buffalo they had killed. We observe large herds of buffalo crossing the river on the ice, the men who were frostbitten are recovering, but the weather is still exceedingly cold, the wind being from the north, and the thermometer at ten and eleven degrees below 0: the rise of the river is one inch and a half.

Tuesday 11. The weather became so intensely cold that we sent for all the hunters who had remained out with Captain Clark's party, and they returned in the evening, several of them frostbitten. The wind was from the north and the thermometer at sunrise stood at twenty-one below 0, the ice in the atmosphere being so thick as to render the weather hazy and give the appearance of two suns reflecting each other. The river continued at a stand. Pocapsahe made us a visit today.

Wednesday, December 12. The wind is still from the north, the thermometer being at sunrise thirty-eight degrees below 0. One of the Ahnahaways brought us down the half of an antelope killed near the fort; we had been informed that all these animals return to the Black Mountains, but there are great numbers of them about us at this season which we might easily kill, but are unwilling to venue out before our constitutions are hardened gradually to the climate. We measured the river on the ice, and find it five hundred yards wide immediately opposite the fort.

Thursday 13. Last night was clear and a very heavy frost covered the old snow, the thermometer at sunrise being twenty degrees below 0, and followed by a fine day. The river falls.

Friday 14. The morning was fine, and the weather having moderated so far, that the mercury stood at 0, Captain Lewis went down with a party to hunt; they proceeded about eighteen miles, but the buffalo having left the banks of the river they saw only two, which were so poor as not to be worth killing, and shot two deer. Notwithstanding the snow we were visited by a large number of the Mandans.

Saturday 15. Captain Lewis finding no game returned to the fort hunting on both sides of the river, but with no success. The wind being from the north, the mercury at sunrise eight degrees below 0, and the snow of last night an inch and a half in depth. The Indian chiefs continue to visit us today with presents of meat.

Sunday 16. The morning is clear and cold, the mercury at sunrise 22 degrees below 0. A Mr. Haney, with two other persons from the British establishment on the Assiniboin, arrived in six days with a letter from Mr. Charles Chaubouilles, one of the company, who with much politeness offered to render us any service in his power.

Monday 17. The weather today was colder than any we had yet experienced, the thermometer at sunrise being 45 degrees below 0, and about eight o'clock it fell to 74 degrees below the freezing point From Mr. Haney, who is a very sensible intelligent man, we obtained much geographical information with regard to the country between the Missouri and Mississippi, and the various tribes of Sioux who inhabit it.

Tuesday 18. The thermometer at sunrise was 32 degrees below 0. The Indians had invited us yesterday to join their chase today, but the seven men whom we sent returned in consequence of the cold, which was so severe last night that we were obliged to have the sentinel relieved every half hour. The northwest traders, however, left us on their return home.

Wednesday 19. The weather moderated, and the river rose a little, so that we were enabled to continue the picketing of the fort. Notwithstanding the extreme cold, we observe the Indians at the village engaged out in the open air at a game which resembled billiards more than any thing we had seen, and which we inclined to suspect may have been acquired by ancient intercourse with the French of Canada. From the first to the second chief's lodge, a distance of about fifty yards, was covered with timber smoothed and joined so as to be as level as the floor of one of our houses, with a battery at the end to stop the rings: these rings were of clay-stone and flat like the chequers for drafts, and the sticks were about four feet long, with two short pieces at one end in the form of a mace, so fixed that the whole will slide along the board. Two men fix themselves at one end, each provided with a stick, and one of them with a ring; they then run along the board, and about half way slide the sticks after the ring.

Thursday 20. The wind was from the N.W., the weather moderate, the thermometer 24 degrees above 0 at sunrise. We availed ourselves of this change to picket the fort near the river.

Friday 21. The day was fine and warm, the wind N.W. by W. The Indian who had been prevented a few days ago from killing his wife came with both his wives to the fort, and was very desirous of reconciling our interpreter, a jealousy against whom, on account of his wife's taking refuge in his house, had been the cause of his animosity. A woman brought her child with an abscess in the lower part of the back, and offered as much corn as she could carry for some medicine; we administered to it, of course, very cheerfully.

Saturday 22. A number of squaws and men dressed like squaws brought corn to trade for small articles with the men. Among other things we procured two horns of the animal called by the French the rock mountain sheep, and known to the Mandans by the name of *ahsahta.* The animal itself is about the size of a small elk or large deer:

the horns winding like those of a ram, which they resemble also in texture, though larger and thicker.

Sunday 23. The weather was fine and warm like that of yesterday: we were again visited by crowds of Indians of all descriptions, who came either to trade or from mere curiosity. Among the rest Kogahami, the Little Raven, brought his wife and son loaded with corn, and she then entertained us with a favorite Mandan dish, a mixture of pumpkins, beans, corn, and chokecherries with the stones, all boiled together in a kettle. and forming a composition by no means unpalatable.

Monday 24. The day continued warm and pleasant, and the number of visitors became troublesome. As a present to three of the chiefs, we divided a fillet of sheep-skin which we brought for spunging into three pieces each of two inches in width; they were delighted at the gift, which they deemed of equal value with a fine horse. We this day completed our fort, and the next morning being Christmas.

Tuesday 25. We were awakened before day by a discharge of three platoons from the party. We had told the Indians not to visit us as it was one of our great medicine days; so that the men remained at home and amused themselves in various ways, particularly with dancing, in which they take great pleasure. The American flag was hoisted for the first time in the fort; the best provisions we had were brought out, and this, with a little brandy, enabled them to pass the day in great festivity.

Wednesday 26. The weather is again temperate, but no Indians have come to see us. One of the northwest traders who came down to request the aid of our Minnetaree interpreter informs us that a party of Minnetarees who had gone in pursuit of the Assiniboins who lately stole their horses had just returned. As is their custom, they came back in small detachments, the last of which brought home eight horses which they had captured or stolen from an Assiniboin camp on Mouse River.

Thursday 27. A little fine snow fell this morning and the air was colder than yesterday, with a high northwest wind. We were fortunate enough to have among our men a good blacksmith, whom we set to work to make a variety of articles: his operations seemed to surprise the Indians who came to see us, but nothing could equal their astonishment at the bellows, which they considered as a very great medicine. Having heretofore promised a more particular account of the Sioux, the following may serve as a general outline of their history:

Almost the whole of that vast tract of country comprised between the Mississippi, the Red River of Lake Winnipeg, the Saskaskawan, and the Missouri, is loosely occupied by a great nation whose primitive name is Darcota, but who are called Sioux by the French, Sues by the English. Their original seats were on the Mississippi, but they have gradually spread themselves abroad and become subdivided into numerous tribes. Of these, what may be considered as the Darcotas are the Mindawarcarton, or Minowakanton, known to the French by the name of the Gens du Lac, or People of the Lake. Their residence is on both sides of the Mississippi near the falls of St. Anthony, and the probable number of their warriors about three hundred. Above them, on the River St. Peter's, is the Wahpatone, a smaller band of nearly two hundred men; and still further up the same river below Yellowwood River are the Wahpatootas or Gens de Feuilles, an inferior band of not more than one hundred men; while the sources of the St. Peter's are occupied by the Sisatoones, a band consisting of about two hundred warriors.

These bands rarely if ever approach the Missouri, which is occupied by their kinsmen the Yanktons and the Tetons. The Yanktons are of two tribes, those of the plains, or rather of the north, a wandering race of about five hundred men, who roam over the plains at the heads of the Jacques, the Sioux, and the Red River; and those of the south, who possess the country between the Jacques and Sioux Rivers and the Desmoine. But the bands of Sioux most known on the Missouri are the Tetons. The first who are met on ascending the Missouri is the tribe called by the French the Tetons of the Boise Brule or Burntwood, who reside on both sides of the Missouri, about White and Teton Rivers, and number two hundred warriors. Above them on the Missouri are the Teton Okandandas, a band of one hundred and fifty men living below the Chayenne River, between which and the Wetarhoo River is a third band, called Teton Minnakenozzo, of nearly two hundred and fifty men; and below the Warrecoune is the fourth and last tribe of Tetons of about three hundred men, and called Teton Saone. Northward of these, between the Assiniboin and the Missouri, are two bands of Assiniboins, one on Mouse River of about two hundred men, and called Assiniboin Menatopa; the other, residing on both sides of White River, called by the French Gens de Feuilles, and amounting to two hundred and fifty men. Beyond these a band of Assiniboins of four hundred and fifty men, and called the Big Devils, wander on the heads of Milk, Porcupine, and Martha's Rivers; while still farther to the north are seen two bands of the same nation, one of five hundred and the other of two hundred, roving on the Saskaskawan. Those Assiniboins are recognized by a similarity of language, and by tradition as descendants or seceders from the Sioux; though often at war are still acknowledged as relations. The Sioux themselves, though scattered, meet annually on the Jacques, those on the Missouri trading with those on the Mississippi.

SOURCE: *The Journals of the Lewis and Clark Expedition.* In *History of the Exploration of Lewis and Clark.* Edited by John B. McMaster. Vol. 1. New York: 1922, pp. 182–206.

SLEEP NOT LONGER, O CHOCTAWS AND CHICKASAWS
(1811, by Tecumseh)

Tecumseh, whose name means "Panther Springing Across the Sky," was born in a small Shawnee village in western Ohio in 1768. The Shawnees were under constant attack from the American settlers streaming into the Ohio Valley and in 1779 were forced to migrate to Missouri. Tecumseh showed early signs of formidable leadership and from a young age felt strongly that any negotiation with the whites was doomed to failure. In 1805, he joined with his brother Tenskwatawa (who had been called "Lalawethika" or "He Makes a Loud Noise" as a baby) to found a settlement which would eventually be called "Prophet's Town." It was there that he began to develop a Native American theology that called for a unification of tribes and a return to a more traditional way of life. In the years leading up to the War of 1812, Tecumseh traveled from the Great Lakes to the Gulf of Mexico in an effort to gain support for his idea of an Indian confederation. It was during this trip that he met with a special council of Choctaws and Chickasaws in what is now Mississippi.

That Tecumseh was keenly aware of the American settlers' genocidal intentions is clear in this impassioned plea for unity and revolt. He claimed that his people would win land and liberty only through radical action. In order to avoid the fate of the enslaved Blacks, he urged the assembly to join his fight which, he said, is backed by British soldiers.

Though Tecumseh's eloquence gained him followers from the Great Plains to Alabama, his was a bloody, losing battle. He was killed at the Battle of the Thames, located in what is now the Province of Ontario, in October 1813. It is not known whether Tecumseh's warriors recovered his remains or, as was common practice, if they were brutally mutilated by the victorious militiamen.

Leah R. Shafer,
Cornell University

See also **Choctaw; Indian Warfare; Wars with Indian Nations: Early Nineteenth Century 1783–1840).**

In view of questions of vast importance, have we met together in solemn council tonight. Nor should we here debate whether we have been wronged and injured, but by what measures we should avenge ourselves; for our merciless oppressors, having long since planned out their proceedings, are not about to make, but have and are still making attacks upon our race who have as yet come to no resolution. Nor are we ignorant by what steps, and by what gradual advances, the whites break in upon our neighbors. Imagining themselves to be still undiscovered, they show themselves the less audacious because you are insensible. The whites are already nearly a match for us all united, and too strong for any one tribe alone to resist; so that unless we support one another with our collective and united forces; unless every tribe unanimously combines to give check to the ambition and avarice of the whites, they will soon conquer us apart and disunited, and we will be driven away from our native country and scattered as autumnal leaves before the wind.

But have we not courage enough remaining to defend our country and maintain our ancient independence? Will we calmly suffer the white intruders and tyrants to enslave us? Shall it be said of our race that we knew not how to extricate ourselves from the three most dreadful calamities—folly, inactivity and cowardice? But what need is there to speak of the past? It speaks for itself and asks, Where today is the Pequod? Where the Narragansetts, the Mohawks, Pocanokets, and many other once powerful tribes of our race? They have vanished before the avarice and oppression of the white men, as snow before a summer sun. In the vain hope of alone defending their ancient possessions, they have fallen in the wars with the white men. Look abroad over their once beautiful country, and what see you now? Naught but the ravages of the paleface destroyers meet our eyes. So it will be with you Choctaws and Chickasaws! Soon your mighty forest trees, under the shade of whose wide spreading branches you have played in infancy, sported in boyhood, and now rest your wearied limbs after the fatigue of the chase, will be cut down to fence in the land which the white intruders dare to call their own. Soon their broad roads will pass over the grave of your fathers, and the place of their rest will be blotted out forever. The annihilation of our race is at hand unless we unite in one common cause against the common foe. Think not, brave Choctaws and Chickasaws, that you can remain passive and indifferent to the common danger, and thus escape the common fate. Your people, too, will soon be as falling leaves and scattering clouds before their blighting breath. You, too, will be driven away from your native land and ancient domains as leaves are driven before the wintry storms.

Sleep not longer, O Choctaws and Chickasaws, in false security and delusive hopes. Our broad domains are fast escaping from our grasp. Every year our white intruders become more greedy, exacting, oppressive and overbearing. Every year contentions spring up between them and our people and when blood is shed we have to make atonement whether right or wrong, at the cost of the lives of our greatest chiefs, and the yielding up of large tracts of our lands. Before the palefaces came among us, we enjoyed the happiness of unbounded freedom, and were acquainted with neither riches, wants nor oppression. How is it now? Wants and oppression are our lot; for are we not controlled in everything, and dare we move without asking, by your leave? Are we not being stripped day by day of the little that remains of our ancient liberty? Do they not even kick and strike us as they do their blackfaces? How long will it be before they will tie us to a post and whip us, and make us work for them in their cornfields as they do them? Shall we wait for that moment or shall we die fighting before submitting to such ignominy?

Have we not for years had before our eyes a sample of their designs, and are they not sufficient harbingers of their future determinations? Will we not soon be driven from our respective countries and the graves of our ancestors? Will not the bones of our dead be plowed up, and their graves be turned into fields? Shall we calmly wait until they become so numerous that we will no longer be able to resist oppression? Will we wait to be destroyed in our turn, without making an effort worthy of our race? Shall we give up our homes, our country, bequeathed to us by the Great Spirit, the graves of our dead, and everything that is dear and sacred to us, without a struggle? I know you will cry with me: Never! Never! Then let us by unity of action destroy them all, which we now can do, or drive them back whence they came. War or extermination is now our only choice. Which do you choose? I know your answer. Therefore, I now call on you, brave Choctaws and Chickasaws, to assist in the just cause of liberating our race from the grasp of our faithless invaders and heartless oppressors. The white usurpation in our common country must be stopped, or we, its rightful owners, be forever destroyed and wiped out as a race of people. I am now at the head of many warriors backed by the strong arm of English soldiers. Choctaws and Chickasaws, you have too long borne with grievous usurpation inflicted by the arrogant Americans. Be no longer their dupes. If there be one here tonight who believes that his rights will not sooner or later be taken from him by the avaricious American palefaces, his ignorance ought to excite pity, for he knows little of the character of our common foe.

And if there be one among you mad enough to undervalue the growing power of the white race among us, let him tremble in considering the fearful woes he will bring down upon our entire race, if by his criminal indifference he assists the designs of our common enemy against our common country. Then listen to the voice of duty, of honor, of nature and of your endangered country. Let us form one body, one heart, and defend to the last warrior our country, our homes, our liberty, and the graves of our fathers.

Choctaws and Chickasaws, you are among the few of our race who sit indolently at ease. You have indeed enjoyed the reputation of being brave, but will you be indebted for it more from report than fact? Will you let the whites encroach upon your domains even to your very door before you will assert your rights in resistance? Let no one in this council imagine that I speak more from malice against the paleface Americans than just grounds of complaint. Complaint is just toward friends who have failed in their duty; accusation is against enemies guilty of injustice. And surely, if any people ever had, we have good and just reasons to believe we have ample grounds to accuse the Americans of injustice; especially when such great acts of injustice have been committed by them upon our race, of which they seem to have no manner of regard, or even to reflect. They are a people fond of innovations, quick to contrive and quick to put their schemes into effectual execution no matter how great the wrong and injury to us; while we are content to preserve what we already have. Their designs are to enlarge their possessions by taking yours in turn; and will you, can you longer dally, O Choctaws and Chickasaws?

Do you imagine that that people will not continue longest in the enjoyment of peace who timely prepare to vindicate themselves, and manifest a determined resolution to do themselves right whenever they are wronged? Far otherwise. Then haste to the relief of our common cause, as by consanguinity of blood you are bound; lest the day be not far distant when you will be left singlehanded and alone to the cruel mercy of our most inveterate foe.

SOURCE: Vanderwerth, W. C. *Indian Oratory: Famous Speeches by Noted Indian Chiefs.* Norman, Okla.: University of Oklahoma Press, 1971.

EXCERPT FROM *GLIMPSE OF NEW MEXICO*
(c. 1820, by Antonio Barreiro)

Antonio Barriero's *Commentaries* observed the commercial and other economic activities of New Spain in the early 1800s. Trade was good and profitable between the region and the "United States of North America," where U.S. merchants brought finished goods to Santa Fe and other trading centers to sell for cash or pelts. But within New Mexico and among the other states of New Spain trade was more tenuous: the economy there depended on barter and continual extensions of credit. Barriero noted that the disparity here was not only one between material success and poverty, but also between civilization and barbarism.

With stable commercial ventures largely unavailable to them, the people of New Spain were isolated from the comforts of civilized life. They were made prey to lawlessness by a legal system too weak to enforce its rules. Further, religion in the region engendered either tragic privation or corrupt greed among its clergy. Because the governors of the region cared only about increasing their own individual power and wealth, inhabitants could find neither legal nor spiritual relief from their travails. No efforts were made to realize the potential of the region's natural and human resources.

Barriero appealed to the Spanish government to initiate a series of reforms aimed at protecting the people of New Spain and guaranteeing to the mother country a lasting source of income and prosperity. Barriero's pleas were ignored. In the Mexican-American War of 1846, the United States took the lands he described here with little resistance.

Mark D. Baumann,
New York University

See also **New Mexico; Santa Fe.**

The commerce of New Mexico must be considered under three aspects, namely: the foreign trade carried on with North America, that carried on with the neighboring states, and the trade which it has internally.

The commerce with the United States of North America is carried on by means of regular caravans which arrive in Santa Fe usually in July. These caravans are composed of ninety or a hundred wagons well loaded with goods and escorted by their respective owners. They elect officers from among themselves to whom they yield obedience on the road. At all times they try to proceed with the greatest care so as not to be surprised by the countless barbarous and warlike Indians who inhabit the dreadful deserts which intervene between New Mexico and Missouri for a distance of more than two hundred and fifty leagues. When a caravan has stopped in the afternoon, they make a circle with the wagons, within which the people and the stock sleep, while a sufficient number of sentinels are on watch all night, in order, when occasion arises, to fire upon the enemy and by all means to save their property.

Generally by July, as I have said, these caravans arrive at Santa Fe, and that is the time when this capital presents a very festive appearance. Then on all sides clothing stores are opened and a considerable number are seen who come to this kind of fair from the pass of the north, from Sonora, and from all parts of the Territory. That is the time when all the Anglo-American merchants are returning who, during the year, have gone to the neighboring states to transact business, and then in short is when one beholds a traffic which is truly pleasing. Goods become extremely cheap, for many merchants "burn their profits" so as to return to the United States in August, and purchases are made with the greatest ease. Upon the invoices from Philadelphia or Saint Louis goods are sold wholesale at an advance of scarcely 80, or 90, or 100%, and indeed they are often sold at an advance of only 50%. These crazy bargains have ruined many merchants, for the losses of the company which came the past year are estimated to have been at least 30 to 40,000 *pesos.*

In August the caravans start back, only those merchants remaining who are interested in the trapping of beaver, of which a considerable exportation is made.

As the exportation of beaver has no duty imposed, the American merchants try upon their return journey to carry beaver instead of money, because thus they secure two advantages: first, that of paying no duties upon the exportation of coin, and second, that of carrying to their own country an effect which is there of great value to them and which here is duty-free.

These caravans originated in 1821 when some adventurers began to enter; but subsequently more formal companies of men were organized, until of late years merchants of means have been coming with ventures on a large scale and under conditions very different from those existing at first. . . .

The Commerce which New Mexico has with the neighboring states.— This also is worthy of attention, as Sonora and Chihuahua are supplied to a large extent by the foreign goods which are imported from here, with the resulting benefit that the Americans who carry on this commerce bring in a considerable amount of money which circulates in this country, both through the payment of duties made upon their return, as well as through the sums which they spend necessarily upon their living.

The New Mexicans also carry on a fairly active commerce with the neighboring States, for yearly they export flocks of sheep, skins, pine-lumber, coarse woolen goods, tobacco and other goods which they sell at good prices. There are persons who have contracts in Durango by which they are to deliver annually 15,000 or more head of sheep which, marketed there, bring nine reales or more. A few persons have the trade in sheep monopolized, so that it cannot be considered as beneficial as the trade in skins, coarse woolens, etc., since the latter trade is well distributed among all classes in New Mexico, especially among the lower and middle classes. The general eagerness found among New Mexicans for commerce with the neighboring States is certainly astonishing. In October especially a multitude of people are seen to set out with this in view and to scatter in all directions. Some head for Chihuahua, others for Pitic or Guaymas; some go even to the fairs of Aguascalientea or San Juan; others to Durango, and others finally as far as the Californias.

The internal commerce of the country.— This is ordinary, and the usual manner of conducting it is by barter. Sheep are held in high esteem, almost more even than money, for the purchase of whatever may be desired. Let me add that such traffic as a regular thing is effected by credit from one year to another, and even for a longer time. I have already spoken to the cheapness of foreign goods; those of the country on the other hand, such as chocolate, rice, sugar, olive oil, almonds, and others of this character, are exceedingly dear and at times very scarce, and furthermore those which are brought here are always of inferior quality.

The commerce which is carried on with the Gentiles.— This also demands our attention. With vermillion, knives, biscuits, ovened bread, powder, awls and other trifles are bought exquisite skins which are resold at a profit and from which [trade] great advantage might be drawn, were the enlightenment of the country different from what it is. Were there revenue and export duties on such rich and abundant peltries, enough could be produced at very little cost to load whole pack-trains. What an immense field in Mexico lies open to industry! What seeds of prosperity are under our hands on every side! Even those most remote places which are now occupied by the barbarians allure us with things of value but with which we are not yet acquainted; those rivers which in their lands teem with valuable beaver; those virgin, untouched fields where fair Nature displays herself in all her beauty; those affable climes which offer to agriculture and to stock-raising their powerful influence; those timber-clad mountains and beautiful marbles which seem to be sketching the plans of magnificient cities, [all these] surely are powerful incentives to make us think seriously upon developing the elements of true happiness which we possess. Revolutionary aspirants! Internal spirits of discord! Cast one single GLANCE OVER YOUR COUNTRY, and hasten to bury yourselves forever in the abysses by reason of the furious remorse which will torment ye when ye shall perceive how this soil, blessed by the adorable hand of Providence, invites the Mexican people with riches and products of every sort, and which they do not enjoy nor even know as yet because of your criminality and perverse designs! . . .

Whoever figures to himself the enormous distance of more than eight hundred leagues at which this Territory lies from its *audiencia;* he who knows the lack of resources with which these unhappy people generally find themselves, for undertaking a ruinous journey even to the capital of Mexico in order there to defend their rights; whoever has a slight conception of the ignorance which reigns in this country, will not require other colors in order to paint vividly the deplorable and doleful state in which the administration of justice finds itself. Should I attempt to unfold any one of the very grave faults from which this most interesting branch suffers, I believe that I should fill many sheets without having done, and so I shall simply indicate some points in passing.

Impunity of crimes.— Never are crimes punished because there is absolutely no one who knows how to draw up a verbal process, to conclude a defense, nor to fill the office of attorney general. It is going on two years that I have been here and in this time I have advised the continuance of numberless cases with the greatest clearness and minuteness, but to date I do not know the result of my advice. I have tried to put to rights the course of other civil proceedings, but I have obtained the same outcome. The vicar general, Don Juan Rafael Rascon, has assured me that in the nearly four years that he has held the vicarate he has been unable to arrange the matters and proceedings of his [ecclesiastical] court. In effect, the appointment of an attorney general is advised, and the judge raises the objection that there is no one who would be able to discharge such an office, so after this fashion one indicates the course of the law, but all are blind for following it. In fine, one cannot recount the obstacles which ignorance presents in New Mexico to the correct administration of justice.

Jails.— There are no other than certain filthy rooms with this appellation in the capital. The prisoners are rewarded instead of punished when they are incarcerated in them, because they pass the time much diverted in merry frolics and chatter; and they take their imprisonment with the greatest ease, for at night they escape to the bailes and by day to other diversions. How reprehensible is such laxness on the part of the judges! The only measures which right now I view as timely are the reestablishment of a learned tribunal for New Mexico, and the enactment of the other measures which the most excellent minister of justice, Don. José Ignacio Espinosa, has introduced in the August chambers.

The spiritual administration finds itself in a truly dismal condition. Nothing is more common than to see numberless sick folk die without confession and extreme unction, and nothing is rarer than to see the eucharist administered to them. Corpses remain unburied many days, and infants are baptized at the cost of a thousand sacrifices. There are unfortunate ones in considerable number who pass most Sundays of the year without hearing mass. The churches are almost destroyed, and most of them are surely unworthy of being called temples of God.

The missions and curacies which do not have pastors are in charge of missionaries and temporary curates and most of these parishioners are visited only a few days in the year. How shall not the poor people who suffer this neglect feel great resentment at seeing that from their crops and herds they have to pay for the maintenance of a priest who does not live with them and who perhaps does not aid them with the consolations of religion in that last hour when they most need them?

There is an absolute deficiency of ministers, for almost all the curacies and missions of the Territory are vacant. The causes which have brought it about that said missions and curacies should have been, and should be, for so extended a time in such great abandonment are very clear; for many ecclesiastics aspire only to hold fat curacies from which to make a fortune, or to maintain a luxury which is surely opposed to the spirit of the Gospel. On the other hand, the curates and missionaries of this Territory have to subsist on a scanty competence; they find themselves separated from cultured intercourse with other people, isolated in these corners of the Republic where only disagreeable objects and oftentimes dangers are near them; they are deprived of the pleasures with which civilized places allure them; they come to live on some miserable ranch and to endure privations which weigh not a little on the spirits of men who are used to a different order of things. And if to those considerations are added the gloomy idea that they have to pass the best of their life in solitude and privation, seeing themselves in the last days of their career without any succor from their poor parishes which from the weariness of years they will now be unable to serve, and therefore reduced to subsist at the expense of charity or off the miserable revenue of some chaplaincy—on these terms, I say, what ecclesiastics will be willing to seek such unhappy lots, unless they be animated by a spirit truly apostolic? It is true that in them they could acquire merits which are very laudable and befitting the obligations of their ministry and of Christian charity, but certain it is that all flee from them.

In order partly to remedy this evil, it would be very fitting that ecclesiastics, when they have served ten years in the cure of souls in these towns with the approbation of the supreme government, should be given preferment for obtaining prebends in the cathedrals of the Republic, for only in this manner would it be possible to induce ecclesiastics of virtue and dignity to come and give their labors on behalf of these unhappy people.

With a saving of revenue and advantages worth considering the missions of this Territory might be secularized, being made into competent curacies which would be sufficient to maintain their rectors in decorum and decency.

It is more than seventy years since a bishop has stepped in New Mexico, and it might be figured that scarcely any age could have an episcopal visit in a country so remote as this, distant more than four hundred leagues from its Metropolis.

The radical way in which to make the spiritual administration is to erect a sacred mitre and a collegiate seminary, as was decreed by the Cortes of Spain on January 26, 1818. With the tithes of New Mexico, now bid off annually at ten or twelve thousand pesos which is scarcely a third of what they produce, there will be sufficient to meet the expenses of the bishop and college. Now the tithes serve only as enrich three or four private parties without profit either to the spiritual welfare of New Mexico or to the temporal good of the Republic.

I will conclude [my notes] upon the ecclesiastical branch, and in summary will say that Christian piety is indignant at seeing the abuses which are committed in New Mexico in the nurture and cure of souls, charity requires a veil to be thrown over many things the relation of which would occasion scandal ... As sole remedy for so many ills, the Territory clamors for the shepherd of her church. *The harvest is plentiful but laborers are lacking. Let us pray the Lord that reapers may enter upon it.*

SOURCE: Excerpt from *Glimpse of New Mexico.* Bloom, Lansing B., "Barreiro's Ojeada Sobre Nuevo-Mexico," *New Mexico Historical Review.* (April 1928): 145–178.

THE MONROE DOCTRINE AND THE ROOSEVELT COROLLARY *(1823–1919)*

In 1823 President James Monroe (1758–1831) declared that the United States would allow no European power to extend its territorial reach throughout the Western Hemisphere. President Theodore Roosevelt (1858–1919) later delivered a series of addresses giving the United States authority to intervene in the affairs of the hemisphere's fledgling republics. In the wake of World War I, President Woodrow Wilson (1856–1924) assured the United States that the Monroe Doctrine would continue to guard the nation's interests and safety.

Monroe's speech appeals to perceived differences between the United States and the nations of Europe: the United States is "comparatively weak and small." Still, the country must defend itself and its interests. Backed by little more than rhetoric, the Monroe Doctrine extended the small nation's reach across half the globe.

Theodore Roosevelt's Corollaries posit that the Doctrine obligates the United States to act as a "police power," to "speak softly and carry a big stick." Careful to allay fears of a colonial expansion by the United States itself, Roosevelt repeatedly assured his listeners that the Doctrine protects interests shared by all humankind—namely, peace and prosperity.

Woodrow Wilson's speech on behalf of the doomed League of Nations Treaty cites the Monroe Doctrine as proof of the nation's resolve and influence. The Doctrine had brought to world affairs a "moral revolution" in the way nations understood their powers abroad and, especially, in the Western Hemisphere.

Mark D. Baumann,
New York University

See also **Cuba, Relations with; Foreign Policy; Isolationism; Latin America, Relations with; Monroe Doctrine; Neutrality; Roosevelt Corollary.**

Annual Message from President James Monroe to the United States Congress, Containing the "Monroe Doctrine," December 2, 1823

At The Proposal of the Russian Imperial Government, made through the minister of the Emperor residing here, a full power and instructions have been transmitted to the minister of the United States at St. Petersburg, to arrange, by amicable negotiation, the respective rights and interests of the two nations on the northwest coast of this continent. A similar proposal has been made by his Imperial Majesty to the Government of Great Britain, which has likewise been acceded to. The Government of the United States has been desirous, by the friendly proceeding, of manifesting the great value which they have invariably attached to the friendship of the Emperor, and their solicitude to cultivate the best understanding with his Government. In the discussions to which this interest has given rise, and in the arrangements by which they may terminate, the occasion has been judged proper for asserting as a principle in which the rights and interests of the United States are involved, that the American continents, by the free and independent condition which they have assumed and maintain, are henceforth not to be considered as subjects for future colonization by any European powers.

It was stated at the commencement of the last session that a great effort was then making in Spain and Portugal to improve the condition of the people of those countries, and that it appeared to be conducted with extraordinary moderation. It need scarcely be remarked that the result has been, so far, very different from what was then anticipated. Of events in that quarter of the globe with which we have so much intercourse, and from which we derive our origin, we have always been anxious and interested spectators. The citizens of the United States cherish sentiments the most friendly in favor of the liberty and happiness of their fellow-men on that side of the Atlantic. In the wars of the European powers in matters relating to themselves we have never taken any part, nor does it comport with our policy so to do. It is only when our rights are invaded or seriously menaced that we resent injuries or make preparation for our defense. With the movements in this hemisphere we are, of necessity, more immediately connected, and by causes which must be obvious to all enlightened and impartial observers. The political system of the allied powers is essentially different in this respect from that of America. This difference proceeds from that which exists in their respective Governments. And to the defense of our own, which has been achieved by the loss of so much blood and treasure, and matured by the wisdom of their most enlightened citizens, and under which we have enjoyed unexampled felicity, this whole nation is devoted. We owe it, therefore, to candor, and to the amicable relations existing between the United States and those powers, to declare that we should consider any attempt on their part to extend their system to any portion of this hemisphere as dangerous to our peace and safety. With the existing colonies or dependencies of any European power we have not interfered and shall not interfere. But with the governments who have declared their independence and maintained it, and whose independence we have, on great consideration and on just principles, acknowledged, we could not view any interposition for the purpose of oppressing them, or controlling in any other manner their destiny, by any European power, in any other light than as the manifestation of an unfriendly disposition toward the United States. In the war between these new governments and Spain we declared our neutrality at the time of their recognition, and to this we have adhered and shall continue to adhere, provided no change shall occur which, in the judgment of the competent authorities of this Government, shall make a corresponding change on the part of the United States indispensable to their security.

The late events in Spain and Portugal show that Europe is still unsettled. Of this important fact no stronger proof can be adduced than that the allied powers should have thought it proper, on any principle satisfactory to themselves, to have interposed by force, in the internal concerns of Spain. To what extent such interposition may be carried, on the same principle, is a question in which all independent powers whose governments differ from theirs are interested, even those most remote, and surely none more so than the United States. Our policy in regard to Europe, which was adopted at an early stage of the wars which have so long agitated that quarter of the globe, nevertheless remains the same, which is, not to interfere in the internal concerns of government for us; to cultivate friendly relations with it, and to any of its powers; to consider the government de facto as the legitimate preserve those relations by a frank, firm, and manly policy, meeting, in all instances, the just claims of every power, submitting to injuries from none. But in regard to these continents, circumstances are eminently and conspicuously different. It is impossible that the allied powers should extend their political system to any portion of either continent without endangering our peace and happiness; nor can anyone believe that our southern brethren, if left to themselves, would adopt it of their own accord. It is equally impossible, therefore, that we should behold such interposition, in any form, with indifference. If we look to the comparative strength and resources of Spain and those new governments, and their distance from each other, it must be obvious that she can never subdue them. It is still the true policy of the United States to leave the parties to themselves, in the hope that other powers will pursue the same course.

The Monroe doctrine finds its recognition in those principles of international law which are based upon the theory that every nation shall have its rights protected and its just claims enforced.

Of course this Government is entirely confident that under the sanction of this doctrine we have clear rights and undoubted claims. Nor is this ignored in the British reply. The prime minister, while not admitting that the Monroe doctrine is applicable to present conditions, states: "In declaring that the United States would resist any such enterprise if it was contemplated, President Monroe adopted a policy which received the entire sympathy of the English Government of that date." He further declares: "Though the language of President Monroe is directed to the attainment of objects which most Englishmen would agree to be salutary, it is impossible to admit that they have been inscribed by any adequate authority in the code of international law." Again he says: "They (Her Majesty's Government) fully concur with the view which President Monroe apparently entertained, that any disturbance of the existing territorial distribution in the hemisphere by any fresh acquisitions on the part of any European state, would be a highly inexpedient change."

In the belief that the doctrine for which we contend was clear and definite, that it was founded upon substantial considerations and involved our safety and welfare, that it was fully applicable to our present conditions and to the state of the world's progress and that it was directly related to the pending controversy and without any conviction as to the final merits of the dispute, but anxious to learn in a satisfactory and conclusive manner whether Great Britain sought, under a claim of boundary, to extend her possessions on this continent without right, or whether she merely sought possession of territory fairly included within her lines of ownership, this Government proposed to the Government of Great Britain a resort to arbitration as the proper means of settling the question to the end that a vexatious boundary dispute between the two contestants might be determined and our exact standing and relation in respect to the controversy might be made clear.

It will be seen from the correspondence herewith submitted that this proposition has been declined by the British Government, upon grounds which in the circumstances seem to me to be far from satisfactory. It is deeply disappointing that such an appeal actuated by the most friendly feelings towards both nations directly concerned, addressed to the sense of justice and to the magnanimity of one of the great powers of the world and touching its relations to one comparatively weak and small, should have produced no better results.

The course to be pursued by this Government in view of the present condition does not appear to admit of serious doubt. Having labored faithfully for many years to induce Great Britain to submit this dispute to impartial arbitration, and having been now finally apprized of her refusal to do so, nothing remains but to accept the situation, to recognize its plain requirements and deal with it accordingly. Great Britain's present proposition has never thus far been regarded as admissible by Venezuela, though any adjustment of the boundary which that country may deem for her advantage and may enter into of her own free will can not of course be objected to by the United States.

Assuming, however, that the attitude of Venezuela will remain unchanged, the dispute has reached such a stage as to make it now incumbent upon the United States to take measures to determine with sufficient certainty for its justification what is the true divisional line between the Republic of Venezuela and British Guiana. The inquiry to that end should of course be conducted carefully and judicially and due weight should be given to all available evidence records and facts in support of the claims of both parties.

In order that such an examination should be prosecuted in a thorough and satisfactory manner I suggest that the Congress make an adequate appropriation for the expenses of a commission, to be appointed by the Executive, who shall make the necessary investigation and report upon the matter with the least possible delay. When such report is made and accepted it will in my opinion be the duty of the United States to resist by every means in its power as a willful aggression upon its rights and interests the appropriation by Great Britain of any lands or the exercise of governmental jurisdiction over any territory which after investigation we have determined of right belongs to Venezuela.

In making these recommendations I am fully alive to the responsibility incurred, and keenly realize all the consequences that may follow.

I am nevertheless firm in my conviction that while it is a grievous thing to contemplate the two great English-speaking peoples of the world as being otherwise than friendly competitors in the onward march of civilization, and strenuous and worthy rivals in all the arts of peace, there is no calamity which a great nation can invite which equals that which follows a supine submission to wrong and injustice and the consequent loss of national self-respect and honor beneath which are shielded and defended a people's safety and greatness.

The Roosevelt Corollary

Annual Message from President Theodore Roosevelt to the United States Congress, December 3, 1901:

. . . More And More the civilized peoples are realizing the wicked folly of war and are attaining that condition of just and intelligent regard for the rights of others which will in the end, as we hope and believe, make world-wide peace possible. The peace conference at The Hague gave definite expression to this hope and belief and marked a stride toward their attainment.

This same peace conference acquiesced in our statement of the Monroe doctrine as compatible with the purposes and aims of the conference.

The Monroe doctrine should be the cardinal feature of the foreign policy of all the nations of the two Americas, as it is of the United States. Just seventy-eight years have passed since President Monroe in his Annual Message announced that "The American continents are henceforth not to be considered as subjects for future colonization by any European power." In other words, the Monroe doctrine is a declaration that there must be no territorial aggrandizement by any non-American power at the expense of any American power or American soil. It is in no wise intended as hostile to any nation in the Old World. Still less is it intended to give cover to any aggression by one New World power at the expense of any other. It is simply a step, and a long step, toward assuring the universal peace of the world by securing the possibility of permanent peace on this hemisphere.

During the past century other influences have established the permanence and independence of the smaller states of Europe. Through the Monroe doctrine we hope to be able to safeguard like independence and secure like permanence for the lesser among the New World nations.

This doctrine has nothing to do with the commercial relations of any American power, save that it in truth allows each of them to form such as it desires. In other words, it is really a guaranty of the commercial independence of the Americans. We do not ask under this doctrine for any exclusive commercial dealings with any other American state. We do not guarantee any state against punishment if it misconducts itself, provided that punishment does not take the form of the acquisition of territory by any non-American power.

Our attitude in Cuba is a sufficient guaranty of our own good faith. We have not the slightest desire to secure any territory at the expense of any of our neighbors. We wish to work with them hand in hand, so that all of us may be uplifted together, and we rejoice over the good fortune of any of them, we gladly hail their material prosperity and political stability, and are concerned and alarmed if any of them fall into industrial or political chaos. We do not wish to see any Old World military power grow up on this continent, or to be compelled to become a military power ourselves. The peoples of the Americas can prosper best if left to work out their own salvation in their own way.

Our people intend to abide by the Monroe doctrine and to insist upon it as the one sure means of securing peace of the Western Hemisphere. The Navy offers us the only means of making our insistence upon the Monroe doctrine anything but a subject of derision to whatever nation chooses to disregard it. We desire the peace which comes as of right to the just man armed; not the peace granted-on terms of ignominy to the craven and the weakling. . . .

Annual Message from President Theodore Roosevelt to the United States Congress, December 2, 1902:

. . . The Canal Will be of great benefit to America, and of importance to all the world. It will be of advantage to us industrially and also as improving our military position.

It will be of advantage to the countries of tropical America. It is earnestly to be hoped that all of these countries will do as some of them have already done with signal success, and will invite to heir shores commerce and improve their material condition by recognizing that stability and order are the prerequisites of our successful development. No independent nation in America need have the slightest fear of aggression from the United States. It behooves each one to maintain order within its own borders and to discharge its just obligations to foreigners. When this is done, they can rest assured that, be they strong or weak, they have nothing to dread from outside interference. More and more the increasing interdependence and complexity of international political and economic relations render it incumbent on all civilized and orderly powers to insist on the proper policing of the world. . . .

Address by President Theodore Roosevelt at Chicago, April 2, 1903:

I Believe in the Monroe Doctrine with all my heart and soul; I am convinced that the immense majority of our fellow-countrymen so believe in it; but I would infinitely prefer to see us abandon it than to see us put it forward and bluster about it, and yet fail to build up the efficient fighting strength which in the last resort can alone make it respected by any strong foreign power whose interest it may ever happen to be to violate it.

There is a homely old adage which runs: "Speak softly and carry a big stick; you will go far." If the American nation will speak softly and yet build and keep at a pitch of the highest training a thoroughly efficient navy the Monroe Doctrine will go far.

Annual Message from President Theodore Roosevelt to the United States Congress, December 6, 1904:

It Is Not True that the United States feels any land hunger or entertains any projects as regards the other nations of the Western Hemisphere save such as are for their welfare. All that this country desires is to see the neighboring countries stable, orderly, and prosperous. Any country whose people conduct themselves well can count upon our hearty friendship. If a nation shows that it knows how to act with reasonable efficiency and decency in social and political matters, if it keeps order and pays its obligations, it need fear no interference from the United States. Chronic wrongdoing, or an impotence which results in a general loosening of the ties of civilized society, may in America, as elsewhere, ultimately require intervention by some civilized nation, and in the Western Hemisphere the adherence of the United States to the Monroe Doctrine may force the United States, however reluctantly, in flagrant cases of such wrongdoing or impotence, to the exercise of an international police power. If every country washed by the Caribbean Sea would show the progress in stable and just civilization which with the aid of the Platt amendment Cuba has shown since our troops left the island, and which so many of the republics in both Americas are constantly and brilliantly showing, all question of interference by this Nation with their affairs would be at an end. Our interests and those of our southern neighbors are in reality identical. They have great natural riches, and if within their borders the reign of law and justice obtains, prosperity is sure to come to them. While they thus obey the primary laws of civilized society they may rest assured that they will be treated by us in a spirit of cordial and helpful sympathy. We would interfere with them only in the last resort, and then only if it became evident that their inability or unwillingness to do justice at home and abroad had violated the rights of the United States or had invited foreign aggression to the detriment of the entire body of American nations. It is a mere truism to say that every nation, whether in America or anywhere else, which desires to maintain its freedom, its independence, must ultimately realize that the right of such independence can not be separated from the responsibility of making good use of it.

In asserting the Monroe Doctrine, in taking such steps as we have taken in regard to Cuba, Venezuela, and Panama, and in endeavoring to circumscribe the theater of war in the Far East, and to secure the open door in China, we have acted in our own interest as well as in the interest of humanity at large.

Annual Message from President Theodore Roosevelt to the United States Congress, December 5, 1905:

One Of The Most effective instruments for peace is the Monroe Doctrine as it has been and is being gradually developed by this Nation and accepted by other nations. No other policy could have been as efficient in promoting peace in the Western Hemisphere and in giving to each nation thereon the chance to develop along its own lines. If we had refused to apply the Doctrine to changing conditions it would now be completely outworn, would not meet any of the needs of the present day, and indeed would probably by this time have sunk into complete oblivion. It is useful at home, and is meeting with recognition abroad, because we have adapted our application of it to meet the growing and changing needs of the Hemisphere. When we announce a policy, such as the Monroe Doctrine, we thereby commit ourselves to the consequences of the policy, and those consequences from time to time alter. It is out of the question to claim a right and yet shirk the responsibility for its exercise. Not only we, but all American Republics who are benefitted by the existence of the Doctrine, must recognize the obligations each nation is under as regards foreign peoples no less than its duty to insist upon its own rights.

That our rights and interests are deeply concerned in the maintenance of the Doctrine is so clear as hardly to need argument. This is especially true in view of the construction of the Panama Canal. As a mere matter of self-defense we must exercise a close watch over the approaches to this canal; and this means that we must be thoroughly alive to our interests in the Caribbean Sea.

There are certain essential points which must never be forgotten as regards the Monroe Doctrine. In the first place we must as a nation make it evident that we do not intend to treat it in any shape or way as an excuse for aggrandizement on our part at the expense of the republics to the south. We must recognize the fact that in some South American countries there has been much suspicion lest we should interpret the Monroe Doctrine as in some way inimical to their interests, and we must try to convince all the other nations of this continent once and for all that no just and orderly government has anything to fear from us. There are certain republics to the south of us which have already reached such a point of stability, order, and prosperity that they themselves, though as yet hardly consciously, are among the guarantors of this Doctrine. These republics we now meet not only on a basis of entire equality, but in a spirit of frank and respectful friendship which we hope is mutual. If all of the republics to the south of us will only grow as those to which I allude have already grown, all need for us to be the especial champions of the Doctrine will disappear, for no stable and growing American Republic wishes to see some great non-American military power acquire territory in its neighborhood. All that this country desires is that the other republics on this Continent shall be happy and prosperous; and they can not be happy and prosperous unless they maintain order within their boundaries and behave with a just regard for their obligations toward outsiders. It must be understood that under no circumstances will the United States use the Monroe Doctrine as a cloak for territorial aggression. We desire peace with all the world, but perhaps most of all with the other peoples of the American Continent. There are of course limits to the wrongs which any self-respecting nation can endure. It is always possible that wrong actions toward this Nation, or toward citizens of this Nation, in some State unable to keep order among its own people, unable to secure justice from outsiders, and unwilling to do justice to those outsiders who treat it well, may result in our having to take action to protect our rights; but such action will not be taken with a view to territorial aggression, and it will be taken at all only with extreme reluctance and when it has become evident that every other resource has been exhausted.

Moreover, we must make it evident that we do not intend to permit the Monroe Doctrine to be used by any nation on this Continent as a shield to protect it from the consequences of its own misdeeds against foreign nations. If a republic to the south of us commits a tort against a foreign nation, such as an outrage against a citizen of that nation, then the Monroe Doctrine does not force us to interfere to prevent punishment of the tort, save to see that the punishment does not assume the form of territorial occupation in any shape. The case is more difficult when it refers to a contractual obligation. Our own Government has always refused to enforce such contractual obligations on behalf of its citizens by an appeal to arms. It is much to be wished that all foreign governments would take the same view. But they do not; and in consequence we are liable at any time to be brought face to face with disagreeable alternatives. On the one hand, this country would certainly decline to go to war to prevent a foreign government from collecting a just debt; on the other hand, it is very inadvisable to permit any foreign power to take possession, even temporarily, of the customhouses of an American Republic in order to enforce the payment of its obligations; for such temporary occupation might turn into a permanent occupation. The only escape from these alternatives may at any time be that we must ourselves undertake to bring about some arrangement by which so much as possible of a just obligation shall be paid. It is far better that this country should put through such an arrangement, rather than allow any foreign country to undertake it. To do so insures the defaulting republic from having to pay debts of an improper character under duress, while it also insures honest creditors of the republic from being passed by in the interest of dishonest or grasping creditors. Moreover, for the United States to take such a position offers the only possible way of insuring us against a clash with some foreign power. The position is, therefore, in the interest of peace as well as in the interest of justice. It is of benefit to our people; it is of benefit to foreign peoples; and most of all it is really of benefit to the people of the country concerned.

This brings me to what should be one of the fundamental objects of the Monroe Doctrine. We must ourselves in good faith try to help upward toward peace and order those of our sister republics which need such help. Just as there has been a gradual growth of the ethical element in the relations of one individual to another, so we are, even though slowly, more and more coming to recognize the duty of bearing one another's burdens, not only as among individuals, but also as among nations.

Annual Message from President Theodore Roosevelt to the United States Congress, December 3, 1906:

. . . Last August an insurrection broke out in Cuba which it speedily grew evident that the existing Cuban Government was powerless to quell. This Government was repeatedly asked by the then Cuban Government to intervene, and finally was notified by the President of Cuba that he intended to resign; that his decision was irrevocable; that none of the other constitutional officers would consent to carry on the Government, and that he was powerless to maintain order. It was evident that chaos was impending, and there was every probability that if steps were not immediately taken by this Government to try to restore order, the representatives of various European nations in the island would apply to their respective governments for armed intervention in order to protect the lives and property of their citizens. Thanks to the preparedness of our Navy, I was able immediately to send enough ships to Cuba to prevent the situation from becoming hopeless; and I furthermore dispatched to Cuba the Secretary of War and the Assistant Secretary of State, in order that they might grapple with the situation on the ground. All efforts to secure an agreement between the contending factions, by which they should themselves come to an amicable understanding and settle upon some modus vivendi—some provisional government of their own—failed. Finally the President of the Republic resigned. The quorum of Congress assembled failed by deliberate purpose of its members, so that there was no power to act on his resignation, and the Government came to a halt. In accordance with the so-called Platt amendment, which was embodied in the constitution of Cuba, I thereupon proclaimed a provisional government for the island, the Secretary of War acting as provisional governor until he could be replaced by Mr. Magoon, the late minister to Panama and governor of the Canal Zone on the Isthmus; troops were sent to support them and to relieve the Navy, the expedition being handled with most satisfactory speed and efficiency. The insurgent chiefs immediately agreed that their troops should lay down their arms and disband; and the agreement was carried out. The provisional government has left the personnel of the old government and the old laws, so far as might be, unchanged, and will thus administer the island for a few months until tranquillity can be restored, a new election properly held, and a new government inaugurated. Peace has come in the island; and the harvesting of the sugar-cane crop, the great crop of the Island, is about to proceed.

When the election has been held and the new government inaugurated in peaceful and orderly fashion the provisional government will come to an end. I take this opportunity of expressing upon behalf of the American people, with all possible solemnity, our most earnest hope that the people of Cuba will realize the imperative need of preserving justice and keeping order in the Island. The United States wishes nothing of Cuba except that it shall prosper morally and materially, and wishes nothing of the Cubans save that they shall be able to preserve order among themselves and therefore to preserve their independence. If the elections become a farce, and if the insurrectionary habit becomes confirmed in the Island, it is absolutely out of the question that the Island should continue independent; and the United States, which has assumed the sponsorship before the civilized world for Cuba's career as a nation, would again have to intervene and to see that the government was managed in such orderly fashion as to secure the safety of life and property. The path to be trodden by those who exercise self-government is always hard, and we should have every charity and patience with the Cubans as they tread this difficult path. I have the utmost sympathy with, and regard for, them; but I most earnestly adjure them solemnly to weigh their responsibilities and to see that when their new government is started it shall run smoothly, and with freedom from flagrant denial of right on the one hand, and from insurrectionary disturbances on the other....

Address by President Woodrow Wilson at San Francisco, September 17, 1919:

...I Want To Say again that Article X is the very heart of the Covenant of the League, because all the great wrongs of the world have had their root in the seizure of territory or the control of the political independence of other peoples. I believe that I speak the feeling of the people of the United States when I say that, having seen one great wrong like that attempted and having prevented it, we are ready to prevent it again.

Those are the two principal criticisms, that we did not do the impossible with regard to Shantung and that we may be advised to go to war. That is all there is in either of those. But they say, "We want the Monroe Doctrine more distinctly acknowledged." Well, if I could have found language that was more distinct than that used, I should have been very happy to suggest it, but it says in so many words that nothing in that document shall be construed as affecting the validity of the Monroe Doctrine. I do not see what more it could say, but, as I say, if the clear can be clarified, I have no objection to its being clarified. The meaning is too obvious to admit of discussion, and I want you to realize how extraordinary that provision is. Every nation in the world had been jealous of the Monroe Doctrine, had studiously avoided doing or saying anything that would admit its validity, and here all the great nations of the world sign a document which admits its validity. That constitutes nothing less than a moral revolution in the attitude of the rest of the world toward America.

What does the Monroe Doctrine mean in that Covenant? It means that with regard to aggressions upon the Western Hemisphere we are at liberty to act without waiting for other nations to act. That is the Monroe Doctrine. The Monroe Doctrine says that if anybody tries to interfere with affairs in the Western Hemisphere it will be regarded as an unfriendly act to the United States—not to the rest of the world—and that means that the United States will look after it, and will not ask anybody's permission to look after it. The document says that nothing in this document must be construed as interfering with that....

SOURCE: *A Compilation of the Messages and Papers of the Presidents, 1789–1897.* Vol. 2. New York: Bureau of National Literature, 1897.

LIFE OF MA-KA-TAI-ME-SHE-KAI-KIAK, OR BLACK HAWK
(c. 1832, by Black Hawk)

The great Sauk war chief Ma-ka-tai-me-she-kai-kiak, or Black Hawk, was born in Illinois near the Mississippi River in 1767. The land on which he was raised was ceded to the United States in 1804 via shady dealings on the part of William Henry Harrison who, it is believed, forced the treaty upon a group of badly intoxicated chiefs who were acting without tribal warrant. Black Hawk's anger over this treaty led him to join Tecumseh's fight for an Indian confederation. After the War of 1812, Black Hawk joined forces with Winnebago prophet White Cloud and the two continued Tecumseh's fight for a unified Indian response to American encroachment.

The Black Hawk War was an attempt by the Sauks (with help from the Winnebagos, Potawatomis, and Mascoutins) to regain their lands in Illinois and southern Wisconsin. Between 1831 and 1832, a series of bloody battles were fought, but though the tribes made small gains they were eventually overcome by a group of Illinois militiamen at the mouth of the Bad Axe River in Wisconsin. Black Hawk and his followers were imprisoned for several years before being allowed to settle in Iowa. After being well received during a 1833 visit to Washington, D.C., Black Hawk decided to tell his story to U.S. interpreter Antoine le Claire. *The Autobiography of Black Hawk* was published in 1833 and is now considered an American classic. This selection details Black Hawk's meeting with Illinois Governor Cole, to whom he makes a case for equitable treatment for his people.

Leah R. Shafer,
Cornell University

***See also* Black Hawk War; Indian Land Cessions; Indians and Alcohol; Sauk.**

The white people brought whisky into our village, made our people drunk, and cheated them out of their horses, guns, and traps! This fraudulent system was carried to such an extent that I apprehended serious difficulties might take place, unless a stop was put to it. Consequently, I visited all the whites and begged them not to sell whisky to my people. One of them continued the practice openly. I took a party of my young men, went to his house, and took out his barrel and broke in the head and poured out the whisky. I did this for fear some of the whites might be killed by my people when drunk.

Our people were treated badly by the whites on many occasions. At one time, a white man beat one of our women cruelly, for pulling a few suckers of corn out of his field, to suck, when hungry. At another time, one of our young men was beat with clubs by two white men for opening a fence which crossed our road, to take his horse through. His shoulder blade was broken, and his body badly bruised, from which he soon after died!

Bad, and cruel, as our people were treated by the whites, not one of them was hurt or molested by any of my band. I hope this will prove that we are a peaceable people—having permitted ten men to take possession of our corn-fields; prevent us from planting corn; burn our lodges; ill-treat our women; and beat to death our men, without offering resistance to their barbarous cruelties. This is a lesson worthy for the white man to learn: to use forbearance when injured.

We acquainted our agent daily with our situation, and through him, the great chief at St. Louis—and hoped that something would be done for us. The whites were complaining at the same time that we were intruding upon their rights! They made themselves out the injured party, and we the intruders! And called loudly to the great war chief to protect their property.

How smooth must be the language of the whites, when they can make right look like wrong, and wrong like right.

During this summer, I happened at Rock Island when a great chief arrived, whom I had known as the great chief of Illinois, [Governor Cole] in company with another chief, who, I have been told, is a great writer (Judge Jas. Hall.) I called upon them and begged to explain to them the grievances, under which me and my people were laboring, hoping that they could do something for us. The great chief, however, did not seem disposed to council with me. He said he was no longer the chief of Illinois—that his children had selected another father in his stead, and that he now only ranked as they did. I was surprised at this talk, as I had always heard that he was a good, brave, and great chief. But the white people never appear to be satisfied. When they get a good father, they hold councils, (at the suggestion of some bad, ambitious man, who wants the place himself,) and conclude, among themselves that this man, or some other equally ambitious, would make a better father than they have, and nine times out of ten they don't get as good a one again.

I insisted on explaining to these two chiefs the true situation of my people. They gave their assent. I arose and made a speech, in which I explained to them the treaty made by Quash-qua-me, and three of our braves, according to the manner the trader and others had explained it to me. I then told them that Quash-qua-me and his party denied, positively, having ever sold my village; and that, as I had never known them to lie, I was determined to keep it in possession.

I told them that the white people had already entered our village, burnt our lodges, destroyed our fences, ploughed up our corn, and beat our people: that they had brought whisky into our country, made our people drunk, and taken from them their horses, guns, and traps; and that I had borne all this injury, without suffering any of my braves to raise a hand against the whites.

My object in holding this council, was to get the opinion of these two chiefs, as to the best course for me to pursue. I had appealed in vain, time after time, to our agent, who regularly represented our situation to the chief at St. Louis, whose duty it was to call upon our Great Father to have justice done to us; but instead of this, we are told that the white people want our country and we must leave it to them!

I did not think it possible that our Great Father wished us to leave our village, where we had lived so long, and where the bones of so many of our people had been laid. The great chief said that, as he was no longer a chief, he could do nothing for us; and felt sorry that it was not in his power to aid us—nor did he know how to advise us. Neither of them could do anything for us; but both evidently appeared very sorry. It would give me great pleasure, at all times, to take these two chiefs by the hand.

That fall I paid a visit to the agent, before we started to our hunting grounds, to hear if he had any good news for me. He had news! He said that the land on which our village stood was now ordered to be sold to individuals; and that, when sold, our right to remain, by treaty, would be at an end, and that if we returned next spring, we would be forced to remove!

We learned during the winter that part of the lands where our village stood had been sold to individuals, and that the trader at Rock Island had bought the greater part that had been sold. The reason was now plain to me why he urged us to remove. His object, we thought, was to get our lands. We held several councils that winter to determine what we should do, and resolved, in one of them, to return to our village in the spring, as usual; and concluded, that if we were removed by force, that the trader, agent, and others, must be the cause; and that, if found guilty of having us driven from our village they should be killed! The trader stood foremost on this list. He had purchased the land on which my lodge stood, and that of our grave yard also! Ne-a-pope promised to kill him, the agent, the interpreter, the great chief at St. Louis, the war chief at fort Armstrong, Rock Island, and Ke-o-kuck—these being the principal persons to blame for endeavoring to remove us.

Our women received bad accounts from the women that had been raising corn at the new village—the difficulty of breaking the new prairie with hoes—and the small quantity of corn raised. We were nearly in the same situation with regard to the latter, it being the first time I ever knew our people to be in want of provision.

I prevailed upon some of Ke-o-kuck's band to return this spring to the Rock river village. Ke-o-kuck would not return with us. I hoped that we would get permission to go to Washington to settle our affairs with our Great Father. I visited the agent at Rock Island. He was displeased because we had returned to our village, and told me that we must remove to the west of the Mississippi. I told him plainly that we would not! I visited the interpreter at his house, who advised me to do as the agent had directed me. I then went to see the trader and upbraided him for buying our lands. He said that if he had not purchased them, some person else would, and that if our Great Father would make an exchange with us, he would willingly give up the land he had purchased to the government. This I thought was fair, and began to think that he had not acted as badly as I had suspected. We again repaired our lodges, and built others, as most of our village had been burnt and destroyed. Our women selected small patches to plant corn, (where the whites had not taken them within their fences,) and worked hard to raise something for our children to subsist upon.

I was told that, according to the treaty, we had no right to remain upon the lands sold, and that the government would force us to leave them. There was but a small portion, however, that had been sold; the balance remaining in the hands of the government, we claimed the right (if we had no other) to "live and hunt upon, as long as it remained the property of the government," by a stipulation in the same treaty that required us to evacuate it after it had been sold. This was the land that we wished to inhabit, and thought we had the best right to occupy.

I heard that there was a great chief on the Wabash, and sent a party to get his advice. They informed him that we had not sold our village. He assured them, then, that if we had not sold the land on which our village stood, our Great Father would not take it from us.

I started early to Malden to see the chief of my British Father, and told him my story. He gave the same reply that the chief on the Wabash had given; and in justice to him, I must say, he never gave me any bad advice: but advised me to apply to our American Father, who, he said, would do us justice. I next called on the great chief at Detroit, and made the same statement to him that I had to the chief of our British Father. He gave the same reply. He said, if we had not sold our lands, and would remain peaceably on them, that we would not be disturbed. This assured me that I was right, and determined me to hold out, as I had promised my people.

I returned from Malden late in the fall. My people were gone to their hunting ground, whither I followed. Here I learned that they had been badly treated all summer by the whites; and that a treaty had been held at Prairie du Chien. Ke-o-kuck and some of our people attended it, and found out that our Great Father had exchanged a small strip of the land that was ceded by Quash-qua-me and his party, with the Pottowattomies, for a portion of their land, near Chicago; and that the object of this treaty was to get it back again; and that the United States had agreed to give them sixteen thousand dollars a year, forever, for this small strip of land—it being less than the twentieth part of that taken from our nation, for one thousand dollars a year! This bears evidence of something I cannot explain. This land they say belonged to the United States. What reason, then, could have induced them to exchange it with the Pottowattomies, if it was so valuable? Why not keep it? Or, if they found that they had made a bad bargain with the Pottowattomies, why not take back their land at a fair proportion of what they gave our nation for it? If this small portion of the land that they took from us for one thousand dollars a year, be worth sixteen thousand dollars a year forever, to the Pottowattomies, then the whole tract of country taken from us ought to be worth, to our nation, twenty times as much as this small fraction. Here I was again puzzled to find out how the white people reasoned; and began to doubt whether they had any standard of right and wrong!

Communication was kept up between myself and the Prophet. Runners were sent to the Arkansas, Red river and Texas—not on the subject of our lands, but a secret mission, which I am not, at present, permitted to explain.

It was related to me, that the chiefs and headmen of the Foxes had been invited to Prairie du Chien, to hold a council to settle the differences existing between them and the Sioux. That the chiefs and headmen, amounting to nine, started for the place designated, taking with them one woman—and were met by the Menomonees and Sioux, near the Ouisconsin and all killed, except one man. Having understood that the whole matter was published shortly after it occurred, and is known to the white people, I will say no more about it.

I would here remark, that our pastimes and sports had been laid aside for two years. We were a divided people, forming two parties. Ke-o-kuck being at the head of one, willing to barter our rights merely for the good opinion of the whites; and cowardly enough to desert our village to them. I was at the head of the other party, and was determined to hold on to my village, although I had been ordered to leave it. But, I considered, as myself and band had no agency in selling our country—and that as provision had been made in the treaty, for us all to remain on it as long as it belonged to the United States, that we could not be forced away. I refused, therefore, to quit my village. It was here, that I was born—and here lie the bones of many friends and relations. For this spot I felt a sacred reverence, and never could consent to leave it, without being forced therefrom.

When I called to mind the scenes of my youth, and those of later days—and reflected that the theatre on which these were acted, had been so long the home of my fathers, who now slept on the hills around it, I could not bring my mind to consent to leave this country to the whites, for any earthly consideration.

SOURCE: Black Hawk. *Life of Black Hawk*. Chicago: R. R. Donnelly and Sons, 1916.

THE STORY OF ENRIQUE ESPARZA
(1836, by Enrique Esparza)

Upon winning independence from Spain in 1821, Mexico opened its sparsely populated northern region to *empresarios,* men who agreed to bring two hundred or more families to settle the land. In return for very cheap land, the new settlers were to become Mexican citizens and embrace the Catholic religion. By 1835, *empresarios* like Moses and Sam Houston had brought over 35,000 settlers to the Texas area. Pro-slavery and hostile to Mexico's laws, Texas settlers took up an armed rebellion against Mexican forces seeking to impose their authority in the region. Beginning on 23 February 1836, Mexican General Santa Anna and a force of three thousand besieged a group of two hundred American and Mexican rebels led by Davy Crockett and Sam Bowie for thirteen days at the Alamo in San Antonio. The Alamo's rebel fighters were all killed, but Texas gained its independence later that year. After a decade of political maneuvering, Congress annexed the Republic of Texas into the union in 1844.

When Gregorio Esparza, a soldier in the U.S. Army in Texas, was ordered to defend the Alamo from General Santa Anna, his wife and six children also sought refuge in the fort. His son, Enrique, eight years old at the time, remembered the siege in newspaper interviews conducted some sixty years later. The younger Esparza's account not only describes the confusion and violence of close combat, but also illuminates social relations in early Texas. Mexican and American rebels shared the same leaders and fought the same enemy. They intermarried and raised families. Nonetheless, race remained a factor, as when a Mexican woman implored her comrades not to reveal to Santa Anna's forces that she had married an American.

Mark D. Baumann,
New York University

See also **Alamo, Siege of the; "Remember the Alamo"; Texas.**

Esparza's Story

My father, Gregorio Esparza, belonged to [Placido] Benavides' company in the American army and I think it was in February 1836 that the company was ordered to Corpus Christi. They had gotten to Gollad when my father was ordered back alone to San Antonio, for what I don't know. When he got here there were rumors that Santa Anna was on the way here and many residents sent their families away. One of my father's friends told him that he could have a wagon and team and all necessary provisions for a trip if he wanted to take his family away. There were six of us besides my father: my mother, whose name was Anita, my elder sister, myself and three younger brothers, one a baby in arms. I was eight years old.

My father decided to take the offer and move the family to San Felipe. Everything was ready when one morning Mr. [John] W. Smith, who was godfather to my youngest brother, came to our house on North Flores Street just above where the Presbyterian Church now is and told my mother to tell my father when he came in that Santa Anna had come.

When my father came my mother asked him what he would do. You know the Americans had the Alamo, which had been fortified a few months before by General [Martin] Cos.

"Well, I'm going to the fort," my father said.

"Well, if you go, I'm going along, and the whole family too."

It took the whole day to move and an hour before sundown we were inside the fort. There was a bridge over the river about where Commerce Street crosses it and just as we got to it we could hear Santa Anna's drums beating on Milam Square; and just as we were crossing the ditch going into the fort Santa Anna fired his salute on Milam Square.

There were a few other families who had gone in. A Mrs. [Juana Navarro] Alsbury and her sister, a Mrs. Victoriana and a family of several girls, two of whom I knew afterwards, Mrs. [Susanna] Dickinson, Mrs. Juana Melton, a Mexican woman who had married an American, also a woman named Concepcion Losoya and her son, Juan, who was a little older than I.

The first thing I remember after getting inside the fort was seeing Mrs. Melton making circles on the ground with an umbrella. I had seen very few umbrellas. While I was walking around about dark I went near a man named [Antonio] Fuentes who was talking at a distance with a soldier. When the latter got near me he said to Fuentes: "Did you know they had cut the water off?"

The fort was built around a square. The present Hugo-Schmeltzer building is part of it. I remember the main entrance was on the south side of the large enclosure. The quarters were not in the church, but on the south side of the fort on either side of the entrance, and were part of the convent. There was a ditch of running water back of the church and another along the west side of Alamo Plaza. We couldn't get to the latter ditch as it was under fire and it was the other one that Santa Anna cut off. The next morning after we had gotten in the fort I saw the men drawing water from a well that was in the convent yard. The well was located a little south of the center of the square. I don't know whether it is there now or not.

On the first night a company of which my father was one went out and captured some prisoners. One of them was a Mexican soldier and all through the siege he interpreted the bugle calls on the Mexican side and in this way the Americans kept posted on the movements of the enemy.

After the first day there was fighting every day. The Mexicans had a cannon somewhere near where Dwyer Avenue now is and every fifteen minutes they dropped a shot into the fort.

The roof of the Alamo had been taken off and the south side filled up with dirt almost to the roof on that side so that there was a slanting embankment up which the Americans could run and take positions. During the fight I saw numbers who were shot in the head as soon as they exposed themselves from the roof. There were holes made in the walls of the fort and the Americans continually shot from these also. We also had two cannon, one at the main entrance and one at the northwest corner of the fort near the post office. The cannon were seldom fired.

Remembers Crockett

I remember Crockett. He was a tall, slim man with black whiskers. He was always at the head. The Mexicans called him Don Benito. The Americans said he was Crockett. He would often come to the fire and warm his hands and say a few words to us in the Mexican language. I also remember hearing the names of Travis and Bowie mentioned, but I never saw either of them that I know of.

After the first few days I remember that a messenger came from somewhere with word that help was coming.

The Americans celebrated it by beating the drums and playing on the flute. But after about seven days fighting there was an armistice of three days and during this time Don Benito had conferences every day with Santa Anna. Badio [Juan A. Badillo], the interpreter, was a close friend of my father and I heard him tell my father in the quarters that Santa Anna had offered to let the Americans go with their lives if they would surrender, but the Mexicans would be treated as rebels.

During the armistice my father told my mother she had better take the children and go, while she could do so safely. But my mother said: "No! If you're going to stay, so am I. If they kill one they can kill us all."

Only one person went out during the armistice, a woman called Trinidad Saucedo.

Don Benito, or Crockett, as the Americans called him, assembled the men on the last day and told them Santa Anna's terms, but none of them believed that anyone who surrendered would get out alive, so they all said as they would have to die anyhow they would fight it out.

The fighting began again and continued every day and every night. One night there was music in the Mexican camp and the Mexican prisoner said it meant the reinforcements had arrived.

We then had another messenger who got through the lines, saying that communication had been cut off and the promised reinforcements could not be sent.

The Last Night

On the last night my father was not out, but he and my mother were sleeping together in headquarters. About two o'clock in the morning there was a great shooting and firing at the northwest corner of the fort and I heard my mother say: "Gregorio, the soldiers have jumped the wall. The fight's begun."

He got up and picked up his arms and went into the fight. I never saw him again. My uncle told me afterwards that Santa Anna gave him permission to get my father's body and that he found it where the thick of the fight had been.

We could hear the Mexican officers shouting to the men to jump over and the men were fighting so close that we could hear them strike each other. It was so dark that we couldn't see anything and the families that were in the quarters just huddled up in the corners. My mother's children were near her. Finally they began shooting through the dark into the room where we were. A boy who was wrapped in a blanket in one corner was hit and killed. The Mexicans fired into the room for at least fifteen minutes. It was a miracle, but none of us children were touched.

By daybreak the firing had almost stopped and through the window we could see shadows of men moving around inside the fort. The Mexicans went from room to room looking for an American to kill. While it was still dark a man stepped into the room and pointed his bayonet at my mother's breast, demanding: "Where's the money the Americans had?"

"If they had any," said my mother, "you may look for it."

Then an officer stepped in and said: "What are you doing? The women and children are not to be hurt."

The officer then told my mother to pick out her own family and get her belongings, and the other women were given the same instructions. When it was broad day the Mexicans began to remove the dead. There were so many killed that it took several days to carry them away.

The families with their baggage were then sent under guard to the house of Don Ramon Musquiz, which was located where Frank Brothers Store now is, on Main Plaza. Here we were given coffee and some food and were told that we would go before the president at two o'clock. On our way to the Musquiz house we passed up Commerce Street and it was crowded as far as Presa Street with soldiers who did not fire a shot during the battle. Santa Anna had many times more troops than he could use.

At three o'clock we went before Santa Anna. His quarters were in a house which stood where Saul Wolfson's store now is. He had a great stack of silver money on a table before him and a pile of blankets. One by one the women were sent into a side room to make their declaration and on coming out were given two dollars and a blanket. While my mother was waiting her turn Mrs. Melton, who had never recognized my mother as an acquaintance and who was considered an aristocrat, sent her brother, Juan Losoya, across the room to my mother to ask the favor that nothing be said to the president about her marriage with an American. My mother told Juan to tell her not to be afraid.

Mrs. Dickinson was there, also several other women. After the president had given my mother her two dollars and blanket, he told her she was free to go where she liked. We gathered what belongings we could together and went to our cousin's place on North Flores Street, where we remained several months.

SOURCE: Esparza, Enrique, "The Story of Enrique Esparza," *San Antonio Express* (22 November 1902).

AMERICANS IN THEIR MORAL, SOCIAL AND POLITICAL RELATIONS
(1837, by Francis J. Grund)

The steady march of Americans toward the Pacific Ocean throughout much of the eighteenth and nineteenth centuries helped to define what many would come to think of as the American character: qualities of individualism, self-determination, free enterprise, and boundless resourcefulness. In fact, Americans had been penetrating the frontier since the founding of Jamestown in 1607, an enterprise that lasted until 1890, when most of the available land had been claimed and settled by homesteaders. The Austrian-born teacher, journalist, and politician Francis J. Grund (1798–1863) offers a glimpse into this restless era of exploration and acquisition in *Americans In Their Moral, Social, and Political Relations.* As much a paean to economic freedom as to political liberty, Grund's book exemplifies much of the enthusiasm and optimism of an age in which pioneers colonized the American West at a rate of only ten miles a year and the U.S. Census often recorded population density along the frontier at two to six people per square mile. A loyal Democrat, Grund later served in the American consulates in France, Belgium, and Germany.

Laura M. Miller,
Vanderbilt University

See also **Frontier; Westward Migration.**

The Settling of the West

Labour is as essential to their [Americans'] well-being as food and raiment to an European. This national characteristic of Americans, together with their love of independence, is a complete commentary on the history of all their settlements, and the progress of manufactures and commerce. Thousands of persons who, as servants, or in other inferior walks of life, might be able to provide for themselves in the large cities, emigrate to the western woods to procure for themselves a larger field of enterprise and useful occupation.

There is no hardship or privation incident to the lives of new settlers which their robust and athletic constitutions would not willingly suffer to gratify their insatiable desire after active and independent labour; there is no pleasure within the range of all a city can afford equal to the proud satisfaction of beholding the daily results of their indefatigable exertions. These phenomena it would be in vain to explain by the mere spirit of adventure.

There are no gold mines in the western states; no active commerce equal to that from which they emigrate; no accumulated wealth to allure their covetousness. The riches of the soil can only be explored by active labour and a series of harassing details, connected with the sacrifice of every convenience of life; the commerce of the explored region is to be created by new roads and lines of communication, which call for new and increased exertion on the part of the settlers; and it is only after a period of many years their sturdy industry can hope for an adequate reward of ease and prosperity. Such prospects are not apt to allure the weak either in body or mind, and require in determination and steadiness of purpose totally incompatible with the vague and loose spirit of adventure. Neither is there any thing in the character of the western people which could give the least foundation to such a suspicion. They are a hardy persevering race, inured to every toil to which human nature can be subjected, and always ready to encounter danger and hardships with a degree of cheerfulness which it is easily perceived is the effect of moral courage and consciousness of power. They are distinguished from the rest of the Americans, and, perhaps, the rest of mankind, by huge athletic frames of body, a peculiar naivete in their manners, and a certain grotesqueness of humour, which, as far as I am acquainted, is not to be found in any other part of the United States.

Their amphibious nature—being obliged to make themselves, at an early period of their lives, familiar with the navigation of the western waters—together with the boldness of their disposition, has won for them the characteristic appellation of "half horse and half alligator;" which, in the language of the western Americans, is full as honourable a term as the preux chevaliers, applied to the chivalry of the middle ages; though they prefer the rifle and the somewhat barbarous amusement of "gouging" to the more knightly combat with spears and lances.

It appears, then, that the universal disposition of Americans to emigrate to the western wilderness, in order to enlarge their dominion over inanimate nature, is the actual result of an expansive power, which is inherent in them, and which, by continually agitating all classes of society, is constantly throwing a large portion of the whole population on the extreme confines of the state, in order to gain space for its development. Hardly is a new state or territory formed before the same principle manifests itself again, and gives rise to a further emigration;

and so is it destined to go on until a physical barrier must finally obstruct its progress. The Americans, who do not pretend to account for this principle at all, are nevertheless aware of its existence, and act and legislate on all occasions as if they were to enjoy the benefits of the next century.

Money and property is accumulated for no other visible purpose than being left to the next generation, which is brought up in the same industrious habits, in order to leave their children a still greater inheritance. The labouring classes of Europe, the merchants, and even the professional men, are striving to obtain a certain competency, with which they are always willing to retire: the Americans pursue business with unabated vigour till the very hour of death, with no other benefits for themselves than the satisfaction of having enriched their country and their children. Fortunes, which on the continent of Europe, and even in England, would be amply sufficient for an independent existence, are in America increased with an assiduity which is hardly equalled by the industrious zeal of a poor beginner, and the term of "rentier" is entirely unknown. The luxurious enjoyments which riches alone can procure are neither known nor coveted in the United States; and the possession of property, far from rendering them indolent, seems to be only an additional stimulus to unremitting exertion....

Every new settlement requires labourers for the construction of roads, canals, &c., to facilitate its communication with the Atlantic states, and every new road and canal increases the commerce of the seaports. But it is not the general prosperity of the people—though of course this must be counted among its happiest results,—it is their useful occupation, and the creation of new and powerful interests, which are of the greatest advantage to the government. Every new colony of settlers contains within itself a nucleus of republican institutions, and revives in a measure the history of the first settlers. Its relation to the Atlantic states is similar to the situation of the early colonies with regard to the mother country, and contains the elements of freedom. Every society which is thus formed must weaken the fury of parties by diminishing the points of contact; while the growing power of the western states becomes a salutary check on the spreading of certain doctrines, which are continually importing from Europe, and to the evil influence of which the Atlantic states are more particularly exposed.

The western states, from their peculiar positions, are supposed to develop all the resources and peculiarities of democratic governments, without being driven to excesses by the opposition of contrary principles. Their number, too, augments the intensity of republican life by increasing the number of rallying points, without which the principle of liberty would be too much weakened by expansion. It is a peculiarly happy feature of the constitution of the United States, that every state has itself an independent government, and becomes thus the repository of its own liberties.

The inhabitant of Arkansas, Illinois, or Indiana, living on the confines of the state and the very skirts of civilization, would, in all probability, be less of a patriot if his attachment to the country were only to be measured by his adherence to the general government. He would be too remote from the centre of action to feel its immediate influence, and not sufficiently affected by the political proceedings of the state to consider them paramount to the local interests of his neighbourhood. Political life would grow fainter in proportion to its remoteness from the seat of legislation, and the energies of the people, instead of being roused by the necessity of action, would degenerate into a passive acknowledgment of the protection offered by the government. This is more or less the case in every country, except England and America, and perhaps the principal reason of their little progress in freedom. Hence the feverish excitement in their capitals and large towns, and the comparative inertness and palsy of the country. Every town and village in America has its peculiar republican government, based on the principle of election, and is, within its own sphere, as free and independent as a sovereign state. On this broad basis rests the whole edifice of American liberty. Freedom takes its root at home, in the native village or town of an American. The county, representing the aggregate of the towns and villages, is but an enlargement of the same principle; the state itself represents the different counties; and the Congress of the United States represents the different states.

In every place, in every walk of life, an American finds some rallying point or centre of political attachment. His sympathies are, first, enlisted by the government of his native village; then, by that of the county; then, by the state itself; and finally, by that of the Union. If he is ambitious, he is obliged to make an humble beginning at home, and figure in his native town or county; thence he is promoted to the dignity of representative or senator of his state; and it is only after he has held these preparatory stations that he can hope to enjoy the honour of representative or senator in the Congress of the nation. Thus the county is the preparatory school for the politician of the state, and the state furnishes him with a proper introduction to national politics.

The advantages of this system are manifold. It creates political action where otherwise all would be passiveness and stupor; it begets attachment to the institutions of the country by multiplying the objects of their political affection, and bringing them within the sphere of every individual; it cools the passions of political parties by offering them frequent opportunities of spending themselves on various subjects and in various directions; it establishes a stronghold of liberty in every village and town, and accustoms all classes of society to a republican government; it enforces submission to laws and institutions which are the type of those of the nation; and it furnishes numerous schools for young politicians, obliging them to remain sufficiently long in each not to enter the university of congress without age and proper experience.

This system, while it lasts—and there are no symptoms of its being speedily abolished—will prevent novices in politics from entering the Senate or House of Representatives of the United States, and reserve the dignity of president for the wisdom of sexagenarians. In France, where no similar freedom and independence exist in the provinces, where the system of centralization is constantly forcing the whole political power into the capital and a few of the large towns, leaving the country without life, motion, or means of defence, all attempts to establish a rational system of liberty were confined to its superstructure, without enlarging its foundation. The most awful lessons of history have been taught to her people in vain; and it seems as if they were the only nation who never profit by experience.

The western states of America are each a nursery of freedom; every new settlement is already a republic in embryo. They extend political life in every direction, and establish so many new fortified points, that the principle of liberty has nothing to dread from a partial invasion of its territory.

Every new state, therefore, is a fresh guarantee for the continuance of the American constitution, and directs the attention of the people to new sources of happiness and wealth. It increases the interest of all in upholding the general government, and makes individual success dependent on national prosperity. But every year which is added to its existence increases its strength and cohesion, by reducing obedience to a habit, and adding to the respect which is due to age. . . .

In the settlements of new districts it is seldom that Europeans are found to be actively engaged. This honour belongs almost exclusively to emigrants from New England, who may most emphatically be called the pioneers of the United States, and to whose enterprising spirit and recklessness of danger may be ascribed most of the valuable improvements of the country. They are, however, satisfied with tracing the road which the others are to follow, and occupying the most important stations: the intervals are afterwards filled up with settlers from other states and from Europe. The character of the New England emigrants has been too well described by Washington Irving for me to attempt to add to it more than is necessary to understand a certain political type, which may be observed in all states to which they have emigrated in large numbers.

The talent of a New Englander is universal. He is a good farmer, an excellent schoolmaster, a very respectable preacher, a capital lawyer, a sagacious physician, an able editor, a thriving merchant, a shrewd pedlar, and a most industrious tradesman. Being thus able to fill all the important posts of society, only a few emigrants from New England are required to imprint a lasting character on a new state, even if their number should be much inferior to that of the other settlers. The states of Ohio and Michigan, and even a large part of the state of New York, offer striking instances of this moral superiority acquired by the people of New England; but it would be wrong thence to conclude that their own habits do not undergo an important metamorphosis, or that, in their new relations in the western states, they merely act as reformers, without being, in turn, influenced by the character of their fellow settlers. The change, however, is altogether for the better. Their patriotism, instead of being confined to the narrow limits of New England,—a fault with which they have been reproached as early as the commencement of the revolutionary war,—partakes there more of a national character. The continued intercourse with strangers from all parts of the world, but more particularly from the different states of the union, serve in no small degree to eradicate from their minds certain prejudices and illiberalities with which they have but too commonly been reproached by their brethren of the south.

Tolerance, the last and most humane offspring of civilization, is, perhaps, the only virtue of which the New Englander is usually parsimonious; but even this seems to improve and to thrive in the western states; and I have no hesitation to say, that, in this respect, the inhabitants of those districts are by far more emancipated than those of the Atlantic states, whatever advantages the latter may possess with regard to refinement of manners. I know of no better specimen of human character than a New Englander transferred to the western states.

To form a correct idea of the rapid increase of cultivated territory in the western states it is only necessary to cast a glance at the unparalleled increase of population. The state of Pennsylvania, which in 1810 contained but 810,091 inhabitants, had in 1830, 1,347,672; increase, 537,581: the population of the state of New York, which in 1810 was but 413,763, had in 1830 already increased to 1,913,508; increase, 1,499,745: the population of Alabama was less than 10,000, but in 1830 already 308,997; increase 298,997, or nearly 2,990 per cent in twenty years: that of Mississippi, which in 1810 amounted to 40,352, was in 1830, 136,800; increase in twenty years 96,448, equivalent to 239 per cent: Tennessee contained in 1810 but 261,727 inhabitants, but in 1830, 684,822; increase 162 per cent nearly: in Kentucky the population increased, in the same time, from 406,511 to 688,844, or by about 70 per cent: that of Ohio advanced, in the same space of time, from 230,760 to 937,637; increase more than 300 per cent: the population of the same state was in 1790 but 3,000; increase in 40 years, 31,154 per cent: Indiana contained in 1810 but 24,520 inhabitants; but in 1830 already 341,582; increase more than 1,293 per cent: but the population of Indiana consisted in 1800 only of 5,641; consequently the total increase in 30 years, or less than a whole generation, is more than 5,955 per cent. Illinois contained in 1810 only 12,282 inhabitants, which number was in 1830 increased to 157,575; equal to about 1,183 per cent: Missouri had in the same space increased to seven times her original population; that of 1810 being 19,833, and that of 1830, 140,074. The population of the eastern and the southern states I have here omitted, because, though on the increase, they present nothing so striking as the rapid growth of the west.

SOURCE: Grund, Francis J. *The Americans in Their Moral, Social, and Political Relations.* Boston: Marsh, Capen and Lyon, 1837.

MEXICAN MINISTER OF WAR'S REPLY TO MANUEL DE LA PEÑA Y PEÑA
(1845, by Pedro María Anaya)

Fearing war with the United States, in 1845 Mexico Minister of Foreign Affairs Manuel de la Peña y Peña asked Minister of War Pedro María Anaya to assess the Mexican military's readiness. In his reply, Anaya advised that Mexico should seek to reconquer lands it held in dispute with the United States. He described Mexico's previous successes defending its territory against a hodgepodge of settlers, speculators, and adventurers. Those who were usurping Mexico's northern reaches in the name of "blinding greed" were no match for Mexican troops. With enough men, guns, and blankets, Anaya wrote, Mexico's "success cannot be in doubt."

In 1846, the United States declared war on Mexico after Mexican soldiers killed American troops along the disputed Texas border. Mexico could not muster the resources Anaya called for in his letter. In 1848, de la Peña y Peña helped negotiate the Treaty of Guadalupe Hidalgo, in which Mexico ceded to the United States all territory north of the Rio Grande River, the very region Anaya had sought to reconquer.

Mark D. Baumann,
New York University

See also **Mexican-American War; Mexico, Relations with; Texas.**

Pedro Maria Anaya, Mexican Minister of War, to Manuel de la Peña y Peña, Mexican Minister of Foreign Affairs

Mexico City, December 2, 1845

This memorandum is written in answer to your note of the 6th of last month regarding the state of relations between our nation and the United States. In your letter you asked me to ascertain the number of troops that would be necessary to undertake a campaign against that country. I hereby comply with the request.

It has always been, and will always be, difficult and costly to transport a considerable number of troops over long distances. The expenses of this enterprise increase in direct proportion to the inconveniences encountered along the way. These inconveniences include topographical obstacles and troubles associated with the simple act of walking; when the enemy in possession of territory that must be traversed is taken into account, more inconveniences appear. The enemy challenges the crossing of rivers and all other natural obstructions and in their defensive position possess an advantage. These general points explain why Mexico's struggle against the usurpers of Texas has from its outset been a most difficult matter.

There are two types of military expeditions. One is carried out with the objective of defeating the enemy's forces, after which the victorious army withdraws. The other is planned with an intention to occupy, settle, and remain in the invaded territory. For the first type, boldness and temporary resources are sufficient, but for the other type constant effort and a steady flow of supplies is required. Under no circumstances should Mexico consider the first type of operation, as it would involve sacrifices which would not result in meaningful victory. Only by reconquering and holding the usurped territory may we achieve success.

At San Jacinto, all conditions favored us. The battle was waged against some miserable settlers, a few hundred adventurers, and a handful of speculators from New Orleans and New York. In itself, that skirmish was not very significant. But the years that followed it were most lamentable and seemingly sanctioned that scandalous usurpation. Now the United States, which claims to respect justice more than any other nation, presents itself on the basis of power alone as the most insolent and shameless usurper in history. Its proximity to the country that has served as its prize facilitated the establishment of its perfidious designs. Blinding greed has enabled that country easily to move armed men, who man for man are no match with our soldiers, to take possession of that fertile territory. With the United States now involved in the usurpation, our problems multiply. Now the matter involves many important considerations that exceed the realm of my official duties.

There are many possible ways to prepare for war with the United States. But I would say that for Upper California we need five battalions and 10 field pieces and for Baja California, one battalion and five field pieces. Guaymas needs one battalion and three pieces; San Blas or Tepic, two battalions and five pieces (the same force is needed for Acapulco); Campeche needs four battalions and eight pieces; Tabasco, one battalion and four pieces; Veracruz, six battalions and 12 pieces; New Mexico, one cavalry regiment; Tampico, four battalions and eight pieces; for the operating army, 16 battalions, six regiments, and 32 pieces; for the reserves, eight battalions, four regiments, and 24 pieces; for the capital of the republic, eight battalions, four regiments, and 24 pieces (these troops could be moved to other areas if needed). All of these add up to 60 battalions, 15 regiments, and 145 pieces (sic).

The three brigades of cavalry that exist by law should be brought up to strength and sent to where needed. The battalion of sappers also should be brought up to strength and assigned, with a competent section of engineers, to the operational army; another battalion of sappers should remain in the reserves. The 35 permanent presidial companies of the frontier, with the 12 active militias, should be brought up to regulations and assigned either to the defense of their own Departments, whether against foreign enemies or savages, or as the light cavalry of the operational army. In addition, it is indispensable to organize the National Guard in all the Departments of the Republic, so that in case it is needed it can aid the army, defend the coasts from enemy attack, and maintain order in the interior.

We should also organize all aspects of transporting artillery, munitions, as well as food and medical supplies in the most efficient and economic manner. All men capable of bearing arms in the Departments of Coahuila and New Mexico should be provided with necessary ammunition and weapons. In sum, the reinforced units which should be on active duty should amount to 65,087 men, of whom 531 would be sappers; 2,640, foot artillerymen; 536, mounted artillerymen; 47,340, infantrymen; 9,450, dragoons; and 4,590, presidial forces. These forces will cost 1,162,539 pesos monthly, which will include expenses for salaries, field rations, costs associated with the artillery trains, the transportation of bridges, munitions, clothing, food, hospital supplies, and miscellaneous items.

As currently constituted, our forces consist of 14,760 infantrymen, 7,550 cavalrymen (including presidial forces), and 1,445 artillerymen. Therefore, there is a need for 32,570 additional infantrymen (sic), 6,490 additional cavalrymen, and 1,731 additional artillerymen.

Troops added to existing forces will have to be clothed. Unfortunately, many of the units already in existence lack even the barest necessities and must also be clothed. Thirteen thousand rifles also need to be purchased since all existing armaments are of poor quality. I understand that there is enough ammunition to start and maintain the campaign for some time.

I have already indicated that my ministry does not have all of the necessary information to make a prudent recommendation regarding war between Mexico and the United States. However, it can supply calculations needed to arrive at a decision. In my personal opinion, if all of the recommendations of this memorandum are forthcoming, our success cannot be in doubt, because the invading nation has only a few disciplined troops, which do not match our forces in spirit or aggressiveness. It can be said without boasting that in the open field Mexican soldiers will be crowned with glory, even though they are a third fewer than the number sent against them by the enemies from the north.

SOURCE: Anaya, Pedro Maria. "Letter Replying to Manuel de la Peña y Peña." In *Origins of the Mexican War: A Documentary Source Book.* Edited by Ward McAfee and J. Cordell Robinson. Vol. 1. Salisbury, N.C.: Documentary Publications, 1982, pp. 143–146.

MESSAGE ON THE WAR WITH MEXICO
(May 11, 1846)

Among President James K. Polk's (1795–1849) plans to expand the nation's territory was the attempted purchase of New Mexico and California from Mexico in 1846. When the sale failed, Polk sent U.S. troops to Texas to provoke long-simmering tensions along the border between the recently annexed territory and Mexico. After sixteen U.S. soldiers were killed in a battle with Mexican forces south of the Nueces River, Polk claimed to Congress that the war "exists by the act of Mexico herself." Congress agreed and formally declared war on Mexico.

The war enabled the United States to seize land where peaceful methods had previously failed: Colonel Stephen Kearny's troops faced little resistance as they first overran New Mexico and then California. Other U.S. forces met fiercer fighting, but the war ended when General Winfield Scott's army captured Mexico City. In 1848 the Treaty of Guadalupe

Hidalgo formally ended the war: the United States obtained California and New Mexico (including the present states of Arizona, Utah, and Nevada) and established the southern border of Texas at the Rio Grande River. In return, Mexico was paid $15 million.

While the Mexican-American War proved the United States' military superiority over its impoverished neighbor to the south, in the end the war brought only new hostilities in the region. The acquisition of new land by warfare was viewed by some as a bald effort to extend slavery into the nation's undeveloped territories. The war further inflamed sectional passions about the future of slavery in the United States, and many who began their military careers in the Mexican-American War, including both Robert E. Lee and Ulysses S. Grant, would fight each other a little more than a decade later in the Civil War.

Mark D. Baumann,
New York University

See also **Mexican-American War; Mexico, Relations with; Texas.**

To the Senate and House of Representatives:

The existing state of the relations between the United States and Mexico renders it proper that I should bring the subject to the consideration of Congress....

In my message at the commencement of the present session I informed you that upon the earnest appeal both of the Congress and convention of Texas I had ordered an efficient military force to take a position "between the Nueces and the Del Norte." This had become necessary to meet a threatened invasion of Texas by the Mexican forces, for which extensive military preparations had been made. The invasion was threatened solely because Texas had determined, in accordance with a solemn resolution of the Congress of the United States, to annex herself to our Union, and under these circumstances it was plainly our duty to extend our protection over her citizens and soil.

This force was concentrated at Corpus Christi, and remained there until after I had received such information from Mexico as rendered it probable, if not certain, that the Mexican Government would refuse to receive our envoy.

Meantime Texas, by the final action of our Congress, had become an integral part of our Union. The Congress of Texas by its act of December 19, 1836, had declared the Rio del Norte to be the boundary of that Republic. Its jurisdiction had been extended and exercised beyond the Nueces. The country between that river and the Del Norte had been represented in the Congress and in the convention of Texas, had thus taken part in the act of annexation itself, and is now included within one of our Congressional districts. Our own Congress had, moreover, with great unanimity, by the act approved December 31, 1845, recognized the country beyond the Nueces as a part of our territory by including it within our own revenue system, and a revenue officer to reside within that district has been appointed by and with the advice and consent of the Senate. It became, therefore, of urgent necessity to provide for the defense of that portion of our country. Accordingly, on the 13th of January last instructions were issued to the general in command of these troops to occupy the left bank of the Del Norte. This river, which is the southwestern boundary of the State of Texas, is an exposed frontier.

The movement of the troops to the Del Norte was made by the commanding general under positive instructions to abstain from all aggressive acts toward Mexico or Mexican citizens and to regard the relations between that Republic and the United States as peaceful unless she should declare war or commit acts of hostility indicative of a state of war....

The Mexican forces at Matamoras assumed a belligerent attitude, and on the 12th of April General Ampudia, then in command, notified General Taylor to break up his camp within twenty-four hours and to retire beyond the Nueces River, and in the event of his failure to comply with these demands announced that arms, and arms alone, must decide the question. But no open act of hostility was committed until the 24th of April. On that day General Arista, who had succeeded to the command of the Mexican forces, communicated to General Taylor that "he considered hostilities commenced and should prosecute them." A party of dragoons of 63 men and officers were on the same day dispatched from the American camp up the Rio del Norte, on its left bank, to ascertain whether the Mexican troops had crossed or were preparing to cross the river, "became engaged with a large body of these troops, and after a short affair, in which some 16 were killed and wounded, appear to have been surrounded and compelled to surrender." ...

The cup of forbearance had been exhausted even before the recent information from the frontier of the Del Norte. But now, after reiterated menaces, Mexico has passed the boundary of the United States, has invaded our territory and shed American blood upon the American soil. She has proclaimed that hostilities have commenced, and that the two nations are now at war.

As war exists, and, notwithstanding all our efforts to avoid it, exists by the act of Mexico herself, we are called upon by every consideration of duty and patriotism to vindicate with decision the honor, the rights, and the interests of our country....

In further vindication of our rights and defense of our territory, I invoke the prompt action of Congress to recognize the existence of the war, and to place at the disposition of the Executive the means of prosecuting the war with vigor, and thus hastening the restoration of peace....

SOURCE: *A Compilation of the Messages and Papers of the Presidents, 1789–1897.* Vol. 4. New York: Bureau of National Literature, 1897.

NATIONAL SONGS, BALLADS, AND OTHER PATRIOTIC POETRY, CHIEFLY RELATING TO THE WAR OF 1846 (1846, compiled by William M'Carty)

The phrase "Manifest Destiny" was first coined in 1845 by newspaperman John O'Sullivan to celebrate the annexation of Texas as evidence of the nation's imperative to settle every corner of a "continent allotted by Providence." A general rubric for the different expansionist sentiments of the middle 1800s, Manifest Destiny envisioned the United States sowing industry, democracy, and freedom in the lands it settled. And while some criticized Manifest Destiny as a pro-slavery tactic, few doubted that in time the United States would spread out to cover all of North America.

Never an official political doctrine, the notion of Manifest Destiny nonetheless made it plausible for the United States to seize upon an 1846 border dispute in Texas as a premise to declare war on Mexico and thereby gain much of California, Nevada, Utah, Arizona, New Mexico, and Texas. The war was initially popular in the United States, and the songs reprinted here show the depth of the nation's expansionist spirit. One song boasts of the nation's willingness to defend its borders, no matter how far-flung. Another song describes the United States' mission to repel European insolence and depredation by leading the rest of the world in the cultivation of freedom. A final song declares that "freedom's pilgrim sons" fight not for individual gain but for the good of all humankind.

These songs, like those of other popular wars, ignore the violence and duplicity with which wars achieve a nation's goals and instead invoke an image of undiluted moral superiority in the nation's political and military actions. That the United States invaded and conquered the territory of another, sovereign nation during the Mexican-American War is understandably left out of these songs.

Mark D. Baumann,
New York University

See also **Mexican-American War; Music: Early American.**

2 Song of The Memphis Volunteers. ***Air—"Lucy Neal."***

ONE mornin' bright and early,
De news came safe to hand,
Dat de Mexicans ten thousand strong,
Had cross'd de Rio Grande!
O, de Rio Grande, O, de Rio Grande,
We would we were upon your banks,
Wid rifle in our hand.
We'd raise de barrel to our eye,
Take trigger in de hand,
Some Memphis thunder soon dey'd hear,
Or leap de Rio Grande.
O, de Rio Grande, &c.
O, Memphis is a mighty place,
Can raise a fightin' band,
Dat soon are ready for a march
To rescue Rio Grande.
O, de Rio Grande, &c.
Wid bosoms to de shock ob war
Boldly we would stand,
And dar present a noble front
On de riber Rio Grande
O, de Rio Grande, &c.
We are waitin' for our orders
To shake our true lub's hand,
To shed a tear—then haste away
To rescue Rio Grande.
O, de Rio Grande, &c.
Now ladies will you remember,
If we fall as soldiers should,
To shed for us a secret tear,

A tear of gratitude.
And now for de Rio Grande,
And now for de Rio Grande,
We would we were already dere,
Wid rifle in our hand.
Our thanks now to de Memphis gals,
For de flags under which we stand,
And when dey hear from us again,
'Twill be from de Rio Grande.
We are bound for de Rio Grande,
We are bound for de Rio Grande,
We would we were already dere,
Wid rifle in our hand.

23 They Wait For Us.
ORIGINAL.

THE Spanish maid, with eye of fire,
At balmy evening turns her lyre
And, looking to the Eastern sky,
Awaits our Yankee chivalry
Whose purer blood and valiant arms,
Are fit to clasp her budding charms.
The *man*, her mate, is sunk in sloth—
To love, his senseless heart is loth:
The pipe and glass and tinkling lute;
A sofa, and a dish of fruit;
A nap, some dozen times by day;
Sombre and sad, and never gay,
He seems accursed for deeds of yore,
When Mexico once smoked with gore:
The blood of many a patriot band,
Shed by invaders of their land,
Who *now*, by quick avenging time,
Are vanquished by the subtile clime,
Which steals upon the manly mind
As comes "miasma" on the wind.
An army of *reformers, we*—
March on to glorious victory;
And on the highest peak of Ande,
Unfurl our banners to the wind, Whose stars shall light the land anew,
And shed rich blessings like the dew

59 Wave, Wave, The Banner High.

Tune—"March to the Battle Field."

WAVE, wave the banner high,
And onward to the field, boys,
By its true blue of the sky,
We ne'er will Texas yield, boys;
Each plain and wood,
Stained by the blood,
Of freedom's pilgrim sons, boys,
There Houston led,
And Crockett bled,
And brav'd the tyrant's guns, boys.
Then wave, wave, &c.
All Europe's haughty powers,
Have owned her a nation,
And we have made her ours,
By the annexation.
A land so fair,
Shall foemen dare,
To crush or to enslave, boys, No, by our veins,
We'll free her plains,
And dig each tyrant's grave, boys.
Then wave, wave, &c.

SOURCE: M'Carty, William, ed. *National Songs, Ballads, and Other Patriotic Poetry, Chiefly Relating to the War of 1846.* Philadelphia: Published by William M'Carty, 1846.

EXCERPT FROM *THE OREGON TRAIL* *(1846, by Francis Parkman)*

Francis Parkman was twenty-two years old when he journeyed on the Oregon Trail. He was a native of Boston, a graduate of Harvard College; a sickly, near-sighted greenhorn. Accompanied by his cousin Quincy Adams Shaw, Parkman went west to study the Plains Indians, whose culture would be a primary source for a projected history of the French-Indian War (1755–1763). Parkman returned from his excursion ill, requiring extensive bed-rest, during which time he wrote *The Oregon Trail*. The book, published in 1847, had an ironic title, as Parkman never reached Oregon, indeed never crossed the Rocky Mountains. His itinerary involved a journey west from the Missouri River overland across the Midwestern prairies to the eastern slopes of the Rockies, which he paralleled south to the neighborhood of Pike's Peak, from which he departed east following the Arkansas River to the prairies of Kansas, which he then crossed, returning to Saint Louis.

The excerpt from *The Oregon Trail* reveals the astonishment of a New Englander used to the tall pine trees and mountains of home, confronting the vast flat sandy plains of the Platte River valley in what is today Nebraska. Parkman echoed earlier explorers who saw the endless prairie before them and could only think to call it "the Great American Desert." All was wild: the climate went from long spells of dry heat to a fierce thunderstorm of the coldest wind and rain. The desert hosted cactus, lizards, and sand—even the Platte was filled with sand. The famous Mountain Men—the white trappers and hunters—were as savage and primitive as the native Pawnee Indians.

Francis Parkman's *The Oregon Trail* is a wonderful tale of the West. But it is, of course, a *tale,* based on actual events romanticized with the imagery of what Parkman expected to see. The experiences and phenomena of the West passed through the mind, and were altered by the pen of a wealthy, sophisticated Bostonian and Harvard man.

Russell Lawson,
Bacone College

See also **Oregon Trail; Pioneers; Westward Migration.**

A low undulating line of sand-hills bounded the horizon before us. That day we rode ten consecutive hours, and it was dusk before we entered the hollows and gorges of these gloomy little hills. At length we gained the summit, and the long expected valley of the Platte lay before us. We all drew rein, and, gathering in a knot on the crest of the hill, sat joyfully looking down upon the prospect. It was right welcome; strange too, and striking to the imagination, and yet it had not one picturesque or beautiful feature; nor had it any of the features of grandeur, other than its vast extent, its solitude, and its wildness. For league after league a plain as level as a frozen lake was outspread beneath us; here and there the Platte, divided into a dozen thread-like sluices, was transversing it, and an occasional clump of wood, rising in the midst like a shadowy island, relieved the monotony of the waste. No living thing was moving throughout the vast landscape, except the lizards that darted over the sand and through the rank grass and prickly pear just at our feet. And yet stern and wild associations gave a singular interest to the view; for here each man lives by the strength of his arm and the valor of his heart. Here the feeble succumb to the brave, with nothing to sustain them in their weakness. Here society is reduced to its original elements, and the whole fabric of art and conventionality is struck rudely to pieces, and men find themselves suddenly brought back to the wants and resources of their original natures.

We had passed the more toilsome and monotonous part of the journey; but four hundred miles still intervened between us and Fort Laramie; and to reach that point cost us the travel of three additional weeks. During the whole of this time we were passing up the center of a long, narrow, sandy plain, reaching like an outstretched belt nearly to the Rocky Mountains. Two lines of sand-hills, broken often into the wildest and most fantastic forms, flanked the valley at the distance of a mile or two on the right and left; while beyond them lay a barren, trackless waste—"the Great American Desert"—extending for hundreds of miles to the Arkansas on the one side and the Missouri on the other. Before us and behind us, the level monotony of the plain was unbroken as far as the eye could reach. Sometimes it glared in the sun, an expanse of hot, bare sand; sometimes it was veiled by long, coarse grass. Huge skulls and whitening bones of buffalo were scattered everywhere; the ground was tracked by myriads of them, and often covered with the circular indentations where the bulls had wallowed in the hot weather. From every gorge and ravine, opening from the hills, descended deep, well-worn paths, where the buffalo issue twice a day in regular procession down to drink in the Platte. The river itself runs through the midst, a thin sheet of rapid, turbid water, half a mile wide, and scarce two feet deep. Its low banks, for the most part without a bush or a tree, are of loose sand, with which the stream is so charged that it grates on the teeth in drinking. The naked landscape is, of itself, dreary and monotonous enough; and yet the wild beasts and wild men that frequent the valley of the Platte make it a scene of interest and excitement to the traveler. Of those who have journeyed there, scarce one, perhaps, fails to look back with fond regret to his horse and his rifle.

Fancy to yourself a long procession of squalid savages approaching our camp. Each was on foot, leading his horse by a rope of bull-hide. His attire consisted merely of a scanty cincture and an old buffalo robe, tattered and begrimed by use, which hung over big shoulders. His head was close shaven, except a ridge of hair reaching over the crown from the center of the forehead, very much like the long bristles on the back of a hyena, and he carried his bow and arrows in his hand, while his meager little horse was laden with dried buffalo meat, the produce of his hunting. Such were the first specimens that we met—and very indifferent ones they were—of the genuine savages of the prairie.

They were the Pawnees whom Kearsley had encountered the day before, and belonged to a large hunting party known to be ranging the prairie in the vicinity. They strode rapidly past, within a furlong of our tents, not pausing or looking toward us, after the manner of Indians when meditating mischief or conscious of ill desert. I went out and met them; and had an amicable conference with their chief, presenting him with half a pound of tobacco, at which unmerited bounty he expressed much gratification. These fellows, or some of their companions, had committed a dastardly outrage upon an emigrant party in advance of us. Two men, out on horseback at a distance, were seized by them, but lashing their horses, they broke loose and fled. At this the Pawnees raised the yell and shot at them, transfixing the hindermost through the back with several arrows, while his companion galloped away and brought in the news to his party. The panic-stricken emigrants remained for several days in camp, not daring even to send out in quest of the dead body.

The reader will recollect Turner, the man whose narrow escape was mentioned not long since; and expect perchance a tragic conclusion to his adventures; but happily none such took place; for a dozen men, whom the entreaties of his wife induced to go in search of him, found him leisurely driving along his recovered oxen, and whistling in utter contempt of the Pawnee nation. His party was encamped within two miles of us; but we passed them that morning, while the men were driving in the oxen, and the women packing their domestic utensils and their numerous offspring in the spacious patriarchal wagons. As we looked back we saw their caravan dragging its slow length along the plain; wearily toiling on its way, to found new empires in the West.

Our New England climate is mild and equable compared with that of the Platte. This very morning, for instance, was close and sultry, the sun rising with a faint oppressive heat; when suddenly darkness gathered in the west, and a furious blast of sleet and hail drove full in our faces, icy cold, and urged with such demoniac vehemence that it felt like a storm of needles. It was curious to see the horses; they faced about in extreme displeasure, holding their tails like whipped dogs, and shivering as the angry gusts, howling louder than a concert of wolves, swept over us. Wright's long train of mules came sweeping round before the storm like a flight of brown snow-birds driven by a winter tempest. Thus we all remained stationary for some minutes, crouching close to our horses' necks, much too surly to speak, though once the Captain looked up from between the collars of his coat, his face blood-red, and the muscles of his mouth contracted by the cold into a most ludicrous grin of agony. He grumbled something that sounded like a curse, directed, as we believed, against the unhappy hour when he first thought of leaving home. The thing was too good to last long; and the instant the puffs of wind subsided we erected our tents, and remained in camp for the rest of a gloomy and lowering day. The emigrants also encamped near at hand. We, being first on the ground, had appropriated all the wood within reach; so that our fire alone blazed cheerily. Around it soon gathered a group of uncouth figures, shivering in the drizzling rain. Conspicuous among them were two or three of the half-savage men who spend their reckless lives in trapping among the Rocky Mountains, or in trading for the Fur Company in the Indian villages. They were all of Canadian extraction; their hard, weather-beaten faces and bushy mustaches looked out from beneath the hoods of their white capotes with a bad and brutish expression, as if their owner might be the willing agent of any villainy. And such in fact is the character of many of these men.

SOURCE: Parkman, Francis. *The California and Oregon Trail: Being Sketches of Prairie and Rocky Mountain Life.* New York: George P. Putnam, 1849.

EXCERPT FROM *MEMORIES OF THE NORTH AMERICAN INVASION* *(c. 1850, by José María Roa Barcena)*

José María Roa Barcena's history of the Mexican-American War notes that the disposition of Texas was long a volatile issue, not least since Mexico's 1829 laws forbidding slavery in the region. With its robust hunger for new land—an appetite whetted in some part by pro-slavery sentiments—the United States was bound to eventually wage war with Mexico. Facing this, Mexico proved a weak opponent. Disorganization in its political and military institutions meant that Mexican soldiers lacked the resources to exploit opportunities with the same effectiveness as their better-equipped American enemies. Still, Roa Barcena praised his country's troops for re-grouping and continuing to fight after each defeat.

A criollo gentleman, Roa Barcena disparaged the "physical inferiority" of his countrymen to partially explain Mexico's poor fortunes. But he more vociferously condemned Mexico's continued lack of national unity. He wondered what might have happened differently if in the years since its independence Mexico had not been at war with itself, but instead had enjoyed strong, competent national leadership. In this light, Roa Barcena praised the United States for its will and discipline during the war. The United States fought only to expand its territory, he observed, not to conquer, enslave, or punish Mexico. Roa Barcena hoped that Mexico would realize this.

Mark D. Baumann,
New York University

See also **Mexican War; Texas.**

Our war with the United States was the double result of inexperience and vanity about our own capacities, on the one hand; and of an ambition unconstrained by concepts of justice and of the abuse of force, on the other.

The rebellion of Texas, more due to the emancipation of the slaves in Mexico than to the fall of the federalist constitution of 1824, would have taken place without the one or the other. It was the result of a plan by the United States, calculated and executed calmly and cold-bloodedly in a manner truly Saxon. It consisted in sending its nationals to colonize lands then belonging to Spain and later to ourselves and in inciting and aiding them to rebel against Mexico, repulsing any counterattack on our part and setting up an independent nation, obtaining in the process the recognition of some nations, and entering finally into the North American confederation as one of its states. Is there calumny or simply happenstance in this? Look at the extensive and illuminating information presented by General Don Manuel de Mier y Terón, who researched in our archives on the subject of the situation and dangers of Texas and of our northern frontier, long before the rebellion of the colonists; consider the initiatives of our Minister of Relations, Don Lucas Alaman, on April 6, 1830, and, most of all, the note of the North American envoy William Shannon of October 14, 1844, which said about the motion for the annexation of Texas then pending in Washington: "This has been a political measure that has been fostered for a long time and been considered indispensable to the security and well-being [of the United States], and consequently, it has been an objective invariably pursued by all parties, and the acquisition of this territory [of Texas] has been a subject of negotiation by almost all the administrations in the last twenty years."

The rebellion of Texas found Mexico flushed with pride over the brilliant results of its war of independence and believing itself capable of any enterprise. With the presumption and boldness that come with youth and inexperience it sent its ill-equipped and ill-provisioned army across immense deserts to the Sabine River to severely punish the rebels, but in the bewilderment of its first defeat this army was forced to retreat to the Rio Grande, as though signaling in anticipation the entire area that we were going to lose, all the way down to this point. Mexico's later and futile shows and preparations aimed at the recovery of Texas, which took place before and during the act of annexation of that state to the American Union, provided that country with a pretext for bringing war upon us, by virtue of which it took over, in the end, the areas above the Rio Grande which remained to us, such as New Mexico and Upper California.

Mexico, if it were to have acted with prevision and wisdom, should have written off Texas in 1835 while fastening into itself and fortifying its new frontiers. It should have recognized as an accepted fact the independence of that colony and, by way of negotiations, should have resolved any differences and settled boundary questions with the United States. It was imprudence and madness not to have done either the one or the other, but one has to agree that such judicious conduct would not have prevented the new territorial losses suffered in 1848. The area between the Rio Grande and Nueces rivers, New Mexico and Upper California, all these too were indispensable to the security and well-being of the United States, as is demonstrated in its diplomatic correspondence, in various allusions in President Polk's messages to Congress, in Trist's note of September 7, 1847, to the Mexican commissioners, and above all by the armed invasions of New Mexico and Upper California, all carried out when the two nations were presumably in a state of peace. Thus the pretext might have been different but the appropriation of those territories would have been the same.

The war with the United States found us in disadvantageous conditions in all respects. To the physical inferiority of our races must be added the weakness of our social and political organization, the general demoralization, the weariness and poverty resulting from twenty-five years of civil war, and an army insufficient in number, composed of forced conscripts, with armaments which were in a large part castoffs sold to us by England, without means of transportation, without ambulances, and without depots. The federation, which in the enemy country was the bond by which the different states united to form one, was here the dismemberment of the old order to constitute many diverse states. In sum, we changed the monetary unity of the peso to centavos while our neighbor combined its small change to make a stronger monetary unit. One of the more deplorable effects of this political organization, weakened and made even more complicated by our racial heterogeneity, could be seen in the indifference and egotism with which many states—while others such as San Luis Potosí made astounding contributions to the defense effort—entrenched themselves in their own sovereignty, denying the resources of money and manpower to the general government which were needed both to face the foreign invasion and to contain and suppress the Indian uprisings. As for our army, its inferiority and deficiency could be seen from that first campaign on the other side of the Rio Grande, which signaled the beginning of the war in 1846. There a detachment of from three to four thousand men, who, because of a rapid and unexpected movement, called Taylor's attention to their advance, had to stop to cross the river in two launches. They were decimated by the artillery of the enemy while our cannon balls could not reach them, and they had to abandon on the field of battle their wounded to the humanity and mercy of the conqueror, while they retired in complete disorder to Matamoros to regroup and await replacements, only to be defeated again at Monterrey.

For a moment it seemed that the fortune of arms had turned toward us. With the impetus and speed with which in 1829 he reached the beaches of Tampico to repel the Spanish invasion, Santa Anna arrived in the country, established general headquarters in San Luis, enlarged and organized his forces, and advanced with them to encounter Taylor at Angostura. He attacked there and forced the enemy to abandon its forward positions. He captured part of their artillery. He made them think that they had been defeated. But at the ultimate hour, the Mexican cavalry failed in its assignment. It was supposed to have advanced from the direction of Saltillo to Buena Vista. Provisions were exhausted, and the Mexicans had to break camp—again with the abandonment of the wounded. A disastrous retreat was begun toward Aguanueva and San Luis, which turned into an absolute rout.

Taylor had been battered and rendered incapable of launching upon any new operations, but the enemy was rich and powerful and could send army after army upon us. While Taylor was rebuilding along his northern line, other North American divisions invaded and conquered New Mexico and the Californias, and we had already lost at Tampico. The army of Major General Scott disembarked and set its batteries against Veracruz and occupied that ruined and heroic plaza at the end of March 1847. The remains of our only army, abandoning its line of defense against Taylor, set out, tattered and burned by the fires of sun and combat, upon a march of hundreds of leagues to Cerro Gordo where, reinforced by some of the units of the National Guard, it defended and finally lost positions that had been badly chosen. This army was broken up and disbanded but not without having made its victory very costly to the enemy.

The defense of the Valley of Mexico constituted the last and most determined of our efforts. A new army, relatively numerous but composed in large part of new and undisciplined troops, occupied the line of fortifications, designed and constructed by Robles and others of our most skilled engineers. Despite the fact that Scott took a deviant route to avoid the firepower placed at El Penon [a heavily fortified position] in his approach to the capital, the plan and all the dispositions for the defense seemed to assure us of a triumph, but human will and arrangements are to no avail if the designs of providence are against them. A knowledgeable and valiant general, placed at the head of a detached division assigned the task of falling upon the rearguard of the enemy when it should attack any point in our line, disobeyed, in his zeal to take the offensive, the orders of the commander in chief. He altered and destroyed the total plan for the defense by occupying and fortifying positions on his own and provoking the battle of Padierna. And Santa Anna, who with the troops at his disposal should have helped him in this battle, adding his weight to Valencia's division (now that the two had exchanged roles), remained a simple spectator of the action, thus allowing it to be lost, though he could have been able to win and should have gained the victory, according to the rules of military science. A glorious page among so many disastrous events was written by the National Guard of the Federal District in its defense of the Convent of Churubusco. Not only here, but in Veracruz, New Mexico, California, Chihuahua, and Tabasco we have seen peaceful citizens take up arms to oppose the foreign invasion and to do battle to the point of exhausting all their strength and resources.

After the first armistice, hostilities were renewed with the battle of Molino del Rey, in which the valiant Echeagaray and his Thirtieth Light saw the backs of the enemy and captured their artillery, which was brought back to our line. Again, this military action, so glorious for us despite its loss, should have been a victory if our commander-in-chief had been there and if the cavalry divisions had attacked at the opportune moment. Chapultepec and the battles at the city gates presented scenes of heroic valor on the part of their defenders and were tinted with foreign blood, but they were, nevertheless, lost, leaving Scott the master of the capital and virtually terminating any further resistance on the part of the Republic.

Such were our campaigns from 1846 to 1848, and in them our army and national guard complied with their duties and presented the uncommon spectacle of rallying to do battle again with the invader, practically the day after each defeat—something which is not done by cowards. No country, where the moral sense is not lacking, could view with indifference in its own annals defenses such as those of Monterrey in Nuevo León, Veracruz and Churubusco; battles such as Buena Vista and Molina del Rey; deaths such as those of Vazquez, Azonos, Martinez de Castro, Fronera, Cano, León, Balderas, and Xicotencatl. And as for the commander-in-chief, Santa Anna, his errors and faults notwithstanding, when the fog of political passions and hatreds has cleared away, who will be able to deny his valor, his energetic vigor, his constancy, his fortitude in the face of the repeated strikes of an always adverse fortune, the marvelous energy with which he roused others to the defense and produced materials and provisions out of nothing and improvised and organized armies, raising himself up like Antaeus' strong and courageous after each reverse. What might not the defense of Mexico have been if there had been some years of interior peace, with an army better organized and armed, and under a political system which would have permitted the chief to dispose freely of all the resistant elements in the nation? One word more about the campaign in order to do proper justice to the enemy: his grave and phlegmatic temperament, his lack of hatred in an adventure embarked upon with the simple intention of extending territory, his discipline, vigorous and severe among the corps of the line, which even extended to the volunteers, with the exception of some of the detached forces that were a veritable scourge, and above all, the noble and kind characters of Scott and Taylor lessened to the extent possible the evils of warfare. And the second of those chiefs cited, who commanded the first of the invading armies, was, once the campaign in the Valley [Mexico City and environs] was ended, the most sincere and powerful of the friends of peace.

Not only was this not dishonorable, but it will figure in the diplomatic annals of the Hispanic American countries as having contributed to the result of a negotiation which only the patriotism and intelligence of Pena y Pena and Couto [Mexican president and Mexican peace commissioner] could have resumed on the agreed-upon conditions, when we were completely at the mercy of the conqueror.

SOURCE: Robinson, Cecil, ed. and trans. Excerpt from "Memories of the North American Invasion." In *The View from Chapultepec: Mexican Writers on the Mexican-American War.* Tucson, Ariz.: University of Arizona Press, 1989, pp. 44–49.

FORT LARAMIE TREATY
(1851)

The years of rapid expansion into the American frontier were marred by fractious battles between forces making way for settlers and the Native Americans already inhabiting the lands. In the period between 1784 and 1894, approximately 720 treaties forcing Native Americans to cede their land were made. The flood of settlers moving west increased substantially with the discovery of gold in California in 1848. In 1851, the United States government, under the direction of Thomas Fitzpatrick, first Indian Agent to the tribes of the upper Platte and Arkansas, called a council of Sioux, Cheyenne, Arapaho, Crown, Assiniboine, Gros Ventre, Mandan, and Arikara Indians at Fort Laramie in present-day Wyoming. Perhaps because Fitzpatrick was a respected champion of Native American rights, the council, which resulted in the Treaty of Fort Laramie, created peace between the often warring tribes and legislated territorial boundaries without requiring the tribes to cede any land. By agreeing to allow the United States government to construct roads and forts, the tribes were afforded protection from "all depredations" by whites and provided with a yearly annuity of $50,000. The agreement covered the lands west of Colorado to the Canadian border and from Nebraska to the Rocky Mountains. Though the Native Americans were not asked to cede rights to their lands, the area was eventually overrun with settlers who paid no heed to the treaty.

Leah R. Shafer,
Cornell University

See also **Blackfeet; Cheyenne; Crow; Indian Land Cessions; Indian Policy, U.S.: 1830–1900; Indian Territory; Indian Treaties; Laramie, Fort, Treaty of (1851); Sioux.**

Articles of a treaty made and concluded at Fort Laramie, in the Indian Territory, between D. D. Mitchell, superintendent of Indian affairs, and Thomas Fitzpatrick, Indian agent, commissioners specially appointed and authorized by the President of the United States, of the first part, and the chiefs, headmen, and braves of the following Indian nations, residing south of the Missouri River, east of the Rocky Mountains, and north of the lines of Texas and New Mexico viz, the Sioux or Dahcotahs, Cheyennes, Arrapahoes, Crows, Assinaboines, Gros-Ventre Mandans, and Arrickaras, parties of the second part, on the seventeenth day of September, A. D. one thousand eight hundred and fifty-one.

ARTICLE 1. The aforesaid nations, parties to this treaty, having assembled for the purpose of establishing and confirming peaceful relations amongst themselves, do hereby covenant and agree to abstain in future from all hostilities whatever against each other, to maintain good faith and friendship in all their mutual intercourse, and to make an effective and lasting peace.

ARTICLE 2. The aforesaid nations do hereby recognize the right of the United States Government to establish roads, military and other posts, within their respective territories.

ARTICLE 3. In consideration of the rights and privileges acknowledged in the preceding article, the United States bind themselves to protect the aforesaid Indian nations against the commission of all depredations by the people of the said United States, after the ratification of this treaty.

ARTICLE 4. The aforesaid Indian nations do hereby agree and bind themselves to make restitution or satisfaction for any wrongs committed, after the ratification of this treaty, by any band or individual of their people, on the people of the United States, whilst lawfully residing in or passing through their respective territories.

ARTICLE 5. The aforesaid Indian nations do hereby recognize and acknowledge the following tracts of country, included within the metes and boundaries hereinafter designated, as their respective territories, viz:

The territory of the Sioux or Dahcotah Nation, commencing the mouth of the White Earth River, on the Missouri River; thence in a southwesterly direction to the forks of the Platte River; thence up the north fork of the Platte River to a point known as the Red Bute, or where the road leaves the river; thence along the range of mountains known as the Black Hills, to the head-waters of Heart River; thence down Heart River to its mouth; and thence down the Missouri River to the place of beginning.

The territory of the Gros Ventre, Mandans, and Arrickaras Nations, commencing at the mouth of Heart River; thence up the Missouri River to the mouth of the Yellowstone River; thence up the Yellowstone River to the mouth of Powder River in a southeasterly direction, to the head-waters of the Little Missouri River; thence along the Black Hills to the head of Heart River, and thence down Heart River to the place of beginning.

The territory of the Assinaboin Nation, commencing at the mouth of Yellowstone River; thence up the Missouri River to the mouth of the Muscle-shell River; thence from the mouth of the Muscle-shell River in a southeasterly direction until it strikes the head-waters of Big Dry Creek: thence down that creek to where it empties into the Yellowstone River, nearly opposite the mouth of Powder River, and thence down the Yellowstone River to the place of beginning.

The territory of the Blackfoot Nation, commencing at the mouth of Muscle-shell River; thence up the Missouri River to its source; thence along the main range of the Rocky Mountains, in a southerly direction, to the head-waters of the northern source of the Yellowstone River; thence down the Yellowstone River to the mouth of Twenty-five Yard Creek; thence across to the head-waters of the Muscle-shell River, and thence down the Muscle-shell River to the place of beginning.

The territory of the Crow Nation, commencing at the mouth of Powder River on the Yellowstone; thence up Powder River to its source; thence along the main range of the Black Hills and Wind River Mountains to the head-waters of the Yellowstone River; thence down the Yellowstone River to the mouth of Twenty-five Yard Creek; thence to the head waters of the Muscle-shell River; thence down the Muscle-shell River to its mouth; thence to the head-waters of Big Dry Creek, and thence to its mouth.

The territory of the Cheyennes and Arrapahoes, commencing at the Red Bute, or the place where the road leaves the north fork of the Platte River; thence up the north fork of the Platte River to its source; thence along the main range of the Rocky Mountains to the head-waters of the Arkansas River; thence down the Arkansas River to the crossing of the Santa Fe road; thence in a northwesterly direction to the forks of the Platte River, and thence up the Platte River to the place of beginning.

It is, however, understood that, in making this recognition and acknowledgement, the aforesaid Indian nations do not hereby abandon or prejudice tiny rights or claims they may have to other lands; and further, that they do not surrender the privilege of hunting, fishing, or passing over any of the tracts of country heretofore described.

ARTICLE 6. The parties to the second part of this treaty having selected principals or head-chiefs for their respective nations, through whom all national business will hereafter be conducted, do hereby bind themselves to sustain said chiefs and their successors during good behavior.

ARTICLE 7. In consideration of the treaty stipulations, and for the damages which have or may occur by reason thereof to the Indian nations, parties hereto, and for their maintenance and the improvement of their moral and social customs, the United States bind themselves to deliver to the said Indian nations the sum of fifty thousand dollars per annum for the term of ten years, with the right to continue the same at the discretion of the President of the United States for a period not exceeding five years thereafter, in provisions, merchandise, domestic animals, and agricultural implements, in such proportions as may be deemed best adapted to their condition by the President of the United States, to be distributed in proportion to the population of the aforesaid Indian nations.

ARTICLE 8. It is understood and agreed that should any of the Indian nations, parties to this treaty, violate any of the provisions thereof, the United States may withhold the whole or a portion of the annuities mentioned in the preceding article from the nation so offending, until in the opinion of the President of the United States, proper satisfaction shall have been made.

In testimony whereof the said D. D. Mitchell and Thomas Fitzpatrick commissioners as aforesaid, and the chiefs, headmen, and braves, parties hereto, have set their hands and affixed their marks, on the day and at the place first above written.

D. D. Mitchell
Thomas Fitzpatrick
Commissioners.

Sioux:

Mah-toe-wha-you-whey, his x mark.
Mah-kah-toe-zah-zah, his x mark.
Bel-o-ton-kah-tan-ga, his x mark.
Nah-ka-pah-gi-gi, his x mark.
Mak-toe-sah-bi-chis, his x mark.
Meh-wha-tah-ni-hans-kah, his x mark.

Cheyennes:

Wah-ha-nis-satta, his x mark.
Voist-ti-toe-vetz, his x mark.
Nahk-ko-me-ien, his x mark.
Koh-kah-y-wh-cum-est, his x mark.

Arrapahoes:

Be-ah-te-a-qui-sah, his x mark.
Neb-ni-bah-seh-it, his x mark.
Beh-kah-jay-beth-sah-es, his x mark.

In the presence of

A. B. Chambers, secretary.
S. Cooper, colonel, U. S. Army.
R. H. Chilton, captain, First Drags.
Thomas Duncan, captain, Mounted Riflemen.
Thos. G. Rhett, brevet captain R. M. R.
W. L. Elliott, first lieutenant R. M. R.
C. Campbell, interpreter for Sioux.
John S. Smith, interpreter for Cheyennes.
Robert Meldrum, interpreter for the Crows.

Crows:

Arra-tu-ri-sash, his x mark.
Doh-chepit-seh-chi-es, his x mark.

Assinaboines:

Mah-toe-wit-ko, his x mark.
Toe-tah-ki-eh-nan, his x mark.

Mandans and Gros Ventres:

Nochk-pit-shi-toe-pish, his x mark.
She-oh-mant-ho, his x mark.

Arickarees:

Koun-hei-ti-shan, his x mark.
Bi-atch-tah-wetch, his x mark.

H. Culbertson, interpreter for Assiniboines and Gros Ventres.

Francois L'Etalie, interpreter for Arickarees.
John Pizelle, interpreter for the Arrapahoes.
B. Gratz Brown.
Robert Campbell.
Edmond F. Chouteau.

SOURCE: "Fort Laramie Treaty of 1851." In *Indian Treaties, 1778–1883.* Compiled by Charles J. Kappler. Washington, DC: 1904, pp. 594–596.

EXCERPT FROM *ACROSS THE PLAINS TO CALIFORNIA IN 1852*
(By Lodisa Frizzell)

A major emigration to the Pacific coast was already underway when President James K. Polk acquired the Oregon Territory in 1844. The discovery of gold in California four years later only increased the stream of new settlers heading west. Women settlers endured great hardships while winning new freedoms borne out of necessity. Lodisa Frizzell's journal, *Across the Plains to California in 1852,* describes her journey toward the Oregon Trail from St. Joseph, Missouri. This selection begins soon after her departure. In it are Frizzell's descriptions of trading and eating with "savages," American Indian toll bridges, graves, and rumors of cholera along the route. She also gave practical advice to her readers "comfortably seated" back east, such as that they should bring buffalo hides rather than cotton quilts and bring an extra horse so someone else in the party could hunt game while the wagon traveled along.

Leah R. Shafer,
Cornell University

See also **Great Plains; Pioneers; Wagon Trains; Westward Migration.**

Chapter III

From St. Joseph to Ft. Kearney

Come now with me gentle reader, and let us cross the plains, I will endeavor to show you whatever is worth seeing, & tell you as much as you will care about hearing, while you are comfortably seated around your own fireside, without fatiegue, or exposure, I will conduct you the whole of this long & weary journey, which I wish if you should ever in reality travel, that you may feel no more fatiegue than you do at the presant moment, but I fear that you would, as you yourself will probably admit before the close of this narative. This is considered th[e] starting point from this river is time reconed, & it matters not how far you have come, this is the point to which they all refer, for the question is never, when did you leave home? but, when did you leave the Mississouri [sic] river? Our team looked bad one ox had died, the roads through Missouri were muddy & bad. It was about 2 o'clock as we started out through the heavy timbered bottom which extends back some 7 or 8 miles from the river, & which was to be the last of any note until we reached the Siera Nevada Mts. It seems hard to believe, but it is nevertheless true, that this immence distance is nearly destitute of timber, particularly near the road. It comenced raining a little, we reached the outskirts of the timber, called the bluffs, as the land raises here, we encamped pitched our tent, soon had a large fire, got supper, turned the cattle out to graze on the grass & bushes, for they were vary hungry & devoured whatever came in their way, they soon filled themselves & they were drove up & tied each one by a rope, to the waggon, or bushes nearby. There were several campfires burning in sight, we at length went to bed, Loyd & I occupied the waggon, while the boys slept in the tent. I had bought rag carpet enough to spread over the ground in the tent which proved excellent for keeping the wet, or sand, from getting on the bedding, which consisted of buffalo robes & blankets, which I considder the best for this journey, as they keep cleaner & do not get damp so easily as cotton quilts.

[May 10—27th day] Stayed in camp to-day unloaded our waggon put every thing that it was possible in sacks leaving our trunk chest, barrels & boxes, which relieved the waggon, of at least, 300 lbs, besides it was much more conveniently packed. Water being handy, we washed up all our things & prepared to start soon in the morning. A boy about 12 years old came to our tent poorly clad, he said he was going back, I asked him several questions, & learned that he had ran away from his folks who lived in the eastern part of Ohio, had got his passage from one Steamboat to another, until he had reached St. Jo. & then had got in with some one to go to California, but he said they would not let him go any further, & sent him back, I gave him something to eat & told him to go back to his parents, I know not where he went but from his tale this was not the first time that he had ran away from home. What a grief to parents must such children be.

[May 11—28th day] Fine morning, started out on the Plain which appeared boundless, stretching away to the south & covered with excellent grass 5 or 6 inches high, but they were not near so level as I had supposed, quite undulating like the waves of the sea when subsiding from a storm. In 6 or 8 ms, we came to where there was a general halt, some dozen teams standing here waiting to cross a deep slue, in which one team & waggon were stuck & were obliged to unload part of their goods, it being difficult to attatch more team to it where it then was, some others taking the precaution doubled theirs before starting in, but noticed that the great difficulty was in the cattle not pulling together, we drove in just above them, passed over, went on our way which for many miles is often in sight of the Mississouri [sic] river and the highlands on the opposite bank to the cultivated fields of which I often turned a "lingiring look" which is the last I have as yet seen, or may see for some time, with one exception which I shall soon relate. We met two or three indians, saw a fresh made grave, a feather bed lying upon it, we afterwards learned that a man & his wife had both died a few days before, & were burried together here, they left 2 small children, which were sent back to St. Joseph by an indian chief. We now came to Wolf creek, a small stream but very steep banks, the indians have constructed a kind of bridge over it, & charged 50 cts per waggon, there were several of them here, quite fine looking fellows, not near so dark as those I had seen, but of the real copper color, said they were of the Sacs & Fox tribes. One was a chief, he was dressed in real indian stile, had his hair shaved off all except the crown lock, which was tied up & ornamented with beads & feathers, he, & one or two others, had various trinkits upon their arms, legs, & heads, but their main dress was their bright red blankets, There were several teams here, which were passing over before us, when one of the teams getting stalled on the opposite bank, which was steep & muddy, a little pert looking indian jumped up comenced talking & jesticulating in great earnest; on inquiring what it was he said? an interpreter nearby said, he was saying to the driver, that if he could not go through there he could not go to California, he had better go back home. We passed over when our turn came, & went a short distance up the stream, & encamped; having come about 20 ms, fine grass here, & some small timber along the banks of this creek, I had a severe headache this evening, our folks having got their supper, they were soon seated around a blazing fire, & were soon joined by several indians, who likewise seated themselves by the fire, & as one of them could speak a little English, they kept up quite a conversation. They said they no steal white mans cattle, they good indian, but the Pawnee he had indian, he steal, no good, Loyd gave them a drink of brandy which when they had tasted, said strong, strong, but smacked their lips as if it was not stronger than they liked. I lay in the waggon looked out upon this group, which as the glare of the fire fell on the grim visages, & bare, brawny arms, & naked bodies; having nothing on the upper part of the body but their loose blanket, & as they move their arms about when speaking, their bodies are half naked most of the time, the contrast was striking between their wild looks & savage dress, to the familiar faces of our own company, & their civilized dress and speech.

[May 12—29th day] I felt quite well this morning, we soon dispatched our breakfast, yoked up our cattle which were as full as ticks, started out into the broad road, or roads, for here there are several tracks, there is plenty of room for horse, or mule teams to go around, which will be quite different when we come to the Mountains, we passed the indian mission, where there are several hundred acers of land cultivated by indians under the superintendince of the missionaries. Rested our teams at noon, took a lunch, went on some 10 miles farther [sic], &

encamped, where there was good grass, but very little water & no wood, we succeeded in boiling the tea kettle, & making some coffee, & having plenty of bread, meat, & crackers, fruit pickles, &c, we done very well for supper, it was quite cold tonight, but slept well till morning.

[May 13—30th day] Started out soon this morning, passed several graves, we hear that it is sickly on the route, that there are cholera, small-pox, & measles, but rumor says so much, that you do not know when to believe her, but the graves prove that some have died, & it must be expected that from such a number, some would die; but it is very sad to part with them here, for the heart can hardly support the addition, of so much grief, for there are few whose hearts are not already pained, by leaving so many behind. We came to another indian toll bridge, which crossed a small ravine, charged but 25 cts, two indians here, went on till near night and encamped for the night, very good place, in a hollow to the left of the road. George caught some small fish with a pinhook.

[May 14—31st day] Soon in the morning we renewed our journey, through a fine rotting prairie, small groves of timber along the water courses, giving the landscape a very picturesque appearance; saw several graves to day, passed where they were burying a man, crossed the little Nimahaw, a fine stream, encamped on the bank. We had not been here long, when a little white calf came up to us out of the bushes, & appeared very hungry; it had probably been left on purpose, though most of them are gennerally killed, but he might have been hid in the bushes, & people are not very tenderhearted on this journey, but he reminded me so much of home I would not let them shoot it; we left it there to be devoured by wolves, or die of hunger, or be killed by some one else.

[May 15—32d day] We renewed our journey, when about noon it commenced to rain we turned down to the right, & encamped, it continuing rainy, we staid till next day; here was a small stream full of little fishes, which if we had had a small sceine, we might have caught any amount; but we had not so much as a fish hook, which we had forgoten to provide.

[May 16—33d day] Crossed the Big Nimahaw, nooned here, there were so many teams here crossing that we had to wait some 2 hours, for many would not go through, until they had doubled their team; but we crossed with our 4 yoke of small cattle, & the largest waggon there, without any difficulty, but a little snug pulling; George said we done it easy; our team is certainly no. 1. This is a fine mill stream, some very good timber on its banks, & as rich prairie around as I ever saw, there is no reason why it should not be settled some day. We passed the junction of the Independence road, there was as many teems in sight, as on ours, & their track looked about the same, Saw a fine sheet iron stove sitting beside the road, took it along cooked in it that night, & then left it; for they are of very little account, unless you could have dry wood. We met a man who was driving several cows, the men in the other waggon recognized 4 of them, belonging to a man from their country, with whom they had intended to travel. They asked the man where was the owner of the cows? & why he was driving them back? he said first that he was the owner, & that he had bought them; but as he could not tell where the man was, nor describe him, they concluded he had no right to them; & finaly he said them four he had found, & they took them away from him; & as one of them gave milk, we were enable[d] to live quite well; & I would advise all to take cows on this trip, if you used the milk only to make bread, for you can do very little with yeast, & the soda & cream tarter I do not like.

[May 17—34th day] We went on through a rich & fertile country, & encamped some 2 ms to the left of the road, in one of the most wild and romantic places I ever saw; the wolves howled around the tent nearly all night, I could not sleep soundly, therefor dreamed of being attacted by bears, & wolves; when the sharp bark of one, close to the waggon, would rouse me from my fitful slumbers but the rest slept so soundly, that they hardly heard them; for people sleep in general very sound, on this trip, for being tired at night, they feel like reposing.

[May 18—35th day] Proceeded onward, crossed the Big Blue river there was a ferry here, but we forded it, although it came near running into our waggon bed; came on some 11, ms. father [sic], & encamped, to the left, down in a hollow where there was small stream; Here a doctor from the same place of those men who were travelling with us, came up, he had started to pack through with 2 horses, but soon getting tired of it, he had let a man have one of the horses, & provisions, to take him through: but he said they soon wanted him to help about every thing & he got tired of it; & offered to go through with them, & cook for them, they concented, as one of their company had gone back which I had forgotten to mention, for we meet some going back every day, some have been sick, some say that they are carrying the mail; but there is most to great a number for that purpose.

[May 19—36th day] Beautiful morning the Dr. said I could ride his horse if I liked, & having my saddle yet, I gladly excepted it; for it is tiresome riding in the waggon all the while, & every waggon should be provided, with at least one good horse, for the company to ride when they are weary, or when they wish to go out & hunt; for it is very hard to go off from the road a hunting, & perhaps kill some game, & then have it to carry & overtake the teams; for as slow a[s] an ox teem may seem to move, they are very hard to catch up with, when you fall behind an hour or two. and you need a horse also, to ride through & drive the team in all bad places, & to get up your cattle without getting your feet wet, by wading in water or dew; if such exposures as these were avoided, I do not think there would be as much sickness as there usually is, along here, for we have not passed less than

100 fresh graves from St. Joseph to the Blue river. See some dead stalk, the wolves have a feast, hope they will not disturb the graves.

[May 20—37th day] We travel about 20 ms. a day our cattle are thriving, look well; but this Gy[p]sy life is anything but agreeable, it is impossible to keep anything clean, & it is with great dificulty that you do what little you have to do. Turned down to the left; tolerable grass only; here we saw the first buffalo sign; the wolves kept barking all night.

[May 21—38th day] Raining some, came 7 or 8 ms, the rain still continuing, we put up for the day, down to the left, near a dry sandy creek, here was a fresh grave; there being some timber along this creek, we soon had a large fire, & prepared our dinner. We have not as yet seen any game, & a fishhook would have been of more service so far, than half a dozen guns, The weather is quite cold, need overcoats, & mittens.

[May 22—39th day] Again we get up the cattle & start on; the land here is poor, the country flat, & grass only in places, the road is very crooked thus far; for the track runs wherever it is nearest level. We encamped on the Little blue, which we had been following up for the last 3 or 4 days, it is a poor place for grass. Some teams turned back a day or two since, & one old lady said we had all better turn back, for if the grass began to give out now, what would become of us if we went on until our teams were not able to take us back; she said she was going back, for she had made a living before she had ever heard of California, & the rest might go on & starve their teams to death if they liked. Saw the heads of [s]everal fine large fish lying here, but could not catch any with a pin hook.

[May 23—40th day] After some difficulty, we got our cattle from the other side of the river, where they had strayed during the night, but when we found they were across, some of the men went over & watched them, which was the first time we had watched them, but being now in the Pawnee country we were a little afraid they might be stolen, but we did not see one of these indians, some said it was because they were afraid of the smallpox. We passed a spot where there was a board put up, & this information upon it, that a man was found here on the 17th, horribly murdered, with wounds of a knife, & buckshot, his shirt was lying there, with the blood & wounds upon it, he was buried near by, it stated by whom &c. I have never learned any more, but I hope the murderer may meet his reward, sooner or later.

[May 24—41st day] The day being clear & still, as we passed over the 16 mile desert, to the head waters of the L. Blue; we saw a mirage, at first we thought we were near a pond of water which we saw just over the ridge, & remarked that the guide had said there was no water here; but when we came near, it was gone, and then suspecting what it was, we looked around (for here you can see any distance in all directions) we saw beautiful streams, bordered with trees, small lakes, with islands, & once on looking back, we saw several men in the road, who looked to be 15 ft tall, & once or twice we saw what appeared to be large & stately buildings. Met a company of fur traders with 16 waggons loaded with buffalo robes, they were very singular in appearance looking like so many huge elephants, & the men, except 2, were half breeds; & indians, & a rougher looking set, I never saw; & their teams which were cattle, looked about used up; quite warm to day, crossed the last branch of the Little Blue, it was dry and good crossing, we went on some 3 miles, and encamped near some small ponds of water, no wood, only what we could find at old camping places; we had brought a little water in our kegs, made some coffe[e], & just as we were done supper, the sun was declining in the west, making thing[s] appear very distinctly on the horizon, when there was an animal discovered, feeding on the plain, not far distant. 2 of our men went in persuit, and after some time, returned with a quarter of fresh meat, which the, said was antelope; but asking them why they did not bring more, & they making rather a vague reply, and not being anyways anxious to have any of it cooked, & from certain sly looks which they exchanged, I began to think something was wrong about it, at length one went out in the morning and found it to be an old sheep left from some drove, which was probably unable to travel, but the sport was that they thinking it was an antelope, and it being so dark that they could not see distinctly, & knowing that they were hard to get a shot at, they crept on their hands & knees for some distance, both fired at the same time, & shot the poor sheep through & through; but to turn the joke, they brought up a piece, to have the Dr. & me cook some of it, but failed. This made us something to joke & laugh about for some time, for it is seldom that you meet with anything for merriment, on this journey.

[May 25—42nd day] We reached the Platte river, after a hard days drive, although the sand hills which were in sight, soon after we started in the morning; did not seem to be, but 2 or 3 ms. distant. Saw several antelope but could not get a shot at them it being so level, There is no wood here, except what is procured from the island, the river was not fordable at this time, but some swam accross on horseback & procured some; but with much difficulty and danger, the current being very swift, & the bottom quicksand; we contented ourselves with a few willow bushes; there were some buffalo chips, but we had not as yet got in the way of using them.

[May 26—43d day] We are about 5, ms below Ft. Karney. Several indians of the Sioux tribe came to our tent, the best looking indians I ever saw, they were tall, strongly made, firm features, light copper color, cleanly in appearance, quite well dressed in red blankets, and highly ornamented, with bows and arrows in their hands. We gave them some crackers & coffee, with which they seemed very much pleased. They signified that they wished to trade, & pointing of to the right, we saw, many

more indians seated on the ground not far distant, with some 20 ponies feeding around them, as we started out there, we saw a train of waggons which were passing, halt, & appear to be perplexed, we soon saw the cause, a huge indian, naked to his waist, with a drawn sword, brandishing it in the road, & seemed to say, "stand & deliver." But when we came up, he signified that he wished to trade, but they wishing to proceed, & not wanting to be detained, they gave him some crackers &c, each waggon as they passed, throwing him something on a blanket, which he had spread on the ground beside the road; but I saw the indians chuckle to one another, upon the success of the old chiefs maneuver. This old chief accompanied us to the rest of the indians, & he gave the doctor a buffalo robe for his vest, which he immediately put on, buttoned it up, and appeared much pleased with his bargain; but not better than the doctor did with his. We also got a very fine robe, for a bridle & mantingals [sic], which were not very new. We struck our tent, moved on up to the fort; there are 2 or 3 good frame building here, saw some children playing in the porch of one of them, suppose there are some families here but the barracks & magazines are mostly built of turf; the place is not inclosed, & presents no striking appearance, but we liked to look at a house as it had been some time since we had seen one, and would be some time before we should see another. They kept a register here, of the number of waggons which passed, there had then passed 2657, & as many waggons pass without touching here, I do not think they can keep a correct account, & I do not think they try to get the number of those that pass on the north side of the river, for it would be difficult to do. Opposite the town, & extending up & down the river for 16 or 18 ms, is an island, it is covered with a fine growth of cottonwood timber, I was struck with its appearance with the mirage which I had seen on the plain, & believe it the same reflected by the atmosphere.

SOURCE: Frizzell, Lodisa. *Across the Plains to California in 1852; Journal of Mrs. Lodisa Frizzell, Edited from the Original Manuscript in the New York Public Library by Victor Hugo Paltsits.* New York: New York Public Library, 1915.

EXCERPT FROM *AN EXPEDITION TO THE VALLEY OF THE GREAT SALT LAKE OF UTAH (1852, by Howard Stansbury)*

Exploration and surveys of lands, for the purpose of establishing townships and planning roads, played a major role in the shaping of the American West. The U.S. Army's Corps of Topographical Engineers was formed early in the nineteenth century. Howard Stansbury, a captain in the Corps, produced a variety of exceptional reports, most notably his popular 1851 survey of the valley of the Great Salt Lake that was published in London in 1852.

Stansbury arrived in the newly established Utah Territory only four years after the Mormons had arrived there to settle. This account covers his meeting with Brigham Young as well as the Mormons' initial reluctance to allow the U.S. government to explore their newly formed community. The report, which was published with illustrations, details vegetation, geological formations, and weather conditions while making observations about Native American culture and encampments.

Leah R. Shafer,
Cornell University

See also **Bridger, Fort; Geophysical Explorations; Great Salt Lake; Salt Lake City; Western Exploration.**

CHAPTER IV.

From Fort Bridger to Great Salt Lake City.

Monday, August 20.—We followed the Mormon road for several miles, and then took a "cut-off" leading more to the north, crossing the dividing ridge between the waters of Muddy Fork, an affluent of Green River, and those of Bear River, which falls into the Great Basin. We crossed the broad valley of Tar-Spring Creek, a tributary of Bear River, where the two roads join. The "cut-off" has been abandoned on account of an almost impassable hill at the dividing ridge. This, and another almost equally steep, are the only objections to this route, the rest of the way being excellent. Leaving the Mormon road at the crossing of Bear River, we followed down its valley six miles, as far as Medicine Butte, an elevated knob in the valley. This is a spot well known among the Indians, as that to which they were formerly in the habit of repairing to consult their oracles, or "medicine-men," who had located their "medicine lodge" in the vicinity of this little mountain. The route of a road to reach the north end of

Salt Lake should pursue a nearly west course from Bridger's Fort to this Butte, a distance of about thirty miles; the country, according to the representations of our guide, who has passed over it many times, being extremely favourable.

At our encampment on Bear River, near this Butte, abundance of speckled trout were caught, resembling in all respects the brook trout of the States, except that the speckles are black instead of yellow. An ox, which had strayed from some unfortunate emigrant, was found on the bank of the stream, in such capital condition that he was shot for food, and such portions as we could not carry with us were most generously presented to a small encampment of Shoshonee Indians, whose wigwams were erected among the bushes on the opposite side of the stream. It was curious to see how perfectly every portion of the animal was secured by them for food, even the paunch and entrails being thoroughly washed for that purpose. The squaws acted as the butchers, and displayed familiar acquaintance with the business, while the men lounged about, leaning lazily upon their rifles, looking listlessly on, as if it were a matter in which they were in no manner interested. They had quite a large number of horses and mules, and their encampment betokened comparative comfort and wealth.

The bottom of Bear River is here four or five miles in breadth, and is partially overflowed in the spring: the snow lies upon it to the depth of four feet in the winter, which prevents the Indians from occupying it during that season of the year, for which it would otherwise be well adapted.

In leaving Fort Bridger, we passed over horizontal lias beds. About six miles to the north of the road, the country appeared to be much broken up, and not solely by the action of water. The strata seemed dislocated and inclined, presenting much the same appearance as those near Laramie. Near this point, Fremont states that he found coal, which probably has been thrown up here. At Ogden's Hole, on the eastern slope of the Wahsatch Mountains, we found the ranges of hills to be composed of the carboniferous strata, thrown up at a very considerable angle; and at Bear River, near our encampment of to-day, they were almost perpendicular, the later strata being deposited by their side in an almost horizontal position, with a very slight dip to the southeast. At this latter point, the older sandstones were cropping out at an angle of 35 degrees; and on the opposite side of the river, the same strata were seen with a dip in the contrary direction, the valley being evidently an anticlinal axis.

Wednesday, August 22.—Crossing the broad valley of Bear River diagonally, we forded that stream, and struck over a point of bluff into a valley, the course of which being too much to the south for our purpose, we passed over to another, and followed it to its head, where it opens upon a long ridge, running to the south-west. Instead of following the ridge, (which I afterward found should have been done,) we crossed over two more ridges into a third valley, in which was a small rapid stream running into Bear River. Fearful of getting too far south, I ascended the western bluff of this stream, in hopes of finding a valley or ridge the course of which would give us more westing; but the country, in that direction, was so much broken that we were forced still farther to the south, and struck upon the heads of Pumbar's Creek, a tributary of the Weber River, which latter discharges its waters into the Great Salt Lake. This valley, our guide insisted, would lead us in the right direction, and it was concluded to follow it down, which we did for about four miles, and bivouacked for the night. We continued down this valley until the middle of the following day, when, instead of the broad open appearance which it had at first presented, it soon began to contract, until it formed a canon, with sides so steep that it was scarcely passable for mules. A blind Indian-trail wound along the hillside, at an elevation of several hundred feet above the stream, into which a single false stop of our mules would instantly have precipitated us. It required no small exertion of nerve to look down from this dizzy height into the yawning gulf beneath. After following the cañon some ten miles, we came to a broad valley coming into it from the left, which the guide declared headed in the ridge from which we had descended yesterday, and to the eastward of the route we had taken. As all prospect of a road by the valley of Pumbar's Creek was now out of the question, I determined to follow up this valley and ascertain whether a route could not be obtained in that direction. This was accordingly done, and we found it to be as the guide had stated. This branch of Pumbar's Creek, which we called Red Chimney Fork, from the remarkable resemblance of one of the projections of the cliffs to that object, we found to have a very moderate descent from the ridge to its mouth, with plenty of room for a road, requiring but little labour to render it a good one. The timber is small and consists of oak, black-jack, aspen, wild-cherry, service-berry, and box-elder of large size. In many places it is quite abundant.

On Pumbar's Creek, the hills were composed of strata of marble and metamorphic sandstone, inclined at an angle of 80 degrees to the north-east. Lower down, the horizontal strata were found lying by the side of these inclined rocks. On Red Chimney Fork, the strata were nearly horizontal, consisting principally of layers of red sandstone conglomerate, formed from metamorphic rocks with calcareous cement, and white sandstone with layers of conglomerate interposed. Near its junction with Pumbar's Creek, strata of slaty shales occurred, cropping out at an angle of 70 degrees.

Below the Red Chimney Fork, the valley of Pumbar's Creek opens sufficiently to allow the passage of a road through the bottom; but, as its course was leading us from our intended direction, we availed ourselves of a ravine, which, a mile below, comes into it from the north-west, and followed this up to its head, thus attaining the height of the general level of the country. The ascent is quite regular, but the road would have to be made all the way up, and a considerable quantity of small cotton-wood timber cut out. The upper strata on this branch appeared to be nearly analogous to those met with on Red Chimney Fork. We followed this ridge or table in a north-west direction for several miles, when we became involved among numerous ravines which ran to the south, and were too deep and abrupt to be available. In order to avoid them, the trace must be thrown so much to the north, that even were a road practicable up to this point, it would be entirely too crooked; and great difficulty, moreover, would have to be encountered in crossing the immense ravines which lay at the eastern base of the ranges bordering the Salt Lake. Some of these ravines run down into Ogden's Creek, and others into Bear River below the point at which we crossed it. Time would not admit of my pursuing the examination farther in this direction. My train had left Fort Bridger several days before me, and would be awaiting my arrival at Great Salt Lake City to commence the survey which was the more immediate object of the expedition. I, therefore, although with the greatest reluctance, concluded to make the best of my way to the lake, passing through Ogden's Hole, and thence crossing the high range dividing it from Salt Lake Valley, by a pass which the guide informed me existed there. We accordingly changed our course, and turning down a steep, narrow ravine for wood and water, encamped. The night was very cold, and ice formed in the buckets nearly an inch thick. We constructed a semicircular barricade of brush to keep off the wind, and, by the aid of a large fire of pine-logs, passed the night very comfortably.

The soil on the ridge passed, over to-day, seemed formed principally from red sandstone, and the boulders are primitive. The country is much better wooded, the timber being willow, aspen, and, in the ravines, tall firs and pines. The geranium was abundant: two or three yellow compositae and asters were observed.

Sunday, August 26.—Morning very cold. Ther. at sunrise, 16 degrees. Our provisions being nearly exhausted, I determined to go on for at least a part of the day, although contrary to my usual practice, this being the first Sabbath on which any travelling has been done since the party left the Missouri. After following some miles down the ravine upon which we had encamped, we struck upon an Indian lodge-trail, leading either to Cache Valley or to Ogden's Hole. This we followed in nearly a southerly direction, crossing many deep hollows and very steep ridges, up which we had to scramble, leading our mules, (it being impossible to ride,) until we struck upon the head of a broad, green, beautiful valley, with an even, gentle descent, which led us, in about three miles, down to Ogden's Creek, just before it makes a canon, previous to entering Ogden's Hole. There we encamped for the remainder of the day, with abundance of excellent grass, wood, and water. The same alternations of red and white sandstone appeared here as were seen on the Red Chimney Fork.

Just before descending into this valley, we had observed from the high ground, the smokes of numerous Indian signal fires, rising in several directions—an intimation that strangers had been discovered in their country. A strict watch was therefore maintained during the night, lest our animals should be stolen. Wild cherries were found in tolerable abundance, and the trail was strewn over with their smaller branches, thrown away by the Indians, who had evidently passed only a day or two before, in considerable numbers.

Monday, August 27.—We followed down Ogden's Creek about a mile, when we found that the broad valley was shut up between two ranges of hills, or rather mountains, leaving a flat, low, level bottom, densely covered in places by willows, through which the stream meanders from side to side, for three miles, washing alternately the base of either range. After passing through this cañon, the ridge separated, and before us lay a most lovely, broad, open valley, somewhat in the shape of a crescent, about fifteen miles long, and from five to seven miles in width, hemmed in on all sides, especially on the south and west, by lofty hills and rocky mountains, upon the tops and sides of which the snow glistened in the rays of the morning sun. The scene was cheering in the highest degree. The valley, rich and level, was covered with grass; springs broke out from the mountains in every direction, and the facilities for irrigation appeared to be very great. Ogden's Creek, breaking through its barriers, flows in a crystal stream at the base of the mountains on the south, for rather more than half the length of the valley, when it forces a passage through the huge range which divides this "gem of the desert" from the Salt Lake Valley, by a cañon wild and almost impassable. On the north, a beautiful little brook, taking its rise in the elevated ground separating this from Cache Valley, washes the base of the western hills, and joins Ogden's Creek just before it enters the cañon, after passing through which the latter discharges its waters into the Weber River, a tributary of the Great Salt Lake. Numerous bright little streams of pure running water were met with in abundance, rendering this the most interesting and delightful spot we had seen during our long and monotonous journey.

Rather more than half-way between the canon of Ogden's Creek and the north end of the valley, a pass is found by which a crossing of the mountain into the Salt Lake Valley can be effected. The ascent of the western side is, for the first four or five hundred yards, very abrupt and rocky, and would require a good deal of grading to render a road practicable; but after this, little or no labour would be necessary, except to cut away the brush, which, in places, is quite thick. The length of the pass is about three miles, and the height of the range through which it makes the cut, from eight hundred to a thousand feet above the valleys on each side. The valley of Ogden's Creek, or Ogden's Hole, (as places of this kind, in the nomenclature of this country, are called,) has long been the rendezvous of the North-west Company, on account of its fine range for stock in the winter, and has been the scene of many a merry reunion of the hardy trappers and traders of the mountains. Its streams were formerly full of beaver, but these have, I believe, entirely disappeared. Some few antelope were bounding over the green, but the appearance of fresh "Indian sign" accounted for their scarcity.

During our ride through the valley we came suddenly on a party of eight or ten Indian women and girls, each with a basket on her back, gathering grass-seeds for their winter's provision. They were of the class of "root-diggers," or, as the guide called them, "snake-diggers." The instant they discovered us, an immediate and precipitate flight took place, nor could all the remonstrances of the guide, who called loudly after them in their own language, induce them to halt for a single moment. Those who were too close to escape by running, hid themselves in the bushes and grass so effectually, that in less time than it has taken to narrate the circumstance, only two of them were to be seen. These were a couple of girls of twelve or thirteen years of age, who, with their baskets dangling at their backs, set off at their utmost speed for the mountains, and continued to run as long as we could see them, without stopping, or so much as turning their heads to look behind them. The whole party was entirely naked. After they had disappeared, we came near riding over two girls of sixteen or seventeen, who had "cached" behind a large fallen tree. They started up, gazed upon us for a moment, waved to us to continue our journey, and then fled with a rapidity that soon carried them beyond our sight.

In the pass through which we entered Ogden's Hole, the carboniferous rocks were again found, thrown up at an angle of 70 degrees or 80 degrees, with a dip to the north-east. On the western side of the high range of hills which extended to the north-west and formed the eastern boundary of Ogden's Hole, the edges of the strata cropped out as if a great fault had been formed at the point of elevation. No debris of primitive rock were discovered, nor was any observed in place during the whole journey from Bridger's Fort. In the pass leading to Salt Lake, through the Wahsatch range, the rock were metamorphic. Some beautiful specimens of marble were observed, and also some white crystalline sandstones. The strata again appeared on the western side of the range, and were inclined to the north-east about 70 degrees. The chain evidently was not formed on a central axis. No fossils were collected during this part of the journey, as we travelled rapidly, and the means of transporting them were necessarily limited.

Descending the pass through dense thickets of small oak-trees, we caught the first glimpse of the Great Salt Lake, the long-desired object of our search, and which it had cost us so many weary steps to reach. A gleam of sunlight, reflected by the water, and a few floating, misty clouds, were all, however, that we could see of this famous spot, and we had to repress our enthusiasm for some more favourable moment. I felt, nevertheless, no little gratification in having at length attained the point where our labours were to commence in earnest, and an impatient longing to enter upon that exploration to which our toils hitherto had been but preliminary.

Emerging from the pass, we entered the valley of the Salt Lake, and descending some moderately high table-land, struck the road from the Mormon settlements to the lower ford of Bear River, whence, in two or three miles, we came to what was called Brown's Settlement, and rode up to quite an extensive assemblage of log buildings, picketed, stockaded, and surrounded by out-buildings and cattle-yards, the whole affording evidence of comfort and abundance far greater than I had expected to see in so new a settlement. Upon requesting food and lodging for the night, we were told to our great surprise that we could not be accommodated, nor would the occupants sell us so much as an egg or a cup of milk, so that we were obliged to remount our horses; and we actually bivouacked under some willows, within a hundred yards of this inhospitable dwelling, turning our animals loose, and guarding them all night, lest, in search of food, they should damage the crops of this surly Nabal. From a neighbouring plantation we procured what we needed; otherwise we should have been obliged to go supperless to bed. I afterward learned that the proprietor had been a sort of commissary or quartermaster in Colonel Cook's Mormon Battalion, in California, and had some reason to expect and to dread a visit from the civil officers of the United States, on account of certain unsettled public accounts; and that he had actually mistaken us for some such functionaries. Subsequent acts of a similar nature, however, fully evinced the ungracious character of the man, strongly contrasted as it was with the frank and generous hospitality we ever received at the hands of the whole Mormon community.

The following day we reached the City of the Great Salt Lake, and found that the train had arrived safely on the 23d, and was now encamped near the Warm Springs on the outskirts of the city, awaiting my coming.

The result of the reconnoissance we had thus completed was such as to satisfy me that a good road can be obtained from Fort Bridger to the head of the Salt Lake; although I incline to the opinion that it should pass farther north than the route taken by me, entering the southern end of Cache Valley, probably by Blacksmith's Fork, and leaving it by the canon formed by Bear River in making its way from that valley into the lake basin. A more minute examination than the pressure of my other duties allowed me time to make will, I think, result in the confirmation of this view and the ultimate establishment of this road. Should such prove to be the case, it will, in addition to shortening the distance, open to the emigration, at the season they would reach it, the inexhaustible resources of Cache Valley, where wood, water, abundance of fish, and the finest range imaginable for any number of cattle, offer advantages for recruiting and rest possessed by no other point that I have seen on either side of the mountains.

Before reaching Great Salt Lake City, I had heard from various sources that much uneasiness was felt by the Mormon community at my anticipated coming among them. I was told that they would never permit any survey of their country to be made; while it was darkly hinted that if I persevered in attempting to carry it on, my life would scarce be safe. Utterly disregarding, indeed giving not the least credence to these insinuations, I at once called upon Brigham Young, the president of the Mormon church and the governor of the commonwealth, stated to him what I had heard, explained to him the views of the Government in directing an exploration and survey of the lake, assuring him that these were the sole objects of the expedition. He replied, that he did not hesitate to say that both he and the people over whom he presided had been very much disturbed and surprised that the Government should send out a party into their country so soon after they had made their settlement; that he had heard of the expedition from time to time, since its outset from Fort Leavenworth; and that the whole community were extremely anxious as to what could be the design of the Government in such a movement. It appeared, too, that their alarm had been increased by the indiscreet and totally unauthorized boasting of an attache of General Wilson, the newly-appointed Indian Agent for California, whose train on its way thither had reached the city a few days before I myself arrived. This person, as I understood, had declared openly that General Wilson had come clothed with authority from the President of the United States to expel the Mormons from the lands which they occupied, and that he would do so if he thought proper. The Mormons very naturally supposed from such a declaration that there must be some understanding or connection between General Wilson and myself; and that the arrival of the two parties so nearly together was the result of a concerted and combined movement for the ulterior purpose of breaking up and destroying their colony. The impression was that a survey was to be made of their country in the same manner that other public lands are surveyed, for the purpose of dividing it into townships and sections, and of thus establishing and recording the claims of the Government to it, and thereby anticipating any claim the Mormons might set up from their previous occupation. However unreasonable such a suspicion may be considered, yet it must be remembered that these people are exasperated and rendered almost desperate by the wrongs and persecutions they had previously suffered in Illinois and Missouri; that they had left the confines of civilization and fled to these far distant wilds, that they might enjoy undisturbed the religious liberty which had been practically denied them; and that now they supposed themselves to be followed up by the General Government with the view of driving them out from even this solitary spot, where they had hoped they should at length be permitted to set up their habitation in peace.

Upon all these points I undeceived Governor Young to his entire satisfaction. I was induced to pursue this conciliatory course, not only in justice to the Government, but also because I knew, from the peculiar organization of this singular community, that, unless the "President" was fully satisfied that no evil was intended to his people, it would be useless for me to attempt to carry out my instructions. He was not only civil governor, but the president of the whole Church of Latter-Day Saints upon the earth, their prophet and their priest, receiving, as they all firmly believed, direct revelations of the Divine will, which, according to their creed, form the law of the church. He is, consequently, profoundly revered by all, and possesses unbounded influence and almost unlimited power. I did not anticipate open resistance; but I was fully aware that if the president continued to view the expedition with distrust, nothing could be more natural than that every possible obstruction should be thrown in our way by a "masterly inactivity." Provisions would not be furnished; information would not be afforded; labour could not be procured; and no means would be left untried, short of open opposition, to prevent the success of a measure by them deemed fatal to their interests and safety. So soon, however, as the true object of the expedition was fully understood, the president laid the subject-matter before the council called for the purpose, and I was informed, as the result of their deliberations, that the authorities were much pleased that the exploration was to be made; that they had themselves contemplated something of the kind, but did not yet feel able to incur the expense; but that any assistance they could render to facilitate our operations would be most cheerfully furnished to the extent of their ability. This pledge, thus heartily given, was as faithfully redeemed; and it gives me pleasure here to acknowledge the warm interest manifested and efficient aid rendered, as well by the president as by all the leading men of the community, both in our personal welfare and in the successful prosecution of the work.

SOURCE: Stansbury, Howard. *An Expedition to the Valley of the Great Salt Lake of Utah: Including a Description of Its Geography, Natural History, and Minerals, and an Analysis of Its Waters; with an Authentic Account of the Mormon Settlement; Illustrated by Numerous Beautiful Plates, from Drawings Taken on the Spot, Also a Reconnoissance [sic] of a New Route through the Rocky Mountains and Two Large and Accurate Maps of That Region.* Philadelphia: Lippincott, Grambo & Co., 1852.

A PIONEER WOMAN'S LETTER HOME
(c. 1856, by Elizabeth Stewart Warner)

The United States pursued an aggressive policy of territorial expansion in the first half of the nineteenth century, leading to settlements being established along the Oregon Trail, which began at the Mississippi River and headed west through the Rocky Mountains. Elizabeth Stewart Warner took the Oregon Trail soon after her marriage in 1853. She gave a vivid account of the hardships faced by women on the journey west. Only days into the journey she watched two young women with children bury their husbands. Women on the journey, many of who came from comfortable backgrounds, faced unprecedented responsibilities and were expected to toil along with the men. The plains crossed by the settlers were dry and water was scarce. Warner wrote, "They talk about the times that tried men souls but if this ware not the times that tried both men and wemon's souls."

Leah R. Shafer,
Cornell University

See also **Pioneers; Westward Migration.**

Dear Friends,

I want to write you a full and true letter, this I promised to do, but I fear I shall fail, not in the truth but in giveing you a full description of the rout and gurny whitch I have neither memory to remember or head to discribe and I did not keep a journal as I intended, but I will try to give you the heads and particulars as well as I can remember. we left and particulars as well as I call remember. we left Pittsburgh, march the 17th 1853, and after a tedous gorney we arived in Saint Jo. april the 5th. We thair bought up our cattle at the verious prices from 65 *dolls* to 85 dollars paid 40 cents per day for the meanest house you could think of human beings living in and we had to steal beg and take watter all over the town we had to pay 10 cts per day for putting our cattles in a yard mud to the knes, and had to drive them more than a mile to watter every day we camped out in the woods and was mutch better of than in Saint Jo. we crossed the Missuri on the fourth of May in the rain. we crosed on a ferry boat and was to cross the next but ther was another familie had got into the boat, before them. david Love and fred was just coming to cross on the same boat they had been over to buy another youlk of cattle but were just one minute to late, and well it was for us all for the boat struck a snag and drowned 7 men a woman was standing on the bank, she said to mother, do you see that man with the red warmer on well that is my husband and while she spoke the boat struck and went down and she had to stand within call of him and see him drownd. O my heart was sore for that woman and three miles from the river we saw another woman with 8 children stand beside the grave of her husband and her oldest son so sick that she could not travel annd had to go up the river 12 miles before they could cross we waited for them at the mishen we then all got together and one of stewart's wagons broke down and wes mended next day we had ben telling him that he ought not to presist in taking such big wagons but he would no advice and when we ware at the mishen the men held a council and determined not to wait for him for they saw he would never keep up. Our wemen protested against it but they started and we were obliged to fowlow and I did not feel so bad when death came and snatched one of us away well we got through and they only made Salt lake about the half way. it was best for us to go on but it was hard to part I do not think that Mother will ever get over it she blames her self for not standing still and she blames us for not doing the same and she blames the men for leaving them. mother says that no consequence could never make her do the like again. But it was shurley best for us to push on we only hea[r]d where they were by Mrs Grilles letter five days ago we thought mother would have been satisfied when she herd whare they ware to a certainy but no we haven't any little Jenett with us and mother clings to the child with a nervous affection whitch I never saw her show to any object before. we then proceded 10 wagons in company to the plat river full for miles in wedth to look at that great flood and think that when we had followed it almost to its cource we would hardley be half way, and it is the easiest half of they way by 20 degrees, it was painful though for faint harts I can tell you. But on we goged each day about 25 or 30 miles and it was a pleasure to travel then we had a very agreeable company not one jarr amongst us had it not been for the thought of anna behind it would have been a pleasure trip indeed. we lost the first ox on sweet watter it was Tom' wheel ox, and what he called one of his main dependence but poor Sam had done his duty and then laid him down to rest, some time after that one of David Loves oxen died and then one of mothers, and when we came to snake river it was every day and every night sombody had lost an ox, we lost four in one day and two nights when we got up in the morning we wemon got the breakfuss and the men went after the cattle, and we thot at last that we could not dare to see them come back for they always came back minus someones cattle. then we came to the new road they talk about the times that tried men souls but if this ware not the times that tried both men and wemon's souls, well thar was a man thair meeting his wife and familie, and he was going the new road, it was a 100 miles nearer, our cattle wer few in number we had enough provisions to do us but no more Thare were a great many wagons gone with that man and thare a great many more going and we thought if it was a nearer and better road we had as much need to go as anybody well on we went until we came to the first camping place and thair we found a paper telling how far to the next camping place and then we came to the blue mountains & these mountains are composed of rocks of a blue coulur and all broken up as eavenly about the size of a pint cup, as if they were broken by the hand of man they were hard on the oxens feet and our feet, for everybody walked here. when we ware crossing the streams the rocks ware larger some times so large they up set the wagons into the wattor. when we had crossed the blue Mountains we came to those hard perplexing lakes. now take the map and look at those lakes which lie between the blue Mountains and the Cascades and you will not see one for every five that theirs on the ground but you will have some little idea. The first one we came to we should have taken the north and instead of that we took the south side and thare we wandered sometimes west. . . .

SOURCE: Schlissel, Lillian. *Women's Diaries of the Westward Journey.* New York: Schocken Books, 1982.

CONSTITUTION OF THE COMMITTEE OF VIGILANTES OF SAN FRANCISCO *(Adopted 15 May 1856)*

The 1848 Gold Rush brought a wealth of prospectors to California. The population of San Francisco, an established outpost since 1776, grew from nine hundred to ten thousand in one year. With the sudden influx of prospectors and great wealth, this city of tents and makeshift buildings was rife with corruption. A popular movement to address this corruption, the San Francisco Vigilantes Committee, was first formed in June 1851. The committee felt that the city did not provide adequate security for either life or property, and they took issue with the courts, the police, the prison-keepers and the city government at large, with particular attention to allegations that ballot boxes were being stolen and stuffed. After the first vigilance committee hanged several men, they disbanded in September 1851, only to reform as the Second Vigilance Committee in 1856.

Leah R. Shafer,
Cornell University

See also **California; Gold Rush; San Francisco; Vigilantes.**

Whereas, has become apparent to the citizens of San Francisco that there is no security for life and property, either under the regulations of society, as it at present exists, or under the laws as now administered; and that by the association together of bad characters, our ballot boxes have been stolen and others substituted, or stuffed with votes that were not polled, and thereby our elections nullified, our dearest rights violated, and no other method left by which the will of the people can be manifested; therefore, the citizens whose names are hereunto attached, do unite themselves into an association for maintenance of peace and good order of society—the preservation of our lives and property, and to insure that our ballot boxes shall hereafter express the actual and unforged will of the majority of our citizens; and we do bind ourselves, each unto the other, by a solemn oath, to do and perform every just and lawful act for the maintenance of law and order, and to sustain the laws when faithfully and properly administered; but we are determined that no thief, burglar, incendiary, assassin, ballot-box stuffer, or other disturbers of the peace, shall escape punishment, either by the quibbles of the law, the insecurity of prisons, the carelessness or corruption of police, or a laxity of those who pretend to administer justice; and to secure the objects of this association, we do hereby agree:

1st. That the name and style of this association shall be the Committee of Vigilance, for the protection of the ballot-box, the lives, liberty and property of the citizens and residents of the City of San Francisco.

2d. That there shall be rooms for the deliberations of the Committee, at which there shall be some one or more members of the Committee appointed for that purpose, in constant attendance at all hours of the day and night, to receive the report of any member of the association, or of any other person or persons of any act of violence done to the person or property of any citizens of San Francisco; and if, in the judgment of the member or members of the Committee present, it be such an act as justifies or demands the interference of this Committee, either in aiding in the execution of the laws, or the prompt and summary punishment of the offender, the Committee shall be at once assembled for the purpose of taking such action as the majority of them, when assembled, shall determine upon.

3d. That it shall be the duty of any member or members of the Committee on duty at the committee rooms, whenever a general assemblage of the Committee be deemed necessary, to cause a call to be made, in such a manner as shall be found advisable.

4th. That whereas, an Executive Committee, has been chosen by the General Committee, it shall be the duty of said Executive Committee to deliberate and act upon all important questions, and decide upon the measures necessary to carry out the objects for which this association was formed.

5th. That whereas, this Committee has been organized into subdivisions, the Executive Committee shall have the power to call, when they shall so determine, upon a board of delegates, to consist of three representatives from each division, to confer with them upon matters of vital importance.

6th. That all matters of detail and government shall be embraced in a code of By-Laws.

7th. That the action of this body shall be entirely and vigorously free from all consideration of, or participation in the merits or demerits, or opinion or acts, of any and all sects, political parties, or sectional divisions in the community; and every class of orderly citizens, of whatever sect, party, or nativity, may become members of this body. No discussion of political, sectional, or sectarian subjects shall be allowed in the rooms of the association.

8th. That no person, accused before this body, shall be punished until after fair and impartial trial and conviction.

9th. That whenever the General Committee have assembled for deliberation, the decision of the majority, upon any question that may be submitted to them by the Executive Committee, shall be binding upon the whole; provided nevertheless, that when the delegates are deliberating upon the punishment to be awarded to any criminals, no vote inflicting the death penalty shall be binding, unless passed by two-thirds of those present and entitled to vote.

10th. That all good citizens shall be eligible for admission to this body, under such regulations as may be prescribed by a committee on qualifications; and if any unworthy persons gain admission, they shall on due proof be expelled; and believing ourselves to be executors of the will of the majority of our citizens, we do pledge our sacred honor, to defend and sustain each other in carrying out the determined action of this committee, at the hazard of our lives and our fortunes.

SOURCE: Lawson, J. D., ed. *American State Trials* Vol. XV. St. Louis: Thomas Law Books, 1914–1936.

EXCERPT FROM *THE VIGILANTES OF MONTANA* *(c. 1860, by Thomas Dimsdale)*

Though gold was mined in the United States as early as 1799, it was not until the great California Gold Rush of 1848 that it became a national preoccupation. After gold was discovered in Montana in the early 1860s, the state became notorious for its lawless, rowdy mining towns. Because such astronomical sums of money were being drawn from the earth, the towns quickly attracted businesses catering to the rough-and-tumble mining crowd: merchants, saloonkeepers, gamblers, and prostitutes.

This selection from Thomas Josiah Dimsdale's 1866 book, *The Vigilantes of Montana,* describes the fun to be had at the "Hurdy-Gurdy" house, where a dance with a professional girl could be purchased for a dollar in gold. The mining camps' preoccupation with the trappings of great wealth are apparent in the pains this author took to describe the elaborate, expensive costumes and habits of both the girls and their buccaneer partners. Though the author mentioned the "shooting scrapes" that resulted from "equal proportions of jealousy, whiskey and revenge," this selection is most interesting in its discussion of the economical opportunities afforded women of various cultures by the professional trade.

Leah R. Shafer,
Cornell University

See also **Frontier; Gold Mines and Mining; Montana.**

The absence of good female society, in any due proportion to the numbers of the opposite sex, is likewise an evil of great magnitude; for men become rough, stern and cruel, to a surprising degree, under such a state of things.

In every frequent street, public gambling houses with open doors and loud music, are resorted to, in broad daylight, by hundreds—it might almost be said—of all tribes and tongues, furnishing another fruitful source of "difficulties," which are commonly decided on the spot, by an appeal to brute force, the stab of a knife, or the discharge of a revolver. Women of easy virtue are to be seen promenading through the camp, habited in the gayest and most costly apparel, and receiving fabulous sums for their purchased favors. In fact, all the temptations to vice are present in full display, with money in abundance to secure the gratification, of the desire for novelty and excitement, which is the ruling passion of the mountaineer.

One "institution," offering a shadowy and dangerous substitute for more legitimate female association, deserves a more peculiar notice. This is the "Hurdy-Gurdy" house. As soon as the men have left off work, these places are opened, and dancing commences. Let the reader picture to himself a large room, furnished with a bar at one end—-where champagne at $12 (in gold) per bottle, and "drinks" at tweny-five to fifty cents, are wholesaled (correctly speaking)—and divided, at the end of this bar, by a railing running from side to side. The outer enclosure is densely crowded (and, on particular occasions, the inner one also) with men in every variety of garb that can be seen on the continent. Beyond the barrier sit the dancing women, called "hurdy-gurdies," sometimes dressed in uniform, but, more generally, habited according to the dictates of individual caprice, in the finest clothes that money can buy, and which are fashioned in the most attractive styles that fancy can suggest. On one side is a raised orchestra. The music suddenly strikes up, and the summons, "Take your partners for the next dance," is promptly answered by some of the male spectators, who paying a dollar in gold for a ticket, approach the ladies' bench, and—in style polite, or otherwise, according to antecedents—invite one of the ladies to dance. The number being complete, the parties take their places, as in any other dancing establishment, and pause for the performance of the introductory notes of the air.

Let us describe a first class dance—"sure of a partner every time"—and her companion. There she stands at the head of the set. She is of middle height, of rather full and rounded form; her complexion as pure as alabaster, a pair of dangerous looking hazel eyes, a slightly Roman nose, and a small and prettily formed mouth. Her auburn hair is neatly banded and gathered in a tasteful, ornamented net, with a roll and gold tassels at the side. How sedate she looks during the first figure, never smiling till the termination of "promenade, eight," when she shows her little white hands in fixing her handsome brooch in its place, and settling her glistening earrings. See how nicely her scarlet dress, with its broad black band round the skirt, and its black edging, sets off her dainty figure. No wonder that a wild mountaineer would be willing to pay—not one dollar, but all that he has in his purse, for a dance and an approving smile from so beautiful a woman.

Her cavalier stands six feet in his boots, which come to the knee, and are garnished with a pair of Spanish spurs, with rowels and bells like young water wheels. His buckskin leggings are fringed at the seams, and gathered at the waist with a U.S. belt, from which hangs his loaded revolver and his sheath knife. His neck is bare, muscular and embrowned by exposure, as is also his bearded face, whose sombre hue is relieved by a pair of piercing dark eyes. His long black hair hangs down beneath his wide felt hat, and, in the corner of his mouth is a cigar, which rolls like the lever of an eccentric, as he chews the end in his mouth. After an amazingly grave salute, "all hands round" is shouted by the prompter, and off bounds the buckskin hero, rising and falling to the rhythm of the dance, with a clumsy agility and a growing enthusiasm, testifying his huge delight. His fair partner, with practised foot and easy grace, keeps time to the music like a clock, and rounds to her place as smoothly and gracefully as a swan. As the dance progresses, he of the buckskins gets excited, and nothing but long practice prevents his partner fom being swept off her feet, at the conclusion of the miner's delight, "set your partners," or "gents to the right." An Irish tune or a hornpipe generally finishes the set, and then the thunder of heel and toe, and some amazing demivoltes are brought to an end by the aforesaid "gents to the right," and "promenade to the bar," which last closes the dance. After a treat, the barkeeper mechanically raps his blower as a hint to "weigh out," the ladies sit down, and with scarcely an interval, a waltz, polka, shottische, mazurka, varsovinne, or another quadrille commences.

All varieties of costume, physique and demeanor can be noticed among the dancers—from the gayest colors and "loudest" styles of dress and manner, to the snugly fitted black silk, and plain white collar, which sets off the neat figure of the blue-eyed, modest looking Anglo-Saxon. Yonder, beside the tall and tastly clad German brunette you see the short curls, rounded tournure and smiling face of an Irish girl; indeed, representatives of almost every dancing nation of white folks may be seen on the floor of the Hurdy-Gurdy house. The earnings of the dancers are very different in amount. That dancer in the low-necked dress, with the scarlet "waist," a great favorite and a really good dancer, counted fifty tickets into her lap before "The last dance, gentlemen," followed by "Only this one before the girls go home," which wound up the performance. Twenty-six dollars is a great deal of money to earn in such a fashion; but fifty sets of quadrilles and four waltzes, two of them for the love of the thing, is very hard work. As a rule, however, the professional "hurdies" are Teutons, and, though first-rate dancers, they are, with some few exceptions, the reverse of good looking.

The dance which is most attended, is one in which ladies to whom pleasure is dearer than fame, represent the female element, and, as may be supposed, the evil only commences at the Dance House. It is not uncommon to see one of these sirens with an "outfit" worth from seven to eight hundred dollars, and many of them invest with merchants and bankers thousands of dollars in gold, the rewards and presents they receive, especially the more highly favored ones, being more in a week than a well-educated girl would earn in two years in an Eastern city.

In the Dance House you can see Judges, the Legislative corps, and every one but the Minister. He never ventures further than to engage in conversation with a friend at the door, and while intently watching the performance, lectures on the evil of such places with considerable force; but his attention is evidently more fixed upon the dancers than on his lecture. Sometimes may be seen gray-haired men dancing, their wives sitting at home in blissful ignorance of the proceeding. There never was a dance house running, for any length of time, in the first days of a mining town, in which "shooting scrapes" do not occur; equal proportions of jealousy, whiskey and revenge being the stimulants thereto. Billiard saloons are everywhere visible, with a bar attached, and hundreds of thousands of dollars are spent there. As might be anticipated, it is impossible to prevent quarrels in these places, at all times, and, in the mountains, whatever weapon is handiest—foot, fist, knife, revolver, or derringer—it is usually used. The authentic, and, indeed, literally exact accounts which follow in the course of this narrative will show that the remarks we have made on the state of society in a new mining country, before a controlling power asserts its sway, are in no degree exaggerated, but fall short of the reality, as all description must.

SOURCE: Dimsdale, Thomas J. *The Vigilantes of Montana, or Popular Justice in the Rocky Mountains.* Virginia City, Mont.: Montana Post Press, D. W. Tilton & Co., 1866.

AMERICAN PARTY PLATFORM *(1856)*

The 1840s and 1850s saw an enormous increase in the numbers of European immigrants, Irish and Germans especially, arriving on American shores and settling in heavily populated urban areas. Many of these immigrants subsequently became active in local politics, much to the vexation of old-stock, "real" Americans. The result was a renaissance in the formation of "nativistic" societies—small, shadowy, anti-foreign, anti-Catholic organizations, a number of which banded together in the early 1850s to form the American Party. Popularly known as "Know-Nothings" (after the response members gave when interrogated about their pro-protestant, pro-native associations), the American Party rode a wave of xenophobia and racism (not to mention political turmoil among the Whigs and Democrats, the major parties of the day) into the mid-1850s. Among the Know-Nothing's dubious political ideas was a call to extend the five-year naturalization period to twenty-one years, as well as a proscription against the holding of elected offices by Catholics and foreigners. Like much of the country, however, the Know-Nothings soon divided over the explosive slavery issue, and the power of the party quickly waned. Their nominee for president in 1856, former President Millard Fillmore, received just twenty-one percent of the popular vote and won only the state of Maryland. Still disdaining urban foreigners, most of who were Democrats, many of the now-erstwhile Know-Nothings allied with the newly formed Republican Party.

Laura M. Miller,
Vanderbilt University

See also **American Party; Know-Nothing Party.**

2. The perpetuation of the Federal Union and Constitution, as the palladium of our civil and religious liberties, and the only sure bulwarks of American Independence.
3. *Americans must rule America;* and to this end *native-born* citizens should be selected for all State, Federal and municipal offices of government employment, in preference to all others. *Nevertheless,*
4. Persons born of American parents residing temporarily abroad, should be entitled to all the rights of native-born citizens.

5. No person should be selected for political station (whether of native or foreign birth), who recognizes any allegiance or obligation of any description to any foreign prince, potentate or power, or who refuses to recognize the Federal and State Constitutions (each within its sphere) as paramount to all other laws, as rules of political action.
6. The unqualified recognition and maintenance of the reserved rights of the several States, and the cultivation of harmony and fraternal good will between the citizens of the several States, and to this end, non-interference by Congress with questions appertaining solely to the individual States, and non-intervention by each State with the affairs of any other State.
7. The recognition of the right of native-born and naturalized citizens of the United States, permanently residing in any territory thereof, to frame their constitution and laws, and to regulate their domestic and social affairs in their own mode, subject only to the provisions of the Federal Constitution, with the privilege of admission into the Union whenever they have the requisite population for one Representative in Congress: *Provided, always*, that none but those who are citizens of the United States, under the Constitution and laws thereof, and who have a fixed residence in any such Territory, ought to participate in the formation of the Constitution, or in the enactment of laws for said Territory or State.
8. An enforcement of the principles that no State or Territory ought to admit others than citizens to the right of suffrage, or of holding political offices of the United States.
9. A change in the laws of naturalization, making a continued residence of twenty-one years, of all not heretofore provided for, an indispensable requisite for citizenship hereafter, and excluding all paupers, and persons convicted of crime, from landing upon our shores; but no interference with the vested rights of foreigners.
10. Opposition to any union between Church and State; no interference with religious faith or worship, and no test oaths for office....
13. Opposition to the reckless and unwise policy of the present Administration in the general management of our national affairs, and more especially as shown in removing "Americans" (by designation) and Conservatives in principle, from office, and placing foreigners and Ultraists in their places; as shown in a truckling subserviency to the stronger, and an insolent and cowardly bravado toward the weaker powers; as shown in reopening sectional agitation, by the repeal of the Missouri Compromise; as shown in granting to unnaturalized foreigners the right of suffrage in Kansas and Nebraska; as shown in its vacillating course on the Kansas and Nebraska question; as shown in the corruptions which pervade some of the Departments of the Government; as shown in disgracing meritorious naval officers through prejudice or caprice: and as shown in the blundering mismanagement of our foreign relations.
14. Therefore, to remedy existing evils, and prevent the disastrous consequences otherwise resulting therefrom, we would build up the "American Party" upon the principles herein before stated....

SOURCE: Greeley, Horace and John F. Cleveland. *A Political Text-book for 1860.* New York: Tribune Association, 1860.

SPEECH OF LITTLE CROW ON THE EVE OF THE GREAT SIOUX UPRISING
(18 August 1862)

Little Crow V, last in a line of great Sioux leaders, was born in 1803 in southeastern Minnesota. In 1851, he signed the Treaty of Mendota that ceded most of the land of the Mdewakanton Sioux to the United States. A persuasive and popular orator, Little Crow widely questioned the terms of this treaty and, citing non-payment of the annuities promised by the U.S. government, incited his people to revolt in 1862. Believing they would find little military resistance from a country mired in civil war, Little Crow led his people in a massive attack upon over two hundred miles of frontier settlements. The uprising was eventually subdued after an unsuccessful attack on Fort Ridgely near what is today Fairfax, Minnesota, and Little Crow was forced to retreat west with his followers. He was shot and killed the following year when he returned to the devastated territory. Little Crow's speech shows he had few illusions about the ability of his people to fight the white man, but that he was determined to engage in battle.

Leah R. Shafer,
Cornell University

See also **Indian Warfare; Sioux; Sioux Uprising in Minnesota; Wars with Indian Nations: Later Nineteenth Century (1840–1900).**

Taoyateduta is not a coward, and he is not a fool! When did he run away from his enemies? When did he leave his braves behind him on the warpath and turn back to his tepee? When he ran away from your enemies, he walked behind on your trail with his face to the Ojibways and covered your backs as a she-bear covers her cubs! Is Taoyateduta without scalps? Look at his war feathers! Behold the scalp locks of your enemies hanging there on his lodgepoles! Do they call him a coward? Taoyateduta is not a coward, and he is not a fool. Braves, you are like little children: you know not what you are doing.

You are full of the white man's devil water. You are like dogs in the Hot Moon when they run mad and snap at their own shadows. We are only little herds of buffalo left scattered; the great herds that once covered the prairies are no more. See!—the white men are like the locusts when they fly so thick that the whole sky is a snowstorm. You may kill one—two—ten; yes, as many as the leaves in the forest yonder, and their brothers will not miss them. Kill one—two—ten, and ten times ten will come to kill you. Count your fingers all day long and white men with guns in their hands will come faster than you can count.

Yes; they fight among themselves—away off. Do you hear the thunder of their big guns? No; it would take you two moons to run down to where they are fighting, and all the way your path would be among white soldiers as thick as tamaracks in the swamps of the Ojibways. Yes; they fight among themselves, but if you strike at them they will all turn on you and devour you and your women and little children just as the locusts in their time fall on the trees and devour all the leaves in one day.

You are fools. You cannot see the face of your chief; your eyes are full of smoke. You cannot hear his voice; your ears are full of roaring waters. Braves, you are little children—you are fools. You will die like the rabbits when the hungry wolves hunt them in the Hard Moon (January). Taoyateduta is not a coward: he will die with you.

SOURCE: "Speech of Little Crow on the Eve of the Great Sioux Uprising, August 18, 1862." Minnesota Historical Society. *Minnesota History.* Vol. 28, no. 3 (September 1962).

EXCERPT FROM *MY ARMY LIFE*
(c. 1866, by Frances C. Carrington)

Fort Phil Kearny was built near present-day Story, Wyoming in 1866 to protect travelers on the Bozeman Trail from attacks by the Sioux. In the first six months of its existence, it was attacked repeatedly by the Sioux, who surrounded the compound with the so-called "Circle of Death." After more than 150 soldiers were killed, the fort was abandoned under the terms of the 1868 Treaty of Fort Laramie.

Frances Carrington was the second wife of Colonel Henry B. Carrington, who oversaw the construction of Fort Phil Kearny. Her memoir, published about forty years after the fort was abandoned, gives a revealing account of the privations and dangers of life in the northern Wyoming encampment. Though under constant attack from both the elements and the Sioux, Mrs. Carrington makes it clear she worked hard to achieve and maintain basic standards of housekeeping and domestic order.

Leah R. Shafer,
Cornell University

See also **Frontier; Wars with Indian Nations: Later Nineteenth Century (1840–1900)**

CHAPTER XII.

Garrison Life Begun.

The sudden change of temperature incident to the high altitude and climate of our new home caused a deep snow to fall during the very night of our arrival, and the tents having been insecurely drawn together, combined with the penetrating wind to supply an extremely novel experience. The snow drifted in, covered my face, and there melting trickled down my cheeks until if I had shed tears they would have been indistinguishable. The cheering proverb, "weeping may endure for a night, but joy cometh in the morning," had neither solace nor comfort for me, just then!

When I arose from fitful slumber and had sufficiently cleared my eyes and face from snow to take my bearings deliberately it was only to find that pillows, bedding, and even the stove and the ground within the tent were also covered. Notwithstanding my misery, there was something actually ludicrous in the situation. I did afterwards intimate to friends that the fancy of thus prematurely donning snow-white robes did not occur to me at that moment, for neither levity nor philosophy could adequately meet the occasion. Shaking out stockings and emptying shoes filled with fine snow was earthly and practical in the extreme.

A soldier from our company had been detailed to make fires and render other domestic service as best he could, and the cook-stove required the first attention both for its heat and its more appetizing functions. That stove proved to be a success. Its warmth soon melted the snow, but in passing from the stove-tent to the mess-chest in the other tent, a slip-shod step became from actual necessity my trying resort. It would seem, and indeed it did seem, as if I had reached the extreme limit of endurance, but no, I had not.

I can speak of it now in calm terms, but at the moment I had such a sensation of actual desperation come over me that with butcher-knife in hand for preparation of something for breakfast I almost threatened then and there to end it all, and I could have settled the question "to be, or not to be" in short order. And then the second thought was of a less morbid vein and I resolved to "take up arms against this sea of trouble" and master the situation.

My first decided action resulted in the manufacture of some very hard biscuit from flour, salt, and water; and then bacon and coffee. All these in course of time were deposited upon the mess-chest for our first morning meal and the bacon and coffee were first served. Then for the biscuit. No hatchet chanced to be conveniently near to aid in separating them in halves, but the work had to be done. Impulsively I seized the butcher-knife, so recently associated with a vague idea of other use, but in the endeavor to do hatchet-work with it the blade slipped and almost severed my thumb, mingling both blood and tears. Had I any doubt of the truth of my statement or the memory thereof I have only to look at the scar which I still wear after the lapse of more than the third of a century.

One morning I started a brisk fire with shavings abundant when a sudden wind blew the sparks under the foundations of the commanding officers quarters where the debris from carpenter work had accumulated, setting the whole on fire and actually threatening the building itself; but quick discovery and prompt action on the part of someone passing by soon extinguished the flame. I suppose that it was thought to be unsafe for such risky experiments as mine in the cooking line, for almost immediately new quarters were assigned me in a large hospital tent recently vacated by the Colonels family, which had moved into their headquarters building then about half finished. The change was a decidedly agreeable one, that of a large tent with a safer cooking arrangement and better protection from future snow and wind blasts.

For some time after that we had no snow and the weather continued fine for weeks, so that in that invigorating climate there was a quick response to the delightful change, at least from a physical point of view. It did not, and could not, bring unalloyed happiness, for Indian alarms were almost constant and attacks upon the wood trains were so frequent that I had a horror of living in a tent, however large or convenient, so near the stockade as the officers line of quarters had been located.

The stockade itself was rapidly nearing completion, notwithstanding all other work went on, and the skirmishing continued to be accepted as a part of the daily discipline and experience. It was made of heavy pine trunks eleven feet in length hewn to a touching surface of four inches, so as to join closely, all pointed, loop-holed, and imbedded in the ground for four feet. Block-houses were at two diagonal corners and one at the water-gate, and massive double gates of double plank, with small sally-wickets and substantial bars and locks opened on three fronts, while the fourth directly behind the officers quarters had but a small sally-port, for the officers use only. My constant fear was that the Indians would work their way over the stockade under cover of the darkness at night. Opening from this, the fort proper, was a rough cottonwood stockade, or corral, known as the quartermasters yard, which contained quarters for teamsters, stock, wagons, hay ricks, and shops for wagon-makers, saddlers, and other general apparatus and conveniences usual in a large frontier fort. I often heard the crack of a rifle, so near that it seemed to be just at the back of my tent. The evident plan of the Indians was to harass the fort constantly by running off stock, to cut off any soldier or citizen who ventured any distance from the gates, and also to entice soldiers from the protection of the stockade and then lead them into some fatal ambush. As yet it was perfectly certain that the leading chiefs had not settled upon any plan to attack the fort itself in mass. Why they did not do so earlier and before the fort was completed is still a mystery.

The mountain scenery about the post was grand, and the beautiful Tongue River Valley, with its countless bright streams, was full of charms. With the Panther Mountains beyond to the westward the Big Horn Mountains to the southward, and the Black Hills, soon after made so famous for golded treasure, to the eastward, surely Fort Phil. Kearney was beautiful for situation. Lowering my gaze to the hills immediately near us, my eyes more frequently rested with pleasure upon Pilot Hill, only a few hundred yards from the fort. This shapely conical summit was the real watch-tower from which the faithful picket guard would signal danger as his watchful eye caught glimpses and his waving flag announced an approaching foe.

As our world revolved in a very small space there were no happenings that were unrelated, and the stories of miners, trappers, and guides were more intensely interesting as told by word of mouth than when filtered through the printed page.

It was my good fortune to meet with old Jim Bridger, already past his three-score and ten, who had been the chief guide to Colonel Carrington in the opening of the country. He was a typical "plainsman" and his name is perpetuated by such types as Fort Bridger and Bridgers Ferry. He had been a chief among the friendly Crows and the guide to Brigham Young in earlier days, and his biography, if written, would make a ponderous volume of tragic and startling events.

Although uneducated, he spoke both Spanish and English, as well as many Indian tongues, and his genial manners and simplicity of bearing commanded respect as well as the attachment and confidence of all who knew him well.

A quaint story is related of Bridger that when Laramie was but a small frontier outpost it was visited by a rich Irish nobleman who was upon a great hunting expedition among the Rockies and had secured Bridger for his guide. His outfit was made up of six wagons, twenty-one carts, twelve yoke of cattle, twelve horses, fourteen dogs and forty servants. He made Laramie the base of his supplies for several months during the hunting season. Bridger was a very revelation of a genuine sportsman to the lordly Irishman, who especially admired him for his honesty, simplicity, and shrewdness, as well as his knowledge of woodcraft and game. The contrast between the Irish gentleman and his train and the rude Bridger, who had depended upon his rifle for his livelihood from early childhood, was at times very amusing. The Irishman would lie in bed until a late hour, then take his hunt and return late at night, but however late he returned he would bring meat and insist upon having a late dinner to which he would invite Bridger. After the meal was over Sir George Gore, for that was his name, was in the habit of reading aloud to draw out Bridgers ideas of the author. On one ocasion when reading from Shakespeare and about Fallstaff, Bridger broke out with the exclamation: "Thats too hyfalutin for me; that thar Fullstuff was a leettle too fond olager beer!" Sir George read the adventures of Baron Munchausen one evening. Bridger shook his head a moment and then remarked, "Ill be dog-goned if I ken swaller everything that Baron sez. I believe hes a liar." A moment afterwards he added, that, "some of his own adventures among the Blackfoot Indians, in old times, would read just as wonderful if they were jest writ down in a book."

He used to tell us stories occasionally at the fort. He ridiculed the frontiersmen for their "gold craze" and laughed himself as he told a hunter once that "there was a diamond out near the Yellowstone Country that was on a mountain and if any one was lucky enough to get the right range it could be seen fifty miles, and one fool offered him a new rifle and a fine horse if he would put him on the right track to go for that diamond."

Bridger would walk about, constantly scanning the opposite hills that commanded a good view of the fort, as if he suspected Indians of having scouts behind every sage clump, or fallen cottonwood; and toward evening, as well as in the early morning, it was not strange that we caught flashes of small hand mirrors, which were used by the Indians in giving signals to other Indians who were invisible from the fort. Indeed all sights and sounds were of constant interest, if not of dread, living so constantly in the region of the senses, keyed to their highest tone by the life external. I often wondered why a post so isolated was not swept away by a rush of mighty numbers of the surrounding savages, to avenge in one vast holocaust the invasion of their finest hunting grounds. Only our strong defenses prevented an assault, and the depletion of our numbers by attacks upon our exposed wood trains seemed to be their sole hope of finding some opportunity by which to find the way to final extermination of the garrison itself.

The nights were made hideous at times by the hungry wolves who gathered in hordes about the slaughter-yard of the quartermaster, without the stockade, and near the Little Piney Creek. The only reassuring comfort was the statement of Bridger and others that Indians were rarely near when many wolves were present, and that they could distinguish the howl of the wolf from the cry of the Indian, by the fact that the former produced no echo. Once indeed, Indians, knowing that the soldiers were accustomed to put poison on the offal at the slaughter-yard to secure the pelts of the wolves for robes, crawled up close to the stockade, crawling under wolf-skins that covered their bodies, and a sentry was actually shot from the banquet that lay along the stockade, by an arrow, before any knowledge of the vicinity of the enemy came to the garrison.

In contrast with howling wolves and screeching savages who on one occasion rode in full view along the summit opposite the fort, waving their blankets and yelling their fierce bravadoes, we had the fine music of our splendid band of forty pieces, which played at guard-mounting in the morning and at dress-parade at sunset, while their afternoon drills and evening entertainments were in strange contrast with the solemn conditions that were constantly suggestive of war and sacrifice of life. If unable to soothe the savage breast, our music did soothe our civilized dread and force cheer in spite of ever present danger.

An Indian superstition maintained that a man killed in the darkness must spend eternity in darkness, and if that enured to our benefit, all right; but it did not deter Indians from making demonstrations by moonlight. On one occasion, just after dark, an alarm called attention to a large fire built on the top of Sullivant Hills, where Indians were visible, dancing about the flames where they were supposed to be taking a substantial meal of basted venison. No alarm was given, but the Colonel turned three howitzers upon the spot, cut fuses for the right time of flight, and all were fired at the same instant. Two spherical case shot exploded just over the fire scattering the bullets which they carried, and the fire was instantly trampled out as the Indians swiftly disappeared. It was a novel surprise to the redman that at a distance of several hundred yards the white soldier could drop into their midst such masterful vollies as eighty-four one-ounce bullets at every discharge. To us who watched the flight and witnessed the flash of the explosion in their very midst there was a satisfaction in the conviction that the Indians would hardly venture to come nearer when the "guns that shoot twice," as they called our howitzers, could do so much fighting even at night at so great a distance.

CHAPTER XIII.

Domesticities and New Friendships.

The residents of Fort Phil. Kearney were not troubled with ennui. While the men were busy in their departments of labor, the ladies were no less occupied in their accustomed activities. "Baking, brewing, stewing, and sewing" was the alliterative expression of the daily routine. With little fresh meat other than juiceless wild game, buffalo, elk, deer, or mountain sheep, and no vegetables, canned stuffs were in immediate and constant requisition. Once, indeed, Mr. Bozeman sent a few sacks of potatoes from his ranch in Montana to headquarters, as precious as grain in the sacks of Israels sons in Egypt; but these were doled out in small quantities to officers families, while the remainder, the major part, was sent to the hospital for men afflicted or threatened with scurvy.

The preparation of edible from canned fruits, meats, and vegetables taxed all ingenuity to evolve some product, independent of mere stewing, for successful results. Calico, flannel, and linsey woolsey, procured from the sutlers store, with gray army blankets as material for little boys overcoats, composed the staple goods required, and ladies garments, evolved after the "hit or miss" style, came in due time without the aid of sewing machines, of which none were at the post. Our buffalo boots were of a pattern emanating from or necessitated by our frontier locality, a counterpart of the leggings worn by the men, except that theirs did not have the shoe attachment. They were made by the company shoemakers of harness leather, to which was attached buffalo skin, with the hair inside, reaching almost to the knee and fastened on the outside with leather straps and brass buttons. The brass buttons were not for ornament, but a necessity in lieu of any other available kind. Nothing could exceed them in comfort, as a means adapted to an end.

There were hours when one could sit down composedly for a bit of sewing in a comfortable chair, with additional pleasure in the possession of a table sufficiently large for the double duty of dining and work table. With the few books I had carried with me for companionship distributed about, there was just a bit of homelikeness in tent life. My cooking experiments were never a great success, especially in the attempt at making pies, though I tried to emulate the ladies of larger experience in the effort. The cook-stove rested upon boards somewhat inclined, which was fatal to pie-making, which I did attempt a few times from canned fruit only to find in due time well developed crusts minus the fruit, which had oozed out gradually during the process, still in evidence of my good intentions, and to be eaten with as much philosophy as one could command with a straight face, disguising laughter, or tears.

Through the kind consideration of Mrs. Carrington, a large double bedstead was made by the carpenters, a luxury indeed, with mattress stuffed with dried grass, army blankets, and a large gay-colored shawl for counterpane, and surely no four-poster of mahogany, with valences of richest texture and downy pillows, and, for that matter, no Chippendale table, with these furniture accessories, could have been more prized during my life at the fort, as a demonstration of the simple life theory in every detail, whether enforced or otherwise.

Often, while reading or sewing quietly by myself, I would be startled by a rustling at my tent door, but fears were soon allayed when I discovered the beautiful head of Mrs. Hortons pet antelope protruding within. Its large, melting eyes would look at me appealingly, and, with sufficient encouragement, it would approach for the accustomed caress and favorite bite to eat.

Of the little children at the fort there were four boys, and many pleasant hours were spent in my tent with Jimmy Carrington, my little favorite, whose loving disposition made him a welcome guest. No picknickers of the pine woods ever enjoyed a repast so much as we did, after our simple preparations, involving a trip to the sutlers store, where cans of sugar were obtained, each with a mysterious-looking little bottle of lemon essence deposited therein, from which we produced lemonade, and this, together with ginger-snaps and nuts, made a "dainty dish fit for a King," never mind about the birds. After the repast was the song. He possessed a remarkably sweet voice, and together we sang familiar Sunday School hymns his mother had taught him, one of which I especially recall, "There is a light in the window for me," and his sweet childish tones sang the words deeply into my heart.

Sunday evening singing at headquarters was a feature of the day. Neither was Sunday morning service neglected, for, though no chapel had as yet been erected, each new building in turn was utilized for the service. With a fine string band to accompany the voices, and sometimes additional instruments, the presence of God was felt and recognized in this impromptu worship. Several of the band were German Catholics and good singers. On one occasion especial pains had been taken by the Colonel to make the music an attractive specialty to interest the men. The chaplain, Rev. David White, was a devout Methodist, of good heart and excellent in teaching the soldiers children at the fort, for there were several, but very unsophisticated in general society matters. On one occasion, when great care had secured the rendition of "Te Deum Laudamus," in which the band took part, he very solemnly asked the Colonel, "Isnt that a

Catholic tune?" and upon answer by the Colonel, "Why, that is one of the oldest and most glorious hymns of the Church all over Christendon," he expressed surprise, but thought himself that "it seemed to be quite religious, but it was new to him."

With a coterie of five ladies at the post, each had four places to visit, and the most was made of it in comparing notes upon the important matters of cooking, sewing, and our various steps of advancement in the different arts, quite independently of prevailing fashions of dress in the States, and yet this did not signify entire emancipation, for the problem was still a little perplexing in the evolution of new ideas, while mutual helpfulness simplified all our efforts. There was often an all-round social dance, games of cards, the "authors game," and other contrivances for recreation and amusement, in addition to the receptions at headquarters, which were spirited and congenial, and, with a band having the deserved reputation of being the finest in the army, their choice music was no small feature in the cheer on the frontier.

SOURCE: Carrington, Frances C. *My Army Life and the Fort Phil. Kearney Massacre, with an Account of the Celebration of "Wyoming Opened."* Philadelphia: Lippincott, 1910.

EXCERPT FROM *ROUGHING IT* *(1872, by Mark Twain)*

Samuel Langhorne Clemens (1835–1910), better known by his pseudonym, Mark Twain, is widely acknowledged to be one of America's most important writers. What is less well known is that he began his writing career while prospecting for gold in the Nevada Territory in 1861. The outbreak of the Civil War forced Twain to cut short his career as a riverboat captain on the Mississippi River, so he went to work for his brother, Orion Clemens, who had recently been appointed secretary of the Nevada Territory. Twain, like most prospectors, was disappointed in his search for gold, so he began to narrate his experiences in a series of comical stories which were printed in Virginia City's *Territorial Enterprise.* Eventually these stories were collected and printed as *Roughing It.* In this selection, Twain narrates the story of his expedition to Humboldt, Nevada, in search of silver.

Leah R. Shafer,
Cornell University

***See also* Frontier; Prospectors; Silver Prospecting and Mining.**

CHAPTER XXVI

By and by I was smitten with the silver fever. "Prospecting parties" were leaving for the mountains every day, and discovering and taking possession of rich silver-bearing lodes and ledges of quartz. Plainly this was the road to fortune. The great "Gould and Curry" mine was held at three or four hundred dollars a foot when we arrived; but in two months it had sprung up to eight hundred. The "Ophir" had been worth only a mere trifle, a year gone by, and now it was selling at nearly four thousand dollars a foot! Not a mine could be named that had not experienced an astonishing advance in value within a short time. Everybody was talking about these marvels. Go where you would, you heard nothing else, from morning till far into the night. Tom So-and-So had sold out of the "Amanda Smith" for $40,000—hadn't a cent when he "took up" the ledge six months ago. John Jones had sold half his interest in the "Bald Eagle and Mary Ann" for $65,000, gold coin, and gone to the States for his family. The widow Brewster had "struck it rich" in the "Golden Fleece" and sold ten feet for $18,000—hadn't money enough to buy a crape bonnet when Sing-Sing Tommy killed her husband at Baldy Johnson's wake last spring. The "Last Chance" had found a "clay casing" and knew they were "right on the ledge"—consequence, "feet" that went begging yesterday were worth a brick house apiece to-day, and seedy owners who could not get trusted for a drink at any bar in the country yesterday were roaring drunk on champagne today and had hosts of warm personal friends in a town where they had forgotten how to bow or shake hands from long-continued want of practice. Johnny Morgan, a common loafer, had gone to sleep in the gutter and waked up worth a hundred thousand dollars, in consequence of the decision in the "Lady Franklin and Rough and Ready" lawsuit. And so on—day in and day out the talk pelted our ears and the excitement waxed hotter and hotter around us.

I would have been more or less than human if I had not gone mad like the rest. Cart-loads of solid silver bricks, as large as pigs of lead, were arriving from the mills every day, and such sights as that gave substance to the wild talk about me. I succumbed and grew as frenzied as the craziest.

Every few days news would come of the discovery of a brand-new mining region; immediately the papers would teem with accounts of its richness, and away the surplus population would scamper to take possession. By the time I was fairly inoculated with the disease, "Esmeralda" had just had a run and "Humboldt" was beginning to shriek for attention. "Humboldt! Humboldt!" was the new cry, and straightway Humboldt, the newest of the new, the richest of the rich, the most marvelous of the marvelous discoveries in silver-land, was occupying two columns of the public prints to "Esmeralda's" one. I was just on the point of starting to Esmeralda, but turned with the tide and got ready for Humboldt. That the reader may see what moved me, and what would as surely have moved him had he been there, I insert here one of the newspaper letters of the day. It and several other letters from the same calm hand were the main means of converting me. I shall not garble the extract, but put it in just as it appeared in the Daily Territorial Enterprise:

> But what about our mines? I shall be candid with you. I shall express an honest opinion, based upon a thorough examination. Humboldt County is the richest mineral region upon God's footstool. Each mountain range is gorged with the precious ores. Humboldt is the true Golconda.
>
> The other day an assay of mere croppings yielded exceeding four thousand dollars to the ton. A week or two ago an assay of just such surface developments made returns of seven thousand dollars to the ton. Our mountains are full of rambling prospectors. Each day and almost every hour reveals new and more startling evidences of the profuse and intensified wealth of our favored county. The metal is not silver alone. There are distinct ledges of auriferous ore. A late discovery plainly evinces cinnabar. The coarser metals are in gross abundance. Lately evidences of bituminous coal have been detected. My theory has ever been that coal is a ligneous formation. I told Col. Whitman, in times past, that the neighborhood of Dayton (Nevada) betrayed no present or previous manifestations of a ligneous foundation, and that hence I had no confidence in his lauded coal-mines. I repeated the same doctrine to the exultant coal-discoverers of Humboldt. I talked with my friend Captain Burch on the subject. My pyrhanism vanished upon his statement that in the very region referred to he had seen petrified trees of the length of two hundred feet. Then is the fact established that huge forests once cast their grim shadows over this remote section. I am firm in the coal faith. Have no fears of the mineral resources of Humboldt County. They are immense—incalculable.

Let me state one or two things which will help the reader to better comprehend certain items in the above. At this time, our near neighbor, Gold Hill, was the most successful silver-mining locality in Nevada. It was from there that more than half the daily shipments of silver bricks came. "Very rich" (and scarce) Gold Hill ore yielded from $100 to $400 to the ton; but the usual yield was only $20 to $40 per ton—that is to say, each hundred pounds of ore yielded from one dollar to two dollars. But the reader will perceive by the above extract, that in Humboldt from one-fourth to nearly half the mass was silver! That is to say, every one hundred pounds of the ore had from two hundred dollars up to about three hundred and fifty in it. Some days later this same correspondent wrote:

> I have spoken of the vast and almost fabulous wealth of this region—it is incredible. The intestines of our mountains are gorged with precious ore to plethora. I have said that nature has so shaped our mountains as to furnish most excellent facilities for the working of our mines. I have also told you that the country about here is pregnant with the finest mill sites in the world. But what is the mining history of Humboldt? The Sheba mine is in the hands of energetic San Francisco capitalists. It would seem that the ore is combined with metals that render it difficult of reduction with our imperfect mountain machinery. The proprietors have combined the capital and labor hinted at in my exordium. They are toiling and probing. Their tunnel has reached the length of one hundred feet. From primal assays alone, coupled with the development of the mine and public confidence in the continuance of effort, the stock had reared itself to eight hundred dollars market value. I do not know that one ton of the ore has been converted into current metal. I do know that there are many lodes in this section that surpass the Sheba in primal assay value. Listen a moment to the calculations of the Sheba operators. They purpose transporting the ore concentrated to Europe. The conveyance from Star City (its locality) to Virginia City will cost seventy dollars per ton; from Virginia to San Francisco, forty dollars per ton; from thence to Liverpool, its destination, ten dollars per ton. Their idea is that its conglomerate metals will reimburse them their cost of original extraction, the price of transportation, and the expense of reduction, and that then a ton of the raw ore will net them twelve hundred dollars. The estimate may be extravagant. Cut it in twain, and the product is enormous, far transcending any previous developments of our racy territory.
>
> A very common calculation is that many of our mines will yield five hundred dollars to the ton. Such fecundity throws the Gould & Curry, the Ophir and the Mexican, of your neighborhood, in the darkest shadow. I have given you the estimate of the value of a single developed mine. Its richness is indexed by its market valuation. The people of Humboldt County are feet crazy. As I write, our towns are near deserted. They look as languid as a consumptive girl. What has become of our sinewy and athletic fellow-citizens? They are coursing through ravines and over mountain-tops. Their tracks are visible in every direction. Occasionally a horseman will dash among us. His steed betrays hard usage. He alights before his adobe dwelling, hastily exchanges courtesies with his townsmen, hurries to an assay office and from thence to the District Recorder's. In the morning, having renewed his provisional supplies, he is off again on his wild and

> unbeaten route. Why, the fellow numbers already his feet by the thousands. He is the horse-leech. He has the craving stomach of the shark or anaconda. He would conquer metallic worlds.

This was enough. The instant we had finished reading the above article, four of us decided to go to Humboldt. We commenced getting ready at once. And we also commenced upbraiding ourselves for not deciding sooner—for we were in terror lest all the rich mines would be found and secured before we got there, and we might have to put up with ledges that would not yield more than two or three hundred dollars a ton, maybe. An hour before, I would have felt opulent if I had owned ten feet in a Gold Hill mine whose ore produced twenty-five dollars to the ton; now I was already annoyed at the prospect of having to put up with mines the poorest of which would be a marvel in Gold Hill.

Chapter XXVII

Hurry, was the word! We wasted no time. Our party consisted of four persons—a black-smith sixty years of age, two young lawyers, and myself. We bought a wagon and two miserable old horses. We put eighteen hundred pounds of provisions and mining-tools in the wagon and drove out of Carson on a chilly December afternoon. The horses were so weak and old that we soon found that it would be better if one or two of us got out and walked. It was an improvement. Next, we found that it would be better if a third man got out. That was an improvement also. It was at this time that I volunteered to drive, although I had never driven a harnessed horse before, and many a man in such a position would have felt fairly excused from such a responsibility. But in a little while it was found that it would be a fine thing if the driver got out and walked also. It was at this time that I resigned the position of driver, and never resumed it again. Within the hour, we found that it would not only be better, but was absolutely necessary, that we four, taking turns, two at a time, should put our hands against the end of the wagon and push it through the sand, leaving the feeble horses little to do but keep out of the way and hold up the tongue. Perhaps it is well for one to know his fate at first, and get reconciled to it. We had learned ours in one afternoon. It was plain that we had to walk through the sand and shove that wagon and those horses two hundred miles. So we accepted the situation, and from that time forth we never rode. More than that, we stood regular and nearly constant watches pushing up behind.

We made seven miles, and camped in the desert. Young Claggett (now member of Congress from Montana) unharnessed and fed and watered the horses; Oliphant and I cut sage-brush, built the fire and brought water to cook with; and old Mr. Ballou, the blacksmith, did the cooking. This division of labor, and this appointment, was adhered to throughout the journey. We had no tent, and so we slept under our blankets in the open plain. We were so tired that we slept soundly.

We were fifteen days making the trip—two hundred miles; thirteen, rather, for we lay by a couple of days, in one place, to let the horses rest. We could really have accomplished the journey in ten days if we had towed the horses behind the wagon, but we did not think of that until it was too late, and so went on shoving the horses and the wagon too when we might have saved half the labor. Parties who met us, occasionally, advised us to put the horses in the wagon, but Mr. Ballou, through whose iron-clad earnestness no sarcasm could pierce, said that that would not do, because the provisions were exposed and would suffer, the horses being "bituminous from long deprivation." The reader will excuse me from translating. What Mr. Ballou customarily meant, when he used a long word, was a secret between himself and his Maker. He was one of the best and kindest-hearted men that ever graced a humble sphere of life. He was gentleness and simplicity itself—and unselfishness, too. Although he was more than twice as old as the eldest of us, he never gave himself any airs, privileges, or exemptions on that account. He did a young man's share of the work; and did his share of conversing and entertaining from the general standpoint of any age—not from the arrogant, overawing summit-height of sixty years. His one striking peculiarity was his Partingtonian fashion of loving and using big words for their own sakes, and independent of any bearing they might have upon the thought he was purposing to convey. He always let his ponderous syllables fall with an easy unconsciousness that left them wholly without offensiveness. In truth, his air was so natural and so simple that one was always catching himself accepting his stately sentences as meaning something, when they really meant nothing in the world. If a word was long and grand and resonant, that was sufficient to win the old man's love, and he would drop that word into the most out-of-the-way place in a sentence or a subject, and be as pleased with it as if it were perfectly luminous with meaning.

We four always spread our common stock of blankets together on the frozen ground, and slept side by side; and finding that our foolish, long-legged hound pup had a deal of animal heat in him, Oliphant got to admitting him to the bed, between himself and Mr. Ballou, hugging the dog's warm back to his breast and finding great comfort in it. But in the night the pup would get stretchy and brace his feet against the old man's back and shove, grunting complacently the while; and now and then, being warm and snug, grateful and happy, he would paw the old man's back simply in excess of comfort; and at yet other times he would dream of the chase and in his sleep tug at the old man's back hair and bark in his ear. The old gentleman complained mildly about these familiarities, at last, and when he got through with his statement he said that such a dog as that was not a proper animal to admit to bed with tired men, because he was "so meretricious in his movements and so organic in his emotions." We turned the dog out.

It was a hard, wearing, toilsome journey, but it had its bright side; for after each day was done and our wolfish hunger appeased with a hot supper of fried bacon, bread, molasses, and black coffee, the pipe-smoking, song-singing, and yarn-spinning around the evening camp-fire in the still solitudes of the desert was a happy, care-free sort of recreation that seemed the very summit and culmination of earthly luxury. It is a kind of life that has a potent charm for all men, whether city or country bred. We are descended from desert-lounging Arabs, and countless ages of growth toward perfect civilization have failed to root out of us the nomadic instinct. We all confess to a gratified thrill at the thought of "camping out."

Once we made twenty-five miles in a day, and once we made forty miles (through the Great American Desert), and ten miles beyond—fifty in all—in twenty-three hours, without halting to eat, drink, or rest. To stretch out and go to sleep, even on stony and frozen ground, after pushing a wagon and two horses fifty miles, is a delight so supreme that for the moment it almost seems cheap at the price.

We camped two days in the neighborhood of the "Sink of the Humboldt." We tried to use the strong alkaline water of the Sink, but it would not answer. It was like drinking lye, and not weak lye, either. It left a taste in the mouth, bitter and every way execrable, and a burning in the stomach that was very uncomfortable. We put molasses in it, but that helped it very little; we added a pickle, yet the alkali was the prominent taste, and so it was unfit for drinking. That coffee we made of this water was the meanest compound man has yet invented. It was really viler to the taste than the unameliorated water itself. Mr. Ballou, being the architect and builder of the beverage, felt constrained to indorse and uphold it, and so drank half a cup, by little sips, making shift to praise it faintly the while, but finally threw out the remainder, and said frankly it was "too technical for him."

But presently we found a spring of fresh water, convenient, and then, with nothing to mar our enjoyment, and no stragglers to interrupt it, we entered into our rest.

Chapter XXVIII

After leaving the Sink, we traveled along the Humboldt River a little way. People accustomed to the monster mile-wide Mississippi, grow accustomed to associating the term "river" with a high degree of watery grandeur. Consequently, such people feel rather disappointed when they stand on the shores of the Humboldt or the Carson and find that a "river" in Nevada is a sickly rivulet which is just the counterpart of the Erie canal in all respects save that the canal is twice as long and four times as deep. One of the pleasantest and most invigorating exercises one can contrive is to run and jump across the Humboldt River till he is overheated, and then drink it dry.

On the fifteenth day we completed our march of two hundred miles and entered Unionville, Humboldt County, in the midst of a driving snow-storm. Unionville consisted of eleven cabins and a liberty pole. Six of the cabins were strung along one side of a deep canon, and the other five faced them. The rest of the landscape was made up of bleak mountain walls that rose so high into the sky from both sides of the canon that the village was left, as it were, far down in the bottom of a crevice. It was always daylight on the mountain-tops a long time before the darkness lifted and revealed Unionville.

We built a small, rude cabin in the side of the crevice and roofed it with canvas, leaving a corner open to serve as a chimney, through which the cattle used to tumble occasionally, at night, and mash our furniture and interrupt our sleep. It was very cold weather and fuel was scarce. Indians brought brush and bushes several miles on their backs; and when we could catch a laden Indian it was well—and when we could not (which was the rule, not the exception), we shivered and bore it.

I confess, without shame, that I expected to find masses of silver lying all about the ground. I expected to see it glittering in the sun on the mountain summit. I said nothing about this, for some instinct told me that I might possibly have an exaggerated idea about it, and so if I betrayed my thought I might bring derision upon myself. Yet I was as perfectly satisfied in my own mind as I could be of anything, that I was going to gather up, in a day or two, or at furthest a week or two, silver enough to make me satisfactorily wealthy—and so my fancy was already busy with plans for spending this money. The first opportunity that offered, I sauntered carelessly away from the cabin, keeping an eye on the other boys, and stopping and contemplating the sky, when they seemed to be observing me; but as soon as the coast was manifestly clear, I fled away as guiltily as a thief might have done and never halted till I was far beyond sight and call. Then I began my search with a feverish excitement that was brimful of expectation—almost of certainty. I crawled about the ground, seizing and examining bits of stone, blowing the dust from them or rubbing them on my clothes, and then peering at them with anxious hope. Presently I found a bright fragment and my heart bounded! I hid behind a boulder and polished it and scrutinized it with a nervous eagerness and a delight that was more pronounced than absolute certainty itself could have afforded. The more I examined the fragment the more I was convinced that I had found the door to fortune. I marked the spot and carried away my specimen. Up and down the rugged mountainside I searched, with always increasing interest and always augmenting gratitude that I had come to Humboldt and come in time. Of all the experiences of my life, this secret search among the hidden treasures of silver-land was the nearest to unmarred ecstasy. It was a delirious revel. By and by, in the bed of a shallow rivulet, I found a deposit of shining yellow scales, and my breath almost forsook me! A gold-mine, and in my simplicity I had been content with vulgar silver! I was so excited that I half believed my overwrought imagination was deceiving me. Then a fear came upon me that people might be observing me and would guess my secret. Moved by this thought, I made a circuit of the place, and ascended a knoll to reconnoiter. Solitude. No creature was near. Then I returned to my mine, fortifying myself against possible disappointment, but my fears were groundless—the shining scales were still there. I set about scooping them out, and for an hour I toiled down the windings of the stream and robbed its bed. But at last the descending sun warned me to give up the quest, and I turned homeward laden with wealth. As I walked along I could not help smiling at the thought of my being so excited over my fragment of silver when a nobler metal was almost under my nose. In this little time the former had so fallen in my estimation that once or twice I was on the point of throwing it away.

The boys were as hungry as usual, but I could eat nothing. Neither could I talk. I was full of dreams and far away. Their conversation interrupted the flow of my fancy somewhat, and annoyed me a little, too. I despised the sordid and commonplace things they talked about. But as they proceeded, it began to arouse me. It grew to be rare fun to hear them planning their poor little economies and sighing over possible privations and distresses when a gold-mine, all our own, lay within sight of the cabin, and I could point it out at any moment. Smothered hilarity began to oppress me, presently. It was hard to resist the impulse to burst out with exultation and reveal everything; but I did resist. I said within myself that I would filter the great news through my lips calmly and be serene as a summer morning while I watched its effect in their faces. I said:

"Where have you all been?"

"Prospecting."

"What did you find?"

"Nothing."

"Nothing? What do you think of the country?"

"Can't tell, yet," said Mr. Ballou, who was an old gold-miner, and had likewise had considerable experience among the silver-mines.

"Well, haven't you formed any sort of opinion?"

"Yes, a sort of a one. It's fair enough here, maybe, but overrated. Seven-thousand-dollar ledges are scarce, though. That Sheba may be rich enough, but we don't own it; and, besides, the rock is so full of base metals that all the science in the world can't work it. We'll not starve, here, but we'll not get rich, I'm afraid."

"So you think the prospect is pretty poor?"

"No name for it!"

"Well, we'd better go back, hadn't we?"

"Oh, not yet—of course not. We'll try it a riffle, first."

"Suppose, now—this is merely a supposition, You know—suppose you could find a ledge that would yield, say, a hundred and fifty dollars a ton—would that satisfy You?"

"Try us once!" from the whole party.

"Or suppose—merely a supposition, of course—suppose you were to find a ledge that would yield two thousand dollars a ton—would that satisfy you?"

"Here—what do you mean? What are you coming at? Is there some mystery behind all this?"

"Never mind. I am not saying anything. You know perfectly well there are no rich mines here—of course you do. Because you have been around and examined for yourselves. Anybody would know that, that had been around. But just for the sake of argument, suppose—in a kind of general way—suppose some person were to tell you that two-thousand-dollar ledges were simply contemptible—contemptible, understand—and that right yonder in sight of this very cabin there were piles of pure gold and pure silver—oceans of it—enough to make you all rich in twenty-four hours! Come!"

"I should say he was as crazy as a loon!" said old Ballou, but wild with excitement, nevertheless.

"Gentlemen," said I, "I don't say anything—I haven't been around, you know, and of course don't know anything—but all I ask of you is to cast your eye on that, for instance, and tell me what you think of it!" and I tossed my treasure before them.

There was an eager scrabble for it, and a closing of heads together over it under the candle-light. Then old Ballou said:

"Think of it? I think it is nothing but a lot of granite rubbish and nasty glittering mica that isn't worth ten cents an acre!"

So vanished my dream. So melted my wealth away. So toppled my airy castle to the earth and left me stricken and forlorn.

Moralizing, I observed, then, that "all that glitters is not gold."

Mr. Ballou said I could go further than that, and lay it up among my treasures of knowledge, that nothing that glitters is gold. So I learned then, once for all, that gold in its native state is but dull, unornamental stuff, and that only low-born metals excite the admiration of the ignorant with an ostentatious glitter. However, like the rest of the world, I still go on underrating men of gold and glorifying men of mica. Commonplace human nature cannot rise above that.

SOURCE: Twain, Mark (Samuel L. Clemens). *Roughing It.* Hartford, Conn.: American Publishing Co., 1872.

ACCOUNT OF THE BATTLE AT LITTLE BIGHORN
(Recalled in 1898 by Two Moon)

Cheyenne Chief Two Moon gave this moving account of the Battle of Little Bighorn to respected writer and Indian sympathizer Hamlin Garland in 1898. In the interview, Two Moon described his experience of the bloody battle on June 25, 1876. Two Moon's people, who had barely escaped the Sand Creek Massacre of 1864, had joined with the Sioux and left their reservations for their annual buffalo hunt in the fall of 1875. Because this exodus violated the terms of their treaties, General Philip H. Sheridan ordered Colonel George A. Custer to capture or disperse the Native American hunting on the upper Yellowstone River. Twelve companies of the U.S. Army Seventh Cavalry moved in and surprised the tribes who were camping and preparing for a great feast. Two Moon's account of the famed battle, which yielded Custer's last stand, makes clear that the Native Americans were fighting a defensive battle. He related the horrifying story of the great battle with stoicism and great dignity, suggesting that war between the Cheyenne, the Sioux, and the White man was an inevitable result of the Great Spirit's lust for human bloodshed. Many accounts exist of the battle in which Custer's men were surrounded and annihilated, but this is one of the few that gives a clear account of the Native American's motivations and experience.

Leah R. Shafer,
Cornell University

***See also* Cheyenne; Indian Warfare; Little Bighorn, Battle of; Sioux; Wars with Indian Nations: Later Nineteenth Century (1840–1900).**

As we topped the low, pine-clad ridge and looked into the hot, dry valley, Wolf Voice, my Cheyenne interpreter, pointed at a little log cabin, toward the green line of alders wherein the Rosebud ran, and said:

"His house—Two Moon."

As we drew near we came to a puzzling fork in the road. The left branch skirted a corner of a wire fence, the right turned into a field. We started to the left, but the waving of a blanket in the hands of a man at the cabin door directed us to the right. As we drew nearer we perceived Two Moon spreading blankets in the scant shade of his low cabin. Some young Cheyennes were grinding a sickle. A couple of children were playing about the little log stables. The barn-yard and buildings were like those of a white settler on the new and arid sod. It was all barren and unlovely—the home of poverty.

As we dismounted at the door Two Moon came out to meet us with hand outstretched. "How?" he said, with the heartiest, long-drawn note of welcome. He motioned us to be seated on the blankets which he had spread for us upon seeing our approach. Nothing could exceed the dignity and sincerity of his greeting.

As we took seats he brought out tobacco and a pipe. He was a tall old man, of a fine, clear brown complexion, big-chested, erect, and martial of bearing. His smiling face was broadly benignant, and his manners were courteous and manly.

While he cut his tobacco Wolf Voice interpreted my wishes to him. I said, "Two Moon, I have come to hear your story of the Custer battle, for they tell me you were a chief there. After you tell me the story, I want to take some photographs of you. I want you to signal with a blanket as the great chiefs used to do in fight."

Wolf Voice made this known to him, delivering also a message from the agents, and at every pause Two Moon uttered deep voiced notes of comprehension. "Ai," "A-ah," "Hoh,"—these sounds are commonly called "grunts," but they were low, long-drawn expulsions of breath, very expressive.

Then a long silence intervened. The old man mused. It required time to go from the silence of the hot valley, the shadow of his little cabin, and the wire fence of his pasture, back to the days of his youth. When he began to speak, it was with great deliberation. His face became each moment graver and his eyes more introspective.

"Two Moon does not like to talk about the days of fighting; but since you are to make a book, and the agent says you are a friend to Grinnell I will tell you about it—the truth. It is now a long time ago, and my words do not come quickly.

"That spring [1876] I was camped on Powder River with fifty lodges of my people—Cheyennes. The place is near what is now Fort McKenney. One morning soldiers charged my camp. They were in command of Three Fingers [Colonel McKenzie]. We were surprised and scattered, leaving our ponies. The soldiers ran all our horses off. That night the soldiers slept, leaving the horses one side; so we crept up and stole them back again, and then we went away.

"We traveled far, and one day we met a big camp of Sioux at Charcoal Butte. We camped with the Sioux, and had a good time, plenty grass, plenty game, good water.

Crazy Horse was head chief of the camp. Sitting Bull was camped a little ways below, on the Little Missouri River.

"Crazy Horse said to me, 'I'm glad you are come. We are going to fight the white man again.' The camp was already full of wounded men, women, and children.

"I said to Crazy Horse, 'All right. I am ready to fight. I have fought already. My people have been killed, my horses stolen; I am satisfied to fight.'"

Here the old man paused a moment, and his face took on a lofty and somber expression.

"I believed at that time the Great Spirits had made Sioux, put them there,"—he drew a circle to the right—"and white men and Cheyennes here,"—indicating two places to the left—"expecting them to fight. The Great Spirits I thought liked to see the fight; it was to them all the same like playing. So I thought then about fighting." As he said this, he made me feel for one moment the power of a sardonic god whose drama was the wars of men.

"About May, when the grass was tall and the horses strong, we broke camp and started across the country to the mouth of the Tongue River. Then Sitting Bull and Crazy Horse and all went up the Rosebud. There we had a big fight with General Crook, and whipped him. Many soldiers were killed—few Indians. It was a great fight, much smoke and dust.

"From there we all went over the divide, and camped in the valley of Little Horn. Everybody thought, 'Now we are out of the white man's country. He can live there, we will live here.' After a few days, one morning when I was in camp north of Sitting Bull, a Sioux messenger rode up and said, 'Let everybody paint up, cook, and get ready for a big dance.'

"Cheyennes then went to work to cook, cut up tobacco, and get ready. We all thought to dance all day. We were very glad to think we were far away from the white man.

"I went to water my horses at the creek, and washed them off with cool water, then took a swim myself. I came back to the camp afoot. When I got near my lodge, I looked up the Little Horn towards Sitting Bull's camp. I saw a great dust rising. It looked like a whirlwind. Soon Sioux horseman came rushing into camp shouting: 'Soldiers come! Plenty white soldiers.'

"I ran into my lodge, and said to my brother-in-law, 'Get your horses; the white man is coming. Everybody run for horses.'

"Outside, far up the valley, I heard a battle cry, Hay-ay, hay-ay! I heard shooting, too, this way [clapping his hands very fast]. I couldn't see any Indians. Everybody was getting horses and saddles. After I had caught my horse, a Sioux warrior came again and said, 'Many soldiers are coming.'

"Then he said to the women, 'Get out of the way, we are going to have hard fight.'

"I said, 'All right, I am ready.'

"I got on my horse, and rode out into my camp. I called out to the people all running about: 'I am Two Moon, your chief. Don't run away. Stay here and fight. You must stay and fight the white soldiers. I shall stay even if I am to be killed.'

"I rode swiftly toward Sitting Bull's camp. There I saw the white soldiers fighting in a line [Reno's men]. Indians covered the flat. They began to drive the soldiers all mixed up—Sioux, then soldiers, then more Sioux, and all shooting. The air was full of smoke and dust. I saw the soldiers fall back and drop into the river-bed like buffalo fleeing. They had no time to look for a crossing. The Sioux chased them up the hill, where they met more soldiers in wagons, and then messengers came saying more soldiers were going to kill the women, and the Sioux turned back. Chief Gall was there fighting, Crazy Horse also.

"I then rode toward my camp, and stopped squaws from carrying off lodges. While I was sitting on my horse I saw flags come up over the hill to the east like that [he raised his finger-tips]. Then the soldiers rose all at once, all on horses, like this [he put his fingers behind each other to indicate that Custer appeared marching in columns of fours]. They formed into three bunches [squadrons] with a little ways between. Then a bugle sounded, and they all got off horses, and some soldiers led the horses back over the hill.

"Then the Sioux rode up the ridge on all sides, riding very fast. The Cheyennes went up the left way. Then the shooting was quick, quick. Pop—pop—pop very fast. Some of the soldiers were down on their knees, some standing. Officers all in front. The smoke was like a great cloud, and everywhere the Sioux went the dust rose like smoke. We circled all round him—swirling like water round a stone. We shoot, we ride fast, we shoot again. Soldiers drop, and horses fall on them. Soldiers in line drop, but one man rides up and down the line—all the time shouting. He rode a sorrel horse with white face and white fore-legs. I don't know who he was. He was a brave man.

"Indians keep swirling round and round, and the soldiers killed only a few. Many soldiers fell. At last all horses killed but five. Once in a while some man would break out and run toward the river, but he would fall. At last about a hundred men and five horsemen stood on the hill all bunched together. All along the bugler kept blowing his commands. He was very brave too. Then a chief was killed. I hear it was Long Hair [Custer], I don't know; and then five horsemen and the bunch of men, may be so forty, started toward the river. The man on the sorrel horse led them, shouting all the time. He wore a buckskin shirt, and had long black hair and mustache. He fought hard with a big knife. His men were all covered with white dust. I couldn't tell whether they were officers or not. One man all alone ran far down toward the river, then round up over the hill. I thought he was going to escape, but a Sioux fired and hit him in the head. He was the last man. He wore braid on his arms [sergeant].

"All the soldiers were now killed, and the bodies were stripped. After that no one could tell which were officers. The bodies were left where they fell. We had no dance that night. We were sorrowful.

"Next day four Sioux chiefs and two Cheyennes and I, Two Moon, went upon the battlefield to count the dead. One man carried a little bundle of sticks. When we came to dead men, we took a little stick and gave it to another man, so we counted the dead. There were 388. There were thirty-nine Sioux and seven Cheyennes killed, and about a hundred wounded.

"Some white soldiers were cut with knives, to make sure they were dead; and the war women had mangled some. Most of them were left just where they fell. We came to the man with big mustache; he lay down the hills toward the river. The Indians did not take his buckskin shirt. The Sioux said, 'That is a big chief. That is Long Hair.' I don't know. I had never seen him. The man on the white-faced horse was the bravest man.

"That day as the sun was getting low our young men came up the Little Horn riding hard. Many white soldiers were coming in a big boat, and when we looked we could see the smoke rising. I called my people together, and we hurried up the Little Horn, into Rotten Grass Valley. We camped there three days, and then rode swiftly back over our old trail to the east. Sitting Bull went back into the Rosebud and down the Yellowstone, and away to the north. I did not see him again.

The old man paused and filled his pipe. His story was done. His mind came back to his poor people on the barren land where the rain seldom falls.

"That was a long time ago. I am now old, and my mind has changed. I would rather see my people living in houses and singing and dancing. You have talked with me about fighting, and I have told you of the time long ago. All that is past. I think of these things now: First, that our reservation shall be fenced and the white settlers kept out and our young men kept in. Then there will be no trouble. Second, I want to see my people raising cattle and making butter. Last, I want to see my people going to school to learn the white man's way. That is all."

There was something placid and powerful in the lines of the chief's broad brow, and his gestures were dramatic and noble in sweep. His extended arm, his musing eyes, his deep voice combined to express a meditative solemnity profoundly impressive. There was no anger in his voice, and no reminiscent ferocity. All that was strong and fine and distinctive in the Cheyenne character came out in the old man's talk. He seemed the leader and the thoughtful man he really is—patient under injustice, courteous even to his enemies.

EXCERPT FROM *HALF A CENTURY*
(1880, by Jane Swisshelm)

Reformer, suffragette and editor Jane Grey Cannon Swisshelm (1815–1884) was born to Scots-Irish covenanters in Pittsburgh, Pennsylvania. Her prodigious talents were apparent from a young age: she took over the local school before her fifteenth birthday. In 1847, she established the *Pittsburgh Saturday Visiter* (sic), the first of her three weekly political and literary papers advocating suffrage, temperance, and abolition. Her views were incendiary and her bold tongue full of racy arguments. Critics attacked her in each of her endeavors. While living in Minnesota, she founded the *Saint Cloud Visitor* and, after critics condemned it, the *Saint Cloud Democrat,* which she referred to here as the *Democrat.* After several years of government service, during which time she became a close friend of Mrs. Abraham Lincoln, Swisshelm retired and began work on her autobiography. Published in 1880, this was *Half a Century.* In this selection, she detailed the productive working relationships made possible by pioneers' associations with the native peoples.

Leah R. Shafer,
Cornell University

***See also* Frontier.**

CHAPTER XLIII.

Frontier Life

The culture which the pale faces introduced into that land of the Dakotas was sometimes curious. The first sermon I heard there was preached in Rockville—a town-site on the Sauk, twelve miles from its confluence with the Mississippi—in a store-room of which the roof was not yet shingled. The only table in the town served as a pulpit; the red blankets from one wagon are converted into cushions for the front pews, which consisted of rough boards laid on trussles. There was only one hymn book, and after reading the hymn, the preacher tendered the book to any one who would lead the singing, but no one volunteered. My scruples about psalms seemed to vanish, so I went forward, took the book, lined out the hymn, and started a tune, which was readily taken up and sung by all present. We were well satisfied with what the day brought us, as we rode home past those wonderful granite rocks which spring up out of the prairie, looking like old hay-ricks in a meadow.

There were people in our frontier town who would have graced any society, and with the elasticity of true culture adapted themselves to all circumstances. At my residence, which adjoined the Democrat office, I held fortnightly receptions, at which dancing was the amusement, and coffee and sandwiches the refreshments. At one of these, I had the honor to entertain Gov. Ramsey, Lieut.-Gov. Donnelly, State Treas. Shaeffer, and a large delegation from St. Paul; but not having plates for seventy people, I substituted squares of white printing paper. When Gov. Ramsey received his, he turned it over, and said:

"What am I to do with this?"

"That is the ticket you are to vote," was the answer.

In our social life there was often a weird mingling of civilization and barbarism. Upon one occasion, a concert was given, in which the audience were in full dress, and all evening in the principal streets of St. Cloud a lot of Chippewas played foot-ball with the heads of some Sioux, with whom they had been at war that day.

In those days, brains and culture were found in shanties. The leaders of progress did not shrink from association with the rule forces of savages and mother nature.

St. Cloud was the advance post of that march of civilization by which the Northern Pacific railroad has since sought to reach the Sascatchewan, a territory yet to be made into five wheat-growing States as large as Illinois. All the Hudson Bay goods from Europe passed our doors, in wagons or on sleds, under the care of the Burbanks, the great mail carriers and express men of Minnesota, and once they brought a young lady who had come by express from Glasgow, Scotland, and been placed under the charge of their agent at New York, and whom they handed over to the officer she had come to marry on the shores of Hudson Bay. But their teams usually came east with little freight, as the furs sent to Europe came down in carts, not one of which had so much iron as a nail in them, and which came in long, creaking trains, drawn by oxen or Indian ponies.

In each train there was generally one gorgeous equipage—a cart painted blue, with a canvas cover, drawn by one large white ox in raw-hide harness. In this coach of state rode the lady of the train—who was generally a half-breed—on her way to do her shopping in St. Paul. Once the lady was a full-blooded Indian, and had her baby with her, neatly dressed and strapped to a board. A bandage across the forehead held the head in place, and every portion of the body was as secure as board and bandages could make them, except the arms from the elbow down, but no danger of the little fellow sucking his thumb. His lady mamma did not have to hold him, for he was stood up in a corner like a cane or umbrella, and seemed quite comfortable as well as content. She had traveled seven weeks, had come seventeen hundred miles to purchase some dresses and trinkets, and would no doubt be a profitable customer to St. Paul merchants, for the lady of the train was a person of wealth and authority, always the wife of the commander-in-chief, and her sentence of death might have been fatal to any man in it.

In these trains were always found Indians filling positions as useful laborers, for the English government never gave premiums for idleness and vagabondism among Indians, by feeding and clothing them without effort on their own part. Their dexterity in turning griddle cakes, by shaking the pan and giving it a jerk which sent the cake up into the air and brought it down square into the pan other side up, would have made Biddy's head whirl to see.

The "Gov. Ramsey" was the first steamboat which ran above the falls of St. Anthony, and in the spring of '59 she was steamed and hawsered up the Sauk Rapids, and ran two hundred miles, until the falls of Pokegamy offered insurmountable barriers to further progress. It was thought impossible to get her down again, there was no business for her, and she lay useless until, the next winter, Anson Northup took out her machinery and drew it across on sleds to the Red River of the North, where it was built into the first steamboat which ever ran on that river.

Before starting on his expedition, Mr. Northup came to the Democrat office to leave an advertisement and ask me to appeal to the public for aid in provisions and feed to be furnished along the route. He was in a Buffalo suit, from his ears to his feet, and looked like a bale of furs. On his head he wore a fox skin cap with the nose lying on the two paws of the animal just between his eyes, the tail hanging down between his shoulders. He was a brave, strong man, and carried out his project, which to most people was wild.

Nothing seemed more important than the cultivation of health for the people, and to this I gave much earnest attention, often expressed in the form of badinage. There were so many young housekeepers that there was much need of teachers. I tried to get the New England women to stop feeding their families on dough—especially hot soda dough—and to substitute well-baked bread as a steady article of diet. In trying to wean them from cake, I told of a time when chaos reigned on earth, long before the days of the mastodons, but even then, New England women were up making cake, and would certainly be found at that business when the last trump sounded. But they bore with my "crotches" very patiently, and even seemed to enjoy them.

SOURCE: Swisshelm, Jane Grey Cannon. *Half a Century.* 2d ed. Chicago: Jansen, McClurg, 1880.

EXCERPT FROM *A CENTURY OF DISHONOR* *(1881, by Helen Hunt Jackson)*

A New Englander by birth, poet and writer Helen Hunt Jackson (1830–1885) was an outspoken and eloquent champion of Native American rights. She was moved to research and publicize the plight of the Native American after hearing Chief Standing Bear of the Poncas tribe speak in Boston about the great sufferings of his people as they were forcibly removed from their native land to a reservation in Oklahoma. Jackson's book, *A Century of Dishonor,* documents the United States government's abuse of treaty rights, their rejection of Indian tribal sovereignty, and details much of the horrific violence committed by white settlers against the native population. In the introduction to her book, a copy of which she sent to every member of Congress, Jackson urged the legislative body to "redeem the name of the United States from the stain of a Century of Dishonor." The book focuses on the history of seven tribes: the Cheyennes, Cherokees, Delawares, Nez Perces, Poncas, Sioux, and Winnebagos. The selection provided here details the sufferings of the Northern Cheyenne as they attempted to hunt on their native land without permission from their Indian Agent. In 1882, President Chester A. Arthur appointed Jackson a commissioner of Indian affairs, but her report about the extreme poverty and deprivation of California's Mission Indians was largely ignored.

Leah R. Shafer,
Cornell University

***See also Century of Dishonor;* Cheyenne; Indian Policy, U.S.: 1830–1900; Indian Removal.**

The winter of 1877 and summer of 1878 were terrible seasons for the Cheyennes. Their fall hunt had proved unsuccessful. Indians from other reservations had hunted the ground over before them, and driven the buffalo off; and the Cheyennes made their way home again in straggling parties, destitute and hungry. Their agent reports that the result of this hunt has clearly proved that "in the future the Indian must rely on tilling the ground as the principal means of support; and if this conviction can be firmly established, the greatest obstacle to advancement in agriculture will be overcome. With the buffalo gone, and their pony herds being constantly decimated by the inroads of horse-thieves, they must soon adopt, in all its varieties, the way of the white man."

The ration allowed to these Indians is reported as being "reduced and insufficient," and the small sums they have been able to earn by selling buffalo-hides are said to have been "of material assistance" to them in "supplementing" this ration. But in this year there have been sold only $657 worth of skins by the Cheyennes and Arapahoes together. In 1876 they sold $17,600 worth. Here is a failing off enough to cause very great suffering in a little community of five thousand people. But this was only the beginning of their troubles. The summer proved one of unusual heat. Extreme heat, chills and fever, and "a reduced and insufficient ration," all combined, resulted in an amount of sickness heart-rending to read of. "It is no exaggerated estimate," says the agent, "to place the number of sick people on the reservation at two thousand. Many deaths occurred which might have been obviated had there been a proper supply of antimalarial remedies at hand. Hundreds applying for treatment have been refused medicine."

The Northern Cheyennes grew more and more restless and unhappy. "In council and elsewhere they profess an intense desire to be sent North, where they say they will settle down as the others have done," says the report; adding, with an obtuseness which is inexplicable, that "no difference has been made in the treatment of the Indians," but that the "compliance" of these Northern Cheyennes has been "of an entirely different nature from that of the other Indians," and that it may be "necessary in the future to compel what so far we have been unable to effect by kindness and appeal to their better natures."

If it is "an appeal to men's better natures" to remove them by force from a healthful Northern climate, which they love and thrive in, to a malarial Southern one, where they are struck down by chills and fever—refuse them medicine which can combat chills and fever, and finally starve them—there indeed, might be said to have been most forcible appeals made to the "better natures" of these Northern Cheyennes. What might have been predicted followed.

Early in the autumn, after this terrible summer, a band of some three hundred of these Northern Cheyennes took the desperate step of running off and attempting to make their way back to Dakota. They were pursued, fought desperately, but were finally overpowered, and surrendered. They surrendered, however, only on the condition that they should be taken to Dakota. They were unanimous in declaring that they would rather die than go back to the Indian Territory. This was nothing more, in fact, than saying that they would rather die by bullets than of chills and fever and starvation.

These Indians were taken to Fort Robinson, Nebraska. Here they were confined as prisoners of war, and held subject to the orders of the Department of the Interior. The department was informed of the Indians' determination never to be taken back alive to Indian Territory. The army officers in charge reiterated these statements, and implored the department to permit them to remain at the North; but it was of no avail. Orders came—explicit, repeated, finally stern—insisting on the return of these Indians to their agency. The commanding officer at Fort Robinson has been censured severely for the course he pursued in his effort to carry out those orders. It is difficult to see what else he could have done, except to have resigned his post. He could not take three hundred Indians by sheer brute force and carry them hundreds of miles, especially when they were so desperate that they had broken up the iron stoves in their quarters, and wrought and twisted them into weapons with which to resist. He thought perhaps he could starve them into submission. He stopped the issue of food; he also stopped the issue of fuel to them. It was midwinter; the mercury froze in that month at Fort Robinson. At the end of two days he asked the Indians to let their women and children come out that he might feed them. Not a woman would come out. On the night of the fourth day—or, according to some accounts, the sixth—these starving, freezing Indians broke prison, overpowered the guards, and fled, carrying their women and children with them. They held the pursuing troops at bay for several days; finally made a last stand in a deep ravine, and were shot down—men, women, and children together. Out of the whole band there were left alive some fifty women and children and seven men, who, having been confined in another part of the fort, had not had the good fortune to share in this outbreak and meet their death in the ravine. These, with their wives and children, were sent to Fort Leavenworth to be put in prison; the men to be tried for murders committed in their skirmishes in Kansas on their way to the north. Red Cloud, a Sioux chief, came to Fort Robinson immediately after this massacre and entreated to be allowed to take the Cheyenne widows and orphans into his tribe to be cared for. The Government, therefore, kindly permitted twenty-two Cheyenne widows and thirty-two Cheyenne children—many of them orphans—to be received into the band of the Ogallalla Sioux.

An attempt was made by the Commissioner of Indian Affairs, in his Report for 1879, to show by tables and figures that these Indians were not starving at the time of their flight from Indian Territory. The attempt only redounded to his own disgrace; it being proved, by the testimony given by a former clerk of the Indian Bureau before the Senate committee appointed to investigate the case of the Northern Cheyennes, that the commissioner had been guilty of absolute dishonesty in his estimates, and that the quantity of beef actually issued to the Cheyenne Agency was hundreds of pounds less than he had reported it, and that the Indians were actually, as they had claimed, "starving."

The testimony given before this committee by some of the Cheyenne prisoners themselves is heart-rending. One must have a callous heart who can read it unmoved.

When asked by Senator [John T.] Morgan [of Alabama], "Did you ever really suffer from hunger?" one of the chiefs replied. "We were always hungry; we never had enough. When they that were sick once in awhile felt as though they could eat something, we had nothing to give them."

"Did you not go out on the plains sometimes and hunt buffalo, with the consent of the agent?"

"We went out on a buffalo-hunt, and nearly starved while out; we could not find any buffalo hardly; we could hardly get back with our ponies; we had to kill a good many of our ponies to eat, to save ourselves from starving."

"How many children got sick and died?"

"Between the fall of 1877 and 1878 we lost fifty children. A great many of our finest young men died, as well as many women."

"Old Crow," a chief who served faithfully as Indian scout and ally under General [George] Crook [commander of Far Western troops since 1868] for years, said: "I did not feel like doing anything for awhile, because I had no heart. I did not want to be in this country. I was all the time wanting to get back to the better country where I was born, and where my children are buried, and where my mother and sister yet live. So I have laid in my lodge most of the time with nothing to think about but that, and the affair up north at Fort Robinson, and my relatives and friends who were killed there. But now I feel as though, if I had a wagon and a horse or two, and some land, I would try to work. If I had something, so that I could do something, I might not think so much about these other things. As it is now, I feel as though I would just as soon be asleep with the rest."

The wife of one of the chiefs confined at Fort Leavenworth testified before the committee as follows: "The main thing I complained of was that we didn't get enough to eat; my children nearly starved to death; then sickness came, and there was nothing good for them to eat; for a long time the most they had to eat was cornmeal and salt. Three or four children died every day for awhile, and that frightened us."

When asked if there were anything she would like to say to the committee, the poor woman replied: "I wish you would do what you can to get my husband released. I am very poor here, and do not know what is to become of me. If he were released he would come down here, and we would live together quietly, and do no harm to anybody, and make no trouble. But I should never get over my desire to get back north; I should always want to get back where my children were born, and died, and were buried. That country is better than this in every respect. There is plenty of good, cool water there—pure water—while here the water is not good. It is not hot there, nor so sickly. Are you going where my husband is? Can you tell when he is likely to be released?"...

It is stated also that there was not sufficient clothing to furnish each Indian with a warm suit of clothing, "as promised by the treaty," and that, "by reference to official correspondence, the fact is established that the Cheyennes and Arapahoes are judged as having no legal rights to any lands, having forfeited their treaty reservation by a failure to settle thereon," and their "present reservation not having been, as yet, confirmed by Congress. Inasmuch as the Indians fully understood, and were assured that this reservation was given to them in lieu of their treaty reservation, and have commenced farming in the belief that there was no uncertainty about the matter it is but common justice that definite action be had at an early day, securing to them what is their right."

It would seem that there could be found nowhere in the melancholy record of the experiences of our Indians a more glaring instance of confused multiplication of injustices than this. The Cheyennes were pursued and slain for venturing to leave this very reservation, which, it appears, is not their reservation at all, and they have no legal right to it. Are there any words to fitly characterize such treatment as this from a great, powerful, rich nation, to a handful of helpless people?

SOURCE: Jackson, Helen Hunt. *A Century of Dishonor; A Sketch of the United States Government's Dealings with Some of the Indian Tribes.* 2d ed. enlarged by addition of report of the needs of the mission Indians of California. Boston: Roberts Brothers, 1888.

A LETTER FROM WOVOKA
(1890)

Wovoka (c. 1856–1932) was a Native American mystic and the father of the Ghost Dance Religion. A member of the Paiutes tribe, Wovoka grew up in the company of white settlers in Nevada. The years he spent working on the ranch of David Wilson earned him the nickname "Jack Wilson," which is how he refers to himself in this selection. At some point in 1889—perhaps during an eclipse of the sun—Wovoka had a spiritual experience that led him to create the mystical Ghost Dance religion.

Wovoka believed that the time of reckoning was nigh and that his people would experience a transformation into bliss early in 1891. Emissaries from the Paiutes carried his message west via a series of letters, including the one selected here. Though the ecstatic religion fell out of popularity soon after the transcendence failed to be achieved, Wovoka's letters were collected and reproduced by ethnologist James Mooney.

Leah R. Shafer,
Cornell University

***See also* Ghost Dance; Indian Dance; Indian Religious Life; Nativist Movements (American Indian Revival Movements); Sioux.**

When you get home you must make a dance to continue five days. Dance four successive nights, and the last night keep up the dance until the morning of the fifth day, when all must bathe in the river and then disperse to their homes. You must all do in the same way.

I, Jack Wilson, love you all, and my heart is full of gladness for the gifts you have brought me. When you get home I shall give you a good cloud [rain?] which will make you feel good. I give you a good spirit and give you all good paint. I want you to come again in three months, some from each tribe there [the Indian Territory].

There will be a good deal of snow this year and some rain. In the fall there will be such a rain as I have never given you before.

Grandfather [a universal title of reverence among Indians and here meaning the messiah] says, when your friends die you must not cry. You must not hurt anybody or do harm to anyone. You must not fight. Do right always. It will give you satisfaction in life. This young man has a good father and mother. [Possibly this refers to Casper Edson, the young Arapaho who wrote down this message of Wovoka for the delegation].

Do not tell the white people about this. Jesus is now upon the earth. He appears like a cloud. The dead are all alive again. I do not know when they will be here; maybe this fall or in the spring. When the time comes there will be no more sickness and everyone will be young again.

Do not refuse to work for the whites and do not make any trouble with them until you leave them. When the earth shakes [at the coming of the new world] do not be afraid. It will not hurt you.

I want you to dance every six weeks. Make a feast at the dance and have food that everybody may eat. Then bathe in the water. That is all. You will receive good words again from me some time. Do not tell lies.

SOURCE: Mooney, James. "A Letter from Wovoka." In *The Ghost-Dance Religion and the Sioux Outbreak of 1890.* 14th Annual Report, Pt. 2. Washington, D.C.: Bureau of American Ethnology, 1896.

WOMEN IN THE FARMERS' ALLIANCE
(1891, by Mary E. Lease)

Farmers interested in combating the railroads' economic control of the Midwestern states formed the National Farmers' Alliance in the 1880s. Speaking out against high shipping costs, outrageous tariffs, and high mortgage rates, the organization quickly garnered significant memberships in Illinois, Kansas, Nebraska, the Dakotas, and Minnesota, among other states. Women, actively involved in farm life, were also actively involved in the movement. Mary Elizabeth Lease, a struggling Kansas farmer and mother of four, was a prominent Alliance leader and speaker. An important figure in the Populist movement, Lease was engaged as an orator across the nation.

This selection is taken from a speech Lease gave in 1891 to the National Council of Women of the United States. A radical speaker—she reportedly urged farmers to "raise less corn and more hell"—Lease argued here for political solidarity in the face of corporate interests. In this speech she stressed Christian-based revolutionary thinking and urged her listeners to become actively involved in the fight against unjust tariffs and oppressive taxation.

Leah R. Shafer,
Cornell University

***See also* Farmer's Alliance.**

"Swing outward, O gates of the morning,
Swing inward, ye doors of the past;
A giant is rousing from slumber,
The people are waking at last."

Madam President, Friends, and Fellow-Citizens,—If God were to give me my choice to live in any age of the world which has flown, or in any age of the world yet to come, I would say, "O God, let me live here and now, in this day and age of the world's history." We are living in a grand and wonderful time; we are living in a day when old ideas, old traditions, and old customs have broken loose from their moorings, and are hopelessly adrift on the great shoreless, boundless sea of human thought; we are living in a time when the gray old world begins to dimly comprehend that there is no difference between the brain of an intelligent woman and the brain of an intelligent man; that there is no difference between the soul-power and the brain-power that nerved the arm of Charlotte Corday to deeds of heroism, and that which swayed old John Brown behind his barricade at Ossawatomie; we are living in a day and age when the women of industrial societies and the Alliance women have become a mighty factor in the politics of this nation; when the mighty dynamite of thought is stirring the hearts of men of this world from centre to circumference, and this thought is crystallizing into action.

Organization is becoming the key-note among the farmers of this nation. The farmers, slow to think and slow to act, are today thinking for themselves; they have been compelled to think. They have been awakened by the load of oppressive taxation, unjust tariffs, and they find themselves standing to-day on the very brink of their own despair. In all the years which have flown, the farmers, in their unswerving loyalty and patriotism to party, have been too mentally lazy to do their own thinking. They have been allowing the unprincipled demagogues of both the old political parties to do their thinking for them, and they have voted poverty and degradation not only upon themselves but upon their wives and their children.

But today these farmers, thank God! are thinking, and also their mothers, wives, and daughters, "their sisters, their cousins, and their aunts." We find, as a result of this mighty thought in the hearts of the people, a movement of the great common people of this nation, and that is the protest of the patient burden-bearers of the world against political superstition, a movement which is an echo of the life of Jesus of Nazareth, a movement that means revolution,—not a revolution such as deluged the streets of Paris with blood in 1793, but the revolution of brain and ballots that shall shake this continent and move humanity everywhere. The voice which is coming up to-day from the mystic cords of the American heart is the same voice which Lincoln heard blending with the guns of Fort Sumter. It is breaking into a clarion cry which will be heard round the world, and thrones will fall and crowns will crumble, and the divine right of kings and capital will fade away like the mists of the morning when the angel of liberty shall kindle the fires of justice in the hearts of men.

An injury to one is the concern of all. Founded upon the eternal principles of truth and right, with special privileges to none, the farmers' movement could not well exclude the patient burden-bearers of the home. And so we find them opening wide the doors of this new and mighty movement, the Farmers' Alliance, admitting women into the ranks of the organization, actually recognizing the fact that they are human beings, and treating them as such, with full privileges of membership and promotion. And the women who have borne the heat and the burden of the day were not slow to accept the newly-offered privileges, undeterred by the fact that the new organization was political, though non-partisan, and they gladly accepted the privileges extended them, until we find today upwards of half a million women in the Farmers' Alliance, who have taken up the study of social and political problems, and are studying and investigating the great issues of the day, fully cognizant of the fact that in the political arena alone can these great problems be satisfactorily settled.

You will wonder, perhaps, why the women of the West are interested so much in this great uprising of the common people, the mightiest uprising that the world has seen since Peter the Hermit led the armies of the East to rescue the tomb of the Saviour from the grasp of the infidel. I will tell you, friends: if you will refer to your old school-maps, you will find that that portion of our country now the valuable, teeming, fruitful West, was twenty-five or thirty years ago marked there as the "Great American Desert, the treeless plain." About that time the women of the East turned their faces towards the boundless, billowy prairies of the West. They accompanied their husbands, sons, and brothers; they came with the roses of health on their cheeks; they left home and friends, school and church, and all which makes life dear to you and me, and turned their faces toward the untried West, willing to brave the dangers of pioneer life upon the lonely prairies with all its privations; their children were born there, and there upon the prairies our little babes lie buried. And after all our years of sorrow, loneliness, and privation, we are being robbed of our farms, of our homes, at the rate of five hundred a week, and turned out homeless paupers, outcasts and wanderers, robbed of the best years of our life and our toil. Do you wonder that women are joining the Farmers' Alliance and the Knights of Labor? Let no one of this audience for one moment suppose that this Alliance movement is but a passing episode of a brief political career. We have come to stay, for we are advocating the principles of truth, right, and justice. Our demands are founded upon the Sermon on the Mount, and that other command, that ye love one another. We seek to put into practical operation the teachings of Christ, who was sent to bring about a better day. Then there shall be no more coal kings nor silver kings, but a better day when there shall be no more millionaires, no more paupers, and no more waifs in our streets.

A SOLDIER'S ACCOUNT OF THE SPANISH-AMERICAN WAR
(1898)

The Spanish-American War evoked much enthusiasm and patriotism across the nation, as newspaper headlines and war hawks trumpeted "Remember the Maine" in an attempt to stir up popular support for the conflict. Invoking the Monroe Doctrine, the United States claimed to desire war with Spain in Cuba in order to rid the Western Hemisphere of a decaying imperial presence, although the American impetus was really much more Machiavellian than that. The United States had to execute an amphibious landing, a task at which it was wholly inexperienced, if it were to wrest control of Cuba from the Spanish. Nonetheless, a poorly trained and inadequately outfitted expeditionary force, which included the First Volunteer Cavalry, embarked in Tampa Bay, Florida for a landing on Cuban shores near the village of Daiquirí.

The First Volunteer Cavalry, nicknamed the "Rough Riders," were a raucous band of men recruited for their shooting and riding abilities by territorial governors in the U.S. West. Colonel Theodore Roosevelt left an important Navy post in Washington, D.C. in order to serve as second in command of the First Volunteer Cavalry, instantly winning the affection and respect of his men. The Rough Riders' most famed exploit occurred at San Juan Hill, where Roosevelt recklessly led his men up a smaller rise, Kettle Hill, and chased the Spanish from their positions. Roosevelt later recalled that "San Juan was the great day of my life."

The Rough Riders' reputation spread more as a result of their swagger and Roosevelt's bumptious personality than any real military accomplishments. As the soldier's account which follows attests, their organization left much to be desired and their energy could be as much a detriment as an asset. The Spanish failed to muster much resistance in Cuba, seeking an armistice prior to an expected clash outside of Santiago.

Paul S. Bartels,
Villanova University

See also **Rough Riders; Spanish-American War.**

One lovely morning a thin, distant, and darker haze appeared off to the south. The shadows on the deck began to shift and we knew we were changing course to round Cape Maisi. We were in sight of Cuba at last!

It was a rugged coast, and in those mountains Cuban soldiers and Spanish troops were fighting. We could see some little settlements on the beaches—from one of these, perhaps, centuries ago, buccaneers had put forth in their crude cockleshells to board a Spanish galley and plunder it for silk and rum and doubloons.

Presently we approached the shore, coming close to a little dock which we later found was Daiquiri, where the Rough Riders were to land. Then, farther on and nearer to Santiago, we came to a little bend in the coastline, sheltered under a hill. This was the cove of Siboney where we were to go ashore. Above the little village and on all the hills and ridges that surrounded it were the little Spanish *fuertes*—blockhouses—that were always built in sight of each other for protection against the Cuban troops in the field. A little farther to the west, we passed the narrow entrance to the Bay of Santiago where Admiral Cervera's fleet lay at anchor. The entrance was almost indistinguishable from the green jungle that rose above it on each side. We could see the pinkish ocher of the ancient forts that guarded it. They looked like the toy forts made for children, or like picturesque defenses of the old-time barons, but Washington knew that they had modern guns as well as the olden bronze cannon. We were three miles off shore, wholly safe, and we gave the Spaniards a review in force—some fifty ships and transports in single column, while our battleships and cruisers fringed the line. Not a shot was fired; it was a demonstration.

We turned slowly back to Guantanamo, and drifted lazily along the coast with the tide, with only here and there a transport turning her engines occasionally to keep her place in the column.

Then we steamed back to the entrance to the Bay of Santiago. This time, the cruisers and battleships began the attack on the forts that guarded the bay. Our transports lay about three miles off, and we had good seats for a perfect panorama. The air was as clear as crystal.

Slowly the battleships and cruisers steamed past the entrance, perhaps two miles off; sometimes it seemed closer. Their turrets would burst into a vast billow of smoke as they scanned the hills with their fire; and occasionally they would turn one into the ancient forts that would burst forth in a blast of shattered brick and dust. We could see shells burst in the jungle. The cruisers steamed slowly from Daiquiri, past Siboney and on past the Santiago forts and into the west, bombarding as they went, and then came back again. The little Spanish blockhouse above Siboney seemed to be hit—yet later, when we landed, it was intact and without a trace of damage. For fifty miles the coast was bombarded, a maneuver to mislead the Spaniards as to where we would land.

It is doubtful if this bombardment had any effect, other than perhaps to delude the Spaniards. They had the whole coast and Cuban mountain range to retire behind—and they did.

Then we prepared to land.

We steamed back to the bight of land where a little beach stretched down from the village of Siboney. Then we drifted with the tide, waiting our turn to land. We watched the little steam launches of the Navy towing strings of ship's boats packed with soldiers and their horse-collar blanket rolls. We envied them. Great Scott, there wouldn't be any Spaniards left by the time we could get ashore! Impatiently we lined the rails and looked at these boatloads of lucky men. We could see the troops form up on shore and then lose themselves in the green that fringed the foothills of the mountains beyond.

The horses and mules were jumped overboard and swam ashore. And not a colonel or a wagon master had the power to tell a ship captain how close in to shore he should come. The transports were under charter merely, and it was the ship captain who could tell the colonel what he, the skipper, would or would not do with his ship. The horses and mules were jumped overboard from a half to a quarter mile off shore—depending upon the skipper's digestion or his judgment—and then swam. Horses by the hundred were drowned.

I have been told by some authorities that if a horse gets water in its ears the animal feels all is lost and will drown. This may have accounted for the heavy loss of horses and mules in the landing.

It was this loss of horses that left each field battery with no spares. Later, when Captain Best's battery was on San Juan and had to be withdrawn, they did not dare risk the horses up in the open on the hill. Two infantry companies were sent over to screen the withdrawal of the guns by the cannoneers. Over twenty infantrymen were casualties in three minutes, though only one artilleryman, a sergeant, was killed. Also, two generals went into the battle of San Juan on foot—an unheard-of thing for those days—and one of them reached the battle line from his headquarters riding on a cargo mule. Horses were reserved for orderlies and messengers and for the immediate staff of General Shafter. Colonel Teddy Roosevelt had a horse but left it behind when the fighting began at Kettle Hill, and fought the rest of the day on foot; but Teddy had a certain way with him.

SOURCE: Post, Charles Johnson. *The Little War of Private Post.* Boston: Little Brown, 1960.

ANTI-IMPERIALIST LEAGUE PLATFORM
(18 October 1899)

Victory in the Spanish-American War reasserted the Monroe Doctrine and established the United States' own sphere of influence in Latin America and the Caribbean. Americans viewed the war as one of liberating peoples from the yoke of Spanish tyranny, while advantageously aligning the former imperial possessions with the United States. Yet when President McKinley urged annexation of the Philippines, a heated debate broke out in America.

The Anti-Imperialist League, an amalgamation of individuals who objected to American intervention abroad for various and sundry reasons, denounced the United States' military involvement in the Philippines. General Emilio Aguinaldo assisted the Americans in defeating the Spanish, all the while hoping to gain Philippine independence once hostilities ceased. However, the possibility of having a strategically located naval base in the Pacific and easy access to the lucrative Chinese market proved irresistible to the McKinley administration.

The anti-imperialists, ranging in composition from Andrew Carnegie to Carl Schurz, feared as much for the ill effects of imperialism on American institutions and ideals as on the subject peoples. They denounced the atrocities committed by the military in the Philippines and argued for national self-determination. Yet a deep-seated racism also informed their opposition, as the anti-imperialists worried that non-white possessions would earn equal admittance into the United States. An influx of foreigners would cause domestic economic strain and give the right to vote to those whom they deemed incapable of such a responsibility. Such concerns were masked by the rhetoric of the 1899 Platform, but the preeminent concern with imperialism's degrading influence on America stands out markedly.

Paul S. Bartels,
Villanova University

See also **Anti-Imperialists; Imperialism; Philippines; Spanish-American War.**

We hold that the policy known as imperialism is hostile to liberty and tends toward militarism, an evil from which it has been our glory to be free. We regret that it has become necessary in the land of Washington and Lincoln to reaffirm that all men, of whatever race or color, are entitled to life, liberty, and the pursuit of happiness. We maintain that governments derive their just powers from the consent of the governed. We insist that the subjugation of any people is "criminal aggression" and open disloyalty to the distinctive principles of our Government.

We earnestly condemn the policy of the present National Administration in the Philippines. It seeks to extinguish the spirit of 1776 in those islands. We deplore the sacrifice of our soldiers and sailors, whose bravery deserves admiration even in an unjust war. We denounce the slaughter of the Filipinos as a needless horror. We protest against the extension of American sovereignty by Spanish methods.

We demand the immediate cessation of the war against liberty, begun by Spain and continued by us. We urge that Congress be promptly convened to announce to the Filipinos our purpose to concede to them the independence for which they have so long fought and which of right is theirs.

The United States have always protested against the doctrine of international law which permits the subjugation of the weak by the strong. A self-governing state cannot accept sovereignty over an unwilling people. The United States cannot act upon the ancient hereby that might makes right.

Imperialists assume that with the destruction of self-government in the Philippines by American hands, all opposition here will cease. This is a grievous error. Much as we abhor the war of "criminal aggression" in the Philippines, greatly as we regret that the blood of the Filipinos is on American hands, we more deeply resent the betrayal of American institutions at home. The real firing line is not in the suburbs of Manila. The foe is of our own household. The attempt of 1861 was to divide the country. That of 1899 is to destroy its fundamental principles and noblest ideals.

Whether the ruthless slaughter of the Filipinos shall end next month or next year is but an incident in a contest that must go on until the Declaration of Independence and the Constitution of the United States are rescued from the hands of their betrayers. Those who dispute about standards of value while the Republic is undermined will be listened to as little as those who would wrangle about the small economies of the household while the house is on fire. The training of a great people for a century, the aspiration for liberty of a vast immigration are forces that will hurl aside those who in the delirium of conquest seek to destroy the character of our institutions.

We deny that the obligation of all citizens to support their Government in times of grave National peril applies to the present situation. If an Administration may with impunity ignore the issues upon which it was chosen, deliberately create a condition of war anywhere on the face of the globe, debauch the civil service for spoils to promote the adventure, organize a truth-suppressing censorship and demand of all citizens a suspension of judgement and their unanimous support while it chooses to continue the fighting, representative government itself is imperiled.

We propose to contribute to the defeat of any person or party that stands for the forcible subjugation of any people. We shall oppose for reelection all who in the White House or in Congress betray American liberty in pursuit of un-American gains. We still hope that both of our great political parties will support and defend the Declaration of Independence in the closing campaign of the century.

We hold, with Abraham Lincoln, that "no man is good enough to govern another man without that man's consent. When the white man governs himself, that is self-government, but when he governs himself and also governs another man, that is more than self-government—that is despotism." "Our reliance is in the love of liberty which God has planted in us. Our defense is in the spirit which prizes liberty as the heritage of all men in all lands. Those who deny freedom to others deserve it not for themselves, and under a just God cannot long retain it."

We cordially invite the cooperation of all men and women who remain loyal to the Declaration of Independence and the Constitution of the United States.

SOURCE: "Anti-Imperialist League Platform." 1899.

GENTLEMEN'S AGREEMENT
(14 March 1907)

In 1906 the San Francisco School Board segregated the city's Japanese students into a school where Chinese students had already been segregated. Deeply insulted, Japanese diplomats lobbied President Theodore Roosevelt to intervene. Roosevelt called the San Francisco mayor and School Board to Washington and negotiated with the Japanese to restrict immigration to the United States in exchange for the desegregation of the San Francisco schools. This diplomatic understanding between the United States and Japan became known as the "Gentlemen's Agreement."

Roosevelt announced the Agreement's immigration restrictions in Executive Order 589. Mindful of the violent anti-Japanese attitudes held in San Francisco and elsewhere, Roosevelt framed his statement in the belief that cheap foreign labor undermines the prospects of native workers. Laborers from Japan (and Korea, which the United States recognized as part of Japan at that time) could no longer enter the United States and its territories.

While prohibiting the immigration of new Japanese laborers, the Gentlemen's Agreement did allow those Japanese already in the United States to bring their parents, wives, and children into the country. Many Japanese and Korean women utilized this provision to immigrate to the United States as "picture brides," marrying immigrant Japanese men they knew only through an exchange of photographs. Such marriages helped Japanese immigrants establish an equitable gender ratio in their communities. Steady birthrates and a strong tradition of familial unity meant that Japanese immigrant communities under the Agreement enjoyed a growth in population previously unmatched by other Asian immigrant groups. Still fearful of a growing "yellow menace" in its midst, the U.S. nativists effectively cut off all Japanese immigration with the Immigration Act of 1924.

Mark D. Baumann,
New York University

See also **Asian Americans; Immigration Restriction; Japanese Americans; Korean Americans; San Francisco.**

Whereas, by the act entitled "An Act to regulate the immigration of aliens into the United States," approved February 20, 1907, whenever the President is satisfied that passports issued by any foreign government to its citizens to go to any country other than the United States or to any insular possession of the United States or to the Canal Zone, are being used for the purpose of enabling the holders to come to the continental territory of the United States to the detriment of labor conditions therein, it is made the duty of the President to refuse to permit such citizens of the country issuing such passports to enter the continental territory of the United States from such country or from such insular possession or from the Canal Zone;

And Whereas, upon sufficient evidence produced before me by the Department of Commerce and Labor, I am satisfied that passports issued by the Government of Japan to citizens of that country or Korea and who are laborers, skilled or unskilled, to go to Mexico, to Canada and to Hawaii, are being used for the purpose of enabling the holders thereof to come to the continental territory of the United States to the detriment of labor conditions therein;

I hereby order that such citizens of Japan or Korea, to-wit: Japanese or Korean laborers, skilled and unskilled, who have received passports to go to Mexico, Canada or Hawaii, and come therefrom, be refused permission to enter the continental territory of the United States.

It is further ordered that the Secretary of Commerce and Labor be, and he hereby is, directed to take, thru Bureau of Immigration and Naturalization, such measures and to make and enforce such rules and regulations as may be necessary to carry this order into effect.

Theodore Roosevelt
The White House,
March 14, 1907
No. 589

SOURCE: *Report of the Commissioner General of Immigration,* 1908.

SLAVERY, CIVIL WAR, AND RECONSTRUCTION

TEXT OF THE PRO-SLAVERY ARGUMENT
(1832, by Thomas Dew)

Thomas Roderick Dew (1802–1846) was an economist, professor of law, and president of the College of William and Mary. His influential *Pro-Slavery Argument* offers theological, historical, and political evidence in a point-by-point refutation of the anti-slavery arguments of his day. Slavery was not a sin, Dew argued, but an established social institution in which God did not meddle: Jesus did not speak against slavery. Nor was slavery immoral, for Dew saw masters treat their slaves with such benevolence and fairness that the slaves responded with joyful obedience. In fact, in Dew's view, the relation between master and slave rivaled that between a parent and child. To those who saw slavery as antithetical to the spirit of democracy Dew responded that the ancient republics of Greece and Rome employed slavery to a much greater degree than the South. It was through the enslavement of Africans that all whites ascended to the same level of social attainment: "color alone here is the badge of distinction." According to Dew, threats to the security and prosperity of the South came from non-Southerners, regarded as strangers and lunatics who did not understand that love bound slaves to their masters. As with the law and other social institutions, slavery would remain the status quo for the course of its natural development—any force exerted to the contrary would result only in bloodshed and violent destruction.

Mark D. Baumann,
New York University

See also **Slavery.**

. . . 1st. It is said slavery is wrong, in the *abstract* at least, and contrary to the spirit of Christianity. To this we answer . . . that any question must be determined by its circumstances, and if, as really is the case, we cannot get rid of slavery without producing a greater injury to both the masters and slaves, there is no rule of conscience or revealed law of God which *can* condemn us. . . . if slavery had commenced even contrary to the laws of God and man, and the sin of its introduction rested upon our hands, and it was even carrying forward the nation by slow degrees to final ruin—yet if it were *certain* that an attept to remove it would only hasten and heighten the final catastrophe . . . then, we would not only not be found to attempt the extirpation, but we would stand guilty of a high offence in the sight of both God and man, if we should rashly make the effort. but the original sin of introduction rests not on our heads, and we shall soon see that all those dreadful calamities which the false prophets of our day are pointing to, will never in all probability occur. With regard to the assertion, that slavery is against the spirit of Christianity, we are ready to admit the general assertion, but deny most positively that there is any thing in the Old or New Testament, which would go to show that slavery, when once introduced, ought at all events to be abrogated, or that the master commits any offence in holding slaves. The children of Israel themselves were slave holders, and were not condemned for it. . . . When we turn to the New Testament, we find not one single passage at all calculated to disturb the conscience of an honest slave holder. No one can read it without seeing and admiring that the meek and humble Saviour of the world in no instance meddled with the established institutions of mankind—he came to save a fallen world, and not to excite the black passions of men and array them in deadly hostility against each other. From no one did he turn away; his plan was offered alike to all—to the monarch and the subject, the rich and the poor—the master and the slave. He was born in the Roman world, a world in which the most galling slavery existed, a thousand times more cruel than the slavery in our own country—and yet he no where encourages insurrection—he nowhere fosters discontent—but exhorts *always* to implicit obedience and fidelity. What a rebuke does the practice of the Redeemer of mankind imply upon the conduct of some of his nominal disciples of the day, who seek to destroy the contentment of the slaves, to rouse their most deadly passions, to break up the deep foundations of society, and to lead on to a night of darkness and confusion! . . .

2dly. *But it is further said that the moral effects of slavery are of the most deleterious and hurtful kind;* and as Mr. Jefferson has given the sanction of his great name to this charge, we shall proceed to examine it with all that respectful deference to which every sentiment of so pure and philanthropic a heart is justly entitled.

"The whole commerce between master and slave," says he, "is a perpetual exercise of the most boisterous passions—the most unremitting despotism on the one part, and degrading submission on the other. Our children see this, and learn to imitate it, for man is an imitative animal—this quality is the germ of education in him. . . ." Now we boldly assert that the fact does not bear Mr. Jefferson out in his conclusions. He has supposed the master in a continual passion—in the constant exercise of the most odious tyranny, and the child, a creature of imitation, looking on and learning. But is not this master sometimes kind and indulgent to his slaves? does he not mete out to them, for faithful service, the reward of his cordial approbation? Is it not his interest to do it? and when thus acting humanely, and speaking kindly, where is the child, the creature of imitation, that he does not look on and learn? We may rest assured, in this intercourse between a good master and his servant, more good than evil *may* be taught the child, the exalted principles of morality and religion may thereby be sometimes indelibly inculcated upon his mind, and instead of being reared a selfish contracted being, with nought but self to look to—he acquires a more exalted benevolence, a greater generosity and elevation of soul, and embraces for the sphere of his generous actions a much wider field. Look to the slave holding population of our country, and you every where find them characterized by noble and elevated sentiment, by humane and virtuous feelings. We do not find among them that cold, contracted, calculating *selfishness*, which withers and repels every thing around it, and lessens or destroys all the multiplied enjoyments of social intercourse. Go into our national councils, and ask for the most generous, the most disinterested, the most conscientious, and the least unjust and oppressive in their principles, and see whether the slave holder will be past by in the selection. . . .

Is it not a fact, known to every man in the South, that the most *cruel masters* are those who have been unaccustomed to slavery. It is well known that northern gentlemen who marry southern heiresses, are much severer masters than southern gentlemen. And yet, if Mr. Jefferson's reasoning were correct, they ought to be much milder: in fact, it follows from his reasoning, that the authority which the father is called on to exercise over his children, must be seriously detrimental; and yet we know that this is not the case; that on the contrary, there is nothing which so much humanizes and softens the heart, as this *very authority;* and there are none, even among those who have no children themselves, so disposed to pardon the follies and indiscretion of youth, as those who have seen most of them, and suffered greatest annoyance. There may be many cruel relentless masters, and there are unkind and cruel fathers too; but both the one and the other make all those around them shudder with horror. We are disposed to think that their example in society tends rather to strengthen, than weaken the principle of benevolence and humanity.

Let us now look a moment to the slave, and contemplate *his* position. Mr. Jefferson has described him as hating, rather than loving his master, and as losing, too, all that *amor patrica* which characterizes the true patriot. We assert again, that Mr. Jefferson is not borne out by the fact. We are well convinced that there is nothing but the mere relations of husband and wife, parent and child, brother and sister, which produce a closer tie, than the relation of master and servant. We have no hesitation in affirming, that throughout the whole slave holding country, the slaves of a good master, are his warmest, most constant, and most devoted friends; they have been accustomed to look up to him as their supporter, director and defender. Every one acquainted with southern slaves, knows that the slave rejoices in the elevation and prosperity of his master; and the heart of no one is more gladdened at the successful debut of young master or miss on the great theatre of the world, than that of either the young slave who has grown up with them, and shared in all their sports, and even partaken of all their delicacies—or the aged one who has looked on and watched them from birth to manhood, with the kindest and most affectionate solicitude, and has ever met from them, all the kind treatment and generous sympathies of feeling tender hearts. Judge Smith in his able speech on Foote's Resolutions in the Senate said, in an emergency he would rely upon his own slaves for his defence—he would put arms into their hands, and he had no doubt they would defend him faithfully. In the late Southampton insurrection, we know that many actually convened their slaves, and armed them for defence, although slaves were here the cause of the evil which was to be repelled. . . .

. . . A merrier being does not exist on the face of the globe, than the negro slave of the United States. *Even* Captain Hall himself, with his thick "crust of prejudice," is obliged to allow that they are happy and contented, and the master much less cruel than is generally imagined. Why then, since the slave is happy, and happiness is the great object of all animated creation, should we endeavor to disturb his contentment by infusing into his mind a vain and indefinite desire for liberty—a something which he cannot comprehend, and which must inevitably dry up the very sources of his happiness....

3dly. *It has been contended that slavery is unfavorable to a republican spirit:* but the whole history of the world proves that this is far from being the case. In the ancient republics of Greece and Rome, where the spirit of liberty glowed with most intensity, the slaves were more numerous than the freemen.... In modern times, too, liberty has always been more ardently desired by slave holding communities.... Burke says, "it is because freedom is to them not only an enjoyment, but a kind of rank and privilege." Another, and perhaps more efficient cause of this, is the perfect spirit of equality so prevalent among the whites of all the slave holding states.... The menial and low offices being all performed by the blacks, there is at once taken away the greatest cause of distinction and separation of the ranks of society. The man to the north will not shake hands familiarly with his servant, and converse, and laugh, and dine with him, no matter how honest and respectable he may be. But go to the south, and you will find that no white man feels such inferiority of rank as to be unworthy of association with those around him. Color alone is here the badge of distinction, the true mark of aristocracy, and all who are white are equal in spite of the variety of occupation....

4thly. *Insecurity of the whites, arising from plots, insurrections, &c., among the blacks.* This is the evil, after all, let us say what we will, which really operates most powerfully upon the schemers and emancipating philanthropists of those sections where slaves constitute the principal property. Now, if we have shown, as we trust we have, that the scheme of deportation is utterly impracticable, and that emancipation, with permission to remain, will produce all these horrors in *still greater degree*, it follows that this evil of slavery, allowing it to exist in all its latitude, would be no argument for legislative action, and therefore we might well rest contented with this issue; but as we are anxious to exhibit this whole subject in its true bearings, and as we do believe that this evil has been most strangely and causelessly exaggerated, we have determined to examine it a moment, and point out its true extent. It seems to us, that those who insist most upon it, commit the enormous error of looking upon every slave in the whole slave-holding country as actuated by the most deadly enmity to the whites, and possessing all that reckless, fiendish temper, which would lead him to murder and assassinate the moment the opportunity occurs.—This is far from being true; the slave, as we have already said, generally loves the master and his family; and few indeed there are, who can coldly plot the murder of men, women, and children; and if they do, there are fewer still who can have the villainy to execute. We can sit down and imagine that all the negroes in the south have conspired to rise on a certain night, and murder all the whites in their respective families; we may suppose the secret to be kept, and that they have the physical power to exterminate; and yet, we say the whole is *morally impossible.* No insurrection of this land can ever occur where the blacks are as much civilized as they are in the United States.... his whole education and course of life are at war with such fell deeds. Nothing, then, but the most subtle and poisonous principles, sedulously infused into his mind, can break his allegiance, and transform him into the midnight murderer.—Any man who will attend to the history of the Southampton massacre, must at once see, that the cause of even the partial success of the insurrectionists, was the very circumstance that there was no extensive plot, and that Nat, a demented fanatic, was under the impression that heaven had enjoined him to liberate the blacks, and had made its manifestations by loud noises in the air, an eclipse, and by the greenness of the sun. It was these signs which determined *him*, and ignorance and superstition, together with implicit confidence in Nat, determined a few others, and thus the bloody work began....

SOURCE: Hart, Albert Bushnell, ed. *American History Told by Contemporaries.* Vol. 3. New York: Macmillan, 1901.

EXCERPT FROM *NOTES ILLUSTRATIVE OF THE WRONG OF SLAVERY (1832, by Mary B. Black Ford)*

Mary B. Black Ford kept a journal recording the cruelty of the slave trade she witnessed in Fredericksburg, Virginia. Fear of social ostracism kept Ford from publicly announcing her antislavery views, but her journal continually calls out the immorality of buying and selling human beings who feel love, loyalty, and fear. She lamented the slaves' loss of freedom, the destruction of their families, and their constant isolation from the protections of the law. When she was unable to convince the mother of a local slave trader to let one of the trader's male slaves say a final farewell to his own mother, Ford underscored how deeply she feels slavery can degrade the moral facilities of even her "own sex."

While Ford dared not publicly advocate emancipation, she could discuss colonization; she brought to a woman she knew pamphlets from the American Colonization Society (ACS). Founded in 1816 in Washington, D.C. to aid the colonization of Africa by free blacks, the ACS enjoyed the support of many in the South. With aid from Congress, the ACS purchased land in West Africa and helped establish the country of Liberia in 1822. By 1885, over fifteen thousand blacks had been transported there by the ACS. Although these were modest successes at best, these colonization efforts sought to allay the seemingly intractable differences between the races by keeping them, literally, an ocean apart.

Mark D. Baumann,
New York University

See also **Antislavery; Slavery.**

Directly across the street from our house in Fredericksburg lives a Negro trader of the name of Finnall. Last summer a young negro man was sold to him who was strongly suspected of the crime of wishing to make his escape to one of the Free States. So his Mistress sold him to this Trader, who confined him in his cellar, not having a jail at hand then. The Mother of this young man was an old woman whom I knew, an excellent and pious woman. This was her only son, her greatest earthly comfort. She would often come to visit him in his cellar. She had sometimes been admitted as far as the iron grated door, but that favour was only granted by the special interposition of the gentleman with whom she lived; after awhile this was denied. Her son remained several months in this confinement; about twilight those confined used to be brought out and walked about the garden for exercise.

When the time drew near for them all to be driven South, the Mother came to the house and every earnestly solicited the young man who had charge of them (the Trader being away), to permit her to see him once more. This was refused!!! She came over the street to our house. When I discovered the cause of her silent grief, for she made no complaint, I asked her if she thought my intercession would do any good. She answered, perhaps it might. So I put on my bonnet and went over with her, she waiting at the gate while I went to the door. The young man I spoke of, I addressed, pleading for permission for the Mother to take leave, face to face, of the Son, but in vain. Though he was quite a youth, his heart seemed quite hardened toward these poor people. I asked him how he would feel were he in the place of the young man now in confinement and his mother waiting to take a last farewell of him. Wearied with my importunities he said he would step in and ask Mrs. Finnall, that she had the liberty to permit it if she chose. I then begged him to see her, hoping from one of my own sex to find that mercy I looked for in vain from a man. I was still standing at the door. She would not come down stairs, but sent me word that she had nothing to do with it. The only reason the young man gave for this unnecessary cruelty was that when Henry saw his Mother it caused him to give himself airs for some time after.

When I found all hope of prevailing with them was over, I fixed my eyes steadily upon the hardhearted being before me and asked him if he did not fear the judgments of an offended God. I warned him that such cruelty could not long go unpunished, and reminded him of the affair at Southampton which had just occurred. He seemed to quail under my rebuke. After it was over I wondered at my own courage but I was entirely carried away by the enthusiasm of my feelings. He had then many human beings, who had committed no crime in close confinement in a damp cellar, I believe handcuffed and chained.

I saw them some weeks after set off, the men chained two & two; the women and little children in large Carryalls, an indulgence not always allowed. The Mother I interceded for was down there. She clasped her son to her bosom, but he was quickly called away by his inhuman driver.

Large droves continually pass here, the men often chained, the women limping after, and their stern Drivers bringing up the rear. Not long since a slave about to be carried off in one of Smith and Finnall's droves cut the sinews of his wrist so as to render his right hand useless.

1833. A call was made not long ago upon the charity of some ladies of my acquaintance in behalf of a negro woman who had been left by a Trader to be confined. The child it appears was his own, though he had left the wretched Mother destitute, depending upon her supporting herself. This she could not do during her confinement, she had not even clothes to put on the poor naked infant but for the charity of these ladies, who felt it more than the hard hearted father. It is one of the most dreadful circumstances of this traffic that the women frequently become the prey of the brutal lust of their oppressors, even those who perhaps have torn them from the arms of a beloved husband and children.

Thank God! that I am permitted to breathe the pure air of Heaven! that no one can deprive me of this privilege unless I have broken through such laws as are essential to the order and well being of Society. Forever praised be His name! that I live in a land where no white man at least can be unjustly thrown into confinement until just cause can be shown why. Thank God!!! that I live in the land where the "Writ of Habeas Corpus" exists for the white man and woman. And may I live to see the time when the poor down trodden negro too shall enjoy this great privilege!

These feelings have been called forth by the delightful sensations I experienced just now (a clear October evening), on walking out, and breathing the fresh air of Heaven. In the midst of these feelings of pleasure, I remembered with shame there are at this moment in the negro jail very near here 3 men whom I can see (when I look that way) through the iron grating of the windows. They belong to Smith and Finnall, traders in human beings, who keep this jail to confine men whose only crime is that they wish to return to their families.

Between Fredericksburg and Mountain, about half way, there is a pleasant little way side inn, white washed, with a pretty green yard before it, where I like to stop to eat my lunch and to enjoy the intelligent conversation of its Mistress, who is deeply interested in the best welfare of our negroes. She is in the habit of circulating pamphlets in favor of the Colonization Society that I leave with her. She told me of her giving one of these to a Negro trader that stopped there with a gang of Slaves he was taking South. Twenty of the men were handcuffed, two and two, a chain passing between them. There were beside women who were not chained. A gentleman there asked one of these women, "Are you willing to go?" She answered, "No, I am not willing." She then said, "Master, do you know why God has sent this cholera among the people?" (It was then raging in this country) He asked her why. She answered by pointing to the twenty men chained together. It is remarkable that the opinion was universal (when the cholera was approaching Virginia) among the negroes, that they should be exempt, because it was a judgment from the Allmighty for our sins in holding them in slavery.

I was greatly struck by an instance of conjugal affection that occurred not long since, and have determined to record it as one among many proofs that such feelings exist among the negroes, notwithstanding the course of treatment pursued by the whites toward them in continually slighting their marriage ties though performed in the most solemn manner.

A woman owned by Mr. Richard Carmichael had her husband (owned by another person), to whom she was much attached, sold to a Negro trader for some slight offence. He was not even allowed to come to town a mile or two to take leave of her, but was carried off immediately. Her distress was so great that she was almost heartbroken. After a short time it settled into a deep melancholy, she was never seen to smile and her mind appeared unsettled. One day when old Mrs. Carmichael called to see her she found her, as she believed, utterly deranged, her pulse low, her flesh perfectly cold, restless, and continuing to exclaim, "No one cares for me. I have no friend. Old Mistress, are you my friend? I have secret, I have a secret." After a while it was discovered that her husband had returned, and this was the secret. She feared it would be discovered and he would be returned to the Trader from whom he had escaped. Some time before she had gone into the cellar about twilight to get wood when he had clasped her in his arms. The suddenness and the joy, together with the apprehension that he would be taken was too much for her and had nearly proved fatal to her reason, perhaps her life. Her husband, in company with another slave, had returned after travelling five hundred miles. They had observed the rout they had gone over narrowly, watching for an opportunity to escape, but had gone five hundred miles before such an one presented itself. They lived on roots and berries, fearing to ask for other food from the risk of being taken up. They secreted themselves during the day and travelled all night. All this danger and hardship encountered for the slender hope of being kept near his wife. Their strong affection interested several persons in his favour who went to see his Master to try what could be done. It proved however that his Master had already repented selling him for he was an excellent Blacksmith, and was glad to make arrangements to keep him at home.

29th February. To day Finnall, the Negro trader who lives diagonally opposite to us, set off with a large gang of Slaves for the Southern Market. There were many women, girls and boys who set off from this place, the men coming afterwards. They are generally chained and handcuffed. Capt. Henry Philips, who lives very near us, has sold to go in this gang, a little girl twelve or thirteen years old, named Melinda, tempted by the price offered, though he is rich. She was a favorite with those who knew her. My good neighbor, Mrs. Stevenson, that when she came to take leave of her "every limb of her delicate frame trembled." The sale had been very sudden. The only reason given for selling her was that Mrs. Philips said she could do her own work. I saw the company of females weeping as they walked before the Drivers, stopping occasionally as they proceeded, to take leave of their friends and relatives as they met them.

Think what it is to be a Slave!!! To be treated not as a Man, but as a personal chattel, a thing that may be bought and sold, to have no right to the fruits of your own labour, no right to your own wife and children, liable at any moment to be seperated at the arbitrary will of another from all that is dearest to you on earth, & whom it is your duty to love & cherish. Deprived by the law of learning to read the Bible, compelled to know that the purity of your wife and daughters is exposed without protection of law to the assault of brutal white men! Think of this, and all the nameless horrors that are concentrated in that one word Slavery.

EXCERPT FROM *RUNNING A THOUSAND MILES FOR FREEDOM* *(1860, by William Craft)*

William and Ellen Craft staged a daring escape from slavery in 1848. Posing as William's sickly master, Ellen's light skin and bandages disguised her identity and buffered them from unwanted inquiries as they fled by boat and train from Macon, Georgia, to Philadelphia. Published in 1860, *Running a Thousand Miles to Freedom* recounts the journey as a series of encounters with numerous characters whose voices depict both the genuine concern and the flip arrogance with which Americans understood slavery. Prominent in this excerpt is the woman "of the 'firstest families'" whose obvious and avowed hatred for her slaves undermined her conviction that she was performing her Christian duty by obstinately refusing to manumit her late husband's slaves.

The Crafts's observant and witty portrayals show the illogic of popular pro-slavery arguments by pitting slave owners' paternalistic ideals against their actual treatment of slaves. Hardly unthinking and ignorant, the former slaves/authors are thoughtful and canny in this excerpt.

Mark D. Baumann,
New York University

See also **Slavery; Underground Railroad.**

We reached Wilmington the next morning, and took the train for Richmond, Virginia. I have stated that the American railway carriages (or cars, as they are called) are constructed differently to those in England. At one end of some of them, in the South, there is a little apartment with a couch on both sides for the convenience of families and invalids; and as they thought my master was very poorly, he was allowed to enter one of these apartments at Petersburg, Virginia, where an old gentleman and two handsome young ladies, his daughters, also got in, and took seats in the same carriage. But before the train started, the gentleman stepped into my car, and questioned me respecting my master. He wished to know what was the matter with him, where he was from, and where he was going. I told him where he came from, and said that he was suffering from a complication of complaints, and was going to Philadelphia, where he thought he could get more suitable advice than in Georgia.

The gentleman said my master could obtain the very best advice in Philadelphia. Which turned out to be quite correct, though he did not receive it from physicians, but from kind abolitionists who understood his case much better. The gentleman also said, "I reckon your master's father hasn't any more such faithful and smart boys as you." "O, yes, sir, he has," I replied, "lots on 'em." Which was literally true. This seemed all he wished to know. He thanked me, gave me a ten-cent piece, and requested me to be attentive to my good master. I promised that I would do so, and have ever since endeavored to keep my pledge. During the gentleman's absence, the ladies and my master had a little cozy chat. But on his return, he said, "You seem to be very much afflicted, sir." "Yes, sir," replied the gentleman in the poultices. "What seems to be the matter with you, sir; may I be allowed to ask?" "Inflammatory rheumatism, sir." "Oh! that is very bad, sir," said the kind gentleman: "I can sympathize with you; for I know from bitter experience what the rheumatism is." If he did, he knew a good deal more than Mr. Johnson.

The gentleman thought my master would feel better if he would lie down and rest himself; and as he was anxious to avoid conversation, he at once acted upon this suggestion. The ladies politely rose, took their extra shawls, and made a nice pillow for the invalid's head. My master wore a fashionable cloth cloak, which they took and covered him comfortably on the couch. After he had been lying a little while the ladies, I suppose, thought he was asleep; so one of them gave a long sigh, and said, in a quiet fascinating tone, "Papa, he seems to be a very nice young gentleman." But before papa could speak, the other lady quickly said, "Oh! dear me, I never felt so much for a gentleman in my life!" To use an American expression, "they fell in love with the wrong chap."

After my master had been lying a little while he got up, the gentleman assisted him in getting on his cloak, the ladies took their shawls, and soon all were seated. They then insisted upon Mr. Johnson taking some of their refreshments, which of course he did, out of courtesy to the ladies. All went on enjoying themselves until they reached Richmond, where the ladies and their father left the train. But, before doing so, the good old Virginian gentleman, who appeared to be much pleased with my master, presented him with a recipe, which he said was a perfect cure for the inflammatory rheumatism. But the invalid not being able to read it, and fearing he should hold it upside down in pretending to do so, thanked the donor kindly, and placed it in his waistcoat pocket. My master's new friend also gave him his card, and requested him the next time he travelled that way to do him the kindness to call, adding, "I shall be pleased to see you, and so will my daughters." Mr. Johnson expressed his gratitude for the proffered hospitality, and said he should feel glad to call on his return. I have not the slightest doubt that he will fulfil the promise whenever that return takes place. After changing trains we went on a little beyond Fredericksburg, and took a steamer to Washington.

At Richmond, a stout elderly lady, whose whole demeanor indicated that she belonged (as Mrs. Stowe's Aunt Chloe expresses it) to one of the "firstest families," stepped into the carriage, and took a seat near my master. Seeing me passing quickly along the platform, she sprang up as if taken by a fit, and exclaimed, "Bless my soul! there goes my nigger, Ned!"

My master said, "No; that is my boy."

The lady paid no attention to this; she poked her head out of the window, and bawled to me, "You Ned, come to me, sir, you runaway rascal!"

On my looking round she drew her head in, and said to my master, "I beg your pardon, sir, I was sure it was my nigger; I never in my life saw two black pigs more alike than your boy and my Ned."

After the disappointed lady had resumed her seat, and the train had moved off, she closed her eyes, slightly raising her hands, and in a sanctified tone said to my master, "Oh! I hope, sir, your boy will not turn out to be so worthless as my Ned has. Oh! I was as kind to him as if he had been my own son. Oh! sir, it grieves me very much to think that after all I did for him he should go off without having any cause whatever."

"When did he leave you?" asked Mr. Johnson.

"About eighteen months ago, and I have never seen hair or hide of him since."

"Did he have a wife?" enquired a very respectable-looking young gentleman, who was sitting near my master and opposite to the lady.

"No, sir; not when he left, though he did have one a little before that. She was very unlike him; she was as good and as faithful a nigger as anyone need wish to have. But, poor thing! she became so ill, that she was unable to do much work; so I thought it would be best to sell her, to go to New Orleans, where the climate is nice and warm."

"I suppose she was very glad to go South for the restoration of her health?" said the gentleman.

"No; she was not," replied the lady, "for niggers never know what is best for them. She took on a great deal about leaving Ned and the little nigger; but, as she was so weakly, I let her go."

"Was she good-looking?" asked the young passenger, who was evidently not of the same opinion as the talkative lady, and therefore wished her to tell all she knew.

"Yes; she was very handsome, and much whiter than I am; and therefore will have no trouble in getting another husband. I am sure I wish her well. I asked the speculator who bought her to sell her to a good master. Poor thing! she has my prayers, and I know she prays for me. She was a good Christian, and always used to pray for my soul. It was through her earliest prayers," continued the lady, "that I was first led to seek forgiveness of my sins, before I was converted at the great camp-meeting."

This caused the lady to snuffle and to draw from her pocket a richly embroidered handkerchief, and apply it to the corner of her eyes. But my master could not see that it was at all soiled.

The silence which prevailed for a few moments was broken by the gentleman's saying, "As your July was such a very good girl, and had served you so faithfully before she lost her health, don't you think it would have been better to have emancipated her?"

"No, indeed I do not!" scornfully exclaimed the lady, as she impatiently crammed the fine handkerchief into a little workbag. "I have no patience with people who set niggers at liberty. It is the very worst thing you can do for them. My dear husband just before he died willed all his niggers free. But I and all our friends knew very well that he was too good a man to have ever thought of doing such an unkind and foolish thing, had he been in his right mind, and, therefore we had the will altered as it should have been in the first place."

"Did you mean, madam," asked my master, "that willing the slaves free was unjust to yourself, or unkind to them?"

"I mean that it was decidedly unkind to the servants themselves. It always seems to me such a cruel thing to turn niggers loose to shift for themselves, when there are so many good masters to take care of them. As for myself," continued the considerate lady, "I thank the Lord my dear husband left me and my son well provided for. Therefore I care nothing for the niggers, on my own account, for they are a great deal more trouble than they are worth; I sometimes wish that there was not one of them in the world, for the ungrateful wretches are always running away. I have lost no less than ten since my poor husband died. It's ruinous, sir!"

"But as you are well provided for, I suppose you do not feel the loss very much," said the passenger.

"I don't feel it at all," haughtily continued the good soul, "but that is no reason why property should be squandered. If my son and myself had the money for those valuable niggers, just see what a great deal of good we could do for the poor, and in sending missionaries abroad to the poor heathen, who have never heard the name of our blessed Redeemer. My dear son who is a good Christian minister has advised me not to worry and send my soul to hell for the sake of niggers; but to sell every blessed one of them for what they will fetch, and go and live in peace with him in New York. This I have concluded to do. I have just been to Richmond and made arrangements with my agent to make clean work of the forty that are left."

"Your son being a good Christian minister," said the gentleman, "it's strange he did not advise you to let the poor Negroes have their liberty and go North."

"It's not at all strange, sir; it's not at all strange. My son knows what's best for the niggers; he has always told me that they were much better off than the free niggers in the North. In fact, I don't believe there are any white laboring people in the world who are as well off as the slaves."

"You are quite mistaken, madam," said the young man. "For instance, my own widowed mother, before she died, emancipated all her slaves, and sent them to Ohio, where they are getting along well. I saw several of them last summer myself."

"Well," replied the lady, "freedom may do for your ma's niggers, but it will never do for mine; and, plague them, they shall never have it; that is the word, with the bark on it."

"If freedom will not do for your slaves," replied the passenger, "I have no doubt your Ned and the other nine Negroes will find out their mistake, and return to their old home."

"Blast them!" exclaimed the old lady, with great emphasis, "if I ever get them, I will cook their infernal hash, and tan their accursed black hides well for them! God forgive me," added the old soul, "the niggers will make me lose all my religion!"

By this time the lady had reached her destination. The gentleman got out at the next station beyond. As soon as she was gone, the young Southerner said to my master, "What a d——d shame it is for that old whining hypocritical humbug to cheat the poor Negroes out of their liberty! If she has religion, may the devil prevent me from ever being converted!"

SOURCE: Craft, William. *Running a Thousand Miles for Freedom: or, The Escape of William and Ellen Craft from Slavery.* London: W. Tweedie, 1860.

ON THE UNDERGROUND RAILROAD
(c. 1850, by Levi Coffin)

Levi Coffin (1789–1877), a Quaker, was from 1826 to 1846 the unofficial leader of the Underground Railroad, an extensive route of abolitionist safe houses harboring escaped slaves and transporting them to freedom. In this account of the escape of twenty-eight slaves from the South to Canada, Coffin describes the myriad dangers facing fugitive slaves and those who helped them. Escapees risked capture and re-enslavement, to be sure, but they also faced starvation, disease, malnutrition, and exposure to the elements on their journey. Coffin also details the logistical complexity required to orchestrate successful passages on the Underground Railroad: a sympathetic white man must conduct the slaves across geographical obstacles to friendly way stations along the route. Ministers, laymen, and women's groups both black and white along the route provide and deliver fresh provisions, clothing, and transportation to the fugitives. Those assisting the slaves faced imprisonment and worse, and Coffin praises their eager willingness to do so.

Mark D. Baumann,
New York University

See also **Slavery; Underground Railroad.**

The fugitives generally arrived in the night, and were secreted among the friendly colored people or hidden in the upper room of our house. They came alone or in companies, and in a few instances had a white guide to direct them.

One company of twenty-eight that crossed the Ohio River at Lawrenceburg, Indiana—twenty miles below Cincinnati—had for conductor a white man whom they had employed to assist them. The character of this man was full of contradictions. He was a Virginian by birth and spent much of his time in the South, yet he hated slavery. He was devoid of moral principle, but was a true friend to the poor slave. . . .

. . . The company of twenty-eight slaves referred to, all lived in the same neighborhood in Kentucky, and had been planning for some time how they could make their escape from slavery. This white man—John Fairfield—had been in the neighborhood for some weeks buying poultry, etc., for market, and though among the whites he assumed to be very pro-slavery, the negroes soon found that he was their friend.

He was engaged by the slaves to help them across the Ohio River and conduct them to Cincinnati. They paid him some money which they had managed to accumulate. The amount was small, considering the risk the conductor assumed, but it was all they had. Several of the men had their wives with them, and one woman a little child with her, a few months old. John Fairfield conducted the party to the Ohio River opposite the mouth of the Big Miami, where he knew there were several skiffs tied to the bank, near a wood-yard. When I asked him afterward if he did not feel compunctions of conscience for breaking these skiffs loose and using them, he replied: "No; slaves are stolen property, and it is no harm to steal boats or anything else that will help them gain their liberty." The entire party crowded into three large skiffs or yawls, and made their way slowly across the river. The boats were overloaded and sank so deep that the passage was made in much peril. The boat John Fairfield was in was leaky, and began to sink when a few rods from the Ohio bank, and he sprang out on the sand-bar, where the water was two or three feet deep, and tried to drag the boat to the shore. He sank to his waist in mud and quicksands, and had to be pulled out by some of the negroes. The entire party waded out through mud and water and reached the shore safely, though all were wet and several lost their shoes. They hastened along the bank toward Cincinnati, but it was now late in the night and daylight appeared before they reached the city. Their plight was a most pitiable one. They were cold, hungry and exhausted; those who had lost their shoes in the mud suffered from bruised and lacerated feet, while to add to their discomfort a drizzling rain fell during the latter part of the night. They could not enter the city for their appearance would at once proclaim them to be fugitives. When they reached the outskirts of the city, below Mill Creek, John Fairfield hid them as well as he could, in ravines that had been washed in the sides of the steep hills, and told them not to move until he returned. He then went directly to John Hatfield, a worthy colored man, a deacon in the Zion Baptist Church, and told his story. He had applied to Hatfield before and knew him to be a great friend to the fugitives—one who had often sheltered them under his roof and aided them in every way he could.

. . . When he arrived, wet and muddy, at John Hatfield's house, he was scarcely recognized. He soon made himself and his errand known, and Hatfield at once sent a messenger to me, requesting me to come to his house without delay, as there were fugitives in danger. I went at once and met several prominent colored men who had also been summoned. While dry clothes and a warm breakfast were furnished to John Fairfield, we anxiously discussed the situation of the twenty-eight fugitives who were lying, hungry and shivering, in the hills in sight of the city.

Several plans were suggested, but none seemed practicable. At last I suggested that some one should go immediately to a certain German livery stable in the city and hire two coaches, and that several colored men should go out in buggies and take the women and children from their hiding-places, then that the coaches and buggies should form a procession as if going to a funeral, and march solemnly along the road leading to Cumminsville, on the west side of Mill Creek. In the western part of Cumminsville was the Methodist Episcopal burying ground, where a certain lot of ground had been set apart for the use of the colored people. They should pass this and continue on the Colerain pike till they reached a right-hand road leading to College Hill. At the latter place they would find a few colored families, living in the outskirts of the village, and could take refuge among them. Jonathan Cable, a Presbyterian minister, who lived near Farmer's College, on the west side of the village, was a prominent abolitionist, and I knew that he would give prompt assistance to the fugitives.

I advised that one of the buggies should leave the procession at Cumminsville, after passing the burying-ground, and hasten to College Hill to apprise friend Cable of the coming of the fugitives, that he might make arrangements for their reception in suitable places. My suggestions and advice were agreed to, and acted upon as quickly as possible, John Hatfield agreeing to apprise friend Cable of the coming of the fugitives. We knew that we must act quickly and with discretion, for the fugitives were in a very unsafe position, and in great danger of being discovered and captured by the police, who were always on the alert for runaway slaves.

While the carriages and buggies were being procured, John Hatfield's wife and daughter, and other colored women of the neighborhood, busied themselves in preparing provisions to be sent to the fugitives. A large stone jug was filled with hot coffee, and this, together with a supply of bread and other provisions, was placed in a buggy and sent on ahead of the carriages, that the hungry fugitives might receive some nourishment before starting. The conductor of the party, accompanied by John Hatfield, went in the buggy, in order to apprise the fugitives of the arrangements that had been made, and have them in readiness to approach the road as soon as the carriages arrived. Several blankets were provided to wrap around the women and children, whom we knew must be chilled by their exposure to the rain and cold. The fugitives were very glad to get the supply of food, the hot coffee especially being a great treat to them, and felt much revived. About the time they finished their breakfast the carriages and buggies drove up and halted in the road, and the fugitives were quickly conducted to them and placed inside. The women in the tight carriages wrapped themselves in the blankets, and the woman who had a young babe muffled it closely to keep it warm, and to prevent its cries from being heard. The little thing seemed to be suffering much pain, having been exposed so long to the rain and cold. All the arrangements were carried out, and the party reached College Hill in safety, and were kindly received and cared for....

When it was known by some of the prominent ladies of the village that a large company of fugitives were in the neighborhood, they met together to prepare some clothing for them. Jonathan Cable ascertained the number and size of the shoes needed, and the clothes required to fit the fugitives for traveling, and came down in his carriage to my house, knowing that the Anti-Slavery Sewing Society had their depository there. I went with him to purchase the shoes that were needed, and my wife selected all the clothing we had that was suitable for the occasion; the rest was furnished by the noble women of College Hill.

I requested friend Cable to keep the fugitives as secluded as possible until a way could be provided for safely forwarding them on their way to Canada. Friend Cable was a stockholder in the Underground Railroad, and we consulted together about the best route, finally deciding on the line by way of Hamilton, West Elkton, Eaton, Paris and Newport, Indiana. West Elkton, twenty-five or thirty miles from College Hill, was the first Underground Railroad depot. That line always had plenty of locomotives and cars in readiness. I agreed to send information to that point, and accordingly wrote to one of my particular friends at West Elkton, informing him that I had some valuable stock on hand which I wished to forward to Newport, and requested him to send three two-horse wagons—covered—to College Hill, where the stock was resting, in charge of Jonathan Cable....

The three wagons arrived promptly at the time mentioned, and a little after dark took in the party, together with another fugitive, who had arrived the night before, and whom we added to the company. They went through to West Elkton safely that night, and the next night reached Newport, Indiana. With little delay they were forwarded on from station to station through Indiana and Michigan to Detroit, having fresh teams and conductors each night, and resting during the day. I had letters from different stations, as they progressed, giving accounts of the arrival and departure of the train, and I also heard of their safe arrival on the Canada shore.

SOURCE: Hart, Albert Bushnell, ed. *American History Told by Contemporaries*. Vol. 4. New York: Macmillan, 1901.

EXCERPT FROM *SOCIOLOGY FOR THE SOUTH* *(1854, by George Fitzhugh)*

George Fitzhugh (1806–1881) was a lawyer and sociologist scientist in Virginia. In *Sociology of the South* he argued that humans, like ants and bees, are social beings driven by natural instinct to join with others to secure their livelihoods. Against social contract theories holding that individuals determine their own social relations, Fitzhugh posited that an individual's station in life is determined by what society deems best for itself. He supported his argument by observing that so-called free societies are marked by unchecked competition in which each must compete against all for mere survival. Thus, in his opinion, the system of free labor practiced in the North was an unhappy and hardscrabble existence running directly counter to humankind's natural impulse for social cooperation.

To Fitzhugh, slave labor presented a more benevolent and efficient system of social organization. In slave societies each individual's social position, from slave to yeoman to master, was bound by obligations to authority. In free societies, he posited, individuals pursued only their own interests: namely, the pursuit of profit. This led to the degeneration of taste and tradition as energies were directed toward technological improvement and expansion of markets and away from the greater social good. In contrast, Fitzhugh wrote, slave societies guarded against the dissolution of civil values by maintaining a view of social relations untainted by the selfish pursuit of individual gains. In Fitzhugh's view, society could not survive unless it embraced slavery.

However extreme his paternalism, Fitzhugh's ideas presented a trenchant critique of economic liberalism by pointing out the manner in which wage labor can degrade humanity.

Mark D. Baumann,
New York University

***See also* Slavery; South, the: The Antebellum South.**

In free society none but the selfish virtues are in repute, because none other help a man in the race of competition. In such society virtue loses all her loveliness, because of her selfish aims. Good men and bad men have the same end in view: self-promotion, self-elevation. The good man is prudent, cautious, and cunning of fence; he knows well, the arts (the virtues, if you please) which enable him to advance his fortunes at the expense of those with whom he deals; he does not "cut too deep;" he does not cheat and swindle, he only makes good bargains and excellent profits. He gets more subjects by this course; everybody comes to him to be bled. He bides his time; takes advantage of the follies, the improvidence and vices of others, and makes his fortune out of the follies and weaknesses of his fellow-men. The bad man is rash, hasty, unskilful and impolitic. He is equally selfish, but not half so prudent and cunning. Selfishness is almost the only motive of human conduct in free society, where every man is taught that it is his first duty to change and better his pecuniary situation.

The first principles of the science of political economy inculcate separate, individual action, and are calculated to prevent that association of labor without which nothing great can be achieved; for man isolated and individualized is the most helpless of animals. We think this error of the economists proceeded from their adoping Locke's theory of the social contract. We believe no heresy in moral science has been more pregnant of mischief than this theory of Locke. It lies at the bottom of all moral speculations, and if false, must infect with falsehood all theories built on it. Some animals are by nature gregarious and associative. Of this class are men, ants and bees. An isolated man is almost as helpless and ridiculous as a bee setting up for himself. Man is born a member of society, and does not form society. Nature, as in the cases of bees and ants, has it ready formed for him. He and society are congenital. Society is the being—he one of the members of that being. He has no rights whatever, as opposed to the interests of society; and that society may very properly make any use of him that will redound to the public good. Whatever rights he has are subordinate to the good of the whole; and he has never ceded rights to it, for he was born its slave, and had no rights to cede.

Government is the creature of society, and may be said to derive its powers from the consent of the governed; but society does not owe its sovereign power to the separate consent, volition or agreement of its members. Like the hive, it is as much the work of nature as the individuals who compose it. Consequences, the very opposite of the doctrine of free trade, result from this doctrine of ours. It makes each society a band of brothers, working for the common good, instead of a bag of cats biting and worrying each other. The competitive system is a system of antagonism and war; ours of peace and fraternity. The first is the system of free society; the other that of slave society. The Greek, the Roman, Judaistic, Egyptian, and all ancient polities, were founded on our theory. The loftiest patrician in those days, valued himself not on selfish, cold individually, but on being the most devoted servant of society and his country. In ancient times, the individual was considered nothing, the State every thing. And yet, under this system, the noblest individuality was evolved that the world has ever seen. The prevalence of the doctrines of political economy has injured Southern character, for in the South those doctrines most prevail. Wealthy men, who are patterns of virtue in the discharge of their domestic duties, value themselves on never intermeddling in public matters. They forget that property is a mere creature of law and society, and are willing to make no return for that property to the public, which by its laws gave it to them, and which guard and protect them in its possession.

All great enterprises owe their success to association of capital and labor. The North is indebted for its great wealth and prosperity to the readiness with which it forms associations for all industrial and commercial purposes. The success of Southern farming is a striking instance of the value of the association of capital and laborers, and ought to suggest to the South the necessity of it for other purposes.

The dissociation of labor and disintegration of society, which liberty and free competition occasion, is especially injurious to the poorer class; for besides the labor necessary to support the family, the poor man is burdened with the care of finding a home, and procuring employment, and attending to all domestic wants and concerns. Slavery relieves our slaves of these cares altogether, and slavery is a form, and the very best form, of socialism. In fact, the ordinary wages of common labor are insufficient to keep up separate domestic establishments for each of the poor, and association or starvation is in many cases inevitable. In free society, as well in Europe as in America, this is the accepted theory, and various schemes have been resorted to, all without success, to cure the evil. The association of labor properly carried out under a common head or ruler, would render labor more efficient, relieve the laborer of many of the cares of household affairs, and protect and support him in sickness and old age, besides preventing the too great reduction of wages by redundancy of labor and free competition. Slavery attains all these results. What else will?

CHAPTER IV.

The Two Philosophies.

In the three preceding chapters we have shewn that the world is divided between two philosophies. The one the philosophy of free trade and universal liberty—the philosophy adapted to promote the interests of the strong, the wealthy and the wise. The other, that of socialism, intended to protect the weak, the poor and the ignorant. The latter is almost universal in free society; the former prevails in the slaveholding States of the South. Thus we see each section cherishing theories at war with existing institutions. The people of the North and of Europe are pro-slavery men in the abstract; those of the South are theoretical abolitionists. This state of opinions is readily accounted for. The people in free society feel the evils of universal liberty and free competition, and desire to get rid of those evils. They propose a remedy, which is in fact slavery; but they are wholly unconscious of what they are doing, because never having lived in the midst of slavery, they know not what slavery is. The citizens of the South, who have seen none of the evils of liberty and competition, but just enough of those agencies to operate as healthful stimulants to energy, enterprise and industry, believe free competition to be an unmixed good.

The South, quiet, contented, satisfied, looks upon all socialists and radical reformers as madmen or knaves. It is as ignorant of free society as that society is of slavery. Each section sees one side of the subject alone; each, therefore, takes partial and erroneous views of it. Social science will never take a step in advance till some Southern slaveholder, competent for the task, devotes a life-time to its study and elucidation; for slavery can only be understood by living in its midst, whilst thousands of books daily exhibit the minutest workings of free society. The knowledge of the numerous theories of radical reform proposed in Europe, and the causes that have led to their promulgation, is of vital importance to us. Yet we turn away from them with disgust, as from something unclean and vicious. We occupy high vantage ground for observing, studying and classifying the various phenomena of society; yet we do not profit by the advantages of our position. We should do so, and indignantly hurl back upon our assailants the charge, the there is something wrong and rotten in our system. From their own mouths we can show free society to be an monstrous abortion, and slavery to be the healthy, beautiful and natural being which they are trying, unconsciously, to adopt.

CHAPTER V.

Negro Slavery.

We have already stated that we should not attempt to introduce any new theories of government and of society, but merely try to justify old ones, so far as we could deduce such theories from ancient and almost universal practices. Now it has been the practice in all countries and in all ages, in some degree, to accommodate the amount and character of government control to the wants, intelligence, and moral capacities of the nations or individuals to be governed. A highly moral and intellectual people, like the free citizens of ancient Athens, are best governed by a democracy. For a less moral and intellectual one, a limited and constitutional monarchy will answer. For a people either very ignorant or very wicked, nothing short of military despotism will suffice. So among individuals, the most moral and well-informed members of society require no other government than law. They are capable of reading and understanding the law, and have sufficient self-control and virtuous disposition to obey it. Children cannot be governed by mere law; first, because they do not understand it, and secondly, because they are so much under the influence of impulse, passion and appetite, that they want sufficient self-control to be deterred or governed by the distant and doubtful penalties of the law. They must be constantly controlled by parents or guardians, whose will and orders shall stand in the place of law for them. Very wicked men must be put into penitentiaries; lunatics into asylums, and the most wild of them into straight jackets, just as the most wicked of the sane are manacled with irons; and idiots must have committees to govern and take care of them. Now, it is clear the Athenian democracy would not suit a negro nation, nor will the government of mere law suffice for the individual negro. He is but a grown up child, and must be governed as a child, not as a lunatic or criminal. The master occupies towards him the place of parent or guardian. We shall not dwell on this view, for no one will differ with us who thinks as we do of the negro's capacity, and we might argue till dooms-day, in vain, with those who have a high opinion of the negro's moral and intellectual capacity.

Secondly. The negro is improvident; will not lay up in summer for the wants of winter; will not accumulate in youth for the exigencies of age. He would become an insufferable burden to society. Society has the right to prevent this, and can only do so by subjecting him to domestic slavery.

In the last place, the negro race is inferior to the white race, and living in their midst, they would be far outstripped or outwitted in the chase of free competition. Gradual but certain extermination would be their fate. We presume the maddest abolitionist does not think the negro's providence of habits and money-making capacity at all to compare to those of the whites. This defect of character would alone justify enslaving him, if he is to remain here. In Africa or the West Indies, he would become idolatrous, savage and cannibal, or be devoured by savages and cannibals. At the North he would freeze or starve.

. . . [A]bolish negro slavery, and how much of slavery still remains. Soldiers and sailors in Europe enlist for life; here, for five years. Are they not slaves who have not only sold their liberties, but their lives also? And they are worse treated than domestic slaves. No domestic affection and self-interest extend their aegis over them. No kind mistress, like a guardian angel, provides for them in health, tends them in sickness, and soothes their dying pillow. Wellington at Waterloo was a slave. He was bound to obey, or would, like admiral Bying, have been shot for gross misconduct, and might not, like a common laborer, quit his work at any moment. He had sold his liberty, and might not resign without the consent of his master, the king. The common laborer may quit his work at any moment, whatever his contract; declare that liberty is an inalienable right, and leave his employer to redress by a useless suit for damages. The highest and most honorable position on earth was that of the slave

Wellington; the lowest, that of the free man who cleaned his boots and fed his hounds. The African cannibal, caught, christianized and enslaved, is as much elevated by slavery as was Wellington. The kind of slavery is adapted to the men enslaved. Wives and apprentices are slaves; not in theory only, but often in fact. Children are slaves to their parents, guardians and teachers. Imprisoned culprits are slaves. Lunatics and idiots are slaves also. Three-fourths of free society are slaves, no better treated, when their wants and capacities are estimated, than negro slaves. The masters in free society, or slave society, if they perform properly their duties, have more cares and less liberty than the slaves themselves. "In the sweat of thy face shalt thou earn thy bread!" made all men slaves, and such all good men continue to be ...

We have a further question to ask. If it be right and incumbent to subject children to the authority of parents and guardians, and idiots and lunatics to committees, would it not be equally right and incumbent to give the free negroes masters, until at least they arrive at years of discretion, which very few ever did or will attain? What is the difference between the authority of a parent and of a master? Neither pay wages, and each is entitled to the services of those subject to him. The father may not sell his child forever, but may hire him out till he is twenty-one. The free negro's master may also be restrained from selling. Let him stand in loco parentis, and call him papa instead of master. Look closely into slavery, and you will see nothing so hideous in it; or if you do, you will find plenty of it at home in its most hideous form....

It is a common remark, that the grand and lasting architectural structures of antiquity were the results of slavery. The mighty and continued association of labor requisite to their construction, when mechanic art was so little advanced, and labor-saving processes unknown, could only have been brought about by a despotic authority, like that of the master over his slaves. It is, however, very remarkable, that whilst in taste and artistic skill the world seems to have been retrograding ever since the decay and abolition of feudalism, in mechanical invention and in great utilitarian operations requiring the wielding of immense capital and much labor, its progress has been unexampled. Is it because capital is more despotic in its authority over free laborers than Roman masters and feudal lords were over their slaves and vassals?

Free society has continued long enough to justify the attempt to generalize its phenomena, and calculate its moral and intellectual influences. It is obvious that, in whatever is purely utilitarian and material, it incites invention and stimulates industry. Benjamin Franklin, as a man and a philosopher, is the best exponent of the working of the system. His sentiments and his philosophy are low, selfish, atheistic and material. They tend directly to make man a mere "featherless biped," well-fed, well-clothed and comfortable, but regardless of his soul as "the beasts that perish.[")]

Since the Reformation the world has as regularly been retrograding in whatever belongs to the departments of genius, taste and art, as it has been progressing in physical science and its application to mechanical construction. Mediaeval Italy rivalled if it did not surpass ancient Rome, in poetry, in sculpture, in painting, and many of the fine arts. Gothic architecture reared its monuments of skill and genius throughout Europe, till the 15th century; but Gothic architecture died with the Reformation. The age of Elizabeth was the Augustan age of England. The men who lived then acquired their sentiments in a world not yet deadened and vulgarized by puritanical cant and levelling demagoguism. Since then men have arisen who have been the fashion and the go for a season, but none have appeared whose names will descend to posterity. Liberty and equality made slower advances in France. The age of Louis XIV was the culminating point of French genius and art. It then shed but a flickering and lurid light. Frenchmen are servile copyists of Roman art, and Rome had no art of her own. She borrowed from Greece; distorted and deteriorated what she borrowed; and France imitates and falls below Roman distortions. The genius of Spain disappeared with Cervantes; and now the world seems to regard nothing as desirable except what will make money and what costs money. There is not a poet, an orator, a sculptor, or painter in the world. The tedious elaboration necessary to all the productions of high art would be ridiculed in this money-making, utilitarian charlatan age. Nothing now but what is gaudy and costly excites admiration. The public taste is debased.

But far the worst feature of modern civilization, which is the civilization of free society, remains to be exposed. Whilst labor-saving processes have probably lessened by one half, in the last century, the amount of work needed for comfortable support the free laborer is compelled by capital and competition to work more than he ever did before, and is less comfortable. The organization of society cheats him of his earnings, and those earnings go to swell the vulgar pomp and pageantry of the ignorant millionaires, who are the only great of the present day. These reflections might seem, at first view, to have little connexion with negro slavery; but it is well for us of the South not to be deceived by the tinsel glare and glitter of free society, and to employ ourselves in doing our duty at home, and studying the past, rather than in insidious rivalry of the expensive pleasures and pursuits of men whose sentiments and whose aims are low, sensual and grovelling.

Human progress, consisting in moral and intellectual improvement, and there being no agreed and conventional standard weights or measures of moral and intellectual qualities and quantities, the question of progress can never be accurately decided. We maintain that man has not improved, because in all save the mechanic arts he reverts to the distant past for models to imitate, and he never imitates what he can excel.

We need never have white slaves in the South, because we have black ones. Our citizens, like those of Rome and Athens, are a privileged class. We should train and educate them to deserve the privileges and to perform the duties which society confers on them. Instead, by a low demagoguism depressing their self-respect by discourses on the equality of man, we had better excite their pride by reminding them that they do not fulfil the menial offices which white men do in other countries. Society does not feel the burden of providing for the few helpless paupers in the South. And we should recollect that here we have but half the people to educate, for half are negroes; whilst at the North they profess to educate all. It is in our power to spike this last gun of the abolitionists. We should educate all the poor. The abolitionists say that it is one of the necessary consequences of slavery that the poor are neglected. It was not so in Athens, and in Rome, and should not be so in the South. If we had less trade with and less dependence on the North, all our poor might be profitable and honorably employed in trades, professions and manufactures. Then we should have a rich and denser population. Yet we but marshal her in the way that she was going. The South is already aware of the necessity of a new policy, and has begun to act on it. Every day more and more is done for education, the mechanic arts, manufactures and internal improvements. We will soon be independent of the North.

We deem this peculiar question of negro slavery of very little importance. The issue is made throughout the world on the general subject of slavery in the abstract. The argument has commenced. One set of ideas will govern and control after awhile the civilized world. Slavery will every where be abolished, or every where be re-instituted. We think the opponents of practical, existing slavery, are estopped by their own admission; nay, that unconsciously, as socialists, they are the defenders and propagandists of slavery, and have furnished the only sound arguments on which its defence and justification can be rested. We have introduced the subject of negro slavery to afford us a better opportunity to disclaim the purpose of reducing the white man any where to the condition of negro slaves here. It would be very unwise and unscientific to govern white men as you would negroes. Every shade and variety of slavery has existed in the world. In some cases there has been much of legal regulation, much restraint of the master's authority; in others, none at all. The character of slavery necessary to protect the whites in Europe should be much milder than negro slavery, for slavery is only needed to protect the white man, whilst it is more necessary for the government of the negro even than for his protection. But even negro slavery should not be outlawed. We might and should have laws in Virginia, as in Louisiana, to make the master subject to presentment by the grand jury and to punishment, for any inhuman or improper treatment or neglect of his slave.

We abhor the doctrine of the "Types of Mankind;" first, because it is at war with scripture, which teaches us that the whole human race is descended from a common parentage; and, secondly, because it encourages and incites brutal masters to treat negroes, not as weak, ignorant and dependent brethren, but as wicked beasts, without the pale of humanity. The Southerner is the negro's friend, his only friend. Let no intermeddling abolitionist, no refined philosophy, dissolve this friendship.

SOURCE: Fitzhugh, George. *Sociology for the South: or, The Failure of Free Society.* Richmond, Va.: A. Morris, 1854.

EXCERPT FROM *THE IMPENDING CRISIS OF THE SOUTH: HOW TO MEET IT* *(1857, by Hinton Rowan Helper)*

Hinton Rowan Helper (1829–1909) was a Southern businessman and diplomat. He served as consul at Buenos Aires during the Civil War, and afterwards devoted his energy trade with South America by promoting a massive railway spanning from the Hudson Bay to the Strait of Magellan. Growing ever despondent as his dream remained unfulfilled, he eventually ended his own life.

Helper's influential *Impending Crisis* raised tempers immediately upon its publication in 1857. In it, he examined how the South lagged behind the North in all aspects of economic life: manufacturing, trade, finance, transportation, the arts, and even agriculture. Everything the South produced it gave to the North and ultimately had to buy back at an exorbitant cost. With no economy of its own, the South had become dependant on the North for even the most meager things in life. Helper identified slavery as the source of the South's economic decay and advocated the total abolition of the practice everywhere, including in his native South and in the new territories. According to Helper, the ruinous nature of slavery was to be found not only in its cruel treatment of Africans, but especially in the slaveholding class's demagogic relations with the poor, illiterate, and free whites of the South. He wrote that poor yeomen were told they are wealthy and free when in fact they were subject to treacherous legislators who sought only to increase their own power at the expense of all Southerners. Helper lamented that the South was "weltering in the cesspool of ignorance and degradation," a cesspool in which he predicted the region would remain as long as slavery remained the rule.

Mark D. Baumann,
New York University

See also **Antislavery; Compromise of 1850;** ***Impending Crisis of the South*****; Slavery; South, the: The Antebellum South.**

The Free and The Slave States.
It is a fact well known to every intelligent Southerner that we are compelled to go to the North for almost every article of utility and adornment, from matches, shoepegs and paintings up to cotton-mills, steamships and statuary; that we have no foreign trade, no princely merchants, nor respectable artists; that, in comparison with the free states, we contribute nothing to the literature, polite arts and inventions of the age; that, for want of profitable employment at home, large numbers of our native population find themselves necessitated to emigrate to the West, whilst the free states retain not only the larger proportion of those born within their own limits, but induce, annually, hundreds of thousands of foreigners to settle and remain amongst them; that almost everything produced at the North meets with ready sale, while, at the same time, there is no demand, even among our own citizens, for the productions of Southern industry; that, owing to the absence of a proper system of business amongst us, the North becomes, in one way or another, the proprietor and dispenser of all our floating wealth, and that we are dependent on Northern capitalists for the means necessary to build our railroads, canals and other public improvements; that if we want to visit a foreign country, even though it may lie directly South of us, we find no convenient way of getting there except by taking passage through a Northern port; and that nearly all the profits arising from the exchange of commodities, from insurance and shipping offices, and from the thousand and one industrial pursuits of the country, accrue to the North, and are there invested in the erection of those magnificent cities and stupendous works of art which dazzle the eyes of the South, and attest the superiority of free institutions!

The North is the Mecca of our merchants, and to it they must and do make two pilgrimages per annum—one in the spring and one in the fall. All our commercial, mechanical, manufactural, and literary supplies come from there. We want Bibles, brooms, buckets and books, and we go to the North; we want pens, ink, paper, wafers and envelopes, and we go to the North; we want shoes, hats, handkerchiefs, umbrellas and pocket knives, and we go to the North; we want furniture, crockery, glassware and pianos, and we go to the North; we want toys, primers, school books, fashionable apparel, machinery, medicines, tombstones, and a thousand other things, and we go to the North for them all. Instead of keeping our money in circulation at home, by patronizing our own mechanics, manufacturers, and laborers, we send it all away to the North, and there it remains; it never falls into our hands again.

In one way or another we are more or less subservient to the North every day of our lives. In infancy we are swaddled in Northern muslin; in childhood we are humored with Northern gewgaws; in youth we are instructed out of Northern books; at the age of maturity we sow our "wild oats" on Northern soil; in middle-life we exhaust our wealth, energies and talents in the dishonorable vocation of entailing our dependence on our children and on our children's children, and, to the neglect of our own interests and the interests of those around us, in giving aid and succor to every department of Northern power; in the decline of life we remedy our eye-sight with Northern spectacles, and support our infirmities with Northern canes; in old age we are drugged with Northern physic; and, finally, when we die, our inanimate bodies, shrouded in Northern cambric, are stretched upon the bier, borne to the grave in a Northern carriage, entombed with a Northern spade, and memorized with a Northern slab!

But it can hardly be necessary to say more in illustration of this unmanly and unnational dependence, which is so glaring that it cannot fail to be apparent to even the most careless and superficial observer. All the world sees, or ought to see, that in a commercial, mechanical, manufactural, financial, and literary point of view, we are as helpless as babes; that, in comparison with the Free States, our agricultural resources have been greatly exaggerated, misunderstood and mismanaged; and that, instead of cultivating among ourselves a wise policy of mutual assistance and co-operation with respect to individuals, and of self-reliance with respect to the South at large, instead of giving countenance and encouragement to the industrial enterprises projected in our midst, and instead of building up, aggrandizing and beautifying our own States, cities and towns, we have been spending our substance at the North, and are daily augmenting and strengthening the very power which now has us so completely under its thumb.

It thus appears, in view of the preceding statistical facts and arguments, that the South, at one time the superior of the North in almost all the ennobling pursuits and conditions of life, has fallen far behind her competitor, and now ranks more as the dependency of a mother country than as the equal confederate of free and independent States. Following the order of our task, the next duty the devolves upon us is to trace out the causes which have conspired to bring about this important charge, and to place on record the reasons, as we understand them,

Why The North Has Surpassed The South.
And now that we have come to the very heart and soul of our subject, we feel no disposition to mince matters, but mean to speak plainly, and to the point, without any equivocation, mental reservation, or secret evasion whatever. The son of a venerated parent, who, while he lived, was a considerate and merciful slaveholder, a native of the South, born and bred in North Carolina, of a family whose home has been in the valley of the Yadkin for nearly a century and a half, a Southerner by instinct and by all the influences of thought, habits, and kindred, and with the desire and fixed purpose to reside permanently within the limits of the South, and with the expectation of dying there also—we feel we that we have the right to express our opinion, however humble or unimportant it may be, on any and every question that affects the public good; and, so help us God, "sink or swim, live or die, survive or perish," we are determined to exercise that right with manly firmness, and without fear, favor or affection. And now to the point. In our opinion, an opinion which has been formed from data obtained by assiduous researches, and comparisons, from laborious investigation, logical reasoning, and earnest reflection, the causes which have impeded the progress and prosperity of the South, which have dwindled our commerce, and other similar pursuits, into the most contemptible insignificance; sunk a large majority of our people in galling poverty and ignorance, rendered a small minority conceited and tyrannical, and driven the rest away from their homes; entailed upon us a humiliating dependence on the Free States; disgraced us in the recesses of our own souls, and brought us under reproach in the eyes of all civilized and enlightened nations—may all be traced to one common source, and there find solution in the most hateful and horrible word, that was ever incorporated into the vocabulary of human economy—Slavery!

Reared amidst the institution of slavery, believing it to be wrong both in principle and in practice, and having seen and felt its evil influences upon individuals, communities and states, we deem it a duty, no less than a privilege, to enter our protest against it, and to use our most strenuous efforts to overturn and abolish it! Then we are an abolitionist? Yes! not merely a freesoiler, but an abolitionist, in the fullest sense of the term. We are not only in favor of keeping slavery out of the territories, but, carrying our opposition to the institution a step further, we here unhesitatingly declare ourself in favor of its immediate and unconditional abolition, in every state in this confederacy, where it now exists! Patriotism makes us a freesoiler; state pride makes us an emancipationist; a profound sense of duty to the South makes us an abolitionist; a reasonable degree of fellow feeling for the negro, makes us a colonizationist. With the free state men in Kansas and Nebraska, we sympathize with all our heart. We love the whole country, the great family of states and territories, one and inseparable, and would have the word Liberty engraved as an appropriate and truthful motto, on the escutcheon of every member of the confederacy. We love freedom, we hate slavery, and rather than give up the one or submit to the other, we will forfeit the pound of flesh nearest our heart. Is this sufficiently explicit and categorical? If not, we hold ourself in readiness at all times, to return a prompt reply to any proper question that may be propounded.

Our repugnance to the institution of slavery, springs from no one-sided idea, or sickly sentimentality. We have not been hasty in making up our mind on the subject; we have jumped at no conclusions; we have acted with perfect calmness and deliberation; we have carefully considered, and examined the reasons for and against the institution, and have also taken into account the probable consequences of our decision. The more we investigate the matter, the deeper becomes the conviction that we are right; and with this to impel and sustain us, we pursue our labor with love, with hope, and with constantly renewing vigor.

That we shall encounter opposition we consider as certain; perhaps we may even be subjected to insult and violence. From the conceited and cruel oligarchy of the South, we could look for nothing less. But we shall shrink from no responsibility, and do nothing unbecoming a man; we know how to repel indignity, and if assaulted, shall not fail to make the blow recoil upon the aggressor's head. The road we have to travel may be a rough one, but no impediment shall cause us to falter in our course. The line of our duty is clearly defined, and it is our intention to follow it faithfully, or die in the attempt.

But, thanks to heaven, we have no ominous forebodings of the result of the contest now pending between Liberty and Slavery in this confederacy. Though neither a prophet nor the son of a prophet, our vision is sufficiently penetrative to divine the future so far as to be able to see that the "peculiar institution" has but a short, and, as heretofore, inglorious existence before it. Time, the righter of every wrong, is ripening events for the desired consummation of our labors and the fulfillment of our cherished hopes. Each revolving year brings nearer the inevitable crisis. The sooner it comes the better; may heaven, through our humble efforts, hasten its advent.

The first and most sacred duty of every Southerner, who has the honor and the interest of his country at heart, is to declare himself an unqualified and uncompromising abolitionist. No conditional or half-way declaration will avail; no mere threatening demonstration will succeed. With those who desire to be instrumental in bringing about the triumph of liberty over slavery, there should be neither evasion, vacillation, nor equivocation. We should listen to no modifying terms or compromises that may be proposed by the proprietors of the unprofitable and ungodly institution. Nothing short of the complete abolition of slavery can save the South from falling into the vortex of utter ruin. Too long have we yielded a submissive obedience to the tyrannical domination of an inflated oligarchy; too long have we tolerated their arrogance and self-conceit; too long have we submitted to their unjust and savage exactions. Let us now wrest from them the scepter of power, establish liberty and equal rights throughout the land, and henceforth and forever guard our legislative halls from the pollutions and usurpations of pro-slavery demagogues.

There are few Southerners who will not be astonished at the disclosures of these statistical comparisons, between the free and the slave States. That the astonishment of the more intelligent and patriotic non-slaveholders will be mingled with indignation, is no more than we anticipate. We confess our own surprise, and deep chagrin, at the result of our investigations. Until we examined into the matter, we thought and hoped the South was really ahead of the North in one particular, that of agriculture; but our thoughts have been changed, and our hopes frustrated, for instead of finding ourselves the possessors of a single advantage, we behold our dear native South stripped of every laurel, and sinking deeper and deeper in the depths of poverty and shame; while, at the same time, we see the North, our successful rival, extracting and absorbing the few elements of wealth yet remaining amongst us, and rising higher and higher in the scale of fame, fortune, and invulnerable power. Thus our disappointment gives way to a feeling of intense mortification, and our soul involuntarily, but justly, we believe, cries out for retribution against the treacherous, slave-driving legislators, who have so basely and unpatriotically neglected the interests of their poor white constituents and bargained away the rights of posterity. Notwithstanding the fact that the white non-slaveholders of the South, are in the majority, as five to one, they have never yet had any part or lot in framing the laws under which they live. There is no legislation except for the benefit of slavery, and slaveholders. As a general rule, poor white per persons are regarded with less esteem and attention than negroes, and though the condition of the latter is wretched beyond description, vast numbers of the former are infinitely worse off. A cunningly devised mockery of freedom is guarantied to them, and that is all. To all intents and purposes they are disfranchised, and outlawed, and the only privilege extended to them, is a shallow and circumscribed participation in the political movements that usher slaveholders into office.

We have not breathed away seven and twenty years in the South, without becoming acquainted with the demagogical manoeuverings of the oligarchy. Their intrigues and tricks of legerdemain are as familiar to us as household words; in vain might the world be ransacked for a more precious junto of flatterers and cajolers. It is amusing to ignorance, amazing to credulity, and insulting to intelligence, to hear them in their blattering efforts to mystify and pervert the sacred principles of liberty, and turn the curse of slavery into a blessing. To the illiterate poor whites—made poor and ignorant by the system of slavery—they hold out the idea that slavery is the very bulwark of our liberties, and the foundation of American independence! For hours at a time, day after day, will they expatiate upon the inexpressible beauties and excellencies of this great, free and independent nation; and finally, with the most extravagant gesticulations and rhetorical flourishes, conclude their nonsensical ravings, by attributing all the glory and prosperity of the country, from Main to Texas, and from Georgia to California, to the "invaluable institutions of the South!" With what patience we could command, we have frequently listened to the incoherent and truth-murdering declamations of these champions of slavery, and, in the absence of a more politic method of giving vent to our disgust and indignation, have involuntarily bit our lips into blisters.

The lords of the lash are not only absolute masters of the blacks, who are bought and sold, and driven about like so many cattle, but they are also the oracles and arbiters of all non-slaveholding whites, whose freedom is merely nominal, and whose unparalleled illiteracy and degradation is purposely and fiendishly perpetuated. How little the "poor white trash," the great majority of the Southern people, know of the real condition of the country is, indeed, sadly astonishing. The truth is, they know nothing of public measures, and little of private affairs, except what their imperious masters, the slave-drivers, condescend to tell, and that is but precious little, and even that little, always garbled and one-sided, is never told except in public harangues; for the haughty cavaliers of shackles and handcuffs will not degrade themselves by holding private converse with those who have neither dimes nor hereditary rights in human flesh.

Whenever it pleases, and to the extent it pleases, a slaveholder to become communicative, poor whites may hear with fear and trembling, but not speak. They must be as mum as dumb brutes, and stand in awe of their August superiors, or be crushed with stern rebukes, cruel oppressions, or downright violence. If they dare to think for themselves, their thoughts must be forever concealed. The expression of any sentiment at all conflicting with the gospel of slavery, dooms them at once in the community in which they live, and then, whether willing or unwilling, they are obliged to become heroes, martyrs, or exiles. They may thirst for knowledge, but there is no Moses among them to smite it out of the rocks of Horeb. The black veil, through whose almost impenetrable meshes light seldom gleams, has long been pendent over their eyes, and there, with fiendish jealousy, the slave-driving ruffians sedulously guard it. Non-slaveholders are not only kept in ignorance of what is transpiring at the North, but they are continually misinformed of what is going on even in the South. Never were the poorer classes of a people, and those classes so largely in the majority, and all inhabiting the same country, so basely duped, so adroitly swindled, or so damnably outraged.

It is expected that the stupid and sequacious masses, the white victims of slavery, will believe, and, as a general thing, they do believe, whatever the slaveholders tell them; and thus it is that they are cajoled into the notion that they are the freest, happiest and most intelligent people in the world, and are taught to look with prejudice and disapprobation upon every new principle or progressive movement. Thus it is that the South, woefully inert and inventionless, has lagged behind the North, and is now weltering in the cesspool of ignorance and degradation.

SOURCE: Helper, H. R. *The Impending Crisis of the South: How to Meet It.* New York: Burdick Brothers, 1857.

A HOUSE DIVIDED
(17 June 1858)

Abraham Lincoln (1809–1865) delivered his famous *A House Divided* speech upon winning the nomination for U.S. Senate in the 1858 Illinois Republican Party Convention. Though he lost to Stephen Douglas, a Democrat, the hard-fought race established Lincoln in the national political scene. He was elected President in 1860. He was assassinated soon after winning a second term at the close of the Civil War.

In this speech Lincoln warned that the nation could not survive half-slave and half-free: it must be one or the other. He then impressed upon his audience the shrewd process proslavery forces employed to spread bondage across the land. The Taney Court's 1851 Dred Scott Decision denied the humanity of slaves and allowed their masters to bring them to states where slavery was previously prohibited. With the Kansas and Nebraska Act of 1854 Congress repealed the 1820 Missouri Compromise by disallowing Congressional prohibitions of slavery in the Territories. Instead, the Act endorsed the doctrine of popular sovereignty, in which the residents of the Territories, not Congress, could determine the future of slavery. Remarking that "individual men may now fill up the Territories with slaves," Lincoln indicted popular sovereignty as a terrible guarantee of slavery's endurance in the country's unincorporated regions and, by extension, the entire nation.

Lincoln concluded with the observation that while these laws and decisions were made by different men, a President, two Senators, and a Chief Justice, the results fitted together perfectly to create a national policy that unequivocally endorsed slavery and its expansion into the Territories. This policy was one that the Republican Party would fight.

Mark D. Baumann,
New York University

See also **Antislavery; Dred Scott Case; House Divided; Lincoln-Douglas Debates; Slavery.**

MR. PRESIDENT AND GENTLEMEN OF THE CONVENTION: If we could first know where we are, and whither we are tending, we could better judge what to do, and how to do it. We are now far into the fifth year since a policy was initiated with the avowed object and confident promise of putting an end to slavery agitation. Under the operation of that policy, that agitation has not only not ceased, but has constantly augmented. In my opinion, it will not cease until a crisis shall have been reached and passed. "A house divided against itself cannot stand." I believe this government cannot endure permanently half slave and half free. I do not expect the Union to be dissolved; I do not expect the house to fall; but I do expect it will cease to be divided. It will become all one thing, or all the other. Either the opponents of slavery will arrest the further spread of it, and place it where the public mind shall rest in the belief that it is in the course of ultimate extinction, or its advocates will push it forward till it shall become alike lawful in all the States, old as well as new, North as well as South.

Have we no tendency to the latter condition?

Let any one who doubts, carefully contemplate that now almost complete legal combination—piece of machinery, so to speak—compounded of the Nebraska doctrine and the Dred Scott decision. Let him consider, not only what work the machinery is adapted to do, and how well adapted, but also let him study the history of its construction, and trace, if he can, or rather fail, if he can, to trace the evidences of design, and concert of action, among its chief architects, from the beginning.

The new year of 1854 found slavery excluded from more than half the States by State Constitutions, and from most of the National territory by Congressional prohibition. Four days later, commenced the struggle which ended in repealing that Congressional prohibition. This opened all the National territory to slavery, and was the first point gained....

While the Nebraska Bill was passing through Congress, a *law case*, involving the question of a negro's freedom, by reason of his owner having voluntarily taken him first into a free State, and then into a territory covered by the Congressional prohibition, and held him as a slave for a long time in each, was passing through the United States Circuit Court for the District of Missouri; and both Nebraska Bill and lawsuit were brought to a decision in the same month of May, 1854. The negro's name was "Dred Scott," which name now designates the decision finally made in the case. Before the then next Presidential election, the law case came to, and was argued in, the Supreme Court of the United States; but the decision of it was deferred until after the election. Still, before the election, Senator Trumbull, on the floor of the Senate, requested the leading advocate of the Nebraska Bill to state *his opinion* whether the people of a Territory can constitutionally exclude slavery from their limits; and the latter answers: "That is a question for the Supreme Court."

The election came. Mr. Buchanan was elected, and the indorsement, such as it was, secured. That was the second point gained.... The Presidential inauguration came, and still no decision of the court; but the incoming President, in his inaugural address, fervently exhorted the people to abide by the forthcoming decision, whatever it might be. Then, in a few days, came the decision.

The reputed author of the Nebraska Bill finds an early occasion to make a speech at this capital indorsing the Dred Scott decision, and vehemently denouncing all opposition to it. The new President, too, seizes the early occasion of the Silliman letter to indorse and strongly construe that decision, and to express his astonishment that any different view had ever been entertained!

At length a squabble springs up between the President and the author of the Nebraska Bill, on the mere question of *fact*, whether the Lecompton Constitution was or was not in any just sense made by the people of Kansas; and in that quarrel the latter declares that all he wants is a fair vote for the people, and that he cares not whether slavery be voted *down* or voted *up*. I do not understand his declaration, that he cares not whether slavery be voted down or voted up, to be intended by him other than as an apt definition of the policy he would impress upon the public mind.... That principle is the only shred left of his original Nebraska doctrine. Under the Dred Scott decision "squatter sovereignty" squatted out of existence, tumbled down like temporary scaffolding; like the mould at the foundry, served through one blast, and fell back into loose sand; helped to carry an election, and then was kicked to the winds. His late joint struggle with the Republicans, against the Lecompton Constitution, involves nothing of the original Nebraska doctrine. That struggle was made on a point—the right of a people to make their own constitution—upon which he and the Republicans have never differed.

The several points of the Dred Scott decision, in connection with Senator Douglas's "care not" policy, constitute the piece of machinery, in its present state of advancement. This was the third point gained. The working points of that machinery are:

Firstly, That no negro slave, imported as such from Africa, and no descendant of such slave, can ever be a citizen of any State, in the sense of that term as used in the Constitution of the United States. This point is made in order to deprive the negro, in every possible event, of the benefit of that provision of the United States Constitution which declares that "The citizens of each State shall be entitled to all privileges and immunities of citizens in the several States."

Secondly, That, "subject to the Constitution of the United States," neither Congress nor a Territorial Legislature can exclude slavery from any United States Territory. This point is made in order that individual men may fill up the Territories with slaves, without danger of losing them as property, and thus to enhance the chances of permanency to the institution through all the future.

Thirdly, That whether the holding a negro in actual slavery in a free State makes him free, as against the holder, the United States courts will not decide, but will leave to be decided by the courts of any slave State the negro may be forced into by the master. This point is made, not to be pressed immediately; but, if acquiesced in for a while, and apparently indorsed by the people at an election, then to sustain the logical conclusion that what Dred Scott's master might lawfully do with Dred Scott, in the free State of Illinois, every other master may lawfully do with any other one, or one thousand slaves, in Illinois, or in any other free State.

Auxiliary to all this, and working hand in hand with it, the Nebraska doctrine, or what is left of it, is to educate and mould public opinion, at least Northern public opinion, not to care whether slavery is voted down or voted up. This shows exactly where we now are; and partially, also, whither we are tending....

Why was the amendment, expressly declaring the right of the people, voted down? Plainly enough now,—the adoption of it would have spoiled the niche for the Dred Scott decision. Why was the court decision held up? Why even a Senator's individual opinion withheld, till after the Presidential election? Plainly enough now,—the speaking out then would have damaged the "perfectly free" argument upon which the election was to be carried. Why the outgoing President's felicitation on the indorsement? Why the delay of a reargument? Why the incoming President's advance exhortation in favor of the decision? These things look like the cautious patting and petting of a spirited horse preparatory to mounting him, when it is dreaded that he may give the rider a fall. And why the hasty after-indorsement of the decision by the President and others?

We cannot absolutely know that all these exact adaptations are the result of preconcert. But when we see a lot of framed timbers, different portions of which we know have been gotten out at different times and places and by different workmen,—Stephen, Franklin, Roger, and James, for instance,—and when we see these timbers joined together, and see they exactly make the frame of a house or a mill, all the tenons and mortises exactly fitting, and all the lengths and proportions of the different pieces exactly adapted to their respective places, and not a piece too many or too few,—not omitting even scaffolding,—or, if a single piece be lacking, we see the place in the frame exactly fitted and prepared yet to bring such piece in,—in such a case, we find it impossible not to believe that Stephen and Franklin and Roger and James all understood one another from the beginning, and all worked upon a common plan or draft drawn up before the first blow was struck....

SOURCE: Lincoln, Abraham. *Writings of Abraham Lincoln.* New York: Lamb, 1905–06.

JOHN BROWN'S LAST SPEECH
(2 November 1859)

John Brown (1800–1859) was an abolitionist who believed God had commanded him to rid the land of slavery. Fanatical in his mission, he sometimes campaigned with violence and terrorism: in the fighting known as "Bleeding Kansas" Brown and his sons killed five pro-slavery settlers in reprisal for the sacking of Lawrence in 1856. Driven from Kansas, Brown returned east. With the support of influential abolitionists he attempted to gather an army of free blacks and fugitive slaves in the mountains of Maryland and Virginia to stage a guerilla campaign against local slaveholders. In 1859, he and a band of twenty-one men seized the U.S. Armory at Harper's Ferry, Virginia. The raid failed miserably and U.S. forces under the command of Colonel Robert E. Lee soon captured Brown and his men. Tried in court, Brown was found guilty of treason and executed by hanging.

In this speech made at the conclusion of his trial, Brown disingenuously speaks against violence and argues that his aims could have been met with no bloodshed on either side. Had his actions suited the interests of "the rich and the powerful," he said, he would have been praised, not condemned. Still, he accepted the verdict of the court; he felt no guilt. He stated that his execution would serve the cause of justice and mix his blood "with the blood of millions" of enslaved Africans. Brown's raid showed to the increasingly fractious nation the extremes some thought necessary to bring about abolition. He was praised as a hero and martyr by many whom might otherwise abhor violence, among them Ralph Waldo Emerson and Henry David Thoreau.

Mark D. Baumann,
New York University

See also **Antislavery; Slave Insurrections.**

I have, may it please the Court, a few words to say.

In the first place, I deny everything but what I have all along admitted,—the design on my part to free the slaves. I intended certainly to have made a clean thing of that matter, as I did last winter, when I went into Missouri and there took slaves without the snapping of a gun on either side, moved them through the country, and finally left them in Canada. I designed to have done the same thing again, on a larger scale. That was all I intended. I never did intend murder, or treason, or the destruction of property, or to excite or incite slaves to rebellion, or to make insurrection.

I have another objection; and that is, it is unjust that I should suffer such a penalty. Had I interfered in the manner which I admit, and which I admit has been fairly proved (for I admire the truthfulness and candor of the greater portion of the witnesses who have testified in this case),—had I so interfered in behalf of the rich, the powerful, the intelligent, the so-called great, or in behalf of any of their friends,—either father, mother, brother, sister, wife, or children, or any of that class,—and suffered and sacrificed what I have in this interference, it would have been all right; and every man in this court would have deemed it an act worthy of reward rather than punishment.

This court acknowledges, as I suppose, the validity of the law of God. I see a book kissed here which I suppose to be the Bible, or at least the New Testament. That teaches me that all things whatsoever I would that men should do to me, I should do even so to them. It teaches me, further, to "remember them that are in bonds, as bound with them." I endeavored to act up to that instruction. I say, I am yet too young to understand that God is any respecter of persons. I believe that to have interfered as I have done—as I have always freely admitted I have done—in behalf of His despised poor, was not wrong, but right. Now, if it is deemed necessary that I should forfeit my life for the furtherance of the ends of justice, and mingle my blood further with the blood of my children and with the blood of millions in this slave country whose rights are disregarded by wicked, cruel, and unjust enactments,—I submit; so let it be done!

Let me say one word further.

I feel entirely satisfied with the treatment I have received on my trial. Considering all the circumstances, it has been more generous than I expected. But I feel no consciousness of guilt. I have stated from the first what was my intention, and what was not. I never had any design against the life of any person, nor any disposition to commit treason, or excite slaves to rebel, or make any general insurrection. I never encouraged any man to do so, but always discouraged any idea of that kind.

Let me say, also, a word in regard to the statements made by some of those connected with me. I hear it has been stated by some of them that I have induced them to join me. But the contrary is true. I do not say this to injure them, but as regretting their weakness. There is not one of them but joined me of his own accord, and the greater part of them at their own expense. A number of them I never saw, and never had a word of conversation with, till the day they came to me; and that was for the purpose I have stated.

Now I have done.

SOURCE: *The Life, Trial, and Execution of Captain John Brown . . . Compiled from Official and Authentic Sources.* New York: R. M. DeWitt, 1859.

THE NAT TURNER INSURRECTION
(1859, by Thomas Hamilton)

Nat Turner (1800–1831) was a slave in Southampton County, Virginia. A precocious child, Turner learned to read at a young age and eventually became a preacher renowned by both blacks and whites. Believing he was called by God to lead his fellow slaves to freedom, Turner staged a violent rebellion in 1831. Under cover of night, he and other slaves killed his master and family before marauding across the countryside. The uprising was swiftly put down the next day, but not before fifty-one whites had been murdered. Turner and some two hundred other slaves, many uninvolved with the violence, were executed in revenge. In the wake of the attacks, the South passed many punitive slaves codes, including bans on literacy among slaves. The Nat Turner Insurrection became for pro and antislavery forces alike a powerful image of the brutality inherent in slavery.

Anglo-African Magazine reprinted Thomas Gray's *Confession of Nat Turner* to mark John Brown's 1859 execution at Harper's Ferry. In his introduction, editor Thomas Hamilton compared the two radicals: both were compelled by conscience and God to free slaves; both were maniacal in their pursuit of emancipation. But where Turner believed freedom possible only with the destruction of the slaveholding race, Brown saw that slaves could be freed without undue bloodshed. While this characterization denied Brown's own use of violence, it served to raise the specter of armed slave rebellion, a fear never far from slaveholders' thoughts. Hamilton remarked that the South was less able to defend itself against insurrection in 1859 than it was in 1831. He posited that Turner would have succeeded were he in Brown's place at Harper's Ferry. Hamilton implored the nation to delay no longer in its decision to emancipate, a choice to be made between hatred and compassion.

Mark D. Baumann,
New York University

See also **Nat Turner's Rebellion; Slave Insurrections.**

There are two reasons why we present our readers with the Confession of Nat Turner. First, to place upon record this most remarkable episode in the history of human slavery, which proves to the philosophic observer, that in the midst of the most perfectly contrived and apparently secure systems of slavery, humanity will out, and engender from its bosom forces, that will contend against oppression, however unsuccessfully: and secondly, that the two methods of Nat Turner and of John Brown may be compared. The one is the mode in which the slave seeks freedom for his fellows, and the other, the mode in which the white man seeks to set the slave free. There are many points of similarity between these two men: they were both idealists; both governed by their views of the teachings of the Bible; both had harbored for years the purpose to which they gave up their lives; both felt themselves swayed as by some divine, or at least, spiritual, impulse; the one seeking in the air, the earth and the heavens, for signs which came at last; and the other, obeying impulses which he believes to have been foreordained from the eternal past; both cool, calm and heroic in prison and in the prospect of inevitable death; both confess with child-like frankness and simplicity the object they had in view—the pure and simple emancipation of their fellow-men; both win from the judges who sentence them, expressions of deep sympathy—and here the parallel ceases. Nat Turner's terrible logic could only see the enfranchisement of one race, compassed by the extirpation of the other; and he followed his gory syllogism with rude exactitude. John Brown, believing that the freedom of the enthralled could only be effected by placing them on an equality with their enslavers, and unable, in the very effort at emancipation, to tyrannize himself, is moved with compassion for tyrants as well as slaves, and seeks to extirpate this formidable cancer, without spilling one drop of christian blood.

These two narratives present a fearful choice to the slaveholders, nay, to this great nation—which of the two modes of emancipation shall take place? The method of Nat Turner or the method of John Brown?

Emancipation must take place, and soon. There can be no long delay in the choice of methods. If John Brown's be not soon adopted by the free North, then Nat Turner's will be by the enslaved South.

Had the order of events been reversed—had Nat Turner been in John Brown's place, at the head of these twenty one men, governed by his inexorable logic and cool daring, the soil of Virginia and Maryland and the far South, would by this time be drenched in blood, and the wild and sanguinary course of these men no earthly power then could stay.

The course which the South is now frantically pursuing, will engender in its bosom and nurse into maturity a hundred Nat Turners, when Virginia is infinitely less able to resist in 1860, than she was in 1831.

So, people of the South, people of the North! men and brethren, choose ye which method of emancipation you prefer—Nat Turner's or John Brown's?

SOURCE: Hamilton, Thomas. *Anglo-African Magazine* (1859).

EXCERPT FROM "THE CRIME AGAINST KANSAS" SPEECH
(1861, by Charles Sumner)

Charles Sumner (1811–1874) was the son of an anti-slavery lawyer in Boston. A skilled orator, he rose to prominence with an incendiary speech denouncing the Mexican-American War in 1845. He was elected to the U.S. Senate five years later.

Sumner's "Crime Against Kansas" speech was delivered to the Senate in 1856. In it, he condemned the Kansas and Nebraska Act of 1854 as a maneuver designed to give proslavery sentiments legislative primacy while denying the illegal, unconstitutional, and, not least, immoral reality of slavery. Authored by Senator Stephen Douglas of Illinois, the Act repealed the Missouri Compromise of 1820 and allowed slavery to enter the Territories. Further, the Act forbade Congress from setting the slave policy of the Territories, leaving the decision instead to the regions' inhabitants, a doctrine known as "popular sovereignty." The pro and antislavery settlers flooding the Territories clashed so often and so violently that the area became known as "Bleeding Kansas." The crime against Kansas, Sumner argued, was the "swindle" perpetuated by the Act upon the people of the nation: slaveholders were allowed to bring slavery to the Territories, while the people there were free to bar its entry. The law's treachery could bring nothing but bloodshed.

Besides Douglas, the speech also indicted Andrew P. Butler, a Senator from South Carolina. Two days after the speech Butler's nephew, Representative Preston Brooks, approached Sumner's desk in the Senate and viciously beat Sumner with a cane. Sumner's injuries kept him away from the Senate for almost three years while he was recuperating. With a keen eye for injustice, Sumner helped the Radical Republicans lead efforts to bring suffrage to the freed slaves during Reconstruction. In 1870, he blocked President Ulysses S. Grant's attempt to annex Santo Domingo, now the Dominican Republic.

Mark D. Baumann,
New York University

See also **Antislavery; Compromise of 1850; Kansas-Nebraska Act.**

I. It belongs to me now, in the first place, to expose the Crime against Kansas, in its origin and extent. Logically, this is the beginning of the argument. I say Crime, and deliberately adopt this strongest term, as better than any other denoting the consummate transgression. I would go further, if language could further go. It is the Crime of Crimes—surpassing far the old crimen majestatis, pursued with vengeance by the laws of Rome, and containing all other crimes, as the greater contains the less. I do not go too far, when I call it the Crime against Nature, from which the soul recoils, and which language refuses to describe. To lay bare this enormity, I now proceed. The whole subject has already become a twice-told tale, and its renewed recital will be a renewal of its sorrow and shame; but I shall not hesitate to enter upon it. The occasion requires it from the beginning.

It has been well remarked by a distinguished historian of our country, that at the Ithuriel touch of the Missouri discussion, the slave interest, hitherto hardly recognized as a distinct element in our system, started up portentous and dilated, with threats and assumptions, which are the origin of our existing national politics. This was in 1820. The discussion ended with the admission of Missouri as a slaveholding State, and the prohibition of Slavery in all the remaining territory west of the Mississippi, and north of 36 degrees 30 minutes, leaving the condition of other territory, south of this line, or subsequently acquired, untouched by the arrangement. Here was a solemn act of legislation, called at the time a compromise, a covenant, a compact, first brought forward in this body by a slaveholder, vindicated by slaveholders in debate, finally sanctioned by slaveholding votes, also upheld at the time by the essential approbation of a slaveholding President, James Monroe, and his Cabinet, of whom a majority were slaveholders, including Mr. Calhoun himself; and this compromise was made the condition of the admission of Missouri, without which that State could not have been received into the Union. The bargain was simple, and was applicable, of course, only to the territory named. Leaving all other territory to await the judgment of another generation, the South said to the North, Conquer your prejudices so far as to admit Missouri as a slave State, and, in consideration of this much-coveted boon, Slavery shall be prohibited forever in all the remaining Louisiana Territory above 36 degrees 30; and the North yielded.

In total disregard of history, the President, in his annual message, has told us that this compromise "was reluctantly acquiesced in by the Southern States." Just the contrary is true. It was the work of slaveholders, and was crowded by their concurring votes upon a reluctant North. At the time it was hailed by slaveholders as a victory. Charles Pinckney, of South Carolina, in an oft-quoted letter, written at three o'clock on the night of its passage, says, "It is considered here by the slaveholding States as a great triumph." At the North it was accepted as a defeat, and the friends of Freedom everywhere throughout the country bowed their heads with mortification. But little did they know the completeness of their disaster. Little did they dream that the prohibition of Slavery in the Territory, which was stipulated as the price of their fatal capitulation, would also at the very moment of its maturity be wrested from them.

Time passed, and it became necessary to provide for this Territory an organized government. Suddenly, without notice in the public press, or the prayer of a single petition, or one word of open recommendation from the President,—after an acquiescence of thirty-three years, and the irreclaimable possession by the South of its special share under this compromise,—in violation of every obligation of honor, compact, and good neighborhood,—and in contemptuous disregard of the out-gushing sentiments of an aroused North, this time-honored prohibition, in itself a Landmark of Freedom, was overturned, and the vast region now known as Kansas and Nebraska was opened to Slavery. It was natural that a measure thus repugnant in character should be pressed by arguments mutually repugnant. It was urged on two principal reasons, so opposite and inconsistent as to slap each other in the face: one being that, by the repeal of the prohibition, the Territory would be left open to the entry of slaveholders with their slaves, without hindrance; and the other being that the people would be left absolutely free to determine the question for themselves, and to prohibit the entry of slaveholders with their slaves, if they should think best. With some, the apology was the alleged rights of slaveholders; with others, it was the alleged rights of the people. With some, it was openly the extension of Slavery; and with others, it was openly the establishment of Freedom, under the guise of Popular Sovereignty. Of course, the measure, thus upheld in defiance of reason, was carried through Congress in defiance of all the securities of legislation; and I mention these things that you may see in what foulness the present Crime was engendered.

It was carried, first, by whipping in to its support, through Executive influence and patronage, men who acted against their own declared judgment, and the known will of their constituents. Secondly, by foisting out of place, both in the Senate and House of Representatives, important business, long pending, and usurping its room. Thirdly, by trampling under foot the rules of the House of Representatives, always before the safeguard of the minority. And fourthly, by driving it to a close during the very session in which it originated, so that it might not be arrested by the indignant voice of the people. Such are some of the means by which this snap judgment was obtained. If the clear will of the people had not been disregarded, it could not have passed. If the Government had not nefariously interposed its influence, it could not have passed. If it had been left to its natural place in the order of business, it could not have passed. If the rules of the House and the rights of the minority had not been violated, it could not have passed. If it had been allowed to go over to another Congress, when the people might be heard, it would have been ended; and then the Crime we now deplore would have been without its first seminal life.

Mr. President, I mean to keep absolutely within the limits of parliamentary propriety. I make no personal imputations; but only with frankness, such as belongs to the occasion and my own character, describe a great historical act, which is now enrolled in the Capitol. Sir, the Nebraska Bill was in every respect a swindle. It was a swindle by the South of the North. It was, on the part of those who had already completely enjoyed their share of the Missouri Compromise, a swindle of those whose share was yet absolutely untouched; and the plea of unconstitutionality set up—like the plea of usury after the borrowed money has been enjoyed—did not make it less a swindle. Urged as a Bill of Peace, it was a swindle of the whole country. Urged as opening the doors to slave-masters with their slaves, it was a swindle of the asserted doctrine of Popular Sovereignty. Urged as sanctioning Popular Sovereignty, it was a swindle of the asserted rights of slave-masters. It was a swindle of a broad territory, thus cheated of protection against Slavery. It was a swindle of a great cause, early espoused by Washington, Franklin, and Jefferson, surrounded by the best fathers of the Republic. Sir, it was a swindle of God-given inalienable rights. Turn it over, look at it on all sides, and it is everywhere a swindle; and, if the word I now employ has not the authority of classical usage, it has, on this occasion, the indubitable authority of fitness. No other word will adequately express the mingled meanness and wickedness of the cheat.

Its character was still further apparent in the general structure of the bill. Amidst overflowing professions of regard for the sovereignty of the people in the Territory, they were despoiled of every essential privilege of sovereignty. They were not allowed to choose their Governor, Secretary, Chief Justice, Associate Justices, Attorney, or Marshal—all of whom are sent from Washington; nor were they allowed to regulate the salaries of any of these functionaries, or the daily allowance of the legislative body, or even the pay of the clerks and door-keepers; but they were left free to adopt Slavery. And this was called Popular Sovereignty! Time does not allow, nor does the occasion require, that I should stop to dwell on this transparent device to cover a transcendent wrong. Suffice it to say, that Slavery is in itself an arrogant denial of Human Rights, and by no human reason can the power to establish such a wrong be placed among the attributes of any just sovereignty. In refusing it such a place, I do not deny popular rights, but uphold them; I do not restrain popular rights, but extend them. And, sir, to this conclusion you must yet come, unless deaf, not only to the admonitions of political justice, but also to the genius of our own constitution, under which, when properly interpreted, no valid claim for Slavery can be set up anywhere in the national territory. The senator from Michigan [Mr. Cass] may say, in response to the senator from Mississippi [Mr. Brown], that Slavery cannot go into the Territory under the constitution, without legislative introduction; and permit me to add, in response to both, that Slavery cannot go there at all. Nothing can come out of nothing; and there is absolutely nothing in the constitution out of which Slavery can be derived, while there are provisions, which, when properly interpreted, make its existence anywhere within the exclusive national jurisdiction impossible.

The offensive provision in the bill was in its form a legislative anomaly, utterly wanting the natural directness and simplicity of an honest transaction. It did not undertake openly to repeal the old Prohibition of Slavery, but seemed to mince the matter, as if conscious of the swindle. It is said that this Prohibition, "being inconsistent with the principle of non-intervention by Congress with Slavery in the States and Territories as recognized by the legislation of 1850, commonly called the Compromise Measures, is hereby declared inoperative and void." Thus, with insidious ostentation, was it pretended that an act, violating the greatest compromise of our legislative history, and setting loose the foundations of all compromise, was derived out of a compromise. Then followed in the Bill the further declaration, which is entirely without precedent, and which has been aptly called "a stump speech in its belly," namely, "it being the true intent and meaning of this act, not to legislate Slavery into any Territory or State, nor to exclude it therefrom, but to leave the people thereof perfectly free to form and regulate their domestic institutions in their own way, subject only to the constitution of the United States." Here were smooth words, such as belong to a cunning tongue, enlisted in a bad cause. But, whatever may have been their various hidden meanings, this at least was evident, that, by their effect, the Congressional Prohibition of Slavery, which had always been regarded as a seven-fold shield, covering the whole Louisiana Territory north of 36 (degree) 30 (minute), was now removed, while a principle as declared, which would render the supplementary Prohibition of Slavery in Minnesota, Oregon, and Washington, "inoperative and void," and thus open to Slavery all these vast regions, now the rude cradles of mighty States. Here you see the magnitude of the mischief contemplated. But my purpose now is with the Crime against Kansas, and I shall not stop to expose the conspiracy beyond.

Mr. President, men are wisely presumed to intend the natural consequences of their conduct, and to seek what their acts seem to promote. Now, the Nebraska Bill, on its very face, openly cleared the way for Slavery, and it is not wrong to presume that its originators intended the natural consequences of such an act, and sought in this way to extend Slavery. Of course, they did. And this is the first stage in the Crime against Kansas.

But this was speedily followed by other developments. The bare-faced scheme was soon whispered, that Kansas must be a slave State. In conformity with this idea was the Government of this unhappy Territory organized in all its departments; and thus did the President, by whose complicity the Prohibition of Slavery had been overthrown, lend himself to a new complicity—giving to the conspirators a lease of connivance, amounting even to copartnership. The Governor, Secretary, Chief Justice, Associate Justices, Attorney, and Marshal, with a whole caucus of other stipendiaries, nominated by the President and confirmed by the Senate, were all commended as friendly to Slavery. No man, with the sentiments of Washington, or Jefferson, or Franklin, found any favor; nor is it too much to say, that, had these great patriots once more come among us, not one of them, with his recorded unretracted opinions on Slavery, could have been nominated by the President or confirmed by the Senate for any post in that Territory. With such auspices the conspiracy proceeded. Even in advance of the Nebraska Bill, secret societies were organized in Missouri, ostensibly to protect her institutions, and afterwards, under the name of "Self-Defensive Associations," and of "Blue Lodges," these were multiplied throughout the western counties of that State, before any counter-movement from the North. It was confidently anticipated, that, by the activity of these societies, and the interest of slaveholders everywhere, with the advantage derived from the neighborhood of Missouri, and the influence of the Territorial Government, Slavery might be introduced into Kansas, quietly but surely, without arousing a conflict; that the crocodile egg might be stealthily dropped in the sunburnt soil, there to be hatched unobserved until it sent forth its reptile monster.

But the conspiracy was unexpectedly balked. The debate, which convulsed Congress, had stirred the whole country. Attention from all sides was directed upon Kansas, which at once became the favorite goal of emigration. The Bill had loudly declared that its object was "to leave the people perfectly free to form and regulate their domestic institutions in their own way;" and its supporters everywhere challenged the determination of the question between Freedom and Slavery by a competition of emigration. Thus, while opening the Territory to Slavery, the Bill also opened it to emigrants from every quarter, who might by their votes redress the wrong. The populous North, stung by a sharp sense of outrage, and inspired by a noble cause, poured into the debatable land, and promised soon to establish a supremacy of numbers there, involving, of course, a just supremacy of Freedom.

Then was conceived the consummation of the Crime against Kansas. What could not be accomplished peaceably, was to be accomplished forcibly. The reptile monster, that could not be quietly and securely hatched there, was to be pushed full-grown into the Territory. All efforts were now given to the dismal work of forcing Slavery on Free Soil. In flagrant derogation of the very Popular Sovereignty whose name helped to impose this Bill upon the country, the atrocious object was now distinctly avowed. And the avowal has been followed by the act. Slavery has been forcibly introduced into Kansas, and placed under the formal safeguards of pretended law. How this was done, belongs to the argument.

In depicting this consummation, the simplest outline, without one word of color, will be best. Whether regarded in its mass or its details, in its origin or its result, it is all blackness, illumined by nothing from itself, but only by the heroism of the undaunted men and women whom it environed. A plain statement of facts will be a picture of fearful truth, which faithful history will preserve in its darkest gallery. In the foreground all will recognize a familiar character, in himself a connecting link between the President and the border ruffian,—less conspicuous for ability than for the exalted place he has occupied,—who once sat in the seat where you now sit, sir; where once sat John Adams and Thomas Jefferson; also, where once sat Aaron Burr. I need not add the name of David R. Atchison. You have not forgotten that, at the session of Congress immediately succeeding the Nebraska Bill, he came tardily to his duty here, and then, after a short time, disappeared. The secret has been long since disclosed. Like Catiline, he stalked into this Chamber, reeking with conspiracy—immo in Senatum venit—and then like Catiline he skulked away—abiit, excessit, evasit, crupit—to join and provoke the conspirators, who at a distance awaited their congenial chief. Under the influence of his malign presence the Crime ripened to its fatal fruits, while the similitude with Catiline was again renewed in the sympathy, not even concealed, which he found in the very Senate itself, where, beyond even the Roman example, a senator has not hesitated to appear as his open compurgator.

And now, as I proceed to show the way in which this Territory was overrun and finally subjugated to Slavery, I desire to remove in advance all question with regard to the authority on which I rely. The evidence is secondary; but it is the best which, in the nature of the case, can be had, and it is not less clear, direct, and peremptory, than any by which we are assured of the campaigns in the Crimea or the fall of Sevastopol. In its manifold mass, I confidently assert that it is such a body of evidence as the human mind is not able to resist. It is found in the concurring reports of the public press; in the letters of correspondents; in the testimony of travellers; and in the unaffected story to which I have listened from leading citizens, who, during this winter, have "come flocking" here from that distant Territory. It breaks forth in the irrepressible outcry, reaching us from Kansas, in truthful tones, which leave no ground of mistake. It addresses us in formal complaints, instinct with the indignation of a people determined to be free, and unimpeachable as the declarations of a murdered man on his dying bed against his murderer. And let me add, that all this testimony finds an echo in the very statute-book of the conspirators, and also in language dropped from the President of the United States.

SOURCE: Sumner, Charles. *The Crime against Kansas. Speech of Hon. Charles Sumner, of Massachusetts. In the Senate of the United States, May 19, 1856.* New York: Greeley & McElrath, 1856.

SOUTH CAROLINA DECLARATION OF CAUSES OF SECESSION *(1860)*

On 20 December 1860, the state of South Carolina sounded the clarion call of secession that rapidly reverberated through the South. The plantation aristocrats, who dominated the state legislature, fearing for the livelihood of their cherished "peculiar institution," voted unanimously to repeal South Carolina's ratification of the U.S. Constitution and thus leave the Union.

While citing what they deemed breaches of the Constitution and states' rights, the legislature denounced newly elected Abraham Lincoln as a representative of a "sectional party" determined to undermine the state's autonomy and tear the very social fabric of the South. Slavery lay at the heart of South Carolina's grievances with the federal government, as Lincoln's election signified the final maneuver of a steadily encroaching Northern hegemony over Southern politics and life. Employing a logic akin to that found in the "social contract" philosophy of John Locke and Jean Jacques Rousseau, the "Declaration of Causes of Secession" argues that the "constitutional compact" between state and nation had "been deliberately broken and disregarded" and thus ceased to be binding.

By 1 February 1861, six more Southern states had followed the lead of the "fire-eating" South Carolinians. Nearly fifty years of turbulence in the relationship between the state of South Carolina and the federal government had finally reached the point of irreconcilable differences. After the nullification campaign of 1832 and near secession in 1836 and 1852, South Carolina took the first official step toward dividing the Union. The new consensus among Southerners regarding secession, which had not existed in 1836 and 1852, placed South Carolina at the spearhead of a steady movement toward civil war.

Paul S. Bartels,
Villanova University

See also **Civil War; Secession; South, the: The Antebellum South; South Carolina.**

The people of the State of South Carolina in Convention assembled, on the 2d day of April, A. D. 1852, declared that the frequent violations of the Constitution of the United States by the Federal Government, and its encroachments upon the reserved rights of the States, fully justified this State in their withdrawal from the Federal Union; but in deference to the opinions and wishes of the other Slaveholding States, she forbore at that time to exercise this right. Since that time these encroachments have continued to increase, and further forbearance ceases to be a virtue.

And now the State of South Carolina having resumed her separate and equal place among nations, deems it due to herself, to the remaining United States of America, and to the nations of the world, that she should declare the immediate causes which have led to this act.

In 1787, Deputies were appointed by the States to revise the articles of Confederation; and on 17th

September, 1787, these Deputies recommended, for the adoption of the States, the Articles of Union, known as the Constitution of the United States.

. . .Thus was established by compact between the States, a Government with defined objects and powers, limited to the express words of the grant. . . .We hold that the Government thus established is subject to the two great principles asserted in the Declaration of Independence; and we hold further, that the mode of its formation subjects it to a third fundamental principle, namely, the law of compact. We maintain that in every compact between two or more parties, the obligation is mutual; that the failure of one of the contracting parties to perform a material part of the agreement, entirely releases the obligation of the other; and that, where no arbiter is provided, each party is remitted to his own judgment to determine the fact of failure, with all its consequences.

In the present case, that fact is established with certainty. We assert that fourteen of the States have deliberately refused for years past to fulfil their constitutional obligations, and we refer to their own statutes for the proof.

The Constitution of the United States, in its fourth Article, provides as follows:

> "No person held to service or labor in one State under the laws thereof, escaping into another, shall, in consequence of any law or regulation therein, be discharged from such service or labor, but shall be delivered up, on claim of the party to whom such service or labor may be due."

This stipulation was so material to the compact that without it that compact would not have been made. The greater number of the contracting parties held slaves, and they had previously evinced their estimate of the value of such a stipulation by making it a condition in the Ordinance for the government of the territory ceded by Virginia, which obligations, and the laws of the General Government, have ceased to effect the objects of the Constitution. The States of Maine, New Hampshire, Vermont, Massachusetts, Connecticut, Rhode Island, New York, Pennsylvania, Illinois, Indiana, Michigan, Wisconsin and Iowa, have enacted laws which either nullify the acts of Congress, or render useless any attempt to execute them. In many of these States the fugitive is discharged from the service of labor claimed, and in none of them has the State Government complied with the stipulation made in the Constitution. The State of New Jersey, at an early day, passed a law in conformity with her constitutional obligation; but the current of Anti-Slavery feeling has led her more recently to enact laws which render inoperative the remedies provided by her own laws and by the laws of Congress. In the State of New York even the right of transit for a slave has been denied by her tribunals; and the States of Ohio and Iowa have refused to surrender to justice fugitives charged with murder, and with inciting servile insurrection in the State of Virginia. Thus the constitutional compact has been deliberately broken and disregarded by the non-slaveholding States; and the consequence follows that South Carolina is released from her obligation. . . .

We affirm that these ends for which this Government was instituted have been defeated, and the Government itself has been destructive of them by the action of the non-slaveholding States. Those States have assumed the right of deciding upon the propriety of our domestic institutions; and have denied the rights of property established in fifteen of the States and recognized by the Constitution; they have denounced as sinful the institution of Slavery; they have permitted the open establishment among them of societies, whose avowed object is to disturb the peace of and eloin the property of the citizens of other States. They have encouraged and assisted thousands of our slaves to leave their homes; and those who remain, have been incited by emissaries, books, and pictures, to servile insurrection.

For twenty-five years this agitation has been steadily increasing, until it has now secured to its aid the power of the common Government. Observing the *forms* of the Constitution, a sectional party has found within that article establishing the Executive Department, the means of subverting the Constitution itself. A geographical line has been drawn across the Union, and all the States north of that line have united in the election of a man to the high office of President of the United States whose opinions and purposes are hostile to Slavery. He is to be intrusted with the administration of the common Government, because he has declared that "Government cannot endure permanently half slave, half free," and that the public mind must rest in the belief that Slavery is in the course of ultimate extinction.

This sectional combination for the subversion of the Constitution has been aided, in some of the States, by elevating to citizenship persons who, by the supreme law of the land, are incapable of becoming citizens; and their votes have been used to inaugurate a new policy, hostile to the South, and destructive of its peace and safety.

On the 4th of March next this party will take possession of the Government. It has announced that the South shall be excluded from the common territory, that the Judicial tribunal shall be made sectional, and that a war must be waged against Slavery until it shall cease throughout the United States.

The guarantees of the Constitution will then no longer exist; the equal rights of the States will be lost. The Slaveholding States will no longer have the power of self-government, or self-protection, and the Federal Government will have become their enemy.

Sectional interest and animosity will deepen the irritation; and all hope of remedy is rendered vain, by the fact that the public opinion at the North has invested a great political error with the sanctions of a more erroneous religious belief.

We, therefore, the people of South Carolina, by our delegates in Convention assembled, appealing to the Supreme Judge of the world for the rectitude of our intentions, have solemnly declared that the Union heretofore existing between this State and the other States of North America is dissolved, and that the State of South Carolina has resumed her position among the nations of the world, as a separate and independent state, with full power to levy war, conclude peace, contract alliances, establish commerce, and to do all other acts and things which independent States may of right do.

SOURCE: Moore, Frank, ed. *The Rebellion Record: A Diary of American Events, With Documents, Narratives, Illustrative Incidents, Poetry, etc.* New York: Putnam, 1861.

BENJAMIN BUTLER'S REPORT ON THE CONTRABANDS OF WAR
(1861, by Benjamin Butler)

In May 1861, three slaves who had been building Confederate fortifications slipped across rebel lines to General Benjamin Franklin Butler's position at Fort Monroe, Virginia. A Confederate colonel appeared the next day under flag of truce demanding that his property be returned under authority of the fugitive slave law. Butler rebuffed him, citing the fact that Virginia's secession from the Union exonerated him from any obligation to respect the law. He labeled the absconders "contraband of war" and promptly set them to work behind his own lines.

Butler had amassed over nine hundred contraband slaves by July and subsequently wrote to Secretary of War Simon Cameron for policy advice. The general asked two important questions: what should be done with the slaves, and second, whether they were free upon arrival in his camp. Butler made his own views rather clear, stating that the runaways were not property but men, women, and children worthy of the freedom "of those made in God's image."

After some hesitation, the administration approved Butler's "contraband" reasoning, but remained reticent on the question of freedom. The administration realized the strategic importance of slave labor in the Confederate Army, thus acting as much—if not more—out of practical concerns as humanitarian motives. The reply to Butler's letter also instructed him that contraband slaves could only be harbored if they had been directly employed by the Confederate armed forces. This hardly amounted to the measures that many Northern abolitionists had begun to call for, but the contraband policy did represent a significant step toward Emancipation and recognizing slavery as the central issue in the war.

Paul S. Bartels,
Villanova University

***See also* Civil War; Contraband, Slaves as; Contraband of War.**

From General Butler

Headquarters, Department of Virginia, Fortress Monroe, July 30th, 1861

Hon. Simon Cameron, Secretary of War

Sir: By an order received on the morning of the 28th July from Major General Dix, by a telegraphic order from Lieutenant-General Scott, I was commanded to forward, of the troops of this department, four regiments, and a half, including Colonel Baker's California regiment, to Washington, via Baltimore. This order reached me at 2 o'clock a.m., by special boat from Baltimore. Believing that it emanated because of some pressing exigency for the defense of Washington, I issued my orders before daybreak for the embarkation of the troops, sending those who were among the very best regiments I had. In the course of the following day they were all embarked for Baltimore, with the exception of some four hundred for whom I had not transportation, although I had all the transport force in the hands of the quartermaster here to aid the Bay line of steamers, which, by the same order from the lieutenant-general, was directed to furnish transportation. Up to, and at the time of the order, I had been preparing for an advance movement, by which I hoped to cripple the resources of the enemy at Yorktown, and especially by seizing a large quantity of negroes who were being pressed into their service in building the intrenchments there. I had five days previously been enabled to mount, for the first time, the first company of light artillery, which I had been empowered to raise, and they had but a single rifled cannon, an iron six-pounder. Of course everything must and did yield to the supposed exigency and the orders. This ordering away the troops from this department, while it weakened the posts at Newport News, necessitated the withdrawal of the troops from Hampton, where I was then throwing up intrenched works to enable me to hold the town with a small force, while I advanced up the York or James River. In the village of Hampton there were a large number of negroes, composed in a great measure of women and children of the men who had fled thither within my lines for protection, who had escaped from marauding parties of rebels, who had been gathering up able-bodied blacks to aid them in constructing their batteries on the James and York Rivers. I had employed the men in Hampton in throwing up intrenchments, and they were working zealously and efficiently at that duty, saving our soldiers from that labor under the gleam of the mid-day sun. The women were earning substantially their own subsistence in washing, marketing, and taking care of the clothes of the soldiers, and rations were being served out to the men who worked for the support of the children. But by the evacuation of Hampton, rendered necessary by the withdrawal of troops, leaving me scarcely five thousand men outside the fort including the force at Newport News, all these black people were obliged to break up their homes at Hampton, fleeing across the creek within my lines for protection and support. Indeed, it was a most distressing sight to see these poor creatures, who had trusted to the protection of the arms of the United States, and who aided the troops of the United States in their enterprise, to be thus obliged to flee from their homes, and the homes of their masters who had deserted them, and become fugitives from fear of the return of the rebel soldiery, who had threatened to shoot the men who had wrought for us, and to carry off the women who had served us to a worse than Egyptian bondage. I have, therefore, now within the peninsula, this side of Hampton Creek, nine hundred negroes, three hundred of whom are able-bodied men, thirty of whom are men substantially past hard labor, one hundred and seventy-five women, two hundred and twenty-five children under the age of ten years, and one hundred and seventy between ten and eighteen years, and many more coming in. The questions which this state of facts present are very embarrassing.

First. What shall be done with them? and, Second. What is their state and condition? Upon these questions I desire the instructions of the department.

The first question, however, may perhaps be answered by considering the last. Are these men, women, and children slaves? Are they free? Is their condition that of men, women, and children, or of property, or is it a mixed relation? What their status was under the constitution and laws, we all know. What has been the effect of a rebellion and a state of war upon that status? When I adopted the theory of treating the able-bodied negro fit to work in the trenches as property liable to be used in aid of rebellion, and so contraband of war, that condition of things was in so far met, as I then and still believe, on a legal and constitutional basis. But now a new series of questions arise. Passing by women, the children, certainly, cannot be treated on that basis; if property, they must be considered the incumbrance rather than the auxiliary of an army, and, of course, in no possible legal relation could be treated as contraband. Are they property? If they were so, they have been left by their masters and owners, deserted, thrown away, abandoned, like the wrecked vessel upon the ocean. Their former possessors and owners have causelessly, traitorously, rebelliously, and, to carry out the figure, practically abandoned them to be swallowed up by the winter storm of starvation. If property, do they not become the property of salvors? But we, their salvors, do not need and will not hold such property, and will assume no such ownership: has not, therefore, all proprietary relation ceased? Have they not become, thereupon, men, women, and children? No longer under ownership of any kind, the fearful relicts of fugitive masters, have they not by their master's acts, and the state of war, assumed the condition, which we hold to be the normal one, of those made in God's image? Is not every constitutional, legal, and normal requirement, as well to the runaway master as their relinquished slaves, thus answered? I confess that my own mind is compelled by this reasoning to look upon them as men and women. If not free born, yet free, manumitted, sent forth from the hand that held them, never to be reclaimed.

Of course, if this reasoning, thus imperfectly set forth, is correct, my duty as a humane man is very plain. I should take the same care of these men, women, and children, houseless, homeless, and unprovided for, as I would of the same number of men, women, and children, who, for their attachment to the Union, had been driven or allowed to flee from the Confederate States. I should have no doubt on this question had I not seen it stated that an order had been issued by General McDowell in his department substantially forbidding all fugitive slaves from coming within his lines, or being harbored there. Is that order to be enforced in all military departments? If so, who are to be considered fugitive whose master runs away and leaves him? Is it forbidden to the troops to aid or harbor within their lines the negro children who are found therein, or is the soldier, when his march has destroyed their means of subsistence, to allow them to starve because he has driven off the rebel masters? Now, shall the commander of a regiment or battalion sit in judgment upon the question, whether any given black man has fled from his master, or his master fled from him? Indeed, how are the free born to be distinguished? Is one any more or less a fugitive slave because he has labored upon the rebel intrenchments? If he has so labored, if I understand it, he is to be harbored. By the reception of which are the rebels most to be distressed, by taking those who have wrought all their rebel masters desired, masked their battery, or those who have refused to labor and left the battery unmasked?

I have very decided opinions upon the subject of this order. It does not become me to criticise it, and I write in no spirit of criticism, but simply to explain the full difficulties that surround the enforcing it. If the enforcement of that order becomes the policy of the government, I, as a soldier, shall be bound to enforce it steadfastly, if not cheerfully. But if left to my own discretion, as you may have gathered from my reasoning, I should take a widely different course from that which it indicates.

In a loyal state, I would put down a servile insurrection. In a state of rebellion I would confiscate that which was used to oppose my arms—and take all that property which constituted the wealth of that state, and furnished the means by which the war is prosecuted, besides being the cause of the war; and if, in so doing, it should be objected that human beings were brought to the free enjoyment of life, liberty, and the pursuit of happiness, such objection might not require much consideration.

Pardon me for addressing the secretary of war directly upon this question, as it involves some political considerations as well as propriety of military action.

(Benj. F. Butler)

SOURCE: Moore, Frank, ed. *The Rebellion Record: A Diary of American Events, with Documents, Narratives, Illustrative Incidents, Poetry, etc., etc.* New York: Putnam, 1861–1868.

A CONFEDERATE BLOCKADE-RUNNER
(1862, by John Wilkinson)

During the time of the American Civil War, the closing of seaports was a matter left in the hands of local officials. In a move to prevent the delivery of supplies and weapons from allies both domestic and foreign, President Abraham Lincoln ordered a blockade by Federal ships of all major Southern U.S. ports. Some historians later regarded this action as a constitutional breach of his authority, since it effectively meant redefining the newly formed Confederate States of America as a hostile, and autonomous, entity. The move gave rise to one of the most romantic figures of the war, the blockade-runner, who slipped past fleets of heavily armed Union ships on moonless nights and often under fire to bring food and medicine to desperate Southern cities. John Wilkinson (1821–1891) was perhaps the most famous of these. A twenty-year veteran of the Navy, Wilkinson attempted to resign his commission when Virginia seceded from the Union, but was upbraided and subsequently dishonorably discharged. Shortly after, he was dispatched to England, where he purchased the steamship *Giraffe,* renamed *Robert E. Lee.* On the night of 28 December 1862, Wilkinson ran his first blockade off the shores of Wilmington, North Carolina. Among his many adventures and narrow escapes, he once created a smoke cloud from the *Lee*'s funnels using low-grade North Carolina coal and coal dust to throw off the doggedly pursuing USS *Iroquois,* fastest of the Federal blockade cruisers. After the war, he resigned himself to life in Nova Scotia, but at last returned to his native Virginia and, in 1877, published a widely read account of his experiences.

Laura M. Miller,
Vanderbilt University

See also **Blockade Runners, Confederate; Civil War.**

The natural advantages of Wilmington for blockade-running were very great, chiefly owing to the fact, that there are two separate and distinct approaches to Cape Fear River, i.e., either by "New Inlet" to the north of Smith's Island, or by the "western bar" to the south of it. This island is ten or eleven miles in length; but the Frying Pan Shoals extend ten or twelve miles further south, making the distance by sea between the two bars thirty miles or more, although the direct distance between them is only six or seven miles. From Smithville, a little village nearly equi-distant from either bar, both blockading fleets could be distinctly seen, and the outward bound blockade-runners could take their choice through which of them to run the gauntlet. The inward bound blockade-runners, too, were guided by circumstances of wind and weather; selecting that bar over which they would cross, after they had passed the Gulf Stream; and shaping their course accordingly. The approaches to both bars were clear of danger, with the single exception of the "Lump" . . . and so regular are the soundings that the shore can be coasted for miles within a stone's throw of the breakers.

These facts explain why the United States fleet were unable wholly to stop blockade-running. It was, indeed, impossible to do so; the result to the very close of the war proves this assertion; for in spite of the vigilance of the fleet, many blockade-runners were afloat when Fort Fisher was captured. In truth the passage through the fleet was little dreaded; for although the blockade-runner might receive a shot or two, she was rarely disabled; and in proportion to the increase of the fleet, the greater would be the danger (we knew,) of their firing into each other. As the boys before the deluge used to say, they would be very apt "to miss the cow and kill the calf," The chief danger was upon the open sea; many of the light cruisers having great speed. As soon as one of them discovered a blockade-runner during daylight she would attract other cruisers in the vicinity by sending up a dense column of smoke, visible for many miles in clear weather. A "cordon" of fast steamers stationed ten or fifteen miles apart *inside the Gulf Stream*, and in the course from Nassau and Bermuda to Wilmington and Charleston, would have been more effectual in stopping blockade-running than the whole United States Navy concentrated off those ports; and it was unaccountable to us why such a plan did not occur to good Mr. Welles; but it was not our place to suggest it. I have no doubt, however, that the fraternity to which I then belonged would have unanimously voted thanks and a service of plate to the Hon. Secretary of the United States Navy for this oversight. I say *inside the Gulf Stream*, because every experienced captain of a blockade-runner made a point to cross "the stream" early enough in the afternoon, if possible, to establish the ship's position by chronometer so as to escape the influence of that current upon his dead reckoning. The lead always gave indication of our distance from the land, but not, of course, of our position; and the numerous salt works along the coast, where evaporation was produced by fire, and which were at work night and day were visible long before the low coast could be seen. Occasionally the whole inward voyage would be made under adverse conditions. Cloudy, thick weather and heavy gales would prevail so as to prevent any solar or lunar observations, and reduce the dead reckoning to mere guess work. In these cases the nautical knowledge and judgment of the captain would be taxed to the utmost. The current of the Gulf Stream varies in velocity and (within certain limits) in direction; and the stream, itself almost as well defined as a river within its banks under ordinary circumstances, is expelled by a strong gale toward the direction in which the wind is blowing, overflowing its banks as it were. The counter current, too, inside of the Gulf Stream is much influenced by the prevailing winds. Upon one occasion, while in command of the R. E. Lee, we had experienced very heavy and thick weather; and had crossed the Stream and struck soundings about midday. The weather then clearing so that we could obtain an altitude near meridian we found ourselves at least forty miles north of our supposed position and near the shoals which extended in a southerly direction off Cape Lookout. It would be more perilous to run out to sea than to continue on our course, for we had passed through the off shore line of blockaders, and the sky had become perfectly clear. I determined to personate a transport bound to Beaufort, which was in the possession of the United States forces, and the coaling station of the fleet blockading Wilmington. The risk of detection was not very great, for many of the captured blockade-runners were used as transports and dispatch vessels. Shaping our course for Beaufort, and slowing down, as we were in no haste to get there, we passed several vessels, showing United States colors to them all. Just as we were crossing through the ripple of shallow water off the "tail" of the shoals, we dipped our colors to a sloop of war which passed three or four miles to the south of us. The courtesy was promptly responded to; but I have no doubt her captain thought me a lubberly and careless seaman to shave the shoals so closely. We stopped the engines when no vessel was in sight; and I was relieved from a heavy burden of anxiety as the sun sank below the horizon; and the course was shaped at full speed for Masonboro' Inlet....

...A blockade-runner did not often pass through the fleet without receiving one or more shots, but these were always preceded by the flash of a calcium light, or by a blue light; and immediately followed by two rockets thrown in the direction of the blockade-runner. The signals were probably concerted each day for the ensuing night, as they appeared to be constantly changed; but the rockets were invariably sent up. I ordered a lot of rockets from New York. Whenever all hands were called to run through the fleet, an officer was stationed alongside of me on the bridge with the rockets. One or two minutes after our immediate pursuer had sent up his rockets, I would direct ours to be discharged at a right angle to our course. The whole fleet would be misled, for even if the vessel which had discovered us were not deceived, the rest of the fleet would be baffled....

The staid old town of Wilmington was turned "topsy turvy" during the war. Here resorted the speculators from all parts of the South, to attend the weekly auctions of imported cargoes; and the town was infested with rogues and desperadoes, who made a livelihood by robbery and murder.... The agents and employés of the different blockade-running companies, lived in magnificent style, paying a king's ransom (in Confederate money) for their household expenses, and nearly monopolizing the supplies in the country market....

SOURCE: Hart, Albert Bushnell, ed. *American History Told by Contemporaries.* Vol. 4. New York: Macmillan, 1901.

LETTER TO PRESIDENT LINCOLN FROM HARRISON'S LANDING
(1862, by General George B. McClellan)

Although Abraham Lincoln has since achieved almost mythical status in American historical and popular memory, in 1861 he entered the White House with remarkably humble credentials and perilously little experience. As a result, Major-General George B. McClellan ("Little Mac") possessed a low opinion of him. In his capacity as the highest-ranking Union officer in the field and commander of the Army of the Potomac, Little Mac considered himself best suited for advising the president as to how the war should be prosecuted.

McClellan's letter from Harrison Landing urged Lincoln not to upset the status quo in antebellum Southern social relations, especially with regard to slavery. Believing the Confederate states could be successfully returned to the fold of the Union through a crushing victory on the battlefield, McClellan failed to recognize deeper problems underlying secession and a movement toward modern warfare. He underestimated the integral role morale at home played in sustaining the Confederate war effort, believing armies and political institutions to be the only Union enemies. And unlike Lincoln, McClellan could not see that slavery lay at the heart of the sectional conflict.

As the course of events would later prove, "total war" and a commitment to abolishing the institution of slavery were necessary before peace could return to a reunited nation. The combatants waged war on the home front as well, and the Southern populace would have to experience the horrors of war firsthand before the Union could break its will to continue the conflict. McClellan's sentiments, on the other hand, depicted a man still attempting to fight a Napoleonic-style war and demonstrated why eventual success would come from replacements like U. S. Grant and William T. Sherman rather than himself. Lincoln worked diligently to devise a masterful grand strategy for victory, and through trial and error found the right personnel to execute it.

Paul S. Bartels,
Villanova University

See also **Civil War.**

Mr. President: . . . I earnestly desire . . . to lay before Your Excellency for your private consideration my general views concerning the existing state of the rebellion. . . . These views amount to convictions, and are deeply impressed upon my mind and heart. Our cause must never be abandoned; it is the cause of free institutions and self-government. The Constitution and the Union must be preserved, whatever may be the cost in time, treasure, and blood. If secession is successful, other dissolutions are clearly to be seen in the future. Let neither military disaster, political faction, nor foreign war shake your settled purpose to enforce the equal operation of the laws of the United States upon the people of every State.

The time has come when the Government must determine upon a civil and military policy covering the whole ground of our national trouble. The responsibility of determining, declaring, and supporting such civil and military policy, and of directing the whole course of national affairs in regard to the rebellion, must now be assumed and exercised by you, or our cause will be lost. The Constitution gives you power sufficient even for the present terrible exigency.

This rebellion has assumed the character of a war. As such it should be regarded, and it should be conducted upon the highest principles known to Christian civilization. It should not be a war looking to the subjugation of the people of any State in any event. It should not be at all a war upon population, but against armed forces and political organizations. Neither confiscation of property, political executions of persons, territorial organization of States, or forcible abolition of slavery should be contemplated for a moment.

In prosecuting the war all private property and unarmed persons should be strictly protected, subject only to the necessity of military operations; all private property taken for military use should be paid or receipted for; pillage and waste should be treated as high crimes, all unnecessary trespass sternly prohibited, and offensive demeanor by the military toward citizens promptly rebuked. Military arrests should not be tolerated, except in places where active hostilities exist, and oaths not required by enactments constitutionally made should be neither demanded nor received. Military government should be confined to the preservation of public order and the protection of political rights.

Military power should not be allowed to interfere with the relations of servitude, either by supporting or impairing the authority of the master, except for repressing disorder, as in other cases. Slaves, contraband under the act of Congress, seeking military protection, should receive it. The right of the Government to appropriate permanently to its own service claims to slave labor should be asserted, and the right of the owner to compensation therefor should be recognized. This principle might be extended, upon grounds of military necessity and security, to all the slaves of a particular State, thus working manumission in such State; and in Missouri, perhaps in Western Virginia also, and possibly even in Maryland, the expediency of such a measure is only a question of time. A system of policy thus constitutional, and pervaded by the influences of Christianity and freedom, would receive the support of almost all truly loyal men, would deeply impress the rebel masses and all foreign nations, and it might be humbly hoped that it would commend itself to the favor of the Almighty.

Unless the principles governing the future conduct of our struggle shall be made known and approved the effort to obtain requisite forces will be almost hopeless. A declaration of radical views, especially upon slavery, will rapidly disintegrate our present armies. The policy of the Government must be supported by concentrations of military power. The national forces should not be dispersed in expeditions, posts of occupation, and numerous armies, but should be mainly collected into masses, and brought to bear upon the armies of the Confederate States. Those armies thoroughly defeated, the political structure which they support would soon cease to exist.

. . . I have written this letter with sincerity toward you and from love for my country.

Very respectfully, your obedient servant,

Geo. B. McClellan,
Major-General, Commanding

SOURCE: McPherson, Edward, ed. *The Political History of the United States of America During the Great Rebellion, from November 6, 1860, to July 4, 1864; etc., etc.* Washington: Philip and Solomons, 1864.

ADDRESS TO PRESIDENT LINCOLN BY THE WORKING-MEN OF MANCHESTER, ENGLAND
(31 December 1862)

In Great Britain, the efforts of Christian humanitarians such as William Wilberforce and Thomas Clarkson, as well as an economy changing from a mercantile system to one of industrial capitalism, eventually led to the cessation of the British slave trade in 1807. The Abolition Act of 1833 brought the total elimination of the institution throughout the Empire. Eager to show their support for President Abraham Lincoln and the Emancipation Proclamation, which would become effective on 1 January 1863, a group of English laborers crafted the entreaty seen here. Their efforts were not without need. Lincoln, who had long favored a system of gradual emancipation to be carried out voluntarily by the states, came slowly to the idea of emancipation by executive order. Primarily viewing the American Civil War as necessary to preserve the Union, Lincoln once told the newspaper editor and recurrent political aspirant Horace Greeley, "If I could save the Union without freeing *any* slave, I would do it; and if I could save it by freeing *all* the slaves, I would do it; and if I could do it by freeing some and leaving others alone, I would also do that." In a response from mid-January 1863, the once-reluctant Lincoln thanked the Manchester writers for encouraging him in his difficult decision to expand the aims of the Civil War.

Laura M. Miller,
Vanderbilt University

See also **Antislavery; Great Britain, Relations with.**

To Abraham Lincoln, President of the United States:

As citizens of Manchester, assembled at the Free-Trade Hall, we beg to express our fraternal sentiments toward you and your country. We rejoice in your greatness as an outgrowth of England, whose blood and language you share, whose orderly and legal freedom you have applied to new circumstances, over a region immeasurably greater than our own. We honor your Free States, as a singularly happy abode for the working millions where industry is honored. One thing alone has, in the past, lessened our sympathy with your country and our confidence in it—we mean the ascendency of politicians who not merely maintained negro slavery, but desired to extend and root it more firmly. Since we have discerned, however, that the victory of the free North, in the war which has so sorely distressed us as well as afflicted you, will strike off the fetters of the slave, you have attracted our warm and earnest sympathy. We joyfully honor you, as the President, and the Congress with you, for many decisive steps toward practically exemplifying your belief in the words of your great founders: "All men are created free and equal." You have procured the liberation of the slaves in the district around Washington, and thereby made the centre of your Federation visibly free. You have enforced the laws against the slave-trade, and kept up your fleet against it, even while every ship was wanted for service in your terrible war. You have nobly decided to receive ambassadors from the negro republics of Hayti and Liberia, thus forever renouncing that unworthy prejudice which refuses the rights of humanity to men and women on account of their color. In order more effectually to stop the slave-trade, you have made with our Queen a treaty, which your Senate has ratified, for the right of mutual search. Your Congress has decreed freedom as the law forever in the vast unoccupied or half unsettled Territories which are directly subject to its legislative power. It has offered pecuniary aid to all States which will enact emancipation locally, and has forbidden your Generals to restore fugitive slaves who seek their protection. You have entreated the slave-masters to accept these moderate offers; and after long and patient waiting, you, as Commander-in-Chief of the Army, have appointed to-morrow, the first of January, 1863, as the day of unconditional freedom for the slaves of the rebel States. Heartily do we congratulate you and your country on this humane and righteous course. We assume that you cannot now stop short of a complete uprooting of slavery. It would not become us to dictate any details, but there are broad principles of humanity which must guide you. If complete emancipation in some States be deferred, though only to a predetermined day, still in the interval, human beings should not be counted chattels. Women must have the rights of chastity and maternity, men the rights of husbands, masters the liberty of manumission. Justice demands for the black, no less than for the white, the protection of law—that his voice be heard in your courts. Nor must any such abomination be tolerated as slave-breeding States, and a slave market—if you are to earn the high reward of all your sacrifices, in the approval of the universal brotherhood and of the Divine Father. It is for your free country to decide whether any thing but immediate and total emancipation can secure the most indispensable rights of humanity against the inveterate wickedness of local laws and local executives. We implore you, for your own honor and welfare, not to faint in your providential mission. While your enthusiasm is aflame, and the tide of events runs high, let the work be finished effectually. Leave no root of bitterness to spring up and work fresh misery to your children. It is a mighty task, indeed, to reorganize the industry not only of four millions of the colored race, but of five millions of whites. Nevertheless, the vast progress you have made in the short space of twenty months fills us with hope that every stain on your freedom will shortly be removed, and that the erasure of that foul blot upon civilization and Christianity—chattel slavery—during your Presidency will cause the name of Abraham Lincoln to be honored and revered by posterity. We are certain that such a glorious consummation will cement Great Britain to the United States in close and enduring regards. Our interests, moreover, are identified with yours. We are truly one people, though locally separate. And if you have any ill-wishers here, be assured they are chiefly those who oppose liberty at home, and that they will be powerless to stir up quarrels between us, from the very day in which your country becomes, undeniably and without exception, the home of the free. Accept our high admiration of your firmness in upholding the proclamation of freedom.

SOURCE: Moore, Frank, ed. *The Rebellion Record: A Diary of American Events, with Documents, Narratives, Illustrative Incidents, Poetry, etc., etc.* New York: Putnam, 1861–1868.

EMANCIPATION PROCLAMATION
(1863)

A seminal document in United States history, the Emancipation Proclamation not only failed to accomplish its stated goal, it also constituted a sharp reversal of the most deeply held convictions of its author. Abraham Lincoln, who viewed the Civil War primarily as a means of preserving the Union, had long favored a system of gradual, voluntary emancipation to be carried out by the states. However, as the abolitionist movement gained support throughout much of the North and in the Congress, the President begin to consider more seriously the idea of total emancipation through executive order. Largely a symbolic gesture of intent, the Proclamation applied only to slaves living in states controlled by the Confederacy, but because Lincoln feared alienating slave-holding border states friendly to the Federal government, did not affect slaves residing in Union-held territory nor those in Confederate regions already retaken by Union soldiers. Despite these very significant limitations, the Emancipation

Proclamation made the freedom of African slaves in the United States a fundamental goal of the Civil War. Lauded by the British and the French, it also served to cut off crucial foreign support from the Confederacy. Before signing it, the formerly reluctant Lincoln is said to have remarked, "I never in my life felt more certain that I was doing right than I do in signing this paper."

Laura M. Miller,
Vanderbilt University

See also **Civil War; Emancipation Proclamation; Slavery.**

Whereas, on the twenty-second day of September, in the year of our Lord one thousand eight hundred and sixty-two, a proclamation was issued by the President of the United States, containing, among other things, the following, to wit:

That on the first day of January, in the year of our Lord one thousand eight hundred and sixty-three, all persons held as slaves within any State, or designated part of a State, the people whereof shall then be in rebellion against the United States, shall be then, thenceforward, and forever free; and the Executive Government of the United States, including the military and naval authority thereof, will recognize and maintain the freedom of such persons, and will do no act or acts to repress such persons, or any of them, in any efforts they may make for their actual freedom.

That the Executive will, on the first day of January aforesaid, by proclamation, designate the States and parts of States, if any, in which the people thereof respectively, shall then be in rebellion against the United States; and the fact that any State, or the people thereof, shall on that day be in good faith represented in the Congress of the United States by members chosen thereto at elections wherein a majority of the qualified voters of such State shall have participated, shall in the absence of strong countervailing testimony, be deemed conclusive evidence that such State, and the people thereof, are not then in rebellion against the United States.

Now, therefore, I, Abraham Lincoln, President of the United States, by virtue of the power in me vested as commander-in-chief of the Army and Navy of the United States, in time of actual armed rebellion against authority and government of the United States, and as a fit and necessary war measure for suppressing said rebellion, do, on this first day of January, in the year of our Lord one thousand eight hundred and sixty-three, and in accordance with my purpose so to do, publicly proclaimed for the full period of one hundred days from the day first above mentioned, order and designate as the States and parts of States wherein the people thereof, respectively, are this day in rebellion against the United States, the following, to wit:

> Arkansas, Texas, Louisiana (except the parishes of St. Bernard, Plaquemines, Jefferson, St. John, St. Charles, St. James, Ascension, Assumption, Terrebonne, Lafourche, St. Mary, St. Martin, and Orleans, including the city of New Orleans), Mississippi, Alabama, Florida, Georgia, South Carolina, North Carolina, and Virginia (except the forty-eight counties designated as West Virginia, and also the counties of Berkley, Accomac, Northampton, Elizabeth City, York, Princess Ann, and Norfolk, including the cities of Norfolk and Portsmouth), and which excepted parts are, for the present, left precisely as if this proclamation were not issued.

And by virtue of the power and for the purpose aforesaid, I do order and declare that all persons held as slaves within said designated States and parts of States are, and henceforward shall be, free; and that the Executive government of the United States, including the military and naval authorities thereof, will recognize and maintain the freedom of said persons.

And I hereby enjoin upon the people so declared to be free to abstain from all violence, unless in necessary self-defence; and I recommend to them that, in all cases when allowed, they labor faithfully for reasonable wages.

And I further declare and make known, that such persons of suitable condition, will be received into the armed service of the United States to garrison forts, positions, stations, and other places, and to man vessels of all sorts in said service.

And upon this act, sincerely believed to be an act of justice, warranted by the Constitution, upon military necessity, I invoke the considerate judgment of mankind and the gracious favor of Almighty God.

In witness whereof, I have hereunto set my hand, and caused the seal of the United States to be affixed.

Done at the city of Washington, this first day of January, in the year of our Lord one thousand eight hundred and sixty-three, and of the Independence of the United States of America the eighty-seventh.

ABRAHAM LINCOLN

L. S.

By the President:
WILLIAM H. SEWARD, Secretary of State

SOURCE: Richardson, James D., ed. *Messages and Papers of the Presidents.* New York: Bureau of National Literature and Art, 1904.

GETTYSBURG ADDRESS
(19 November 1863)

Often simply called "The Speech" among speechwriters, Abraham Lincoln's "Gettysburg Address" is not only a marvel of concinnity and plainspoken grace, but also a model of a message that transcends the mundane and immediate to touch on points universal and grand. Delivered on 19 November 1863 at the dedication of the Soldiers Cemetery on the grounds of the Battle of Gettysburg (Pennsylvania), during which some seven thousand Americans killed one another, Lincoln's 272-word address was not even the keynote. The honor of delivering that fell to the noted public orator Edward Everett, whose impassioned, classical rhetoric rang across the recently cleared battlefield for almost two hours. Shortly after, Everett would tell Lincoln, "I should be glad if I could flatter myself that I came as near to the central idea of the occasion in two hours as you did in two minutes." Lincoln's speech came at an opportune moment, one many historians consider a turning point in the American Civil War, and it was instantly regarded as a profound work of American political and literary genius.

Laura M. Miller,
Vanderbilt University

See also **Civil War; Gettysburg Address.**

FOURSCORE and seven years ago our fathers brought forth on this continent a new nation, conceived in liberty, and dedicated to the proposition that all men are created equal. Now we are engaged in a great civil war, testing whether that nation, or any nation so conceived and so dedicated, can long endure. We are met on a great battlefield of that war. We have come to dedicate a portion of that field as a final resting-place for those who here gave their lives that the nation might live. It is altogether fitting and proper that we should do this. But, in a larger sense, we cannot dedicate—we cannot consecrate—we cannot hallow—this ground. The brave men, living and dead, who struggled here have consecrated it, far above our poor power to add or detract. The world will little note, nor long remember, what we say here, but it can never forget what they did here. It is for us the living, rather, to be dedicated here to the unfinished work which they who fought here have thus far so nobly advanced. It is rather for us to be here dedicated to the great task remaining before us—that from these honored dead we take increased devotion to that cause for which they gave the last full measure of devotion—that we here highly resolve that these dead shall not have died in vain—that this nation, under God, shall have a new birth of freedom and that government of the people, by the people, for the people, shall not perish from the earth.

SOURCE: Lincoln, Abraham. *Writings of Abraham Lincoln.* New York: Lamb, 1905–06.

HEAD OF CHOCTAW NATION REAFFIRMS HIS TRIBE'S POSITION
(21 October 1863)

After April 1861, both Union and Confederate troops were desperate for soldiers, so they recruited among the Native Americans living on the western frontier. Though most of the nations had been forced to relocate to the Indian Territory earlier in the century, many retained loyalties with their native regions, particularly the Choctaws, Creeks, Seminoles, Chickasaws, and Cherokees, who were from the south.

The Confederate Native Americans, however, fared little better in the Civil War than they did during their own wars with the settlers. As Choctaw leader Chief P. P. Pitchlynn described in this letter, the Native American troops were widely neglected and frequently robbed. His letter illuminates the difficult position of the Native American allied to the Southern cause. After the war, tribes who fought for the South were punished with further relocations and injustices.

Leah R. Shafer,
Cornell University

See also **Choctaw; Civil War; Indians in the Civil War.**

Col. Eakin—Editor Telegraph—Dear sir:

Inasmuch as reports are in circulation prejudicial to me as a Southern man and Choctaw, I solicit a place in your columns that I may place myself right before your public. I am represented by some as a Union man, by others as favoring a treaty of union with the Lincoln Government, and by others as being, at best, lukewarm in the Southern cause. To these several reports I can truthfully affirm that there is no truth in them whatever. As regards the first point in the charge, I reply that I am a Southern man by birth, education, association and interest. As to favoring or suggesting a treaty with the Lincoln Government, the charge is as untrue as it is unjust or impracticable. We have consulted with each other in regard to our situation. The Federal forces were advancing without opposition—destruction and desolation following in their wake. What is to be the fate of the Choctaw people if their neighbors and friends from Arkansas and Texas forsake them in this their day of trial and gloom? Reports were current that the white forces would be withdrawn from this department. Will the Confederates leave them to the Federal mercy and merciless jayhawkers? This Nation is the only abiding place for the poor Choctaws. For unlike the white man, there are no sister States to which he can emigrate. In view of such state of affairs, it was suggested, as the last resort, that permission be solicited of the Confederate States for the Choctaws to make an armistice. But in no instance, and under no conditions whatever, did the Choctaws intend to switch without the consent of the Confederate States; nor did they intend to act on that suggestion only as a means of preserving a home for the poor Choctaws, and, also, as securing a temporary abiding place to those unfortunates of other tribes amongst us. But so long as our neighbors and allies stood by us in defense of our common cause, I have urged, in speeches to the Choctaws, that they should unitedly peril their lives and their all in defence of the South. If I have appeared lukewarm, it has grown out of denunciations which the interference in the affairs of this department by Confederate commanders, unconnected with it, have provoked. It is well known that arms, clothing and money intended for the Indian allies were used elsewhere. Such interference has caused the Indian allies to think that they were treated with indifference and neglect. And it also greatly embarrassed the commanders in this department in their operations against the enemy. Had I been a Union man, these things would have passed with indifference; but a desire to see justice done the Choctaw people cause me to "cry aloud and spare not." Furthermore, the constitution of my mind and not its convictions may have caused me to appear lukewarm to the casual observer; yet while others have been hot I have been warm; while some have been blatant for Southern rights I have been consistent and hopeful; while some have professed zeal for the cause and love for its defenders I have furnished sons for the battle, kept an open door and free table for the Southern soldiers. My desire to sustain my consistency before the better class of Southern people induces me to thus publicly notice and give character to irresponsible reports.

Very respectfully,

P. P. Pitchlynn

LETTERS FROM WIDOWS TO LINCOLN ASKING FOR HELP
(1861 and 1864)

In many cases the Civil War caused as much hardship for those left on the home front as for the men who marched off to battle. A woman who was entirely dependent upon her husband's support had to survive on the army pay he could spare and whatever help she could muster from family and neighbors. The loss of a husband and father exacerbated already tenuous conditions at home for families. With so many men dead or permanently disabled as a result of military service, the Northern government passed the Pension Act of 1862. The war widowed approximately 180,000 women, leaving many wives and children dependent upon an $8 monthly allowance. By 1866, nearly $16 million had been disbursed to 300,000 veterans and 220,000 dependents in what became one of the nation's first national entitlement programs.

Paul S. Bartels,
Villanova University

See also **Army, Union; Civil War.**

A "Widder Wumman" wants "Wurk"

Frederick, June 17, 1864

tu Abraham linkun President of the U. States at Washington—Deer Sur: I take mi pen in hand to aske yu about the munney cumming to me frum my husband Daniel Spielman who was a solger in the 2d Mariland Ridgment in company C who was kill in a fite with the rebs last fal near Boonsborrow M.D. I haint got no pay as was cummin toe him and none of his bounty munney and now Mr. President I am a pore widder wumman and have to munney and have borrered all what I lived on last winter and this summer toe—Now Mr. President I can soe and cook and wash and du enny kind of wurk but cant get none—see if you cant git me a plaice in one of your hospittles and I will goe rite to wurk—but I dont want to leve mi little gurl so I want to git a plaice what I can take her toe—I no yu du what is rite and yu will se tu me a pore widder wumman whose husband fote in your army your younion army Mr. President—So Mr. President I sign myself your servant to command

Catherine Spielman

A Plea for "Some Help"

Chester [Penn.] July 8th 1861

Mr. Linkin

I have called on you for some help I am a widir woman with sixth children I was doing pirty well but since this war bisness commence it has cost me a good bit of truble I am willing to do with less for the sake of are union to stand I want you please to help me a little as I stand badly in need of som help please to rite and lit me know direct your letter to

Mrs. Sarah H Vandegrift

Chester

I shall put it to a good use.

There is no record of a reply to this plea.

PRISONER AT ANDERSONVILLE
(1864, by John Ransom)

Amicable relations between the Confederacy and the Union regarding prisoner exchanges broke down by 1863. Following the Emancipation Proclamation and the introduction of African-Americans into Union ranks, many Confederates refused to give captured black soldiers quarter. Lincoln's administration demanded that Blacks receive equal treatment as Whites when taken prisoner, refusing to exchange captured men until the terms were met. Prison camps swelled in numbers by 1864, as the two sides remained at an impasse.

The South had great difficulty in providing for the rapidly increasing number of detained Union soldiers within their borders. Georgia's Andersonville prison featured particularly horrible conditions. Originally built to accommodate 15,000 men, its population grew to 33,000 by August 1864. Along with congestion within the prison, starvation, inadequate clothing and shelter, poor sanitary conditions, disease, and depression afflicted those interned at Andersonville. Despite abundant wood in the surrounding pine forest, prisoners were not allowed to build huts in which to live. They languished outside in the oppressive heat of the summer months, as only the extremely ill received shelter inside the camp hospital.

An appalling total of 13,000 men perished at Andersonville, with countless others emaciated beyond recognition by the time of their release. Captain Henry Wirz, who served as commandant of the prison, faced charges for war crimes following the war and was hanged in an attempt to find a scapegoat. Assessing blame for the atrocities at Andersonville remains difficult, as the Confederate Army and the Southern population teetered on the brink of collapse and material depravation by 1864. Unsuccessful negotiations for prisoner exchange also were partially to blame. Many prisoners, such as John Ransom (whose diary follows), did not understand why their own government failed to come to their aid.

Paul S. Bartels,
Villanova University

See also **Andersonville Prison; Civil War; Prison Camps, Confederate; Prisoners of War.**

July 6
Boiling hot, camp reeking with filth, and no sanitary privileges; men dying off over a hundred and forty per day. Stockade enlarged, taking in eight or ten more acres, giving us more room and stumps to dig up for wood to cook with.

Mike Hoare is in good health; not so Jimmy Devers. Jimmy has now been a prisoner over a year, and poor boy, will probably die soon.

Have more mementoes than I can carry, from those who have died, to be given to their friends at home. At least a dozen have given me letters, pictures, &c. to take North. Hope I shan't have to turn them over to someone else.

July 7
The court was gotten up by our men and from our own men; judge, jury, council. Had a fair trial, and were even defended, but to no purpose. It is reported that six have been sentenced to be hung, while a good many others are condemned to lighter punishment, such as setting in the stocks, strung up by the thumbs, thumbscrews, head hanging.

The court has been severe but just.

Mike goes out tomorrow to take some part in the court proceeding.

The prison seems a different place altogether; still, dread disease is here, and mowing down good and true men. Would seem to me that three or four hundred died each day, though officially but one hundred and forty odd is told. About twenty-seven thousand, I believe, are here now in all. No new ones for a few days.

Rebel visitors, who look at us from a distance. It is said the stench keeps all away who have no business here and can keep away. Washing business good. Am negotiating for a pair of pants. Dislike fearfully to wear dead men's clothes, and haven't, to any great extent.

July 8
O, how hot, and O how miserable. The news that six have been sentenced to be hanged is true, and one of them is Moseby.

The camp is thoroughly under control of the police now, and it is a heavenly boon. Of course, there is some robbery, but not as before. Swan, of our mess, is sick with scurvy. I am gradually swelling up and growing weaker.

Guards shoot now very often. Boys, as guards, are the most cruel. It is said that if they kill a Yankee they are given a thirty days' furlough. Guess they need them as soldiers too much to allow of this.

The swamp now is fearful. Water perfectly reeking with prison offal and poison. Still men drink it and die. Rumors that the six will be hung inside. Bread today, and it is so coarse as to do more hurt than good to a majority of the prisoners.

The place still gets worse. Tunneling is over with; no one engages in it now that I know of. The prison is a success as regards safety; no escape except by death, and very many take advantage of that way.

A man who has preached to us (or tried to) is dead. Was a good man, I verily believe, and from Pennsylvania.

Our quartette of singers a few rods away is disbanded. One died, one nearly dead, one a policeman and the other cannot sing alone, and so, where we used to hear and enjoy good music evenings, there is nothing to attract us from the groans of the dying.

Having formed a habit of going to sleep as soon as the air got cooled off and before fairly dark, I wake up at two or three o'clock and stay awake. I then take in all the horrors of the situation. Thousands are groaning, moaning and crying, with no bustle of the daytime to drown it. Guards every half hour call out the time and post, and there is often a shot to make one shiver as if with the ague. Must arrange my sleeping hours to miss getting up early in the morning.

Have taken to building air castles of late on being exchanged. Getting loony, I guess, same as all the rest.

July 9
Battese brought me some onions, and if they ain't good, then no matter; also a sweet potato. One-half the men here would get well if they only had something in the vegetable line to eat, or acids. Scurvy is about the most loathsome disease, and when dropsy takes hold with the scurvy, it is terrible. I have both diseases, but keep them in check, and it only grows worse slowly. My legs are swollen, but the cords are not contracted much, and I can still walk very well.

Our mess all keep clean, in fact are obliged to, or else turned adrift. We want none of the dirty sort in our mess. Sanders and Rowe enforce the rules, which is not much work, as all hands are men who prefer to keep clean.

I still do a little washing, but more particularly hair cutting, which is easier work. You should see one of my hair cuts. Knobby! Old prisoners have hair a foot long or more, and my business is to cut it off, which I do without regard to anything except to get it off.

I should judge there are one thousand rebel soldiers guarding us and perhaps a few more, with the usual number of officers.

A guard told me today that the Yanks were "gittin' licked," and they didn't want us exchanged, just as soon we should die here as not. A Yank asked him if he knew what exchange meant; said he knew what shootin' meant, and as he began to swing around his old shooting iron, we retreated in among the crowd.

Someone stole Battese's wash board, and he is mad; is looking for it. May bust up the business. Think Hub Dakin will give me a board to make another one. Sanders owns the jack-knife of this mess, and he don't like to lend it either; borrow it to carve on roots for pipes.

Actually take solid comfort "building castles in the air," a thing I have never been addicted to before. Better than getting blue and worrying myself to death. After all, we may get out of this dodrotted hole. Always an end of some sort to such things.

July 10
Have bought of a new prisoner quite a large (thick, I mean) blank book, so as to continue my diary. Although it's a tedious and tiresome task, am determined to keep it up. Don't know of another man in prison who is doing likewise. Wish I had the gift of description, that I might describe this place. Know that I am not good at such things.

Nothing can be worse or nastier than the stream drizzling its way through this camp. On all four sides of us are high walls and tall trees, and there is apparently no wind or breeze to blow away the stench, and we are obliged to breathe and live in it. Dead bodies lay around all day in the broiling sun, by the dozen and even hundreds. It's too horrible for me to describe in fitting language.

Only those who are here will ever know what Andersonville is.

July 13
Can see in the distance the cars go poking along by this station, with wheezing old engines snorting along. As soon as night comes a great many are blind, caused by sleeping in the open air, with moon shining in the face.

Many holes are dug and excavations made in camp. Near our quarters is a well, about five or six feet deep, and the poor blind fellows fall into this pit-hole. None seriously hurt, but must be shaken up. Half of the prisoners have no settled place for sleeping, wander and lay down wherever they can find room.

Have two small gold rings on my finger, worn ever since I left home. Have also a small photograph album with eight photographs in. Relics of civilization.

Should I get these things through to our lines they will have quite a history. When I am among the Rebels I wind a rag around my finger to cover up the rings, or else take them and put them in my pocket. Bad off as I have been, have never seen the time yet that I would part with them. Were presents to me, and the photographs had looked at about one-fourth of the time since imprisonment.

One prisoner made some buttons here for his little boy at home, and gave them to me to deliver, as he was about to die. Have them sewed on to my pants for safe keeping.

July 17
Cords contracting in my legs, and very difficult for me to walk—after going a little way have to stop and rest, and am faint. Am urged by some to go to the hospital, but don't like to do it; mess say had better stay where I am, and Battese says shall not go, and that settles it.

Jimmy Devers anxious to be taken to the hospital but is persuaded to give it up. Tom McGill, another Irish friend, is past all recovery; is in another part of the prison. Many old prisoners are dropping off now, this fearful hot weather; knew that July and August would thin us out, cannot keep track of them in my disabled condition.

A fellow named Hubbard, with whom I have conversed a good deal, is dead; a few days ago was in very good health, and it's only a question of a few days now with any of us.

Succeeded in getting four small onions about as large as hickory nuts, tops and all, for two dollars, Confederate money. Battese furnished the money but won't eat an onion; ask him if he is afraid it will make his breath smell. It is said that two or three onions or a sweet potato eaten raw daily will cure the scurvy.

What a shame that such things are denied us, being so plenty the world over. Never appreciated such things before, but shall hereafter. Am talking as if I expected to get home again. I do.

July 18

Time slowly dragging along. Cut some wretch's hair almost every day. Have a sign out, "Hair Cutting," as well as "Washing," and by the way, Battese has a new washboard, made from a piece of the scaffold lumber.

About half the time do the work for nothing; in fact, not more than one in three or four pays anything—expenses not much though, don't have to pay any rent.

All the mess keep their hair cut short, which is a very good advertisement. My eyes getting weak, with other troubles. Can just hobble around. Death rate more than ever, reported one hundred and sixty-five per day.

Jimmy Devers most dead, and begs us to take him to the hospital, and guess will have to. Every morning the sick are carried to the gate in blankets and on stretchers, and the worst cases admitted to the hospital.

Probably out of five or six hundred, half are admitted. Do not think any live after being taken there; are past all human aid. Four out of every five prefer to stay inside and die with their friends rather than go to the hospital.

Hard stories reach us of the sick out there, and I am sorry to say, the cruelty emanates from our own men, who act as nurses. These dead beats and bummer nurses are the same bounty jumpers the United States authorities have had so much trouble with.

July 19
There is no such thing as delicacy here. Nine out of ten would as soon eat with a corpse for a table as any other way. In the middle of last night I was awakened by being

kicked by a dying man. He was soon dead. In his struggles he had floundered clear into our bed. Got up and moved the body off a few feet, and again went to sleep.

July 20
My teeth are all loose, and it is with difficulty I can eat. Jimmy Devers was taken out to die today. I hear that McGill is also dead. John McGuire died last night. Both were Jackson men and old acquaintances.

Mike Hoare is still policeman and is sorry for me. Does what the can. And so we have seen the last of Jimmy. A prisoner of war one year and eighteen days. Struggled hard to live through it, if ever anyone did. Ever since I can remember, have known him. John McGuire also, I have always known. Everybody in Jackson, Michigan, will remember him as living on the east side of the river near the wintergreen patch, and his father before him. They were one of the first families to settle that country. His people are well to do, with much property. Leaves a wife and one boy. Tom McGill is also a Jackson boy, and a member of my own company. Thus you will see that three of my acquaintances died the same day, for Jimmy cannot live until night, I don't think. Not a person in the world but would have thought either one of them would kill me a dozen times enduring hardships. Pretty hard to tell about such things.

Small squad of poor deluded Yanks turned inside with us, captured at Petersburg. It is said the talk of winning recent battles.

Battese has traded for an old watch and Mike will try to procure vegetables for it from the guard. That is what will save us, if anything.

July 22

A petition is gotten up, signed by all the Sergeants in the prison, to be sent to Washington, District Columbia, *begging* to be released. Captain Wirtz has consented to let three representatives go for that purpose. Rough that it should be necessary for us to *beg* to be protected by our Government.

July 25
Rowe getting very bad. Sanders ditto. Am myself much worse, and cannot walk. And with difficulty stand up. Legs drawn up like a triangle, mouth in terrible shape, and dropsy worse than all. A few more days.

At my earnest solicitation was carried to the gate this morning, to be admitted to the hospital. Lay in the sun some hours to be examined, and finally my turn came and I tried to stand up, but was so excited I fainted away. When I came to myself I lay along with a row of dead on the outside. Raised up and asked a Rebel for a drink of water, and he said, "Here, you Yank, if you ain't dead yet, get inside there!" And with his help was put inside again.

Told a man to go to our mess, and tell them to come to the gate, and pretty soon Battese and Sanders came and carried me back to our quarters; and here I am, completely played out. Battese flying around to buy me something good to eat. Can't write much more. Exchange rumors.

July 26
Ain't dead yet. Actually laugh when I think of the Rebel who thought if I wasn't dead I had better get inside. Can't walk a step now. Shall try for the hospital no more. Had an onion.

Marine Hospital, Savannah, Ga., September 15
A great change has taken place since I last wrote in my diary. Am in heaven now, compared with the past. At about midnight, September 7th, our detachment was ordered outside at Andersonville, and Battese picked me up and carried me to the gate.

The men were being let outside in ranks of four, and counted as they went out. They were very strict about letting none go but the well ones, or those who could walk. The Rebel Adjutant stood upon a box by the gate, watching very close. Pitch-pine knots were burning in the near vicinity to give light.

As it came our turn to go, Battese got me in the middle of the rank, stood me up as well as I could stand, and with himself on one side and Sergeant Rowe on the other, began pushing our way through the gate. Could not help myself a particle, and was so faint that I hardly knew what was going on.

As we were going through the gate the Adjutant yelled out: "Here, here! Hold on there, that man can't go, hold on there!"

And Battese crowding right along outside. The Adjutant struck over the heads of the men and tried to stop us, but my noble Indian friend kept straight ahead, hallooing: "He all right, he well, he go!"

And so I got outside, the Adjutant having too much to look after to follow me. After we were outside, I was carried to the railroad in the same coverlid which I fooled the Rebel out of when captured, and which I presume has saved my life a dozen times.

SOURCE: Ranson, John L. *Andersonville Diary.* Auburn, N.Y.: 1881.

ROBERT E. LEE'S FAREWELL TO HIS ARMY
(10 April 1865)

Robert E. Lee's surrender to U.S. Grant at the Appomattox Courthouse on 9 April 1865 effectively ended the American Civil War. A well-respected military strategist and organizer with experience in the war with Mexico, in 1861 Lee was asked by General Winfield Scott to take command of the armies of the Union to put down a rebellion by a number of southern states. An avowed anti-secessionist who had freed his slaves long before, Lee nonetheless remained loyal to his native Virginia and refused, instead offering his services to the newly elected president of the Confederate States of America, Jefferson Davis. Following the war, he became president of Washington University, later renamed Washington and Lee in his honor. In many parts of the north and south today, Robert E. Lee remains a much-admired figure, not only for his military acumen, but also as a model of grace and poise, even in defeat. Oddly enough, his petition for reinstatement of citizenship was somehow inadvertently mislaid, and it was not until more than a hundred years later, during the administration of Gerald Ford, that Robert E. Lee once again became a citizen of the United States of America.

Laura M Miller,
Vanderbilt University

***See also* Army, Confederate; Army of Northern Virginia; Virginia; Civil War.**

Headquarters, Army of Northern Virginia,

April 10, 1865.

After four years of arduous service, marked by unsurpassed courage and fortitude, the Army of Northern Virginia has been compelled to yield to overwhelming numbers and resources. I need not tell the survivors of so many hard-fought battles, who have remained steadfast to the last, that I have consented to this result from no distrust of them; but, feeling that valour and devotion could accomplish nothing that could compensate for the loss that would have attended the continuation of the contest, I have determined to avoid the useless sacrifice of those whose past services have endeared them to their countrymen. By the terms of the agreement, officers and men can return to their homes and remain there until exchanged. You will take with you the satisfaction that proceeds from the consciousness of duty faithfully performed; and I earnestly pray that a merciful God will extend to you His blessing and protection. With an increasing admiration of your constancy and devotion to your country, and a grateful remembrance of your kind and generous consideration of myself, I bid you an affectionate farewell.

R. E. Lee, General.

SOURCE: Lee, Robert E., Jr. *Recollections and Letters of General Robert E. Lee.* New York: Doubleday, 1904.

LINCOLN'S SECOND INAUGURAL ADDRESS
(4 March 1865)

President Abraham Lincoln consistently remarked that his days looked to be numbered in 1864; offensives had bogged down and the Northern populace had grown weary of high casualties and the exigencies of a grueling war. Breakthroughs at Atlanta, in the Shenandoah Valley, and outside Petersburg, Virginia late that year, however, turned the tide of opinion at home and carried Lincoln to victory in his bid for reelection.

The strain of four years of conflict discernibly showed on the president's face, yet his resolve may have never shone brighter than in his *Second Inaugural Address.* Though brief, Lincoln's 4 March 1865 speech marked perhaps his greatest oratory effort and rightfully earned Charles Francis Adams Jr.'s remark that it represented "the historical keynote of this war." Frederick Douglass pronounced it "a sacred effort," although the speech's seeming ambiguity puzzled many contemporaries.

Lincoln surprisingly attributes little direct blame for the conflict, instead surmising that God was punishing the entire nation for two hundred and fifty years of slavery. He refers to God twelve times and quotes three separate passages of scripture in one span of twenty-five lines alone, giving the temporal conflict a moral tone and decidedly spiritual character.

Much had been accomplished by March 1865, but Lincoln outlined the work left to be done both militarily and socially. He offered an impressionistic plan for peace and reconciliation—a plan Lincoln likely thought he would survive to see through to fruition. His last major speech, the *Second Inaugural Address* ranks among the greatest addresses of its kind ever given.

Paul S. Bartels,
Villanova University

See also **Civil War; Lincoln's Second Inaugural Address.**

Fellow-Countrymen:

At this second appearing to take the oath of the Presidential office there is less occasion for an extended address than there was at the first. Then a statement somewhat in detail of a course to be pursued seemed fitting and proper. Now, at the expiration of four years, during which public declarations have been constantly called forth on every point and phase of the great contest which still absorbs the attention and engrosses the energies of the nation, little that is new could be presented. The progress of our arms, upon which all else chiefly depends, is as well known to the public as to myself, and it is, I trust, reasonably satisfactory and encouraging to all. With high hope for the future, no prediction in regard to it is ventured.

On the occasion corresponding to this four years ago all thoughts were anxiously directed to an impending civil war. All dreaded it, all sought to avert it. While the inaugural address was being delivered from this place, devoted altogether to saving the Union without war, urgent agents were in the city seeking to destroy it without war-seeking to dissolve the Union and divide effects by negotiation. Both parties deprecated war, but one of them would make war rather than let the nation survive, and the other would accept war rather than let it perish, and the war came.

One-eighth of the whole population were colored slaves, not distributed generally over the Union, but localized in the southern part of it. These slaves constituted a peculiar and powerful interest. All knew that this interest was somehow the cause of the war. To strengthen, perpetuate, and extend this interest was the object for which the insurgents would rend the Union even by war, while the Government claimed no right to do more than to restrict the territorial enlargement of it. Neither party expected for the war the magnitude or the duration which it has already attained. Neither anticipated that the cause of the conflict might cease with or even before the conflict itself should cease. Each looked for an easier triumph, and a result less fundamental and astounding. Both read the same Bible and pray to the same God, and each invokes His aid against the other. It may seem strange that any men should dare to ask a just God's assistance in wringing their bread from the sweat of other men's faces, but let us judge not, that we be not judged. The prayers of both could not be answered. That of neither has been answered fully. The Almighty has His own purposes. "Woe unto the world because of offenses; for it must needs be that offenses come, but woe to that man by whom the offense cometh." If we shall suppose that American slavery is one of those offenses which, in the providence of God, must needs come, but which, having continued through His appointed time, He now wills to remove, and that He gives to both North and South this terrible war as the woe due to those by whom the offense came, shall we discern therein any departure from those divine attributes which the believers in a living God always ascribe to Him? Fondly do we hope, fervently do we pray, that this mighty scourge of war may speedily pass away. Yet, if God wills that it continue until all the wealth piled by the bondsman's two hundred and fifty years of unrequited toil shall be sunk, and until every drop of blood drawn with the lash shall be paid by another drawn with the sword, as was said three thousand years ago, so still it must be said "the judgments of the Lord are true and righteous altogether."

With malice toward none, with charity for all, with firmness in the right as God gives us to see the right, let us strive on to finish the work we are in, to bind up the nation's wounds, to care for him who shall have borne the battle and for his widow and his orphan, to do all which may achieve and cherish a just and lasting peace among ourselves and with all nations.

SOURCE: Nicolay, John G. and John Hay, eds. *Complete Works of Abraham Lincoln.* New and enlarged ed. New York: Lamb, 1905.

CONGRESS DEBATES THE FOURTEENTH AMENDMENT
(1866)

Lincoln's Emancipation Proclamation abolished the institution of slavery, but as Reconstruction began it became apparent that legal measures needed to be taken in order to protect the rights of freedmen. With President Andrew Johnson proving hostile to any legislation designed to ensure protection and equality for freedmen, the Republican majority in Congress decided to pass a constitutional amendment that would grant citizenship to African Americans while, in theory, shielding them from discriminatory state laws. An amendment to the Constitution would not be in jeopardy of repeal, like the Civil Rights Act, and it would be beyond the reach of presidential veto power.

The debate over the Fourteenth Amendment in congress, however, raged over states' rights issues and the meaning of citizenship and equal protection under the law. In a series of alterations and compromises, any extension of suffrage to freedman was dropped from the amendment. As the daunting project of reconstructing the union lay before them, the Republican Party needed a common ground on which to unite while demonstrating strong federal action to protect freedmen's rights. Unfortunately the common ground and compromise created a thoroughly ambiguous amendment, leading to many subsequent legal debates over what the original intent of universalist language such as "equal protection of the laws" really meant.

The following excerpts from the congressional debates over the Fourteenth Amendment cover the draft proposed by John A. Bingham of Ohio, which was tabled in early March 1866, and the May debates over numerous drafts and proposals. Final approval of the amendment in the House came on 13 June, compelling Pennsylvania Senator Thaddeus Stevens to remark: "Do you inquire why I accept so imperfect a proposition? I answer, because I live among men and not among angels."

Paul S. Bartels,
Villanova University

See also **Constitution of the United States; Due Process of Law; Equal Protection of the Law; State Sovereignty.**

February 27, 1866

MR. HALE. What is the effect of the amendment which the committee on reconstruction propose for the sanction of this House and the States of the Union? I submit that it is in effect a provision under which all State legislation, in its codes of civil and criminal jurisprudence and procedure, affecting the individual citizen, may be overridden, may be repealed or abolished, and the law of Congress established instead. I maintain that in this respect it is an utter departure from every principle ever dreamed of by the men who framed our Constitution.

MR. STEVENS. Does the gentleman mean to say that, under this provision, Congress could interfere in any case where the legislation of a State was equal, impartial to all? Or is it not simply to provide that, where any State makes a distinction in the same law between different classes of individuals, Congress shall have power to correct such discrimination and inequality? Does this proposition mean anything more than that?

MR. HALE. I will answer the gentleman. In my judgment it does go much further than the remarks of the gentleman would imply: but even if it goes no further than that—and I will discuss this point more fully before I conclude—it is still open to the same objection, that it proposes an entire departure from the theory of the Federal Government in meddling with these matters of State jurisdiction at all.

Now, I say to the gentleman from Pennsylvania [Mr. Stevens] that reading the language in its grammatical and legal construction it is a grant of the fullest and most ample power to Congress to make all laws "necessary and proper to secure to all persons in the several States protection in the rights of life, liberty, and property," with the simple proviso that such protection shall be equal. It is not a mere provision that when the States undertake to give protection which is unequal Congress may equalize it: it is a grant of power in general terms—a grant of the right to legislate for the protection of life, liberty and property, simply qualified with the condition that it shall be equal legislation. That is my construction of the proposition as it stands here. It may differ from that of other gentlemen.

MR. ELDRIDGE. Mr. Speaker, let me go a little further here. If it be true that the construction of this amendment, which I understand to be claimed by the gentlemen from Ohio, [Mr. Bingham] who introduced it, and which I infer from his question is claimed by the gentleman from Pennsylvania. [Mr. Stevens:] if it be true that that is the true construction of this article, is it not even then introducing a power never before intended to be conferred upon Congress. For we all know it is true that probably every State in this Union fails to give equal protection to all persons within its borders in the rights of life, liberty, and property. It may be a fault in the States that they do not do it. A reformation may be desirable, but by the doctrines of the school of politics in which I have been brought up, and which I have been taught to regard was the best school of political rights and duties in this Union, reforms of this character should come from the States, and not be forced upon them by the centralized power of the Federal Government.

Take a single case by way of illustration, and I take it simply to illustrate the point, without expressing any opinion whatever on the desirability or undesirability of a change in regard to it. Take the case of the rights of married women: did any one ever assume that Congress was to be invested with the power to legislate on that subject, and to say that married women, in regard to their rights of property, should stand on the same footing with men and unmarried women? There is not a State in the Union where disability of married women in relation to the rights of property does not to a greater or less extent still exist. Many of the States have taken steps for the partial abolition of that distinction in years past, some to a greater extent and others to a less. But I apprehend there is not to-day a State in the Union where there is not a distinction between the rights of married women, as to property, and the rights of femmes sole and men.

MR. STEVENS. If I do not interrupt the gentleman I will say a word. When a distinction is made between two married people or two femmes sole, then it is unequal legislation: but where all of the same class are dealt with in the same way then there is no pretense of inequality.

MR. HALE. The gentleman will pardon me: his argument seems to me to be more specious than sound. The language of the section under consideration gives to all persons equal protection. Now, if that means you shall extend to one married woman the same protection you extend to another, and not the same you extend to unmarried women or men, then by parity of reasoning it will be sufficient if you extend to one negro the same rights you do to another, but not those you extend to a white man. I think, if the gentleman from Pennsylvania claims that the resolution only intends that all of a certain class shall have equal protection, such class legislation may certainly as easily satisfy the requirements of this resolution in the case of the negro as in the case of the married woman. The line of distinction is, I take it, quite as broadly marked between negroes and white men as between married and unmarried women.

MR. HALE. It is claimed that this constitutional amendment is aimed simply and purely toward the protection of "American citizens of African descent" in the States lately in rebellion. I understand that to be the whole intended practical effect of the amendment.

MR. BINGHAM. It is due to the committee that I should say that it is proposed as well to protect the thousands and tens of thousands and hundreds of thousands of loyal white citizens of the United States whose property, by State legislation, has been wrested from them under confiscation, and protect them also against banishment.

MR. HALE. I trust that when the gentlemen comes to reply, he will give me as much of his time as he takes of mine. As he has the reply. I do not think he ought to interject his remarks into my speech. I will modify my statement and say that this amendment is intended to apply solely to the eleven States lately in rebellion, so far as any practical benefit to be derived from it is concerned. The gentleman from Ohio can correct me if I am again in error.

MR. BINGHAM. It is to apply to other States also that have in their constitutions and laws to-day provisions in direct violation of every principle of our Constitution.

MR. ROGERS. I suppose this gentleman refers to the State of Indiana!

MR. BINGHAM. I do not know: it may be so. It applies unquestionably to the State of Oregon.

MR. HALE. Then I will again modify my correction and say that it is intended to apply to every State which, in the judgment of the honorable member who introduced this measure, has failed to provide equal protection to life, liberty, and property. And here we come to the very thing for which I denounce this proposition, that it takes away from these States the right to determine for themselves what their institutions shall be.

February 28, 1866

MR. BINGHAM. Excuse me. Mr. Speaker, we have had some most extraordinary arguments against the adoption of the proposed amendment.

But, say the gentleman, if you adopt this amendment you give to Congress the power to enforce all the rights of married women in the several States. I beg the gentleman's pardon. He need not be alarmed at the condition of married women. Those rights which are universal and independent of all local State legislation belong, by the gift of God, to every woman, whether married or single. The rights of life and liberty are theirs whatever States may enact. But the gentleman's concern is as to the right of property in married women.

Although this word property has been in your bill of rights from the year 1789 until this hour, who ever heard it intimated that anybody could have property protected in any State until he owned or acquired property there according to its local law or according to the law of some other State which he may have carried thither? I undertake to say no one. As to real estate, every one knows that its acquisition and transmission under every interpretation ever given to the word property, as used in the Constitution of the country, are dependent exclusively upon the local law of the States, save under a direct grant of the United States. But suppose any person has acquired property not contrary to the laws of the State, but in accordance with its law, are they not to be equally protected in the enjoyment of it, or are they to be denied all protection? That is the question, and the whole question, so far as that part of the case is concerned.

Mr. Speaker. I speak in behalf of this amendment in no party spirit, in no spirit of resentment toward any State or the people of any State, in no spirit of innovation, but for the sake of a violated Constitution and a wronged and wounded country whose heart is now smitten with a strange, great sorrow. I urge the amendment for the enforcement of these essential provisions of your Constitution, divine in their justice, sublime in their humanity, which declare that all men are equal in the rights of life and liberty before the majesty of American law.

Representatives, to you I appeal, that hereafter, by your act and the approval of the loyal people of this country, every man in every State of the Union, in accordance with the written words of your Constitution, may, by the national law, be secured in the equal protection of his personal rights. Your Constitution provides that no man, no matter what his color, no matter beneath what sky he may have been born, no matter in what disastrous conflict or by what tyrannical hand his liberty may have been cloven down, no matter how poor, no matter how friendless, no matter how ignorant, shall be deprived of life or liberty or property without due process of law—law in its highest sense, that law which is the perfection of human reason, and which is impartial, equal, exact justice; that justice which requires that every man shall have his right: that justice which is the highest duty of nations as it is the imperishable attribute of the God of nations.

MR. HALE. Before the gentleman takes his seat will he allow me to ask a single question pertinent to this subject?

MR. BINGHAM. Yes sir.

MR. HALE. I desire after hearing the gentleman's argument, in which I have been much interested as a very calm, lucid, and logical vindication of the amendment, to ask him, as an able constitutional lawyer, which he has proved himself to be, whether in his opinion this proposed amendment to the Constitution does not confer upon Congress a general power of legislation for the purpose of securing to all persons in the several States protection of life, liberty, and property, subject only to the qualification that that protection shall be equal.

MR. BINGHAM. I believe it does in regard to life and liberty and property as I have heretofore stated it: the right to real estate being dependent on the State law except when granted by the United States.

MR. HALE. Excuse me. If I understand the gentleman, he now answers that it does confer a general power to legislate on the subject in regard to life and liberty, but not in regard to real estate. I desire to know if he means to imply that it extends to personal estate.

MR. BINGHAM. Undoubtedly it is true. Let the gentleman look to the great Mississippi case, Slaughter and another, which is familiar doubtless, to all the members of the House, and he will find that under the Constitution the personal property of a citizen follows its owner, and is entitled to be protected in the State into which he goes.

MR. HALE. The gentleman misapprehends my point, or else I misapprehend his answer. My question was whether this provision, if adopted, confers upon Congress general powers of legislation in regard to the protection of life, liberty, and personal property.

MR. BINGHAM. It certainly does this: it confers upon Congress power to see to it that the protection given by the laws of the United States shall be equal in respect to life and liberty and property to all persons.

MR. HALE. Then will the gentleman point me to that clause or part of this resolution which contains the doctrine he here announces?

MR. BINGHAM. The words "equal protection" contain it, and nothing else.

May 8, 1866

MR. STEVENS. Let us now refer to the provisions of the proposed amendment. The first section prohibits the States from abridging the privileges and immunities of citizens of the United States, or unlawfully depriving them of life, liberty, or property, or of denying to any person within their jurisdiction the "equal" protection of the laws.

I can hardly believe that any person can be found who will not admit that every one of these provisions is just. They are all asserted, in some form or other, in our DECLARATION or organic law. But the Constitution limits only the action of Congress, and is not a limitation on the States. This amendment supplies that defect, and allows Congress to correct the unjust legislation of the States, so far that the law which operates upon one man shall operate equally upon all. Whatever law punishes a white man for a crime shall punish the black man precisely in the same way and to the same degree. Whatever law protects the white man shall afford "equal" protection to the black man. Whatever means of redress is afforded to one shall be afforded to all. Whatever law allows the white man to testify in court shall allow the man of color to do the same. These are great advantages over their present codes. Now different degrees of punishment are inflicted, not on account of the magnitude of the crime, but according to the color of the skin. Now color disqualifies a man from testifying in courts, or being tried in the same way as white men. I need not enumerate these partial and oppressive laws. Unless the Constitution should restrain them those States will all, I fear, keep up this discrimination, and crush to death the hated freedmen. Some answer, "Your civil rights bill secures the same things." That is party true, but a law is repealable by a majority. And I need hardly say that the first time that the South with their copperhead allies obtain the command of Congress it will be repealed. The veto of the President and their votes on the bill are conclusive evidence of that.

MR. GARFIELD. Sir. I believe that the right to vote, if it be not indeed one of the natural rights of all men, is so necessary to the protection of their natural rights as to be indispensable, and therefore equal to natural rights. I believe that the golden sentence of John Stuart Mill, in one of his greatest works, ought to be written on the constitution of every State, and on the Constitution of the United States as the greatest and most precious of truths. "That the ballot is put into the hands of men, not so much to enable them to govern others as that he may not be misgoverned by others." I believe that suffrage is the shield, the sword, the spear, and all the panoply that best befits a man for his own defense in the great social organism to which he belongs. And I profoundly regret that we have not been enabled to write it and engrave it upon our institutions, and imbed it in the imperishable bulwarks of the Constitution as a part of the fundamental law of the land. But I am willing, as I said once before in this presence, when I cannot get all I wish to take what I can get. And therefore I am willing to accept the propositions that the committee have laid before us, though I desire one amendment which I will mention presently.

I am glad to see this first section here which proposes to hold over every American citizen, without regard to color, the protecting shield of law. The gentleman who has just taken his seat [Mr. Finck] undertakes to show that because we propose to vote for this section we therefore acknowledge that the civil rights bill was unconstitutional. He was anticipated in that objection by the gentleman from Pennsylvania [Mr. Stevens]. The civil rights bill is now a part of the law of the land. But every gentleman knows it will cease to be a part of the law whenever the sad moment arrives when that gentleman's party comes into power. It is precisely for that reason that we propose to lift that great and good law above the reach of political strife, beyond the reach of the plots and machinations of any party, and fix it in the serene sky, in the eternal firmament of the Constitution, where no storm of passion can shake it and no cloud can obscure it. For this reason, and not because I believe the civil rights bill unconstitutional, I am glad to see that first section here.

MR. THAYER. With regard to the second section of the proposed amendment to the Constitution, it simply brings into the Constitution what is found in the bill of rights of every State of the Union. As I understand it, it is but incorporating in the Constitution of the United States the principle of the civil rights bill which has lately become a law, and that, not as the gentleman from Ohio [Mr, Finck] suggested, because in the estimation of this House that law cannot be sustained as constitutional, but in order, as was justly said by the gentleman from Ohio who last addressed the House [Mr. Garfield.] that that provision so necessary for the equal administration of the law, so just in its operation, so necessary for the protection of the fundamental rights of citizenship, shall be forever incorporated in the Constitution of the United States. But, sir, that subject has already been fully discussed. I have upon another occasion expressed my views upon it, and I do not propose to detain the House with any further remarks of my own upon it.

May 10, 1866

MR. BINGHAM. The necessity for the first section of this amendment to the Constitution, Mr. Speaker, is one of the lessons that have been taught to your committee and taught to all the people of this country by the history of the past four years of terrific conflict—that history in which God is, and in which He teaches the profoundest lessons to men and nations. There was a want hitherto, and there remains a want now, in the Constitution of our country, which the proposed amendment will supply. What is that? It is the power in the people, the whole people of the United States, by express authority of the Constitution to do that by congressional enactment which hitherto they have not had the power to do, and have never even attempted to do; that is, to protect by national law the privileges and immunities of all the citizens of the Republic and the inborn rights of every person within its jurisdiction whenever the same shall be abridged or denied by the unconstitutional acts of any State.

Allow me, Mr. Speaker, in passing, to say that this amendment takes from no State any right that ever pertained to it. No State ever had the right, under the forms of law or otherwise, to deny to any freeman the equal protection of the laws or to abridge the privileges or immunities of any citizen of the Republic, although many of them have assumed and exercised the power, and that without remedy. The amendment does not give, as the second section shows, the power to Congress of regulating suffrage in the several States.

The second section excludes the conclusion that by the first section suffrage is subjected to congressional law: save, indeed, with this exception, that as the right in the people of each State to a republican government and to choose their Representatives in Congress is of the guarantees of the Constitution, by this amendment a remedy might be given directly for a case supposed by Madison, where treason might change a State government from a republican to a despotic government, and thereby deny suffrage to the people. Why should any American citizen object to that? But, sir, it has been suggested, not here, but elsewhere, if this section does not confer suffrage the need of it is not perceived. To all such I beg leave again to say, that many instances of State injustice and oppression have already occurred in the State legislation of this Union, of flagrant violations of the guaranteed privileges of citizens of the United States, for which the national Government furnished and could furnish by law no remedy whatever. Contrary to the express letter of your Constitution, "cruel and unusual punishments" have been inflicted under State laws within this Union upon citizens, not only for crimes committed, but for sacred duty done, for which and against which the Government of the United States had provided no remedy and could provide none.

Sir, the words of the Constitution that "the citizens of each State shall be entitled to all privileges and immunities of citizens in the several States" include, among other privileges, the right to bear true allegiance to the Constitution and laws of the United States, and to be protected in life, liberty, and property. Next, sir, to the allegiance which we all owe to God our Creator, is the allegiance which we owe to our common country.

The time was in our history, thirty-three years ago, when, in the State of South Carolina, by solemn ordinance adopted in a convention held under the authority of State law, it was ordained, as a part of the fundamental law of that State, that the citizens of South Carolina, being citizens of the United States as well, should abjure their allegiance to every other government or authority than that of the State of South Carolina.

That ordinance contained these words:

> "The allegiance of the citizens of this State is due to the State: and no allegiance is due from them to any other Power or authority: and the General Assembly of said State is hereby empowered from time to time, when they may deem it proper, to provide for the administration to the citizens and officers of the State, or such of the said officers, as they may think fit, of suitable oaths or affirmations, binding them to the observance of such allegiance, and abjuring all other allegiance; and also to define what shall amount to a violation of their allegiance, and to provide the proper punishment for such violation."

There was also, as gentlemen know, an attempt made at the same time by that State to nullify the revenue laws of the United States. What was the legislation of Congress in that day to meet this usurpation of authority by that State, violative alike of the rights of the national Government and of the rights of the citizen?

In that hour of danger and trial to the country there was as able a body of men in this Capitol as was ever convened in Washington, and of these were Webster, Clay, Benton, Silas Wright, John Quincy Adams, and Edward Livingston. They provided a remedy by law for the invasion of the rights of the Federal Government and for the protection of its officials and those assisting them in executing the revenue laws. (See 4 Statutes-at-Large, 632–33.) No remedy was provided to protect the citizen. Why was the act to provide for the collection of the revenue passed, and to protect all acting under it, and no protection given to secure the citizen against punishment for fidelity to his country? But one answer can be given. There was in the Constitution of the United States an express grant of power to the Federal Congress to lay and collect duties and imposts and to pass all laws necessary to carry that grant of power into execution. But, sir, that body of great and patriotic men looked in vain for any grant of power in the Constitution by which to give protection to the citizens of the United States resident in South Carolina against the infamous provision of the ordinance which required them to abjure the allegiance which they owed their country. It was an opprobrium to the Republic that for fidelity to the

United States they could not by national law be protected against the degrading punishment inflicted on slaves and felons by State law. That great want of the citizen and stranger, protection by national law from unconstitutional State enactments, is supplied by the first section of this amendment. That is the extent that it hath, no more; and let gentlemen answer to God and their country who oppose its incorporation into the organic law of the land.

May 23, 1866

MR. HOWARD. The first clause of this section relates to the privileges and immunities of citizens of the United States as such, and as distinguished from all other persons not citizens of the United States.

It would be a curious question to solve what are the privileges and immunities of citizens of each of the States in the several States. I do not propose to go at any length into that question at this time. It would be a somewhat barren discussion. But it is certain the clause was inserted in the Constitution for some good purpose. It has in view some results beneficial to the citizens of the several States, or it would not be found there; yet I am not aware that the Supreme Court have ever undertaken to define either the nature or extent of the privileges and immunities thus guaranteed. Indeed, if my recollection serves me, that court, on a certain occasion not many years since, when this question seemed to present itself to them, very modestly declined to go into a definition of them, leaving questions arising under the clause to be discussed and adjudicated when they should happen practically to arise. But we may gather some intimation of what probably will be the opinion of the judiciary by referring to a case adjudged many years ago in one of the circuit courts of the United States by Judge Washington: and I will trouble the Senate but for a moment by reading what that very learned and excellent judge says about these privileges and immunities of the citizens of each State in the several States. It is the case of Corfield v. Coryell.

Such is the character of the privileges and immunities spoken of in the second section of the fourth article of the Constitution. To these privileges and immunities, whatever they may be—for they are not and cannot be fully defined in their entire extent and precise nature—to these should be added the personal rights guaranteed and secured by the first eight amendments of the Constitution; such as the freedom of speech and of the press; the right of the people peaceably to assemble and petition the Government for a redress of grievances, a right appertaining to each and all the people; the right to keep and to bear arms; the right to be exempted from the quartering of soldiers in a house without the consent of the owner; the right to be exempt from unreasonable searches and seizures, and from any search or seizure except by virtue of a warrant issued upon a formal oath or affidavit: the right of an accused person to be informed of the nature of the accusation against him, and his right to be tried by an impartial jury of the vicinage; and also the right to be secure against excessive bail and against cruel and unusual punishments.

Now, sir, here is a mass of privileges, immunities, and rights, some of them secured by the second section of the fourth article of the Constitution, which I have recited, some by the first eight amendments of the Constitution; and it is a fact well worthy of attention that the course of decision of our courts and the present settled doctrine is, that all these immunities, privileges, rights, thus guaranteed by the Constitution or recognized by it, are secured to the citizen solely as a citizen of the United States and as a party in their courts. They do not operate in the slightest degree as a restraint or prohibition upon State legislation. States are not affected by them, and it has been repeatedly held that the restriction contained in the Constitution against the taking of private property for public use without just compensation is not a restriction upon State legislation, but applies only to the legislation of Congress.

Now, sir, there is no power given in the Constitution to enforce and to carry out any of these guarantees. They are not powers granted by the Constitution to Congress, and of course do not come within the sweeping clause of the Constitution authorizing Congress to pass all laws necessary and proper for carrying out the foregoing or granted powers, but they stand simply as a bill of rights in the Constitution, without power on the part of Congress to give them full effect; while at the same time the States are not restrained from violating the principles embraced in them except by their own local constitutions, which may be altered from year to year. The great object of the first section of this amendment is, therefore, to restrain the power of the States and compel them at all times to respect these great fundamental guarantees. How will it be done under the present amendment? As I have remarked, they are not powers granted to Congress, and therefore it is necessary, if they are to be effectuated and enforced, as they assuredly ought to be, that additional power should be given to Congress to that end. This is done by the fifth section of this amendment, which declares that "the Congress shall have power to enforce by appropriate legislation the provisions of this article." Here is a direct affirmative delegation of power to Congress to carry out all the principles of all these guarantees, a power not found in the Constitution.

The last two clauses of the first section of the amendment disable a State from depriving not merely a citizen of the United States, but any person, whoever he may be, of life, liberty, or property without due process of law, or from denying to him the equal protection of the laws of the State. This abolishes all class legislation in the States and does away with the injustice of subjecting one caste of persons to a code not applicable to another. It prohibits the hanging of a black man for a crime for which the white man is not to be hanged. It protects the black man in his fundamental rights as a citizen with the same shield which it throws over the white man. Is it not time, Mr. President, that we extend to the black man, I had almost called it the poor privilege of the equal protection of the law? Ought not the time to be now passed when one measure of justice is to be meted out to a member of one caste while another and a different measure is meted out to the member of another caste, both castes being alike citizens of the United States, both bound to obey the same laws, to sustain the burdens of the same Government, and both equally responsible to justice and to God for the deeds done in the body?

But, sir, the first section of the proposed amendment does not give to either of these classes the right of voting. The right of suffrage is not, in law, one of the privileges or immunities thus secured by the Constitution. It is merely the creature of law. It has always been regarded in this country as the result of positive local law, not regarded as one of those fundamental rights lying at the basis of all society and without which a people cannot exist except as slaves, subject to a despotism.

As I have already remarked, section one is a restriction upon the States, and does not, of itself, confer any power upon Congress. The power which Congress has, under this amendment, is derived, not from that section, but from the fifth section, which gives it authority to pass laws which are appropriate to the attainment of the great object of the amendment. I look upon the first section, taken in connection with the fifth, as very important. It will, if adopted by the States, forever disable every one of them from passing laws trenching upon those fundamental rights and privileges which pertain to citizens of the United States, and to all persons who may happen to be within their jurisdiction. It establishes equality before the law, and it gives to the humblest, the poorest, the most despised of the race the same rights and the same protection before the law as it gives to the most powerful, the most wealthy, or the most haughty. That, sir, is republican government, as I understand it, and the only one which can claim the praise of a just Government. Without this principle of equal justice to all men and equal protection under the shield of the law, there is no republican government and none that is really worth maintaining.

May 30, 1866

MR. DOOLITTLE. As I understand, a member from Ohio, Mr. Bingham, who in a very able speech in the House maintained that the civil rights bill was without any authority in the Constitution, brought forward a proposition in the House of Representatives to amend the Constitution so as to enable Congress to declare the civil rights of all persons, and that the constitutional amendment, Mr. Bingham being himself one of the committee of fifteen, was referred by the House to that committee, and from the committee it has been reported. I say I have a right to infer that it was because Mr. Bingham and others of the House of Representatives and other persons upon the committee had doubts, at least, as to the constitutionality of the civil rights bill that this proposition to amend the Constitution now appears to give it validity and force. It is not an imputation upon any one.

MR. GRIMES. It is an imputation upon every member who voted for the bill, the inference being legitimate and logical that they violated their oaths and knew they did so when they voted for the civil rights bill.

MR. DOOLITTLE. The Senator goes too far. What I say is that they had doubts.

MR. FESSENDEN. I will say to the Senator one thing: whatever may have been Mr. Bingham's motives in bringing it forward, he brought it forward some time before the civil rights bill was considered at all and had it referred to the committee, and it was discussed in the committee long before the civil rights bill was passed. Then I will say to him further, that during all the discussion in the committee that I heard nothing was ever said about the civil rights bill in connection with that. It was placed on entirely different grounds.

MR. DOOLITTLE. I will ask the Senator from Maine this question: if Congress, under the Constitution now has the power to declare that "all persons born in the United States, and not subject to any foreign Power, excluding Indians not taxed, are hereby declared to be citizens of the United States," what is the necessity of amending the Constitution at all on this subject?

MR. FESSENDEN. I do not choose that the Senator shall get off from the issue he presented. I meet him right there on the first issue. If he wants my opinion upon other questions, he can ask it afterward. He was saying that the committee of fifteen brought this proposition forward for a specific object.

MR. DOOLITTLE. I said the committee of fifteen brought it forward because they had doubts as to the constitutional power of Congress to pass the civil rights bill.

MR. FESSENDEN. Exactly: and I say, in reply, that if they had doubts, no such doubts were stated in the committee of fifteen, and the matter was not put on that ground at all. There was no question raised about the civil rights bill.

MR. DOOLITTLE. Then I put the question to the Senator: if there are no doubts, why amend the Constitution on that subject?

MR. FESSENDEN. That question the Senator may answer to suit himself. It has no reference to the civil rights bill.

MR. DOOLITTLE. That does not meet the case at all. If my friend maintains that at this moment the Constitution of the United States, without amendment, gives all the power you ask, why do you put this new amendment into it on that subject?

MR. HOWARD. If the Senator from Wisconsin wishes an answer, I will give him one such as I am able to give.

MR. DOOLITTLE. I was asking the Senator from Maine.

MR. HOWARD. I was a member of the same committee, and the Senator's observations apply to me equally with the Senator from Maine. We desired to put this question of citizenship and the right of citizens and freedmen under the civil rights bill beyond the legislative power of such gentlemen as the Senator from Wisconsin, who would pull the whole system up by the roots and destroy it, and expose the freedmen again to the oppressions of their old masters.

SOURCE: *Congressional Register*, 1866.

PRESIDENT ANDREW JOHNSON'S CIVIL RIGHTS BILL VETO
(1866)

Emancipation and the Thirteenth Amendment provided former slaves with freedom, but no laws protected them from the quasi-slavery of the Black Codes and similar state legislation. In an attempt to offer freedmen equal protection under the law and freedom in seeking employment, Congress passed the Civil Rights Bill of 1866. The Bill bound state governments to obey a federal law ensuring that freedmen be conferred full citizenship in the United States. Congress aimed it at the Southern states, but the Civil Rights Bill actually undermined discriminatory laws in many Northern states as well. Moderate and Radical Republicans in Congress formed a coalition championing the Bill, along with the establishment of a Freedmen's Bureau, as pillars of Reconstruction.

President Andrew Johnson exercised his right to veto the Civil Rights Bill, however, temporarily derailing the transition toward Radical Reconstruction. In so doing, Johnson ended all hope of cooperation between Congress and himself. The President sank into political isolation, wielding little authority outside of his negative power to veto. Johnson's veto message denounced the Bill as unconstitutionally subordinating state law to federal law, while confounding what he saw as a positive redefinition of interracial economic and social relationships already taking place in the South. He deemed the bill "fraught with evil," and in decidedly racist language derided freedmen as unfit to receive and exercise the rights of American citizenship.

By striking down what New York Senator Henry J. Raymond lauded as "one of the most important bills ever presented to this House for its action," Johnson rang the death knell of his political career. To add further insult to the President's injury, Congress rammed the Bill through with the necessary majority anyway, marking the first time a major piece of legislation passed over a veto in American history.

Paul S. Bartels,
Villanova University

See also **Citizenship; Civil Rights Act of 1866; Reconstruction.**

By the first section of the bill all persons born in the United States and not subject to any foreign power, excluding Indians not taxed, are declared to be citizens of the United States. This provision comprehends the Chinese of the Pacific States, Indians subject to taxation, the people called gypsies, as well as the entire race designated as blacks.... Every individual of these races born in the United States is by the bill made a citizen....

The grave question presents itself whether, when eleven of the thirty-six States are unrepresented in Congress at the present time, it is sound policy to make our entire colored population and all other excepted classes citizens of the United States. Four millions of them have just emerged from slavery into freedom. Can it be reasonably supposed that they possess the requisite qualifications to entitle them to all the privileges and immunities of citizens of the United States? Have the people of the several States expressed such a conviction? ... The policy of the Government from its origin to the present time seems to have been that persons who are strangers to and unfamiliar with our institutions and our laws should pass through a certain probation, at the end of which, before attaining the coveted prize, they must give evidence of their fitness to receive and to exercise the rights of citizens as contemplated by the Constitution of the United States. The bill in effect proposes a discrimination against large numbers of intelligent, worthy, and patriotic foreigners, and in favor of the negro....

A perfect equality of the white and colored races is attempted to be fixed by Federal law in every State of the Union over the vast field of State jurisdiction covered by these enumerated rights. In no one of these can any State ever exercise any power of discrimination between the different races. In the exercise of State policy over matters exclusively affecting the people of each State it has frequently been thought expedient to discriminate between the two races. By the statutes of some of the States, Northern as well as Southern, it is enacted, for instance, that no white person shall intermarry with a negro or mulatto....

I do not say that this bill repeals State laws on the subject of marriage between the two races....

I cite this discrimination, however, as an instance of the State policy as to discrimination, and to inquire whether if Congress can abrogate all State laws of discrimination between the two races in the matter of real estate, of suits, and of contracts generally Congress may not also repeal the State laws as to the contract of marriage between the two races. Hitherto every subject embraced in the enumeration of rights contained in this bill has been considered as exclusively belonging to the States. They all relate to the internal police and economy of the respective States. They are matters which in each State concern the domestic condition of its people, varying in each according to its own peculiar circumstances and the safety and well-being of its own citizens....

If, in any State which denies to a colored person any one of all those rights, that person should commit a crime against the laws of a State—murder, arson, rape, or any other crime—all protection and punishment through the courts of the State are taken away, and he can only be tried and punished in the Federal courts.... So that over this vast domain of criminal jurisprudence provided by each State for the protection of its own citizens and for the punishment of all persons who violate its criminal laws, Federal law, whenever it can be made to apply, displaces State law.... This section of the bill undoubtedly comprehends cases and authorizes the exercise of powers that are not, by the Constitution, within the jurisdiction of the courts of the United States....

I do not propose to consider the policy of this bill. To me the details of the bill seem fraught with evil. The white race and the black race of the South have hitherto lived together under the relation of master and slave—capital owning labor. Now, suddenly, that relation is changed, and as to ownership capital and labor are divorced. They stand now each master of itself. In this new relation, one being necessary to the other, there will be a new adjustment, which both are deeply interested in making harmonious....

This bill frustrates this adjustment. It intervenes between capital and labor and attempts to settle questions of political economy through the agency of numerous officials whose interest it will be to foment discord between the two races, for as the breach widens their employment will continue, and when it is closed their occupation will terminate.

In all our history, in all our experience as a people living under Federal and State law, no such system as that contemplated by the details of this bill has ever before been proposed or adopted. They establish for the security of the colored race safeguards which go infinitely beyond any that the General Government has ever provided for the white race. In fact, the distinction of race and color is by the bill made to operate in favor of the colored and against the white race. They interfere with the municipal legislation of the States, with the relations existing exclusively between a State and its citizens, or between inhabitants of the same State—an absorption and assumption of power by the General Government which, if acquiesced in, must sap and destroy our federative system of limited powers and break down the barriers which preserve the rights of the States. It is another step, or rather stride, toward centralization and the concentration of all legislative powers in the National Government. The tendency of the bill must be to resuscitate the spirit of rebellion and to arrest the progress of those influences which are more closely drawing around the States the bonds of union and peace.

SOURCE: Richardson, James D., ed. *A Compilation of the Messages and Papers of the Presidents 1789–1897.* Washington: Bureau of National Literature, 1896–1899.

BLACK CODE OF MISSISSIPPI
(25 November 1865)

With the fall of the Confederacy came the harsh reality of Emancipation for white Southerners. Social relations, politics, organization of labor, and the Southern economy would feel the effects of the dissolution of slavery. President Andrew Johnson took personal leadership of Reconstruction, however, granting pardons to former champions of secession and Confederate politicians and allowing them to earn election to political positions. The state governments, full of elite white Southerners, grudgingly accepted that de facto slavery had come to an end and thus began to create legislation that would keep a de jure form of slavery intact.

Mississippi and South Carolina were the first states to produce "Black Codes," legislation aimed at maintaining as many vestiges of slave society as possible. The Mississippi Black Code, perhaps the harshest of its kind, sought to restrict newly freed African-Americans' economic mobility and options while ensuring their continued subordinate status in social relations. The Code extended legal sanction of marriage, granted the right to own property, and allowed Blacks to testify in a court of law. Still, its main impetus centered on restricting freedmen to agricultural work, ensuring their perpetual status as a static economic and social underclass, and barring miscegenation and interracial marriage.

In the maze of semantics and sometimes vague, confusing language, a thinly veiled iniquity informs the Code. With the move toward Radical Reconstruction in 1866, Southern lawmakers were forced to abandon the Black Codes. Radical Republicans in Congress realized that Emancipation and Reconstruction would be farcical if social and economic restrictions were foisted upon the freedmen. The Reconstruction Act of 1867 disbanded the Southern state governments and imposed military rule until federal protections such as the Fourteenth Amendment could be impressed upon the Southern population.

Paul S. Bartels,
Villanova University

See also **Black Codes; Mississippi; Reconstruction; South, the: The New South**

An Act to Confer Civil Rights on Freedmen, and for other Purposes

Section 1. . . . All freedmen, free negroes and mulattoes may sue and be sued, implead and be impleaded, in all the courts of law and equity of this State, and may acquire personal property, and choses in action, by descent or purchase, and may dispose of the same in the same manner and to the same extent that white persons may: Provided, That the provisions of this section shall not be so construed as to allow any freedman, free negro or mulatto to rent or lease any lands or tenements except in incorporated cities or towns, in which places the corporate authorities shall control the same.

Section 2. All freedmen, free negroes and mulattoes may intermarry with each other, in the same manner and under the same regulations that are provided by law for white persons: Provided, that the clerk of probate shall keep separate records of the same.

Section 3. All freedmen, free negroes or mullatoes who do now and have herebefore lived and cohabited together as husband and wife shall be taken and held in law as legally married, and the issue shall be taken and held as legitimate for all purposes; and it shall not be lawful for any freedman, free negro or mulatto to intermarry with any white person; nor for any person to intermarry with any freedman, free negro or mulatto; and any person who shall so intermarry shall be deemed guilty of felony, and on conviction thereof shall be confined in the State penitentiary for life; and those shall be deemed freedmen, free negroes and mulattoes who are of pure negro blood, and those descended from a negro to the third generation, inclusive, though one ancestor in each generation may have been a white person.

Section 4. In addition to cases in which freedmen, free negroes and mulattoes are now by law competent witnesses, freedmen, free negroes or mulattoes shall be competent in civil cases, when a party or parties to the suit, either plaintiff or plaintiffs, defendant or defendants; also in cases where freedmen, free negroes and mulattoes is or are either plaintiff or plaintiffs, defendant or defendants. They shall also be competent witnesses in all criminal prosecutions where the crime charged is alleged to have been committed by a white person upon or against the person or property of a freedman, free negro or mulatto: Provided, that in all cases said witnesses shall be examined in open court, on the stand; except, however, they may be examined before the grand jury, and shall in all cases be subject to the rules and tests of the common law as to competency and credibility.

Section 5. Every freedman, free negro and mulatto shall, on the second Monday of January, one thousand eight hundred and sixty-six, and annually thereafter, have a lawful home or employment, and shall have written evidence thereof as follows, to wit: if living in any incorporated city, town, or village, a license from the mayor thereof; and if living outside of an incorporated city, town, or village, from the member of the board of police of his beat, authorizing him or her to do irregular and job work; or a written contract, as provided in Section 6 in this act; which license may be revoked for cause at any time by the authority granting the same.

Section 6. All contracts for labor made with freedmen, free negroes and mulattoes for a longer period than one month shall be in writing, and a duplicate, attested and read to said freedman, free negro or mulatto by a beat, city or county officer, or two disinterested white persons of the county in which the labor is to be performed, of which each party shall have one: and said contracts shall be taken and held as entire contracts, and if the laborer shall quit the service of the employer before the expiration of his term of service, without good cause, he shall forfeit his wages for that year up to the time of quitting.

Section 7. Every civil officer shall, and every person may, arrest and carry back to his or her legal employer any freedman, free negro, or mulatto who shall have quit the service of his or her employer before the expiration of his or her term of service without good cause; and said officer and person shall be entitled to receive for arresting and carrying back every deserting employee aforesaid the sum of five dollars, and ten cents per mile from the place of arrest to the place of delivery; and the same shall be paid by the employer, and held as a set off for so much against the wages of said deserting employee: Provided, that said arrested party, after being so returned, may appeal to the justice of the peace or member of the board of police of the county, who, on notice to the alleged employer, shall try summarily whether said appellant is legally employed by the alleged employer, and has good cause to quit said employer. Either party shall have the right of appeal to the county court, pending which the alleged deserter shall be remanded to the alleged employer or otherwise disposed of, as shall be right and just; and the decision of the county court shall be final.

Section 8. Upon affidavit made by the employer of any freedman, free negro or mulatto, or other credible person, before any justice of the peace or member of the board of police, that any freedman, free negro or mulatto legally employed by said employer has illegally deserted said employment, such justice of the peace or member of the board of police issue his warrant or warrants, returnable before himself or other such officer, to any sheriff, constable or special deputy, commanding him to arrest said deserter, and return him or her to said employer, and the like proceedings shall be had as provided in the preceding section; and it shall be lawful for any officer to whom such warrant shall be directed to execute said warrant in any county in this State; and that said warrant may be transmitted without endorsement to any like officer of another county, to be executed and returned as aforesaid; and the said employer shall pay the costs of said warrants and arrest and return, which shall be set off for so much against the wages of said deserter.

Section 9. If any person shall persuade or attempt to persuade, entice, or cause any freedman, free negro or mulatto to desert from the legal employment of any person before the expiration of his or her term of service, or shall knowingly employ any such deserting freedman, free negro or mulatto, or shall knowingly give or sell to any such deserting freedman, free negro or mulatto, any food, raiment, or other thing, he or she shall be guilty of a misdemeanor, and, upon conviction, shall be fined not less than twenty-five dollars and not more than two hundred dollars and costs; and if the said fine and costs shall not be immediately paid, the court shall sentence said convict to not exceeding two months imprisonment in the county jail, and he or she shall moreover be liable to the party injured in damages: Provided, if any person shall, or shall attempt to, persuade, entice, or cause any freedman, free negro or mulatto to desert from any legal employment of any person, with the view to employ said freedman, free negro or mulatto without the limits of this State, such costs; and if said fine and costs shall not be immediately paid, the court shall sentence said convict to not exceeding six months imprisonment in the county jail.

Section 10. It shall be lawful for any freedman, free negro, or mulatto, to charge any white person, freedman, free negro or mulatto by affidavit, with any criminal offense against his or her person or property, and upon such affidavit the proper process shall be issued and executed as if said affidavit was made by a white person, and it shall be lawful for any freedman, free negro, or mulatto, in any action, suit or controversy pending, or about to be instituted in any court of law equity in this State, to make all needful and lawful affidavits as shall be necessary for the institution, prosecution or defense of such suit or controversy.

Section 11. The penal laws of this state, in all cases not otherwise specially provided for, shall apply and extend to all freedman, free negroes and mulattoes. . . .

An Act to Regulate the Relation of Master and Apprentice, as Relates to Freedmen, Free Negroes, and Mulattoes

Section 1. It shall be the duty of all sheriffs, justices of the peace, and other civil officers of the several counties in this State, to report to the probate courts of their respective counties semiannually, at the January and July terms of said courts, all freedmen, free negroes, and mulattoes, under the age of eighteen, in their respective counties, beats, or districts, who are orphans, or whose parent or parents have not the means or who refuse to provide for and support said minors; and thereupon it shall be the duty of said probate court to order the clerk of said court to apprentice said minors to some competent and suitable person on such terms as the court may direct, having a particular care to the interest of said minor: Provided, that the former owner of said minors shall have the preference when, in the opinion of the court, he or she shall be a suitable person for that purpose.

Section 2. The said court shall be fully satisfied that the person or persons to whom said minor shall be apprenticed shall be a suitable person to have the charge and care of said minor, and fully to protect the interest of said minor. The said court shall require the said master or mistress to execute bond and security, payable to the State of Mississippi, conditioned that he or she shall furnish said minor with sufficient food and clothing; to treat said minor humanely; furnish medical attention in case of sickness; teach, or cause to be taught, him or her to read and write, if under fifteen years old, and will conform to any law that may be hereafter passed for the regulation of the duties and relation of master and apprentice: Provided, that said apprentice shall be bound by indenture, in case of males, until they are twenty-one years old, and in case of females until they are eighteen years old.

Section 3. In the management and control of said apprentices, said master or mistress shall have the power to inflict such moderate corporeal chastisement as a father or guardian is allowed to infliction on his or her child or ward at common law: Provided, that in no case shall cruel or inhuman punishment be inflicted.

Section 4. If any apprentice shall leave the employment of his or her master or mistress, without his or her consent, said master or mistress may pursue and recapture said apprentice, and bring him or her before any justice of the peace of the county, whose duty it shall be to remand said apprentice to the service of his or her master or mistress; and in the event of a refusal on the part of said apprentice so to return, then said justice shall commit said apprentice to the jail of said county, on failure to give bond, to the next term of the county court; and it shall be the duty of said court at the first term thereafter to investigate said case, and if the court shall be of opinion that said apprentice left the employment of his or her master or mistress without good cause, to order him or her to be punished, as provided for the punishment of hired freedmen, as may be from time to time provided for by law for desertion, until he or she shall agree to return to the service of his or her master or mistress: Provided, that the court may grant continuances as in other cases: And provided further, that if the court shall believe that said apprentice had good cause to quit his said master or mistress, the court shall discharge said apprentice from said indenture, and also enter a judgment against the master or mistress for not more than one hundred dollars, for the use and benefit of said apprentice, to be collected on execution as in other cases.

Section 5. If any person entice away any apprentice from his or her master or mistress, or shall knowingly employ an apprentice, or furnish him or her food or clothing without the written consent of his or her master or mistress, or shall sell or give said apprentice spirits without such consent, said person so offending shall be guilty of a misdemeanor, and shall, upon conviction there of before the county court, be punished as provided for the punishment of persons enticing from their employer hired freedmen, free negroes or mulattoes.

Section 6. It shall be the duty of all civil officers of their respective counties to report any minors within their respective counties to said probate court who are subject to be apprenticed under the provisions of this act, from time to time as the facts may come to their knowledge, and it shall be the duty of said court from time to time as said minors shall be reported to them, or otherwise come to their knowledge, to apprentice said minors as hereinbefore provided.

Section 9. It shall be lawful for any freedman, free negro, or mulatto, having a minor child or children, to apprentice the said minor child or children, as provided for by this act.

Section 10. In all cases where the age of the freedman, free negro, or mulatto cannot be ascertained by record testimony, the judge of the county court shall fix the age. . . .

An Act to Amend the Vagrant Laws of the State

Section 1. All rogues and vagabonds, idle and dissipated persons, beggars, jugglers, or persons practicing unlawful games or plays, runaways, common drunkards, common night-walkers, pilferers, lewd, wanton, or lascivious persons, in speech or behavior, common railers and brawlers, persons who neglect their calling or employment, misspend what they earn, or do not provide for the support of themselves or their families, or dependents, and all other idle and disorderly persons, including all who neglect all lawful business, habitually misspend their time by frequenting houses of ill-fame, gaming-houses, or tippling shops, shall be deemed and considered vagrants, under the provisions of this act, and upon conviction thereof shall be fined not exceeding one hundred dollars, with all accruing costs, and be imprisoned, at the discretion of the court, not exceeding ten days.

Section 2. All freedmen, free negroes and mulattoes in this State, over the age of eighteen years, found on the second Monday in January, 1866, or thereafter, with no lawful employment or business, or found unlawfully assembling themselves together, either in the day or night time, and all white persons assembling themselves with freedmen, free negroes or mulattoes, or usually associating with freedmen, free negroes or mulattoes, on terms of equality, or living in adultery or fornication with a freed woman, freed negro or mulatto, shall be deemed vagrants, and on conviction thereof shall be fined in a sum not exceeding, in the case of a freedman, free negro or mulatto, fifty dollars, and a white man two hundred dollars, and imprisonment at the discretion of the court, the free negro not exceeding ten days, and the white man not exceeding six months.

Section 3. All justices of the peace, mayors, and aldermen of incorporated towns, counties, and cities of the several counties in this State shall have jurisdiction to try all questions of vagrancy in their respective towns, counties, and cities, and it is hereby made their duty, whenever they shall ascertain that any person or persons in their respective towns, and counties and cities are violating any of the provisions of this act, to have said party or parties arrested, and brought before them, and immediately investigate said charge, and, on conviction, punish said party or parties, as provided for herein. And it is hereby made the duty of all sheriffs, constables, town constables, and all such like officers, and city marshals, to report to some officer having jurisdiction all violations of any of the provisions of this act, and in case any officer shall fail or neglect any duty herein it shall be the duty of the county court to fine said officer, upon conviction, not exceeding one hundred dollars, to be paid into the county treasury for county purposes.

Section 4. Keepers of gaming houses, houses of prostitution, prostitutes, public or private, and all persons who derive their chief support in the employments that militate against good morals, or against law, shall be deemed and held to be vagrants.

Section 5. All fines and forfeitures collected by the provisions of this act shall be paid into the county treasury for general county purposes, and in case of any freedman, free negro or mulatto shall fail for five days after the imposition of any or forfeiture upon him or her for violation of any of the provisions of this act to pay the same, that it shall be, and is hereby, made the duty of the sheriff of the proper county to hire out said freedman, free negro or mulatto, to any person who will, for the shortest period of service, pay said fine and forfeiture and all costs: Provided, a preference shall be given to the employer, if there be one, in which case the employer shall be entitled to deduct and retain the amount so paid from the wages of such freedman, free negro or mulatto, then due or to become due; and in case freedman, free negro or mulatto cannot hire out, he or she may be dealt with as a pauper.

Section 6. The same duties and liabilities existing among white persons of this State shall attach to freedmen, free negroes or mulattoes, to support their indigent families and all colored paupers; and that in order to secure a support for such indigent freedmen, free negroes, or mulattoes, it shall be lawful, and is hereby made the duty of the county police of each county in this State, to levy a poll or capitation tax on each and every freedman, free negro, or mulatto, between the ages of eighteen and sixty years, not to exceed the sum of one dollar annually to each person so taxed, which tax, when collected, shall be paid into the county treasurer's hands, and constitute a fund to be called the Freedman's Pauper Fund, which shall be applied by the commissioners of the poor for the maintenance of the poor of the freedmen, free negroes and mulattoes of this State, under such regulations as may be established by the boards of county police in the respective counties of this State.

Section 7. If any freedman, free negro, or mulatto shall fail or refuse to pay any tax levied according to the provisions of the sixth section of this act, it shall be *prima facie* evidence of vagrancy, and it shall be the duty of the sheriff to arrest such freedman, free negro, or mulatto, or such person refusing or neglecting to pay such tax, and proceed at once to hire for the shortest time such delinquent taxpayer to any one who will pay the said tax, with accruing costs, giving preference to the employer, if there be one.

Section 8. Any person feeling himself or herself aggrieved by judgment of any justice of the peace, mayor, or alderman in cases arising under this act, may within five days appeal to the next term of the county court of the proper county, upon giving bond and security in a sum not less than twenty-five dollars nor more than one hundred and fifty dollars, conditioned to appear and prosecute said appeal, and abide by the judgment of the county court; and said appeal shall be tried *de novo* in the county court, and the decision of the said court shall be final. . . .

SOURCE: *Laws of the State of Mississippi, Passed at Regular Session of the Mississippi Legislature, Held in . . . Jackson, October, November, and December, 1865.* Jackson, Miss.: 1866.

POLICE REGULATIONS OF SAINT LANDRY PARISH, LOUISIANA
(1865)

Like the Black Codes, police regulations restricted the freedoms and personal autonomy of freedmen after the Civil War in the South. The Saint Landry Parish, Louisiana police regulations offer merely one example of the lengths Southern legislatures went to in preserving as much of the master-slave dynamic as possible. Louisiana possessed a large free black population prior to the Civil War, concentrated primarily in New Orleans, and offered more rights and freedoms to them than many Northern states. A virulent racism still pervaded the state, however, as freedmen were characterized as children in need of care and supervision by White employers, clergymen, and public officials. Some Louisiana politicians desired to expel all Blacks from the state following the war, but a commitment to maintaining as much of the antebellum status quo as possible prevailed. Slavery and the ideology on which it was based had ceased to exist only in name.

The regulations strove to hinder freedmen's ability to move about freely, binding them as much to the direct oversight and authority of the employer as possible. In many cases the employer was actually the employee's former master, effectively negating any real differences from slavery. The regulations sought to limit economic freedom and ensure that each former slave was in constant employment of "some White person," therefore effectively proscribing any chance of upward economic mobility and autonomy. In addition, laws enacted to keep freedmen from meeting "after sunset" and from preaching "to congregations of colored people" betrayed a deep-seated fear of African-American political and social organization that would pose a threat to White authority and order.

Paul S. Bartels,
Villanova University

See also **Black Codes; Louisiana; Reconstruction; South, the: The New South.**

Police Regulations of St. Landry Parish, Louisiana, by Louisiana Legislature

Sec. 1. Be it ordained by the police jury of the parish of St. Landry, That no negro shall be allowed to pass within the limits of said parish without special permit in writing from his employer....

Sec. 2. ... Every negro who shall be found absent from the residence of his employer after ten o'clock at night, without a written permit from his employer, shall pay a fine of five dollars, or in default thereof, shall be compelled to work five days on the public road, or suffer corporeal punishment as hereinafter provided.

Sec. 3. ... No negro shall be permitted to rent or keep a house within said parish. Any negro violating this provision shall be immediately ejected and compelled to find an employer....

Sec. 4. ... Every negro is required to be in the regular service of some white person, or former owner, who shall be held responsible for the conduct of said negro. But said employer or former owner may permit said negro to hire his own time by special permission in writing, which permission shall not extend over seven days at any one time....

Sec. 5. ... No public meetings or congregations of negroes shall be allowed within said parish after sunset; but such public meetings and congregations may be held between the hours of sunrise and sunset, by the special permission in writing of the captain of patrol, within whose beat such meetings shall take place. This prohibition, however, is not to prevent negroes from attending the usual church services, conducted by white ministers and priests....

Sec. 6. ... No negro shall be permitted to preach, exhort, or otherwise declaim to congregations of colored people, without a special permission in writing from the president of the policy jury....

Sec. 7. ... No negro who is not in the military service shall be allowed to carry fire-arms, or any kind of weapons, within the parish, without the special written permission of his employers, approved and indorsed by the nearest and most convenient chief of patrol....

Sec. 8. ... No negro shall sell, barter, or exchange any articles of merchandise or traffic within said parish without the special written permission of his employer, specifying the article of sale, barter or traffic....

WOMEN'S RIGHTS

EXCERPT FROM "ON THE EQUALITY OF THE SEXES"
(1790, by Judith Sargent Murray)

Women in early America enjoyed few freedoms or legal rights. Once a woman married—and there were few that did not—she ceded her existence as a legal citizen to her husband in a consolidation that was referred to as "couverture." Those few rights a woman did have were discarded in the years following the American Revolution when the "dower," or a woman's right to one-third of her husband's property, was abolished. However, the reform spirit of the nation's early years did lead to the development of educational opportunities for middle- and upper-middle-class white women. Judith Sargent Murray's (1751–1820) articulate essay, "On the Equality of the Sexes," published in 1790, argues against the notion that women are naturally intellectually inferior. After citing women's ingenuity and accomplishment in social and sartorial circles, she asks why these talents could not be applied to other realms of knowledge, like those denied the uneducated woman. We can read in her lucid reserve a righteous anger: she sees women's radical disenfranchisement as a crime against not just half the world's population but against humanity at large.

Leah R. Shafer,
Cornell University

See also **Equality, Concept of; Gender and Gender Roles.**

Is it upon mature consideration we adopt the idea, that nature is thus partial in her distributions? Is it indeed a fact, that she hath yielded to one half of the human species so unquestionable a mental superiority? I know that to both sexes elevated understandings, and the reverse, are common. But, suffer me to ask, in what the minds of females are so notoriously deficient, or unequal. May not the intellectual powers be ranged under their four heads—imagination, reason, memory and judgement. The province of imagination has long since been surrendered up to us, and we have been crowned undoubted sovereigns of the regions of fancy. Invention is perhaps the most arduous effort of the mind; this branch of imagination hath been particularly ceded to us, and we have been time out of mind invested with that creative faculty. Observe the variety of fashions (here I bar the contemptuous smile) which distinguish and adorn the female world; how continually are they changing, insomuch that they almost render the whole man's assertion problematical, and we are ready to say, there is something new under the sun. Now, what a playfulness, what an exuberance of fancy, what strength of inventive imagination, doth this continual variation discover? Again, it hath been observed, that if the turpitude of the conduct of our sex, hath been ever so enormous, so extremely ready are we that the very first thought presents us with an apology so plausible, as to produce our actions even in an amiable light. Another instance of our creative powers, is our talent for slander; how ingenious are we at inventive scandal? what a formidable story can we in a moment fabricate merely from the force of a prolifick imagination? how many reputations, in the fertile brain of a female, have been utterly despoiled? how industrious are we at improving a hint? suspicion how easily do we convert into conviction, and conviction, embellished by the power of eloquence, stalks abroad to the surprise and confusion of unsuspecting innocence. Perhaps it will be asked if I furnish these facts as instances of excellency in our sex. Certainly not; but as proofs of a creative faculty, of a lively imagination. Assuredly great activity of mind is thereby discovered, and was this activity properly directed, what beneficial effects would follow. Is the needle and kitchen sufficient to employ the operations of a soul thus organized? I should conceive not. Nay, it is a truth that those very departments leave the intelligent principle vacant, and at liberty for speculation. Are we deficient in reason? We can only reason from what we know, and if opportunity of acquiring knowledge hath been denied us, the inferiority of our sex cannot fairly be deduced from thence. Memory, I believe, will be allowed us in common, since every one's experience must testify, that a loquacious old woman is as frequently met with, as a communicative old man; their subjects are alike drawn from the fund of other times, and the transactions of their youth, or of maturer life, entertain, or perhaps fatigue you, in the evening of their lives. "But our judgment is not so strong—we do not distinguish so well." Yet it may be questioned, from what doth this superiority, in thus discriminating faculty of the soul, proceed. May we not trace its source in the difference of education, and continued advantages? Will it be said that the judgment of a male of two years old, is more sage than that of a female's of the same age? I believe the reverse is generally observed to be true. But from that period what partiality! how is the one exalted and the other depressed, by the contrary modes of education which are adopted! the one is taught to aspire, and the other is early confined and limited. As their years increase, the sister must be wholly domesticated, while the brother is led by the hand through all the flowery paths of science. Grant that their minds are by nature equal, yet who shall wonder at the apparent superiority, if indeed custom becomes second nature; nay if it taketh place of nature, and that it doth the experience of each day will evince. At length arrived at womanhood, the uncultivated fair one feels a void, which the employments allotted her are by no means capable of filling. What can she do? to books, she may not apply; or if she doth, to those only of the novel kind, lest she merit the appellation of a learned lady; and what ideas have been affixed to this term, the observation of many can testify. Fashion, scandal and sometimes what is still more reprehensible, are then called in to her relief; and who can say to what lengths the liberties she takes may proceed. Meantime she herself is most unhappy; she feels the want of a cultivated mind. Is she single, she in vain seeks to fill up time from sexual employments or amusements. Is she united to a person whose soul nature made equal to her own, education hath set him so far above her, that in those entertainments which are productive of such rational felicity, she is not qualified to accompany him. She experiences a mortifying consciousness of inferiority, which embitters every enjoyment. Doth the person to whom her adverse fate hath consigned her, possess a mind incapable of improvement, she is equally wretched, in being so closely connected with an individual whom she cannot but despise. Now, was she permitted the same instructors as her brother, (with an eye however to their particular departments) for the employment of a rational mind an ample field would be opened. In astronomy she might catch a glimpse of the immensity of the Deity, and thence she would form amazing conceptions of the august and supreme Intelligence. In geography she would admire Jehova in the midst of his benevolence; thus adapting this globe to the various wants and amusements of its inhabitants. In natural philosophy she would adore the infinite majesty of heaven, clothed in condescension; and as she traversed the reptile world, she would hail the goodness of a creating God. A mind, thus filled, would have little room for the trifles with which our sex are, with too much justice, accused of amusing themselves, and they would thus be rendered fit companions for those, who should one day wear them as their crown. Fashions, in their variety, would then give place to conjectures, which might perhaps conduce to the improvement of the literary world; and there would be no leisure for slander or detraction. Reputation would not then be blasted, but serious speculations would occupy the lively imaginations of the sex. Unnecessary visits would be precluded, and that custom would only be indulged by way of relaxation, or to answer the demands of consanguinity and friendship. Females would become discreet, their judgments would be invigorated, and their partners for life being circumspectly chosen, an unhappy Hymen would then be as rare, as is now the reverse.

Will it be urged that those acquirements would supersede our domestick duties, I answer that every requisite in female economy is easily attained; and, with truth I can add, that when once attained, they require no further mental attention. Nay, while we are pursuing the needle, or the superintendency of the family, I repeat, that our minds are at full liberty for reflection; that imagination may exert itself in full vigor; and that if a just foundation early laid, our ideas will then be worthy of rational beings. If we were industrious we might easily find time to arrange them upon paper, or should avocations press too hard for such an indulgence, the hours allotted for conversation would at least become more refined and rational. Should it still be vociferated, "Your domestick employments are sufficient"—I would calmly ask, is it reasonable, that a candidate for immortality, for the joys of heaven, an intelligent being, who is to spend an eternity in contemplating the works of Deity, should at present be so degraded, as to be allowed no other ideas, than those which are suggested by the mechanism of a pudding, or the sewing of the seams of a garment? Pity that all such censurers of female improvement do not go one step further, and deny their future existence; to be consistent they surely ought.

Yes, ye lordly, ye haughty sex, our souls are by nature equal to yours; the same breath of God animates, enlivens, and invigorates us; and that we are not fallen lower than yourselves, let those witness who have greatly towered above the various discouragements by which they have been so heavily oppressed; and though I am unacquainted with the list of celebrated characters on either side, yet from the observations I have made in the contracted circle in which I have moved, I dare confidently believe, that from the commencement of time to the present day, there hath been as many females, as males, who, by the mere force of natural powers, have merited the crown of applause; who thus unassisted, have seized the wreath of fame. I know there are who assert, that as the animal powers of the one sex are superiour, of course their mental faculties also must be stronger; thus attributing strength of mind to the transient organization of this earth born tenement. But if this reasoning is just, man must be content to yield the palm to many of the brute creation, since by not a few of his brethren of the field, he is far surpassed in bodily strength. Moreover, was this argument admitted, it would prove too much, for occular demonstration evinceth, that there are many robust masculine ladies, and effeminate gentlemen. Yet I fancy that Mr. Pope, though clogged with an enervated body, and distinguished by a diminutive stature, could nevertheless lay claim to greatness of soul; and perhaps there are many other instances which might be adduced to combat so unphilosophical an opinion. Do we not often see, that when the clay built tabernacle is well nigh dissolved, when it is just ready to mingle with the parent oil, the immortal inhabitant aspires to, and even attaineth heights the most sublime, and which were before wholly unexplored. Besides, were we to grant that animal strength proved anything, taking into consideration the accustomed impartiality of nature, we should be induced to imagine, that she had invested the female mind with superiour strength as an equivalent for the bodily powers of man. But waving this however palpable advantage, for equality only, we wish to contend.

Constantia

SOURCE: Murray, Judith S. "On the Equality of the Sexes," *The Massachusetts Magazine*, March and April, 1790.

HUMAN RIGHTS NOT FOUNDED ON SEX
(2 October 1837, by Angelina Grimké)

The temperance and abolition movements of the mid-nineteenth century counted an increasingly large number of women among their ranks. When these ardently involved reformers were denied the right to speak publicly—because it was believed that women should not speak before audiences of men—some broke off to form women's rights groups. Angelina and Sarah Grimké were Quaker sisters whose deep involvement in the abolition movement taught them about organizing, publicizing, and creating a platform. When they found themselves shouted out of public meetings they turned to the press to express their views. Sarah's letters about the grave injustice of female oppression were eventually published in the collection *On the Province of Women.*

In this letter to a friend, Angelina recommended her sister's book while stating unequivocally that women are the moral equals of men. Grimké believed that women, like men, deserve the same rights as any other moral, human creature. She saw the male-dominated culture's refusal to recognize this fundamental truth as an evil and tyrannical disavowal of God-given rights. She quoted the Bible in support of what she calls the "grand equalizing principle" and argued that the arrangement of society is "a violation of human rights" and "a rank usurpation of power."

Leah R. Shafer,
Cornell University

***See also:* Gender and Gender Roles; Human Rights; Women's Rights Movement: The Nineteenth Century.**

East Boylston, Mass. 10*th mo.* 2*d*, 1837.

Dear Friend: In my last, I made a sort of running commentary upon thy views of the appropriate sphere of woman, with something like a promise, that in my next, I would give thee my own.

The investigation of the rights of the slave has led me to a better understanding of my own. I have found the Anti-Slavery cause to be the high school of morals in our land—the school in which *human rights* are more fully investigated, and better understood and taught, than in any other. Here a great fundamental principle is uplifted and illuminated, and from this central light, rays innumerable stream all around. Human beings have *rights*, because they are *moral* beings: the rights of *all* men grow out of their moral nature; and as all men have the same moral nature, they have essentially the same rights. These rights may be wrested from the slave, but they cannot be alienated: his title to himself is as perfect *now*, as is that of Lyman Beecher: it is stamped on his moral being, and is, like it, imperishable. Now if rights are founded in the nature of our moral being, then the *mere circumstance of sex* does not give to man higher rights and responsibilities, than to woman. To suppose that it does, would be to deny the self-evident truth, that the 'physical constitution is the mere instrument of the moral nature.' To suppose that it does, would be to break up utterly the relations, of the two natures, and to reverse their functions, exalting the animal nature into a monarch, and humbling the moral into a slave; making the former a proprietor, and the latter its property. When human beings are regarded as *moral* beings, *sex*, instead of being enthroned upon the summit, administering upon rights and responsibilities, sinks into insignificance and nothingness. My doctrine then is, that whatever it is morally right for man to do, it is morally right for woman to do. Our duties originate, not from difference of sex, but from the diversity of our relations in life, the various gifts and talents committed to our care, and the different eras in which we live.

This regulation of duty by the mere circumstance of sex, rather than by the fundamental principle of moral being, has led to all that multifarious train of evils flowing out of the anti-christian doctrine of masculine and feminine virtues. By this doctrine, man has been converted into the warrior, and clothed with sternness, and those other kindred qualities, which in common estimation belong to his character as a *man;* whilst woman has been taught to lean upon an arm of flesh, to sit as a doll arrayed in 'gold, and pearls, and costly array,' to be admired for her personal charms, and caressed and humored like a spoiled child, or converted into a mere drudge to suit the convenience of her lord and master. Thus have all the diversified relations of life been filled with 'confusion and every evil work.' This principle has given to man a charter for the exercise of tyranny and selfishness, pride and arrogance, lust and brutal violence. It has robbed woman of essential rights, the right to think and speak and act on all great moral questions, just as men think and speak and act; the right to share their responsibilities, perils and toils; the right to fulfill the great end of her being, as a moral, intellectual and immortal creature, and of glorifying God in her body and her spirit which are His. Hitherto, instead of being a help meet to man, in the highest, noblest sense of the term, as a companion, a co-worker, an equal; she has been a mere appendage of his being, an instrument of his convenience and pleasure, the pretty toy with which he wiled away his leisure moments, or the pet animal whom he humored into playfulness and submission. Woman, instead of being regarded as the equal of man, has uniformly been looked down upon as his inferior, a mere gift to fill up the measure of his happiness. In 'the poetry of romantic gallantry,' it is true, she has been called 'the last *best* gift of God to man;' but I believe I speak forth the words of truth and soberness when I affirm, that woman never was given to man. She was created, like him, in the image of God, and crowned with glory and honor; created only a little lower than the angels,—not, as is almost universally assumed, a little lower than man; on her brow, as well as on his, was placed the 'diadem of beauty,' and in her hand the sceptre of universal dominion. Gen: i. 27, 28. 'The last *best gift* of God to man!' Where is the scripture warrant for this 'rhetorical flourish, this splendid absurdity?' Let us examine the account of her creation. 'And the rib which the Lord God had taken from man, made he a woman, and brought her unto the man.' Not as a gift—for Adam immediately recognized her *as a part of himself*—('his is now bone of my bone, and flesh of my flesh')—a companion and equal, not one hair's breadth beneath him in the majesty and glory of her moral being; not placed under his authority as a *subject*, but by his side, on the same platform of human rights, under the government of God only. This idea of woman's being 'the last best gift of God to man,' however pretty it may sound to the ears of those who love to discourse upon 'the poetry of romantic gallantry, and the generous promptings of chivalry,' has nevertheless been the means of sinking her from an *end* into a mere *means*—of turning her into an *appendage* to man, instead of recognizing her as *a part of man*—of destroying her individuality, and rights, and responsibilities, and merging her moral being in that of man. Instead of *Jehovah* being *her* king, *her* lawgiver, and *her* judge, she has been taken out of the exalted scale of existence in which He placed her, and subjected to the despotic control of man.

I have often been amused at the vain efforts made to define the rights and responsibilities of immortal beings as *men* and *women.* No one has yet found out just *where* the line of separation between them should be drawn, and for this simple reason, that no one knows just how far below man woman is, whether she be a head shorter in her moral responsibilities, or head and shoulders, or the full length of his noble stature, below him, i.e. under his feet. Confusion, uncertainty, and great inconsistencies, must exist on this point, so long as woman is regarded in the least degree inferior to man; but place her where her Maker placed her, on the same high level of human rights with man, side by side with him, and difficulties vanish, the mountains of perplexity flow down at the presence of this grand equalizing principle. Measure her rights and duties by the unerring standard of *moral being*, not by the false weights and measures of a mere circumstance of her human existence, and then the truth will be self-evident, that whatever it is *morally* right for a man to do, it is *morally* right for a woman to do. I recognize no rights but *human* rights—I know nothing of men's rights and women's rights; for in Christ Jesus, there is neither male nor female. It is my solemn conviction, that, until this principle of equality is recognised and embodied in practice, the church can do nothing effectual for the permanent reformation of the world. Woman was the first transgressor, and the first victim of power. In all heathen nations, she has been the slave of man, and Christian nations have never acknowledged her rights. Nay more, no Christian denomination or Society has ever acknowledged them on the broad basis of humanity. I know that in some denominations, she is permitted to preach the gospel; not from a conviction of her rights, nor upon the ground of her equality as a *human being*, but of her equality in spiritual gifts —for we find that woman, even in these Societies, is allowed no voice in framing the Discipline by which she is to be governed. Now, I believe it is woman's right to have a voice in all the laws and regulations by which she is to be *governed*, whether in Church or State; and that the present arrangements of society, on these points, are *a violation of human rights, a rank usurpation of power*, a violent seizure and confiscation of what is sacredly and inalienably hers—thus inflicting upon woman outrageous wrongs, working mischief incalculable in the social circle, and in its influence on the world producing only evil, and that continually. *If* Ecclesiastical and Civil governments are ordained of God, *then* I contend that woman has just as much right to sit in solemn counsel in Conventions, Conferences, Associations and General Assemblies, as man—just as much right to it upon the throne of England, or in the Presidential chair of the United States.

Dost thou ask me, if I would wish to see woman engaged in the contention and strife of sectarian controversy, or in the intrigues of political partizans? I say no! never—never. I rejoice that she does not stand on the same platform which man now occupies in these respects; but I mourn, also, that he should thus prostitute his higher nature, and vilely cast away his birthright. I prize the purity of *his* character as highly as I do that of hers. As a moral being, *whatever it is morally wrong for her to do, it is morally wrong for him to do.* The fallacious doctrine of male and female virtues has well nigh ruined all that is morally great and lovely in his character: he has been quite as deep a sufferer by it as woman, though mostly in different respects and by other processes. As my time is engrossed by the pressing responsibilities of daily public duty, I have no leisure for that minute detail which would be required for the illustration and defence of these principles. Thou wilt find a wide field opened before thee, in the investigation of which, I doubt not, thou wilt be instructed. Enter this field, and explore it: thou wilt find in it a hid treasure, more precious than rubies—a fund, a mine of principles, as new as they are great and glorious.

Thou sayest, 'an ignorant, a narrow-minded, or a stupid woman, cannot feel nor understand the rationality, the propriety, or the beauty of this relation'—i. e. subordination to man. Now, verily, it does appear to me, that nothing but a narrow-minded view of the subject of human rights and responsibilities can induce any one to believe in *this subordination to a fallible* being. Sure I am, that the signs of the times clearly indicate a vast and rapid change in public sentiment, on this subject. Sure I am that she is not to be, as she has been, '*a mere second-hand agent*' in the regeneration of a fallen world, but the acknowledged equal and co-worker with man in this glorious work. Not that 'she will carry her measure by tormenting when she cannot please, or by petulant complaints or obtrusive interference, in matters which are out of her sphere, and which she cannot comprehend.' But just in proportion as her moral and intellectual capacities become enlarged, she will rise higher and higher in the scale of creation, until she reaches that elevation prepared for her by her Maker, and upon whose summit she was originally stationed, only 'a little lower than the angels.' Then will it be seen that nothing which concerns the well-being of mankind is either beyond her sphere, or above her comprehension: *Then* will it be seen 'that America will be distinguished above all other nations for well educated women, and for the influence they will exert on the general interests of society.'

But I must close with recommending to thy perusal, my sister's Letters on the Province of Woman, published in the New England Spectator, and republished by Isaac Knapp of Boston. As she has taken up this subject so fully, I have only glanced at it. That thou and all my country-women may better understand the true dignity of woman, is the sincere desire of

Thy Friend,
A. E. GRIMKÉ

SOURCE: Grimké, Angelina Emily. *Letters to Catherine E. Beecher, in Reply to An Essay on Slavery and Abolitionism, Addressed to A. E. Grimké.* Revised by the author. Boston: Isaac Knapp, 1838.

WHEN WOMAN GETS HER RIGHTS MAN WILL BE RIGHT
(c. 1860, by Sojourner Truth)

Sojourner Truth, born and raised a slave, was perhaps the most outspoken and impressive voice in the women's rights movement. Born in 1797 to slaves on a Dutch plantation, and badly treated throughout her youth, Truth (née Isabella Baumfree) was sold four times before fleeing slavery in 1826. She became actively involved in the social reform movement when she moved to New York around 1829. After living in a variety of progressive utopian communities, including the Northampton Industrial Association, where she met and was influenced by Frederick Douglass, Truth began singing, preaching, praying, and evangelizing wherever she could find an audience. At a time when even white women were rarely allowed to speak publicly, Truth stands out as an accomplished orator and leader in both the abolition and women's rights movements. This selection echoes the message of Truth's famous "Ain't I a woman?" speech given at a women's rights convention in Akron, Ohio, in 1851. In the speech, Truth used her slave background to reject the prevailing notion that women were less capable than men, saying, "I have ploughed, planted, and gathered into barns and ain't I a woman?" She expanded upon this declaration of equality here in a discussion of unfair labor practice. It can be noted that her argument that able women deserve to be paid the same as able men has not, even a hundred years later, been fully addressed.

Leah R. Shafer,
Cornell University

***See also* Women's Rights Movement: The Nineteenth Century.**

My Friends, I am rejoiced that you are glad, but I don't know how you will feel when I get through. I come from another field—the country of the slave. They have got their rights—so much good luck. Now what is to be done about it? I feel that I have got as much responsibility as anybody else. I have as good rights as anybody. There is a great stir about colored men getting their rights, but not a word about the colored women; and if colored men get their rights, and not colored women get theirs, there will be a bad time about it. So I am for keeping the thing going while things are stirring; because if we wait till it is still, it will take a great while to get it going again. White women are a great deal smarter and know more than colored women, while colored women do not know scarcely anything. They go out washing, which is about as high as a colored woman gets, and their men go about idle, strutting up and down; and when the women come home, they ask for their money and take it all, and then scold because there is no food. I want you to consider on that, chil'n. I want women to have their rights. In the courts women have no right, no voice; nobody speaks for them. I wish woman to have her voice there among the pettifoggers. If it is not a fit place for women, it is unfit for men to be there. I am above eighty years old; it is about time for me to be going. But I suppose I am kept here because something remains for me to do; I suppose I am yet to help break the chain. I have done a great deal of work—as much as a man, but did not get so much pay. I used to work in the field and bind grain, keeping up with the cradler; but men never doing no more, got twice as much pay. So with the German women. They work in the field and do as much work, but do not get the pay. We do as much, we eat as much, we want as much. I suppose I am about the only colored woman that goes about to speak for the rights of the colored woman, I want to keep the thing stirring, now that the ice is broken. What we want is a little money. You men know that you get as much again as women when you write, or for what you do. When we get our rights, we shall not have to come to you for money, for then we shall have money enough of our own. It is a good consolation to know that when we have got this we shall not be coming to you any more. You have been having our right so long, that you think, like a slave-holder, that you own us. I know that it is hard for one who has held the reins for so long to give up; it cuts like a knife. It will feel all better when it closes up again. I have been in Washington about three years, seeing about those colored people. Now colored men have a right to vote; and what I want is to have colored women have the right to vote. There ought to be equal rights more than ever, since colored people have got their freedom.

I know that it is hard for men to give up entirely. They must run in the old track. I was amused how men speak up for one another. They cannot bear that a woman should say anything about the man, but they will stand here and take up the time in man's cause. But we are going, tremble or no tremble. Men are trying to help us. I know that all—the spirit they have got; and they cannot help us much until some of the spirit is taken out of them that belongs among the women. Men have got their rights, and women has not got their rights. That is the trouble. When woman gets her rights man will be right. How beautiful that will be. Then It will be peace on earth and good will to men. But it cannot be until it be right . . . It will come . . . Yes, it will come quickly. It must come. And now when the waters is troubled, and now is the time to step into the pool. There is a great deal now with the minds, and now is the time to start forth . . . The great fight was to keep the rights of the poor colored people. That made a great battle. And now I hope that this will be the last battle that will be in the world. Let us finish up so that there be no more fighting. I have faith in God and there is truth in humanity. Be strong women! Blush not! Tremble not! I want you to keep a good faith and good courage. And I am going round after I get my business settled and get more equality. People in the North, I am going round to lecture on human rights. I will shake every place I go to.

WHAT IF I AM A WOMAN?
(1833, by Maria W. Stewart)

Maria W. Stewart (1803–1879) was the first American-born black woman to publicly lecture and publish on political themes. After a religious conversion following the death of her husband, she began to speak and write for women's rights and racial justice. Stewart published a number of pamphlets and gave several notable public lectures in the 1830s. Though her controversial views were incendiary in the exclusionary political climate of early nineteenth-century America (she urged enslaved Blacks to rise up in revolution in order to gain freedom), she achieved a surprising measure of social prominence. After she retired from public life, she worked as a teacher in New York, Baltimore, and Washington, D.C.

In this selection, Stewart called upon Biblical precedent in an argument for the equality of women. If women have historically been leaders, prophets, and lawmakers, she argued, should they not be so now at the eventful beginning of the nineteenth century?

Leah R. Shafer,
Cornell University

See also **Gender and Gender Roles; Women's Rights Movement: The Nineteenth Century.**

... To begin my subject. "Ye have heard that it hath been said whoso is angry with his brother without cause shall be in danger of the judgment; and whoso shall say to his brother Raca, shall be in danger of the council. But whosoever shall say, thou fool, shall be in danger of hell fire." For several years my heart was in continual sorrow. Then I cried unto the Lord my troubles. And thus for wise and holy purposes best known to himself, he has raised me in the midst of my enemies to vindicate my wrongs before this people, and to reprove them for sin as I have reasoned to them of righteousness and judgment to come. "For as the heavens are higher than the earth, so are his ways above our ways, and his thoughts above our thoughts. I believe, that for wise and holy purposes best known to himself, he hath unloosed my tongue and put his word into my mouth in order to confound and put all those to shame that rose up against me. For he hath closed my face with steel and lined my forehead with brass. He hath put his testimony within me and engraven his seal on my forehead. And with these weapons I have indeed set the fiends of earth and hell at defiance."

What if I am a woman; is not the God of ancient times the God of these modern days? Did he not raise up Deborah to be a mother and a judge in Israel? Did not Queen Esther save the lives of the Jews? And Mary Magdalene first declare the resurrection of Christ from the dead?

... Again: Holy women ministered unto Christ and the apostles; and women of refinement in all ages, more or less, have had a voice in moral, religious, and political subjects.

Again: Why the Almighty hath imparted unto me the power of speaking thus I cannot tell.

... But to convince you of the high opinion that was formed of the capacity and ability of woman by the ancients, I would refer you to "Sketches of the Fair Sex." Read to the fifty-first page, and you will find that several of the northern nations imagined that women could look into futurity, and that they had about them an inconceivable something approaching to divinity. ... A belief that the Deity more readily communicates himself to women, has at one time or other prevailed in every quarter of the earth: not only among the Germans and the Britons, but all the people of Scandinavia were possessed of it. Among the Greeks, women delivered the oracles. The respect the Romans paid to the Sybils is well known. The Jews had their prophetesses. The prediction of the Egyptian women obtained much credit at Rome, even unto the emperors. And in most barbarous nations all things that have the appearance of being supernatural, the mysteries of religion, the secrets of physic, and the rights of magic, were in the possession of women.

If such women as are here described have once existed, be no longer astonished, then, my brethren and friends, that God at this eventful period should raise up your own females to strive by their example, both in public and private, to assist those who are endeavoring to stop the strong current of prejudice that flows so profusely against us at present. No longer ridicule their efforts; it will be counted for sin. For God makes use of feeble means sometimes to bring about his most exalted purposes.

In the fifteenth century, the general spirit of this period is worthy of observation. We might then have seen women preaching and mixing themselves in controversies. Women occupying the chairs of philosophy and justice; women haranguing in Latin before the Pope; women writing in Greek and studying in Hebrew; nuns were poetesses and women of quality divines. ... Women in those days devoted their leisure hours to contemplation and study. The religious spirit which has animated women in all ages showed itself at this time. It has made them, by turns, martyrs, apostles, warriors, and concluded in making them divines and scholars.

Why cannot a religious spirit animate us now? Why cannot we become divines and scholars? Although learning is somewhat requisite, yet recollect that those great apostles, Peter and James, were ignorant and unlearned. They were taken from the fishing-boat, and made fishers of men.

In the thirteenth century, a young lady of Bologne devoted herself to the study of the Latin language and of the laws. At the age of twenty-three she pronounced a funeral oration in Latin in the great church of Bologne; and to be admitted as an orator, she had neither need of indulgence on account of her youth or of her sex. At the age of twenty-six she took the degree of doctor of laws, and began publicly to expound the Institutes of Justinian. At the age of thirty-four, her great reputation raised her to a chair (where she taught the law to a prodigious concourse of scholars from all nations.) She joined the charms and accomplishments of a woman to all the knowledge of a man. And such was the power of her eloquence, that her beauty was only admired when her tongue was silent.

What if such women as are here described should rise among our sable race? And it is not impossible, for it is not the color of the skin that makes the man or the woman, but the principle formed in the soul. Brilliant wit will shine, come from whence it will; and genius and talent will not hide the brightness of its lustre.. . .

SOURCE: *Spiritual Narratives.* New York: Oxford, 1988.

SENECA FALLS DECLARATION OF RIGHTS AND SENTIMENTS

(1848, National Women's Party Convention)

Young American abolitionists Elizabeth Cady Stanton (1815–1902) and Lucretia Coffin Mott (1793–1880) met in 1840 at the World Anti-Slavery convention held in London. When the women found themselves barred from the proceedings, they vowed to form a woman's rights movement. Eight years later, the women called a "convention to discuss the social, civil, and religious condition and rights of woman." The first women's rights convention was held at Seneca Falls, New York, in July 1848. In anticipation of the event, Stanton and Mott crafted a "Declaration of Rights and Sentiments" which they modeled after the Declaration of Independence. Their Declaration demanded (among other things): equal treatment under the law; equal education and access to employment; the right to hold property, sue, and hold guardianship of children; and, most contentiously, the right to vote. Though many of the women in attendance feared demands for suffrage, believing this would turn men's opinion against them forever, the resolution was eventually passed. Unfortunately for these pioneering champions of equality, few if any would live the more than seventy years before their resolution would be made into law with the passage, in 1920, of the Nineteenth Amendment which gave women the right to vote.

Leah R. Shafer,
Cornell University

See also **Declaration of Sentiments; Seneca Falls Convention; Suffrage: Woman's Suffrage; Women's Rights Movement: The Nineteenth Century.**

Declaration of Sentiments.

When, in the course of human events, it becomes necessary for one portion of the family of man to assume among the people of the earth a position different from that which they have hitherto occupied, but one to which the laws of nature and of nature's God entitle them, a decent respect to the opinions of mankind requires that they should declare the causes that impel them to such a course.

We hold these truths to be self-evident: that all men and women are created equal; that they are endowed by their Creator with certain inalienable rights; that among these are life, liberty, and the pursuit of happiness; that to secure these rights governments are instituted, deriving their just powers from the consent of the governed. Whenever any form of government becomes destructive of these ends, it is the right of those who suffer from it to refuse allegiance to it, and to insist upon the institution of a new government, laying its foundation on such principles, and organizing its powers in such form, as to them shall seem most likely to effect their safety and happiness. Prudence indeed, will dictate that governments long established should not be changed for light and transient causes; and accordingly all experience hath shown that mankind are more disposed to suffer, while evils are sufferable, than to right themselves by abolishing the forms to which they were accustomed. But when a long train of abuses and usurpations, pursuing invariably the same object evinces a design to reduce them under absolute despotism, it is their duty to throw off such government, and to provide new guards for their future security. Such has been the patient sufferance of the women under this government, and such is now the necessity which constrains them to demand the equal station to which they are entitled.

The history of mankind is a history of repeated injuries and usurpations on the part of man toward woman, having in direct object the establishment of an absolute tyranny over her. To prove this, let facts be submitted to a candid world.

He has never permitted her to exercise her inalienable right to the elective franchise.

He has compelled her to submit to laws, in the formation of which she had no voice.

He has withheld from her rights which are given to the most ignorant and degraded men—both natives and foreigners.

Having deprived her of this first right of a citizen, the elective franchise, thereby leaving her without representation in the halls of legislation, he has oppressed her on all sides.

He has made her, if married, in the eye of the law, civilly dead.

He has taken from her all right in property, even to the wages she earns.

He has made her, morally, an irresponsible being, as she can commit many crimes with impunity, provided they be done in the presence of her husband. In the covenant of marriage, she is compelled to promise obedience to her husband, he becoming, to all intents and purposes, her master—the law giving him power to deprive her of her liberty, and to administer chastisement.

He has so framed the laws of divorce, as to what shall be the proper causes, and in the case of separation, to whom the guardianship of the children shall be given, as to be wholly regardless of the happiness of women—the law, in all cases, going upon a false supposition of the supremacy of man, and giving all power into his hands.

After depriving her of all rights as a married woman, if single, and the owner of property, he has taxed her to support a government which recognizes her only when her property can be made profitable to it.

He has monopolized nearly all the profitable employments, and from those she is permitted to follow, she receives but a scanty remuneration. He closes against her all the avenues to wealth and distinction which he considers most honorable to himself. As a teacher of theology, medicine, or law, she is not known.

He has denied her the facilities for obtaining a thorough education, all colleges being closed against her.

He allows her in Church, as well as State, but a subordinate position, claiming Apostolic authority for her exclusion from the ministry, and, with some exceptions, from any public participation in the affairs of the Church.

He has created a false public sentiment by giving to the world a different code of morals for men and women, by which moral delinquencies which exclude women from society, are not only tolerated, but deemed of little account in man.

He has usurped the prerogative of Jehovah himself, claiming it as his right to assign for her a sphere of action, when that belongs to her conscience and to her God.

He has endeavored, in every way that he could, to destroy her confidence in her own powers, to lessen her self-respect, and to make her willing to lead a dependent and abject life.

Now, in view of this entire disfranchisement of one-half the people of this country, their social and religious degradation—in view of the unjust laws above mentioned, and because women do feel themselves aggrieved, oppressed, and fraudulently deprived of their most sacred rights, we insist that they have immediate admission to all the rights and privileges which belong to them as citizens of the United States.

In entering upon the great work before us, we anticipate no small amount of misconception, misrepresentation, and ridicule; but we shall use every instrumentality within our power to effect our object. We shall employ agents, circulate tracts, petition the State and National legislatures, and endeavor to enlist the pulpit and the press in our behalf. We hope this Convention will be followed by a series of Conventions embracing every part of the country.

[Resolutions]

Whereas, The great precept of nature is conceded to be, that "man shall pursue his own true and substantial happiness." Blackstone in his Commentaries remarks, that this law of Nature being coeval with mankind, and dictated by God himself, is of course superior in obligation to any other. It is binding over all the globe, in all countries and at all times; no human laws are of any validity if contrary to this, and such of them as are valid, derive all their force, and all their validity, and all their authority, mediately and immediately, from this original; therefore,

Resolved, That such laws as conflict, in any way, with the true and substantial happiness of woman, are contrary to the great precept of nature and of no validity, for this is "superior in obligation to any other."

Resolved, That all laws which prevent woman from occupying such a station in society as her conscience shall dictate, or which place her in a position inferior to that of man, are contrary to the great precept of nature, and therefore of no force or authority.

Resolved, That woman is man's equal—was intended to be so by the Creator, and the highest good of the race demands that she should be recognized as such.

Resolved, That the women of this country ought to be enlightened in regard to the laws under which they live, that they may no longer publish their degradation by declaring themselves satisfied with their present position, nor their ignorance, by asserting that they have all the rights they want.

Resolved, That inasmuch as man, while claiming for himself intellectual superiority, does accord to woman moral superiority, it is pre-eminently his duty to encourage her to speak and teach, as she has an opportunity, in all religious assemblies.

Resolved, That the same amount of virtue, delicacy, and refinement of behavior that is required of woman in the social state, should also be required of man, and the same transgressions should be visited with equal severity on both man and woman.

Resolved, That the objection of indelicacy and impropriety, which is so often brought against woman when she addresses a public audience, comes with a very ill-grace from those who encourage, by their attendance, her appearance on the state, in the concert, or in feats of the circus.

Resolved, That woman has too long rested satisfied in the circumscribed limits which corrupt customs and a perverted application of the Scriptures have marked out for her, and that it is time she should move in the enlarged sphere which her great Creator has assigned her.

Resolved, That it is the duty of the women of this country to secure to themselves their sacred right to the elective franchise.

Resolved, That the equality of human rights results necessarily from the fact of the identity of the race in capabilities and responsibilities.

Resolved, therefore, That, being invested by the Creator with the same capabilities, and the same consciousness of responsibility for their exercise, it is demonstrably the right and duty of woman, equally with man, to promote every righteous cause by every righteous means; and especially in regard to the great subjects of morals and religion, it is self-evidently her right to participate with her brother in teaching them, both in private and in public, by writing and by speaking, by any instrumentalities proper to be used, and in any assemblies proper to be held; and this being a self-evident truth growing out of the divinely implanted principles of human nature, any custom or authority adverse to it, whether modern or wearing the hoary sanction of antiquity, is to be regarded as a self-evident falsehood, and at war with mankind.

SOURCE: Anthony, Susan B., Elizabeth Cady Stanton, and Matilda Joslyn Gage, eds. *The History of Woman Suffrage.* Rochester, N.Y.: S. Anthony, 1889.

EXCERPT FROM *PATH BREAKING*
(1914, by Abigail Scott Duniway)

Women living in the American west had very different lives from their urban, East Coast counterparts. Pioneering women's integral role in developing frontier economies led to a measure of progressivism unknown in the already settled states: for example, in 1890 Wyoming was admitted into the Union as the first state giving women the right to vote. Abigail Scott Duniway (1834–1915) was a women's rights activist and newspaper editor living in the Pacific Northwest. Her paper the *New Northwest,* published between 1871 and 1887, was a stalwart supporter of suffrage and other issues of human equality.

In the selection here Duniway described the forming of the Oregon State Equal Suffrage Association and her participation in a lecture tour with Susan B. Anthony. The two women encountered shut-outs, jeering detractors, and the wrath of the church, but also won supporters to the cause, leading Anthony to remark, "If you want any cause to prosper, just persecute it." The story of Duniway's life as an activist was published in her 1914 autobiography *Path Breaking,* from which this excerpt is taken.

Leah R. Shafer,
Cornell University

See also **Suffrage: Woman's Suffrage.**

CHAPTER V.

Brings Miss Anthony to Oregon.

Among the many incidents I recall, which led me into the Equal Suffrage movement and crowd upon my memory as I write, was one which calls for special mention, and ought not to be omitted here. I had grown dispirited over an accumulation of petty annoyances in the store, when a woman entered suddenly, and throwing back a heavy green berage veil, said. "Mrs. Duniway, I want you to go with me to the court house!" I replied rather curtly, I fear: "The court house is a place for men." The visitor, whose eyes were red with weeping, explained that the county court had refused to accept the terms of her annual settlement, as administratrix of her husband's estate. But her lawyer had told her to get some merchant to accompany her to the court house, to bear testimony to the manner of settling her accounts. "Can't you get some man to go with you?" I asked, with growing sympathy. "I have asked several, but they all say they are too busy," was her tearful response. A sudden impulse seized me, and, calling one of the girls from the work room to wait upon customers, I started with the widow to the court house, feeling half ashamed, as I walked the street, to meet any one who might guess my errand. The woman kept up a running conversation as we proceeded, her words often interrupted by sobs. "Only think!" she cried, in a broken voice, "my husband—if he had lived and I had died—could have spent every dollar we had earned in twenty years of married life, and nobody would have cared what became of my children. I wasn't supposed to have any children. My girls and I have sold butter, eggs, poultry, cord wood, vegetables, grain and hay—almost enough to pay taxes and meet all of our bills, but after I've earned the means to pay expenses I can't even buy a pair of shoestrings without being lectured by the court for my extravagance!" By this time I was so deeply interested that I shouldn't have cared if all the world knew I was going to the court house. I felt a good deal as the man must have felt "who whipped another man for saying his sister was cross-eyed."

When arraigned for misconduct before the court he said: "Your Honor, my sister isn't cross-eyed. I haven't any sister. It was the principle of the thing that stirred me up!"

The court had adjourned for recess as I entered the room and I felt much relieved, as I knew the officers and didn't feel afraid to meet them when off duty. The urbane judge, who was still occupying his revolving chair, leaned back and listened to my story. When I had finished, he put his thumbs in the armholes of his vest and said, with a patronizing air: "Of course, Mrs. Duniway, as you are a lady, you are not expected to understand the intricacies of the law." "But we are expected to know enough to foot the bills, though," I retorted with more force than elegance. The widow's lawyer beckoned us to him and said, with a merry twinkle in his eye. "I guess there won't be any more trouble with the county court or the commissioners this year." As we were returning to the store the widow said: "I have to pay that lawyer enough every year to meet all my taxes, if I wasn't compelled to administer on my husband's estate."

In relating this incident to my husband at night, I added: "One-half of the women are dolls, the rest of them are drudges, and we're all fools!" He placed his hand on my head, as I sat on the floor beside his couch, and said: "Don't you know it will never be any better for women until they have the right to vote?" "What good would that do?" I asked, as a new light began to break across my mental vision. "Can't you see," he said earnestly, "that women do half of the work of the world? And don't you know that if women were voters there would soon be lawmakers among them? And don't you see that, as women do half the work of the world, besides bearing all the children, they ought to control fully half of the pay?" The light permeated my very marrow bones, filling me with such hope, courage and determination as no obstacle could conquer and nothing but death could overcome.

Early in the month of November, in the year 1870, shortly after many such practical experiences as related above, which led me to determine to remove from Albany to Portland, to begin the publication of my weekly newspaper, "The New Northwest," I met one day at the home of my estimable neighbor, the late Mrs. Martha J. Foster, and our mutual friend, Mrs. Martha A. Dalton, of Portland, to whom I announced my intention. My friends heartily agreed with my idea as to Equal Rights for Women, but expressed their doubts as to the financial success of the proposed newspaper enterprise. After much discussion and finding my determination to begin the work unshaken, the three of us met at my home and decided to form the nucleus of a State Equal Suffrage Association.

A little local Equal Suffrage Society had previously been organized in Salem, with Colonel C. A. Reed as president and Judge G. W. Lawson as secretary. I at once communicated with these gentlemen, stating our purpose, and, as I was going to San Francisco on business in the approaching holidays, I was favored by them with credentials as a delegate to the California Woman Suffrage convention, to meet in Sacramento the following Spring. No record of our preliminary meeting to form the State Society of Oregon Suffragists was preserved of which Mrs. Dalton or myself had knowledge. The minutes were left with Mrs. Foster, who, like Colonel Reed and Judge Lawson, long ago passed to the higher life. But I promised Mrs. Dalton, who visited me at this writing, in October, 1913, and has since passed away, to make special mention of that initial meeting in these pages, little dreaming that ere this history should see the light; she would have preceded me to the unseen world, leaving me the sole survivor of our compact of 1870.

Mrs. Dalton became one of the charter members of the State Equal Suffrage Association at the time of its permanent organization in Portland, in 1873, and continued a member of its executive committee up to the time of her death. While she was not a public speaker, and was not given to writing essays, she was always ready to attend to any kind of detail work, such as other and less enterprising women might easily be tempted to shirk. Her occupation, as a successful music teacher, afforded her extensive acquaintance among the leading people of Portland, many of whom confided their family or personal grievances to her, to whom she was always a sympathetic friend. As I pause to drop a sympathetic tear to her memory as I add this paragraph, I feel comforted, because I know that in the course of nature I, too, shall join the great majority in the rapidly approaching bye and bye.

The first number of "The New Northwest" was issued on the 5th of May, 1871. As I look backward over the receded years, and recall the incidents of this venture, in the management of which I had had no previous training, I cannot but wonder at my own audacity, which can be compared to the spirit of adventure which led the early pioneers to cross, or try to cross, the unknown plains, with helpless families in covered wagons, drawn by teams of oxen. It is true that I did not encounter the diseases and deaths of the desert, in making that venture, nor meet attacks from wild beasts and wilder savages, but I did encounter ridicule, ostracism and financial obstacles, over which I fain would draw the veil of forgetfulness. While I did not regret meeting insults and misrepresentation on my own account, I did suffer deeply because of my budding family, who naturally resented the slander and downright abuse I suffered from ambitious editors, to all of whose attacks I replied in my own paper, in such a way as to bring to my defense the wiser comments of successful men, among whom I number many of our most prominent citizens of today; while among my detractors, I cannot recall a single one who has placed on record a single important deed redounding to his public or private credit.

Of the many men and women, who have honestly differed from me in the past, I have no word of censure. To my good brother, the late Mr. Harvey W. Scott, three years my junior, editor of the "Oregonian," then a rising journalist, universally honored in his later years, I owe a debt of lasting gratitude, for much assistance, editorial and otherwise, during the stormy years of my early efforts to secure a footing in my inexperienced attempts at journalism. It was through his influence and that of his honored partner, Mr. H. L. Pittock, that I was favored often with railway transportation across the Continent; and, although my brother did not editorially espouse my mission, as I believe he would have done if I had not been his sister, he many a time gladdened my heart by copying incidents of woman's hardships from my "New Northwest" into his own columns, thus indirectly championing, or at least commending, my initial efforts to secure Equal Rights for women.

To my faithful, invalid husband, the late Mr. Ben C. Duniway, but for whose sterling character as a man I could not have left our growing family in the home while I was away, struggling for a livelihood and the support of my newspaper, nor could I have reached the broader field, which now crowns my life with the success for which I toiled in my early itinerancy, I owe undying gratitude.

To the 61,265 affirmative votes cast for the Equal Suffrage Amendment, at the November election of 1912, and the more than an equal number of women; who rejoice with me over the culmination of my life's endeavors, I turn with words and thoughts of love and thankfulness. Many will live to see the beneficent results of their patriotism and foresight, long after I shall have joined the silent majority. Others may see their cherished ambitions fade, and will lay their failure to their discovery that all women cannot be made to vote or think according to their dictation, any more than all men can be so made, or led or driven.

First and foremost, among my many Eastern coworkers, who had come to San Francisco on a lecture tour with Elizabeth Cady Stanton in the spring of 1871 (shortly after I had launched my newspaper), I am proud to mention Susan B. Anthony. This wonderful woman had up to that time been an object of almost universal ridicule, being caricatured as a "cross, cranky old maid," an avowed "man-hater" and a "dangerous agitator." I was seriously disappointed when Miss Anthony came alone, by steamer, to Oregon, as I had arranged for, and hoped much from, a visit by Mrs. Stanton as an offset to the caricatures that Miss Anthony's visit had previously occasioned elsewhere. Messrs. Mitchell and Dolph, prominent young attorneys of Portland—both afterwards United States Senators—had obligingly provided me with steamer passes for both ladies; but when Miss Anthony came alone, and I called upon her at her hotel in the early morning, after her arrival at midnight, I was delighted to find her a most womanly woman, gentle voiced, logical, full of business, and so fertile in expedients as to disarm all apprehension as to the financial results of her visit. She decided, at once, that I must become her business manager during her sojourn of two months or more, in Oregon and Washington; that I must preside, and make introductory speeches at all of her meetings, advertise her thoroughly through "The New Northwest," and print and circulate numerous "dodgers" in her behalf, securing meanwhile such favorable recognition from the general press as I could obtain in our wanderings.

How vividly I recall my first experience before a Portland audience! No church was open to us anywhere, and the old Orofino Theatre was our only refuge. I went in fear and trembling before a cold, curious and critical crowd, half bent with weariness resulting from long, continuous mental and physical overwork, and said in a faltering voice, "The movement that arose in the East nearly twenty years ago, to demand Equal Rights for Women, and appeared, at first, as a shadow not larger than a woman's hand, has grown and spread from the

Atlantic Coast, till it pauses tonight in farthest Oregon, almost in hearing of the Pacific Ocean. Keeping ahead of that shadow is the illustrious visitor, who illuminates it wherever she goes with the freedom spirit of her devotion. This distinguished visitor is my world renowned coadjutor, Susan B. Anthony of Everywhere, who will now address you."

Nobody was more astonished over the effect of that little impromptu speech than myself, and from that time to this I have never been without more invitations to lecture than I could fill. Miss Anthony spoke as one inspired, and many who came to scoff remained to praise. Her assistance in increasing the circulation of "The New Northwest" was wonderful. The newspapers were filled with generous words of approval of ourselves and of our work, wherever we went, and "The New Northwest" gave Miss Anthony many whole pages of free advertisement for many weeks.

From Portland we went to Salem, Albany and other Willamette Valley towns, meeting success everywhere. Returning, we visited Olympia and addressed the Territorial Legislature of Washington, which was then in session, and were accorded a most gracious hearing. We had had similar success in Seattle and Port Townsend, but were ordered from the home of a Port Gamble citizen, whose wife had invited us to the house in the absence of her husband, who, returning unexpectedly, treated us as tramps. I wanted to stay it out and conquer the head of the family with a little womanly tact, but Miss Anthony hurried me off with her to the hotel. We spoke in the evening to a crowded house, making no allusion to the incident, which had spread through the milling town like wild fire.

We continued finding friends wherever we went, and remained long enough in Seattle to organize a Woman Suffrage Association with a staff of influential officers. No official record of this organization is obtainable, but I copy from the editorial correspondence of "The New Northwest" the names of H. L. Yesler, Mayor of Seattle; Mrs. Yesler, Reverend and Mrs. John F. Damon, Mrs. Mary Olney Brown, Reverend and Mrs. Daniel Bagley and Mr. and Mrs. Amos Brown. A Suffrage Society was also formed in Olympia, under the leadership of Mrs. A. H. H. Stuart, Mrs. C. P. Hale, Hon. Elwood Evans, Mrs. Clara E. Sylvester and Mr. J. M. Murphy, editor of "The Washington Standard."

When we returned to Portland, the winter rains were deluging the earth. The stage carrying us from Olympia to the Columbia River at Kalama, led us through the blackness of darkness in the night time, giving Miss Anthony a taste of pioneering under difficulties that remained with her as a memory to her dying day.

We had previously visited Walla Walla, enjoying the hospitality of Captain J. C. Ainsworth's Company of Columbia River Steamers, and stopping at The Dalles, where my personal friends, Mr. and Mrs. Joseph Wilson and Mrs. C. C. Donnell, secured the Congregational Church for our meeting, much to the disgust of the pastor, to whom our supposed-to-be-inferior sex was his only audible objection.

The steamer stopped for an hour at Umatilla, where Miss Anthony happened to meet the son of an old lady friend of Rochester, New York, an humble bar keeper of the village, whose only way to exhibit his hospitality was to offer her a drink of white wine of which she politely took a sip and gave him back the glass with a gentle "Thank you." The news of this trivial incident preceded us to Walla Walla, and was made the excuse by the preachers for denying us the use of any pulpit in the little city; and we were compelled to speak in a little room in the rear of a saloon, the Pixley Sisters having previously engaged the only theatre. The next Sunday, the preachers who had closed the churches against us, solemnly denounced the Equal Suffrage Movement, giving as one of their reasons therefor, the fact that we had lectured in the dance hall, but failing to tell the other side of the story.

No suffrage organization was effected in Walla Walla, but the interest our visit created was much enhanced by the prohibitory action of the clergy. Many influential families entertained us in their homes. "If you want any cause to prosper, just persecute it," said Miss Anthony—and she was right.

When the Annual State Fair of Oregon convened at Salem, Miss Anthony camped with my family on the grounds, her first experience at camping out. There was no assembly hall at that time on the Fair Grounds, and we held an open-air meeting in the shade of the pavilion, where the shrieking of whistles and blare of drums and brass instruments, combined with the spieling of sideshow promoters, compelled us to speak with a screeching accent, but brought us much commendation from a large and intelligent audience, and secured us many subscriptions to "The New Northwest."

The autumn rains were in their glory in Portland before Miss Anthony finally left us, going by stage to Sacramento, and lecturing at stopover stations along the way. She informed me regularly of the incidents of her journey by letter, and I particularly recall her favorable mention of Dr. Barthenia Owens, of Roseburg (now Dr. Owens-Adair), who arranged a successful meeting for her at the Douglas County Court House and entertained her in her home. The Doctor is now a retired physician, and like Dr. Mary A. Thompson, of Portland, the original, though only "irregular" path-breaker for women practitioners, is honored now by the medical profession, which formerly denounced and ridiculed all such women as "freaks."

SOURCE: Duniway, Abigail Scott. *Path Breaking: An Autobiographical History of the Equal Suffrage Movement in the Pacific Coast States.* Portland, Oreg.: James, Kerns & Abbott, 1914.

INDUSTRY AND LABOR

CIVIL DISOBEDIENCE
(1846, by Henry David Thoreau)

From 4 July 1845 to 6 September 1847, the writer Henry David Thoreau lived in solitude on Walden Pond in Massachusetts, in a cabin he built himself. The cabin was situated on a plot of land given to him by his friend and mentor Ralph Waldo Emerson. It was Thoreau's aim to demonstrate he could live in the woods without the benefits of industrial society. It was during this time that the United States went to war with Mexico, a conflict bitterly opposed by the growing antislavery movement. Like other abolitionists, Thoreau was horrified by the war, believing it a Southern attempt to expand and extend the institution of slavery. To protest the war, Thoreau refused to pay his poll tax. (He had actually failed to pay his poll tax for three successive years; it was only in 1846 that he linked it to the larger issues of war and slavery). For this action, Thoreau was arrested and jailed. Within hours, his aunt paid the tax and the following day he was released. In total, he spent one night in jail.

From this experience came his famous essay, "Civil Disobedience." Of the essay, the historian Robert D. Cross has written: "Thoreau makes a powerful case for the duty of an individual not to violate his own convictions by acquiescence; there are times when the individual must not only say no but act on his refusal. . . . He shared Emerson's horror of becoming embroiled in mass crusades, however elevated the avowed purpose. Yet when the state, or any part of it, commits what a man deeply believes is absolute wrong, Thoreau would sanction any form of resistance."

Robert Jakoubek,
Independent Scholar

***See also* Civil Disobedience.**

I HEARTILY accept the motto—"That government is best which governs least;" and I should like to see it acted up to more rapidly and systematically. Carried out, it finally amounts to this, which also I believe,—"That government is best which governs not at all;" and when men are prepared for it, that will be the kind of government which they will have. Government is at best but an expedient; but most governments are usually, and all governments are sometimes, inexpedient. The objections which have been brought against a standing army, and they are many and weighty, and deserve to prevail, may also at last be brought against a standing government. The standing army is only an arm of the standing government. The government itself, which is only the mode which the people have chosen to execute their will, is equally liable to be abused and perverted before the people can act through it. Witness the present Mexican war, the work of comparatively a few individuals using the standing government as their tool; for in the outset, the people would not have consented to this measure. . . .

All men recognize the right of revolution; that is, the right to refuse allegiance to, and to resist, the government, when its tyranny or its inefficiency are great and unendurable. But almost all say that such is not the case now. But such was the case, they think, in the Revolution of '75. If one were to tell me that this was a bad government because it taxed certain foreign commodities brought to its ports, it is most probable that I should not make an ado about it, for I can do without them. All machines have their friction; and possibly this does enough good to counter-balance the evil. At any rate, it is a great evil to make a stir about it. But when the friction comes to have its machine, and oppression and robbery are organized, I say, let us not have such a machine any longer. In other words, when a sixth of the population of a nation which has undertaken to be the refuge of liberty are slaves, and a whole country is unjustly overrun and conquered by a foreign army, and subjected to military law, I think that it is not too soon for honest men to rebel and revolutionize. What makes this duty the more urgent is that fact that the country so overrun is not our own, but ours is the invading army.

. . .No man with a genius for legislation has appeared in America. They are rare in the history of the world. There are orators, politicians, and eloquent men, by the thousand; but the speaker has not yet opened his mouth to speak who is capable of settling the much-vexed questions of the day. We love eloquence for its own sake, and not for any truth which it may utter, or any heroism it may inspire. Our legislators have not yet learned the comparative value of free trade and of freed, of union, and of rectitude, to a nation. They have no genius or talent for comparatively humble questions of taxation and finance, commerce and manufactures and agriculture. If we were left solely to the wordy wit of legislators in Congress for our guidance, uncorrected by the seasonable experience and the effectual complaints of the people, America would not long retain her rank among the nations. For eighteen hundred years, though perchance I have no right to say it, the New Testament has been written; yet where is the legislator who has wisdom and practical talent enough to avail himself of the light which it sheds on the science of legislation.

The authority of government, even such as I am willing to submit to—for I will cheerfully obey those who know and can do better than I, and in many things even those who neither know nor can do so well—is still an impure one: to be strictly just, it must have the sanction and consent of the governed. It can have no pure right over my person and property but what I concede to it. The progress from an absolute to a limited monarchy, from a limited monarchy to a democracy, is a progress toward a true respect for the individual. Even the Chinese philosopher was wise enough to regard the individual as the basis of the empire. Is a democracy, such as we know it, the last improvement possible in government? Is it not possible to take a step further towards recognizing and organizing the rights of man? There will never be a really free and enlightened State until the State comes to recognize the individual as a higher and independent power, from which all its own power and authority are derived, and treats him accordingly. I please myself with imagining a State at last which can afford to be just to all men, and to treat the individual with respect as a neighbor; which even would not think it inconsistent with its own repose if a few were to live aloof from it, not meddling with it, nor embraced by it, who fulfilled all the duties of neighbors and fellow men. A State which bore this kind of fruit, and suffered it to drop off as fast as it ripened, would prepare the way for a still more perfect and glorious State, which I have also imagined, but not yet anywhere seen.

SOURCE: Thoreau, Henry David. Collected under this title in *A Yankee in Canada, with Anti-Slavery and Reform Papers.* Boston: Ticknor and Fields, 1866.

MILL WORKER'S LETTER ON HARDSHIPS IN THE TEXTILE MILLS
(5 November 1848, by Mary Paul)

After the American Revolution, Britain's control of the textile industry left the United States economically dependent upon imported cloth. The first mechanized textile mill was not built in the United States until 1790, when British immigrant Samuel Slater built a water-powered mill for Moses Brown in Pawtucket, Rhode Island. The dangerous and complicated mill work was first done by middle-class white women seeking economic independence, but by the late nineteenth century, wages dropped and the jobs were taken over by immigrants and freed slaves arriving from the South.

Mary S. Paul's letter home describes the conditions at the mills in Lowell, Massachusetts, where she worked as a warper. In 1848, the year of her letter, wages were cut in all of the Lowell mills. Paul made $2.00 a week after room and board.

Leah R. Shafer,
Cornell University

***See also* Industrial Revolution; Textiles.**

Lowell Nov 5th 1848

Dear Father

Doubtless you have been looking for a letter from me all the week past. I would have written but wished to find whether I should be able to stand it—to do the work that I am now doing. I was unable to get my old place in the cloth room on the Suffolk or on any other corporation. I next tried the dressrooms on the Lawrence Cor[poration], but did not succe[e]d in getting a place. I almost concluded to give up and go back to Claremont, but thought I would try once more. So I went to my old overseer on the Tremont Cor. I had no idea that he would want one, but he did, and I went to work last Tuesday—warping—the same work I used to do. It is very hard indeed and sometimes I think I shall not be able to endure it. I never worked so hard in my life but perhaps I shall get used to it. I shall try hard to do so for there is no other work that I can do unless I spin and that I shall not undertake on any account. I presume you have heard before this that the wages are to be reduced on the 20th of this month. It is true and there seems to be a good deal of excitement on the subject but I can not tell what will be the consequence. The companies pretend they are losing immense sums every day and therefore they are obliged to lessen the wages, but this seems perfectly absurd to me for they are constantly making repairs and it seems to me that this would not be if there were really any danger of their being obliged to stop the mills.

It is very difficult for any one to get into the mill on any corporation. All seem to be very full of help. I expect to be paid about two dollars a week but it will be dearly earned. I cannot tell how it is but never since I have worked in the mill have I been so very tired as I have for the last week but it may be owing to the long rest I have had for the last six months. I have not told you that I do not board on the Lawrence. The reason of this is because I wish to be nearer the mill and I do not wish to pay the extra \$.12–1/2 per week (I should not be obliged to do it if I boarded at 15) and I know that they are not able to give it me. Beside this I am so near I can go and see them as often as I wish. So considering all things I think I have done the best I could. I do not like here very well and am very sure I never shall as well as at Mother Guilds. I can now realize how very kind the whole family have ever been to me. It seems like going home when I go there which is every day. But now I see I have not told you yet where I do board. It is at No. 5 Tremont Corporation. Please enlighten all who wish for information. There is one thing which I forgot to bring with me and which I want very much. That is my rubbers. They hang in the back room at uncle Jerrys. If Olive comes down here I presume you can send them by her, but if you should not have the opportunity to send them do not trouble yourself about them. There is another thing I wish to mention—about my fare down here. If you paid it all the way as I understand you did there is something wrong about it. When we stopped at Concord to take the cars, I went to the ticket office to get a ticket which I knew I should be obliged to have. When I called for it I told the man that my fare to Lowell was paid all the way and I wanted a ticket to Lowell. He told me if this was the case the Stagedriver would get the ticket for me and I supposed of course he would. But he did not, and when the ticket master called for my ticket in the cars, I was obliged to give him a dollar. Sometimes I have thought that the fare might not have been paid beside farther than Concord. If this is the case all is right. But if it is not, then I have paid a dollar too much and gained the character of trying to cheat the company out of my fare, for the man thought I was lying to him. I suppose I want to know how it is and wish it could be settled for I do not like that any one should think me capable of such a thing, even though that person be an utter stranger. But enough of this. The Whigs of Lowell had a great time on the night of the 3rd. They had an immense procession of men on foot bearing torches and banners got up for the occasion. The houses were illuminated (Whigs houses) and by the way I should think the whole of Lowell were Whigs. I went out to see the illuminations and they did truly look splendid. The Merrimack house was illuminated from attic to cellar. Every pane of glass in the house had a half candle to it and there were many others lighted in the same way. One entire block on the Merrimack Cor[poration] with the exception of one tenement which doubtless was occupied by a free soiler who would not illuminate on any account whatever.

(Monday Eve) I have been to work today and think I shall manage to get along with the work. I am not so tired as I was last week. I have not yet found out what wages I shall get but presume they will be about \$2.00 per week exclusive of board. I think of nothing further to write excepting I wish you to prevail on Henry to write to me, also tell Olive to write and Eveline when she comes.

Give my love to uncle Jerry and aunt Betsey and tell little Lois that "Cousin Carra" thanks her very much for the apple she sent her. Her health is about the same that it was when she was at Claremont. No one has much hope of her ever being any better.

Write soon. Yours affectionately

Mary S Paul

Mr. Bela Paul

P.S. Do not forget to direct to No. 5 Tremont Cor and tell all others to do the same.

SOURCE: Larcom, Lucy. *A New England Girlhood.* Boston: Houghton Mifflin, 1892.

EXCERPT FROM *THE PRINCIPLES OF SCIENTIFIC MANAGEMENT* *(1911, by Frederick Winslow Taylor)*

Frederick Winslow Taylor (1856–1915) was a mechanical engineer and inventor who began studying the physical motions steel workers used in their jobs in the late nineteenth century. These studies revolutionized labor practices in the United States.

In this excerpt from *The Principles of Scientific Management* (1911), Taylor identifies "soldiering," the practice of deliberately working slowly and inefficiently, and "loafing" as the greatest evils facing humankind. Seen as an instinct shared by workers in any industrial employment, soldiering robs businesses of prosperity by keeping labor costs high and productivity low. Spurred by custom and peer pressure, employees consistently hold down productivity by taking advantage of their employer's ignorance of how quickly tasks can be performed. For Taylor, this deception was "more or less hypocritical." It prevents workers and managers from realizing the benefits of mutual cooperation by maintaining antagonism between the two parties. A selfish exercise in waste, soldiering is as much a moral problem as it is an economic one. As a remedy, Taylor implored managers to employ scientific methods to counter the fallacious and sentimental attitudes of the "rule of thumb."

By introducing the scientific method to business management Taylor hoped to arm employers with the expert knowledge necessary to enable employees to conquer the immoral human instinct to soldier. This belief in the efficacy of scientific expertise to overcome perceived human failings and usher in new social standards of cooperation and mutual benefit was a common theme of reform in the Progressive Era. And while some of Taylor's prescriptions may now seem dated, his goal of maximum prosperity achieved through maximum productivity still resonates. As do his methods: his pioneering time-and-motion studies of individual tasks have since been adopted by coaches and trainers to improve athletic performance. Ironically, sports are one activity Taylor explicitly identifies as free from the scourge of soldiering.

Mark D. Baumann,
New York University

See also **Productivity, Concept of; Scientific Management.**

Fundamentals of Scientific Management

The principal object of management should be to secure the maximum prosperity for the employer, coupled with the maximum prosperity for each employé.

The words "maximum prosperity" are used, in their broad sense, to mean not only large dividends for the company or owner, but the development of every branch of the business to its highest state of excellence, so that the prosperity may be permanent.

In the same way maximum prosperity for each employé means not only higher wages than are usually received by men of his class, but, of more importance still, it also means the development of each man to his state of maximum efficiency, so that he may be able to do, generally speaking, the highest grade of work for which his natural abilities fit him, and it further means giving him, when possible, this class of work to do.

It would seem to be so self-evident that maximum prosperity for the employer, coupled with maximum prosperity for the employé, ought to be the two leading objects of management, that even to state this fact should be unnecessary. And yet there is no question that, throughout the industrial world, a large part of the organization of employers, as well as employés, is for war rather than for peace, and that perhaps the majority on either side do not believe that it is possible so to arrange their mutual relations that their interests become identical.

The majority of these men believe that the fundamental interests of employés and employers are necessarily antagonistic. Scientific management, on the contrary, has for its very foundation the firm conviction that the true interests of the two are one and the same; that prosperity for the employer cannot exist through a long term of years unless it is accompanied by prosperity for the employé, and *vice versa;* and that it is possible to give the workman what he most wants—high wages—and the employer what he wants—a low labor cost—for his manufactures.

It is hoped that some at least of those who do not sympathize with each of these objects may be led to modify their views; that some employers, whose attitude toward their workmen has been that of trying to get the largest amount of work out of them for the smallest possible wages, may be led to see that a more liberal policy toward their men will pay them better; and that some of those workmen who begrudge a fair and even a large profit to their employers, and who feel that all of the fruits of their labor should belong to them, and that those for whom they work and the capital invested in the business are entitled to little or nothing, may be led to modify these views.

No one can be found who will deny that in the case of any single individual the greatest prosperity can exist only when that individual has reached his highest state of efficiency; that is, when he is turning out his largest daily output.

The truth of this fact is also perfectly clear in the case of two men working together. To illustrate: if you and your workman have become so skilful that you and he together are making two pairs of shoes in a day, while your competitor and his workman are making only one pair, it is clear that after selling your two pairs of shoes you can pay your workman much higher wages than your competitor who produces only one pair of shoes is able to pay his man, and that there will still be enough money left over for you to have a larger profit than your competitor.

In the case of a more complicated manufacturing establishment, it should also be perfectly clear that the greatest permanent prosperity for the workman, coupled with the greatest prosperity for the employer, can be brought about only when the work of the establishment is done with the smallest combined expenditure of human effort; plus nature's resources, plus the cost for the use of capital in the shape of machines, buildings, etc. Or, to state the same thing in a different way: that the greatest prosperity can exist only as the result of the greatest possible productivity of the men and machines of the establishment—that is, when each man and each machine are turning out the largest possible output; because unless your men and your machines are daily turning out more work than others around you, it is clear that competition will prevent your paying higher wages to your workmen than are paid to those of your competitor. And what is true as to the possibility of paying high wages in the case of two companies competing close beside one another is also true as to whole districts of the country and even as to nations which are in competition. In a word, that maximum prosperity can exist only as the result of maximum productivity. Later in this paper illustrations will be given of several companies which are earning large dividends and at the same time paying from 30 per cent. to 100 per cent. higher wages to their men than are paid to similar men immediately around them, and with whose employers they are in competition. These illustrations will cover different types of work, from the most elementary to the most complicated.

If the above reasoning is correct, it follows that the most important object of both the workmen and the management should be the training and development of each individual in the establishment, so that he can do (at his fastest pace and with the maximum of efficiency) the highest class of work for which his natural abilities fit him.

These principles appear to be so self-evident that many men may think it almost childish to state them. Let us, however, turn to the facts, as they actually exist in this country and in England. The English and American peoples are the greatest sportsmen in the world. Whenever an American workman plays baseball, or an English workman plays cricket, it is safe to say that he strains every nerve to secure victory for his side. He does his very best to make the largest possible number of runs. The universal sentiment is so strong that any man who fails to give out all there is in him in sport is branded as a "quitter," and treated with contempt by those who are around him.

When the same workman returns to work on the following day, instead of using every effort to turn out the largest possible amount of work, in a majority of the cases this man deliberately plans to do as little as he safely can—to turn out far less work than he is well able to do—in many instances to do not more than one-third to one-half of a proper day's work. And in fact if he were to do his best to turn out his largest possible day's work, he would be abused by his fellow-workers for so doing, even more than if he had proved himself a "quitter" in sport. Underworking, that is, deliberately working slowly so as to avoid doing a full day's work, "soldiering," as it is called in this country, "hanging it out," as it is called in England, "ca canae," as it is called in Scotland, is almost universal in industrial establishments, and prevails also to a large extent in the building trades; and the writer asserts without fear of contradiction that this constitutes the greatest evil with which the working-people of both England and America are now afflicted.

It will be shown later in this paper that doing away with slow working and "soldiering" in all its forms and so arranging the relations between employer and employé that each workman will work to his very best advantage and at his best speed, accompanied by the intimate cooperation with the management and the help (which the workman should receive) from the management, would result on the average in nearly doubling the output of each man and each machine. What other reforms, among those which are being discussed by these two nations, could do as much toward promoting prosperity, toward the diminution of poverty, and the alleviation of suffering? America and England have been recently agitated over such subjects as the tariff, the control of the large corporations on the one hand, and of hereditary power on the other hand, and over various more or less socialistic proposals for taxation, etc. On these subjects both peoples have been profoundly stirred, and yet hardly a voice has been raised to call attention to this vastly greater and more important subject of "soldiering," which directly and powerfully affects the wages, the prosperity, and the life of almost every working-man, and also quite as much the prosperity of every industrial establishment in the nation.

The elimination of "soldiering" and of the several causes of slow working would so lower the cost of production that both our home and foreign markets would be greatly enlarged, and we could compete on more than even terms with our rivals. It would remove one of the fundamental causes for dull times, for lack of employment, and for poverty, and therefore would have a more permanent and far-reaching effect upon these misfortunes than any of the curative remedies that are now being used to soften their consequences. It would insure higher wages and make shorter working hours and better working and home conditions possible.

Why is it, then, in the face of the self-evident fact that maximum prosperity can exist only as the result of the determined effort of each workman to turn out each day his largest possible day's work, that the great majority of our men are deliberately doing just the opposite, and that even when the men have the best of intentions their work is in most cases far from efficient?

There are three causes for this condition, which may be briefly summarized as:

First. The fallacy, which has from time immemorial been almost universal among workmen, that a material increase in the output of each man or each machine in the trade would result in the end in throwing a large number of men out of work.

Second. The defective systems of management which are in common use, and which make it necessary for each workman to soldier, or work slowly, in order that he may protect his own best interests.

Third. The inefficient rule-of-thumb methods, which are still almost universal in all trades, and in practising which our workmen waste a large part of their effort.

This paper will attempt to show the enormous gains which would result from the substitution by our workmen of scientific for rule-of-thumb methods.

To explain a little more fully these three causes:

First. The great majority of workmen still believe that if they were to work at their best speed they would be doing a great injustice to the whole trade by throwing a lot of men out of work, and yet the history of the development of each trade shows that each improvement, whether it be the invention of a new machine or the introduction of a better method, which results in increasing the productive capacity of the men in the trade and cheapening the costs, instead of throwing men out of work make in the end work for more men.

The cheapening of any article in common use almost immediately results in a largely increased demand for that article. Take the case of shoes, for instance. The introduction of machinery for doing every element of the work which was formerly done by hand has resulted in making shoes at a fraction of their former labor cost, and in selling them so cheap that now almost every man, woman, and child in the working-classes buys one or two pairs of shoes per year, and wears shoes all the time, whereas formerly each workman bought perhaps one pair of shoes every five years, and went barefoot most of the time, wearing shoes only as a luxury or as a matter of the sternest necessity. In spite of the enormously increased output of shoes per workman, which has come with shoe machinery, the demand for shoes has so increased that there are relatively more men working in the shoe industry now than ever before.

The workmen in almost every trade have before them an object lesson of this kind, and yet, because they are ignorant of the history of their own trade even, they still firmly believe, as their fathers did before them, that it is against their best interests for each man to turn out each day as much work as possible.

Under this fallacious idea a large proportion of the workmen of both countries each day deliberately work slowly so as to curtail the output. Almost every labor union has made, or is contemplating making, rules which have for their object curtailing the output of their members, and those men who have the greatest influence with the working-people, the labor leaders as well as many people with philanthropic feelings who are helping them, are daily spreading this fallacy and at the same time telling them that they are overworked.

A great deal has been and is being constantly said about "sweat-shop" work and conditions. The writer has great sympathy with those who are overworked, but on the whole a greater sympathy for those who are *under paid.* For every individual, however, who is overworked, there are a hundred who intentionally underwork—greatly underwork—every day of their lives, and who for this reason deliberately aid in establishing those conditions which in the end inevitably result in low wages. And yet hardly a single voice is being raised in an endeavor to correct this evil.

As engineers and managers, we are more intimately acquainted with these facts than any other class in the community, and are therefore best fitted to lead in a movement to combat this fallacious idea by educating not only the workmen but the whole of the country as to the true facts. And yet we are practically doing nothing in this direction, and are leaving this field entirely in the hands of the labor agitators (many of whom are misinformed and misguided), and of sentimentalists who are ignorant as to actual working conditions.

Second. As to the second cause for soldiering—the relations which exist between employers and employés under almost all of the systems of management which are in common use—it is impossible in a few words to make it clear to one not familiar with this problem why it is that the *ignorance of employers* as to the proper time in which work of various kinds should be done makes it for the interest of the workman to "soldier."

The writer therefore quotes herewith from a paper read before The American Society of Mechanical Engineers, in June, 1903, entitled "Shop Management," which it is hoped will explain fully this cause for soldiering:

"This loafing or soldiering proceeds from two causes. First, from the natural instinct and tendency of men to take it easy, which may be called natural soldiering. Second, from more intricate second thought and reasoning caused by their relations with other men, which may be called systematic soldiering.

"There is no question that the tendency of the average man (in all walks of life) is toward working at a slow, easy gait, and that it is only after a good deal of thought and observation on his part or as a result of example, conscience, or external pressure that he takes a more rapid pace.

"There are, of course, men of unusual energy, vitality, and ambition who naturally choose the fastest gait, who set up their own standards, and who work hard, even though it may be against their best interests. But these few uncommon men only serve by forming a contrast to emphasize the tendency of the average.

"This common tendency to 'take it easy' is greatly increased by bringing a number of men together on similar work and at a uniform standard rate of pay by the day.

"Under this plan the better men gradually but surely slow down their gait to that of the poorest and least efficient. When a naturally energetic man works for a few days beside a lazy one, the logic of the situation is unanswerable. 'Why should I work hard when that lazy fellow gets the same pay that I do and does only half as much work?'

"A careful time study of men working under these conditions will disclose facts which are ludicrous as well as pitiable.

"To illustrate: The writer has timed a naturally energetic workman who, while going and coming from work, would walk at a speed of from three to four miles per hour, and not infrequently trot home after a day's work. On arriving at his work he would immediately slow down to a speed of about one mile an hour. When, for example, wheeling a loaded wheelbarrow, he would go at a good fast pace even up hill in order to be as short a time as possible under load, and immediately on the return walk slow down to a mile an hour, improving every opportunity for delay short of actually sitting down. In order to be sure not to do more than his lazy neighbor, he would actually tire himself in his effort to go slow.

"These men were working under a foreman of good reputation and highly thought of by his employer, who, when his attention was called to this state of things, answered: 'Well, I can keep them from sitting down, but the devil can't make them get a move on while they are at work.'

"The natural laziness of men is serious, but by far the greatest evil from which both workmen and employers are suffering is the *systematic soldiering* which is almost universal under all of the ordinary schemes of management and which results from a careful study on the part of the workmen of what will promote their best interests.

"The writer was much interested recently in hearing one small but experienced golf caddy boy of twelve explaining to a green caddy, who had shown special energy and interest, the necessity of going slow and lagging behind his man when he came up to the ball, showing him that since they were paid by the hour, the faster they went the less money they got, and finally telling him that if he went too fast the other boys would give him a licking.

"This represents a type of *systematic soldiering* which is not, however, very serious, since it is done with the knowledge of the employer, who can quite easily break it up if he wishes.

"The greater part of the *systematic soldiering*, however, is done by the men with the deliberate object of keeping their employers ignorant of how fast work can be done.

"So universal is soldiering for this purpose that hardly a competent workman can be found in a large establishment, whether he works by the day or on piece work, contract work, or under any of the ordinary systems, who does not devote a considerable part of his time to studying just how slow he can work and still convince his employer that he is going at a good pace.

"The causes for this are, briefly, that practically all employers determine upon a maximum sum which they feel it is right for each of their classes of employees to earn per day, whether their men work by the day or piece.

"Each workman soon finds out about what this figure is for his particular case, and he also realizes that when his employer is convinced that a man is capable of doing more work than he has done, he will find sooner or later some way of compelling him to do it with little or no increase of pay.

"Employers derive their knowledge of how much of a given class of work can be done in a day from either their own experience, which has frequently grown hazy with age, from casual and unsystematic observation of their men, or at best from records which are kept, showing the quickest time in which each job has been done. In many cases the employer will feel almost certain that a given job can be done faster than it has been, but he rarely cares to take the drastic measures necessary to force men to do it in the quickest time, unless he has an actual record proving conclusively how fast the work can be done.

"It evidently becomes for each man's interest, then, to see that no job is done faster than it has been in the past. The younger and less experienced men are taught this by their elders, and all possible persuasion and social pressure is brought to bear upon the greedy and selfish men to keep them from making new records which result in temporarily increasing their wages, while all those who come after them are made to work harder for the same old pay.

"Under the best day work of the ordinary type, when accurate records are kept of the amount of work done by each man and of his efficiency, and when each man's wages are raised as he improves, and those who fail to rise to a certain standard are discharged and a fresh supply of carefully selected men are given work in their places, both the natural loafing and systematic soldiering can be largely broken up. This can only be done, however, when the men are thoroughly convinced that there is no intention of establishing piece work even in the remote future, and it is next to impossible to make men believe this when the work is of such a nature that they believe piece work to be practicable. In most cases their fear of making a record which will be used as a basis for piece work will cause them to soldier as much as they dare.

"It is, however, under piece work that the art of systematic soldiering is thoroughly developed; after a workman has had the price per piece of the work he is doing lowered two or three times as a result of his having worked harder and increased his output, he is likely entirely to lose sight of his employer's side of the case and become imbued with a grim determination to have no more cuts if soldiering can prevent it. Unfortunately for the character of the workman, soldiering involves a deliberate attempt to mislead and deceive his employer, and thus upright and straightforward workmen are compelled to become more or less hypocritical. The employer is soon looked upon as an antagonist, if not an enemy, and the mutual confidence which should exist between a leader and his men, the enthusiasm, the feeling that they are all working for the same end and will share in the results is entirely lacking.

"The feeling of antagonism under the ordinary piece-work system becomes in many cases so marked on the part of the men that any proposition made by their employers, however reasonable, is looked upon with suspicion, and soldiering becomes such a fixed habit that men will frequently take pains to restrict the product of machines which they are running when even a large increase in output would involve no more work on their part."

Third. As to the third cause for slow work, considerable space will later in this paper be devoted to illustrating the great gain, both to employers and employés, which results from the substitution of scientific for rule-of-thumb methods in even the smallest details of the work of every trade. The enormous saving of time and therefore increase in the output which it is possible to effect through eliminating unnecessary motions and substituting fast for slow and inefficient motions for the men working in any of our trades can be fully realized only after one has personally seen the improvement which results from a thorough motion and time study, made by a competent man.

To explain briefly: owing to the fact that the workmen in all of our trades have been taught the details of their work by observation of those immediately around them, there are many different ways in common use for doing the same thing, perhaps forty, fifty, or a hundred ways of doing each act in each trade, and for the same reason there is a great variety in the implements used for each class of work. Now, among the various methods and implements used in each element of each trade there is always one method and one implement which is quicker and better than any of the rest. And this one best method and best implement can only be discovered or developed through a scientific study and analysis of all of the methods and implements in use, together with accurate, minute, motion and time study. This involves the gradual substitution of science for rule of thumb throughout the mechanic arts.

This paper will show that the underlying philosophy of all of the old systems of management in common use makes it imperative that each workman shall be left with the final responsibility for doing his job practically as he thinks best, with comparatively little help and advice from the management. And it will also show that because of this isolation of workmen, it is in most cases impossible for the men working under these systems to do their work in accordance with the rules and laws of a science or art, even where one exists.

The writer asserts as a general principle (and he proposes to give illustrations tending to prove the fact later in this paper) that in almost all of the mechanic arts the science which underlies each act of each workman is so great and amounts to so much that the workman who is best suited to actually doing the work is incapable of fully understanding this science, without the guidance and help of those who are working with him or over him, either through lack of education or through insufficient mental capacity. In order that the work may be done in accordance with scientific laws, it is necessary that there shall be a far more equal division of the responsibility between the management and the workmen than exists under any of the ordinary types of management. Those in the management whose duty it is to develop this science should also guide and help the workman in working under it, and should assume a much larger share of the responsibility for results than under usual conditions is assumed by the management.

The body of this paper will make it clear that, to work according to scientific laws, the management must take over and perform much of the work which is now left to the men; almost every act of the workman should be preceded by one or more preparatory acts of the management which enable him to do his work better and quicker than he otherwise could. And each man should daily be taught by and receive the most friendly help from those who are over him, instead of being, at the one extreme, driven or coerced by his bosses, and at the other left to his own unaided devices.

This close, intimate, personal cooperation between the management and the men is of the essence of modern scientific or task management.

SOURCE: Taylor, Frederick Winslow. *Principles of Scientific Management.* New York: Harper, 1911.

EXCERPT FROM *THE THEORY OF THE LEISURE CLASS* *(1899, by Thorstein Veblen)*

Thorstein Veblen (1857–1929) was an iconoclastic economist. He was among the first faculty to teach at the University of Chicago and the New School for Social Research in New York.

In *The Theory of the Leisure Class,* Veblen observed how economic tasks are differentiated among members of a society as their social arrangements become more complex. According to Veblen, this differentiation of tasks brought with it the development of a marked antipathy toward the productive, industrial tasks necessary for humankind's day-to-day existence. Eventually there emerged a leisure class exempt from productive labor and thereby able to dictate an era's social timbre, he wrote. Even those who worked for a living are in the thrall of such counter-productive social values as "conspicuous consumption," the phrase Veblen coined to describe social practices serving no purpose other than to display one's wealth and distance from productive labor.

In this excerpt Veblen found the evolution of leisure class's social power in its ability to seize the work of others by violence, by "force and fraud." He posited that the leisure class attacked all segments of society, but it preyed especially on the work of women. As Veblen repeatedly noted, women perform many of the tasks necessary to keep a people and their economy alive but are actively disparaged for their efforts. Notable for his astute conception of history as a study of the manner in which human perceptions of the world vary according to a social group's material attainment, Veblen saw some manifestation of the leisure class in nearly all stages of human development.

Initially received as satire, *The Theory of the Leisure Class* nonetheless draws keen insights to the social mechanisms of industrial society. That the least productive livelihoods are lauded at the expense of the most necessary is troubling. That this hierarchy maintains itself through "force and fraud," through the exploitation of the weak by the strong, is terrifying.

Mark D. Baumann,
New York University

See also **Class; Feudalism; Gender and Gender Roles.**

The institution of a leisure class is found in its best development at the higher stages of the barbarian culture; as, for instance, in feudal Europe or feudal Japan. In such communities the distinction between classes is very rigorously observed; and the feature of most striking economic significance in these class differences is the distinction maintained between the employments proper to the several classes. The upper classes are by custom exempt or excluded from industrial occupations, and are reserved for certain employments to which a degree of honour attaches. Chief among the honourable employments in any feudal community is warfare; and priestly service is commonly second to warfare. If the barbarian community is not notably warlike, the priestly office may take the precedence, with that of the warrior second. But the rule holds with but slight exceptions that, whether warriors, or priests, the upper classes are exempt from industrial employments, and this exemption is the economic expression of their superior rank. Brahmin India affords a fair illustration of the industrial exemption of both these classes. In the communities belonging to the higher barbarian culture there is a considerable differentiation of sub-classes within what may be comprehensively called the leisure class; and there is a corresponding differentiation of employments between these subclasses. The leisure class as a whole comprises the noble and the priestly classes, together with much of their retinue. The occupations of the class are correspondingly diversified; but they have the common economic characteristic of being non-industrial. These non-industrial upper-class occupations may be roughly comprised under government, warfare, religious observances, and sports.

At an earlier, but not the earliest, stage of barbarism, the leisure class is found in a less differentiated form. Neither the class distinctions nor the distinctions between leisure-class occupations are so minute and intricate. The Polynesian islanders generally show this stage of the development in good form, with the exception that, owing to the absence of large game, hunting does not hold the usual place of honour in their scheme of life. The Icelandic community in the time of the Sagas also affords a fair instance. In such a community there is a rigorous distinction between classes and between the occupations peculiar to each class. Manual labour, industry, whatever has to do directly with the everyday work of getting a livelihood, is the exclusive occupation of the inferior class. This inferior class includes slaves and other dependents, and ordinarily also all the women. If there are several grades of aristocracy, the women of high rank are commonly exempt from industrial employment, or at least from the more vulgar kinds of manual labour. The men of the upper classes are not only exempt, but by prescriptive custom they are debarred, from all industrial occupations. The range of employments open to them is rigidly defined. As on the higher plane already spoken of, these employments are government, warfare, religious observances, and sports. These four lines of activity govern the scheme of life of the upper classes, and for the highest ranks—the kings or chieftains—these are the only kinds of activity that custom or the common sense of the community will allow. Indeed, where the scheme is well developed even sports are accounted doubtfully legitimate for the members of the highest rank. To the lower grades of the leisure class certain other employments are open, but they are employments that are subsidiary to one or another of these typical leisure-class occupations. Such are, for instance, the manufacture and care of arms and accoutrements and of war canoes, the dressing and handling of horses, dogs, and hawks, the preparation of sacred apparatus, etc. The lower classes are excluded from these secondary honourable employments, except from such as are plainly of an industrial character and are only remotely related to the typical leisure-class occupations.

If we go a step back of this exemplary barbarian culture, into the lower stages of barbarism, we no longer find the leisure class in fully developed form. But this lower barbarism shows the usages, motives, and circumstances out of which the institution of a leisure class has arisen, and indicates the steps of its early growth. Nomadic hunting tribes in various parts of the world illustrate these more primitive phases of the differentiation. Any one of the North American hunting tribes may be taken as a convenient illustration. These tribes can scarcely be said to have a defined leisure class. There is a differentiation of function, and there is a distinction between classes on the basis of this difference of function, but the exemption of the superior class from work has not gone far enough to make the designation "leisure class" altogether applicable. The tribes belonging on this economic level have carried the economic differentiation to the point at which a marked distinction is made between the occupations of men and women, and this distinction is of an invidious character. In nearly all these tribes the women are, by prescriptive custom, held to those employments out of which the industrial occupations proper develop at the next advance. The men are exempt from these vulgar employments and are reserved for war, hunting, sports, and devout observances. A very nice discrimination is ordinarily shown in this matter.

This division of labour coincides with the distinction between the working and the leisure class as it appears in the higher barbarian culture. As the diversification and specialisation of employments proceed, the line of demarcation so drawn comes to divide the industrial from the non-industrial employments. The man's occupation as it stands at the earlier barbarian stage is not the original out of which any appreciable portion of later industry has developed. In the later development it survives only in employments that are not classed as industrial,—war, politics, sports, learning, and the priestly office. The only notable exceptions are a portion of the fishery industry and certain slight employments that are doubtfully to be classed as industry; such as the manufacture of arms, toys, and sporting goods. Virtually the whole range of industrial employments is an outgrowth of what is classed as woman's work in the primitive barbarian community.

The work of the men in the lower barbarian culture is no less indispensable to the life of the group than the work done by the women. It may even be that the men's work contributes as much to the food supply and the other necessary consumption of the group. Indeed, so obvious is this "productive" character of the men's work that in the conventional economic writings the hunter's work is taken as the type of primitive industry. But such is not the barbarian's sense of the matter. In his own eyes he is not a labourer, and he is not to be classed with the women in this respect; nor is his effort to be classed with the women's drudgery, as labour or industry, in such a sense as to admit of its being con-founded with the latter. There is in all barbarian communities a profound sense of the disparity between man's and woman's work. His work may conduce to the maintenance of the group, but it is felt that it does so through an excellence and an efficacy of a kind that cannot without derogation be compared with the uneventful diligence of the women.

At a farther step backward in the cultural scale—among savage groups—the differentiation of employments is still less elaborate and the invidious distinction between classes and employments is less consistent and less rigorous. Unequivocal instances of a primitive savage culture are hard to find. Few of those groups or communities that are classed as "savage" show no traces of regression from a more advanced cultural stage. But there are groups—some of them apparently not the result of retrogression—which show the traits of primitive savagery with some fidelity. Their culture differs from that of the barbarian communities in the absence of a leisure class and the absence, in great measure, of the animus or spiritual attitude on which the institution of a leisure class rests. These communities of primitive savages in which there is no hierarchy of economic classes make up but a small and inconspicuous fraction of the human race. As good an instance of this phase of culture as may be had is afforded by the tribes of the Andamans, or by the Todas of the Nilgiri Hills. The scheme of life of these groups at the time of their earliest contact with Europeans seems to have been nearly typical, so far as regards the absence of a leisure class. As a further instance might be cited the Ainu of Yezo, and, more doubtfully, also some Bushman and Eskimo groups. Some Pueblo communities are less confidently to be included in the same class. Most, if not all, of the communities here cited may well be cases of degeneration from a higher barbarism, rather than bearers of a culture that has never risen above its present level. If so, they are for the present purpose to be taken with allowance, but they may serve none the less as evidence to the same effect as if they were really "primitive" populations.

These communities that are without a defined leisure class resemble one another also in certain other features of their social structure and manner of life. They are small groups and of a simple (archaic) structure; they are commonly peaceable and sedentary; they are poor; and individual ownership is not a dominant feature of their economic system. At the same time it does not follow that these are the smallest of existing communities, or that their social structure is in all respects the least differentiated; nor does the class necessarily include all primitive communities which have no defined system of individual ownership. But it is to be noted that the class seems to include the most peaceable—perhaps all the characteristically peaceable—primitive groups of men. Indeed, the most notable trait common to members of such communities is a certain amiable inefficiency when confronted with force or fraud.

The evidence afforded by the usages and cultural traits of communities at a low stage of development indicates that the institution of a leisure class has emerged gradually during the transition from primitive savagery to barbarism; or more precisely, during the transition from a peaceable to a consistently warlike habit of life. The conditions apparently necessary to its emergence in a consistent form are: (1) the community must be of a predatory habit of life (war or the hunting of large game or both); that is to say, the men, who constitute the inchoate leisure class in these cases, must be habituated to the infliction of injury by force, and stratagem; (2) subsistence must be obtainable on sufficiently easy terms to admit of the exemption of a considerable portion of the community from steady application to a routine of labour. The institution of a leisure class is the outgrowth of an early discrimination between employments, according to which some employments are worthy and others unworthy. Under this ancient distinction the worthy employments are those which may be classed as exploit; unworthy are those necessary everyday employments into which no appreciable element of exploit enters.

This distinction has but little obvious significance in a modern industrial community, and it has, therefore, received but slight attention at the hands of economic writers. When viewed in the light of that modern common sense which has guided economic discussion, it seems formal and insubstantial. But it persists with great tenacity as a commonplace preconception even in modern life, as is shown, for instance, by our habitual aversion to menial employments. It is a distinction of a personal kind—of superiority and inferiority. In the earlier stages of culture, when the personal force of the individual counted more immediately and obviously in shaping the course of events, the element of exploit counted for more in the everyday scheme of life. Interest centred about this fact to a greater degree. Consequently a distinction proceeding on this ground seemed more imperative and more definitive then than is the case to-day. As a fact in the sequence of development, therefore, the distinction is a substantial one and rests on sufficiently valid and cogent grounds.

The ground on which a discrimination between facts is habitually made changes as the interest from which the facts are habitually viewed changes. Those features of the facts at hand are salient and substantial upon which the dominant interest of the time throws its light. Any given ground of distinction will seem insubstantial to any one who habitually apprehends the facts in question from a different point of view and values them for a different purpose. The habit of distinguishing and classifying the various purposes and directions of activity prevails of necessity always and everywhere; for it is indispensable in reaching a working theory or scheme of life. The particular point of view, or the particular characteristic that is pitched upon as definitive in the classification of the facts of life depends upon the interest from which a discrimination of the facts is sought. The grounds of discrimination, and the norm of procedure in classifying the facts, therefore, progressively change as the growth of culture proceeds; for the end for which the facts of life are apprehended changes, and the point of view consequently changes also. So that what are recognised as the salient and decisive features of a class of activities or of a social class at one stage of culture will not retain the same relative importance for the purposes of classification at any subsequent stage.

But the change of standards and points of view is gradual only, and it seldom results in the subversion of entire suppression of a standpoint once accepted. A distinction is still habitually made between industrial and non-industrial occupations; and this modern distinction is a transmuted form of the barbarian distinction between exploit and drudgery. Such employments as warfare, politics, public worship, and public merry-making, are felt, in the popular apprehension, to differ intrinsically from the labour that has to do with elaborating the material means of life. The precise line of demarcation is not the same as it was in the early barbarian scheme, but the broad distinction has not fallen into disuse.

The tacit, common-sense distinction to-day is, in effect, that any effort is to be accounted industrial only so far as its ultimate purpose is the utilisation of non-human things. The coercive utilisation of man by man is not felt to be an industrial function; but all effort directed to enhance human life by taking advantage of the non-human environment is classed together as industrial activity. By the economists who have best retained and adapted the classical tradition, man's "power over nature" is currently postulated as the characteristic fact of industrial productivity. This industrial power over nature is taken to include man's power over the life of the beasts and over all the elemental forces. A line is in this way drawn between mankind and brute creation.

In other times and among men imbued with a different body of preconceptions, this line is not drawn precisely as we draw it to-day. In the savage or the barbarian scheme of life it is drawn in a different place and in another way. In all communities under the barbarian culture there is an alert and pervading sense of antithesis between two comprehensive groups of phenomena, in one of which barbarian man includes himself, and in the other, his victual. There is a felt antithesis between economic and non-economic phenomena, but it is not conceived in the modern fashion; it lies not between man and brute creation, but between animate and inert things.

It may be an excess of caution at this day to explain that the barbarian notion which it is here intended to convey by the term "animate" is not the same as would be conveyed by the word "living." The term does not cover all living things, and it does cover a great many others. Such a striking natural phenomenon as a storm, a disease, a waterfall, are recognised as "animate"; while fruits and herbs, and even inconspicuous animals, such as house-flies, maggots, lemmings, sheep, are not ordinarily apprehended as "animate" except when taken collectively. As here used the term does not necessarily imply an indwelling soul or spirit. The concept includes such things as in the apprehension of the animistic savage or barbarian are formidable by virtue of a real or imputed habit of initiating action. This category comprises a large number and range of natural objects and phenomena. Such a distinction between the inert and the active is still present in the habits of thought of unreflecting persons, and it still profoundly affects the prevalent theory of human life and of natural processes; but it does not pervade our daily life to the extent or with the far-reaching practical consequences that are apparent at earlier stages of culture and belief.

To the mind of the barbarian, the elaboration and utilisation of what is afforded by inert nature is activity on quite a different plane from his dealings with "animate" things and forces. The line of demarcation may be vague and shifting, but the broad distinction is sufficiently real and cogent to influence the barbarian scheme of life. To the class of things apprehended as animate the barbarian fancy imputes an unfolding of activity directed to some end. It is this teleological unfolding of activity that constitutes any object or phenomenon an "animate" fact. Wherever the unsophisticated savage or barbarian meets with activity that is at all obtrusive, he construes it in the only terms that are ready to hand—the terms immediately given in his consciousness of his own actions. Activity is, therefore assimilated to human action, and active objects are in so far assimilated to the human agent. Phenomena of this character—especially those whose behaviour is notably formidable or baffling—have to be met in a different spirit and with proficiency of a different kind from what is required in dealing with inert things. To deal successfully with such phenomena is a work of exploit rather than of industry. It is an assertion of prowess, not of diligence.

Under the guidance of this naive discrimination between the inert and the animate, the activities of the primitive social group tend to fall into two classes, which would in modern phrase be called exploit and industry. Industry is effort that goes to create a new thing, with a new purpose given it by the fashioning hand of its maker out of passive ("brute") material while exploit, so far as it results in an outcome useful to the agent, is the conversion to his own ends of energies previously directed to some other end by another agent. We still speak of "brute matter" with something of the barbarian's realisation of a profound significance in the term.

The distinction between exploit and drudgery coincides with a difference between the sexes. The sexes differ, not only in stature and muscular force, but perhaps even more decisively in temperament, and this must early have given rise to a corresponding division of labour. The general range of activities that come under the head of exploit falls to the males as being the stouter, more massive, better capable of a sudden and violent strain, and more readily inclined to self assertion, active emulation, and aggression. The difference in mass, in physiological character, and in temperament may be slight among the members of the primitive group; it appears, in fact, to be relatively slight and inconsequential in some of the more archaic communities with which we are acquainted—as for instance the tribes of the Andamans. But so soon as a differentiation of function has well begun on the lines marked out by this difference in physique and animus, the original difference between the sexes will itself widen. A cumulative process of selective adaptation to the new distribution of employments will set in, especially if the habitat or the fauna with which the group is in contact is such as to call for a considerable exercise of the sturdier virtues. The habitual pursuit of large game requires more of the manly qualities of massiveness, agility, and ferocity, and it can therefore scarcely fail to hasten and widen the differentiation of functions between the sexes. And so soon as the group comes into hostile contact with other groups, the divergence of function will take on the developed form of a distinction between exploit and industry.

In such a predatory group of hunters it comes to be the able-bodied men's office to fight and hunt. The women do what other work there is to do—other members who are unfit for man's work being for this purpose classed with the women. But the men's hunting and fighting are both of the same general character. Both are of a predatory nature; the warrior and the hunter alike reap where they have not strewn. Their aggressive assertion of force and sagacity differs obviously from the women's assiduous and uneventful shaping of materials; it is not to be accounted productive labour but rather an acquisition of substance by seizure. Such being the barbarian man's work, in its best development and widest divergence from women's work, any effort that does not involve an assertion of prowess comes to be unworthy of the man. As the tradition gains consistency, the common sense of the community erects it into a canon of conduct; so that no employment and no acquisition is morally possible to the self respecting man at this cultural stage, except such as proceeds on the basis of prowess—force or fraud. When the predatory habit of life has been settled upon the group by long habituation, it becomes the able bodied man's accredited office in the social economy to kill, to destroy such competitors in the struggle for existence as attempt to resist or elude him, to overcome and reduce to subservience those alien forces that assert themselves refractorily in the environment. So tenaciously and with such nicety is this theoretical distinction between exploit and drudgery adhered to that in many hunting tribes the man must not bring home the game which he has killed, but must send his woman to perform that baser office.

SOURCE: Veblen, Thorstein. *The Theory of the Leisure Class: An Economic Study in the Evolution of Institutions.* New York: Macmillan, 1899.

IN THE SLUMS
(1890, by Jacob Riis)

The rapid industrialization of post-Civil War America, coupled with massive influxes of immigrants into urban areas, resulted in the appearance of blighted residential districts or slums. Primitive sanitary facilities, windowless tenement rooms, and massive overcrowding were only a few of the many problems suffered by the urban poor at the turn of the century.

When Jacob Riis (1848–1914) came to America from Denmark in 1870 he held a number of low-wage jobs before becoming a journalist, so he was well acquainted with the horrors and depravations of slum life. His zeal for reform led him to publish widely on the problems of the urban poor. Riis, who eventually became a close ally of Theodore Roosevelt, exposed the contamination of New York City's water supply, lobbied against child labor, forced the destruction of dangerous tenements, argued for public parks, and performed countless other deeds in the service of public health and welfare. His book, *How the Other Half Lives* (1890), was a watershed publication in the field of public service. In it, short descriptive essays are accompanied by startling photographs of the devastating squalor in immigrant neighborhoods. In this selection, Riis describes life inside the tenement houses.

Leah R. Shafer,
Cornell University

See also **Housing; Poverty; Tenements.**

... In the dull content of life bred on the tenement-house dead level there is little to redeem it, or to calm apprehension for a society that has nothing better to offer its toilers; while the patient efforts of the lives finally attuned to it to render the situation tolerable, and the very success of these efforts, serve only to bring out in stronger contrast the general gloom of the picture by showing how much farther they might have gone with half a chance. Go into any of the "respectable" tenement neighborhoods—the fact that there are not more than two saloons on the corner, nor over three or four in the block will serve as a fair guide—where live the great body of hard-working Irish and German immigrants and their descendants, who accept naturally the conditions of tenement life, because for them there is nothing else in New York; be with and among its people until you understand their ways, their aims, and the quality of their ambitions, and unless you can content yourself with the scriptural promise that the poor we shall have always with us, or with the menagerie view that, if fed, they have no cause of complaint, you shall come away agreeing with me that, humanly speaking, life there does not seem worth the living. Take at random one of these uptown tenement blocks, not of the worst nor yet of the most prosperous kind, within hail of what the newspapers would call a "fine residential section." These houses were built since the last cholera scare made people willing to listen to reason. The block is not like the one over on the East Side in which I actually lost my way once. There were thirty or forty rear houses in the heart of it, three or four on every lot, set at all sorts of angles, with odd, winding passages, or no passage at all, only "runways" for the thieves and toughs of the neighborhood. These yards are clear. There is air there, and it is about all there is. The view between brick walls outside is that of a stony street; inside, of rows of unpainted board fences, a bewildering maze of clothes-posts and lines; underfoot, a desert of brown, hard-baked soil from which every blade of grass, every stray weed, every speck of green, has been trodden out, as must inevitably be every gentle thought and aspiration above the mere wants of the body in those whose moral natures such home surroundings are to nourish. In self-defence, you know, all life eventually accommodates itself to its environment, and human life is no exception. Within the house there is nothing to supply the want thus left unsatisfied. Tenement-houses have no asthetic resources. If any are to be brought to bear on them, they must come from the outside. There is the common hall with doors opening softly on every landing as the strange step is heard on the stairs, the air-shaft that seems always so busy letting out foul stenches from below that it has no time to earn its name by bringing down fresh air, the squeaking pumps that hold no water, and the rent that is never less than one week's wages out of the four, quite as often half of the family earnings.

Why complete the sketch? It is drearily familiar already. Such as it is, it is the frame in which are set days, weeks, months, and years of unceasing toil, just able to fill the mouth and clothe the back. Such as it is, it is the world, and all of it, to which these weary workers return nightly to feed heart and brain after wearing out the body at the bench, or in the shop. To it come the young with their restless yearnings. . . . These in their coarse garments—girls with the love of youth for beautiful things, with this hard life before them—who shall save them from the tempter? Down in the street the saloon, always bright and gay, gathering to itself all the cheer of the block, beckons the boys. In many such blocks the census-taker found two thousand men, women, and children, and over, who called them home....

With the first hot nights in June police despatches, that record the killing of men and women by rolling off roofs and window-sills while asleep, announce that the time of greatest suffering among the poor is at hand. It is in hot weather, when life indoors is well-nigh unbearable with cooking, sleeping, and working, all crowded into the small rooms together, that the tenement expands, reckless of all restraint. Then a strange and picturesque life moves upon the flat roofs. In the day and early evening mothers air their babies there, the boys fly their kites from the house-tops, undismayed by police regulations, and the young men and girls court and pass the growler. In the stifling July nights, when the big barracks are like fiery furnaces, their very walls giving out absorbed heat, men and women lie in restless, sweltering rows, panting for air and sleep. Then every truck in the street, every crowded fire-escape, becomes a bedroom, infinitely preferable to any the house affords. A cooling shower on such a night is hailed as a heaven-sent blessing in a hundred thousand homes.

Life in the tenements in July and August spells death to an army of little ones whom the doctor's skill is powerless to save. When the white badge of mourning flutters from every second door, sleepless mothers walk the streets in the gray of the early dawn, trying to stir a cooling breeze to fan the brow of the sick baby. There is no sadder sight than this patient devotion striving against fearfully hopeless odds. Fifty "summer doctors," especially trained to this work, are then sent into the tenements by the Board of Health, with free advice and medicine for the poor. Devoted women follow in their track with care and nursing for the sick. Fresh-air excursions run daily out of New York on land and water; but despite all efforts the grave-diggers in Calvary work over-time, and little coffins are stacked mountains high on the deck of the Charity Commissioners' boat when it makes its semi-weekly trips to the city cemetery....

That ignorance plays its part, as well as poverty and bad hygienic surroundings, in the sacrifice of life is of course inevitable....

No doubt intemperance bears a large share of the blame for it; judging from the stand-point of the policeman perhaps the greater share.... Even if it were all true, I should still load over upon the tenement the heaviest responsibility. A single factor, the scandalous scarcity of water in the hot summer when the thirst of the million tenants must be quenched, if not in that in something else, has in the past years more than all other causes encouraged drunkenness among the poor. But to my mind there is a closer connection between the wages of the tenements and the vices and improvidence of those who dwell in them than, with the guilt of the tenement upon our heads, we are willing to admit even to ourselves. Weak tea with a dry crust is not a diet to nurse moral strength....

Perhaps of all the disheartening experiences of those who have devoted lives of unselfish thought and effort, and their number is not so small as often supposed, to the lifting of this great load, the indifference of those they would help is the most puzzling. They will not be helped. Dragged by main force out of their misery, they slip back again on the first opportunity, seemingly content only in the old rut. The explanation was supplied by two women of my acquaintance in an Elizabeth Street tenement, whom the city missionaries had taken from their wretched hovel and provided with work and a decent home somewhere in New Jersey. In three weeks they were back, saying that they preferred their dark rear room to the stumps out in the country. But to me the oldest . . . made the bitter confession: "We do get so kind o' downhearted living this way, that we have to be where something is going on, or we just can't stand it." And there was sadder pathos to me in her words than in the whole long story of their struggle with poverty; for unconsciously she voiced the sufferings of thousands, misjudged by a happier world, deemed vicious because they are human and unfortunate.

SOURCE: Hart, Albert Bushnell, ed. *American History Told by Contemporaries*. Vol. 4. New York: Macmillan, 1901.

THE PULLMAN STRIKE AND BOYCOTT
(June, 1894)

A graphic example of the often-tumultuous relationship between American capitalist enterprise and organized labor, the Pullman Strike began after the economic panic of 1893, when the Pullman Palace Car Company of Chicago, Illinois, cut workers' wages without also lowering food and housing costs in its company town. When union representatives were fired for protesting the company's decision, the head of the American Railway Union, former Indiana state legislator Eugene V. Debs, ordered a general strike in the servicing of Pullman cars. Some 50,000 workers heeded his call, and soon rail traffic throughout much of the country virtually ceased. Desperate, railroad owners turned to United States Attorney General Richard Olney, director of the Burlington and Santa Fe lines, who quickly issued a blanket injunction declaring the strike illegal. Two days later, on July 4th, President Grover Cleveland ordered Federal troops to Chicago. During the resulting violence, several strikers were killed. Riots erupted as far away as Oakland, California, but ultimately the government's actions were successful. With trains moving again under armed guard, the boycott broke down, and its leaders, Eugene Debs and three others, were jailed for disobeying the injunction.

Laura M. Miller,
Vanderbilt University

See also **American Railway Union; Pullman Strike.**

Statement of the Strikers

Mr. President and Brothers of the American Railway Union: We struck at Pullman because we were without hope. We joined the American Railway Union because it gave us a glimmer of hope. Twenty thousand souls, men, women, and little ones, have their eyes turned toward this convention today, straining eagerly through dark despondency for a glimmer of the heaven-sent message you alone can give us on this earth.

In stating to this body our grievances, it is hard to tell where to begin. You all must know that the proximate cause of our strike was the discharge of two members of our Grievance Committee the day after George M. Pullman, himself, and Thomas H. Wickes, his second vice-president, had guaranteed them absolute immunity. The more remote causes are still imminent. Five reductions in wages, in work, and in conditions of employment swept through the shops at Pullman between May and December 1893. The last was the most severe, amounting to nearly 40 percent, and our rents had not fallen. We owed Pullman $70,000 when we struck May 11. We owe him twice as much today. He does not evict us for two reasons: one, the force of popular sentiment and public opinion; the other, because he hopes to starve us out, to break through in the back of the American Railway Union, and to deduct from our miserable wages when we are forced to return to him the last dollar we owe him for the occupancy of his houses.

Rents all over the city in every quarter of its vast extent have fallen, in some cases to one-half. Residences, compared with which ours are hovels, can be had a few miles away at the prices we have been contributing to make a millionaire a billionaire. What we pay $15 for in Pullman is leased for $8 in Roseland; and remember that just as no man or woman of our 4,000 toilers has ever felt the friendly pressure of George M. Pullman's hand, so no man or woman of us all has ever owned or can ever hope to own one inch of George M. Pullman's land. Why, even the very streets are his. His ground has never been platted of record, and today he may debar any man who has acquiring rights as his tenant from walking in his highways. And those streets; do you know what he has named them? He says after the four great inventors in methods of transportation. And do you know what their names are? Why, Fulton, Stephenson, Watt, and Pullman.

Water which Pullman buys from the city at 8 cents a thousand gallons he retails to us at 500 percent advance and claims he is losing $400 a month on it. Gas which sells at 75 cents per thousand feet in Hyde Park, just north of us, he sells for $2.25. When we went to tell him our grievances, he said we were all his "children."

Pullman, both the man and the town, is an ulcer on the body politic. He owns the houses, the schoolhouses, and churches of God in the town he gave his once humble name. The revenue he derives from these, the wages he pays out with one hand—the Pullman Palace Car Company—he takes back with the other—the Pullman Land Association. He is able by this to bid under any contract car shop in this country. His competitors in business, to meet this, must reduce the wages of their men. This gives him the excuse to reduce ours to conform to the market. His business rivals must in turn scale down; so must he. And thus the merry war—the dance of skeletons bathed in human tears—goes on; and it will go on, brothers, forever unless you, the American Railway Union, stop it; end it; crush it out.

Our town is beautiful. In all these thirteen years no word of scandal has arisen against one of our women, young or old. What city of 20,000 persons can show the like? Since our strike, the arrests, which used to average four or five a day, had dwindled down to less than one a week. We are peaceable; we are orderly; and but for the kindly beneficence of kindly hearted people in and about Chicago we would be starving. We are not desperate today because we are not hungry, and our wives and children are not begging for bread. But George M. Pullman, who ran away from the public opinion that has arisen against him, like the genii from the bottle in the *Arabian Nights*, is not feeding us. He is patiently seated beside his millions waiting for what? To see us starve.

We have grown better acquainted with the American Railway Union these convention days, and as we have heard sentiments of the noblest philanthropy fall from the lips of our general officers—your officers and ours—we have learned that there is a balm for all our troubles, and that the box containing it is in your hands today, only awaiting opening to disseminate its sweet savor of hope.

George M. Pullman, you know, has cut our wages from 30 to 70 percent. George M. Pullman has caused to be paid in the last year the regular quarterly dividend of 2 percent on his stock and an extra slice of 1 1/2 percent, making 9 1/2 percent on $30 million of capital. George M. Pullman, you know, took three contracts on which he lost less than $5,000. Because he loved us? No. Because it was cheaper to lose a little money in his freight car and his coach shops than to let his workingmen go, but that petty loss, more than made up by us from money we needed to clothe our wives and little ones, was his excuse for effecting a gigantic reduction of wages in every department of his great works, of cutting men and boys and girls with equal zeal, including everyone in the repair shops of the Pullman Palace cars on which such preposterous profits have been made.

George M. Pullman will tell you, if you could go to him today, that he was paying better wages than any other car shops in the land. George M. Pullman might better save his breath. We have worked too often beside graduates from other establishments not to know that, work for work and skill for skill, no one can compete with us at wages paid for work well done. If his wage list showed a trifle higher, our efficiency still left us heavily the loser. He does not figure on our brain and muscle. He makes his paltry computation in dollars and cents.

We will make you proud of us, brothers, if you will give us the hand we need. Help us make our country better and more wholesome. Pull us out of our slough of despond. Teach arrogant grinders of the faces of the poor that there is still a God in Israel, and if need be a Jehovah—a God of battles. Do this, and on that last great day you will stand, as we hope to stand, before the great white throne "like gentlemen unafraid."

Statement of the Company

In view of the proposed attempt of the American Railway Union to interfere with public travel on railway lines using Pullman cars, in consequence of a controversy as to the wages of employees of the manufacturing department of the company, the Pullman Company requests the publication of the following statement of the facts, in face of which the attempt is to be made.

In the first week of May last, there were employed in the car manufacturing department at Pullman, Illinois, about 3,100 persons. On May 7, a committee of the workmen had an interview by arrangement with Mr. Wickes, vice-president, at which the principal subject of discussion related to wages, but minor grievances as to shop administration were also presented, and it was agreed that another meeting should be held on the 9th of May, at which all the grievances should be presented in writing. The second meeting was held. As to the complaints on all matters except wages, it was arranged that a formal and thorough investigation should be made by Mr. Wickes, to be begun the next day, and full redress was assured to the committee as to all complaints proved to be well founded.

The absolute necessity of the last reduction in wages, under the existing condition of the business of car manufacturing, had been explained to the committee, and they were insisting upon a restoration of the wage scale of the first half of 1893, when Mr. Pullman entered the room and addressed the committee, speaking in substance as follows:

"At the commencement of the very serious depression last year, we were employing at Pullman 5,816 men and paying out in wages there $305,000 a month. Negotiations with intending purchasers of railway equipment that were then pending for new work were stopped by them, orders already given by others were canceled, and we were obliged to lay off, as you are aware, a large number of men in every department; so that by November 1, 1893, there were only about 2,000 men in all departments, or about one-third of the normal number. I realized the necessity for the most strenuous exertions to procure work immediately, without which there would be great embarrassment, not only to the employees and their families at Pullman but also to those living in the immediate vicinity, including between 700 and 800 employees who had purchased homes and to whom employment was actually necessary to enable them to complete their payments.

"I canvassed the matter thoroughly with the manager of the works and instructed him to cause the men to be assured that the company would do everything in its power to meet the competition which was sure to occur because of the great number of large car manufacturers that were in the same condition and that were exceedingly anxious to keep their men employed. I knew that if there was any work to be let, bids for it would be made upon a much lower basis than ever before.

"The result of this discussion was a revision in piecework prices, which, in the absence of any information to the contrary, I supposed to be acceptable to the men under the circumstances. Under these conditions, and with lower prices upon all materials, I personally undertook the work of the lettings of cars, and, by making lower bids than other manufacturers, I secured work enough to gradually increase our force from 2,000 up to about 4,200, the number employed, according to the April payrolls, in all capacities at Pullman.

"This result has not been accomplished merely by reduction in wages, but the company has borne its full share by eliminating from its estimates the use of capital and machinery, and in many cases going even below that and taking work at considerable loss, notably the 55 Long Island cars, which was the first large order of passenger cars let since the great depression and which was sought for by practically all the leading car builders in the country. My anxiety to secure that order so as to put as many men at work as possible was such that I put in a bid at more than $300 per car less than the actual cost to the company. The 300 stock cars built for the Northwestern Road and the 250 refrigerator cars now under construction for the same company will result in a loss of at least $12 per car, and the 25 cars just built for the Lake Street elevated road show a loss of $79 per car. I mention these particulars so that you may understand what the company has done for the mutual interests and to secure for the people at Pullman and vicinity the benefit of the disbursement of the large sums of money involved in these and similar contracts, which can be kept up only by the procurement of new orders for cars; for, as you know, about three-fourths of the men must depend upon contract work for employment.

"I can only assure you that if this company now restores the wages of the first half of 1893, as you have asked, it would be a most unfortunate thing for the men because there is less than sixty days of contract work in sight in the shops under all orders, and there is absolutely no possibility, in the present condition of affairs throughout the country, of getting any more orders for work at prices measured by the wages of May 1893. Under such a scale the works would necessarily close down and the great majority of the employees be put in idleness, a contingency I am using my best efforts to avoid.

"To further benefit the people of Pullman and vicinity, we concentrated all the work that we could command at that point by closing our Detroit shops entirely and laying off a large number of men at our other repair shops, and gave to Pullman the repair of all cars that could be taken care of there.

"Also, for the further benefit of our people at Pullman, we have carried on a large system of internal improvements, having expended nearly $160,000 since August last in work which, under normal conditions, would have been spread over one or two years. The policy would be to continue this class of work to as great an extent as possible, provided, of course, the Pullman men show a proper appreciation of the situation by doing whatever they can to help themselves to tide over the hard times which are so seriously felt in every part of the country.

"There has been some complaint made about rents. As to this I would say that the return to this company on the capital invested in the Pullman tenements for the last year and the year before was 3.82 percent. There are hundreds of tenements in Pullman renting from $6 to $9 per month, and the tenants are relieved from the usual expenses of exterior cleaning and the removal of garbage, which is done by the company. The average amount collected from employees for gas consumed is about $2 a month. To ascertain the exact amount of water used by tenants, separate from the amount consumed by the works, we have recently put in meters, by which we find that the water consumed by the tenants, if paid for at the rate of 4 cents per 1,000 gallons, in accordance with our original contract with the village of Hyde Park, would amount to about $1,000 a month, almost exactly the rate which we have charged the tenants, this company assuming the expense of pumping. At the increased rate the city is now charging us for water, we are paying about $1,500 a month in excess of the amount charged to the tenants. The present payrolls at Pullman amount to about $7,000 a day."

On the question of rents, while, as stated above, they make a manifestly inadequate return upon the investment, so that it is clear they are not, in fact, at an arbitrarily high figure, it may be added that it would not be possible in a business sense so to deal with them.

The renting of the dwellings and the employment of workmen at Pullman are in no way tied together. The dwellings and apartments are offered for rent in competition with those of the immediately adjacent towns of Kensington, Roseland, and Gano. They are let alike to Pullman employees and to very many others in no way connected with the company, and, on the other hand, many Pullman employees rent or own their homes in those adjacent towns. The average rental at Pullman is at the rate of $3 per room per month. There are 1,200 tenements, of varying numbers of rooms, the average monthly rental of which is $10; of these there are 600 the average monthly rental of which is $8. In very many cases, men with families pay a rent seemingly large for a workman, but which is in fact reduced in part, and often wholly repaid, by the subrents paid by single men as lodgers.

On May 10, the day after the second conference above mentioned, work went on at Pullman as usual, and the only incident of note was the beginning by Mr. Wickes, assisted by Mr. Brown, the general manager of the company, of the promised formal investigation at Pullman of the shop complaints.

A large meeting of employees had been held the night before at Kensington, which, as was understood by the company, accepted the necessity of the situation preventing an increase of wages; but at a meeting of the local committee held during the night of May 10, a strike was decided upon, and, accordingly, the next day about 2,500 of the employees quit their work, leaving about 600 at work, of whom very few were skilled workmen. As it was found impracticable to keep the shops in operation with a force thus diminished and disorganized, the next day those remaining were necessarily laid off, and no work has since been done in the shops.

The payrolls at the time amounted to about $7,000 a day and were reduced $5,500 by the strike, so that during the period of a little more than six weeks which has elapsed the employees who quit their work have deprived themselves and their comrades of earnings of more than $200,000.

It is an element of the whole situation worthy of note that at the beginning of the strike the Pullman Savings Bank had on deposit in its savings department $488,000, of which about nine-tenths belonged to employees at Pullman, and that this amount has since been reduced by the sum of $32,000.

While deploring the possibility of annoyance to the public by the threats of irresponsible organizations to interrupt the orderly ministration to the comfort of travelers on railway lines, aggregating 125,000 miles in length, the Pullman Company can do no more than explain its situation to the public.

It has two separate branches of business, essentially distinct from each other. One is to provide sleeping cars, which are delivered by it under contract to the various railway companies, to be run by them on their lines as a part of their trains for the carriage of their passengers, over the movements of which this company has no control. Contract arrangements provide for the making of all repairs to such cars by the railway companies using them—as to certain repairs absolutely and as to all others upon the request of the Pullman Company, which ordinarily finds it most convenient to use its own manufacturing facilities to make such repairs. The other, and a distinct branch of the business of the Pullman Company, is the manufacture of sleeping cars for the above-mentioned use of railway companies and the manufacture for sale to railway companies of freight cars and ordinary passenger cars, and of streetcars, and this business is almost at a standstill throughout the United States.

The business of manufacturing cars for sale gives employment to about 70 percent of the shop employees. The manufacture of sleeping cars for use by railway companies under contract, and which, under normal conditions, gives employment to about 15 percent of the shop employees, cannot be resumed by the company to an important extent for a very long time; for, out of the provision made for the abnormal travel last year, the company now has about 400 sleeping cars in store ready for use, but for which there is no need in the existing conditions of public travel.

It is now threatened by the American Railway Union officials that railway companies using Pullman sleeping cars shall be compelled to deprive their passengers of sleeping-car accommodations unless the Pullman Company will agree to submit to arbitration the question as to whether or not it shall open its manufacturing shops at Pullman and operate them under a scale of wages which would cause a daily loss to it of one-fourth the wages paid.

SOURCE: 53rd Congress, 3rd Session. Senate Document No. 7.

WOMEN IN INDUSTRY (BRANDEIS BRIEF)
(1903, by Louis D. Brandeis)

The progressive reform movement of the early twentieth century grew out of the social health and welfare crises caused by rapid urbanization and industrialization. In 1908, future Supreme Court Justice Louis D. Brandeis defended before the court a 1903 Oregon law that forbade women from working longer than ten hours a day. The case, Muller v. Oregon, represented laundry owner Curt Muller's appeal of a $10 fine he received when one of his foremen forced Mrs. E. Gotcher to work longer than ten hours. The law stood. In his groundbreaking brief, Brandeis referred only briefly to legal precedent, providing instead voluminous sociological evidence to support his claim that "women are fundamentally weaker than men in all that makes for endurance." Brandeis, a millionaire corporate lawyer who was moved in mid-life to become "the people's lawyer" and fight for social and legal reforms, was a leader in the progressive movement. The National Consumer's League, a middle-class workers' organization which enlisted Brandeis for the Oregon case, was so impressed with his sociological study that it published it in book form as *Women in Industry*, from which this excerpt is taken.

Leah R. Shafer,
Cornell University

See also **Government Regulation of Business; *Lochner v. New York;* Minimum-Wage Legislation; *Muller v. Oregon;* Wages and Hours of Labor, Regulation of; Women in Public Life, Business, and Professions.**

Decision of the United States Supreme Court in Curt Muller vs. State of Oregon Upholding the Constitutionality of the Oregon Ten Hour Law for Women and Brief for the State of Oregon

Brief for the Defendant in Error

This case presents the single question whether the Statute of Oregon, approved Feb. 19, 1903, which provides that "no female [shall] be employed in any mechanical establishment or factory or laundry" "more than ten hours during any one day," is unconstitutional and void as violating the Fourteenth Amendment of the Federal Constitution.

The decision in this case will, in effect, determine the constitutionality of nearly all the statutes in force in the United States, limiting the hours of labor of adult women,—namely:

Massachusetts

First enacted in 1874 (chap. 221), now embodied in Revised Laws, chap. 106, sec. 24, as amended by Stat. 1902, chap. 435, as follows:

No woman shall be employed in laboring in a manufacturing or mechanical establishment more than ten hours in any one day, except as hereinafter provided in this section, unless a different appointment in hours of labor is made for the sole purpose of making a shorter day's work for one day of the week; and in no case shall the hours of labor exceed fifty-eight in a week.... (Held constitutional in *Comm. v. Hamilton Mfg. Co.*, 120 Mass. 383.)

Rhode Island

First enacted in 1885 (chap. 519, sec. 1), now embodied in Stat. 1896, chap. 198, sec. 22 (as amended by Stat. 1902, chap. 994), as follows:

... No woman shall be employed in laboring in any manufacturing or mechanical establishment more than fifty-eight hours in any one week; and in no case shall the hours of labor exceed ten hours in any one day, excepting when it is necessary to make repairs or to prevent the interruption of the ordinary running of the machinery, or when a different apportionment of the hours of labor is made for the sole purpose of making a shorter day's work for one day of the week.

Louisiana

First enacted in 1886 (Act No. 43), and amended by Acts of 1902 (No. 49); now embodied in Revised Laws (1904, p. 989, sec. 4):

... No woman shall be employed in any factory, warehouse, workshop, telephone or telegraph office, clothing, dressmaking, or millinery establishment, or in any place where the manufacture of any kind of goods is carried on, or where any goods are prepared for manufacture, for a longer period than an average of ten hours in any day, or sixty hours in any week, and at least one hour shall be allowed in the labor period of each day for dinner.

Connecticut

First enacted in 1887 (chap. 62, sec. 1), now embodied in General Statutes, Revision 1902, sec. 4691, as follows:

... No woman shall be employed in laboring in any manufacturing, mechanical, or mercantile establishment more than ten hours in any day, except when it is necessary to make repairs to prevent the interruption of the ordinary running of the machinery, or where a different apportionment of the hours of labor is made for the sole purpose of making a shorter day's work for one day of the week.... In no case shall the hours exceed sixty in a week.

Maine

First enacted in 1887 (chap. 139, sec. 1), now re-enacted in Revised Statues, 1903, chap. 40, sec. 48, as follows:

... No woman shall be employed in laboring in any manufacturing or mechanical establishment in the State more than ten hours in any day, except when it is necessary to make repairs to prevent the interruption of the ordinary running of the machinery, or when a different apportionment of the hours of labor is made for the sole purpose of making a shorter day's work for one day of the week; and in no case shall the hours of labor exceed sixty in a week.

There is a further provision that any woman "may lawfully contract for such labor or number of hours in excess of ten hours a day, not exceeding six hours in any one week or sixty hours in any one year, receiving additional compensation therefor."

New Hampshire

First enacted in 1887 (chap. 25 sec. 1), now re-enacted by Stat. 1907, chap. 94, as follows:

No woman ... shall be employed in a manufacturing or mechanical establishment for more than nine hours and forty minutes in one day except in the following cases: I. To make a shorter day's work for one day in the week. II. To make up time lost on some day in the same week in consequence of the stopping of machinery upon which such person was dependent for employment. III. When it is necessary to make repairs to prevent interruption of the ordinary running of the machinery. In no case shall the hours of labor exceed fifty-eight in one week.

Maryland

First enacted in 1888 (chap. 455), now embodied in Public General Law, Code of 1903, art. 100, sec. 1:

No corporation or manufacturing company engaged in manufacturing either cotton or woollen yarns, fabrics or domestics of any kind, incorporated under the law of this State, and no officer, agent or servant of such named corporation, ... and no agent or servant of such firm or person shall require, permit, or suffer its, his, or their employees in its, his, or their service, or under his, its, or their control, to work for more than ten hours during each or any day of twenty-four hours for one full day's work, and shall make no contract or agreement with such employees or any of them providing that they or he shall work for more than ten hours for one day's work during each or any day of twenty-four hours, and said ten hours shall constitute one full day's work.

Section 2 makes it possible for male employees to work longer either to make repairs, or by express agreement.

Virginia

First enacted in 1890 (chap. 193, sec. 1), now embodied in Virginia Code (1904), chap. 178a, sec. 3657b, as follows:

No female shall work as an operative in any factory or manufacturing establishment in the State more than ten hours in any one day of twenty-four hours. All contracts made or to be made for the employment of any female ... as an operative in any factory or manufacturing establishment to work more than ten hours in any one day of twenty-four hours shall be void.

Pennsylvania

First enacted in 1897 (No. 26), and re-enacted in Laws of 1905, No. 226, as follows:

Section 1, That the term "establishment," where used for the purpose of this act, shall mean any place within this Commonwealth other than where domestic, coal-mining, or farm labor is employed; where men, women, and children are engaged, and paid a salary or wages, by any person, firm, or corporation, and where such men, women, or children are employees, in the general acceptance of the term.

Section 3. . . . No female shall be employed in any establishment for a longer period than sixty hours in any one week, nor for a longer period than twelve hours in any one day.

(Certain exceptions covering Saturday and Christmas.)

(Held constitutional in Comm. Beatty, 15 Pa. Superior Ct. 5.)

New York

First enacted in 1899 (chap. 192. sec. 77), now embodied in Stat. 1907, chap. 507, sec. 77, sub-division 3:

. . . No woman shall be employed or permitted to work in any factory in this State ... more than six days or sixty hours in any one week; nor for more than ten hours in one day. . . .

A female sixteen years of age or upwards ... may be employed in a factory more than ten hours a day; (a) regularly in not to exceed five days a week in order to make a short day or holiday on one of the six working days of the week; provided that no such person shall be required or permitted to work more than twelve hours in any one day or more than sixty hours in any one week, etc.

Nebraska

First enacted in 1899 (chap. 107), now embodied in Complied Statutes (1905, sec. 7955a):

No female shall be employed in any manufacturing, mechanical, or mercantile establishment, hotel, or restaurant in this State more than sixty hours during any one week, and ten hours shall constitute a day's labor. The hours of each day may be so arranged as to permit the employment of such female at any time from six o'clock A.M. to ten o'clock P.M.; but in no case shall such employment exceed ten hours in any one day.

(Held constitutional in Wenham v. State, 65 Neb. 400.)

Washington

Enacted in 1901, Stat. 1901, chap. 68, sec. 1, as follows:

No female shall be employed in any mechanical or mercantile establishment, laundry, hotel, or restaurant in this State more than ten hours during any day.

The hours of work may be so arranged as to permit the employment of females at any time so that they shall not work more than ten hours during the twenty-four.

(Held constitutional in State v. Buchanan, 29 Wash. 603.)

Argument

The legal rules applicable to this case are few and are well established, namely:

First: The right to purchase or to sell labor is a part of the "liberty" protected by the Fourteenth Amendment of the Federal Constitution.

Lochner v. New York, 198 U.S. 45, 53.

Second: The right to "liberty" is, however, subject to such reasonable restraint of action as the States may impose in the exercise of the police power for the protection of health, safety, morals, and the general welfare.

Lochner v. New York, 198 U.S. 45, 53, 67.

Third: The mere assertion that a statute restricting "liberty" relates, though in a remote degree, to the public health, safety, or welfare does not render it valid. The act must have a "real or substantial relation to the protection of the public health and the public safety."

Jacobson v. Mass, 197 U.S. 11, 31.

It must have "a more direct relation, as a means to an end, and the end itself must be appropriate and legitimate."

Lochner v. New York, 198 U.S. 45, 56, 57, 61.

Fourth: Such a law will not be sustained if the Court can see that it has no real or substantial relation to public health, safety, or welfare, or that it is "an unreasonable, unnecessary and arbitrary interference with the right of the individual to his personal liberty or to enter into those contracts in relation to labor which may seem to him appropriate or necessary for the support of himself and his family."

But "If the end which the Legislature seeks to accomplish be one to which its power extends, and if the means employed to that end, although not the wisest or best, are yet not plainly and palpably unauthorized by law, then the Court cannot interfere. In other words, when the validity of statute is questioned, the burden of proof, so to speak, is upon those" who assail it.

Lochner v. New York, 198 U.S. 45–68.

Fifth: The validity of the Oregon statute, must therefore be sustained unless the Court can find that there is no "fair ground, reasonable in and of itself, to say that there is material danger to the public health (or safety), or to the health (or safety) of the employees (or to the general welfare), if the hours of labor are not curtailed."

Lochner v. New York, 198 U.S. 45, 61.

The Oregon statute was obviously enacted for the purpose of protecting the public health, safety, and welfare. Indeed it declares:

"Section 5. Inasmuch as the female employees in the various establishments are not protected from overwork, an emergency is hereby declared to exist, and this act shall be in full force and effect from and after its approval by the Governor."

The facts of common knowledge of which the Court may take judicial notice —

See *Holden v. Hardy*, 169 U.S. 366

Jacobson v. Mass, 197 U.S. 11

Lochner v. New York, 198 U.S. 481.

establish, we submit, conclusively, that there is reasonable ground for holding that to permit women in Oregon to work in a "mechanical establishment, or factory, or laundry" more than ten hours in one day is dangerous to the public health, safety, morals, or welfare.

Long hours of labor are dangerous for women primarily because of their special physical organization. In structure and function women are differentiated from men. Besides these anatomical and physiological differences, physicians are agreed that women are fundamentally weaker than men in all that makes for endurance: in muscular strength, in nervous energy, in the powers of persistent attention and application. Overwork, therefore, which strains endurance to the utmost, is more disastrous to health of women than of men, and entails upon them more lasting injury.

Such being their physical endowment, women are affected to a far greater degree than men by the growing strain of modern industry.

The evil of overwork before as well as after marriage upon childbirth is marked and disastrous.

When the health of women has been injured by long hours, not only is the working efficiency of the community impaired, but the deterioration is handed down to succeeding generations ... The overwork of future mothers thus directly attacks welfare of the nation.

In order to establish enforceable restrictions upon working hours of women, the law must fix a maximum working day.

We submit that in view of the facts above set forth and of legislative action extending over a period of more than sixty years in the leading countries of Europe, and in twenty States, it cannot be said that the Legislature of Oregon had no reasonable ground for believing that the public health, safety, or welfare did not require a legal limitation on women's work in manufacturing and mechanical establishments and laundries to ten hours in one day.

Louis D. Brandeis
Counsel for State of Oregon

SOURCE: From *Women in Industry: Decision of the United States Supreme Court in Curt Miller v. State of Oregon, Upholding the Constitutionality of the Oregon Ten Hour Law for Women and Tried for the State of Oregon.* New York: National Consumer's League, 1908 (reprint).

CONDITIONS IN MEATPACKING PLANTS
(1906, by Upton Sinclair)

The explosive growth of American industry in the late nineteenth century caused a similar expansion in the work force. Working conditions in the new urban industrial zones were wretched, and a progressive reform movement soon grew out of the need to address the health and welfare of the American worker. In 1905, Upton Sinclair (1878–1968), a young socialist journalist and novelist, received a $500 advance to write a novel about abuses in the meat processing industry and spent seven weeks investigating the subject in Chicago. His novel, *The Jungle* (1906), a shocking exposé of the unsanitary and dangerous conditions in the plants, was an immediate best-seller and incited President Roosevelt to enact a series of food safety laws. Though Sinclair had hoped to excite interest in the difficult lives of the workers, the public was much more interested in the disgusting details about meat production. "I aimed at the public's heart," Sinclair said, "and by accident I hit it in the stomach." He would go on to be one of the most prolific writers in American literature, publishing over eighty books, pamphlets, and studies. This selection from *The Jungle* provides a stomach-turning description of what exactly goes into sausage.

Leah R. Shafer,
Cornell University

See also **Food and Cuisines; *Jungle, The;* Meatpacking.**

It was only when the whole ham was spoiled that it came into the department of Elzbieta. Cut up by the two-thousand-revolutions-a-minute flyers, and mixed with half a ton of other meat, no odor that ever was in a ham could make any difference. There was never the least attention paid to what was cut up for sausage; there would come all the way back from Europe old sausage that had been rejected, and that was mouldy and white—it would be dosed with borax and glycerine, and dumped into the hoppers, and made over again for home consumption. There would be meat that had tumbled out on the floor, in the dirt and sawdust, where the workers had tramped and spit uncounted billions of consumption germs. There would be meat stored in great piles in rooms; and the water from leaky roofs would drip over it, and thousands of rats would race about on it. It was too dark in these storage places to see well, but a man could run his hand over these piles of meat and sweep off handfuls of the dried dung of rats. These rats were nuisances, and the packers would put poisoned bread out for them; they would die, and then rats, bread, and meat would go into the hoppers together. This is no fairy story and no joke; the meat would be shovelled into carts, and the man who did the shovelling would not trouble to lift out a rat even when he saw one—there were things that went into the sausage in comparison with which a poisoned rat was a tidbit. There was no place for the men to wash their hands before they ate their dinner, and so they made a practice of washing them in the water that was to be ladled into the sausage. There were the butt-ends of smoked meat, and the scraps of corned beef, and all the odds and ends of the waste of the plants, that would be dumped into old barrels in the cellar and left there. Under the system of rigid economy which the packers enforced, there were some jobs that it only paid to do once in a long time, and among these was the cleaning out of the waste-barrels. Every spring they did it; and in the barrels would be dirt and rust and old nails and stale water—and cart load after cart load of it would be taken up and dumped into the hoppers with fresh meat, and sent out to the public's breakfast. Some of it they would make into "smoked" sausage—but as the smoking took time, and was therefore expensive, they would call upon their chemistry department, and preserve it with borax and color it with gelatine to make it brown. All of their sausage came out of the same bowl, but when they came to wrap it they would stamp some of it "special," and for this they would charge two cents more a pound.

SOURCE: Sinclair, Upton. *The Jungle.* New York: Doubleday, 1906.

BARTOLOMEO VANZETTI'S LAST STATEMENT
(21 August 1927)

Bartolomeo Vanzetti (1888–1927) and Nicola Sacco (1881–1927) were Italian immigrants and anarchists sentenced to death for a payroll holdup and murder in Massachusetts in 1920. Legal scholars generally consider the case a miscarriage of justice: the defense was inept, the prosecution was openly prejudicial, the judge repeatedly attacked and profaned the defendants outside the courtroom, evidence was fabricated, and witnesses were perjured, among other things. Though Sacco and Vanzetti eventually received support from an increasingly international group of liberal activists, labor organizers, and concerned citizens, the prevailing spirit of the times condemned them as dangerous communists and they were executed on August 23, 1927.

Vanzetti's letter to his compatriot's son, Dante, is the last in a series of letters written by the two men during their seven years in prison. In the letter, Vanzetti stresses that the men were not criminals but principled lovers of liberty. He decries the corrupt prejudices behind his conviction and urges Dante to follow in his father's struggle against the "exploitation and oppression of the man by the man."

Leah R. Shafer,
Cornell University

***See also* Anarchists; Sacco-Vanzetti Case.**

My Dear Dante:

I still hope, and we will fight until the last moment, to revindicate our right to live and to be free, but all the forces of the State and of the money and reaction are deadly against us because we are libertarians or anarchists.

I write little of this because you are now and yet too young to understand these things and other things of which I would like to reason with you.

But, if you do well, you will grow and understand your father's and my case and your father's and my principles, for which we will soon be put to death.

I tell you now that all that I know of your father, he is not a criminal, but one of the bravest men I ever knew. Some day you will understand what I am about to tell you. That your father has sacrificed everything dear and sacred to the human heart and soul for his fate in liberty and justice for all. That day you will be proud of your father, and if you come brave enough, you will take his place in the struggle between tyranny and liberty and you will vindicate his (our) names and our blood.

If we have to die now, you shall know, when you will be able to understand this tragedy in its fullest, how good and brave your father has been with you, your father and I, during these eight years of struggle, sorrow, passion, anguish and agony.

Even from now you shall be good, brave with your mother, with Ines, and with Susie—brave, good Susie—and do all you can to console and help them.

I would like you to also remember me as a comrade and friend to your father, your mother and Ines, Susie and you, and I assure you that neither have I been a criminal, that I have committed no robbery and no murder, but only fought modestily to abolish crimes from among mankind and for the liberty of all.

Remember Dante, each one who will say otherwise of your father and I, is a liar, insulting innocent dead men who have been brave in their life. Remember and know also, Dante, that if your father and I would have been cowards and hypocrits and rinnegetors of our faith, we would not have been put to death. They would not even have convicted a lebbrous dog; not even executed a deadly poisoned scorpion on such evidence as that they framed against us. They would have given a new trial to a matricide and habitual felon on the evidence we presented for a new trial.

Remember, Dante, remember always these things; we are not criminals; they convicted us on a frame-up; they denied us a new trial; and if we will be executed after seven years, four months and seventeen days of unspeakable tortures and wrong, it is for what I have already told you; because we were for the poor and against the exploitation and oppression of the man by the man.

The documents of our case, which you and other ones will collect and preserve, will prove to you that your father, your mother, Ines, my family and I have sacrificed by and to a State Reason of the American Plutocratic reaction.

The day will come when you will understand the atrocious cause of the above written words, in all its fullness. Then you will honor us.

Now Dante, be brave and good always. I embrace you.

P.S. I left the copy of *An American Bible* to your mother now, for she will like to read it, and she will give it to you when you will be bigger and able to understand it. Keep it for remembrance. It will also testify to you how good and generous Mrs. Gertrude Winslow has been with us all. Good-bye Dante.

Bartolomeo

SOURCE: Frankfurter, Marion Denman, and Gardner Jackson, eds. *The Letters of Sacco and Vanzetti.* New York: Octagon Books, 1971.

WORLD WAR I

EXCERPT FROM "THE WAR IN ITS EFFECT UPON WOMEN" *(1916, by Helena Swanwick)*

The cost of the Great War (World War I) in Europe was the needless loss of nearly an entire generation of young men, but in many regards, the social conventions of the time, exemplified in the infamous, government concocted "Little Mother" letter, required women to accept their losses quietly. A dedicated pacifist and supporter of universal suffrage, among the most outspoken opponents of Britain's participation in World War I, Helena Swanwick defied this thinking. As active after the war as during it, she later served in the League of Nations Union and was a member of the Empire's delegation to the League in 1929, though she remained always a harsh critic of the watered-down and self-serving Treaty of Versailles. Her many writings, salient, strong, and fiercely argued, would prove a powerful influence on a generation of women across the ocean in the United States, as well as in her native England. Depressed by failing health and the rise of fascism on the continent, she committed suicide in 1939, shortly before the outbreak of World War II.

Laura M. Miller,
Vanderbilt University

***See also* Gender and Gender Roles; World War I.**

How has the war affected women? How will it affect them? Women, as half the human race, are compelled to take their share of evil and good with men, the other half. The destruction of property, the increase of taxation, the rise of prices, the devastation of beautiful things in nature and art—these are felt by men as well as by women. Some losses doubtless appeal to one or the other sex with peculiar poignancy, but it would be difficult to say whose sufferings are the greater, though there can be no doubt at all that men get an exhilaration out of war which is denied to most women. When they see pictures of soldiers encamped in the ruins of what was once a home, amidst the dead bodies of gentle milch cows, most women would be thinking too insistently of the babies who must die for need of milk to entertain the exhilaration which no doubt may be felt at "the good work of our guns." When they read of miles upon miles of kindly earth made barren, the hearts of men may be wrung to think of wasted toil, but to women the thought suggests a simile full of an even deeper pathos; they will think of the millions of young lives destroyed, each one having cost the travail and care of a mother, and of the millions of young bodies made barren by the premature death of those who should have been their mates. The millions of widowed maidens in the coming generation will have to turn their thoughts away from one particular joy and fulfilment of life. While men in war give what is, at the present stage of the world's development, the peculiar service of men, let them not forget that in rendering that very service they are depriving a corresponding number of women of the opportunity of rendering what must, at all stages of the world's development, be the peculiar service of women. After the war, men will go on doing what has been regarded as men's work; women, deprived of their own, will also have to do much of what has been regarded as men's work. These things are going to affect women profoundly, and one hopes that the reconstruction of society is going to be met by the whole people—men and women—with a sympathetic understanding of each other's circumstances. When what are known as men's questions are discussed, it is generally assumed that the settlement of them depends upon men only; when what are known as women's questions are discussed, there is never any suggestion that they can be settled by women independently of men. Of course they cannot. But, then, neither can "men's questions" be rightly settled so. In fact, life would be far more truly envisaged if we dropped the silly phrases "men's and women's questions;" for, indeed, there are no such matters, and all human questions affect all humanity.

Now, for the right consideration of human questions, it is necessary for humans to understand each other. This catastrophic war will do one good thing if it opens our eyes to real live women as they are, as we know them in workaday life, but as the politician and the journalist seem not to have known them. When war broke out, a Labour newspaper, in the midst of the news of men's activities, found space to say that women would feel the pinch, because their supply of attar of roses would be curtailed. It struck some women like a blow in the face. When a great naval engagement took place, the front page of a progressive daily was taken up with portraits of the officers and men who had won distinction, and the back page with portraits of simpering mannequins in extravagantly fashionable hats; not frank advertisement, mind you, but exploitation of women under the guise of news supposed to be peculiarly interesting to the feeble-minded creatures. When a snapshot was published of the first women ticket collectors in England, the legend underneath the picture ran "Superwomen"! It took the life and death of Edith Cavell to open the eyes of the Prime Minister to the fact that there were thousands of women giving life and service to their country. "A year ago we did not know it," he said, in the House of Commons. Is that indeed so? Surely in our private capacities as ordinary citizens, we knew not only of the women whose portraits are in the picture papers (mostly pretty ladies of the music hall or of society), but also of the toiling millions upon whose courage and ability and endurance and goodness of heart the great human family rests. Only the politicians did not know, because their thoughts were too much engrossed with faction fights to think humanly; only the journalists would not write of them, because there was more money in writing the columns which are demanded by the advertisers of feminine luxuries. Anyone who has conducted a woman's paper knows the steady commercial pressure for that sort of "copy."

The other kind of women are, through the war, becoming good "copy." But women have not suddenly become patriotic, or capable, or self-sacrificing; the great masses of women have always shown these qualities in their humble daily life. Now that their services are asked for in unfamiliar directions, attention is being attracted to them, and many more people are realising that, with extended training and opportunity, women's capacity for beneficent work would be extended....

SOURCE: Swanwick, Helena. "The War in Its Effect upon Women," 1916. Reprinted in *World War I and European Society: A Sourcebook.* Edited by Marilyn Shevin-Coetzee and Frans Coetzee. Lexington, Mass: D.C. Heath, 1995.

LYRICS OF "OVER THERE"
(1917, by George M. Cohan)

Penned by George M. Cohan during the earliest days of the United States' involvement in the Great War (World War I), "Over There" stands as an artifact of a more innocent time. By 1917, the war in Europe had entered its third year, and the levels of bloodshed and cruel devastation unleashed by this new mechanized conflict had reached unimaginable levels. (During the Battle of the Somme in France, some sixty thousand British soldiers were killed in a single day. That was unimaginable, except that another sixty thousand had already been killed in April at Ypres, mostly by gas. Tens of thousands more died at Loos when the British's own chlorine canisters blew back into their trenches.) But for the so-called doughboys of the United States Army, something like Old World esprit de corps was still possible. "Over There" was the greatest of the wartime propaganda songs, made famous by the singer Noya Bayes, and recorded dozens of times, once by the opera star Enrico Caruso. By 1918, and the end of hostilities in the European theater, more than a hundred thousand Americans had lost their lives. In 1940, President Franklin D. Roosevelt awarded Cohan a special Medal of Honor for his contribution to the cause in World War I.

Laura M. Miller,
Vanderbilt University

See also **Music: Popular; World War I.**

Johnnie get your gun, get your gun, get your gun,
Take it on the run, on the run, on the run;
Hear them calling you and me;
Every son of liberty.
Hurry right away, no delay, go today,
Make your daddy glad, to have had such a lad,

Tell your sweetheart not to pine,
To be proud her boy's in line.

Chorus:

Over there, over there,
Send the word, send the word over there,
That the Yanks are coming, the Yanks are coming,
The drums rum-tumming everywhere.
So prepare, say a prayer,
Send the word, send the word to beware,
We'll be over, we're coming over,
And we won't come back till it's over over there.

Johnnie get your gun, get your gun, get your gun,
Johnnie show the Hun, you're a son-of-a-gun,
Hoist the flag and let her fly,
Like true heroes do or die.
Pack your little kit, show your grit, do your bit,
Soldiers to the ranks from the towns and the tanks,
Make your mother proud of you,
And to liberty be true.

SOURCE: Cohan, George M. "Over There." New York: Leo Feist, 1917.

EXCERPT FROM *PEACE AND BREAD IN TIME OF WAR* *(1917, by Jane Addams)*

A lifelong pacifist, co-founder of Hull House, and eventual Nobel Peace Prize recipient, Jane Addams (b. 1860) was also America's, possibly the world's, most outspoken opponent of the Great War (World War I). As described in these pages from one of her most famous works, such dedication to progressive causes, however, did not always endear her to her philosophical opponents, who derided and ridiculed her commitment to peace, as well as Hull House's widely known tolerance of radical organizations. Among her many accomplishments, the tireless Addams was the first woman to be named president of the National Conference of Social Work, was the author of various books and articles, sat on the board of innumerable international peace organizations, and helped found the American Civil Liberties Union. On the occasion of her death by cancer on 21 May 1935, by which time public opinion was more favorable, her obituary in the *New York Times* honored Jane Addams as the best-known and best-loved woman in the world.

Laura M. Miller,
Vanderbilt University

See also **Antiwar Movements; Pacifism; Peace Movements; World War I.**

From the very beginning of the great war, as the members of our group gradually became defined from the rest of the community, each one felt increasingly the sense of isolation which rapidly developed after the United States entered the war into that destroying effect of "aloneness," if I may so describe the opposite of mass consciousness. We never ceased to miss the unquestioning comradeship experienced by our fellow citizens during the war, nor to feel curiously outside the enchantment given to any human emotion when it is shared by millions of others. The force of the majority was so overwhelming that it seemed not only impossible to hold one's own against it, but at moments absolutely unnatural, and one secretly yearned to participate in "the folly of all mankind." Our modern democratic teaching has brought us to regard popular impulses as possessing in their general tendency a valuable capacity for evolutionary development. In the hours of doubt and self-distrust the question again and again arises, has the individual or a very small group, the right to stand out against millions of his fellow countrymen? Is there not a great value in mass judgment and in instinctive mass enthusiasm, and even if one were right a thousand times over in conviction, was he not absolutely wrong in abstaining from this communion with his fellows? The misunderstanding on the part of old friends and associates and the charge of lack of patriotism was far easier to bear than those dark periods of faint-heartedness. We gradually ceased to state our position as we became convinced that it served no practical purpose and, worse than that, often found that the immediate result was provocative....

The pacifist was constantly brought sharply up against a genuine human trait with its biological basis, a trait founded upon the instinct to dislike, to distrust and finally to destroy the individual who differs from the mass in time of danger. Regarding this trait as the basis of self-preservation it becomes perfectly natural for the mass to call such an individual a traitor and to insist that if he is not for the nation he is against it. To this an estimated nine million people can bear witness who have been burned as witches and heretics, not by mobs, for of the people who have been "lynched" no record has been kept, but by order of ecclesiastical and civil courts.

There were moments when the pacifist yielded to the suggestion that keeping himself out of war, refusing to take part in its enthusiasms, was but pure quietism, an acute failure to adjust himself to the moral world. Certainly nothing was clearer than that the individual will was helpless and irrelevant. We were constantly told by our friends that to stand aside from the war mood of the country was to surrender all possibility of future influence, that we were committing intellectual suicide, and would never again be trusted as responsible people or judicious advisers. Who were we to differ with able statesmen, with men of sensitive conscience who also absolutely abhorred war, but were convinced that this war for the preservation of democracy would make all future wars impossible, that the priceless values of civilization which were at stake could at this moment be saved only by war? But these very dogmatic statements spurred one to alarm. Was not war in the interest of democracy for the salvation of civilization a contradiction of terms, whoever said it or however often it was repeated?

Then, too, we were always afraid of fanaticism, of preferring a consistency of theory to the conscientious recognition of the social situation, of a failure to meet life in the temper of a practical person. Every student of our time had become more or less a disciple of pragmatism and its great teachers in the United States had come out for the war and defended their positions with skill and philosophic acumen. There were moments when one longed desperately for reconciliation with one's friends and fellow citizens; . . . Solitude has always had its demons, harder to withstand than the snares of the world, and the unnatural desert into which the pacifist was summarily cast out seemed to be peopled with them. We sorely missed the contagion of mental activity, for we are all much more dependent upon our social environment and daily newspaper than perhaps any of us realize. . . .

The consciousness of spiritual alienation was lost only in moments of comradeship with the like minded, which may explain the tendency of the pacifist in war time to seek his intellectual kin, his spiritual friends, wherever they might be found in his own country or abroad.

It was inevitable that in many respects the peace cause should suffer in public opinion from the efforts of groups of people who, early in the war, were convinced that the country as a whole was for peace and who tried again and again to discover a method for arousing and formulating the sentiment against war. . . .

We also read with a curious eagerness the steadily increasing number of books published from time to time during the war, which brought a renewal of one's faith or at least a touch of comfort. These books broke through that twisting and suppressing of awkward truths, which was encouraged and at times even ordered by the censorship. Such manipulation of news and motives was doubtless necessary in the interest of war propaganda if the people were to be kept in a fighting mood. . . .

On the other hand there were many times when we stubbornly asked ourselves, what after all, has maintained the human race on this old globe despite all the calamities of nature and all the tragic failings of mankind, if not faith in new possibilities, and courage to advocate them. Doubtless many times these new possibilities were declared by a man who, quite unconscious of courage, bore the "sense of being an exile, a condemned criminal, a fugitive from mankind." Did every one so feel who, in order to travel on his own proper path had been obliged to leave the traditional highway? The pacifist, during the period of the war could answer none of these questions but he was sick at heart from causes which to him were hidden and impossible to analyze. He was at times devoured by a veritable dissatisfaction with life. Was he thus bearing his share of blood-guiltiness, the morbid sense of contradiction and inexplicable suicide which modern war implies? We certainly had none of the internal contentment of the doctrinaire, the ineffable solace of the self-righteous which was imputed to us. No one knew better than we how feeble and futile we were against the impregnable weight of public opinion, the appalling imperviousness, the coagulation of motives, the universal confusion of a world at war. There was scant solace to be found in this type of statement: "The worth of every conviction consists precisely in the steadfastness with which it is held," perhaps because we suffered from the fact that we were no longer living in a period of dogma and were therefore in no position to announce our sense of security! We were well aware that the modern liberal having come to conceive truth of a kind which must vindicate itself in practice, finds it hard to hold even a sincere and mature opinion which from the very nature of things can have no justification in works. The pacifist in war time is literally starved of any gratification of that natural desire to have his own decisions justified by his fellows.

That, perhaps, was the crux of the situation. We slowly became aware that our affirmation was regarded as pure dogma. We were thrust into the position of the doctrinnaire, and although, had we been permitted, we might have cited both historic and scientific tests of our so-called doctrine of Peace, for the moment any sanction even by way of illustration was impossible.

It therefore came about that ability to hold out against mass suggestion, to honestly differ from the convictions and enthusiasms of one's best friends did in moments of crisis come to depend upon the categorical belief that a man's primary allegiance is to his vision of the truth and that he is under obligation to affirm it. . . .

SOURCE: Addams, Jane. *Peace and Bread in Time of War.* 1922. Reprint, New York: King's Crown Press, 1945, pp. 140–151. Reprinted in *America's Major Wars: Crusaders, Critics, and Scholars.* Vol. 2 (1898–1972).

LETTERS FROM THE FRONT, WORLD WAR I
(1918, by Quentin Roosevelt)

These diary pages, penned by Theodore Roosevelt's son, Quentin, offer a glimpse into the earliest days of mechanized warfare and the mind of an adventurous young American engaged in it. Aerial combat in the Great War (World War I) was a crude affair. Targets had to be located visually, and a reliance on small arms was not unusual. Pilots often dropped bricks on targets below. By 1918, the war had dragged on in Europe for four years, exacting a death toll heretofore unheard of in the annals of war. Even the intrepid and good-natured Quentin, who memorized eye charts before his enlistment physical so that his poor eyesight would not keep him out of the newly formed United States Air Force, was no match for its ferocity. On July 14, just days after he penned the pages here, he was shot down and killed behind enemy lines by a pair of German fighter planes. Only twenty years old, he was buried near Reims, France, and later re-interred at Normandy.

Laura M. Miller,
Vanderbilt University

***See also* World War I.**

June 8, 1918

I've had so much happening to me, tho, in the last ten days, that I have not had time to think even, which is just as well. Ham and I had almost begun to think we were permanently stuck in Issoudun, when with no warning, we were ordered up to Orly, which is just outside of Paris. No one knew anything about the orders, and Ham and I felt sure that it meant our first step out to the front. Once the orders came, tho, we only had twelve hours time to settle everything up and leave. You can imagine how we hurried, with all the goodbyes to be said and packing, and paying bills. I thought we never would get away, but finally it was thru, and we got in the truck and started to leave for the main camp to get our clearance papers. Then they did one of the nicest things I've ever had happen. Our truck driver instead of going out the regular way, took us down the line of hangars and as we went past all the mechanics were lined up in front and cheered us goodbye. As we passed the last hangar one of the sergeants yelled, after us, "Let us know if you're captured and we'll come after you." So I left with a big lump in my throat, for its nice to know that your men have liked you.

July 6, 1918

Yesterday our flight officer was sent out to patrol at thirty-five hundred metres over about a ten kilometre sector where some sort of straightening the line action was going on. Our orders were not to cross the line, or fight unless forced to. For about fifteen minutes we chased up and down, up and down, with no more excitement than scaring a few *reglage* planes back into Germany. I was busy watching below us—I was flying right—when I saw our leader give the alert signal. I hadn't seen anything below, so I looked ahead and there up about a thousand metres, on the German side I saw a patrol of six Boche. We started climbing at once, and I was having a horrid time, for while the rest of the formation closed in I dragged farther and farther behind. I have a bad motor, so that when the rest hurry up they leave me. There I was, with only the slim consolation that the leader was probably keeping his eye on me. We climbed on, and I did my darndest to keep up and at the same time keep an eye on the Boche who remained comfortably on top. The next thing I knew, a shadow came across my plane, and there, about two hundred metres above me, and looking as big as all outdoors was a Boche. He was so near I could make out the red stripes around his fuselage. I'm free to confess that I was scared blue. I was behind the rest of the formation, and he had all the altitude. So I pushed on the stick, prayed for motor, and watched out of the corner of my eye to see his elevators go down, and have his tracers shooting by me. However, for some reason he didn't attack, instead he took a few general shots at the lot and then swung back to his formation. Our only explanation is that he didn't want to fight in our lines,—he had every kind of advantage over us. Lord, but I was glad when he left. When I got back they decided to pull my motor, so I was given another plane for this morning, which belongs to a fellow who's sick.

We went out on patrol again, this time at five thousand and started over across, hunting for trouble. A couple of kilometres inside the line we spotted six of them about a thousand metres below us. We circled and came back between them and the sun, and dove on them. They never saw us until we started shooting so we had them cold. I had miserable luck—I had my man just where I wanted, was piquing down on him, (he was a monoplane) and after getting good and close, set my sight on him and pulled the trigger. My gun shot twice and then jammed. It was really awfully hard luck, for I couldn't fix it. The feed box had slipped, so she only fired one shot at a time, and then quit. I did everything I could, but finally had to give up and come home, as we were about fifteen kilometres their side of the line. As the papers put it, tho', "a successful evening was had by all." We got three of them— They weren't the circus of course. We lost one man, tho', and we aren't sure how. We rather think his motor must have gone dead on him, and forced him to land in Germany. So things are looking more interesting around here, and I've had my first real fight. I was doubtful before,—for I thought I might get cold feet, or something, but you don't. You get so excited that you forget everything except getting the other fellow, and trying to dodge the tracers, when they start streaking past you.

July 11, 1918

I got my first real excitement on the front for I think I got a Boche. The Operations Officer is trying for confirmation on it now. I was out on high patrol with the rest of my squadron when we got broken up, due to a mistake in formation. I dropped into a turn of a *vrille*—these planes have so little surface that at five thousand you can't do much with them. When I got straightened out I couldn't spot my crowd any where, so, as I had only been up an hour, I decided to fool around a little before going home, as I was just over the lines. I turned and circled for five minutes or so, and then suddenly,—the way planes do come into focus in the air, I saw three planes in formation. At first I thought they were Boche, but as they paid no attention to me I finally decided to chase them, thinking they were part of my crowd, so I started after them full speed. I thought at the time it was a little strange, with the wind blowing the way it was, that they should be going almost straight into Germany, but I had plenty of gas so I kept on.

They had been going absolutely straight and I was nearly in formation when the leader did a turn, and I saw to my horror that they had white tails with black crosses on them. Still I was so near by them that I thought I might pull up a little and take a crack at them. I had altitude on them, and what was more they hadn't seen me, so I pulled up, put my sights on the end man, and let go. I saw my tracers going all around him but for some reason he never even turned, until all of a sudden his tail came up and he went down in a *vrille.* I wanted to follow him but the other two had started around after me, so I had to cut and run. However, I could half watch him looking back, and he was still spinning when he hit the clouds three thousand meters below. Of course he may have just been scared, but I think he must have been hit, or he would have come out before he struck the clouds. Three thousand meters is an awfully long spin.

I had a long chase of it for they followed me all the way back to our side of the lines, but our speed was about equal so I got away. The trouble is that it was about twenty kilometers inside their lines, and I am afraid, too far to get confirmation.

At the moment every one is very much pleased in our Squadron for we are getting new planes. We have been using Nieuports, which have the disadvantage of not being particularly reliable and being inclined to catch fire.

SOURCE: Roosevelt, Kermit, ed. *Quentin Roosevelt: A Sketch with Letters.* New York: Scribners, 1922.

THE FOURTEEN POINTS
(8 January 1918)

Frustrated by the European Allies' unwillingness to specify their terms for peace in the Great War (later called World War I), President Woodrow Wilson outlined his own plan, later called simply the Fourteen Points, to a joint session of Congress on 8 January 1918. Essentially a foreign policy manifestation of American Progressivism, Wilson's vision of a "Peace Without Victory" articulated modern ideas of free trade, fair dealing, and self-determination, as well as the belief that morality, and not merely self-interest, ought to guide foreign affairs. The speech made Wilson an international hero, a towering figure on a crusade to restore the hope of progressives dashed on the tortured battlefields of the Great War. Unfortunately, the "general association of nations" called for in Wilson's last point was not to be. By 1919, the Congress had become fearful that membership in the League of Nations would subvert its power to declare war and might eventually entrap the United States in another foreign conflict. Wilson's European allies were often as reluctant, and soon the beleaguered president was forced to compromise on point after point. The Treaty of Versailles, which ended hostilities in the Great War, contains little either of the spirit or the matter of Wilson's original vision. Without the support of the United States, the League of Nations failed, and Wilson's fear of another war in Europe, this one more terrible than the last, was a mere twenty years away.

Laura M. Miller,
Vanderbilt University

See also **Fourteen Points; Peace Conferences; Versailles, Treaty of; World War I.**

Gentlemen of the Congress:

. . . It will be our wish and purpose that the processes of peace, when they are begun, shall be absolutely open and that they shall involve and permit henceforth no secret understandings of any kind. The day of conquest and aggrandizement is gone by; so is also the day of secret covenants entered into in the interest of particular governments and likely at some unlooked-for moment to upset the peace of the world. It is this happy fact, now clear to the view of every public man whose thoughts do not still linger in an age that is dead and gone, which makes it possible for every nation whose purposes are consistent with justice and the peace of the world to avow now or at any other time the objects it has in view.

We entered this war because violations of right had occurred which touched us to the quick and made the life of our own people impossible unless they were corrected and the world secured once for all against their recurrence. What we demand in this war, therefore, is nothing peculiar to ourselves. It is that the world be made fit and safe to live in; and particularly that it be made safe for every peace-loving nation which, like our own, wishes to live its own life, determine its own institutions, be assured of justice and fair dealing by the other peoples of the world as against force and selfish aggression. All the peoples of the world are in effect partners in this interest, and for our own part we see very clearly that unless justice be done to others it will not be done to us. The program of the world's peace, therefore, is our program; and that program, the only possible program, as we see it, is this:

I. Open covenants of peace, openly arrived at, after which there shall be no private international understandings of any kind but diplomacy shall proceed always frankly and in the public view.

II. Absolute freedom of navigation upon the seas, outside territorial waters, alike in peace and in war, except as the seas may be closed in whole or in part by international action for the enforcement of international covenants.

III. The removal, so far as possible, of all economic barriers and the establishment of an equality of trade conditions among all the nations consenting to the peace and associating themselves for its maintenance.

IV. Adequate guarantees given and taken that national armaments will be reduced to the lowest point consistent with domestic safety.

V. A free, open-minded, and absolutely impartial adjustment of all colonial claims, based upon a strict observance of the principle that in determining all such questions of sovereignty the interests of the populations concerned must have equal weight with the equitable claims of the government whose title is to be determined.

VI. The evacuation of all Russian territory and such a settlement of all questions affecting Russia as will secure the best and freest cooperation of the other nations of the world in obtaining for her an unhampered and unembarrassed opportunity for the independent determination of her own political development and national policy and assure her of a sincere welcome into the society of free nations under institutions of her own choosing; and, more than a welcome, assistance also of every kind that she may need and may herself desire. The treatment accorded Russia by her sister nations in the months to come will be the acid test of their good will, of their comprehension of her needs as distinguished from their own interests, and of their intelligent and unselfish sympathy.

VII. Belgium, the whole world will agree, must be evacuated and restored, without any attempt to limit the sovereignty which she enjoys in common with all other free nations. No other single act will serve as this will serve to restore confidence among the nations in the laws which they have themselves set and determined for the government of their relations with one another. Without this healing act the whole structure and validity of international law is forever impaired.

VIII. All French territory should be freed and the invaded portions restored, and the wrong done to France by Prussia in 1871 in the matter of Alsace-Lorraine, which has unsettled the peace of the world for nearly fifty years, should be righted, in order that peace may once more be made secure in the interest of all.

IX. A readjustment of the frontiers of Italy should be effected along clearly recognizable lines of nationality.

X. The peoples of Austria-Hungary, whose place among the nations we wish to see safe-guarded and assured, should be accorded the freest opportunity of autonomous development.

XI. Rumania, Serbia, and Montenegro should be evacuated; occupied territories restored; Serbia accorded free and secure access to the sea; and the relations of the several Balkan states to one another determined by friendly counsel along historically established lines of allegiance and nationality; and international guarantees of the political and economic independence and territorial integrity of the several Balkan states should be entered into.

XII. The Turkish portions of the present Ottoman Empire should be assured a secure sovereignty, but the other nationalities which are now under Turkish rule should be assured an undoubted security of life and an absolutely unmolested opportunity of autonomous development, and the Dardanelles should be permanently opened as a free passage to the ships and commerce of all nations under international guarantees.

XIII. An independent Polish state should be erected which should include the territories inhabited by indisputably Polish populations, which should be assured a free and secure access to the sea, and whose political and economic independence and territorial integrity should be guaranteed by international covenant.

XIV. A general association of nations must be formed under specific covenants for the purpose of affording mutual guarantees of political independence and territorial integrity to great and small states alike.

In regard to these essential rectifications of wrong and assertions of right we feel ourselves to be intimate partners of all the governments and peoples associated together against the Imperialists. We cannot be separated in interest or divided in purpose. We stand together until the end.

For such arrangements and covenants we are willing to fight and to continue to fight until they are achieved; but only because we wish the right to prevail and desire a just and stable peace such as can be secured only by removing the chief provocations to war, which this program does not remove. We have no jealousy of German greatness, and there is nothing in this program that impairs it. We grudge her no achievement or distinction of learning or of pacific enterprise such as have made her record very bright and very enviable. We do not wish to injure her or to block in any way her legitimate influence or power. We do not wish to fight her either with arms or with hostile arrangements of trade if she is willing to associate herself with us and the other peace-loving nations of the world in covenants of justice and law and fair dealing. We wish her only to accept a place of equality among the peoples of the world,—the new world in which we now live,—instead of a place of mastery.

Neither do we presume to suggest to her any alteration or modification of her institutions. But it is necessary, we must frankly say, and necessary as a preliminary to any intelligent dealings with her on our part, that we should know whom her spokesmen speak for when they speak to us, whether for the Reichstag majority or for the military party and the men whose creed is imperial domination.

We have spoken now, surely, in terms too concrete to admit of any further doubt or question. An evident principle runs through the whole program I have outlined. It is the principle of justice to all peoples and nationalities, and their right to live on equal terms of liberty and safety with one another, whether they be strong or weak. Unless this principle be made its foundation no part of the structure of international justice can stand. The people of the United States could act upon no other principle; and to the vindication of this principle they are ready to devote their lives, their honor, and everything that they possess. The moral climax of this the culminating and final war for human liberty has come, and they are ready to put their own strength, their own highest purpose, their own integrity and devotion to the test.

SOURCE: Wilson, Woodrow. "Fourteen Points" speech to Congress. Reprinted in *Major Problems in the Gilded Age and the Progressive Era: Documents and Essays,* edited by Leon Fink. Lexington, Mass: D.C. Heath, 1993.

DEDICATING THE TOMB OF THE UNKNOWN SOLDIER
(1921, by Kirke E. Simpson)

More than 100,000 Americans lost their lives during the United States's two-year involvement in World War I. Three years after the signing of the Treaty of Versailles and the end of hostilities in Europe, in a solemn ceremony President Warren G. Harding dedicated a monument to unidentifiable, "unknown" soldiers killed during the war. For progressives, World War I represented the shattering failure of the ideal of civilized reform and enlightenment. For isolationists, it was the confirmation of their deepest fears, the beginning of a new era of intercontinental mechanized warfare the likes of which the world had never seen. Thousands—ordinary citizens, foreign dignitaries, and American politicians alike—attended the dedication described here. Former President Woodrow Wilson, himself instrumental in crafting the peace, was present. Many years later, the unidentified remains of dead soldiers from World War II and the Korean conflict were buried with the monument's original inhabitant. A casualty of the Vietnam War was interred alongside them in 1973, but when advances in forensic science allowed for his identification, his remains were disinterred and turned over to his family. The age of the unknown soldier, it would seem, had come to an end.

Laura M. Miller,
Vanderbilt University

See also **Unknown Soldier, Tomb of the.**

Under the wide and starry skies of his own homeland America's unknown dead from France sleeps tonight, a soldier home from the wars.

Alone, he lies in the narrow cell of stone that guards his body; but his soul has entered into the spirit that is America. Wherever liberty is held close in men's hearts, the honor and the glory and the pledge of high endeavor poured out over this nameless one of fame will be told and sung by Americans for all time.

Scrolled across the marble arch of the memorial raised to American soldier and sailor dead, everywhere, which stands like a monument behind his tomb, runs this legend: "We here highly resolve that these dead shall not have died in vain."

The words were spoken by the martyred Lincoln over the dead at Gettysburg. And today with voice strong with determination and ringing with deep emotion, another President echoed that high resolve over the coffin of the soldier who died for the flag in France.

Great men in the world's affairs heard that high purpose reiterated by the man who stands at the head of the American people. Tomorrow they will gather in the city that stands almost in the shadow of the new American shrine of liberty dedicated today. They will talk of peace; of the curbing of the havoc of war.

They will speak of the war in France, that robbed this soldier of life and name and brought death to comrades of all nations by the hundreds of thousands. And in their ears when they meet must ring President Harding's declaration today beside that flag-wrapped, honor-laden bier:

> "There must be, there shall be, the commanding voice of a conscious civilization against armed warfare."

Far across the seas, other unknown dead, hallowed in memory by their countrymen, as this American soldier is enshrined in the heart of America, sleep their last. He, in whose veins ran the blood of British forebears, lies beneath a great stone in ancient Westminster Abbey; he of France, beneath the Arc de Triomphe, and he of Italy under the altar of the fatherland in Rome....

And it seemed today that they, too, must be here among the Potomac hills to greet an American comrade come to join their glorious company, to testify their approval of the high words of hope spoken by America's President. All day long the nation poured out its heart in pride and glory for the nameless American. Before the first crash of the minute guns roared its knell for the dead from the shadow of Washington Monument, the people who claim him as their own were trooping out to do him honor. They lined the long road from the Capitol to the hillside where he sleeps tonight; they flowed like a tide over the slopes about his burial place; they choked the bridges that lead across the river to the fields of the brave, in which he is the last comer....

As he was carried past through the banks of humanity that lined Pennsylvania Avenue a solemn, reverent hush held the living walls. Yet there was not so much of sorrow as of high pride in it all, a pride beyond the reach of shouting and the clamor that marks less sacred moments in life.

Out there in the broad avenue was a simpler soldier, dead for honor of the flag. He was nameless. No man knew what part in the great life of the nation he had died as Americans always have been ready to die, for the flag and what it means. They read the message of the pageant clear, these silent thousands along the way. They stood in almost holy awe to take their own part in what was theirs, the glory of the American people, honored here in the honors showered on America's nameless son from France.

Soldiers, sailors, and marines—all played their part in the thrilling spectacles as the cortege rolled along. And just behind the casket, with its faded French flowers on the draped flag, walked the President, the chosen leader of a hundred million, in whose name he was chief mourner at his bier. Beside him strode the man under whom the fallen hero had lived and died in France, General Pershing, wearing only the single medal of

Victory that every American soldier might wear as his only decoration.

Then, row on row, came the men who lead the nation today or have guided its destinies before. They were all there, walking proudly, with age and frailties of the flesh forgotten. Judges, Senators, Representatives, highest officers of every military arm of government, and a trudging little group of the nation's most valorous sons, the Medal of Honor men. Some were gray and bent and drooping with old wounds; some trim and erect as the day they won their way to fame. All walked gladly in this nameless comrade's last parade.

Behind these came the carriage in which rode Woodrow Wilson, also stricken down by infirmities as he served in the highest place in the nation, just as the humble private riding in such state ahead had gone down before a shell of bullet. For the dead man's sake, the former President had put aside his dread of seeming to parade his physical weakness and risked health, perhaps life, to appear among the mourners for the fallen.

There was handclapping and a cheer here and there for the man in the carriage, a tribute to the spirit that brought him to honor the nation's nameless hero, whose commander-in-chief he had been.

After President Harding and most of the high dignitaries of the government had turned aside at the White House, the procession, headed by its solid blocks of soldiery and the battalions of sailor comrades, moved on with Pershing, now flanked by secretaries Weeks and Denby, for the long road to the tomb. It marched on, always between the human borders of the way of victory the nation had made for itself of the great avenue; on over the old bridge that spans the Potomac, on up the long hill to Fort Myer, and at last to the great cemetery beyond, where soldier and sailor folk sleep by the thousands. There the lumbering guns of the artillery swung aside, the cavalry drew their horses out of the long line and left to the foot soldiers and the sailors and marines the last stage of the journey.

Ahead, the white marble of the amphitheater gleamed through the trees. It stands crowning the slope of the hills that sweep upward from the river, and just across was Washington, its clustered buildings and monuments to great dead who have gone before, a moving picture in the autumn haze.

People in thousands were moving about the great circle of the amphitheater. The great ones to whom places had been given in the sacred enclosure and the plain folk who had trudged the long way just to glimpse the pageant from afar, were finding their places. Everywhere within the pillared enclosure bright uniforms of foreign soldiers appeared. They were laden with the jeweled order of rank to honor an American private soldier, great in the majesty of his sacrifices, in the tribute his honors paid to all Americans who died.

Down below the platform placed for the casket, in a stone vault, lay wreaths and garlands brought from England's King and guarded by British soldiers. To them came the British Ambassador in the full uniform of his rank to bid them keep safe against that hour.

Above the platform gathered men whose names ring through history—Briand, Foch, Beatty, Balfour, Jacques, Diaz, and others—in a brilliant array of place and power. They were followed by others, Baron Kato from Japan, the Italian statesmen and officers, by the notables from all countries gathered here for tomorrow's conference, and by some of the older figures in American life too old to walk beside the approaching funeral train.

Down around the circling pillars the marbled box filled with distinguished men and women, with a cluster of shattered men from army hospitals, accompanied by uniformed nurses. A surpliced choir took its place to wait the dead.

Faint and distant, the silvery strains of a military band stole into the big white bowl of the amphitheater. The slow cadences and mourning notes of a funeral march grew clearer amid the roll and mutter of the muffled drums.

At the arch where the choir awaited the heroic dead, comrades lifted his casket down and, followed by the generals and the admirals, who had walked beside him from the Capitol, he was carried to the place of honor. Ahead moved the white-robed singers, chanting solemnly.

Carefully, the casket was placed above the banked flowers, and the Marine Band played sacred melodies until the moment the President and Mrs. Harding stepped to their places beside the casket; then the crashing, triumphant chorus of The Star Spangled Banner swept the gathering to its feet again.

A prayer, carried out over the crowd over the amplifiers so that no word was missed, took a moment or two, then the sharp, clear call of the bugle rang "Attention!" and for two minutes the nation stood at pause for the dead, just at high noon. No sound broke the quiet as all stood with bowed heads. It was much as though a mighty hand had checked the world in full course. Then the band sounded, and in a mighty chorus rolled up in the words of America from the hosts within and without the great open hall of valor.

President Harding stepped forward beside the coffin to say for America the thing that today was nearest to the nation's heart, that sacrifices such as this nameless man, fallen in battle, might perhaps be made unnecessary down through the coming years. Every word that President Harding spoke reached every person through the amplifiers and reached other thousands upon thousands in New York and San Francisco.

Mr. Harding showed strong emotion as his lips formed the last words of the address. He paused, then with raised hand and head bowed, went on in the measured, rolling periods of the Lord's Prayer. The response that came back to him from the thousands he faced, from the other thousands out over the slopes beyond, perhaps from still other thousands away near the Pacific, or close-packed in the heart of the nation's greatest city, arose like a chant. The marble arches hummed with a solemn sound.

Then the foreign officers who stand highest among the soldiers or sailors of their flags came one by one to the bier to place gold and jeweled emblems for the brave above the breast of the sleeper. Already, as the great prayer ended, the President had set the American seal of admiration for the valiant, the nation's love for brave deeds and the courage that defies death, upon the casket.

Side by side he laid the Medal of Honor and the Distinguished Service Cross. And below, set in place with reverent hands, grew the long line of foreign honors, the Victoria Cross, never before laid on the breast of any but those who had served the British flag; all the highest honors of France and Belgium and Italy and Rumania and Czechoslovakia and Poland.

To General Jacques of Belgium it remained to add his own touch to these honors. He tore from the breast of his own tunic the medal of valor pinned there by the Belgian King, tore it with a sweeping gesture, and tenderly bestowed it on the unknown American warrior.

Through the religious services that followed, and prayers, the swelling crowd sat motionless until it rose to join in the old, consoling Rock of Ages, and the last rite for the dead was at hand. Lifted by his hero-bearers from the stage, the unknown was carried in his flag-wrapped, simple coffin out to the wide sweep of the terrace. The bearers laid the sleeper down above the crypt, on which had been placed a little soil of France. The dust his blood helped redeem from alien hands will mingle with his dust as time marches by.

The simple words of the burial ritual were said by Bishop Brent; flowers from war mothers of America and England were laid in place.

For the Indians of America Chief Plenty Coos came to call upon the Great spirit of the Red Men, with gesture and chant and tribal tongue, that the dead should not have died in vain, that war might end, peace be purchased by such blood as this. Upon the casket he laid the coupstick of his tribal office and the feathered war bonnet from his own head. Then the casket, with its weight of honors, was lowered into the crypt.

A rocking blast of gunfire rang from the woods. The glittering circle of bayonets stiffened to a salute to the dead. Again the guns shouted their message of honor and farewell. Again they boomed out; a loyal comrade was being laid to his last, long rest.

High and clear and true in the echoes of the guns, a bugle lifted the old, old notes of taps, the lullaby for the living soldier, in death his requiem. Long ago some forgotten soldier-poet caught its meaning clear and set it down that soldiers everywhere might know its message as they sink to rest:

Fades the light;
And afar
Goeth day, cometh night,
And a star,
Leadeth all, speedeth all,
To their rest.

The guns roared out again in the national salute. He was home, The Unknown, to sleep forever among his own.

SOURCE: Simpson, Kirke L. Associated Press report on the Dedication of the Tomb of the Unknown Soldier (11 November 1921).

THE GREAT DEPRESSION

ADVICE TO THE UNEMPLOYED IN THE GREAT DEPRESSION
(11 June 1932, by Henry Ford)

The decade before the Great Depression was one of unprecedented economic growth. The rise of new industries, such as automobile manufacturing, created jobs and newfound prosperity for working and middle-class American families. Automobile industry giant Henry Ford (1863–1947), whose company, Ford Motor Company, designed and implemented the first continuously moving assembly line, was a prominent leader in the new industrial order.

The stock market crash of 1929 and the deepening post-war economic crisis overseas devastated the rapidly growing American economy, however, and many industrial workers were forced out of their jobs. Ford regarded himself as a groundbreaking advocate for fair labor management policies, such as the institution, in 1914, of an eight-hour workday, and saw himself as a champion of economic independence. In light of these beliefs, in this passage Ford urged the unemployed not to depend upon benefactors or charity for their survival. Hard, self-directed work, he believed, will keep the worker profitably employed until the economic situation turns around.

Leah R. Shafer,
Cornell University

See also **Great Depression; Unemployment.**

I have always had to work, whether anyone hired me or not. For the first forty years of my life, I was an employee. When not employed by others, I employed myself. I found very early that being out of hire was not necessarily being out of work. The first means that your employer has not found something for you to do; the second means that you are waiting until he does.

We nowadays think of work as something others find for us to do, call us to do, and pay us to do. No doubt our industrial growth is largely responsible for that. We have accustomed men to think of work that way.

In my own case, I was able to find work for others as well as myself. Outside my family life, nothing has given me more satisfaction than to see jobs increase in number and in profit to the men who handle them. And, beyond question, the jobs of the world today are more numerous and profitable in wages than they were even eighteen year ago.

But something entirely outside the workshops of the nation has affected this hired employment very seriously. The word "unemployment" has become one of the most dreadful words in the language. The condition itself has become the concern of every person in the country.

When this condition arrived, there were just three things to be done. The first, of course, was to maintain employment at the maximum by every means known to management. Employment—hire—was what the people were accustomed to; they preferred it; it was the immediate solution of the difficulty. In our plants we used every expedient to spread as much employment over as many employees as was possible. I don't believe in "make work"—the public pays for all unnecessary work—but there are times when the plight of others compels us to do the human thing even though it be but a makeshift; and I am obliged to admit that, like most manufacturers, we avoided layoffs by continuing work that good business judgment would have halted. All of our nonprofit work was continued in full force and much of the shop work. There were always tens of thousands employed—the lowest point at Dearborn was 40,000—but there were always thousands unemployed or so meagerly employed that the situation was far from desirable.

When all possible devices for providing employment have been used and fall short, there remains no alternative but self-help or charity.

I do not believe in routine charity. I think it a shameful thing that any man should have to stoop to take it, or give it. I do not include human helpfulness under the name of charity. My quarrel with charity is that it is neither helpful nor human. The charity of our cities is the most barbarous thing in our system, with the possible exception of our prisons. What we call charity is a modern substitute for being personally kind, personally concerned, and personally involved in the work of helping others in difficulty. True charity is a much more costly effort than money-giving. Our donations too often purchase exemption from giving the only form of help that will drive the need for charity out of the land.

Our own theory of helping people has been in operation for some years. We used to discuss it years ago—when no one could be persuaded to listen. Those who asked public attention to these matters were ridiculed by the very people who now call most loudly for someone to do something.

Our own work involves the usual emergency relief, hospitalization, adjustment of debt, with this addition—we help people to alter their affairs in commonsense accordance with changed conditions, and we have an understanding that all help received should be repaid in reasonable amounts in better times. Many families were not so badly off as they thought; they needed guidance in the management of their resources and opportunities. Human nature, of course, presented the usual problems. Relying on human sympathy many develop a spirit of professional indigence. But where cooperation is given, honest and self-respecting persons and families can usually be assisted to a condition which is much less distressing than they feared.

One of our responsibilities, voluntarily assumed—not because it was ours but because there seemed to be no one else to assume it—was the care of a village of several hundred families whose condition was pretty low. Ordinarily, a large welfare fund would have been needed to accomplish anything for these people. In this instance, we set the people at work cleaning up their homes and backyards, and then cleaning up the roads of their town, and then plowing up about 500 acres of vacant land around their houses. We abolished everything that savored of "handout" charity, opening instead a modern commissary where personal I O U's were accepted, and a garment-making school, and setting the cobblers and tailors of the community to work for their neighbors. We found the people heavily burdened with debt, and we acted informally as their agents in apportioning their income to straighten their affairs. Many families are now out of debt for the first time in years. There has appeared in this village, not only a new spirit of confidence in life but also a new sense of economic values and an appreciation of economic independence which we feel will not soon be lost.

None of these things could have been accomplished by paying out welfare funds after the orthodox manner. The only true charity for these people was somehow to get under their burdens with them and lend them the value of our experience to show them what can be done by people in their circumstances.

Our visiting staff in city work has personally handled thousands of cases in the manner above described. And while no institution can shoulder all the burden, we feel that merely to mitigate present distress is not enough—we feel that thousands of families have been prepared for a better way of life when the wheels of activity begin turning again.

But there is still another way, a third way, so much better than the very best charitable endeavor that it simply forbids us to be satisfied with anything less. That is the way of Self-Help.

SOURCE: Ford, Henry. "On Unemployment." *Literary Digest* (11–18 June 1932).

LETTER TO FRANKLIN ROOSEVELT ON JOB DISCRIMINATION
(20 December 1933, by Frances M. Kubicki)

Massive unemployment and layoffs were among the most devastating effects of America's Great Depression. Unemployment rose from 1.5 million in 1926 to 2.7 million in 1929, and one hundred thousand Americans lost their jobs every week between October 1929 and March 1933. President Franklin Roosevelt's New Deal offered relief in the form of public works projects, federal banking insurance, the development of social security, and the passage of the National Recovery Act (NRA), among other things. Passed in June 1933, the NRA attempted to alleviate unemployment by establishing regulatory business codes. Though the NRA was successful, disenfranchised populations of American workers, such as single women, continued to struggle for fair labor practices. In this letter to President Roosevelt, Frances Kubicki explains the particular difficulties faced by the single working woman.

Leah Shafer,
Cornell University

See also **Discrimination: Sex; Women in Public Life, Business, and Professions.**

Kansas City, Missouri.
December 20th, 1933.

President Franklin D. Roosevelt,
Washington, D. C.
United States of America.

Dear Mister President;
Having long been an admirer of your integrity and wisdom, I am taking the liberty of writing to you of a problem which is getting more serious each day.

I am thirty seven years old, and for fourteen years held the position of assistant bookkeeper in a large department store in Kansas City. Recently, this company changed hands, the new president bringing in an efficiency engineer. This man put in a new system in the office, which required bookkeeping machines and calculators. So far, there has been eight of us to lose our jobs.

No consideration was given as to who needed jobs, in fact is seemed that those who needed them most, were fired. Not one married woman in that office was fired, and each and every one of them has a husband employed. This deplorable condition seems to be prevalent in this city and other cities of this country. Every-where I go to look for a job I find these women, some of them my friends, working—and I have found that nine cases out of ten their husbands have good jobs. I do believe there are about ten percent of these cases where husbands are out of work.

I understand that some employers say that the married woman is more efficient. Naturally, the half-starved, worried, single woman hasn't a chance with a well-kept married woman who has two incomes to meet her greedy demands. I have come in contact with quite a few single women since I have been out of work, and many of them are eating only one or two meals a day. My heart aches for these women, Mr. President, and I know you would feel the same way, if you knew this condition as it really exists.

The greedy type of married woman does not only cheat her single sisters, but she makes conditions worse for the single and married men who are out of work. They are also a stumbling-block to the boy and girl out of school. The people of Kansas City are greatly incensed over this, but of course it is up to the employers to act-and only a few of them have done so. So far, the N. R. A. has done nothing about it. It seems to me, Mr. President, that it could be handled through this source.

Wishing you and yours a Glorious Christmas and a Merry New Year, I am

Sincerely,
Miss Frances M. Kubicki,

FIRESIDE CHAT ON THE BANK CRISIS
(12 March 1933)

The months surrounding the October 1929 stock market crash saw that market lose $30 billion dollars in value. By the time Franklin D. Roosevelt (1882–1945) was inaugurated on March 4, 1933, the American banking system had collapsed. The frantic public was withdrawing its savings in record numbers and the banks, already strapped by the stock market crash, were incapable of supplying enough currency to meet the public's needs. On the day after he was inaugurated, President Roosevelt, invoking the 1917 Trading with the Enemy Act, closed all American banks for a "bank holiday." While the banks were closed, Congress developed a program of rehabilitation for the banks and the Federal Reserve released extra currency. On March 12, 1933, the day before the banks were to reopen, President Roosevelt delivered his first "fireside chat" radio address to the American public. In his reassuring address, Roosevelt outlined the steps the government was taking to secure currency and bring equilibrium back to the banks. The chat, which reached an estimated sixty million people, restored public confidence and led to a short-term restabilizing of the American economy.

Leah Shafer,
Cornell University

See also **Banking; Federal Reserve System; Radio.**

I want to talk for a few minutes with the people of the United States about banking—with the comparatively few who understand the mechanics of banking but more particularly with the overwhelming majority who use banks for the making of deposits and the drawing of checks. I want to tell you what has been done in the last few days, why it was done, and what the next steps are going to be. I recognize that the many proclamations from State Capitols and from Washington, the legislation, the Treasury regulations, etc., couched for the most part in banking and legal terms should be explained for the benefit of the average citizen. I owe this in particular because of the fortitude and good temper with which everybody has accepted the inconvenience and hardships of the banking holiday. I know that when you understand what we in Washington have been about I shall continue to have your cooperation as fully as I have had your sympathy and help during the past week.

First of all let me state the simple fact that when you deposit money in a bank the bank does not put the money into a safe deposit vault. It invests your money in many different forms of credit-bonds, commercial paper, mortgages and many other kinds of loans. In other words, the bank puts your money to work to keep the wheels of industry and of agriculture turning around. A comparatively small part of the money you put into the bank is kept in currency—an amount which in normal times is wholly sufficient to cover the cash needs of the average citizen. In other words the total amount of all the currency in the country is only a small fraction of the total deposits in all of the banks.

What, then, happened during the last few days of February and the first few days of March? Because of undermined confidence on the part of the public, there was a general rush by a large portion of our population to turn bank deposits into currency or gold.—A rush so great that the soundest banks could not get enough currency to meet the demand. The reason for this was that on the spur of the moment it was, of course, impossible to sell perfectly sound assets of a bank and convert them into cash except at panic prices far below their real value.

By the afternoon of March 3 scarcely a bank in the country was open to do business.

Proclamations temporarily closing them in whose or in part had been issued by the Governors in almost all the states.

It was then that I issued the proclamation providing for the nation-wide bank holiday, and this was the first step in the Government's reconstruction of our financial and economic fabric.

The second step was the legislation promptly and patriotically passed by the Congress confirming my proclamation and broadening my powers so that it became possible in view of the requirement of time to entend (sic) the holiday and lift the ban of that holiday gradually. This law also gave authority to develop a program of rehabilitation of our banking facilities. I want to tell our citizens in every part of the Nation that the national Congress—Republicans and Democrats alike—showed by this action a devotion to public welfare and a realization of the emergency and the necessity for speed that it is difficult to match in our history.

The third stage has been the series of regulations permitting the banks to continue their functions to take care of the distribution of food and household necessities and the payment of payrolls.

This bank holiday while resulting in many cases in great inconvenience is affording us the opportunity to supply the currency necessary to meet the situation. No sound bank is a dollar worse off than it was when it closed its doors last Monday. Neither is any bank which may turn out not to be in a position for immediate opening. The new law allows the twelve Federal Reserve banks to issue additional currency on good assets and thus the banks which reopen will be able to meet every legitimate call. The new currency is being sent out by the Bureau of Engraving and Printing in large volume to every part of the country. It is sound currency because it is backed by actual, good assets.

As a result we start tomorrow, Monday, with the opening of banks in the twelve Federal Reserve bank cities—those banks which on first examination by the Treasury have already been found to be all right. This will be followed on Tuesday by the resumption of all their functions by banks already found to be sound in cities where there are recognized clearing houses. That means about 250 cities of the United States.

On Wednesday and succeeding days banks in smaller places all through the country will resume business, subject, of course, to the Government's physical ability to complete its survey. It is necessary that the reopening of banks be extended over a period in order to permit the banks to make applications for necessary loans, to obtain currency needed to meet their requirements and to enable the Government to make common sense checkups. Let me make it clear to you that if your bank does not open the first day you are by no means justified in believing that it will not open. A bank that opens on one of the subsequent days is in exactly the same status as the bank that opens tomorrow.

I know that many people are worrying about State banks not members of the Federal Reserve System. These banks can and will receive assistance from members banks and from the Reconstruction Finance Corporation. These state banks are following the same course as the national banks except that they get their licenses to resume business from the state authorities, and these authorities have been asked by the Secretary of the Treasury to permit their good banks to open up on the same schedule as the national banks. I am confident that the state banking departments will be as careful as the National Government in the policy relating to the opening of banks and will follow the same broad policy. It is possible that when the banks resume a very few people who have not recovered from their fear may again begin withdrawals. Let me make it clear that the banks will take care of all needs—and it is my belief that hoarding during the past week has become an exceedingly unfashionable pastime. It needs no prophet to tell you that when the people find that they can get their money—that they can get it when they want it for all legitimate purposes—the phantom of fear will soon be laid. People will again be glad to have their money where it will be safely taken care of and where they can use it conveniently at any time. I can assure you that it is safer to keep your money in a reopened bank than under the mattress.

The success of our whole great national program depends, of course, upon the cooperation of the public—on its intelligent support and use of a reliable system.

Remember that the essential accomplishment of the new legislation is that it makes it possible for banks more readily to convert their assets into cash than was the case before. More liberal provision has been made for banks to borrow on these assets at the Reserve Banks and more liberal provision has also been made for issuing currency on the security of those good assets. This currency is not fiat currency. It is issued only on adequate security—and every good bank has an abundance of such security.

One more point before I close. There will be, of course, some banks unable to reopen without being reorganized. The new law allows the Government to assist in making these reorganizations quickly and effectively and even allows the Government to subscribe to at least a part of new capital which may be required.

I hope you can see from this elemental recital of what your government is doing that there is nothing complex, or radical in the process.

We had a bad banking situation. Some of our bankers had shown themselves either incompetent or dishonest in their handling of the people's funds. They had used the money entrusted to them in speculations and unwise loans. This was of course not true in the vast majority of our banks but it was true in enough of them to shock the people for a time into a sense of insecurity and to put them into a frame of mind where they did not differentiate, but seemed to assume that the acts of a comparative few had tainted them all. It was the Government's job to straighten out this situation and do it as quickly as possible—and the job is being performed.

I do not promise you that every bank will be reopened or that individual losses will not be suffered, but there will be no losses that possibly could be avoided; and there would have been more and greater losses had we continued to drift. I can even promise you salvation for some at least of the sorely pressed banks. We shall be engaged not merely in reopening sound banks but in the creation of sound banks through reorganization. It has been wonderful to me to catch the note of confidence from all over the country. I can never be sufficiently grateful to the people for the loyal support they have given me in their acceptance of the judgment that has dictated our course, even though all of our processes may not have seemed clear to them.

After all there is an element in the readjustment of our financial system more important than currency, more important than gold, and that is the confidence of the people. Confidence and courage are the essentials of success in carrying out our plan. You people must have faith; you must not be stampeded by rumors or guesses. Let us unite in banishing fear. We have provided the machinery to restore our financial system; it is up to you to support and make it work.

It is your problem no less than it is mine. Together we cannot fail.

SOURCE: *Fireside Chat on the Bank Crisis.* Courtesy of Franklin D. Roosevelt Library, Hyde Park, N.Y.

EXCERPT FROM *LAND OF THE SPOTTED EAGLE (1933, by Luther Standing Bear)*

For many Americans in the early twentieth century, the problems of Native Americans too often seemed distant concerns. A hereditary chief of the Dakotas, and one of the first students to attend the Carlisle Indian School in Pennsylvania, Luther Standing Bear (born Ota Kte) was an advocate for reform in the United States government's often neglectful policies toward Native Americans. Much of his writing addresses the inequities and injustices of a system that consigned Indians to life on reservations without adequate schools, housing, or medicine. The author of four books about the effects of governmental negligence on Indian life, Luther Standing Bear was a member of the National League for Justice to the American Indian, a former star in Buffalo Bill's Wild West Show, and an actor in several Hollywood motion pictures. A year after the publication of *The Land of the Spotted Eagle,* Congress passed the Indian Reorganization Act (1934), legislation designed to return to Native Americans control of reservation resources, reduce disproportionately high unemployment rates, and restore the administrative authority of individual tribes.

Laura M. Miller,
Vanderbilt University

See also **Carlisle Indian School; Indian Policy, U.S.: 1900–2000; Indian Political Life; Indian Reorganization Act; Wild West Show.**

What the Indian Means to America

THE feathered and blanketed figure of the American Indian has come to symbolize the American continent. He is the man who through centuries has been moulded and sculped by the same hand that shaped its mountains, forests, and plains, and marked the course of its rivers.

The American Indian is of the soil, whether it be the region of forests, plains, pueblos, or mesas. He fits into the landscape, for the hand that fashioned the continent also fashioned the man for his surroundings. He once grew a naturally as the wild sunflowers; he belongs just as the buffalo belonged.

With a physique that fitted, the man developed fitting skills—crafts which today are called American. And the body had a soul, also formed and moulded by the same master hand of harmony. Out of the Indian approach to existence there came a great freedom—an intense and absorbing love for nature; a respect for life; enriching faith in a Supreme Power; and principles of truth, honesty, generosity, equity, and brotherhood as a guide to mundane relations.

Becoming possessed of a fitting philosophy and art, it was by them that native man perpetuated his identity; stamped it into the history and soul of this country—made land and man one.

By living—struggling, losing, meditating, imbibing, aspiring, achieving—he wrote himself into ineraceable evidence—an evidence that can be and often has been ignored, but never totally destroyed. Living—and all the intangible forces that constitute that phenomenon—are brought into being by Spirit, that which no man can alter. Only the hand of the Supreme Power can transform man; only Wakan Tanka can transform the Indian. But of such deep and infinite graces finite man has little comprehension. He has, therefore, no weapons with which to slay the unassailable. He can only foolishly trample.

The white man does not understand the Indian for the reason that he does not understand America. He is too far removed from its formative processes. The roots of the tree of his life have not yet grasped the rock and soil. The white man is still troubled with primitive fears; he still has in his consciousness the perils of this frontier continent, some of its fastnesses not yet having yielded to his questing footsteps and inquiring eyes. He shudders still with the memory of the loss of his forefathers upon its scorching deserts and forbidding mountain-tops. The man from Europe is still a foreigner and an alien. And he still hates the man who questioned his path across the continent.

But in the Indian the spirit of the land is still vested; it will be until other men are able to divine and meet its rhythm. Men must be born and reborn to belong. Their bodies must be formed of the dust of their forefathers' bones.

The attempted transformation of the Indian by the white man and the chaos that has resulted are but the fruits of the white man's disobedience of a fundamental and spiritual law. The pressure that has been brought to bear upon the native people, since the cessation of armed conflict, in the attempt to force conformity of custom and habit has caused a reaction more destructive than war, and the injury has not only affected the Indian, but has extended to the white population as well. Tyranny, stupidity, and lack of vision have brought about the situation now alluded to as the 'Indian Problem.'

There is, I insist, no Indian problem as created by the Indian himself. Every problem that exists today in regard to the native population is due to the white man's cast of mind, which is unable, at least reluctant, to seek understanding and achieve adjustment in a new and a significant environment into which it has so recently come.

The white man excused his presence here by saying that he had been guided by the will of his God; and in so saying absolved himself of all responsibility for his appearance in a land occupied by other men.

Then, too, his law was a written law; his divine decalogue reposed in a book. And what better proof that his advent into this country and his subsequent acts were the result of divine will! He brought the Word! There ensued a blind worship of written history, of books, of the written word, that has denuded the spoken word of its power and scaredness. The written word became established as a criterion of the superior man—a symbol of emotional fineness. The man who could write his name on a piece of paper, whether or not he possessed the spiritual fineness to honor those words in speech, was by some miraculous formula a more highly developed and sensitized person than the one who had never had a pen in hand, but whose spoken word was inviolable and whose sense of honor and truth was paramount. With false reasoning was the quality of human character measured by man's ability to make with an implement a mark upon paper. But granting this mode of reasoning be correct and just, then where are to be placed the thousands of illiterate whites who are unable to read and write? Are they, too, 'savages'? Is not humanness a matter of heart and mind, and is it not evident in the form of relationship with men? Is not kindness more powerful than arrogance; and truth more powerful than the sword?

True, the white man brought great change. But the varied fruits of his civilization, though highly colored and inviting, are sickening and deadening. And if it be the part of civilization to maim, rob, and thwart, then what is progress?

I am going to venture that the man who sat on the ground in his tipi meditating on life and its meaning, accepting the kinship of all creatures, and acknowledging unity with the universe of things was infusing into his being the true essence of civilization. And when native man left off this form of development, his humanization was retarded in growth.

Another most powerful agent that gave native man promise of developing into a true human was the responsibility accepted by parenthood. Mating among Lakotas was motivated, of course, by the same laws of attraction that motivate all beings; however, considerable thought was given by parents of both boy and girl to the choosing of mates. And a still greater advantage accrued to the race by the law of self-mastery which the young couple voluntarily placed upon themselves as soon as they discovered they were to become parents. Immediately, and for some time after, the sole thought of the parents was in preparing the child for life. And true civilization lies in the dominance of self and not in the dominance of other men.

How far this idea would have gone in carrying my people upward and toward a better plane of existence, or how much of an influence it was in the development of their spiritual being, it is not possible to say. But it had its promises. And it cannot be gainsaid that the man who is rising to a higher estate is the man who is putting into his being the essence of humanism. It is self-effort that develops, and by this token the greatest factor today in dehumanizing races is the manner in which the machine is used—the product of one man's brain doing the work for another. The hand is the tool that has built man's mind; it, too, can refine it.

The Savage

After subjugation, after dispossession, there was cast the last abuse upon the people who so entirely resented their wrongs and punishments, and that was the stamping and the labeling of them as savages. To make this label stick has been the task of the white race and the greatest salve that it has been able to apply to its sore and troubled conscience now hardened through the habitual practice of injustice.

But all the years of calling the Indian a savage has never made him one; all the denial of his virtues has never taken them from him; and the very resistance he has made to save the things inalienably his has been his saving strength—that which will stand him in need when justice does make its belated appearance and he undertakes rehabilitation.

All sorts of feeble excuses are heard for the continued subjection of the Indian. One of the most common is that he is not yet ready to accept the society of the white man—that he is not yet ready to mingle as a social entity.

This, I maintain, is beside the question. The matter is not one of making-over the external Indian into the likeness of the white race—a process detrimental to both races. Who can say that the white man's way is better for the Indian? Where resides the human judgment with the competence to weigh and value Indian ideals and spiritual concepts; or substitute for them other values?

Then, has the white man's social order been so harmonious and ideal as to merit the respect of the Indian, and for that matter the thinking class of the white race? Is it wise to urge upon the Indian a foreign social form? Let none but the Indian answer!

Rather, let the white brother face about and cast his mental eye upon a new angle of vision. Let him look upon the Indian world as a human world; then let him see to it that human rights be accorded to the Indians.

And this for the purpose of retaining for his own order of society a measure of humanity.

The Indian School of Thought

I say again that Indians should teach Indians; that Indians should serve Indians, especially on reservations where the older people remain. There is a definite need of the old for the care and sympathy of the young and they are today perishing for the joys that naturally belong to old Indian people. Old Indians are very close to their progeny. It was their delightful duty to care for and instruct the very young, while in turn they looked forward to being cared for by sons and daughters. These were the privileges and blessings of old age.

Many of the grievances of the old Indian, and his disagreements with the young, find root in the far-removed boarding-school which sometimes takes the little ones at a very tender age. More than one tragedy has resulted when a young boy or girl has returned home again almost an utter stranger. I have seen these happenings with my own eyes and I know they can cause naught but suffering. The old Indian cannot, even if he wished, reconcile himself to an institution that alienates his young. And there is something evil in a system that brings about an unnatural reaction to life; when it makes young hearts callous and unheedful of the needs and joys of the old.

The old people do not speak English and they never will be English-speaking. To place upon such people the burden of understanding and functioning through an office bound up with the routine and red tape of the usual Government office is silly and futile, and every week or so I receive letters from the reservation evidencing this fact. The Indian's natural method of settling questions is by council and conference. From time immemorial, for every project affecting their material, social, and spiritual lives, the people have met together to 'talk things over.'

To the end that young Indians will be able to appreciate both their traditional life and modern life they should be doubly educated. Without forsaking reverence for their ancestral teachings, they can be trained to take up modern duties that relate to tribal and reservation life. And there is no problem of reservation importance but can be solved by the joint efforts of the old and the young Indians.

There certainly can be no doubt in the public mind today as to the capacity of the younger Indians in taking on white modes and manners. For many years, and particularly since the days of General Pratt, the young Indian has been proving his efficiency when entering the fields of white man's endeavor and has done well in copying and acquiring the ways of the white man.

The Indian liked the white man's horse and straightway became an expert horseman; he threw away his age-old weapons, the bow and arrow, and matched the white man's skill with gun and pistol; in the field of sports—games of strength and skill—the Indian enters with no shame in comparison; the white man's beads the Indian woman took, developed a technique and an art distinctly her own with no competitor in design; and in the white man's technique of song and dance the Indian has made himself a creditable exponent.

However, despite the fact that Indian schools have been established over several generations, there is a dearth of Indians in the professions. It is most noticeable on the reservations where the numerous positions of consequence are held by white employees instead of trained Indians. For instance, why are not the stores, post-offices, and Government office jobs on the Sioux Reservation held by trained Indians? Why cannot Sioux be reservation nurses and doctors; and road-builders too? Much road work goes on every summer, but the complaint is constant that it is always done by white workmen, and in such manner as to necessitate its being done again in a short time. Were these numerous positions turned over to trained Indians, the white population would soon find reservation life less attractive and less lucrative.

With school facilities already fairly well established and the capability of the Indian unquestioned, every reservation could well be supplied with Indian doctors, nurses, engineers, road- and bridge-builders, draughtsmen, architects, dentists, lawyers, teachers, and instructors in tribal lore, legends, orations, song, dance, and ceremonial ritual. The Indian, by the very sense of duty, should become his own historian, giving his account of the race—fairer and fewer accounts of the wars and more of state-craft, legends, languages, oratory, and philosophical conceptions. No longer should the Indian be dehumanized in order to make material for lurid and cheap fiction to embellish street-stands. Rather, a fair and correct history of the native American should be incorporated in the curriculum of the public school.

Caucasian youth is fed, and rightly so, on the feats and exploits of their old-world heroes, their revolutionary forefathers, their adventurous pioneer trail-blazers, and in our Southwest through pageants, fiestas, and holidays the days of the Spanish *conquistador* is kept alive.

But Indian youth! They, too, have fine pages in their past history; they, too, have patriots and heroes. And it is not fair to rob Indian youth of their history, the stories of their patriots, which, if impartially written, would fill them with pride and dignity. Therefore, give back to Indian youth all, everything in their heritage that belongs to them and augment it with the best in the modern schools. I repeat, doubly educate the Indian boy and girl.

What a contrast this would make in comparison with the present unhealthy, demoralized place the reservation is today, where the old are poorly fed, shabbily clothed, divested of pride and incentive; and where the young are unfitted for tribal life and untrained for the world of white man's affairs except to hold an occasional job!

Why not a school of Indian thought, built on the Indian pattern and conducted by Indian instructors? Why not a school of tribal art?

Why should not America be cognizant of itself; aware of its identity? In short, why should not America be preserved?

There were ideals and practices in the life of my ancestors that have not been improved upon by the present-day civilization; there were in our culture elements of benefit; and there were influences that would broaden any life. But that almost an entire public needs to be enlightened as to this fact need not be discouraging. For many centuries the human mind labored under the delusion that the world was flat; and thousands of men have believed that the heavens were supported by the strength of an Atlas. The human mind is not yet free from fallacious reasoning; it is not yet an open mind and its deepest recesses are not yet swept free of errors.

But it is now time for a destructive order to be reversed, and it is well to inform other races that the aboriginal culture of America was not devoid of beauty. Furthermore, in denying the Indian his ancestral rights and heritages the white race is but robbing itself. But America can be revived, rejuvenated, by recognizing a native school of thought. The Indian can save America.

The Living Spirit of the Indian—His Art

The spiritual health and existence of the Indian was maintained by song, magic, ritual, dance, symbolism, oratory (or council), design, handicraft, and folk-story.

Manifestly, to check or thwart this expression is to bring about spiritual decline. And it is in this condition of decline that the Indian people are today. There is but a feeble effort among the Sioux to keep alive their traditional songs and dances, while among other tribes there is but a half-hearted attempt to offset the influence of the Government school and at the same time recover from the crushing and stifling regime of the Indian Bureau.

One has but to speak of Indian verse to receive uncomprehending and unbelieving glances. Yet the Indian loved verse and into this mode of expression went his deepest feelings. Only a few ardent and advanced students seem interested; nevertheless, they have given in book form enough Indian translations to set forth the character and quality of Indian verse.

Oratory receives a little better understanding on the part of the white public, owing to the fact that oratorical compilations include those of Indian orators.

Hard as it seemingly is for the white man's ear to sense the differences, Indian songs are as varied as the many emotions which inspire them, for no two of them are alike. For instance, the Song of Victory is spirited and the notes high and remindful of an unrestrained hunter or warrior riding exultantly over the prairies. On the other hand, the song of the *Cano unye* is solemn and full of urge, for it is meant to inspire the young men to deeds of valor. Then there are the songs of death and the spiritual songs which are connected with the ceremony of initiation. These are full of the spirit of praise and worship, and so strong are some of these invocations that the very air seems as if surcharged with the presence of the Big Holy.

The Indian loved to worship. From birth to death he revered his surroundings. He considered himself born in the luxurious lap of Mother Earth and no place was to him humble. There was nothing between him and the Big Holy. The contact was immediate and personal, and the blessings of Wakan Tanka flowed over the Indian like rain showered from the sky. Wakan Tanka was not aloof, apart, and ever seeking to quell evil forces. He did not punish the animals and the birds, and likewise He did not punish man. He was not a punishing God. For there was never a question as to the supremacy of an evil power over and above the power of Good. There was but one ruling power, and that was *Good.*

Of course, none but an adoring one could dance for days with his face to the sacred sun, and that time is all but done. We cannot have back the days of the buffalo and beaver; we cannot win back our clean blood-stream and superb health, and we can never again expect that beautiful *rapport* we once had with Nature. The springs and lakes have dried and the mountains are bare of forests. The plow has changed the face of the world. Wiwila is dead! No more may we heal our sick and comfort our dying with a strength founded on faith, for even the animals now fear us, and fear supplants faith.

And the Indian wants to dance! It is his way of expressing devotion, of communing with unseen power, and in keeping his tribal identity. When the Lakota heart was filled with high emotion, he danced. When he felt the benediction of the warming rays of the sun, he danced. When his blood ran hot with success of the hunt or chase, he danced. When his heart was filled with pity for the orphan, the lonely father, or bereaved mother, he danced. All the joys and exaltations of life, all his gratefulness and thankfulness, all his acknowledgments of the mysterious power that guided life, and all his aspirations for a better life, culminated in one great dance—the Sun Dance.

Today we see our young people dancing together the silly jazz—dances that add nothing to the beauty and fineness of our lives and certainly nothing to our history, while the dances that record the life annals of a people die. It is the American Indian who contributes to this country its true folk-dancing, growing, as we did, out of the soil. The dance is far older than his legends, songs, or philosophy.

Did dancing mean much to the white people they would better understand ours. Yet at the same time there is no attraction that brings people from such distances as a certain tribal dance, for the reason that the white mind senses its mystery, for even the white man's inmost feelings are unconsciously stirred by the beat of the tomtom. They are heart-beats, and once all men danced to its rhythm.

When the Indian has forgotten the music of his forefathers, when the sound of the tomtom is no more, when noisy jazz has drowned the melody of the flute, he will be a dead Indian. When the memory of his heroes are no longer told in story, and he forsakes the beautiful white buckskin for factory shoddy, he will be dead. When from him has been taken all that is his, all that he has visioned in nature, all that has come to him from infinite sources, he then, truly, will be a dead Indian. His spirit will be gone, and though he walk crowded streets, he will, in truth, be—*dead!*

But all this must not perish; it must live, to the end that America shall be educated no longer to regard native production of whatever tribe—folk-story, basketry, pottery, dance, song, poetry—as curios, and native artists as curiosities. For who but the man indigenous to the soil could produce its song, story, and folk-tale; who but the man who loved the dust beneath his feet could shape it and put it into undying, ceramic form; who but he who loved the reeds that grew beside still waters, and the damp roots of shrub and tree, could save it from seasonal death, and with almost superhuman patience weave it into enduring objects of beauty—into timeless art!

Regarding the 'civilization' that has been thrust upon me since the days of reservation, it has not added one whit to my sense of justice; to my reverence for the rights of life; to my love for truth, honesty, and generosity; nor to my faith in Wakan Tanka—God of the Lakotas. For after all the great religions have been preached and expounded, or have been revealed by brilliant scholars, or have been written in books and embellished in fine language with finer covers, man—all man—is still confronted with the Great Mystery.

So if today I had a young mind to direct, to start on the journey of life, and I was faced with the duty of choosing between the natural way of my forefathers and that of the white man's present way of civilization, I would, for its welfare, unhesitatingly set that child's feet in the path of my forefathers. I would raise him to be an Indian!

SOURCE: Standing Bear, Luther. *Land of the Spotted Eagle.* Boston: Houghton Mifflin, 1933.

LIVING IN THE DUST BOWL
(1934, by Anne Marie Low)

The settlement of the Great Plains states in the late nineteenth and early twentieth century provided the growing nation with agricultural riches and a bustling farm economy, but the rapid development of previously arid lands into massive wheat fields had a detrimental effect upon the land itself. Where buffalo grass had previously provided nutrients and kept soil anchored to the ground, the newly plowed wheat fields left the soil exposed to the elements. In the summer of 1934, with conditions exacerbated by a long drought, winds began to whip the sun-baked soil into thick, dark, low-riding clouds of dust. In April, Kansas, Texas, Oklahoma, Colorado, and New Mexico were all hit with a devastating dust storm. The dust clouds assaulted everything, destroying crops, killing livestock, and suffocating settlers. It is estimated that in April and May of 1934, more than 650,000,000 tons of topsoil were blown off the plains. In this selection, Ann Marie Low, a young woman whose family farm was in North Dakota, writes in her diary about the dust storm. When we read that Low had to wash the washing machine before she could wash clothes, we begin to appreciate the extraordinary difficulties faced by those trying to survive the storm.

Leah R. Shafer,
Cornell University

See also **Dust Bowl; Great Plains.**

April 25, 1934, Wednesday
Last weekend was the worst dust storm we ever had. We've been having quite a bit of blowing dirt every year since the drought started, not only here, but all over the Great Plains. Many days this spring the air is just full of dirt coming, literally, for hundreds of miles. It sifts into everything. After we wash the dishes and put them away, so much dust sifts into the cupboards we must wash them again before the next meal. Clothes in the closets are covered with dust.

Last weekend no one was taking an automobile out for fear of ruining the motor. I rode Roany to Frank's place to return a gear. To find my way I had to ride right beside the fence, scarcely able to see from one fence post to the next.

Newspapers say the deaths of many babies and old people are attributed to breathing in so much dirt.

May 21, 1934, Monday
Saturday Dad, Bud, and I planted an acre of potatoes. There was so much dirt in the air I couldn't see Bud only a few feet in front of me. Even the air in the house was just a haze. In the evening the wind died down, and Cap came to take me to the movie. We joked about how hard it is to get cleaned up enough to go anywhere.

The newspapers report that on May 10 there was such a strong wind the experts in Chicago estimated 12,000,000 tons of Plains soil was dumped on that city. By the next day the sun was obscured in Washington, District of Columbia, and ships 300 miles out at sea reported dust settling on their decks.

Sunday the dust wasn't so bad. Dad and I drove cattle to the Big Pasture. Then I churned butter and baked a ham, bread, and cookies for the men, as no telling when Mama will be back.

May 30, 1934, Wednesday
Ethel got along fine, so Mama left her at the hospital and came to Jamestown by train Friday. Dad took us both home.

The mess was incredible! Dirt had blown into the house all week and lay inches deep on everything. Every towel and curtain was just black. There wasn't a clean dish or cooking utensil. There was no food. Oh, there were eggs and milk and one loaf left of the bread I baked the weekend before. I looked in the cooler box down the well (our refrigerator) and found a little ham and butter. It was late, so Mama and I cooked some ham and eggs for the men's supper because that was all we could fix in a hurry. It turned out they had been living on ham and eggs for two days.

Mama was very tired. After she had fixed starter for bread, I insisted she go to bed and I'd do all the dishes.

It took until 10 o'clock to wash all the dirty dishes. That's not wiping them—just washing them. The cupboards had to be washed out to have a clean place to put them.

Saturday was a busy day. Before starting breakfast I had to sweep and wash all the dirt off the kitchen and dining room floors, wash the stove, pancake griddle, and dining room table and chairs. There was cooking, baking, and churning to be done for those hungry men. Dad is 6 feet 4 inches tall, with a big frame. Bud is 6 feet 3 inches and almost as big-boned as Dad. We say feeding them is like filling a silo.

Mama couldn't make bread until I carried water to wash the bread mixer. I couldn't churn until the churn was washed and scalded. We just couldn't do anything until something was washed first. Every room had to have dirt almost shoveled out of it before we could wash floors and furniture.

We had no time to wash clothes, but it was necessary. I had to wash out the boiler, wash tubs, and the washing machine before we could use them. Then every towel, curtain, piece of bedding, and garment had to be taken outdoors to have as much dust as possible shaken out before washing. The cistern is dry, so I had to carry all the water we needed from the well.

That evening Cap came to take me to the movie, as usual. Ixnay. I'm sorry I snapped at Cap. It isn't his fault, or anyone's fault, but I was tired and cross. Life in what the newspapers call "the Dust Bowl" is becoming a gritty nightmare.

SOURCE: Low, Ann Marie. *Dust Bowl Diary*. Lincoln: University of Nebraska Press, 1984.

FORD MEN BEAT AND ROUT LEWIS
(26 May 1937, newspaper account)

The automobile industry was the leading industry in the American economy in the 1920s and 1930s, with about ten percent of Americans' annual income going to car-related items, including gasoline. As such, the industry took a great hit during the Great Depression and large numbers of employees were laid off. Believing their only chance for job security lay in unionization, automobile workers began to organize in the late 1930s. All major auto manufacturers at the time (General Motors, Chevrolet, and Ford) were opposed to unionization and employed violence and spies in an effort to resist, but the Ford Service Department, headed by Harry Bennett, was most notorious for its ill treatment. On May 26, 1937, United Automobile Workers (UAW) union organizers Dick Frankensteen and Walter Reuther and their supporters were viciously attacked as they attempted to distribute pamphlets to Ford employees. Though Ford claimed the organizers had set up the incident to gain sympathy, the attack solidified support for the UAW, which eventually won the right to unionize Ford plants in 1941.

Leah R. Shafer,
Cornell University

***See also* American Federation of Labor–Congress of Industrial Organizations; Automobile Industry; Ford Motor Company; Trade Unions; United Automobile Workers of America.**

16 HURT IN BATTLE

C.I.O. Leader, 7 Women Are Among Injured at Dearborn Plant

FORD PROPERTY CLEARED

Fight Blocks Distribution of Leaflets—Union and Company Blame Each Other

NLRB INVESTIGATION BEGUN

County Prosecutor Also Taker Action—U. A. W. A. Asks National Demonstrations

Day's Strike Developments

Ford workers beat union organizers and chased them from the Ford Company property in the first battle of the C. I. O. drive at the Rouge plant. Sixteen were reported injured, including seven women. National Labor Board and Wayne County prosecutor began investigations as the company charged a "frame-up" by the union. . . .

Strikes in twenty-seven plants of Republic Steel, Youngstown Sheet and Tube and Inland Steel, employing nearly 80,000 men, and called by S. W. O. C., began at 11 o'clock last night. . . .

The A. F. of L. decided to organize a new maritime department to combat the C. I. O. in shipping centers and offered an industrial union charter to a Chevrolet group in Indianapolis....

The Ford plant at Richmond, Calif., was closed by a strike called by the U. A. W. A. Pickets barred company officials and office workers from the factory and 1,800 workers were made idle....

Battle at Ford Plant

Special to The New York Times.

DETROIT, May 26.—An outburst of violence, in which union representatives were beaten, kicked and driven away, marked today the first attempt of the United Automobile Workers of America to organize the employees of the Ford Motor Company.

Richard T. Frankensteen, directing the membership drive in behalf of the auto affiliate of the Committee for Industrial Organization, and Walter Reuther, president of the West Side local of the automobile workers' union, were set upon by a group of employees at No. 4 gate of the Ford Rouge plant in Dearborn. With two other men who had accompanied them to oversee the distribution of union handbills, they were knocked down repeatedly, kicked, and finally forced away from the gate, despite efforts of Frankensteen to fight off his assailants.

Subsequent fighting, in which employees routed union representatives who had come to distribute leaflets, resulted in the injury of twelve more persons, seven of them women, the union stated.

"It was the worst licking I've ever taken," Frankensteen declared. "They bounced us down the concrete steps of an overpass we had climbed. Then they would knock us down, stand us up, and knock us down again."

Both Frankensteen and Reuther, together with several of the other victims, were treated by physicians.

Accuses Ford Service Men

Members of the Ford service department participated in the attack in an effort to block any union contact with the workers, the union charged in a statement issued later. Spokesmen for the Ford Company denied this, however, and said that the attack had been provoked when the union representatives shouted "scabs" at Ford workmen, in an effort, the company said, to provoke a clash that could be brought to the attention of the Senate's La Follette civil liberties investigation.

Two investigations of the outbreak were under way tonight, one by representatives of the National Labor Relations Board; the other by Duncan C. McCrea, Wayne County prosecutor.

In addition, the union, at headquarters guarded by a watchman with a shotgun, was endeavoring to get an inquiry on charges that the Ford company has violated the Wagner act.

Investigators for the Senate Civil Liberties subcommittee, reported at the scene to watch distribution of the union leaflets, were said to have witnessed the fighting. Frankensteen stated that he had telephoned a report of the outbreak to Governor Murphy of Michigan.

Michigan House Urged to Act

A resolution calling for an investigation by the Michigan House of Representatives was introduced in that body by Representative John F. Hamilton of Detroit.

Clergymen and other persons interested in labor problems had also been invited to be present as observers, but it was not learned how many of these had attended. One of this number, the Rev. Raymond Prior Sanford of Chicago, said that he had witnessed the fighting and had noted one incident in which policemen told workers who had surrounded a group of women union representatives not to molest the women.

The police, however, made no attempt to interfere with the workers, Mr. Sanford stated. While at the scene, the clergyman had declined to comment on the melee, replying, "Ask me somewhere else."

The drive to unionize the plants of the Ford company will not be halted, Frankensteen asserted. As part of the campaign, an appeal went out from union headquarters for support in a plan to organize demonstrations at all Ford service stations throughout the country as a protest, the leader said, against the attack on the union members.

Frankensteen declared:

"If Mr. Ford thinks this will stop us, he's got another think coming. We'll go back there with enough men to lick him at his own game."

Photographers With the Group

With two organizers, Robert Cantor and J. J. Kennedy, Frankensteen and Reuther had climbed on the overpass of the Rouge plant at Gate 4, with a group of newspaper photographers following near them. Frankensteen explained that he thought the spot a good one from which to observe the work of distributing leaflets by other representatives of the union, including women, who had come by auto and by street car.

As the fighting started, some fifty employes, many of them in work clothes, rushed forward and began beating Frankensteen and his party before the four had left the overpass. Frankensteen, 30 years old, of strong build and a former football player, sought for a moment to stand up against his nearest assailants but went down under the weight of numbers.

After he had been driven from the overpass, he attempted several times to fight back. For this reason, witness said, he apparently was more severely pummeled than the others.

Women Forced Back Into Cars

Meanwhile, others of the workmen rushed out and blocked the persons who had arrived to distribute leaflets, entitled "Unionism, Not Fordism." The women of the union party, distinguished by the green berets and arm bands of the U. A. W. A. "emergency brigade," had arrived by street car just as the fighting started.

Parties of workmen surrounded them, forcing them back into the cars, which took them from the scene. The seven women injured, according to the union, were kicked in some cases, stepped on in others, and in others, beaten.

Most of the women, however, alighted from the street cars at near-by stops, stood in the safety islands and distributed their leaflets by throwing them into the automobiles of Ford workers who passed on their way from the plant. The men who had come in automobiles to distribute handbills were unceremoniously bundled into their cars, after some allegedly were beaten, and were forced to drive away.

One organizer received a traffic summons because he left the area with his car so crowded with union men who had been forced into it by the Ford employes, the union said, that police decided he was driving improperly.

Otherwise, Dearborn police who were in the vicinity appeared only to have watched the fighting and to have kept crowds from collecting.

There were no reports of injuries among the Ford employees. So far as could be learned, the only victims of the fighting besides the unionists were several of the photographers at the scene, some of whom were halted by employees and forced to give up their exposed plates.

The outbreak occurred at 2 P. M., at the hour of changing shifts in the great plant, which employs 90,000 men, and was over in fifteen minutes. A half hour later, however, four more union members, evidently tardy, drove up in a sedan, parked on Ford property, and the driver, getting out, asked:

"Now, just where do we have to stand to pass out these handbills, boys?"

One of a group of Ford employees standing at the spot struck the driver in the face. The driver climbed back into the car and drove away.

Harry H. Bennett, head of the Ford company's personnel department, issued this statement after he had made an investigation of the disturbance:

"The affair was deliberately provoked by union officials. They feel, with or without justification, the La Follette Civil Liberties Committee sympathizes with their aims and they simply wanted to trump up a charge of Ford brutality that they could take down to Washington and flaunt before the Senatorial committee.

Charges Taunts by Union Men

"I know definitely no Ford service men or plant police were involved in any way in the fight. As a matter of fact, the service men had issued instructions the union people could come and distribute their pamphlets at the gates so long as they didn't interfere with employees at work.

"The union men were beaten by regular Ford employees who were on their way to work on the afternoon shift. The union men called them scabs and cursed and taunted them. A Negro who works in the foundry was goaded and cursed so viciously by one union organizer that he turned and struck him. That was the first blow struck, and then the workmen and the union men milled around a few minutes, punching at each other and the union men withdrew.

"I would be glad to testify before any official investigating committee and I would have no trouble convincing them that the union cold-bloodedly framed and planned today's disturbance."

Besides Frankensteen, Reuther, Kennedy and Cantor, the names of some of the injured were made public by the union as follows:

Tony Marinovich, kicked, choked and beaten: Estelle Michalek, kicked in the stomach; Catherine Gelles, kicked in the stomach; Marion Bascom, knocked down; Tillie Kaptn, arms wrenched; Julia Swierk, knocked down and kicked.

Maurice Sugar, attorney for the union, announced that a complaint had been filed with the National Labor Relations Board to bring about an investigation of the labor practices of the Ford Company, if possible. The union also made known that it had sent a telegram to all members of Congress, urging that immediate action be taken as a result of the beatings of the organizers. The leaflet which the organizers sought to distribute outlined the union program for the Ford plants as follows:

"Higher wages and better working conditions; stop speed-up by union supervision; 6-hour day, $8 minimum pay; job security through seniority rights; end the Ford service system; union recognition."

Permission to distribute the leaflets had been obtained previously from the Dearborn City Council. Mr. Bennett had said earlier today that the Ford Company would make no effort to halt the distributions, but had added that he did not know "what our men will do about it."

A group of employees, known as the Knights of Dearborn, and described as a social organization, had previously protested to the council against the granting of a permit to the union to distribute the handbills.

SOURCE: *New York Times*, 26 May 1937.

EXCERPT FROM *POWER*
(1938, by Arthur Arent)

Arthur Arent's play *Power* was created for the Federal Theatre Project (FTP), which was a project of Franklin D. Roosevelt's Works Progress Administration (WPA). The FTP was created in 1935 to provide employment for out-of-work theatre professionals and to produce affordable, accessible, progressive theatre in each state. Before the House Un-American Activities Committee cut its funding in 1939, the FTP performed innovative theatre for over twenty-five million Americans.

Power was a one of the FTP's popular "Living Newspaper" productions: plays that addressed contemporary issues in an accessible style. The Tennessee Valley Authority (TVA), which is the subject of this play, was a public works project also started by the Roosevelt Administration. The TVA built a series of dams on the Tennessee River that provided cheap electric power and rehabilitated the social and economic welfare of the historically impoverished Tennessee Valley.

Leah Shafer,
Cornell University

See also **Electric Power and Light Industry; Electrification, Household; Hydroelectric Power; Public Utilities; Tennessee Valley Authority; Waterpower.**

SCENE FIFTEEN
(The Tennessee Valley)

CHARACTERS
Prologue

LOUDSPEAKER

A-Farmer and wife
WIFE
FARMER

B-City man and wife
HUSBAND
WIFE

C-Farmer and Electric Company Manager
MANAGER
FARMER

D-City Man and Public Utilities Commissioner
COMMISSIONER
MAN

E-Parade and TVA Song
CLERK
PARADERS

PROLOGUE
(*Movies of Tennessee Valley come on scrim. They are integrated with the following* LOUDSPEAKER *announcements:*)

LOUDSPEAKER: In the Tennessee Valley.... Parts of seven States, 40,000 square miles, two million people. All living in a region blighted by the misuse of land, and by the wash of small streams carrying away the fertile topsoil. In these cabins, life has changed but little since some pioneer wagon broke down a century ago, and for them this became the promised land. Occupations—when they exist at all—are primitive, a throwback to an earlier America. Here stand the results of poor land, limited diet, insufficient schooling, inadequate medical care, no plumbing, industry, agriculture or electrification! (*Front traveler curtain opens. Light comes up very slowly on* FARMER *and* WIFE, *left, while movies are still on*) Meanwhile, the entire country seeks cheap electric power, and the demand for a cost yardstick comes from every section. In the Tennessee Valley, 1933. (*Scrim goes up.*)

SCENE FIFTEEN-A
(*Farmer and Wife*)
(FARMER *seated at cut-out table on which is a lighted kerosene lamp. He is reading;* WIFE *is kneeling, measuring a knitted sock to his foot, carrying out the action as seen in the last movie flash.*)

WIFE: [FICTIONAL CHARACTER] Beats me how you see to read in that light.

FARMER: [IBID.] What's the matter with it?

WIFE: What's the matter with it? You're squinting down your nose like you had a bug on the end of it!

FARMER: Same light I been usin' for the last twenty years.

WIFE: Yeah, and look at you now. Them glasses are thick enough to fry eggs under if we ever got any sun in this dump!

FARMER (*QUIETLY*): Andy Jackson used a lamp like this, Nora.

WIFE: Then it was just too bad for Andy. Besides, they didn't have electricity in them days.

FARMER: (*FOLDING PAPER AND PUTTING IT DOWN:*) Maybe I better read durin' the day.

WIFE: How?

FARMER: What d'you mean, how?

WIFE: How you gonna read when you're out there plowin' from sunup to dark?

FARMER: Maybe I better quit readin.

WIFE: That's right. Don't do nothing about it. Just give in and don't make no fuss, and everybody'll love you.

FARMER: What you want me to do, Nora? The wick's up as high as it'll go.

WIFE: Never mind the wick! How about a couple of nice little electric lights around here?

FARMER: Now, we been all over that before. And there ain't nothin' I can do about it.

WIFE: Ain't there?

FARMER: You heard what Joe Frank said. His farm's bigger'n mine. He can use more lights, and the company told him, nothin' doin'.

WIFE: So, you and Joe are gettin' up a little club to read in the daytime, eh? (*She rises*) Suppose they told you you couldn't have any air, would you stop breathin'?

FARMER: What's that got to do with it?

WIFE: Light's just as important as air.

FARMER: Sure it is, but . . .

WIFE: Don't "but" me! Why don't you go out and do somethin' about it?

FARMER: Nora, if they don't want to string lights out to my farm I can't make 'em.

(FARMER: *rises* .)

WIFE: Who said you can't? Who says you can't go up there and raise holy blazes until they give 'em to you! Tell 'em you're an American citizen! Tell 'em you're sick and tired of lookin' at fans and heaters and vacuums and dish-washin' machines in catalogues, that you'd like to *use* 'em for a change! Tell 'em . . . (*She stops*) . . . What the hell do you think Andy Jackson you're always talkin' about would do in a case like this! (*As he stands, convinced, she claps his hat on his head, and gives him a push*) Now go on out and tell 'em somethin'!

(FARMER: *exits*.)

Blackout

SCENE FIFTEEN-B

(*City Man and Wife*)

LOUDSPEAKER: In nearby Chattanooga. (*Lights come up on* HUSBAND and WIFE *City dwellers are seated at table on which is an electric lamp. He reads and she peels potatoes.*)

HUSBAND: Well, here it is. First of the month. (*Picks up envelope from table, reads bill, emits a long whistle*) Six ninety-two! Say, what do you do with the juice around here, eat it?

WIFE (*FLIPPANTLY*): No, darling. We burn it.

HUSBAND: But good Lord, I only pay thirty-five dollars a month rent for this whole house!

WIFE: What's that got to do with it?

HUSBAND: It seems all out of proportion, one-fifth for electricity. If this keeps up I'll have to cut down my life insurance.

WIFE: That'll be nice.

HUSBAND: Of course, if I had the kind of wife who turned the lights off when she walked out of a room I wouldn't have to. (*Rises, stands left of table.*)

WIFE: I did that once and you almost broke your leg going back into it.

HUSBAND: Well, we've got to cut down. Our bills shouldn't be more than three dollars a month.

WIFE: That's what I say.

HUSBAND: Don't say anything, do something about it!

WIFE: All right, let's throw out the radio.

HUSBAND: How can I hear any football games if you do that? Let's stop using the vacuum.

WIFE: And me get down on my hands and knees? Not on your life!

HUSBAND: How about the washing machine? You used to send the stuff out.

WIFE: Yeah, and your shirts came back without cuffs. Remember?

HUSBAND: Well, we've got to do something. You got any ideas?

WIFE: I got one.

HUSBAND: What is it?

WIFE: Did it ever occur to you that maybe those electric companies are charging too much?

HUSBAND: Sure it did. But what can I do about it? Bump my head against the wall?

WIFE: No, but you can complain to the State Electric Commission.

HUSBAND: Look, dear. I'm just one little consumer. How can I fight a utility?

WIFE: Tell the Commission. That's what they're there for.

HUSBAND: Why, they won't even listen to me.

WIFE (*RISES*): Make em. Tell em that your taxes are paying their salaries. Tell em that that's what they're there for, to regulate things. Tell 'em you're sick and tired of making dividends for somebody else and it's about time the little fellow got a look-in some place. And tell 'em . . . (*She stops*) . . . tell 'em you'll be damned if you'll give up listening to those football games on Saturday afternoon! (*She thrusts hat at him*) Now get goin'! (*He does.*)

Blackout

SCENE FIFTEEN-C

(*Farmer and Electric Company Manager*)

(*Lights come up on desk.* MANAGER *of Electric Company is seated at desk.* FARMER, *left of desk, stands.*)

FARMER: [FICTIONAL CHARACTER] My God, I've got to have lights, I tell you!

MANAGER: [Ibid.] Certainly, Mr. Parker. You can have all the lights you want. All you've got to do is pay for the cost of poles and wires.

FARMER: But I haven't got four hundred dollars! And my farm's mortgaged up to the hilt already. (*Desperately*) Can't you see? If I could only get juice I could get me an electric churn and make enough money to pay for the poles!

MANAGER: I'm sorry, Mr. Parker, but that's the way we operate. I'm afraid I can't do a thing for you.

FARMER: And I got to go on livin' the rest of my life with a kerosene lamp and a hand churn like my grandfather did when he came here?

MANAGER: Until you can raise the cost of the equipment.

FARMER (*DESPERATELY*): Isn't there anybody else I can talk to?

MANAGER: I'm the manager here. There's nobody else.

FARMER: Isn't there any other company I can go to?

MANAGER: We're the only one in this part of the State.

FARMER: Then when you turn me down I'm finished?

MANAGER: That's right. (*A pause.*)

FARMER: By God, the Government ought to do something about this!

Blackout

SCENE FIFTEEN-D

(*City Man and Commissioner*)

(*Lights up on desk.* COMMISSIONER seated, MAN *standing, right of desk.*)

MAN: [FICTIONAL CHARACTER] Mr. Commissioner, my electric bills are too high!

COMMISSIONER: [IBID.] Have you had your meter tested?

MAN: Yes, I've had it tested twice. The meter's all right, but the bills are too high just the same.

COMMISSIONER: Mr. Clark, you're not paying one cent more for your electricity than anybody else.

MAN: I know that! That's what the trouble is, we're *all* paying too much!

COMMISSIONER: Mr. Clark, the company that sells you is working on a margin of seven to eight per cent. We consider that a fair profit. And so will you, if you're a business man.

MAN: Look, Mr. Commissioner. I'm not asking you to argue with me on behalf of the utilities. I am a taxpayer! I'm paying your salary I want you to go and argue with them! What's the Commission for, if it's not to help guys like me?

COMMISSIONER: Mr. Clark, the law permits any private enterprise to make a fair return on its investment.

MAN: It does, eh?

COMMISSIONER: And the law permits any company to charge any rate so long as that fair profit is maintained.

MAN: It does, eh? Well, tell me this: If laws like that are made for utilities, why aren't laws made to help people like me?

(*General lighting on entire stage reveals* FARMER, *his*, WIFE, *and* CITY WIFE *in their former positions.*)

FARMER'S WIFE: *And me!*

CITY WIFE: *And me!*

FARMER: *And me!*

Blackout

SCENE FIFTEEN-E

Parade . . .

LOUDSPEAKER: May 18th, 1933. The United States Government answers. [New York Times, May 19, 1933.]

(*Lights pick up* CLERK *of senate.*)

CLERK (*READS*): The Tennessee Valley Authority is created for the purpose of: one, flood control of the Tennessee River Basin; two, elimination of soil erosion, and three, the social and economic rehabilitation of the swampland and hill people of this district; four, *the generation and distribution of cheap electric power and the establishment of a cost yardstick.* (*As the* CLERK *reaches the words "the social and economic rehabilitation" orchestra plays the TVA song very softly. When the* CLERK *reaches the words "cost yardstick" lights fade on him. A motion picture of TVA activities and water flowing over the Norris Dam appears on the scrim, and through the scrim and on projection curtain upstage. A parade of men and women comes on stage behind scrim, singing the TVA song. Many of them carry lanterns. Red, yellow and amber side lights pick up the parade. They circle the stage and continue the song until act curtain falls, which comes down on movie of second large waterfall.*). . . .

Curtain

Movie continues on front curtain until end of film.

SOURCE: Arent, Arthur. *Power.* Washington, DC.: Records of the Federal Theatre Project, National Archives, 1937.

PROCLAMATION ON IMMIGRATION QUOTAS
(28 April 1938)

The rapid proliferation of agricultural and industrial capitalism in the United States attracted huge numbers of European immigrants. Overcrowding on the continent and the ready availability of jobs in America intensified the immigration explosion. In the 1890s, only a few hundred thousand southern and eastern Europeans arrived each year. In less than two decades, however, that number had increased dramatically, with more than a million immigrants pouring into the United States between 1906 and 1914. By 1920 America was the destination of nearly 60 percent of the world's immigrants, a number that would hold until 1930. Those opposed to the country's open-door policy for European immigrants included some in organized labor, who believed that cheap (usually exploited) foreign workers weakened the bargaining power of unions, as well as Nativists, white Protestants who feared that the unchecked influx of Jews and Catholics would pollute the American bloodline and steal political and civil authority from old-stock Americans. Finally, with the country suffering the aftershocks of the Great Depression, President Roosevelt signed legislation restricting the number of Europeans allowed into the United States (somewhat stricter limitations had already been placed on Asians). The decision was a sweeping reversal of traditional U.S. policy. Although future legislation, for example the McCarran-Walter Act of 1952 (the so-called Immigration and Nationality Act), would alter and eventually outlaw quotas based on race or place of origin, the United States still maintains immigration limits. The Immigration and Naturalization Service, which pursues and deports illegal aliens, is the country's largest law enforcement agency.

Laura M. Miller,
Vanderbilt University

See also **Immigration; Immigration and Naturalization Service; Immigration Restriction; McCarran-Walter Act; Nativists.**

Immigration Quotas
By the President of the United States of America

A Proclamation
WHEREAS the Acting Secretary of State, the Secretary of Commerce, and the Secretary of Labor have reported to the President that pursuant to the duty imposed and the authority conferred upon them in and by sections 11 and 12 of the Immigration Act approved May 26, 1924 (43 Stat. 161), they jointly have made the revision provided for in section 12 of the said act and have fixed the quota of each respective nationality in accordance therewith to be as hereinafter set forth:

NOW, THEREFORE, I, FRANKLIN D. ROOSEVELT, President of the United States of America, acting under and by virtue of the power in me vested by the aforesaid act of Congress, do hereby proclaim and make known that the annual quota of each nationality effective for the remainder of the fiscal year ending June 30, 1938, and for each fiscal year thereafter, has been determined in accordance with the law to be, and shall be, as follows:

National Origin Immigration Quotas

Afghanistan (100)
Albania (1000)
Andorra (100)
Arabian peninsula (except Muscat, Aden Settlement and Protectorate, and Saudi Arabia; 100)
Australia (including Tasmania, Papua, and all islands appertaining to Australia; 100)
Belgium (1,304)
Bhutan (100)
Bulgaria (100)
Cameroons (British mandate; 100)
Cameroun (French mandate; 100)
China (100)
Czechoslovakia (2,874)
Danzig, Free City of (100)
Denmark (1,181)
Egypt (100)
Estonia (116)
Ethiopia (Abyssinia; 100)
Finland (569)
France (3,086)
Germany (27,370)
Great Britain and Northern Ireland (65,721)
Greece (307)
Hungary (869)
Iceland (100)
India (100)
Iran (100)
Iraq (100)
Ireland (Eire; 17,853)
Italy (5,802)
Japan (100)
Latvia (236)
Liberia (100)
Liechtenstein (100)
Lithuania (386)
Luxemburg (100)
Monaco (100)
Morocco (French and Spanish zones and Tangier; 100)
Muscat (Oman; 100)
Nauru (British mandate; 100)
Nepal (100)
Netherlands (3,153)
New Guinea, Territory of (including appertaining islands; Australian mandate; 100)
New Zealand (100)
Norway (2,377)
Palestine (with Trans-Jordan; British mandate; 100)
Poland (6,524)
Portugal (440)
Ruanda and Urundi (Belgian mandate; 100)
Rumania (377)
Samoa, Western (mandate of New Zealand; 100)
San Marino (100)
Saudi Arabia (100)
Siam (100)
South Africa, Union of (100)
South-West Africa (mandate of the Union of South Africa; 100)

Spain (252)
Sweden (3,314)
Switzerland (1,707)
Syria and the Lebanon (French mandate; 123)
Tanganyika Territory (British mandate; 100)
Togoland (British mandate; 100)
Togoland (French mandate; 100)
Turkey (226)
Union of Soviet Socialist Republics (2,712)
Yap and other Pacific islands under Japanese mandate (100)
Yugoslavia (845)

The immigration quotas assigned to the various countries and quote areas are designed solely for purposes of compliance with the pertinent provisions of the Immigration Act of 1924 and are not to be regarded as having any significance extraneous to this object.

This proclamation shall take effect immediately, and shall supersede Proclamation No. 2048 of June 16, 1933.

IN WITNESS WHEREOF, I have hereunto set my hand and caused the seal of the United States to be affixed.

DONE at the City of Washington this 28th day of April, in the year of our Lord nineteen hundred and thirty-eight and of the Independence of the United States of America the one hundred and sixty-second.

FRANKLIN D. ROOSEVELT

WORLD WAR II

"AMERICA FIRST" SPEECH
(23 April 1941, by Charles Lindbergh)

Prior to the Japanese bombing of Pearl Harbor, a debate raged across America over the possibility of intervention in the war. The Germans had invaded France and Britain seemed on the verge of defeat at the hands of Hitler, but a strong isolationist impulse remained in the United States. "America First," a prominent anti-interventionist organization, believed that America needed to focus on its own defense rather than engage in a futile attempt to battle the Axis Powers. Trusting that the Western Hemisphere could be made safe from outside threats, America First members urged energy to be channeled into what they termed "Fortress America."

One of the most prominent spokesmen for America First, Charles A. Lindbergh vehemently argued that no successful air attack could ever be carried out against America. As the first man to make the transatlantic flight, Lindbergh brought instant credibility to the organization. He had served as a key intelligence source for the U.S. government, performing extensive inspections of the German, Russian, British, and French air forces. His investigations into foreign air power, which included test flights of Luftwaffe airplanes, led him to conclude that America could rest easy about the possibility of a German air threat.

Lindbergh's isolationism was partly influenced by his Swedish-born father's opposition to Wilsonian foreign policy during World War I. The elder Lindbergh believed that American involvement in the war was linked to Wall Street and amounted to an effort to further pad the pocketbooks of financiers and captains of industry. Charles Lindbergh, on the other hand, argued more from the standpoint that America was incapable of military victory in the European theater. He, like other America First adherents, believed that the fate of Europe would not adversely affect the quality of life in the United States regardless of who emerged victorious. Lindbergh's speech on 23 April 1941 was merely one of many that he gave across the country, but his popularity would wane after anti-Semitism crept into an 11 September speech of that year in Des Moines, Iowa. He soon became branded as a modern "copperhead." Subsequently, President Franklin D. Roosevelt waged a public campaign against Lindbergh and America First.

Paul S. Bartels,
Villanova University

***See also* America First Committee; Isolationism; World War II.**

There are many viewpoints from which the issues of this war can be argued. Some are primarily idealistic. Some are primarily practical. One should, I believe, strive for a balance of both. But, since the subjects that can be covered in a single address are limited, tonight I shall discuss the war from a viewpoint which is primarily practical. It is not that I believe ideals are unimportant, even among the realities of war; but if a nation is to survive in a hostile world, its ideals must be backed by the hard logic of military practicability. If the outcome of war depended upon ideals alone, this would be a different world than it is today.

I know I will be severely criticized by the interventionists in America when I say we should not enter a war unless we have a reasonable chance of winning. That, they will claim, is far too materialistic a viewpoint. They will advance again the same arguments that were used to persuade France to declare war against Germany in 1939. But I do not believe that our American ideals and our way of life will gain through an unsuccessful war. And I know that the United States is not prepared to wage war in Europe successfully at this time. We are no better prepared today than France was when the interventionists in Europe persuaded her to attack the Siegfried Line.

I have said before and I will say again that I believe it will be a tragedy to the entire world if the British Empire collapses. That is one of the main reasons why I opposed this war before it was declared and why I have constantly advocated a negotiated peace. I did not feel that England and France had a reasonable chance of winning. France has now been defeated; and despite the propaganda and confusion of recent months, it is now obvious that England is losing the war. I believe this is realized even by the British government. But they have one last desperate plan remaining. They hope that they may be able to persuade us to send another American Expeditionary Force to Europe and to share with England militarily as well as financially the fiasco of this war.

I do not blame England for this hope, or for asking for our assistance. But we now know that she declared a war under circumstances which led to the defeat of every nation that sided with her, from Poland to Greece. We know that in the desperation of war England promised to all those nations armed assistance that she could not send. We know that she misinformed them, as she has misinformed us, concerning her state of preparation, her military strength, and the progress of the war.

In time of war, truth is always replaced by propaganda. I do not believe we should be too quick to criticize the actions of a belligerent nation. There is always the question whether we, ourselves, would do better under similar circumstances. But we in this country have a right to think of the welfare of America first, just as the people in England thought first of their own country when they encouraged the smaller nations of Europe to fight against hopeless odds. When England asks us to enter this war she is considering her own future and that of her Empire. In making our reply, I believe we should consider the future of the United States and that of the Western Hemisphere.

It is not only our right but it is our obligation as American citizens to look at this war objectively and to weigh our chances for success if we should enter it. I have attempted to do this, especially from the standpoint of aviation; and I have been forced to the conclusion that we cannot win this war for England, regardless of how much assistance we extend.

I ask you to look at the map of Europe today and see if you can suggest any way in which we could win this war if we entered it. Suppose we had a large army in America, trained and equipped. Where would we send it to fight? The campaigns of the war show only too clearly how difficult it is to force a landing, or to maintain an army, on a hostile coast.

Suppose we took our Navy from the Pacific and used it to convoy British shipping. That would not win the war for England. It would, at best, permit her to exist under the constant bombing of the German air fleet. Suppose we had an air force that we could send to Europe. Where could it operate? Some of our squadrons might be based in the British Isles, but it is physically impossible to base enough aircraft in the British Isles alone to equal in strength the aircraft that can be based on the continent of Europe.

I have asked these questions on the supposition that we had in existence an army and an air force large enough and well enough equipped to send to Europe; and that we would dare to remove our Navy from the Pacific. Even on this basis, I do not see how we could invade the continent of Europe successfully as long as all of that continent and most of Asia is under Axis domination. But the fact is that none of these suppositions are correct. We have only a one-ocean Navy. Our Army is still untrained and inadequately equipped for foreign war. Our air force is deplorably lacking in modern fighting planes.

When these facts are cited, the interventionists shout that we are defeatists, that we are undermining the principles of democracy, and that we are giving comfort to Germany by talking about our military weakness. But everything I mention here has been published in our newspapers and in the reports of congressional hearings in Washington. Our military position is well known to the governments of Europe and Asia. Why, then, should it not be brought to the attention of our own people?

I say it is the interventionists in America, as it was in England and in France, who give comfort to the enemy. I say it is they who are undermining the principles of democracy when they demand that we take a course to which more than 80 percent of our citizens are opposed. I charge them with being the real defeatists, for their policy has led to the defeat of every country that followed their advice since this war began. There is no better way to give comfort to an enemy than to divide the people of a nation over the issue of foreign war. There is no shorter road to defeat than by entering a war with inadequate preparation. Every nation that has adopted the interventionist policy of depending on someone else for its own defense has met with nothing but defeat and failure.

When history is written, the responsibility for the downfall of the democracies of Europe will rest squarely upon the shoulders of the interventionists who led their nations into war, uninformed and unprepared. With their shouts of defeatism and their disdain of reality, they have already sent countless thousands of young men to death in Europe. From the campaign of Poland to that of Greece, their prophecies have been false and their policies have failed. Yet these are the people who are calling us defeatists in America today. And they have led this country, too, to the verge of war.

There are many such interventionists in America, but there are more people among us of a different type. That is why you and I are assembled here tonight. There is a policy open to this nation that will lead to success—a policy that leaves us free to follow our own way of life and to develop our own civilization. It is not a new and untried idea. It was advocated by Washington. It was incorporated in the Monroe Doctrine. Under its guidance the United States became the greatest nation in the world.

It is based upon the belief that the security of a nation lies in the strength and character of its own people. It recommends the maintenance of armed forces sufficient to defend this hemisphere from attack by any combination of foreign powers. It demands faith in an independent American destiny. This is the policy of the America First Committee today. It is a policy not of isolation but of independence; not of defeat but of courage. It is a policy that led this nation to success during the most trying years of our history, and it is a policy that will lead us to success again.

We have weakened ourselves for many months, and, still worse, we have divided our own people by this dabbling in Europe's wars. While we should have been concentrating on American defense we have been forced to argue over foreign quarrels. We must turn our eyes and our faith back to our own country before it is too late. And when we do this a different vista opens before us. Practically every difficulty we would face in invading Europe becomes an asset to us in defending America. Our enemy, and not we, would then have the problem of transporting millions of troops across the ocean and landing them on a hostile shore. They, and not we, would have to furnish the convoys to transport guns and trucks and munitions and fuel across 3,000 miles of water. Our battleships and submarines would then be fighting close to their home bases. We would then do the bombing from the air and the torpedoing at sea. And if any part of an enemy convoy should ever pass our Navy and our air force, they would still be faced with the guns of our coast artillery and behind them the divisions of our Army.

The United States is better situated from a military standpoint than any other nation in the world. Even in our present condition of unpreparedness no foreign power is in a position to invade us today. If we concentrate on our own defenses and build the strength that this nation should maintain, no foreign army will ever attempt to land on American shores.

War is not inevitable for this country. Such a claim is defeatism in the true sense. No one can make us fight abroad unless we ourselves are willing to do so. No one will attempt to fight us here if we arm ourselves as a great nation should be armed. Over 100 million people in this nation are opposed to entering the war. If the principles of democracy mean anything at all, that is reason enough for us to stay out. If we are forced into a war against the wishes of an overwhelming majority of our people, we will have proved democracy such a failure at home that there will be little use fighting for it abroad.

The time has come when those of us who believe in an independent American destiny must band together and organize for strength. We have been led toward war by a minority of our people. This minority has power. It has influence. It has a loud voice. But it does not represent the American people.

During the last several years I have traveled over this country from one end to the other. I have talked to many hundreds of men and women, and I have letters from tens of thousands more who feel the same way as you and I. Most of these people have no influence or power. Most of them have no means of expressing their convictions except by their vote, which has always been against this war. They are the citizens who have had to work too hard at their daily jobs to organize political meetings. Hitherto, they have relied upon their vote to express their feelings; but now they find that it is hardly remembered except in the oratory of a political campaign.

These people, the majority of hardworking American citizens, are with us. They are the true strength of our country. And they are beginning to realize, as you and I, that there are times when we must sacrifice our normal interests in life in order to insure the safety and the welfare of our nation.

Such a time has come. Such a crisis is here. That is why the America First Committee has been formed—to give voice to the people who have no newspaper or newsreel or radio station at their command; to the people who must do the paying and the fighting and the dying if this country enters the war.

Whether or not we do enter the war rests upon the shoulders of you in this audience; upon us here on this platform; upon meetings of this kind that are being held by Americans in every section of the United States today. It depends upon the action we take and the courage we show at this time. If you believe in an independent destiny for America, if you believe that this country should not enter the war in Europe, we ask you to join the America First Committee in its stand. We ask you to share our faith in the ability of this nation to defend itself, to develop its own civilization, and to contribute to the progress of mankind in a more constructive and intelligent way than has yet been found by the warring nations of Europe. We need your support, and we need it now. The time to act is here.

SOURCE: *New York Times*, 24 April 1941.

WAR AGAINST JAPAN
(8 December 1941)

The attack on Pearl Harbor sent a shock wave through the country, representing what Franklin D. Roosevelt so cogently labeled "a date which will live in infamy." America had been rudely awakened out of its isolationist slumber by a masterful Japanese strike. The attack not only severely disabled the Pacific Fleet stationed at Hawaii, but also shattered Americans' naive belief that they were invulnerable to attack. More than 2,400 American servicemen lost their lives, as the Japanese destroyed 160 aircraft and sunk four battleships and three destroyers.

With the country simultaneously seething with fury and stricken with grief, Roosevelt provided the even-handed leadership necessary to overcome the crisis. His radio message to the American people in the wake of Pearl Harbor objectively assessed the damage and hinted at the course of action that the nation would follow in response. Roosevelt portrayed the Japanese as dishonorable, describing their attack as "dastardly" and pointing to diplomats' "false statements" and deception in diplomatic negations. Being a masterful politician, Roosevelt knew that rhetoric could be a powerful tool in mobilizing the nation.

The president adroitly used radio as a means of mass communication throughout the war with his intimate "fireside chats," giving Americans hope and rallying them to ultimate victory. On 8 December 1941 America found itself suddenly and irreversibly at war, but Roosevelt's voice filled the airwaves with the steady resolve needed to calm the people and mobilize them for what lay ahead.

Paul S. Bartels,
Villanova University

See also **Japan, Relations with; Pearl Harbor; World War II.**

Yesterday, December 7, 1941—a date which will live in infamy—the United States of America was suddenly and deliberately attacked by naval and air forces of the Empire of Japan.

The United States was at peace with that nation and, at the solicitation of Japan, was still in conversation with its Government and its Emperor looking toward the maintenance of peace in the Pacific. Indeed, one hour after Japanese air squadrons had commenced bombing in the American Island of Oahu, the Japanese Ambassador to the United States and his colleague delivered to our Secretary of State a formal reply to a recent American message. And while this reply stated that it seemed useless to continue the existing diplomatic negotiations, it contained no threat or hint of war of armed attack.

It will be recorded that the distance of Hawaii from Japan makes it obvious that the attack was deliberately planned many days or even weeks ago. During the intervening time the Japanese Government has deliberately sought to deceive the United States by false statements and expressions of hope for continued peace.

The attack yesterday on the Hawaiian Islands has caused severe damage to American naval and military forces, I regret to tell you that very many American lives have been lost. In addition American ships have been reported torpedoed on the high seas between San Francisco and Honolulu.

Yesterday the Japanese Government also launched an attack against Malaya.

Last night Japanese forces attacked Hong Kong.

Last night Japanese forces attacked Guam.

Last night Japanese forces attacked the Philippine Islands.

Last night the Japanese attacked Wake Island.

And this morning the Japanese attacked Midway Island.

Japan has, therefore, undertaken a surprise offensive extending throughout the Pacific area. The facts of yesterday and today speak for themselves. The people of the United States have already formed their opinions and well understand the implications to the very life and safety of our nation.

As Commander-in-Chief of the Army and Navy I have directed that all measures be taken for our defense. But always will our whole nation remember the character of the onslaught against us.

No matter how long it may take us to overcome this premeditated invasion, the American people in their righteous might will win through to absolute victory.

I believe that I interpret the will of the Congress and of the people when I assert that we will not only defend ourselves to the uttermost but will make it very certain that this form of treachery shall never again endanger us.

Hostilities exist. There is no blinking at the fact that our people, our territory and our interests are in grave danger.

With confidence in our armed forces—with the unbounding determination of our people—we will gain the inevitable triumph—so help us God.

I ask that the Congress declare that since the unprovoked and dastardly attack by Japan on Sunday, December seventh, 1941, a state of war has existed between the United States and the Japanese Empire.

WOMEN WORKING IN WORLD WAR II
(1941, by Peggy Terry)

Since government programs during the Great Depression had concentrated mainly on creating jobs for men, the outbreak of the Second World War brought tremendous labor shortages to the United States. By 1941, huge numbers were abandoning civilian life to serve in the military, leaving women like Peggy Terry to fill their places. For the first time in American history, millions of women took an active role in war, building bombs, planes, and ships in factories like Henry Ford's massive Willow Run plant outside Detroit which at the height of its production turned out B-24 bombers at the rate of one an hour. Hundreds of thousands more served in women's military auxiliary organizations like the WACs or WAVES. Inspired in part by propaganda posters like the one featuring Rosie the Riveter, a strong, fierce-countenanced factory worker who exhorted her fellow women to "Get The Job Done," the women of the Unites States responded as no one would have imagined possible. At the beginning of the war, the United States was a third-rate military power, barely mechanized and still cocooned in the separatism brought on by the Great War in Europe, but by 1945, it was a dominant global force, producing more weapons, military vehicles, and ammunition than the rest of the world combined.

Laura M. Miller,
Vanderbilt University

***See also* Women in Public Life, Business, and Professions; World War II.**

The first work I had after the Depression was at a shell-loading plant in Viola, Kentucky. It is between Paducah and Mayfield. They were large shells: anti-aircraft, incendiaries, and tracers.

We painted red on the tips of the tracers. My mother, my sister, and myself worked there. Each of us worked a different shift because we had little ones at home. We made the fabulous sum of thirty-two dollars a week. (Laughs.) To us it was just an absolute miracle. Before that, we made nothing.

You won't believe how incredibly ignorant I was. I knew vaguely that a war had started, but I had no idea what it meant.

Didn't you have a radio?

Gosh, no. That was an absolute luxury. We were just moving around, working wherever we could find work. I was eighteen. My husband was nineteen. We were living day to day. When you are involved in stayin' alive, you don't think about big things like a war. It didn't occur to us that we were making these shells to kill people. It never entered my head.

There were no women foremen where we worked. We were just a bunch of hillbilly women laughin' and talkin'. It was like a social. Now we'd have money to buy shoes and a dress and pay rent and get some food on the table. We were just happy to have work.

I worked in building number 11. I pulled a lot of gadgets on a machine. The shell slid under and powder went into it. Another lever you pulled tamped it down. Then it moved on a conveyer belt to another building where the detonator was dropped in. You did this over and over.

Tetryl was one of the ingredients and it turned us orange. Just as orange as an orange. Our hair was streaked orange. Our hands, our face, our neck just turned orange, even our eyeballs. We never questioned. None of us ever asked, What is this? Is this harmful? We simply didn't think about it. That was just one of the conditions of the job. The only thing we worried about was other women thinking we had dyed our hair. Back then it was a disgrace if you dyed your hair. We worried what people would say.

We used to laugh about it on the bus. It eventually wore off. But I seem to remember some of the women had breathing problems. The shells were painted a dark gray. When the paint didn't come out smooth, we had to take rags wet with some kind of remover and wash that paint off. The fumes from these rags—it was like breathing cleaning fluid. It burned the nose and throat. Oh, it was difficult to breathe. I remember that.

Nothing ever blew up, but I remember the building where they dropped in the detonator. These detonators are little black things about the size of a thumb. This terrible thunderstorm came and all the lights went out. Somebody knocked a box of detonators off on the floor. Here we were in the pitch dark. Somebody was screaming, "Don't move, anybody!" They were afraid you'd step on the detonator. We were down on our hands and knees crawling out of that building in the storm. (Laughs.) We were in slow motion. If we'd stepped on one . . .

Mamma was what they call terminated—fired. Mamma's mother took sick and died and Mamma asked for time off and they told her no. Mamma said, "Well, I'm gonna be with my mamma. If I have to give up my job, I will just have to." So they terminated Mamma. That's when I started gettin' nasty. I didn't take as much baloney and pushing around as I had taken. I told 'em I was gonna quit, and they told me if I quit they would blacklist me wherever I would go. They had my fingerprints and all that. I guess it was just bluff, because I did get other work.

I think of how little we knew of human rights, union rights. We knew Daddy had been a hell-raiser in the mine workers' union, but at that point it hadn't rubbed off on any of us women. Coca-Cola and Dr. Pepper were allowed in every building, but not a drop of water. You could only get a drink of water if you went to the cafeteria, which was about two city blocks away. Of course you couldn't leave your machine long enough to go get a drink. I drank Coke and Dr. Pepper and I hated 'em. I hate 'em today. We had to buy it, of course. We couldn't leave to go to the bathroom, 'cause it was way the heck over there.

We were awarded the navy E for excellence. We were just so proud of that E. It was like we were a big family, and we hugged and kissed each other. They had the navy band out there celebrating us. We were so proud of ourselves.

First time my mother ever worked at anything except in the fields—first real job Mamma ever had. It was a big break in everybody's life. Once, Mamma woke up in the middle of the night to go to the bathroom and she saw the bus going down. She said, "Oh my goodness, I've overslept." She jerked her clothes on, throwed her lunch in the bag, and was out on the corner, ready to go, when Boy Blue, our driver, said, "Honey, this is the wrong shift." Mamma wasn't supposed to be there until six in the morning. She never lived that down. She would have enjoyed telling you that.

My world was really very small. When we came from Oklahoma to Paducah, that was like a journey to the center of the earth. It was during the Depression and you did good having bus fare to get across town. The war just widened my world. Especially after I came up to Michigan. My grandfather went up to Jackson, Michigan, after he retired from the railroad. He wrote back and told us we could make twice as much in the war plants in Jackson. We did. We made ninety dollars a week. We did some kind of testing for airplane radios.

Ohh, I met all those wonderful Polacks. They were the first people I'd ever known that were any different from me. A whole new world just opened up. I learned to drink beer like crazy with 'em. They were all very union-conscious. I learned a lot of things that I didn't even know existed.

SOURCE: Terry, Peggy. From an interview in *"The Good War": An Oral History of World War Two.* By Studs Terkel. New York: Pantheon Books, 1984.

HOBBY'S ARMY
(c. 1943)

During World War II, some 150,000 women served in the Women's Army Corps. Their leader, the capable and astute Colonel Oveta Culp Hobby (1905–1995), had already served as Parliamentarian of the Texas legislature, authored a book, and worked for ten years at the *Houston Post* before she was asked to help establish the WAC. On 5 July 1943, she was sworn in as its first leader. Hobby personally established procedures for recruitment and training, and sometimes almost single-handedly led the fight for the acceptance of women in the armed forces. Living in a society that believed women belonged in the home, the Colonel once touched off a brief national debate when, at a press conference early in her commission, she announced that any WAC who became pregnant would be summarily discharged. Newspapers writers, most of who had concentrated before on what sort of headgear the "girls" would wear and whether makeup was permitted, were taken aback. The *Dallas Times Herald* reported that Hobby's actions would adversely affect the birthrate and "hurt us twenty years from now, when we get ready to fight the next war." Throughout it all, Hobby led the WACs with firm resolve and professionalism, installing women in some four hundred non-combat military posts both at home and abroad. Due to poor health, she resigned from the service in July 1945, having received the Distinguished Service Medal, the only WAC to be so honored. Following the war, she became the first secretary of the Department of Health, Education, and Welfare in the cabinet of President Dwight D. Eisenhower.

Laura M. Miller,
Vanderbilt University

See also **Women in Military Service; World War II.**

In England this week, the U.S. Women's Army Corps had the pleasantly apprehensive experience of being inspected by the Corps' Commanding Officer. Trim Colonel Oveta Culp Hobby, head woman of the WACs, found everything in order.

She saw erect, well-dressed girls drawn up for parade. In the clammy English dawn, she saw WACs in maroon bathrobes (with boy friends' unit insignia sewn in their sleeves) dashing from tin barracks and scuttling across the mud—heading for the "ablution hut" to start the day with a shivery wash-up.

There was not much glamor in it, Hobby's army had found out. Living quarters were either huts heated by a single, stove, or some drafty English country house. Only a few hundred WACs working in London were lucky enough to live in greater comfort. The pay was low. The hours were long. Discipline was strict. Sometimes there were bombings.

G.I. Jane. By last week, 1,170 WACs, dubbed "G.I. Janes" in the European Theater of Operations, were undergoing these rigors. Most of them were at General Dwight Eisenhower's headquarters and English Air Force Stations, where they plotted, teleprinted, operated switchboards, made maps, assessed combat films, "sweated out" missions in flight control rooms.

With dignity and firm morale, they had survived difficulties due to early mistakes in organization and many other unforeseen obstacles. They had caught on with a speed which amazed U.S. and British officers. They had distinguished themselves as nice-looking, hard-working, cheerful girls. Commanding officers recognized their work by pleading for more of them.

They managed to have some fun; they took in the sights, had more dates than they had ever had in their lives. During occasional air raids, some achieved the WAC ambition: to bolt from barracks, crouch in a slit trench and duck back to bed at the "all clear" without really waking up. Instead of, "What's cooking?" they said, "Nervous in the service?"

From three whole WAC battalions only three Janes had gone A.W.O.L. Chief gripe was "Why should we stay behind when the boys open the second front?"

Chief wonderment was over the tales from home that WAC recruiting had fallen down. They favored conscription for women. They asked: "What's the matter with them? Don't they want to live?"

The Colonel indeed had reason to be proud of her overseas troops, 3,000 of whom were serving in England, North Africa, Egypt, New Caledonia, India.

Like G.I. Joe. At home the women in Hobby's army had turned in an equally good record. The Army had anticipated emotional outbursts, resentment at having to take orders, squawks about living in barracks, feuds and cliques and general troubles with the unpredictable (to men) nature of women. Now at Fort des Moines, oldest of the three training centers, officers were quick to say that the Army's fears were generally groundless.

Women had turned out to be more awed than men by the military structure. Colonel Frank U. McCoskrie, who occasionally inspected a line-up, asking questions, once snapped at a WAC recruit: "Who is the commandant?" Back came the answer: "Colonel Frank U. McCoskrie." To the next WAC he said: "What's in that barracks bag?" Gulped the stiff-legged little private: "Colonel Frank U. McCoskrie." But except for a greater respect for authority and a greater capacity for bustling industry, they were not much different from G.I. Joes. In the evenings, off duty they talked about home, their dates, their husbands and sweethearts.

Like G.I. Joes, a few got in serious jams. A few overstayed leave. A few got fed up and went on mild benders. But for the most, behavior was average young female. They put wet towels in each other's beds and tied knots in pajama legs. They griped about red tape, uniforms that did not fit hats not "as cute" as the Marine women's. They might refer to an unpopular officer privately as "that bitch." To the surprise of most males, they got along together just as well as men.

Statement of a Difference. Essential difference between Jane and Joe was pointed out by a Fort Des Moines recruit who was being loaded into an already jampacked Army truck. "Hey, sergeant," she protested, "having a heart, this bus is full." Said they tough male sergeant: "Lady, I been getting 18 men into these trucks and I sure as hell can get 18 WACs in." Wailed the squeezed WAC: "But men are broad in the shoulders."

Graduated from training, WACs now fill 239 different kinds of jobs and in some cases have filled them better than men. Among other things, WACs are opticians, surgical technicians, chemists, surveyors, electricians, radio repairmen, control-tower operators, boiler inspectors, riveters, welders, tractor mechanics, balloon-gas handlers, dog trainers.

Chief gripe of WACs at home is now that they are stuck. Said Corporal Sara Sykes at Fort Oglehorpe: "We practically drool when we hear of someone going overseas." They complain that C.O.s do not always give them enough to do. Old soldiers fear that the busy WACs are on the way to end forever the enlisted soldiers' time-honored practice of "gold bricking."

On performance, the WACs had proved themselves. The failure was not theirs but the nation's: U.S. women still refused to join up. That was Colonel Hobby's headache—and to a lesser degree it has become the headache of Captain Mildred H. McAfee of the WAVES, Commander Dorothy C. Stratton of the SPARS and Lieut. Colonel Ruth Cheney Streeter of the Marine Women's Reserve.

Shoulder to Shoulder. Before she went to England, Colonel Hobby sat in her office in the Pentagon Building and with an air of patent unhappiness parried questions about the failure of woman recruiting. Beside her sat the Army Bureau of Public Relations' Major Francis Frazier—"to protect her," he said.

In the beginning Hobby had confidently proclaimed: "Women will come marching—shoulder to shoulder—to serve their country. . . . I predict that all America will be proud of them." Last week she said pensively: "I don't think it is so strange that there are no more women in uniform. Add up all the services, WACs, WAVES, SPARS, Marines and the various nursing corps and you get a sizable number of women who volunteered. I don't think it's a bad figure."

The figure was 172,822 out of the nearly 50,000,000 women: about one woman in every 3000. By comparison with this "not-bad" figure:

Of some 4,000,000 Canadian women, 31,367 have volunteered for the Army, Navy, Air Force women's services and the nursing corps: about one out of every 150.

Despite the Colonel's assertion that the U.S. could not raise a volunteer army of 400,000 men, . . . 677,000 men were voluntarily serving in the country's armed forces before the draft.

In Britain, where there is a generally approved national conscription (set up as much to distribute woman power as to compel service), out of some 8,670,000 women registered for national service, 7,750,000 have full-time war jobs. At least 2,500,000 of them are in the military services.

In Russia, millions serve in home-guard units for air-raid defense. Numberless women joined the Partisans during the Nazi occupation. The Government has decorated 4,575 women for valor on the battlefield. Six women have won the Government's highest award.

U.S. women are ready to point out that Russia's war is on her own soil, that British homes' have been bombed; if U.S. women had to defend their homes they would join just as valorously; if they could even take a more active part in the war, they would join.

The simple fact remains that women who took on the prosaic, behind-the-lines jobs open to them released U.S. men for the fighting fronts, just as English and Russian women have done. The enemy realizes this better than the U.S. women. Last week the Berlin radio gloated over "totally inadequate" women's Army enlistments in the U.S.

Diminishing Return. The history of WAC recruiting has been one of diminishing returns. In May 1942, when Hobby's army was the WAACs, a kind of stepsister to the Army, but not an integral part of it, it looked as if women would indeed come marching "shoulder to shoulder." The Army had set the WAAC quota at a cautious 25,000. The first day 13,208 applied.

There were some vexations. The country was inclined to laugh. Catholic Bishop James E. Cassidy of Fall River deplored the idea as a "serious menace to the home and foundation of a true Christian and democratic country." Even Army officers joined in inconsidered and harmful wise-cracks among their friends. But the women kept coming in at a gratifying rate, until by last January 20,943 had joined.

In the months that followed, however, recruiting began to slide. The Army upped the quota to 150,000; enrollment by last summer was less than half that. In the fall the WAACs became the WACs, and a full-fledged branch of the Army, with soldier's privileges of insurance, pensions, dependency allotments and overseas pay.

Given the chance to get out, 14,950 women took it. By last week Hobby's army had only recovered the strength it had lost during the debacle. Today Hobby has requests from field commanders for 600,000 WACs. She has only 63,000 to supply. For the second time in her successful life Oveta Culp Hobby has been really balked.

Miss Spark-Plug. When the chief WAC was a little girl in curls she read aloud from the *Congressional Record* to her father, Lawyer Isaac William Culp, of Killeen, Tex. She thought at first she would like to be a foreign missionary. Later she thought she might go on the stage.

In the end she studied law, got her degree from the University of Texas, became parliamentarian of the Texas Legislature and wrote a book on parliamentary law. At 22, Oveta codified Texas' banking laws. At 24, she ran for the State Legislature and was beaten—the first setback in a face-ever-forward career.

When she was 25, she married William Pettus Hobby. She had met him first when she was around 13 and he was Governor of Texas. Mr. Hobby published the Houston *Post*. She plunged into newspaper work—at the *Post*. For six months she studied formats, cleaned out old files; for two years she was book editor; for three years she wrote editorials and a series of articles on the constitutions of the world. At 32, she became the *Post*'s executive vice president. *Post* colleagues called her "Miss Spark-Plug."

On the side she acted in amateur theatricals, collected Georgian silver and rare books (she describes herself as "bookish"). Her chief sport was riding horseback. Once she was thrown, but climbed back to the nearest horse as soon as she got out of the hospital. She had a "planned life."

She became executive director of station KPRC, a director of the Cleburne National Bank, a member of the Board of Regents at Texas State Teachers College, president of the Texas League of Women Voters, Texas chairman of the Women's Committee for the New York World's Fair. In 1941, the War Department appointed her boss of a new women's publicity bureau set up to sell the Army to the wives and mothers of the men. A year later final honors crowned her: the Army invited her to be chief of the WAACs. Mrs. Hobby moved on Washington.

Lawyer Culp's Little Girl. People in Houston observed that even if Oveta Culp Hobby had started as a private she would have soon become the colonel anyhow. She promised that "our staff will offer a reservoir of woman power on which the Army can call," and dug in for the duration. Sixty-five-year-old Mr. Hobby stayed behind in the large brick house in Houston to run the paper.

Mrs. Hobby's Washington apartment was elegant with antiques. (Friends who sublet let it for a while kept their young son in the bathroom most of the time because they were afraid he would break something.) As busy as she was, Isaac William Culp's little girl never lost her style, her poise, her figure. Guests admired the way she appeared on sweltering nights looking cool and handsome in dinner dresses with ruffles. She thought she looked best in yellow and chartreuse. She always had a weakness for absurd headgear and courageously indulged it.

Now she spares herself no work. Husband Hobby has to go to Washington if he wants to see her. She is at her office before 9 o'clock, gets home around 7:30 to have dinner with her seven-year-old daughter Jessica (William, 12, lives with his father). Frequently in the evening she pores over a stack of work. In her busy, private moments among the soft tan Chinese hangings of her living room, she must often wonder, as many a WAC does: What is the matter with U.S. women?

The Answer. One of the answers is: U.S. men—who have always preferred their women in the home. Women themselves have plenty of excuses and confused rationalizations:

"WACs waste time in bedmaking, drilling, marching. A woman can get more accomplished as an ordinary civilian worker. WAC hats are terrible. They were designed for Mrs. Hobby. She's the only one they look smart on. The WACs might make woman with a scientific background into the cook. The Army gives the WACs no real responsibility. There is no glamor in the WACs, or in the WAVES or the SPARS or the Marines. They are segregated from men. The pay is awful."

The truth might be: the majority of U.S. women are unmoved by any great sense of personal responsibility for helping fight this war. Colonel Hobby could beat her iron-grey, smartly coiffured head against that blank wall until she was groggy. She could launch advertising campaigns, promise recruits they could pick their own post, camp or station, get Army generals themselves to appeal to U.S. young women to help. The U.S.'s young women were not listening.

SOURCE: Reproduced in *Time*, 17 January 1944.

TOTAL VICTORY
(1945)

The untimely death of President Franklin D. Roosevelt on 12 April 1945 left Vice President Harry S. Truman to finish the war as commander-in-chief. Hitler initially responded with elation upon hearing the news of Roosevelt's demise. He saw parallels with how Frederick the Great had seemed doomed with the Russians threatening Berlin in 1762. The death of Tsarina Elizabeth saved Prussia, however, because her successor decided to make peace rather than finish the war. Hitler hoped that Truman would prove as malleable as the tsarina's heir, but could not have been more misguided in his optimism. Quite the opposite occurred; Truman held to the policy of unconditional surrender and aided the Soviets in bringing the war in Europe to a decisive end.

Truman did not have the luxury of savoring the victory in Europe for long, as Japan stubbornly persevered in the Pacific theater. Rather than risking a costly amphibious invasion of Japan, Truman decided to drop the Atomic Bombs on Hiroshima and Nagasaki. Soon after the twin catastrophes, Japan offered its unconditional surrender on 14 August 1945. Truman effectively proved his mettle as a decisive wartime leader, although some would eventually question his decision to use atomic force.

Truman's "Total Victory" speech memorialized the sacrifices of Roosevelt and the countless American service men and women who saw the conflict through to a victorious conclusion. He spoke of optimism for the future and a transition back to peacetime life for the whole country. Truman wanted the next generation of Americans to never have to experience the life of the "foxhole and the bomber," fearing that "Civilization cannot survive another total war." Yet his hope for a world at peace would soon be in jeopardy, as relations with the Soviet Union continued to erode. A bipolar world emerged out of the ashes of World War II, rather than the "cooperation among all nations" that Truman desired.

Paul S. Bartels,
Villanova University

***See also* Unconditional Surrender; World War II.**

I am speaking to you, the Armed Forces of the United States, as I did after V Day in Europe, at a moment of history. The war, to which we have devoted all the resources and all the energy of our country for more than three and a half years, has now produced total victory over all our enemies.

This is a time for great rejoicing and a time for solemn contemplation. With the destructive force of war removed from the world, we can now turn to the grave task of preserving the peace which you gallant men and women have won. It is a task which requires our most urgent attention. It is one in which we must collaborate with our allies and the other nations of the world. They are determined as we are that war must be abolished from the earth, if the earth, as we know it, is to remain. Civilization cannot survive another total war.

I think you know what is in the hearts of our countrymen this night. They are thousands of miles away from most of you. Yet they are close to you in deep gratitude and in a solemn sense of obligation. They remember—and I know they will never forget—those who have gone from among you, those who are maimed, those who, thank God, are still safe after years of fighting and suffering and danger.

And I know that in this hour of victory their thoughts—like yours—are with your departed Commander-in-Chief Franklin D. Roosevelt. This is the hour for which he so gallantly fought and so bravely died.

I think I know the American soldier and sailor. He does not want gratitude or sympathy. He had a job to do. He did not like it. But he did it. And how he did it!

Now, he wants to come back home and start again the life he loves—a life of peace and quiet, the life of the civilian.

But he wants to know that he can come back to a good life. He wants to know that his children will not have to go back to the life of the fox-hole and the bomber, the battleship and the submarine.

I speak in behalf of all your countrymen when I pledge to you that we shall do everything in our power to make those wishes come true.

For some of you, I am sorry to say military service must continue for a time. We must keep an occupation force in Japan, just as we are cleaning out the militarism of Germany. The United Nations are determined that never again shall either of those countries be able to attack its peaceful neighbors.

But the great majority of you will be returned to civilian life as soon as the ships and planes can get you here. The task of moving so many men and women thousands of miles to their homes is a gigantic one. It will take months to accomplish. You have my pledge that we will do everything possible to speed it up. We want you back with us to make your contribution to our country's welfare and to a new world of peace.

The high tide of victory will carry us forward to great achievements in the era which lies ahead. But we can perform them only in a world which is free from the threat of war. We depend on you, who have known war in all its horror, to keep this nation aware that only through cooperation among all nations can any nation remain wholly secure.

On this night of total victory, we salute you of the Armed Forces of the United States—wherever you may be. What a job you have done! We are all waiting for the day when you will be home with us again.

Good luck and God bless you.

"WAR AND THE FAMILY" SPEECH
(c. 1945, by Margaret Culkin Banning)

In 1941, approximately forty percent of American families were living beneath the poverty level and birth and marriage rates were stagnant. After the United States entered World War II, however, all of these trends reversed. Ten million American men were conscripted into the armed forces and many rushed to marry before they were shipped off. The stepped-up demand for military production meant that women entered the workforce in record numbers and the basic composition of the American family was radically changed.

Margaret Banning was one of many social reformers investigating the effect these changes had on the composition and conduct of the American family. In this speech, she draws attention to the way that World War II created a diversity of alliances modeled on the family structure and drew attention from the plight of the individual to the plight of the family unit. She urged her listeners to work together, disregard traditional gender roles, and focus their energies on sustaining the unified family model engendered by the necessities of war.

Leah R. Shafer,
Cornell University

See also **Family; World War II.**

The fate of the family is one of the things that the world is fighting over. The issue is sometimes lost in the mazes of geo-politics. On the other hand, it is sometimes greatly oversentimentalized, which is a pity. For in an unparalleled war like this, it is important that as many men and women as possible be sufficiently impersonal to realize that they are fighting not merely to preserve their own homes or to protect their own relatives. If it gives courage or stimulus to a soldier to so limit the object of the war, or if it gives comfort to his wife or mother, no one will gainsay them. But the danger is that this limitation of outlook may lead to bewilderment or lack of satisfaction later on, when in peace the family may still face problems and changes.

When we talk realistically of the preservation of the family as an object of the Allied Nations' joined struggle, what we mean is that we fight for the right of each nation to preserve and develop the family in its own way. It means that we fight for the right of the individual to relate his human relationships to supernatural ones if he is inspired to do so. That Christian nations will have methods and patterns for the family and enhance it with supernatural values that will be ignored or disbelieved in non-Christian nations is obvious.

Most of us watched the shaping of German family life under Hitler with intense dismay. A few were deceived by a front of athletics and virility. A few were reactionary enough to believe that Hitler had the right idea about keeping women in the home. This was prewar and there was nothing that outsiders could do about it, any more than we could prevent the mad teaching in Japan that a young man's greatest glory is to die in battle. But such things became our business very definitely when the arrogant attempt to impose curiously ideas on the rest of the world came from both East and West within a few years.

So the fight of nations to preserve their own kind of family life and the privilege of religions to influence and support family ties are both motives and objects in this war. In this country its preservation is a most important object, for the whole social organization of the United States is based on the family and if this war harms or disintegrates that unit, we shall find ourselves completely loose at the roots.

It is very easy and worse than useless to try to generalize about the effects of the war on the family. So many things are true as to its effect and they seem to contradict one another. And some things are true, but not true often enough to be significant. For example, the war breaks up families. But it brings families closer together. It is very hard on children, causing neglect and danger to them. Yet it makes people and their governments very conscious of the needs of children, very much in the mood to contribute to their protection and welfare and, as notably in England, the children of the poor get more care in wartime than ever before.

Some say in rounded phrases that we are at war to preserve the traditional family. Others insist that we are at war because of a deep world urge to improve the conditions surrounding the family.

So what have we? We have a war, rooted in great processes of change, but projected and promoted and flung at the world by those who would destroy the right to have such private human relationships as our kind of family.

The Allied Nations are going to win this war sooner or later, and so we can confident that, after disappointments and deaths, after many more individual families have been torn away and maimed and destroyed by the losses of war, we shall in the end retain the right to set up the family. And when that happens, it may be important to remind ourselves that the right will be variously exercised and that neither China nor Russia had the American idea of family in mind when they were fighting so superbly. They had their own ideas, and a right to them. If we have the same right, and if freedom of speech and freedom of religion are maintained, our task limits itself to a close consideration of what war has done to the family in the United States of America, and what we want the subsequent peace to do for it.

Let us look first at what the war had done to the family right around us, within our immediate vision. Certainly, even in separation, it has brought a new appreciation of family ties within the group. The boy who took home for granted and was often rather bored with it, who went out whenever he could get out, finds himself on a desert in Africa dreaming of home. Not of the pool hall on the corner, but of little family things, of what he had to eat and what fun it was to quarrel with his sister, and what a swell mother he has. The wife, who was restless because her husband seemed rather commonplace and irritating, finds that now that he is gone to war her life is empty. Bride after bride finds her married life condensed, as far as she can be certain of it at least, to a few weeks or even days. The mother and father who used to scold Johnny for being careless or negligent, find that now that he is in the wars, even his faults are dear to them.

The family is not only more dear to its own members but it is more valued by the government. Not for political reasons but because health and stability in young men and women are so closely related to family habits and training. The soft spots of dissipated circles, of degenerate or illiterate communities, show up very quickly, when we begin closely to appraise our youth.

And as the United States was sobered by war and began to detach itself from frivolities and ephemeral values, family units began to stand out as something to tie to. Tired of rattling around in the wide and undefined spaces conjured up by phrases about "a better world," people began to pin their minds to the family unit as a place to begin. It is the best metaphor for an idea burgeoning everywhere. If you doubt this, look at Broadway, look at the book counters, and listen to the internationalists!

The sophisticated are crowding to see "The Skin of Our Teeth," an obscure play representing the course of the human family. The optimistic are reading and seeing Saroyan's larger-and-better-than-life family. The radios tell problem stories of families in unending succession to untiring audiences. The best-selling novels are no longer the stories of the experiences of one individual, but stories of the course of families that repeat their faults and build up their strength. We hear on every side the phrase "family of nations." It is an understandable unit.

So the first thing that the war has done to the family is to give it not only a fresh popularity but a deepened honor.

Some other effects are not so cheering. In spite of this resurgence of admiration for family life, the family has suffered more in this war than in previous wars. The impacts against it have been three. Two have been the classic ones of separation and of deprivation. The other we may call participation, and though it is not entirely new to this war, it is new in scope. The first two impacts are obvious enough. The third results from the fact that in total war every sound adult, man or woman, is due to participate in the war effort.

In all other involved countries, separation and deprivation and participation as well have been carried to extents which are far greater than they are here within the United States. We may perhaps know and suffer as much separation as other peoples before the war is over. But a like measure of deprivation is unlikely, and certainly unnecessary, for our resources, properly managed, would outlast those of any other fighting country for needs of sustenance. The impact of family participation we are beginning to feel more and more, as women become involved in the war effort.

If I may, I would like to clear away one detail that might clutter this discussion. There has been an attempt here and there, sometimes for sensational reasons, sometimes based on true concern, to debate the point as to whether or not it is wise for women who have young children to go into industry. On this point there are no two opinions. That is not only true in this country but also in Great Britain, and in all the other countries where it is possible to do anything about it. No one, either in authority in any government that I know anything about, or in private life, wants to take a young mother way from her children or to encourage her to leave them. All over the world, governments wish young mothers to continue the patriotic duty of bringing children into the world and of giving them personal care.

But life, even in peace time, is not so simple or easy to regulate as our preferences. And the events of war do not wait upon perfected national arrangements at home. The facts are that in many places women with small children are working—in factories because jobs are suddenly available and wages good—because no other labor is available and war orders must be filled. Because there is no place to house mobile labor. Also, because of a shortage of labor, women are working as laundresses, scrubwomen, and in all kinds of jobs. And I believe that our first concern at this point should not be to stand on theory, but to win the war, and to see simultaneously that, whether the theory is right or wrong, the children of a working mother must be cared for. In that way we shall prevent irreparable damage being done to the family during the war.

At the end of the war the family will find that it has been affected perhaps by only one of these impacts, perhaps by all of them. It is to be hoped that every family will have felt the deprivations of war, and have been strengthened by sacrifice of luxury, of money and of unnecessary foods. Heaven knows that our prayers go up all the time that as few separations as possible will be permanent. The final effect, that of full participation, on the family, may serve—and I hope it will—to give it a new power in the future.

Let us think for a minute or two of the differences the family may expect for itself after the war.

First of all, the family will be physically safe again, except from normal risks. The air raid placards can be taken down. But it will be a long time before the home feels as safe as it has in the past, if ever. Families will know now that if the world is not safely governed there is no real remoteness from the bombers and the flame thrower, and no permanent safety for women and children, except in international cooperation.

Second, the family will be encouraged to increase itself because, as every nation knows now, there is a grave danger of a falling birthrate. Mr. Churchill said, in his recent Sunday broadcast to the world, that England must produce more children. Many a sound and thoughtful article in this country points out the same thing.

Third, the family should be able to have a better and more comfortable home. Abilities that are preoccupied now with war material will turn to better housing, to supplying comforts and conveniences for everyone.

Fourth, the family will have more earning capacity than before because in many instances the wife, as well as the husband, the girl as well as the boy; has learned a new trade during the war.

Finally, as I think we all know in our hearts as well as from our observation, there will be a danger of reaction from the present emotional drawing together within the family, from the nobility of purpose and from the establishment of real values, which we feel exists today. There is a let-down that camp-follows after wars, always seeking to corrupt the peace.

Now if we truly and gravely seek to keep what we have gained, to get the most out of the changes for good the war can bring, and to minimize its evil effects, our task as women is before us. It is large but not too large so that we can not see the details of our personal jobs.

We should then insist on safety for the families of the future. Safety from war, which will always be total war from now on.

We should encourage in every possible way the increase of families in accordance with government wish and human desire. But we should insist that government see to it that there are no neglected children, and no vitiating childhoods in the whole breadth of this country, and no burdens on mothers which make them unfit for their jobs. These things go together. I have known in my life few people who didn't want children, who did not think it was their human or sacred duty to have them. There will be no open protest if society in the future does not do its share in helping motherhood, but there will be a definite absenteeism from motherhood.

It is our immediate business to help steady the great numbers of marriages in which the beginning of married life has been abnormal because of separation of husband and wife, to urge continuance and adjustment when thee marriages falter. We all know these cases. This is personal work, where advice will help but a job and a place to rent will help even more.

I think we should see to it that no capacity which a woman has gained during the war should be wasted or lost. All these feed into the family strength. Sometimes these capacities may be kept alive by retraining after the childbearing period is over, sometimes they may serve to make a mother a better mother to her sons and daughters and a better companion to her husband.

The Hitler pattern of the family failed in this war. He sent women to the kitchens and nurseries, but he took their growing sons from them and he lessened their husbands' respect for them. When he had to take them from the kitchens to the factories again, as he had to, he found the women were incompetent, faulty in spirit and effort. Our pattern for family life after this war should be the direct converse. Men and women should share their whole lives more completely than they ever have in the past, understanding that sex is the fusion of the family and not a dividing line.

My great hope for the post-war family is that it will apply what it has learned and waste nothing.

THE JAPANESE INTERNMENT CAMPS
(1942)

In 1942, President Franklin Roosevelt, citing concerns about wartime security, issued executive order 9066 which forced upwards of 110, 000 Japanese-Americans to relocate to a number of "relocation centers," or concentration camps, on the West Coast. These Japanese-Americans, a majority being American citizens, were confined in makeshift rural camps for up to four years before being allowed to resettle. Basic issues of constitutional liberty and due process were blatantly violated by this order, which forcefully detained

American citizens who had neither broken any laws nor shown any signs of disloyalty. It is now believed that racism and hysteria, rather than actual threat, led to the internment of the Japanese. In the selection here, a young girl narrates her family's experience of being thrown out of their house and moved into a horse stable in Santa Anita before being transported to a camp in Jerome, Arkansas.

Leah Shafer,
Cornell University

See also **Asian Americans; Internment, Wartime; Japanese-American Incarceration; Japanese Americans; World War II.**

The war became real for me when the two FBI agents came to our home in Long Beach. It was a few months after December 7. It was a rainy Saturday morning. My three sisters, my mother, and myself were at home doing the chores. I was twelve.

A black car came right into the driveway. One man went into the kitchen. As I watched, he looked under the sink and he looked into the oven. Then he went into the parlor and opened the glass cases where our most treasured things were. There were several stacks of *shakuhachi* sheet music. It's a bamboo flute. My father played the *shakuhachi* and my mother played the *koto.* At least once a month on a Sunday afternoon, their friends would come over and just enjoy themselves playing music. The man took the music.

I followed the man into my mother and father's bedroom. Strangers do not usually go into our bedrooms when they first come. As I watched, he went into the closet and brought out my father's golf clubs. He turned the bag upside down. I was only concerned about the golf balls, because I played jacks with them. He opened the *tansu,* a chest of drawers. My mother and sisters were weeping.

My father was at work. He took care of the vegetable and fruit sections for two grocery stores. He was brought home by the agents. He was taken to a camp in Tujunga Canyon. My grandmother and I went to visit him. It was a different kind of visit. There was a tall barbed-wire fence, so we were unable to touch each other. The only thing we could do was see each other. My father was weeping.

Our family moved to my grandmother's house—my mother's mother. At least six of my uncles were at home, so it was very crowded. My next recollection is that my mother, my three little sisters, and I were on this streetcar. My mother had made a little knapsack for each of us, with our names embroidered. We had a washcloth, a towel, soap, a comb. Just enough for us to carry. It was the first time we took a streetcar. Because we always went by my father's car.

We went to Santa Anita. We lived in a horse stable. We filled a cheesecloth bag with straw—our mattress. The sides of the room did not go up to the ceiling, so there was no privacy at all. They were horse stalls. We'd have fun climbing up. The floors were asphalt. I do remember what we called stinky bugs. They were crunchy, like cockroaches, large, black. Oh, it's really—(Laughs, as she shakes her head.) We had apple butter. To this day, I cannot taste apple butter.

She shows her internee's record, which she had saved all these years: her name, birthdate, internment date, places of internment. At the bottom of the sheet, in large print: KEEP FREEDOM IN YOUR FUTURE WITH U.S. SAVINGS BONDS.

Our teachers were young Nisei internees. There was a lot of rotation among them. The schooling was informal. Oh, I learned how to play cards there.

In the mornings, a man would knock on the door. There was a sort of bed check at night. There were searchlights always going.

All during this time, I was writing letters to Attorney General Biddle. I was asking him to release my father. I said we are four growing girls. We need our father here. Period.

We left Santa Anita in October 1942. It was a very long train with many, many cars. The stops were made at night with all the shades drawn. We wound up in Jerome, Arkansas. It was in the swamps. The toilet facilities had not yet been finished. The minute we got off, we had to go to the bathroom. I was standing in line, next thing I know people were looking down at me. I had fainted.

PACHUCOS IN THE MAKING
(1943, by George I. Sanchez)

The early 1940s saw an increase in institutionalized discrimination against minorities in the United States. Mexican Americans in Los Angeles faced segregation and racism even as they gained a new level of prosperity from defense-industry jobs. The political climate was charged with racist dogma and the Los Angeles press fostered unreasonable fears about the danger presented by gangs of young "zoot suit"-wearing Mexicans calling themselves "pachucos."

On June 3, 1943, a fight between some pachucos and a group of sailors ignited several nights of rioting. Over the next five days, hundreds of sailors cruised the Mexican districts, brutally beating anyone they saw wearing a zoot suit, as well as many others. The police and other local authorities looked the other way and the rioting continued until downtown Los Angeles was declared off-limits to military personnel on June 9. George I. Sanchez's essay questions the democratic ideals of a society that allows blatantly racist policies to guide its citizens. He argues that segregatory attitudes and practices, not racial disposition, led the young Chicanos to form gangs.

Leah R. Shafer,
Cornell University

See also **Discrimination: Race; Hispanic Americans; Los Angeles; Mexican Americans; Segregation.**

Widespread attention has been drawn to the Los Angeles, California, gangs of zoot-suited, socially maladjusted, "Mexican" youngsters known as "pachucos." Mixed with the intelligent efforts and genuine concern of some public officials and laymen over the disgraceful situation which has been allowed to develop in the Los Angeles area, there is also much sanctimonious "locking of barn doors after the horses have been stolen" sort of expression and action by those whose past lack of interest and whose official negligence bred the juvenile delinquency which now plagues that city's officialdom, hinders the program of the armed forces, and embarrasses the United States before Latin America and the world.

The seed for the pachucos was sown a decade or more ago by unintelligent educational measures, by discriminatory social and economic practices, by provincial smugness and self-assigned "racial" superiority. Today we reap the whirlwind in youth whose greatest crime was to be born into an environment which, through various kinds and degrees of social ostracism and prejudicial economic subjugation, made them a caste apart, fair prey to the cancer of gangsterism. The crimes of these youths should be appropriately punished, yes. But what of the society which is an accessory before and after the fact?

Almost ten years ago, I raised this issue in an article in the Journal of Applied Psychology: "The frequent prostitution of democratic ideals to the cause of expediency, politics, vested interests, ignorance, class and 'race' prejudice, and to indifference and inefficiency is a sad commentary on the intelligence and justice of a society that makes claims to those very progressive democratic ideals. The dual system of education presented in 'Mexican' and 'white' schools, the family system of contract labor, social and economic discrimination, educational negligence on the part of local and state authorities, 'homogeneous grouping' to mask professional inefficiency—all point to the need for greater insight into a problem which is inherent in a 'melting pot' society. The progress of our country is dependent upon the most efficient utilization of the heterogeneous masses which constitute its population—the degree to which the 2,000,000 or more Spanish-speaking people, and their increment, are permitted to develop is the extent to which the nation should expect returns from that section of its public."

When the pachuco "crime wave" broke last year, I communicated with the Office of War Information: "I understand that a grand jury is looking into the 'Mexican' problem in Los Angeles and that there seems to be considerable misunderstanding as to the causes of the gang activities of Mexican youth in that area. I hear also that much ado is being made about 'Aztec forebears,' 'blood lust,' and similar claptrap in interpreting the behavior of these citizens. It would be indeed unfortunate if this grand jury investigation were to go off on a tangent, witchhunting in anthropological antecedents for causes which, in reality, lie right under the noses of the public service agencies in Los Angeles County."

Subsequent developments have borne out the fears implied above. And still, in June of this year, the Los Angeles City Council could think of no better answer to the deep-rooted negligence of public service agencies than to deliberate over an ordinance outlawing zoot suits! The segregatory attitudes and practices, and the vicious economic exploitation directed against the "Mexican" in California in the past—not zoot suits—are responsible for the pachucos of today.

The pseudo-science of the Los Angeles official who is quoted as reporting to the Grand Jury on the Sleepy Lagoon murder case that Mexican youths are motivated to crime by certain biological or "racial" characteristics would be laughable if it were not so tragic, so dangerous, and, worse still, so typical of biased attitudes an misguided thinking which are reflected in the practices not only of California communicates but also elsewhere in this country.

The genesis of pachuquismo is an open book to those who care to look into the situations facing Spanish-speaking people in many parts of the Southwest. Arizona Colorado, Texas, and, to a much lesser degree, even New Mexico have conditions analogous to those which have nurtured the California riots. In some communities in each of these states, "Mexican" is a term of opprobrium applied to anyone with a Spanish name—citizen and alien alike, of mestizo blood or of "pure white" Spanish colonial antecedents. In many place these people are denied service in restaurants, barbershops, and stores. Public parks and swimming pools some of which were built by federal funds, are often closed to them. Some churches, court houses, and public hospitals have been known to segregate them from "whites." Separate, and usually shockingly inferior, segregated "Mexican" schools have been set up for their children. Discriminatory employment practices and wage scales, even in war industries (the President's Executive Order 8802 and his Committee on Fair Employment Practice to the contrary notwithstanding), are still used to "keep the 'Mexican' in his place." ...

A pathetic letter from a descendant of the colonial settlers of Texas states: "Do you think there is any hope of getting our problems solved? We wish you would do something to help us. We are being mistreated here every time we turn around. We are not allowed in cafes movies, restaurants. Even Latin Americans in United States Army uniforms are sometimes told they can't see a show because the Mexican side is full. In the public schools our children are segregated. They are given only half a day's school because of the teacher shortage, while the other have full-time classes. There is no teacher shortage for them. Please tell us if there is anything to do about it. We wrote a letter to the Office of Civilian defense, Washington, D.C. But we haven't heard from them. We don't know if that is the right place to write to or not."

Many communities provide a separate school for children of Spanish name. These "Mexican schools," are established ostensibly for "pedagogical reasons," thinly veiled excuses which do not conform with either the science of education or the facts in the case. Judging from current practice, these pseudo-pedagogical reasons call for short school terms, ramshackle school buildings, poorly paid and untrained teachers, and all varieties of prejudicial discrimination. The "language handicap" reason, so glibly advanced as the chief pedagogical excuse for the segregation of these school children, is extended to apply to all Spanish-name youngsters regardless of the fact that some of them know more English and more about other school subjects than the children from whom they are segregated. In addition some of these Spanish-name children know no Spanish whatsoever, coming from homes where only English has been spoken for two generations or more....

On July 12, 1941, before the pachuco question had become a matter of general interest, a Spanish American from California summarized the situation this way: The so-called 'Mexican Problem' is not in fact a Mexican problem. It is a problem foisted by American mercenary interests upon the American people. It is an American problem made in the U.S.A. He was protesting the movement then on foot to permit the indiscriminate and wholesale importation of laborers from Mexico. In response to such protests steps were taken by the governments of the United States and Mexico to protect both the imported alien and the residents of this area from the evils inherent in such letting down of the bars, evils of which ample evidence was furnished during World War I under similar circumstances. Today, however, the pressure of vested interests is finding loopholes in that enlightened policy and, again, the bars are rapidly being let down.

Si Casady of McAllen, Texas, in an editorial in the Valley Evening Monitor hits the nail on the head when he says: "... there is a type of individual who does not understand and appreciate the very real dangers inherent in racial discrimination. This type of individual does not understand that his own right to enjoy life, his own liberty, the very existence of this nation and all the other free nations of the world depend utterly and completely on the fundamental principle that no man, because of race, has any right to put his foot upon the neck of any other man. The racial discrimination problem has been daintily out of sight for so long in the [Rio Grande] Valley that it cannot now be solved overnight. Instead of dragging it out into the sunlight where it could be left lying until all the nauseous fumes of hypocrisy and bigotry had dissipated, we have showed the problem down into the cellar like an idiot child, hoping the neighbors would not notice its existence." ...

The establishment of segregated schools for "Mexicans" lays the foundation for most of the prejudice and discrimination. Local and state educational authorities have the power to institute satisfactory remedies. There is no legal requirement in any state calling for the organization of such schools. There are all sorts of legal mandates to the contrary. Forthright action by school authorities could remove these blots on American education in a very brief period of time. As an illustration of how this may be done in Texas, consider this provision adopted by the State Legislature in 1943: "The State Board of Education with the approval of the State Superintendent of Public Instruction shall have the authority to withhold the per capita apportionment to any school district at any time that a discrimination between groups of white scholastics exists."

The exclusion of "Mexicans" from public places solely on the basis of "race" (legally, they are "white"), can be stopped through the enforcement of such provisions as that embodied in the legislative Concurrent Resolution adopted in Texas a few months ago: "1. All persons of the Caucasian Race within the jurisdiction of this State are entitled to the full and equal accommodations, advantages, facilities, and privileges of all public places of business or amusement, subject only to the conditions and limitations established by law, and rules and regulations applicable alike to all persons of the Caucasian Race. 2. Whoever denies to any person the full advantages, facilities, and privileges enumerated in the preceding paragraph or who aids or incites such denial or whoever makes any discrimination, distinction, or restriction except for good cause applicable alike to all persons of the Caucasian Race, respecting accommodations, advantages, facilities, and privileges of all public places of business, or whoever aids or incites such discrimination, distinction, or restriction shall be considered as violating the good neighbor policy of our State." Vigorous action by the public officials in enforcing this mandate in Texas, and similar legal provisions in other states, would go far in solving this fundamental phase of the whole "Mexican" question.

These illustrations of specific remedial action could be multiplied by reference to legal mandates as to suffrage, jury service, practices in war industries, etc. Public officials—local, state, and federal—have in their hands the power to correct the discriminatory practices which lie at the root of prejudicial attitudes and actions on the part of some sectors of the public. I have the fullest confidence that the great majority of Americans would applaud the enforcement of those legal mandates.

The Spanish-speaking people of the United States need to be incorporated into, and made fully participating members of, the American way of life. The "Mexican" needs education, he needs vocational training and placement in American industry on an American basis, he needs active encouragement to participate in civic affairs and to discharge his civic obligations, and he needs constant protection by public officials from the pitfalls into which his cultural differences may lead him or into which he may be forced by unthinking sectors of the public.

SOURCE: Sanchez, George I., "Pachucos in the Making," *Common Ground* (Autumn 1943).

THE COLD WAR

EXCERPT FROM "AMERICAN DIPLOMACY"
(1947, by George Kennan)

In 1947, with the Cold War between the United States and the Soviet Union well underway, there appeared in the Council of Foreign Relations' magazine *Foreign Affairs* an article written by George Kennan. Kennan, a U.S. diplomat and Soviet specialist from 1926–1950, used the pseudonym of "Mister X"—following the advice of his boss, George Marshall, that "planners don't talk"—and postulated a policy toward the USSR known as "containment."

Kennan claimed that the behavior of the Soviet Union in its international relations was determined by its fundamental antagonism toward the capitalist West. The ultimate goal of Soviet power was worldwide domination, said Kennan, but this domination would come in its own good time, according to Soviet theorists, given capitalism's inherent "seeds of destruction." Soviet policy, in the meantime, was to cooperate with the West when convenient, "badger" its enemies, and take no "premature" risks. Monolithic in structure, the Soviet hierarchy deemed itself infallible, properly stern in discipline, and pragmatically flexible—and its minions were trained to ignore reasonable pleas from the West.

Thus, in the face of this patient implacability, the best recourse for the United States was to enact a "vigilant containment" of what Kennan saw as Russia's expansionist aims and for the United States to likewise remain patient and respond forcefully at every geographical point at which the Soviets applied pressure.

Kennan's real intent in the article was to argue for the political containment of the Soviet Union, such as through the Marshall Plan. To Kennan's dismay, the article was misinterpreted as a call for military containment; a misinterpretation for which Kennan later took full responsibility, admitting his writing "was at best ambiguous."

P. M. Carpenter,
University of Illinois at Urbana-Champaign

See also **Foreign Policy; Russia, Relations with; "X" Article.**

Of the original ideology [communism], nothing has been officially junked. Belief is maintained in the basic badness of capitalism, in the inevitability of its destruction, in the obligation of the proletariat to assist in that destruction and to take power into its own hands. But stress has come to be laid primarily on those concepts which relate most specifically to the Soviet regime itself: to its position as the sole truly Socialist regime in a dark and misguided world, and to the relationships of power within it.

The first of these concepts is that of the innate antagonism between capitalism and Socialism. We have seen how deeply that concept has become imbedded in foundations of Soviet power. It has profound implications for Russia's conduct as a member of international society. It means that there can never be on Moscow's side any sincere assumptions of a community of aims between the Soviet Union and powers which are regarded as capitalism. It must invariably be assumed in Moscow that the aims of the capitalist world are antagonistic to the Soviet regime and, therefore, to the interests of the peoples it controls. If the Soviet Government occasionally sets its signature to documents which would indicate the contrary, this is to be regarded as a tactical maneuver permissible in dealing with the enemy (who is without honor) and should be taken in the spirit of caveat emptor. Basically, the antagonism remains. It is postulated. And from it flow many of the phenomena which we find disturbing in the Kremlin's conduct of foreign policy: the secretiveness, the lack of frankness, the duplicity, the war suspiciousness, and the basic unfriendliness of purpose. These phenomena are there to stay, for the foreseeable future. There can be variations of degree and of emphasis. When there is something the Russians want from us, one of the other of these features of their policy may be thrust temporarily into the background; and when that happens there will always be Americans who will leap forward with gleeful announcements that "the Russians have changed," and some who will even try to take credit for having brought about such changes. But we should not be misled by tactical maneuvers. These characteristics of Soviet policy, like the postulate from which they flow, are basic to the internal nature of Soviet power, and will be with us, whether in the foreground or the background, until the internal nature of Soviet power is changed.

This means that we are going to continue for a long time to find the Russians difficult to deal with. It does not mean that they should be considered as embarked upon a do-or-die program to overthrow our society by a given date. The theory of the inevitability of the eventual fall of capitalism has the fortunate connotation that there is no hurry about it. The forces of progress can take their time in preparing the final coup de grace. Meanwhile, what is vital is that the "Socialist fatherland"—that oasis of power which has been already won for Socialism in the person of the Soviet Union—should be cherished and defended by all good Communists at home and abroad, its fortunes promoted, its enemies badgered and confounded. The promotion of premature, "adventuristic" revolutionary projects abroad which might embarrass Soviet power in any way would be an inexcusable, even counter-revolutionary act. The cause of Socialism is the support and promotion of Soviet power, as defined in Moscow.

This brings us to the second of the concepts important to contemporary Soviet outlook. That is the infallibility of the Kremlin. The Soviet concept of power, which permits no focal points of organization outside the Party itself, requires that the Party leadership remain in theory the sole repository of truth. For if truth were to be found elsewhere, there would be justification for its expression in organized activity. But it is precisely that which the Kremlin cannot and will not permit.

The leadership of the Communist Party is therefore always right, and has been always right ever since in 1929 Stalin formalized his personal power by announcing that decisions of the Politburo were being taken unanimously.

On the principle of infallibility there rests the iron discipline of the Communist Party. In fact, the two concepts are mutually self-supporting. Perfect discipline requires recognition of infallibility. Infallibility requires the observance of discipline. And the two together go far to determine the behaviorism of the entire Soviet apparatus of power. But their effect cannot be understood unless a third factor be taken in account: namely, the fact that the leadership is at liberty to put forward for tactical purposes any particular thesis which it finds useful to the cause at any particular moment and to require the faithful and unquestioning acceptance of that thesis by the members of the movement as a whole. This means that truth is not constant but is actually created, for all intents and purposes, by the Soviet leaders themselves. It may vary from week to week, from month to month. It is nothing absolute and immutable—nothing which flows from objective reality. It is only the most recent manifestation of the wisdom of those in whom the ultimate wisdom is supposed to reside, because they represent the logic of history. The accumulative effect of these factors is to give to the whole subordinate apparatus of Soviet power an unshakeable stubbornness and steadfastness in its orientation. This orientation can be changed at will by the Kremlin but by no other power. Once a given party line has been laid down on a given issue of current policy, the whole Soviet governmental machine, including the mechanism of diplomacy, moves inexorably along the prescribed path, like a persistent toy automobile wound up and headed in a given direction, stopping only when it meets with some unanswerable force. The individuals who are the components of this machine are unamenable to argument or reason which comes to them from outside sources. Their whole training has taught them to mistrust and discount the glib persuasiveness of the outside world. Like the white dog before the phonograph, they hear only the "master's voice." And if they are to be called off from the purposes last dictated to them, it is the master who must call them off. Thus the foreign representative cannot hope that his words will make any impression on them. The most that he can hope is that they will be transmitted to those at the top, who are capable of changing the party line. But even those are not likely to be swayed by any normal logic in the words of the bourgeois representative. Since there can be no appeal to common purposes, there can be no appeal to common mental approaches. For this reason, facts speak louder than words to the ears of the Kremlin; and words carry the greatest weight when they have the ring of reflecting, or being backed by, facts of unchallengeable validity.

But we have seen that the Kremlin is under no ideological compulsion to accomplish its purposes in a hurry. Like the Church, it is dealing in ideological concepts which are of long-term validity, and it can afford to be patient. It has no right to risk the existing achievements of the revolution for the sake of vain baubles of the future. The very teachings of Lenin himself require great caution and flexibility in the pursuit of Communist purposes. Again, these precepts are fortified by the lessons of Russian history: of centuries of obscure battles between nomadic forces over the stretches of a vast unfortified plain. Here caution, circumspection, flexibility and deception are the valuable qualities; and their value finds natural appreciation in the Russian or the oriental mind. Thus the Kremlin has no compunction about retreating in the face of superior force. And being under the compulsion of no timetable, it does not get panicky under the necessity for such retreat. Its political action is a fluid stream which moves constantly, wherever it is permitted to move, toward a given goal. Its main concern is to make sure that it has filled every nook and cranny available to it in the basin of world power. But if it finds unassailable barriers in its path, it accepts these philosophically and accommodates itself to them. The main thing is that there should always be pressure, increasing constant pressure toward the desired goal. There is no trace of any feeling in Soviet psychology that that goal must be reached at any given time.

These considerations make Soviet diplomacy at once easier and more difficult to deal with than the diplomacy of the individual aggressive leaders like Napoleon and Hitler. On the one hand it is more sensitive to contrary force, more ready to yield on individual sectors of the diplomatic front when that force is felt to be too strong, and thus more rational in the logic and rhetoric of power. On the other hand it cannot be easily defeated or discouraged by a single victory on the part of its opponents. And the patient persistence by which it is animated means that it can be effectively countered not by sporadic acts which represent momentary whims of democratic opinion but only intelligent long-range policies on the part of Russia's adversaries—policies no less steady in their purpose, and no less variegated and resourceful in their application, than those of the Soviet Union itself.

In these circumstances it is clear that the main element of any United States policy toward the Soviet Union must be that of a long-term, patient but firm and vigilant containment of Russian expansive tendencies. It is important to note, however, that such a policy has nothing to do with outward histrionics: with threats or blustering or superfluous gestures of outward "toughness." While the Kremlin is basically flexible in its reaction to political realities, it is by no means unamenable to considerations of prestige. Like almost any other government, it can be placed by tactless and threatening gestures in a position where it cannot afford to yield even though this might be dictated by its sense of realism. The Russian leaders are keen judges of human psychology, and as such they are highly conscious that loss of temper and of self-control is never a source of strength in political affairs. They are quick to exploit such evidences of weakness. For these reasons, it is a sine qua non of successful dealing with Russia that the foreign government in question should remain at all times cool and collected and that its demands on Russian policy should be put forward in such a manner as to leave the way open for a compliance not too detrimental to Russian prestige.

In light of the above, it will be clearly seen that the Soviet pressure against the free institutions of the Western world is something that can be contained by the adroit and vigilant application of counter-force at a series of constantly shifting geographical and political points, corresponding to the shifts and maneuvers of Soviet policy, but which cannot be charmed or talked out of existence. The Russians look forward to a duel of infinite duration, and they see that already they have scored great successes. It must be borne in mind that there was a time when the Communist Party represented far more of a minority in the sphere of Russian national life than Soviet power today represents in the world community. . . .

The issue of Soviet-American relations is in essence a test of the over-all worth of the United States as a nation among nations. To avoid destruction the United States need only measure up to its own best traditions and prove itself worthy of preservation as a great nation.

Surely, there was never a fairer test of national quality than this. In the light of these circumstances, the thoughtful observer of Russian-American relations will find no cause for complaint in the Kremlin's challenge to American society. He will rather experience a certain gratitude to a Providence which, by providing the American people with this implacable challenge, has made their entire security as a nation dependent on their pulling themselves together and accepting the responsibilities of moral and political leadership that history plainly intended them to bear.

SOURCE: Kennan, George Frost. "American Diplomacy, 1900–1950." Reprinted by permission of *Foreign Affairs*.

THE TESTIMONY OF WALTER E. DISNEY BEFORE THE HOUSE COMMITTEE ON UN-AMERICAN ACTIVITIES
(24 October 1947)

Originally a special committee of the House of Representatives under the leadership of Texas Democrat Martin Dies, Jr., the House Un-American Activities Committee was established in 1938 to investigate and impede the infiltration of Axis propaganda in the United States. By the mid-1940s, however, with much of the country in the grip of a Red Scare, HUAC had become a standing committee with much of its focus centered on the investigation of Union leaders, New Deal liberals, and leftist intellectuals. Inevitably, the committee trained its eye on Hollywood and the entertainment industry, where it discovered insinuations of Communist activity even in the animation studios of Walter Elias Disney, producer of *Snow White, Dumbo,* and other well-known children's films. But not all witnesses were as forthcoming as Disney. In 1947, the committee accused ten directors and screenwriters of having Communist affiliations. When called to testify, however, the so-called Hollywood Ten, the director Edward Dmytryk and the writer Ring Lardner, Jr. among them, refused to comply, thus incurring contempt of Congress charges, jail time, and perhaps worst of all, the addition of their names to a growing catalog of "blacklisted" artists. Both civil libertarians and ordinary citizens protested the committee's strong-arm tactics as well as its frequent presumption of a suspect's guilt. Nevertheless, HUAC continued its activities throughout the 1940s and 1950s and would become a model for the permanent investigations subcommittee of the Government Operations Committee headed by Wisconsin Senator Joseph McCarthy. Renamed the House Internal Security Committee in 1969, HUAC was at last abolished in 1975.

Laura M. Miller,
Vanderbilt University

***See also* Anticommunism; Blacklisting; Cold War; House Committee on Un-American Activities; McCarthyism.**

[ROBERT E.] STRIPLING [CHIEF INVESTIGATOR]: Mr. Disney, will you state your full name and present address, please?

WALTER DISNEY: Walter E. Disney, Los Angeles, California.

RES: When and where were you born, Mr. Disney?

WD: Chicago, Illinois, December 5, 1901.

RES: December 5, 1901?

WD: Yes, sir.

RES: What is your occupation?

WD: Well, I am a producer of motion-picture cartoons.

RES: Mr. Chairman, the interrogation of Mr. Disney will be done by Mr. Smith.

THE CHAIRMAN [J. PARNELL THOMAS]: Mr. Smith.

[H. A.] SMITH: Mr. Disney, how long have you been in that business?

WD: Since 1920.

HAS: You have been in Hollywood during this time?

WD: I have been in Hollywood since 1923.

HAS: At the present time you own and operate the Walt Disney Studio at Burbank, California?

WD: Well, I am one of the owners. Part owner.

HAS: How many people are employed there, approximately?

WD: At the present time about 600.

HAS: And what is the approximate largest number of employees you have had in the studio?

WD: Well, close to 1,400 at times.

HAS: Will you tell us a little about the nature of this particular studio, the type of pictures you make, and approximately how many per year?

WD: Well, mainly cartoon films. We make about twenty short subjects, and about two features a year.

HAS: Will you talk just a little louder, Mr. Disney?

WD: Yes, sir.

HAS: How many, did you say?

WD: About twenty short subject cartoons and about two features per year.

HAS: Where are these films distributed?

WD: All over the world.

HAS: In all countries of the world?

WD: Well, except the Russian countries.

HAS: Why aren't they distributed in Russia, Mr. Disney?

WD: Well, we can't do business with them.

HAS: What do you mean by that?

WD: Oh, well, we have sold them some films a good many years ago. They bought the Three Little Pigs [1933] and used it through Russia. And they looked at a lot of our pictures, and I think they ran a lot of them in Russia, but then turned them back to us and said they didn't want them, they didn't suit their purposes.

HAS: Is the dialogue in these films translated into the various foreign languages?

WD: Yes. On one film we did ten foreign versions. That was Snow White and the Seven Dwarfs.

HAS: Have you ever made any pictures in your studio that contained propaganda and that were propaganda films?

WD: Well, during the war we did. We made quite a few-working with different government agencies. We did one for the Treasury on taxes and I did four anti-Hitler films. And I did one on my own for air power.

HAS: From those pictures that you made, have you any opinion as to whether or not the films can be used effectively to disseminate propaganda?

WD: Yes, I think they proved that.

HAS: How do you arrive at that conclusion?

WD: Well, on the one for the Treasury on taxes, it was to let the people know that taxes were important in the war effort. As they explained to me, they had 13,000,000 new taxpayers, people who had never paid taxes, and they explained that it would be impossible to prosecute all those that were delinquent and they wanted to put this story before those people so they would get their taxes in early. I made the film, and after the film had its run the Gallup poll organization polled the public and the findings were that twenty-nine percent of the people admitted that had influenced them in getting their taxes in early and giving them a picture of what taxes will do.

HAS: Aside from those pictures you made during the war, have you made any other pictures, or do you permit pictures to be made at your studio containing propaganda?

WD: No; we never have. During the war we thought it was a different thing. It was the first time we ever allowed anything like that to go in the films. We watch so that nothing gets into the films that would be harmful in any way to any group or any country. We have large audiences of children and different groups, and we try to keep them as free from anything that would offend anybody as possible. We work hard to see that nothing of that sort creeps in.

HAS: Do you have any people in your studio at the present time that you believe are Communist or Fascist, employed there?

WD: No; at the present time I feel that everybody in my studio is one-hundred-percent American.

HAS: Have you had at any time, in your opinion, in the past, have you at any time in the past had any Communists employed at your studio?

WD: Yes; in the past I had some people that I definitely feel were Communists.

HAS: As a matter of fact, Mr. Disney, you experienced a strike at your studio, did you not?

WD: Yes.

HAS: And is it your opinion that that strike was instituted by members of the Communist Party to serve their purposes?

WD: Well, it proved itself so with time, and I definitely feel it was a Communist group trying to take over my artists and they did take them over.

CHAIRMAN: Do you say they did take them over?

WD: They did take them over.

HAS: Will you explain that to the committee, please?

WD: It came to my attention when a delegation of my boys, my artists, came to me and told me that Mr. Herbert Sorrell

HAS: Is that Herbert K. Sorrell?

WD: Herbert K. Sorrell, was trying to take them over. I explained to them that it was none of my concern, that I had been cautioned to not even talk with any of my boys on labor. They said it was not a matter of labor, it was just a matter of them not wanting to go with Sorrell, and they had heard that I was going to sign with Sorrell, and they said that they wanted an election to prove that Sorrell didn't have the majority, and I said that I had a right to demand an election. So when Sorrell came, I demanded an election. Sorrell wanted me to sign on a bunch of cards that he had there that he claimed were the majority, but the other side had claimed the same thing. I told Mr. Sorrell that there is only one way for me to go and that was an election and that is what the law had set up, the National Labor Relations Board was for that purpose. He laughed at me and he said that he would use the Labor Board as it suited his purposes and that he had been sucker enough to go for that Labor Board ballot and he had lost some election—I can't remember the name of the place—by one vote. He said it took him two years to get it back. He said he would strike, that that was his weapon. He said, "I have all of the tools of the trade sharpened," that I couldn't stand the ridicule or the smear of a strike. I told him that it was a matter of principle with me, that I couldn't go on working with my boys feeling that I had sold them down the river to him on his say-so, and he laughed at me and told me I was naive and foolish. He said, you can't stand this strike, I will smear you, and I will make a dust bowl out of your plant.

CHAIRMAN: What was that?

WD: He said he would make a dust bowl out of my plant if he chose to. I told him I would have to go that way, sorry, that he might be able to do all that, but I would have to stand on that. The result was that he struck. I believed at that time that Mr. Sorrell was a Communist because of all the things that I had heard and having seen his name appearing on a number of Commie front things. When he pulled the strike, the first people to smear me and put me on the unfair list were all of the Commie front organizations. I can't remember them all, they change so often, but one that is clear in my mind is the League of Women Shoppers, The People's World, The Daily Worker, and the PM magazine in New York. They smeared me. Nobody came near to find out what the true facts of the thing were. And I even went through the same smear in South America, through some Commie periodicals in South America, and generally throughout the world all of the Commie groups began smear campaigns against me and my pictures.

JOHN MCDOWELL: In what fashion was that smear, Mr. Disney, what type of smear?

WD: Well, they distorted everything, they lied; there was no way you could ever counteract anything that they did; they formed picket lines in front of the theaters, and, well, they called my plant a sweatshop, and that is not true, and anybody in Hollywood would prove it otherwise. They claimed things that were not true at all and there was no way you could fight it back. It was not a labor problem at all because—I mean, I have never had labor trouble, and I think that would be backed up by anybody in Hollywood.

HAS: As a matter of fact, you have how many unions operating in your plant?

CHAIRMAN: Excuse me just a minute. I would like to ask a question.

HAS: Pardon me.

CHAIRMAN: In other words, Mr. Disney, Communists out there smeared you because you wouldn't knuckle under?

WD: I wouldn't go along with their way of operating. I insisted on it going through the National Labor Relations Board. And he told me outright that he used them as it suited his purposes.

CHAIRMAN: Supposing you had given in to him, then what would have been the outcome?

WD: Well, I would never have given in to him, because it was a matter of principle with me, and I fight for principles. My boys have been there, have grown up in the business with me, and I didn't feel like I could sign them over to anybody. They were vulnerable at that time. They were not organized. It is a new industry.

CHAIRMAN: Go ahead, Mr. Smith.

HAS: How many labor unions, approximately, do you have operating in your studios at the present time?

WD: Well, we operate with around thirty-five—I think we have contacts with thirty.

HAS: At the time of this strike you didn't have any grievances or labor troubles whatsoever in your plant?

WD: No. The only real grievance was between Sorrell and the boys within my plant, they demanding an election, and they never got it.

HAS: Do you recall having had any conversations with Mr. Sorrell relative to Communism?

WD: Yes, I do.

HAS: Will you relate that conversation?

WD: Well, I didn't pull my punches on how I felt. He evidently heard that I had called them all a bunch of Communists—and I believe they are. At the meeting he leaned over and he said, "You think I am a Communist, don't you," and I told him that all I knew was what I heard and what I had seen, and he laughed and said, "Well, I used their money to finance my strike of 1937," and he said that he had gotten the money through the personal check of some actor, but he didn't name the actor. I didn't go into it any further. I just listened.

HAS: Can you name any other individuals that were active at the time of the strike that you believe in your opinion are Communists?

WD: Well, I feel that there is one artist in my plant, that came in there, he came in about 1938, and he sort of stayed in the background, he wasn't too active, but he was the real brains of this, and I believe he is a Communist. His name is David Hilberman.

HAS: How is it spelled?

WD: H-i-l-b-e-r-m-a-n, I believe. I looked into his record and I found that, number 1, that he had no religion and, number 2, that he had spent considerable time at the Moscow Art Theatre studying art direction, or something.

HAS: Any others, Mr. Disney?

WD: Well, I think Sorrell is sure tied up with them. If he isn't a Communist, he sure should be one.

HAS: Do you remember the name of William Pomerance, did he have anything to do with it?

WD: Yes, sir. He came in later. Sorrell put him in charge as business manager of cartoonists and later he went to the Screen Actors as their business agent, and in turn he put in another man by the name of Maurice Howard, the present business agent. And they are all tied up with the same outfit.

HAS: What is your opinion of Mr. Pomerance and Mr. Howard as to whether or not they are or are not Communists?

WD: In my opinion they are Communists. No one has any way of proving those things.

HAS: Were you able to produce during the strike?

WD: Yes, I did, because there was a very few, very small majority that was on the outside, and all the other unions ignored all the lines because of the setup of the thing.

HAS: What is your personal opinion of the Communist Party, Mr. Disney, as to whether or not it is a political party?

WD: Well, I don't believe it is a political party. I believe it is an un-American thing. The thing that I resent the most is that they are able to get into these unions, take them over, and represent to the world that a group of people that are in my plant, that I know are good, one-hundred-percent Americans, are trapped by this group, and they are represented to the world as supporting all of those ideologies, and it is not so, and I feel that they really ought to be smoked out and shown up for what they are, so that all of the good, free causes in this country, all the liberalisms that really are American, can go out without the taint of communism. That is my sincere feeling on it.

HAS: Do you feel that there is a threat of Communism in the motion-picture industry?

WD: Yes, there is, and there are many reasons why they would like to take it over or get in and control it, or disrupt it, but I don't think they have gotten very far, and I think the industry is made up of good Americans, just like in my plant, good, solid Americans. My boys have been fighting it longer than I have. They are trying to get out from under it and they will in time if we can just show them up.

HAS: There are presently pending before this committee two bills relative to outlawing the Communist Party. What thoughts have you as to whether or not those bills should be passed?

WD: Well, I don't know as I qualify to speak on that. I feel if the thing can be proven un-American that it ought to be outlawed. I think in some way it should be done without interfering with the rights of the people. I think that will be done. I have that faith. Without interfering, I mean, with the good, American rights that we all have now, and we want to preserve.

HAS: Have you any suggestions to offer as to how the industry can be helped in fighting this menace?

WD: Well, I think there is a good start toward it. I know that I have been handicapped out there in fighting it, because they have been hiding behind this labor setup, they get themselves closely tied up in the labor thing, so that if you try to get rid of them they make a labor case out of it. We must keep the American labor unions clean. We have got to fight for them.

HAS: That is all of the questions I have, Mr. Chairman.

CHAIRMAN: Mr. Vail.

R. B. VAIL: No questions.

CHAIRMAN: Mr. McDowell.

J. MCDOWELL: No questions.

WD: Sir?

JM: I have no questions. You have been a good witness.

WD: Thank you.

CHAIRMAN: Mr. Disney, you are the fourth producer we have had as a witness, and each one of those four producers said, generally speaking, the same thing, and that is that the Communists have made inroads, have attempted inroads. I just want to point that out because there seems to be a very strong unanimity among the producers that have testified before us. In addition to producers, we have had actors and writers testify to the same. There is no doubt but what the movies are probably the greatest medium for entertainment in the United States and in the world. I think you, as a creator of entertainment, probably are one of the greatest examples in the profession. I want to congratulate you on the form of entertainment which you have given the American people and given the world and congratulate you for taking time out to come here and testify before this committee. He has been very helpful. Do you have any more questions, Mr. Stripling?

HAS: I am sure he does not have any more, Mr. Chairman.

RES: No; I have no more questions.

CHAIRMAN: Thank you very much, Mr. Disney.

SOURCE: "Testimony of Walter E. Disney, Hearings Before the Committee on Un-American Activities," House of Representatives, 80th Congress, First Session (Friday, 24 October 1947).

A PERSONAL NARRATIVE OF THE KOREAN WAR
(1950, by Bob Roy)

Korea was divided during the last week of World War II when a Soviet effort to occupy the country was stopped by American troops at the thirty-eighth parallel of the Korean peninsula. The two sides agreed to work toward establishing an independent state while occupying the territories. By 1947, however, the Cold War was already entrenched and the North Koreans established themselves as the Democratic People's Republic (DPR), a Soviet satellite. The newly formed United Nations sponsored the creation of the Republic of Korea (ROK) in the south during the following year.

On June 25, 1950, DPR troops, trained and armed by the Soviets, crossed the parallel and attacked. The ROK army was ill-trained and poorly equipped and as a result suffered grievous losses until U.N. forces, headed by American troops, arrived in early July to shore up defenses. This personal narrative, written by an eighteen-year-old American soldier arriving in one of the first waves, illustrates the atrocious fighting characteristic of this dead-end conflict.

Mark D. Baumann,
New York University

See also **Korean War.**

When we heard the news of the invasion we didn't pay any attention to it. The officers did, but we didn't.

On the last day of June we got paid, and as usual the whole camp cleared out except for the guys who had duty. Everybody else went into town and stayed until the midnight curfew. At midnight we all came in to the barracks pretty well feeling our oats. We'd just gotten to bed when one of our lieutenants came in, threw on the lights and said, "Pack your gear. We're headed for Korea."

That's when we knew the war was on.

A lot of the guys were writing letters, hoping to get them out somehow, because the families weren't notified. Nobody knew we were going. And of course nobody knew what the hell was going to happen when we got there.

We landed near Pusan on the first of July, and it took us four days to get into position. First we were put on a train and went as far as Taejon. At Taejon we loaded onto trucks, and from there we moved a little farther north each day. I had no idea where we were going. All I knew was we were headed for the front, wherever the hell that was. I was only a PFC, and when they tell you to go somewhere, you go. You don't ask questions.

What I remember most about those four days was not getting any sleep. And the flies. The flies would carry you away. We were in this little Korean village, before we went up to our final position, and Marguerite Higgins showed up and started interviewing us, and the flies . . . we were spitting them out of our mouths as we talked.

And the stench. The Koreans put human excrement in their rice paddies, and God did it smell.

About seven in the morning I decided to open a can of C rations, and that's when we saw the tanks. I just dropped the can. What the hell was this? Nobody told us about any tanks.

Before I fired the first round I counted thirty-five tanks coming down the road. Everybody was shitting their pants. From what I understand now, the South Koreans had been running from the tanks, and they wanted somebody up there who wasn't going to run. But at the time we weren't told that. We weren't told anything. We were all eighteen, nineteen years old, a bunch of cocky guys. We didn't know what to expect, and we didn't think too much about it. I think if I'd been thirty years old I would've turned around and run.

We didn't realize what we'd gotten into until we saw those tanks. But by then we were in it.

We had no armor-piercing shells, so we tried to stop them by hitting the tracks. We would've been better off throwing Molotov cocktails at them. Some rounds were duds, some were even smoke rounds. We could see them bounce right off the tanks.

We fired as fast as we could. As soon as we'd get a round into the breech we'd cover our ears and let it go, get another one in, fire that one . . . but they went right through us, right on down the road.

A round from one of the tanks hit right in front of my gun. I saw it coming. I saw the turret turn. We worked as fast as we could to try and get off another round, but the tank shot first, and all five of us were thrown back over the hill from the concussion and the earth hitting us in the face. Our ears were ringing. We were all disoriented, couldn't function at all for five or ten minutes.

But the gun was all right. The lieutenant, he wanted us to go back and get it. The tank was still there, with its turret pointed right at us. I said to him, "I'm not going up there until that tank moves." I disobeyed a direct order. I said, "If you want that gun, you go get it."

He didn't go. The gun just sat there, and the tank waited there for a while, and we kept peeking over the hill, watching the tank, until it moved farther down the road.

We stayed there for a while longer and just watched the tanks. A few had stopped alongside the road and were firing into our positions, into the infantry, but none of them stayed around for long. Then our officers moved us across the road and behind a hill where the mortars were.

By this time, eight, nine in the morning, it was raining like hell. The mortars were right behind us, firing for all they were worth. The North Korean infantry had come down the road in trucks, and had gotten out of the trucks and started moving around our flanks. I didn't actually see the North Koreans deploy, because our view was blocked by the hill in front of us, but we knew their infantry must have come up behind the tanks because the mortars and our own infantry were all firing like crazy.

Me, I couldn't see anything to shoot at. So we got under a poncho, me and another guy, and we sat there smoking a cigarette.

An officer came by and yelled down at us, "What the hell are you doing?"

"We're having a smoke."

He says, "You're about to die."

"Yeah," we said, "we're havin' our last smoke."

That's the way it was for us. That was our state of mind. We'd been told how the North Koreans were a ragtag army, couldn't fight worth a shit, couldn't shoot straight, all that baloney. And what did we know? A bunch of kids? We just believed what we were told. And it was raining like hell. And our ammo's no good.

We had nothing at all to fight with.

We'd been in trouble from the beginning, only now we knew it.

Hell, it was even worse than we knew. By now all the radios were out. The tanks had run over the communications wire, and the ones in the jeeps got wet from the rain and just stopped working. The infantry was strung out along the ridge, and we were just behind them, and there was no communication between any of the units.

I heard Brad Smith give the order to withdraw. He was up on the hill behind us. He stood up there and gave the order verbally. Just yelled it out. I don't remember exactly what he said, if he said "Every man for himself," but they were words to that effect.

So we got the word, but I found out later that one platoon never did get the word to pull out. They were left there all by themselves. Some of those guys eventually got out, and some didn't.

As soon as we heard the withdrawal order we took off down the hill and crossed the road, but by now the North Koreans had gotten behind us. They had the high ground, and I was down in a rice paddy and all friggin' hell broke loose. It sounded like a bunch of bees. Friggin' bullets bouncing all over the place.

Normally what you do when you have to withdraw is you set up a rendezvous point. Then you retreat in an orderly fashion toward that point. But there was never any rendezvous point. Nobody told us anything. So we all took off on our own.

I was with a squad of guys who all got captured. Every one of them except me. I went over a railroad embankment, running like a bastard, because the North Koreans were still firing at us from the hills. Everybody was with me when I went over the embankment, but after running three or four hundred yards I turned around and, Jesus, I'm all alone.

I'm in the middle of all these rice paddies, and I'm thinking, Where the hell is everybody?

I found out, forty years later, that everybody else went down the *right* side of the railroad tracks. They went due south, where the North Korean tanks were, and they got captured. Most of them spent the war as POWs. I went down the left side, kind of southeast, because I wasn't about to go where those tanks were.

We were on the Kum River waiting to be relieved by the 19th Infantry when General Walker showed up. He stood next to his jeep and gave us a talk. "If they come across this river," he says, "you guys are to stay here and fight to the death." Then he jumps in his jeep and takes off.

And we're all saying, "Yeah, sure."

They got tanks, and we got nothing to knock them out with. I still had only a .45 at the time, and I think six rounds of ammunition.

You've got to understand what it feels like to be in combat and not have enough ammunition, or have a weapon that don't work. The feeling of helplessness. What I'm saying is, it's easy to sit back and say, Well, those guys ran. Sure we ran. But what did we have to fight with?

You read about a lot of the wounded and litter cases being left behind. But I saw guys who should've gotten medals. I saw guys carrying other guys who had been shot in the legs. There were a lot of guys trying to help other people out. I saw a buddy of mine stay behind to lay down covering fire, and I don't know to this day if he got out of there. Everybody was trying to help out the best they could.

We were sent over there to delay the North Koreans. We delayed them seven hours. Don't ask me if it was worth it. We were a bunch of kids and we were just trying to do our jobs.

SOURCE: Roy, Bob. From "First Blood," in *No Bugles, No Drums: An Oral History of the Korean War.* By Rudy Tomedi. John Wiley & Sons, 1993.

"WAR STORY"
(c. 1950–1953, by Elaine H. Kim)

Within a few months of their initial engagement in the Korean conflict, U.N. troops were able to push the North Koreans' front back across the thirty-eighth parallel. American forces, headed by General Douglas MacArthur, pursued the North Korean forces into the communist-controlled territory that instigated the introduction of thousands of Chinese troops into the war. For the next three years, bloody battles raged in and around Seoul.

In this selection, Korean-American writer Elaine Kim narrates her half-sister's family's narrow escape from persecution in Seoul during the initial months of the conflict. The detailed retelling of their flight is accompanied by Kim's meditations on what it means to be Korean American. The differences between her half-sister's life during war and Kim's relatively prosperous existence in America illuminate Kim's experience of living with *han,* "the anguished feeling of being far from what you wanted, a longing that never went away, but ate and slept with you every day of your life."

Mark D. Baumann,
New York University

See also **Asian Americans; Korea, Relations with; Korean Americans; Korean War.**

To most Americans the 1950–53 war in Korea is not familiar or interesting, not like the Second World War or the war in Vietnam. Not many Americans know that the United States has been shaping the destiny of everyone on the Korean peninsula since the turn of the century—handing Korea over to Japan by secret agreement in 1909 and helping the Soviet Union divide the country in half along political lines at the end of

World War II. Even today, most Americans might be surprised to know how much American "aid" has gone into creating and propping up regimes that are supportive of American military and economic interests in Korea. Traditionally, Korea and Koreans have not been of much concern to the average American. What finally brought Korea into the consciousness of the American people was the war, in which American troops participated.

The morning the war began, my parents were still in bed when I got up. My parents never slept late; it was the only time I can remember getting up before they did. I wondered why they lay in bed and, as if to answer my unspoken question, they told me that war has broken out in Korea.

I had just finished fourth grade at a small town primary school in Maryland and was eager for a summer of bare feet and playing jacks. None of my friends had ever heard of Korea; they often accused me of making up the word "Korean" because I must have really been Chinese Japanese after all. But Korea was important to me because my parents and all the people they knew never seemed to think or talk of anything else.

We had many relatives in Korea then, as we do now. Our family, like so many Korean families, is scattered across the world. My uncle joined the resistance movement against Japan in China, and my aunt joined the Communist movement in North Korea. My half-brother was taken to Japan by other Koreans during the Second World War. Not one of my father's blood relatives ever immigrated to America after he came in 1926, so I have first cousins in China, Japan, North and South Korea, but none in America. We were the estranged branch of the family, living among Westerners who had never even heard of Korea.

Throughout my life, it has seemed to me that being Korean meant living with *han* every day. *Han*, the anguished feeling of being far from what you wanted, a longing that never went away, but ate and slept with you every day of your life, has no exact equivalent in English. It must be a Korean feeling, born from and nurtured by what Korea and Koreans have faced over the centuries: longing for the end of the brutal Japanese rule, longing for the native place left behind when you went into exile, longing for your loved ones after being separated by war or the new boundary in your homeland, longing for the reunification of Korea as one nation of people who can trace their common roots back several millennia.

Han is by no means a hopeless feeling, however. It is something like rage. You can see it sometimes in people's eyes. South Korean poet Kim Chi Ha shows it to us in "Groundless Rumors," which is about a day worker who, jailed and executed for daring to curse his oppression, is said to roll his limbless trunk back and forth between the walls of his cell in protest. The sound strikes fear into the hearts of the powerful and lights a "strange fire" in the eyes of the oppressed everywhere.

Liberation from Japanese rule was the holy cause of Korean people my parents' age. Like many other resisters, my father left Korea for Japan as a teenager, just after Korea was annexed. He left behind his new bride who was pregnant at the time with my half-sister. Except for a brief summer visit, he did not return to his native place, not even when his wife died of consumption. Instead, he left Japan on a boat bound for America. He stayed twenty years with a student visa and had various restaurant jobs before he started to work for the U.S. and South Korean governments in Washington, D.C. He and my mother, the daughter of an immigrant Korean sugar plantation worker in Hawaii, met in Chicago and married in New York, where my older brother and I were born.

I never saw our half-sister until I visited Korea at age twenty. My Korean isn't fluent and she can't speak English, but after a year of living with her and her family, I was able to understand most of what she said and say pretty much what I wanted to to her. Because we are sisters, I am always haunted by her stories, feeling that we were like a pair of twins separated by accident. I could have been the one imprisoned for "anti-Japanese thoughts," the one married off to a man I had never met, the one drinking in the fragrance of cucumbers I could not afford to eat. I might have known nothing about American racism. In turn, she could have been the "Chink" or the "Jap" on the school playground, the one with the full stomach and the saddle shoes, diagraming English sentences for homework, ears stinging from being asked by teachers to stand in front of the room to tell her classmates "what you are."

Perhaps this mysterious feeling of being interchangeable has forged the bond welding many Americans in a nation of immigrants to the people who remained at home. This is my half-sister's story.

On 25 June 1950, when the war began, I was at church with your two little nephews when I noticed people running around outside in the streets, shouting that people from the North had crossed the 38th parallel. I didn't worry much, since I had witnessed so many shooting incidents when I lived near the 38th parallel. No one believed that our country would be divided for long, just as no one guessed that there would be such a terrible war to bring death and destruction everywhere.

The announcer on the radio said that people were being killed or captured in the streets, but I was sure there wouldn't be any fighting in Seoul. I did worry about your *hyungbu* [her husband, my brother-in-law], who had a job as a reservoir and irrigation worker near the DMZ [demilitarized zone]. Under the Japanese, we Koreans had been out of work except for the worst menial jobs because the Japanese had taken all the middle- and high-level jobs. Now that Japan had surrendered, he finally had work, and we were glad even though it meant he had to live far from home for the time being. I had returned with the children to Father-in-law's house in Seoul to escape the cross-fire in the region. But even though there were rumors that the fighting was coming closer and closer to Seoul and many people were packing up to flee across the Han River, I still didn't think anything would happen and had no thoughts of fleeing further south, since I was physically separated from my husband.

A day or two later, he arrived at our gate, so exhausted by his three-day walk to Seoul without food or sleep that he collapsed, speechless, on the floor. He wouldn't budge, even though there were gunshots all around and most our neighbors had already fled across the river. Father-in-law was jumping up and down screaming that everyone else was gone, but *hyungbu* said he couldn't move even if his life depended on it.

We finally ran out in the rain, carrying only some rice and our children on our backs, heading for his aunt's house, where we all sat around worrying about what to do. We thought that at least it would be better to be together. I had heard somewhere that bullets don't penetrate cotton comforters, so I wrapped the children up in the blankets. They were hot and I couldn't sleep, but *hyungbu*, still exhausted from his walk to Seoul, snored all night long.

When we peered outside the next morning, we saw red flags everywhere. The people from the North had arrived. On the radio, the South Korean president was telling everyone, "Don't worry, everything is all right. The North Koreans will never be able to penetrate Seoul." Later, we found out that the president had already fled, leaving behind a tape-recorded message. After he had safely crossed the Han River, the South Korean military blew up the bridge in his wake, even though many refugees on the bridge were killed.

We decided to go back home, figuring that no matter where we were the situation would be the same. The problem was that the North Korean soldiers were looking for young men to induct into their Righteous Brave Army. The North Koreans had access to all the census information and government documents, so they knew how many young men were in each household. Each night they would bang on people's gates looking for young men, who would be hiding under the floorboards or somewhere else out of sight. We would lie, saying that the young men had gone to the countryside to buy food and hadn't returned. The soldiers would ask the neighborhood children to tell them where their fathers were, and some of them would reply, "He's hiding under the floorboards." Then the men would be discovered and drafted. They didn't ask your nephew Sung-hi, though. Anyway, we had instructed him never to tell.

Since the United States was bombing everything during the day, all work had to be done under cover of night, and one person from each household was required to come out to detonate bombs and rebuild wreckage. The North Koreans were not harsh with us because our neighborhood was poor. They said I didn't have to work with a baby on my back and that Father-in-law was too old to work.

I had two bags of rice, which I hid with the linens. Rice was hard to come by then: none of the stores were open, and it was several months before the rice harvest. We bought potatoes and barley and ate that, mixed with a little rice. People were making stew from zucchini leaves and whatever vegetables they could get, boiling them with some barley in lots of water.

When *hyungbu* could no longer bear hiding under the floorboards and urinating into a bowl, he decided to try fleeing to the countryside to his relative's house. We had no idea that things were even worse there. He couldn't go alone because people were being grabbed off the streets, so he dressed up as an old farmer and took Sung-hi on his back, thinking that no one would try to take him into the army if he had a child with him. If he had gone to *Uijungbu* after all, I probably would never have seen him again, since his relatives there had become Communists, and he might have ended up in North Korea. We would have been a divided family like so many others who were separated when the borders closed and all traffic between North and South Korea stopped permanently. If he had been caught along the way, perhaps our son would have become one of those orphans crying by the side of the road.

It happened that the construction company *hyungbu* had been working in was run by men sympathetic with North Korea. Someone came to our house and told me that the people working in that company would not be drafted into the North Korean army. Instead, they would receive identification cards showing them to be draft exempt. Overjoyed, I ran all the way over the *Miari* hill to catch up with *hyungbu*, who was trudging along very slowly because he was really heartsick at leaving in the first place.

We were elated at first, but after he had worked for about one month, we began getting scared. The United Nations forces were coming closer and closer to Seoul, and we thought we'd get into trouble for cooperating with North Koreans. *Hyungbu* stopped going to work and, sure enough, when the South Korean soldiers re-entered Seoul in late September, they arrested and imprisoned all of the people who had cooperated with North Koreans, including *hyungbu*'s co-workers. Many people were murdered at that time. Now *hyungbu* was hiding from the *South* Korean soldiers. This time, we pretended he was sick. We had him lie down next to a medicine distiller. Because he was so thin and pale, people really believed that he was ill.

By now everyone was talking about how Korea would be reunited under UN forces. We had to go on living: it was autumn, so I went ahead and made winter *kimchee* and bought firewood for the winter. But in November the UN and South Korean forces were driven back down from North Korea. The South Korean army tried to draft all the young men, many of whom were hiding or running away. *Hyungbu* was tired of hiding and decided that since he was a citizen of South Korea, it was his duty to volunteer. But how he suffered for it!

The enlisted men had to walk to Taegu [250 miles away]. They were a ragged bunch, with blankets hung over their shoulders like hoboes or beggars. What kind of an "army" was that? The road was difficult and the weather was freezing and the men had to sell their watches and possessions to buy food along the way.

In Taegu *hyungbu* failed the physical examination. Those who failed were considered of little use and unable to fight, so they were poorly fed and had to live in barns. Many men were said to have died from exposure, malnutrition, and diseases carried by vermin. Somehow, though, *hyungbu* survived. He organized people to gather wood to sell so that they could buy food. Everyone cooperated with each other, even making trips into Taegu to buy medicine for the sick among them. Finally, these men just deserted and tried to get back to their families.

Meanwhile, I was in Seoul with the babies and Father-in-law. I didn't know how we were going to flee from the battle zone. But one of *hyungbu*'s relatives had connections with a cargo train, so we got a place on top of some big drums filled with gasoline. Even though it was dangerous, everyone wanted to get a place on top of the train. We were so happy that we could get a ride, since Father-in-law was much too old to walk. Rice prices had plummeted in Seoul, so I bought two large bags of rice to carry with us. The train would go for a few hours and then stop for a few hours. Sometimes it would stop on top of some mountain and not move the whole night. We were afraid to get down to urinate, for fear the train would take off without us or that we would lose our places. It took us over a week to get to Pusan.

It was December, so it was very cold. We used our comforters for cover from the snow and freezing rain, but the wet comforters kept freezing. It was hot and sweaty under them, but if we lifted them, we would catch a chill; somehow the baby caught pneumonia. Not having any food, I tried to nurse him, but I was not producing any milk because I wasn't eating anything myself. My nipples got torn from his desperate sucking, and I was sore from his clawing little hands. He was burning up with fever by the time we finally reached Pusan, and I thought that the child was going to die.

The first thing I did in Pusan was rush to the hospital for some penicillin for the baby. We didn't have any place to sleep. Rooms were expensive, and Pusan was filled to overflowing with refugees from Seoul and other places. We were among the last to arrive—we learned that North Korean soldiers had re-entered Seoul just after we left—and we couldn't find a place to stay, so we were sleeping in the streets.

I had earlier vowed to myself that no matter how badly off I was, I would never seek out Small Uncle [Father's younger brother], because he had told us that he had no way to leave Seoul. We found out later that he had gone to Pusan in a truck sponsored by the bank where he worked. He took with him not only his entire family but even all his home furnishings. Now, with my child almost dead, there was nothing I could do but go to the bank branch in Pusan to find Uncle, who was surprised and a little embarrassed to see me. He took me to the place where he was staying with his family: it was a huge house, big enough to hold many families. The floors were heated and the people were cooking and eating almost normally, very unlike refugees. Some of the other bank employees had brought their relatives with them. It was clear that Uncle could have brought us with him. War brings out the worst in people. You never know, not even about your own relatives, until something dreadful happens . . .

Meanwhile, Father [in the United States] had put notices in the newspapers asking after us. We couldn't even wash our faces on top of those oil drums on the cargo train; how could we read the newspaper? Uncle saw one of the notices and contacted Father, who sent us a little money. Since we were living with him then, Uncle took all the money. Father asked me to write to him, and when I told him about how Uncle had left us in Seoul, fleeing with his family and belongings to Pusan, Father was furious. I got into trouble with Uncle, but I was glad that someone knew what had happened to us.

I was surprised to see so many young men in Pusan. I had thought they would enlist in the South Korean army as they were supposed to and as *hyungbu* had. How naive we were! The young men had run away from the draft to Pusan.

Since his father was not around, your little nephew went around calling every man he saw "Daddy." I kept hearing about how many men were dying, and I didn't know whether my husband was one of them. One day, your older nephew ran into our house crying, "Mommy, Mommy, there's a beggar coming this way who looks just like Daddy!" Sure enough, it was *hyungbu*, dirty, emaciated, and dressed in rags and tatters. The new, thick pants he had been wearing when he left several months before were torn and infested with lice and fleas. We burned those clothes, and he washed and got a haircut so that he looked like a human being again. We prepared to move into our household. Like a fool, I gave all the rice I had brought and the money I had to Uncle, so we started off on our own with nothing. People were just constructing shacks here and there with dirt floors and straw mats for walls. We too built one of these.

Hyungbu found work at the docks loading and unloading cargo, but the contractor took the workers' pay and disappeared. We were in real trouble then: the only food we could afford was bean sprouts. We couldn't even buy soy sauce, so we boiled the sprouts and ate them with a little salt. It wasn't even like eating.

When fall came, Father's friend got *hyungbu* a job. We were paid in barley, but it was better than not having any work at all. Your little nephew would see the autumn persimmons that the street vendors were selling and say, "Mommy, wouldn't it be nice to have some of those soft persimmons?" I would just tell him I'd buy him some later. He remembered my promise for a long time, and he kept reminding me about it. But people were lucky to be eating anything at all back then.

That winter, Father-in-law died. We couldn't even afford to take him to the hospital.

There should never be wars. It's the most blameless ones who are sacrificed. There was a young woman living in the shack next to us who cried all day long. It turns out that she had to leave one of her little girls behind on the road while she was fleeing. Many children were left at the side of the road or dropped into rivers if they started to cry or make noise while their parents were trying to flee under cover of night. Everyone in the group would argue that it was better for one child to die than for a whole group to be discovered and prevented from escaping. How can a mother go on living after she has thrown away her baby?

During the war, Father came to Pusan from America. Today, people can travel so easily between Korea and America, but in those days, arriving from America was like arriving from another planet. I had seen him only once before, when I was about six years old. I remember running in from playing outside to find a strange man eating on the *maru* (wooden floor veranda). People said, "That is your father." He had returned from Japan during the summer for just one visit to Cholwon. Too shy and scared to greet him, I ran out the back door. Now twenty-five years later, it was so strange to see him—he didn't seem like a father, he looked so young. I bowed to him, and he said, "Who bows to their own father?" He wanted to come to our house, and when he saw our shack, he was shocked. He didn't have much money himself, but he gave us $100, which was a huge sum then; we rented a room for six months with it. Your niece was born in the middle of the night while we were living our refugee life in Pusan. *Hyungbu* had gotten a construction job, so we had some income until the end of the war, when we returned to Seoul to try to rebuild our lives.

Now that the children are all grown up, I often think about how it was never easy. We worked so hard to send them all to school and see each one of them marry and start a family. Some people want their children to marry on auspicious days of the astrological calendar, but our children married on patriotic days, like Liberation Day or the birthdate of Korea's mythical founder.

On the small plot of land we live on in the outskirts of Seoul, we spend our time now growing vegetables of all kinds—tomatoes, cabbage, squash, onions, garlic, and corn—and taking care of our fruit trees. Now that *hyungbu* is retired, we have time to visit with three grandsons and three granddaughters. I have to work hard, since your older nephew and his family live with us. These days parents-in-law have to bend over backwards to get their children to live with them. In my time daughters-in-law had to do all the housework, but nowadays the mothers-in-law have to do everything just to keep their sons living with them. We don't have any social security or retirement income, so we have to get help from the children. In return, we try to do our best for them. I can say that we have a happy life now.

During the war, everyone was talking about how we Koreans were all going to be killed somehow, either by American bombers or by North Koreans, whom we heard were killing people everywhere. Actually, they were punishing rich people and high officials, but we didn't know what would happen to people like us. Father was trying to figure out a way to bring me to America. People would say to my sons, "Yeah! If you go to your Grandpa, you won't have to die like us." But I was afraid to go: I didn't know where my husband was then; I felt I couldn't leave my old father-in-law; I couldn't speak any English; and I had two small children. Besides, Father was a stranger to me, since I had only met him twice! So I said I didn't want to leave.

Later on I sometimes regretted missing the chance to go to America. Who knows how things would have turned out? Maybe my children would have been able to study and become successful, because in America it seems possible to get somewhere by working hard. In Korea, no matter how hard you try and how much you work, you don't necessarily get anywhere at all. Just think, if my husband or my sons had worked as hard in America as they have in Korea, they might have received a real reward for their effort. On the other hand, maybe American life would have ruined my children. It seems that people in America don't think very much about their parents or their families. And what if my own grandchildren couldn't even speak to me in our language? Or what if *hyungbu* and I had returned to Korea, leaving our children in America like so many older people do? We haven't much money and wouldn't be able to see our children and grandchildren often like we do now. And after all, we do love our country.

We are Koreans and we want to remain Koreans. My second son says that he'd rather live in the filthiest and poorest Korean place than in the most luxurious American place, just because he wants to live in his own country. Even though we aren't as comfortable, we like living in our own country. There's no place like your own country. During the past ten or fifteen years, many people have been leaving for the States and Canada. Of course ordinary people can't emigrate, since you need money to emigrate. The people who really need to emigrate so they can work to eat can't afford to go. The ones who leave are pretty well off. They sneak money out with them so they can start businesses, make money, and live out their dream of being like kings and queens in foreign countries. Sometimes these days, people in Korea criticize those who leave for America, saying they have deserted their motherland, taking all their wealth with them and leaving the problems for someone else to solve.

When my sister says this about Korean immigrants deserting their homeland, she only reinforces my own concern for the well-being of Koreans, both in America and in Korea. As a Korean American, I support movements for democratic reforms in South Korea, am critical of Japanese and U.S. exploitation of Korea, and cherish a vibrant hope for national reunification. At the same time, I live and work in the United States, and I feel I must find ways to work against racism and toward our community's strength, health, and self-sufficiency.

I often think about what it would have been like for my sister and her family to have immigrated to America, just as I wonder what my life would be like now if I had been born and raised in Korea. I always conclude that things turned out better this way. I probably would not have finished school in Korea—how could I have passed those excruciatingly difficult college entrance exams? In fact, I would probably have been married off at the "appropriate time" and pressed into a role that Korean women of my generation rarely escaped, a role that many women born and raised in the United States would find difficult and unattractive. But although my sister does not enjoy the same material possessions Americans do, she is still happy because she stayed in the country she loved, among her friends and family members, speaking her native language, instead of living as a stranger in an adopted land.

Nonetheless, there is a branch of the family she can visit in America. The last time we parted—she has visited America four times now, and I have lived at her house in Korea—I teased her about how she always weeps as if we were never going to meet again, even though we see each other every few years. She didn't shed a tear when she left Oakland this time.

SOURCE: Kim, Elaine H. "War Story." In *Making Waves: An Anthology of Writings By and About Asian American Women by Asian Women United of California*. Edited by Asian Women United of California. Boston: Beacon Press, 1989.

THE HISTORY OF GEORGE CATLETT MARSHALL
(14 June 1951, by Senator Joseph McCarthy)

In a speech delivered in Wheeling, West Virginia in early 1950, Joseph Raymond McCarthy (1908–57) achieved national notoriety when he claimed that the United States State Department had been virtually overrun by card-carrying members of the Communist party. By taking advantage of Cold War paranoia, McCarthy, an unremarkable Republican senator from Wisconsin, managed to parlay his unsubstantiated accusations into a virtual second career. Despite the fact that the State Department was exonerated in a Senate investigation, McCarthy repeated his accusations and added new ones. When the Republicans seized control of Congress in 1953, McCarthy became chairman of the Senate permanent investigations subcommittee of the Government Operations Committee. Inspired in part by the House Committee on Un-American Activities (HUAC) investigations in the House of Representatives, McCarthy and his allies, Roy Cohn and David Schine, set about searching for Communist influence at the highest levels of the American Government. Their biggest target was Secretary of Defense, author of the Marshall Plan, and eventual Noble Peace Prize recipient, George Catlett Marshall. After having slandered Marshall and President Truman, McCarthy, spurred on by many of his Republican colleagues, turned his eye toward Secretary of the Army Robert T. Stevens and his aides. During a series of highly publicized televised hearings, the public at last got a look at Joseph McCarthy. For days, they watched as he made wild accusations, browbeat witnesses, and evaded repeated requests to produce tangible evidence. Unable to prove Stevens or the Army guilty of subversion, McCarthy was undone. His influence with the public shattered, the once unknown Senator from Wisconsin was censured by the Senate during the winter of 1954.

Laura M. Miller,
Vanderbilt University

See also **Anticommunism; Cold War; House Committee on Un-American Activities; Marshall Plan; McCarthyism.**

How can we account for our present situation unless we believe that men high in this Government are concerting to deliver us to disaster? This must be the product of a great conspiracy, a conspiracy on a scale so immense as to dwarf any previous such venture in the history of man. A conspiracy of infamy so black that, when it is finally exposed, its principals shall be forever deserving of the maledictions of all honest men.

Who constitutes the highest circles of this conspiracy? About that we cannot be sure. We are convinced that Dean Acheson, who steadfastly serves the interests of nations other than his own, the friend of Alger Hiss, who supported him in his hour of retribution, who contributed to his defense fund, must be high on the roster. The President? He is their captive. I have wondered, as have you, why he did not dispense with so great a liability as Acheson to his own and his party's interests. It is now clear to me. In the relationship of master and man, did you ever hear of man firing master? Truman is a satisfactory front. He is only dimly aware of what is going on.

I do not believe that Mr. Truman is a conscious party to the great conspiracy, although it is being conducted in his name. I believe that if Mr. Truman had the ability to associate good Americans around him, be would have behaved as a good American in this most dire of all our crises.

It is when we return to an examination of General Marshall's record since the spring of 1942 that we approach an explanation of the carefully planned retreat from victory, Let us again review the Marshall record, as I have disclosed it from all the sources available and all of them friendly. This grim and solitary man it was who, early in World War II, determined to put his impress upon our global strategy, political and military.

It was Marshall, who, amid the din for a "second front now" from every voice of Soviet inspiration, sought to compel the British to invade across the Channel in the fall of 1942 upon penalty of our quitting the war in Europe.

It was Marshall who, after North Africa had been secured, took the strategic direction of the war out of Roosevelt's hands and—who fought the British desire, shared by Mark Clark, to advance from Italy into the eastern plains of Europe ahead of the Russians.

It was a Marshall-sponsored memorandum, advising appeasement of Russia In Europe and the enticement of Russia into the far-eastern war, circulated at Quebec, which foreshadowed our whole course at Tehran, at Yalta, and until now in the Far East.

It was Marshall who, at Tehran, made common cause with Stalin on the strategy of the war in Europe and marched side by side with him thereafter.

It was Marshall who enjoined his chief of military mission in Moscow under no circumstances to "irritate" the Russians by asking them questions about their forces, their weapons, and their plans, while at the same time opening our schools, factories, and gradually our secrets to them in this count.

It was Marshall who, as Hanson Baldwin asserts, himself referring only to the "military authorities," prevented us having a corridor to Berlin. So it was with the capture and occupation of Berlin and Prague ahead of the Russians.

It was Marshall who sent Deane to Moscow to collaborate with Harriman in drafting the terms of the wholly unnecessary bribe paid to Stalin at Yalta. It was Marshall, with Hiss at his elbow and doing the physical drafting of agreements at Yalta, who ignored the contrary advice of his senior, Admiral Leahy, and of MacArtbur and Nimitz in regard to the folly of a major land invasion of Japan; who submitted intelligence reports which suppressed more truthful estimates in order to support his argument, and who finally induced Roosevelt to bring Russia into the Japanese war with a bribe that reinstated Russia in its pre-1904 imperialistic position in Manchuria—an act which, in effect, signed the death warrant of the Republic of China.

It was Marshall, with Acheson and Vincent eagerly assisting, who created the China policy which, destroying China, robbed us of a great and friendly ally, a buffer against the Soviet imperialism with which we are now at war.

It was Marshall who, after long conferences with Acheson and Vincent, went to China to execute the criminal folly of the disastrous Marshall mission.

It was Marshall who, upon returning from a diplomatic defeat for the United States at Moscow, besought the reinstatement of forty millions in lend-lease for Russia.

It was Marshall who, for 2 years suppressed General Wedemeyer's report, which is a direct and comprehensive repudiation of the Marshall policy.

It was Marshall who, disregarding Wedemeyer's advices on the urgent need for military supplies, the likelihood of China's defeat without ammunition and equipment, and our "moral obligation" to furnish them, proposed instead a relief bill bare of military support.

It was the State Department under Marshall, with the wholehearted support of Michael Lee and Remington in the Commerce Department, that sabotaged the \$125,000,000 military-aid bill to China in 1948.

It was Marshall who fixed the dividing line for Korea along the thirty-eighth parallel, a line historically chosen by Russia to mark its sphere of interest in Korea.

It is Marshall's strategy for Korea which has turned that war into a pointless slaughter, reversing the dictum of Von Clausewitz and every military theorist since him that the object of a war is not merely to kill but to impose your will on the enemy.

It is Marshall-Acheson strategy for Europe to build the defense of Europe solely around the Atlantic Pact nations, excluding the two great wells of anti-Communist manpower in Western Germany and Spain and spurning the organized armies of Greece and Turkey—another case of following the Lattimore advice of "let them fall but don't let it appear that we pushed them."

It is Marshall who, advocating timidity as a policy so as not to annoy the forces of Soviet imperialism in Asia, had admittedly put a brake on the preparations to fight, rationalizing his reluctance on the ground that the people are fickle and if war does not come, will hold him to account for excessive zeal.

What can be made of this unbroken series of decisions and acts contributing to the strategy of defeat? They cannot be attributed to incompetence. If Marshall were merely stupid, the laws of probability would dictate that part of his decisions would serve this country's interest. If Marshall is innocent of guilty intention, how could he be trusted to guide the defense of this country further? We have declined so precipitously in relation to the Soviet Union in the last 6 years. How much swifter may be our fall into disaster with Marshall at the helm? Where Will all this stop? That is not a rhetorical question: Ours is not a rhetorical danger. Where next will Marshall carry us? It is useless to suppose that his nominal superior will ask him to resign. He cannot even dispense with Acheson.

What is the objective of the great conspiracy? I think it is clear from what has occurred and is now occurring: to diminish the United States in world affairs, to weaken us militarily, to confuse our spirit with talk of surrender in the Far East and to impair our will to resist evil. To what end? To the end that we shall be contained, frustrated and finally: fall victim to Soviet intrigue from within and Russian military might from without. Is that farfetched? There have been many examples in history of rich and powerful states which have been corrupted from within, enfeebled and deceived until they were unable to resist aggression....

It is the great crime of the Truman administration that it has refused to undertake the job of ferreting the enemy from its ranks. I once puzzled over that refusal. The President, I said, is a loyal American; why does he not lead in this enterprise? I think that I know why he does not. The President is not master in his own house. Those who are master there not only have a desire to protect the sappers and miners—they could not do otherwise. They themselves are not free. They belong to a larger conspiracy, the world-wide web of which has been spun from Moscow. It was Moscow, for example, which decreed that the United States should execute its loyal friend, the Republic of China. The executioners were that well-identified group headed by Acheson and George Catlett Marshall.

How, if they would, can they, break these ties, how return to simple allegiance to their native land? Can men sullied by their long and dreadful record afford us leadership in the world struggle with the enemy? How can a man whose every important act for years had contributed to the prosperity of the enemy reverse himself? The reasons for his past actions are immaterial. Regardless of why he has done what be did, be has done it and the momentum of that course bears him onward....

The time has come to halt this tepid, milk-and-water acquiescence which a discredited administration, ruled by disloyalty, sends down to us. The American may belong to an old culture, he may be beset by enemies here and abroad, he may be distracted by the many words of counsel that assail him by day and night, but he is nobody's fool. The time has come for us to realize that the people who sent us here expect more than time-serving from us. The American who has never known defeat in war, does not expect to be again sold down the river in Asia. He does not want that kind of betrayal. He has had betrayal enough. He has never failed to fight for his liberties since George Washington rode to Boston in 1775 to put himself at the head of a band of rebels unversed in war. He is fighting tonight, fighting gloriously in a war on a distant American frontier made inglorious by the men he can no longer trust at the head of our affairs.

The America that I know, and that other Senators know, this vast and teeming and beautiful land, this hopeful society where the poor share the table of the rich as never before in history, where men of all colors, of all faiths, are brothers as never before in history, where great deeds have been done and great deeds are yet to do, that America deserves to be led not to humiliation or defeat, but to victory.

The Congress of the United States is the people's last hope, a free and open forum of the people's representatives. We felt the pulse of the people's response to the return of MacArthur. We know what it meant. The people, no longer trusting their executive, turn to us, asking that we reassert the constitutional prerogative of the Congress to declare the policy for the United States.

The time has come to reassert that prerogative, to oversee the conduct of this war, to declare that this body must have the final word on the disposition of Formosa and Korea. They fell from the grasp of the Japanese empire through our military endeavors, pursuant to a declaration of war made by the Congress of the United States on December 8, 1941. If the Senate speaks, as is its right, the disposal of Korea and Formosa can be made only by a treaty which must be ratified by this body. Should the administration dare to defy such a declaration, the Congress has abundant recourses which I need not spell out.

SOURCE: "The History of George Catlett Marshall." In *The Congressional Record: Proceedings and Debates of the 82nd Congress, First Session.* Volume 97, Part 5 (28 May 1951–27 June 1951): 6556–6603.

GENERAL DOUGLAS MACARTHUR'S SPEECH TO CONGRESS
(19 April 1951)

Douglas MacArthur (1880–1964) was a leading American general in World War II. The youngest army chief of staff in U.S. history, he was a military adviser for the Philippines before Franklin D. Roosevelt named him Commander of the Allied Forces in the Southwest Pacific in 1942. Two years later he took command of all Allied forces in the Pacific, and when the Japanese surrendered in 1945, he became sole administrator of the occupation government in Japan.

In 1950, the Republic of Korea, known as South Korea, was invaded from the north. Fearing communist expansion, the United Nations authorized the United States to organize armed forces to aid the republic. In addition to his occupation work, MacArthur then became U.N. commander in Korea. When China offered support to the North Korean invaders, MacArthur called for a tougher prosecution of the war. He proposed to institute a naval blockade of China and invade North Korea to destroy enemy bases there. President Harry S. Truman, however, was afraid that such aggressive action would provoke a much larger war. After MacArthur made several public statements in conflict with U.S. and U.N. policy, Truman relieved him of the Korean command, creating a nationwide controversy. MacArthur defended his policies in this speech to Congress. Later the recipient of many honors, MacArthur received a unanimous joint resolution of tribute from Congress in 1962.

Bettina Drew

See also **Korean War.**

. . . The Communist threat is a global one. Its successful advance in one sector threatens the destruction of every other sector. You cannot appease or otherwise surrender to communism in Asia without simultaneously undermining our efforts to halt its advance in Europe. . . .

. . . While I was not consulted prior to the President's decision to intervene in support of the Republic of Korea, that decision, from a military standpoint, proved a sound one, as we hurled back the invader and decimated his forces. Our victory was complete and our objectives within reach when Red China intervened with numerically superior ground forces. This created a new war and an entirely new situation—a situation not contemplated when our forces were committed against the North Korean invaders—a situation which called for new decisions in the diplomatic sphere to permit the realistic adjustment of military strategy. Such decisions have not been forthcoming.

While no man in his right mind would advocate sending our ground forces into continental China and such was never given a thought, the new situation did urgently demand a drastic revision of strategic planning if our political aim was to defeat this new enemy as we had defeated the old.

Apart from the military need as I saw it to neutralize the sanctuary protection given the enemy north of the Yalu, I felt that military necessity in the conduct of the war made mandatory:

1. The intensification of our economic blockade against China;
2. The imposition of a naval blockade against the China coast;
3. Removal of restrictions on air reconnaissance of China's coastal areas of Manchuria;
4. Removal of restrictions on the forces of the Republic of China on Formosa with logistical support to contribute to their effective operations against the common enemy.

For entertaining these views, all professionally designed to support our forces committed to Korea and bring hostilities to an end with the least possible delay and at a saving of countless American and Allied lives, I have been severely criticized in lay circles, principally abroad, despite my understanding that from a military standpoint the above views have been fully shared in past by practically every military leader concerned with the Korean campaign, including our own Joint Chiefs of Staff.

I called for reinforcements, but was informed that reinforcements were not available. I made clear that if not permitted to destroy the enemy buildup bases north of the Yalu; if not permitted to utilize the friendly Chinese force of some 600,000 men on Formosa; if not permitted to blockade the China coast to prevent the Chinese Reds from getting succor from without; and if there were to be no hope of major reinforcements, the position of the command from the military standpoint forbade victory. We could hold in Korea by constant maneuver and at an approximate area where our supply line advantages were in balance with the supply line disadvantages of the enemy, but we could hope at best for only an indecisive campaign, with its terrible and constant attrition upon our forces if the enemy utilized his full military potential. I have constantly called for new political decisions essential to a solution. Efforts have been made to distort my position. It has been said that I was in effect a warmonger. Nothing could be further from the truth. I know war as few other men now living know it, and nothing to me is more revolting. I have long advocated its complete abolition as its very destructiveness on both friend and foe has rendered it useless as a means of settling international disputes.

SOURCE: "Gen. Douglas MacArthur's 'Old Soldiers Never Die' Address to Congress, 19 April 1951." "Words and Deeds in American History: Selected Documents Celebrating the Manuscript Division's First 100 Years." Library of Congress. http://memory.loc.gov.

CENSURE OF SENATOR JOSEPH MCCARTHY
(2 December 1954)

By 1954 the investigative excesses of Wisconsin senator Joseph McCarthy had run their course. Once a virtually unknown Senator from Wisconsin, McCarthy ascended to national prominence by claiming he had proof that "card-carrying" members of the Communist party had infiltrated the U.S. State Department. Also serving as head of the Senate's Government Operations Committee and its permanent investigations subcommittee, McCarthy exceeded his limits when he set his sights on the United States Army. During days of nationally televised hearings, the American public watched as McCarthy, who many of them had previously only read about, browbeat and bullied witness after witness without ever producing a shred of tangible evidence to support his damning accusations. For McCarthy, the result was catastrophic. Public support, even among those who believed in his cause, dwindled and virtually disappeared. By the end of the year the Senate issued the condemnation seen here, which passed by a vote of 65–22. With the so-called Red Scare on the wane and the Democrats once again in control of the Senate, Joseph McCarthy was relegated to the role of political nonentity until his death in 1957.

Laura M. Miller,
Vanderbilt University

See also **Anticommunism; Cold War; McCarthyism.**

Resolved, That the Senator from Wisconsin, Mr. McCarthy, failed to cooperate with the Subcommittee on Privileges and Elections of the Senate Committee on Rules and Administration in clearing up matters referred to that subcommittee which concerned his conduct as a Senator and affected the honor of the Senate and, instead, repeatedly abused the subcommittee and its members who were trying to carry out assigned duties, thereby obstructing the constitutional processes of the Senate, and that this conduct of the Senator from Wisconsin, Mr. McCarthy, is contrary to senatorial traditions and is hereby condemned.

Sec 2. The Senator from Wisconsin, Mr. McCarthy, in writing to the chairman of the Select Committee to Study Censure Charges (Mr. Watkins) after the Select Committee had issued its report and before the report was presented to the Senate charging three members of the Select Committee with "deliberate deception" and "fraud" for failure to disqualify themselves; in stating to the press on November 4, 1954, that the special Senate session that was to begin November 8, 1954, was a "lynch-party"; in repeatedly describing this special Senate session as a "lynch bee" in a nationwide television and radio show on November 7, 1954; in stating to the public press on November 13, 1954, that the chairman of the Select Committee (Mr. Watkins) was guilty of "the most unusual, most cowardly things I've ever heard of" and stating further: "I expected he would be afraid to answer the questions, but didn't think he'd be stupid enough to make a public statement;" and in characterizing the said committee as the "unwitting handmaiden," "involuntary agent" and "attorneys-in-fact" of the Communist Party and in charging that the said committee in writing its report "imitated Communist methods—that it distorted, misrepresented, and omitted in its effort to manufacture a plausible rationalization" in support of its recommendations to the Senate, which characterizations and charges were contained in a statement released to the press and inserted in the Congressional Record of November 10, 1954, acted contrary to senatorial ethics and tended to bring the Senate into dishonor and disrepute, to obstruct the constitutional processes of the Senate, and to impair its dignity; and such conduct is hereby condemned.

SOURCE: "Censure of Senator Joseph McCarthy," 83rd Congress, 2nd Session, Senate Resolution 301 (2 December 1954).

EXCERPT FROM *THE BLUE BOOK OF THE JOHN BIRCH SOCIETY* (c. 1960)

Though the 1960s are remembered as the era of left-wing radicalism, they also saw the development of the John Birch Society, a radical-right group formed in the name of anti-communism. Founded in 1958 by ultraconservative businessman Robert H. W. Welch Jr., the society takes its name from John Birch, a Fundamentalist Baptist missionary killed by Chinese Communists after World War II ended. Hailing Birch as the first casualty in the war against communism, the society aims to fight communism by whatever means necessary.

The Blue Book of the John Birch Society is the group's manifesto. The society believes in a radical reduction of the federal government and the abandonment of the Federal Reserve System, among other things. The book attacks the civil rights movement for sowing subversion in the United States. In this excerpt, collectivism is described as a devious cancer growing on the healthy body of the American public.

Leah R. Shafer,
Cornell University

See also **Anti-communism; John Birch Society.**

But Let's Look Deeper . . .

Now if the danger from the Communist conspiracy were all we had to worry about, it would be enough. But every thinking and informed man senses that, even as cunning, as ruthless, and as determined as are the activists whom we call Communists with a capital "C," the conspiracy could never have reached its present extensiveness, and the gangsters at the head of it could never have reached their present power, unless there were tremendous weaknesses in the whole body of our civilization—weaknesses to make the advance of such a disease so rapid and its ravages so disastrous. And this feeling is easily confirmed by observation. But to analyze and understand these weaknesses we have to go deeply into both the political history and the philosophical history of the human race. By your leave—or perhaps I should say without it—I am going to attempt that analysis. For we definitely need this understanding also, as background to the suggestions of program and of action which will eventually follow. I shall keep this exploration from being dry and boring, to the best of my ability. And I shall keep it as short as I well can.

In my opinion, the first great basic weakness of the United States, and hence its susceptibility to the disease of collectivism, is simply the age of the *Western European* civilization. And I am not being cryptic, clever, nor facetious, as I hope soon to make clear. Some of you will already have recognized, in fact, that I am drawing a corollary to the conclusions usually connected with the name of Oswald Spengler. In actual fact there were many other scholars who, during the first decades of this century, supplied what were probably sounder studies and interpretations of the cyclic theory of cultures than did Spengler. But the concept has become so associated with his name that we might as well accept that identification. So let me put "Spengler's theory" in simple language, as concisely as I can.

Oswald Spengler was a very learned but very conceited German who wrote a book, first published in 1918, I believe, of which the title in the English translation was *The Decline of the West.* A lot of its direct effectiveness was spoiled by the almost nauseating displays of erudition in which the book abounds. Chief Justice Oliver Wendell Holmes once called it "a marvelous humbug of a book," which description actually reveals more about that eternal sophomore, Holmes, than it does about the ostentatious scholar, Spengler.

And despite the way that Spengler overplayed his hand and overproved his point, a rather strange thing has happened. The so-called liberal scholars of the world completely demolished Spengler's arguments at once. And then they have kept right on returning to the task, and demolishing Spengler's thesis *finally and for good,* every year or two for the past forty years. For the convincing way in which Spengler's explanation fits the known facts of human history just would not let his conclusion be downed and forgotten—any more than the convincing way in which Darwin's general theory fitted the known facts of animal life would let Darwin's theory be suppressed and ignored two generations earlier.

Until at last the international socialists, with the Fabians and Labor Party bosses in England taking the lead, made one grand and lasting effort to have Spengler discredited by being overshadowed. They took a meretricious hack named Arnold J. Toynbee, who just by the intrinsic evidence of his own pages is one of the worst charlatans that ever lived; they had Toynbee interpret and rewrite history in such fashion as specifically to supplant Spengler's cyclic theory of cultures with Toynbee's half-baked nonsense; and then they—the whole liberal establishment, especially of England and America—gave Toynbee such favorable publicity and such a terrific build-up as no other historian, not even the socialist H. G. Wells, has ever enjoyed before. The result has been that today at least one thousand people are familiar with Toynbee's history, and have even read a few pages of it, to each one who has read Spengler and knows what he tried to say.

Those who are familiar with the way in which Stalin won out in his contest with Trotsky, in the years 1924 to 1929, will recognize the similarity of the technique used. Stalin, who was in complete charge of all media of communication in Russia during those years, never actually suppressed, nor even refused to allow to be published, any pamphlets by, or favorable to, Trotsky. He merely held the press run and distribution of all such pamphlets down to a few thousand, on the ground that the demand didn't justify any more; while pamphlets by himself or others, condemning Trotsky, were printed and distributed in huge quantities all over Russia. Incidentally, it is the same typically Communist technique which was used by the Fund for the Republic, when they printed and distributed thirty-five thousand copies of Erwin Griswold's straining pedantry in defense of the Fifth Amendment pleaders; and then printed and distributed *one thousand* copies of Dickerman Williams' answer to Griswold's nonsense, in order to show how fair-minded they were.

But I am getting off the track. Which is that, due to all this huge build-up of Arnold Toynbee as a philosopher-historian, almost any American or Englishman who happened to take a notion, for some reason, to go digging into world history from a philosophical viewpoint—or just from sheer curiosity—would certainly turn to Toynbee, would never have heard of Spengler, and hence would have no chance to learn Spengler's ideas. And all of this introduction to those ideas has not been wasted, I hope. For it does emphasize this fact. *Spengler's theory is absolutely fatal to the acceptance of socialism or any form of collectivism as a forward step, or as a form of progress, in man's sociological arrangements.* For in Spengler's view collectivism is a disease of society, concomitant with decay, and remarkably similar to cancer in the individual.

Basically, when you dig through the chaff and the dressing in Spengler enough to get at his thought, he held that a societal development which we ordinarily classify as a civilization is an organic culture, which goes through a life cycle just the same as any of the individual organisms which we see whole and with which we are more familiar. It has been many years since I have read Spengler, so I do not know how far I am wandering from his own specific or exact thinking, in trying to present his central theme. There is certainly more Welch than there is Spengler in what follows. But the easiest way to make the theme clear is to illustrate the life of a civilization as a parallel to the life of an individual man.

You then find, that of the some twenty-one or twenty-two civilizations which we know enough about to discuss intelligently, some were struck down while in middle age and reasonable health, by an enemy, as was the Neo-Babylonian civilization by Cyrus, for instance; just the same as an individual man might be shot by an enemy, or run over by a streetcar. Another, like the Carthaginian, never was able to attain its full normal growth and strength, because of the overwhelming competition, for sustenance and *lebensraum*, of a too close, too powerful, and too greedy rival, namely Rome—which must have been the case for many a man, in the barbarian settings of our evolution. And another, like the Assyrian, could almost be said to have died of a heart attack, it went to pieces so suddenly and so completely in the middle stage of an apparently successful and healthy existence. There were factors of weakness inside the body which caused it to drop almost exactly like a man whose heart suddenly kicks up and then quits altogether twenty minutes later.

The real point, however, is this. An individual human being may die of any number of causes. But if he escapes the fortuitous diseases, does not meet with any fatal accident, does not starve to death, does not have his heart give out, but lives in normal health to his three score years and ten and then keeps on living—if he escapes or survives everything else and keeps on doing so, he will eventually succumb to the degenerative disease of cancer. For death must come, and cancer is merely death coming by stages, instead of all at once. And exactly the same thing seems to be true of those organic aggregations of human beings, which we called cultures or civilizations.

The individual cells in a human body die and are replaced by new ones constantly. Only when and where cancer attacks a part of the body are the dead ones not replaced by new cells which contribute their share of strength to the body as a whole. The individual human beings in an organic culture die and are replaced constantly by new ones. But even if the culture escapes enemy conquest and accidents of nature and starvation and all the fortuitous diseases—such as the internal bleeding which almost destroyed Europe at the time of the Reformation and the Thirty Years War—death will still come eventually, and usually a lingering death, through the degenerative disease of collectivism. For collectivism destroys the value to the organism of the individual cells—that is, the individual human beings—without replacing them with new ones with new strength. The Roman Empire of the West, for instance, started dying from the cancer of collectivism from the time Diocletian imposed on it his New Deal. And while it was given the *coup de grace* by the barbarians a hundred and seventy-five years later, it had already been so weakened by this cancer that the city of Rome itself had been an easy prey to Alaric more than sixty years before its final fall.

Now how really exact or how valid this parallel between the lives of human individuals and the lives of their well integrated aggregations may be, I don't know. I certainly do not have either the knowledge or the inclination to support whatever belief Spengler may have had that there was actually a biological compulsion for a social organism to follow a life cycle similar to that of the individual. But no such rigid crystallization of the thought is at all necessary. For whether fatalistically determined by biological principles or not, there is an analogy between the two which is inescapable. And even if it is nothing more than a useful analogy, subject to all of the flaws and possible exceptions which may mar any analogy, it leads automatically to conclusions which are devastating to socialist theory. For it is perfectly evident, right in the cases of the very civilizations that we know most about, that both the Greek and the Roman civilizations did perish of the cancer of collectivism, and that the civilization of Western Europe is doing so today.

Now it is even possible to establish a fairly accurate time ratio for this analogy or parallel. It runs about twenty to one. In other words a civilization fourteen hundred years old would be at the physical stage in its life cycle, roughly, of a man of seventy. And with that yardstick in mind we can now come at last to take the look at Western Europe which I have been trying to make worthwhile; and after that the look at America which is the real goal of all this preparation.

The civilization of Western Europe arose out of the ashes of the Roman Empire of the West. If we try to establish any approximation to a birthdate, the analogy becomes sloppy. For actually the parallel is much closer to that of an oak tree which has been felled, but which still scatters acorns that sprout long afterwards. But if we still stick to the analogy of a man nevertheless, we might consider that, after a long gestation period, an entity which could eventually become Western European civilization was born in the time of Charlemagne. The boy had reached the strutting, stick-throwing stage at the time of the Crusades; the stage of growing intellectual curiosity in the Renaissance; the stage of youthful adventure in the ocean explorations of the fifteenth century; and then three centuries, or the equivalent of fifteen years for a man, of the most solid accomplishments of a hard-working, hard-thinking middle age.

None of these comparisons will quite hold water, and I don't know whether Spengler could have postulated some that would or not. But after all shortcomings of the allegory are recognized, the fact remains that Western Europe of the last half of the nineteenth century was remarkably similar to a man of some sixty-five years of age who had led an extremely busy life of great stresses and strains, but an extremely successful life, nevertheless, of mental growth, physical accomplishments, and material acquisitions. The old man had weathered every danger, had stood all the bludgeonings of fate, and had come out, at that age, with a tremendous accumulation of knowledge, experience, material possessions, and prestige among his neighbors—the other civilizations or societal organizations of the rest of the planet.

In fact, in my amateurish opinion, the last half of the nineteenth century A.D., like the first half of the sixth century B.C. before it, was the high-water mark up to its time of human civilization, accomplishment, and hope for the future. And it was Western Europe which made that last half of the nineteenth century the period of the highest level to which man has yet climbed in his struggle to reach an enlightened and humane life.

But, as so often happens for the individual, by the time Western Europe had the knowledge, the wealth, and the ability to get the most out of life, it was ready to die. The truth is that, by a cycle which seems inevitable whether it is a biological reality or only an analogy, Western Europe was worn out. And under those circumstances the degenerative disease of collectivism, the cancer of social organizations, began its peripheral infiltration.

Not only the early beginnings of the disease, but the certainty of its slowly increasing ravages, and the eventual fatal effect of its ultimately advanced stages, were clearly visible to the genius of Herbert Spencer as early as the middle of the century. And by the time Bismarck, forming that alliance of the autocratic top of society with the greedy masses at the bottom, which is so commonplace in history, began to crystallize the nebulous theories of the Marxists and other modern socialists into the welfare legislation of Germany of the 1880's; by that time the disease was starting to eat its way further into the body in disastrous fashion. Its ravages continued, increased, and spread, until today Western Europe is so sick and weakened from the collectivism in its body and veins that it can never recover.

This doesn't mean that, in the normal course of events, Europe will soon become a desolate waste, while the monuments of its former kings lie toppled and forgotten where the lone and level sands stretch far away. Even when an individual is dying of cancer, there are periods of apparent recovery or improvement, and even times when some organs of the body seem as strong, healthy, and invulnerable to the disease as ever. Also, I must emphasize again that there are many points—such as the doubtful transmissibility of cancer itself to individuals, through either contagion or environment—at which there are apparent flaws in the analogy which would take more time than we can spare here to put in their proper light. And sticking to the historical parallels for the minute, rather than the biological one, it is clear that even hundreds of years after the fall of the Assyrian, Neo-Babylonian, and Persian civilizations in the Tigris-Euphrates stretches of Western Asia, the subjects of the Sassanid dynasty and other lesser offsprings of those once great civilizations led lives that were perhaps happy, and that certainly were important to themselves. I am sure that, likewise, it will be a long time before the lizards run undisturbed over the toppled ruins of the Arc de Triomphe, or London Bridge is allowed to fall, unreconstructed, into the waters of the Thames.

But our analysis does mean that the entity which was Western Europe; the social organism which was so closely knit and so well integrated despite its national boundaries, languages, and jealousies; the Western Europe whose parts were so intertwined that Napoleon of France could marry the daughter of the emperor of Austria to help one of his brothers to rule Spain and another brother to rule Holland; the Western Europe which could spare the strength to spread its pioneers to colonize the uninhabited lands, and its pukka sahibs to bring civilized rule to the settled natives, on all the continents of earth— *that* Western Europe of the nineteenth century can never come back. It is either dying before our eyes, or is already dead. For the vigor of its muscles and the strength of its whole body have been sapped beyond recovery by the cancer of collectivism.

Now, lest I seem to be putting too much dependence in an analogy which is full of holes, let me just very briefly make a more matter-of-fact approach towards the same conclusion. For regardless of any organic cycles which may be involved, it is perfectly visible and incontrovertible that the rugged pioneer settlers of a new land want as little government as possible; that as the new society becomes more settled, as population grows, as commerce and/or industry increase, as the society grows older, more and more government creeps in. And then, because demagogues find it to their personal advantage, they use trickery, persuasion, and bribery of the people with their own money, to make the rate of increase in the quantity and reach of government far greater than the rate of increase in either the population or the justifiable need for government. So that by the time any society which has been so originated and fashioned has reached a thick population, comparative wealth and considerable age, enough government has already been imposed on the people to constitute the beginnings of collectivism.

This happened to the people who settled the islands and founded the city-states of Greece. It happened to their descendants who settled the Italian peninsula and founded the Roman Empire. It happened to *their* spiritual descendants who built the Western European civilization. And it is certainly happening to *their* descendants who founded and have built the American Republic.

With the next inevitable stage, after advanced collectivism has destroyed the vigor of any such society—which is its break-up into feudal units and the accompanying serfdom—we are not concerned here. But what we are concerned with is the time usually involved in these successive developments. It is this question of the speed of the movement around the arc, from pioneer to serf, or of the various stages of the movement, to which this whole present discussion has been leading. And purely for the sake of simplicity and clarity, I hope you will let me go back to my analogy, even if you now regard it only as a figure of speech.

For the whole point is that the Greek civilization was at least many centuries old—that is, many centuries removed from its pioneer days—before Pericles started it on the road to death, at the very height of its glory, through making the government increasingly responsible for its citizens, instead of its citizens being responsible for, and watchdogs over, their government. Rome was already over a thousand years from the days of Romulus and Remus when Diocletian's reign signalized the advance of collectivism beyond the point of any possible recovery. Western Europe was, by a most conservative method of figuring its age, at least eleven to twelve hundred years old before the disease of collectivism began to bring it to its deathbed. Or we even know enough today to go back in the other direction, where we find that the first Babylonian civilization also was at least a thousand years old before collectivism had become sufficiently prevalent for Hammurabi to formalize it as the New Deal of his era.

Now—in view of all of that, take a look at what has happened to America. It's true that the same thing has also happened to most of the other former British colonies, such as Canada, Australia, and New Zealand, but that is not our concern here; and there was a little more justification for it anyway, because they remained more closely tied to England. But the United States was not only a new and completely independent country. It was, by any measure of appraisal, the seat of a whole new civilization.

There are few parallels in history more striking than the way Italy was settled by Greek pioneers, who simply took over from the aborigines already there, and developed the new nation and new civilization of Rome, and the way America was settled by pioneers from Western Europe who developed a new nation and a new civilization here. In its earlier centuries America not only did not regard itself as a part of the European organism at all, but became fiercely proud of its differences from Europe, and of its indigenously vigorous customs, culture, and destiny of its own. The American civilization was every bit as much of an entirely new and different civilization from the old and ancestral one of Western Europe, as was Rome a new civilization distinct from Greece.

And this American civilization, at the turn of the present century, was only three hundred years old. It had the strength and vigor and promise of a healthy young man in his late teens. There was no reason on earth for any such organism to be attacked by, and start succumbing to, the cancerous disease of collectivism at that stage of its young manhood, with its whole life span of accomplishment before it. And any of the natural or fortuitous attempts of the disease to get a foothold in the American social body—such as the virus implanted by Edward Bellamy with his *Looking Backward*, or by Upton Sinclair with his *Jungle*, or even the more pretentious concoctions of Thorstein Veblen—would have been so easily repulsed by the strong and growing organism that none of them would have left even a scar.

But we have the cancerous disease of collectivism firmly implanted now, nevertheless. We have people feeling that nothing should be done by them, but everything for them by the government. Its disastrous ravages are quite far advanced. And we have it, basically, because of too long and too close an association with a parent that was dying of the disease; that was old enough and weakened enough for the virus to be rampantly active throughout this parent's whole environment.

When Woodrow Wilson, cajoled and guided even then by the collectivists of Europe, took us into the first World War, while solemnly swearing that he would never do so, he did much more than end America's great period of happy and wholesome independence of Europe. He put his healthy young country in the same house, and for a while in the same bed, with this parent who was already yielding to the collectivist cancer. We never got out of that house again. We were once more put back even in the same bed by Franklin D. Roosevelt, also while lying in his teeth about his intentions, and we have never been able to get out of that *bed* since.

In the meantime, the closer our relationship with this parent civilization has become, and the more exposed to the unhealthy air and the raging virus of the sick room we have been, the sicker and more morbidly diseased has the patient become. Until now, there is a tremendous question whether, even if we did not have the Communist conspirators deliberately helping to spread the virus for their own purposes, we could recover from just the natural demagogue-fed spread of that virus when it is already so far advanced. With the Communists skillfully using and encouraging the disease as a means of weakening us, the outlook leads ever more irresistibly to despondency and despair. And we simply cannot overlook or underrate the prevalence of this disease in our vitals—entirely aside from the way the Communists agitate the affected parts and make the disease worse—in any sound thinking or constructive plans for the future of America.

But—if I thought all hope were gone I wouldn't be here, and neither would you. Let's leave the Communist disease-carriers out of the picture for a minute. I knew a man who, when he was around fifty, and still otherwise a very healthy fifty, was found by the doctors to have cancer already far advanced in one side of his jaw. They took that side of his jaw, and practically half his face, right away from him at once. And when I first got to know him, at least ten years later, he had a very peculiar looking face, it is true; but otherwise he was a grand example of both mental and physical health for a man of sixty-five; and he was very happily teaching his lifetime subject as a professor at one of our most famous universities. Probably all of you have known somewhat similar cases. And it is certain that in those very rare cases where a healthy young man of twenty-five does, in some way, contract cancer, a sufficiently accurate diagnosis and sufficiently drastic surgery can restore him to health and enable him to go on and live out a normal, active, successful and happy life. But it can't be done by half measures.

Now what I have been trying so long and so hard to say comes to this. We have got to stop the Communists, for many reasons. One reason is to keep them from agitating our cancerous tissues, reimplanting the virus, and working to spread it, so that we never have any chance of recovery. And stopping the Communists is the most urgently important task before us, which we are going to talk about plenty at this meeting. But even in stopping them, or in our efforts to do so, we cannot forget for a minute the disease which has enabled them to go so far, weaken us so much, and become so dangerous to us. Nor can we forget for a minute the imperative need of excising and stopping the disease itself, while we are stopping and after we have stopped the Communists, or we shall merely die a somewhat slower and more lingering national death than if we let the Communists destroy us in the first place.

Push the Communists back, get out of the bed of a Europe that is dying with this cancer of collectivism, and breathe our own healthy air of opportunity, enterprise, and freedom; then the cancer we already have, even though it is of considerable growth, can be cut out. And despite the bad scars and the loss of some muscles, this young, strong, great new nation, restored to vigor, courage, ambition, and self-confidence, can still go ahead to fulfill its great destiny, and to become an even more glorious example for all the earth than it ever was before. It should be centuries from now before the natural time comes for the decline of America, and for the highest torch of civilization to be taken over by the rising newer nations to the West. But we do have to achieve the sufficiently drastic surgery; and that of course is a Herculean task. We shall return to a study of it when we come to the more positive part of this program.

SOURCE: Welch, R. *The Blue Book of the John Birch Society.* Reprinted, 1995.

EISENHOWER'S FAREWELL ADDRESS
(17 January 1961)

After leading the Allied invasion of Europe and serving as the Supreme Commander of Allied Forces in Europe during World War II and later as the Army Chief of Staff, Dwight D. Eisenhower (1890–1969) was elected to the presidency on the Republican ticket in 1952. The first Republican to be elected to the highest office in twenty years, he was tremendously popular. Negotiating a truce in Korea, Eisenhower created the International Atomic Energy Agency, which helped sixty-two countries pool atomic information and materials for peaceful purposes. In addition, he organized eight countries into the Southeast Asia Treaty Organization (SEATO) to resist Communist aggression, and urged Congress to pass internal security laws which in effect outlawed the Communist Party. After Fidel Castro seized property owned by American companies in Cuba, Eisenhower broke off diplomatic relations with the island in 1961. That January, as John F. Kennedy was about to be inaugurated, Eisenhower gave a farewell speech to the nation that reflected his preoccupation with international relations and world peace. While calling attention to what he saw as the ongoing threat posed by Communism, he also warned Americans to be careful to limit the increasing power of what he called "the military-industrial complex," the pairing of huge military forces with the vast new domestic arms industry. Eisenhower's own military career gave great weight to this message.

Bettina Drew

See also **Arms Race and Disarmament; Military-Industrial Complex.**

My fellow Americans:

Three days from now, after half a century in the service of our country, I shall lay down the responsibilities of office as, in traditional and solemn ceremony, the authority of the Presidency is vested in my successor. . . .

We now stand ten years past the midpoint of a century that has witnessed four major wars among great nations. Three of them involved our own country. Despite these holocausts America is today the strongest, the most influential and most productive nation in the world. Understandably proud of this pre-eminence we yet realize that America's leadership and prestige depend, not merely upon our unmatched material progress, riches and military strength, but on how we use our power in the interests of world peace and human betterment.

Throughout America's adventure in free government, our basic purposes have been to keep the peace; to foster progress in human achievement, and to enhance liberty, dignity and integrity among people and among nations. To strive for less would be unworthy of a free and religious people. Any failure traceable to arrogance, or our lack of comprehension or readiness to sacrifice would inflict upon us grievous hurt both at home and abroad.

Progress toward these noble goals is persistently threatened by the conflict now engulfing the world. It commands our whole attention, absorbs our very beings. We face a hostile ideology—global in scope, atheistic in character, ruthless in purpose, and insidious in method. Unhappily the danger it poses promises to be of indefinite duration. To meet it successfully, there is called for, not so much the emotional and transitory sacrifices of crisis, but rather those which enable us to carry forward steadily, surely, and without complaint the burdens of a prolonged and complex struggle—with liberty the stake. Only thus shall we remain, despite every provocation, on our charted course toward permanent peace and human betterment. . . .

A vital element in keeping the peace is our military establishment. Our arms must be mighty, ready for instant action, so that no potential aggressor may be tempted to risk his own destruction.

Our military organization today bears little relation to that known by any of my predecessors in peacetime, or indeed by the fighting men of World War II or Korea.

Until the latest of our world conflicts, the United States had no armaments industry. American makers of plowshares could, with time and as required, make swords as well. But now we can no longer risk emergency improvisation of national defense; we have been compelled to create a permanent armaments industry of vast proportions. Added to this, three and a half million men and women are directly engaged in the defense establishment. We annually spend on military security more than the net income of all United States corporations.

This conjunction of an immense military establishment and a large arms industry is new in the American experience. The total influence—economic, political, even spiritual—is felt in every city, every statehouse, every office of the federal government. We recognize the imperative need for this development. Yet we must not fail to comprehend its grave implications. Our toil, resources, and livelihood are all involved; so is the very structure of our society.

In the councils of government, we must guard against the acquisition of unwarranted influence, whether sought or unsought, by the military-industrial complex. The potential for the disastrous rise of misplaced power exists and will persist.

We must never let the weight of this combination endanger our liberties or democratic processes. We should take nothing for granted. Only an alert and knowledgeable citizenry can compel the proper meshing of the huge industrial and military machinery of defense with our peaceful methods and goals, so that security and liberty may prosper together.

Akin to, and largely responsible for the sweeping changes in our industrial-military posture, has been the technological revolution during recent decades.

In this revolution, research has become central; it also becomes more formalized, complex, and costly. A steadily increasing share is conducted for, by, or at the direction of, the federal government....

The prospect of domination of the nation's scholars by federal employment, project allocations, and the power of money is ever present—and is gravely to be regarded.

Yet, in holding scientific research and discovery in respect, as we should, we must also be alert to the equal and opposite danger that public policy could itself become the captive of a scientific-technological elite.

It is the task of statesmanship to mold, to balance, and to integrate these and other forces, new and old, within the principles of our democratic system—ever aiming toward the supreme goals of our free society.

Another factor in maintaining balance involves the element of time. As we peer into society's future, we—you and I, and our government—must avoid the impulse to live only for today, plundering, for our own ease and convenience, the precious resources of tomorrow. We cannot mortgage the material assets of our grandchildren without risking the loss also of their political and spiritual heritage. We want democracy to survive for all generations to come, not to become the insolvent phantom of tomorrow.

Down the long lane of the history yet to be written America knows that this world of ours, ever growing smaller, must avoid becoming a community of dreadful fear and hate, and be, instead, a proud confederation of mutual trust and respect.

Such a confederation must be one of equals. The weakest must come to the conference table with the same confidence as do we, protected as we are by our moral, economic, and military strength. That table, though scarred by many past frustrations, cannot be abandoned for the certain agony of the battlefield.

Disarmament, with mutual honor and confidence, is a continuing imperative. Together we must learn how to compose differences, not with arms, but with intellect and decent purpose. Because this need is so sharp and apparent I confess that I lay down my official responsibilities in this field with a definite sense of disappointment. As one who has witnessed the horror and the lingering sadness of war—as one who knows that another war could utterly destroy this civilization which has been so slowly and painfully built over thousands of years—I wish I could say tonight that a lasting peace is in sight.

Happily, I can say that war has been avoided. Steady progress toward our ultimate goal has been made. But, so much remains to be done. As a private citizen, I shall never cease to do what little I can to help the world advance along that road....

SOURCE: *New York Times*, 18 January 1961.

"VOICE FROM MOON: THE EAGLE HAS LANDED" *(1969)*

The National Aeronautical and Space Administration (NASA) was established in 1958, the year after the Soviet Union shocked the world with the launch of its Sputnik satellite. When Soviet cosmonaut Yuri Gagarin became the first human to orbit the Earth in 1961, President John F. Kennedy announced that the U.S. would put a man on the moon and bring him back alive "before the decade is out."

The Apollo 11 lunar module touched down on the moon on 20 July 1969. A worldwide audience watched on live television as first Neil Armstrong and then Edwin "Buzz" Aldrin carefully climbed out of the module onto the lunar surface. Orbiting above them in the command module was the mission's third crew member, Michael Collins. These transcripts of the mission, originally published in the *New York Times,* describe how Armstrong, Aldrin, Collins, and the Houston Command Center worked together to negotiate the landing. In their communications they address the mundane but threatening events that have plagued explorers since humans have set out for the unknown: equipment problems, communication errors, and the difficulty of physical movement on unfamiliar terrain. And, like earlier explorers, the astronauts indulge in romantic, if factual, descriptions of the land's topography. But perhaps most striking in this account is the acknowledgement that individual acts of daring result from the collective action of many different people. A symbol of the United States's ingenuity, technological expertise, and financial resources in the Cold War, the last mission to the moon was launched in 1972.

Mark Baumann,
New York University

See also **Moon Landing; Space Program.**

EAGLE (THE LUNAR MODULE): Houston, Tranquility Base here. The Eagle has landed.

HOUSTON: Roger, Tranquility, we copy you on the ground. You've got a bunch of guys about to turn blue. We're breathing again. Thanks a lot.

TRANQUILITY BASE: Thank you.

HOUSTON: You're looking good here.

TRANQUILITY BASE: A very smooth touchdown.

HOUSTON: Eagle, you are stay for T1. [The first step in the lunar operation.] Over.

TRANQUILITY BASE: Roger. Stay for T1.

HOUSTON: Roger and we see you venting the ox.

TRANQUILITY BASE: Roger.

COLUMBIA (THE COMMAND AND SERVICE MODULE): How do you read me?

HOUSTON: Columbia, he has landed Tranquility Base. Eagle is at Tranquility. I read you five by. Over.

COLUMBIA: Yes, I heard the whole thing.

HOUSTON: Well, it's a good show.

COLUMBIA: Fantastic.

TRANQUILITY BASE: I'll second that.

APOLLO CONTROL: The next major stay-no stay will be for the T2 event. That is at 21 minutes 26 seconds after initiation of power descent.

COLUMBIA: Up telemetry command reset to reacquire on high gain.

HOUSTON: Copy. Out.

APOLLO CONTROL: We have an unofficial time for that touchdown of 102 hours, 45 minutes, 42 seconds and we will update that.

HOUSTON: Eagle, you loaded R2 wrong. We want 10254.

TRANQUILITY BASE: Roger. Do you want the horizontal 55 15.2?

HOUSTON: That's affirmative.

APOLLO CONTROL: We're now less than four minutes from our next stay-no stay. It will be for one complete revolution of the command module. One of the first things that Armstrong and Aldrin will do after getting their next stay-no stay will be to remove their helmets and gloves.

HOUSTON: Eagle, you are stay for T2. Over.

TRANQUILITY BASE: Roger. Stay for T2. We thank you.

HOUSTON: Roger, sir.

APOLLO CONTROL: That's stay for another two minutes plus. The next stay-no stay will be for one revolution.

TRANQUILITY BASE: Houston, that may have seemed like a very long final phase but the auto targeting was taking us right into a football field-sized crater with a large number of big boulders and rocks for about one or two crater diameters around it. And it required us to fly manually over the rock field to find a reasonably good area.

HOUSTON: Roger. We copy. It was beautiful from here, Tranquility. Over.

TRANQUILITY BASE: We'll get to the details of what's around here but it looks like a collection of just about every variety of shape, angularity, granularity, about every variety of rock you could find. The colors vary pretty much depending on how you are looking relative to the zero phase length. There doesn't appear to be too much of a general color at all. However, it looks as though some of the rocks and boulders, of which there are quite a few in the near area—it looks as though they're going to have some interesting colors to them. Over.

HOUSTON: Roger. Copy. Sounds good to us, Tranquility. We'll let you press on through the simulated countdown and we'll talk to you later. Over.

TRANQUILITY BASE: Okay, this one-sixth G is just like an airplane.

HOUSTON: Roger, Tranquility. Be advised there are lots of smiling faces in this room and all over the world. Over.

TRANQUILITY BASE: There are two of them up here.

HOUSTON: Roger. It was a beautiful job, you guys.

COLUMBIA: And don't forget one in the command module.

TRANQUILITY BASE: Roger.

Remark by Collins

APOLLO CONTROL: That last remark from Mike Collins at an altitude of 60 miles. The comments on the landing, on the manual take-over came from Neil Armstrong. Buzz Aldrin followed that with a description of the lunar surface and the rocks and boulders that they are able to see out the window of the LM.

COLUMBIA: Thanks for putting me on relay, Houston. I was missing all the action.

HOUSTON: Roger. We'll enable relay.

COLUMBIA (4:30 P.M.): I just got it, I think.

HOUSTON: Roger, Columbia. This is Houston. Say something; they ought to be able to hear you. Over.

COLUMBIA: Roger. Tranquility Base. It sure sounded great from up here. You guys did a fantastic job.

TRANQUILITY BASE: Thank you. Just keep that orbiting base ready for us up there, now.

COLUMBIA: Will do.

APOLLO CONTROL: That request from Neil Armstrong.

APOLLO CONTROL: We've just gotten a report from the telcom here in mission control that LM systems look good after that landing. We're about 26 minutes now from loss of signal from the command module.

HOUSTON: Tranquility Base, Houston. All your consumables are solid. You're looking good in every respect. We copy the DPS venting. Everything is copacetic. Over.

TRANQUILITY BASE: Thank you, Houston. Houston, the guys that bet that we wouldn't be able to tell precisely where we are are the winners today. We were a little busy worrying about program alarms and things like that in the part of the descent where we would normally be picking out our landing spot; and aside from a good look at several of the craters we came over in the final descent, I haven't been able to pick out the things on the horizon as a reference as yet.

HOUSTON: Rog, Tranquility. No sweat. We'll figure out—we'll figure it out. Over.

TRANQUILITY BASE: You might be interested to know that I don't think we noticed any difficulty at all in adapting to one-sixth G. It seems immediately natural to live in this environment.

HOUSTON: Roger, Tranquility. We copy. Over.

APOLLO CONTROL: Neil Armstrong reporting there is no difficulty adapting to the one-sixth gravity of the moon.

TRANQUILITY BASE: [Unintelligible] . . . window, with relatively level plain cratered with fairly a large number of craters of the 5- to 50-foot variety. And some ridges, small, 20 to 30 feet high, I would guess. And literally thousands of little one- and two-foot craters around the area. We see some angular blocks out several hundred feet in front of us that are probably two feet in size and have angular edges. There is a hill in view just about on the ground track ahead of us. Difficult to estimate, but might be a half a mile or a mile.

HOUSTON: Roger, Tranquility. We copy. Over.

COLUMBIA: Sounds like it looks a lot better than it did yesterday. At that very low sun angle, it looked rough as a cob then.

TRANQUILITY BASE: It really was rough, Mike, over the targeted landing area. It was extremely rough, cratered and large numbers of rocks that were probably some many larger than 5 or 10 feet in size.

COLUMBIA: When in doubt, land long.

TRANQUILITY BASE: Well, we did.

Question on Landing

COLUMBIA: Do you have any idea whether they landed left or right of center line—just a little bit long. Is that all we know?

HOUSTON: Apparently that's about all we can tell. Over.

COLUMBIA: Okay, thank you.

TRANQUILITY BASE: Okay. I'd say the color of the local surface is very comparable to that we observed from orbit at this sun angle—about 10 degrees sun angle or that nature. It's pretty much without color. It's gray and it's very white as you look into the zero phase line. And it's considerably darker gray, more like an ashen gray, as you look out 90 degrees to the sun. Some of the surface rocks in close here that have been fractured or disturbed by the rocket engine plume are coated with this light gray on the outside. But where they've been broken, they display a dark, very dark, gray interior and it looks like it could be country basalt.

HOUSTON: Tranquility, Houston. Please vent fuel and ox again. Over. It's building back up.

TRANQUILITY BASE: Okay, ox going now.

HOUSTON: Tranquility, Houston. You can open both fuel and ox vent now. Over.

TRANQUILITY BASE: Houston, Tranquility. Standing by for go AGS to the line and lunar line. Over.

HOUSTON: Stand by.

HOUSTON: Tranquility, Houston. You're go for the AGS the line and the lunar line. Over.

TRANQUILITY BASE: Roger.

HOUSTON: Tranquility, Houston. Please vent the fuel. It's increasing rapidly. Over.

TRANQUILITY BASE: We show 30 psi in the fuel and 30 on the oxydizer.

HOUSTON: Roger, we're reading somewhat different than that. Stand by.

TRANQUILITY BASE: The fuel temperature is reading 64 in the descent two and the oxydizer off scale low. Descent one is showing 61 in the fuel and 65 in the oxydizer.

HOUSTON: Roger, stand by.

HOUSTON: Tranquility, Houston. Please take the fuel vent switch and hold it open. Over.

TRANQUILITY BASE: Okay. We're holding it open, indicating about 24 psi on board.

HOUSTON: Roger.

TRANQUILITY BASE: Now indicating 20 psi in fuel.

HOUSTON: Roger.

TRANQUILITY BASE: And 22 in the ox.

HOUSTON: Roger.

TRANQUILITY BASE: Now indicating 15 psi in both tanks.

HOUSTON: Roger.

HOUSTON: Tranquility, Houston. If you haven't done so, you can release the fuel vent switch. Over.

TRANQUILITY BASE: Roger.

HOUSTON: Tranquility, Houston. We have indication that we've frozen up the descent fuel helium heat exchanger and with some fuel trapped in the line between air and the valves and the pressure we're looking at is increasing there. Over.

TRANQUILITY BASE: Roger. Understand.

HOUSTON: Tranquility Base, Houston. If you have not done so, please close both fuel and ox vents now.

TRANQUILITY BASE: They're closed.

HOUSTON: Thank you, sir.

TRANQUILITY BASE: From the surface we could not see any stars out the window, but on my overhead patch I'm looking at the earth. It's big and bright, beautiful. Buzz is going to give a try at seeing some stars through the optics.

HOUSTON: Roger, Tranquility. We understand must be a beautiful sight. Over.

APOLLO CONTROL: We would like to point out that the fuel pressure problem that has been called to the attention of the crew is in the descent system. It is apparently downstream of the tanks where a small amount of fluid has been trapped in a line and we don't expect it to cause any problem. The line should be able to take far more pressure than the fluid would exert. In the event that there was an overpressurization, we would expect that the line would spring a small leak, the pressure would drop rapidly. Again I would point out that we do not see this as a significant problem.

'Going Over the Hill'

HOUSTON: Columbia, Houston. Two minutes to LOS [loss of signal]. You're looking great. Going over the hill. Over.

COLUMBIA: Okay. Thank you. Glad to hear it's looking good. Do you have a suggested attitude for me? This one here seems all right.

HOUSTON: Stand by.

COLUMBIA: Let me know when it's lunch time, will ya?

HOUSTON: Say again?

HOUSTON: Columbia, Houston. You got a good attitude right there.

APOLLO CONTROL: This is Apollo Control. We've had loss of signal now from the command module. Of course, we'll maintain constant communication with the lunar module on the lunar surface. We have some heart rates for Neil Armstrong during that powered descent to lunar surface. At the time the burn was initiated, Armstrong's heart rate was 110. At touchdown on the lunar surface, he had a heart rate of 156 beats per minute, and the flight surgeon reports that his heart rate is now in the 90's. We do not have biomedical data on Buzz Aldrin.

APOLLO CONTROL (5:04 P.M.): We have an update on that touchdown time on the lunar surface. This still is not the final official time, which we'll get from readout of data. But the refined time is 102 hours, 45 minutes, 40 seconds, which would have been 12 minutes, 36 seconds after initiating the powered descent. That was 102 hours, 45 minutes, 40 seconds for touchdown and a total time of powered descent 12 minutes, 36 seconds. And we would expect those numbers to change perhaps a little bit when we get final data readout.

HOUSTON: Tranquility Base, Houston. If you want me to, I can give you a hack on the mission time every 30 minutes. Over.

HOUSTON: Tranquility, Houston. I'm counting down to T3 time. If you'd like to give me a hack, we can set up an event timer. Over.

TRANQUILITY BASE: Okay. How about counting up.

HOUSTON: Roger, you want it counting up? Stand by.

HOUSTON: Tranquility, Houston. On my mark 6230. Mark 6230 from pass TDI.

TRANQUILITY BASE: What we're looking for, Charlie, is time counting up to T2 that will be equal to 60 minutes or T3 equal to 60 minutes—T3.

HOUSTON: Roger. We'll have it for you.

HOUSTON: Tranquility Base, Houston. Reset the event timer to 0 and on my mark at 103 3941. Will give you a hack and it will be in one hour. Over.

TRANQUILITY BASE: Roger.

HOUSTON: And we got about almost 3 minutes to go, Neil. Over.

TRANQUILITY BASE: Okay.

HOUSTON: Tranquility Base, stand by on the event timer.

HOUSTON: Tranquility Base, on my mark start your event timer, 5, 4, 3, 2, 1, Mark.

TRANQUILITY BASE: Roger. We got it. Thank you.

HOUSTON: Rog, Neil.

Statement by Paine

APOLLO CONTROL (5:17 P.M.): There will be a brief statement from Dr. Thomas Paine, NASA administrator, in the Building 1 auditorium at 4:30 [Houston time]. We also have updated information on the landing point. It appears that the spacecraft Eagle touched down at .799 degrees north or just about on the lunar equator and 23.46 degrees east longitude, which would have put it about four miles from the targeted landing point downrange. We're now 54 minutes—or rather 27 minutes from reacquisition of the command module and of course we're in constant contact with the lunar module of the surface. At this point, all LM systems continue to look very good.

APOLLO CONTROL (5:29 P.M.): We will be taking the release line down briefly for a statement from Dr. Thomas Paine, NASA administrator. We will be recording any further conversations with the spacecraft and will play those back following the statement.

APOLLO CONTROL (5:42 P.M.): We understand there's been a brief delay in the statement from NASA administrator Thomas Paine. We will catch up with the tape-recorded conversation that we've had with Eagle on the lunar surface at this time.

TRANQUILITY BASE: Down 86 plus 0538 plus all zeros and the last one was 0012 and what's the sign of that, please?

HOUSTON: Tranquility, Houston. The delta VY is minus all zeros. The delta VZ is plus 0012. Over.

TRANQUILITY BASE: Roger plus 0012.

HOUSTON: Good readback.

TRANQUILITY BASE: Houston, Tranquility Base. The diskeys yours and up data link to ??.

HOUSTON: Roger, thank you, Tranquility. Hello, Tranquility Base, Houston. On my mark it will be 37 minutes to T3. Over.

TRANQUILITY BASE: Okay.

HOUSTON: Stand by. Mark 37 minutes till T3.

TRANQUILITY BASE: Okay. Thank you.

HOUSTON: Tranquility, this is Houston. It's your computer. We've got the load in. You can start your P57.

TRANQUILITY BASE: Roger, thank you. Houston, Tranquility Base. Did somebody down there have a mike buskeyed. Over.

HOUSTON: Stand by, we'll check.

TRANQUILITY BASE: Houston, Tranquility Base. Does somebody down there have a life button keyed? Over.

HOUSTON: Stand by. We'll check. Tranquility, Houston. Do you still hear it now? Over.

TRANQUILITY BASE: No, I still hear it. Sounds like somebody is banging some chairs around in the back room.

HOUSTON: Roger, that's a VOGA you hear for the CSM to keep the noise down on the loop. Maybe we got a missed relay or something. Stand by.

APOLLO CONTROL: Ladies and gentlemen, I'd like to at this time introduce the administrator of the National Aeronautics and Space Administration, Dr. Thomas O. Paine. I have a short statement then we'll be glad to accept questions. Dr. Paine.

Report to the President

DR. PAINE: Immediately after the lunar touchdown I called the White House from Mission Control and gave the following report to the President:

Mr. President, it is my honor on behalf of the entire NASA team to report to you that the Eagle has landed on the Sea of Tranquility and our astronauts are safe and looking forward to starting the exploration of the moon. We then discussed the gripping excitement and wonder that has been present in the White House and in Mission Control during the final minutes of this historic touchdown. I emphasized to the President the fact that we still had many difficult steps ahead of us in the Apollo 11 mission, but that at the same time a giant step had been made with our successful landing.

President Nixon asked me to convey to all of the NASA team and its associated industrial and university associates his personal congratulations on the success of the initial lunar landing and gave us his good wishes for the continuing success of this mission.

APOLLO CONTROL (6:01 P.M.): During the news conference with the NASA Administrator, Dr. Thomas Paine, we had conversation with both Eagle and Columbia and we'll play that tape for you now:

HOUSTON: Tranquility Base, on my mark 25 minutes until T3. Stand by. Mark 25 minutes until T3.

TRANQUILITY BASE: Roger. Thank you, Charlie.

COLUMBIA: HOUSTON, how do you read me?

HOUSTON: Columbia, we read you about 3 by. You might be advised we have an update for you on the P22 for the LM. We estimate he landed about four miles downrange. Your T1 times are updated and the T2 if you are ready to copy it. Over.

HOUSTON: Hello, Tranquility Base. We copy the now 93. You can torque him. Over.

COLUMBIA: Is that four miles?

HOUSTON: Stand by, we'll have a map location.

TRANQUILITY BASE: Houston, do you have an updated LM wait for us? Over.

HOUSTON: Affirmative. Stand by on the data.

HOUSTON: LM weight 10,906.

HOUSTON: Columbia with a latitude and longitude over 2 update for LM position. Over.

COLUMBIA: Go ahead.

HOUSTON: Roger, Columbia. It's plus .799 for the lat plus 11.730 for the longitude over 2 over.

COLUMBIA: Thank you.

HOUSTON: Hello Tranquility Base. You are stay for T3. We have some surface block data if you're ready to copy. Over.

TRANQUILITY BASE: Roger. Understand we're stay for T3. Stand by. Okay, Houston, go ahead with your block data.

HOUSTON: Roger. Hello Columbia, Houston. Columbia we don't want you to transmit, Mike. We just want you in that position in case you want to talk to Tranquility.

HOUSTON: Tranquility, Houston, say again. Over.

TRANQUILITY BASE: Roger. I have a fairly good-sized difference between battery volts on five and six. Six is reading 33.5 and five is reading 36.5. Is that what you expect? Over.

HOUSTON: Tranquility. They are both coming up in voltage. No problem. We're still go. Over.

Praise Is Returned

HOUSTON: Hello Tranquility Base, Houston. You can start your power down now. Over.

TRANQUILITY BASE: Roger.

HOUSTON: Tranquility Base, the white team is going off now and the maroon team take over. We appreciate the great show; it was a beautiful job, you guys.

TRANQUILITY BASE: Roger. Couldn't ask for better treatment from all the way back there.

TRANQUILITY BASE: Houston, our recommendation at this point is planning an EVA [Extra Vehicular Activity] with your concurrence starting at about 8 o'clock this evening, Houston time. That is about three hours from now.

HOUSTON: Stand by.

TRANQUILITY BASE: We will give you some time to think about that.

HOUSTON: Tranquility Base, Houston. We thought about it. We will support it. We'll go at that time.

TRANQUILITY BASE: Roger.

HOUSTON: You guys are getting prime time on TV there.

TRANQUILITY BASE: I hope that little TV set works. We'll see.

HOUSTON: Roger. Was your 8 o'clock Houston time in reference to opening the hatch or starting the prep for EVA at that time. Over.

TRANQUILITY BASE: At the hatch, it will be.

HOUSTON: That's what we thought. Thank you, much.

TRANQUILITY BASE (6:02 P.M.): It might be a little later than that. But—in other words, start the prep in about an hour or so.

HOUSTON: Tranquility Base, Houston. That's fine. We're ready to support you any time, Neil. Over.

TRANQUILITY BASE: Right.

HOUSTON: Right. Columbia, we see the noun 49. Stand by.

HOUSTON: Columbia, Houston. We got the data. We'd like a verb 34. Over.

COLUMBIA: Roger, Stand-by one, Charlie, for . . .

HOUSTON: Roger, Columbia. How did Tranquility look down there to you? Over.

COLUMBIA (6:03 P.M.): Well the area looked smooth. But I was unable to see him. I just picked out a distinguishable crater nearby and marked on it.

HOUSTON: Roger.

COLUMBIA: Looks like a nice area, though.

HOUSTON: Hello Columbia, Houston. I understand you could not see Tranquility. What were you marking on? Over.

COLUMBIA: Houston, Columbia. I say again. I could not see him. Auto optics pointed at a spot very close to the coordinates which you gave me. So I picked out a tiny crater in that area and marked on it so that I'll be able to have repeatable data. But I was unable to see him.

HOUSTON: Roger. Copy.

APOLLO CONTROL: You heard that last exchange and there is a very strong indication we might have an early EVA, with the hatch open perhaps at 8 o'clock, Houston time. One other item of significance: The pressure rise in descent propellant line downstage of the tanks has relieved. All aspects of the mission looking very good at this time.

HOUSTON (6:05 P.M.): Hello Tranquility Base, Houston. On our dips venting and that fuel problem, our heat exchangers, it's cleared up. It appears that the ice has melted and we're in good shape now. Out.

APOLLO CONTROL (6:31 P.M.): We expect Capsule Communicator Owen Garrett to pass along data to spacecraft Columbia momentarily. We are standing by for that. Meanwhile I think we should discuss a little further the projected EVA. Our current plan is to have crew members aboard the Eagle eat and relax for a little while prior to starting EVA prep. We won't know with certainty or have a reasonable time hack until about an hour before the scheduled event. Right now it looks like it could occur at 8 o'clock, Houston time. We have conversation going now with the spacecraft and we'll pick that up. Following is replay of tape of astronaut conversations recorded during the news briefing and press conference.

APOLLO CONTROL: At 105 hours, 30 minutes now into the mission Apollo 11. The spacecraft Columbia now out of range with Mission Control Center Houston, passing over the far side of the moon. As it passed out of sight we read an apolune of 63 nautical miles, a perilune of 56 nautical miles, a velocity of 5,367 feet per second. We've had conversation both with Tranquility Base and Columbia during this span of time. Also, as will come up in the course of that conversation, Lunar Module pilot Buzz Aldrin delivers a message to people everywhere listening. We'll play those tapes for you now.

'They'll Need Some Lunch'

HOUSTON: Columbia, we will have a stat vector update for you a little later. We're not prepared with it right now. And on another subject. From Tranquility Base they are prepared to begin the EVA early. They expect to begin depress operations in about three hours.

COLUMBIA: I guess they'll need some lunch before they go.

HOUSTON: We'd like your PRD readouts when possible and we've checked over your EM data and it's all okay.

COLUMBIA: Columbia's on the high-gain.

HOUSTON: Roger, Columbia. You're sounding much better now. Request accept and will uplink another stat vector. Over.

COLUMBIA: Roger. Accept.

HOUSTON: Suggest you put bat A on your bat relay buss. Over.

HOUSTON: Columbia, we're through with your computer. You can go to block.

COLUMBIA: Roger. Block.

HOUSTON: Tranquility Base. Over.

TRANQUILITY BASE: Go ahead, Houston.

HOUSTON: We've reviewed the checklist. About the only change in order to advance EVA that we've found is that you'll want to delay your hydroxide change and go after the EVA rather than before. Over.

TRANQUILITY BASE: Roger. We'd just as soon make the change and jettison the old one. Over.

HOUSTON: We would like to delay that LIOH change until after the EVA. There is a possibility you could jettison the canister when you jettison your pliss. Over.

TRANQUILITY BASE: All right. We'll plan it that way.

HOUSTON: Roger, Tranquility.

HOUSTON: Columbia. Over.

COLUMBIA: This is Columbia.

HOUSTON: We show your evap out temperature running low. Request you go to manual temperature control and bring it up. You can check the procedures in ECS Manual 17. Over.

COLUMBIA: Roger.

TRANQUILITY BASE: This is the LM pilot. I'd like to take this opportunity to ask every person listening in, whoever, wherever they may be, to pause for a moment and contemplate the events of the past few hours and to give thanks in his or her own way. Over.

HOUSTON: Roger, Tranquility Base.

APOLLO CONTROL (7:15 P.M.): You heard that statement in our taped transmission from lunar module pilot Buzz Aldrin. Our projected time for Extra Vehicular Activity at this point is still very preliminary. I repeat, it could come as soon as 8 P.M., Houston time. We won't know for sure about the time with reasonable certainty until about an hour before the event. Meanwhile, we'll soon be progressing toward man's first step on the lunar surface. We have an interesting phenomena here in the Mission Control Center, Houston, something that we've never seen before. Our visual of the lunar module—our visual display now standing still, our velocity digitals for our Tranquility Base now reading zero. Reverting, if we could, to the terminology of an earlier form of transportation—the railroad—what we're witnessing now is man's very first trip into space with a station-stop along the route.

HOUSTON: Tranquility Base, Houston. We'd like some estimate of how far along you are with your eating and when you may be ready to start your EVA prep.

TRANQUILITY BASE: I think that we'll be ready to start EVA prep in about a half hour or so.

TRANQUILITY BASE: We are beginning our EVA prep.

HOUSTON: Tranquility Base, this is Houston. Roger copy your beginning EVA prep. Break. Break. Columbia. Columbia. This is Houston, reading you loud and clear. Over.

COLUMBIA: You're loud and clear. The waste water dump is down to 10 per cent. I have a question on the B 22. Do you want me to do another B 22, or was all that information just for my own use in tracking the LM for photographic purposes?

HOUSTON: Columbia, this is Houston. We request that you perform another B 22. We'd like you to let the auto optics take care of the tracking and devote your energies to trying to pick out the LM on the lunar surface. If you can find the LM, of course, we're looking for marks on it. Tracking of geographical features doesn't do us at all that much good. Over.

COLUMBIA: Okay.

COLUMBIA (7:45 P.M.): Okay, I'll do it. And on the ECS system the—whatever the problem was seems to have gone away without any changing of J52 sensors, or anything like that. My evaporator outlet temp is up about 50 now and it's quite comfortable in the cockpit. So we'll talk more about that one later.

HOUSTON: Roger, Columbia. Did you shift into manual control, or did the problem resolve itself under auto control? Over.

COLUMBIA: The problem went away under auto.

After Years of Anticipation, an Astronaut Tells About His Walk on the Moon

HOUSTON: Roger. It's the best type. Out.

COLUMBIA: I did cycle out of auto into manual back into auto.

HOUSTON (7:55 P.M.): Tranquility Base. Tranquility Base. This is Houston. Over.

TRANQUILITY BASE: Go ahead, Houston.

HOUSTON: Tranquility, this is Houston. We need a second set of PRD ratings so that we may establish a rate. Over.

COLUMBIA (8:09 P.M.): Houston, Columbia. I'm coming up from . . . Do you have any topographical cues that might help me out here. I'm tracking between two craters. One of them is . . . that would be long at 11 o'clock. The other would be short and behind him at 5 o'clock. These are great big old craters, depressions.

HOUSTON: Columbia, this is Houston. The best we can do on top features is to advise you to look to the west of the irregularly shaped crater and then work on down to the southwest of it. Over.

HOUSTON: Columbia, Houston. Another possibility is the southern rim of the southern of the two old-looking craters. Over.

COLUMBIA: Houston, Columbia. I kept my eyes glued to the . . . that time, hoping I'd get a flash of vector light off the LM but I was unable see in my scan areas that you suggested.

HOUSTON: Roger. On that southern of the old craters there is a small bright crater on the southern rim. One plot would put him slightly to the west of that small bright crater about 500 to 1,000 feet. Do you see anything down there? Over.

COLUMBIA: It's gone past now, Bruce. But I scanned that area that you're talking about very closely and, no, I did not see anything.

HOUSTON: Roger. Out.

HOUSTON: Columbia, this is Houston. Over.

COLUMBIA: Here I am.

HOUSTON: Columbia, this is Houston. On your LAM 2 map, we'd like to confirm the topographical area in which you were looking on this last period of sightings. As we understand you, you were looking in the vicinity of Papa 7 to November 8. Is that correct?

COLUMBIA: Stand by.

HOUSTON: Roger.

HOUSTON (8:17 P.M.): Columbia, go ahead.

COLUMBIA: One of the craters I was talking about is located exactly at 56.7.

HOUSTON: Roger, we found that one.

COLUMBIA: The other one's located at 7.2 two-thirds of the way from . . .

HOUSTON: Roger, we believe you were looking a little too far to the west and south.

COLUMBIA: Roger, I was looking where . . . was tracking on the average and I understand it should have been more to the north and more to the west; actually, a tiny bit outside the circle.

HOUSTON: More to the north and a little more to the east. The feature that I was describing to you, the small bright crater on the rim of the large fairly old crater, would be about Mike .8 and 8.2.

HOUSTON: Tranquility Base, this is Houston. Can you give us some idea where you are in the surface checklist at the present time.

TRANQUILITY BASE: They were at the top of page 27.

COLUMBIA: Roger. Finally got you back on. I've been unsuccessfully trying to get you on the high gain and I've got command to reset the process. How do you read me now?

HOUSTON: Roger. I hear you loud with background noise.

COLUMBIA: Omni Delta and you were cut out and I never got your coordinance or estimated LM position.

HOUSTON: Estimated LM position is latitude plus .799, longitude over 2 plus 11.730.

COLUMBIA: What I'm interested is in direct coordinance on that map reading.

COLUMBIA: Could you enable the S-band relay at least one way from Eagle to Columbia, so I can hear what's going on?

HOUSTON: Roger. There's not much going on at the present time, Columbia. I'll see what I can do about the relay. . . .

HOUSTON: Columbia, this is Houston. Are you aware that Eagle plans the EVA about four hours early?

COLUMBIA: Affirmative. I haven't had any word from those guys and I thought I'd be hearing them through your S-band relay.

APOLLO CONTROL (8:48 P.M.): We'll still have acquisition of Columbia for another eight minutes. All systems in Eagle still looking good. Cabin pressure 4.86 pounds, showing a temperature of 63 degrees in the Eagle's cabin.

COLUMBIA: During the next pass I'd appreciate the S-band relay mode.

HOUSTON: We're working on that. There haven't been any transmissions from Tranquility Base since we last talked to you.

APOLLO CONTROL: We've had loss of signal on Columbia. The clock here at Control Center counting down to depressurization time on Eagle shows we're 36 minutes, 39 seconds away from that event. We believe the crew is pretty well on the time line in the EVA preparation.

APOLLO CONTROL (9:36 P.M.): This latest report the crew is—they're getting the electrical checkout—indicates they are about 40 minutes behind the time line. We will acquire Columbia in six minutes.

TRANQUILITY BASE: How do you read now?

HOUSTON: Okay. I, think that's going to be better.

HOUSTON: We have acquisition of Columbia.

HOUSTON: Roger, Columbia. Reading you loud and clear on the high gain. We have enabled the one-way Nixon relay that you requested. The crew of Tranquility Base is currently donning PLSSes [portable life support systems]. Com checks out.

COLUMBIA: Sounds okay.

TRANQUILITY BASE (9:45 P.M.): Houston, Tranquility. You'll find that the area around the ladder is in a complete dark shadow, so we're going to have some problem with TV. But I'm sure you'll see the—you'll get a picture from the lighted horizon.

HOUSTON: Neil, Neil, this is Houston. I can hear you trying to transmit. However, your transmission is beaking up.

TRANQUILITY BASE: Neil's got his antenna up now. Let's see if he comes through any better now.

TRANQUILITY BASE: Okay, Houston, this is Neil. How do you read?

HOUSTON: Neil, this is Houston, reading you beautifully.

TRANQUILITY BASE: My antenna's scratching the roof. Do we have a go for cabin depress?

COLUMBIA: They hear everything but that.

TRANQUILITY BASE: Houston, this is Tranquility. We're standing by for go for cabin depress.

HOUSTON: You are go for cabin depressurization. Go for cabin depressurization.

COLUMBIA (10 P.M.): I don't know if you guys can read me on VHF, but you sure sound good down there.

TRANQUILITY BASE: Okay, the vent window is clear. I remove lever from the engine cover.

HOUSTON: Buzz, you're coming through loud and clear, and Mike passes on the word that he's receiving you and following your progress with interest.

TRANQUILITY BASE: Lock system, decks, exit check, blue locks are checked, lock locks, red locks, perch locks, and on this side the perch locks and lock locks—both sides, body locks, and the calm.

HOUSTON (10:17 P.M.): Columbia, this is Houston. Do you read?

COLUMBIA: Read you loud and clear.

HOUSTON: Were you successful in spotting the LM on that pass?

COLUMBIA: Negative. I checked both locations and it's no dice.

APOLLO CONTROL (10:25 P.M.): In the control center a clock has been set up to record the operating time on Neil Armstrong's total life support system. EVA will be counted from that time.

TRANQUILITY BASE: Cabin repress closed. Now comes the gymnastics. Air pressure going toward zero. Standby LM suit circuit 36 to 43. That's verified. FIT GA pressure about 4.5, 4.75 and coming down. We'll open the hatch when we get to zero. Do you want to bring down one of your visors now or leave them up? We can put them down if we need them. We have visor down.

APOLLO CONTROL (10:33 P.M.): Coming up on five minutes of operation of Neil Armstrong's portable life support system now.

HOUSTON (10:37): Neil, this is Houston, what's your status on hatch opening?

TRANQUILITY BASE: Everything is go here. We're just waiting for the cabin pressure to bleed to a low enough pressure to open the hatch. It's about .1 on our gauge now. (Aldrin) I'd hate to tug on that thing. Alternative would be to open that one too.

HOUSTON: We're seeing a relatively static pressure on your cabin. Do you think you can open the hatch at this pressure?

TRANQUILITY BASE: We're going to try it. The hatch is coming open. (Aldrin): Hold it from going closed and I'll get the valve turner. I'd better get up first.

ALDRIN: Your window cleared yet?

ARMSTRONG: It was, yeah.

ALDRIN: Mine hasn't cleared yet.

(Following Is Conversation Between Armstrong and Aldrin): Okay. Bical pump secondary circuit breaker open. Back to lean—this way. Radar circuit breakers open. Well, I'm looking head-on at it. I'll get it. Okay. My antenna's out. Right. Okay, now we're ready to hook up the LEC. Okay. Now we need to hook this. Your visor. Yep. Your back is up against the perch. Now you're clear. Over toward me. Straight down, to your left a little bit. Plenty of room. You're lined up nicely. Toward me a little bit. Down. Okay. Now you're clear. You're catching the first hinge. The what hinge? All right, move. Roll to the left. Okay now you're clear. You're lined up on the platform. Put your left foot to the right a little bit. Okay that's good. More left. Good.

'I'm on the Porch'

ARMSTRONG: Okay, Houston, I'm on the porch.

HOUSTON: Roger, Neil.

HOUSTON: Columbia, Columbia, This is Houston. One minute, 30 seconds LOS, all systems go, Over.

ALDRIN: Halt where you a minute. Neil.

ARMSTRONG AND ALDRIN: Okay. Everything's nice and straight in here. Okay, can you pull the door open a little more? Right.

HOUSTON: We're getting a picture on the TV.

ALDRIN: You've got a good picture, huh?

HOUSTON: There's a great deal of contrast in it and currently it's upside down on monitor. But we can make out a fair amount of detail.

ARMSTRONG: Okay, will you verify the position, the opening I ought to have on the camera.

HOUSTON: The what? We can see you coming down the ladder now.

ARMSTRONG: Okay. I just checked getting back up to that first step. It didn't collapse too far. But it's adequate to get back up. It's a pretty good little jump.

ARMSTRONG: I'm at the foot of the ladder. The LM foot beds are only depressed in the surface about one or two inches, although the surface appears to be very, very fine-grained as you get close to it. It's almost like a powder. It's very fine. I'm going to step off the LM now. That's one small step for man, one giant leap for mankind.

The surface is fine and powdery. I can pick it up loosely with my toe. It does adhere in fine layers like powdered charcoal to the sole and the sides of my boots. I only go in a small fraction of an inch, maybe an eighth of an inch but I can see the footprints of my boots and the treads in the fine sandy particles.

There seems to be no difficulty in moving around this and we suspect that it's even perhaps easier than the simulations of 1/6 G that we performed in various simulations on the ground. Actually no trouble to walk around.

No Crater from Descent

The descent engine did not leave a crater of any size. It has about one foot clearance on the ground. We're essentially on a very level place here. I can see some evidence of rays emananting from the descent engine, but a very insignificant amount. Okay, Buzz, are we ready to bring down the camera?

ALDRIN: I'm all ready. I think it's squared away and in good shape. But you'll have to pay out all the LEC. Looks like it's coming out nice and evenly. It's quite dark here in the shadow and a little hard for me to see if I have good footing. I'll work my way over into the sunlight here without looking directly into the sun.

ARMSTRONG: Looking up at the LM, I'm standing directly in the shadow now looking up at . . . in the windows and I can see everything quite clearly. The light is sufficiently bright backlighted into the front of the LM that everything is clearly visible. I'll step out and take some of my first pictures here.

ALDRIN: Are you going to get the contingency sample? Okay. That's good.

ARMSTRONG: The contingency sample is down and it's up. Like it's a little difficult to dig through the crust. It's very interesting. It's a very soft surface but here and there where I plug with the contingency sample collector I run into very hard surface but it appears to be very cohesive material of the same sort. I'll try to get a rock in here.

HOUSTON: Oh, that looks beautiful from here, Neil.

ARMSTRONG: It has a stark beauty all its own. It's like much of the high desert of the United States. It's different but it's very pretty out here. Be advised that a lot of the rock samples out here, the hard rock samples have what appears to be vesicles in the surface.

ARMSTRONG: This has been about six or eight inches into the surface. It's easy to push on it. I'm sure I could push it in farther but it's hard for me to bend down farther than that.

ALDRIN: Ready for me to come out?

ARMSTRONG: Yeah. Just stand by a second, I'll move this over the handrail.

ALDRIN: Okay?

ARMSTRONG: All right, that's got it. Are you ready?

ALDRIN: All set.

ARMSTRONG: Okay. You saw what difficulties I was having. I'll try to watch your PLSS from underneath here. The toes are about to come over the sill. Now drop your PLSS down. There you go, you're clear. And laterally you're good. About an inch clearance on top of your PLSS. You need a little bit of arching of the back to come down.

ALDRIN: How far are my feet from the ...

ARMSTRONG: You're right at the edge of the porch.

ALDRIN: Small little foot movement. Porch. Arching of the back ... without any trouble at all.

ALDRIN: Now I want to back up and partially close the hatch—making sure not to lock it on my way out.

ARMSTRONG: Good thought....

ALDRIN: That's our home for the next couple of hours; we want to take care of it. I'm on the top step. It's a very simple matter to hop down from one step to the next.

ARMSTRONG: Yes, I found that to be very comfortable, and walking is also very comfortable, Houston. You've got three more steps and then a long one.

ALDRIN: I'm going to leave that one foot up there and both hands down to about the fourth rung up.

ARMSTRONG: A little more. About another inch, there you got it. That's a good step.

ALDRIN: About a three footer. Beautiful view.

ARMSTRONG: Ain't that somethin'?

SOURCE: *New York Times.*

CIVIL RIGHTS

THE ARREST OF ROSA PARKS
(1 December 1955)

The 1 December 1955 refusal of Rosa Louise McCauley Parks (1913–) to surrender her seat to a white man on a municipal bus would have far-reaching implications, not only for her fellow citizens of Montgomery, Alabama, but for all Americans as well. A seamstress and secretary of the local branch of the National Association for the Advancement of Colored People (NAACP), Parks, with this simple act of defiance, touched off the year-long Montgomery bus boycott which would become a model for future nonviolent protests and marked the emergence of the Reverend Martin Luther King, Jr. as a civil rights leader of national prominence. Fired from her job due to her notoriety, Parks relocated to Detroit in 1957 and resumed her activities in the civil rights movement, of which she became an enduring and much-loved figure. Her memoirs appeared in 1992, and in 1999, Parks was awarded the Congressional Gold Medal, the highest national honor bestowed by the Congress upon civilians.

Laura M. Miller,
Vanderbilt University

See also **Civil Rights Movement; Segregation.**

Having to take a certain section [on a bus] because of your race was humiliating, but having to stand up because a particular driver wanted to keep a white person from having to stand was, to my mind, most inhumane.

More than seventy-five, between eighty-five and I think ninety, percent of the patronage of the buses were black people, because more white people could own and drive their own cars than blacks.

I happened to be the secretary of the Montgomery branch of the NAACP as well as the NAACP Youth Council adviser. Many cases did come to my attention that nothing came out of 'cause the person that was abused would be too intimidated to sign an affidavit, or to make a statement. Over the years, I had had my own problems with the bus drivers. In fact, some did tell me not to ride their buses if I felt that I was too important to go to the back door to get on. One had evicted me from the bus in 1943, which did not cause anything more than just a passing glance.

On December 1, 1955, I had finished my day's work as a tailor's assistant in the Montgomery Fair department store and I was on my way home. There was one vacant seat on the Cleveland Avenue bus, which I took, alongside a man and two women across the aisle. There were still a few vacant seats in the white section in the front, of course. We went to the next stop without being disturbed. On the third, the front seats were occupied and this one man, a white man, was standing. The driver asked us to stand up and let him have those seats, and when none of us moved at his first words, he said, "You all make it light on yourselves and let me have those seats." And the man who was sitting next to the window stood up, and I made room for him to pass by me. The two women across the aisle stood up and moved out.

When the driver saw me still sitting, he asked if I was going to stand up and I said, "No, I'm not."

And he said, "Well, if you don't stand up, I'm going to call the police and have you arrested."

I said, "You may do that."

He did get off the bus, and I still stayed where I was. Two policemen came on the bus. One of the policemen asked me if the bus driver had asked me to stand and I said yes.

He said, "Why don't you stand up?"

And I asked him, "Why do you push us around?"

He said, "I do not know, but the law is the law and you're under arrest."

SOURCE: Parks, Rosa. "The Montgomery Bus Boycott, 1955–1956: 'Like a Revival Starting'." In *Voices of Freedom: An Oral History of the Civil Rights Movement from the 1950s through the 1980s*. By Henry Hampton, Steve Fayer, and Sarah Flynn. New York: Bantam Books, 1990.

STUDENT NONVIOLENT COORDINATING COMMITTEE FOUNDING STATEMENT *(1960)*

On 1 February 1960, four African American college students staged a sit-in at a segregated Woolworth's lunch counter in Greensboro, North Carolina, thus firing the opening salvo in what would become a widespread national movement. Eager to coordinate the resulting sit-in movement rapidly spreading through the southern United States, Southern Christian Leadership Conference (SCLC) officer Ella Baker gathered student protest leaders in Raleigh, North Carolina, for an Easter weekend strategy session. It was during these meetings that the Student Nonviolent Coordinating Committee (SNCC) was born. A potent force for social change, the SNCC organized or participated in numerous nonviolent segregation protests, voter registration drives, and Freedom Rides throughout much of the turbulent 1960s. Often running afoul of local authorities, SNCC members willingly accepted jail time as the consequence of their activities, and employed a "jail, no bail" strategy intended to dramatically demonstrate the depth of their convictions. The late 1960s, however, brought a philosophical change to the SNCC. Many members, frustrated by the seeming intransigence of racial injustice, began to advocate a more radical approach to achieving the organization's goals. Elected chairman in 1966, Stokely Carmichael espoused "Black Power" and a belief in Black separatism, a move that frustrated many of SNCC's mainstream political allies. By the end of the decade, the organization had switched its focus from grass-roots community activism to an emphasis on sometimes-unpopular ideological issues. By the early 1970s, already largely irrelevant in American politics, the SNCC ceased to exist.

Laura M. Miller,
Vanderbilt University

See also **Civil Rights Movement; Student Nonviolent Coordinating Committee.**

We affirm the philosophical or religious ideal of nonviolence as the foundation of our purpose, the presupposition of our belief, and the manner of our action.

Nonviolence, as it grows from the Judeo-Christian tradition, seeks a social order of justice permeated by love. Integration of human endeavor represents the crucial first step towards such a society.

Through nonviolence, courage displaces fear. Love transcends hate. Acceptance dissipates prejudice; hope ends despair. Faith reconciles doubt. Peace dominates war. Mutual regards cancel enmity. Justice for all overthrows injustice. The redemptive community supersedes immoral social systems.

By appealing to conscience and standing on the moral nature of human existence, nonviolence nurtures the atmosphere in which reconciliation and justice become actual possibilities.

Although each local group in this movement must diligently work out the clear meaning of this statement of purpose, each act or phase of our corporate effort must reflect a genuine spirit of love and good-will.

AN INTERVIEW WITH FANNIE LOU HAMER
(1965)

The daughter of poor Mississippi sharecroppers and the youngest of nineteen, Fannie Lou Hamer, the woman who was "sick and tired of being sick and tired," did not become active in the American civil rights movement until she was forty-four years old. During her struggle for her right to vote, Hamer was intimidated, jailed, beaten, fired from her job, and shot at, but she persevered, and by 1963 she had become a field secretary for the Student Nonviolent Coordinating Committee (SNCC) and a political leader in her community. When, as co-founder and vice-president of the Mississippi Freedom Democratic Party, she and others challenged the Mississippi Democratic Party's decision to send an all-white delegation to the National Convention, the plight of countless black Americans was brought to public attention. A tireless crusader for human rights and an inspiration for Americans of all colors, Hamer would go on to receive a number of honorary degrees from colleges and universities, and even to run for Congress. Suffering from cancer, diabetes, and heart disease, she died on 14 March 1977 in a hospital not far from her home in Ruleville, Mississippi.

Laura M. Miller,
Vanderbilt University

See also **Civil Rights Movement; Mississippi; Suffrage: African American Suffrage; Voter Registration; White Citizens Councils.**

Life in Mississippi

O'DELL: Mrs. Hamer, it's good to see you again. I understand you have been to Africa since we last talked? I would like for you to talk about your African trip today.

HAMER: It was one of the proudest moments in my life.

O'DELL: That is a marvelous experience for any black American particularly for anyone who has lived here all of his life. Then, too, we want to talk about some of your early childhood experiences which helped to make you the kind of person you are and provided the basis for your becoming so active in the Freedom Movement.

HAMER: I would like to talk about some of the things that happened that made me know that there was something wrong in the south from a child. My parents moved to Sunflower County when I was two years old. I remember, and I will never forget, one day—I was six years old and I was playing beside the road and this plantation owner drove up to me and stopped and asked me "could I pick some cotton." I told him I didn't know and he said, "Yes, you can. I will give you things that you want from the commissary store," and he named things like crackerjacks and sardines—and it was a huge list that he called off. So I picked the 30 pounds of cotton that week, but I found out what actually happened was he was trapping me into beginning the work I was to keep doing and I never did get out of his debt again. My parents tried so hard to do what they could to keep us in school, but school didn't last but four months out of the year and most of the time we didn't have clothes to wear. My parents would make huge crops of sometimes 55 to 60 bales of cotton. Being from a big family where there were 20 children, it wasn't too hard to pick that much cotton. But my father, year after year, didn't get too much money and I remember he just kept going. Later on he did get enough money to buy mules. We didn't have tractors, but he bought mules, wagons, cultivators and some farming equipment. As soon as he bought that and decided to rent some land, because it was always better if you rent the land, but as soon as he got the mules and wagons and everything, somebody went to our trough—a white man who didn't live very far from us—and he fed the mules Paris Green, put it in their food and it killed the mules and our cows. That knocked us right back down. And things got so tough then I began to wish I was white. We worked all the time, just worked and then we would be hungry and my mother was clearing up a new ground trying to help feed us for $1.25 a day. She was using an axe, just like a man, and something flew up and hit her in her eye. It eventually caused her to lose both of her eyes and I began to get sicker and sicker of the system there. I used to see my mother wear clothes that would have so many patches on them, they had been done over and over and over again. She would do that but she would try to keep us decent. She still would be ragged and I always said if I lived to get grown and had a chance, I was going to try to get something for my mother and I was going to do something for the black man of the south if it would cost my life; I was determined to see that things were changed. My mother got down sick in 53 and she lived with me, an invalid, until she passed away in 1961. And during the time she was staying with me sometime I would be worked so hard I couldn't sleep at night . . .

O'DELL: What kind of work were you doing?

HAMER: I was a timekeeper and sharecropper on the same plantation I was fired from. During the time she was with me, if there was something I had to do without, I was determined to see that she did have something in her last few years. I went almost naked to see that my mother was kept decent and treated as a human being for the first time in all of her life. My mother was a great woman. To look at her from the suffering she had gone through to bring us up—20 children: 6 girls and 14 boys, but still she taught us to be decent and to respect ourselves, and that is one of the things that has kept me going, even after she passed. She tried so hard to make life easy for us. Those are the things that forced me to try to do something different and when this Movement came to Mississippi I still feel it is one of the greatest things that ever happened because only a person living in the State of Mississippi knows what it is like to suffer; knows what it is like to be hungry; knows what it is like to have no clothing to wear. And these people in Mississippi State, they are not "down"; all they need is a chance. And I am determined to give my part not for what the Movement can do for me, but what I can do for the Movement to bring about a change in the State of Mississippi. Actually, some of the things I experienced as a child still linger on; what the white man has done to the black people in the south!

One of the things I remember as a child: There was a man named Joe Pulliam. He was a great Christian man; but one time, he was living with a white family and this white family robbed him of what he earned. They didn't pay him anything. This white man gave him $150 to go to the hill, (you see, I lived in the Black Belt of Mississippi) . . . to get another Negro family. Joe Pulliam knew what this white man had been doing to him so he kept the $150 and didn't go. This white man talked with him then shot him in the shoulder and Joe Pulliam went back into the house and got a Winchester and killed this white man. The other white fellow that was with him he "outrun the word of God" back to town. That gave this Negro a chance to go down on the bayou that was called Powers Bayou and he got in a hollowed-out stump where there was enough room for a person. He got in there and he stayed and was tracked there, but they couldn't see him and every time a white man would peep out, he busted him. He killed 13 white men and wounded 26 and Mississippi was a quiet place for a long time. I remember that until this day and I won't forget it. After they couldn't get him, they took gas—one man from Clarksdale used a machine gun—(Bud Doggins)—they used a machine gun and tried to get him like that and then they took gas and poured it on Powers Bayou. Thousands of gallons of gas and they lit it and when it burned up to the hollowed-out stump, he crawled out. When they found him, he was unconscious and he was lying with his head on his gun but the last bullet in the gun had been snapped twice. They dragged him by his heels on the back of a car and they paraded about with that man and they cut his ears off and put them in a showcase and it stayed there a long, long time—in Drew, Mississippi. All of those things, when they would happen, would make me sick in the pit of my stomach and year after year, everytime something would happen it would make me more and more aware of what would have to be done in the State of Mississippi.

O'DELL: What do you think will have to be done?

HAMER: The only thing I really feel is necessary is that the black people, not only in Mississippi, will have to actually upset this applecart. What I mean by that is, so many things are under the cover that will have to be swept out and shown to this whole world, not just to America. This thing they say of "the land of the free and the home of the brave" is all on paper. It doesn't really mean anything to us. The only way we can make this thing a reality in America is to do all we can to destroy this system and bring this out to the light that has been under the cover all these years. That's why I believe in Christianity because the Scriptures said: "The things that have been done in the dark will be known on the house tops."

Now many things are beginning to come out and it was truly a reality to me when I went to Africa, to Guinea. The little things that had been taught to me about the African people, that they were "heathens," "savages," and they were just downright stupid people. But when I got to Guinea, we were greeted by the Government of Guinea, which is Black People—and we stayed at a place that was the government building, because we were the guests of the Government. You don't know what that meant to me when I got to Guinea on the 12th of September. The President of Guinea, Sekou Toure, came to see us on the 13th. Now you know, I don't know how you can compare this by me being able to see a President of a country when I have just been there two days; and here I have been in America, born in America, and I am 46 years pleading with the President for the last two to three years to just give us a chance-and this President in Guinea recognized us enough to talk to us.

O'DELL: How many were in your delegation?

HAMER: It was eleven of us during that time, and I could get a clear picture of actually what had happened to the black people of America. Our foreparents were mostly brought from West Africa, the same place that we visited in Africa. We were brought to America and our foreparents were sold; white people bought; white people changed their names . . . and actually . . . here, my maiden name is supposed to be Townsend; but really, what is my maiden name . . . ? What is my name? This white man who is saying "it takes time." For three hundred and more years they have had "time," and now it is time for them to listen. We have been listening year after year to them and what have we got? We are not even allowed to think for ourselves. "I know what is best for you," but they don't know what is best for us! It is time now to let them know what they owe us, and they owe us a great deal. Not only have we paid the price with our names in ink, but we have also paid in blood. And they can't say that black people can't be intelligent, because going back to Africa, in Guinea, there are almost 4 million people there and what he, President Toure, is doing to educate the people: as long as the French people had it they weren't doing a thing that is being done now. I met one child there eleven years old, speaking three languages. He could speak English, French and Malinke. Speaking my language actually better than I could. And this hypocrisy—they tell us here in America. People should go there and see. It would bring tears in your eyes to make you think of all those years, the type of brain-washing that this man will use in America to keep us separated from our own people. When I got on that plane, it was loaded with white people going to Africa for the Peace Corps. I got there and met a lot of them, and actually they had more peace there in Guinea than I have here. I talked to some of them. I told them before they would be able to clean up somebody else's house you would have to clean up yours; before they can tell somebody else how to run their country, why don't they do something here. This problem is not only in Mississippi. During the time I was in the Convention in Atlantic City, I didn't get any threats from Mississippi. The threatening letters were from Philadelphia, Chicago and other big cities.

O'DELL: You received threatening letters while you were at the Convention?

HAMER: Yes. I got pictures of us and they would draw big red rings around us and tell what they thought of us. I got a letter said, "I have been shot three times throught the heart. I hope I see your second act." But this white man who wants to stay white, and to think for the Negro, he is not only destroying the Negro, he is destroying himself, because a house divided against itself cannot stand and that same thing applies to America. America that is divided against itself cannot stand, and we cannot say we have all of this unity they say we have when black people are being discriminated against in every city in America I have visited.

I was in jail when Medgar Evers was murdered and nothing, I mean nothing has been done about that. You know what really made me sick? I was in Washington, D.C. at another time reading in a paper where the U.S. gives Byron de la Beckwith—the man who is charged with murdering Medgar Evers—they were giving him so much money for some land and I ask "Is this America?" We can no longer ignore the fact that America is NOT the "land of the free and the home of the brave." I used to question this for years—what did our kids actually fight for? They would go in the service and go through all of that and come right out to be drowned in a river in Mississippi. I found this hypocrisy is all over America.

The 20th of March in 1964, I went before the Secretary of State to qualify to run as an official candidate for Congress from the 2nd Congressional District, and it was easier for me to qualify to run than it was for me to pass the literacy test to be a registered voter. And we had four people to qualify and run in the June primary election be we didn't have enough Negroes registered in Mississippi. The 2nd Congressional District where I ran, against Jamie Whitten, is made up of 24 counties. Sixty-eight per cent of the people are Negroes, only 6–8 per cent are registered. And it is not because Negroes don't want to register. They try and they try and they try. That's why it was important for us to set up the "Freedom Registration" to help us in the Freedom Democratic Party.

O'DELL: This was a registration drive organized by the Movement?

HAMER: Yes. The only thing we took out was the Constitution of the State of Mississippi and the interpretation of the Constitution. We had 63,000 people registered on the Freedom Registration form. And we tried from every level to go into the regular Democratic Party medium. We tried from the precinct level. The 16th of June when they were holding precinct meetings all across the state, I was there and there was eight of us there to attend the meeting, and they had the door locked at 10 o'clock in the morning. So we had our own meeting and elected our permanent chairman and secretary and regulars and alternates and we passed a resolution as the law requires and then mailed it to Oscar Townsend, our permanent chairman. This is what's happening in the State of Mississippi. We had hoped for a change, but these people (Congressmen) go to Washington and stay there for 25 and 30 years and more without representing the people of Mississippi. We have never been represented in Washington. You can tell this by the program the federal government had to train 2,400 tractor drivers. They would have trained Negro and white together, but this man, Congressman Jamie Whitten, voted against it and everything that was decent. So, we've got to have somebody in Washington who is concerned about the people of Mississippi.

After we testified before the Credentials Committee in Atlantic City, their Mississippi representative testified also. He said I got 600 votes but when they made the count in Mississippi, I was told I had 388 votes. So actually it is no telling how many votes I actually got.

O'DELL: In other words, a Mr. Collins came before the Credentials Committee of the Democratic National Convention and actually gave away the secret in a sense, because the figure he gave was not the same figure he gave you as an official candidate?

HAMER: That's right. He also said I had been allowed to attend the precinct meeting which was true. But he didn't say we were locked out of the polling place there and had to hold our meeting on the lawn.

O'DELL: So now you have a situation where you had the basis for a Freedom Democratic Party. You have had four candidates to run for Congress. You had a community election where 63,000 of our folk showed their interest in the election. How do you size up the situation coming out of Atlantic City? What impressions did you get from your effort in Atlantic City to be seated, and how do you feel the people back home are going to react to this next period you are going into?

HAMER: The people at home will work hard and actually all of them think it was important that we hade the decision that we did make not to compromise; because we didn't have anything to compromise for. Some things I found out in the National Convention I wasn't too glad I did find out. But we will work hard, and it was important to actually really bring this out to the open, the things I will say some people knew about and some people didn't; this stuff that has been kept under the cover for so many years. Actually, the world and America is upset and the only way to bring about a change is to upset it more.

O'DELL: What was done about the beating you and Miss Annelle Ponder, your colleague in the citizenship school program, experienced while in jail? Was any action taken at all?

HAMER: The Justice Department filed a suit against the brutality of the five law officials and they had this trial. The trial began the 2nd of December 1963 and they had white jurors from the State of Mississippi, and the Federal Judge Clayton made it plain to the jurors that they were dealing with "nigras" and that "who would actually accuse such upstanding people like those law officials"—be careful what they was doing because they are law-abiding citizens and were dealing with agitators and niggers. It was as simple as that? And those police were cleared. They were on the loose for about a week before I left for Atlantic City. One of those men was driving a truck from the State Penitentiary. One night he passed my house and pointed me out to one of the other men in the State Penitentiary truck and that same night I got a threat: "We got you located Fannie Lou and we going to put you in the Mississippi River." A lot of people say why do they let the hoodlums do that? But it is those people supposed to have class that are doing the damage in Mississippi. You know there was a time, in different places, when people felt safe going to a law official. But I called them that day and got the answer back, "You know you don't look to us for help."

O'DELL: This threat: the man called you up and said "we've got you spotted;" I gather from that that the river has some special meaning to us living there in Mississippi?

HAMER: Yes. So many people have been killed and put in the Mississippi River. Like when they began to drag the river for Mickey and Chaney and Andy. Before he was to go to Oxford, Ohio, Mickey was telling me his life had been threatened and a taxi driver had told him to be careful because they was out to get him.

When they (the sailors) began to drag the river and found other people and I actually feel like they stopped because they would have been shook up to find so many if they had just been fishing for bodies. The Mississippi is not the only river. There's the Tallahatchie and the Big Black. People have been put in the river year after year, these things been happening.

O'DELL: The general policy of striking fear in people's hearts. In other words, it is like lynchings used to be. They used to night ride . . .

HAMER: They still night ride. The exact count was 32 churches they had burned down in the State of Mississippi and they still ride at night and throw bombs at night. You would think they would cut down with Mrs. Chaney. But since they murdered James Chaney, they have shot buckshot at his mother's house. And hate won't only destroy us. It will destroy these people that's hating as well. And one of the things is, they are afraid of getting back what they have been putting out all of these years. You know the Scripture says "be not deceived for God is not mocked; whatsoever a man sow that shall he also reap." And one day, I don't know how they're going to get it, but they're going to get some of it back. They are scared to death and are more afraid now than we are.

O'DELL: How active is the White Citizen's Council? Has it the kind of outlet through TV and radio and so forth that Negroes are aware of its presence?

HAMER: They announce their programs. In fact, one day I was going to Jackson and I saw a huge sign that U.S. Senator John Stennis was speaking that night for the White Citizens Council in Yazoo City and they also have a State Charter that they may set up for "private schools." It is no secret.

O'DELL: Does it seem to be growing? Is the white community undergoing any change as a result of all the pressure that has been put now with Mississippi Summer Project and the killing of the three civil rights workers. What effect is it having on the white community?

HAMER: You can't ever tell. I have talked to two or three whites that's decent in the State of Mississippi, but you know, just two or three speaking out. I do remember, one time, a man came to me after the students began to work in Mississippi and he said the white people were getting tired and they were getting tense and anything might happen. Well, I asked him "how long he thinks we had been getting tired"? I have been tired for 46 years and my parents was tired before me and their parents were tired, and I have always wanted to do something that would help some of the things I would see going on among Negroes that I didn't like and I don't like now.

O'DELL: Getting back just for a minute to Atlantic City. You all were in the national spotlight because there was nothing else happening in the Democratic National Convention other than your challenge to the Mississippi delegation and I would like to go back to that and pull together some of the conclusions you might have drawn form that experience.

HAMER: In coming to Atlantic City, we believed strongly that we were right. In fact, it was just right for us to come to challenge the seating of the regular Democratic Party from Mississippi. But we didn't think when we got there that we would meet people, that actually the other leaders of the Movement would differ with what we felt was right. We would have accepted the Green proposal. But, when we couldn't get that, it didn't make any sense for us to take "two votes at large." What would that mean to Mississippi? What would it have meant to us to go back and tell the Mississippi people? And actually, I think there will be great leaders emerging from the State of Mississippi. The people that have the experience to know and the people not interested in letting somebody pat you on the back and tell us "I think it is right." And it is very important for us not to accept a compromise and after I got back to Mississippi, people there said it was the most important step that had been taken. We figured it was right and it was right, and if we had accepted that compromise, then we would have been letting the people down in Mississippi. Regardless of leadership, we have to think for ourselves!

O'DELL: In other words, you had two battles on your hands when you went to Atlantic City?

HAMER: Yes. I was in one of the meetings when they spoke about accepting two votes and I said I wouldn't dare think about anything like this. So, I wasn't allowed to attend the other meetings. It was quite an experience.

O'DELL: There will be other elections and other conventions and the people in Mississippi should be a little stronger.

HAMER: I think so.

O'DELL: Well, it's good to know that the people you have to work with every day are with you.

HAMER: Yes, they are with us one hundred per cent.

O'DELL: That's encouraging because it makes the work that much easier. Is there any final thing you want to say that is part of this historic statement of life in Mississippi for yourself as a person who lives there?

HAMER: Nothing other than we will be working. When I go back to Mississippi we will be working as hard or harder to bring about a change, but things are not always pleasant there.

O'DELL: You will probably have the support of more people than you have ever had, all around the country.

HAMER: Yes, actually since the Convention I have gotten so many letters that I have tried to answer but every letter said they thought this decision, not to accept the compromise, was so important. There wasn't one letter I have gotten so far that said we should have accepted the compromise—not one.

O'DELL: So, those are people who are interested in your work, and as you get back into the main swing of things you will be keeping in touch with those people so that they should be asked to help in any way they can regardless of where they live. It is national and international public pressure that is needed.

HAMER: I don't know about the press, but I know in the town where I live everybody was aware that I was in Africa, because I remember after I got back some of the people told me that Mayor Dura of our town said he just wished they would boil me in tar. But, that just shows how ignorant he is, I didn't see any tar over there. But I was treated much better in Africa than I was treated in America. And you see, often I get letters like this: "Go back to Africa."

Now I have just as much right to stay in America—in fact, the black people have contributed more to America than any other race, because our kids have fought here for what was called "democracy"; our mothers and fathers were sold and bought here for a price. So all I can say when they say "go back to Africa," I say "when you send the Chinese back to China, the Italians back to Italy, etc., and you get on that Mayflower from whence you came, and give the Indians their land back, who really would be here at home?" It is our right to stay here and we will stay and stand up for what belongs to us as American citizens, because they can't say that we haven't had patience.

O'DELL: Was there a lot of interest in your trip among the African people that you met?

HAMER: Yes. I saw how the Government was run there and I saw where black people were running the banks. I saw, for the first time in my life, a black stewardess walking through a plane and that was quite an inspiration for me. It shows what black people can do if we only get the chance in America. It is there within us. We can do things if we only get the chance. I see so many ways America uses to rob Negroes and it is sinful and America can't keep holding on, and doing these things. I saw in Chicago, on the street where I was visiting my sister-in-law, this "Urban Renewal" and it means one thing: "Negro removal." But they want to tear the homes down and put a parking lot there. Where are those people going? Where will they go? And as soon as Negroes take to the street demonstrating, one hears people say, "they shouldn't have done it." The world is looking at America and it is really beginning to show up for what it is really like. "Go Tell It on the Mountain." We can no longer ignore this, that America is not "the land of the free and the home of the brave."

SOURCE: Interview with Fannie Lou Hamer. *Freedomways: a quarterly review of the Negro freedom movement* (Spring 1965).

"BLACK POWER" SPEECH
(28 July 1966, by Stokely Carmichael)

When James Meredith was shot by a sniper during his one-man "March Against Fear," Stokely Carmichael (1941–1998) and others, the Reverend Martin Luther King, Jr. among them, vowed to complete the march in his name, only to be arrested by police in Greenwood, Mississippi. It was upon his release that Carmichael made the speech presented here calling for black Americans to reject the values of a society that he felt were preventing them from reaching their full potential. The message, delivered in no-nonsense, plain-spoken English, represented a rejection of the teachings and style of the Reverend King, whose advocacy of nonviolent civil disobedience and the belief that blacks and whites had to work together toward racial reconciliation Carmichael himself had once championed in the Student Nonviolent Coordinating Committee (SNCC).

A controversial figure and an inspiration for frustrated black Americans, Carmichael was jailed during civil rights activities some twenty-seven times, once in Jackson, Mississippi, for forty-nine days. He would go on to join the militant Black Panthers, a move that would lead the National Association for the Advancement of Colored People (NAACP) and the Southern Christian Leadership Conference (SCLC) to publicly denounce his ideas as dangerous and racist. In 1969, his passport having been confiscated then returned ten months later by the United States Government, Carmichael changed his name to Kwame Ture and relocated to Guinea, West Africa, where he served as aide to the prime minister. He was still living there when he died of cancer on 15 November 1998.

Laura M. Miller,
Vanderbilt University

See also **Black Nationalism; Black Panthers; Black Power; Military Service and Minorities: African Americans; Student Nonviolent Coordinating Committee.**

This is 1966 and it seems to me that it's "time out" for nice words. It's time black people got together. We have to say things nobody else in this country is willing to say and find the strength internally and from each other to say the things that need to be said. We have to understand the lies this country has spoken about black people and we have to set the record straight. No one else can do that but black people.

I remember when I was in school they used to say, "If you work real hard, if you sweat, if you are ambitious, then you will be successful." I'm here to tell you that if that was true, black people would own this country, because we sweat more than anybody else in this country. We have to say to this country that you have lied to us. We picked your cotton for $2.00 a day, we washed your dishes, we're the porters in your bank and in your building, we are the janitors and the elevator men. We worked hard and all we get is a little pay and a hard way to go from you. We have to talk not only about what's going on here but what this country is doing across the world. When we start getting the internal strength to tell them what should be told and to speak the truth as it should be spoken, let them pick the sides and let the chips fall where they may.

Now, about what black people have to do and what has been done to us by white people. If you are born in Lowndes County, Alabama, Swillingchit, Mississippi, or Harlem, New York, and the color of your skin happens to be black you are going to catch it. The only reason we have to get together is the color of our skins. They oppress us because we are black and we are going to use that blackness to get out of the trick bag they put us in. Don't be ashamed of your color.

A few years ago, white people used to say, "Well, the reason they live in the ghetto is they are stupid, dumb, lazy, unambitious, apathetic, don't care, happy, contented," and the trouble was a whole lot of us believed that junk about ourselves. We were so busy trying to prove to white folks that we were everything they said we weren't that we got so busy being white we forgot what it was to be black. We are going to call our black brother's hand.

Now, after 1960, when we got moving, they couldn't say we were lazy and dumb and apathetic and all that anymore so they got sophisticated and started to play the dozens with us. They called conferences about our mamas and told us that's why we were where we were at. Some people were sitting up there talking with Johnson while he was talking about their mamas. I don't play the dozens with white folks. To set the record straight, the reason we are in the bag we are in isn't because of my mama, it's because of what they did to my mama. That's why I'm where I'm at. We have to put the blame where it belongs. The blame does not belong on the oppressed but on the oppressor, and that's where it is going to stay.

Don't let them scare you when you start opening your mouth—speak the truth. Tell them, "Don't blame us because we haven't ever had the chance to do wrong." They made sure that we have been so blocked-in we couldn't move until they said, "Move." Now there are a number of things we have to do. The only thing we own in this country is the color of our skins and we are ashamed of that because they made us ashamed. We have to stop being ashamed of being black. A broad nose, a thick lip and nappy hair is us and we are going to call that beautiful whether they like it or not. We are not going to fry our hair anymore but they can start wearing their hair natural to look like us.

We have to define how we are going to move, not how they say we can move. We have never been able to do that before. Everybody in this country jumps up and says, "I'm a friend of the civil rights movement. I'm a friend of the Negro." We haven't had the chance to say whether or not that man is stabbing us in the back or not. All those people who are calling us friends are nothing but treacherous enemies and we can take care of our enemies but God deliver us from our "friends." The only protection we are going to have is from each other. We have to build a strong base to let them know if they touch one black man driving his wife to the hospital in Los Angeles, or one black man walking down a highway in Mississippi or if they take one black man who has a rebellion and put him in jail and start talking treason, we are going to disrupt this whole country.

We have to say, "Don't play jive and start writing poems after Malcolm is shot." We have to move from the point where the man left off and stop writing poems. We have to start supporting our own movement. If we can spend all that money to send a preacher to a Baptist convention in a Cadillac then we can spend money to support our own movement.

Now, let's get to what the white press has been calling riots. In the first place don't get confused with the words they use like "anti-white," "hate," "militant" and all that nonsense like "radical" and "riots." What's happening is rebellions not riots and the extremist element is not RAM. As a matter of fact RAM is a very reactionary group, reacting against the pressures white people are putting on them. The extremists in this country are the white people who force us to live the way we live. We have to define our own ethic. We don't have to (and don't make any apologies about it) obey any law that we didn't have a part to make, especially if that law was made to keep us where we are. We have the right to break it.

We have to stop apologizing for each other. We must tell our black brothers and sisters who go to college, "Don't take any job for IBM or Wall Street because you aren't doing anything for us. You are helping this country perpetuate its lies about how democracy rises in this country." They have to come back to the community, where they belong and use their skills to help develop us. We have to tell the doctors, "You can't go to college and come back and charge us $5.00 and $10.00 a visit. You have to charge us 50 cents and be thankful you get that." We have to tell our lawyers not to charge us what they charge but to be happy to take a case and plead it free of charge. We have to define success and tell them the food Ralph Bunche eats doesn't feed our hungry stomachs. We have to tell Ralph Bunche the only reason he is up there is so when we yell they can pull him out. We have to do that, nobody else can do that for us.

We have to talk about wars and soldiers and just what that means. A mercenary is a hired killer and any black man serving in this man's army is a black mercenary, nothing else. A mercenary fights for a country for a price but does not enjoy the rights of the country for which he is fighting. A mercenary will go to Vietnam to fight for free elections for the Vietnamese but doesn't have free elections in Alabama, Mississippi, Georgia, Texas, Louisiana, South Carolina and Washington, D.C.

A mercenary goes to Vietnam and gets shot fighting for his country and they won't even bury him in his own hometown. He's a mercenary, that's all. We must find the strength so that when they start grabbing us to fight their war we say, "Hell no."

We have to talk about nonviolence among us, so that we don't cut each other on Friday nights and don't destroy each other but move to a point where we appreciate and love each other. That's the nonviolence that has to be talked about. The psychology the man has used on us has turned us against each other. He says nothing about the cutting that goes on Friday night but talk about raising one fingertip towards him and that's when he jumps up. We have to talk about nonviolence among us first.

We have to study black history but don't get fooled. You should know who John Hullett is, and Fannie Lou Hamer is, who Lerone Bennett is, who Max Stanford is, who Lawrence Landry is, who May Mallory is and who Robert Williams is. You have to know these people yourselves because you can't read about them in a book or in the press. You have to know what Mr. X said from his own lips not the *Chicago Sun-Times.* That responsibility is ours. The Muslims call themselves Muslims but the press calls them black Muslims. We have to call them Muslims and go to their mosque to find out what they are talking about firsthand and then we can talk about getting together. Don't let that man get up there and tell you, "Oh, you know those Muslims preach nothing but hate. You shouldn't be messing with them." "Yah, I don't mess with them, yah, I know they bad." The man's name is the Honorable Elijah Muhammad and he represents a great section of the black community. Honor him.

We have to go out and find our young blacks who are cutting and shooting each other and tell them they are doing the cutting and shooting to the wrong people. We have to bring them together and spend the time if we are not just shucking and jiving. This is 1966 and my grandmother used to tell me, "The time is far spent." We have to move this year.

There is a psychological war going on in this country and it's whether or not black people are going to be able to use the terms they want about their movement without white people's blessing. We have to tell them we are going to use the term "Black Power" and we are going to define it because Black Power speaks to us. We can't let them project Black Power because they can only project it from white power and we know what white power has done to us. We have to organize ourselves to speak from a position of strength and stop begging people to look kindly upon us. We are going to build a movement in this country based on the color of our skins that is going to free us from our oppressors and we have to do that ourselves.

We have got to understand what is going on in Lowndes County, Alabama, what it means, who is in it and what they are doing so if white people steal that election like they do all over this country then the eyes of black people all over this country will be focused there to let them know we are going to take care of business if they mess with us in Lowndes County. That responsibility lies on all of us, not just the civil rights workers and do-gooders.

If we talk about education we have to educate ourselves, not with Hegel or Plato or the missionaries who came to Africa with the Bible and we had the land and when they left we had the Bible and they had the land. We have to tell them the only way anybody eliminates poverty in this country is to give poor people money. You don't have to Headstart, Uplift and Upward-Bound them into your culture. Just give us the money you stole from us, that's all. We have to say to people in this country, "We don't really care about you. For us to get better, we don't have to go to white things. We can do it in our own community, ourselves if you didn't steal the resources that belong there." We have to understand the Horatio Alger lie and that the individualist, profit-concept nonsense will never work for us. We have to form cooperatives and use the profits to benefit our community. We can't tolerate their system.

When we form coalitions we must say on what grounds we are going to form them, not white people telling us how to form them. We must build strength and pride amongst ourselves. We must think politically and get power because we are the only people in this country that are powerless. We are the only people who have to protect ourselves from our protectors. We are the only people who want a man called Willis removed who is a racist, that have to lie down in the street and beg a racist named Daley to remove the racist named Willis. We have to build a movement so we can see Daley and say, "Tell Willis to get hat," and by the time we turn around he is gone. That's Black Power.

Everybody in this country is for "Freedom Now" but not everybody is for Black Power because we have got to get rid of some of the people who have white power. We have got to get us some Black Power. We don't control anything but what white people say we can control. We have to be able to smash any political machine in the country that's oppressing us and bring it to its knees. We have to be aware that if we keep growing and multiplying the way we do in ten years all the major cities are going to be ours. We have to know that in Newark, New Jersey, where we are sixty percent of the population, we went along with their stories about integrating and we got absorbed. All we have to show for it is three councilmen who are speaking for them and not for us. We have to organize ourselves to speak for each other. That's Black Power. We have to move to control the economics and politics of our community . . .

THE VIETNAM WAR

EXCERPT FROM *THE PENTAGON PAPERS* *(1963–1964)*

The Pentagon Papers are a forty-seven-volume, seven-thousand-page archive of sealed Department of Defense (DOD) files, diplomatic papers and important presidential orders about the United States' involvement in Vietnam. DOD aide Daniel Ellsberg, who felt that the American public should know what was going on behind the government's closed doors, published selections from the papers in the *New York Times*. The papers covered U.S. actions and involvement in Vietnam between the years 1945 and 1968.

Ellsberg was immediately charged by the Nixon Administration with espionage, theft, and conspiracy, but was eventually freed of charges when it was revealed that government operatives had broken into Ellsberg's psychiatrist's office in an attempt to discredit him. A Supreme Court case, *The New York Times v. United States* (1971) ruled that the publication of the papers was constitutional, claiming the government's attempt to keep the papers secret infringed upon the First Amendment. Once published, the papers fueled the already strong antiwar movement by underscoring the relative impossibility of concluding the war in a manner favorable to the Americans.

Mark D. Baumann,
New York University

See also **Pentagon Papers; Vietnam War.**

"McNamara Report to Johnson on the Situation in Saigon in '63"

Memorandum, "Vietnam Situation," from Secretary of Defense Robert S. McNamara to President Lyndon B. Johnson, Dec. 21, 1963.

In accordance with your request this morning, this is a summary of my conclusions after my visit to Vietnam on December 19–20.

1. Summary. The situation is very disturbing. Current trends, unless reversed in the next 2–3 months, will lead to neutralization at best and more likely to a Communist-controlled state.
2. The new government is the greatest source of concern. It is indecisive and drifting. Although Minh states that he, rather than the Committee of Generals, is making decisions, it is not clear that this is actually so. In any event, neither he nor the Committee are experienced in political administration and so far they show little talent for it. There is no clear concept on how to re-shape or conduct the strategic hamlet program; the Province Chiefs, most of whom are new and inexperienced, are receiving little or no direction because the generals are so preoccupied with essentially political affairs. A specific example of the present situation is that General [name illegible] is spending little or no time commanding III Corps, which is in the vital zone around Saigon and needs full-time direction. I made these points as strongly as possible to Minh, Don, Kim, and Tho.
3. The Country Team is the second major weakness. It lacks leadership, has been poorly informed, and is not working to a common plan. A recent example of confusion has been conflicting USOM and military recommendations both to the Government of Vietnam and to Washington on the size of the military budget. Above all, Lodge has virtually no official contact with Harkins. Lodge sends in reports with major military implications without showing them to Harkins, and does not show Harkins important income traffic. My impression is that Lodge simply

does not know how to conduct a coordinated administration. This has of course been stressed to him both by Dean Rusk and myself (and also by John McCone), and I do not think he is consciously rejecting our advice; he has just operated as a loner all his life and cannot readily change now.

Lodge's newly-designated deputy, David Nes, was with us and seems a highly competent team player. I have stated the situation frankly to him and he has said he would do all he could to constitute what would in effect be an executive committee operating below the level of the Ambassador.

As to the grave reporting weakness, both Defense and CIA must take major steps to improve this. John McCone and I have discussed it and are acting vigorously in our respective spheres.

4. Viet Cong progress has been great during the period since the coup, with my best guess being that the situation has in fact been deteriorating in the countryside since July to a far greater extent than we realized because of our undue dependence on distorted Vietnamese reporting. The Viet Cong now control very high proportions of the people in certain key provinces, particularly those directly south and west of Saigon. The Strategic Hamlet Program was seriously over-extended in those provinces, and the Viet Cong has been able to destroy many hamlets, while others have been abandoned or in some cases betrayed or pillaged by the government's own Self Defense Corps. In these key provinces, the Viet Cong have destroyed almost all major roads, and are collecting taxes at will.

As remedial measures, we must get the government to re-allocate its military forces so that its effective strength in these provinces is essentially doubled. We also need to have major increases in both military and USOM staffs, to sizes that will give us a reliable, independent U.S. appraisal of the status of operations. Thirdly, realistic pacification plans must be prepared, allocating adequate time to secure the remaining government-controlled areas and work out from there.

This gloomy picture prevails predominantly in the provinces around the capital and in the Delta. Action to accomplish each of these objectives was started while we were in Saigon. The situation in the northern and central areas is considerably better, and does not seem to have deteriorated substantially in recent months. General Harkins still hopes these areas may be made reasonably secure by the latter half of next year.

In the gloomy southern picture, an exception to the trend of Viet Cong success may be provided by the possible adherence to the government of the Cao Dai and Hoa Hao sects, which total three million people and control key areas along the Cambodian border. The Hoa Hao have already made some sort of agreement, and the Cao Dai are expected to do so at the end of this month. However, it is not clear that their influence will be more than neutralized by these agreements, or that they will in fact really pitch in on the government's side.

5. Infiltration of men and equipment from North Vietnam continues using (a) land corridors through Laos and Cambodia; (b) the Mekong River waterways from Cambodia; (c) some possible entry from the sea and the tip of the Delta. The best guess is that 1000–1500 Viet Cong cadres entered South Vietnam from Laos in the first nine months of 1963. The Mekong route (and also the possible sea entry) is apparently used for heavier weapons and ammunition and raw materials which have been turning up in increasing numbers in the south and of which we have captured a few shipments.

To counter this infiltration, we reviewed in Saigon various plans providing for cross-border operations into Laos. On the scale proposed, I am quite clear that these would not be politically acceptable or even militarily effective. Our first need would be immediate U-2 mapping of the whole Laos and Cambodian border, and this we are preparing on an urgent basis.

One other step we can take is to expand the existing limited but remarkably effective operations on the Laos side, the so-called Operation HARDNOSE, so that it at least provides reasonable intelligence on movements all the way along the Laos corridor; plans to expand this will be prepared and presented for approval in about two weeks.

As to the waterways, the military plans presented in Saigon were unsatisfactory, and a special naval team is being sent at once from Honolulu to determine what more can be done. The whole waterway system is so vast, however, that effective policing may be impossible.

In general, the infiltration problem, while serious and annoying, is a lower priority than the key problems discussed earlier. However, we should do what we can to reduce it.

6. Plans for Covert Action into North Vietnam were prepared as we had requested and were an excellent job. They present a wide variety of sabotage and psychological operations against North Vietnam from which I believe we should aim to select those that provide maximum pressure with minimum risk. In accordance with your direction at the meeting, General Krulak of the JCS is chairing a group that will lay out a program in the next ten days for our consideration.

7. Possible neutralization of Vietnam is strongly opposed by Minh, and our attitude is somewhat suspect because of editorials by the New York Times and mention by Walter Lippmann and others. We reassured them as strongly as possible on this—and in somewhat more general terms on the neutralization of Cambodia. I recommend that you convey to

Minh a Presidential message for the New Year that would also be a vehicle to stress the necessity of strong central direction by the government and specifically by Minh himself.

8. U.S. resources and personnel cannot usefully be substantially increased. I have directed a modest artillery supplement, and also the provision of uniforms for the Self Defense Corps, which is the most exposed force and suffers from low morale. Of greater potential significance, I have directed the Military Departments to review urgently the quality of the people we are sending to Vietnam. It seems to have fallen off considerably from the high standards applied in the original selections in 1962, and the JCS fully agree with me that we must have our best men there.

Conclusion. My appraisal may be overly pessimistic. Lodge, Harkins, and Minh would probably agree with me on specific points, but feel that January should see significant improvement. We should watch the situation very carefully, running scared, hoping for the best, but preparing for more forceful moves if the situation does not show early signs of improvement.

"'64 Memo by Joint Chiefs of Staff Discussing Widening of the War"

Memorandum from Gen. Maxwell D. Taylor, Chairman of the Joint Chiefs of Staff to Secretary of Defense McNamara, Jan. 22, 1964, "Vietnam and Southeast Asia."

1. National Security Action Memorandum No. 273 makes clear the resolve of the President to ensure victory over the externally directed and supported communist insurgency in South Vietnam. In order to achieve that victory, the Joint Chiefs of Staff are of the opinion that the United States must be prepared to put aside many of the self-imposed restrictions which now limit our efforts, and to undertake bolder actions which may embody greater risks.
2. The Joint Chiefs of Staff are increasingly mindful that our fortunes in South Vietnam are an accurate barometer of our fortunes in all of Southeast Asia. It is our view that if the US program succeeds in South Vietnam it will go far toward stabilizing the total Southeast Asia situation. Conversely, a loss of South Vietnam to the communists will presage an early erosion of the remainder of our position in that subcontinent.
3. Laos, existing on a most fragile foundation now, would not be able to endure the establishment of a communist—or pseudo neutralist—state on its eastern flank. Thailand, less strong today than a month ago by virtue of the loss of Prime Minister Sarit, would probably be unable to withstand the pressures of infiltration from the north should Laos collapse to the communists in its turn. Cambodia apparently has estimated that our prospects in South Vietnam are not promising and, encouraged by the actions of the French, appears already to be seeking an accommodation with the communists. Should we actually suffer defeat in South Vietnam, there is little reason to believe that Cambodia would maintain even a pretense of neutrality.
4. In a broader sense, the failure of our programs in South Vietnam would have heavy influence on the judgments of Burma, India, Indonesia, Malaysia, Japan, Taiwan, and Republic of Korea, and the Republic of the Philippines with respect to US durability, resolution, and trustworthiness. Finally, this being the first real test of our determination to defeat the communist was of national liberation formula, it is not unreasonable to conclude that there would be a corresponding unfavorable effect upon our image in Africa and in Latin America.
5. All of this underscores the pivotal position now occupied by South Vietnam in our world-wide confrontation with the communists and the essentiality that the conflict there would be brought to a favorable end as soon as possible. However, it would be unrealistic to believe that a complete suppression of the insurgency can take place in one or even two years. The British effort in Malaya is a recent example of a counterinsurgency effort which required approximately ten years before the bulk of the rural population was brought completely under control of the government, the police were able to maintain order, and the armed forces were able to eliminate the guerilla strongholds.
6. The Joint Chiefs of Staff are convinced that, in keeping with the guidance in NSAM 273, the United States must make plain to the enemy our determination to see the Vietnam campaign through to a favorable conclusion. To do this, we must prepare for whatever level of activity may be required and, being prepared, must then proceed to take actions as necessary to achieve our purposes surely and promptly.
7. Our considerations, furthermore, cannot be confined entirely to South Vietnam. Our experience in the war thus far leads us to conclude that, in this respect, we are not to now giving sufficient attention to the broader area problems of Southeast Asia. The Joint Chiefs of Staff believe that our position in Cambodia, our attitude toward Laos, our actions in Thailand, and our great effort in South Vietnam do not comprise a compatible and integrated US policy for Southeast Asia. US objectives in Southeast Asia cannot be achieved by either economic, political, or military measures alone. All three fields must be integrated into a single, broad US program for Southeast Asia. The measures recommended in this memorandum are a partial contribution to such a program.

8. Currently we and the South Vietnamese are fighting the war on the enemy's terms. He has determined the locale, the timing, and the tactics of the battle while our actions are essentially reactive. One reason for this is the fact that we have obliged ourselves to labor under self-imposed restrictions with respect to impeding external aid to the Viet Cong. These restrictions include keeping the war within the boundaries of South Vietnam, avoiding the direct use of US combat forces, and limiting US direction of the campaign to rendering advice to the Government of Vietnam. These restrictions, while they may make our international position more readily defensible, all tend to make the task in Vietnam more complex, time-consuming, and in the end, more costly. In addition to complicating our own problem, these self-imposed restrictions may well now be conveying signals of irresolution to our enemies—encouraging them to higher levels of vigor and greater risks. A reversal of attitude and the adoption of a more aggressive program would enhance greatly our ability to control the degree to which escalation will occur. It appears probable that the economic and agricultural disappointments suffered by Communist China, plus the current rift with the Soviets, could cause the communists to think twice about undertaking a large-scale military adventure in Southeast Asia.

9. In advertising to actions outside of South Vietnam, the Joint Chiefs of Staff are aware that the focus of the counterinsurgency battle lies in South Vietnam itself, and that the war must certainly be fought and won primarily in the minds of the Vietnamese people. At the same time, the aid now coming to the Viet Cong from outside the country in men, resources, advice, and direction is sufficiently great in the aggregate to be significant—both as help and as encouragement to the Viet Cong. It is our conviction that if support of the insurgency from outside South Vietnam in terms of operational direction, personnel, and material were stopped completely, the character of the war in South Vietnam would be substantially and favorably altered. Because of this conviction, we are wholly in favor of executing the covert actions against North Vietnam which you have recently proposed to the President. We believe, however, that it would be idle to conclude that these efforts will have a decisive effect on the communist determination to support the insurgency; and it is our view that we must therefore be prepared fully to undertake a much higher level of activity, not only for its beneficial tactical effect, but to make plain our resolution, both to our friends and to our enemies.

10. Accordingly, the Joint Chiefs of Staff consider that the United States must make ready to conduct increasingly bolder actions in Southeast Asia; specifically as to Vietnam to:

    a. Assign to the US military commander responsibilities for the total US program in Vietnam.

    b. Induce the Government of Vietnam to turn over to the United States military commander, temporarily, the actual tactical direction of the war.

    c. Charge the United States military commander with complete responsibility for conduct of the program against North Vietnam.

    d. Overfly Laos and Cambodia to whatever extent is necessary for acquisition of operational intelligence.

    e. Induce the Government of Vietnam to conduct overt ground operations in Laos of sufficient scope to impede the flow of personnel and material southward.

    f. Arm, equip, advise, and support the Government of Vietnam in its conduct of aerial bombing of critical targets in North Vietnam and in mining the sea approaches to that country.

    g. Advise and support the Government of Vietnam in its conduct of large-scale commando raids against critical targets in North Vietnam.

    h. Conduct aerial bombing of key North Vietnam targets, using US resources under Vietnamese cover, and with the Vietnamese openly assuming responsibility for the actions.

    i. Commit additional US forces, as necessary, in support of the combat action within South Vietnam.

    j. Commit US forces as necessary in direct actions against North Vietnam.

11. It is our conviction that any or all of the foregoing actions may be required to enhance our position in Southeast Asia. The past few months have disclosed that considerably higher levels of effort are demanded of us if US objectives are to be attained.

12. The governmental reorganization which followed the coup d'etat in Saigon should be completed very soon, giving basis for concluding just how strong the Vietnamese Government is going to be and how much of the load they will be able to bear themselves. Additionally, the five-month dry season, which is just now beginning, will afford the Vietnamese an opportunity to exhibit their ability to reverse the unfavorable situation in the critical Mekong Delta. The Joint Chiefs of Staff will follow these important developments closely and will recommend to you progressively the execution of such of the above actions as are considered militarily required, providing, in each case, their detailed assessment of the risks involved.

13. The Joint Chiefs of Staff consider that the strategic importance of Vietnam and of Southeast Asia warrants preparations for the actions above and recommend that the substance of this memorandum be discussed with the Secretary of State.

STATEMENT BY COMMITTEE SEEKING PEACE WITH FREEDOM IN VIETNAM *(1967)*

The Committee Seeking Peace with Freedom in Vietnam was a group of prominent American business people, educators, scientists, government officials, and religious leaders who supported American actions in Vietnam. The committee felt that popular opposition to the war in Vietnam did not, in fact, represent the feelings of America's "silent center": a majority of "independent and responsible men and women who have consistently opposed rewarding international aggressors."

This statement, published in the *New York Times* in 1967, advocates a "noncompromising resistance to aggression" in Vietnam. The committee believes that communism will spread if unchecked and that it is in the best interests of all Americans to support the fight against totalitarian regimes. Though the bipartisan group was actively supported by the Johnson administration, it failed to affect the influence of the rapidly growing peace movement.

Mark D. Baumann,
New York University

See also **Antiwar Movements; Peace Movements; Vietnam War.**

We are a group of concerned citizens who seek peace with freedom in Vietnam.

We do so in the conviction that our own vital national interests are at stake in that troubled land. We are not ashamed to admit that our primary motivation is self-interest—the self-interest of our own country in this shrinking world. America cannot afford to let naked aggression or the suppression of freedom go unchallenged. To Americans, peace and freedom are inseparable.

Our committee is national and nonpartisan—it is composed of Democrats, Republicans and independents, and of "liberals," "moderates" and "conservatives" drawn from all sections and all sectors of our country.

Concern With Principle

We believe in the great American principle of civilian control and a civilian Commander in Chief. And we strongly support our commitment in Vietnam and the policy of noncompromising, although limited, resistance to aggression. All four of the post-World War II American Presidents—Truman, Eisenhower, Kennedy and Johnson—have proclaimed America's basic purpose of defending freedom. We are not supporters of a President or of an Administration; we are supporters of the office of the Presidency.

As a committee, we shall strive to stay above partisan politics, political personalities and transitory opinion polls. Our concern is not with politics or popularity, but with principle.

We are opposed to surrender, however, camouflaged. Yet nothing we advocate can be interpreted as unnecessarily risking a general war in Asia or a nuclear war in the world. We favor a sensible road between capitulation and the indiscriminate use of raw power.

A Small Country

We believe that, in this, we speak for the great "silent center" of American life, the understanding, independent and responsible men and women who have consistently opposed rewarding international aggressors from Adolf Hitler to Mao Tse-tung. And we believe that the "silent center" should now be heard.

A great test is taking place in Vietnam—that test is whether or not the rulers of one territory can cheaply and safely impose a government and a political system upon their neighbors by internal subversion, insurrection, infiltration and invasion. These are the tactics of the Communist "wars of liberation," which depend for success upon achieving their goals at an endurable price and a bearable risk.

Our objective in Vietnam is to make the price too high and the risk too great for the aggressor. This is why we fight.

Vietnam is a small country and we Americans had little contact with it until after World War II. It still seems isolated and remote to many of us, although all of our Presidents for 30 years have had to concern themselves with our national interests in East Asia. For better perspective, we must turn our sights to the edge of East Asia, that enormous area of peninsulas and islands from Korea and Japan south to Taiwan and the Philippines, then west across Southeast Asia to Burma, then southeast to Malaysia, Indonesia, Australia and New Zealand.

That area contains 370 million people—approximately twice the population of the United States. Each of these nations is different from the others but they have one thing in common—all of them are free from external domination. Will this be true if we abandon Vietnam? Or will Peking and Hanoi, flushed with success, continue their expansionist policy through many other "wars of liberation," each conducted at a price which they can endure and a risk which they can bear? We believe they would.

Loud and Clear

Never in over a century has there been as much loud and violent opposition expressed in America to a conflict in which our fighting men are heavily and heroically engaged. Our committee specifically affirms and supports the right of opponents of our national policy to criticize that effort and to offer alternatives consistent with our national interest and security. However, we are concerned that voices of dissent have, thus far, received attention far out of proportion to their actual numbers.

Our objective as a committee is not to suppress the voices of such opposition. Our objective is to make sure that the majority voice of America is heard—loud and clear—so that Peking and Hanoi will not mistake the strident voices of some dissenters for American discouragement and a weakening of will. And, at the same time, we want to give renewed assurance to our fighting men that their sacrifices are neither in vain nor unappreciated—or unwanted—by the great bulk of their fellow citizens.

We want the aggressors to know that there is a solid, stubborn, dedicated, bipartisan majority of private citizens in America who approve our country's policy of patient, responsible, determined resistance which is dependent for its success on having the enemy realize that we shall keep the pressure on and not back down, that the peace we insist upon is a peace with freedom and, thus, with honor.

Today, America is a great world power, shedding its blood and expending its treasure in a distant country for the simple privilege of withdrawing in peace as soon as that country is guaranteed the effective right of self-determination. We ask nothing for ourselves and insist upon nothing for South Vietnam except that it be free to chart its own future, no matter what course it may choose. Surely this is a noble and worthy objective consistent with all that is best in American life and tradition.

Our committee has been formed to rally and articulate the support of the concerned, independent thinking, responsible citizens in America who favor our nation's fundamental commitment to peace with freedom.

Will you join with us?

List of the Members

Membership roster of Citizens Committee for Peace With Freedom in Vietnam:

TRUMAN, HARRY S.—33d President of the United States.

EISENHOWER, DWIGHT D.—34th President of the United States.

ACHESON, DEAN—Former Secretary of State.

ALEXANDER, HOLMES—Syndicate columnist.

ARNOLD, THURMAN—Former Assistant Attorney General in charge of Antitrust Division.

BANDLER, NED—Business executive.

BARNETT, FRANK R.—President, National Strategy Information Center, Inc.

BARON, MURRAY—Industrial consultant.

BEIRNE, JOSEPH W.—President, Communications Workers of America.

BRADLEY, General of the Army OMAR N.—Former chairman, Joint Chiefs of Staff.

BREIT, Dr. GREGORY—Donner Professor of Physics, Yale University.

BROWN, Dr. J. DOUGLAS—Professor of Economics, Princeton University. Former dean of the faculty.

BROWN, EDMUND G.—Former Governor of California.

BURNS, Dr. JAMES MacGREGOR—James Phinney Baster Professor of History and Public Affairs and chairman, Department of Political Science, Williams College.

BYRNES, JAMES F.—Former Secretary of State.

CABOT, THOMAS D.—Chairman of the board, Cabot Corporation, Boston. Former director, Office of International Security Affairs, Department of State.

CHERNE, LEO—Executive director, the Research Institute of America, Inc.

CLAY, Gen. LUCIUS D.—Senior partner, Lehman Brothers.

CONANT, Dr. JAMES B.—Former president, Harvard University. Former Ambassador to Germany.

CONNELLY, MARC—Playwright.

DARDEN, COLGATE—Former president, University of Virginia.

DAVIS, THURSTON N., S.J.—Editor in chief, America.

DOUGLAS, PAUL H.—Former Senator from Illinois.

DRAPER, Gen. WILLIAM H.—Partner, Draper, Gaither & Anderson.

DRUMMOND, ROSCOE—Syndicated columnist.

ELLISON, RALPH—Author.

EMMETT, CHRISTOPHER—Chairman, American Friends of the Captive Nations.

ENGEL, IRVING M.—Attorney-at-law. Past president, American Jewish Committee.

FARLAND, JOSEPH S.—Former Ambassador to the Dominican Republic and to the Republic of Panama.
FARRELL, JAMES T.—Author.
FISHER, JOHN M.—President, American Research Foundation, Chicago.
GASTON, A. G.—President, Booker T. Washington Insurance Company, Birmingham.
GATES, THOMAS S.—Chairman, Morgan Guaranty Trust Company, former Secretary of Defense.
GIDEONSE, Dr. HARRY D.—Chancellor, New School for Social Research.
GULLION, Dr. EDMUND A.—Dean, Fletcher School of Law and Diplomacy, Tufts University.
GUNDERSON, Mrs. ROBERT—Former Civil Service Commissioner.
HACKER, LOUIS M.—Historian and professor of economics, Columbia University.
HANDLIN, Dr. OSCAR—Director, Charles Warren Center for Studies in American History, Harvard University.
HANES, JOHN W. Jr.—Investment banker. Former Assistant Secretary of State.
HARRIS, Dr. HUNTINGTON—Business executive.
HECHT, Rabbi ABRAHAM B.—President, Rabbinical Alliance of America.
HOFFER, ERIC—Author and long-shoreman.
JONES, Dr. FRANK—Physician and surgeon.
KELLER, W. W.—President, Phillips Petroleum Company.
KEGGI, Dr. KRISTAPS J.—Assistant professor of orthopedic surgery, Yale University.
KING, WILSON—Farmer.
LAPP, Dr. RALPH E.—Nuclear physicist and author.
LIEBMAN, MORRIS I.—Attorney-at-law, Chicago.
DE LIMA, OSCAR—Business executive. Chairman, executive committee, United Nations Association.
LINDSAY, HOWARD—Playwright, producer and actor.
LOCKE, EDWIN ALLEN Jr.—President, Modern Homes Construction Company.
LODGE, GEORGE C.—University official. Former Assistant Secretary of Labor.
LOOMIS, HENRY—Former director, Voice of America.
LORD, Mrs. OSWALD B.—Former United States representative on Human Rights Commission, United Nations.
LUCEY, ARCHBISHOP ROBERT E.—San Antonio prelate.
McCALEB, CLAUDE B.—Book company executive.
McDOUGAL, MYRES S.—Sterling Professor of Law, Yale University.
McGILL, RALPH—Syndicated columnist.
MARSHALL, BRIG. Gen. S. L. A.—Military historian.
MARTIN, C. V.—President, Carson Pirie Scott & Co.
MEANY, GEORGE—President, American Federation of Labor and Congress of Industrial Organizations.
MICHAEL, FRANZ—Associate director, Institute for Sino-Soviet Studies, George Washington University.
NASH, Dr. PHILLFO—Consulting anthropologist. Former Commissioner of Indian Affairs.
NEVINS, ALLAN—Historian.
NEWMAN, RALPH G.—Author, publisher and columnist.
RANDALL, Mrs. ANN HAGEN—Television producer and former foreign correspondent.
REID, WHITELAW—Business executive.
ROBINSON, PROF. JAMES A.—Director, Mershon Center for Education in National Security, Ohio State University.
ROOSEVELT, KERMIT—President, Kermit Roosevelt & Associates.
ROSE, Dr. FRANK—President, University of Alabama.
ROWE, JAMES H. Jr.—Former assistant to President Roosevelt and former Assistant Attorney General.
RUBIN, RABBI SCHULEN—New York City.
SACKS, PROF. I. MILTON—Dean of the undergraduate school, Brandeis University.
SALTONSTALL, LEVERETT—Former Senator from Massachusetts.
SALTZMAN, CHARLES E.—Investment banker. Former Under Secretary of State.
SCALAPINO, ROBERT A.—Professor of political science, University of California.
SLABURY, Dr. PAUL—Professor of political science, University of California.
SEIZTZ, Dr. FREDERICK—President, National Academy of Sciences.
SHUSTER, Dr. GEORGE N.—President emeritus, Hunter College.
SMITH, HOWARD E.—News analyst, commentator and author.
SMITHIES, Dr. ARTHUR—Nathaniel Ropes Professor of Political Economy, Harvard University.
DE SOLA POOL, Dr. NHIEL—Professor of political science Center for International Studies, Massachusetts Institute of Technology.
SONNE, H. CHRISTIAN—Chairman, National Planning Association.
STEPHENS, CHARLES J.—Student, University of California, Berkeley.

STOUT, REX—Author.

STRAUSS, Miss ANNA LORD—Former president, League of Women Voters of the United States.

STRAUSS, LEWIS L.—Former chairman of the Atomic Energy Commission.

STULBERG, LOUIS—President, International Ladies' Garment Workers' Union.

SWEARINGEN, RODGER—Professor of international relations, University of Southern California.

SWIG, BENJAMIN H.—Chairman of the board, Fairmont Hotel Company.

TATUM, Dr. E. L.—Nobel laureate in medicine and physio-Professor, Rockefeller University.

TAYLOR, Prof. GEORGE E.—Director, Far Eastern and Russian Institute, University of Washington.

THACHER, JAMES—Attorney-at-law.

TRAGER, FRANK N.—Professor of international affairs, New York University

TYROLER, CHARLES 2d—President, Quadri-Science, Inc.

UREY, Dr. HAROLD C.—Nobel laureate in chemistry. Professor of chemistry at large, University of California.

VAN DUSEN, Dr. HENRY P.—Clergyman, educator and author. Chairman, Foundation for Theological Education in Southeast Asia.

WASHBURN, ABBOTT—Former deputy director, United States Information Agency.

WHITE, ROBERT P.—Student, University of Oklahoma.

WHITNEY, JOHN HAY—Former Ambassador to Britain.

WIGNER, EUGENE P.—Nobel laureate in physics. Professor of physics, Princeton University.

WILLIAMS, T. HARRY—Boyd Professor of History, Louisiana State University.

WILSON, JOSEPH C.—Chairman of the board, Xerox Corporation.

SOURCE: *New York Times*, 1967.

LYNDON B. JOHNSON'S SPEECH DECLINING TO SEEK RE-ELECTION
(31 March 1968)

The administration of President Lyndon B. Johnson (1908–1973) had supported a gradual escalation of American involvement in the Vietnam crisis. After the disastrous Tet Offensive in 1968, however, Johnson and his advisors concluded that a cutback in the bombing of North Vietnam was a better course of action. In a surprisingly dramatic televised speech to the nation on March 31, Johnson announced that he was no longer seeking re-election so that he could work full-time on achieving peace in Vietnam.

The speech not only introduced a fundamental shift in the administration's Vietnam policies, but also served a larger political purpose. By aligning himself with the movement for peace, Johnson undercut the ability of presidential candidate Robert F. Kennedy to critique Johnson's war policies; he also failed to give an expected endorsement of his party's other candidate, Hubert Humphrey.

Mark D. Baumann,
New York University

***See also* Vietnam War.**

The President's Address to the Nation Announcing Steps To Limit the War in Vietnam and Reporting His Decision Not To Seek Reelection. *March* 31, 1968

Good evening, my fellow Americans:

Tonight I want to speak to you of peace in Vietnam and Southeast Asia.

No other question so preoccupies our people. No other dream so absorbs the 250 million human beings who live in that part of the world. No other goal motivates American policy in Southeast Asia.

For years, representatives of our Government and others have traveled the world—seeking to find a basis for peace talks.

Since last September, they have carried the offer that I made public at San Antonio.

That offer was this:

That the United States would stop its bombardment of North Vietnam when that would lead promptly to productive discussions—and that we would assume that North Vietnam would not take military advantage of our restraint.

Hanoi denounced this offer, both privately and publicly. Even while the search for peace was going on, North Vietnam rushed their preparations for a savage assault on the people, the government, and the allies of South Vietnam.

Their attack—during the Tet holidays—failed to achieve its principal objectives.

It did not collapse the elected government of South Vietnam or shatter its army—as the Communists had hoped.

It did not produce a "general uprising" among the people of the cities as they had predicted.

The Communists were unable to maintain control of any of the more than 30 cities that they attacked. And they took very heavy casualties.

But they did compel the South Vietnamese and their allies to move certain forces from the countryside into the cities.

They caused widespread disruption and suffering. Their attacks, and the battles that followed, made refugees of half a million human beings.

The Communists may renew their attack any day.

They are, it appears, trying to make 1968 the year of decision in South Vietnam—the year that brings, if not final victory or defeat, at least a turning point in the struggle.

This much is clear:

If they do mount another round of heavy attacks, they will not succeed in destroying the fighting power of South Vietnam and its allies.

But tragically, this is also clear: Many men—on both sides of the struggle—will be lost. A nation that has already suffered 20 years of warfare will suffer once again. Armies on both sides will take new casualties. And the war will go on.

There is no need for this to be so.

There is no need to delay the talks that could bring an end to this long and this bloody war.

Tonight, I renew the offer I made last August—to stop the bombardment of North Vietnam. We ask that talks begin promptly, that they be serious talks on the substance of peace. We assume that during those talks Hanoi will not take advantage of our restraint.

We are prepared to move immediately toward peace through negotiations.

So, tonight, in the hope that this action will lead to early talks, I am taking the first step to deescalate the conflict. We are reducing—substantially reducing—the present level of hostilities.

And we are doing so unilaterally, and at once.

Tonight, I have ordered our aircraft and our naval vessels to make no attacks on North Vietnam, except in the area north of the demilitarized zone where the continuing enemy buildup directly threatens allied forward positions and where the movements of their troops and supplies are clearly related to that threat.

The area in which we are stopping our attacks includes almost 90 percent of North Vietnam's population, and most of its territory. Thus there will be no attacks around the principal populated areas, or in the food-producing areas of North Vietnam.

Even this very limited bombing of the North could come to an early end—if our restraint is matched by restraint in Hanoi. But I cannot in good conscience stop all bombing so long as to do so would immediately and directly endanger the lives of our men and our allies. Whether a complete bombing halt becomes possible in the future will be determined by events.

Our purpose in this action is to bring about a reduction in the level of violence that now exists.

It is to save the lives of brave men—and to save the lives of innocent women and children. It is to permit the contending forces to move closer to a political settlement.

And tonight, I call upon the United Kingdom and I call upon the Soviet Union—as cochairmen of the Geneva Conferences, and as permanent members of the United Nations Security Council—to do all they can to move from the unilateral act of deescalation that I have just announced toward genuine peace in Southeast Asia.

Now, as in the past, the United States is ready to send its representatives to any forum, at any time, to discuss the means of bringing this ugly war to an end.

I am designating one of our most distinguished Americans, Ambassador Averell Harriman, as my personal representative for such talks. In addition, I have asked Ambassador Llewellyn Thompson, who returned from Moscow for consultation, to be available to join Ambassador Harriman at Geneva or any other suitable place—just as soon as Hanoi agrees to a conference.

I call upon President Ho Chi Minh to respond positively, and favorably, to this new step toward peace.

But if peace does not come now through negotiations, it will come when Hanoi understands that our common resolve is unshakable, and our common strength is invincible.

Tonight, we and the other allied nations are contributing 600,000 fighting men to assist 700,000 South Vietnamese troops in defending their little country.

Our presence there has always rested on this basic belief: The main burden of preserving their freedom must be carried out by them—by the South Vietnamese themselves.

We and our allies can only help to provide a shield behind which the people of South Vietnam can survive and can grow and develop. On their efforts—on their determination and resourcefulness—the outcome will ultimately depend.

That small, beleaguered nation has suffered terrible punishment for more than 20 years.

I pay tribute once again tonight to the great courage and endurance of its people. South Vietnam supports armed forces tonight of almost 700,000 men—and I call your attention to the fact that this is the equivalent of more than 10 million in our own population. Its people maintain their firm determination to be free of domination by the North.

There has been substantial progress, I think, in building a durable government during these last 3 years. The South Vietnam of 1965 could not have survived the enemy's Tet offensive of 1968. The elected government of South Vietnam survived that attack—and is rapidly repairing the devastation that it wrought.

The South Vietnamese know that further efforts are going to be required:

—to expand their own armed forces,

—to move back into the countryside as quickly as possible,

—to increase their taxes,

—to select the very best men that they have for civil and military responsibility,

—to achieve a new unity within their constitutional government, and

—to include in the national effort all those groups who wish to preserve South Vietnam's control over its own destiny.

Last week President Thieu ordered the mobilization of 135,000 additional South Vietnamese. He plans to reach—as soon as possible—a total military strength of more than 800,000 men.

To achieve this, the Government of South Vietnam started the drafting of 19-year-olds on March 1st. On May 1st, the Government will begin the drafting of 18-year-olds.

Last month, 10,000 men volunteered for military service—that was two and a half times the number of volunteers during the same month last year. Since the middle of January, more than 48,000 South Vietnamese have joined the armed forces—and nearly half of them volunteered to do so.

All men in the South Vietnamese armed forces have had their tours of duty extended for the duration of the war, and reserves are now being called up for immediate active duty.

President Thieu told his people last week:

"We must make greater efforts and accept more sacrifices because, as I have said many times, this is our country. The existence of our nation is at stake, and this is mainly a Vietnamese responsibility."

He warned his people that a major national effort is required to root out corruption and incompetence at all levels of government.

We applaud this evidence of determination on the part of South Vietnam. Our first priority will be to support their effort.

We shall accelerate the reequipment of South Vietnam's armed forces—in order to meet the enemy's increased firepower. This will enable them progressively to undertake a larger share of combat operations against the Communist invaders.

On many occasions I have told the American people that we would send to Vietnam those forces that are required to accomplish our mission there. So, with that as our guide, we have previously authorized a force level of approximately 525,000.

Some weeks ago—to help meet the enemy's new offensive—we sent to Vietnam about 11,000 additional Marine and airborne troops. They were deployed by air in 48 hours, on an emergency basis. But the artillery, tank, aircraft, medical, and other units that were needed to work with and to support these infantry troops in combat could not then accompany them by air on that short notice.

In order that these forces may reach maximum combat effectiveness, the Joint Chiefs of Staff have recommended to me that we should prepare to send—during the next 5 months—support troops totaling approximately 13,500 men.

A portion of these men will be made available from our active forces. The balance will come from reserve component units which will be called up for service.

The actions that we have taken since the beginning of the year

—to reequip the South Vietnamese forces,

—to meet our responsibilities in Korea, as well as our responsibilities in Vietnam,

—to meet price increases and the cost of activating and deploying reserve forces,

—to replace helicopters and provide the other military supplies we need,

all of these actions are going to require additional expenditures.

The tentative estimate of those additional expenditures is $2.5 billion in this fiscal year, and $2.6 billion in the next fiscal year.

These projected increases in expenditures for our national security will bring into sharper focus the

Nation's need for immediate action: action to protect the prosperity of the American people and to protect the strength and the stability of our American dollar.

On many occasions I have pointed out that, without a tax bill or decreased expenditures, next year's deficit would again be around $20 billion. I have emphasized the need to set strict priorities in our spending. I have stressed that failure to act and to act promptly and decisively would raise very strong doubts throughout the world about America's willingness to keep its financial house in order.

Yet Congress has not acted. And tonight we face the sharpest financial threat in the postwar era—a threat to the dollar's role as the keystone of international trade and finance in the world.

Last week, at the monetary conference in Stockholm, the major industrial countries decided to take a big step toward creating a new international monetary asset that will strengthen the international monetary system. I am very proud of the very able work done by Secretary Fowler and Chairman Martin of the Federal Reserve Board.

But to make this system work the United States just must bring its balance of payments to—or very close to—equilibrium. We must have a responsible fiscal policy in this country. The passage of a tax bill now, together with expenditure control that the Congress may desire and dictate, is absolutely necessary to protect this Nation's security, to continue our prosperity, and to meet the needs of our people.

What is at stake is 7 years of unparalleled prosperity. In those 7 years, the real income of the average American, after taxes, rose by almost 30 percent—a gain as large as that of the entire preceding 19 years.

So the steps that we must take to convince the world are exactly the steps we must take to sustain our own economic strength here at home. In the past 8 months, prices and interest rates have risen because of our inaction.

We must, therefore, now do everything we can to move from debate to action—from talking to voting. There is, I believe—I hope there is—in both Houses of the Congress—a growing sense of urgency that this situation just must be acted upon and must be corrected.

My budget in January was, we thought, a tight one. It fully reflected our evaluation of most of the demanding needs of this Nation.

But in these budgetary matters, the President does not decide alone. The Congress has the power and the duty to determine appropriations and taxes.

The Congress is now considering our proposals and they are considering reductions in the budget that we submitted.

As part of a program of fiscal restraint that includes the tax surcharge, I shall approve appropriate reductions in the January budget when and if Congress so decides that that should be done.

One thing is unmistakably clear, however: Our deficit just must be reduced. Failure to act could bring on conditions that would strike hardest at those people that all of us are trying so hard to help.

These times call for prudence in this land of plenty. I believe that we have the character to provide it, and tonight I plead with the Congress and with the people to act promptly to serve the national interest, and thereby serve all of our people.

Now let me give you my estimate of the chances for peace:

—the peace that will one day stop the bloodshed in South Vietnam,

—that will permit all the Vietnamese people to rebuild and develop their land,

—that will permit us to turn more fully to our own tasks here at home.

I cannot promise that the initiative that I have announced tonight will be completely successful in achieving peace any more than the 30 others that we have undertaken and agreed to in recent years.

But it is our fervent hope that North Vietnam, after years of fighting that have left the issue unresolved, will now cease its efforts to achieve a military victory and will join with us in moving toward the peace table.

And there may come a time when South Vietnamese—on both sides—are able to work out a way to settle their own differences by free political choice rather than by war.

As Hanoi considers its course, it should be in no doubt of our intentions. It must not miscalculate the pressures within our democracy in this election year.

We have no intention of widening this war.

But the United States will never accept a fake solution to this long and arduous struggle and call it peace.

No one can foretell the precise terms of an eventual settlement.

Our objective in South Vietnam has never been the annihilation of the enemy. It has been to bring about a recognition in Hanoi that its objective—taking over the South by force—could not be achieved.

We think that peace can be based on the Geneva Accords of 1954—under political conditions that permit the South Vietnamese—all the South Vietnamese—to chart their course free of any outside domination or interference, from us or from anyone else.

So tonight I reaffirm the pledge that we made at Manila—that we are prepared to withdraw our forces from South Vietnam as the other side withdraws its forces to the north, stops the infiltration, and the level of violence thus subsides.

Our goal of peace and self-determination in Vietnam is directly related to the future of all of Southeast Asia—where much has happened to inspire confidence during the past 10 years. We have done all that we knew how to do to contribute and to help build that confidence.

A number of its nations have shown what can be accomplished under conditions of security. Since 1966, Indonesia, the fifth largest nation in all the world, with a population of more than 100 million people, has had a government that is dedicated to peace with its neighbors and improved conditions for its own people. Political and economic cooperation between nations has grown rapidly.

I think every American can take a great deal of pride in the role that we have played in bringing this about in Southeast Asia. We can rightly judge—as responsible Southeast Asians themselves do—that the progress of the past 3 years would have been far less likely—if not completely impossible—if America's sons and others had not made their stand in Vietnam.

At Johns Hopkins University, about 3 years ago, I announced that the United States would take part in the great work of developing Southeast Asia, including the Mekong Valley, for all the people of that region. Our determination to help build a better land—a better land for men on both sides of the present conflict—has not diminished in the least. Indeed, the ravages of war, I think, have made it more urgent than ever.

So, I repeat on behalf of the United States again tonight what I said at Johns Hopkins—that North Vietnam could take its place in this common effort just as soon as peace comes.

Over time, a wider framework of peace and security in Southeast Asia may become possible. The new cooperation of the nations of the area could be a foundation-stone. Certainly friendship with the nations of such a Southeast Asia is what the United States seeks—and that is all that the United States seeks.

One day, my fellow citizens, there will be peace in Southeast Asia.

It will come because the people of Southeast Asia want it—those whose armies are at war tonight, and those who, though threatened, have thus far been spared.

Peace will come because Asians were willing to work for it—and to sacrifice for . . . and to die by the thousands for it.

But let it never be forgotten: Peace will come also because America sent her sons to help secure it.

It has not been easy—far from it. During the past 4 1/2 years, it has been my fate and my responsibility to be Commander in Chief. I have lived—daily and nightly—with the cost of this war. I know the pain that it has inflicted. I know, perhaps better than anyone, the misgivings that it has aroused.

Throughout this entire, long period, I have been sustained by a single principle: that what we are doing now, in Vietnam, is vital not only to the security of Southeast Asia but it is vital to the security of every American.

Surely we have treaties which we must respect. Surely we have commitments that we are going to keep.

Resolutions of the Congress testify to the need to resist aggression in the world and in Southeast Asia.

But the heart of our involvement in South Vietnam—under three different Presidents, three separate administrations—has always been America's own security.

And the larger purpose of our involvement has always been to help the nations of Southeast Asia become independent and stand alone, self-sustaining, as members of a great world community—at peace with themselves, and at peace with all others.

With such an Asia, our country—and the world—will be far more secure than it is tonight.

I believe that a peaceful Asia is far nearer to reality because of what America has done in Vietnam. I believe that the men who endure the dangers of battle—fighting there for us tonight—are helping the entire world avoid far greater conflicts, far wider wars, far more destruction, than this one.

The peace that will bring them home someday will come. Tonight I have offered the first in what I hope will be a series of mutual moves toward peace.

I pray that it will not be rejected by the leaders of North Vietnam. I pray that they will accept it as a means by which the sacrifices of their own people may be ended. And I ask your help and your support, my fellow citizens, for this effort to reach across the battlefield toward an early peace.

Finally, my fellow Americans, let me say this:

Of those to whom much is given, much is asked. I cannot say and no man could say that no more will be asked of us.

Yet, I believe that now, no less than when the decade began, this generation of Americans is willing to "pay any price, bear any burden, meet any hardship, support any friend, oppose any foe to assure the survival and the success of liberty."

Since those words were spoken by John F. Kennedy, the people of America have kept that compact with mankind's noblest cause.

And we shall continue to keep it.

Yet, I believe that we must always be mindful of this one thing, whatever the trials and the tests ahead. The ultimate strength of our country and our cause will lie not in powerful weapons or infinite resources or boundless wealth, but will lie in the unity of our people.

This I believe very deeply.

Throughout my entire public career I have followed the personal philosophy that I am a free man, an

American, a public servant, and a member of my party, in that order always and only.

For 37 years in the service of our Nation, first as a Congressman, as a Senator, and as Vice President, and now as your President, I have put the unity of the people first. I have put it ahead of any divisive partisanship.

And in these times as in times before, it is true that a house divided against itself by the spirit of faction, of party, of region, of religion, of race, is a house that cannot stand.

There is division in the American house now. There is divisiveness among us all tonight. And holding the trust that is mine, as President of all the people, I cannot disregard the peril to the progress of the American people and the hope and the prospect of peace for all peoples.

So, I would ask all Americans, whatever their personal interests or concern, to guard against divisiveness and all its ugly consequences.

Fifty-two months and 10 days ago, in a moment of tragedy and trauma, the duties of this office fell upon me. I asked then for your help and God's, that we might continue America on its course, binding up our wounds, healing our history, moving forward in new unity, to clear the American agenda and to keep the American commitment for all of our people.

United we have kept that commitment. United we have enlarged that commitment.

Through all time to come, I think America will be a stronger nation, a more just society, and a land of greater opportunity and fulfillment because of what we have all done together in these years of unparalleled achievement.

Our reward will come in the life of freedom, peace, and hope that our children will enjoy through ages ahead.

What we won when all of our people united just must not now be lost in suspicion, distrust, selfishness, and politics among any of our people.

Believing this as I do, I have concluded that I should not permit the Presidency to become involved in the partisan divisions that are developing in this political year.

With America's sons in the fields far away, with America's future under challenge right here at home, with our hopes and the world's hopes for peace in the balance every day, I do not believe that I should devote an hour or a day of my time to any personal partisan causes or to any duties other than the awesome duties of this office—the Presidency of your country.

Accordingly, I shall not seek, and I will not accept, the nomination of my party for another term as your President.

But let men everywhere know, however, that a strong, a confident, and a vigilant America stands ready tonight to seek an honorable peace—and stands ready tonight to defend an honored cause—whatever the price, whatever the burden, whatever the sacrifice that duty may require.

Thank you for listening.

Good night and God bless all of you.

NOTE: The President spoke at 9 p.m. in his office at the White House. The address was broadcast nationally.

SOURCE: *U.S. Department of State Bulletin*, 15 April 1968.

VIETNAMIZATION AND SILENT MAJORITY
(3 November 1969, by Richard M. Nixon)

By the time that Richard M. Nixon (1913–1994) was inaugurated as president in 1969, the Vietnam War had been going on for four years and over thirty thousand Americans had been killed in action. Vocal antiwar activists were demanding an end to American occupation of South Vietnam and there were no workable plans for peace under discussion. On November 3, 1969, Nixon addressed the nation with a promise to work toward withdrawing American troops and negotiating a "peace with honor."

In the speech, Nixon outlined a plan for decreasing American troops while training and arming South Vietnamese soldiers to continue the battle against the communists in the North. Previous administrations, he said, "Americanized" the war in Vietnam. He called instead for a "Vietnamization" of the struggle. Though he said the choice to not withdraw all American forces immediately may have seemed wrong, he promised that the tougher choice, instituting a policy to help the South Vietnamese defend their own freedom, would bring greater chances for a lasting solution to this conflict and other similar conflicts in the future.

Mark D. Baumann,
New York University

See also **Vietnam War; Vietnamization.**

Good evening, my fellow Americans:

Tonight I want to talk to you on a subject of deep concern to all Americans and to many people in all parts of the world—the war in Vietnam.

I believe that one of the reasons for the deep division about Vietnam is that many Americans have lost confidence in what their Government has told them about our policy. The American people cannot and should not be asked to support a policy which involves the overriding issues of war and peace unless they know the truth about that policy.

Tonight, therefore, I would like to answer some of the questions that I know are on the minds of many of you listening to me.

How and why did America get involved in Vietnam in the first place?

How has this administration changed the policy of the previous administration?

What has really happened in the negotiations in Paris and on the battlefront in Vietnam?

What choices do we have if we are to end the war?

What are the prospects for peace?

Now, let me begin by describing the situation I found when I was inaugurated on January 20.

—The war had been going on for 4 years.

—31,000 Americans had been killed in action.

—The training program for the South Vietnamese was behind schedule.

—540,000 Americans were in Vietnam with no plans to reduce the number.

—No progress had been made at the negotiations in Paris and the United States had not put forth a comprehensive peace proposal.

—The war was causing deep division at home and criticism from many of our friends as well as our enemies abroad.

In view of these circumstances there were some who urged that I end the war at once by ordering the immediate withdrawal of all American forces.

From a political standpoint this would have been a popular and easy course to follow. After all, we became involved in the war while my predecessor was in office. I could blame the defeat which would be the result of my action on him and come out as the peacemaker. Some put it to me quite bluntly: This was the only way to avoid allowing Johnson's war to become Nixon's war.

But I had a greater obligation than to think only of the years of my administration and of the next election. I had to think of the effect of my decision on the next generation and on the future of peace and freedom in America and in the world.

Let us all understand that the question before us is not whether some Americans are for peace and some Americans are against peace. The question at issue is not whether Johnson's war becomes Nixon's war. The great question is: How can we win America's peace?

Well, let us turn now to the fundamental issue. Why and how did the United States become involved in Vietnam in the first place?

Fifteen years ago North Vietnam, with the logistical support of Communist China and the Soviet Union, launched a campaign to impose a Communist government on South Vietnam by instigating and supporting a revolution.

In response to the request of the Government of South Vietnam, President Eisenhower sent economic aid and military equipment to assist the people of South Vietnam in their efforts to prevent a Communist takeover. Seven years ago, President Kennedy sent 16,000 military personnel to Vietnam as combat advisers. Four years ago, President Johnson sent American combat forces to South Vietnam.

Now, many believe that President Johnson's decision to send American combat forces to South Vietnam was wrong. And many others—I among them—have been strongly critical of the way the war has been conducted. But the question facing us today is: Now that we are in the war, what is the best way to end it?

In January I could only conclude that the precipitate withdrawal of American forces from Vietnam would be a disaster not only for South Vietnam but for the United States and for the cause of peace.

For the South Vietnamese, our precipitate withdrawal would inevitably allow the Communists to repeat the massacres which followed their takeover in the North 15 years before.

—They then murdered more than 50,000 people and hundreds of thousands more died in slave labor camps.

—We saw a prelude of what would happen in South Vietnam when the Communists entered the city of Hue last year. During their brief rule there, there was a bloody reign of terror in which 3,000 civilians were clubbed, shot to death, and buried in mass graves.

—With the sudden collapse of our support, these atrocities of Hue would become the nightmare of the entire nation—and particularly for the million and a half Catholic refugees who fled to South Vietnam when the Communists took over in the North.

For the United States, this first defeat in our Nation's history would result in a collapse of confidence in American leadership, not only in Asia but throughout the world.

Three American Presidents have recognized the great stakes involved in Vietnam and understood what had to be done.

In 1963, President Kennedy, with his characteristic eloquence and clarity, said: "... we want to see a stable government there, carrying on a struggle to maintain its national independence.

"We believe strongly in that. We are not going to withdraw from that effort. In my opinion, for us to withdraw from that effort would mean a collapse not only of South Viet-Nam, but Southeast Asia. So we are going to stay there."

President Eisenhower and President Johnson expressed the same conclusion during their terms of office.

For the future of peace, precipitate withdrawal would thus be a disaster of immense magnitude.

—A nation cannot remain great if it betrays its allies and lets down its friends.

—Our defeat and humiliation in South Vietnam without question would promote recklessness in the councils of those great powers who have not yet abandoned their goals of world conquest.

—This would spark violence wherever our commitments help maintain the peace—in the Middle East, in Berlin, eventually even in the Western Hemisphere.

Ultimately, this would cost more lives.

It would not bring peace; it would bring more war.

For these reasons, I rejected the recommendation that I should end the war by immediately withdrawing all of our forces. I chose instead to change American policy on both the negotiating front and battlefront. In order to end a war fought on many fronts, I initiated a pursuit for peace on many fronts.

In a television speech on May 14, in a speech before the United Nations, and on a number of other occasions I set forth our peace proposals in great detail.

—We have offered the complete withdrawal of all outside forces within 1 year.

—We have proposed a cease-fire under international supervision.

—We have offered free elections under international supervision with the Communists participating in the organization and conduct of the elections as an organized political force. And the Saigon Government has pledged to accept the result of the elections.

We have not put forth our proposals on a take-it-or-leave-it basis. We have indicated that we are willing to discuss the proposals that have been put forth by the other side. We have declared that anything is negotiable except the right of the people of South Vietnam to determine their own future. At the Paris peace conference, Ambassador Lodge has demonstrated our flexibility and good faith in 40 public meetings.

Hanoi has refused even to discuss our proposals. They demand our unconditional acceptance of their terms, which are that we withdraw all American forces immediately and unconditionally and that we overthrow the Government of South Vietnam as we leave.

We have not limited our peace initiatives to public forums and public statements. I recognized, in January, that a long and bitter war like this usually cannot be settled in a public forum. That is why in addition to the public statements and negotiations I have explored every possible private avenue that might lead to a settlement.

Tonight I am taking the unprecedented step of disclosing to you some of our other initiatives for peace—initiatives we undertook privately and secretly because we thought we thereby might open a door which publicly would be closed.

I did not wait for my inauguration to begin my quest for peace.

—Soon after my election, through an individual who is directly in contact on a personal basis with the leaders of North Vietnam, I made two private offers for a rapid, comprehensive settlement. Hanoi's replies called in effect for our surrender before negotiations.

—Since the Soviet Union furnishes most of the military equipment for North Vietnam, Secretary of State Rogers, my Assistant for National Security Affairs, Dr. Kissinger, Ambassador Lodge, and I, personally, have met on a number of occasions with representatives of the Soviet Government to enlist their assistance in getting meaningful negotiations started. In addition, we have had extended discussions directed toward that same end with representatives of other governments which have diplomatic relations with North Vietnam. None of these initiatives have to date produced results.

—In mid-July, I became convinced that it was necessary to make a major move to break the deadlock in the Paris talks. I spoke directly in this office, where I am now sitting, with an individual who had known Ho Chi Minh [President, Democratic Republic of Vietnam] on a personal basis for 25 years. Through him I sent a letter to Ho Chi Minh.

I did this outside of the usual diplomatic channels with the hope that with the necessity of making statements for propaganda removed, there might be constructive progress toward bringing the war to an end. Let me read from that letter to you now.

"Dear Mr. President:

"I realize that it is difficult to communicate meaningfully across the gulf of four years of war. But precisely because of this gulf, I wanted to take this opportunity to reaffirm in all solemnity my desire to work for a just peace. I deeply believe that the war in Vietnam has gone on too long and delay in bringing it to an end can benefit no one—least of all the people of Vietnam. . . .

"The time has come to move forward at the conference table toward an early resolution of this tragic war. You will find us forthcoming and open-minded in a common effort to bring the blessings of peace to the brave people of Vietnam. Let history record that at this critical juncture, both sides turned their face toward peace rather than toward conflict and war."

I received Ho Chi Minh's reply on August 30, 3 days before his death. It simply reiterated the public position North Vietnam had taken at Paris and flatly rejected my initiative.

The full text of both letters is being released to the press.

—In addition to the public meetings that I have referred to, Ambassador Lodge has met with Vietnam's chief negotiator in Paris in 11 private sessions.

—We have taken other significant initiatives which must remain secret to keep open some channels of communication which may still prove to be productive.

But the effect of all the public, private, and secret negotiations which have been undertaken since the bombing halt a year ago and since this administration came into office on January 20, can be summed up in one sentence: No progress whatever has been made except agreement on the shape of the bargaining table.

Well now, who is at fault?

It has become clear that the obstacle in negotiating an end to the war is not the President of the United States. It is not the South Vietnamese Government.

The obstacle is the other side's absolute refusal to show the least willingness to join us in seeking a just peace. And it will not do so while it is convinced that all it has to do is to wait for our next concession, and our next concession after that one, until it gets everything it wants.

There can now be no longer any question that progress in negotiation depends only on Hanoi's deciding to negotiate, to negotiate seriously.

I realize that this report on our efforts on the diplomatic front is discouraging to the American people, but the American people are entitled to know the truth—the bad news as well as the good news—where the lives of our young men are involved.

Now let me turn, however, to a more encouraging report on another front.

At the time we launched our search for peace I recognized we might not succeed in bringing an end to the war through negotiation. I, therefore, put into effect another plan to bring peace—a plan which will bring the war to an end regardless of what happens on the negotiating front.

It is in line with a major shift in U.S. foreign policy which I described in my press conference at Guam on July 25. Let me briefly explain what has been described as the Nixon Doctrine—a policy which not only will help end the war in Vietnam, but which is an essential element of our program to prevent future Vietnams.

We Americans are a do-it-yourself people. We are an impatient people. Instead of teaching someone else to do a job, we like to do it ourselves. And this trait has been carried over into our foreign policy.

In Korea and again in Vietnam, the United States furnished most of the money, most of the arms, and most of the men to help the people of those countries defend their freedom against Communist aggression.

Before any American troops were committed to Vietnam, a leader of another Asian country expressed this opinion to me when I was traveling in Asia as a private citizen. He said: "When you are trying to assist another nation defend its freedom, U.S. policy should be to help them fight the war but not to fight the war for them."

Well, in accordance with this wise counsel, I laid down in Guam three principles as guidelines for future American policy toward Asia:

—First, the United States will keep all of its treaty commitments.

—Second, we shall provide a shield if a nuclear power threatens the freedom of a nation allied with us or of a nation whose survival we consider vital to our security.

—Third, in cases involving other types of aggression, we shall furnish military and economic assistance when requested in accordance with our treaty commitments. But we shall look to the nation directly threatened to assume the primary responsibility of providing the manpower for its defense.

After I announced this policy, I found that the leaders of the Philippines, Thailand, Vietnam, South Korea, and other nations which might be threatened by Communist aggression, welcomed this new direction in American foreign policy.

The defense of freedom is everybody's business—not just America's business. And it is particularly the responsibility of the people whose freedom is threatened. In the previous administration, we Americanized the war in

Vietnam. In this administration, we are Vietnamizing the search for peace.

The policy of the previous administration not only resulted in our assuming the primary responsibility for fighting the war, but even more significantly did not adequately stress the goal of strengthening the South Vietnamese so that they could defend themselves when we left.

The Vietnamization plan was launched following Secretary Laird's visit to Vietnam in March. Under the plan, I ordered first a substantial increase in the training and equipment of South Vietnamese forces.

In July, on my visit to Vietnam, I changed General Abrams' orders so that they were consistent with the objectives of our new policies. Under the new orders, the primary mission of our troops is to enable the South Vietnamese forces to assume the full responsibility for the security of South Vietnam.

Our air operations have been reduced by over 20 percent.

And now we have begun to see the results of this long overdue change in American policy in Vietnam.

—After 5 years of Americans going into Vietnam, we are finally bringing American men home. By December 15, over 60,000 men will have been withdrawn from South Vietnam—including 20 percent of all of our combat forces.

—The South Vietnamese have continued to gain in strength. As a result they have been able to take over combat responsibilities from our American troops.

Two other significant developments have occurred since this administration took office.

—Enemy infiltration, infiltration which is essential if they are to launch a major attack, over the last 3 months is less than 20 percent of what it was over the same period last year.

—Most important—United States casualties have declined during the last 2 months to the lowest point in 3 years.

Let me now turn to our program for the future.

We have adopted a plan which we have worked out in cooperation with the South Vietnamese for the complete withdrawal of all U.S. combat ground forces, and their replacement by South Vietnamese forces on an orderly scheduled timetable. This withdrawal will be made from strength and not from weakness. As South Vietnamese forces become stronger, the rate of American withdrawal can become greater.

I have not and do not intend to announce the timetable for our program. And there are obvious reasons for this decision which I am sure you will understand. As I have indicated on several occasions, the rate of withdrawal will depend on developments on three fronts.

One of these is the progress which can be or might be made in the Paris talks. An announcement of a fixed timetable for our withdrawal would completely remove any incentive for the enemy to negotiate an agreement. They would simply wait until our forces had withdrawn and then move in.

The other two factors on which we will base our withdrawal decisions are the level of enemy activity and the progress of the training programs of the South Vietnamese forces. And I am glad to be able to report tonight progress on both of these fronts has been greater than we anticipated when we started the program in June for withdrawal. As a result, our timetable for withdrawal is more optimistic now than when we made our first estimates in June. Now, this clearly demonstrates why it is not wise to be frozen in on a fixed timetable. We must retain the flexibility to base each withdrawal decision on the situation as it is at that time rather than on estimates that are no longer valid.

Along with this optimistic estimate, I must—in all candor—leave one note of caution.

If the level of enemy activity significantly increases we might have to adjust our timetable accordingly.

However, I want the record to be completely clear on one point.

At the time of the bombing halt just a year ago, there was some confusion as to whether there was an understanding on the part of the enemy that if we stopped the bombing of North Vietnam they would stop the shelling of cities in South Vietnam. I want to be sure that there is no misunderstanding on the part of the enemy with regard to our withdrawal program.

We have noted the reduced level of infiltration, the reduction of our casualties, and are basing our withdrawal decisions partially on those factors.

If the level of infiltration or our casualties increase while we are trying to scale down the fighting, it will be the result of a conscious decision by the enemy.

Hanoi could make no greater mistake than to assume that an increase in violence will be to its advantage. If I conclude that increased enemy action jeopardizes our remaining forces in Vietnam, I shall not hesitate to take strong and effective measures to deal with that situation.

This is not a threat. This is a statement of policy, which as Commander in Chief of our Armed Forces, I am making in meeting my responsibility for the protection of American fighting men wherever they may be.

My fellow Americans, I am sure you can recognize from what I have said that we really only have two choices open to us if we want to end this war.

—I can order an immediate, precipitate withdrawal of all Americans from Vietnam without regard to the effects of that action.

—Or we can persist in our search for a just peace through a negotiated settlement if possible, or through continued implementation of our plan for Vietnamization if necessary—a plan in which we will withdraw all of our forces from Vietnam on a schedule in accordance with our program, as the South Vietnamese become strong enough to defend their own freedom.

I have chosen this second course.

It is not the easy way.

It is the right way.

It is a plan which will end the war and serve the cause of peace—not just in Vietnam but in the Pacific and in the world.

In speaking of the consequences of a precipitate withdrawal, I mentioned that our allies would lose confidence in America.

Far more dangerous, we would lose confidence in ourselves. Oh, the immediate reaction would be a sense of relief that our men were coming home. But as we saw the consequences of what we had done, inevitable remorse and divisive recrimination would scar our spirit as a people.

We have faced other crises in our history and have become stronger by rejecting the easy way out and taking the right way in meeting our challenges. Our greatness as a nation has been our capacity to do what had to be done when we knew our course was right.

I recognize that some of my fellow citizens disagree with the plan for peace I have chosen. Honest and patriotic Americans have reached different conclusions as to how peace should be achieved.

In San Francisco a few weeks ago, I saw demonstrators carrying signs reading: "Lose in Vietnam, bring the boys home."

Well, one of the strengths of our free society is that any American has a right to reach that conclusion and to advocate that point of view. But as President of the United States, I would be untrue to my oath of office if I allowed the policy of this Nation to be dictated by the minority who hold that point of view and who try to impose it on the Nation by mounting demonstrations in the street.

For almost 200 years, the policy of this Nation has been made under our Constitution by those leaders in the Congress and the White House elected by all of the people. If a vocal minority, however fervent its cause, prevails over reason and the will of the majority, this Nation has no future as a free society.

And now I would like to address a word, if I may, to the young people of this Nation who are particularly concerned, and I understand why they are concerned, about this war.

I respect your idealism.

I share your concern for peace.

I want peace as much as you do.

There are powerful personal reasons I want to end this war. This week I will have to sign 83 letters to mothers, fathers, wives, and loved ones of men who have given their lives for America in Vietnam. It is very little satisfaction to me that this is only one-third as many letters as I signed the first week in office. There is nothing I want more than to see the day come when I do not have to write any of those letters.

—I want to end the war to save the lives of those brave young men in Vietnam.

—But I want to end it in a way which will increase the chance that their younger brothers and their sons will not have to fight in some future Vietnam someplace in the world.

—And I want to end the war for another reason. I want to end it so that the energy and dedication of you, our young people, now too often directed into bitter hatred against those responsible for the war, can be turned to the great challenges of peace, a better life for all Americans, a better life for all people on this earth.

I have chosen a plan for peace. I believe it will succeed.

If it does succeed, what the critics say now won't matter. If it does not succeed, anything I say then won't matter.

I know it may not be fashionable to speak of patriotism or national destiny these days. But I feel it is appropriate to do so on this occasion.

Two hundred years ago this Nation was weak and poor. But even then, America was the hope of millions in the world. Today we have become the strongest and richest nation in the world. And the wheel of destiny has turned so that any hope the world has for the survival of peace and freedom will be determined by whether the American people have the moral stamina and the courage to meet the challenge of free world leadership.

Let historians not record that when America was the most powerful nation in the world we passed on the other side of the road and allowed the last hopes for peace and freedom of millions of people to be suffocated by the forces of totalitarianism.

And so tonight—to you, the great silent majority of my fellow Americans—I ask for your support.

I pledged in my campaign for the Presidency to end the war in a way that we could win the peace. I have initiated a plan of action which will enable me to keep that pledge.

The more support I can have from the American people, the sooner that pledge can be redeemed; for the more divided we are at home, the less likely the enemy is to negotiate at Paris.

Let us be united for peace. Let us also be united against defeat. Because let us understand: North Vietnam cannot defeat or humiliate the United States. Only Americans can do that.

Fifty years ago, in this room and at this very desk, President Woodrow Wilson spoke words which caught the imagination of a war-weary world. He said: "This is the war to end war." His dream for peace after World War I was shattered on the hard realities of great power politics and Woodrow Wilson died a broken man.

Tonight I do not tell you that the war in Vietnam is the war to end wars. But I do say this: I have initiated a plan which will end this war in a way that will bring us closer to that great goal to which Woodrow Wilson and every American President in our history has been dedicated—the goal of a just and lasting peace.

As President I hold the responsibility for choosing the best path to that goal and then leading the Nation along it.

I pledge to you tonight that I shall meet this responsibility with all of the strength and wisdom I can command in accordance with your hopes, mindful of your concerns, sustained by your prayers.

Thank you and goodnight.

NOTE: The President spoke at 9:32 p.m. in his office at the White House. The address was broadcast on radio and television.

On November 3, 1969, the White House Press Office released an advance text of the address.

SOURCE: *U.S. Department of State Bulletin*, 24 November 1969.

EXCERPTS FROM *DEAR AMERICA: LETTERS HOME FROM VIETNAM (1967–1979)*

The twentieth century was a decade of war: of the hundred million war-related deaths worldwide since 1700, over 90 percent occurred in the twentieth century. Due in part to escalating advances in military technology, twentieth-century modern combat was exponentially more devastating than any previous incarnation. Also, new "total war" strategies radically increased civilian casualties and military "battle fatigue."

Those who experienced modern combat firsthand were more often than not psychologically traumatized: American combat veterans of the Vietnam War, in particular, exhibited "traumatic stress syndrome" in large numbers. Bernard Edelman's collection of letters home from American women and men in Vietnam provides us with a firsthand glimpse into the minds of the traumatized young soldiers and others. The two letters selected here are from U.S. soldiers about to return home and in both, the young men express their anxiety about integrating themselves back into "normal" life.

Mark D. Baumann,
New York University

***See also* Vietnam War.**

Going Home—PFC David Bowman, Co. B, 1st Bn., 8th Cav., 1st Cav. Div., An Khe/Phong Dien, 1967–1968

Dear Civilians, Friends, Draft Dodgers, etc.:

In the very near future, the undersigned will once more be in your midst, dehydrated and demoralized, to take his place again as a human being with the well-known forms of freedom and justice for all; engage in life, liberty and the somewhat delayed pursuit of happiness. In making your joyous preparations to welcome him back into organized society you might take certain steps to make allowances for the past twelve months. In other words, he might be a little Asiatic from Vietnamesitis and Overseasitis, and should be handled with care. Don't be alarmed if he is infected with all forms of rare tropical diseases. A little time in the "Land of the Big PX" will cure this malady.

Therefore, show no alarm if he insists on carrying a weapon to the dinner table, looks around for his steel pot when offered a chair, or wakes you up in the middle of the night for guard duty. Keep cool when he pours gravy on his dessert at dinner or mixes peaches with his Seagrams VO. Pretend not to notice if he acts dazed, eats with his fingers instead of silverware and prefers C-rations to steak. Take it with a smile when he insists on digging up the garden to fill sandbags for the bunker he is building. Be tolerant when he takes his blanket and sheet off the bed and puts them on the floor to sleep on.

Abstain from saying anything about powdered eggs, dehydrated potatoes, fried rice, fresh milk or ice cream. Do not be alarmed if he should jump up from the dinner table and rush to the garbage can to wash his dish with a toilet brush. After all, this has been his standard. Also, if it should start raining, pay no attention to him if he pulls off his clothes, grabs a bar of soap and a towel and runs outdoors for a shower.

When in his daily conversation he utters such things as "Xin loi" and "Choi oi" just be patient, and simply leave quickly and calmly if by some chance he utters "didi" with an irritated look on his face because it means no less than "Get the h—— out of here." Do not let it shake you up if he picks up the phone and yells "Sky King forward, Sir" or says "Roger out" for good-by or simply shouts "Working."

Never ask why the Jones' son held a higher rank than he did, and by no means mention the word "extend." Pretend not to notice if at a restaurant he calls the waitress "Numbuh 1 girl" and uses his hat as an ashtray. He will probably keep listening for "Homeward Bound" to sound off over AFRS. If he does, comfort him, for he is still reminiscing. Be especially watchful when he is in the presence of women—*especially* a beautiful woman.

Above all, keep in mind that beneath that tanned and rugged exterior there is a heart of gold (the only thing of value he has left). Treat him with kindness, tolerance, and an occasional fifth of good liquor and you will be able to rehabilitate that which was once (and now a hollow shell) the happy-go-lucky guy you once knew and loved.

Last, but not least, send no more mail to the APO, fill the ice box with beer, get the civvies out of mothballs, fill the car with gas, and get the women and children off the streets—BECAUSE THE KID IS COMING HOME!!!!!

Love,
Dave

Going Home—Sp/4 Peter Roepcke, from Glendale, New York

20 April 1970

Hi doll,

I don't know who will get home first, me or this letter. But I thought I would write anyway. It was so good to hear your voice [last night]. The connections were weak, but still the same you sounded great. I can still hear you saying, "I can't believe it." You sounded so happy, and it sounded like you did not believe that I only busted a few bones.

I got a call through to my parents a little while after I talked to you. My mother did not believe that I was coming home. But I finally got through to her. And, boy, was she happy. She said she was sorry that I got hurt, but also glad—you know, glad that it was only this and not something worse.

You don't know how close I have been to getting killed or maimed. Too many times I have seen guys near me get hit and go home in a plastic bag. Like I have said before, someone was looking over me.

Well, it is all over now. Now it's time to forget. But it's hard to forget these things. I close my eyes and try to sleep, but all I can see is Jenkins lying there with his brains hanging out or Lefty with his eyes shot out. You know these guys—we have lived with them for a long time. We know their wives or girlfriends. Then you stop to think it could be me. Hell, I don't know why I am writing all this. But it feels better getting it out of my mind.

So, doll, in titi time I will be with you again. . . .

Well, honey, I will close for now. Until I see you again,

I love you.

Your,
Pete

SOURCE: Bowman, David, and Peter Roepcke. *Dear America: Letters Home From Vietnam.* Edited by Bernard Edelman. New York: Norton, 1985, pp. 280–282, p. 287.

NIXON'S LETTER TO NGUYEN VAN THIEU
(17 December 1972)

As part of his plan to extricate the United States from the Vietnam War, President Richard M. Nixon convinced intransigent South Vietnamese President Nguyen Van Thieu that America would provide his government with massive military and economic aid. When the Paris Peace Accord was signed on January 17, 1973, however, there was no clear resolution of the major political issue of who would rule South Vietnam. In spite of the implications of support that President Nixon made in this letter to Thieu, written a little over a month before the Peace Accord was signed, the United States failed to provide either military or economic aid. Thieu's regime could not hold up under the pressure from North Vietnam, and within two years of the Peace Accord, he resigned.

Mark D. Baumann,
New York University

See also **Diplomacy, Secret; Vietnam War.**

Dear Mr. President:

I have again asked General Haig to visit you in Saigon. He will inform you of my final considered personal judgment of the state of the ceasefire negotiations and of the prospects we now face.

Over the last two months—through my personal letters through my extensive personal discussions with your emissary, through communications via Dr. Kissinger, General Haig, and Ambassador Bunker, and through daily consultations in Paris—I have kept you scrupulously informed of the progress of the negotiations. I have sought to convey to you my best judgment of what is in our mutual interest. I have given you every opportunity to join with me in bringing peace with honor to the people of South Vietnam.

General Haig's mission now represents my final effort to point out to you the necessity for joint action and to convey my irrevocable intention to proceed, preferably with your cooperation but, if necessary, alone.

Recent events do not alter my conclusion. Although our negotiations with Hanoi have encountered certain obstacles, I want you to have no misunderstanding with regard to three basic issues: First we may still be on the verge of reaching an acceptable agreement at any time. Second, Hanoi's current stalling is prompted to a great degree by their desire to exploit the public dissension between us. As Hanoi obviously realizes, this works to your grave disadvantage. Third, as I have informed Hanoi, if they meet our minimum remaining requirements, I have every intention of proceeding rapidly to a settlement.

You are also aware of certain military actions which will have been initiated prior to General Haig's arrival. As he will explain to you, these actions are meant to convey to the enemy my determination to bring the conflict to a rapid end—as well as to show what I am prepared to do in case of violation of the agreement, I do not want you to be left, under any circumstances, with the mistaken impression that these actions signal a willingness or intent to continue U.S. military involvement if Hanoi meets the requirements for a settlement which I have set.

If the present lack of collaboration between us continues and if you decide not to join us in proceeding now to a settlement, it can only result in a fundamental change in the character of our relationship. I am convinced that your refusal to join us would be an invitation to disaster—to the loss of all that we together have fought for over the past decade. It would be inexcusable above all because we will have lost a just and honorable alternative.

I have asked General Haig to obtain your answer to this absolutely final offer on my part for us to work together in seeking a settlement along the lines I have approved or to go our separate ways. Let me emphasize in conclusion that General Haig is not coming to Saigon for the purpose of negotiating with you. The time has come for us to present a united front in negotiating with our enemies, and you must decide now whether you desire to continue to work together or whether you want me to seek a settlement with the enemy which serves U.S. interests alone.

Sincerely,

SOURCE: Courtesy of the Gerald Ford Library.

THE CHRISTMAS BOMBING OF HANOI WAS JUSTIFIED
(1 February 1973, interview with Henry A. Kissinger)

In December 1972, when the already tortuous peace talks between the United States and the Communist-backed government in North Vietnam began to break down, the Nixon administration responded by initiating "Operation Linebacker," the so-called "Christmas Bombing" of Hanoi, Ho Chi Minh's capital of North Vietnam. From 18 December to 30 December 1972, waves of American B-52s dropped nearly forty thousand tons of bombs on the mostly evacuated city. Although the administration defended its actions as essential to the attainment of a cease-fire, reaction from much of the country and the world was shock and outrage. Many accused Nixon and his National Security Advisor Henry Kissinger of enacting a policy of revenge and frustration. The destruction of several residential neighborhoods as well as the French embassy only stood to confirm these suspicions. At home, the president's approval rating plummeted, but some three weeks later, negotiations between divided Vietnam and the United States resumed in Paris. On 17 January 1973, the Paris Peace Accord was signed, and America's long direct involvement in the Vietnam War at last came to an end.

Laura M. Miller,
Vanderbilt University

See also **Vietnam War.**

On December 18, 1972, the United States launched a massive bombing attack on Hanoi in response to stalled peace negotiations. The "Christmas bombing" created much shock and anger in the United States and was denounced as an immoral terrorist act against the North Vietnamese civilian population. (Civilian casualties of the twelve-day campaign have been estimated at about fifteen hundred; the number was relatively low because American pilots took measures to minimize such casualties and the North Vietnamese government had evacuated much of Hanoi and other areas prior to the bombing.) At that time neither President Richard M. Nixon nor members of his administration made any public defense or explanation of the December bombing campaign.

The following viewpoint on the Christmas bombing of Hanoi and other parts of North Vietnam is taken from an interview by television journalist Marvin Kalb with Henry A. Kissinger on February 1, 1973. As national security adviser to Nixon, Kissinger shaped foreign policy more than any other person save Nixon himself. Beginning in 1969, while public peace negotiations were being held in Paris between delegations representing the governments of North Vietnam, South Vietnam, the National Liberation Front (NLF) rebels in South Vietnam, and the United States, Kissinger engaged in secret talks with a series of North Vietnamese envoys, including Le Duc Tho. These talks eventually resulted in the Paris Peace Accords, signed by the four official negotiating parties on January 27, 1973. The accords called for the United States to withdraw all of its military forces and marked the end of American participation in the Vietnam War. In his interview with Kalb, Kissinger defends the December 1972 bombings as part of the effort to convince both North and South Vietnam of the desirability and necessity for a peace agreement.

KALB: Dr. Kissinger, let's move the clock back about one month, at a time when the United States was engaged in a very extensive bombing program in the Hanoi-Haiphong area. We've never heard any explanation about why that was really necessary. Could you give us your own feeling on that?

KISSINGER: The decision to resume bombing in the middle of December was perhaps the most painful, the most difficult and certainly the most lonely that the President has had to make since he is in—has been in office. It was very painful to do this at that particular season, when the expectation for peace had been so high, and only six weeks before his inauguration. It was very difficult to do it under circumstances when the outcome was not demonstrable. There were really three parts to it. One: should we resume bombing? Two: if we resume bombing, with what weapons? That involved the whole issue of the B-52. And three: should we talk to the American people?—which was really implied in your question: there's never been an explanation.

With respect to the first part—why did the President decide to resume bombing—we had come to the conclusion that the negotiations as they were then being conducted were not serious; that for whatever reason, the North Vietnamese at that point had come to the conclusion that protracting the negotiations was more in their interest than concluding them. It was not a case that we made certain demands that they rejected. It was a case that no sooner was one issue settled than three others emerged, and as soon as one approached a solution, yet others came to the forefront. At the same time, the more difficult Hanoi was, the more rigid Saigon grew, and we could see a prospect, therefore, where we would be caught between the two contending Vietnamese parties with no element introduced that would change their opinion, with a gradual degeneration of the private talks between Le Duc Tho and me into the same sort of propaganda that the public talks . . . had reached. And therefore it was decided to try to bring home, really to both Vietnamese parties, that the continuation of the war had its price. And it was not generally recognized that when we started the bombing again of North Vietnam, we also sent General [Alexander] Haig to Saigon to make very clear what—that this did not mean that we would fail to settle on the terms that we had defined as reasonable. So we really moved in both directions simultaneously.

Once the decision was made to resume bombing, we faced the fact that it was in the rainy season and that really the only plane that could act consistently was the B-52, which was an all-weather plane. The—You mentioned the Hanoi-Haiphong area. But major efforts were made to avoid residential areas, and the casualty figures which were released by the North Vietnamese of something like a thousand tend to support that many—that this was the case, because many of these casualties must have occurred in the target areas and not in civilian residential areas.

KALB: Yet a lot of the civilian areas were hit, apparently. There were pictures of that and—

KISSINGER: Well, you can never tell when a picture is made how vast the surrounding area of destruction is, but of course some civilian areas must have been hit. And I'm—I don't want to say that it was not a very painful thing to have to do.

Now, why did the President decide not to speak to the American people? The President can speak most effectively when he announces a new departure in policy and indicates what can be done to bring that particular departure to a conclusion. He could have done only two things in such a speech—which was considered. One is to explain why the negotiations had stalemated, and two, to explain under what circumstances he would end the bombing. The first would have broken the confidentiality of the negotiations, even more than was the case anyway through the exchanges that were going on publicly. And the second would have made the resumption of talks an issue of prestige and might have delayed it. And therefore the President decided that if this action succeeded, then the results would speak for themselves in terms of a settlement, and if a settlement was not reached, then he would have to give an accounting to American people—to the American people of all the actions that led to the continuing stalemate. Now, whatever the reason, once the Viet—once the talks were resumed a settlement was reached fairly rapidly. And I have—we have never made an assertion as to what produced it, but you asked why was the decision made to resume bombing, and this was the reasoning that led to it.

KALB: Dr. Kissinger, isn't the assumption that you're leaving with us that without that kind of heavy bombing the North Vietnamese would not have become serious—your term—and that therefore one could conclude that it was the bombing that brought the North Vietnamese into a serious frame of mind? I ask the question only because they've been bombed so repeatedly and for so many years and still stuck to their guns and their position. What was so unique about this?

KISSINGER: Well, that it came at the end of a long process—

KALB: Mm-hmm.

KISSINGER: —in which they too had suffered a great deal. But I don't think—at this moment, when I am preparing to go to Hanoi—it would serve any useful purpose for me to make any—to speculate about what caused them to make this decision.... And at this moment, I think, it is important to understand that the decision was not made lightly, that it was made in the interest of speeding the end of the war, and that now that the war has ended, I think, it is best to put the acrimony behind us.

SOURCE: "The Christmas Bombing of Hanoi Was Justified." Interview with Henry A. Kissinger. CBS News (1 February 1973). Courtesy, CBS News Archives.

THE FALL OF SAIGON
(April, 1975, by Stephen Klinkhammer)

The end of America's direct involvement in the Vietnam War also meant the end of South Vietnam's hopes for victory against the Communist North. Led by President Nguyen Van Thieu, South Vietnam had come to rely heavily on support from the United States, which reached its peak in 1969 with some 550,000 U.S. soldiers stationed in Southeast Asia. With that support gone, Thieu's government was forced to abandon the military defense of several key outlying areas. Contributing to the South's woes was an economic crisis brought on by the war and Thieu's growing unpopularity. When the North mounted a major offensive in 1975, the situation quickly became desperate. President Thieu resigned his office and fled to Taiwan as the capitol of the South, Saigon, fell to the North Vietnamese virtually without opposition. The following day, the government of the South surrendered, Saigon was renamed Ho Chi Minh City, and the divided country of Vietnam was whole once again.

Laura M. Miller,
Vanderbilt University

See also **Vietnam War.**

The evacuation of Saigon, the whole thing, was called Operation New Wind or Fresh Wind or Fresh Breeze or something like that. We got to the aircraft carrier *Midway*, and as soon as we got off the helicopter—since I was a surgical tech, my hair was always under a cap and it was rather long, about halfway down my ears—the CO, who was up in the tower, comes down and says, "Get those guys down for haircuts." So right away he gets on us for haircuts. The *Midway* was our base of operations. Our surgical equipment, all the green crates, never did catch up to us. That's known throughout the military, that they never catch up with you, and the *Midway* didn't have an operating room. This is about April 10 or 11.

We were real close to shore at that time, right off Saigon. We heard that we were taking on a whole bunch of civilians. We would be flying in and out with refugees, with American personnel, with reporters. The Tan Son Nhut airport was being bombed with big rockets. You could see the explosions from the sea. We were flying in and taking on refugees, and they were flying out whatever they could. With the refugees there were worms, women going into labor, TB and wounded lying on the choppers because there were a lot of shells coming in. There were a couple dead or dying on the chopper whom we couldn't save. We were landing in Tan Son Nhut. That was our staging point, where everybody was loading.

There were people coming out in boats, half-sinking boats. There were people who had their own airplanes who were flying out. There were all these choppers we had left there; they were using these to fly out, the Vietnamese. The flight deck was so full of choppers that we had to push them overboard because there was no room, we couldn't get our own choppers in. We were flying the big medevac choppers. We had an overload, packing in about twenty-five at a time, both Vietnamese and American. It was total chaos. The Purple Heart Trail, the road that came into Saigon from the paddies west of the city, was so jammed, from the air I could see columns of people that were at least twenty miles long. A lot of children crying. Some had clothes they picked off dead bodies. Most were barefoot. There were oxcarts and they were hauling what they had. There were wounded men on both sides of the road with battle dressings on. The NVA was lobbing these rockets all over the place, they were wiping out civilians ... There were piles of wounded on the back of ambulances. They were dropping the rockets right into the crowds of fleeing people. There were trucks, buses, anything they could get into. Saigon was the last stand, the capital, where the American embassy was.

A lot of American Marines were activated and had put up a perimeter guard around Tan Son Nhut. The NVA was still lobbing these rockets in. In fact, when I took off we were also flying out from the American embassy—a lot of people had been told to go there instead of Tan Son Nhut. It was really a mess. These rockets are lobbing in and a C-130 took off full of people going out to one of the aircraft carriers and it was blown out of the sky ... that was all over the runway. There were corpses, there were burned-out tanks that people had used to come in, there were pieces of bodies lying in the fields and on the streets. It was just bananas, total chaos. It was one mass of humanity being pushed to where people were being trampled. People screaming, "I want a place on this chopper!" and not being able to communicate because of the language barrier and because they would not listen.

They were raiding the American Exchange. The image I have is this one guy holding up one of those ten-packs of Kellogg's cereal and he's waving it. They were throwing American money up in the air ... totally berserk ... total chaos. We were trying to get the wounded first. They were piled in these old ambulances. The refugees were coming up from the Delta as well as from the North. We were trying to get the wounded out first and a lot of them we just couldn't.

Each time we went in, a bunch of Marines would get out and cover the landing zone as we tried to get the wounded on first, but sometimes they were just overwhelmed. They had orders to shoot if they couldn't maintain order. They shot mostly over the heads. I didn't see any of the Marines shoot any civilians. The Marines set up a defensive perimeter and would return fire at the enemy, but like the rest of the war, you never saw the NVA. The ARVN were running, they were coming in, they were bypassing civilians, shooting civilians, trying to get out first all the time. The best way to describe it was every man for himself. There were pregnant women going into labor right there on the goddamn landing zone. I delivered a baby right on the chopper. And I also delivered two more on the ships. It was just bananas.

We ended up with three thousand civilians aboard the *Midway*. We had taken all of our squadrons off because they had been there for offensive purposes. The civilians all stayed where the squadrons used to be. There were people sleeping on the floors, all over. Of course, they didn't know what a bathroom was. They were packed in, I'll tell you that. So we'd all take turns walking duty and if someone was puking or if someone had diarrhea or worms, we'd treat that.

On April 30 Saigon fell. South Vietnam had fallen. The Vice-President, Ky, flew out to the *Midway* in his own Cessna. Ky had with him an immense amount of gold bars. A lot of these people, some of the higher-ups in the ARVN and so on, had with them a lot of American money. We confiscated everything from civilians when they came on board. There were pounds and pounds of pure heroin, pounds and pounds of nice marijuana, which I really wanted to sample. People had little cherry-bomb grenades. We picked up guns. A lot of canned fish had to be tossed out. A lot of fever, they had a lot of malaria. So we had these three thousand people packed in there. That was the best we could do. We had a twenty-four-hour watch on a couple of kids down in the sick bay who had 104-degree temperatures. We had an interpreter down there and a bunch of families stayed with him. There were dead bodies we were bagging and bagging. There were still people fleeing Saigon in small boats.

The Vietnamese were scared. I have to put myself in their place—leaving my home, not being sure where I'm going to go, what's going to happen to me. They were very calm, almost in shock. We fed them and had interpreters tell them what to do, and I think the interpreters helped a lot. We had gunnery sergeants, old Marines, who spoke the language. I knew enough to get by, enough to say, "What's wrong with you?" or "I need this" or "I need that." They were basically very calm, sleeping on the hangar deck. They were treated very nice. They were in, I guess you could call it, shock—just a panic, the intensity of the five- or ten-day span there.... The adrenaline runs for so long, then it all stops. The war's ending cut you off just like that. You say okay, but the adrenaline is still running.

I have cried my ass off. I don't have any tears left. I first started letting it out in April of 1977. It took two years. I did that because I just couldn't handle being a soldier anymore.... I got out of the Navy in June of '76, but I still acted like one. I guess I still do in a way. I still sleep with one eye open, you know. And I wake up with bad dreams that I have of taking fire and watching people being murdered and being a part of that process. In fact, around this time of year—Christmas time —it gets really heavy for some reason. My wife knows it. Sometimes she feels inadequate because she doesn't know how to deal with that. I get really upset and I have to cry a lot and talk. Once I start it's like for three or four hours. I'm completely exhausted. I cry myself to sleep wherever I am, or I need to go out by myself. People feel inadequate. My wife feels inadequate. I tell her, "There's nothing you can do that can be any more adequate than just to be here." There is no understanding. My mind isn't mature enough. It wasn't then and it isn't now and it's never going to be able to understand murder.

It's a dull pain, you know. Just a whole lot of knowledge that I think I've gained, and I think I've grown from it. And I have to deal with that maturity, too, in myself. I grew up real fast. Real fast. It seems like a whole block of my life that I can't account for and I want to find that block because I know it's important. I have a certain pride, too, because I was a damn good medic—I have problems with that. I think a lot of times that it's my fault, and it's not my fault—there is no blame. The actual emotions are a fact. I'm a fresh veteran, I'm really not that old —I'm twenty-five, I'm just out. And there's still a lot of things that I'm real close to in there. A lot of that system I didn't mind. But the people I know say, "Steve, forget it. It's over." The last thing I need is pity. The last thing I need is someone to feel sorry for me.

My mother told my brother, "Leave Steve alone, he's not the same anymore." This was after my first tour in 'Nam. I guess I was changed and didn't know it. You're the last person to see yourself change. And the fact that you're not going to get any pats on the back, you're not going to get a parade, you're not going to get anything but spit on and misunderstood and blamed—I still feel that sometimes. Maybe I could have done better.

People want me to bury it. I can't bury it. I did learn something and I'm not sure what. But I know it's affected me a whole lot. And I think it's in a good way and I think I've really grown from that, because I don't want to see it happen again and I really care about people. To really try to help people to work through the problems of their own.

SOURCE: Klinkhammer, Stephen. "The Fall of Saigon." In *Everything We Had: An Oral History of the Vietnam War by Thirty-Three American Soldiers Who Fought It.* Edited by Al Santoli. New York: Random House, 1981.

PARDON FOR VIETNAM DRAFT EVADERS
(21 January 1977, by Jimmy Carter)

One of the many divisive issues related to America's involvement in Vietnam arose after the end of the war. One day after assuming office, newly elected President Jimmy Carter fulfilled his controversial campaign pledge to pardon those who had unlawfully avoided military service either by not registering for the draft or by fleeing to another country. For Carter, the pardon was necessary to heal the wounds brought on by the disruptive conflict. Not everyone agreed, however. Some veterans' groups considered Carter's action an insult to those who had willingly served, many of whom had lost their lives. Meanwhile, several pro-pardon groups like Americans for Amnesty complained that by excluding deserters, Carter had not gone far enough. What was certain was that the pardon allowed what the administration said were hundreds of thousands of draft dodgers to return to their homes without fear of prosecution.

Laura M. Miller,
Vanderbilt University

See also **Conscription and Recruitment; Vietnam War.**

Proclamation 4483

Acting pursuant to the grant of authority in Article II, Section 2, of the Constitution of the United States. I, Jimmy Carter, President of the United States, do hereby grant a full, complete and unconditional pardon to: (1) all persons who may have committed any offense between August 4, 1964 and March 28, 1973 in violation of the Military Selective Service Act or any rule or regulation promulgated thereunder; and (2) all persons heretofore convicted, irrespective of the date of conviction, of any offense committed between August 4, 1964 and March 28, 1973 in violation of the Military Selective Service Act, or any rule or regulation promulgated thereunder, restoring to them full political, civil and other rights.

This pardon does not apply to the following who are specifically excluded therefrom:

(1) All persons convicted of or who may have committed any offense in violation of the Military Selective Service Act, or any rule or regulation promulgated thereunder, involving force or violence; and

(2) All persons convicted of or who may have committed any offense in violation of the Military Selective Service Act, or any rule or regulation promulgated thereunder, in connection with duties or responsibilities arising out of employment as agents, officers or employees of the Military Selective Service system.

IN WITNESS WHEREOF, I have unto set my hand this 21st day of January, in the year of our Lord nineteen hundred and seventy-seven, and of the Independence of the United States of America the two hundred and first.

Executive Order 11967

The following actions shall be taken to facilitate Presidential Proclamation of Pardon of January 21, 1977:

1. The Attorney General shall cause to be dismissed with prejudice to the government all pending indictments for violations of the Military Selective Service Act alleged to have occurred between August 4, 1964 and March 28, 1973 with the exception of the following:
   (a) Those cases alleging acts of force or violence deemed to be serious by the Attorney General as to warrant continued prosecution; and
   (b) Those cases alleging acts in violation of the Military Selective Service Act by agents, employees or officers of the Selective Service System arising out of such employment.
2. The Attorney General shall terminate all investigations now pending and shall not initiate further investigations alleging violations of the Military Selective Service Act between August 4, 1964 and March 28, 1973, with the exception of the following:
   (a) Those cases involving allegations of force or violence deemed to be so serious by the Attorney General as to warrant continued investigation, or possible prosecution; and
   (b) Those cases alleging acts in violation of the Military Selective Service Act by agents, employees or officers of the Selective Service System arising out of such employment.
3. Any person who is or may be precluded from reentering the United States under 8 U.S.C. 1182(a)(22) or under any other law, by reason of having committed or apparently committed any violation of the Military Selective Service Act shall be permitted as any other alien to reenter the United States.

The Attorney General is directed to exercise his discretion under 8 U.S.C. 1182 (d)(5) or other applicable law to permit the reentry of such persons under the same terms and conditions as any other alien.

This shall not include anyone who falls into the exceptions of paragraphs 1 (a) and (b) and 2 (a) and (b) above.

4. Any individual offered conditional clemency or granted a pardon or other clemency under Executive Order 11803 or Presidential Proclamation 4313, dated September 16, 1974, shall receive the full measure of relief afforded by this program if they are otherwise qualified under the terms of this Executive Order.

SOURCE: Proclamation 4483, Executive Order 11967.

THE LATE TWENTIETH CENTURY

NOW STATEMENT OF PURPOSE
(1966, by National Organization for Women)

The Civil Rights Act of 1964 not only prohibited racial discrimination but also proscribed discrimination based on sex. Yet in the implementation of the Act, extension of equality to women lagged behind advancements experienced by African Americans. Women continued to be spurned from equal economic and political participation, trapped under a glass ceiling of socially constructed gender roles. The expectation of women serving the role of wife and mother in American society hindered any tangible progress.

The National Organization for Women (NOW) was formed in response to what many women saw as neglect of the concerns and condition of women during the Civil Rights Movement. Betty Friedan's groundbreaking work, *The Feminine Mystique,* had given a voice to widely held feelings in 1963 and NOW sought to mobilize an increasingly conscious female population. NOW resolved to fight the iniquities of women being consistently marginalized in politics, paid only a percentage of what men earned, and all but barred from the professions and higher education.

NOW not only targeted the surface-level problems, but denounced the ideology that created them. In the 1966 Statement of Purpose, NOW expounded upon its rejection of traditionally conceived gender roles in which the man acted in the public sphere while the woman was relegated to a life of domesticity. NOW did not shy away from controversy, advocating such measures as the creation of nationwide childcare facilities that would alleviate women from having to sacrifice ten to fifteen years of their life in childrearing. The organization postulated that women possessed the same abilities to contribute on every level of society as men, and NOW sought to help blaze a trail for equal opportunity in education, politics, and the workplace.

Paul S. Bartels,
Villanova University

See also **Discrimination: Sex; Equal Employment Opportunity Commission; Equal Rights Amendment; Gender and Gender Roles; National Organization of Women; Women in Public Life, Business, and Professions; Women's Rights Movement: The Twentieth Century.**

We, men and women who hereby constitute ourselves as the National Organization for Women, believe that the time has come for a new movement toward true equality for all women in America, and toward a fully equal partnership of the sexes, as part of the world-wide revolution of human rights now taking place within and beyond our national borders.

The purpose of NOW is to take action to bring women into full participation in the mainstream of American society now, exercising all the privileges and responsibilities thereof in truly equal partnership with men.

We believe the time has come to move beyond the abstract argument, discussion and symposia over the status and special nature of women which has raged in America in recent years; the time has come to confront, with concrete action, the conditions that now prevent women from enjoying the equality of opportunity and freedom of choice which is their right as individual Americans, and as human beings.

NOW is dedicated to the proposition that women first and foremost are human beings, who, like all other people in our society, must have the chance to develop their fullest human potential. We believe that women can achieve such equality only by accepting to the full the challenges and responsibilities they share with all other people in our society, as part of the decision-making mainstream of American political, economic and social life.

We organize to initiate or support action, nationally or in any part of this nation, by individuals or organizations, to break through the silken curtain of prejudice and discrimination against women in government, industry, the professions, the churches, the political parties, the judiciary, the labor unions, in education, science, medicine, law, religion and every other field of importance in American society.

Enormous changes taking place in our society make it both possible and urgently necessary to advance the unfinished revolution of women toward true equality, now. With a life span lengthened to nearly seventy-five years, it is no longer either necessary or possible for women to devote the greater part of their lives to child bearing; yet childbearing and rearing—which continues to be a most important part of most women's lives—is still used to justify barring women from equal professional and economic participation and advance.

Today's technology has reduced most of the productive chores which women once performed in the home and in mass production industries based upon routine unskilled labor. This same technology has virtually eliminated the quality of muscular strength as a criterion for filling most jobs, while intensifying American industry's need for creative intelligence. In view of this new industrial revolution created by automation in the mid-twentieth century, women can and must participate in old and new fields of society in full equality—or become permanent outsiders.

Despite all the talk about the status of American women in recent years, the actual position of women in the United States has declined, and is declining, to an alarming degree throughout the 1950's and 1960's. Although 46.4 percent of all American women between the ages of eighteen and sixty-five now work outside the home, the overwhelming majority—75 percent—are in routine clerical, sales, or factory jobs, or they are household workers, cleaning women, hospital attendants. About two-thirds of Negro women workers are in the lowest paid service occupations. Working women are becoming increasingly—not less—concentrated on the bottom of the job ladder. As a consequence, full-time women workers today earn on the average only 60 percent of what men earn, and that wage gap has been increasing over the past twenty-five years in every major industry group. In 1964, of all women with a yearly income, 89 percent earned under $5,000 a year; half of all full-time year-round women workers earned less than $3,690; only 1.4 percent of full-time year-round women workers had an annual income of $10,000 or more.

Further, with higher education increasingly essential in today's society, too few women are entering and finishing college or going on to graduate or professional school. Today women earn only one in three of the B.A.'s and M.A.'s granted, and one in ten of the Ph.D.'s.

In all the professions considered of importance to society, and in the executive ranks of industry and government, women are losing ground. Where they are present it is only a token handful. Women comprise less than 1 percent of federal judges; less than 4 percent of all lawyers; 7 percent of doctors. Yet women represent 53 percent of the U.S. population. And increasingly men are replacing women in the top positions in secondary and elementary schools, in social work, and in libraries—once thought to be women's fields.

Official pronouncements of the advance in the status of women hide not only the reality of this dangerous decline, but the fact that nothing is being done to stop it. The excellent reports of the President's Commission on the Status of Women and of the state commissions have not been fully implemented. Such commissions have power only to advise. They have no power to enforce their recommendations, nor have they the freedom to organize American women and men to press for action on them. The reports of these commissions have, however, created a basis upon which it is now possible to build.

Discrimination in employment on the basis of sex is now prohibited by federal law, in Title VII of the Civil Rights Act of 1964. But although nearly one-third of the cases brought before the Equal Employment Opportunity Commission during the first year dealt with sex discrimination and the proportion is increasing dramatically, the commission has not made clear its intention to enforce the law with the same seriousness on behalf of women as of other victims of discrimination. Many of these cases were Negro women, who are the victims of the double discrimination of race and sex. Until now, too few women's organizations and official spokesmen have been willing to speak out against these dangers facing women. Too many women have been restrained by the fear of being called "feminist."

There is no civil rights movement to speak for women, as there has been for Negroes and other victims of discrimination. The National Organization for Women must therefore begin to speak.

WE BELIEVE that the power of American law, and the protection guaranteed by the U.S. Constitution to the civil rights of all individuals, must be effectively applied and enforced to isolate and remove patterns of sex discrimination, to ensure equality of opportunity in employment and education, and equality of civil and political rights and responsibilities on behalf of women, as well as for Negroes and other deprived groups.

We realize that women's problems are linked to many broader questions of social justice; their solution will require concerted action by many groups. Therefore, convinced that human rights for all are indivisible, we expect to give active support to the common cause of equal rights for all those who suffer discrimination and deprivation, and we call upon other organizations committed to such goals to support our efforts toward equality for women.

WE DO NOT ACCEPT the token appointment of a few women to high-level positions in government and industry as a substitute for a serious continuing effort to recruit and advance women according to their individual abilities. To this end, we urge American government and industry to mobilize the same resources of ingenuity and command with which they have solved problems of far greater difficulty than those now impeding the progress of women.

WE BELIEVE that this nation has a capacity at least as great as other nations, to innovate new social institutions which will enable women to enjoy true equality of opportunity and responsibility in society, without conflict with their responsibilities as mothers and homemakers. In such innovations, America does not lead the Western world, but lags by decades behind many European countries. We do not accept the traditional assumption that a woman has to choose between marriage and motherhood, on the one hand, and serious participation in industry or the professions on the other. We question the present expectation that all normal women will retire from job or profession for ten or fifteen years, to devote their full time to raising children, only to reenter the job market at a relatively minor level. This in itself is a deterrent to the aspirations of women, to their acceptance into management or professional training courses, and to the very possibility of equality of opportunity or real choice, for all but a few women. Above all, we reject the assumption that these problems are the unique responsibility of each individual woman, rather than a basic social dilemma which society must solve. True equality of opportunity and freedom of choice for women requires such practical and possible innovations as a nationwide network of child-care centers, which will make it unnecessary for women to retire completely from society until their children are grown, and national programs to provide retraining for women who have chosen to care for their own children full time.

WE BELIEVE that it is as essential for every girl to be educated to her full potential of human ability as it is for every boy—with the knowledge that such education is the key to effective participation in today's economy and that, for a girl as for boy, education can only be serious where there is expectation that it will be used in society. We believe that American educators are capable of devising means of imparting such expectations to girl students. Moreover, we consider the decline in the proportion of women receiving higher and professional education to be evidence of discrimination. This discrimination may take the form of quotas against the admission of women to colleges and professional schools; lack of encouragement by parents, counselors and educators; denial of loans or fellowships; or the traditional or arbitrary procedures in graduate and professional training geared in terms of men, which inadvertently discriminate against women. We believe that the same serious attention must be given to high school dropouts who are girls as to boys.

WE REJECT the current assumptions that a man must carry the sole burden of supporting himself, his wife, and family, and that a woman is automatically entitled to lifelong support by a man upon her marriage, or that marriage, home and family are primarily woman's world and responsibility—hers, to dominate, his to support. We believe that a true partnership between the sexes demands a different concept of marriage, an equitable sharing of the responsibilities of home and children and of the economic burdens of their support. We believe that proper recognition should be given to the economic and social value of homemaking and child care. To these ends, we will seek to open a reexamination of laws and mores governing marriage and divorce, for we believe that the current state of "half-equality" between the sexes discriminates against both men and women, and is the cause of much unnecessary hostility between the sexes.

WE BELIEVE that women must now exercise their political rights and responsibilities as American citizens. They must refuse to be segregated on the basis of sex into separate-and-not-equal ladies' auxiliaries in the political parties, and they must demand representation according to their numbers in the regularly constituted party committees—at local, state, and national levels—and in the informal power structure, participating fully in the selection of selection of candidates and political decision-making, and running for office themselves.

IN THE INTERESTS OF THE HUMAN DIGNITY OF WOMEN, we will protest and endeavor to change the false image of women now prevalent in the mass media, and in the texts, ceremonies, laws, and practices of our major social institutions. Such images perpetuate contempt for women by society and by women for themselves. We are similarly opposed to all policies and practices—in church, state, college, factory, or office—which, in the guise of protectiveness, not only deny opportunities but also foster in women self-denigration, dependence, and evasion of responsibility, undermine their confidence in their own abilities and foster contempt for women.

NOW WILL HOLD ITSELF INDEPENDENT OF ANY POLITICAL PARTY in order to mobilize the political power of all women and men intent on our goals. We will strive to ensure that no party, candidate, President, senator, governor, congressman, or any public official who betrays or ignores the principle of full equality between the sexes is elected or appointed to office. If it is necessary to mobilize the votes of men and women who believe in our cause, in order to win for women the final right to be fully free and equal human beings, we so commit ourselves.

WE BELIEVE THAT women will do most to create a new image of women by *acting* now, and by speaking out in behalf of their own equality, freedom, and human dignity—not in pleas for special privilege, nor in enmity toward men, who are also victims of the current half-equality between the sexes—but in an active, self-respecting partnership with men. By so doing, women will develop confidence in their own ability to determine actively, in partnership with men, the conditions of their life, their choices, their future and their society.

SOURCE: National Organization for Women. From *NOW Statement of Purpose*, 1966. This is a historical document and does not reflect the current language or priorities of the organization.

EXCERPT FROM "CHICANO NATIONALISM: THE KEY TO UNITY FOR LA RAZA"
(1970, by Rodolfo "Corky" Gonzáles)

Rodolfo "Corky" Gonzáles was an influential leader of the Chicano movement in the 1960s and 1970s. Born in Denver, Colorado, Gonzáles was a nationally ranked featherweight boxer before becoming involved in local social service programs. In 1966 he founded the Crusade for Justice, a Denver-based organization that assisted Chicano youth with a school, social center, and a store. In 1969, Gonzales organized the first Chicano Youth Liberation Conference; at the second conference, he began to advocate a Chicano political party, which he called *La Raza Unida* Party. In this essay, Gonzales claims that Chicano pride and "nationalism" will lead to a stronger party. He wants a united movement working against the system to fight racism, discrimination, and the emulation of Chicano stereotypes within the community itself.

Leah R. Shafer,
Cornell University

See also **Hispanic Americans; Nationalism.**

What are the common denominators that unite the people? The key common denominator is nationalism. When I talk about nationalism, some people run around in their intellectual bags, and they say this is reverse racism. The reverse of a racist is a humanitarian. I specifically mentioned what I felt nationalism was, Nationalism becomes *la familia.* Nationalism comes first out of the family, then into tribalism, and then into alliances that are necessary to lift the burden of all suppressed humanity.

Now, if you try to climb up a stairway, you have to start with the first step. You can't jump from the bottom of this floor to the top of those bleachers. If you can, then you must be "super-*macho.*" (I don't talk about superman.) But, you can't, so you start using those tools that are necessary to get from the bottom to the top. One of these tools is nationalism. You realize that if Chavez, or any popular figure in the Mexicano scene decides to run, and if he ran for any party, as popular as, he is, then out of nationalism we would even vote for an idiot. If his name was Sanchez, if his name was Gonzalez, you would walk in and vote for him, whether you know him or not, because you are nationalistic. And we have elected too many idiots in the past out of nationalism, right?

Now, let's take that common denominator, that same organizing tool of nationalism, and utilize it to work against the system. Let's use it to work against the two parties that I say are like an animal with two heads eating out of the same trough, that sits on the same boards of directors of the banks and corporations, that shares in the same industries that make dollars and profits off wars. To fight this thing, you look for the tools.

Now, if Tony is a socialist, if my brother here is an independent, if my sister is a Republican—she might hit on me later—if one of the others is a Democrat and one is a communist, and one from the Socialist Labor Party, what do we have in common politically? Nothing. We've been fighting over parties across the kitchen table, wives are Republicans and husbands are Democrats, sometimes, and we argue over a bunch of garbage. And the same Republicans and Democrats are having cocktails together at the same bar and playing golf together and kissing each other behind the scenes.

So you tell me then, what is the common denominator that will touch the *barrio,* the *campos* and the ranchitos? Are we going to go down there with some tremendous words of intellectualism which they cannot relate to, when they relate on the level of, "We need food. We need health care for our children. I need someone to go down to juvenile court with my son. There is no job for my husband." And the revolution of 15 or 20 years from now is not going to feed a hungry child today....

All right, how do we start this? We start it and call it an independent Chicano political organization. We can use it as Tony mentioned also, under the FCC code, we can use it as a forum to preach and teach. We can gain the same amount of radio and TV time as any phony candidate. We proved it in Colorado. I ran for mayor as an independent, and I campaigned two weeks. Two weeks, because we were busy directing a play and busy in civil rights actions. But, we had the same amount of time on TV as anybody else, and on radio. We were able to start to politicize people. We were able to start to tell about an idea. We were able, even, to sue the mayor and the top candidates for violating the city charter, for spending more money than the city provided for under its constitution. We had that mayor and the most powerful Republicans and Democrats sitting on their asses down in the courtroom. Our method was to take them to court, to take them to task, to show the public that they were corrupt. And we proved that they were liars, over and over again.

We must start off by creating the structure—the concilio—by calling a congress sometime this spring, bringing together all those people that believe that it can be done. We understand that when we organize in an area where we are a majority, we can control. Where we are a minority, we will be a pressure group. And we will be a threat.

We understand the need to take action in the educational system. We understand that we need actions such as the "blow-outs," because the youth are not afraid of anything. Because the youth are ready to move. The whole party will be based on the actions of the young, and the support of the old.

Secondly, in the communities where we are a majority, we can then control and start to reassess taxes, to start charging the exploiters for what they have made off our people in the past. You can also incorporate the community to drive out the exploiters, to make them pay the freight for coming into the community, and sign your own franchises. You can de-annex a community as easily as they annex a *barrio* and incorporate it. You can create your own security groups, and place a gun here to protect the people, not to harass them, but to protect them from the Man who is going to come in from the outside. You can also create your own, economic base by starting to understand that we can share instead of cut each others' throats.

Now what are the tools? We said nationalism, which means that we have to be able to identify with our past, and understand our past, in order that we can dedicate ourselves to the future, dedicate ourselves to change. And we have to understand what humanism really is. We can tie the cultural thing into it, but we also have to tie in the political and the economic. We tie these things together, and we start to use the common denominator of nationalism.

Now for those Anglo supporters, don't get up-tight. For the Black brothers, they are practicing the same thing right now. And we understand it and respect it. And we are for meaningful coalitions with organized groups.

We have to start to consider ourselves as a nation. We can create a congress or a *concilio*. We can understand that we are a nation of *Aztlan*. We can understand and identify with Puerto Rican liberation. We can understand and identify with Black liberation. We can understand and identify with white liberation from this oppressing system once we organize around ourselves.

Where they have incorporated themselves to keep us from moving into their neighborhoods, we can also incorporate ourselves to keep them from controlling our neighborhoods. We have to also understand economic revolution, of driving the exploiter out. We have to understand political change. And we have to understand principle. And the man who says we can do it within the system—who says, "Honest, you can, look at me, I have a $20,000-a-year job"—he's the man who was last year's militant and this year's OEO employee [Office of Economic Opportunity]. And now he's keeping his mouth shut and he ain't marching any more. We have to understand that he is not a revolutionary, that he's a counter-revolutionary. He's not an ally, he becomes an enemy because he's contaminated.

You can't walk into a house full of disease with a bottle full of mercurochrome and cure the disease without getting sick yourself. That's what we say about the lesser of the two evils. If four grains of arsenic kill you, and eight grains of arsenic kill you, which is the lesser of two evils? You're dead either way.

We have to understand that liberation comes from self-determination, and to start to use the tools of nationalism to win over our *barrio* brothers, to win over the brothers who are still believing that *machismo* means getting a gun and going to kill a communist in Vietnam because they've been jived about the fact that they will be accepted as long as they go get themselves killed for the *gringo* captain; who still think that welfare is giving them something and don't understand that the one who is administering the welfare is the one that's on welfare, because, about 90 percent of the welfare goes into administration; and who still do not understand that the war on poverty is against the poor, to keep them from reacting.

We have to win these brothers over, and we have to do it by action. Whether it be around police brutality, the educational system, whether it be against oppression of any kind—you create an action, you create a blowout, and you see how fast those kids get politicized. Watch how fast they learn the need to start to take over our own communities. And watch how fast they learn to identify with ourselves, and to understand that we need to create a nation.

We can create a thought, an idea, and we can create our own economy. You don't hear of any "yellow power" running around anywhere. Because they base their power around their church, their house, their community. They sell Coca Cola, but their profits go to their own people, you see, so that they have an economic base. We are strangers in our own church. We have got gachupin [traditional terms of contempt for Spaniards who ruled Mexico for 400 years] priests from Spain in our communities, telling us *vamos a hechar unos quatros pesos en la canasta* [let's throw four pesos in the collection dish]. And then he tells you, "I'm your religious leader," and he tries to tell you how to eat, where to go, who to sleep with and how to do it right—while he's copping everything else out. You know, we're tired of this kind of leadership.

You have to understand that we can take over the institutions within our community. We have to create the community of the Mexicano here in order to have any type of power. As much as the young ladies have created power in their own community. But they have to share it with the rest of us. They have to be able to bring it together. And we are glad when they sit down instead of retreating. It means that we're all one people. It means that we're all one *Raza* and that we will, work together and we will walk out of here in a positive fashion.

SOURCE: Gonzáles, Rudolfo "Corky." "Chicano Nationalism: The Key to Unity for La Raza." *The Militant.* (30 March 1970).

NIXON'S WATERGATE INVESTIGATION ADDRESS *(30 April 1973)*

On 17 June 1972, employees of the Committee for the Reelection of the President (CRP) were caught breaking into the Democratic National Committee headquarters in the Watergate apartment complex in Washington, D.C. The CRP employees had broken in so they could replace one of the variety of surveillance tools they had planted on a previous occasion. The cover-up and destruction of incriminating evidence began almost immediately, as the CRP employees were closely tied to key members of Nixon's administration. Ultimately, investigation of the crimes and their cover-up led to impeachment charges against President Nixon, who resigned the Presidency on 4 August 1974.

In this speech, Nixon accepted "responsibility" for the Watergate event, but not explicitly. By noting the resignations of several distinguished members of his staff, Nixon revealed that the scandal reached to the highest levels of government. Though he was later on the verge of being indicted for obstructing the investigation, Nixon claimed that he was committed to seeking justice and finding out the truths behind the break-in.

Leah R. Shafer,
Cornell University

See also **Nixon, Resignation of; Political Scandals; Watergate.**

Good evening:

I want to talk to you tonight from my heart on a subject of deep concern to every American.

In recent months, members of my Administration and officials of the Committee for the Re-Election of the President—including some of my closest friends and most trusted aides—have been charged with involvement in what has come to be known as the Watergate affair. These include charges of illegal activity during and preceding the 1972 Presidential election and charges that responsible officials participated in efforts to cover up that illegal activity.

The inevitable result of these charges has been to raise serious questions about the integrity of the White House itself. Tonight I wish to address those questions.

Last June 17, while I was in Florida trying to get a few days rest after my visit to Moscow, I first learned from news reports of the Watergate break-in. I was appalled at this senseless, illegal action, and I was shocked to learn that employees of the Re-Election Committee were apparently among those guilty. I immediately ordered an investigation by appropriate Government authorities. On September 15, as you will recall, indictments were brought against seven defendants in the case.

As the investigations went forward, I repeatedly asked those conducting the investigation whether there was any reason to believe that members of my Administration were in any way involved. I received repeated assurances that there were not. Because of these continuing reassurances, because I believed the reports I was getting, because I had faith in the persons from whom I was getting them, I discounted the stories in the press that appeared to implicate members of my Administration or other officials of the campaign committee.

Until March of this year, I remained convinced that the denials were true and that the charges of involvement by members of the White House Staff were false. The comments I made during this period, and the comments made by my Press Secretary in my behalf, were based on the information provided to us at the time we made those comments. However, new information then came to me which persuaded me that there was a real possibility that some of these charges were true, and suggesting further that there had been an effort to conceal the facts both from the public, from you, and from me.

As a result, on March 21, I personally assumed the responsibility for coordinating intensive new inquiries into the matter, and I personally ordered those conducting the investigations to get all the facts and to report them directly to me, right here in this office.

I again ordered that all persons in the Government or at the Re-Election Committee should cooperate fully with the FBI, the prosecutors, and the grand jury. I also ordered that anyone who refused to cooperate in telling the truth would be asked to resign from Government service. And, with ground rules adopted that would preserve the basic constitutional separation of powers between the Congress and the Presidency, I directed that members of the White House Staff should appear and testify voluntarily under oath before the Senate committee which was investigating Watergate.

I was determined that we should get to the bottom of the matter, and that the truth should be fully brought out—no matter who was involved.

At the same time, I was determined not to take precipitate action and to avoid, if at all possible, any action that would appear to reflect on innocent people. I wanted to be fair. But I knew that in the final analysis, the integrity of this office—public faith in the integrity of this office—would have to take priority over all personal considerations.

Today, in one of the most difficult decisions of my Presidency, I accepted the resignations of two of my closest associates in the White House—Bob Haldeman, John Ehrlichman—two of the finest public servants it has been my privilege to know.

I want to stress that in accepting these resignations, I mean to leave no implication whatever of personal wrongdoing on their part, and I leave no implication tonight of implication on the part of others who have been charged in this matter. But in matters as sensitive as guarding the integrity of our democratic process, it is essential not only that rigorous legal and ethical standards be observed but also that the public, you, have total confidence that they are both being observed and enforced by those in authority and particularly by the President of the United States. They agreed with me that this move was necessary in order to restore that confidence.

Because Attorney General Kleindienst—though a distinguished public servant, my personal friend for 20 years, with no personal involvement whatever in this matter—has been a close personal and professional associate of some of those who are involved in this case, he and I both felt that it was also necessary to name a new Attorney General.

The Counsel to the President, John Dean, has also resigned.

As the new Attorney General, I have today named Elliot Richardson, a man of unimpeachable integrity and rigorously high principle. I have directed him to do everything necessary to ensure that the Department of Justice has the confidence and the trust of every law-abiding person in this country.

I have given him absolute authority to make all decisions bearing upon the prosecution of the Watergate case and related matters. I have instructed him that if he should consider it appropriate, he has the authority to name a special supervising prosecutor for matters arising out of the case.

Whatever may appear to have been the case before, whatever improper activities may yet be discovered in connection with this whole sordid affair, I want the American people. I want you to know beyond the shadow of a doubt that during my term as President, justice will be pursued fairly, fully, and impartially, no matter who is involved. This office is a sacred trust and I am determined to be worthy of that trust.

Looking back at the history of this case, two questions arise:

How could it have happened?

Who is to blame?

Political commentators have correctly observed that during my 27 years in politics I have always previously insisted on running my own campaigns for office.

But 1972 presented a very different situation. In both domestic and foreign policy, 1972 was a year of crucially important decisions, of intense negotiations, of vital new directions, particularly in working toward the goal which has been my overriding concern throughout my political career—the goal of bringing peace to America, peace to the world.

That is why I decided, as the 1972 campaign approached, that the Presidency should come first and politics second. To the maximum extent possible, therefore, I sought to delegate campaign operations to remove the day-to-day campaign decisions from the President's office and from the White House. I also, as you recall, severely limited the number of my own campaign appearances.

Who, then, is to blame for what happened in this case?

For specific criminal actions by specific individuals, those who committed those actions must, of course, bear the liability and pay the penalty.

For the fact that alleged improper actions took place within the White House or within my campaign organization, the easiest course would be for me to blame those to whom I delegated the responsibility to run the campaign. But that would be a cowardly thing to do.

I will not place the blame on subordinates—on people whose zeal exceeded their judgment and who may have done wrong in a cause they deeply believed to be right.

In any organization, the man at the top must bear the responsibility. That responsibility, therefore, belongs here, in this office. I accept it. And I pledge to you tonight, from this office, that I will do everything in my power to ensure that the guilty are brought to justice and that such abuses are purged from our political processes in the years to come, long after I have left this office.

Some people, quite properly appalled at the abuses that occurred, will say that Watergate demonstrates the bankruptcy of the American political system. I believe precisely the opposite is true. Watergate represented a series of illegal acts and bad judgments by a number of individuals. It was the system that has brought the facts to light and that will bring those guilty to justice—a system that in this case has included a determined grand jury, honest prosecutors, a courageous judge, John Sirica, and a vigorous free press.

It is essential now that we place our faith in that system—and especially in the judicial system. It is essential that we let the judicial process go forward, respecting those safeguards that are established to protect the innocent as well as to convict the guilty. It is essential that in reacting to the excesses of others, we not fall into excesses ourselves.

It is also essential that we not be so distracted by events such as this that we neglect the vital work before us, before this Nation, before America, at a time of critical importance to America and the world.

Since March, when I first learned that the Watergate affair might in fact be far more serious than I had been led to believe, it has claimed far too much of my time and my attention.

Whatever may now transpire in the case, whatever the actions of the grand jury, whatever the outcome of any eventual trials, I must now turn my full attention—and I shall do so—once again to the larger duties of this office. I owe it to this great office that I hold, and I owe it to you—to my country.

I know that as Attorney General, Elliot Richardson will be both fair and he will be fearless in pursuing this case wherever it leads. I am confident that with him in charge, justice will be done.

There is vital work to be done toward our goal of a lasting structure of peace in the world—work that cannot wait, work that I must do.

Tomorrow, for example, Chancellor Brandt of West Germany will visit the White House for talks that are a vital element of "The Year of Europe," as 1973 has been called. We are already preparing for the next Soviet-American summit meeting later this year.

This is also a year in which we are seeking to negotiate a mutual and balanced reduction of armed forces in Europe, which will reduce our defense budget and allow us to have funds for other purposes at home so desperately needed. It is the year when the United States and Soviet negotiators will seek to work out the second and even more important round of our talks on limiting nuclear arms and of reducing the danger of a nuclear war that would destroy civilization as we know it. It is a year in which we confront the difficult tasks of maintaining peace in Southeast Asia and in the potentially explosive Middle East.

There is also vital work to be done right here in America: to ensure prosperity, and that means a good job for everyone who wants to work; to control inflation, that I know worries every housewife, everyone who tries to balance a family budget in America; to set in motion new and better ways of ensuring progress toward a better life for all Americans.

When I think of this office—of what it means—I think of all the things that I want to accomplish for this Nation, of all the things I want to accomplish for you.

On Christmas Eve, during my terrible personal ordeal of the renewed bombing of North Vietnam, which after 12 years of war finally helped to bring America peace with honor, I sat down just before midnight. I wrote out some of my goals for my second term as President.

Let me read them to you.

"To make it possible for our children, and for our children's children, to live in a world of peace.

"To make this country be more than ever a land of opportunity—of equal opportunity, full opportunity for every American.

"To provide jobs for all who can work, and generous help for those who cannot work.

"To establish a climate of decency and civility, in which each person respects the feelings and the dignity and the God-given rights of his neighbor.

"To make this a land in which each person can dare to dream, can live his dreams—not in fear, but in hope—proud of his community, proud of his country, proud of what America has meant to himself and to the world."

These are great goals. I believe we can, we must work for them. We can achieve them. But we cannot achieve these goals unless we dedicate ourselves to another goal.

We must maintain the integrity of the White House, and that integrity must be real, not transparent. There can be no whitewash at the White House.

We must reform our political process—ridding it not only of the violations of the law but also of the ugly mob violence and other inexcusable campaign tactics that have been too often practiced and too readily accepted in the past, including those that may have been a response by one side to the excesses or expected excesses of the other side. Two wrongs do not make a right.

I have been in public life for more than a quarter of a century. Like any other calling, politics has good people and bad people. And let me tell you, the great majority in politics—in the Congress, in the Federal Government, in the State government—are good people. I know that it can be very easy, under the intensive pressures of a campaign, for even well-intentioned people to fall into shady tactics—to rationalize this on the grounds that what is at stake is of such importance to the Nation that the end justifies the means. And both of our great parties have been guilty of such tactics in the past.

In recent years, however, the campaign excesses that have occurred on all sides have provided a sobering demonstration of how far this false doctrine can take us. The lesson is clear: America, in its political campaigns, must not again fall into the trap of letting the end, however great that end is, justify the means.

I urge the leaders of both political parties, I urge citizens, all of you, everywhere, to join in working toward a new set of standards, new rules and procedures to ensure that future elections will be as nearly free of such abuses as they possibly can be made. This is my goal. I ask you to join in making it America's goal.

When I was inaugurated for a second time this past January 20, I gave each member of my Cabinet and each member of my senior White House Staff a special 4-year calendar, with each day marked to show the number of days remaining to the Administration. In the inscription on each calendar, I wrote these words: "The Presidential term which begins today consists of 1,461 days—no more, no less. Each can be a day of strengthening and renewal for America; each can add depth and dimension to the American experience. If we strive together, if we make the most of the challenge and the opportunity that these days offer us, they can stand out as great days for America, and great moments in the history of the world."

I looked at my own calendar this morning up at Camp David as I was working on this speech. It showed exactly 1,361 days remaining in my term. I want these to be the best days in America's history, because I love America. I deeply believe that America is the hope of the world. And I know that in the quality and wisdom of the leadership America gives lies the only hope for millions of people all over the world that they can live their lives in peace and freedom. We must be worthy of that hope, in every sense of the word. Tonight, I ask for your prayers to help me in everything that I do throughout the days of my Presidency to be worthy of their hopes and of yours.

God bless America and God bless each and every one of you.

"CONSTITUTIONAL FAITH" SPEECH
(25 July 1974, by Rep. Barbara Jordan)

The scandal that followed the discovery of the burglary of the offices of the Democratic National Committee at the Watergate complex on 17 June 1972 changed the face of American politics. As damning evidence against the Nixon administration mounted over the next year, the House Judiciary Committee began an investigation into the President's conduct. By early 1974, the committee was holding hearings about impeaching the President. Each of the thirty-eight members of the committee was given fifteen minutes to state their views before a television audience on 25 July.

Representative Barbara Jordan (1936–1996) from Texas was among those members who felt strongly that the President's actions had grievously violated the Constitution. Jordan, who was the first African American woman to be elected to Congress from the South, was known for her legislative acumen, her oratorical excellence, and her unflappable personal integrity. In her now-famous speech, Jordan revealed an impressive knowledge of the Constitution while damning the President, saying, "I am not going to sit here and be an idle spectator to the diminution, the subversion, the destruction of the Constitution."

Leah R. Shafer,
Cornell University

See also **Impeachment; Nixon, Resignation of; Watergate.**

Mr. Chairman, I join my colleague, Mr. Rangel, in thanking you for giving the junior members of this committee the glorious opportunity of sharing the pain of this inquiry. Mr. Chairman, you are a strong man and it has not been easy but we have tried as best we can to give you as much assistance as possible.

Earlier today we heard the beginning of the Preamble to the Constitution of the United States, "We, the people." It is a very eloquent beginning. But when that document was completed on the seventeenth of September in 1787 I was not included in that "We, the people." I felt somehow for many years that George Washington and Alexander Hamilton just left me out by mistake. But through the process of amendment, interpretation and court decision I have finally been included in "We, the people."

Today, I am an inquisitor. I believe hyperbole would not be fictional and would not overstate the solemnness that I feel right now. My faith in the Constitution is whole, it is complete, it is total. I am not going to sit here and be an idle spectator to the diminution, the subversion, the destruction of the Constitution.

"Who can so properly be the inquisitors for the nation as the representatives of the nation themselves?" (Federalist, number 65). The subject of its jurisdiction are those offenses which proceed from the misconduct of public men. That is what we are talking about. In other words, the jurisdiction comes from the abuse or violation of some public trust. It is wrong, I suggest, it is a misreading of the Constitution for any member here to assert that for a member to vote for an article of impeachment means that that member must be convinced that the president should be removed from office. The Constitution doesn't say that. The powers relating to impeachment are an essential check in the hands of this body, the legislature, against and upon the encroachment of the executive. In establishing the division between the two branches of the legislature, the House and the Senate, assigning to the one the right to accuse and to the other the right to judge, the framers of this Constitution were very astute. They did not make the accusers and the judges the same person.

We know the nature of impeachment. We have been talking about it awhile now. "It is chiefly designed for the president and his high ministers" to somehow be called into account. It is designed to "bridle" the executive if he engages in excesses. "It is designed as a method of national inquest into the conduct of public men." (Hamilton, Federalist, number 65). The framers confined in the Congress the power if need be, to remove the President in order to strike a delicate balance between a president swollen with power and grown tyrannical; and preservation of the independence of the executive. The nature of impeachment is a narrowly channeled exception to the separation of powers maxim, the federal convention of 1787 said that. It limited impeachment to high crimes and misdemeanors and discounted and opposed the term, "maladministration." "It is to be used only for great misdemeanors," so it was said in the North Carolina ratification convention. And in the Virginia ratification convention: "We do not trust our liberty to a particular branch. We need one branch to check the others."

The North Carolina ratification convention: "No one need be afraid that officers who commit oppression will pass with immunity."

"Prosecutions of impeachments will seldom fail to agitate the passions of the whole community," said Hamilton in the Federalist Papers, number 65. "And to divide it into parties more or less friendly or inimical to the accused." I do not mean political parties in that sense.

The drawing of political lines goes to the motivation behind impeachment; but impeachment must proceed within the confines of the constitutional term, "high crime and misdemeanors."

Of the impeachment process, it was Woodrow Wilson who said that "nothing short of the grossest offenses against the plain law of the land will suffice to give them speed and effectiveness. Indignation so great as to overgrow party interest may secure a conviction; but nothing else can."

Common sense would be revolted if we engaged upon this process for petty reasons. Congress has a lot to do. Appropriations, tax reform, health insurance, campaign finance reform, housing, environmental protection, energy sufficiency, mass transportation. Pettiness cannot be allowed to stand in the face of such overwhelming problems. So today we are not being petty. We are trying to be big because the task we have before us is a big one.

This morning in a discussion of the evidence we were told that the evidence which purports to support the allegations of misuse of the CIA by the president is thin. We are told that that evidence is insufficient. What that recital of the evidence this morning did not include is what the president did know on June 23, 1972. The president did know that it was Republican money, that it was money from the Committee for the Re-election of the President, which was found in the possession of one of the burglars arrested on June 17.

What the president did know on June 23 was the prior activities of E. Howard Hunt, which included his participation in the break-in of Daniel Ellsberg's psychiatrist, which included Howard Hunt's participation in the Dita Beard ITT affair, which included Howard Hunt's fabrication of cables designed to discredit the Kennedy administration.

We were further cautioned today that perhaps these proceedings ought to be delayed because certainly there would be new evidence forthcoming from the president of the United States. There has not even been an obfuscated indication that this committee would receive any additional materials from the president. The committee subpoena is outstanding and if the president wants to supply that material, the committee sits here.

The fact is that on yesterday, the American people waited with great anxiety for eight hours, not knowing whether their president would obey an order of the Supreme Court of the United States.

At this point I would like to juxtapose a few of the impeachment criteria with some of the president's actions.

Impeachment criteria: James Madison, from the Virginia ratification convention. "If the president be connected in any suspicious manner with any person and there be grounds to believe that he will shelter him, he may be impeached."

We have heard time and time again that the evidence reflects payment to the defendants of money. The president had knowledge that these funds were being paid and that these were funds collected for the 1972 presidential campaign.

We know that the president met with Mr. Henry Petersen twenty-seven times to discuss matters related to Watergate and immediately thereafter met with the very persons who were implicated in the information Mr. Petersen was receiving and transmitting to the president. The words are, "If the President be collected in any suspicious manner with any person and there be grounds to believe that he will shelter that person, he may be impeached."

Justice Story: "Impeachment is intended for occasional and extraordinary cases where a superior power acting for the whole people is put into operation to protect their rights and rescue their liberties from violations."

We know about the Huston plan. We know about the break-in of the psychiatrist's office. We know that there was absolute complete direction in August 1971 when the president instructed Ehrlichman to "do whatever is necessary." This instruction led to a surreptitious entry into Dr. Fielding's office.

"Protect their rights." "Rescue their liberties from violation. "

The South Carolina ratification convention impeachment criteria: Those are impeachable "who behave amiss or betray their public trust."

Beginning shortly after the Watergate break-in and continuing to the present time the president has engaged in a series of public statements and actions designed to thwart the lawful investigation by government prosecutors. Moreover, the president has made public announcements and assertions bearing on the Watergate case which the evidence will show he knew to be false.

These assertions, false assertions, impeachable, those who misbehave. Those who "behave amiss or betray their public trust."

James Madison again at the constitutional convention: "A president is impeachable if he attempts to subvert the Constitution."

The Constitution charges the president with the task of taking care that the laws be faithfully executed, and yet the president has counseled his aides to commit perjury, willfully disregarded the secrecy of grand jury proceedings, concealed surreptitious entry, attempted to compromise a federal judge while publicly displaying his cooperation with the processes of criminal justice.

"A president is impeachable if he attempts to subvert the Constitution."

If the impeachment provision in the Constitution of the United States will not reach the offenses charged here, then perhaps that eighteenth century Constitution should be abandoned to a twentieth century paper shredder. Has the president committed offenses and planned and directed and acquiesced in a course of conduct which the Constitution will not tolerate? That is the question. We know that. We know the question. We should now forthwith proceed to answer the question. It is reason, and not passion, which must guide our deliberations, guide our debate, and guide our decision.

PROCLAMATION 4311: NIXON PARDONED
(8 September 1974)

Reaction to the pardon of former President Richard Nixon by Gerald Ford was largely negative. By 1974, most Americans were convinced of Nixon's participation in the Watergate break-ins and the elaborate cover-up that followed. In a televised address to the American people, Ford cited the good of the nation, the sure-to-be insurmountable difficulty in achieving a fair trial for Nixon, and even the health of the disgraced president as reasons for his decision. Dire political consequences were the result. Appointed to the Vice-Presidency following the resignation of Spiro T. Agnew, Ford was the first person to become President of the United States without having first been elected President or Vice-President. Many Americans came to believe that the promise of a full pardon was what Ford exchanged for his promotion to the second highest office in the land. By the election of 1976, hounded by the press for misstatements about Soviet influence in Eastern Europe, and endlessly ridiculed on television shows like NBC's *Saturday Night Live,* Ford had very little appeal to the American people, or even his own party, as a viable candidate. He was beaten by a political unknown, former Georgia governor Jimmy Carter, who successfully pinned the sins of the Nixon administration, and its aftermath, to the short presidency of Gerald Ford.

Laura M. Miller,
Vanderbilt University

See also **Nixon, Resignation of; Watergate.**

By the President of the United States of America a Proclamation

Now, THEREFORE, I, GERALD R. FORD, President of the United States, pursuant to the pardon power conferred upon me by Article II, Section 2, of the Constitution, have granted and by these presents do grant a full, free, and absolute pardon unto Richard Nixon for all offenses against the United States which he, Richard Nixon, has committed or may have committed or taken part in during the period from January 20, 1969 through August 9,1974.

IN WITNESS WHEREOF, I have hereunto set my hand this eighth day of September, in the year of our Lord nineteen hundred and seventy-four, and of the Independence of the United States of America the one hundred and ninety-ninth.

GERALD R. FORD

ADDRESS ON THE ENERGY CRISIS
(15 July 1979)

By the late 1960s, the American economy had become dependent upon oil imports, largely from the Middle East. The Nixon administration was the first to call for energy policies decreasing independence on foreign oil when the Organization of Petroleum Exporting Countries (OPEC) raised prices during the Arab oil embargo of 1973–1974. A second oil crisis was triggered in the summer of 1979 when the Shah of Iran was deposed and OPEC again raised prices. Oil prices soared and there were major shortages at gas stations across the country.

In response, President Jimmy Carter gave a speech exhorting Americans to conserve energy and renew their faith in America. The speech set goals for the reduction of American use of foreign oil by setting import quotas, developing alternative fuel sources, mandating utility regulations, and establishing conservation programs. The American public and energy interests, however, were reluctant to either reduce or conserve, and by the close of the 1970s, almost half of the American economy relied on imported oil.

Leah R. Shafer,
Cornell University

See also **Energy, Renewable; Oil Crises.**

. . . I want to speak to you first tonight about a subject even more serious than energy or inflation. I want to talk to you right now about a fundamental threat to American democracy.

I do not mean our political and civil liberties. They will endure. And I do not refer to the outward strength of America, a nation that is at peace tonight everywhere in the world, with unmatched economic power and military might.

The threat is nearly invisible in ordinary ways. It is a crisis of confidence. It is a crisis that strikes at the very heart and soul and spirit of our national will. We can see this crisis in the growing doubt about the meaning of our own lives and in the loss of a unity of purpose for our Nation.

The erosion of our confidence in the future is threatening to destroy the social and the political fabric of America.

The confidence that we have always had as a people is not simply some romantic dream or a proverb in a dusty book that we read just on the Fourth of July. It is the idea which founded our Nation and has guided our development as a people. Confidence in the future has supported everything else—public institutions and private enterprise, our own families, and the very Constitution of the United States. Confidence has defined our course and has served as a link between generations. We've always believed in something called progress. We've always had a faith that the days of our children would be better than our own.

Our people are losing that faith, not only in government itself but in the ability as citizens to serve as the ultimate rulers and shapers of our democracy. As a people we know our past and we are proud of it. Our progress has been part of the living history of America, even the world. We always believed that we were part of a great movement of humanity itself called democracy, involved in the search for freedom, and that belief has always strengthened us in our purpose. But just as we are losing our confidence in the future, we are also beginning to close the door on our past.

In a nation that was proud of hard work, strong families, close-knit communities, and our faith in God, too many of us now tend to worship self-indulgence and consumption. Human identity is no longer defined by what one does, but by what one owns. But we've discovered that owning things and consuming things does not satisfy our longing for meaning. We've learned that piling up material goods cannot fill the emptiness of lives which have no confidence or purpose.

The symptoms of this crisis of the American spirit are all around us. For the first time in the history of our country a majority of our people believe that the next 5 years will be worse than the past 5 years. Two-thirds of our people do not even vote. The productivity of American workers is actually dropping, and the willingness of Americans to save for the future has fallen below that of all other people in the Western world.

As you know, there is a growing disrespect for government and for churches and for schools, the news media, and other institutions. This is not a message of happiness or reassurance, but it is the truth and it is a warning.

These changes did not happen overnight. They've come upon us gradually over the last generation, years that were filled with shocks and tragedy.

We were sure that ours was a nation of the ballot, not the bullet, until the murders of John Kennedy and Robert Kennedy and Martin Luther King, Jr. We were taught that our armies were always invincible and our causes were always just, only to suffer the agony of Vietnam. We respected the Presidency as a place of honor until the shock of Watergate.

We remember when the phrase "sound as a dollar" was an expression of absolute dependability, until 10 years of inflation began to shrink our dollar and our savings. We believed that our Nation's resources were limitless until 1973 when we had to face a growing dependence on foreign oil.

These wounds are still very deep. They have never been healed.

Looking for a way out of this crisis, our people have turned to the Federal Government and found it isolated from the mainstream of our Nation's life. Washington, District of Columbia, has become an island. The gap between our citizens and our Government has never been so wide. The people are looking for honest answers, not easy answers; clear leadership, not false claims and evasiveness and politics as usual.

What you see too often in Washington and elsewhere around the country is a system of government that seems incapable of action. You see a Congress twisted and pulled in every direction by hundreds of well-financed and powerful special interests.

You see every extreme position defended to the last vote, almost to the last breath by one unyielding group or another. You often see a balanced and a fair approach that demands sacrifice, a little sacrifice from everyone, abandoned like an orphan without support and without friends.

Often you see paralysis and stagnation and drift. You don't like it, and neither do I. What can we do?

First of all, we must face the truth, and then we can change our course. We simply must have faith in each other, faith in our ability to govern ourselves, and faith in the future of this Nation. Restoring that faith and that confidence to America is now the most important task we face. It is a true challenge of this generation of Americans. . . .

We know the strength of America. We are strong. We can regain our unity. We can regain our confidence. We are the heirs of generations who survived threats much more powerful and awesome than those that challenge us now. Our fathers and mothers were strong men and women who shaped a new society during the Great Depression, who fought world wars, and who carved out a new charter of peace for the world.

We ourselves are the same Americans who just 10 years ago put a man on the Moon. We are the generation that dedicated our society to the pursuit of human rights and equality. And we are the generation that will win the war on the energy problem and in that process rebuild the unity and confidence of America. . . .

Energy will be the immediate test of our ability to unite this Nation. . . .

The energy crisis is real. It is worldwide. It is a clear and present danger to our Nation. These are facts and we simply must face them.

What I have to say to you now about energy is simple and vitally important.

> Point one: I am tonight setting a clear goal for the energy policy of the Unites States. Beginning this

moment, this Nation will never use more foreign oil than we did in 1977—never. . . .

Point two: To ensure that we meet these targets, I will use my Presidential authority to set import quotas. I'm announcing tonight that for 1979 and 1980, I will forbid the entry into this country of one drop of foreign oil more than these goals allow. These quotas will ensure a reduction in imports even below the ambitious levels we set at the recent Tokyo summit.

Point three: To give us energy security, I am asking for the most massive peacetime commitment of funds and resources in our Nation's history to develop America's own alternative sources of fuel—from coal, from oil shale, from plant products for gasohol, from unconventional gas, from the Sun.

> I propose the creation of an energy security corporation to lead this effort to replace 2 1/2 million barrels of imported oil per day by 1990. The corporation will issue up to $5 billion in energy bonds, and I especially want them to be in small denominations so that average Americans can invest directly in America's energy security. . . .

Point four: I'm asking Congress to mandate, to require as a matter of law, that our Nation's utility companies cut their massive use of oil by 50 percent within the next decade and switch to other fuels, especially coal, our most abundant energy source.

Point five: To make absolutely certain that nothing stands in the way of achieving these goals, I will urge Congress to create an energy mobilization board which, like the War Production Board in World War II, will have the responsibility and authority to cut through the redtape, the delays, and the endless roadblocks to completing key energy projects.

> We will protect our environment. But when this Nation critically needs a refinery or a pipeline, we will build it.

Point six: I'm proposing a bold conservation program to involve every State, county, and city and every average American in our energy battle. This effort will permit you to build conservation into your homes and your lives at a cost you can afford.

I ask Congress to give me authority for mandatory conservation and for standby gasoline rationing. To further conserve energy, I'm proposing tonight an extra $10 billion over the next decade to strengthen our public transportation systems. And I'm asking you for your good and for your Nation's security to take no unnecessary trips, to use carpools or public transportation whenever you can, to park your car one extra day per week, to obey the speed limit, and to set your thermostats to save fuel. Every act of energy conservation like this is more than just common sense—I tell you it is an act of patriotism. . . .

SOURCE: *Weekly Compilation of Presidential Documents*, 20 July 1979.

INTERROGATION OF AN IRAN HOSTAGE *(1979)*

On November 4, 1979, a crowd of almost five hundred Iranian militants, enraged by the United States's decision to admit exiled Muhammad Reza Shah Pahlevi for cancer treatment, seized the American embassy in Tehran, taking hostage the nearly ninety people inside. The next 444 days, a glimpse into which is presented here, would represent the greatest foreign policy challenge of the Carter administration. In fact, the conflict had begun early in the 1960s with the Shah undertaking a program of "Westernization." These broad social and economic reforms were marred by riots and mass persecution of the ruling regime's political and philosophical opponents, the Ayatollah Ruhollah Khomeini among them. Carter's first reaction to the embassy seizure was to freeze Iranian assets in the United States and order the immediate cessation of oil imports from Iran. Not until April of 1980 was a military rescue attempt mounted, called Operation Eagle Claw. However, helicopter engine trouble at a staging area and a fatal mid-air collision during withdrawal left eight Americans dead, and the failed operation resulted in a major embarrassment for the Carter administration. Preoccupied with the crisis and blamed by many frustrated voters for the lack of resolution, Carter was defeated by former California governor and movie star Ronald Reagan in the landslide presidential election of 1980. Finally, with the help of Algerian intermediaries, on January 20, 1981 the United States agreed to release some $8 billion in frozen Iranian assets, bringing the hostage crisis to an end at last.

Laura M. Miller,
Vanderbilt University

See also **Hostage Crises; Iran Hostage Crisis.**

Their routine for the interrogations was to take me down to this room that was as cold as the weather outside, and this was December—the dead of winter. I mean, it was colder than a bear in there. The militants took me down to this room and left me sitting there in my bare feet and a T-shirt for two or three hours. That was the routine. Then at about the time I was good and blue, they came in all dressed up warmly and started asking questions. By this time, I was one nervous guy. I was jumping and moving just to keep warm. This went on for several days, and I was really afraid that I was going to get pneumonia or something like that. I figured they would purposely let me die rather than give me any kind of medical treatment.

They'd leave me sitting in that room and go away. I knew damn well they'd gone off to bed. Every now and then one guy would come into the room and look at me. They didn't want me sleeping. He'd look at me and then back out. Once I started dozing, and he hit me with a rifle butt. It was obvious that they were trying to wear me down both emotionally and physically.

It became very obvious to me that somebody they had previously questioned had done some talking, because they were telling me things that were not in the files. They had information they should not have had. But how were they getting this information? Was it being extracted, or was it being freely volunteered? That was something I didn't know. But it was a godamn startling fact when they came in and started telling me what it was that I knew. They were hitting poop that was accurate, and they knew it. I thought, "Goddamn, they're coming in with something, and there's no way I can mislead them. They have got the file plus supplementary information." That was a nerve-racking session. All I could do was sit there and wonder, "What's going to happen next?" They would ask the same questions over and over and over and over again. It was like: "You're going to stay here until you get it right." I guess they were looking for me to make a mistake and trip over my own words.

Specifically, they were interested in a number of things. One of the big things they wanted was to know about any Iranians we had been working with or had been in contact with. The key to their thinking seemed to be that if an American had been in Iran for a reasonable length of time, then that American was automatically a CIA spy. Second, any Iranians that any Americans dealt with were automatically as guilty as the "CIA spies." The militants who took over the embassy believed that an Iranian who gave us any kind of help or information had done a horrible thing. It was obvious that they were going to go after these people. If you named names or gave them identities, then you could really get some of the Iranians in trouble, because the hard-core militants considered them collaborators, and they wanted to get them. Of course, I had been in contact with a lot of Iranians. Since I was a representative of the army, there were a lot of things about the Iranian army that we were interested in—officially, legally, and legitimately so. One thing of interest was that the Iranians did purchase some Russian equipment, so we were interested in any sort of Iranian army equipment, particularly if it was a Russian brand of mousetrap. But the militants didn't understand this sort of thing. They were convinced that everything we did was done to undermine the revolution. So I felt it was important not to give them the identities of any Iranians I had dealt with, because they considered those people to be collaborators and traitors.

SOURCE: Wells, Tim. *444 Days: The Hostages Remember.* San Diego: Harcourt Brace, 1985.

EXCERPT FROM *THE NEW RIGHT: WE'RE READY TO LEAD* *(1980, by Richard A. Viguerie)*

In part because of the increasing tensions of the Cold War, conservatism in American politics rose sharply in the late 1970s and early 1980s. With the election of Ronald Reagan as president in 1980, the "New Right" emerged as a powerful political force with a rapidly growing number of constituents. Many of these supporters had been solicited through the painstaking work of conservative Virginia advertising executive Richard Viguerie. Viguerie created a database of over twenty million persons who had donated to conservative causes, which he used to solicit money and support for conservative candidates in massive direct-mail fund-raisers. Viguerie's book, *The New Right: We're Ready to Lead* (1980), decries the "liberal" control of mass media and claims that the majority of Americans are good, god-fearing Christians who support the conservative agenda. Though the rallying cries of the New Right were devoted mostly to social issues, the administration they supported concentrated its efforts on right-wing economic and foreign policy agendas.

Leah R. Shafer,
Cornell University

See also **Conservatism; Mass Media; Neoconservatism.**

We're just beginning. And the future is wide open.

As the Bible says, there is a time for everything under heaven—a time to be born, and a time to die; a time to break down, and a time to build up; a time to keep silent, and a time to speak; a time of war, and a time of peace.

I think it is a time to lead.

We've already made such tremendous gains that some people assume we must have already fulfilled our basic potential. Frankly, I might have thought so too—except for one thing. We've surpassed our early goals by so much that I've learned to quit expecting to run up against a final limit.

It isn't just the liberals who have been shocked by our successes. Even some of our conservative allies have been stunned. They're glad, of course, but they can't quite believe it's really happening.

Perhaps if I had been in the foxholes for 30 years as a lot of conservatives have, if I had been shot at and shelled and torn apart and suffered as many defeats as they've suffered, I might have a defeatist attitude too.

But life teaches you to be ready for anything—even success.

And we're ready. We of the New Right believe that we will prevail.

Several years ago, Phyllis Schlafy asked Dr. Fred Schwarz what did he think was the Communists' greatest asset, and before he could reply Phyllis answered her own question. She said she felt the Communists' greatest asset was their total conviction that they will win.

There isn't a Communist leader in the world worth his salt who doesn't feel that Communism is the wave of the future.

That's what conservatives have going for them now. New Right conservatives believe that we will govern America. And we believe that freedom is the wave of the future.

A lot of older conservatives did not see themselves as winning and governing America. They saw themselves as sometimes influencing those who governed, but they did not see themselves as governing.

When Martin Luther nailed his 95 theses to the church door, he didn't know he was launching the biggest revolution in the history of Europe. Like everyone else in his time, he assumed that there would always be one all-inclusive Church.

But within a few years the entire face of the continent was changed. I believe that something similar, on a smaller scale, is now happening in America.

Like Luther, American conservatives didn't set out to make radical changes—just to restore some basic principles. But we've found that the ancient truths require new actions.

Our new reality has been achieved—though only partially so far—in the New Right, a network nearly as vast and complex as all the new Reformed churches that sprang up in Europe in Luther's time. If the Reformation could occur so swiftly in the age of the printing press and the horse-drawn carriage, think of how fast

America can change in the age of television, computers, and jet planes!

Think of the established media as being like the medieval Church, and you begin to grasp why people are alarmed by the New Right. People are used to getting their messages from certain familiar sources: the major networks, the newspapers and wire services, the schools and universities, the pollsters and experts.

CBS may be a private organization, but there is something so official-seeming about Walter Cronkite.

I don't just mean that the established media are liberal in their orientation. That's only part of it, and maybe not even the most important part.

It's something different. People are used to being guided by these media not only in what to think, but in what to think *about.* They expect the media not to dictate opinion (which most people in the media conscientiously try to avoid doing) but to announce the agenda.

The pollsters are willing to let you give your own answers, but you're probably accustomed to letting them choose the questions.

The result of this is that what we call "public opinion" is highly artificial. It may tell you in a general way what most people feel about the items on the liberal agenda. It doesn't answer the deeper question of how they feel about the agenda itself.

They may care very little about things the liberals feel strongly about, like the Equal Rights Amendment. They may hide their real feelings and give the answers they think the pollsters expect, because they think it's "unenlightened," or "bad taste," or may be seen as a sign of a "lack of compassion" to give non-liberal answers. They may not even realize there are *non-liberal* answers. So the responses people give to the polls are often formalistic and misleading.

For all these reasons, polls can be used to make it appear there is a national mandate for liberal policies, when in fact there just isn't. Don't think it doesn't happen!

Columnist Joseph Sobran has defined public opinion as "what everyone thinks everyone else thinks." That's an apt way of describing the barrier the New Right has had to break down.

Public opinion of this kind has another serious defect. It doesn't include all the things people may think and talk and care about when they're among themselves, without any liberal supervision around—the things the liberals would often prefer not to hear about anyway, and even discourage people from mentioning in public.

As the years have passed and the media have grown in influence, something else has grown too: a widening gap between "public opinion" and the real concerns of Americans.

It isn't just a gap. It's become a real tension, as the liberal program has been imposed often in direct opposition to what the American people would really prefer.

As I said at the beginning of this book, the media have given very little attention to subjects like school prayer and Communist aggression. A study by Dr. Ernest Lefever of Georgetown University found that the CBS Evening News had devoted only *one minute* to the Soviet arms buildup over a *two-year period!* And naturally enough, TV has given very little coverage to one of its own "pocketbook issues": immorality on TV.

Is it any wonder the New Right has sought to break free of the established mass communications system with its own independent channels of communication?

And is it any wonder we make them and the people who have innocently relied on them a little uneasy?

Our power is the ignored and untapped power of millions of ordinary Americans who want to hear another side and make some contribution of their own. We're trying to answer a profound need in American life. The results speak for themselves.

The American people believe in the separation of church and state. They don't believe in the segregation of traditional morality and public life.

Many who were alarmed by us at first are discovering that while we may be a little unorthodox, they basically agree with us. This has even been known to happen to liberals! Some of them too have come to feel that while tolerance is a fine thing, enough is enough.

One of the few conservatives who rejected the attitude that the nation was somehow doomed to eternal liberalism was the late Professor Willmoore Kendall. He long ago perceived that liberalism was riding for a fall, and that it was placing intolerable strains on the patience of the American people and on their deepest traditions.

Kendall predicted that when all the pockets of resistance to the liberal program had had enough, they would get in touch with each other and fight back. And in the showdown, he added, liberalism would lose.

That's exactly what is happening today.

Conservatism isn't the special philosophy of a fringe group. It's the American mainstream. That's why we *know* we're going to win.

Today, as Jeffrey Hart has observed, it's the liberal *New York Times*, not the conservative *National Review*, that seems like the "fringe" publication.

The liberals have done a good job of impersonating a mainstream, and they have succeeded in winning an extension for their unnatural dominance in public life.

They should have lost in 1974, and in 1976. But each time they succeeded in improvising, with issues like Watergate and with a Southern presidential candidate who was able to patch together the old Democratic coalition for a last hurrah, while the Republican Party failed to provide conservative leadership.

But deep down, they knew it wasn't solid. Today, some of the hard-core liberals know their time is up, and many of their own faithful are defecting. They can't pretend we aren't here, as they did for so many years. At the moment they are pretending we pose a threat to the Constitution they have so badly abused, but this is only a desperate, rear-guard action to rally their remaining troops.

It won't last. In a few months—a few years, at most—they will have to concede defeat and step aside. The 1980 elections were a big victory for conservatives. We won a battle, not the war.

But our final triumph won't happen automatically. All the conditions are favorable. But we still have to *make* it happen, just as much as when we set out, many years ago, to fight our first lonely battles.

There won't be a formal surrender. Pockets of liberal resistance will remain for a long time—after all, they've ruled the roost for at least half a century. The framers of our constitutional system created a wonderfully durable and complex political order, one that has withstood many determined assaults, and no single party—not even conservatives—can or should take it over all at once.

And let's not forget the many positive contributions of liberals themselves. For all their excesses, they have helped America to see and correct blind spots with respect to blacks, women, prisoners, and various other victims of injustice. We want liberals out of power. We don't want them out of the country.

Meanwhile, there is work to be done.

Conservatives have a lot of good ideas to make America a better place to live and work in. But I can't say it enough: the basic ingredient now is *leadership.* That's what the New Right has to offer. But we can't get too much of it. There has never been a leadership surplus.

I feel that most of the problems the cause of freedom faces in America and in the world today arise from a lack of leadership. Most of them could be corrected if we had a few more good leaders.

If you think about it, this country is here today because of a few dozen people. If there had been no Washington, no Franklin, no Jefferson, no Adams, plus

20 others some 200 years ago we might still be a colony of Great Britain.

Starting in the early 1930s, we did not graduate from the universities or colleges future conservative leaders.

For some reason, we conservatives skipped an entire generation of leaders.

As a result, in the 1950s, 1960s and 1970s the Left had their Humphreys, Stevensons, Kennedys, Rockefellers, Javits, Mondales and Reuthers.

But the right had very few leaders during these three decades.

We did have a fair number of people who were well-known and articulate, good writers, good debaters, who had charisma.

And most people would think that they were leaders. But only in the last few years did I come to understand that most were spokesmen. They were not leaders.

A leader will make things happen, he will start a new organization or a new magazine. He will call meetings, suggest assignments, then call a follow-up meeting to review the progress.

A leader realizes that winners have plans and losers have excuses.

There is a big difference between a spokesman and a leader. It's not that a spokesman is not important; it's just that you need both spokesmen *and* leaders. But for many years conservatives had spokesmen but very few leaders.

But starting in the 1950s and early 1960s we started to produce from our universities and colleges those who have gone on to provide the critically needed conservative leadership.

First came Bill Buckley, Bill Rusher, Stan Evans, and Phyllis Schlafly, then, in rapid succession, Howard Phillips, Carol and Bob Bauman, Jesse Helms, Jerry Falwell, Jameson Campaigne, Orrin Hatch, Mickey Edwards, Paul Weyrich, James Robison, Morton Blackwell, Terry Dolan and many, many others.

While the conservative leadership gap is being filled, the liberals are rapidly losing their leadership. And it will be at least ten years before the kids who were in the streets marching against the war in Vietnam will be old enough to provide leadership for the Left.

It appears to me that the 1980s will see the liberals suffering from a serious leadership gap.

This provides an enormous opportunity for the conservatives to take charge of the major institutions in America while the left is not playing with a full team.

However, we need lots more leaders—and at all levels, not just in Washington.

I'd like *you*, personally, to give some serious thought to becoming a leader. You might think about becoming a candidate for the school board, city council, state legislature or Congress. Or perhaps you might seek a position in your local Democratic or Republican organization.

Don't sell yourself short by thinking you don't have the talent or ability or background to run for or hold public office.

Very few people who hold public office are genuine giants. They are people for the most part like you and me—engineers, housewives, doctors, concerned parents, salesmen.

Don't make the mistake of waiting for a committee of the leading citizens of your community to plead with you to run for Congress, or mayor, or city council, or the board of education.

Occasionally, it does work that way. But if Jimmy Carter had waited for a committee to plead with him, he'd still be waiting in Plains, Georgia.

Orrin Hatch, a Salt Lake City attorney with no political experience, decided to make his plunge in 1976. He now represents Utah in the U.S. Senate.

Gordon Humphrey, an Allegheny Airlines co-pilot who had never run for public office, decided to provide some leadership in 1978. Gordon did not have the support of any big name New Hampshire political leaders, only his own friends, his associates from The New Hampshire Conservative Caucus and a few New Right national leaders. He now represents New Hampshire in the U.S. Senate.

There are many more Orrin Hatches and Gordon Humphreys in America—conservatives who can and must make a contribution now to their country.

For the past 50 years, conservatives have stressed almost exclusively economic and foreign policy. The New Right shares the same basic beliefs of other conservatives in economics and foreign policy matters, but we feel that conservatives cannot become the dominant political force in America until we stress the issues of concern to ethnic and blue collar Americans, born-again Christians, pro-life Catholics and Jews.

Some of these issues are busing, quotas, crime, abortion, pornography, education and traditional Biblical moral values.

However, there are certain qualities that the New Right has that previous conservatives didn't have.

As a general rule, New Right conservatives are young. They are aggressive, sharp, tough, work long hours, meet often, develop strategy, plans and tactics, cooperate with Democrats, Independents and Republicans, use and understand new technology. Their day is filled with activities designed to replace liberals with conservatives in all major American institutions.

They are conservatives who are tired of losing and are personally committed to bringing freedom to America and the world in the near future. And they have a firm conviction that they will succeed.

What keeps conservatives like Jesse Helms, that dedicated, tireless "conscience of the Senate" going? He has the following motto on a plaque in his Senate office, and I've adopted it as a guide for my life:

"*God does not require me to succeed, but He does require me to try.*"

Frankly, I think He requires all of us to try.

As I said at the very beginning of this book, the left is old and tired. We in the New Right are young and vigorous.

Many of the liberals' leaders like Adlai Stevenson, Nelson Rockefeller, Hubert Humphrey, Robert and Jack Kennedy are gone. Our leaders are coming into their own.

The liberals had a lot of victories over the last 50 years. But they've grown soft and sluggish. They have lost confidence in themselves and in their ideas.

We're lean, determined and hungry—to gain victories for conservatism and to renew our great country.

Yes, the tide is turning. It is turning our way—freedom's way.

SOURCE: Viguerie, Richard A. *The New Right: We're Ready to Lead.* Falls Church, Va.: Viguerie Co., 1981.

DEMING'S 14 POINTS FOR MANAGEMENT
(c. 1982, by W. Edwards Deming)

The American economy was in a state of decline when Ronald Reagan was elected president in 1980. The declining status of American industry, called "deindustrialization," led to a sustained period of "stagflation," during which the economy suffered from both stagnation and inflation. One industry particularly hard-hit by deindustrialization was the U.S. auto industry, which was being crushed by high-quality, low-priced vehicles from Japan. Ironically, American consultants, such as W. Edwards Deming (1900–1993), who had invigorated Japan's post-war economy by advocating quality and worker involvement as the greatest priorities of business, had built the Japanese industries. In the 1980s, American businesses turned to Deming's theories to help them navigate the new challenges of the global economy. Deming's *14 Points for Management,* which advocated giving power of production to workers, was highly popular among American business leaders.

Leah R. Shafer,
Cornell University

See also: **Industrial Management**

The 14 points are the basis for transformation of American industry. It will not suffice merely to solve problems, big or little. Adoption and action on the 14 points are a signal that the management intend to stay in business and aim to protect investors and jobs. Such a system formed the basis for lessons for top management in Japan in 1950 and in subsequent years. The 14 points apply anywhere, to small organizations as well as to large ones, to the service industry as well as to manufacturing. They apply to a division within a company.

1. Create constancy of purpose toward improvement of product and service, with the aim to become competitive and to stay in business, and to provide jobs.
2. Adopt the new philosophy. We are in a new economic age. Western management must awaken to the challenge, must learn their responsibilities, and take on leadership for change.
3. Cease dependence on inspection to achieve quality. Eliminate the need for inspection on a mass basis by building quality into the product in the first place.
4. End the practice of awarding business on the basis of price tag. Instead, minimize total cost. Move toward a single supplier for any one item, on a long-term relationship of loyalty and trust.
5. Improve constantly and forever any system of production and service, to improve quality and productivity, and thus constantly decrease costs.
6. Institute training on the job.
7. Institute leadership. The aim of supervision should be to help people and machines and gadgets to do a better job. Supervision of management is in need of overhaul, as well as supervision of production workers.
8. Drive out fear, so that everyone may work effectively for the company.
9. Break down barriers between departments. People in research, design, sales, and production must work as a team, to foresee problems of production and in use that may be encountered with the product or service.

10. Eliminate slogans, exhortations, and targets for the work force asking for zero defect and new levels of productivity. Such exhortations only create adversarial relationships, as the bulk of the causes of low quality and low productivity belong to the system and thus lie beyond the power of the work force.

11a. Eliminate work standards (quotas) on the factory floor. Substitute leadership.

b. Eliminate management by objective. Eliminate management by numbers, numerical goals. Substitute leadership.

12a. Remove barriers that rob the hourly worker of his right to pride of workmanship. The responsibility of supervisors must be changed from sheer numbers to quality.

b. Remove barriers that rob people in management and in engineering of their right to pride of workmanship. This means, *inter alia*, abolishment of the annual or merit rating and of management by objective.

13. Institute a vigorous program of education and self-improvement.

14. Put everybody in the company to work to accomplish the transformation. The transformation is everybody's job.

SOURCE: *Out of the Crisis.* Cambridge, Mass.: MIT Center for Advanced Engineering, 1986; MIT Press, 2000.

EXCERPT FROM *THE NEW AMERICAN POVERTY* *(1984, by Michael Harrington)*

High inflation, little economic growth, and rising unemployment were rampant in the early 1980s. Trade imbalances, energy crises, and the decline of American industrial production all contributed to the increases in poverty, homelessness, and crime that characterize the decade. While the Reagan administration heralded an era of perceived prosperity and power, the poor population was growing at an astronomical rate and social programs designed to help them were being cut in an effort to reduce the deficit.

Michael Harrington's 1984 book, *The New American Poverty*, was part of the widespread media attention being given to social welfare problems in the early 1980s. The book illustrates the ineffectiveness of government programs designed to address poverty by drawing attention to statistics revealing the desperate plight of poor Americans. In this excerpt, Harrington discusses the new face of rural poverty in the South and the escalating Social Security crisis.

Leah R. Shafer,
Cornell University

See also **Old Age; Poverty; Rural Life; Social Security.**

I was on my way to give a speech at Starkville, Mississippi, and since I was working on this book I decided that I would be a poverty tourist. I told my faculty contact at Mississippi State University that I preferred to drive from Jackson to Starkville. I didn't tell him that I hoped to see, and even photograph, some obvious rural poverty. But I knew that welfare was the main source of income in thirty-one of Mississippi's eighty-two counties, that half of the five-year-olds in the state were not in pre-schools (although the state is now moving to change that), and that 35 percent of the Mississippians who tried to enlist in the Air Force were rejected. Wouldn't it be quite simple to get such a social problem to pose for a picture?

In *The Other America* I had written that poverty in general—and rural poverty in particular—lies off the beaten track. It is not obvious, which is precisely one of the reasons it is so often tenacious. As we drove from the Jackson Airport, I became uncomfortably aware that I should have heeded my own forgotten advice. The outskirts of Jackson could have been the outskirts of any city in the United States: the motels, the fast-food places, the low-rise business, that plastic homogeneity of Any City, U.S.A. Then we went down the Natchez Trail Highway, a pretty road lined with the ubiquitous pine trees of the South. There was a lovely reservoir named for a former racist governor, and then came small homes and apparently prosperous farms.

As we talked, my old knowledge slowly began to come back to me. The Delta is where the heavy concentration of blacks is found; shacks are not to be found on major arteries, because they can't pay the rent commanded by such important roads. But then it turned out that even some of the superficial well-being was not quite as it seemed. The chicken sheds at the seemingly prosperous farms were not owned by the farmers but advanced to them, along with the chickens and the feed, by entrepreneurs. Even the affluent farm owner, I remembered, is normally squeezed between the corporate input sector of the agricultural economy—the banks, the manufacturers of agricultural implements—and the corporate output sector—the processors, distributors, and giant export companies.

Social structure, I understood once again, was not to be seen; it had to be perceived. My act of stupidity on the road to Starkville might be paradigmatic of the attitude of the entire society toward rural poverty. Our eyes are so totally controlled by the stereotypes in our minds that we cannot see what we see.

For instance, it is well known that the American South is in the Sun Belt, which has been growing, and that it is better off than the Frost Belt of the North, which is in crisis. The fact is that the South, with less than a third of the population, accounted for 49.3 percent of the American poor in 1959 and 41.9 percent in 1978. Even that relative decline has to be put into a context, since part of it is explained by the fact that, though white out-migration stopped in a state like Mississippi during the sixties, black out-migration continued. As we have already seen, some of the worst aspects of black poverty in the cities of the North are consequences of the shocked lives of the black economic refugees from the South.

When one looks at the poverty rate in the non-urban parts of the South, however, there seems to have been real progress: from 33.2 percent in 1959, down to 13.5 percent in 1978. But the bulk of that improvement (from 33.2 percent to 17.9 percent) was made in the sixties, and in the mid-seventies the poverty percentage actually increased as a result of the recession of 1974–75. Since the statistics do not as yet reflect the economic catastrophe of 1981–82, the numbers are likely to have already gone up. But when it comes to the black and non-urban South, one does not have to be sensitive to statistical nuances to get a sense of the incredible deprivation: In 1978—a relatively "good" year—37.2 percent of the people living there were poor.

I finally got some sense of that reality on my visit to Starkville. The student who drove me to the local airport for the return trip took me down some back roads, and there were the broken-down houses that I had thought would be on the main highways for all to see. There was also a trailer camp, one of the important assembly points for the poor and the almost-poor. Indeed, when one looks at the 1980 census figures for "mobile home and trailer" percentages, they are very high in Mississippi, North Carolina, South Carolina, Tennessee, and West Virginia. And if one examines the states where more than 20 percent of the population had less than 125 percent of the poverty level, one finds that they are Alabama, Arkansas, Georgia, Kentucky, Louisiana, North Carolina, South Carolina, and Tennessee. Mississippi, as is so often the case, is the poorest of all, with 31.5 percent of the people below that level. Yet I could not see that last fact with my presumably trained eyes.

But then, if one looks not at the South in general, but at the poor black South, the reality becomes even more grim. The National Association of the Southern Poor describes the Black Belt as the area between Virginia and Louisiana with counties in which the black population ranges from 30 to 82 percent. Typically, Northampton County, North Carolina, had a per capita income of $2,673 a year at the end of the seventies, which was about one-third of the national average, and the three hundred other counties of the Black Belt had similar rates. These figures should not, however, be seen as shocking. Right before the Reagan cuts, the state of Mississippi provided a family of four on welfare with $120 a month—or $1,440 a year.

"The life of the people in the area reflects the very low income," the association's report continues. "They live in houses insulated by cardboard with tin roofs, in converted stables or chicken coops. Many have no toilets, indoors or out. Often they must transport water from long distances. Most babies are born without the assistance of any medical advice. The sleep of residents is sometimes disturbed by children crying from hunger; and our organization has witnessed hunger pacified by sugar and water for entire households, including babies, for periods of up to ten days."

The South, particularly the Southeast but even the Southwest, is not a happy Sun Belt with an affluent economy even in good times Rather, a part of its growth has been based precisely on low-wage, anti-union practices. North Carolina, for instance, is a more industrialized state than many think; in 1980 it ranked seventeenth in value added by manufacture. It was, however, forty-ninth in the percentage of union membership (only South Carolina was lower). All of this is not to say that the South made no gains during the relatively good times of the fifties and sixties. It did. It is to say that economic growth will have less of an impact there than it did historically in the industrial heartland—unless, that is, the American labor movement can finally make a major breakthrough into the region.

But what, one might ask, do unionism and industry have to do with *rural* America? A great deal. Here, again, stereotypes inhibit the eyes.

In 1945, at the end of World War II, there were about six million farms in the United States. By 1970 there were half that number, and their average size had almost doubled. In human terms, 24.9 percent of the American population was composed of farmers in 1930, 2.6 percent in 1981. What these statistics describe is the elimination of most of the subsistence farms as well as of most of the farm hands. Rural poverty, then, is often not farm poverty.

There are, for instance, sections of New York State that are "Appalachian." In part that adjective has to do with the landscape and the economy; in part it has to do with the fact that the definition of Appalachia in the 1960s was an exercise in politics having to do with the spending of money rather than the work of scholarly geographers. In Janet Fitchen's analysis of one of the small towns in this New York Appalachia, social decay "proceeded unrelentingly, with much the same inexorable sweep as was the case in the chestnut blight, which struck the same region and wiped out whole hillsides of stately and useful trees."

In the early twentieth century, agricultural decline, out-migration, debt-ridden farms, and people without skills adjusted to the industrial labor market. At the same time, the legendary social structure of rural America was subverted. The hamlets were impoverished, underpopulated, unable to carry out their traditional functions as centers of a vibrant, friendly community life. The people became members of the working poor, holding low-paying jobs in factories, in the highway department, in the low-skill, left-over jobs of an area that was no longer agricultural and not yet urban. That was much the same pattern I had encountered in Maine, where the subsistence farmers, the clammers, and the berry pickers had been driven by gentrification into the mill towns. It exists in Vermont where, only a few miles away from a fashionable ski resort, there are enclaves of bitter poverty.

The migrant workers face a different kind of poverty than do the exhausted agricultural areas of the Northeast. For one thing, they are extremely hard to count. For instance, the *Statistical Abstract* follows the legal definitions and, in effect, assumes that no Mexican agricultural laborers entered the United States after 1965. That is one improbable reason why it estimates migrants in 1979 at a mere 217,000. The best count, according to Richard Margolis, who wrote an excellent survey for *Rural America*, was made by the Department of Agriculture in 1977, which said that this labor force was one-third white, one-third Hispanic, one-third black, Oriental, and Native American. Margolis puts the total number at "more than one million women, men, and children who travel from place to place, yet have no place to call their own."

But then, where does one take note of the similar, but different, poverty of the Chicanos living in that thirties-style "tourist court" I saw in a tiny Nebraska town? There is a Chicano community of ex-migrants in East Kearney, Nebraska, a town of 20,000 people. It is on the "wrong side" of the Union Pacific Railroad tracks, in a neighborhood that spectacularly lives up to one of the classic patterns of poverty in the United States: bad roads for poor people. There are not simply muddy streets and trailer parks; there are no sidewalks. And yet the people living under these conditions have more stability and even amenities than do the migrants themselves. There are places, Margolis found, where at the height of the season a dozen people are stuffed into a single trailer and charged ten dollars a head per week.

There are even a few places where there is a minimum of decency for migrants. Farmworker Village is a 276-unit public housing project in Immokalee, Florida, built in the mid-seventies to show that, with money and imagination, migrants don't have to be treated like animals. It is both an exception and a "Potemkin village" for the government (Potemkin was a minister under Catherine the Great who rigged up villages with phony facades to prove that progress was being made), an exception to the rule. Yet the point has been made: There could be decent housing for these people; we just don't care.

It might seem strange to include a brief discussion of the poverty of the aging in a book that talks of new forms of misery. Isn't it clear that in this area there has been unambiguous and irreversible progress? Yes and maybe.

The "yes" part is clear enough. In 1959, 35.2 percent of people over sixty-five were poor; in 1980, 15.7 percent. Indeed, between 1970 and 1983, the income of older Americans went up faster than that of those under sixty-five. One of the reasons for this change is that social security coverage was extended from 60 percent of the aging in 1960 to 92 percent in 1981. Another reason is that, during the sixties and the seventies, the benefit levels were increased and then indexed. The aging, then, were probably better protected against inflation in the seventies and early eighties than was any other group. So, yes, there has been progress and those who fought for it should be proud of their accomplishment. Now come the qualifications—and the possibility that the aging could indeed become the new poor, not so much in the near future (although that is possible, too) but in the early twenty-first century.

First, the qualifications. If it is true that "only" 15.7 percent of the aging are poor—a mere 3,853,000 human beings in their "golden years"—another 25 percent are on, or just above, the poverty line. In the Miami Beach area, where there are so many social security recipients, one watches them waiting outside of cheap restaurants to take advantage of specials, or sitting in front of shabby hotels. Many are not poor—that is a gain—but are within the magnetic field of insecurity and faced with all of the health problems that age brings. Older blacks and widows more than seventy years old are particularly at risk. *The Wall Street Journal* quotes an expert: "We're just giving them enough so they'll starve better." Second, the optimistic statistics do not emphasize the fact that more than 10 percent of those over sixty-five are getting Medicaid—even though more than half of them (1,700,000 people) are technically above the poverty line.

If the conservative proposals designed to assign a cash value to in-kind income prevail, the portion of the aging poor having their nursing-home bills paid for by Medicaid will be suddenly promoted into the middle class. On the other hand, there are those who attack the medical care programs for the aging on the grounds that they go far beyond the intentions of the original Social Security Act. In fact, Franklin Roosevelt's Committee on Economic Security, which proposed the social security bill, had said that the "second major step" in the social security process should be not simply health care for the aging, but the application of social insurance principles to the problem of health itself. And there are still major problems for divorced women, particularly those in their fifties who have spent their lives as homemakers. In fact, older women as a group are almost twice as likely to be impoverished as men.

The point is, progress has indeed been made, but it is not quite as unambiguous as some think. And the progress is not universally welcomed, either. This act surfaced in the debate over the social security "crisis" of 1982–83. In early 1982, former Commerce Secretary Peter Peterson made the famous discovery that public expenditures for the poor were only a fraction of the outlays for the aging. To deal with the budgetary crisis, he said, it was necessary to think about cuts in this area. At the same time, it became known that some of the social security trust funds were in trouble. The air was filled with dire predictions of a breakdown in the system.

Peterson's point constitutes an ongoing danger, i.e., that some politician will, particularly at the end of the century, decide to balance the budget on the backs of the aging. But before looking at that possibility, it is important to understand that the crisis of the eighties was not a crisis of social security but of the American economy. During the seventies, both inflation and unemployment rose to very high levels. This put a special burden on social security. Unemployed workers do not pay social security (or any other) taxes; and benefits were indexed to correct for inflation. The system's revenues went down and its expenditures went up because the economy as a whole was in a period of "stagflation," which was inexplicable in terms of the conventional Keynesian wisdom.

This brings us to an ABC that is sometimes forgotten. Many Americans think that social security is a form of insurance, like a private policy. In fact, the system is not "funded" at all. That is, the government does not take—nor has it ever taken—the payments, invest them, and then pay the claims out of the monies actually earned, minus a charge for administration. Rather, it uses the taxes of the current working generation to pay the benefits of the retired generation. Unemployment among the young is thus a problem for the old. Moreover, the benefits are not proportioned to payments as an insurance policy. Two groups in particular, the rich and the poor, get welfare from the system, the poor because there is a certain minimum level of support, no matter what has been paid in, the rich because they are only taxed on a small portion of their income and therefore get maximum benefits at a very cheap (relative) price.

In the eighties, the "crisis" was a function of the mismanagement of the economy. If America had been operating at full employment with stable prices, the "crisis" would hardly have existed. As it was, that "breakdown" of the system was resolved by a compromise with one clearly reactionary factor. In addition to some sensible reforms, such as taxing the benefits of retired individuals receiving $20,000 a year and couples getting $25,000, the law postponed the July 1983 cost-of living adjustment to January 1984. That "one time" postponement will affect benefits for years to come, and could even push some of the marginal people under the poverty line. Congressman Claude Pepper and AFL-CIO leader Lane Kirkland fought that provision and did eventually win some extra help for people receiving Supplemental Security Income. But still, a principle had been breached, i.e., there had been a slight rollback in the real income of people over sixty-five. They were penalized for Washington's inability to manage the economy.

What makes this particularly disturbing is that the real crisis will occur shortly after the turn of the century. In 1980 there were roughly five people of working age for every person sixty-five or older; by the year 2030, when the "baby boom" generation (1945–60) has retired, there are expected to be two and a half people between twenty and sixty-four for every retiree over sixty-five. On all but the most pessimistic analysis, the system will run a surplus until 2015, or even 2025, but then there is a danger of significant deficits. Mind you, all demographic projections are speculative; the baby boom itself came as a surprise.

This gets to a central point, one that the best people in the political movement of the aging have understood: To protect, and deepen, the antipoverty gains of the social security system requires that the society face up to structural economic problems.

The movement itself is one of the most exciting political developments in the United States in years. The original Social Security Act was, in part, a response to the organization of the aging by Dr. Townsend in the thirties. His plan, interestingly enough, was supposed to stimulate the entire economy, since the aging would agree to spend their benefits in the month they received them and thus help prime the pump for all. But after the agitation of the thirties there seemed to be relative quiet until sometime in the sixties or early seventies. I first encountered this new trend in Denver at a meeting of the Western Gerontological Society in the mid-seventies. There was a large audience, part of it made up of doctors and social workers, but part composed of the militant aging themselves. As people lined up at the microphone to criticize or applaud speakers, the confident and aggressive tone reminded me of the best days of the civil rights movement.

There was, for example, a very palpable response to the psychiatrist who attacked diagnoses of "senility" which allowed government to abandon expensive attempts to restore the aging to a meaningful life and permitted them to prescribe cheap tranquilizers for a vegetablized existence instead. In 1981, Ronald Reagan made a tentative suggestion to cut back on some social security benefits, and it was this same movement of the aging that rose up in protest and helped persuade every Republican in the United States Senate to reject the President's proposal. Reagan promptly backed down.

In October 1983, when I spoke at a Gray Panthers meeting in Seattle, what impressed me most was the understanding of the way in which the problems of the aging are linked to the fate of the economy as a whole. The conference was co-sponsored by the Washington AFL-CIO, and it had attracted activists of all ages. When I spoke of how the aging had to support the full employment of the young, there was an enthusiastic response.

Most of the older people in Denver and Seattle and at other meetings were not poor. They were middle class. But they were and are the front line of the forces defending the biggest single gain of the poor in the past twenty years, one that even Ronald Reagan has not yet dared to attack. If they build the kind of alliances talked of in Seattle, it is possible that this progress will continue for the indefinite future. But if the American economy continues to malfunction for another decade or so, it could well be that some unscrupulous politician will notice the figures that so intrigued Peter Peterson. When asked why he robbed banks Willie Sutton said, "Because that's where the money is." And if a reactionary politician looks around for cuts, his eye will eventually alight upon social security. Because that's where most of the social spending is.

Finally, what about the 15.7 percent of the aging who, despite the gains, still are poor? It would be simplicity itself to raise coverage to 100 percent of the people over sixty-five and increase benefits so that everyone has enough to meet necessities. We have been sitting on the 15-percent laurel for a decade now (actually there has been a slight increase in the poverty of the aging since 1975). But why, in what is potentially the richest society in human history, should people in the twilight of their lives have to pinch the pennies of necessity? This is not a possibility of future poverty but a present reality, and it can be abolished anytime we decide to do so. We showed in the sixties and seventies that it is easy enough. If we care.

SOURCE: Harrington, Michael. *The New American Poverty.* New York: Holt, Rinehart, and Winston, 1984.

REPORT ON THE IRAN-CONTRA AFFAIR
(13 November 1987)

In 1985, high-ranking officials in the Ronald Reagan administration began selling arms clandestinely to Iran for its war with America-supported Iraq. The money from these arms sales was laundered in Israel and diverted to the Contras, rebels fighting the elected communist government in Nicaragua. The U.S. officials concealed knowledge of the arms sales and, when questioned, shredded and destroyed key evidence. The scandal marred the Reagan and George H. W. Bush administrations.

The *Report on the Iran-Contra Affair,* the result of Congressional hearings, is emphatic in its denunciation of these activities, claiming the "common ingredients of the Iran and Contra policies were secrecy, deception, and disdain for the law." The report strongly states that it is unconstitutional for foreign policy decisions to be made by the President alone. Only "policies formed through consultation and the democratic process," will eventually succeed.

Leah R. Shafer,
Cornell University

See also **Contra Aid; Diplomacy, Secret; Hostage Crises; Iran-Contra Affair; National Security Council.**

By Executive Order and National Security Decision Directive issued by President Reagan, all covert operations must be approved by the President personally and in writing. By statute, Congress must be notified about each covert action. The funds used for such actions, like all government funds, must be strictly accounted for.

The covert action directed by [Lt. Col. Oliver] North, however, was not approved by the President in writing. Congress was not notified about it. And the funds to support it were never accounted for. In short, the operation functioned without any of the accountability required of Government activities. It was an evasion of the Constitution's most basic check on Executive action—the power of the Congress to grant or deny funding for Government programs. . . .

. . . [Robert] McFarlane [National Security Advisor] told Congressional Committees that he had no knowledge of contributions made by a foreign country, Country 2, to the Contras, when in fact McFarlane and the President had discussed and welcomed $32 million in contributions from that country. In addition, [Elliot] Abrams initially concealed from Congress—in testimony given to several Committees—that he had successfully solicited a contribution of $10 million from Brunei.

North conceded at the Committees' public hearings that he had participated in making statements to Congress that were "false," "misleading," "evasive and wrong," . . .

The Coverup

The sale of arms to Iran was a "significant anticipated intelligence activity." By law, such an activity must be reported to Congress "in a timely fashion" pursuant to Section 501 of the National Security Act. If the proposal to sell arms to Iran had been reported, the Senate and House Intelligence Committees would likely have joined Secretaries Shultz and Weinberger in objecting to this initiative. But [John] Poindexter [new National Security Advisor] recommended—and the President decided—not to report the Iran initiative to Congress.

Indeed, the Administration went to considerable lengths to avoid notifying Congress. . . .

After the disclosure of the Iran arms sales on November 3, 1986, the American public was still not told the facts. The President sought to avoid any comment on the ground that it might jeopardize the chance of securing the remaining hostages' release. But it was impossible to remain silent, and inaccurate statements followed.

In his first public statement on the subject on November 6, 1986, the President said that the reports concerning the arms sales had "no foundation." A week later, on November 13, the President conceded that the United States had sold arms, but branded as "utterly false" allegations that the sales were in return for the release of the hostages. The President also maintained that there had been no violations of Federal law. . . .

The common ingredients of the Iran and Contra policies were secrecy, deception, and disdain for the law. A small group of senior officials believed that they alone knew what was right. They viewed knowledge of their actions by others in the Government as a threat to their objectives. They told neither the Secretary of State, the Congress, nor the American people of their actions. When exposure was threatened, they destroyed official documents and lied to Cabinet officials, to the public, and to elected representatives in Congress. They testified that they even withheld key facts from the President.

The United States Constitution specifies the process by which laws and policy are to be made and executed. Constitutional process is the essence of our democracy, and our democratic form of Government is the basis of our strength. Time and again we have learned that a flawed process leads to bad results, and that a lawless process leads to worse.

Policy Contradictions and Failures

The Administration's departure from democratic processes created the conditions for policy failure and led to contradictions which undermined the credibility of the United States.

The United States simultaneously pursued two contradictory foreign policies—a public one and a secret one:

- The public policy was not to make any concessions for the release of hostages lest such concessions encourage more hostage-taking. At the same time, the United States was secretly trading weapons to get the hostages back.
- The public policy was to ban arms shipments to Iran and to exhort other Governments to observe this embargo. At the same time, the United States was secretly selling sophisticated missiles to Iran and promising more.
- The public policy was to improve relations with Iraq. At the same time, the United States secretly shared military intelligence on Iraq with Iran, and North told the Iranians, in contradiction to United States policy, that the United States would help promote the overthrow of the Iraqi head of government. . . .
- The public policy was to observe the "letter and spirit" of the Boland Amendment's proscriptions against military or paramilitary assistance to the Contras. At the same time, the NSC staff was secretly assuming direction and funding of the Contras' military effort.
- The public policy, embodied in agreements signed by [C.I.A.] Director [William] Casey, was for the Administration to consult with the Congressional oversight committees about covert activities in a "new spirit of frankness and cooperation." At the same time, the CIA and the White House were secretly withholding from those Committees all information concerning the Iran initiative and the Contra support network.
- The public policy, embodied in Executive Order 12333, was to conduct covert operations solely through the CIA or other organs of the intelligence community specifically authorized by the President. At the same time, although the NSC was not so authorized, the NSC staff secretly became operational and used private, non-accountable agents to engage in covert activities. . . .

Confusion

There was confusion and disarray at the highest levels of Government. . . .

- One National Security Adviser understood that the Boland Amendment applied to the NSC; another thought it did not. Neither sought a legal opinion on the question.

- The President incorrectly assured the American people that the NSC staff was adhering to the law and that the Government was not connected to the Hasenfus airplane. His staff was in fact conducting a "full service" covert operation to support the Contras which they believed he had authorized....

Dishonesty and Secrecy

The Iran-Contra Affair was characterized by pervasive dishonesty and inordinate secrecy.

North admitted that he and other officials lied repeatedly to Congress and to the American people about the Contra covert action and Iran arms sales, and that he altered and destroyed official documents. North's testimony demonstrates that he also lied to members of the Executive branch, including the Attorney General and officials of the State Department, CIA and NSC.

Secrecy became an obsession. Congress was never informed of the Iran or the Contra covert actions, notwithstanding the requirement in the law that Congress be notified of all covert actions in a "timely fashion."

Poindexter said that Donald Regan, the President's Chief of Staff, was not told of the NSC staff's fundraising activities because he might reveal it to the press. Secretary Shultz objected to third-country solicitation in 1984 shortly before the Boland Amendment was adopted; accordingly, he was not told that, in the same time period, the National Security Adviser had accepted an $8 million contribution from Country 2—even though the State Department had prime responsibility for dealings with that country. Nor was the Secretary of State told by the President in February 1985 that the same country had pledged another $24 million—even though the President briefed the Secretary of State on his meeting with the head of state at which the pledge was made. Poindexter asked North to keep secrets from Casey; Casey, North, and Poindexter agreed to keep secrets from Schultz.

Poindexter and North cited fear of leaks as a justification for these practices. But the need to prevent public disclosure cannot justify the deception practiced upon Members of Congress and Executive branch officials by those who knew of the arms sales to Iran and to the Contra support network....

... North ordered the intelligence agencies not to disseminate intelligence on the Iran initiative to the Secretaries of State and Defense. Poindexter told the Secretary of State in May 1986 that the Iran initiative was over, at the very time the McFarlane mission to Tehran was being launched. Poindexter also concealed from Cabinet officials the remarkable nine-point agreement negotiated by Hakim with the Second Channel. North assured the FBI liaison to the NSC as late as November 1986 that the United States was not bargaining for the release of hostages but seizing terrorists to exchange for hostages—a complete fabrication. The lies, omissions, shredding, attempts to rewrite history—all continued, even after the President authorized the Attorney General to find out the facts.

It was not operational security that motivated such conduct—not when our own Government was the victim. Rather, the NSC staff feared, correctly, that any disclosure to Congress or the Cabinet of the arms-for-hostages and arms-for-profit activities would produce a storm of outrage.

As with Iran, Congress was misled about the NSC staff's support for the Contras during the period of the Boland Amendment, although the role of the NSC staff was not secret to others. North testified that his operation was well known to the press in the Soviet Union, Cuba, and Nicaragua. It was not a secret from Nicaragua's neighbors, with whom the NSC staff communicated throughout the period. It was not a secret from the third countries—including a totalitarian state—from whom the NSC staff sought arms or funds. It was not a secret from the private resupply network which North recruited and supervised....

Privatization

The NSC staff turned to private parties and third countries to do the Government's business. Funds denied by Congress were obtained by the Administration from third countries and private citizens. Activities normally conducted by the professional intelligence services—which are accountable to Congress—were turned over to [Retired Air Force Major General Richard] Secord and [Albert] Hakim [involved in Iranian arms negotiations, with Secord].

The solicitation of foreign funds by an Administration to pursue foreign policy goals rejected by Congress is dangerous and improper. Such solicitations, when done secretly and without Congressional authorization, create a risk that the foreign country will expect and demand something in return. McFarlane testified that "any responsible official has an obligation to acknowledge that every country in the world will see benefit to itself by ingratiating itself to the United States." North, in fact, proposed rewarding a Central American country with foreign assistance funds for facilitating arms shipments to the Contras. And Secord, who had once been in charge of the U.S. Air Force's foreign military sales, said "where there is a quid, there is a quo."

Moreover, under the Constitution only Congress can provide funds for the Executive branch. The Framers intended Congress's "power of the purse" to be one of the principal checks on Executive action. It was designed, among other things, to prevent the Executive from involving this country unilaterally in a foreign conflict. The Constitutional plan does not prohibit a President from asking a foreign state, or anyone else, to contribute funds to a third party. But it does prohibit such solicitation where the United States exercises control over their receipt and expenditure. By circumventing Congress's power of the purse through third-country and private contributions to the Contras, the Administration undermined a cardinal principle of the Constitution.

Further, by turning to private citizens, the NSC staff jeopardized its own objectives. Sensitive negotiations were conducted by parties with little experience in diplomacy, and with financial interests of their own. The diplomatic aspect of the mission failed—the United States today has no long-term relationship with Iran and no fewer hostages in captivity. . . .

Covert operations of this Government should only be directed and conducted by the trained professional services that are accountable to the President and Congress. Such operations should never be delegated, as they were here, to private citizens in order to evade Governmental restrictions.

Lack of Accountability

The confusion, deception, and privatization which marked the Iran-Contra Affair were the inevitable products of an attempt to avoid accountability. Congress, the Cabinet, and the Joint Chiefs of Staff were denied information and excluded from the decision-making process. Democratic procedures were disregarded.

Officials who make public policy must be accountable to the public. But the public cannot hold officials accountable for policies of which the public is unaware. . . .

Congress was told almost nothing—and what it was told was false.

Deniability replaced accountability. Thus, Poindexter justified his decision not to inform the President of the diversion on the ground that he wanted to give the President "deniability." Poindexter said he wanted to shield the President from political embarrassment if the diversion became public.

This kind of thinking is inconsistent with democratic governance. "Plausible denial," an accepted concept in intelligence activities, means structuring an authorized covert operation so that, if discovered by the party against whom it is directed, United States involvement may plausibly be denied. That is a legitimate feature of authorized covert operations. In no circumstance, however, does "plausible denial" mean structuring an operation so that it may be concealed from—or denied to—the highest elected officials of the United States Government itself.

The very premise of democracy is that "we the people" are entitled to make our own choices on fundamental policies. But freedom of choice is illusory if policies are kept, not only from the public, but from its elected representatives.

. . . In the Iran-Contra Affair, secrecy was used to justify lies to Congress, the Attorney General, other Cabinet officers, and the CIA. It was used not as a shield against our adversaries, but as a weapon against our own democratic institutions. . . .

The NSC was created to provide candid and comprehensive advice to the President. It is the judgment of these Committees that the NSC staff should never again engage in covert operations.

Disdain for Law

In the Iran-Contra Affair, officials viewed the law not as setting boundaries for their actions, but raising impediments to their goals. When the goals and the law collided, the law gave way:

- The covert program of support for the Contras evaded the Constitution's most significant check on Executive power: the President can spend funds on a program only if he can convince Congress to appropriate the money.

  When Congress enacted the Boland Amendment, cutting off funds for the war in Nicaragua, Administration officials raised funds for the Contras from other sources— foreign Governments, the Iran arms sales, and private individuals; and the NSC staff controlled the expenditures of these funds through power over the Enterprise. Conducting the covert program in Nicaragua with funding from the sale of U.S. Government property and contributions raised by Government officials was a flagrant violation of the Appropriations Clause of the Constitution.
- In addition, the covert program of support for the Contras was an evasion of the letter and spirit of the Boland Amendment. The President made it clear that while he opposed restrictions on military or paramilitary assistance to the Contras, he recognized that compliance with the law was not optional. "[W]hat I might personally wish or what our Government might wish still would not justify us violating the law of the land," he said in 1983.

A year later, members of the NSC staff were devising ways to continue support and direction of Contra activities during the period of the Boland Amendment. What was previously done by the CIA—and now prohibited by the Boland Amendment—would be done instead by the NSC staff.

The President set the stage by welcoming a huge donation for the Contras from a foreign Government—a contribution clearly intended to keep the Contras in the field while U.S. aid was barred. The NSC staff thereafter solicited other foreign Governments for military aid, facilitated the efforts of U.S. fundraisers to provide lethal assistance to the Contras, and ultimately developed and directed a private network that conducted, in North's words, a "full-service covert operation" in support of the Contras.

This could not have been more contrary to the intent of the Boland legislation. . . .

Numerous other laws were disregarded:

- North's full-service covert operation was a "significant anticipated intelligence activity" required to be disclosed to the Intelligence Committees of Congress under Section 501 of the National Security Act. No such disclosure was made.
- By Executive order, a covert operation requires a personal determination by the President before it can be conducted by an agency other than the CIA. It requires a written Finding before any agency can carry it out. In the case of North's full-service covert operation in support of the Contras, there was no such personal determination and no such Finding. In fact, the President disclaims any knowledge of this covert action.
- False statements to Congress are felonies if made with knowledge and intent. Several Administration officials gave statements denying NSC staff activities in support of the Contras which North later described in his testimony as "false," and "misleading, evasive, and wrong."
- The application of proceeds from U.S. arms sales for the benefit of the Contra war effort violated the Boland Amendment's ban on U.S. military aid to the Contras and constituted a misappropriation of Government funds derived from the transfer of U.S. property....

Congress and the President

The Constitution of the United States gives important powers to both the President and the Congress in the making of foreign policy....

Yet, in the Iran-Contra Affair, Administration officials holding no elected office repeatedly evidenced disrespect for Congress's efforts to perform its Constitutional oversight role in foreign policy:

- Poindexter testified, referring to his efforts to keep the covert action in support of the Contras from Congress: "I simply did not want any outside interference."
- North testified: "I didn't want to tell Congress anything" about this covert action.
- [Elliot] Abrams [Assistant Secretary of State] acknowledged in his testimony that, unless Members of Congressional Committees asked "exactly the right question, using exactly the right words, they weren't going to get the right answers," regarding solicitation of third-countries for Contra support.
- And numerous other officials made false statements to, and misled, the Congress.

Several witnesses at the hearings stated or implied that foreign policy should be left solely to the President to do as he chooses, arguing that shared powers have no place in a dangerous world. But the theory of our Constitution is the opposite: policies formed through consultation and the democratic process are better and wiser than those formed without it. Circumvention of Congress is self-defeating, for no foreign policy can succeed without the bipartisan support of Congress....

... Democratic government is not possible without trust between the branches of government and between the government and the people. Sometimes that trust is misplaced and the system falters. But for officials to work outside the system because it does not produce the results they seek is a prescription for failure.

Who Was Responsible?

Who was responsible for the Iran-Contra Affair?...

At the operational level, the central figure in the Iran-Contra Affair was Lt. Col. North, who coordinated all of the activities and was involved in all aspects of the secret operations. North, however, did not act alone.

North's conduct had the express approval of Admiral John Poindexter, first as Deputy National Security Adviser and then as National Security Adviser. North also had at least the tacit support of Robert McFarlane, who served as National Security Adviser until December 1985.

In addition, for reasons cited earlier, we believe that the late Director of Central Intelligence, William Casey, encouraged North, gave him direction, and promoted the concept of an extra-legal covert organization....

The Attorney General [Edwin Meese] recognized on November 21, 1986, the need for an inquiry. His staff was responsible for finding the diversion memorandum, which the Attorney General promptly made public. But as described earlier, his fact-finding inquiry departed from standard investigative techniques. The Attorney General saw Director Casey hours after the Attorney General learned of the diversion memorandum, yet he testified that he never asked Casey about the diversion. He waited two days to speak to Poindexter, North's superior, and then did not ask him what the President knew. He waited too long to seal North's offices. These lapses placed a cloud over the Attorney General's investigation. ...

Nevertheless, the ultimate responsibility for the events in the Iran-Contra Affair must rest with the President. If the President did not know what his National Security Advisers were doing, he should have. It is his responsibility to communicate unambiguously to his subordinates that they must keep him advised of important actions they take for the Administration. The Constitution requires the President to "take care that the laws be faithfully executed." This charge encompasses a responsibility to leave the members of his Administration in no doubt that the rule of law governs....

Several of the President's advisers pursued a covert action to support the Contras in disregard of the Boland Amendment and of several statutes and Executive orders requiring Congressional notification. Several of these same advisers lied, shredded documents, and covered up their actions. These facts have been on the public record for months. The actions of those individuals do not comport with the notion of a country guided by the rule of law. But the President has yet to condemn their conduct.

The President himself told the public that the U.S. Government had no connection to the Hasenfus airplane. [Eugene Hasenfus, an American mercenary, had been captured when his plane, part of a C.I.A.-supported supply network, had been shot down.] He told the public that early reports of arms sales for hostages had "no foundation." He told the public that the United States had not traded arms for hostages. He told the public that the United States had not condoned the arms sales by Israel to Iran, when in fact he had approved them and signed a Finding, later destroyed by Poindexter, recording his approval. All of these statements by the President were wrong.

Thus, the question whether the President knew of the diversion is not conclusive on the issue of his responsibility. The President created or at least tolerated an environment where those who did know of the diversion believed with certainty that they were carrying out the President's policies.

This same environment enabled a secretary [Fawn Hall] who shredded, smuggled, and altered documents to tell the Committees that "sometimes you have to go above the written law," and it enabled Admiral Poindexter to testify that "frankly, we were willing to take some risks with the law." It was in such an environment that former officials of the NSC staff and their private agents could lecture the Committees that a "rightful cause" justifies any means, that lying to Congress and other officials in the executive branch itself is acceptable when the ends are just, and that Congress is to blame for passing laws that run counter to Administration policy. What may aptly be called the "cabal of the zealots" was in charge.

In a Constitutional democracy, it is not true, as one official maintained, that "when you take the King's shilling, you do the King's bidding." The idea of monarchy was rejected here 200 years ago, and since then, the law—not any official or ideology—has been paramount. For not instilling this precept in his staff, for failing to take care that the law reigned supreme, the President bears the responsibility.

Fifty years ago Supreme Court Justice Louis Brandeis observed: "Our Government is the potent, the omnipresent teacher. For good or for ill, it teaches the whole people by its example. Crime is contagious. If the Government becomes a law-breaker, it breeds contempt for law, it invites every man to become a law unto himself, it invites anarchy."

The Iran-Contra Affair resulted from a failure to heed this message.

EXCERPT FROM *MAYA IN EXILE: GUATEMALANS IN FLORIDA* *(1990, by Allan F. Burns)*

In the early 1980s Guatemala was engaged in a bloody civil war between rural, leftist guerrillas and the right-wing military forces of the government. The government's "scorched-earth policy of rural destruction" forced over 600,000 rural Maya Indians into exile in Mexico and the United States. Though at least one-third of these refugees is estimated to be living in the United States, few have been granted political asylum. The Mayans' immigrant experience reflects many of the difficulties faced by refugees fleeing late-twentieth-century conflicts.

Many of the Mayan refugees settled in the rural, agricultural area of southeast Florida, which is among America's most multicultural states. By examining how new Mayan immigrants found work and housing, cultural anthropologist Allan F. Burns studied the ways that the Mayan people adapted to their new environment. In his book, *Maya in Exile: Guatemalans in Florida,* from which this excerpt is taken, Burns says that Mayans in Florida endeavor to retain their language and other cultural expressions while integrating themselves into American life.

Leah R. Shafer,
Cornell University

See also **Florida; Guatemala, Relations with; Immigration; Political Exiles to the United States; Refugees.**

Escape and Arrival

The number of Maya people who have to come to the United States as refugees is difficult to assess. Since 1981 the number of Guatemalan refugees inside and outside Guatemala has been estimated as being as high as 600,000, with up to 200,000 in the United States (Zolberg, Suhrke, and Aguayo 1989:212). Of these, only a very few have been given political asylum. Between

1983 and 1986, when the first wave of close to 100,000 Guatemalans fled to the United States, only 14 petitions for political asylum were granted while 1,461 were denied (United States President's Advisory Committee for Refugees 1986:9). The numbers of people applying for either temporary or permanent worker status, those receiving legal papers through one of the provisions of the Immigration and Reform Control Act of 1986, and those here illegally have not been assessed.

Nor are there accurate figures for the number of Mayas in Florida. According to one newspaper account in late 1988, there were probably between fifteen and twenty thousand Maya in the state at that time (Palm Beach Post, Dec. 12, 1988). Of this number, probably close to five thousand live in Indiantown during the harvest season. Other communities with significant Maya populations include West Palm Beach, Homestead, Boynton Beach, Immokalee, and Okeechobee. These communities each have between five hundred and several thousand Maya immigrants. Small groups composed of individuals and families are found in most other agricultural communities in the state. But Indiantown is the historic, cultural, and numeric center of the Maya in the state. Indiantown and Los Angeles are considered the two major centers of Maya immigration in the United States.

As we saw in Chapter One, the violence in Guatemala in the 1980s was overwhelming for many Maya groups. Hundreds of villages were destroyed, lands were appropriated, and people were tortured and murdered with a ferocity that traumatized much of the indigenous population. The Maya of northwestern Guatemala were caught between the military forces of the government and the guerilla movement. The guerilla movement sought food, recruits, and ideological legitimacy from the Maya. The military sought to destroy the subsistence base of the guerrilla movement by a scorched-earth policy of rural destruction.

Not all Maya were caught by the military violence, nor were all communities in Guatemala affected. Some groups were able simply to stay isolated and outside of the zones of conflict. Others sided with the government in order to save their villages. Still others stood up to both the government forces and the guerrillas and were left alone. But many were not so fortunate. The area of the Cuchumatan Mountains was especially susceptible to both guerilla and military campaigns through the 1980s. This chapter focuses on the stories of some of the people from this region who have now come to the United States.

The Maya who fled this modern devastation of their culture their homes, and their families did not know where they were going or what they would find. Once in Mexico they set up temporary camps, which were soon raided by the Guatemalan military (Carmack 1988). Forty-two thousand of them were given refugee status by the Mexican government and put in camps near the Guatemalan border. When the Guatemalan army made several attacks on the camps in 1982 and 1983, several thousand were taken to isolated lands in the states of Campeche and Quintana Roo, Mexico.

One community leader, Joaquim Can, recounted the forced journey between the camps in Chiapas and Campeche:

ALLAN BURNS: What was it like to travel from the camps in Chiapas to Campeche?

JOAQUIM CAN: They brought us in big school buses from Chiapas. It took several weeks to bring us all here. I remember that at night they would put us in big warehouses and we had to all sleep on the floor next to each other. It was crowded and many people died, especially children and those who had infections. There was no sanitation and no way to care for those of us who were sick. Many people died.

In Campeche, the refugees constructed stick shacks with corrugated cardboard roofs. In 1989, when I interviewed residents of the camps, the same cardboard was there, only now the rains and storms had opened many houses to the elements. Despite the pathetic conditions, however, people preferred to live here than to live near the border or return to Guatemala.

Those who could fled farther north, through Mexico and into the United States. They crossed deserts at night, where they saw the bodies of people who had gotten lost in the wilderness of the border, and eventually they arrived in Phoenix and other cities. Once in the United States many applied for political asylum, while the majority entered the illegal alien world.

Receiving political asylum has been an important hope for many of the Maya. During the early years of the Maya immigration to the United States and especially to Florida, American Friends Service Committee and Florida Rural Legal Services worked to secure documentation for political asylum cases. As more and more Maya arrived in the United States, however, asylum hearings turned hopeless; only a small handful of applicants achieved legal status through these means. Application for political asylum was still a viable strategy in the short term, however, since it enabled those Maya who applied for the status to receive temporary work permits. This temporary status allowed people to work legally and have access to hospitals and other facilities.

One of the problems with applying for political asylum status for the Maya was the fear that had been engendered in Guatemala and in the United States concerning government institutions. Refugees feared that providing their names or any information about their families to a lawyer or an immigration judge would lead to their immediate deportation to Guatemala. For this reason, individuals were loath to step into the limelight of a court hearing, especially when it became well known that asylum application hearings seemed always to lead to denial.

The case of one woman, Maria Gonzalez, is illustrative of the summary nature of the hearings. Paralegals wrote up their experience with the case in a letter to the public after her immigration hearing:

> From the first defendant, Juan Francisco, the judge heard of the brutal massacre of eleven men, including his father and two brothers, in his village of Ixcanac. Juan was away working on a coffee plantation during the massacre and received a warning from his mother never to return. Another defendant, Carlos Juan, spoke of the killings in the town of San Rafael by guerrillas of the people who did not support their movement. Maria Ana, the last defendant to be heard described in detail how she witnessed the army massacre of El Mul in which eleven men were killed, and on the stand Maria described to the court how many soldiers stormed into her home and brutally beat and hacked her father and two brothers to death with machetes. The soldiers also beat women and children, stole villagers' animals and possessions, and burned homes to the ground.
>
> The contention of the authorities all along has been that the Kanjobal people have come here for economic reasons rather than fleeing political violence. Another position of the government is that the refugees should have gone to UN-sponsored refugee camps in Mexico rather than continue on to the United States. Judge Foster told the defense attorneys that it was not enough that one's family had been killed for one to prove persecution and qualify for asylum.
>
> In many ways the trials showed the cultural conflicts between a Maya people . . . and the court. An example was Maria. Confident in the telling of the brutality she experienced, she nonetheless is not even sure of the months of the year, is unschooled in numbers and mathematics, and during her long flight she was often sick and unable to document how long she remained in each place. So afraid was she by what she had witnessed that she assumed a false name in Guatemala to protect herself, and continued using it when caught by the immigration authorities and put in detention in the United States. (Camposeco, Silvestre, and Davey 1986)

It is difficult to convince the U.S. immigration authorities of the reality of the violence and fear that are at the heart of the Maya immigration to the United States, and attitudes about work and being a productive member of society contribute to misunderstanding as well. Maya people take great pride in their dedication and commitment to work. Their abilities to work well in diverse places such as the mountains of Guatemala, coastal coffee plantations, and now the migrant streams of the United States are a source of pride. To work hard and long is a value assumed to be appreciated in any country. When Maya women or men are asked why they are here in the United States, it is much more common for them to say that they came to work than to say that they came to escape repression. The violence, the betrayal of families and communities by neighbors, and the brutality of the Guatemalan government during the 1980s are issues that are simultaneously overwhelming and difficult to express. It is much easier to tell someone that you came to the United States because you are a good worker, in the hope that this virtue will be better received than will a sad story of your homeland. A newspaper article titled "Strangers in a Strange Land" (*Palm Beach Post*, Aug. 19, 1990) quoted a Maya who was learning English. The first phrase he proudly spoke was, "I need a good work."

The irony of this is that identifying oneself as a good worker or in immigration terms, an "economic refugee," is the one sure way not to have a chance at gaining legal status through political asylum. Economic refugees are popularly seen as workers who take jobs from U.S. citizens, even though this is not so and as unskilled laborers, even though many of the Maya once held positions as shopkeepers, cooperative officials, and school teachers. Economic refugees are seen as a drain on the U.S. economy because of the remittances they send back home. As George Waldroup, the assistant district director of the INS in Miami, said in a newspaper interview, "Most of these claims are based on economic need, but there is no such thing as economic asylum" (*Palm Beach Post*, Aug. 22, 1990).

A final problem with political asylum as a strategy for achieving legal status in the United States is the time that it takes for Maya people to travel from Guatemala to the United States. The United States is not a country of "first asylum" for most of the Maya. A very few have managed to fly directly to the United States, but the vast majority who come by land often spend months or even years moving surreptitiously through Mexico. Sometimes individuals spend a year or more in Mexico earning enough money to move slowly toward the U.S. border. Once here, they continue with the same strategies of being unobtrusive migrant workers.

Jose Xunche, a recent arrival to Florida, had spent several years in Mexico, working in the oil fields of Tabasco and in a restaurant in Mexico City, before coming to the United States:

ALLAN BURNS: When was the last time you were in Guatemala?

JOSE XUNCHE: I left on January 10, 1982, and went to Mexico for two years. I heard that the military was going to come into our hamlet. I came back in 1984. I lived near Rio Azul and every day the army would come there with a truck of guerrilla captives. They would stand at the bridge, cut them up with machetes, and throw them into the river. Half of them weren't dead but they just threw them in with the dead ones. I couldn't stay, so I left and made my way up here.

Rodrigo Antonio, another immigrant, talked with Julian Arturo, a University of Florida anthropology student from Colombia, about his journey from Guatemala through Mexico:

> Well, it was for the war. There in Guatemala. In my town, I am from San Miguel. But I am from Guatemala. Well, then, when there was war there it was hard for us to leave. Also we didn't have any money. Then finally I left there, fleeing. I left without hardly saying goodbye to my family because of the fear I had of the army, the ones that were killing people. It was of the government, as we say. The guerilla was also active, killing people once in a while. But it was the army that I feared more; I feared that they would come and kill me. For example, if you went out to work there and the army came upon you, it was really easy for them to kill you, because the army could do it there. The guerilla was up in the mountains, but the army could come upon you on the road or in the milpas or wherever. This is what happened to my best friend. He was in his milpa and the army came upon him and killed him there. This is what happened to him. That's why it frightens you to live there. And that's how I came here. I hardly said goodbye to my family because I left so quickly. I came here.

Since recording this interview, Rodrigo has returned to Guatemala to bring his wife and children to the United States.

Rodrigo's matter-of-fact telling of the personal terror in Guatemala is common in refugee accounts of terrorism. For him and others, the conditions in Guatemala can be described, but the killings and destruction of villages need no stress when told to others. Victor Montejo's *Testimony: Death of a Guatemalan Village* (1987) has a similar style of unexaggerated description: "Before going down to rescue the captives I had learned of the death of one patrol member: the boy of fourteen. . . . It was now two thirty, and the day had begun to cloud over. The bullet-riddled bodies of the dead civil defenders remained where they had fallen. No one, not even the widows, dared to leave the group to weep over the bodies of their husbands" (Montejo 1987:29).

In Rodrigo Antonio's case, the journey through Mexico to California and subsequently to Florida was in itself traumatic. After staying in Mexico City for several months, Rodrigo and a group of four companions (three men and a woman) made their way by train to the U.S. border:

RODRIGO ANTONIO: Well, we got there to Mexicali and we got a ticket for Tijuana. We got to Tijuana and we arrived—how do you say it?—real nervous. There were two women with us as well.

JULIAN ARTURO: Two women with you?

RODRIGO ANTONIO: Yes, two women with their husbands. They were almost dead. When we were on the train, we couldn't even get up. People just walked over us, because we felt so weak for lack of food. When we got to Tijuana, we still had a few pesos. The brother of the coyote [a person who brings people across the border for money] found us and we went to his house. There we bathed, ate some eggs, then we went to buy a few beers, so that was the end of that money. That was the last dollar I had; we spent it on beer with that coyote. We were in the hands of one of those coyotes, in his house.

I went with the coyote myself. The migra [Immigration and Naturalization Service agents] was there in front of a church. I was really tired and hungry. But when I saw the migra, I didn't worry about being tired or hungry, nothing! Thanks to God the church had something, a little park with flowers and everything. That's where I hid.

JULIAN ARTURO: The Mexican migra or the United States?

RODRIGO ANTONIO: The United States migra! We were in the United States, in Chula Vista, in California. We had already passed on to California. And the migra chased me, but thanks to the little park that was in front of the church, I was able to get away. I hid in the flowers and then escaped out the fence to a road that was in front with a lot of cars. I was running behind the coyote. We got to another house where they had—how do you call them, those things to carry horses?

JULIAN ARTURO: Horse trailers.

RODRIGO ANTONIO: Horse trailers. An old one was parked there by the side of the house. The migra was still after us, but I was hidden in there, in the trailer. I waited while the migra stopped looking. After a while they came back, but I was still hidden in there. Luckily there was a little hill there. That's where I hid myself. I lost the coyote; I was all alone; everyone else, including the coyote, was gone.

Rodrigo Antonio's story is similar to that of many of the Maya who have come to the United States. California is often the first place that they try to find work, as it is the place where most Mexican coyotes, the people who are paid for bringing people across the border, know well. Connover's book *Coyote* (1987) presents a powerful story of what it is like to come across the United States—Mexican border with the help of the coyotes.

Rodrigo describes his life in both California and Florida almost as if they were neighboring villages:

RODRIGO ANTONIO: Yes, one of my cousins left when I was in California, the other later. I was by myself. I went up north by myself. The other one stayed in Fort Myers. There a lot of people in Alabama. Too many people. We didn't get anything for our work. It was really hot. Everyone was sweating a lot, even the women who were working there in the sun. We were all sweaty. It was like it was raining; you couldn't even go to the bathroom. And we didn't get anything for it. So after this I went to Michigan.

JULIAN ARTURO: And did you do well there?

RODRIGO ANTONIO: Yes. I went with a woman friend up there to Michigan. We got up there and began picking cherries. We went in June. In one week we made three hundred dollars. "Ay, here there is money," I said. We stayed there for the entire cherry harvest, three weeks. Then we picked apricots, cucumbers. It was really good there. I had work there usually every day. After the apricots, then we picked apples. Then after the apple harvest, when it gets cold in November, we came back here again.

JULIAN ARTURO: Where did you go?

RODRIGO ANTONIO: First I spent a few days in Fort Myers; then I came here to Indiantown.

JULIAN ARTURO: How did you know about Indiantown?

RODRIGO ANTONIO: I had a friend there who had a car, and he brought me here once to visit some friends who live here. I knew about Indiantown because when I was living in Fort Myers I came here to visit now and again. I knew how it was here. I had friends who gave me a ride here.

One of the first places the Guatemalan Maya can find to live in Indiantown is in the apartment complexes built to house migrant workers. These apartment buildings are privately owned but are called "camps" like the farmworker housing found in the citrus and vegetable farms of the area.

JULIAN ARTURO: Did you come to one of the camps, like Blue Camp when you came?

RODRIGO ANTONIO: No, I always came here to Seminole Street. Near the house of Luis. That's where my friend lives. I picked oranges.

When Rodrigo Antonio returned to Guatemala to find his family, he found himself conscripted into the "civil patrol," one of the more burdensome organizations now instituted in many of the villages such as San Miguel, where Rodrigo was born. These patrols are made up of local men who are expected to give up their time to defend the villages from guerrilla soldiers. A list of every adult man is made in each village, and the men take turns doing "guard service." Suspicious strangers are reported to military authorities by these patrols, and often jealousies or old conflicts between families are settled by a patrol member's telling the military government that the other party is "subversive." In this way the current system installed by the Guatemalan government to lessen the threat of guerrilla insurgency has been transformed into a means for indulging feuds and personal conflicts. Some men pay others to take their turn at patrol. Many who now work in the United States send back money for years to pay a neighbor or relative to do their patrol duty.

RODRIGO ANTONIO: When I went back, it had changed a lot. It wasn't at all like it was when the war was going on. Now there is the patrol. You have to be a part of the patrol and not miss a day. When I went back, I had to patrol three times a week. You can't work at all. You have to be on patrol so much that you can't get any work done.

JULIAN ARTURO: They don't let you work?

RODRIGO ANTONIO: No. There is no time to work. You have to patrol when it's your turn.

JULIAN ARTURO: In the camps?

RODRIGO ANTONIO: No, in our town. We are, as we say, guarding our town. The army is there making sure we do.

JULIAN ARTURO: So you can't work more than four days a week?

RODRIGO ANTONIO: Yes, you can't work five days, just four days a week. Most of the time you can only work two or three days a week. You see, that is why the people are so ... in poverty now. It's because of the patrols, the war. Lots of things have been destroyed.

As we have seen, because political asylum was the most viable strategy for staying in the United States, the Maya like Rodrigo who came here were encouraged to apply for it, even though it was seldom granted. The year or more that it took for cases to go through the appeals process at least gave applicants a period of relative safety when they could legally find jobs and live without fear of deportation. With support from the Indian Law Resource Center in Washington, Jerónimo Camposeco began working with lawyers and other advocates to advance as many political asylum cases as possible through the court systems. The strategy taken by Jerónimo and other advocates was to be forthright about the presence of the Maya in the United States. The filing of political asylum applications provided people with legal status as long as the process of deciding on the individual cases continued. The Maya did not want to remain "undocumented aliens," illegal people. They wanted a chance to maintain their families until it was safe for them to return to Guatemala.

The case of Jerónimo Camposeco is indicative of this process.

ALLAN BURNS: Were you working there in the seventies on a school project or what?

JERONIMO CAMPOSECO: Yes, I was a teacher there in the parochial school teaching little kids. I was teaching them how to write and literacy. And many of these refugees here were my students.

ALLAN BURNS: Were you teaching them to write in Maya as well as in Spanish?

JERONIMO CAMPOSECO: Yes I was, because they don't speak Spanish. I was teaching Maya, in Kanjobal language. It's a Maya language, one of the many Maya languages in Guatemala.

ALLAN BURNS: So you devised an alphabet that could be used.

JERONIMO CAMPOSECO: Yes, we have an alphabet. We are using the modern alphabet of the modern script, but we have to have some changes in the alphabet.

We need to learn and then to teach the children. In other words, we teach the children in the modern alphabet, because when they are going to school, they can read in Spanish also. So this is a good help for them. Not only [because to] learn from their own language . . . is more easy, but because if you impose the Spanish since the beginning then. . . . There is a program of the government that is called "Castellanización" that is for the little Indians to learn Spanish before starting school. What I did was teach directly in the Indian language.

ALLAN BURNS: Did the people accept that; did you have a lot of students?

JERONIMO CAMPOSECO: Yes, it was very . . . they accepted that, because they didn't have to do big . . . they didn't have problems to understand the teacher; because they trusted the teacher because the teacher speaks the language. Of course the teacher was another Indian like them.

ALLAN BURNS: You grew up in Jacaltenango, speaking Jacaltec.

JERONIMO CAMPOSECO: Yes, Jacaltenango is a village not too far from San Miguel. We are only divided by two rivers and a mountain. So the Kanjobals go to the market place in Jacaltenango every Sunday carrying their . . . they make, from the maguey fiber, crafts like bags and ropes and all those good things. And also pottery, and also wood for construction. They are very good for those kinds of things like carpentry. . . . So I learned Kanjobal because my father was some kind of instructor also and he had many deals with the Kanjobal.

In the 1970s, Native Americans from New York and Pennsylvania contacted the Maya of Guatemala as part of a pan-Indian movement that crossed national boundaries. Jerónimo and several others from the northwestern highlands were invited to speak and perform marimba music in reservations across the United States and Canada.

ALLAN BURNS: But how did you end up here in Indiantown; why did you leave Guatemala?

JERONIMO CAMPOSECO: Because I could learn Spanish. I am an Indian like everybody else. Since I was a kid I helped my father in the fields, working in the lands and working to grow milpa and bringing wood to myself. And so I had the opportunity to go to the school. Later I worked at the National Indian Institute. We were a team of people there, and we were connected with the North American Indians. And some of them were working with us in the villages, because in 1976 was an earthquake, and so some just came to work. And some of them stayed there after the earthquake until 1980. And this work, for the government, for the paramilitary groups and the death squads, and even the army was looking for all the people who were working to try to have a better life in the countryside. Because we are the people in Guatemala, we are very poor. You know that since colonial times the people in power took our lands—we only have tiny lands in the mountains, and the good lands are in the lowlands in the hands of the companies. Exporting all the products like sugar cane, coffee, bananas, but there is nothing for our consumption, so I teach the Indians how to develop their own lands.

ALLAN BURNS: Did the army come for you?

JERONIMO CAMPOSECO: Yes. First of all the army came and killed some of my friends and my co-workers.

Even a North American Indian was killed by the army; his name was Kayuta Clouds. He was tortured. And because we worked together, the death squads found my name in a letter I sent to him inviting him to come to Guatemala. And so the American Embassy called to my office saying that I need to be careful because some people are looking for me because they found the body of Kay. After that they were looking for me. So I went to my house and told my wife and my children that I am leaving because the death squads are looking for me. So I escaped to Mexico. My family went to another house. There was a store next to my house. The people there saw three men in a car looking for me, but fortunately my family and I were not there. So I could escape to the United States. And I came to Pennsylvania because there is a place where my friends there, American Indians, farm. And so they gave me refuge there for six months. My family came later, and they joined me in Pennsylvania.

When the Maya of Florida immigrated to the United States in the early 1980s, like many groups of people before them they found the new language, customs, and communities both fascinating and frightening. On the one hand, they found a haven from the disarray of Guatemala, a community that was hospitable to their plight and their work ethic. One woman, Maria Andrés, put it quite succinctly:

MARIA ANDRES: Well, we left Guatemala for the problem that was there, for the war. We wanted to save ourselves in Guatemala, so we came to this land. We looked for each other here in this land. We like living here in this land. Now we don't want to go back to Guatemala.

ALLAN BURNS: What year did you come here?

MARIA ANDRES: In '80 or '81.

ALLAN BURNS: Did you come directly to Indiantown?

MARIA ANDRES: No. We first came to Los Angeles. We came to Los Angeles first. We can't live in our own country, because they are killing a lot of people there. It's because of that. We don't want to die; we want to live in peace, and so we came here. That is the problem that we have.

ALLAN BURNS: And are these your two daughters?

MARIA ANDRES: Yes, one is a niece, but her mother was killed, so she's here with me.

ALLAN BURNS: Did they come with you?

MARIA ANDRES: One of them, yes; the other arrived earlier.

ALLAN BURNS: When did your mother die?

EUGENIA FRANCISCO (THE NIECE): In '79.

ALLAN BURNS: Did she die here or where?

EUGENIA FRANCISCO: In Guatemala. There was an accident.

ALLAN BURNS: And here in the United States, how is life for women?

MARIA ANDRES: No, we don't have problems here. We just want to work here. We just want to live and work here.

ALLAN BURNS: What did you do in Guatemala?

MARIA ANDRES: There in Guatemala, we didn't work. We were in the house, taking care of it and raising our children. That's what we did in our houses.

ALLAN BURNS: Were you making things of clay?

MARIA ANDRES: No, it was others who did that. Where we lived we didn't. We made food for those who worked, the campesinos. That is what we were doing. Now, we have to go and look for work elsewhere, well, because here there isn't any work. We won't be able to work anymore here. We'll leave and then we'll return here again after the work.

ALLAN BURNS: Where will you go?

MARIA ANDRES: To New York.

ALLAN BURNS: To New York?

MARIA ANDRES: All of us, the whole family will go. We are taking the number of the center here with us in case our application comes up and they have to call us for an appointment. If they do, we'll come by plane for the appointment for political asylum. That's what we're going to do.

ALLAN BURNS: What do you need here in Indiantown?

MARIA ANDRES: If the president would let us, we would buy a little land here so we could live better.

Maria Andrés and others from Guatemala came to Florida and found jobs, first in the citrus groves, later in construction and the service industries. They found their friends who had fled several years earlier, and some went back to bring wives and children. With the passing of years, their children learned English and some went to college. Others moved away from Indiantown to see other parts of the United States and to see what it means to be a Maya American.

The narratives of the violence of Guatemala, the flight to the United States, and the difficulties of staying in the United States legally now make up a new oral history among the Maya of the United States. The narratives are not just stories of a journey, but are at the intersection of personal history and political adaptation. People like Maria Andrés who are not practiced in public speaking have had to talk about events that are personally tragic and that run counter to the prevailing beliefs of U.S. citizens and immigration authorities. Their stories are met with incredulity, an incredulity often fueled by the legal expectation of precision with regard to dates and locations. The narratives have been honed through interactions with lawyers working for political asylum, but even when dates and places are precisely given, new challenges are brought forward. Sometimes it is the challenge of time itself: after a few years threats and persecution are thought to disappear, and dangers experienced a few years ago are not seen as real today. Sometimes the challenge is to the veracity of the asylum seekers, as when an immigration hearing judge doubts that a gentle Maya person could recall such tragic events in a voice without emotion.

SOURCE: Burns, Allen F. *Maya in Exile: Guatemalans in Florida.* Philadelphia: Temple University Press, 1993.

ADDRESS TO THE NATION: ALLIED MILITARY ACTION IN THE PERSIAN GULF

(16 January 1991)

Almost one hundred years after the Spanish-American war, the United States found itself in another "splendid little war"—one fought partly to reunify the country after its experience in Vietnam, much the way scholars have claimed the earlier Spanish-American War helped heal the divisions of America's Civil War. President George H. W. Bush's nationally televised speech announcing the beginning of the air war on 16 January 1991 (17 January in the Middle East) explains and seeks to justify the steps taken by the United States, the United Nations, and the Coalition toward a war with Iraq for the liberation of Kuwait. In the speech, Bush focuses on the moral obligations of the international community to help bring about a New World Order based on justice and the rule of law. Though he concedes that U.S. involvement in Kuwait's liberation is also about the control of oil resources, Bush downplays domestic anxiety about the cost and availability of oil, placing fiscal concerns in the light of potential damage to the economies of Third World nations and emerging democracies. The air war's purpose was threefold: first, to gain air supremacy; then to destroy all targets that supported

Iraq's command and control structure, ruining Saddam Hussein's ability to lead his forces; and finally to harass and degrade the capacity of Iraq's army to function effectively in the field against U.S.-led Coalition ground forces. After nullifying Iraq's air force and air defense systems, Coalition fighters and bombers moved on to economic and military targets. They then began attacking Iraq's ground forces in Kuwait and Iraq in a heavy bombing campaign that represents the first instance in the history of warfare in which a combatant force was defeated primarily through the use of overwhelming air power.

Tony Aiello,
Cornell University

***See also* Persian Gulf War.**

Just 2 hours ago, allied air forces began an attack on military targets in Iraq and Kuwait. These attacks continue as I speak. Ground forces are not engaged.

This conflict started August 2d when the dictator of Iraq invaded a small and helpless neighbor. Kuwait—a member of the Arab League and a member of the United Nations—was crushed; its people, brutalized. Five months ago, Saddam Hussein started this cruel war against Kuwait. Tonight, the battle has been joined.

This military action, taken in accord with United Nations resolutions and with the consent of the United States Congress, follows months of constant and virtually endless diplomatic activity on the part of the United Nations, the United States, and many, many other countries. Arab leaders sought what became known as an Arab solution, only to conclude that Saddam Hussein was unwilling to leave Kuwait. Others traveled to Baghdad in a variety of efforts to restore peace and justice. Our Secretary of State, James Baker, held an historic meeting in Geneva, only to be totally rebuffed. This past weekend, in a last-ditch effort, the Secretary-General of the United Nations went to the Middle East with peace in his heart—his second such mission. And he came back from Baghdad with no progress at all in getting Saddam Hussein to withdraw from Kuwait.

Now the 28 countries with forces in the Gulf area have exhausted all reasonable efforts to reach a peaceful resolution—have no choice but to drive Saddam from Kuwait by force. We will not fail.

As I report to you, air attacks are underway against military targets in Iraq. We are determined to knock out Saddam Hussein's nuclear bomb potential. We will also destroy his chemical weapons facilities. Much of Saddam's artillery and tanks will be destroyed. Our operations are designed to best protect the lives of all the coalition forces by targeting Saddam's vast military arsenal. Initial reports from General Schwarzkopf are that our operations are proceeding according to plan.

Our objectives are clear: Saddam Hussein's forces will leave Kuwait. The legitimate government of Kuwait will be restored to its rightful place, and Kuwait will once again be free. Iraq will eventually comply with all relevant United Nations resolutions, and then, when peace is restored, it is our hope that Iraq will live as a peaceful and cooperative member of the family of nations, thus enhancing the security and stability of the Gulf.

Some may ask: Why act now? Why not wait? The answer is clear: The world could wait no longer. Sanctions, though having some effect, showed no signs of accomplishing their objective. Sanctions were tried for well over 5 months, and we and our allies concluded that sanctions alone would not force Saddam from Kuwait.

While the world waited, Saddam Hussein systematically raped, pillaged, and plundered a tiny nation, no threat to his own. He subjected the people of Kuwait to unspeakable atrocities—and among those maimed and murdered, innocent children.

While the world waited, Saddam sought to add to the chemical weapons arsenal he now possesses, an infinitely more dangerous weapon of mass destruction—a nuclear weapon. And while the world waited, while the world talked peace and withdrawal, Saddam Hussein dug in and moved massive forces into Kuwait.

While the world waited, while Saddam stalled, more damage was being done to the fragile economies of the Third World, emerging democracies of Eastern Europe, to the entire world, including to our own economy.

The United States, together with the United Nations, exhausted every means at our disposal to bring this crisis to a peaceful end. However, Saddam clearly felt that by stalling and threatening and defying the United Nations, he could weaken the forces arrayed against him.

While the world waited, Saddam Hussein met every overture of peace with open contempt. While the world prayed for peace, Saddam prepared for war.

I had hoped that when the United States Congress, in historic debate, took its resolute action, Saddam would realize he could not prevail and would move out of Kuwait in accord with the United Nation resolutions. He did not do that. Instead, he remained intransigent, certain that time was on his side.

Saddam was warned over and over again to comply with the will of the United Nations: Leave Kuwait, or be driven out. Saddam has arrogantly rejected all warnings. Instead, he tried to make this a dispute between Iraq and the United States of America.

Well, he failed. Tonight, 28 nations—countries from 5 continents, Europe and Asia, Africa, and the Arab League—have forces in the Gulf area standing shoulder to shoulder against Saddam Hussein. These countries had hoped the use of force could be avoided. Regrettably, we now believe that only force will make him leave.

Prior to ordering our forces into battle, I instructed our military commanders to take every necessary step to prevail as quickly as possible, and with the greatest degree of protection possible for American and allied service men and women. I've told the American people before that this will not be another Vietnam, and I repeat this here tonight. Our troops will have the best possible support in the entire world, and they will not be asked to fight with one hand tied behind their back. I'm hopeful that this fighting will not go on for long and that casualties will be held to an absolute minimum.

This is an historic moment. We have in this past year made great progress in ending the long era of conflict and cold war. We have before us the opportunity to forge for ourselves and for future generations a new world order—a world where the rule of law, not the law of the jungle, governs the conduct of nations. When we are successful—and we will be—we have a real chance at this new world order, an order in which a credible United Nations can use its peacekeeping role to fulfill the promise and vision of the U.N.'s founders.

We have no argument with the people of Iraq. Indeed, for the innocents caught in this conflict, I pray for their safety. Our goal is not the conquest of Iraq. It is the liberation of Kuwait. It is my hope that somehow the Iraqi people can, even now, convince their dictator that he must lay down his arms, leave Kuwait, and let Iraq itself rejoin the family of peace-loving nations.

Thomas Paine wrote many years ago: "These are the times that try men's souls." Those well-known words are so very true today. But even as planes of the multinational forces attack Iraq, I prefer to think of peace, not war. I am convinced not only that we will prevail but that out of the horror of combat will come the recognition that no nation can stand against a world united, no nation will be permitted to brutally assault its neighbor.

No President can easily commit our sons and daughters to war. They are the Nation's finest. Ours is an all-volunteer force, magnificently trained, highly motivated. The troops know why they're there. And listen to what they say, for they've said it better than any President or Prime Minister ever could.

Listen to Hollywood Huddleston, Marine lance corporal. He says, "Let's free these people, so we can go home and be free again." And he's right. The terrible crimes and tortures committed by Saddam's henchmen against the innocent people of Kuwait are an affront to mankind and a challenge to the freedom of all.

Listen to one of our great officers out there, Marine Lieutenant General Walter Boomer. He said: "There are things worth fighting for. A world in which brutality and lawlessness are allowed to go unchecked isn't the kind of world we're going to want to live in."

Listen to Master Sergeant J. P. Kendall of the 82d Airborne: "We're here for more than just the price of a gallon of gas. What we're doing is going to chart the future of the world for the next 100 years. It's better to deal with this guy now than 5 years from now."

And finally, we should all sit up and listen to Jackie Jones, an Army lieutenant, when she says, "If we let him get away with this, who knows what's going to be next?"

I have called upon Hollywood and Walter and J. P. and Jackie and all their courageous comrades-in-arms to do what must be done. Tonight, America and the world are deeply grateful to them and to their families. And let me say to everyone listening or watching tonight: When the troops we've sent in finish their work, I am determined to bring them home as soon as possible.

Tonight, as our forces fight, they and their families are in our prayers. May God bless each and every one of them, and the coalition forces at our side in the Gulf, and may He continue to bless our nation, the United States of America.

Note: President Bush spoke at 9:01 p.m. from the Oval Office at the White House. In his address, he referred to President Saddam Hussein of Iraq; Secretary of State James A. Baker III; United Nations Secretary-General Javier Perez de Cuellar de la Guerra; and Gen. H. Norman Schwarzkopf, commander of the U.S. forces in the Persian Gulf. The address was broadcast live on nationwide radio and television.

SOURCE: Bush, George H. W. *Speech Announcing the War against Iraq (16 January 1991).*

GULF WAR STORY
(1991, interview with David Eberly)

On 16 January 1991 President George H. W. Bush announced the commencement of the air war against Iraq. By the time the Gulf War ended on 28 February, more than 116,000 Coalition air sorties had been flown. Iraq's air force and air defenses were in ruins, its command and control centers largely destroyed, and its ground forces in Iraq and Kuwait bombed to the point that they offered little resistance once the ground war began on 24 February. It was the first time in history that a war was won mainly through the use of overwhelming air power. But as this interview with David Eberly, a captured U.S. pilot, shows, victory did not come without a price. Coalition air forces lost seventy-five aircraft, including sixty-three U.S. warplanes. In all, twenty men serving in the U.S. Air Force died in action. Most American prisoners of war later testified to brutal treatment by the Iraqis; such treatment was graphically illustrated when Iraq released photographs of bruised and beaten Coalition pilots who had been shot down and captured in the early days of the air war. Ultimately, twenty-three Americans from all service branches would be captured and later repatriated. Iraqi prisoners of war numbered more than 71,000—so many that they slowed the speed of the ground assaults into Kuwait and Iraq as Coalition forces struggled to process and gather the surrendering combatants.

Tony Aiello,
Cornell University

***See also* Persian Gulf War.**

[Eberly's story begins at the point where he has spent several days in the desert, successfully avoiding Iraqi detection; he is just about to be captured.]

DE: Well we crouched down in some small scrub there ... up together in what bit of cover we had, which was merely an aluminium blanket, and we waited and as the sky cleared and the stars came out even more. The wind picked up, and we were sweating a bit from having walked probably seven and a half miles. We began to get extremely cold to the point that we were shaking and, having not eaten for about three days now and having ... very little water, our physical strength was ... we weren't in the best shape at all. So we decided that we would wait ... for the rescue, and I made the decision that if we were going to wait out for the rescue rather than go on into Syria, we needed to at least get out of the cold because we were liable to go into shock from the cold and lose consciousness. So we backtracked a couple of hundred yards to what we thought was a deserted building and ... we approached that building again listening, looking, all senses out.

As I approached the building in the complete darkness, I saw a slight flicker of a candle in a window and, much like the pink panther in a movie, I began to take a couple of steps backward as quietly as I could.... I hadn't taken more than about two or three steps back ... I was maybe 10 feet from ... the actual building, and it simply erupted. There was automatic weapons fire around all sides of the building.... There was automatic weapons fire from the roof, and I found myself in the middle of a fourth of July celebration of fire crackers, and yet we weren't really celebrating. We were actually post mortem celebrating not our freedom but the end of our freedom. The yelling and the firing finally subsided ... it was foolish to get up and run ... that's not a point at which you run and die for your country. They eventually decided that we were not a threat, and they came up and grabbed us and half way drug us into the building.... The first sensation I had was of the warmth of the building. They took us inside into a small room threw us down on a cot.... As I went through the door, I happened to see a picture on the wall, and my mind tried, without looking at the picture, to recreate the image as, 'I am now face to face with the enemy.' Throughout the portion that they were firing at us, they were chanting Iraq, Syria, Iraq, Syria, and so I felt ... it could go either way ... then the picture came clear in my mind and the picture on the wall was Saddam Hussein and I knew that it was the enemy.

INTERVIEWER: Can you describe to me how you were blindfolded, what they were asking you and what they then did?

DE: During the interrogations we were always blindfolded. Always somewhat shackled or handcuffed, and on one particular interrogation early on in the prison experience, being dealt with by professionals I guess you would say, they were pursuing a line of questioning with regard to the army ground attack plan, and they had gotten fed up with me it was ... and said if you don't co-operate we're going to take you downtown and let some of the people deal with you whose wives and children that you've killed. And it got to a point of disgust where, although blindfolded, I could tell there was a 9mm being cocked and then I felt the business end of the 9mm up against my head ... cold steel, just like you see in the movies. And I guess they gave me one last chance and it was a point at which I basically drew my line in the sand and they pulled the trigger. From then on that ploy was useless; I'd seen that act and it wasn't going to work.

INTERVIEWER: What were you thinking though that ...

DE: Well, I visualised the side of my head coming out against the wall. And then the trigger pulled and nothing happened just the click.

INTERVIEWER: What does that type of experience do to you?

DE: It's one that gives you pause to reflect, and I guess you among the many things you remember throughout your life, you can always remember the sound of the click of that gun going off.

INTERVIEWER: Could you recall for me what it was like when you were in your cell and the place was bombed?

DE: The night of the 23rd February we had spent ... nearly four weeks in a maximum security prison.

DE: This particular night was not ... much different than any others. I had no watch and couldn't see a clock, but somewhere around the 8 o'clock time frame body time, you would hear the air raid sirens go off. Normally I would stop pacing I'd sit down against ... one of the side walls in the cell, and for that particular night, for some reasons, I had put my blanket up over my head sort of in ET fashion although I walked around like that much of the time just to keep warm. And then I hear the front end of a low altitude fighter coming in. And it's very easy to determine when a fighter's pointed at you; it's a very distinct sound, and hearing a crackling sound and then a concussion from the building ... is one of those that ... is very hard to describe. But the building seems to, I mean you become almost floating in air, and the feeling of being hit or the building that you're in is being hit is, again, an awesome feeling. The building swayed, and the concussion ... goes beyond simply popping your ears. As I sat there ... trying to again realise if I was dead or alive, I could almost envision that the ceiling was going to come in on me, or at any time I was going to fall through the floor several levels. And then you hear the second aeroplane, and you know that you haven't died, but now you're waiting and what are the odds on the next bomb taking you out. And it followed to the third aeroplane and, ... knowing that most formations fly four ships, you are in long wait for that fourth one ... It turned out that it was an extra long time before the fourth hit, but the place had become very chaotic by then. Yelling and screaming, the Iraqi guards had left; they had actually started running with the air raid siren two nights before, and so on this night, yes, they had run, and we were left.... After the first bomb hit, the guys were yelling get us out of here, and then we began to yell after the fourth bomb, sounding off our names. Who's there? Have you heard from this guy? Who is it? ... It was chaotic.

INTERVIEWER: Who do you remember shouting at each other? What voices did you hear? What names did you hear? What do you remember about that?

DE: I suppose my mind was flooded with, 'what are our chances now to escape' and in the yelling, my mind was pre-occupied with if somebody's out in the corridor, and I could hear somebody walking out there. Although picture yourself in a strange place; it's completely dark and all you know is the inside of your cell and the path that you've been led on to be interrogated. So we're in an unknown ... I thought, if we can get out of the doors, we're going to need transportation, we're going to need to hijack some kind of bus, we're going to need some weapons and we need somebody that can speak Arabic to get out of here and then we're going to need to figure our where we are. So my mind was flooded with what can we do now if we can get free.

INTERVIEWER: Was your cell door blown open?

DE: No, it wasn't. Mine was not and of course I guess that's why I wasn't preoccupied with running up and down the hall way in the dark trying to locate other people. I heard a couple of other voices and one humorous story. We had no idea who was there, we had no idea there'd been the slamming of the doors, how many people were in these particular cells, and so people would yell out there name and even spell it if it was an unusual name and at one point ... somebody said, 'who's that out in the hall?' and ... I remember Jeff S.... saying, well it's me and I'm trying to find some keys. And then another voice came up and said something about, 'Whose that down there' and the voices came back 'Well it's so and so, we're from CBS,' and with that I thought holy smoke, how did they ever co-ordinate to have press coverage at the bombing of this.... Very quickly ... the voice came back and said 'No, we're in a cell just like you are' and it turned out to be Bob Simon, Roberto Alvarez and the others who were, in fact, held with us.

DE: My release came as an absolute surprise. I mean the timing of it, I'd never given up hope that I knew we'd be released. In fact, Griff and I early on said ... if we can just stay alive, someday we'll be home. So it was Tuesday morning, and they ... began to feed us a little bit in this fourth prison. It had been a rainy night, cold and damp as usual, and in this particular prison there was no protection from that through any sort of glass or whatever. It was . . . the elements affected us a lot . . . and I had decided that . . . to sleep in, as you, might say that morning.

DE: The steel door came creaking open, as it always did, with . . . a rust sound, and there in the lie of the doorway was . . . an older man in a rather fresh military uniform carrying a clip board. So I wasn't sure at first whether to stand up or stay . . . sitting down, but I decided I'll stand up. Because you have to be careful not to be too aggressive. And I stood up and walked over toward him. He had two other guards with him, and I said, 'Why do you want to know?'. And he simply said I'm here to take you home. And I looked at him, and I could tell from his eyes that he was telling the truth, that it wasn't another ploy, it wasn't another game to try to get me to talk one way or the other and I put my arms around him in a rather European fashion and slapped him a couple of times on the back and he did the same. But he could tell that . . . after all the tough guy interrogation, those little words had pretty well broken me, and he whispered in my ear 'Just remember you're a man' and so I pattered him again on the back and mustered and stepped back and he said 'Just wait, just five minutes' and he left.

INTERVIEWER: You really . . . ?

DE: Well it got to me. You know the facade that I'd put on with every one of these guys, both the good guys and the bad guys, and the routines that they go through and he was somebody that, looking in his eyes, there wasn't any doubt he was there to take us home. And it was one of those just let your guard down for a second. But he could tell that . . . I knew he meant it.

SOURCE: *Frontline.* "The Gulf War. An In-Depth Examination of the 1990–1991 Persian Gulf Crisis." Available at http://www.pbs.org/wgbh/pages/frontline.

GULF WAR LETTER
(March 1991)

After forty-one days and nights of aerial bombardment, the U.S.-led Coalition began its ground war against Iraq on 23 February 1991. Saudi and other Arab forces, U.S. Marines, and the U.S. Seventh Corps pushed directly into Kuwait. To their left, other Coalition units, spearheaded by the U.S. Eighteenth Airborne Corps and 101st Air Assault Division, made a wide flanking movement through the supposedly impassable desert, advancing north from Saudi Arabia into Iraq before turning east toward Basra to encircle and trap the Iraqi army as it attempted to escape from Kuwait. Already demoralized by the air campaign, Iraq's defenders were caught completely off guard by the surprise and speed of the Coalition attack. Although a few stood and fought, most quickly fled or surrendered. By the time of the cease-fire five days later, the Coalition ground forces had advanced hundreds of miles with less than twenty hours of sleep. It was the fastest and deepest advance made by any army into enemy territory in the history of warfare. Kuwait was restored to its aristocratic ruling family, but Saddam Hussein, managing to crush rebellions in the south and Kurdish uprisings in the north, held on to Iraq. This letter, by a teenaged enlisted man of the U.S. Eighteenth Airborne Corps, provides an ordinary soldier's perspective on speed and violence of the ground war. As the writer relates, not only the Iraqis were confused by the pace of the assault. The letter also clearly reveals the overwhelming ground and aerial firepower available to the Coalition. Indeed, estimates of Iraqi losses in the fighting range from 25,000 to 100,000 or more. In contrast, only 234 Coalition soldiers were killed in action, with 479 wounded and 57 missing.

John W. I. Lee,
University of California at Santa Barbara

See also **Persian Gulf War.**

2/22?–3/5

Karen,

Okay, the Soviets have just about approved a peace resolution with Iraq. The US hates the resolution and has decided it's time to start the ground war. We were told we'd probably leave today, but possibly tomorrow. I say tomorrow at the earliest. Whenever it is, it won't be very fun.

Randy just beat me for the first time ever at chess. I turned around and beat him back. Uh oh, Carlos is here. He's making me stop, so we can play. Be back in a few.

"Be back in a few"? Sure. That was written around 7 or 8 days ago. It is now the 1st of March and as far as I can tell, the war is over.

So, what was it like? This'll take awhile. On the first day we rolled out, nothing significant happened. We drove all night and I slept maybe an hour or two. It was the second day that things started happening. We started moving at first light after stopping at around 4:30am. We came to a position and dug in. We were there for maybe an hour when someone yelled, "There they go!" I looked up and saw a rocket streaking across the sky. That launcher fired six rockets. As soon as it stopped firing, another launcher started. It was Carlos' and it fired all twelve of its rockets. I was in awe. It was the first time I had ever seen one fired and it was awesome. All of us were jumping around and smiling and laughing. I looked at Mark and said, "Ya know, we just killed a whole lot of motherfuckers." He nodded and said, "I know." First platoon also fired 6 rockets for a total of 24. Our target was a field artillery command center. The forward observer who called in the mission said simply that we had annihilated the target. Our war had started.

Nothing happened again until 3:30–4am of the 3rd day. We fired a night mission and put a hell of a lot of rockets downrange at different targets. By the time the sky started to lighten we were done and preparing to move. Why were we moving? Well, it had been discovered that we were in Iraq and elements of the Republican Guard had been sent our way. We moved and we moved fast. As were hauling ass, we passed one of the targets we had fired upon. It didn't seem like anything had happened to them—the vehicles; I could see no people. You see, what makes our rockets so deadly is that each rocket has a payload of 644 submunitions that look and explode sort of like a grenade. The rocket comes apart over the target and the submunitions are spread over an area, falling like rain. Due to this, you don't really get the blown up vehicles and buildings that cannon-artillery has. You get a swiss cheese effect. The vehicles are destroyed, but from a distance, you can't really tell. Anyway, as we're moving away from the Republican Guard, we came upon about 20 Iraqi soldiers and took them prisoner. Processing them took about 4–5hrs. We started moving again—east towards Kuwait City or as the commander put it: "East. We're just going east. I don't have a grid [location], the colonel doesn't have a grid, nobody has a fucking grid. We're just going east and watching all these motherfuckers surrender." As we convoyed east, we saw dozens of blown and burning vehicles and hundreds of Iraqi soldiers walking west waving white material in their hands. This is still the third day. Okay, here's the exciting part.

We're moving east behind a "maneuver brigade" of infantry. They're armed with Bradley fighting vehicles, Apache helicopters, M-1 tanks and other various armored vehicles. We, for some reason, caught up with and started to pass the maneuver brigade—something we *aren't* supposed to do. They halt us and we stop at the front of their group of vehicles. As we're waiting, we're watching the fighting around and to the front of us—all you can see and hear are the explosions. I'm near the front of the convoy and I see the Bradley at the front open fire. I thought he was firing at something far to our front. Suddenly, everyone yells take cover and "hits the dirt." I lock and load my M-16 and watch as the turret of the Bradley begins to turn as it continues firing. "Something is coming at us," I say out loud. Across the street, on the right side of our convoy, I see a truck. Tracer rounds are streaking from it and it's taking hits from the Bradley. Everyone opens fire on it. Someone fires a grenade at it and the truck rocks with the impact. It is now taking fire from about 40 soldiers and the Bradley's 25mm machine gun/cannon. The truck fishtails, swerves to the left, and flips twice. It isn't more than 30 meters from me. I lift my rifle and put it from "safe" to "semi." An Iraqi soldier jumps out of the truck and into my sights. I take careful aim, but don't fire. He's confused and shaken, has no weapon, and is trying to surrender. Sorry, I can't shoot someone under those circumstances. A lot of people around me thought different and continued to shoot at him and the truck. Luckily, he wasn't hit. Another guy jumped out of the wreck with a rifle and kneeled down behind a wheel. He didn't last long. He probably got hit more than 40 times. I didn't fire a single round. We captured 4 and killed 8. The driver had no face and his chest was full of holes, one Iraqi had to have his foot amputated with a bayonet and died anyway, one had a mangled leg, one was shot down, and the other 2 were uninjured. About 10 minutes after we had ceased fire to take prisoners, we looked up and saw a *large* number of Iraqi vehicles and foot-soldiers coming at us. We turned around and retreated, leaving them to the infantry. We didn't go too far—about 5 kilometers. We turned into an area, set up, and started firing on the forces coming at our front. We fired nearly a hundred rockets. It was dark by now. After firing, we set up a perimeter and started to catch some sleep. Five hours later, we were up and preparing to move—it is now day four—when fire missions started coming up "over the boards." Karen, it was incredible. The next group of fire missions was just incredible. We fired from about 4–5am. Over a hundred rockets were fired. The only reason we stopped was because the cease-fire came down from the president. It turned out that we wiped out 80% of Saddam Hussein's Republican Guard who had come out of nowhere. If we hadn't been there, we were told the battle would been one of the worst battles the American forces had encountered yet. Our rockets thoroughly ruined their last offensive. It is now the 6th day and we're waiting to go to Kuwait City. We were told that we can expect to be home within 3–5 days of arriving there or 2 weeks from today. Cheney has stated nearly all American forces will be out by April 1st. As far as we know, Saddam is agreeing to all 12 UN resolutions, though there is still limited resistance from elements of his own forces. An

Iraqi colonel stated under interrogation that he wished we would "stop the rain." He was referring to us—MLRS. I believe it's over and that I'll be home soon.

It is now March 5. A lot has happened and a lot is waiting to happen. I just read what I'd written on the 1st. It sounds like I enjoyed what happened. I didn't. I can't explain what I feel about what happened. My battery was responsible for thousands of Iraqi casualties (dead and injured). Thousands. We fired 350+ of the 550+ rockets that were shot by my unit. Everyone is saying that MLRS and the Apache helicopters won the war for us. I just want to go home. I've seen combat. I've seen dead soldiers. It's time to go home. I'm not proud of what I took part in, but I am glad of the fact that my efforts had a lot to do with the *absolutely incredibly* small numbers of American dead. Mixed feelings. Also, upon rereading the beginning of this letter, I realized that I left out a whole day of fighting. We moved so much and slept so little in those 4 or 5 days that everything is blurred. It's very weird.

Well, the "war" is over. I survived.

Peace and love,
Tony

SOURCE: Aiello, Tony. Previously unpublished letter, dated 22 February/5 March 1991.

CLINTON'S ROSE GARDEN STATEMENT
(11 December 1998)

What began as an illicit sexual affair between President William Jefferson Clinton and a young White House intern named Monica Lewinsky would soon erupt into a national firestorm. Amid partisan mudslinging, relentless accusations of malfeasance and mendacity, and an ongoing, tortuous independent investigation, President Clinton was at last forced to retract his protestations of innocence and confess his guilt. Never before had the private life of a sitting American president been the focus of such intense international scrutiny. For many, the scandal represented the regrettable culmination of America's amoral fascination with public confession and all things prurient. Others saw it as part of a Republican smear campaign against a popular president who had unseated the incumbent George H. W. Bush in the election of 1992. Whatever its origin, the Clinton-Lewinsky scandal had taken on a life of its own. On 11 December, shortly after the House Judiciary Committee approved the first of three articles of impeachment, President Clinton appeared in the White House Rose Garden to once again express his sense of shame and wrongdoing.

Laura M. Miller,
Vanderbilt University

See also **Clinton Scandals; Impeachment Trial of Bill Clinton.**

Good afternoon.

As anyone close to me knows, for months I have been grappling with how best to reconcile myself to the American people, to acknowledge my own wrongdoing and still to maintain my focus on the work of the presidency.

Others are presenting my defense on the facts, the law and the Constitution. Nothing I can say now can add to that.

What I want the American people to know, what I want the Congress to know is that I am profoundly sorry for all I have done wrong in words and deeds.

I never should have misled the country, the Congress, my friends or my family. Quite simply, I gave in to my shame. I have been condemned by my accusers with harsh words.

And while it's hard to hear yourself called deceitful and manipulative, I remember Ben Franklin's admonition that our critics are our friends, for they do show us our faults.

Mere words cannot fully express the profound remorse I feel for what our country is going through and for what members of both parties in Congress are now forced to deal with. These past months have been a torturous process of coming to terms with what I did. I understand that accountability demands consequences, and I'm prepared to accept them.

Painful as the condemnation of the Congress would be, it would pale in comparison to the consequences of the pain I have caused my family. There is no greater agony.

Like anyone who honestly faces the shame of wrongful conduct, I would give anything to go back and undo what I did.

But one of the painful truths I have to live with is the reality that that is simply not possible. An old and dear friend of mine recently sent me the wisdom of a poet who wrote, "The moving finger writes and having writ, moves on. Nor all your piety nor wit shall lure it back to cancel half a line. Nor all your tears wash out a word of it."

So nothing, not piety, nor tears, nor wit, nor torment can alter what I have done. I must make my peace with that.

I must also be at peace with the fact that the public consequences of my actions are in the hands of the American people and their representatives in the Congress.

Should they determine that my errors of word and deed require their rebuke and censure, I am ready to accept that.

Meanwhile, I will continue to do all I can to reclaim the trust of the American people and to serve them well.

We must all return to the work, the vital work, of strengthening our nation for the new century. Our country has wonderful opportunities and daunting challenges ahead. I intend to seize those opportunities and meet those challenges with all the energy and ability and strength God has given me.

That is simply all I can do—the work of the American people.

Thank you very much.

SOURCE: Clinton, William J. Rose Garden Statement. Associated Press (11 December 1998).

RESPONSES TO SUPREME COURT DECISION IN *BUSH V. GORE* *(13 December 2001)*

On 7 November 2000, the American people went to the polls to elect a new president. As election night wore on, the extreme closeness of the race between Vice President Al Gore, the Democratic candidate, and Texas Governor George W. Bush, the Republican candidate, became apparent. Although Gore won the popular vote by a small margin, ultimately the outcome hinged on Florida's twenty-five electoral votes. Election night ended with no conclusive result in Florida, after the television networks had reversed their pronouncements several times and Gore himself had offered, and then retracted, a concession.

Given the closeness of the vote, Florida state election law called for an automatic recount. Amid controversy over potentially misleading punch-card ballots and charges that many African Americans were denied rightful access to the polls, several Florida counties conducted manual recounts. Against the objections of Bush's lawyers and Florida's secretary of state, Katharine Harris—an appointee of Governor Jeb Bush, George W. Bush's brother—the Florida Supreme Court permitted the recounts to proceed.

The case reached the U.S. Supreme Court after Bush's legal team sought an injunction against further vote counts. On 9 December the Supreme Court ruled 5 to 4 to stop the manual recounts until the court considered arguments by both candidates' lawyers. On 11 December, Bush's lawyers argued that the Florida Supreme Court had no constitutional authority to order a manual recount, whereas Gore's lawyers contended that the U.S. Supreme Court had no jurisdictional authority to intervene in a state election. Siding with the Bush campaign, the U.S. Supreme Court, again split 5–4, declared the Florida Supreme Court's action unconstitutional. The recounts did not resume, and Florida's electoral votes—and the Presidency—went to Bush. For the first time in the country's history, a presidential election had been decided by the U.S. Supreme Court. The documents below contain Gore's and Bush's responses to the Court's ruling.

Paul Rosier,
Villanova University

See also Bush v. Gore; **Elections, Presidential: 2000.**

Concession by Vice President Al Gore

Good evening.

Just moments ago, I spoke with George W. Bush and congratulated him on becoming the 43rd president of the United States, and I promised him that I wouldn't call him back this time.

I offered to meet with him as soon as possible so that we can start to heal the divisions of the campaign and the contest through which we just passed.

Almost a century and a half ago, Senator Stephen Douglas told Abraham Lincoln, who had just defeated him for the presidency, "Partisan feeling must yield to patriotism. I'm with you, Mr. President, and God bless you."

Well, in that same spirit, I say to President-elect Bush that what remains of partisan rancor must now be put aside, and may God bless his stewardship of this country.

Neither he nor I anticipated this long and difficult road. Certainly neither of us wanted it to happen. Yet it came, and now it has ended, resolved, as it must be resolved, through the honored institutions of our democracy.

Over the library of one of our great law schools is inscribed the motto, "Not under man but under God and law." That's the ruling principle of American freedom, the source of our democratic liberties. I've tried to make it my guide throughout this contest as it has guided America's deliberations of all the complex issues of the past five weeks.

Now the U.S. Supreme Court has spoken. Let there be no doubt, while I strongly disagree with the court's decision, I accept it. I accept the finality of this outcome which will be ratified next Monday in the Electoral College. And tonight, for the sake of our unity of the people and the strength of our democracy, I offer my concession.

I also accept my responsibility, which I will discharge unconditionally, to honor the new president elect and do everything possible to help him bring Americans together in fulfillment of the great vision that our Declaration of Independence defines and that our Constitution affirms and defends.

Let me say how grateful I am to all those who supported me and supported the cause for which we have fought. Tipper and I feel a deep gratitude to Joe and Hadassah Lieberman [Joseph Lieberman, U.S. Senator from Connecticut and Gore's running mate] who brought passion and high purpose to our partnership and opened new doors, not just for our campaign but for our country.

This has been an extraordinary election. But in one of God's unforeseen paths, this belatedly broken impasse can point us all to a new common ground, for its very closeness can serve to remind us that we are one people with a shared history and a shared destiny.

Indeed, that history gives us many examples of contests as hotly debated, as fiercely fought, with their own challenges to the popular will.

Other disputes have dragged on for weeks before reaching resolution. And each time, both the victor and the vanquished have accepted the result peacefully and in the spirit of reconciliation.

So let it be with us.

I know that many of my supporters are disappointed. I am too. But our disappointment must be overcome by our love of country.

And I say to our fellow members of the world community, let no one see this contest as a sign of American weakness. The strength of American democracy is shown most clearly through the difficulties it can overcome.

Some have expressed concern that the unusual nature of this election might hamper the next president in the conduct of his office. I do not believe it need be so.

President-elect Bush inherits a nation whose citizens will be ready to assist him in the conduct of his large responsibilities.

I personally will be at his disposal, and I call on all Americans—I particularly urge all who stood with us to unite behind our next president. This is America. Just as we fight hard when the stakes are high, we close ranks and come together when the contest is done.

And while there will be time enough to debate our continuing differences, now is the time to recognize that that which unites us is greater than that which divides us.

While we yet hold and do not yield our opposing beliefs, there is a higher duty than the one we owe to political party. This is America and we put country before party. We will stand together behind our new president.

As for what I'll do next, I don't know the answer to that one yet. Like many of you, I'm looking forward to spending the holidays with family and old friends. I know I'll spend time in Tennessee and mend some fences, literally and figuratively.

Some have asked whether I have any regrets and I do have one regret: that I didn't get the chance to stay and fight for the American people over the next four years, especially for those who need burdens lifted and barriers removed, especially for those who feel their voices have not been heard. I heard you and I will not forget.

I've seen America in this campaign and I like what I see. It's worth fighting for and that's a fight I'll never stop.

As for the battle that ends tonight, I do believe as my father once said, that no matter how hard the loss, defeat might serve as well as victory to shape the soul and let the glory out.

So for me this campaign ends as it began: with the love of Tipper and our family; with faith in God and in the country I have been so proud to serve, from Vietnam to the vice presidency; and with gratitude to our truly tireless campaign staff and volunteers, including all those who worked so hard in Florida for the last 36 days.

Now the political struggle is over and we turn again to the unending struggle for the common good of all Americans and for those multitudes around the world who look to us for leadership in the cause of freedom.

In the words of our great hymn, "America, America": "Let us crown thy good with brotherhood, from sea to shining sea."

And now, my friends, in a phrase I once addressed to others, it's time for me to go.

Thank you and good night, and God bless America.

Remarks by Governor George W. Bush

Thank you all.

[Applause]

Thank you very much. Thank you.

Thank you very much. Good evening, my fellow Americans. I appreciate so very much the opportunity to speak with you tonight.

Mr. Speaker, Lieutenant Governor, friends, distinguished guests, our country has been through a long and trying period, with the outcome of the presidential election not finalized for longer than any of us could ever imagine.

Vice President Gore and I put our hearts and hopes into our campaigns. We both gave it our all. We shared similar emotions, so I understand how difficult this moment must be for Vice President Gore and his family.

He has a distinguished record of service to our country as a congressman, a senator and a vice president.

This evening I received a gracious call from the vice president. We agreed to meet early next week in Washington and we agreed to do our best to heal our country after this hard-fought contest.

Tonight I want to thank all the thousands of volunteers and campaign workers who worked so hard on my behalf.

I also salute the vice president and his supports for waging a spirited campaign. And I thank him for a call that I know was difficult to make. Laura and I wish the vice president and Senator Lieberman and their families the very best.

I have a lot to be thankful for tonight. I'm thankful for America and thankful that we were able to resolve our electoral differences in a peaceful way.

I'm thankful to the American people for the great privilege of being able to serve as your next president.

I want to thank my wife and our daughters for their love. Laura's active involvement as first lady has made Texas a better place, and she will be a wonderful first lady of America.

[Applause]

I am proud to have Dick Cheney by my side, and America will be proud to have him as our next vice president.

[Applause]

Tonight I chose to speak from the chamber of the Texas House of Representatives because it has been a home to bipartisan cooperation. Here in a place where Democrats have the majority, Republicans and Democrats have worked together to do what is right for the people we represent.

We've had spirited disagreements. And in the end, we found constructive consensus. It is an experience I will always carry with me, an example I will always follow.

I want to thank my friend, House Speaker Pete Laney, a Democrat, who introduced me today. I want to thank the legislators from both political parties with whom I've worked.

Across the hall in our Texas capitol is the state Senate. And I cannot help but think of our mutual friend, the former Democrat lieutenant governor, Bob Bullock. His love for Texas and his ability to work in a bipartisan way continue to be a model for all of us.

[Applause]

The spirit of cooperation I have seen in this hall is what is needed in Washington, D.C. It is the challenge of our moment. After a difficult election, we must put politics behind us and work together to make the promise of America available for every one of our citizens.

I am optimistic that we can change the tone in Washington, D.C.

I believe things happen for a reason, and I hope the long wait of the last five weeks will heighten a desire to move beyond the bitterness and partisanship of the recent past.

Our nation must rise above a house divided. Americans share hopes and goals and values far more important than any political disagreements.

Republicans want the best for our nation, and so do Democrats. Our votes may differ, but not our hopes.

I know America wants reconciliation and unity. I know Americans want progress. And we must seize this moment and deliver.

Together, guided by a spirit of common sense, common courtesy and common goals, we can unite and inspire the American citizens.

Together, we will work to make all our public schools excellent, teaching every student of every background and every accent, so that no child is left behind.

Together we will save Social Security and renew its promise of a secure retirement for generations to come.

Together we will strengthen Medicare and offer prescription drug coverage to all of our seniors.

Together we will give Americans the broad, fair and fiscally responsible tax relief they deserve.

Together we'll have a bipartisan foreign policy true to our values and true to our friends, and we will have a military equal to every challenge and superior to every adversary.

Together we will address some of society's deepest problems one person at a time, by encouraging and empowering the good hearts and good works of the American people.

This is the essence of compassionate conservatism and it will be a foundation of my administration.

These priorities are not merely Republican concerns or Democratic concerns; they are American responsibilities.

During the fall campaign, we differed about the details of these proposals, but there was remarkable consensus about the important issues before us: excellent schools, retirement and health security, tax relief, a strong military, a more civil society.

We have discussed our differences. Now it is time to find common ground and build consensus to make America a beacon of opportunity in the 21st century.

I'm optimistic this can happen. Our future demands it and our history proves it. Two hundred years ago, in the election of 1800, America faced another close presidential election. A tie in the Electoral College put the outcome into the hands of Congress.

After six days of voting and 36 ballots, the House of Representatives elected Thomas Jefferson the third president of the United States. That election brought the first transfer of power from one party to another in our new democracy.

Shortly after the election, Jefferson, in a letter titled "Reconciliation and Reform," wrote this. "The steady character of our countrymen is a rock to which we may safely moor; unequivocal in principle, reasonable in manner. We should be able to hope to do a great deal of good to the cause of freedom and harmony."

Two hundred years have only strengthened the steady character of America. And so as we begin the work of healing our nation, tonight I call upon that character: respect for each other, respect for our differences, generosity of spirit, and a willingness to work hard and work together to solve any problem.

I have something else to ask you, to ask every American. I ask for you to pray for this great nation. I ask for your prayers for leaders from both parties. I thank you for your prayers for me and my family, and I ask you to pray for Vice President Gore and his family.

I have faith that with God's help we as a nation will move forward together as one nation, indivisible. And together we will create and America that is open, so every citizen has access to the American dream; an America that is educated, so every child has the keys to realize that dream; and an America that is united in our diversity and our shared American values that are larger than race or party.

I was not elected to serve one party, but to serve one nation.

The president of the United States is the president of every single American, of every race and every background.

Whether you voted for me or not, I will do my best to serve your interests and I will work to earn your respect.

I will be guided by President Jefferson's sense of purpose, to stand for principle, to be reasonable in manner, and above all, to do great good for the cause of freedom and harmony.

The presidency is more than an honor. It is more than an office. It is a charge to keep, and I will give it my all.

Thank you very much and God bless America.

[Applause]

GEORGE W. BUSH, ADDRESS TO A JOINT SESSION OF CONGRESS AND THE AMERICAN PEOPLE *(20 September 2001)*

On the morning of 11 September 2001, a small group of terrorists from countries in the Middle East hijacked four American commercial airliners with the intention of using them as weapons of terror. Two of the passenger jets, loaded with fuel for cross-country flights, crashed into the twin towers of New York's World Trade Center, causing the enormous structures to collapse. Shortly after, another plane smashed into the Pentagon in Washington, D.C., and the fourth crashed in an empty field near Pittsburgh, Pennsylvania. In all, 3,213 people were killed, including the 265 people aboard the four planes and 343 firefighters who had rushed into the World Trade Center after the planes struck. The fires in the lower Manhattan rubble would burn for three months. Days later, on 20 September, with the country still badly shaken and the American economy on the verge of a free fall, President George W. Bush delivered a televised address to a joint session of Congress. The address identified the most likely perpetrators of the attack, a group of Islamic extremists led by a wealthy Saudi named Osama bin

Laden, and demanded their immediate extradition by Afghanistan's ruling Taliban faction. For President Bush, who had been awarded the presidency by the Supreme Court following a controversial election in which he lost the popular vote, the speech was a watershed moment, in which he saw his administration not only defined, but also justified. For many Americans, the president's address had a galvanizing effect, for it put a face and a name on a once-anonymous enemy. Bush's demands for the swift delivery of the Al Qaeda terrorists, however, would go unmet by the Taliban. On 7 October, the United States launched an attack on Afghanistan and in the matter of a few weeks, overthrew the Taliban's rule and installed a new provisional government led by Hamid Karzhai.

Laura M. Miller,
Vanderbilt University

***See also* 9/11 Attacks; Pentagon; Terrorism; World Trade Center.**

THE PRESIDENT: Mr. Speaker, Mr. President Pro Tempore, members of Congress, and fellow Americans: In the normal course of events, Presidents come to this chamber to report on the state of the Union. Tonight, no such report is needed. It has already been delivered by the American people.

We have seen it in the courage of passengers, who rushed terrorists to save others on the ground—passengers like an exceptional man named Todd Beamer. And would you please help me to welcome his wife, Lisa Beamer, here tonight. *[Applause]*

We have seen the state of our Union in the endurance of rescuers, working past exhaustion. We have seen the unfurling of flags, the lighting of candles, the giving of blood, the saying of prayers—in English, Hebrew, and Arabic. We have seen the decency of a loving and giving people who have made the grief of strangers their own.

My fellow citizens, for the last nine days, the entire world has seen for itself the state of our Union—and it is strong. *[Applause]*

Tonight we are a country awakened to danger and called to defend freedom. Our grief has turned to anger, and anger to resolution. Whether we bring our enemies to justice, or bring justice to our enemies, justice will be done. *[Applause]*

I thank the Congress for its leadership at such an important time. All of America was touched on the evening of the tragedy to see Republicans and Democrats joined together on the steps of this Capitol, singing "God Bless America." And you did more than sing; you acted, by delivering $40 billion to rebuild our communities and meet the needs of our military.

Speaker Hastert, Minority Leader Gephardt, Majority Leader Daschle and Senator Lott, I thank you for your friendship, for your leadership and for your service to our country. *[Applause]*

And on behalf of the American people, I thank the world for its outpouring of support. America will never forget the sounds of our National Anthem playing at Buckingham Palace, on the streets of Paris, and at Berlin's Brandenburg Gate.

We will not forget South Korean children gathering to pray outside our embassy in Seoul, or the prayers of sympathy offered at a mosque in Cairo. We will not forget moments of silence and days of mourning in Australia and Africa and Latin America.

Nor will we forget the citizens of 80 other nations who died with our own: dozens of Pakistanis; more than 130 Israelis; more than 250 citizens of India; men and women from El Salvador, Iran, Mexico and Japan; and hundreds of British citizens. America has no truer friend than Great Britain. *[Applause]* Once again, we are joined together in a great cause—so honored the British Prime Minister has crossed an ocean to show his unity of purpose with America. Thank you for coming, friend. *[Applause]*

On September the eleventh, enemies of freedom committed an act of war against our country.

Americans have known wars—but for the past 136 years, they have been wars on foreign soil, except for one Sunday in 1941. Americans have known the casualties of war—but not at the center of a great city on a peaceful morning. Americans have known surprise attacks—but never before on thousands of civilians. All of this was brought upon us in a single day—and night fell on a different world, a world where freedom itself is under attack.

Americans have many questions tonight. Americans are asking: Who attacked our country? The evidence we have gathered all points to a collection of loosely affiliated terrorist organizations known as al Qaeda. They are the same murderers indicted for bombing American embassies in Tanzania and Kenya, and responsible for bombing the USS Cole.

Al Qaeda is to terror what the mafia is to crime. But its goal is not making money; its goal is remaking the world—and imposing its radical beliefs on people everywhere.

The terrorists practice a fringe form of Islamic extremism that has been rejected by Muslim scholars and the vast majority of Muslim clerics—a fringe movement that perverts the peaceful teachings of Islam. The terrorists' directive commands them to kill Christians and Jews, to kill all Americans, and make no distinction among military and civilians, including women and children.

This group and its leader—a person named Osama bin Laden—are linked to many other organizations in different countries, including the Egyptian Islamic Jihad and the Islamic Movement of Uzbekistan. There are thousands of these terrorists in more than 60 countries. They are recruited from their own nations and neighborhoods and brought to camps in places like Afghanistan, where they are trained in the tactics of terror. They are sent back to their homes or sent to hide in countries around the world to plot evil and destruction.

The leadership of al Qaeda has great influence in Afghanistan and supports the Taliban regime in controlling most of that country. In Afghanistan, we see al Qaeda's vision for the world.

Afghanistan's people have been brutalized—many are starving and many have fled. Women are not allowed to attend school. You can be jailed for owning a television. Religion can be practiced only as their leaders dictate. A man can be jailed in Afghanistan if his beard is not long enough.

The United States respects the people of Afghanistan—after all, we are currently its largest source of humanitarian aid—but we condemn the Taliban regime. *[Applause]* It is not only repressing its own people, it is threatening people everywhere by sponsoring and sheltering and supplying terrorists. By aiding and abetting murder, the Taliban regime is committing murder.

And tonight, the United States of America makes the following demands on the Taliban: Deliver to United States authorities all the leaders of al Qaeda who hide in your land. *[Applause]* Release all foreign nationals, including American citizens, you have unjustly imprisoned. Protect foreign journalists, diplomats and aid workers in your country. Close immediately and permanently every terrorist training camp in Afghanistan, and hand over every terrorist, and every person in their support structure, to appropriate authorities. *[Applause]* Give the United States full access to terrorist training camps, so we can make sure they are no longer operating.

These demands are not open to negotiation or discussion. *[Applause]* The Taliban must act, and act immediately. They will hand over the terrorists, or they will share in their fate.

I also want to speak tonight directly to Muslims throughout the world. We respect your faith. It's practiced freely by many millions of Americans, and by millions more in countries that America counts as friends. Its teachings are good and peaceful, and those who commit evil in the name of Allah blaspheme the name of Allah. *[Applause]* The terrorists are traitors to their own faith, trying, in effect, to hijack Islam itself. The enemy of America is not our many Muslim friends; it is not our many Arab friends. Our enemy is a radical network of terrorists, and every government that supports them. *[Applause]*

Our war on terror begins with al Qaeda, but it does not end there. It will not end until every terrorist group of global reach has been found, stopped and defeated. *[Applause]*

Americans are asking, why do they hate us? They hate what we see right here in this chamber—a democratically elected government. Their leaders are self-appointed. They hate our freedoms—our freedom of religion, our freedom of speech, our freedom to vote and assemble and disagree with each other.

They want to overthrow existing governments in many Muslim countries, such as Egypt, Saudi Arabia, and Jordan. They want to drive Israel out of the Middle East. They want to drive Christians and Jews out of vast regions of Asia and Africa.

These terrorists kill not merely to end lives, but to disrupt and end a way of life. With every atrocity, they hope that America grows fearful, retreating from the world and forsaking our friends. They stand against us, because we stand in their way.

We are not deceived by their pretenses to piety. We have seen their kind before. They are the heirs of all the murderous ideologies of the 20th century. By sacrificing human life to serve their radical visions—by abandoning every value except the will to power—they follow in the path of fascism, and Nazism, and totalitarianism. And they will follow that path all the way, to where it ends: in history's unmarked grave of discarded lies. *[Applause]*

Americans are asking: How will we fight and win this war? We will direct every resource at our command—every means of diplomacy, every tool of intelligence, every instrument of law enforcement, every financial influence, and every necessary weapon of war—to the disruption and to the defeat of the global terror network.

This war will not be like the war against Iraq a decade ago, with a decisive liberation of territory and a swift conclusion. It will not look like the air war above Kosovo two years ago, where no ground troops were used and not a single American was lost in combat.

Our response involves far more than instant retaliation and isolated strikes. Americans should not expect one battle, but a lengthy campaign, unlike any other we have ever seen. It may include dramatic strikes, visible on TV, and covert operations, secret even in success. We will starve terrorists of funding, turn them one against another, drive them from place to place, until there is no refuge or no rest. And we will pursue nations that provide aid or safe haven to terrorism. Every nation, in every region, now has a decision to make. Either you are with us, or you are with the terrorists. *[Applause]* From this day forward, any nation that continues to harbor or support terrorism will be regarded by the United States as a hostile regime.

Our nation has been put on notice: We are not immune from attack. We will take defensive measures against terrorism to protect Americans. Today, dozens of federal departments and agencies, as well as state and local governments, have responsibilities affecting homeland security. These efforts must be coordinated at the highest level. So tonight I announce the creation of a Cabinet-level position reporting directly to me—the Office of Homeland Security.

And tonight I also announce a distinguished American to lead this effort, to strengthen American security: a military veteran, an effective governor, a true patriot, a trusted friend—Pennsylvania's Tom Ridge. *[Applause]* He will lead, oversee and coordinate a comprehensive national strategy to safeguard our country against terrorism, and respond to any attacks that may come.

These measures are essential. But the only way to defeat terrorism as a threat to our way of life is to stop it, eliminate it, and destroy it where it grows. *[Applause]*

Many will be involved in this effort, from FBI agents to intelligence operatives to the reservists we have called to active duty. All deserve our thanks, and all have our prayers. And tonight, a few miles from the damaged Pentagon, I have a message for our military: Be ready. I've called the Armed Forces to alert, and there is a reason. The hour is coming when America will act, and you will make us proud. *[Applause]*

This is not, however, just America's fight. And what is at stake is not just America's freedom. This is the world's fight. This is civilization's fight. This is the fight of all who believe in progress and pluralism, tolerance and freedom.

We ask every nation to join us. We will ask, and we will need, the help of police forces, intelligence services, and banking systems around the world. The United States is grateful that many nations and many international organizations have already responded—with sympathy and with support. Nations from Latin America, to Asia, to Africa, to Europe, to the Islamic world. Perhaps the NATO Charter reflects best the attitude of the world: An attack on one is an attack on all.

The civilized world is rallying to America's side. They understand that if this terror goes unpunished, their own cities, their own citizens may be next. Terror, unanswered, can not only bring down buildings, it can threaten the stability of legitimate governments. And you know what—we're not going to allow it. *[Applause]*

Americans are asking: What is expected of us? I ask you to live your lives, and hug your children. I know many citizens have fears tonight, and I ask you to be calm and resolute, even in the face of a continuing threat.

I ask you to uphold the values of America, and remember why so many have come here. We are in a fight for our principles, and our first responsibility is to live by them. No one should be singled out for unfair treatment or unkind words because of their ethnic background or religious faith. *[Applause]*

I ask you to continue to support the victims of this tragedy with your contributions. Those who want to give can go to a central source of information, libertyunites .org, to find the names of groups providing direct help in New York, Pennsylvania, and Virginia.

The thousands of FBI agents who are now at work in this investigation may need your cooperation, and I ask you to give it.

I ask for your patience, with the delays and inconveniences that may accompany tighter security; and for your patience in what will be a long struggle.

I ask your continued participation and confidence in the American economy. Terrorists attacked a symbol of American prosperity. They did not touch its source. America is successful because of the hard work, and creativity, and enterprise of our people. These were the true strengths of our economy before September 11th, and they are our strengths today. *[Applause]*

And, finally, please continue praying for the victims of terror and their families, for those in uniform, and for our great country. Prayer has comforted us in sorrow, and will help strengthen us for the journey ahead.

Tonight I thank my fellow Americans for what you have already done and for what you will do. And ladies and gentlemen of the Congress, I thank you, their representatives, for what you have already done and for what we will do together.

Tonight, we face new and sudden national challenges. We will come together to improve air safety, to dramatically expand the number of air marshals on domestic flights, and take new measures to prevent hijacking. We will come together to promote stability and keep our airlines flying, with direct assistance during this emergency. *[Applause]*

We will come together to give law enforcement the additional tools it needs to track down terror here at home. *[Applause]* We will come together to strengthen our intelligence capabilities to know the plans of terrorists before they act, and find them before they strike. *[Applause]*

We will come together to take active steps that strengthen America's economy, and put our people back to work.

Tonight we welcome two leaders who embody the extraordinary spirit of all New Yorkers: Governor George Pataki and Mayor Rudolph Giuliani. *[Applause]* As a symbol of America's resolve, my administration will work with Congress, and these two leaders, to show the world that we will rebuild New York City. *[Applause]*

After all that has just passed—all the lives taken, and all the possibilities and hopes that died with them—it is natural to wonder if America's future is one of fear. Some speak of an age of terror. I know there are struggles ahead, and dangers to face. But this country will define our times, not be defined by them. As long as the United States of America is determined and strong, this will not be an age of terror; this will be an age of liberty, here and across the world. *[Applause]*

Great harm has been done to us. We have suffered great loss. And in our grief and anger we have found our mission and our moment. Freedom and fear are at war. The advance of human freedom—the great achievement of our time, and the great hope of every time— now depends on us. Our nation—this generation—will lift a dark threat of violence from our people and our future. We will rally the world to this cause by our efforts, by our courage. We will not tire, we will not falter, and we will not fail. *[Applause]*

It is my hope that in the months and years ahead, life will return almost to normal. We'll go back to our lives and routines, and that is good. Even grief recedes with time and grace. But our resolve must not pass. Each of us will remember what happened that day, and to whom it happened. We'll remember the moment the news came—where we were and what we were doing. Some will remember an image of a fire, or a story of rescue. Some will carry memories of a face and a voice gone forever.

And I will carry this: It is the police shield of a man named George Howard, who died at the World Trade Center trying to save others. It was given to me by his mom, Arlene, as a proud memorial to her son. This is my reminder of lives that ended, and a task that does not end. *[Applause]*

I will not forget this wound to our country or those who inflicted it. I will not yield; I will not rest; I will not relent in waging this struggle for freedom and security for the American people.

The course of this conflict is not known, yet its outcome is certain. Freedom and fear, justice and cruelty, have always been at war, and we know that God is not neutral between them. *[Applause]*

Fellow citizens, we'll meet violence with patient justice—assured of the rightness of our cause, and confident of the victories to come. In all that lies before us, may God grant us wisdom, and may He watch over the United States of America.

Thank you. *[Applause]*

SOURCE: Bush, George W. Address to a Joint Session of Congress and the American People. Washington, D.C., Office of the Press Secretary, (20 September 2001).

ACKNOWLEDGMENTS

Excerpts of primary source documents were reproduced from the copyrighted sources below; permission of rights holders is gratefully acknowledged.

Asian Women United of California. *Making Waves: An Anthology of Writings by and about Asian American Women by Asian Women United of California.* Boston: Beacon Press. Reproduced by permission of Beacon Press.

Burns, Allen F. From "Escape and Arrival" as it appears in *Maya in Exile: Guatemalans in Florida.* Reprinted by permission of Temple University Press. ©1993 by Temple University. All rights reserved.

CBS News Archives.

Edelman, Bernard, ed. *Dear America: Letters Home from Vietnam.* New York: Norton, 1985. ©The New York Vietnam Veterans Memorial Commission.

Fink, Leon, ed. *Major Problems in the Gilded Age and the Progressive Era: Documents and Essays.* Lexington, Mass.: D. C. Heath, 1993.

Frankfurter, Marion Denman, and Gardner Jackson, eds. *The Letters of Sacco and Vanzetti.* New York: Octagon Books, 1971.

Freedomways: A Quarterly Journal of the Negro Freedom Movement. Spring 1965.

Gonzalez, Rudolfo "Corky." "Chicano Nationalism: The Key to Unity for La Raza." *The Militant.* 30 March 1970.

Hampton, Henry, Steve Fayer, and Sarah Flynn. *Voices of Freedom: An Oral History of the Civil Rights Movement from the 1950s through the 1980s.* New York: Bantam Books, 1990. © 1990 by Blackside, Inc. All rights reserved. Reproduced by permission of Blackside, Inc.

Harrington, Michael. *The New American Poverty.* New York: Holt, Rinehart, and Winston, 1984.

Kennan, George Frost. "American Diplomacy, 1900-1950." © 1951 by the Council on Foreign Relations, Inc. Reprinted by permission of *Foreign Affairs.*

Low, Ann Marie. *Dust Bowl Diary.* Lincoln, Neb.: University of Nebraska Press, 1984. © 1984 by the University of Nebraska Press. All rights reserved. Reproduced by permission of the publisher.

McAfee, Ward, and J. Cordell Robinson, eds. *Origins of the Mexican War: A Documentary Source Book.* Vol. 1. Salisbury, N.C.: Documentary Publications, 1982.

Minnesota Historical Society. *Minnesota History.* Vol. 28, no. 3. September 1962.

National Organization of Women. *NOW Statement of Purpose.* 1966. Reproduced by permission of the National Organization of Women.

New York Times. 26 May 1937; 24 April 1941; 18 January 1961.

Out of the Crisis. Cambridge, Mass.: MIT Center for Advanced Engineering Study, 1986. Reprinted by MIT Press, 2000.

Standing Bear, Luther. *Land of the Spotted Eagle.* University of Nebraska Press, 1978. Copyright renewed by Ray Jones.

PBS. *Frontline.*

Post, Charles Johnson. *The Little War of Private Post.* Boston: Little Brown, 1960.

Robinson, Cecil, ed. and trans. *The View from Chapultepec: Mexican Writers on the Mexican-American War.* Tucson, Ariz.: University of Arizona Press, 1989.

Sanchez, George I. "Pachucos in the Making." *Common Ground.* Autumn 1943.

Santoli, Al, comp. *Everything We Had: An Oral History of the Vietnam War by Thirty-three American Soldiers Who Fought It.* New York: Random House, 1981. © 1981 by Albert Santoli and Vietnam Veterans of America. All rights reserved. Reproduced with permission of Al Santoli.

Schlissel, Lillian. *Women's Diaries of the Westward Journey.* New York: Schocken Books, 1982.

Shevin-Coetzee, Marilyn, and Frans Coetzee. *World War I and European Society: A Sourcebook.* Lexington, Mass.: D. C. Heath, 1995.

Terkel, Studs. *The Good War.* New York: Pantheon Books, 1984. © 1984 by Studs Terkel. All rights reserved. Reproduced by permission of Donadio and Ashworth, Inc.

Tibesar, Antonine, ed. *Writings of Junipero Serra.* Vol. 1. Washington, D.C.: Academy of American Franciscan History, 1955.

Time. 17 January 1944.

Tomedi, Rudy. *No Bugles, No Drums: An Oral History of the Korean War.* New York: John Wiley & Sons, 1993. Reproduced by permission of the author.

Viguerie, Richard. *The New Right: We're Ready to Lead.* Falls Church, Va.: Viguerie Co., 1981. Reproduced by permission.

Welch, R. *The Blue Book of the John Birch Society.* Reprinted 1995.

Wells, Tim. Excerpt from *444 Days: The Hostages Remember.* ©1985 by Tim Wells, reprinted by permission of Harcourt, Inc. This material may not be reproduced in any form or by any means without the prior written permission of the publisher.

ISBN 0-684-80531-6

90000

9 780684 805313